VICTORIAN BRITAIN

AN ENCYCLOPEDIA

Sally Mitchell
EDITOR

Michael J. Herr
EDITORIAL AND RESEARCH ASSISTANT

ADVISORY EDITORS

Josef L. Altholz
N. Merrill Distad
Joel H. Kaplan
Laura Stempel Mumford
M. Jeanne Peterson
Ward M. Stanley
Nicholas Temperley

Garland Publishing, Inc.
NEW YORK & LONDON   1988

Library of Congress Cataloging-in-Publication Data

Victorian Britain: an encyclopedia/Sally Mitchell, editor . . . [et al.].
    p. cm.—(Garland reference library of social science; vol. 438)
    Includes index.
    ISBN 0-8240-1513-4 (alk. paper)
    1. Great Britain—History—Victoria, 1837–1901—Dictionaries.
   2. Great Britain—Civilization—19th century—Dictionaries.
    I. Mitchell, Sally, 1937–   . II. Series: Garland reference library
of social science; v. 438.
DA550.V53   1988
941.081′03′21—dc19   87-29947

Printed on acid-free, 250-year-life paper

Manufactured in the United States of America

VICTORIAN BRITAIN

GARLAND REFERENCE LIBRARY
OF SOCIAL SCIENCE
(VOL. 438)

CONTENTS

LIST OF ILLUSTRATIONS

PREFACE

Queen Victoria reigned for sixty-four years; her empire ultimately covered one-fourth of the earth's surface. Between 1837 and 1901 science, education, politics, communications, medicine, mass culture, the physical fabric of life, and the legal status of workers and of all women were profoundly transformed. Furthermore, as the last people who had been adult Victorians faded from the scene and the era of post-Victorian debunking passed, increasing attention has been paid to the massive records left by an age of growing literacy and cheap publishing. In addition to reworking the conventional matter of academic study, scholars in the last thirty years have opened new areas of inquiry into popular culture, the woman question, the material conditions of daily life, and the contribution of individuals who stood outside the Victorian mainstream.

It is clearly presumptuous for a book in one volume to call itself an encyclopedia of Victorian Britain—yet the very breadth of Victorian change suggests the uses of a single-volume reference work. In an age of massive transformations in almost every area of life, subjects that are now compartmentalized in separate scholarly disciplines could be thoroughly intertwined. At the beginning of Victoria's reign, for example, the various scientific societies had overlapping memberships; by its end most scientists were specialists, and nonprofessionals no longer expected to understand their debates. During most of the century, however, the interested amateur—even the self-educated amateur—might well be simultaneously collecting fossils, engaged in religious controversy, working with a charity that had political goals, and practicing art or journalism. Poems and novels embodied scientific controversies, politicians and public servants wrote fiction, and the names of polymaths such as Annie Besant and William Morris crop up in a wide variety of contexts.

Victorian Britain: An Encyclopedia is intended to serve as an overview and point of entry to the complex interdisciplinary field of Victorian studies. The signed articles, which cover persons, events, institutions, topics, groups, and artifacts in Great Britain between 1837 and 1901, have been written by authorities in the field and contain bibliographies to provide guidance for further research. For undergraduates and general readers, the encyclopedia will be a ready source of names, dates, and explanations. For graduate students and scholars it should be particularly useful as a starting point to explore fields that are not their own: art historians for example, know where to look for information about the arts and crafts movement, but novel-readers or students of economics or religion or engineering who need to know something about the arts and crafts movement will find a brief explanation and a list of the authoritative sources that art historians would use.

Matters of selection and proportion are always a problem for the editor of a reference book. Entries on major figures—about whom information can be found in dozens of standard sources—are deliberately brief in order to leave room for fields that are not so well represented in older works. The entries are restricted to persons and topics whose major work or influence fell within Queen Victoria's reign. In literature, for example, writers whose important books were published before 1837 or after 1901 are generally excluded even though one or two works may have been written during the Victorian period. Articles on concepts or institutions cover only the significant Victorian changes, developments, and influence. The entries focus on Britain, including Ireland, with attention to the colonies and empire as significant aspects of Victorian experience at home.

The disappearance of the Victorian assumptions that control the previous sentence raises certain problems which I have negotiated in ways that are not always consistent. There are, for example, significant political differences between the terms "Indian Mutiny" and

"Sepoy Rebellion" or "Boer War," "Anglo-Boer War," and "South African War." For the convenience of readers, I have alphabetized under the older usages of "Indian Mutiny" and "Boer War," although the text of these and other articles largely preserves the authors' choice of language. On the other hand, I have followed modern practice in referring to public figures—both women and men—by surname alone and without title. And although I have done some editing, I have not imposed a uniform "reference work" style; signed articles were used so that contributors could express their own judgment and opinions.

The alphabetical sequence of titles is a compromise between my sense of where users will expect to find certain information and my desire to keep related entries in the same general vicinity. Thus what might have been "Technical Education" appears as "Education, Technical" so that it will be a neighbor to the other broad articles on education, although "Mechanics Institutes," "Public Schools," "Oxford University," and "Cambridge University" are separate topics in their respective portions of the alphabet. Cross-references are provided in boldface within the entries or as "see also" topics at the end of an entry when there is significant further discussion of a topic or its context. Use the index if you do not find what you are looking for—or even if you do. The index includes mentions too minor for cross-references; thus, for example, the article "New Woman" does not cross-reference everyone referred to by that term, but the index entry lists all of the articles in which it appears.

The bibliography for each entry includes the secondary sources that are considered standard, the most authoritative recent work, and (where they exist) those books or articles that contain extensive bibliographies. The guide to research materials that appears at the end of the volume provides more general help for locating information on special figures or on topics that do not appear in the encyclopedia. It also suggests ways to tap the wealth of Victorian primary sources that (in some cases) have not yet been well mined.

Over the three years that elapsed between the stage of trying to figure out how one figures out what goes in an encyclopedia and the production of a final manuscript, Merrill Distad has been a splendid source of ideas, advice, and suggestions, which I did not always take. For help in locating appropriate contributors, my thanks go to the advisory editors, to Joanne Shattock of the Victorian Studies Centre at the University of Leicester, and to all of the other people who passed along names—particularly those who provided the names of graduate students doing new research that might otherwise not have been located. *Victorian Studies*, the Research Society for Victorian Periodicals, the Midwest Victorian Studies Association, and the Victorian Studies Association of Western Canada allowed me to use their directories and mailing lists. Phil Lapsansky at the Library Company of Philadelphia provided valuable help in securing illustrations. Gary Kuris at Garland Publishing supplied advice that was always prompt, sensible, and friendly. Temple University supported the project with two faculty summer research grants and a grant-in-aid to pay the reproduction fee for some illustrations; the English Department and its Graduate Committee provided an extraordinarily competent research assistant, Michael J. Herr, whose work has been invaluable.

Sally Mitchell

CHRONOLOGY

1837

Victoria becomes queen (June 20)

Prime minister: Viscount Melbourne, April 18, 1835–August 30, 1841 (Whig)

Registrar General's Office established, registration of births made compulsory

Charles Dickens, *Pickwick Papers* (1836–1837)
Oliver Twist (1837–1839)

Houses of Parliament built (1837–1867)

First telegraph equipment patented

Feargus O'Connor founds the *Northern Star*

Anthony Panizzi becomes keeper of the Department of Printed Books at the British Museum

Benjamin Disraeli elected member of Parliament for Maidstone

New Zealand Association (for colonization) founded

Severe smallpox epidemic (1837–1840)

1838

Great Western Railway opens (designed by I. K. Brunel); Great Western paddle steamer crosses Atlantic in under twenty days

Euston Station built

Manchester incorporated as city with local government

Anti-Corn-Law League organized

Afghan Wars (1838–1842)

Public Records Office established

Charles Lyell, *Elements of Geology*

Regulation of licensing hours begins: pubs are closed from midnight Saturday until noon Sunday

1839

Custody of Infants Act gives woman separated from husband right to petition Chancery for right to see her children and for their temporary custody if they are under seven

Educational Committee of the Privy Council Office established; first government agency for supervising education and distributing grants to schools run by the National Society (Anglican) and the British and Foreign Schools Society (Nonconformist)

First Chartist petition presented to Parliament

British Consulate at Jerusalem opens

"Opium War" (1839–1842)

Photographic experiments of Talbot and Daguerre become known

Admiralty orders first iron naval steamer, the *Dover*

Sarah Ellis, *The Women of England*

Catherine Sinclair, *Holiday House*

1840

Queen Victoria marries Prince Albert of Saxe-Coburg-Gotha

Penny post established

Vaccination Act provides free smallpox vaccination to poor

World Antislavery Convention in London refuses to seat women in American delegation

Nottingham laceworkers strike

New Zealand annexed

1841

Prime Minister: Robert Peel, August 30, 1841–June 27, 1846 (Conservative)

"Hungry forties": depression (1841–1842)

Treaty with Austria, France, Russia, and Prussia for suppression of African slave trade

London Library established

Punch begins publication

Chemical Society founded

1842

Railway links Manchester and London

Most major thoroughfares in London are lit by gas

Mines and Collieries Act forbids underground employment in mines for women, girls, and boys under ten

Miners Association of Great Britain formed (union)

Second peak of Chartist agitation

Committee on Health of Towns recommends closing city churchyards

Pentonville model prison opens

Crime rate highest of the century

London Police establish detective department

Nelson's Column built (Trafalgar Square)

China cedes Hong Kong to Britain

Illustrated London News begins publication

1843

Young England coalition forms in Parliament

Free Church of Scotland secedes from established Church of Scotland

National Temperance Society founded

Theatre Regulation Act allows spoken drama at theaters other than Drury Lane and Covent Garden

Thomas Hood, "The Song of the Shirt"

John Ruskin, *Modern Painters*, vol. 1

Thomas Carlyle, *Past and Present*

John Stuart Mill, *A System of Logic*

Charles Dickens, *A Christmas Carol*

Custom of sending Christmas cards begins

1844

Great Western Railway reaches Paddington

J. M. W. Turner, *Rain Steam, and Speed—the Great Western Railway*

Rochdale Equitable Pioneers (cooperative) established

Imprisonment for debt prohibited if amount owed is under 20 pounds

Bank Charter Act begins process that will eventually give the Bank of England a monopoly on the issue of banknotes

Robert Chambers, *The Vestiges of the Natural History of Creation* (proposes a theory of evolution)

Thomas Hood, "The Bridge of Sighs"

P. T. Barnum exhibits Tom Thumb in London

1845

Irish potato crop fails; beginning of the great famine

Benjamin Disraeli, *Sibyl; or the Two Nations*

Friedrich Engels, *The Condition of the Working Class in England*

John Henry Newman converts to Roman Catholicism

Anglican Sisters of the Holy Cross founded

Lunacy Act requires counties to provide asylums

Sikh War (1845–1846)

Eliza Acton, *Modern Cookery for Private Families*

1846

Prime Minister: Lord John Russell, June 30, 1846–February 21, 1852 (Whig)

Corn Laws suspended

"Railway Mania" transforms transportation

Lord Shaftesbury becomes president of the Ragged School Union

Pupil-teacher system established

Robert Liston performs amputation on anaesthetized patient at University College, London

Leben Jesu translated by George Eliot

Hans Christian Andersen's tales translated into English

Edward Lear, *The Book of Nonsense*

G. W. M. Reynolds, *The Mysteries of London* (1846–1848)

1847

Working day in textile mill limited to ten hours for women and children

United Presbyterian Church of Scotland formed

Royal Opera House, Covent Garden, opens

Juvenile Offenders Act makes it possible to dismiss minor charges

Band of Hope (juvenile temperance organization) founded

George Boole, *The Mathematical Analysis of Logic*

Angela Burdett-Coutts establishes Urania Cottage for reformation of prostitutes

William Makepeace Thackeray, *Vanity Fair* (1847–1848)

Emily Brontë, *Wuthering Heights*

Charlotte Brontë, *Jane Eyre*

Alfred Tennyson, *The Princess*

Varney the Vampyre

1848

Cholera epidemic (1848–1849)

Public Health Act; first General Board of Health established

St. John's House (Anglican order) founded to train nurses

Queen's College opens higher education to women

Final Chartist petition presented to Parliament

F. D. Maurice, Charles Kingsley, and J. M. Ludlow begin to form group that became known as Christian socialists

Unsuccessful rebellion in Ireland

Pre-Raphaelite Brotherhood formed

John Stuart Mill, *Principles of Political Economy*

Elizabeth Gaskell, *Mary Barton*

1849

Corn Laws abolished

Agricultural crisis (1849–1853)

Bedford College for Women established

Charles Dickens, *David Copperfield*

1850

Frances Buss founds North London Collegiate School for Girls

Restoration of Roman Catholic hierarchy; Cardinal Wiseman becomes first Archbishop of Westminster

Christian socialists begin tailors' cooperative

Oxford University establishes law school

Public Libraries Act

Alfred Tennyson becomes poet laureate

William Wordsworth, *The Prelude*

Elizabeth Barrett Browning, *Sonnets from the Portuguese*

1851

Great Exhibition (Crystal Palace)

Michael Faraday discovers electromagnetic induction

William Thomson (later Lord Kelvin) publishes first and second laws of thermodynamics

Cambridge University adds degree examination in natural sciences

"The Enfranchisement of Women," by Harriet Taylor Mill, published in *Westminster Review*

Liverpool Children's Hospital established

Amalgamated Society of Engineers (union)

Owens College, Manchester, admits first class

Gold discovered in New South Wales and Victoria, Australia

First formal chess competition in London

John Ruskin, *The King of the Golden River*

1852

Prime minister: Earl of Derby, February 23, 1852–December 17, 1852 (Conservative)
    Earl of Aberdeen, December 19, 1852–January 30, 1855 (Aberdeen Coalition)

New Houses of Parliament opened

Duke of Wellington dies

Burmese War (1852–1853)

Register of Pharmacists established

Spiritualism introduced to England

1853

Smallpox vaccination becomes compulsory

Cholera epidemic (1853–1854)

John Snow administers chloroform to Queen Victoria for Prince Leopold's birth

Duty on advertisements abolished

Cheltenham Ladies' College established

Ticket-of-leave (parole) system established

Amalgamated Association of Operative Cotton Spinners (union)

Charlotte Brontë, *Villette*

1854

Crimean War (1854–1856)

Earl of Cardigan leads charge of light brigade at Balaclava

Construction of London underground begins

Christian socialists establish Working Men's College, London

Reformatories established for offenders under sixteen

Caroline Norton, *English Laws for Women in the Nineteenth Century*

Coventry Patmore, *The Angel in the House* (1854–1856)

Charles Dickens, *Hard Times*

1855

Prime minister: Viscount Palmerston, February 6, 1855–February 21, 1858 (Palmerston Government)

Stamp tax abolished (repeal of duties on newspapers)

Barbara Leigh Smith Bodichon forms Married Women's Property Committee

Metropolitan Board of Works (London) established to provide sewers

Herbert Spencer, *Principles of Psychology*

Fall of Sebastapol

Edward James Loder's opera *Raymond and Agnes*

Australian colonies become self-governing

1856

New Zealand achieves responsible self-government

Rubber teats for nursing bottles become available

William Sterndale Bennett becomes conductor of the Philharmonic Society and professor of music at Cambridge

Anthony Panizzi becomes principal librarian at British Museum

1857

Matrimonial Causes Act makes divorce available without special act of Parliament

Victoria names Albert prince consort

Indian Mutiny (1857–1858)

Sentence of transportation abolished, although some long-term convicts still sent to Australia

Obscene Publications Act

End of Gretna Green elopements: twenty-one days' residence in Scotland required for marriage

British Museum reading room opens

National Association for the Promotion of Social Science formed

Matthew Arnold becomes professor of poetry at Oxford University (1857–1867)

George Eliot, *Scenes of Clerical Life*

Thomas Hughes, *Tom Brown's School Days*

1858

Prime minister: Earl of Derby, February 21, 1858–June 11, 1859 (Conservative)

Papers by Charles Darwin and Alfred Russel Wallace, read at meeting of Linnean Society, propose theory of evolution

Medical Act sets up General Medical Council and establishes register of qualified practitioners

Emancipation of Jews from legal disabilities begins when Lionel de Rothschild is seated in Parliament without taking oath "by the true faith of a Christian"

"Great Stink" caused by sewage in Thames; London metropolitan drainage system begun

English Woman's Journal established

Halle Orchestra founded in Manchester

1859

Prime minister: Viscount Palmerston, June 12, 1859–October 18, 1865 (Liberal)

Charles Darwin, *On the Origin of Species Through Natural Selection*

Samuel Smiles, *Self-Help*

John Stuart Mill, *On Liberty*

London building workers' strike (1859–1860)

Reforms in conditions of naval service initiated

Elizabeth Blackwell has name placed on register of qualified physicians

I. K. Brunel's *Great Eastern*, the largest ship of the century

Alfred Tennyson, *Idylls of the King* (1869–1874)

George Eliot, *Adam Bede*

Macmillan's Magazine begins publication

Dog shows established at Newcastle

1860

Nightingale Training School for Nurses established

Emily Faithfull founds Victoria Press

Essays and Reviews

John Ruskin, *Unto This Last*

George Eliot, *The Mill on the Floss*

Wilkie Collins, *The Woman in White*

Cornhill Magazine begins publication

Establishment of Battersea Dog's Home, the first animal shelter

1861

Prince Albert dies of typhoid

Duty on paper abolished

Maria Rye establishes Female Middle-Class Emigration Society

H.M.S. *Warrior*, first iron-hulled warship, has both steam and full sail power

Hymns Ancient and Modern

Isabella Beeton, *Book of Household Management*

Charles Dickens, *Great Expectations*

Ellen Price Wood, *East Lynne*

Francis Palgrave, *Golden Treasury*

1862

Thames Embankment begun; Westminster Bridge built

Revised education code begins payment by results

Cotton famine caused by U.S. Civil War; 500,000 people in textile districts receive poor relief or private charity

John Ruskin, *Unto This Last*

Christina Rossetti, *Goblin Market and Other Poems*

Mary Elizabeth Braddon, *Lady Audley's Secret*

1863

Steam-powered subway begins operation on Metropolitan Line

Cambridge Local Examinations experimentally opened to girls

Cooperative Wholesale Society established

Football Association founded; Cambridge University Football rules standardize soccer

Charles Kingsley, *The Water Babies*

1864

Octavia Hill buys three slum houses to begin plan of model lodgings

Contagious Disease Acts passed to register and examine prostitutes in port and garrison towns

Early English Text Society formed

John Henry Newman, *Apologia pro vita sua*

Algernon Charles Swinburne, *Atalanta in Calydon*

1865

Prime minister: Earl Russell, October 29, 1865–June 26, 1866 (Liberal)

Barbara Bodichon forms Women's Suffrage Committee

Reform League founded to press for franchise for working-class men

Steam tonnage in Lloyd's Register of Shipping exceeds sailing ships

Joseph Lister promotes use of antiseptics to prevent infection during childbirth

Commons Preservation Society founded

Lewis Carroll, *Alice's Adventures in Wonderland*

1866

Prime minister: Earl of Derby, June 28, 1866–February 25, 1868 (Conservative)

Women's suffrage petition presented to Parliament by John Stuart Mill

Atlantic telegraph cable completed

Emily Davies founds London School Mistresses Association

Metropolitan Fire Brigade comes under public control

Last major cholera epidemic

Aunt Judy's Magazine begins publication

Algernon Swinburne, *Poems and Ballads*

1867

Second Reform Bill extends vote to all male householders in boroughs

W. E. Gladstone becomes leader of Liberal party

Agricultural Gangs Act forbids mixed sexes and children under eight on public gangs

Abyssinian War (1867–1868)

Dominion of Canada created

Diamonds discovered in South Africa

Last convict ship sent to Western Australia

Matthew Arnold, "Dover Beach"

Hesba Stretton, *Jessica's First Prayer*

First women's golf club formed

1868

Prime minister: Benjamin Disraeli, February 27, 1868–December 1, 1868 (Conservative) W. E. Gladstone, December 3, 1868–February 17, 1874 (Liberal)

Trades Union Congress established

Ursula Mellor Bright and Elizabeth Wolstone-

holme Elmy form Married Women's Property Committee

London University admits women to examinations

Eliza Lynn Linton, "The Girl of the Period"

Last public hanging

Church rates abolished

Robert Browning, *The Ring and the Book*

Wilkie Collins, *The Moonstone*

1869

Suez Canal opens

Single, property-owning women achieve vote in municipal elections

Josephine Butler founds Ladies' National Association for Repeal of the Contagious Diseases Acts

Emily Davies establishes women's residence at Cambridge that will become Girton College

First group of women medical students admitted at Edinburgh (but eventually not permitted to finish required courses)

J. S. Mill, *The Subjection of Women*

Disestablishment of Anglican church in Ireland

Charitable Organization Society founded

Metaphysical Society formed; T. H. Huxley coins term "agnosticism"

Poor Law Amendmant Act makes it an offense for parents to neglect children under fourteen; Maria Rye begins large-scale efforts to send homeless children to colonies

Headmasters Conference (public schools) founded

Imprisonment for debt abolished

Sea Birds Preservation Act (first legislation to protect wildlife)

Nature (science journal) begins publication

Matthew Arnold, *Culture and Anarchy*

Francis Galton, *Hereditary Genius*

1870

W. E. Forster's Education Act establishes principle that elementary education shall be available to all children in England and Wales

First Married Women's Property Act: women have right to their own wages earned after marriage, certain investments, and legacies under 200 pounds

Women eligible to serve as Poor Law guardians and members of school boards; Emily Davies takes seat on London School Board

Home Government Association founded in Ireland (in 1873 becomes Home Rule League)

United Synagogue Act formalizes authority of chief rabbi and organization of member congregations

Open competitive examinations for the civil service instituted

Increased pace of British Empire expansion begins

Thomas Barnardo opens first home for orphans

Charles Dickens dies

During the decade, birth rate peaks at 36.3/1,000

1871

Trade unions legalized

Engineering workers win strike for nine-hour day

Purchase of army commissions abolished

Religious tests for university matriculation and graduation ended

Cavendish Laboratories established at Cambridge University

Women's Education Union founded

Rugby Football Union established

Stanley and Livingstone meet at Lake Tanganyika

Charles Darwin, *Descent of Man*

George Eliot, *Middlemarch* (1871–1872)

First of Bracebridge Hemyng's "Jack Harkaway" stories published in *Boys of England*

1872

Voting by secret ballot instituted

Maria Shirreff Grey founds Girls' Public Day School Company (later Trust)

Slade School of Art opened to women

Infant Life Protection Act regulates baby farming

Peak in amount of land under tillage; in mid-1870s golden age of British agriculture ends

Agricultural Labourers Union founded

Thomas Cook offers tour around the world

Samuel Butler, *Erewhon*

1873

East India Company dissolved

James Clerk Maxwell, *Treatise on Electricity and Magnetism*

H.M.S. *Devastation*: turret warship wholly powered by steam (no auxiliary sails)

Jane Hughes Senior appointed first woman inspector of workhouses and pauper schools

Mary Ward and others establish lectures for ladies in Oxford

New Shakespeare Society founded

John Stuart Mill, *Autobiography*

Walter Pater, *Studies in the History of the Renaissance*

1874

Prime minister: Benjamin Disraeli, February 20, 1874–April 21, 1880 (Conservative)

Repeal of patronage for Church of Scotland

Factory Act establishes fifty-six hour work week

Helen Blackburn becomes president of National Woman's Suffrage Society

Emma Paterson founds Women's Protective and Provident League

London Medical College for Women established

John Richard Green, *A Short History of the English People*

James Thompson, *A City of Dreadful Night*

Safety bicycle patented

1875

Peaceful picketing legalized

Emma Paterson and Edith Simcox are first women delegates to TUC Congress

Judicature Act establishes formal court of appeal

Age of consent raised to thirteen

Women clerks hired by National Savings Bank

Bedford Park is first planned "Garden Suburb"

Trial by Jury—first Gilbert and Sullivan success

1876

Medical licensing bodies given the power to examine women; Irish College of Physicians is the first to open its examinations

British Women's Temperance Association established

Invention of the telephone

Post office establishes women's clerical branch

Cruelty to Animals Act creates licensing procedures and guidelines for animal research

1877

Annie Besant and Charles Bradlaugh tried for publishing inexpensive book on birth control

Society for the Protection of Ancient Buildings created

Library Association founded

Transvaal annexed

Wimbledon Club standardizes rules of lawn tennis

Anna Sewell, *Black Beauty*

1878

Salvation Army formed

Ebbw Vale colliery accident kills 269 miners

Zulu War (1878-1879)

Women admitted to lectures at Oxford; Maria Grey Training College for Teachers established; University of London degrees opened to women

James O'Grady, *History of Ireland: The Heroic Period* retells myths and heroic tales

Henry Irving becomes manager of Lyceum Theatre

Electric lights installed in machine rooms of the *Times*

Thomas Hardy, *The Return of the Native*

1879

Louis Pasteur identifies the organisms that cause puerperal fever

Suicide no longer considered homicide

George Grove, *Dictionary of Music and Musicians* (4 vols., 1879-1880)

Somerville Hall and Lady Margaret Hall established at Oxford

George Meredith, *The Egoist*

Boy's Own Paper begins publication

1880

Prime minister: W. E. Gladstone, April 23, 1880-June 9, 1885 (Liberal)

Elementary education made compulsory ages seven to ten

First South African War (1880-1881)

William Archer's translation of *The Pillar of Society* is first London performance of Ibsen

Ouida, *Moths*

During this decade, gaslights begin to be installed in newly built homes

1881

Irish Land Acts provide some land reforms in Ireland

New civil service grade of woman clerk established

Women allowed to take Cambridge honours exams

H. M. Hyndman founds (Social) Democratic Federation

Flogging abolished in army

Savoy Theatre opens, the first to be lit by electricity

William Poel produces first quarto *Hamlet* for New Shakespeare Society

1882

Married Women's Property Act: women have right to all their property earned or acquired before or after marriage

Entail of property restricted

Egyptian war; Britain occupies Cairo

Society for Psychical Research founded

Suicides permitted daylight burial

First shipment of meat in cold storage from New Zealand

Robert Louis Stevenson, *Treasure Island*

1883

Corrupt Practices Act limits electoral expenditure

Oxford founds professorship in classical archaeology

Finsbury Technical Institute established

First electric tram in operation

Olive Schreiner, *The Story of an African Farm*

1884

Third Reform Bill extends franchise to all male householders

Fabian Society founded

Octavia Hill takes charges of houses for Ecclesiastical Commission

London Society for Prevention of Cruelty to Children formed

Louisa Twining elected to Kensington Board of Guardians

Toynbee Hall Settlement founded at Whitechapel

Steam turbine for generation of electricity invented

Britain signs International Patent Convention

Victoria University, Manchester, opens (coeducational)

First section of *Oxford English Dictionary* published

First ladies' singles championship in tennis held

1885

Prime minister: Marquis of Salisbury, June 23, 1885–January 28, 1886 (Conservative)

Football League formed to control professional soccer matches

Criminal Law Amendment Act raises age of consent for girls to sixteen and makes sexual acts between males an offense

Gold discovered in Transvaal

Khartoum falls, General Gordon killed

James McNeill Whistler's "Ten O'Clock" lecture, a manifesto of "art for art's sake"

Dictionary of National Biography (1885–1900)

1886

Prime minister: W. E. Gladstone, February 1, 1886–July 20, 1886 (Liberal)
           Marquis of Salisbury, July 25, 1886–August 11, 1892 (Conservative)

Irish Home Rule bill defeated in the House of Commons

Infant Custody Act: mother gains right to custody of child if father dies (previously, his will could name any guardian)

Contagious Disease Acts repealed

Riots in Trafalgar Square protest unemployment

Robert B. Cunningham Graham becomes first avowed socialist M.P.

Mansfield College established as Oxford University's first college for Nonconformists

Remington Typewriter Company establishes dealerships in Britain

First safety bicycles manufactured for sale at Coventry

Robert Louis Stevenson, *The Strange Case of Dr. Jekyll and Mr. Hyde*

Marie Corelli, *A Romance of Two Worlds*

1887

Celebration of Queen Victoria's Golden Jubilee

"Bloody Sunday" riots in Trafalgar Square, November 13

Arthur Conan Doyle, *A Study in Scarlet*

1888

London County Council created

First large electric power station built in London

Strike by matchworkers at Bryant and May's

Charter granted to British East Africa Company

"Jack the Ripper" murders

Arts and Crafts Exhibition Society formed

Nellie Melba makes debut at Covent Garden

Mrs. Humphry Ward, *Robert Elsmere*

Oscar Wilde, *The Happy Prince and Other Tales*

Rudyard Kipling, *Plain Tales from the Hills*

1889

London Dock Strike

Miners Federation of Great Britain established

Beckton gasworkers achieve eight-hour day

An act for the prevention of cruelty to children allows neglected or abused children to be removed from their parents

Technical Instruction Act

W. B. Yeats's *The Wanderings of Oisin and Other Poems* begins Irish literary renaissance

Andrew Lang, *Blue Fairy Book*

1890

Eleanor Marx organizes first English May Day celebration

Subways electrified

Forth bridge completed

Alfred Marshall, *Principles of Economics*

William Morris, *News from Nowhere*

James Frazer, *The Golden Bough*

William Booth, *In Darkest England and the Way Out*

1891

Fees abolished in most state elementary schools

United States agrees to end sanction of literary piracy

Shopworkers union formed; admits men and women equally

Oscar Wilde, *Picture of Dorian Gray*

Thomas Hardy, *Tess of the d'Urbervilles*

George Gissing, *New Grub Street*

1892

Prime minister: W. E. Gladstone, August 15, 1892–March 2, 1894 (Liberal)

James Kier Hardie elected to Parliament as Independent Labour delegate

Sidney Webb and five other Fabians elected to London County Council

Israel Zangwill, *Children of the Ghetto*

G. B. Shaw's *Widower's Houses* performed

Oscar Wilde, *Lady Windermere's Fan*

1893

Irish Home Rule Bill defeated in House of Lords

Gaelic League founded

Miners strike successfully resists 25 percent pay cut

Education (Blind and Deaf Children) Act establishes special schools

New Zealand becomes first country in world with universal adult suffrage

Oxford University abolishes requirement that women attending lectures be chaperoned

George Gissing, *The Odd Women*

1894

Prime minister: Earl of Rosebery, March 5, 1894–June 21, 1895 (Liberal)

Manchester Ship Canal opens

Local Government Act guarantees local franchise to married women

Emmeline Pankhurst elected to Chorlton Board of Guardians

Mudie's and Smith's libraries ban three-volume novel

George Moore, *Esther Waters*

Oscar Wilde's *Salomé*, with illustrations by Aubrey Beardsley, published in England

Rudyard Kipling, *Jungle Book*

1895

Prime minister: Marquis of Salisbury, June 25, 1895–July 11, 1902 (Conservative)

Jameson Raid attempts to overthrow Transvaal government

London School of Economics founded

Oscar Wilde sentenced to prison

All-England Women's Hockey Association formed

Grant Allen, *The Woman Who Did*

H. G. Wells, *The Time Machine*

Thomas Hardy, *Jude the Obscure*

1896

Cinema begins at Empire Theatre

A. E. Housman, *A Shropshire Lad*

Arthur Morrison, *A Child of the Jago*

Daily Mail (halfpenny evening newspaper)

1897

Queen Victoria's Diamond Jubilee

Workmen's Compensation Act

Millicent Garrett Fawcett becomes president of National Union of Women's Suffrage Societies

National Portrait Gallery opens

Sarah Grand, *The Beth Book*

First volume of Havelock Ellis, *Studies in the Psychology of Sex*

Bram Stoker, *Dracula*

1898

West Ham becomes first council to be controlled by Labour

Thomas Hardy, *Wessex Poems*

1899

Boer War (1899–1902)

First milk depot offering sterilized milk for infant feeding

First motor bus in service

W. B. Yeats's *The Countess Cathleen* performed

1900

Boxer Rebellion in China

Emmeline Pankhurst elected to Manchester School Board

Free Church of Scotland and United Presbyterian Church of Scotland unite

Joseph Conrad, *Lord Jim*

1901

Queen Victoria dies, January 22

Commonwealth of Australia comes into being

Factory Act forbids employment of children under twelve in any factory or workshop

Rudyard Kipling, *Kim*

Edward Elgar, *Pomp and Circumstance*

Beatrix Potter, *The Tale of Peter Rabbit*

THE ENCYCLOPEDIA

ABORTION

The termination of a pregnancy by any means was punishable as a felony in Victorian Britain. Despite the illegality and the difficulty of procuring a safe or effective abortifacient, women clearly regarded abortion as an acceptable means of fertility control. Traditional methods adopted by Victorian women included herbal remedies, such as tansy, squill, ergot, and pennyroyal, as well as hot baths and vigorous exercise. More dangerous practices involved the use of knitting needles or other sharp instruments to induce miscarriages. By the end of the century, working-class women in the Midlands had begun using white lead as an abortifacient. While lead was easy to obtain and effective if taken in large enough quantities, it had serious and sometimes lethal side effects.

Married working-class women were probably the most frequent users of traditional means of abortion. Middle-class women also sought abortions from midwives or medical men willing to ignore the law and used the many medicines that were advertised as cures for "female complaints" but were often thinly disguised abortifacients. In one famous case, the Chrimes brothers, makers of Lady Montrose's Female Tabules, were charged with blackmailing 12,000 women who had bought their ineffective abortifacients. The extent of the demand for such worthless concoctions is one indication of the number of Victorian women seeking to control their reproductive lives.

ANN R. HIGGINBOTHAM

Bibliography

Knight, Patricia. "Women and Abortion in Victorian and Edwardian England." *History Workshop*, vol. 4, pp. 57-68.

McLaren, Angus. *Birth Control in Nineteenth-Century England*. 1978.

Sauer, R. "Infanticide and Abortion in Nineteenth-Century Britain." *Population Studies*, vol. 32, pp. 81-93.

Smith, F. B. *The People's Health, 1830-1910*. 1979.

Taylor, Alfred S. *The Principles and Practice of Medical Jurisprudence*. 1894. 2 vols.

Whitley, William F. "Criminal Abortion and Abortifacients." *Public Health*, February 28, 1915, pp. 104-106.

. . . . .

ABRAHAMS, ISRAEL (1858-1924)

Israel Abrahams used academic scholarship both to provide sympathetic portrayals of Jews and Judaism, particularly Rabbinic Judaism, for Christian audiences and to persuade fellow Jews of the legitimacy of religious reform. He was appointed reader in Rabbinics at Cambridge in 1902, succeeding Solomon Schechter.

Abrahams was instrumental in establishing the Jewish Historical Society of England (1893), which documented the roots of Jewry in Britain. Although his work was characterized by an apologetic tone, Abrahams distinguished himself as a social historian of medieval Jewry and as a bulwark of intellectual Judaism in England. His combination of scholarship and theology twice led to his consideration for presidency of Hebrew Union College, the leading Reform rabbinical school in the United States. He utilized the critical study of the past to legitimate ritual changes such as mixed pews and prayer without a head covering, and lent an academic stature to the nascent Jewish Religious Union, as Liberal Judaism was known in England.

Despite Abraham's partisan theological stance, he maintained strong links with other segments of Anglo-Jewry. He collaborated in scholarship with his father-in-law, the Orthodox minister Simeon Singer. Although an anti-Zionist, as were most Liberal Jews in England, Abrahams supported the concept of a Jewish university in Jerusalem. Abrahams aimed particularly to inculcate beliefs and dogma and to restore religious feeling rather than to advance the cause of biblical criticism. Although essentially a scholar, Abrahams perceived scholarship as a tool for Jewish renewal.

STEVEN BAYME

Bibliography

Hyamson, Albert M. *Israel Abrahams: A Memoir.* 1940.

Loewe, Herbert M. J. *Israel Abrahams: A Biographical Sketch.* 1944.

See also JEWRY AND JUDAISM

· · · · ·

ACADEMIC PAINTING

Academic painting in Victorian England was characterized by a variety of style and genre unparalleled in Europe. This was due to the liberal policies of the Royal Academy of Arts (founded 1768), which departed from the European example of strong theoretical principles and strict hierarchy of genre. The annual summer academy exhibitions provided artists with a showcase for the purchase of their work. Those that attracted the largest crowds and subsequently a buyer, or the purchase of rights to engrave for popular sale, were judged the most successful. Therefore academic painting in Britain was a matter not so much of style and content as it was of the influence of popularity and changing taste.

The audience for academic painting was the newly rich middle class who regarded collecting as a demonstration of taste. Selection policy was liberal; submission was not limited to members of the academy. An artist therefore was concerned with drawing the attention of a potential purchaser amid the up to 2,000 works on exhibition. Placement in the installation was of primary significance. The best place was eye level or "on the line," a ledge located eight feet above the ground. In the National Gallery at Trafalgar Square (1837-1868) large pictures could be hung only above the line; a smaller format therefore ensured better location. After the move to Burlington House (1869), the line was eliminated and large-scale pictures came into fashion. The truest test of success was the placement of a rail to keep the public at a safe distance, a precaution first implemented for David Wilkie's *Chelsea Pensioners* (Victoria and Albert Museum) in 1822.

Although technical standards demanded expert draftsmanship and fine surface finish, subject and style reflected changing taste. During the presidential tenure of Martin Archer Shee (1830–1850), the sentimental genre of **William Mulready** (1786–1863) and **Edwin Landseer** (1802–1873) shared popularity with the extravagant literary themes of Daniel Maclise (1806–1870) and the austere history painting of William Dyce (1806–1864). Academy pictures during the presidency of Charles Lock Eastlake (1850–1865) revealed a strong interest in modern life and moral genre as seen in the works of **Augustus Leopold Egg** (1816–1863), Thomas Faed (1826–1900), and Henry Nelson O'Neil (1817–1880). **John Everett Millais's** (1829–1896) *Order of Release* (1853; Tate Gallery) required a police guard to hold back the crowds. The rail was employed for William Powell Frith's (1819–1909) *Derby Day* (1858; Tate Gallery), a picture of unusual scale and meticulous detail acclaimed for its realism. Also popular were chivalric works based on literature, often painted in the Pre-Raphaelite style and submitted by nonmembers.

The terms of Francis Grant (1866–1878) and Frederic, Lord Leighton (1878–1896) saw three major trends. Sentimental historical genre paintings such as Millais's *The Boyhood of Raleigh* (1870; Tate Gallery) enjoyed popularity in the early years. Of increasing interest was social realism, seen in the works of Luke Fildes (1843–1927), **Hubert von Herkomer** (1849–1914), and Frank Holl (1845–1888). The stellar works of the Leighton era were grand, neoclassical visions such as those of Edward Poynter (1836–1919), *A Visit to Aesculapius* (1880; Tate Gallery); Leighton, *Captive Andromache* (1888; Manchester City Art Gallery); and Lawrence Alma-Tadema (1836–1912), *The Roses of Helioga-*

bolus (1896; private collection). The only rival in sentimental genre was Millais's *Bubbles* (1896; A. & F. Pears), which was the first academic painting to be purchased for use in advertising. Preferences for neoclassicism and social realism continued through Millais's brief presidency in 1896 and that of Poynter (1896–1918).

Academic painting in Victorian Britain was a reflection of popular taste. Unlike European academies, the Royal Academy never employed strong policy opposing progressive trends. Although artists such as Dante Gabriel Rossetti (1828–1882) never exhibited at the Royal Academy and Edward Burne-Jones (1833–1898) exhibited only once, this was by choice, not by proscription. The whole panoply of Victorian art can be found in Victorian academic painting.

DEBRA N. MANCOFF

Bibliography

Arts Council of Great Britain. *Great Victorian Pictures*. 1978.

Forbes, Christopher. *The Royal Academy (1837–1901) Revisited*. 1975.

Graves, Algernon. *The Royal Academy of Arts: A Complete Dictionary of Contributors and Their Work from Its Foundation in 1769 to 1904*. 1905. 8 vols.

Hutchison, Sidney C. *The History of the Royal Academy, 1768–1968*. 1968.

See also GENRE PAINTING;
HISTORY PAINTING; ROYAL
ACADEMY OF ARTS

· · · · ·

ACTON, WILLIAM
(1813–1875)

A medical practitioner specializing in sex and sexual diseases, William Acton published *A Complete Practical Treatise on Venereal Diseases* in 1841. His *Prostitution: Considered in Its Moral, Social and Sanitary Aspects* appeared in 1857. He published a second edition of the *Treatise* in 1851 under

the title *A Practical Treatise on the Diseases of the Urinary and Generative Organs* and a third, abridged version in 1857 under yet another title: *The Functions and Disorders of the Re-productive Organs*, with further editions in 1865, 1871, and 1875. Acton's medical writings reflect little research or originality; they rely heavily on the publications of other medical writers. They nevertheless brought him a growing reputation.

Educated at St. Bartholomew's Hospital, London, and at the Venereal Hospitals in Paris, Acton was qualified as surgeon and apothecary and practiced in London from the 1830s onward. He was surgeon to the Islington Dispensary. He was married, apparently late in life, for he had infant children when he was fifty years old. His estate, valued at nearly 25,000 pounds, suggests that his practice was lucrative.

Acton exemplifies the power of self-promotion in Victorian medical practice. His venereal specialization and the content and style of his writings suggest that he was a medical "freebooter." His widely quoted writings on sexuality should not, therefore, be uncritically accepted, nor is it safe to consider him a typical Victorian doctor or a spokesman for the medical profession.

M. JEANNE PETERSON

Bibliography

Marcus, Steven. *The Other Victorians: A Study of Sexuality and Pornography in Mid-Nineteenth-Century England*. 1964.

Peterson, M. Jeanne. "Dr. Acton's Enemy: Medicine, Sex, and Society in Victorian England." *Victorian Studies*, vol. 29, pp. 569–590.

———.*The Medical Profession in Mid-Victorian London*. 1978.

· · · · ·

ACTORS AND THE
ACTING PROFESSION

At the beginning of Victoria's reign actors were regarded as social outcasts, however much individual performers might be publicly lionized. Moreover, female actors were judged by harsh moral standards and their position as professional women ran counter to Victorian ideals of womanhood. At midcentury the position of actors had not changed, but by 1880, abetted by the fact that many of their number now came from solid middle-class origins, actors could earn a substantial livelihood from their craft and society was able to accept, through the personal examples of Madge Kendal, **Marie Wilton Bancroft**, **Mrs. Patrick Campbell**, **Ellen Terry**, and Lily Langtry, that the profession could encompass the respectable and the glamorous.

Until the 1870s the actor's life both in London and the provinces was precarious. The only training was that provided by provincial stock companies which demanded up to fifteen hours a day of rehearsal and performance with a nightly change of program. The system demanded extreme versatility. Actors had to be willing to accept low wages (from 15 to 30 shillings per week), to take any roles the manager thought fit to assign, to provide the necessary personal costumes, makeup, and props, and to endure primitive lodgings and backstage conditions. Star performers, however, remained throughout the period a breed apart. Even in the 1830s star actors in London could earn 50 to 100 pounds per week, and leading actors in the provinces by the 1850s were able to earn 200 to 300 pounds per year.

Perhaps the most dramatic changes in acting conditions arose at the end of the 1860s with the establishment of long-running productions which, together with seasonal contracts, allowed actors more leisure time and a greater security of employment. At the same time, the popularity and proliferation of music halls, which by 1866 allowed versatile performers to earn 20 to 30 pounds a night with short turns at various venues, measurably increased employment opportunities. This popularity, however, brought the question of status sharply into focus. Increasingly, from 1870 actors sought to emphasize their social respectability and their claims to salaried professional status. Though many succeeded in attaining social respectability—as evidenced by the knighthoods granted to **Henry Irving** (1895) and **Squire Bancroft** (1897)—the other aims were frustrated by the financial chasm between stars and rank-and-file performers, by the absence of formal training institutions, and by the increasing exclusive-

ness of London's actor-managers. Only in 1891, with the formation of the Actors Association, was any formal attempt made to professionalize actors. This organization, however, proved merely to serve the interests of well-heeled West End managers; not until 1919 was the association reorganized as a trade union.

Though the overall status of the profession was low, the history of Victorian theater is marked by a series of significant actor-managements in the provinces and London. **William Charles Macready**, as manager of Covent Garden (1837–1839) and of Drury Lane (1841–1843), attempted to raise the moral tone of the patent theaters and reform rehearsal practices and production techniques. At the same time **Madame Vestris** was concluding her management of the "minor" Olympic Theatre. Since 1830 her productions of Planché's extravaganzas and vaudeville comedies had been characterized by attention to scenic detail and the performances of an acting company which included John Liston, the most popular low comedian of the early period, and Charles James Mathews, whose restrained acting style anticipated developments in realistic performance.

After the removal of the patent theater monopoly in 1843, Samuel Phelps began his management of Sadler's Wells Theatre (1844–1864). As an actor, Phelps was immensely versatile. Known for his restraint in performance, he was able to establish a coherent house style for his company. His example was followed by **Charles Kean**, especially during his management of the Princess's Theatre (1851–1859). Kean was identified with French-derived melodrama and spectacular Shakespearean revivals performed with antiquarian authenticity and a detailed realistic acting style.

Stage reform and the movement toward ensemble acting were further advanced by the Bancrofts during their management of the Prince of Wales's Theatre (1865–1879). The arrival of realistically motivated behavior on stage was hastened as well by the influence of foreign actors like Charles Fechter, Adelaide Ristory, Edwin Booth, and Tomasso Salvini, though often their extravagantly emotional performances and innovations in costume or business caused considerable critical hostility.

Although by 1860 there was a distinct tendency toward a quieter acting style, broad comic performances persisted at theaters like the Haymarket under the managements of Benjamin Webster (1837–1853) and John Buckstone (1853–1878), and traditional melodramatic acting could still be enjoyed at the Adelphi under the Webster–Madame Celeste management (1844–1858) and the Surrey under the Shepherd-Creswick management (1848–1869). Furthermore, despite the move toward ensemble, the preeminence of star performers remained undiminished throughout the period. In fact, 1880 to the end of the Victorian period can be identified as the era of the great actor-managers. From 1860 the development of music hall entertainers and variety artists, some of whom moved fluidly between straight drama and the musical theater, emphasized the continuing diversity within British acting.

Theaters in the second half of the period started to identify themselves by their dramatic fare. Performers as well were identified by their particular style of playing. Henry Irving combined unexpected idosyncratic details of character with physical expressiveness and stage business, paying particular attention to the totality of his role. In this he was complemented by Ellen Terry's admired grace and sense of spontaneity. **Herbert Beerbohm Tree** was identified as a character actor, particularly powerful in extravagant, sinister roles.

Just as distinctive were actors who concentrated on the polite comedies and society dramas of the end of the century and whose pedigree derived from the pioneering work of the Bancrofts in fostering quiet "natural" acting and meticulous stage management. Among them were **John Hare**, Madge Kendal, **Charles Wyndham** (whose forte was light urbane comedy and who was arguably the first matinee idol), and **George Alexander**, whose management of the St. James's Theater made it the most genteel in London, purveying society drama and sophisticated comedy. Among the actresses of the late Victorian period, Mrs. Patrick Campbell was preeminent in ironic comedy and society drama, and it was she, together with Janet Achurch and Elizabeth Robins, who brought Ibsen to public attention.

The development of acting in the Victorian period therefore can be roughly traced along two parallel lines. On the one hand, as a reaction to the unashamedly self-centered artifice of the pre-Victorian period, actors increasingly sought a quieter, integrated performance style usually labeled "natural" but which owed nothing to "naturalism." On the other hand, the tradition of the star performer refused to die and actively militated against ensemble playing or self-effacement. The two lines coexisted and on occasions came together. The history of Victorian acting, however, is more often than not one of diversity and the active promotion of personal idiosyncrasy.

VICTOR EMELJANOW

Bibliography

Archer, William. *Masks or Faces?* 1888.

Baker, Michael. *The Rise of the Victorian Actor.* 1978.

Donaldson, Frances. *The Actor-Managers.* 1970.

Downer, Alan. "Players and Painted Stage: Nineteenth Century Acting." *PMLA*, vol. 61, pp. 522–576.

Fitzgerald, Percy H. *The Art of Acting.* 1892.

Kent, Christopher. "Image and Reality: The Actress and Society." In Martha Vicinus, ed., *A Widening Sphere: Changing Roles of Victorian Women.* 1977.

Lewes, George H. *On Actors and the Art of Acting.* 1875.

Mullin, Donald, ed. *Victorian Actors and Actresses in Review: A Dictionary of Contemporary Views.* 1983.

Sanderson, Michael. *From Irving to Olivier: A Social History of the Acting Profession in England, 1880–1983.* 1984.

See also THEATERS AND STAGING

· · · · ·

ADAMS, SARAH FLOWER (1805–1848)

Sarah Flower Adams is known chiefly for the hymn "Nearer, My God, to Thee." She wrote a poetic drama, *Vivia Perpetua* (1841), about a woman martyr. Her lyrics and hymns appear in Victorian collections. She contributed to the

Monthly Repository (1832–1836), wrote "poetical notices" for the *Westminster Review,* and published a historical poem, "The Royal Progress," in the *Illuminated Magazine* (1845).

Adams belonged to the circle amiably satirized by Leigh Hunt in "Blue-Stocking Revels" (1837). Centered on W. J. Fox, it included her sister Eliza Flower, Harriet Taylor, (later **Harriet Taylor Mill**) **Harriet Martineau,** and Margaret and Mary Gillies. Adams was the daughter of Benjamin Flower, editor of the *Cambridge Intelligencer.* His unconventional upbringing of his motherless girls is described in Harriet Martineau's *Five Years of Youth* (1831). She married W. B. Adams, a railway engineer of fiercely radical persuasion, the "Junius Redivivus" of the *Monthly Repository.*

Adams is particularly interesting in this circle of radicals for expressing their shared perception of the importance of aesthetic emotion in religious feeling and their corresponding equation of nature and art as agents in moral life. The themes are combined in "York Minster and the Forest Bugle" (*Monthly Repository,* 1836). Her work is idealistic and delicate, but the liberating democratic tendencies are confined by the necessarily adversarial position of the dissenting radical.

SHELAGH HUNTER

Bibliography

Garnett, Richard. *The Life of W. J. Fox: Public Teacher and Social Reformer, 1786–1864.* 1910.

Miles, Alfred H. and others. *The Poets and the Poetry of the Century.* 1892–1897. 10 vols.

Mineka, Francis. *The Dissidence of Dissent: The Monthly Repository, 1806–1838.* 1944.

Taylor, Emily. *Memories of Some Contemporary Poets: With Selections from Their Writings.* 1868.

. . . . .

ADLER, NATHAN M.
(1803–1890)

A German-born rabbi, Nathan M. Adler was elected in 1844 as chief rabbi of Britain, succeeding Solomon Hirschell. He served until 1879 when, citing ill health, he appointed his son Hermann Adler as delegate chief rabbi.

Adler's tenure signified a transformation of the chief rabbinate. Previously the incumbent had functioned as the rabbi of London's leading synagogues. Adler centralized the institution as the official "address" of Anglo-Judaism. Under his tutelage Parliament in 1870 adopted the United Synagogue Act, formalizing the authority of the chief rabbi among the federated member congregations of the United Synagogue, following the model of the Anglican church. In 1855 Adler established Jews' College as a training ground for Jewish ministers. Among the clergy he possessed a virtual monopoly of rabbinical authority.

Most controversial were Adler's battles with English Reform Judaism. He excommunicated Reform and banned marriages with Reform Jews. The needs of communal unity, however, necessitated compromise. In 1849 he lifted the ban on Reform Jews (thereby permitting marriages), although it remained on Reform congregations. He even consented to certain changes within the United Synagogue itself, notably shortening the sabbath service and introducing an English sermon. These changes were consonant with Adler's distinctive blend of modernity and tradition.

Apparently he questioned his own achievements. In 1885 he warned Jews to avoid Britain, citing both economic difficulties and those of maintaining Jewish traditions. Yet he did symbolize a new era in which the chief rabbi articulated the "Victorian compromise" of being both Englishman and Jew.

STEVEN BAYME

Bibliography

Gartner, Lloyd. *The Jewish Immigrant in England.* 2nd ed., 1973.

Williams, Bill. *The Making of Manchester Jewry.* 1976.

See also JEWRY AND JUDAISM

. . . . .

ADVICE MANUALS

Advice manuals provide information and guidance on a wide range of topics, including household management, etiquette, success in careers, health, child care, fashion, education, entertainment, and conduct or morals. Advice manuals are written for a largely middle-class readership, and thus differ from self-help books, which attempt to help working-class people improve their political and social status through self-education.

Advice manuals have a long history as courtesy books, cookery books, domestic conduct manuals and guides for raising children. In the nineteenth century, with rising rates of literacy, increased social mobility, and a population shift to urban areas, advice manuals became extremely popular. The growing middle class confronted new standards and styles of living at a time when religious and family tradition were losing their usefulness and prestige. Women, for example, often wanted to improve on the ways of their mothers and grandmothers, who in any case were often too far away to give advice. Isabella Beeton's *Book of Household Management* (1861) sold over 60,000 copies in its first year.

Advice manuals are useful to scholars because they provide insights into values and details of ordinary life not always supplied by histories or novels, but there is some question as to how accurately they reflect reality. Some manuals are relevant to studies of feminism, since they address themselves to the nature and duties of the sexes, but they tend to be conservative in their outlook. Furthermore, advice (in general) is prescriptive, reflecting what authors believe people should do rather than describing their usual behavior. Some typical advice manuals of the nineteenth century include: Thomas Bull's *Hints to Mothers, for the Management of Health During the Period of Pregnancy, and in the Lying-In Room* (1837); *Cassell's Household Guide* (1871); William Cobbett's *Cottage Economy* (1822) and *Advice to Young Men* (1829); Sarah Ellis's *The Women of England* (1838), *The Daughters of England* (1842), *The Wives of England* (1843), and *The Mothers of England* (1843); Harriet Martineau's *How to Observe Morals and Manners* (1838); John Maynard's *Matrimony: Or, What Marriage Life Is, and How to Make the Best of It* (1866); and Alexis Soyer's *Shilling Cookery for the People* (1855).

MICAEL M. CLARKE

Bibliography

Branca, Patricia. *Silent Sisterhood: Middle-Class Women in the Victorian Home.* 1975.

Kanner, Barbara. "The Women of England in a Century of Social Change, 1815–1914: A Select Bibliography." In Martha Vicinus, ed., *Suffer and Be Still: Women in the Victorian Age.* 1972.

———. "The Women of England . . . A Select Bibliography, Part 2." In Martha Vicinus, ed., *A Widening Sphere: Changing Roles of Victorian Women.* 1977.

. . . . .

AESTHETIC MOVEMENT

Although critics disagree upon its exact dates, the aesthetic movement in England began in the early 1850s, flourished in the 1870s and 1880s, and modulated into the **decadence** of the 1890s. While it lasted, the cultivation of taste in beauty received widespread attention. The movement seems to have begun as a rebellion against the mass production and mass education of the industrial age, against the strict moral standards of Victorianism and the ugliness of polluting factories and cheap, poorly designed products. Aesthetes sought to experience art in their lives, sought to escape from their surroundings and from materialists, whom they called philistines, in the perfection of art.

Aesthetic artists declared their individuality by expressing their own visions of beauty; they declared independence from society by producing "pure" art. "Pure" art, concerned with the formal qualities of design and composition, was independent of moral, philosophical, and cultural concerns. In addition, it dealt with any subject matter, including the sexual, morbid, or perverse. Aesthetic art was **art for art's sake**; indeed, this phrase, which Walter Pater translated from the French *l'art pour l'art*, became the aesthetes' slogan.

Aesthetic artists also strove to define the abstract quality of beauty and to set standards for taste. They declared that beauty could be achieved in all forms of art, both fine and applied; consequently, attention to all the arts—including furnishing, clothing, book production, and housing, as well as painting and literature—was a characteristic of the movement.

One foundation of aestheticism was the teachings of art critic **John Ruskin** (1819–1900). Rebelling against industrial ugliness, Ruskin urged artists to "return to nature." Further, he rejected conventions and stereotypes in art, promoting individual self-expression. In his monthly pamphlet *Fors Clavigera* (1871), Ruskin published a criticism of **James MacNeil Whistler**'s "Nocturne"—declaring it to be a pot of paint flung in the public's face—which led to the libel trial of *Whistler vs. Ruskin* (1878). This trial had important implications for the movement: while Whistler asserted the artist's independence from society, declaring art to be a specialized field, Ruskin asserted the artist's responsibility to communicate with society. Although Whistler won the suit, he was awarded only one shilling in damages.

The Pre-Raphaelite Brotherhood, also inspired by Ruskin's precepts, articulated many principles which would become associated with aestheticism. Their journal, *The Germ, or Thoughts Towards Nature in Poetry, Literature, and Art* (January–May 1850) was, like the later journals associated with the movement, an effort to unite art and letters. Edited by William Michael Rossetti, the *Germ* stressed artists' needs to express their own thoughts, based not on convention or stereotype but on experience and study of nature. Its contributors included Thomas Woolner, Coventry Patmore, Ford Madox Brown, Christina Rossetti, William Michael Rossetti, and Dante Gabriel Rossetti. Each of the four issues had an etching, done (respectively) by William Holman Hunt, James Collinson, Brown, and Richard Deverell.

Influenced by the Pre-Raphaelites, **William Morris** (1834–1896) and his friend **Edward Burne-Jones** founded "the brotherhood" in the mid-fifties. The brotherhood printed the *Oxford and Cambridge Magazine, Conducted by Members of the Two Universities* (although most contributors were from the Oxford group). Morris financed the journal; William Fulford was its editor. The *Oxford and Cambridge Magazine* printed many of Morris's early poems and tales, and its articles not only criticized industrial England but also promoted medieval feudalism.

Morris later established a design firm whose practitioners, including Brown, Burne-Jones, D. G. Rossetti, and Philip Webb, produced designs for tapestries, wallpapers, furniture, stained glass, and domestic utensils. Morris designed more than eighty patterns for textiles and wallpapers; he also taught his workers outmoded techniques in his attempt to retrieve the feudal age. Morris's home, Red House, which was designed by Webb in the medieval style, became a standard for Victorian homes. The movement also initiated the Queen Anne style, which appeared not only in schools and private houses but also in the Bedford Park Estate (1877).

Another innovation in decorative arts and design was Japanism. Oriental art, introduced to the British at the International Exhibition of 1862 and made widely available at Liberty's import shop, stressed line, shape, and color, and demonstrated beauty of design in goods for ordinary household use. Aesthetic homes were a mixture of Morris designs, Queen Anne styles, and Japanism, with red brick, tall chimneys, curved gables, sash windows, and sunflower and Japanese motifs for exteriors; and with tertiary colors, dados, Morris rush chairs and wallpaper, blue-and-white porcelain, Japanese fans, and peacock feathers for their interiors.

The movement led to the founding of various decorative art organizations and guilds. The Century Guild, which "intended to render all branches of art the sphere no longer of the tradesman but of the artist," founded the *Hobby Horse* (1886–1892, with a premature 1884 issue). The *Hobby Horse* was the first of a series of illustrated journals of the 1880s and 1890s, such as the *Dome* and the *Butterfly*. It was also the first journal to reflect a serious interest in book production, giving new status to illustration and the graphic arts. And through such contributors as Matthew Arnold, J. A. Symonds, Katherine Tynan, Christina Rossetti, and Oscar Wilde, it especially filled the hiatus between the Pre-Raphaelite journals and the journals of the 1890s.

The *Yellow Book* (1894–1897) had contributions from writers including Henry James, George Egerton, George Gissing, Ella D'Arcy, John Oliver Hobbes, Ernest Dowson, William Butler Yeats, and H. G. Wells, and from artists such as John Singer Sargent, Joseph Pennell, Max Beerbohm, and Aubrey Beardsley. The art was independent of the text, and the *Yellow Book* was the first journal with a changing cover design. Henry Harland and

Beardsley, its editors, promoted self-expression by refusing to "tremble at the frown of Mrs. Grundy"; offered avant-garde work (Beerbohm's "A Defense of Cosmetics"; John Davidson's "A Ballad of a Nun"; Beardsley's black-and-white drawings); and included a debate between Arthur Waugh and Hugh Crackenthorpe on morality in art.

The body of the *Yellow Book*'s work, however, was conservative, and the periodical lost its reputation for expressing the new movement in the tangle of polarized opinion that surrounded **Oscar Wilde**'s trial. Wilde was a prominent figure in the aesthetic movement, giving it publicity both through his appearance in satires by W. S. Gilbert and George du Maurier and through his tour of America (1881). When Wilde was arrested for homosexuality, public outcry arose also against Beardsley, who was associated with Wilde only because he had illustrated Wilde's *Salomé* (1893). The publishers of the *Yellow Book* nevertheless dismissed Beardsley as art editor.

Arthur Symonds seized the opportunity to make Beardsley art editor of the *Savoy* (January–December 1896), a rival periodical. The *Savoy* contained work by G. B. Shaw, Joseph Conrad, Ford Madox Ford, Yeats, Beardsley, Charles Conder, William Rothenstein, and Whistler. Frankness in literature was espoused in Havelock Ellis's article on *Jude the Obscure*, and freedom in art in Vincent O'Sullivan's "On the Kind of Fiction Called Morbid." The continuing public reaction against Wilde—and Beardsley—led the booksellers Smith and Company to ban the *Savoy* from their stands, and the journal soon folded due to lack of public support.

BONNIE JEAN ROBINSON

Bibliography

Aslin, Elizabeth. *The Aesthetic Movement: Prelude to Art Nouveau*. 1969.

Buckley, Jerome. *The Victorian Temper: A Study in Literary Culture*. 1969.

Dowling, Linda. *Aestheticism and Decadence: A Selective Annotated Bibliography*. 1977.

Gaunt, William. *The Aesthetic Adventure*. 1945.

Hamilton, Walter. *The Aesthetic Movement in England*. 1882.

Mix, Katherine. *A Study in Yellow: The Yellow Book and Its Contributors*. 1960.

Spencer, Robin. *The Aesthetic Movement: Theory and Practice*. 1972.

Stetz, M. and M. Samuels Lasner. *England in the 1880s*. 1988.

See also ARTS AND CRAFTS MOVEMENT

. . . . .

AGNOSTICISM

The term "agnosticism" refers to a particular form of scepticism that flourished in England from the 1860s until the turn of the century. Although originally articulated by Christian theologians and philosophers, agnostic arguments became a favorite weapon of liberal, scientifically minded Victorians who were hostile to the dominance of the aristocracy and to the Church of England in intellectual matters, and intent on challenging the traditional role of conservatives and the Anglican clergy as providers of social and political leadership.

The term was first coined in 1869 during the early meetings of the illustrious Metaphysical Society by **Thomas Henry Huxley** (1825–1895), an influential biologist famous for his vigorous defense of evolutionary theory. During its existence from 1869 to 1880, the Metaphysical Society met nine times a year in London to hear prepared papers and discuss ultimate questions. Members represented every shade of theological opinion. Huxley did not feel fully sympathetic toward the atheists, materialists, positivists, or empiricists in the society, or toward the positions of the theists, pantheists, idealists, or Christians. He invented the title "agnostic" in order to distinguish himself from the modern-day gnostics, whether unbelievers or believers, who had pretensions to transcendental insight.

To Huxley, the new term meant that human knowledge is limited to the phenomenal realm. He looked to epistemological arguments developed by Christian philosophers Immanuel Kant (1724–1804), **William Hamilton** (1788–1856), and Henry Longueville Mansel (1820–1871) that outlined the limits of knowledge that arose from the inherent structure of the human mind. Although often directed at claims to certain knowledge of God, agnosticism could equally find baseless the concept of knowledge of self, or of a material, external world. Agnostics considered that any manifestation of a transcendental or noumenal realm was beyond the limits of human knowledge.

Huxley's beliefs were shared by many Victorian intellectuals. Even before Huxley coined the term, **Herbert Spencer** (1820-1903) systematically outlined the agnostic position in "The Unknowable," the opening section of his *First Principles* (1862). Immensely influential among unbelievers, "The Unknowable" was regarded as the new agnostic bible. **Leslie Stephen** (1832-1904) professed his agnosticism in "An Agnostic's Apology" (1876). John Tyndall (1820-1893), professor of natural philosophy at the Royal Institution, and William Kingdom Clifford (1845-1879), professor in applied mathematics at University College, London, did not call themselves agnostics, but both wrote controversial works articulating the agnostic position: Tyndall's "Belfast Address" (1874) and Clifford's "The Ethics of Belief" (1877) and "The Ethics of Religion" (1877) in his *Lectures and Essays* (1879). Men who claimed to be agnostics but were not major contributors to the initial development of Victorian agnosticism included **John Morley** (1838-1923), **Francis Galton** (1822-1911), Edward Clodd (1840-1930), Samuel Laing (1812-1897), Frederick James Gould (1855-1938) and Richard Bithell (b. 1821). Charles Darwin (1809-1882) talked of passing through an agnostic phase of thought after publishing *The Origin of Species* (1859).

Agnostics often found their conception of the limits of knowledge useful for undermining the conservative-Anglican establishment. They criticized apologists of the old order for grounding the legitimacy of English institutions on a pretended insight into divine will. Agnostics could contrast this vain attempt to exceed the limits of knowledge with the scientific naturalists' humble reliance on empirical methods to justify political, social, ethical, and religious beliefs. Agnostic arguments were also valuable aids in professionalizing science. The notion of the limits of knowledge

was an effective tool to define the boundaries of science and attack those within and outside the profession who brought improper theological concepts into science. But although contemporaries often saw agnosticism as destructive, many agnostics fancied themselves as constructive theists who offered a genuine type of religion as an alternative to a complacent and decaying Christianity.

Agnosticism represented a response to specific social, political, and intellectual conditions and was framed in opposition to the conservative Anglican order. For this reason agnosticism was symbiotically linked to the Victorian era. For many agnostics, their creed also encapsulated the individual's uncertainty when confronting a world convulsed by change. It seemed to them that an admission of ignorance was the only honest position possible for the thoughtful nineteenth-century person.

BERNARD LIGHTMAN

Bibliography

Cockshut, A. O. J. *The Unbelievers: English Agnostic Thought, 1840-1890.* 1966.

Dockrill, D. W. "The Origin and Development of Nineteenth Century English Agnosticism." *Historical Journal*, vol. 1, pp. 3-31.

Flint, Robert. *Agnosticism.* 1903.

Lightman, Bernard. *The Origins of Agnosticism: Victorian Unbelief and the Limits of Knowledge.* 1987.

Turner, Frank Miller. *Between Science and Religion: The Reaction to Scientific Naturalism in Late Victorian England.* 1974.

See also FREETHOUGHT

· · · · ·

AGRICULTURAL LABORERS

At the beginning of Victoria's reign the majority of her subjects were country folk. In 1851 there were 1,250,000 British agricultural workers; one-fourth of all employed males worked in agriculture. Life for these people was restricted, harsh, and tenuous. By 1901 the number of agricultural laborers had decreased to 600,000, and their condition had somewhat improved.

England was unique in nineteenth-century Europe in that it had no peasants. Its rural population had been proletarianized in the eighteenth century. The parliamentary enclosures, which between 1750 and 1850 turned six million acres into private holdings, completed the transformation of agrarian working people into a completely dependent group. Previously, middle-sized farms had been worked principally by servants who lived in the farmer's house. Extra hands for harvest and planting were drawn from smallholders, who supplemented their own produce with seasonal work. Inflation of food prices and the development of a permanent surplus of agricultural labor were key factors in the shift to casual labor. Farm servants were regarded as an economic burden; they consumed food the whole year even in slack times.

Although parliamentary enclosure initially increased the demand for hired labor, it ultimately deprived small producers of their ability to support themselves. The predominance of grain production on the engrossed farms minimized the need for year-round regular work. The traditional lengthy labor contracts (generally one year) gave way to weekly, daily, and even hourly employment.

Living conditions among rural working people declined between 1750 and 1850. The new agrarian proletarians lived in rented, often wretched housing some distance from the farms where they worked. Their diet consisted principally of bread, tea, and potatoes. Extra labor at harvest enabled the family to earn enough for rent payments and special purchases such as shoes. The harvest was followed by a feast provided by the farmer. This feast along with occasional fairs provided rare moments of release and plenty for the rural workers. During winter, laborers were at the mercy of Poor Law administrators.

The threat to employment raised by threshing machines spurred agricultural workers to act in self-defense in 1816, 1822, and especially 1830. The uprising in 1830 spread westward from Kent until twenty counties were affected. Violence was at first directed primarily at threshing machines, but subsequent

hangings and transportation engendered widespread incendiarism and cattle maiming. Sporadic reactive violence continued into the next decades.

In the 1850s the average weekly wage for an adult male agricultural laborer was approximately 11 shillings, augmented by some payments in kind, such as beer, cider, and potatoes. Farm workers in the north usually fared better than those in the south because higher wages in the industrial towns forced northern farmers to compete for labor.

At midcentury women, depending on the nature of their work, were paid from sixpence to a shilling a day. Children were paid about a shilling a week. Some women and children were organized into gangs by contractors who hired out their services to farmers. The Agricultural Gangs Act of 1867 prohibited the employment on public gangs of children under eight and the mixing of sexes on gangs. In the latter part of the century there was a decline in female and child labor. By the 1880s women generally only performed seasonal work. An 1873 law made it illegal to employ children under eight on farms, but casual employment of children to pick and harvest continued until the end of the century.

In 1871 agricultural laborers began organizing in Herefordshire, Kent, and Warwickshire. In 1872 Joseph Arch organized the National Agricultural Labourers Union. Arch and his followers, inspired by the example of industrial workers, hoped to take advantage of the labor shortage in the countryside caused by internal and external migration. The union enrolled 100,000 members within a year and was responsible for considerable improvement in wages. Though the union largely collapsed after 1875 during the agricultural depression brought on by bad weather and American imports, wages never again fell to their preunion level.

BERNARD A. COOK

Bibliography

Ashby, Mabel K. *Joseph Ashby of Tysoe, 1859–1919: A Study of English Village Life.* 1961.

Hammond, John L. and Barbara Hammond. *The Village Labourer, 1760–1832.* 1911.

Hasbach, Wilhelm. *A History of the English Agricultural Labourer.* 1908.

Paying Hop-Pickers. Illustrated London News, 5 October 1867. Library Company of Philadelphia

Hobsbawm, Eric and George Rudé. *Captain Swing: A Social History of the Great English Agricultural Uprising of 1830.* 1968.

Horn, Pamela. *Labouring Life in the Victorian Countryside.* 1976.

Huggett, Frank E. *A Day in the Life of a Victorian Farm Worker.* 1972.

Jefferies, Richard. *The Toilers of the Field.* 1892.

. . . . .

AGRICULTURE

At the beginning of the nineteenth century agriculture produced about one-third of the British national income. Though no longer dominant in the economy, agriculture was the indispensable British industry. Until mid-century, cost and inadequate transportation prevented the nation from being regularly fed by imports. In the 1830s, 90 percent of British food was grown in the United Kingdom.

The basic structure of nineteenth-century British agriculture came into existence before the start of the industrial revolution. Land was concentrated in the hands of a small number of landowners. By the 1870s, 4,000 proprietors owned one-fourth of the land in the entire United Kingdom. Tenant farmers rented and operated the land in fairly large units. The average farm rented by a farmer in the nineteenth century was 110 acres. Finally, 1,500,000 men, women, and children worked the land as agricultural laborers, farm servants, and shepherds.

The demand of an expanding and increasingly urban population fueled the agricultural economy, but agricultural prices, and as a consequence agricultural prosperity, fluctuated considerably. Landowners and farmers measured their prosperity against the abnormal profits of the war period from 1795 to 1815. Though prices were considerably higher in the postwar period than they had been before the wars with France, there was a dramatic decline from their wartime high.

Between 1815 and 1850 British farmers believed that they were threatened. They had taken advantage of easy credit to expand their operations in expectation that the boom prices would endure. Marginal land had been leased at inflationary rates, and farmers had developed expensive habits of consumption. Agriculture's answer to this perceived threat was to maintain prices by exploiting the control that landed interests exercised in Parliament to pass the protectionist **Corn Laws** of 1815-1846. The Corn Laws provided artificial protection for high food prices and, therefore, high rents. Farmers also sought to cut their costs at the expense of their laborers.

Despite the panic of agricultural interests, prices remained relatively stable until improvements in agricultural methods increased productivity, primarily (at this period) through nonmechanical methods. The final phase of parliamentary enclosure brought former waste or pasture lands into cultivation. There was a systematic employment of the best traditional methods and of eighteenth-century innovations in crops and methods of rotation.

The industrial revolution and science affected agriculture only after the late 1830s. The Royal Agricultural Society (1838) and the Rothamsted experimental station (1843) promoted new techniques. Underdraining, which spread during the 1820s, was abetted by the introduction of clay drainage pipes in 1843. Commercial fertilization was promoted with the patenting of superphosphate in 1842 and the import of Peruvian guano in the 1840s. Markets were widened, though not yet threatened, by innovations in transportation.

Although the threshing machine had been introduced at the end of the eighteenth century, there was little mechanization of agriculture before midcentury. Thereafter machines were increasingly used to economize on labor costs and thus offset rising rents. In 1870, 80 percent of the grain harvest was threshed mechanically. By the end of the century, when mechanization was regarded as a cost-cutting solution to foreign competition, most grain was harvested mechanically by reaping machines and self-binders.

After midcentury, agriculture, although still the greatest single employer of British labor, no longer played a pivotal role in the British economy. Its proportion of the gross national income fell from one-third to one-fifth. The repeal of the Corn Laws in 1846 was symbolic of the growing ascendancy of manufacturing and commerce. When capital was available, free trade stimulated investment to improve the soil and methods of cultivation. Indebted or entailed landowners, however, were unable to respond effectively.

The impact of free trade was exacerbated by a series of bad harvests in 1848, 1850, 1852, and 1853. The agricultural crisis of 1849 to 1853 was one of the century's worst. External factors, however, rescued British grain farming from this nadir. California gold stimulated a rise in prices. The Crimean War and the American Civil War gave respites from competition. The prosperity of British industry and the rise in industrial workers' earnings increased demand for agricultural products. Acreage devoted to grain decreased as land was shifted to pasturage and fodder crops. As a result, the price of wheat remained steady for a generation. There was a twenty-year-long period of prosperity for landlords and farmers, the era of Victorian "high" farming.

This "golden age" of British agriculture came to an end in the 1870s. Prosperity was followed by a disastrous agricultural slump, the result of bad weather combined with cheap imports flooding in from the plains of temperate countries. Improved transportation enabled foreign imports to undersell British agriculture in its home market.

British farming was vulnerable because it had concentrated upon its least competitive product, grain. Because grain producers suffered while livestock, dairy farming, orchards, and market gardening remained lucrative, tillage contracted from its 1872 "golden age" peak of 9.6 million acres to 6.5 in 1913. Pasturage during the same period rose from 17.1 million acres to 21.5. The transition was traumatic for some, but by the reign of Edward, British agriculture was moderately stable.

BERNARD A. COOK

Bibliography

Chambers, Jonathan D. and G. E. Mingay. *The Agricultural Revolution, 1750-1880.* 1966.

Hobsbawm, Erich. *Industry and Empire.* 1982.

Jones, E. L. *The Development of English Agriculture, 1815-1873.* 1968.

Mingay, G. E. *Enclosure and the Small Farmer in the Age of the Industrial Revolution.* 1968.

Orwin, Cristabel S. and Edith H. Whetham. *The History of British Agriculture, 1846–1914.* 1964.

. . . . .

AGUILAR, GRACE
(1816–1847)

One of the earliest Anglo-Jewish novelists, Grace Aguilar also wrote short stories (*Records of Israel,* 1844, later incorporated into *Home Scenes and Heart Studies,* 1853) and essays (*The Spirit of Judaism,* 1842; *Women of Israel,* 1845; *The Jewish Faith,* 1846; *Sabbath Thoughts and Sacred Communings,* 1853). Her first work was a translation from the French of Orobio de Castro's *Israel Defended* (1838). Of her six novels, the popular *The Vale of Cedars; or, the Martyr* (1850) examines Jewish life.

A descendant of Sephardic Jews, Aguilar was acutely aware of the difficulties of being raised in a non-Jewish environment and of receiving a religious education from books translated into English by Christians. During her brief life, she directed her work to a non-Jewish audience. Her essays explain Judaism. Her fiction, written when Jews were working to remove their legal disabilities, minimizes doctrinal differences between Christians and Jews and deftly exploits historical settings to plead for English tolerance of Jews.

Aguilar's non-Jewish audience, for the first time, learned from a Jew about the way Jewish rituals and beliefs shape Jewish life. Christians accepted her as an authentic spokesperson for Judaism. Her work stresses the Jewish woman's historical importance, but it also reveals the acculturing influence of contemporary English life on Jews.

LINDA GERTNER ZATLIN

Bibliography

Abrahams, Beth-Zion. "Grace Aguilar: A Centenary Tribute." *Transactions of the Jewish Historical Society of England,* vol. 16, pp. 137–148.

Zatlin, Linda Gertner. *The Nineteenth-Century Anglo-Jewish Novel.* 1981.

See also ANGLO-JEWISH NOVEL

. . . . .

AINSWORTH, WILLIAM HARRISON
(1805–1882)

William Harrison Ainsworth achieved recognition as a historical romance novelist and an influential editor. The adventures of highwayman Dick Turpin in *Rookwood* (1834) and the escapades of *Jack Sheppard* (1839) secured his popularity among young male readers. Both works, illustrated by George Cruikshank, were considered "**Newgate novels**"—fiction dealing sympathetically with criminal heroes. Influenced by Walter Scott and public taste, Ainsworth concentrated on serial romances concerned with historical events, including *Guy Fawkes* (1841) and *Windsor Castle* (1843), which were also illustrated by Cruikshank.

Ainsworth, born in Manchester, entered publishing in 1824. Ridiculed by *Punch* for his vanity, he began *Ainsworth's Magazine* (1842–1854) to showcase his fiction. In the mid-nineteenth century he could not adjust his romances to the shift toward domestic fiction. To maintain his rank in London's literary world he abandoned *Ainsworth's* in 1854, focusing on the *New Monthly Magazine* (1845–1870) and *Bentley's Miscellany* (1854–1868). His editorial success depended upon his lavish entertainment of contributors, most notably William Thackeray. His move to Brighton (1854) reduced his contact with London literati. With popularity and influence declining, he relinquished both editorships by 1870.

Although Ainsworth outlived his popularity, *Rookwood* and *Jack Sheppard* remain central works of Newgate fiction. Recent criticism has reappraised his historical novels. Despite wooden characterization and formulaic plots, these romances capture the flavor of life in foreign and domestic settings during significant historical periods.

CATHERINE J. GOLDEN

Bibliography

Ellis, Stewart M. *William Harrison Ainsworth and His Friends.* 1911.

Worth, George J. *William Harrison Ainsworth.* 1972.

See also HISTORICAL NOVEL

. . . . .

ALBERT, PRINCE CONSORT (1819–1861)

Albert (Francis Charles Augustus Albert Emmanuel), the German prince who married his first cousin Queen **Victoria** at twenty and died at forty-two, was one of the most accomplished and versatile men of his age. Instigator of the international **Exhibition of 1851**, he was also chancellor of Cambridge University (effecting radical reforms), patron of the arts and sciences, architect of Osborne House and Balmoral, model farmer, friend of industry and the working classes, and a statesman working behind the scenes for the good of his adopted country.

Born at Rosenau in the same year as Victoria, Albert was the younger son of the duke of Saxe-Coburg-Gotha by his brief marriage to Princess Louise of Saxe-Gotha-Altenburg. A precocious, responsive boy, he studied at Brussels, where his uncle Leopold was king of Belgium, and later at the University of Bonn. Complementing his study of natural science, philosophy, and political economy with painting and music, he exemplified the current Germanic zest for learning. Leopold, who would have shared the English throne had his wife Charlotte lived, championed Albert's union with Victoria, daughter of his sister, the duchess of Kent. Albert's good looks and sweetness won the queen, and their marriage, despite storms, was a love match, producing nine children.

A practical man, Albert patiently weaned Victoria away from her attachment to Lord Melbourne and the Whig party, knowing that they must be nonpartisan to secure the constitutional monarchy, though he himself was later drawn to Robert Peel, the Tory minister.

Prince Albert at Twenty-four.
From a miniature by Robert Thorburn ARA, engraved by Francis Hallo. Reproduced by permission of the Bodleian Library, Oxford (shelfmark 210 j 484 the frontispiece).

As Victoria's advisor and private secretary, he impressed successive prime ministers, even cocksure Lord Palmerston, with his foresight. Though not proclaimed prince consort until 1859, he headed bodies for the arts, sciences, industry, agriculture, and even the army, where he declined the position of commander in chief. Just before he died in 1861 of overwork and fever, he probably prevented war with America by softening Lord John Russell's inflammatory letter to Washington over a federal warship boarding the British *Trent*.

Albert helped stabilize the British monarchy when midcentury revolutions were sweeping away crowned heads in Europe. His uprightness and family life set standards for the nation. He cultivated artists and men of learning, had Mendelssohn perform at court, and enriched the royal collection with medieval and early Renaissance art. Periodic suspicions of his national loyalty wounded him, and he was not the unbending German often portrayed but a lover of fun, a good mimic, a detester of joyless Sundays, and a devoted father. He perhaps imposed too rigorous a regime on his eldest son and ruined his own health by failure to delegate responsibility. Yet he earned Disraeli's tribute: "This German prince . . . governed England for 21 years with a wisdom and energy none of our kings have ever shown."

TAMIE WATTERS

Bibliography

Albert, Consort of Queen Victoria. *Letters of the Prince Consort, 1831-1861,* 1938. Ed. Kurt Jagow.

——. *The Principal Speeches and Addresses.* 1862.

Bennett, Daphne. *King Without a Crown.* 1977.

Bolitho, Hector. *Albert, the Good.* 1932.

Fulford, Roger T. *The Prince Consort.* 1949.

Grey, Charles. *The Early Years of His Royal Highness the Prince Consort.* 1867.

Martin, Theodore. *The Life of His Royal Highness the Prince Consort.* 1875-1880. 5 vols.

See also ROYAL FAMILY; VICTORIA, QUEEN OF ENGLAND

· · · · ·

ALEXANDER, GEORGE (1858-1918)

George Alexander made his professional acting debut in Nottingham in 1879. Two years later he appeared for the first time with Henry Irving's company at the Lyceum. During the next decade Alexander acted for Irving as well as John Hare and the Kendals at the St. James's Theatre. In 1884 he joined Irving's second North American tour performing the roles of Valentine (*Faust*), Claudio, and Macduff. Alexander's brief management of the Avenue Theatre (1890) was followed by a lengthy and successful association with the St. James's (1891-1918).

Under Alexander's regime the St. James's became a glittering center for London theatergoers, identified particularly with the fashionable society plays of Oscar Wilde and Arthur Wing Pinero. In the first years of his management Alexander produced and acted

in Wilde's *Lady Windermere's Fan* (1892) and Pinero's *The Second Mrs. Tanqueray* (1893), establishing in the latter piece the reputation of Mrs. Patrick Campbell. Later premieres included Henry Arthur Jones's *The Masqueraders* (1894) and Wilde's *The Importance of Being Earnest* (1895), with Alexander as an elegant Jack Worthing. In the first decade of the twentieth century Alexander once more joined forces with Pinero to present three of that playwright's most effective social dramas, *His House in Order* (1906), *The Thunderbolt* (1908), and *Mid-Channel* (1909). Alexander was knighted in 1911.

JOEL H. KAPLAN

Bibliography

Mason, A. E. W. *Sir George Alexander and the Saint James' Theatre.* 1935.

· · · · ·

ALLEN, GRANT (1848-1899)

A man of science as well as letters, Charles Grant Blairfindie Allen wrote on popular science for various periodicals during the late 1870s and early 1880s, turning to fiction during the late 1880s. Some of his work was published under the pseudonyms J. Arbuthnot Wilson, Cecil Power, and Olive Pratt Raynor. *The Woman Who Did* (1895), a novel about a woman who rejected the formal marriage tie, caused a contemporary public stir.

Allen was the son of an Irish clergyman who emigrated to Canada in 1840. In 1861 the family moved to France, where Allen attended the Collège Impérial at Dieppe. He was graduated from Merton College, Oxford, in 1871, and after some schoolmastering became professor of mental and moral philosophy at a college in Spanish Town, Jamaica, designed to educate blacks. When the school failed he returned to England and began his science writing. He was married twice, once during undergraduate days to a woman who died and, in 1873, to Ellen Jerrard, by whom he had one son.

Physiological Aesthetics (1877), dedicated to Herbert Spencer, did not sell, but Allen's work in *Cornhill, St. James's Gazette,* and

London was successful. He also wrote "The Colour Sense" (1879) and three volumes of popular science essays published between 1881 and 1883.

Allen's early fiction was published in *Belgravia, Cornhill,* and *Gentleman's Magazine.* Between 1884 and 1899 he published more than fifty volumes on varied subjects, the most memorable being *The Woman Who Did* (1895), which was regarded in its day as a risqué commentary on the marriage tie in the manner of Thomas Hardy's *Jude the Obscure* (1896) or George Gissing's *The Odd Women* (1893)—though its events could well have been taken from the simple didactic romances whose moral is "don't." During the final two decades of his life Allen continued to write extensively on the physical and natural sciences for periodicals; on *The Evolution of the Idea of God* (1897); and, latterly, on Italian art. He died on October 28, 1899, clearly a man who had been, first and foremost, a commerical and professional author.

ROSEMARY T. VAN ARSDEL

Bibliography

Clodd, Edward. *Grant Allen: A Memoir.* 1900.

· · · · ·

AMUSEMENTS AND RECREATION: MIDDLE CLASS

Nineteenth-century historians, painters, and novelists usually depicted the middle-class Victorian family at leisure in the drawing room or parlor playing chess, backgammon, dominoes, cards, or some other popular table game; singing around the piano; or reciting poetry or reading a novel aloud to the gathering. All of these scenes are accurate, for the Victorians did, indeed, entertain themselves within the family. Inexpensive upright pianos were within the means of most middle-class families, and the cost of sheet music, magazines, and books fell with the abolition of taxes on paper in 1861. Above all, reading, especially novel reading—either by oneself or to others—dominated the recreation of the Victorians. As Trollope declared in 1870, "We

have become a novel-reading people, from the Prime Minister down to the last-appointed scullery maid." The rental figures from Mudie's Select Library, the growth of municipal libraries after the Ewart's Acts of 1845 and 1850, and the reviews in the periodicals attest to that fact. The *Athenaeum*, for example, reviewed over 10,000 novels between 1840 and 1870. In addition, newspapers, monthly magazines, and low-priced editions of fiction and nonfiction fed the Victorians' appetite for reading material.

Outside of the home the Victorian engaged more in spectator team sports, such as cricket, soccer, and rugby football, than in participatory ones, but many still enjoyed archery (men and women playing separately), horseback riding, cycling, and the game that Mrs. Horton, a character in Elizabeth Eiloart's 1870 novel *From Thistles— Grapes?*, called the foremost invention of the nineteenth century: croquet. Until it was eclipsed by lawn tennis in the 1870s, croquet reigned supreme as the one game "where men and women can meet without man being effeminate or women masculine" (Rhoda Broughton, *Cometh Up as a Flower*, 1867). Concomitantly, the nineteenth century saw the rise of organized choral societies and brass bands, especially in urban areas outside of London. Recruited not only from churches and chapels but also from labor societies and other organizations, participants formed companies and competed with each other.

The Victorians also had an appetite for the curious and the exotic. As Thomas Hood declared: "There are three things the public will always clamor for, sooner or later; namely, novelty, novelty, novelty." They found such in the strolling entertainers with dancing bears or dressed-up monkeys, the fire-eaters and the jugglers; the Chinese shade shows, such as the popular *Woodchopper's Frolic*, which told a story with a white sheet, a lantern and cutout paper characters; the Punch and Judy shows; the Harlequin Pantomimes, which utilized historical or contemporary events to entertain; the annual fairs, such as London's Bartholomew Fair, which were occasions for extended holidays; and Vauxhall Gardens and Cremorne Gardens in Chelsea. At their heyday in the eighteenth century, these pleasure gardens still drew large crowds until they finally closed in 1859 and 1877, respectively.

A Saturday Half Holiday.
Illustrated London News, *15 July 1871. Library Company of Philadelphia.*

Also popular were music halls with their singers, dancers, acrobats, animal trainers, impersonators, and their star performers—by the 1870s London alone had 347 music halls; theaters with their mostly melodramatic and sensational plays and great personalities; and public parks which opened in most of the major cities in the nineteenth century, with some, such as Hampstead Heath, offering fare similar to that of the pleasure gardens.

The event, however, that changed the leisure patterns of the Victorians was the development of the railroad. Before the coming of the railroads it was not unusual for a member of the middle classes never to have been more than twenty miles from home. The railroad was not only a novelty to ride, but it brought the entire island into the reach of the middle class. Extremely popular were Wordsworth's Lake District, Walter Scott's Highlands, and the bathing machines, shells, souvenir shops, libraries, and beaches of Bridlington, Brighton, and other seaside resorts, where the Victorians even played croquet and rode horses on the beach. Informal day and weekend excursions and formally planned trips by tour agents (Thomas Cook and his rivals) became pleasurable ways to spend one's leisure time. The railroad made it possible for middle-class Victorian families not only to leave their drawing rooms for prolonged holidays away from home but also to travel into all parts of England, Wales, and Scotland for new kinds of experiences and adventures.

WILLIAM H. SCHEUERLE

Bibliography

Bailey, Peter. *Leisure and Class in Victorian England.* 1978.

Cruse, Amy. *The Victorians and Their Reading.* 1935.

Cunningham, Hugh. *Leisure in the Industrial Revolution. c. 1780–c. 1880.* 1980.

Malcomson, R. W. *Popular Recreations in English Society, 1700–1850.* 1973.

Victorian Studies, vol. 21, no. 1. (Special issue on leisure.)

· · · · ·

AMUSEMENTS AND RECREATION: WORKING CLASS

It was, until recently, assumed that the industrial revolution destroyed a vigorous, preindustrial popular culture; that, in terms of recreation, the years 1800 to 1840 were marked by gloom; and that only in the 1890s did a new, recognizably "modern," world of entertainment emerge. Historians now suggest that while popular culture was indeed transformed in this period, the transformation was more complicated than was once believed.

The industrial and French revolutions gave rise to concerns about establishing a work discipline and maintaining social order. Popular pastimes that tended to subvert these aims were thus discouraged. In the countryside the gentry withdrew support from games and carnivals, while in the towns employers and authorities clamped down on wakes, fairs, and blood sports. Workers defended their right to enjoy these pleasures, and the attempt at suppression merely drove many of them underground.

The 1820s and 1830s witnessed a dramatic increase in working-class recreational activity. Many preindustrial fairs continued to flourish, while in the workplace an active shop-floor culture developed. Self-taught artisans built a vigorous radical culture through their mutual improvement societies and political organizations, while Methodists encouraged a working-class religious culture which also emphasized the importance of self-help and mutual improvement. In addition, new opportunities for recreation were offered in the towns by publicans and entrepreneurs who presided over the growth of singing saloons, concert rooms, penny theaters, and public houses.

Middle-class observers became worried by forms of recreational activity that threatened to escape their control. By the 1840s they suggested the need for counterattractions. Their programs of "rational recreation" included mechanics' institutes, temperance cafés, the Pleasant Sunday Afternoon associations and, for working-class youths, the Band of Hope movement. In the 1880s, believing that the regulation of popular culture was a

Rational Recreation and the August Bank Holiday:
Blackpool, 1900.
Clarion, *4 August 1900.*

crucial component of social reform, they encouraged workers to participate in socially mixed cultural institutions like settlement houses.

Many workers accepted the activities offered by reformers while rejecting the patronage that accompanied them. Moreover, from the 1870s rising real wages and shorter working hours meant that workers—primarily regularly employed males—could choose from a number of recreational options unavailable earlier in the century. The development of the Bank Holiday (1871) and the Saturday half-holiday solidified the division between work and leisure, while the excursion train encouraged the growth of resorts like Blackpool. Investment in music halls, football teams, and the popular press also led to the emergence of an entertainment industry which served to redefine working-class culture.

Socialists complained about the new pleasures of the worker, as did conservative middle-class reformers. Thus, despite enormous changes in the nature of working-class recreation, popular culture remained a contested issue.

CHRIS WATERS

Bibliography

Bailey, Peter. *Leisure and Class in Victorian England: Rational Recreation and the Contest for Control, 1830-1885.* 1978; rpt. 1987.

Cunningham, Hugh. *Leisure in the Industrial Revolution, c. 1780-c. 1880.* 1980.

Golby, John M. and A. W. Purdue. *The Civilization of the Crowd: Popular Culture in England 1750-1900.* 1984.

Harrison, Brian. *Drink and the Victorians: The Temperance Question in England, 1815-1872.* 1971.

Meller, Helen E. *Leisure and the Changing City, 1870-1914.* 1976.

Storch, Robert D., ed. *Popular Culture and Custom in Nineteenth-Century England.* 1982.

Walton, John K. and James Walvin, eds. *Leisure in Britain, 1780–1939.* 1983.

Walvin, James. *Leisure and Society, 1830–1950.* 1978.

Yeo, Eileen and Stephen Yeo, eds. *Popular Culture and Class Conflict, 1590–1914: Explorations in the History of Labour and Leisure.* 1981.

See also BAND OF HOPE; BANDS AND BAND MUSIC; BROADSIDES AND CHAPBOOKS; BICYCLE; CHORAL MUSIC; MECHANICS' INSTITUTES; MUSIC HALL; PENNY THEATERS; POPULAR SHOWS AND EXHIBITIONS; RACING AND RACEHORSES; RUGBY FOOTBALL; SOCCER; SPORTS; TRAVEL AND HOLIDAYS; WORKING-CLASS CLUBS AND ASSOCIATIONS

. . . . .

ANDERSON, ELIZABETH GARRETT (1836–1917)

Elizabeth Garrett Anderson was the second woman to become a fully accredited physician in England. Her determination to study medicine was fired by **Elizabeth Blackwell**'s success in having her name placed on the British medical register in 1859. Blackwell, however, had attended medical school in America; no British school was open to women. After several years of unofficial training and private tuition, Anderson received her license in 1865 by passing the Society of Apothecaries' qualifying examinations. In 1869 she was placed on the medical register, and in 1870 received an M.D. from the Sorbonne. Supported throughout by her father, by educator Emily Davies, and by the circle of feminists surrounding Barbara Leigh Smith, Anderson's struggle had nevertheless been se-

vere. She later combined her exacting career with marriage (1871) and three children.

Anderson began practicing in 1866 at a small dispensary for women, which developed into the New Hospital for Women and Children (1872) and became Elizabeth Garrett Anderson Hospital after her death. In 1874 she helped to establish London Medical College for Women, where she taught for twenty-three years and served as dean from 1883 to 1903. She served on the London School Board (1870) and developed fitness programs for girls' schools. Also a suffragist and an avid supporter of the women's movement (except in its protest against the Contagious Diseases Acts), she wrote in leading periodicals to defend intellectual rigor in female education against the recurring charge that strenuous mental activity harmed women. The first woman dean of a medical college and the first woman member of the British Medical Association, Anderson also became the first woman mayor in England when she was elected mayor of Aldeburgh, her hometown, upon her retirement in 1908.

SUZANNE GRAVER

Bibliography

Anderson, Louisa Garrett. *Elizabeth Garrett Anderson.* 1939.

Bell, E. Moberly. *Storming the Citadel: The Rise of the Woman Doctor.* 1953.

Manton, Jo. *Elizabeth Garrett Anderson.* 1965.

See also MEDICAL EDUCATION

. . . . .

ANESTHESIA

The discovery of anesthetic agents and their incorporation into medical practice permitted a dramatic turning in the history of medicine. During the early nineteenth century, Humphry Davy (1778–1829), Michael Faraday (1791–1867), and Henry Hill Hickman (1800–1830) experimented with nitrous oxide, ether, and carbon dioxide, respectively. The English chemist Davy introduced the possibility of using nitrous oxide in surgical operations as early as 1800; Samuel Taylor Coleridge was among the first to trust in Davy's proposal. Hickman, a surgeon of Shifnal in Shropshire, commiserated with patients who underwent surgery, especially the destitute. By 1823 Hickman had rendered small animals unconscious with carbon dioxide asphyxiation before performing amputation. Ignored and rejected by the Royal Society of London (of which Davy was president), Hickman's work was overshadowed by Davy's recommendation of nitrous oxide anesthesia.

Experiments on the other side of the Atlantic contributed to the development of practical anesthesia. Ether had served as a stimulant before Crawford Williamson Long (1815–1878) administered it to James Venables in Jefferson, Georgia, on March 30, 1842 as an aid in the surgical removal of a neck tumor. By December of 1844, Horace Wells (1815–1848) had employed nitrous oxide in his dental practice. On October 16, 1846, William Thomas Green Morton (1819–1868) anesthetized Golbert Abbott with ether for the surgical removal of a neck tumor at the Massachusetts General Hospital.

News of the successful demonstration of surgical anesthesia in Boston quickly reached English surgeons. On December 21, 1846, at University College, London, the most influential English surgeon of his era, Robert Liston (1794–1847), amputated a leg and removed an ingrown toenail from anesthetized patients. Soon James Syme (1799–1870) and James Young Simpson (1811–1870) were employing ether anesthesia in Scotland. Simpson, an obstetrician, quickly turned to chloroform because ether was found to irritate the nasal passages and throat.

Pivotal acceptance of anesthesia, overturning objections from Christian clergymen, occurred when John Snow administered chloroform to Queen Victoria during the birth of Prince Leopold in 1853. More effective than the arguments of Simpson and other medical authorities, Victoria's action immediately set the stage for the anesthetic application of chloroform for the next 60 years. In reviewing the contribution of English and American physicians and celebrating the conquest over surgical pain, William Osler (1849–1919) called anesthesia "the greatest single gift ever made to suffering humanity."

FRANK JOHN PAPATHEOFANIS

Bibliography

Cartwright, Frederick F. *The English Pioneers of Anaesthesia*. 1952.

Raper, Howard R. *Man Against Pain: The Epic of Anesthesia*. 1945.

· · · · ·

ANGLO-CATHOLICISM see HIGH CHURCH

· · · · ·

ANGLO-INDIAN LITERATURE

Anglo-Indian literature—or that literature by English writers in India, and mainly about English life in India—became noteworthy only at the end of the eighteenth century. Until then Anglo-Indian writing was confined mainly to travel books meant to satisfy English curiosity about the exotic East. But by the late nineteenth century, especially after the enormous success of **Rudyard Kipling**, India exerted a powerful influence on the minds of Anglo-Indian writers. The English reading public after about 1880 enjoyed a vast—if largely mediocre—body of fiction developed in Indian settings.

Kipling's most important Indian works are *Plain Tales from the Hills* (1888), *Soldiers Three and Other Stories* (1888), *Wee Willie Winkie and Other Child Stories* (1888), *Life's Handicap* (1891), and *Kim* (1901). *Kim* and the ninety-six stories in the other volumes vividly dramatize Kipling's observations of Anglo-Indian character and society. Roughly a quarter of his stories treat purely Indian topics, as in "The Story of Muhammad Din" and "The Gate of the Hundred Sorrows" from *Plain Tales from the Hills*.

Kipling popularized the Anglo-Indian genre and inspired many others to exploit its variety and exotic appeal. Flora Annie Steel is best remembered for her novels *The Potter's Thumb* (1894), *Voices in the Night* (1900), *Hosts of the Lord* (1900), and an important collection of tales, *In The Permanent Way and Other Stories* (1897). Bithia Mary Croker published thirty-one novels between 1882 and 1919. One of her best is *Diana Barrington* (1888), the romantic story of a jungle girl's marriage to an English officer. Many of Kipling's most prolific successors—such as E. W. Savi, Maud Diver, and Alice Perrin—published their works in the first three decades of the twentieth century.

Some Anglo-Indian writers preferred other subjects than the popular but comparatively pallid chronicling of Anglo-Indian social life. In *David Leslie* (1879) and *Trangression* (1899), S. S. Thornborn depicted the adventures of British administrators on India's dangerous northwest frontier, and William Hunter used an early nineteenth-century setting for *The Old Missionary* (1895). Alexander Allardyce analyzed Indian psychology in *The City of Sunshine* (1877), and George Chesney dramatized aspects of the Sepoy mutiny of 1857–1858 in *The Dilemma* (1876).

Anglo-Indian poetry never achieved the wide popularity of the fiction. Edwin Arnold's *The Light of Asia* (1879), a blank verse epic about the Buddha, was accused of distorting Buddhism. Alfred Lyall treated Indian politics and religion in verse form, and Charles Kelly wrote poetry about the mutiny. Mary Leslie took Indian natural history as the subject of her poems; William Waterfield found his inspiration in Indian myths; and Henry George Keene presented the diversity of Indian culture.

With the exception of the giant figure of Kipling, Anglo-Indian literature never attained high distinction in the nineteenth century. But India played a large role in the imagination of empire-conscious British readers, and writers who responded to the challenge found a ready audience.

FRANK DAY

Bibliography

Greenberger, Allen J. *The British Image of India: A Study in the Literature of Imperialism, 1880–1960.* 1969.

Oaten, Edward F. *A Sketch of Anglo-Indian Literature.* 1908.

Parry, Benita. *Delusions and Discoveries: Studies on India in the British Imagination, 1880–1930.* 1972.

Singh, Bhupal. *A Survey of Anglo-Indian Fiction.* 1934.

See also EDEN, EMILY
. . . . .

ANGLO-IRISH LIFE AND SOCIETY

The Protestant landlords of English origin who dominated Ireland's political and cultural life from the seventeenth century until the early twentieth were known as the Anglo-Irish. Their "plantation" in Ireland in order to subdue the Irish and exploit the land was initiated by Mary I, pursued by both Elizabeth I and James I, and energetically completed by Oliver Cromwell during the Commonwealth.

The resultant Anglo-Irish society functioned as a powerful political, economic, cultural, and religious enclave within Ireland until the end of the nineteenth century. Because these people's allegiance was to the British Crown and because their language and religion were not those of their tenants, the English model of the feudal system that they were meant to replicate in Ireland never flourished; with a few significant exceptions, the Anglo-Irish landlords were a destructive rather than a constructive and nurturing aristocracy. By the Victorian era, political and economic challenges to the Anglo-Irish hegemony were becoming frequent and threatening, and by 1903 Anglo-Irish privilege had been almost entirely dismantled.

The world that the Anglo-Irish lost is epitomized in Brendan Behan's description of the Anglo-Irishman as "a Protestant with a horse." Living in splendid "Big Houses," the life of the Protestant ascendancy was intensely social and sporting. Big House families visited one another throughout the year to pursue their favorite activities: bird shooting and fox hunting in the fall and winter, lawn tennis, croquet, sailing, and gardening in the spring and summer. When in Dublin the landlords frequented the Kildare Street Club; they sent their sons to English universities or to Trinity College, Dublin, and did not bother to formally educate their daughters for whom the annual Viceregal balls at Dublin Castle functioned as the matrimonial market. Amateur theatricals, the Continental tour and, in later years, the Dublin Horse Show complete the picture of Anglo-Irish social life. Hence about the only thing this social class fully shared and suffered with the native Irish was the weather.

Anglo-Irish power steadily declined during the Victorian period. It is estimated that the famines of the 1840s ruined one-third of the landlords, and reform agitation both outside and within Parliament throughout the remainder of the century diminished the power of the rest: the disestablishment of the Church of Ireland (1869), the founding of the National Land League (1879), the granting of total manhood suffrage (1884), and a series of land acts insuring tenants' rights and providing funds to facilitate tenant purchase, the most important of which occurred in 1881, 1885, and 1903.

Paradoxically the Anglo-Irish furnished many of the thinkers and writers associated with Ireland's cultural heritage as well as the majority of the political figures in Ireland's struggle for independence from the late seventeenth century through the nineteenth; accordingly, any general assessment of the Anglo-Irish must emphasize their cultural importance. From the ranks of the Anglo-Irish landholders or their descendants came Bishop Berkeley (1685–1753), Richard Brinsley Sheridan (1751–1816), Maria Edgeworth (1767–1849), **George Bernard Shaw** (1856–1950), and **W. B. Yeats** (1865–1939). Central to Ireland's evolution as an independent nation are Henry Grattan (1746–1820), Wolfe Tone (1763–1798), Robert Emmett (1778–1803), Isaac Butt (1813–1879), and **Charles Stewart Parnell** (1846–1891).

VIRGINIA K. BEARDS

Bibliography

Beckett, J. C. *The Making of Modern Ireland, 1603–1923.* 1966.

Curtis, Edmund. *A History of Ireland.* 1936.

Fleming, Lionel. *Head or Harp.* 1965.

O'Brien, Conor Cruise. *States of Ireland.* 1972.

O'Faolain, Sean. *The Irish: A Character Study.* 1956.

Somerville, Edith. *Irish Memories.* 1917.

White, Terence de Vere. *The Anglo-Irish.* 1972.

See also IRISH LITERATURE; IRISH NATIONALISM

· · · · ·

ANGLO-JEWISH NOVEL

The Anglo-Jewish novel is a body of didactic fiction written about Jewish life by writers who did not formally renounce Judaism, and can be best discussed against a sociopolitical background. Institutionalized anti-Semitism, which extended back to the expulsion of the Jews from England in 1290, continued throughout the nineteenth century. The passage of the Catholic Emancipation Act in 1830, however, signaled to the Jews that they could work to remove legal and civil restrictions. While some focused on politics, others turned to art. For the first time, Jews responded in fiction to nine centuries of pejorative images in Christian English literature. After 1870, in addition, Jewish novelists confronted tensions within the Anglo-Jewish community.

The earliest fiction was published during the 1840s, when legal and civil constraints were still in force. Jewish life in England was not controlled by ministers of the interior as it was in other European countries, nor was qualification for civil rights dependent upon conversion to Christianity. While their emancipation in 1858 was basically unconditional, Jews were forced to struggle to revoke each law that kept them from participating fully in England's civil life. Eschewing the political arena, the earliest novelists responded to the social bigotry that accompanied English resistance to the full acceptance of Jews. Celia and Marian Moss (*The Romance of Jewish History*, 1840; *Tales of Jewish History*, 1843) and **Grace Aguilar** (*The Vale of Cedars; or, the Martyr*, 1850) cautiously plead for tolerance, framing their stories in previous centuries in order to idealize Jewish characters and minimize doctrinal differences between Christians and Jews without provoking anti-Semitic sensibilities. Later novels that consider English anti-Semitism—Isidore G. Ascher's *The Doom of Destiny* (1895); Samuel Gordon's *The Queen's Quandary* (1903) and *The Ferry of Fate* (1906); and Cecily Ullman Sidgwick's *The Devil's Cradle*

(1918), *Iron Cousins* (1919), and *Refugee* (1934)—are set contemporaneously but in foreign countries and implicitly, like Aguilar's, flatter British tolerance of Jews. Novelists also reacted to the methodical attempt to eradicate Judaism by converting the Jews, a process formally advocated by the Society for Promoting Christianity Among the Jews, founded in 1809. Charlotte Montefiore (*Caleb Asher*, 1845), Matthias Levy (*The Hasty Marriage: A Sketch of Modern Jewish Life*, 1857), Oswald John Simon (*The World and the Cloister*, 1890), and **Benjamin Farjeon** (*Aaron the Jew*, 1894) all exhort Jews not to succumb to conversionist rhetoric.

In contrast to the apologetic intent of the early novelists, those writing during the last third of the century addressed themselves to tensions within the Jewish community. Emily Marian Harris (*Estelle,* 1878; *Benedictus*, 1887) portrays the drift into assimilation, while Gordon (*Sons of the Covenant*, 1900) depicts communal work as the way to avoid it. Associated with assimilation were two issues: work ethics and intermarriage. The example of Judaic ethics governing business affairs was offered by Farjeon (*Solomon Isaacs*, 1877; *Aaron the Jew*, 1894) and **Israel Zangwill** (*The King of Schnorrers*, 1894). Samuel Phillips (*Caleb Stukely*, 1844), Leonard Merrick (*Violet Moses*, 1891), and Julia Frankau (*Dr. Phillips; A Maida Vale Idyll*, 1887; *Pigs in Clover*, 1903; *The Sphinx's Lawyer*, 1906) show nonreligious Jews as venal social climbers. **Amy Levy** (*Reuben Sachs; A Sketch*, 1888), Sidgwick (*Lesser's Daughter*, 1894; *Grasshoppers*, 1895), Farjeon (*Pride of Race*, 1900), and Gordon (*Unto Each Man His Own*, 1904) demonstrate that assimilated Jews compounded their problems by marrying Christians.

Another type of internal tension was the integration of the flood of immigrants from eastern Europe after 1880. The spectrum of Jewish response ranges from Frankau's derision of the immigrant (*A Babe in Bohemia*, 1889) to Zangwill's sympathy (*Children of the Ghetto*, 1892; *Ghetto Tragedies*, 1893; *Ghetto Comedies*, 1907).

Throughout the century, Anglo-Jewish novelists addressed Christians and Jews. Their novels are informed by their consciousness of the Jew's position in Victorian England, a position shaped largely by anti-Semitism. Thus, many of these novels attempt to counter stereotypes of Jews in English literature. With the exception of Zangwill's work, these novels present little of the moral vision, prophecy, or characterization that raises fiction to the level of art; they do provide insight into the Victorian Jew's changing position in English society and delineate seemingly unresolvable tensions within the Anglo-Jewish community.

LINDA GERTNER ZATLIN

Bibliography

Zatlin, Linda Gertner. *The Nineteenth-Century Anglo-Jewish Novel*. 1981.

See also JEWRY AND JUDAISM

· · · · ·

ANGLO-WELSH LITERATURE

Anglo-Welsh literature is a phenomenon of the twentieth century; in its strictest definition the phrase means literature written in Wales by English-speaking Welsh persons. Used more liberally, and retrospectively, the term has been taken to include such writers as Henry Vaughan and George Herbert of the seventeenth century, George Eliot, born Marian Evans (1819–1880), Gerard Manley Hopkins (1844–1889) and William Morris (1834–1896), whose connection with or commitment to Wales is nominal or tangential.

The clearest distinction is to be made between Anglo-Welsh and Welsh literature, that written in the Welsh language, whose origins are ancient, dating from the late sixth-century poets Aneirin and Taliesin, the unknown authors of the medieval prose romances known as *The Mabinogion*, Dafydd ap Gwilym (c. 1325–1380), and so forth. Welsh poetry written to the prescribed and complex rules of medieval bards is perpetuated in the annual Welsh cultural festival known as the *Eisteddfod*, an event reintroduced to Welsh life in 1819 by "Iolo Morganwg" (Edward Williams, 1747–1826), replete with druidic pageantry of questioned authenticity.

The Romantic revival of interest in antiquity and Celtic studies is evidenced in Lady Charlotte Guest's translation of *The Mabino-*

gion (1838–1849), George Borrow's *Wild Wales* (1862), and Matthew Arnold's *On the Study of Celtic Literature* (1867). The Welsh poet Lewis Morris (1833–1907), a contender for the laureateship at Tennyson's death in 1892, was influential in the founding of the University of Wales at Aberystwyth (1872).

In the early twentieth century, the poets W. H. Davies (1871–1940), Edward Thomas (1878–1917), and Wilfred Owen (1893–1918) achieved reputation beyond the borders of Wales, while Caradoc Evans (1878–1945) stirred local controversy with his short stories of Welsh rural life. The wish to perceive and develop a distinct Welsh cultural presence and the study of Welsh and Anglo-Welsh literature have grown stronger as the proportion of English speakers among the Welsh population has reached virtually 100 percent (including the one-quarter or more who are bilingual).

SAMUEL REES

Bibliography

Garlick, Raymond and Roland Mathias, eds. *Anglo-Welsh Poetry, 1480–1980.* 1984.

Jones, Brynmor, ed. *A Bibliography of Anglo-Welsh Literature.* 1970.

Jones, Glyn. *The Dragon Has Two Tongues.* 1968.

Jones, Gwyn, ed. *The Oxford Book of Welsh Verse in English.* 1977.

Parry, Thomas. *A History of Welsh Literature.* 1955. Trans. Sir Idris Bell.

Stephens, Meic, ed. *The Oxford Companion to the Literature of Wales.* 1986.

See also CELTIC REVIVAL

· · · · ·

ANIMAL PROTECTION

Legislative efforts to protect domesticated animals began with Martin's Act (1822), sponsored by Richard Martin (1754–1834), which prohibited cruelty to cattle and horses. In 1835 the act was extended to cover all domesticated animals, including dogs and cats, and to attempt to eliminate bull and dog baiting and cockfighting. Use of dogcarts was prohib-

ited in 1854 and acts passed between 1878 and 1894 protected animals in transit. Such animal protective legislation has been interpreted as an imposition of urban values on rural residents: the acts were introduced into a society that was reducing its historic proximity to animals raised for work or slaughter while pioneering in the new mass phenomenon of animals as pets. The acts can also be seen as unfairly directed at lower-class amusements, while ignoring blood sports patronized by the upper classes. Their passage may have been motivated as much by concern about the effects of brutality upon human perpetrators as upon the animal victims. Landmarks in the changing attitude toward animals include the first dog show, at Newcastle in 1859; the first animal shelter, the Battersea Dogs' Home in 1860; the founding of the Kennel Club (1873) to regulate pedigrees; the development of bird watching, as distinct from bird shooting, in the 1880s; and the eruption of wild bird feeding as a popular pursuit during the severe winter of 1890–1891.

To support the effective enforcement of Martin's Act, the Society for the Prevention of Cruelty to Animals was founded in 1824. Its license to adopt the preface "Royal" (RSPCA) in 1840 indicated personal support by Queen Victoria. Its first major triumph, the suppression in 1838, with the aid of troops, of the annual bull-running at Stamford, presaged its later policy of close cooperation with the government. Under the management of John Colam (1827–1910), secretary from 1861 to 1905, the RSPCA became a nationwide organization, with 254 branches by 1901. It sponsored and publicized legislation and, through a corps of RSPCA constables (120 by 1897), brought prosecutions (71,657 in the 1890s) against violators of protective legislation. From 1869 it published *Animal World.* It interested itself in the regulation of slaughterhouses and supported the professionalization of veterinary science. Its success was largely due to discretion in refusing to outdistance public opinion significantly; zealots were encouraged to form separate specialized organizations. **Angela Burdett-Coutts** (1814–1906) became the influential president of the RSPCA's Ladies' Committee in 1870. Women gave 64 percent of the RSPCA's nineteenth-century legacies and constituted 69 percent of its subscribers in 1900.

Action against vivisection was supported by Cardinal **Henry Edward Manning**, who brought to English Catholicism a sympathy for animals rare in the Continental Church, by **Lord Shaftesbury**, and, with tenacious insistence, by the Queen. The resulting Cruelty to Animals Act (1876), regulating but not outlawing experimentation on animals, represented a victory for the moderate position adopted by the RSPCA and a defeat for those who, under the leadership of **Frances Power Cobbe** (1822–1904) and her Victoria Street Society (1875), undertook agitation for total abolition.

JOHN RANLETT

Bibliography

French, Richard D. *Antivivisection and Medical Science in Victorian Society.* 1975.

Harrison, Brian. "Animals and the State in Nineteenth-Century England." In Brian Harrison, *Peaceable Kingdom: Stability and Change in Modern Britain.* 1982.

Lansbury, Coral. *The Old Brown Dog: Women, Workers, and Vivisection in Edwardian England.* 1985.

Moss, Arthur W. *Valiant Crusade: The History of the R.S.P.C.A.* 1961.

Turner, James. *Reckoning with the Beast: Animals, Pain, and Humanity in the Victorian Mind.* 1980.

See also WILDLIFE PROTECTION

· · · · ·

ANNUALS AND GIFT BOOKS

Literary annuals were introduced into England in 1823 by Rudolph Ackermann. His *Forget-Me-Not* of that year inspired a swarm of British imitators, so that by 1831 over sixty different "keepsake" books of uneven literary merit vied for the annual Christmas trade. By about 1855 the commercial potential of these "butterfly books" had been exhausted and the gift book craze was over.

Many of the less successful annuals were aimed at specific audiences—juvenile, parochial, sectarian—or their emphases were non-literary, as with the numerous botanical and geographical annuals. The more popular annuals, however, catered to the literary tastes and moral values of the affluent middle class, and were lavishly turned out. Ranking artists and engravers were commissioned to illustrate the poetic fragments of several hundred regular contributors including such established writers as Scott, Wordsworth, Coleridge, and Lamb.

Although most of the leading poets of the period contributed at least once to the annuals, the letterpress of most annuals was dominated by such "specialist" gift book versifiers as Barry Cornwall, L. E. L., Felicia Hemans, and the countess of Blessington, as well as by a host of amateur poets—clergymen, lords, ladies, and children of the nobility.

The various "Winter Wreaths" and "Amethysts" offer cheer and comfort for every human grief and are free from the slightest hint of impropriety. All reflect conventional views on hearth and homeland, morality and mortality, and nearly all feature the same spectrum of sentimental literary stereotypes: the deepening of married love, the wages of sin, the virtues of the country life, and the blessings of poverty. The diction and imagery are as formulaic as the sentiments. It is little wonder that the annuals became favorite gifts at birthdays and weddings as well as at Christmastime.

By 1850 many publishers had been forced to abandon the publication of gift books as a consequence of commercially suicidal expenditures on the vanity features of the product. Nevertheless, over a period of three decades the gift books had sold more than two million copies.

LLOYD SIEMENS

Bibliography

Altick, Richard. *The English Common Reader: A Social History of the Mass Reading Public, 1800–1900.* 1957.

Boyle, Andrew. *An Index to the Annuals, 1820–1850.* 1967.

Faxon, Frederick. *Literary Annuals and Gift Books.* Rev. ed., 1973.

Siemens, Lloyd. "The Poet as Huckster: Some Victorians in the Toyshop of Literature." *English Language Notes,* vol. 16, pp. 129–144.

· · · · ·

ANTHROPOLOGY

The Victorian era was a remarkably rich period for the growth and popularization of scientific research, for the extension of the sphere of scientific inquiry, and for the development of new scientific disciplines. One of the most important new fields was anthropology.

Anthropology was a synthesis of previously separate study areas linked by a common theoretical framework. Unlike Continental usage, where "anthropology" referred to purely physical research on human variation and origins, in Britain the term came to include both cultural and physical studies. It subsumed **ethnology** and ethnography, **archaeology**, comparative **philology**, historical jurisprudence, **folklore**, and physical anthropology or somatology. Anthropology's object, according to E. B. Tylor (1832–1917), Britain's most influential anthropologist, was to collect and coordinate data gleaned through its various departments "so as to elaborate as completely as may be the synopsis of man's bodily and mental nature, and the theory of his whole course of life and action from his first appearance on earth." The various subfields of the new science were united by a comprehensive theory of physical and cultural evolution.

Theories of cultural evolution predated Darwinian evolutionary thought and were not the consequence of applying biological theory to the social realm. Nevertheless, the success of Darwinian evolution as an explanatory system did make evolution more popular among social theoreticians. Furthermore, biological evolution explained the origin of racial variation and generally put to rest the question of whether human races had a single or multiple origins (monogenesis vs. polygenesis).

Social evolution was hypothesized to be the result of slow incremental change from simplicity and homogeneity to complexity and heterogeneity. Everything from the structure of language to social organization became more complex and differentiated as time passed. Development was unilinear, but proceeded at different rates among different peoples. Change was a graduated process moving from savagery—the lowest form of which was characterized by the culture of Brazilian Indians and Australian aborigines—through barbarism, to civilization, the highest form of which was to be found among European industrialized peoples. Each stage was subclassified into low, middle, and high, with the criteria of classification being a combination of social organization, language, and material culture. The study of contemporary primitives and the remains of prehistoric peoples allowed the course of upward progress to be charted. Consequently, any people's place on the developmental path could be pinpointed through analysis of their cultural traits.

The focus of anthropological activity in Great Britain was the (Royal) Anthropological Institute, founded in 1871. The institute merged two previously competing societies, the Ethnological Society of London (1843) and the Anthropological Society of London (1863). While the ESL had as its research focus the pursuit of linguistic ethnology, with the implicit goal of demonstrating the unity of humankind, the ASL centered on the study of human races. The Anthropological Society followed Robert Knox's dictum that "race is everything." It mapped out a research program of racial classification and analysis aimed at demonstrating the importance of race in the production of civilization. The death in 1869 of James Hunt, founder and leader of the ASL, allowed intersocietal disagreements to be set aside. A circle of young Darwinians centered around John Lubbock (1834–1913), and including T. H. Huxley, George Busk, Augustus Franks, A. R. Wallace, E. B. Tylor, J. D. Hooker, George Rolleston, and William Spottiswoode, had taken leadership of the ESL in the early 1860s. The Lubbock circle dominated the amalgamated society after 1871 and helped move anthropology into the British scientific mainstream.

Anthropology remained an armchair science throughout the nineteenth century. The writings of such important thinkers as E. B. Tylor, R. R. Marett, Augustus Pitt-Rivers, Henry Sumner Maine, James G. Frazer, C. H. Read, and others were based upon observations and notes collected from explorers, travelers, and printed sources. A. C. Haddon (1855–1940) was the first major anthropologist to do his own field work, leading an expedition to the Torres Straits from 1898 to 1899.

Tylor was the first British anthropologist to receive a university appointment, becoming keeper of the Oxford University Museum in

1883 and reader in anthropology the following year. A. C. Haddon initiated anthropology lectures at Cambridge in the 1890s. Both Tylor's and Haddon's teaching was primarily ethnological. Physical anthropology was more frequently represented within anatomy and biology departments. Museums were also important centers for anthropological employment and research. Nevertheless, anthropology remained an avocation rather than a profession throughout the Victorian era.

DAVID K. VAN KEUREN

Bibliography

Burrow, J. W. *Evolution and Society: A Study in Victorian Social Theory.* 1966.

Kuklick, Henrika. *The Savage Within: The Social Context of British Anthropological Thought, 1885–1945.* 1989.

Stocking, George R., Jr. *Victorian Anthropology.* 1987.

See also RACE

. . . . .

ANTI–CORN–LAW LEAGUE (1838–1846)

The Anti–Corn-Law League was an organization of free traders and radicals which agitated for the total and immediate repeal of the corn and provision laws. Leaguers believed that the unrestricted import of cereal grain and other foodstuffs was the key to a commercial policy that would lead to economic growth and political progress. The league was a symbol for free trade, laissez-faire economics, and other liberal causes, and it opposed monopoly, protectionism, and aristocratic misrule.

The league was organized by the Manchester Anti–Corn-Law Association in late 1838 and had local associations in Britain's major northern industrial cities and in London. The league's leaders, including **Richard Cobden**, **John Bright**, and J. B. Smith, were predominantly manufacturers from Manchester, which remained the center of the movement

and the home of Free-Trade Hall. A number of philosophical radicals, including **Francis Place** and Joseph Hume, headed the metropolitan association in London. Several journalists and Nonconformists were also prominent in the league.

The league first concentrated upon the "enlightenment of the public mind" on the issue of the Corn Laws. It sent out lecturers, collected signatures on petitions, held mass meetings, and published its own newspapers and a host of tracts, pamphlets, and books. Several league leaders were returned to Parliament, and C. P. Villiers annually introduced motions and resolutions calling for an end to protection. After 1842, when George Wilson became head of the league's executive council, the league broadened its activities to include enrollment of additional members, increased attention to fund raising, and registration of electors.

The league created the climate of public opinion which made possible the repeal of the Corn Laws in 1846 by the Peel ministry. It became the most effective political pressure group and propaganda machine that Britain had ever seen, and it proved a model for other reform agitations.

RICHARD FRANCIS SPALL, JR.

Bibliography

McCord, Norman. *The Anti–Corn-Law League, 1838–1846.* 1958.

See also CORN LAWS; FREE TRADE; MANCHESTER SCHOOL

. . . . .

ANTIQUARIANISM

During the Victorian period, local antiquarian societies proliferated, particularly at mid-century, and a split developed between those antiquarians who became professional students of the past (field archaeologists and some local historians) and simple collectors. Antiquarians were typically self-made members of the middle class, some of them women. Even those Victorians who were not professional students of the past interpreted contemporary society with reference to ideas about societies that had preceded them.

The activities of the venerable London Society of Antiquaries reflect these trends. As early as 1855, John Ruskin urged the society to institute a conservation fund to preserve monuments of the past. John Evans, who became president of the society in 1885, was the preeminent numismatist of the period and the director of a family paper-making firm—neither university educated nor aristocratic. In 1900 the society formally encouraged the presentation of papers detailing field work, particularly in prehistory, at the expense of exhibitions of individual collections. Those collections that were displayed were more and more often archaeological artifacts in provincial museums established by local antiquarian societies. England never established a national museum for British antiquities, though Scotland supported one by 1858.

Victorian interest in the past was painstaking and often scholarly; it was also subjective, providing a way for Victorians to interpret their own society. Ecclesiology, the science of church building and decoration, is a case in point. The study of old rural churches became a popular pastime, the Cambridge Camden Society (founded in 1839) providing an exhaustive checklist of architectural features for the student to observe. This interest coincided with the high point of Tractarianism: ancient—especially Gothic—churches were appreciated for their atmosphere conducive to **High Church** ritual and liturgy. The Cambridge Camden Society supported restoration of medieval churches, sometimes modifying them to fit a modern idea of Gothic sanctity; William Morris, later in the century, attacked their policies and lobbied for responsible preservation practices.

Victorian literary, artistic, and social life all used the past to comment on the present. At the Eglinton Tournament (1839), in which a large portion of England's upper class recreated a medieval joust in the rain, the aristocracy used the Middle Ages to reaffirm its own conservative values. Similarly, the **Gothic revival** in architecture, embraced by wealthy estate owners, harked back to a feudal order. When Morris founded the most influential design firm of the century in 1861, he derived his ideals of craft from medieval guilds.

Later in the century classical culture, particularly Greek aesthetics, became the reference point for young artists like Lawrence Alma-Tadema and George Moore, who used formal elements of Greek art to disavow the values of the generation that had preceded them. The artists of the 1890s deliberately rejected the association of form and substance whereas the medievalism of midcentury had been used precisely to establish that association—yet in both cases, antiquarian interest was placed in the service of a contemporary agenda, the most characteristic nineteenth-century use of the past.

LAURA NOVO

Bibliography

Evans, Joan. *A History of the Society of Antiquaries.* 1956.

Jenkyns, Richard. *The Victorians and Ancient Greece.* 1980.

Piggott, Stuart. *Ruins in a Landscape: Essays in Antiquarianism.* 1976.

White, James F. *The Cambridge Movement: The Ecclesiologists and the Gothic Revival.* 1962.

See also ARCHAEOLOGY; CLASSICAL SCHOLARSHIP; MEDIEVALISM; PLANCHÉ, JAMES ROBINSON

. . . . .

ANTISLAVERY MOVEMENT

British antislavery, although obscured by the momentous efforts of its American counterpart and by other reform traditions in England, remained a viable popular movement through the 1860s. One hundred auxiliaries functioned between 1839 and 1869, of which one-third were women's groups.

The British Emancipation Bill of 1833, prohibiting slavery in the British colonies, ended the era of English antislavery which had concentrated on using political means to achieve limited objectives. From 1833 until the early 1850s British antislavery more closely reflected developments in American abolitionism, with a concurrent increase in dissension within the movement and a rankling political ineffectiveness. New agitation revolved around Joseph Sturge (1793-1859) and the British and Foreign Antislavery Society which he formed in 1833. This organization sought to expand British antislavery into a general, worldwide crusade with ambitious plans for eliminating the Atlantic slave trade. Two World Antislavery Conventions, held in London in 1840 and 1843, marked the high point of English idealism and Anglo-American antislavery cooperation, but attracted only limited public attention. (Indeed, the first convention is best remembered for the vehement British opposition to the seating of American women delegates.)

By the 1850s the sense of urgency dwindled; abolitionists redirected their efforts among various other middle-class social reform endeavors. Traditional support among the Quakers decreased, the leadership was crippled by the bitter debate over free-trade versus slave-grown goods, and the movement was attacked as a hypocritical delusion by more radical agitators. Despite the lack of tangible results in the early Victorian era, British antislavery remained an intriguing if ambivalent mixture of moral and religious idealism and practical limitations.

KAREN I. HALBERSLEBEN

Bibliography

Temperley, Howard. *British Antislavery, 1833-1870.* 1972.

Fladeland, Betty. *Men and Brothers: Anglo-American Antislavery Cooperation.* 1972.

Coupland, Sir Reginald. *The British Anti-Slavery Movement.* 1933.

See also SLAVE TRADE; UNITARIANISM

. . . . .

APOTHECARIES

The institutional structure of the medical profession in the early nineteenth century was tripartite, with three legally recognized groups of medical practitioners: physicians, surgeons, and apothecaries. The apothecaries, lowest in the hierarchy, were represented by the Worshipful Society of Apothecaries (formed in 1617).

Although apothecaries won the legal right to prescribe as well as dispense medicines in the Rose case of 1703, dispensing remained an important part of the apothecary's duties, especially following the Apothecaries Act of 1815. The apothecary was required by law to dispense the prescriptions of physicians and so remained in a subordinate position.

The description of medical structure, however, obscures important changes that had taken place by the early nineteenth century. Especially in the provinces, it became commonplace for medical men to diversify their practice; with increased numbers and greater competition, few could survive by practicing only one branch of medicine. Distinctions blurred, and practitioners often took the examination of the Royal College of Surgeons along with that of the Society of Apothecaries, described themselves as surgeon-apothecaries, and provided a less specialized and more general medicine.

General practice thus came into being through demands for wider medical experience, the need of practitioners to extend their practice to make a living, and the move of orthodox medicine toward professional status. A distinction was made between the consultant (a product of the growth of hospitals) and the general practitioner. Professional status was solidified by the Medical Registration Act of 1858, which set up the General Medical Council and directed medicine toward a more uniform standard of qualification and practice. By the mid-nineteenth century relatively few medical men described themselves simply as apothecaries; most used the designation surgeon-apothecary or general practitioner.

PHILIP SWAN

Bibliography

Brown, P. S. "The Providers of Medical Treatment in Mid-Nineteenth-Century Bristol." *Medical History,* vol. 24, pp. 297-314.

Holloway, S. W. F. "The Apothecaries' Act, 1815: A Reinterpretation." *Medical History,* vol. 10, pp. 107-129.

Peterson, M. Jeanne. *The Medical Profession in Mid-Victorian London.* 1978.

Waddington, Ivan. *The Medical Profession in the Industrial Revolution.* 1984.

See also MEDICAL EDUCATION; MEDICAL PRACTICE

· · · · ·

ARCHAEOLOGY

In the early nineteenth century, interest in the remote past was an antiquarian hobby practiced largely by rural clergy; by 1900 archaeology was a science, a component in the sweeping Victorian reassessment of the age and nature of the past, a university subject and a profession.

Archaeology developed quickly for many reasons: the aftermath of romantic nationalism encouraged popular interest in a distant national past; the development of land for industrial purposes uncovered potential archaeological sites and created a capitalist class with leisure and means to study them; a new network of railways gave access to sites and meetings of societies devoted to antiquities and archaeology; and European imperialism made it safe and profitable for the British to explore Egypt, Mesopotamia, and Palestine.

But most important for the development of archaeology was the intellectual climate of midcentury Britain. The concept of prehistory, essential for any systematic study of the remote past, could not exist until traditional assumptions about the age of humanity, based on a literal interpretation of the Bible, were replaced. Charles Lyell's *Principles of Geology* (1830–1833) and his promotion of the principle of uniformitarianism, the higher criticism of the Bible, and Charles Darwin's work on evolution all contributed to the rise of archaeology.

Archaeological study within Britain developed from local antiquarian societies active before the nineteenth century. These societies produced systematic regional histories and organized expeditions to view pre-Roman ruins; often the study of British antiquities was a cheap substitute for classically trained enthusiasts who could not afford to travel abroad. Early in the century there was little understanding of the depth of the British past; in John Akerman's *Archaeological Index* (1847) everything pre-Roman was classified as Celtic, and the British public considered these civilizations barbaric and undeveloped.

In 1843 the British Archaeological Association was formed and in 1849 *Notes and Queries*, a popular journal for the study of antiquities, was founded. In 1858 William Pengelly (1812–1894) began work at Brixham, discovering human tools alongside the remains of extinct animals that provided evidence of humanity's great age. In 1863 Lyell published *The Geological Evidences of the Antiquity of Man* and the following year John Evans (1823–1908) showed that the pre-Roman past deserved serious scholarly attention with his *The Coins of the Ancient Britons.* In 1865 John Lubbock (1834–1913) published *Pre-Historic Times*, popularizing the term "prehistory" and dividing the Stone Age into Paleolithic and Neolithic periods. The three-age system of dating prehistory (Stone, Bronze, and Iron ages), introduced in Denmark in 1819, was finally gaining credence in Britain.

When Lubbock learned in 1871 that Avebury, an important prehistoric site, was about to be built on, he bought it; not until 1882, with the first Monuments Protection Act, was there any national attempt to preserve archaeological sites. Excavation became progressively more scientific, particularly when Augustus Pitt-Rivers (1827–1900) inherited Cranborne Chase, a site of prehistoric and Roman antiquities, and began excavating in 1880.

The preeminent Victorian archaeologist working in Britain, Pitt-Rivers was one of the first to realize that the mundane find was often the most significant. He recorded the characteristics and stratigraphic location of everything he found, feeling that through the remains of their daily lives the development of prehistoric societies could be shown. A believer in evolution, he perceived archaeology as science rather than treasure seeking and opened a museum of finds on his estate for the education of the public.

In 1888 the Society of Antiquaries undertook the excavation of the Roman town of Silchester with Pitt-Rivers in charge. Archaeology was so popular, largely because of work being done abroad, that the project was financed partly through subscription and the public frequently visited the excavation in progress.

British interest in archaeology abroad was strong from the first. The eighteenth-century grand tour had introduced many upper-class young men to the classical world, and the British acquisition of the Elgin marbles (1803-1812) encouraged interest, though primarily esthetic rather than scholarly. Napoleon's occupation of Egypt produced spectacular archaeological finds, including the Rosetta stone in 1799, captured by the British in 1801 and sent to England.

The first important British expedition came in 1845 when Austen Henry Layard (1817-1894) began excavations in Nimrud, which he then thought to be Nineveh. His book *Nineveh and Its Remains* (1849), published in an abridged popular version in 1851, became the first archaeological best seller, partly because of Layard's particular site: the places he uncovered were familiar and exciting to all classes of British through their reading of the Old Testament. The Crimean War stopped Mesopotamian excavation in 1855, but in 1872 George Smith (1840-1876), working in the Assyrian Department at the British Museum, translated tablets which gave the Chaldean account of the Biblical Flood; the *Daily Telegraph* sponsored an expedition to look for a missing section, evidence of the widespread appeal of Near Eastern excavation.

Heinrich Schliemann (1822-1890) began his search for Troy in 1868, revitalizing European interest in Greece, which had waned after the early part of the century. His great appeal to classicists was his conviction that Homer could lead him to Troy as, in fact, he did. Schliemann uncovered Bronze Age Troy as well as Mycenae; he misidentified Homeric Troy, but many British, including William Gladstone, believed along with him that he had found it. Gladstone, a fervent Hellenist, wrote the introduction to the English translation of Schliemann's *Mycenae* (1878), and British interest in Schliemann's frequent dispatches to the *Times* and *Daily Telegraph* was high. Arthur Evans (1851-1941), son of John Evans, discovered a third prehistoric civilization in Greece when he uncovered Knossos on Crete in 1900.

The most important British archaeologist working abroad near the end of the century was Flinders Petrie (1853-1942), whose excavations in Egypt and Palestine established the scientific archaeological techniques of the twentieth century. Petrie first visited Egypt in 1880, making precise observations of Giza, though he was not allowed to excavate; his measurements provided useful evidence about Egyptian engineering skills. Egypt's appeal to the British was enhanced by its combined classical and Biblical associations, and in 1883 Amelia Blandford Edwards (1831-1892) founded the Egypt Exploration Fund, employing Petrie to work abroad.

Petrie made important prehistoric finds, particularly of pottery fragments. Egyptian archaeology had previously concentrated on large spectacular finds, and a persistent mystery for Europeans was how the Egyptians had suddenly emerged, evidently fully developed. Like Pitt-Rivers, Petrie excavated meticulously, in this case uncovering a wealth of prehistoric Egyptian remains that allowed scholars to reconstruct a developing Egyptian past. Petrie also invented sequence dating, organizing finds in relation to one another and their stratigraphic locations, thus providing an absolute record of chronology at a particular site; sometimes chronological dating is possible when remains are cross-referenced with similar ones whose date is known.

In 1883 Oxford was founding a professorship in classical archaeology and in 1884, when Arthur Evans was appointed keeper of the Ashmolean Museum, a massive renovation was begun to turn the museum from a poorly classified collection of antiquarian and fine art objects to a center for archaeological research. In 1893 Petrie accepted the first Edwards Chair of Egyptology at University College, London. By the end of the century, archaeology was an institutionalized field of study and profession.

LAURA NOVO

Bibliography

Daniel, Glyn. *150 Years of Archaeology.* 1975.

Evans, Joan. *Time and Chance: The Story of Arthur Evans and His Forebears.* 1943.

Hudson, Kenneth. *A Social History of Archaeology: The British Experience.* 1981.

Kendrick, Thomas. "The British Museum and British Antiquities." *Antiquity,* vol. 28, pp. 132-142.

Layard, Austen Henry. *Nineveh and Its Remains.* 1849.

Petrie, Flinders. *70 Years in Archaeology.* 1932.

Wortham, John David. *The Genesis of British Egyptology, 1549–1906.* 1971.

See also CLASSICAL SCHOLARSHIP

· · · · ·

Postlewait, Thomas. *Prophet of the New Drama: William Archer and the Ibsen Campaign.* 1986.

————, ed. *William Archer on Ibsen: The Major Essays, 1889–1919.* 1984.

Schmid, Hans B. *The Dramatic Criticism of William Archer.* 1964.

· · · · ·

ARCHER, WILLIAM
(1856–1924)

Author of *English Dramatists of To-day* (1882), *Henry Irving, Actor and Manager* (1883), and *About the Theatre* (1886), William Archer first established himself as a leading drama critic in his reviews for the *London Figaro* (1879–1881) and the *World* (1884–1906). His theories of acting and dramatic construction are set forth in *Masks or Faces?* (1888) and *Play-Making* (1912). In *The Old Drama and the New* (1923) Archer praises the craftsmanship of selected Victorian playwrights at the expense of their seventeenth-century predecessors.

Archer's belief in the intellectual potential of theater appears in his early championing of the new drama. His translation of *The Pillars of Society* (*Quicksands*, 1880) provided London audiences with their first opportunity to see a play by Ibsen, and was followed by productions of his English texts of *A Doll's House* (1889), *Ghosts* (1891), *The Master Builder* (1893), *An Enemy of the People* (1893), *Little Eyolf* (1896), *John Gabriel Borkman* (1897), and *When We Dead Awaken* (1903). From 1906–1912 his *Collected Works of Henrik Ibsen* appeared.

Archer also tried his hand at playwriting, collaborating with Bernard Shaw upon a piece that eventually became *Widowers' Houses* (1892). Archer's farsighted plans for the establishment of a national theater are recorded in *A National Theatre: Scheme and Estimates* (1907), coauthored with Harley Granville-Barker. His most successful play was, ironically, *The Green Goddess* (1919), a traditional melodrama.

SHEILA STOWELL

Bibliography

Archer, Charles. *William Archer: His Life, Work and Friendships.* 1931.

ARCHITECTURAL COMPETITIONS

Formal competition was a process by which architects or building designs were selected during the nineteenth century. By 1900 virtually all large public buildings and many small private ones were products of architectural competitions, from the Houses of Parliament (1835) and the Crystal Palace (1850) to a railway drinking fountain for 25 pounds (1877). More than 2,500 competitions were advertised in England's principal architectural journal, the weekly *Builder*, between its founding in 1842 and 1900. In this era of tremendous building activity, competitions attracted both architects with established practices, who had free labor in the form of pupils to prepare their drawings, and those just starting out, whose first commission might come from an open competition.

The typical competition began with a committee who advertised for designs. Upon application, architects were given instructions and a specified time to prepare drawings. The committee then reviewed the plans (with or without the help of an architect hired as an assessor) and selected a winner, who received the advertised premium. This did not insure the commission, and sometimes the winning architect had to stand by while another built his design.

Distress about competition abuses served to unite architects and underline the need for a strong professional organization. On its founding in 1834, the Institute of British Architects (later RIBA) immediately addressed the competition problem. Their report of 1839 is the first official document regarding architectural competitions in England. This was followed by recommendations from the Architectural Association (1850), the General Conference of Architects (1872), and an architects' memorial (1880), in which 1,300 architects pledged refusal to participate in any competition without a professional assessor. When the competition process came firmly under the control of the profession in the twentieth century, and hence more favorable to architects, it also became less attractive to the building committees who had enjoyed a large selection of designs for only the price of the premium.

JOAN BASSIN

Bibliography

Bassin, Joan. *Architectural Competitions in Nineteenth-Century England.* 1984.

Harper, Roger H. *Victorian Architectural Competitions: An Index to British and Irish Architectural Competitions in The Builder, 1943-1900.* 1983.

Summerson, John. *Victorian Architecture in England: Four Studies in Evaluation.* 1970.

· · · · ·

ARCHITECTURE

The Victorian period in British architecture is characterized by great dichotomies and is especially affected by the industrial revolution and the artistic and social reactions to it. As imperial England became a world leader in industry, commerce, and manufacturing, the enriched middle class and the nouveau riche expressed their status architecturally in lavish and gargantuan country houses, magnificent and conspicuous public buildings, and elaborate pleasure parks. At the same time, the squalor of housing and workplaces for the laboring classes offered visible evidence of the other side of Victorian experience. The railroad, the coal mine (providing energy), the tenant and country houses, and the new iron and glass architecture in burgeoning cities all contributed to the composite of Victorian living and working environments.

Victorian architecture, therefore, extended from magnificent estate buildings, urbane residences, and public monuments of increasing technological sophistication to crowded tenements, row houses, and rural hovels. Reacting to the latter, guilt and enlightened social

thinking conspired from midcentury to create paternalistic model factory towns (Saltaire, Yorkshire, 1854), planned communities and model estate villages (Edensor, begun 1839 at Chatsworth, Derbyshire), and utopian towns and suburbs (Bedford Park, London, 1875, or Bourneville, Worcestershire, 1895). Some representative architectural structures of nineteenth-century Britain give an indication of the dichotomies, enthusiasm, individualism, and energy of the age: Harlaxton Manor (1838-1855); Manchester Town Hall (1868-1877); Birmingham or Newcastle terrace housing; Blackpool; Sydenham; St. Katherine's Dock; Leamington Spa; Covent Garden Market; the Grand Hotel of Scarborough (1863-1867); the London "Underground" (opened 1863); and the Firth of Forth Bridge (1882-1890). The architectural face of Great Britain was under the influence of both technology and reformism; every level of society was affected by dramatic change.

Progressive builders looked forward to twentieth-century modern architecture in developing new building types, new materials for construction, and revolutionary structural advances in metal frame and glass. But at the same time the architecture of the modern nation and its empire was often clothed in an unabashed eclectic historicism, unsurpassed in any period before or since.

Joseph Paxton's Crystal Palace (1850-1851) expressed unqualified modern functionalism with its constructional techniques of mass assemblage and standardized parts. At the very same time, however, Paxton was clothing his Mentmore Towers (1851-1854), Buckinghamshire, in a sixteenth-century Elizabethan revival garb. Victorian mastodons such as Mentmore sought to disguise technological advances beneath anachronistic architectural styles; wrought iron riveted girders supported Mentmore's ridge-and-furrow roof and spanned the forty-foot central hall. The house also boasted a hot water central heating system.

Architects such as S. S. Teulon (1812-1873) at Tortworth Court, Gloucestershire (1849-1852); **Richard Norman Shaw** (1831-1912) at Cragside, Northumberland (1870-1884); or Edward Middleton Barry (1830-1880) at Wykehurst, Sussex (1871-1874) created High Victorian country houses with significant advances in residential comfort made possible by advances in technology. Tortworth Court pioneered in its use of gas lighting. Cragside was one of the first houses in the world to be lit by electricity. Wykehurst had cavity wall construction, double-framed fireproof floors of iron and concrete, warm air heating, and internal water pipes supplying hot water to all floors and protected from freezing by running through hot air flues; ventilation flues, elevators for luggage and coal, and a bathroom for each bedroom suite. At the same moment, Robert Kerr (1823-1904) was building Bear Wood in Berkshire (1865-1874), where he installed twenty-two water closets and five bathrooms.

Works of engineering occasionally encountered the battle of styles. **Isambard Kingdom Brunel** (1806-1859), John Fowler (1817-1898), and other heroic engineers built extraordinary bridges which directly expressed their engineering function. R. M. Ordish (1824-1886) and Horace Jones (1819-1887), on the other hand, clothed London bridges such as the Albert Bridge (1872-1873) or Tower Bridge (1886-1894) in **Gothic revival** frill or High Victorian castellation.

The juxtaposition of technology and art is best exemplified by one of the new building types of the Victorian age: the railroad station. St. Pancras Station, with its Midland Grand Hotel (1868-1874), was designed by the leading Gothic revivalist, **George Gilbert Scott** (1811-1878), and provided travelers to London with a major urban monument; it was High Victorian Gothic at its best, designed by the architect of the unsurpassed Albert Memorial in Kensington Park. But behind St. Pancras terminal and hotel was the train shed (1863-1869), in which Ordish and W. H. Barlow (1812-1902) expressed the simple functionalism of engineering: it was (and remains) a vast metallic shelter for long rows of parallel trains disgorging commuters and freight with equal dispatch. In the encounter between art and technics at St. Pancras, there was no question in the building where engineering stopped and art took over.

But elsewhere, traditional forms and new technologies brought different results. Victorians in Britain excelled, architecturally, in responding to the new programmatic demands of their world. They built workhouses, asylums, and prisons which extended eighteenth-century models to more enlightened and humane architectural solutions. Victorian social, cultural, and philanthropic groups built halls and meeting places; the private gentleman's club and atheneum of earlier years gave rise to the public library. Colleges, hospitals, and prisons all felt the impact of philanthropic reformism, technological innovation, and historicism. Increasingly more splendid government buildings reflected the growing administrative bureaucracy and announced that the cities, in spite of their visible ills, were among the best policed, best serviced, and best governed in Europe.

Other building types reflected new technologies put to new functions. Commercial retail shops coalesced to create the modern shopping arcade, and cast iron warehouses, cast and wrought iron shop fronts, and innovative factory designs stepped forward toward the twentieth century. Less obvious was the technology informing hotels, theaters, and museums. Their forms emulated the sophistication, richness, and grandeur that the lower and middle classes associated with the gentry and with wealth. Many of these building types were as rare or unknown to the eighteenth century as they were common to the twentieth, and it is characteristic of Victorian Britain that they are among its most noteworthy architectural works.

One reaction against the industrial revolution and the new technology was led by **A. W. N. Pugin** (1812-1852), **John Ruskin** (1819-1900), and **William Morris** (1834-1896). In *Contrasts; or, A Parallel Between the Noble Edifices of the Fourteenth and Fifteenth Centuries and Similar Buildings of the Present Day* (1836), Pugin promoted architecture as an act of religious devotion rather than of business; he rejected classicism as paganist (he would later claim that Gothic was "the only true Christian architecture"); and he contrasted the good architecture of medieval villages to the bad architecture of industrial cities. Ruskin's *Seven Lamps of Architecture* (1849) and *The Stones of Venice* (3 vols., 1851-1853) continued to argue the moral imperative, insisting that architecture was a higher art than mere building; although inherently functional, architecture added "characters venerable or beautiful but otherwise unnecessary." The new iron and glass architecture, he said, was "eternally separated from all good and great things." The High

Victorian movement, with its "aesthetic," "Queen Anne," and "arts and crafts" successors, reflected and extended Ruskin's prescriptions for good design. William Morris emphasized the social implication of the Ruskinian view, arguing that the value, pleasure, and worth in art, including architecture, lay in its labor, its evidence of craft and handiwork.

Later Victorian styles, in religious, public, and domestic architecture alike, found new meaning in the employment of ornament, color, and honest (natural) building materials. With the arts and crafts movement, architecture became a moral act; and the comfortable middle-class houses created by some of the followers of William Morris are among the most noteworthy achievements of the age.

ROBERT M. CRAIG

Bibliography

Davey, Peter. *Architecture of the Arts and Crafts Movement.* 1980.

Dixon, Roger and Stefan Muthesius. *Victorian Architecture.* 1978.

Ferriday, Peter, ed. *Victorian Architecture.* 1964.

Girouard, Mark. *Sweetness and Light: The "Queen Anne" Movement, 1860–1900.* 1977.

——— *The Victorian Country House.* 1979.

Hitchcock, Henry–Russell. *Early Victorian Architecture in Britain.* 1954. 2 vols.

Muthesius, Stefan. *The High Victorian Movement in Architecture, 1850–1870.* 1972.

Pevsner, Nikolaus. *Studies in Art, Architecture and Design: Victorian and After.* 1968; rpt. 1982.

Stamp, Gavin and Andre Goulancourt. *The English House, 1860–1914: The Flowering of English Domestic Architecture.* 1986.

Summerson, John. *Victorian Architecture in England: Four Studies in Evaluation.* 1970.

See also AESTHETIC MOVEMENT; ARTS AND CRAFTS MOVEMENT; EDINBURGH; GOTHIC REVIVAL; HOUSING; SUBURBS AND PLANNED COMMUNITIES

· · · · ·

ARCTIC AND ANTARCTIC EXPLORATION

From the close of the Napoleonic Wars to the eve of World War I, Great Britain was committed to polar exploration. The early phase sought to attain the North Pole and navigate the Northwest Passage. After the loss of the final expedition by John Franklin (1786–1847), other nations played an increasing role in the North. In the Antarctic, the midcentury discoveries of James Clark Ross (1800–1862) remained highlights until the tragedy of Robert Falcon Scott's (1868–1912) last expedition.

Polar exploration fascinated the Victorian public. From "The Rime of the Ancient Mariner" to *Frankenstein,* pre-Victorians incorporated the Arctic into their imaginative literature. Tennyson later wrote a heroic poem for Franklin's cenotaph, and Landseer's painting of 1866, "Man Proposes, God Disposes," expressed a grim facet of the polar regions.

The voyages of Captain Cook (1728–1779) had opened the door to both Arctic and Antarctic discovery. At the end of the Napoleonic Wars the Royal Navy was free to explore the northern oceans which, according to reports from whalers, were then unusually ice free. Lord Melville determined to send two polar expeditions, one under Franklin and David Buchan by the Spitsbergen route, the other commanded by John Ross (1777–1856) through Baffin Bay. The expeditions were to combine geographical and scientific exploration and serve as vehicles for national prestige.

Ross failed to discern a passage via Lancaster Sound. A series of further expeditions followed, including the more successful voyages of William Parry (1790–1855) in 1819 and 1821. Ross returned to the Arctic in the steam-driven *Victory* in 1831; during the voyage his nephew James Clark Ross discovered the north magnetic pole. Meanwhile, Frederick William Beechey commanded an expedition to Bering Strait, failing by a relatively modest margin to meet up with John Franklin's overland expedition (1825–1827).

Franklin's last expedition set out in 1845; searches began in 1847, and news of the expedition's fate was first brought back by John Rae of the Hudson's Bay Company. For the next two decades, the Royal Navy was chary of Arctic exploration. In 1875 another naval

Arctic expedition, commanded by George Strong Nares (1831–1915) on H.M.S. *Alert*, reached the north of Smith Sound, demonstrated the existence of a polar ocean, had serious trouble with scurvy, and returned a year early. When it came to the International Polar Year of 1882–1883, British participation was minimal.

In the Antarctic, however, James Clark Ross, accompanied by a number of scientists, led a productive expedition in 1839–1843, discovering the Victoria Barrier (now the Ross Ice Shelf), a subsequent gateway to the fastnesses of Antarctica. H.M.S. *Challenger*, commanded by Nares, crossed the Antarctic Circle in 1874 in the course of a major oceanographic and hydrographic voyage. At the century's end, Sir Clements Markham (1830–1916) of the Royal Geographic Society lobbied for further Antarctic expeditions, and the new century began with the expeditions of Scott. The last, ending in tragedy, has entered into heroic mythology.

TREVOR H. LEVERE

Bibliography

Cooke, Alan and Clive Holland. *The Exploration of Northern Canada, 500 to 1920: A Chronology.* 1978.

Kirwan, Laurence P. *The White Road: A Survey of Polar Exploration.* 1959.

Thomson, George Malcolm. *The Northwest Passage.* 1975.

. . . . .

ARISTOCRACY AND GENTRY

The aristocracy and gentry had in common the ownership of enough land to maintain an appropriate establishment, provide generous hospitality, and engage in voluntary public service without the need to work for money. An increasingly strict observance of precedence and etiquette differentiated the ranks of nobility from one another and from the monied professional and middle classes. Although the titled class lost political and economic power over the course of the century, its social prestige remained, and a belief in breeding enabled even its poorer members to retain the deference considered their due. Careful conformity to the customs of the upper class could supply social mobility. Probably fewer people entered the titled class than seemed to, but the availability of a route upward was a distinguishing feature of the English aristocratic system.

The gentry included all persons who owned landed property and were qualified to apply for a coat of arms, which permitted the use of Esquire, an inheritable title, after their names. The publishers of *Burke's Landed Gentry* required that those listed own at least 300 acres. By Victorian times, however, almost any male who considered himself a gentleman was apt to write "Esquire" after his name, whether or not he owned land. "Squire" was used by custom to refer to the head of a landed estate who was active in local affairs.

Knights (titles not inheritable) and baronets (titles inheritable) came next in rank. They were addressed as Sir and their wives as Lady. Knights and baronets are technically commoners; they do not sit in the House of Lords but may be elected to the Commons.

The five ranks of the peerage, in order from least to highest, are: baron/baroness, viscount/viscountess, earl/countess, marquess/marchioness, duke/duchess. The forms of proper address in various circumstances were complex, but in general a duke or duchess was referred to by exact title and addressed as "your Grace," while those of the four lesser ranks were known as "Lord ———" and "Lady ———."

Only the current holder of the title in each family was noble. Children and siblings were commoners, although the heir was allowed the courtesy of using the next subsidiary title. Thus, the eldest son of a duke could be called a marquess. Younger sons of dukes and marquesses were called "Lord"; daughters of dukes, marquesses, and earls were "Lady," followed by both Christian name and surname (thus distinguishing them from the wives of knights and baronets, who were addressed as "Lady," followed by surname only). Younger sons of earls and all sons and daughters of barons and viscounts could use Honourable before their names. Before the law they were like other citizens—tried in ordinary courts and liable to arrest for debt. Because of primogeniture, younger sons had to seek careers in the army, government, law, or church and to mix with professional men. The nobility was not a completely separate body, as in other countries.

So important was land to maintaining nobility that until 1885, estates were granted if necessary when new peerages were created (as they often were) as political rewards. Landed gentlemen justified their privileges by taking on obligations to improve their estates and maintain their tenants through bad times, and by local public service as magistrates, justices of the peace, local Poor Law guardians, and supporters of voluntary schools. Their wives did charitable works. Until 1888, when county councils began to replace the squires, they were the primary local government.

The nobility lost considerable power when the Reform Act of 1832 took away much of their borough patronage. Their influence in national politics remained very strong, however; even after the Reform Act of 1867, tenant farmers usually voted with their landlords. Since heirs of peers could sit in the Commons, the views of landed men were influential in the legislature. It has been calculated that 220 men in the 1865 House of Commons were baronets or the sons or grandsons of peers.

Social life was regulated by rules of etiquette that endowed the pursuit of pleasure with serious purpose, as well as demonstrating breeding and so restricting the social circle. The round of hunts, balls, house parties, and London seasons nourished social connections of important economic and political consequence and—no less important—encouraged marriages and friendships that preserved the position of the ruling class.

By purchasing a large estate, sending his children to the prominent **public schools**, and adopting proper accent and behavior, it was possible for a man of wealth to gain acceptance by the gentry and even the aristocracy for his descendants if not wholly for himself. Widespread knowledge of these methods and the aping of some upper-class attitudes have given the impression that more people moved up than actually did. Those who succeeded were more likely to be bankers and professionals than manufacturers or merchants. Not until 1881 were daughters of a chemical manufacturer presented at court,

causing a sensation. But later in the 1880s and 1890s industrialists themselves were being enobled.

By this time real political power had been transferred to other groups. Repeal of the Corn Laws (which had protected the price of grain) in 1846 removed the economic buffer the landed classes had enjoyed. Many subsequently improved their estates, but the agricultural losses of the 1870s and 1880s were disastrous for landed proprietors who depended entirely on tenants' rents. Wiser people invested in overseas trade or the rising industries and railways whose owners were gaining the real power in the land. By 1885 these men, not the landed interest, were in the majority of the House of Commons. The social preeminence of the gently born began to give way.

SIDNEY JOHNSON

Bibliography

Bagehot, Walter. *The English Constitution.* 1867.

Pine, L. G. *The Story of Titles.* 1969.

Stone, Lawrence and Jeanne C. Stone. *An Open Elite? England 1540-1880.* 1984.

Thompson, F. M. L. *English Landed Society in the Nineteenth Century.* 1963.

See also CHURCH OF ENGLAND PARISH LIFE; CLASS; COUNTRY SOCIETY; SOCIAL SEASON; SOCIETY, ETIQUETTE AND CUSTOMS OF

· · · · ·

ARMY

The Victorian army played a major role in expanding "Greater Britain" overseas, while at home, from the **Crimean War** on, it was the subject of a good deal of reform activity. Moreover, it existed in a society experiencing the changes that historians associate with "modernization." But the army that plunged into World War I was in many respects the same army that Wellington had commanded at Waterloo a century earlier.

The Victorian army's primary mission was to defend British colonies and overseas outposts from both internal insurrection and external encroachment. In practice, its role was often less defensive than offensive and expansionist. During the Palmerstonian era it advanced the sphere of British rule, particularly in **India**, while the need to protect the route to this colony led in 1854 to the Crimean War against Russia's expansion into the Turkish Empire. During the "century of peace" after Waterloo, this was to be the only war fought by the British army against a major power. Yet Britain continued to be involved in countless small wars, and from the 1870s on played an ever more active role in the "scramble for empire" in sub-Saharan Africa. Thus the army was an essential tool of British foreign policy, and its success seemed based upon combining traditional tactics with improvisation, and upon the esprit de corps and heroism of the troops and their commanders. Its history overseas seemed to confirm that what had worked at Waterloo continued to work. This was precisely what a people devoting their energy to industry and commerce wanted to believe—that an army could be had "on the cheap."

Retrenchment in spending on the army had set in immediately after the end of the occupation of France in 1818. From over 43 million pounds, expenditure sank to average under 10 million during the following decades. Troop manpower was reduced by half, increased to over 200,000 during the Crimean War, and then reduced again. Although three-quarters of the army were infantrymen, they were largely displaced to overseas garrison duty. Colonial crises seriously depleted home battalions, leaving few troops available to help suppress civil disorder and protect against foreign invaders. Although domestic peace keeping became less crucial with the establishment of police forces on a national basis in midcentury, periodic invasion scares continued. However, in accordance with the "blue-water school" of thought (which held that the navy was an insular nation's first line of defense), such panics led to strengthening the navy rather than the army.

The army remained for the most part an unpopular institution partly because of its class and ethnic composition. Soldiers seemed un-English because so many were Irish and Catholic. Because the rank and file were recruited largely from unemployed, unskilled rural laborers or, by the century's closing decades, from the urban poor, they were considered unreliable.

Meanwhile, poor pay, hard conditions of service, and lack of prestige assured lower-class recruits. Throughout the century the private soldier's basic daily pay did not exceed one shilling—a paltry wage even by contemporary standards. Living conditions were little better. Moved constantly from barracks to barracks and with only six in every hundred allowed to marry "on the strength," soldiers could hardly establish domestic ties. **Prostitution** and **venereal disease** flourished, and quarters were crowded, unventilated, and without sanitary facilities. The mortality rate of the pre-Crimean army was substantially higher than that of the civilian population.

Military discipline was equally harsh. For serious crimes the punishment was death by hanging or firing squad. For all other offenses, including the most trivial, the lash was administered. The scale and severity of military floggings were exceptional by all contemporary standards; yet the lash was not fully abolished until 1881.

Army life was a monotonous routine of parades, drills, and menial labor. Victorian soldiers received virtually no formal military training. Not until the Edwardian era were annual maneuvers held on a divisional scale. The Victorian army remained essentially a collection of unrelated regiments.

Commissioned officers were largely drawn from the landed classes. Particularly for younger sons of the **aristocracy and gentry**, the military offered an appropriate and prestigious career. Commissions and promotions of officers were purchased rather than won by education or merit. The purchase system was defended on the grounds that it ensured that officers would be gentlemen who enjoyed the natural respect of the class which made up the rank and file. Opposition to change in this and other military matters was powerful because members of Parliament and officers were of the same class and often the same families.

Military reverses and defeats in the Crimean War (1854–1856) led to a temporary collapse of national complacency. As the soldier's sufferings were publicized by the press, he became for the first time the focal point of public attention. Reforms forwarded by **Florence Nightingale** and by Sidney Herbert as war secretary led to some improvement in medical and sanitary conditions. Additionally, the Contagious Diseases Acts passed during the 1860s attempted to address the fact that one-third of the troops were hospitalized because of venereal disease. These acts instituted the compulsory hospitalization and incarceration of suspected prostitutes in garrison towns. However, challenged by a strong, popular abolitionist movement, they were repealed in 1886.

The officer class was less affected by post-Crimean changes. Sidney Herbert's efforts did strengthen the Royal Military College at Sandhurst and the Royal Military Academy at Woolwich, and also led to the establishment of the Staff College at Camberley to which admission was gained by competitive examination. However, so long as commissions and promotions were based on purchase, most officers had little incentive to pursue more than a **public school** education. In 1872 the purchase system was finally abolished by the Liberal war secretary, Edward Cardwell. But officers' pay remained so low and their messing expenses so high that they continued to be primarily drawn from the independently wealthy.

Cardwell's reforming ministry (1868–1874) set out to address the continuing problem of recruitment and the lack of a reliable reserve, which had become even more pressing because of the **Indian Mutiny** of 1857. After the revolt of the sepoy troops, the ratio of British to Indian soldiers in the Indian Army was substantially and permanently increased, creating a tremendous manpower strain on the troops available for home duties. Although the auxiliary forces of militia and yeomanry had been augmented by a volunteer force established in 1859, the home defense force did not constitute a reliable reserve. Cardwell, however, faced not only the political necessity of controlling military expenditure, but also the stumbling block of civil-military conflict over who was to rule the army—Parliament or the Crown. This underlying controversy helps to explain why, in spite of a good deal of military reform activity between the Crimean and Anglo-Boer Wars, little fundamental change was actually achieved.

At the close of the eighteenth century, command of the army had been entrusted to the commander in chief as representative of the Crown. This personage and his staff were housed at Whitehall and were known as the Horse Guards. The commander in chief had authority over the discipline and military efficiency of the infantry and cavalry. But responsibility for all other military matters was divided among some thirteen different departments staffed by civilians responsible to Parliament. Through the secretary-at-war, who served as the army's representative in the House of Commons and had to approve all military expenditures, Parliament's ultimate authority was based on its control of the purse strings.

Since the various departments functioned as essentially autonomous units, the system impeded military efficiency. It also inhibited military reform, since all changes were treated in light of their effect on the balance of military-civil power. Hence the efforts of successive commanders in chief to increase the army's manpower were frustrated by the politicians' wish to hold down military expenditure, while civilian efforts to reform the army were frustrated by a Horse Guards intent upon ruling its own affairs.

The first major reorganization of this administrative structure began when the Crimean War exposed its disastrous results for troops. The separation of functions under many different departments was ended and all were placed under the authority of a consolidated War Department headed by a secretary of state for war. Subsequently, Cardwell's War Office Act of 1870 combined the Horse Guards and the War Office into a single department under the control of the war secretary. But the net effect essentially consolidated the dual system: the war secretary remained in charge of supply and finance, and the commander in chief controlled the army's internal administration and its preparation for military duties. Though technically responsible to the war secretary, in practice the commander in chief continued to function independently.

By the closing decades of the century, Continental armies had constituted general staffs as central strategic and coordinating bodies, but in Britain no general staff could be created so long as the office of commander in chief remained. Military education and professionalization of the officer class could make little headway while military policy remained a matter of "muddling through" and decision by crisis. The longevity of Queen Victoria's cousin, the duke of Cambridge, as commander in chief protected the office from attempts to abolish it or substantially reduce its authority. Additionally, efforts to establish a general staff were blocked by liberal and radical politicians who feared the taint of Continental militarism and worried about increasing military expenditure.

By century's end the successive reorganizations of the War Department had clearly established parliamentary control of the army—and thereby furthered the perception of the officer class that it was increasingly isolated from decisions. Lord Wolseley's succession to the office of commander in chief failed to usher in a new era for the army in spite of his leadership of the "Ashanti ring" of military reformers. On taking office in 1895, he discovered that the newly established War Office Council left him with overall responsibility for military affairs but without effective control. During his tenure of office (to 1904), civil-military relations in the War Office continued to deteriorate. The humiliating military reverses of the **Boer War** (1899–1902) exposed the disastrous results of the breakdown of communication in the army's higher command.

The war also revealed the fundamental weakness of an army which remained ill trained and so undermanned that it resorted to bringing raw recruits from home to combat an enemy that never fielded more than 50,000 troops. Cardwell's 1870 Army Enlistment Act had replaced long-service with short-service enlistment, in which a soldier normally did six years of active service and six in the reserve. Additionally, Cardwell had hoped to attract more and better recruits by his Localization Act, which connected regiments to specific territorial areas. However, home battalions continued to be moved regularly from barracks to barracks and depleted by overseas drafts, which necessitated further lowerings of recruiting standards. By the close of the century the empire had vastly outstripped the army's ability to perform its assigned roles of defending the homeland, maintaining overseas garrisons, and dispatching expeditionary forces as needed. Complacency was preserved by the general consensus that expeditionary forces would have colonial rather than Continental destinations. Not until the early twentieth century was this faith shaken by the evident increase of international tensions and the menace of German naval strength.

In that new context the Edwardian war secretary, Richard Burdon Haldane, would reorganize the army into a Field Force and a Territorial Force. Additionally, since the office of commander in chief was finally abolished in 1904, Haldane was able to establish the general staff on a firm basis in 1906 and to promote military-civilian cooperation. But with the outbreak of World War I the war secretary, Lord Kitchener, would again place the army under the direction of a single military person.

In sum, the history of the British army during the century that followed Waterloo is characterized above all by a continuity, traditionalism, and conservatism. So long as the troops were kept busy overseas and out of sight, a profoundly civilianist society could keep them out of mind. The army's successful performance fostered public complacency and encouraged the "small war mentality" of military men, which worked against the development of a modern military machine. Traditional British suspicion of the potential for military tyranny worked in tandem with the Victorian urge to economize in military expenditure through the vehicle of parliamentary control of the army. Since in this context the choice seemed to be between a constitutional army and an efficient army, reform was piecemeal and the army remained small, amateurish, and ill administered. Thus, from one perspective, political control of the army, encouraged by the development of democracy and party politics, weakened national security. But so long as the Victorians continued to believe in an international order in which moral law was sovereign, they remained free to maintain a critical perspective on the army's place in a liberal state.

PATRICIA MORTON

Bibliography

Barnet, Correlli. *Britain and Her Army, 1509–1970.* 1970.

Bond, Brian. *The Victorian Army and the Staff College*. 1972.

Farwell, Byron. *For Queen and Country*. 1981.

Gooch, John. *The Prospect of War: Studies in British Defence Policy, 1847-1942*. 1981.

Hamer, W. S. *The British Army: Civil-Military Relations, 1885-1905*. 1970.

Harries-Jenkins, Gwyn. *The Army in Victorian Society*. 1977.

Skelley, Alan Ramsay. *The Victorian Army at Home*. 1977.

Spiers, Edward M. *The Army and Society, 1815-1914*. 1980.

See also EMPIRE AND IMPERIALISM; WARS AND MILITARY ENGAGEMENTS

. . . . .

ARNOLD, MATTHEW (1822-1888)

Of the great Victorian poets and prose writers, Matthew Arnold is, perhaps, the figure most representative of his age. His self-divisions are at once quintessentially Victorian and peculiarly modern. He was an optimistic school inspector who believed in the spiritual efficacy of cultural institutions and a melancholy poet consumed by a sense of human futility. He was an eloquent spokesman for the virtues of "sweetness and light" and an inveterate pessimist haunted by the "blankness" and "barrenness" of life. He is equally distinguished for his essays, which strenuously defend an "ideal order of conduct and beauty," and for his elegaic poems which bewail the spiritual drift and metaphysical anguish of an age in which the Christian tradition seemed increasingly remote from contemporary problems.

The son of the famous Oxford preacher and pedagogue **Thomas Arnold** and his wife Mary Penrose, Matthew followed in his father's footsteps by becoming professor of poetry at Oxford University between 1857 and 1867 and an inspector of schools between 1851 and 1886. In both positions he endeavored to apply his father's high moral standards. Because of his lapsed faith, however, Arnold placed an increasingly higher premium on culture's role in counterbalancing middle-class self-centeredness. In books and essays such as *Culture and Anarchy* (1869), "Literature and Science" (1882), "The Study of Poetry" (1888), and "The Function of Criticism at the Present Time" (1865), Arnold extolled the value of humanistic studies and tried to create a climate favorable to the reception of "the best that has been thought and known." Moreover, Arnold recognized the need to harmonize the legacy of "Hebraism" (which he designated as "strictness of conscience") with the spirit of "Hellenism" (or "spontaneity of consciousness"). Though Arnold questioned the supernatural claims of Christianity in books like *St. Paul and Protestantism* (1870) and *God and the Bible* (1875), he wished to preserve the aesthetic and ethical elements of the Christian message.

Arnold's substitute for religion was **poetry**; and hence his critical standards became increasingly rigorous. In "The Study of Poetry" he adduces critical "touchstones" which enable the reader to discriminate between poetry of secondary value (because of its merely "personal" or "historic" significance) and poetry of "high seriousness" which blends verbal expression with a "criticism of life." Oscillating between a theory of poetry that emphasized the application of great ideas to life and a recognition that poetry is an autonomous art and not merely a platform for expressing noble sentiments, Arnold was frequently involved in self-contradictory utterances. In the preface to the 1853 volume of his own *Poems*, he rejected many of his most successful works—especially *Empedocles on Aetna* (1852)—because they failed to inculcate tonic sentiments and expressed a morbid and irresolvable anxiety in the face of an ambiguous universe.

Urbane, assured, and even something of a dandy in his prose, Arnold is the opposite in his poetry. Like Tennyson, he was a writer with two voices: one affirmed the popular Victorian belief in human progress; the other lamented the loss of a stable system of ordered and hierarchic values. His words from "Stanzas from the Grande Chartreuse" (1855), in which he describes himself as "Wandering between two worlds, one dead, /

The other powerless to be born," epitomize his sense of having arrived too late to adhere with any conviction to the formulas of traditional Christianity and too early to embrace with any enthusiasm the demythologized system of ethics destined, in his opinion, to take its place.

His most popular poem, which may be read as a concentrated extract of Arnold's poetic sensibility as well as a distillation of Victorian disquietude, is "Dover Beach" (1867). Lyrically, it is his most successful work. The haunting evocation of the cliffs of Dover, the restless movement of the tides, the "grating roar of pebbles" and "the eternal note of sadness" create a visual and auditory counterpart to the poet's dread in facing a world deprived of meaning and significance. Similarly, in "The Scholar-Gipsy" (1853), "The Buried Life" (1852), and "Thyrsis" (1866), the note of homesickness and disquietude is sustained in an exquisite minor key. Even human love was for Arnold of momentary duration, providing, at best, no more than an intermittent and tantalizing release from alienated introspection.

In the end, Arnold was compelled to give up writing poetry. The discrepancy between his inconsolable spirit and his philosophy of education was too discordant to sustain. After 1858 the poet is almost entirely superseded by the active cultural campaigner and the tireless exponent of civilizational standards.

STEPHEN GURNEY

Bibliography

Buckler, William E. *On the Poetry of Matthew Arnold.* 1982.

Bush, Douglas. *Matthew Arnold: A Survey of His Poetry and Prose.* 1971.

Eliot, T. S. "Matthew Arnold." In T. S. Eliot, *The Use of Poetry and the Use of Criticism.* 1933.

———. "Arnold and Pater." In T. S. Eliot, *Selected Essays.* 1932.

Honan, Park. *Matthew Arnold: A Life.* 1981.

James, D. G. *Matthew Arnold and the Decline of English Romanticism.* 1961.

Johnson, Edward D. H. *The Alien Vision of Victorian Poetry.* 1952.

Super, R. H., ed. *The Complete Prose Works of Matthew Arnold.* 1960–1977. 6 vols.

Tinker, C. B. and H. F. Lowry, eds. *The Poetry of Matthew Arnold.* 1940.

Trilling, Lionel. *Matthew Arnold.* 1949.

See also LITERARY CRITICISM

· · · · ·

ARNOLD, THOMAS (1795–1842)

Through his triumphant headmastership at Rugby (1828-1842), Thomas Arnold—doctor of divinity and classical scholar—gave the mid-Victorian **public school** its image as a training ground in Christian character, self-government, and public service. Championing a unified Christian state, of which the school was a microcosm, Arnold urged social and church reforms in *The Christian Duty of Granting the Claims of the Roman Catholics* (1829) and *Principles of Church Reform* (1833), and in contributions to newspapers, including his own short-lived *Englishman's Register* (1831). These views lost him a bishopric, and his attack on Newmanites in "The Oxford Malignants" (*Edinburgh Review*, April 1836) almost cost him his headmastership. But the sense of history evident in his *Thucydides* (1830-1835) and *History of Rome* (1838-1842) brought him Oxford's Regius Professorship of Modern History in 1841.

Arnold's world outlook sprang from his early fascination with foreign ships at his birthplace in West Cowes, Isle of Wight, where his father was customs keeper. Educated at Winchester and then at Oxford, where he excelled in classics at Corpus Christi College and afterward held a fellowship at Oriel College, Arnold spent nine years at Laleham coaching boys for Oxford prior to his Rugby appointment in 1828. His home life with his wife Mary Penrose and their nine children (the poet **Matthew Arnold** was the eldest) was reputedly one of "industrious peace." The family vacationed in Westmorland where Arnold built idyllic Fox How near Wordsworth's Rydal Mount.

At thirty-three Arnold was chosen Rugby's headmaster out of one hundred applicants, with the autonomy he demanded, because the trustees were worried about slipping enrollment despite new buildings. Oriel's provost predicted that "if Mr. Arnold were elected he would change the face of education all through the public schools of England." Rugby, founded for local boys in 1567, had become (like Eton and Winchester) one of the fee-paying boarding schools known as public schools, institutions then plagued with bullying and immorality. Raising fees, Arnold hand picked his masters for their love of learning and Christian character, furnished boys with individual beds, abolished lodging houses under dames, expelled irredeemable bullies, and inculcated Christian principles by his example and his stirring Sunday afternoon sermons. He then entrusted the running of the school to the senior boys. He infused new life into the primarily classical curriculum by stimulating inquiry into ideas and issues, emphasizing history and geography, and adding mathematics, French, and German. A school newspaper, debating and dramatic societies, and games were begun. Enrollment rose from 116 to Arnold's limit of 300 as Rugbeians became known for their purposefulness and took university prizes and scholarships.

Arnold, a man of "buoyant vigor," inspired exceptional works from three former pupils: his son Matthew's "Rugby Chapel" (1867), A. P. Stanley's *The Life and Correspondence of Thomas Arnold* (1844), and Thomas Hughes's *Tom Brown's School Days* (1857). In *Eminent Victorians* (1918) Lytton Strachey on slim and fabricated evidence distorts Arnold into a stern patriarch who warped the consciences of morally sensitive boys like Arthur Hugh Clough. Admittedly, Arnold made too much of sin for modern taste, but he was on the side of his boys and equipped them to cope with life.

TAMIE WATTERS

Bibliography

Arnold, Thomas. *Sermons*. Rev. ed., 1878. Ed. W. E. Forster, 6 vols.

Stanley, A. P. *The Life and Correspondence of Thomas Arnold*. 1844, 2 vols.

Wymer, Norman. *Dr. Arnold of Rugby*. 1953.

· · · · ·

ART CRITICISM

Three distinct discourses can be identified in Victorian art criticism: the associational, the pragmatic, and the aesthetic. The first was an emotional response to the morally edifying aspects of art that was based on the eighteenth-century philosophical theories of Hume, Locke, and Hartley. The second was a more scientific method of criticism which emphasized close observation of facts. Finally, the aesthetic approach, in reaction against the literary and moral tenor of the first two branches of criticism, stressed the primacy of beauty alone.

The theory of associations was first applied to art by Archibald Alison in his *Essays on the Nature and Principles of Taste* (1790), in which he maintained that the imagination was a key ingredient in the perception of beauty because it led the viewer to pleasurable sensations which were then directed by chains of ideas toward a greater moral sensibility. Adopted by such prominent proponents as Charles Lamb and William Hazlitt, Alison's ideas remained in the forefront of art criticism until well into the nineteenth century.

The more scientific climate of the 1840s, however, did not support the vagueness of associationism. **William Makepeace Thackeray** regularly mocked subjective practices in *Fraser's Magazine* and **John Ruskin** campaigned against excessive emotionalism in art criticism, although both were guilty of indulging in what they condemned—Ruskin most memorably in his impassioned description of Turner's *Slave Ship* in the first volume of *Modern Painters* in 1843. Ruskin's originality lay in his acute observation of botanical, geological, and meteorological phenomena which he used as the foundation for his moral and aesthetic theories.

Although not as grandiloquent as Ruskin, other critics, such as F. G. Stephens of the *Athenaeum* and P. G. Hamerton of the *Portfolio* were more consistent in applying objective standards to art. Unlike most other major critics of the period, Ruskin, Stephens, and Hamerton had training as artists and could write knowledgeably about technique. But it was the pen rather than the brush that dictated most of what was written about art in the periodicals—as late as 1887, the *National Review* observed that "nine-tenths, most certainly seven-tenths, of our art-writers are literary men." Most critics emphasized narrative rather than pictorial values—even Ruskin argued (in *Modern Painters*, vol. 3, 1856) that painting should "take its proper place beside literature."

Ruskin's archenemy, the **aesthetic movement** painter **James McNeill Whistler**, signaled the break with referential meaning in art when he defended his nocturnes as "an arrangement of line, form, and color first," in his celebrated libel suit against Ruskin in 1878. Whistler's pronouncement had been anticipated by **Algernon Charles Swinburne** in his 1866 essay on William Blake; Swinburne declared that art should never be the "handmaid of religion, exponent of duty, servant of fact, pioneer of morality." Similarly, **Walter Pater** diminished the narrative import of art when he defined aesthetic criticism in his preface to *Studies in the History of the Renaissance* (1873) as the expression of impressions of beauty which should be experienced, not analyzed. Aesthetic criticism ushered in the modern era of art appreciation represented by the formalist criticism of Clive Bell and Roger Fry in the early years of the twentieth century.

DIANNE SACHKO MACLEOD

Bibliography

Kallich, Martin. *The Association of Ideas and Critical Theory in Eighteenth-Century England.* 1970.

Landow, George P. *The Aesthetic and Critical Theories of John Ruskin.* 1971.

Levine, George and William Madden, eds. *The Art of Victorian Prose.* 1968.

Olmstead, John Charles. *Victorian Painting: Essays and Reviews.* 1980–1985. 3 vols.

Roberts, Helene. "Art Reviewing in the Early Nineteenth-Century Art Periodicals." *Victorian Periodicals Newsletter*, no. 19, pp. 9–20.

Shattock, Joanne and Michael Wolff. *The Victorian Periodical Press.* 1982.

Warner, Eric and Graham Hough, eds. *Strangeness and Beauty: An Anthology of Aesthetic Criticism, 1840–1910.* 1983. 2 vols.

· · · · ·

ART FOR ART'S SAKE

At its most vocal in the 1880s, the doctrine of art for art's sake sought to free artists from all moral constraints and duties regarding their art. Art was to exist for the sake of its own inherent (but consciously amplified) beauty. The movement, essentially amoral, inevitably led to the **decadence** of the 1890s.

French aestheticism was the strongest influence on the movement. However, the English aesthetes, unlike their populist French cousins, were careful to impart only such tenets as supported an artistic elitism. Some of this elitism was reaction against a stifling middle-class culture, but some was a careless snobbery that served to blind an indignant public to the more serious philosophy behind the movement.

Art for art had been explored by mid-Victorian writers, most notably John Ruskin (1819–1900), while some artists of the Pre-Raphaelite Brotherhood touched on its implications. However, the movement's best spokesmen were **James McNeill Whistler** (1834–1903), **Oscar Wilde** (1854–1900), and, unwittingly, **Walter Pater** (1839–1894). Pater, in the unguarded conclusion of *The Renaissance* (1873), seemed to sanction the cultivation of artistic sensations for their own sakes. Wilde carried this credo, which solidified into the aesthetic movement, to London and the provinces. Whistler's 1885 "Ten O'Clock" lecture gave art for art's sake its most lucid manifesto, just as his paintings best demonstrated the theory in practice.

CYNTHIA J. NOWAK

Bibliography

Buckley, Jerome H. *The Victorian Temper.* 1952.

Whistler, James Abbott McNeill. *The Gentle Art of Making Enemies.* 1890.

See also **AESTHETIC MOVEMENT; FIN DE SIÈCLE**

· · · · ·

ART NOUVEAU

Art nouveau (new art) was an artistic and decorative phenomenon of the 1890s, principally in France and Belgium, that had its En-

John Thirtle in The Studio, *May 1896. Reproduced from* Art Nouveau: An Anthology of Design and Illustration from The Studio, *ed. Edmund V. Gillon, Jr., Dover Publications Inc.*

glish counterpart in the work of **William Morris** (1834-1896) and, more notably, **Aubrey Beardsley** (1872-1898). Influenced by the English **arts and crafts movement**, of which Morris was an early and guiding proponent, by such **Pre-Raphaelites** as **Dante Gabriel Rossetti** (1828-1882) and **Edward Burne-Jones** (1833-1898), and by impressionist and symbolist painting, art nouveau took in all aspects of the decorative arts with a particular emphasis on ornament, chiefly of vegetation with long tendrils. One notable English influence on this predominantly French movement was Morris's Kelmscott Press (founded in 1890), which produced highly decorated and illustrated volumes. As a movement, art nouveau was especially remarkable in the 1890s, culminating with the Universal Exposition at Paris in 1900.

The importation of art nouveau from France came primarily through the medium of British writers influenced by their French travels. Oscar Wilde (1854-1900) adapted his *Salomé* (1891) from an opera by Jules Massenet (1881) and had Beardsley illustrate its published version (1894). The black-and-white erotic drawings contain figures of bizarre proportion, some willowy figures placed jarringly in the same frame with monstrously shaped dwarves, and fanciful tracery. In Beardsley the art nouveau movement found an advocate and an adapter. He introduced the term to the British public in the first issue of the *Studio* (1893) and found for the movement a wider if not wholly sympathetic audience in the illustrations for the *Yellow Book* (1894) and its successor, the *Savoy* (1896), where it formed a part of the well-established **aesthetic movement** that became, in the 1890s, the decadent movement.

Not confined to painting and drawing, art nouveau manifested itself in the design of furniture, stained glass windows, jewelry, clothing, tableware, household ornaments, and commercial and residential buildings. Of the many artists and artisans who worked in this popular and pervasive style in Britain, William Morris and his circle and **Charles Rennie Mackintosh** (1868-1928) of Glasgow are notable examples of talented workers in many media.

The emphasis on line and its ornamental value in ubiquitous curvilinear motifs and the filmy visionary and sometimes grotesque treatments of figures, flora, and fauna are hallmarks of art nouveau. Like other artistic movements of the age it emphasizes style and romantic content; it may justly be considered a late flowering of **romanticism**.

JOHN J. CONLON

Bibliography

Battersby, Martin. *The World of Art Nouveau.* 1969.

Jullian, Philippe. *Dreamers of Decadence: Symbolist Painters of the 1890s.* 1971.

Kempton, Richard. *Art Nouveau: An Annotated Bibliography.* 1977.

Milner, John. *Symbolists and Decadents.* 1971.

Richard, J. M. and Nikolaus Pevsner, eds. *The Anti-Rationalists.* 1973.

Schmutzler, Robert. *Art Nouveau.* 1962.

Selz, Peter and Mildred Constantine, eds. *Art Nouveau: Art and Design at the Turn of the Century.* 1959.

See also DECADENCE

· · · · ·

ARTHURIAN LEGEND

In Victorian Britain the Arthurian legends provided political, social, moral, religious, and aesthetic idealism. The chief source of the legendary history was Thomas Malory's *Morte d'Arthur* (1485). Lady Charlotte Guest's translations of the Welsh *Mabinogion* (1838-1849), George Ellis's *Specimens of Early English Metrical Romances* (1805), and John Dunlop's *History of Fiction* (1814) were also used. That chivalric virtues were relevant to contemporary life was acknowledged in the decoration of the new Palace of Westminster. In 1847 William Dyce was commissioned to paint the Queen's Robing Room with Malorian scenes associating Arthur, Launcelot, Gawain, Tristram, and Galahad with Hospitality, Generosity, Mercy, Courtesy, and Religion. Arthur appeared as exemplary ruler in Edward Bulwer-Lytton's *King Arthur* (1848) and Alfred Tennyson's *Idylls of the King* (1859), a work which established the "Matter of Britain" as a popular vehicle for moral instruction and mythopoeic invention.

Pre-Raphaelite interest began in 1857 with woodcuts which Dante Gabriel Rossetti and Holman Hunt contributed to Moxon's edition of Tennyson's 1842 *Poems* and with the Oxford Union frescoes painted by Rossetti, William Morris, Edward Burne-Jones, Val Prinsep, Spencer Stanhope, and Hungerford Pollen. The frescoes proved ephemeral, but the subject persisted in Morris's poetry—*The Defence of Guenevere* (1858)—and in drawings and paintings by Morris, Rossetti, Burne-Jones, Elizabeth Siddall, Arthur Hughes, Frederick Sandys, and James Archer, where beautiful, sensuous women demand emotional response.

Arthurian characters could be used for ethical instruction, psychological revelation, and aesthetic indulgence. Launcelot, whom Tennyson condemned as a source of corruption, became the model English gentleman, an idealization effected by obscuring his adultery and emphasizing his courage, honesty, and sportsmanship. The tragic love of Tristram and Isolde inspired Matthew Arnold's "Tristram and Iseult" (1852), Algernon Swinburne's *Tristram of Lyonesse* (1882), Lawrence Binyon's "Tristram's End" (1901), and stained glass windows executed by Morris, Marshall, Faulkner and Co. for a Bradford merchant. The grail legends, rejected after the Reformation as Catholic, resurfaced to express Victorian aspirations. Tennyson's "Sir Galahad" (1842) and "The Holy Grail" (1870), Morris's "Sir Galahad" (1858), Robert Stephen Hawker's *Quest of the Sangraal* (1864), and Thomas Westwood's *Quest of the Sancgreall* (1868) poetically investigated mystical experience. George Frederic Watts's popular oil "Sir Galahad" (1862) presented an upper-class ideal of manliness. Sensuous and symbol-studded religiosity characterized Rossetti's grail paintings, Burne-Jones's grail tapestries, and Aubrey Beardsley's "The Achieving of the Sangreal" (1892), a drawing which led to his illustrating the Dent Malory. In short, the legends provided images to express good government, social responsibility, purity, piety, beauty, and love.

MURIEL WHITAKER

Bibliography

Banham, Joanna and Jennifer Harris, eds. *William Morris and the Middle Ages.* 1984.

Girouard, Mark. *The Return to Camelot: Chivalry and the English Gentleman.* 1981.

Taylor, Beverly and Elisabeth Brewer. *The Return of King Arthur.* 1983.

See also MEDIEVALISM

· · · · ·

ARTISTS' MODELS

Many Victorian artists worked from the nude and then painted in drapery. Given the nudity and the general beliefs about the morals of artists, female models were thought to be little better than prostitutes. For pretty working-class girls modeling was a way up the social scale: from ragged clothes and crowded rooms to good clothes and outings. Many women by drudgery from morning to night earned less than five shillings weekly; modeling commanded one shilling per hour. A successful model, furthermore, gained an entree into the world of art which could sometimes be put to independent use.

W. H. Deverell discovered red-haired Elizabeth Eleanor Siddall (1829–1862) working in a milliner's shop off Leicester Square in 1849. She was used widely by the Pre-Raphaelites. **Dante Gabriel Rossetti** trained her to paint and secured her **John Ruskin**'s patronage; her work reveals more originality and energy than has generally been acknowledged. Rossetti ultimately married Siddall in 1860. She died in 1862 from an overdose of laudanum.

Fanny Cornforth (1824–1906) was described as "sumptuously blonde, coarsely good-natured, of Rubens-like sexuality"; she was probably a prostitute when befriended by Rossetti, to whom she became model, mistress, and later housekeeper. Annie Miller (1835–1925) was found by **William Holman Hunt** in a Chelsea slum and was intended to become his wife after suitable education, for which he invested time and money. She modeled widely and became the mistress of Lord Ranelagh, but married his cousin T. R. Thomson.

While in Oxford to paint murals in the Union, Rossetti and Burne-Jones saw Jane Burden (1839–1914) in a theater. Altogether a different sort of beauty than the variety then fashionable, Burden had a pale complexion, heavy brows, and hair apparently "forged from some strange metal thread by thread." Her sensual appearance lent itself to Rossetti's style. In 1859 she married **William Morris** and evidently made unacknowledged contributions to Morris's design of embroideries and tapestries. Titian-haired Dorothy Dene (1859–1899), discovered by H. G. Schmalz in 1879, eventually became Lord Leighton's chief model and, as his protégée, a successful actress.

Among male models, Italians were popular. Gaetano Meo (1850–1925) was a Sicilian who hiked to London with his brother. Mentioned to Rossetti by his barber, Meo was in great demand for his classic profile and curly hair. After painting lessons from Alma Tadema and Hunt, he became an accomplished mosaicist.

Although relatively well paid, modeling was not easy. L. S. Canziani had a model pose without rest for nine hours. Pre-Raphaelite "faithfulness to nature" could make heavy demands: Siddall, posing for **John Everett Millais**'s *Ophelia* (1852), caught a severe cold in a bath of cold water, and Miller was forced to hold an extremely uncomfortable half-rising position for Hunt's *The Awakening Conscience* (1854). The trained model who had the necessary adaptability, discipline, and stamina—and who took an intelligent interest in the artist's work—was far more than simply a pretty face.

PAUL A. B. WRIGHT

Bibliography

Garland, Madge. "Fair Face in Many Guises." *Country Life*, vol. 175, pp. 604–605.

Marsh, Jan. *Pre-Raphaelite Sisterhood.* 1985.

· · · · ·

ARTS AND CRAFTS MOVEMENT

The "arts and crafts movement," dedicated to a reform of the decorative arts and the conditions of their production, includes a broad range of figures and developments in the last two decades of the nineteenth century. The central organization of the movement, the Arts and Crafts Exhibition Society, though formally constituted in 1888, had its origin four years earlier, when three artists—George Clausen, **William Holman Hunt**, and **Walter Crane**—expressed their dissatisfaction with the exhibition policy of the **Royal Academy** and proposed in a letter to the leading London dailies that a national exhibition be organized to present to the public all of the arts and crafts. Upon the organization of this exhibition at the New Gallery, the title "The Combined Arts" was suggested, but the alternative, "Arts and Crafts," proposed by the bookbinder Thomas Cobden-Sanderson, was preferred. An earlier organization important to the movement was the firm of Morris, Marshall, Faulkner and Co., established by **William Morris** in 1861.

A variety of social and intellectual forces lay behind the rise of the arts and crafts movement. Among the most important was the perception that mechanization and competitive commerce had accelerated the decline of traditional design and craftwork which had begun with the Protestant Reformation. Thomas Carlyle lamented in 1829 that "on every hand, the living artisan is driven from his workship, to make way for a speedier, inanimate one." The most influential reflection upon the condition of work and worker in the industrial regime was **John Ruskin**'s "The Nature of Gothic" from volume two of *The Stones of Venice* (1853). Ruskin analyzed machine production in terms of its tendency to subdivide the labor process, thus depriving workers of creative exertion and alienating them from the finished product. When Morris reprinted "The Nature of Gothic" at the Kelmscott Press in 1892, he evaluated it as "one of the very few necessary and inevitable utterances of this century," which had pointed the way to social and artistic reform.

Several leaders of the movement followed Ruskin in proposing that the problems of industrial manufacture could be resolved by subordinating mechanical means to human and by restoring the goals of creative fulfillment in work and beauty in the finished product. The study of the artistic and archaeological record of preindustrial (especially medieval) culture, of the records of medieval guilds, and of manuals such as Cennini's *Libro dell'arte* confirmed their belief that modern craftwork had degenerated and their conviction that reform needed to be sustained by tradition. This partly explains the medieval outlook of the arts and crafts movement. But it should also serve as a reminder that in the late nineteenth century the continuity of artistic tradition was perceived by many as having been irreparably broken, necessitating a return to the integral culture of the Middle Ages; and (furthermore) that subsequent history has offered no viable alternative for reintegrating art with daily life.

A practical incentive for reform came from the **Exhibition of 1851**, which many believed revealed the ugliness and shoddiness of manufactured goods. In 1861 the firm of Morris, Marshall, Faulkner and Co. began to employ established artists associated with the **Pre-Raphaelite Brotherhood** to design decorative objects; their aim was to unite all of the visual arts in the service of a beautiful and harmonious physical environment. The firm and its successor, Morris and Co. (1875), achieved relative financial success and an impressive standard in its manufacture of furniture, fabric, tapestry, carpets, wallpaper, stained glass, and ceramics.

Other productive organizations took as their model the medieval guild and workshop. These included the Century Guild, founded by **Arthur Heygate Mackmurdo** and Selwyn Image in 1882; the Art Workers' Guild, whose founders in 1888 included William Lethaby, Walter Crane, and Lewis F. Day; the Guild and School of Handicraft, founded by **Charles R. Ashbee** in 1888; and the Birmingham Guild, founded in 1890. The comprehensive program of the Guild and School of Handicraft details most of the concerns of these organizations. As proposed by Ashbee, it included the following principles: elevating the craftworker above the system and restoring freedom and spontaneity to craftwork; assumption by the architect of the role of "master builder," uniting and coordinating all the arts and crafts; reorganizing the craft workshop on a cooperative basis; reinstituting an organized system of apprenticeship; recovering and transmitting craft knowledge and technique; regulating the role of machinery in production, particularly by means of worker control of the productive system; upholding standards of production; and orienting the productive system to the general social welfare.

The practical consequence of such guide-

lines was a reform of design that eschewed excessive and inappropriate ornamentation, and was instead governed by a respect for the object's function and for the nature of the material and tools used to produce it. Eclectic use of styles culled arbitrarily from the past was discouraged. The results, in the best productions of the arts and crafts revival, demonstrated a remarkable variety and inventiveness, and included the rich effect of Morris and Co. stained glass, carpets, and tapestries; the economical elegance of buildings by Charles F. A. Voysey; the organic vitality of book cover decorations and wallpapers by Mackmurdo that anticipate **art nouveau**; and the felicitous integration of word and image in the magnificent Kelmscott Chaucer. The movement may justly claim to have reformed, and set standards of judgment for, later crafts in a wide variety of media.

The influence of the arts and crafts movement arises not only from its productive achievement but also from its examination of the history of crafts and its analysis of the problems created by mechanization and modern commerce. That influence was most fruitful in Holland, Germany, Austria, and the United States, where the ideals of the movement assumed a new vitality and were given new forms of expression after they had ceased to be an active force in Britain.

LARRY D. LUTCHMANSINGH

Bibliography

Anscombe, Isabelle and Charlotte Gere. *Arts and Crafts in Britain and America*. 1978.

Arts and Crafts Exhibition Society. *Arts and Crafts Essays*. 1893.

Callen, Anthea. *Women Artists of the Arts and Crafts Movement*. 1979.

Cobden-Sanderson, Thomas J. *The Arts and Crafts Movement*. 1905.

Davey, Peter. *Arts and Crafts Architecture*. 1980.

Fine Art Society Ltd. *The Arts and Crafts Movement: Artists, Craftsmen and Designers, 1890–1930*. 1973.

Lambourne, Lionel. *Utopian Craftsmen: The Arts and Crafts Movement from the Cotswolds to Chicago*. 1980.

Naylor, Gillian. *The Arts and Crafts Movement.* 1971.

Pevsner, Nikolaus. *Pioneers of Modern Design: From William Morris to Walter Gropius.* 1986.

See also AESTHETIC MOVEMENT; EMBROIDERY; MEDIEVALISM

· · · · ·

ASHBEE, CHARLES ROBERT
(1863–1942)

Charles Robert Ashbee was an architect, designer, and town planner associated with the **arts and crafts movement**. His outstanding achievement was the Guild and School of Handicraft (1888), though he also achieved distinction as a designer in metal.

After taking his degree in history at King's College, Cambridge, Ashbee was articled to the architect G. F. Bodley. While a resident of Toynbee Hall in London's East End, he started a Ruskin reading class and undertook a decorative scheme with some fellow residents. This experience inspired in Ashbee the vision of a craft revival centered around a "school" or "guild" and led to the establishment of the Guild and School of Handicraft, which engaged in several crafts, notably metalwork, jewelry, and printing. Moving to Chipping Campden in 1902, the guild undertook a remarkable experiment in education and craft production under communal conditions, but within six years financial difficulties drove it into liquidation.

Ashbee's architectural works included several houses at Cheyne Walk, London: no. 37, the "Magpie and Stump" (1894, later destroyed), nos. 72 and 73 (1897), and nos. 38 and 39 (1899); the Norman Chapel at Broad Campden (1906); and Byways, at Yarnton, near Oxford (1907).

Ashbee's interest in typography and book design was furthered when, after acquiring much of the Kelmscott Press in 1898, he founded Essex House Press. His foreign travel included visits to the United States, Egypt, and Palestine, where he was involved in the replanning of Jerusalem and restoration of

some of its monuments between 1917 and 1924.

LARRY D. LUTCHMANSINGH

Bibliography

Ashbee, Charles R. *Craftsmanship in Competitive Industry.* 1908.

——. *An Endeavour Towards the Teaching of John Ruskin and William Morris.* 1901.

——. *A Few Chapters in Workshop Reconstruction and Citizenship.* 1894.

——. *The Manual of the Guild and School of Handicraft.* 1892.

——. *Where the Great City Stands.* 1917.

Cheltenham Art Gallery and Museum. *C. R. Ashbee and the Guild of Handicraft.* 1981.

Crawford, Alan. *C. R. Ashbee: Architect, Designer and Romantic Socialist.* 1985.

MacCarthy, Fiona. *The Simple Life: C. R. Ashbee in the Cotswolds.* 1981.

· · · · ·

ASTRONOMY

In Victorian Britain astronomy, conceived primarily as "astrometrics" or the measurement of the positions of the planets and stars, was a mature, practically important science grounded theoretically in Newton's celestial mechanics. Its most striking developments lay in "astrophysics," whereby light from the stars could be made to yield otherwise inaccessible information on the composition and motion of heavenly bodies.

The establishment of the Royal Astronomical Society (1820) and the appointment of George Biddell Airy (1801–1892) as astronomer royal and director of the Royal Observatory in 1835 gave a new boost to the science. The Royal Observatory performed many practically important tasks such as checking chronometers, producing lunar tables used in navigation, and maintaining Greenwich mean time. During Airy's long tenure, new telescopes incorporated enormous increases in precision, and automatic registering devices greatly reduced observational error. But the Royal Observatory was not the source of major new discoveries or developments. Airy was widely blamed for his slow confirmation of John Couch Adams's (1818–1892) prediction of the existence of a planet beyond Uranus, which allowed the Frenchman Leverrier to claim the discovery of Neptune.

Amateurs were often the source of novel developments. Nebulae (faint patches of light, some resolved into clusters of stars) could only be observed with very powerful telescopes. **J. F. W. Herschel** (1792–1871) greatly extended the number of nebulae observed by his father William (1738–1822). The telescopes of William Parsons, earl of Rosse (1800–1867) further extended the catalogue of nebulae. Rosse succeeded in resolving nebulae which William Herschel had observed only as luminous patches of light, and discovered a spiral variety which was later important in solving the riddle of the nebulae. These findings gave new popularity to William Herschel's early speculation that the solar system was part of the "island universe" of the Milky Way and that the nebulae were other island universes.

Rosse's observations also bore upon a set of ideas about the evolution of the solar system, nebulae, and the universe at large developed by Laplace and William Herschel and known as the "nebular hypothesis." **Robert Chambers's** advocacy of the hypothesis in *Vestiges of the Natural History of Creation* (1844) stimulated much controversy about whether the universe was evolving by natural law and, if so, how God's role in creation should be understood. Astronomy was a debating ground for evolutionary naturalism before the Darwinism with which it is usually associated.

New discoveries and techniques enabled astronomers to establish the composition and radial motion of astronomical objects. Gradually a new specialty of "astrophysics" was established. Analysis of the solar spectrum by Fraunhofer and Kirchhoff showed how emission and absorption lines in its spectrum gave information about the nature and physical state of a body. In Britain, Norman Lockyer (1836–1920) and William Huggins (1824–1910) used the spectroscope with the telescope to analyze solar prominences. Huggins also obtained the first spectrum of a nebula in 1864. In some cases spectra revealed nebulae as clusters of stars, in others they suggested a gaseous composition which created skepticism about the island universe theory.

Spectroscopists examining the sun had found that a version of the Doppler principle enabled them to interpret shifts in spectral lines from their usual position as a measure of local movements of solar matter. In 1868 Huggins made the first determination of the radial motion of a star. The shifts in spectral lines involved in such measurements, however, were generally too small to be reliably determined by visual methods. The photographic recording of spectra (spectrography) eventually enabled measurement of the radial motion of nebulae.

Though first used in the 1840s, astronomical photography was not widely accepted until the 1880s. The astrophysicist found photography an indispensable technique. Its astrometric uses were also gradually acknowledged, especially when improvements in the sensitivity of photographic materials allowed the photographic plate to "see" more than the human eye. Photography thus became a technique of discovery, not just of record.

The professionalism of German and American astronomers and their increasingly superior technology was to give them leadership in the cosmological revolution of the early twentieth century, but astronomers in Victorian Britain contributed much to laying the foundations upon which our current view of the universe is constructed.

DAVID PHILIP MILLER

Bibliography

Clerke, Agnes M. *A Popular History of Astronomy During the Nineteenth Century.* 1885.

Dreyer, John L. E. and H. H. Turner, eds. *History of the Royal Astronomical Society, 1820–1920.* 1923.

Gingerich, Owen, ed. *The General History of Astronomy,* vol. 4: *Astrophysics and Twentieth-Century Astronomy to 1950: Part A.* 1984.

Herrmann, Dieter. *The History of Astronomy from Herschel to Hertzsprung.* 1984. Trans. Kevin Krisciunas.

Hoskin, Michael. *Stellar Astronomy: Historical Studies.* 1982.

Lankford, John. "Amateurs and Astrophysics: A Neglected Aspect in the Development of a Scientific Specialty." *Social Studies of Science,* vol. 11, pp. 275–303.

Meadows, A. J. *Greenwich Observatory: The Royal Observatory at Greenwich and Herstmonceux*, vol. 2. 1975.

—— *Science and Controversy: A Biography of Sir Norman Lockyer.* 1972.

· · · · ·

ATHLETIC SPORTS

British society had always been sports-minded but it became much more so during the nineteenth century since the Victorians firmly believed that athletic activity was essential for the proper development of both the mind and the body. Hence the emergence of several athletic clubs in nineteenth-century Britain, including the famous Birchfield and Moseley Harriers who produced many outstanding runners. Athletic contests were also encouraged and popularized in the second half of the century by the leading public schools and universities. The Royal Military Academy at Woolwich staged its first athletic competition in 1849, and the annual Oxford and Cambridge athletic rivalry was inaugurated in 1864. The Amateur Athletic Association was established in 1880, under the presidency of the earl of Jersey, to control British athletic sports. It soon became the most important athletic body throughout the world and did more than any other single group to promote international competition. It played a prominent role in reviving the ancient Greek Olympic tradition and organizing the 1896 and 1900 Olympics.

The Victorians made significant progress in track and field and remained consistently superior to the Europeans, but they gradually fell behind the United States, whose athletic stars held most of the major world records in 1900. The North Americans, in fact, have traditionally dominated track events in modern Olympic competition. The Victorians made difficulties for themselves by adhering too strictly to the laws governing amateurism, which the Americans interpreted more liberally. The result was that professionals and amateurs seldom competed against each other in Britain, and the British amateurs were thus deprived of the opportunity to hone their skills by performing at the highest level.

Even so, a cursory glance at athletic records during the last four decades of the nineteenth century clearly shows that British skills improved considerably. When Oxford and Cambridge staged their inaugural competition, F. H. Gooch won the high jump with a leap of 5'5", and the long jump with 18'. Such marks were soon eclipsed. By the end of the Victorian age, British athletes were long jumping more than 23', and high jumping over 6'4". Few athletes had been able to run the mile in less than 5 minutes during the 1860s, but the great Walter George trimmed the world record to 4:12.8 before the turn of the century. Irish athletes, like Patrick Davin, Patrick Leahy, Peter O'Connor, and Dan Shanahan consistently dominated the jumping events after 1880. Among the greatest of Victorian sprinters were Charles Bradley, Edgar Bredin, and Alfred Downer. Bradley and Downer created a sensation in the 1890s by running 100 yards in less than 10 seconds. But it was the incredible Walter George who blazed the most glorious trail, establishing a series of durable world records for one mile, two miles, and three miles during the 1880s.

KEITH A. P. SANDIFORD

Bibliography

Jamieson, David A. *Fifty Years of Athletics.* 1933.

Lovesey, Peter. *The Official Centenary History of the Amateur Athletic Association.* 1979.

Mandell, Richard D. *The First Modern Olympics.* 1976.

Shearman, Montague. *Athletics and Football.* 1889.

Watman, Melvyn. *History of British Athletics.* 1968.

See also SPORT

· · · · ·

ATLANTIC CABLE

The Atlantic cable, a telegraph cable stretching over 2,000 miles of sea floor between Ireland and Newfoundland, was successfully laid in August 1866 as a cooperative venture by the British and American governments and by private backers. The project was largely the work of the New York engineer Cyrus Field (1819–1892).

The cable itself consisted of copper wires wound into seven strands and insulated with gutta percha, a natural plastic formed from the sap of a Malayan tree. It was further wound with tarred hemp, and the whole was sheathed in a casing of heavy iron wires.

Initial attempts in 1857 failed when the cable broke several times in midocean. In 1858 two ships successfully laid the cable, but excessive voltage ruined the insulation, and within a month the cable was dead. After the American Civil War, I. K. Brunel's huge ship the *Great Eastern* was employed. An attempt in 1865 failed, but in 1866 the cable was successfully laid between Valentia, Ireland, and Trinity Bay, Newfoundland, making communication between the old world and the new a matter of minutes rather than days.

PHILLIP THURMOND SMITH

Bibliography

Bright, Charles. *The Story of the Atlantic Cable.* 1903.

Derry, T. K. and Trevor Williams. *A Short History of Technology.* 1961.

Finn, Bernard S. *Submarine Telegraphy: The Grand Victorian Technology.* 1973.

Headrick, Daniel. *The Tools of Empire. Technology and European Imperialism in the Nineteenth Century,* 1981.

. . . . .

AUSTRALIA

Although sighted by seventeenth-century Spanish and Dutch explorers, Australia was not opened to European expansion until Captain James Cook's voyages along the east coast (1768–1771). Following the loss in 1783 of the American colonies which had occasionally served as a prison, Australia's isolated position made it an ideal penal colony. By an order in council in December 1786, its eastern half was annexed and in January 1788, eleven ships of the First Fleet carrying about 1,100 prisoners (about four men to each woman) arrived at Botany Bay. A week later the captain, Arthur Phillip, moved the settlement to Sydney Harbor and named it New South Wales. Convicts supplied the labor under government supervision or private enterprise. They were allowed some hours a day to work on their own and earn money or were assigned to private employers who paid them either in food or money with which they could buy other commodities, including rum imported from India.

With only the Colonial Office above them and no representative institutions, the governors ruled with a free hand from 1788 until 1821—a period known as the "age of tyrants." Following the departure of Captain Phillips in 1792, the governors were "assisted" in keeping order by the new South Wales Corps, who became so notoriously corrupted by their lucrative trade in Indian rum, among other items, that they earned the name "the Rum Corps."

The age of tyrants saw a division between the "emancipists," convicts who had served their time and earned their freedom, and the "exclusionists," jailers who had never been in the penal system and tried to exclude the "felonry" from polite society. Captain William Bligh (of the *Bounty* mutiny) arrived as governor in 1806 and took the part of the emancipists. In 1809 the exclusionists, led by John MacArthur (who would introduce sheep raising), overthrew and imprisoned Bligh. The British government intervened and replaced Bligh in 1810 with Lt. Col. Lachlan McQuarry who remained until 1821. The "Rum Corps" was disbanded and replaced with McQuarry's Highland Regiment. In 1813 a way was found through the Blue Mountains, revealing the "outback" where sheep could be raised. Following the Napoleonic Wars, the first free settlers began to arrive, and by 1821 New South Wales was no longer a prison farm, although transportation would continue until 1842.

The children born of convict parents were called "national" children or "currency lads and lasses" because, like the makeshift local currency, they were of local manufacture. Although the penal system tended to corrupt both the prisoners and the jailers, the national children were notable for their higher morality. A report by J. T. Bigge in 1823 attested that they "neither inherit the vices nor feelings of their parents." They often took charge of the Blue Mountain trade as wagoners providing free and experienced labor.

A "pastoral ascendancy" from 1821 to 1855 saw a transition to responsible government. In 1823 a legislative council was established with nine members appointed by the governor. When transportation ended in 1842, the council was enlarged to thirty-six members, twenty-four elected and twelve nominated. The property qualifications were high, so the twenty-four elected members represented those who wanted to exclude free settlers.

Meanwhile, Robert Peel had established Western Australia in the 1830s to be colonized along the lines of Edward Gibbon Wakefield's scheme for "systematic colonization." According to this scheme, the government would sell land at a sufficient price to discourage wasteful free grants of land to the indigent. Part of the proceeds would then be used to encourage further emigration. Although forty acres of land could be had for three pounds, the few settlers who came soon went to eastern Australia, so a petition for convicts resulted in a renewal of transportation from 1850 until 1868. Even so, western Australia languished until the gold rush of the 1890s.

Southern Australia, like the west, had little connection with the east and no experience with convictism. It was also a "Wakefield province." Land was sold at five pounds an acre and the colony attracted middle-class settlers who tended to be Nonconformists and so puritanical that its capital, Adelaide, became "the city of churches."

Victoria, a region that simply broke away from New South Wales in 1850, was recognized as a separate colony. Queensland resulted from a new convict settlement established in 1824 on Morton Bay. In 1859 it also separated from New South Wales. In 1850 when Victoria separated, the British Government, reacting to the successful experiment with responsible government in Canada, asked the Australian colonies for draft constitutions. In 1855 the Australian colonies became self-governing and in 1900 were federated as the Commonwealth of Australia.

It is the outback that has shaped the Australian personality. The vast distances and scant rainfall and the fact that most sheep stations were owned by one man or company employing many hands who were emancipists or national children rather than free settlers helped to generate the sense of solidarity or "mateship" against the common enemy, the "shepherd kings" who employed them. This was transferred later to urban life in a dislike of affectation, a distaste for forces of authority such as the police or military, and a related contempt for the "new chums" or free settlers. A shortage of clergy tended to foster an indifference to religion and sometimes even hostility since the clergy, like secular authority, was associated with the hostile "establishment" of the shepherd kings. The certainty of full employment made it possible to wander from one employer to another and the harsh environment placed a premium on improvisation and on practical virtues, hospitality, and sharing. When gold was discovered in 1851, the rush of free settlers did not adulterate these values. Rather, the bushmen were usually the first at the diggings and took in the "new chums" who then accepted the values of the bushmen.

Australia has been remarkable for its extremely low crime rate. There was some cattle rustling, often viewed as a minor infraction since cattle were seen as a common property. The peaceful character of Australian life owes much to the absence of racial tensions. The indigenous population was primitive, peaceable, and incapable of any organized resistance to white settlement. As whites moved in they were detribalized and, in some views, completely demoralized. There has been only one major political upheaval in all of Australia's history: in 1854 gold miners at the Eureka stockade revolted against the authorities for charging high license fees.

JOAN MICKELSON GAUGHAN

Bibliography

Blainey, Geoffrey. *The Tyranny of Distance.* 1968.

Clark, Charles Manning. *A Short History of Australia.* 1963.

Hancock, William Keith. *Australia.* 1930.

Pike, Douglas, *Australia: The Quiet Continent.* 1962.

Ward, Russel. *Australia.* 1965.

· · · · ·

AUTOBIOGRAPHY

In the nineteenth century, autobiography established itself as a popular genre with definite conventions. Discussions of ancestry, childhood, education and religious beliefs combined with a peculiarly public self-examination to reflect Victorian interest in education and developmental psychology and the debate between science and religion. Major intellectual figures such as **John Stuart Mill, John Henry Newman, John Ruskin, Charles Darwin, Harriet Martineau,** and **Anthony Trollope** undertook autobiographies as a matter of course, almost as a public service. Other genres were infused with autobiographical elements. Popular autobiographical novels include *David Copperfield* (1849–1850), *The Mill on the Floss* (1860), *Villette* (1853), *Tom Brown's School Days* (1857), *Marius the Epicurean* (1883), and *The Way of All Flesh* (1903). Two of the century's most influential works, **Thomas Carlyle**'s *Sartor Resartus* (1833–1834) and William Wordsworth's *The Prelude* (1850) were autobiographical. Indeed, the first recorded use of the term "autobiography" appears in the December 1809 *Quarterly Review.*

Although autobiography demands self-examination, not all Victorians were comfortable with confession. By the middle of the century, the romantic poets' concern with self seemed excessive and dangerous. Byron, Shelley, and (especially) their followers appeared paralyzed by depression and inward focus, whereas the Victorians saw themselves as doers as well as thinkers. However, because evangelical religion stressed self-examination and the eighteenth-century psychological novel emphasized motivation, Victorian autobiographers felt compelled to explain themselves and offer reasons for their behavior or beliefs.

They tend, however, to emphasize a "public" self and reason, rather than emotion or inner psychology. Mill's *Autobiography* (1873), for example, concentrates almost exclusively on his unusual education. Although he confesses suffering severe depression, Mill presents himself as a thinking machine, programmed to be logical, helpful, and modest. He discusses his ennui because he considers it an important and unforeseen outcome of his education, not because he wants to reveal his inner self. His family also appears only in terms of his education. He mentions siblings because he tutored them, his mother because he feels her influence did not sufficiently affect the children's upbringing, and, of course, his father, who dominates the first half of the book as he dominated the first half of Mill's life. Harriet Taylor, his colleague and eventual wife, is described as his last educator. Whatever is not related to Mill's education, no matter what it may have meant to him personally, is simply suppressed.

Mill's autobiography is also a forum for his philosophical, political, religious, and social beliefs. Martineau's *Autobiography* (edited by Maria Weston Chapman, 1877) dilates at length on her economic views and discusses her move from the intense religious fervor of her teens to agnosticism in adulthood. Newman's *Apologia pro Vita Sua* (1864) provides the most detailed examination of its author's religious beliefs. Darwin (*Life and Letters of Charles Darwin,* 1887) defends both religious and scientific views. The dominant concerns of the nineteenth century—politics, economics, religion, science, and education—are all discussed at great length and with painstaking care in its autobiographies.

Another primary focus is work. Victorian autobiographers seem to follow Carlyle's dictum to "Produce! Produce!" as they explain how they found their life's work and then how it dominated their adult existence, frequently to the exclusion of all other concerns. Trollope (*An Autobiography,* 1883) admires his mother's ability to work despite inconvenience and personal tragedy, which no doubt influenced his inflexible rules for unremitting authorship. Martineau describes writing pamphlets, sometimes from daybreak to midnight. **Margaret Oliphant** confesses in her *Autobiography* (1899) the conflict between her desire to write and her duties to her ailing family. Ruskin (*Praeterita,* 1885–1900), on the other hand, sacrifices without qualms any personal or familial concerns to his work.

A fourth concern of Victorian autobiography is the influence of childhood experiences upon the adult. Ruskin mentions that because he had no toys as a child he amused himself by studying the patterns in the carpet, and so his aesthetic appreciation was formed early in life. Martineau and Trollope detail unhappy childhoods and claim that insecurity influenced their adult behavior. Mill again is a prime example, for his childhood was the test case for Benthamite principles and James Mill's ideas on eduction.

Also of interest to Victorian scholars are the autobiographies written early in the century—especially *Confessions of an English Opium-Eater* (1822) by Thomas de Quincey (1785-1859) and *The Autobigraphy of Leigh Hunt* (1850)—and those late in the century such as **George Moore's** *Confessions of a Young Man* (1888), which was the first of several autobiographies chronicling different periods of his life. Throughout the century, futhermore, autobiographies were written by lesser-known people. Those engaged in picturesque occupations were especially popular. James Dawson Burn's *The Autobiography of a Beggar Boy* (1855) was a best seller. Many working-class political leaders wrote autobiographies, usually to plead their causes and win converts to political radicalism. The best known include Samuel Bamford's *Passages in the Life of a Radical* (1844) and *Early Days* (1849), **Thomas Cooper's** *Life of Thomas Cooper Written by Himself* (1872), and William Lovett's *The Life and Struggles of William Lovett* (1876).

Victorian autobiographies must be approached with care. Some autobiographers (including Newman and Moore) published several editions, sometimes with substantial revisions. Also, those first published posthumously were frequently bowdlerized by relatives, as in the cases of Mill and Darwin. However, most major works can be found in good modern editions with footnotes to aid in the comparison of various versions.

NAN HACKETT

Bibliography

Buckley, Jerome Hamilton. *The Turning Key: Autobiography and the Subjective Impulse Since 1800.* 1984.

Landow, George. *Approaches to Victorian Autobiography.* 1979.

Shumaker, Wayne. *English Autobiography: Its Emergence, Materials and Form.* 1954.

Vincent, David. *Bread, Knowledge and Freedom: A study of Nineteenth-Century Working-Class Autobiography.* 1981.

. . . . .

BABBAGE, CHARLES (1792-1871)

Often referred to as the father of the modern computer, Charles Babbage was both more and less than this. He made important contributions in mathematical pedagogy by encouraging scientific organizations and as an advocate of the sytematic use of science in industry, but his "analytic engine" was never completed and differed in principle from today's computers in being decimal rather than binary.

Babbage was born into an affluent Devonshire family and entered Cambridge in 1810. Here he quickly acquired a great reputation and, although he did not complete the mathematical tripos, allied himself with George Peacock and **John Herschel** to campaign for revitalized mathematics teaching. He devoted much of his life to eliminating errors in mathematical and astronomical tables. He became a fellow of the Royal Society in 1816 and from 1828–1839 was the sinecurist professor of mathematics at Cambridge.

Babbage's first "difference engine" (1827) compiled and printed tables of logarithms from 1 to 108,000. His more complex "analytical machine" was capable of undertaking any type of calculation. Though Babbage invested a great deal of his fortune in this invention, it was only after his death that his son sorted out the paper plans and built the device. Babbage was never as successful as he wished in receiving government backing, which prompted him to campaign for closer links between science, technology, and production (*On the Economy of Machinery and Manufactures*, 1832). He also helped form new scientific societies, notably the Astronomical Society (1820) and the Statistical Society of London (1834). His objections to the Royal Society and contemporary English society (*Reflections on the Decline of Science in England*, 1830) inaugurated an important debate and encouraged the formation of the British Association a year later.

MICHAEL SHORTLAND

Bibliography

Babbage, Charles. *Passages from the Life of a Philosopher*. 1864.

Babbage, Henry P. *Babbage's Calculating Engines*. 1889.

Hyman, Anthony. *Charles Babbage: Pioneer of the Computer*. 1982.

Morrison, Philip and Emily Morrison, eds. *Charles Babbage and his Calculating Engines*. 1961.

Moseley, Maboth. *Irascible Genius: A Life of Charles Babbage, Inventor*. 1964.

See also LOVELACE, ADA

· · · · ·

BABY FARMING

Baby farming was the popular nineteenth-century term for the professional adoption or fostering of infants. The high mortality rate of these infants was the target of the Infant Life Protection Act (1872), the first British legislation designed to protect children in private homes.

The sensational trials of women accused of adopting illegitimate children only to kill them (Charlotte Winsor in 1865 and Margaret Waters and Sarah Ellis in 1870) drew much public attention to baby farming. In 1870 members of the Harveian Medical Society, led by J. B. Curgenven (1831-1903), Charles Drysdale (1829-1907), and Ernest Hart (1835-1898), formed the Infant Life Protection Society to campaign for legislation to prevent **infanticide**, which public health officials and physicians believed to be on the increase. The hearings of the Select Committee on the Protection of Infant Life (1871) revealed that poverty and social ostracism forced single mothers to place their infants with foster parents. In particular, witnesses criticized the bastardy clauses of the New Poor Law (1834), which refused outdoor relief to unmarried mothers and made it very difficult

for them to obtain support from their children's fathers.

The Infant Life Protection Act required the licensing of private maternity homes and the registration of all people who cared for two or more children for more than one day. Feminists, notably **Lydia Becker** (1827-1890) and members of the Manchester branch of the National Association for Women's Suffrage, criticized the legislation because it interferred with women's individual liberty but did not force men to take responsibility for their sexuality. In any case, the legislation had little impact on the professional fostering of infants, since local authorities did little to enforce it.

ALISA KLAUS

Bibliography

Behlmer, George. *Child Abuse and Moral Reform in England, 1870-1908*. 1982.

· · · · ·

BACTERIOLOGY

Bacteriology as a separate discipline began to emerge in the last third of the nineteenth century. The British, like the French and Germans, worked on several major lines of research: the origin of microbial life forms; the germ theory of disease; and, later, during the "golden age of bacteriology" (1880-1900), the explication of specific disease agents. The British did more than their foreign colleagues in two other areas: water bacteriology and tropical disease.

Before 1870 only two notable studies in bacteriology occurred in Britain. John Goodsir (1814-1867) discovered and named the genus *Sarcina* (1842) when bacteria were virtually inexplicable entities. The anesthetist John Snow (1813-1858)—who twice administered chloroform to Queen Victoria—did his classic work on the waterborne **cholera** epidemic of 1854 in Broad Street, London. Water bacteriology was later well developed by Alexander Cruikshank Houston (1865-1933) (sewage disposal) and Percy Faraday Frankland (1858-1946) (water treatment).

A central issue from 1870 to about 1877 was the development of an explanation for the origin of microbes. Especially in France many supported the view that the creatures arose spontaneously without benefit of preexisting parents. In England, Henry Charlton Bastian (1837–1915) was foremost among the spontaneous origin school. Bastian was opposed by most British scientists of established reputation, such as John Scott Burdon-Sanderson (1828–1905), a pupil of Goodsir and later Regius Professor at Oxford. John Tyndall (1820–1893) also opposed Bastian between 1870 and 1877; Bastian, however, never recanted his belief, even on his deathbed.

Another theme, inextricably tied to the origin debate, was the investigation of the germ theory of disease. Edgar March Crookshank (1858–1928), a student of both Lister and the German pioneer Robert Koch, established England's first bacteriology laboratory. Alexander Ogston (1844–1929) of Aberdeen studied under the masters of Europe and, in 1882, discovered and named the genus *Staphylococcus*, a major pathogen. Preeminent among the medical bacteriologists, however, was **Joseph Lister** (1827–1912), who revolutionized surgery by his use of antisepsis.

The Indian Medical Service continued the tradition of disease agent discovery. The work of David Bruce (1855–1931) on Malta fever and insect-borne diseases and, earlier, of Timothy Richards Lewis (1841–1886), pioneer in the study of cholera, relapsing fever, and other parasitic diseases, were products of the IMS.

At the turn of the century immunology saw a rapid development by Continental workers. Notable British were fewer in number, but included Marc Armand Ruffer (1859–1916), who was the first to manufacture antitoxins in England (1894), and Almrath Edward Wright (1861–1947), who pioneered typhoid injection and, as mentor to Alexander Fleming, led bacteriology into its post-Victorian successes.

DONALD J. McGRAW

Bibliography

Bulloch, William. *The History of Bacteriology.* 1938.

Collard, Patrick. *The Development of Microbiology.* 1976.

. . . . .

BALFE, MICHAEL WILLIAM (1808–1870)

Michael William Balfe, an Irish musician who settled in London, was composer of *The Bohemian Girl* (1843), the most successful Victorian opera before Sullivan's.

The son of a dancing master, he was taken to Italy by an Italian count, where his baritone voice was trained and he learned the current operatic style. From 1833 he pursued a successful career as a composer, chiefly in London but also in Paris, where he wrote three French operas on commission. His first English opera, *The Siege of Rochelle* (1835), brought instant fame and the rare honor of a commission from Her Majesty's Theatre for an Italian opera, *Falstaff* (1838). A long train of English operas followed. Balfe also wrote ballads, and more serious Longfellow and Tennyson songs (notably "Come into the garden, Maud," 1855).

Balfe's operas suffered from third-rate librettos by writers such as Alfred Bunn (c. 1797–1860). The secret of his success was his gift for vocal melody, whether in elaborate Italianate arias and duets, or in the more characteristically English ballads, like "I dreamt that I dwelt in marble halls" from *The Bohemian Girl.* On occasion, however, as in *Falstaff* and in *Satanella* (1858), he succeeded in composing truly dramatic scenes.

NICHOLAS TEMPERLEY

Bibliography

Kenney, Charles. *A Memoir of Michael William Balfe.* 1875.

. . . . .

BALFOUR, ARTHUR JAMES (1848–1930)

Conservative politician Arthur James Balfour served as chief secretary for Ireland (1887–1891), first lord of the Treasury (1891–1892 and 1895–1902), prime minister (1902–1905), first lord of the Admiralty (1915–1916), foreign secretary (1916–1919), and lord president of the Council (1919–1922 and 1925–1929). He was Conservative leader in the House of Commons from 1891 to 1902 and party leader from 1902 until 1911. In 1922 he was created first earl of Balfour.

Balfour's family provided his most important political connection: his uncle, **Lord Salisbury**, led the **Conservative party** (1885–1902). Balfour was associated with the Fourth party (1880–1885). He made his political reputation as Irish secretary, demonstrating unexpected firmness, and passing two Land Purchase Acts (1888 and 1891). When W. H. Smith collapsed in 1891, Balfour was the obvious successor as Conservative leader in the House of Commons. After an unsteady first four years, his skills in debate made him a dominant figure.

Balfour's interest in philosophy resulted in several books, including *A Defense of Philosophic Doubt* (1879). He was not by nature an initiator of legislation. The one measure associated with his name is the Education Act (1902). Its passage was a parliamentary triumph which made him the inevitable prime minister when Salisbury retired. Balfour had a consistent interest in foreign and defense policy, establishing the Committee of Imperial Defence (1902). Although his government was destroyed by internal crises, Balfour survived to enjoy a significant second career after he resigned the party leadership in 1911.

STUART BALL

Bibliography

Dugdale, Blanche. *Arthur James Balfour.* 1936. 2 vols.

Egremont, Max. *Balfour: A Life of Arthur James Balfour.* 1980.

Mackay, Ruddock. *Balfour, Intellectual Statesman.* 1985.

Zebel, Sydney Herbert. *Balfour: A Political Biography.* 1973.

. . . . .

BALLAD (DRAWING-ROOM)

The ballad was a type of middle-class popular song. Ballads might be launched by famous singers like **Jenny Lind** (1820–1887), or Emma Lajeunesse Albani (1847–1930), but their destination was the drawing room. Their sale as sheet music was so lucrative that singers were paid royalties to introduce them in a concert or opera: hence the term *royalty ballad.*

Ballads cover a wide range of subject matter, though the treatment is often shallow. Few deal with the realities of Victorian life; instead, they invite escape into dream worlds, or reassert older, purer values. The most popular of all was "Home, Sweet Home," which had first appeared in the opera *Clari* (1823) by Henry Bishop (1786–1855), but reached the millions only when Lind took it up in her London tours of the late 1840s.

The earlier "national song" had transformed Celtic folksong into such genteel romantic artifacts as Thomas Moore's "The Last Rose of Summer" (1813). From this source came the ballad's sentiment, folklike simplicity, and strophic form. More complex songs like **Arthur Sullivan**'s "Lost Chord" became ballads by popular acclamation.

Sentimentality, or emotional expression out of proportion to the matter at hand, is a pervasive characteristic of Victorian ballads. The strong emotion often conveyed by this music perhaps has its source not in the scenes depicted, but in pent-up feelings denied natural expression by the social custom of the time.

NICHOLAS TEMPERLEY

Bibliography

Simpson, Harold. *A Century of Ballads, 1810–1910.* 1910.

Temperley, Nicholas. "Ballroom and Drawing-Room Music." In *The Athlone History of Music in Britain,* vol. 5. 1981.

Turner, Michael, ed. *The Parlour Song Book.* 1972.

. . . . .

BANCROFT, SQUIRE (1841–1926) AND MARIE WILTON (1839–1921)

As actor-managers, Squire Bancroft and his wife Marie Wilton were most notable for their successful staging of the drawing-room comedies of **T. W. Robertson**, for technical innovations such as practical scenery, and for their consistent efforts to raise the standing of the acting profession.

Bancroft, who had no familial connections with the stage, began his theatrical career in 1861 with a Birmingham stock company. For the next four years he appeared in Dublin and the leading provincial theaters, playing a wide variety of roles. Wilton, whom Bancroft met during this period, had appeared on the stage since early childhood, often playing boys' roles, with such distinguished actors as W. C. Macready and Charles Kean. She made her London debut in *Belphegor* (1856) at the Lyceum and quickly found success at the Strand in a series of burlesque extravaganzas by H. J. Byron. At twenty-six Wilton entered into management with Byron by renting the Queen's Theatre, a property so decrepit that it was popularly named the "dust hole." In 1865 she invited Bancroft to join the company as her leading man at the refurbished and renamed Prince of Wales Theatre; they were married two years later. Their first production, staged the same year, featured Bancroft in Wooler's *A Winning Hazard*.

It was, however, with the works of T. W. Robertson that they achieved their greatest success. Robertson's distinctive emphasis on domestic and social realism coincided perfectly with the aims of the Bancrofts; their introduction of practical scenery, primarily in the form of the box set, closely mirrored the thematic content of Robertson's plays. The success of works such as *Caste* (1867), with its delicate mixture of naturalism and decorum, raised new possibilities for mid-Victorian theater. The high wages that the couple paid their company, coupled with the knighthood conferred on Squire Bancroft in 1897, did much to raise the standing of their profession. They retired from the stage in 1885.

LAUREN SMITH

Bibliography

Nicoll, Allardyce. *A History of English Drama*, vol. 5. 1959.

· · · · ·

BAND OF HOPE

The Band of Hope was a temperance organization for working-class children founded in Leeds in 1847. At the movement's height late in the century over three million children were enrolled in local bands affiliated with churches, chapels, and secular temperance societies.

All members took a pledge of total abstinence and were taught the "evils of drink." They also learned the virtues of thrift, cleanliness, hard work, and self-control. Coming primarily from upwardly mobile working-class families, these temperance children were reaching for a place in the lower middle class through clerical or other white-collar occupations where these lessons would serve them well. The Band of Hope's recreational as well as educational activities played an important role in training children to socially acceptable pursuits at a time when child labor was being curtailed and children had more free time.

But the movement's main purpose was to raise a "race free from drink." The members were enrolled from the age of six and met at least once a week to listen to lectures and participate in activities. Music played an important role; many Band of Hope choirs sang at public events and competed with one another in local and national competitions.

In addition, books, journals, and articles were published in support of temperance reform. Stories about men and women who were successful in business and industry provided suitable role models for the members. Most Band of Hope children would become adult members of the chapelgoing community, placing them squarely on the "right" side of society, opposing the drinkers on the "pub" side.

LILIAN LEWIS SHIMAN

Bibliography

Shiman, Lilian Lewis. "The Band of Hope Movement: Respectable Recreation for Working-Class Children." *Victorian Studies*, vol. 17, pp. 49–74.

See also TEMPERANCE MOVEMENT

· · · · ·

BANDS AND BAND MUSIC

Brass band music was one of the few areas in which Britain enjoyed acknowledged musical supremacy in the nineteenth century. The band festivals and competitions were an important focus of working-class recreation and aspiration.

Military bands of woodwind, brass, and percussion, played by professionals in uniform, found a peacetime role after Waterloo in parades, street processions, and concerts. Standards of performance were raised after the foundation of the Royal Military School of Music at Kneller Hall (1857).

Meanwhile, out-of-work musicians from the many disbanded regiments joined with church bands and volunteers to form civilian bands in a few northern towns, soon imitated all over northern England. By 1850, most of them were all-brass bands. They were encouraged by industrialists and landed gentry. In 1845 came the first organized brass band contest, at the home of Clifford Constable. The London festival of 1860 marked the expansion of the movement into southern England: an audience of 27,000 heard some 115 bands playing, first in competition, then all together for a gigantic performance that included Handel's "Hallelujah Chorus." By 1900 more than 20,000 amateur brass players were taking part in the festivals. Music for brass bands broadened from the military march and quickstep to include dances, overtures, and arrangements of orchestral, operatic, and choral classics.

An offshoot of the movement was the Salvation Army bands, which played hymns and religious songs in the open air and in the streets, and aroused the admiration of George Bernard Shaw. There were 10,000 Salvation Army band musicians by 1900 in the United Kingdom alone.

Band music was popular and largely working class, but was not a free expression of popular taste. It was always under paternalistic auspices, whether military, philanthropic, or religious.

NICHOLAS TEMPERLEY

Bibliography

Russell, John and John Elliot. *The Brass Band Movement.* 1936.

Van Ess, Donald. "Band Music." In *The Athlone History of Music in Britain*, vol. 5. 1981.

· · · · ·

BANKING

During the second half of the nineteenth century, the Bank of England developed as a central bank, and bank deposit money (checks) began to gain acceptance. The London financial system—the most highly organized and largest in the world—consisted of the Bank of England; the London joint-stock banks; the large private banks, discount houses, and bill brokers; the large mercantile houses; and the stock exchange. London and the country were linked through inland bills of exchange.

Originally, bills were orders for payment drawn by farmers and industrialists on the London merchants who ordered their produce. These bills were sold (discounted) through London bill brokers, giving the issuers ready cash and those who purchased the bills a profit when they were later redeemed at face value. With industrial development, bills became the means for obtaining credit. Well-known merchants could draw bills of exchange on London banks on the strength of their reputations alone. Since this method of financing was restricted to established merchants, these merchants served as intermediaries and often became commercial bankers—country bankers. After 1826 the Bank of England and joint-stock banks opened branches in competition with country banks, so that by the second half of the century country banking was in the hands of the sounder joint-stock banks.

Victoria's reign commenced amid an economic controversy between the "currency school" and the "banking school" concerning the appropriate method to control business cycles. The currency school argued that price level fluctuations were caused by variations in the amount of bank notes and coin in circulation. Therefore, if paper currency were backed by a 100 percent gold standard, neither the bank nor the government could cause a price inflation by "overissue" of currency.

The banking school recognized that checks and circulating bills of exchange—in addition to coins and bank notes—served as means of payment. If the number of bank notes issued could not meet the demand generated by the level of economic activity, the volume of checks and bills would expand to fill the gap. Moreover, they argued, the quantity of bank notes in circulation was the result rather than the cause of price level changes. Thomas Tooke (1774–1858), a leading spokesman for the banking school, argued that borrowing by merchants during economic expansion increased deposits and checks drawn on these deposits. The increase in checks created a higher price level, which induced the public to withdraw money from the banks in the form of bank notes, thus increasing the amount of paper in circulation. Falling prices caused money to be deposited into banks, reducing paper in circulation. The banking school concluded that prices were influenced most heavily by the volume of lending and discounting undertaken by the banks. Overissue could be prevented if the banks investigated the credit history of potential borrowers and discounted only "real bills"—bills drawn to finance inventories of goods rather than speculative ventures.

The Bank Charter Act (1844), influenced by the currency school, separated the Bank of England into the issue department and the banking department. The issue department was permitted to issue fourteen million pounds in notes backed by government securities; further expansion demanded a 100 percent specie (gold and silver) reserve. The banking department functioned as a commercial bank, using Bank of England notes earned through business activity as its reserves. No other bank could expand its note issue in excess of the amount it had in circulation in 1844, and if any bank gave up its note issue, the Bank of England could add two-thirds of the amount given up to its uncovered circulation. Thus, gradually, bank notes issued by the Bank of England replaced those issued by other banks and became the standard paper currency.

The act of 1844 encouraged the proliferation of checking. While unable to limit the growth of the money supply defined to include checks, the Bank of England was nevertheless prevented from adjusting the uncovered note issue to counteract financial panics. In the crises of 1847 and 1857, the government prevented complete financial collapse only by suspending the act.

After the 1850s the Bank of England gradually developed the policies required to modulate economic fluctuations. By 1875 the Bank of England was such a large holder of bills that it had virtual control of the rate of discount, and therefore over the level of economic activity. It could lower the rate to encourage borrowing, or raise it to discourage borrowing. By 1900 the bank had ceased to compete with the great joint-stock banks for bills, and hence its rate of discount ceased to be any indication of the real discount rate, which was determined by the business decisions of the largest commercial banks. Nevertheless, the major commercial banks accepted the Bank of England's leadership, since it was the ultimate depository of the reserves of the entire banking system, the government's banker, and the "lender of last resort." Commercial bank operations depended upon the stability of the Bank of England.

The discount houses and bill brokers acted as intermediaries between the great banks and the holders. While banks generally held bills until maturity, brokers turned them over at a profit. They met informally, and published the rates they would allow, which were comparable to the terms offered depositors by the banks. The brokers worked with money borrowed for a short term. Most of their money was borrowed from banks, but they also lent to and borrowed from stock exchange money brokers on low-risk securities.

The London money market became a most efficient organization during the Victorian period. Loanable capital was gathered up from savers throughout the country and distributed to those investors with the most profitable projects. Virtually all savings were held in bank deposits, and checking grew in importance. Walter Bagehot's *Lombard Street* (1873) articulated, for the first time, the principles of central banking and the role of the Bank of England as guardian of the financial markets and "lender of the last resort."

E. L. FORGET

Bibliography

Bagehot, Walter. *Lombard Street*. 1873; rpt. 1915.

Clapham, John H. *The Bank of England*. 1944. 2 vols.

Mints, Lloyd W. *A History of Banking Theory.* 1945.

Pressnell, L. S. and John Orbell. *A Guide to the Historical Records of British Banking.* 1985.

· · · · ·

BANKRUPTCY

Bankruptcy was something of a cultural obsession for the Victorian middle class: lists of failures were chronicled in the daily newspapers, bankruptcy reform was endlessly debated in Parliament, and the threat of economic failure haunted the popular imagination in paintings, melodramas, and novels.

Statistics of bankruptcy are flawed and liable to misinterpretation because of frequent changes in the laws. (For example, those not defined as "traders" were until 1861 considered insolvent debtors rather than bankrupts, and treated under a different set of laws.) But it seems clear that bankruptcy had increased greatly in the last half of the eighteenth century and continued to do so in Victoria's reign. Parliamentary commissions in the 1840s estimated the loss by economic failure at about fifty million pounds annually.

Throughout the period, great outrage was expressed in Parliament and in contemporary journals over the number of bankrupts, who seemed to challenge the era's most cherished notions about hard work and success—and the importance of commercial honor and paying one's debts. Nevertheless, despite much public rhetoric stigmatizing bankruptcy as a disgrace and demanding harsh legislation, the Victorians were forced by the economic realities of the new industrial economy to make some provision for those who had failed. Bankruptcy had become a necessary refuge for the marginal entrepreneurs of capitalism, and major reform bills in 1825, 1831, 1842, 1849, 1861, and 1883 ameliorated their condition, abolished imprisonment for debt and eventually established official control over the procedure.

BARBARA WEISS

Bibliography

Marriner, Sheila. "English Bankruptcy Records and Statistics Before 1850." *The Economic History Review*, vol. 33 (series 2), pp. 351–366.

Mathias, Peter. *The First Industrial Nation.* 1969.

Thompson, James H. *The Principles of Bankruptcy Law.* 1967

Weiss, Barbara. *The Hell of the English: Bankruptcy and the Victorian Novel.* 1986.

See also DEBT, IMPRISONMENT FOR

· · · · ·

BANKS, ISABELLA VARLEY (1821–1897)

Isabella Varley Banks (also known as Mrs. G. Linnaeus Banks) wrote poetry, short stories, and novels, including *The Manchester Man* (1876), which depicts working-class life in Manchester in the first quarter of the nineteenth century and gives a good picture of the riots of 1819. Its popularity was long-lived and eventually there was a fourth edition (1881) and a one-volume edition. This and other novels dealing with Manchester life earned her the title "the Lancashire novelist."

Banks was born at Cheetham, near Manchester, to James Varley, a chemist, and his wife Amelia Daniels. In early life she was a schoolmistress at Cheetham, joined the **Anti–Corn-Law League** (1842), and married journalist George Linnaeus Banks (December 27, 1846), whom she assisted in his editorial work, both in Birmingham and London.

At the London Shakespeare tercentenary Banks baptized a memorial oak presented by Queen Victoria and delivered an address. She was also skilled at knitting and needlework and produced an original fancywork pattern each month from 1850 to 1895.

Banks was often aided by the Royal Literary Fund (365 pounds by 1882); Anthony Trollope suggested that her reward in literary life had fallen far short of her desserts. Often compared with **Elizabeth Gaskell** in subject matter, Banks will be remembered chiefly for her pictures of Manchester working life.

ROSEMARY T. VAN ARSDEL

Bibliography

Burney, Edward L. *Mrs. G. Linnaeus Banks.* 1969.

The Illustrated London News, May 15, 1897.

Manchester Faces and Places, December 1892.

Manchester Guardian, May 6, 1897.

. . . . .

BAPTISTS

Granted a form of semilegality by the Toleration Act of 1689, the two traditions of Baptist life in Britain faced severe internal pressures during the eighteenth century. The majority of the older General or Arminian Baptists were drawn towards Socinianism or Unitarianism, while many (though not all) of the Particular Baptists espoused a form of hyper-Calvinism that was opposed to all evangelical activity.

The evangelical revival, which brought about the birth of the Methodists and of the Evangelical party within the Church of England, also revived the moribund life of old dissent. In particularly, two regional groups influenced by the revival came to Baptist convictions, one in Leicestershire and adjacent counties associated with Samuel Deacon (1746-1816) and another in the West Riding associated with Dan Taylor (1738-1816). Attempts to work with the existing General Baptists failed. A separate New Connexion of General Baptists was formed under Dan Taylor's leadership in June 1770 which centered its work in emerging industrial communities.

The evangelical revival also had an impact upon the Particular Baptists. Andrew Fuller (1754-1815) published *The Gospel Worthy of All Acceptation* (1785), which emphasized the missionary implications of Calvinist theology. The Baptist Missionary Society (1792) was the first of the foreign mission societies founded in Britain in the late eighteenth century. Within five years there was a Baptist Itinerant Society for home mission work and a period of new growth among the churches. Although religious statistics are difficult to verify, the following figures have been suggested for Baptists in the United Kingdom: 37,000 in 1800; 125,000 in 1837; and 373,000 in 1901.

Such growth produced problems as well as promise, especially when associated with a primitive spirit of ecumenical cooperation. When people agreed about evangelistic enterprise, should polity be allowed to divide evangelical Christendom? In local terms, this narrowed down to debate about admission to Holy Communion and, later in the century, about the terms of membership in a Baptist church. Robert Hall (1764-1831) argued that "no man or set of men are entitled to prescribe as an indispensable condition of communion, what the New Testament has not enjoined as a condition of salvation." The conservative Joseph Kinghorn (1766-1832) disagreed, urging that Holy Communion be closed to all except those baptized or believers, although he was otherwise prepared to cooperate with other evangelical Christians. The children of the old hyper-Calvinism, now known as Strict (and Particular) Baptists, were led in the north by William Gadsby (1773-1844), who fiercely upheld the older views of Strict Communion and Particular Redemption. In midcentury they secured new and vital leadership from a number of Anglican seceders including J. C. Philpot, William Tiptaft, and other Anglican clergymen.

The Strict Baptists rejected not only the new missionary theology but also the whole apparatus of denominationalism which had been launched at the beginning of the nineteenth century. The Baptists established a General Union of Baptist Ministers and Churches in 1813, founded colleges at Horton, Abergavenny, and Stepney in the years 1806-1810, and created a vehicle for communication in the *Baptist Magazine* (1810). The various regional associations came into new life, and soon no church was complete without its **Sunday School**.

Superficially, the two most prominent Baptist preachers of Victorian Britain, Charles Haddon Spurgeon (1834-1892) and John Clifford (1836-1923), might seem to represent the unresolved tensions between Particular and General Baptists. Yet Spurgeon, though holding firmly to old verities, was fully aware of the need to woo new worshippers. His Metropolitan Tabernacle was very much an "institutional church" with a battery of organizations and agencies to meet the social and spiritual needs of South Londoners. John Clifford held "advanced" views, became a Fabian author, and led the movement of passive resistance in opposing rate aid for denominational education at the beginning of the twentieth century. But for all their differences, Spurgeon and Clifford were equally committed to the Baptists' concern for personal evangelism as the principal task of each local congregation.

J. H. Y. BRIGGS

Bibliography

Baptist Quarterly. 1922-.

Payne, Ernest A. The Baptist Union: A Short History. 1959.

Underwood, A. C. A History of the English Baptists. 1947.

See also EVANGELICAL MOVEMENT; THEOLOGY

· · · · ·

BARNARDO, THOMAS
(1845-1905)

A prominent social reformer and medical missionary, Thomas Barnardo was known primarily for his child rescue work and for the children's homes that bear his name. Like many of his contemporaries, his work in **ragged schools** (attended by children whose abject physical condition rendered them unacceptable to the schools of the working poor) sensitized him to the deplorable plight of so many of England's youth, and evoked at an early age a commitment to their cause. The first of his many homes was opened in Stepney, for boys, in 1870, and he soon extended his child rescuing work to include neglected girls. Financed by Samuel Smith, philanthropist and influential M.P. for Liverpool, Barnardo embarked in 1882 on his massive scheme to send children to Canada. Criticized for his methods of obtaining children to emigrate, he confessed to practicing "philanthropic abduction" as a means of rescuing children, but defended his actions in light of the intolerable conditions in which he found them. Although he expended considerable effort ministering and bringing medical relief to residents of all ages in London's East End, his legacy rests on his claim that he had never turned away any child from his homes, irrespective of background or condition.

TREVOR J. PHILLIPS

Bibliography

Bagnell, Kenneth. The Little Immigrants. 1980.

Wagner, Gillian. Barnardo. 1979.

See also CHILD SAVING

· · · · ·

BARRIE, J. M.
(1860-1937)

The ninth child of a Scottish handloom weaver, James Matthew Barrie became a spectacularly successful author by marketing a talent for sentimental humor. Like many other writers of his generation, he broke into literature via journalism. He began his career as a freelance journalist while studying at Edinburgh University, and after completing his M.A. he worked for the Nottingham Journal. When he arrived in London in 1885, he was already a contributor to the St. James's Gazette and several other metropolitan papers. In his novel When a Man's Single (1888), Barrie revealed his formula for success in journalism: his knack for spinning clever copy out of incidents in everyday life. (H. G. Wells later copied that method to launch his own literary career.)

Barrie also found a market for mawkish sketches of Scottish rural life, laced with an almost insulting dialect humor. His Auld Licht Idylls (1888) and A Window in Thrums (1889) gave rise to the "Kailyard School," a subgenre of Scots cabbage patch literature.

A Freudian analysis of Barrie's play Dear Brutus (1917) was published as early as 1922, and psychological critics have since uncovered a jungle of Victorian neuroses in his life and work. His attachment to his mother, Margaret Ogilvy (1819-1895), was consuming: and he was deeply scarred by the tragic deaths of an older brother, a sister, and the fiancé of another sister. Barrie's marriage (1894) to the actress Mary Ansell (1861-1948) was childless and ended in divorce in 1909. Out of these complexes emerged Barrie's distinctive literary themes: he venerated virgin mothers, he fixated on children "lost" in eternal **childhood**, and he escaped from his anxieties by fabricating island fantasy worlds.

Barrie used these devices to produce a string of commercial successes. *Walker, London* (1892), set on a houseboat, was his first theatrical triumph; and *Margaret Ogilvy* (1896) was a worshipful portrait of his mother. He also wrote a series of sticky-sweet novels: *The Little Minister* (1891), *Sentimental Tommy* (1896), and *Tommy and Grizel* (1900).

In the new century, Barrie would employ these themes with more deftness and sophistication, particularly in *The Admirable Crichton* (1902), a sharp satire on the class system. *Peter Pan* (1904) had a triumphant opening night and went on to become one of the most popular plays of all time. Clearly, in refusing to grow up, Barrie had touched a chord among Victorian and Edwardian audiences.

JONATHAN ROSE

Bibliography

Birkin, Andrew. *J. M. Barrie and the Lost Boys.* 1979.

Blake, George. *Barrie and the Kailyard School.* 1951.

Dunbar, Janet. *J. M. Barrie: The Man Behind the Image.* 1970.

. . . . .

BARRY, CHARLES
(1795–1860)

Charles Barry was a major architect: his greatest work was the New Palace at Westminster (1840–1860), and he introduced the Renaissance Italianate style into Britain. He received the Gold Medal (1850), was knighted (1852), and is buried in Westminster Abbey.

Articled to surveyors in Lambeth, Barry later traveled for three years in Europe and the Middle East; he was the first British architect to visit Egypt. Setting up practice in London in 1820, he led the early **Gothic revival** with seven churches built under the authority of the Church Building Act (1818). His best surviving church is St. Peter's, Brighton (1823–1828).

Barry worked in all styles. His Royal Institution of Fine Arts (1824; now the Manchester City Art Gallery) is a fine example of Greek revival. He remodeled Dunrobin Castle (1844–1848) in the Scottish Baronial style and Highclere Castle (1842–c.1850) in the Elizabethan mode. He reworked Dance's classical Royal College of Surgeons (1833–1837).

Barry's favorite style was Renaissance Italianate, which he introduced with the Travellers' Club (1829–1832), at the time a startling building. The Reform Club (1837–1841), inspired by the Palazzo Farnese in Rome, was acclaimed for its "grandeur and gusto." Barry's Italianate style was widely copied and became characteristic of secular buildings for the next quarter-century. Among the best examples of Barry's Italianate style are Trentham Hall (1834–1844; demolished 1910), Cliveden House (1850), and Bridgewater House (1845–1850). His last building, the Halifax Town Hall (1859–1862), was completed by E. M. Barry.

Barry's name will be remembered primarily for the Gothic New Palace of Westminster. Winning the competition for a new Parliament building in 1835, he was preoccupied with the project until his death. The building brilliantly combines classical symmetry with Gothic drama. As the symbol of Britain, it has become one of the world's best known buildings.

There has, however, been controversy about whether the building was designed by Barry or **A. W. N. Pugin**, his assistant. Their sons carried on an unseemly public debate about the matter after the deaths of their fathers. Recent studies confirm that Barry was responsible for the overall design and that Pugin planned and executed the interior decor.

Barry was also a landscape architect. He surrounded his country houses with Italianate gardens, which became popular, and designed the northern side of Trafalgar Square. Although lack of taste in his later works has often been criticized, Barry pleased contemporaries and intimately reflected the changing taste of the early Victorian era. The Palace of Westminster is as surely his monument as St. Paul's is Wren's.

WILSON J. HOFFMAN

Bibliography

Barry, Alfred. *The Life and Works of Sir Charles Barry.* 1867; rpt. 1972.

Fleetwood-Hesketh, Peter. "Sir Charles Barry." In Peter Ferriday, ed., *Victorian Architecture.* 1964.

Whiffen, Marcus. *The Architecture of Sir Charles Barry in Manchester and Neighbourhood.* 1950.

Wodehouse, Lawrence. *British Architects, 1840–1976: A Guide to Information Sources.* 1978.

See also LANDSCAPE ARCHITECTURE AND DESIGN

· · · · ·

BEALE, DOROTHEA
(1831–1906)

Principal of the prestigious pioneer girls' public school Cheltenham Ladies' College from 1858–1906, Dorothea Beale was important in the movement to change education for middle-class girls and women. Her edited version (1869) of those sections of the Taunton Commission Report (1868–1869) dealing with the inadequacies of girls' schools publicized the commission's evidence and lent weight to the arguments of reformers.

The daughter of Miles Beale, a London surgeon, and his wife Dorothea Margaret Complin, Beale was one of the first students of Queen's College for Women, and soon became a mathematics teacher. Dissatisfied with the declining importance of women visitors at Queen's College, she left in 1856 to take up another post. In 1858, she became head of Cheltenham Ladies' College, a post that she held until her death.

Beale became a schoolteacher from a sense of religious vocation, believing that women, like men, should use the talents God had given them. With an evangelical zeal, she saw education as a means of improving society. Although choosing to remain unmarried, Beale emphasized that sound education for women enhanced home and family life, while education for idleness and trivial pursuits harmed both individuals and society.

At Cheltenham Ladies' College languages and science gradually replaced "accomplishments" in the curriculum, and the school day was reorganized, reforms later copied by

many of the new girls' public schools. Beale encouraged the professional training of women teachers in her essays and lectures, and by training programs at Cheltenham, by founding St. Hilda's College, Oxford (1893), and by supporting the professional associations of headmistresses (founded in 1874) and assistant mistresses (founded in 1884). She also served as a vice-president of the Central Society for Women's Suffrage.

Although disliking competitive examinations in principle, Beale helped ensure that the new schools for middle-class girls provided high-quality academic education and good teaching by professional trained women.

ROSAMUND BILLINGTON

Bibliography

Beale, Dorothea. *History of the Ladies' College, 1853–1904.* 1905.

Burstyn, Joan. *Victorian Education and the Ideal of Womanhood.* 1980.

Clarke, A. K. *History of the Ladies' College, 1853–1953.* 1954.

Kamm, Josephine. *How Different from Us: A Biography of Miss Buss and Miss Beale.* 1958.

Raikes, Elizabeth. *Dorothea Beale of Cheltenham.* 1908.

See also EDUCATION, WOMEN'S

· · · · ·

BEARDSLEY, AUBREY VINCENT
(1872–1898)

The most significant English visual artist of the 1890s, Aubrey Beardsley's work appeared almost entirely in the form of illustrations for books (Oscar Wilde's *Salomé*, 1894) and periodicals (*The Yellow Book*, 1894–1895).

From childhood Beardsley manifested symptoms of the tuberculosis which would kill him in his twenty-sixth year. After formal education at Brighton Grammar School (1884–1889) he moved to London to work as an insurance clerk.

Encouraged by **Edward Burne-Jones**, Beardsley devoted his free hours to drawing. His early efforts echo Burne-Jones's taste for unnaturally elongated figures and stylized vegetative forms, as in the illustrations for Malory's *Le Morte d'Arthur* (1893–1894).

Beardsley collected Japanese woodblock prints, and a trip to Paris in 1892, where he received the encouragement of Puvis de Chavannes, confirmed his inclination to abandon chiaroscuro, using instead large areas of flat black or white, set off against each other asymmetrically, counterpointed by tiny, finely drawn contiguous details. Over the pictorial space sweep long, curving lines, so perfect the viewer wonders how a human hand could draw them, which Beardsley uses to render not only form, but volume, distance, and emotion.

This new style climaxes in the *Salomé* illustrations which also carry to an extreme Beardsley's fascination for the grotesque and for a sexuality tinged with homoeroticism, sadism, and necrophilia. Influenced by the aestheticism of the 1890s, Beardsley rejected conventional moral imperatives, convinced that art is principally about itself, about line, mass, and visual balance. His outrageous images, created for mechanical reproduction, are best seen on the pages of a book, and so constitute a high art available to anyone.

In his last working year Beardsley continued stylistic experimentation, adopting rococo mannerisms for his *Rape of the Lock* illustrations (1896), wittily replicating the effects of eighteenth-century engraving through elaborate stippling and hatching.

During his lifetime Beardsley's work suffered vitriolic attacks from the establishment press, but after his death it influenced illustrators and designers from Chicago to St. Petersburg, who found in him one of the central exponents of **art nouveau**.

JOHN PFORDRESHER

Bibliography

Weintraub, Stanley. *Aubrey Beardsley: Imp of the Perverse.* 1976.

Wilson, Simon. *Beardsley.* 1983.

· · · · ·

BECKER, LYDIA ERNESTINE (1827–1890)

A leader in the women's suffrage movement, Lydia Ernestine Becker was a botanist, edited the *Women's Suffrage Journal* (1870–1890), and served on the Manchester School Board.

She was the daughter of Mary and Hannibal Leigh Becker (who owned a calico printing works and later a chemical plant). Living in the country as a young woman, Becker was interested in botany and astronomy. She published *Botany for Novices* (1864) and, in 1865, read a paper on fungus before the British Association.

Becker moved to Manchester in 1865, where she founded the Manchester Ladies' Literary Society, with indifferent success. A paper by **Barbara Leigh Smith Bodichon** in 1866 attracted her to the **suffrage** question. In 1867 she became secretary of the newly formed Manchester Women's Suffrage Committee, which merged with other suffrage organizations and became the powerful and influential Manchester National Society for Women's Suffrage. Becker remained as secretary. "Female Suffrage," published in the March 1867 issue of the *Contemporary Review*, gained her national visibility. Three important publications followed: "Some Supposed Differences in the Minds of Men and Women with Regard to Educational Necessities," read at the British Association Congress in Norwich, 1868; "Political Disabilities of Women," *Westminster Review*, vol. 97, January 1872; and "Liberty, Equality, Fraternity: A Reply to Mr. Fitzjames Stephen's Strictures on Mr. J. S. Mill's Subjection of Women," a pamphlet.

Becker was elected to the first Manchester School Board in 1870 and returned in seven consecutive elections as an unsectarian member, with special interest in female teachers and girl students. She will be remembered for her pioneer work in woman's suffrage; for keeping news of the movement circulating during the largely hostile 1870s; for her courageous stance as editor of *Women's Suffrage Journal*; and also for her efforts in school board work, one of the first public offices to open to women in the nineteenth century.

ROSEMARY T. VAN ARSDEL

Bibliography

Blackburn, Helen. *Women's Suffrage.* 1902.

Holmes, Marion. *Lydia Becker.* 1913.

Illustrated London News, August 2, 1890, p. 154.

Times, July 21, 1890, p. 9.

Women's Suffrage Journal, August 1890. (Memorial number.)

·   ·   ·   ·   ·

BEGGARS AND VAGRANTS

Although Victorian beggars were not necessarily vagrants, and many vagrants never begged, all such persons were subject to the penalties of the Vagrancy Act of 1824, which labeled them variously "idle and disorderly persons," or "rogues and vagabonds," and empowered their imprisonment at hard labor. Both beggars and vagrants were notorious features of the mid-Victorian social landscape, and while visible, obnoxious begging had largely disappeared by 1900, vagrancy remained an intractable problem well into the twentieth century.

The beggars of midcentury London are celebrated in **Henry Mayhew**'s vivid descriptions. Their colorful dodges ("lays"), cant language, and astonishing numbers gave a peculiar character to metropolitan street life. Most—and by all accounts the most successful—street beggars were children; they were commonly rented or purchased for their ability to exploit the convention of the suffering waif. But the armies of urchins who plagued London and the provincial cities and towns in 1850 almost vanished in the following decades. New schools took many: industrial and reformatory schools, Poor Law district and separate workhouse schools, and board schools after the 1870 Education Act. The shrunken **child labor** pool meant that more casual employment was available for those children who remained at large. Moreover, from the 1860s there developed a stern new

public attitude toward beggars and almsgiving. The Charity Organization Society (1869) and similar agencies argued with great effect that indiscriminate charity demoralized the poor. They sought to coordinate and reduce private giving and official relief, and so revive honest labor, foresight, and thrift. Later still, in the 1880s and 1890s, **poverty** came increasingly to be identified as a national problem susceptible only to collective, even state, remedies; this further eroded the custom of casual handouts. In this ever more hostile environment there were few beggars about, and end-of-century commentators seldom perceived them as a serious social affliction.

Vagrancy proved far more difficult to eradicate. Except in times of unusual distress like the Irish and cotton famines, there were basically two sorts of vagrants: artisans and seasonal harvesters who sought work, and "professional" vagrants who avoided work. Contrary to the prevailing myth of the ubiquitous carefree or criminal tramp, many—often most—who regularly tramped were work seekers. Throughout the Victorian era **Poor Law** authorities could not decide whether to discriminate in favor of those honest work seekers, or to treat all vagrants as shirkers deserving strictly punitive treatment in **workhouse** casual wards. And if the central Poor Law authorities enjoined brief detention and a task of work, local authorities often sought to move vagrants on quickly, sparing local ratepayers. Lack of uniformity in local administration brought an additional dilemma. Where local workhouse regimes were harsh, vagrants wandered and slept in the open, alarming householders; where regimes were soft, multitudes came into the casual wards, burdening ratepayers. No sort of policy or administration seemed to influence the incidence and cost of vagrancy, and the muddled report of the 1904 Departmental Committee on Vagrancy signaled the failure of decades of shifting directives aimed at this obstinate social problem. Far more instrumental in affecting the numbers of vagrants were the requirements of industrial capitalism and the mechanization of agriculture, which by the end of the century had significantly reduced the numbers of tramping artisans and harvesters.

MARK NEUMAN

Bibliography

Hobsbawm, E. J. "The Tramping Artisan." In Eric Hobsbawm, *Labouring Men: Studies in the History of Labour.* 1964.

Jones, Gareth Stedman. *Outcast London.* 1971.

Mayhew, Henry. *London Labour and the London Poor.* 1861–1862; rpt. 1968. 4 vols.

Vorspan, Rachel. "Vagrancy and the New Poor Law in Late Victorian and Edwardian England." *English Historical Review,* vol. 92, pp. 59–81.

Webb, Sidney and Beatrice Webb. *English Poor Law History.* Part 2: *The Last Hundred Years.* Vol. 1 1929; rpt. 1963.

See also WORKHOUSE *(illus.)*

• • • • •

Today Bennett is valued above all for the delicacy of his piano pieces. Their style bears a family resemblance to that of Mendelssohn, but has its own individuality and reflects the composer's high artistic purpose. A modest revival of his songs, chamber music, and orchestral music is now under way.

NICHOLAS TEMPERLEY

Bibliography

Bennett, James Sterndale. *The Life of William Sterndale Bennett.* 1907.

Temperley, Nicholas, ed. *The London Pianoforte School, 1766–1860.* Vols. 17, 18: *Works for Pianoforte Solo by William Sterndale Bennett.* 1985.

• • • • •

BENNETT, WILLIAM STERNDALE (1816–1875)

William Sterndale Bennett, composer, pianist, and conductor (knighted 1871), was the most distinguished musician of the early Victorian period.

He lost both parents in infancy, and was raised by his grandfather, a choral singer in Cambridge college chapels. He studied at the Royal Academy of Music. Invited by Felix Mendelssohn to Leipzig in 1835, he was acclaimed as a sensitive artist of the new German romantic school. Robert Schumann hailed him as a coming genius. In this youthful period Bennett composed major symphonies, overtures, piano concertos, songs, and, above all, pieces for piano solo.

In London Bennett was increasingly occupied with teaching, to which administrative duties were eventually added: he became an instructor at the Royal Academy (1837), conductor of the **Philharmonic Society** (1856), professor of music at Cambridge (1856), and principal of the Royal Academy (1866). During his later years he occasionally produced large works for public consumption—the cantata *The May Queen* (1858), the Symphony in G minor (1864), and the oratorio *The Woman of Samaria* (1867); but he never recovered the fecundity of his early years.

BESANT, ANNIE WOOD (1847–1933)

Annie Besant, Anglican minister's wife turned radical activist and pamphleteer, embodied the dilemmas and concerns of the Victorian freethinker, the Victorian socialist, and the Victorian woman.

After rejecting Christian orthodoxy for its moral as well as intellectual untenability, Besant left both her marriage and the church in 1873. Guided by a commitment to truth, justice, equality and moral progress, she wavered on whether these issues could best be addressed through the intellect, through political and economic structures, or through the spirit.

Associated with the freethinkers from 1874–1886, she occupied leadership in the National Secular Society, the Freethought Publishing Company, and the *National Reformer.* In her socialist stage from 1884–1889 she edited *Our Corner* (1883–1888). In later years she espoused **Theosophy** under the tutelage of **Madame Blavatsky**. Besant wrote pamphlets on land reform, political equality, marriage and property arrangements for women, prostitution, socialism, imperialism, Ireland, and Theosophy. She also wrote for the *National Reformer,* often under the pseudonym "Ajax."

Besant was best known in Victorian England for her advocacy of **birth control**. In addition to serving as secretary for the Malthusian League, she was tried under the Obscene Publications Act in 1877 (along with Charles Bradlaugh) for printing Knowlton's *The Fruits of Philosophy*, a work discussing contraception. Although the indictment was dismissed on appeal, Besant was declared unfit to parent and lost custody of her daughter in 1878.

Much of Besant's later life was spent in India, where she promoted Indian independence. She is significant for her early articulation of national and international issues that would become major themes for early twentieth-century reformers.

SHIRLEY A. MULLEN

Bibliography

Besant, Annie. *The Ancient Wisdom: An Outline of Theosophical Teachings*. 1897.

———. *Annie Besant: An Autobiography*. 1893.

Dinnage, Rosemary. *Annie Besant*. 1986.

Nethercot, Arthur H. *The First Five Lives of Annie Besant*. 1960.

———. *The Last Four Lives of Annie Besant*. 1963.

Saville, John, ed. *A Selection of the Social and Political Pamphlets of Annie Besant*. 1970.

See also MATCHWORKERS

· · · · ·

BEVINGTON, LOUISA SARAH
(1845-?)

Louisa Bevington was a poet and essayist in the service of evolutionary science. *Key Notes* (1876), originally published under the pseudonym "Arbor Leigh," contained verses philosophically based in the theory of **evolution**; this volume was reissued under Bevington's name in 1879. Charles Darwin, who had not read a volume of poetry in fifteen years, expressed satisfaction with *Key Notes* which, like most of Bevington's work, found favor chiefly in scientific rather than literary circles.

Bevington even took an evolutionist approach to the amelioration of social ills such as wife beating. In 1881 she contributed an article to the *Fortnightly Review* defending evolutionary morality. "The Poet's Tear," from her 1882 collection *Poems, Lyrics, and Sonnets*, expressed the view that human suffering is useful because it is the source of art. No further poetry or prose by Bevington appeared in England after she married a Munich artist and moved to Germany in 1883.

KATHLEEN HICKOK
· · · · ·

BIBLICAL CRITICISM

Biblical criticism refers to the methods and results of applying to the Bible the techniques of historical and literary analysis that might be used to interpret any written work. It includes the attempt to establish the most reliable texts (the so-called "lower criticism") and to place biblical interpretation on an objective, scientific basis (the so-called "higher criticism"). Modern biblical criticism had its main impetus in the German universities of the eighteenth and nineteenth centuries, where academic freedom, concern for intellectual rigor, and the importance attached to the Bible encouraged these pursuits. The German school concentrated on such concerns as the contents, composition, and editing of the Pentateuch; the composite nature of such prophetic books as Isaiah and Zechariah; the literary relationships among the four Gospels; the authorship of much of the Hebrew Bible and New Testament; and the historical backgrounds of various books and the literary genres among and within them.

While such analysis was not entirely new, the British public was at first largely unaware of it and its possible consequences for religious faith. Since the literal accuracy of the Bible, including the historicity of the Gospel accounts of Jesus, was involved, the issues raised by biblical criticism were profound and potentially troubling for many people. Samuel Taylor Coleridge (1772-1834) synthesized and endorsed many conclusions of the German scholarship of his day, and through his influence and that of younger followers such as Thomas Arnold (1795-1842) and Julius Charles Hare (1795-1855), Broad Church Anglicanism was receptive to this scholarship. In most of British Christianity, however, the Bible was viewed as an inspired, authoritative, and infallible revelation that proved the absolute validity of Christian faith, which was the cement of all morality. Thus any analysis that questioned the literal accuracy or plenary inspiration of the Bible seemed to threaten belief systems and encourage moral anarchy. The contemporary issue of literalism versus geological evidence and Darwinism made those clergy who advocated Biblical criticism seem a heinous fifth column of the Enemy.

The publication of *Essays and Reviews* (1860) brought the issues into the open. Written almost entirely by clergy associated with Oxford, it was intended to establish a place for biblical criticism within the Church of England. Quite conservative compared to contemporary German studies, it nevertheless provoked a stormy opposition. Following closely on this controversy was the publication of the first two volumes of *The Pentateuch and Book of Joshua Critically Examined* (1862-1863) by John William Colenso (1814-1883). Like some German scholars before him, Colenso concluded that little of the Pentateuch was from the time of Moses and that the historicity of both Moses and Joshua was dubious. He applied his mathematical skills to show that such biblical numbers as 600,000 fighting men plus women, children, and slaves in the Sinai desert were unlikely to be accurate. That he was the Anglican bishop of Natal intensified the outrage of literalists and even such moderates as Frederick Denison Maurice. The results of biblical researches also came to the attention of the British public through the succession of rationalized "lives of Jesus," especially David Friedrich Strauss's (1808-1874) *Das Leben Jesu* (1835; translated by George Eliot, 1846), Ernest Renan's (1823-1892) *Vie de Jésus* (1863), and **John Robert Seeley's** (1834-1895) anonymous *Ecce Homo* (1865), all of which played down the miraculous elements in the Gospels and emphasized the purely human ones. A more balanced approach to biblical criticism characterized the scholarship of Brooke Foss Westcott (1825-1901), Joseph Barber Lightfoot (1828-1889), and Fenton John Anthony Hort (1828-1892), whose openness to sound criticism was combined with respect for the texts with which they worked and helped bridge the perceived gulf between science and religion.

While the methods and conclusions of biblical scholarship were anathema to many in Victorian Britain, they did not lack positive support. Theological liberals and moderates welcomed them in their struggles with what they saw as narrow and dogmatic literalism, however much they deplored extreme forms of that scholarship. The absorption of biblical criticism into the mainstream of British Christianity is evidenced by the fact that one of the authors of *Essays and Reviews*, Frederick Temple (1821-1902), became archbishop of Canterbury before the end of the century (1896).

E. CLEVE WANT

Bibliography

De Vries, Simon J. "Biblical Criticism, History of." In *The Intepreter's Dictionary of the Bible*, vol. 1. 1962.

Distad, N. Merrill. *Guessing at Truth: The Life of Julius Charles Hare*. 1979.

Grant, Robert M. with David Tracy. *A Short History of the Interpretation of the Bible*. 1984.

Grobel, Kendrick. "Biblical Criticism." In *The Interpreter's Dictionary of the Bible*, vol. 1. 1962.

Harding, Anthony John. *Coleridge and the Inspired Word*. 1985.

Reardon, Bernard M. G. *From Coleridge to Gore: A Century of Religious Thought in Britain*. 1971.

Rogerson, John. *Old Testament Criticism in the Nineteenth Century: England and Germany*. 1984.

Sanders, Charles Richard. *Coleridge and the Broad Church Movement: Studies in S. T. Coleridge, Dr. Arnold of Rugby, J. C. Hare, Thomas Carlyle and F. D. Maurice*. 1942.

Terrien, Samuel. "History of the Interpretation of the Bible: III. Modern Period." In *The Interpreter's Bible*. vol. 1. 1952.

See also CHURCH OF ENGLAND; THEOLOGY

. . . . .

BICYCLE

Though the Scotsman Kirkpatrick Macmillan invented the first self-propelled bicycle (1839), his design never really caught on; not until 1861, when the Michaux family of Paris produced its wood-and-iron "boneshaker" did the first widely adopted cycle appear. In Britain, during the early 1870s, the Michaux machine was transformed by James Starley; his "ordinary" or "penny-farthing" bicycle was characterized by large front and small back wheels and long-lasting tangential spokes. Further refinements included the safety bicycle of 1874, with an endless chain and wheels of equal size; the pneumatic tire of 1888; and the introduction of gears (1901).

The ninth edition of the *Encyclopedia Britannica* (1892) notes a rapid growth in the popularity of cycling "during the past two years." According to Constance Everett-Green there was a marked shift between April and June of 1895; suddenly, during the latter month, it was eccentric among the fashionable *not* to cycle. The fad lasted through 1897, leaving several marks on British culture. To some extent interest in the bicycle cut across classes: sudden and widespread enthusiasm created an important manufacturing industry catering to a mass market. H. G. Wells's *The Wheels of Chance* (1896) has for its hero the shop assistant Hoopdriver, who discovers new mobility on a bike. But particularly attracted to this pastime were young people of the middle classes with advanced views, money, and leisure time. Bicycling allowed new and less supervised forms of contact between the sexes. It was taken up extensively by women seeking independence; there were controversies about proper female dress for cycling. A popular association between bicycling and controversial social positions is suggested by stories of male hostility to female riders passing through working-class neighborhoods. In the preface to *Too True to Be Good* (1932) George Bernard Shaw (an enthusiastic cyclist in his youth, once colliding with Bertrand Russell) complained that newspapers could not distinguish between "a bicycle accident and the collapse of civilization." During the 1890s, however, bicycles often did seem tied to the fortunes of civilization.

RICHARD MAXWELL

Bibliography

Caunter, Cyril Francis. *The History and Development of Cycles*. 1955, 1958. 2 vols.

Rubinstein, David. "Cycling in the 1890s." *Victorian Studies*, vol. 21, pp. 47–71.

Woodforde, John. *The Story of the Bicycle*. 1970.

· · · · ·

BIOCHEMISTRY

With origins as diverse as botany and zoology, biochemistry emerged as a subdiscipline of **physiology** in the late nineteenth century. This new discipline introduced a fresh intellectual rationale and developed experimental methodologies which redefined biological processes at the molecular level. Biochemistry originated in the laboratories of the British universities.

Chemical physiology was established in Britain through the efforts of William Sharpey (1802–1880). At University College, London, Sharpey encouraged his student W. D. Halliburton to teach an advanced course in chemical physiology (1884–1890) and establish research laboratories apart from the physiologists'. Sharpey's approach and influence spread to Cambridge, Edinburgh, Glasgow, Kings College, and Oxford, where professorships in biochemistry were established between 1895 and 1905. Michael Foster, at Cambridge, assumed a major role in establishing the "Cambridge school" of biochemistry; Frederick Gowland Hopkins (1861–1947), a product of Cambridge, was the first academic biochemist in Britain. The only exception to the origin of biochemistry from the physiological departments occurred at Liverpool where in 1902 the biochemistry chair was founded in the School of Hygiene and Public Health.

Hopkins and his co-workers were the first to begin to define the nature of the cellular protoplasm. Within a cell, nature's chemical enterprises occurred by unknown mechanisms. Chemical methods and tools were directed toward probing cellular mysteries. Hopkins (and the new discipline of biochemistry) received singular distinction with the award of the 1929 Nobel Prize for physiology or medicine.

The German chemist Paul Ehrlich (1854–

1915) was interested not only in the normal operation of cells but also in the causes of cell destruction and death. Based on observations made by Hopkins and the British biochemical community in addition to those of German biochemists, Ehrlich formulated his "magic bullet" hypothesis which envisioned the synthesis of chemical reagents that would be directed against specific biochemical processes. Thus the Victorian exploration of biochemistry permitted the initiation and development of the chemotherapeutic era.

FRANK JOHN PAPATHEOFANIS

Bibliography

Kohler, Robert E. *From Medical Chemistry to Biochemistry: The Making of a Biomedical Discipline.* 1982.

· · · · ·

BIOLOGICAL SCIENCE

The science of biology developed during the nineteenth century in a spectacular yet peculiar fashion. It promoted knowledge of living creatures beyond all anticipation, but accumulated that knowledge in a casual way. It achieved great success in solving problems bequeathed by former ages and in proposing some grand unifying theories. Nevertheless, biology failed on the whole to respond to the needs of medicine, to the agricultural revolution, or to the demands of industries (such as textiles, food, and drink) which depended on animal and vegetable products.

The term "biology" dates from 1800; it was first used by Karl Friedrich Burdach (1776–1847) to denote the study of human beings within the combined perspectives of psychology, physiology, and anthropology. Two years later Jean Baptiste Lamarck (1744–1829) described biology in his *Hydrogéologie* (1802) as one of the divisions of "terrestrial physics" that included "all which pertains to living bodies." In coining the term, Lamarck intended to inaugurate a new area of research. Almost immediately, however, that area became crisscrossed by competing interests. Biological science encompassed a wide range of separate, if closely linked, domains, of which half a dozen may be mentioned.

First, taxonomy compared external characteristics of closely allied living forms. It was advanced in Britain by J. D. Hooker (1817–1911) and **Charles Darwin** (1809–1882), among others. Second, morphology or comparative anatomy considered the internal structure of contrasting forms; Robert Brown (1773–1858) and Richard Owen (1804–1892) were the British pioneers in this domain. Third, paleontology studied the comparative anatomy of fossils and was led by Owen and, in paleobotany, by W. C. Williamson (1816–1895). Embryology, which dealt with the formation of parts in the embryo, was undertaken with greatest success abroad. Fifth, physiology was concerned with animal function and was advanced in significant ways by Claude Bernard (1813–1878) and Charles Bell (1774–1842). Finally, evolutionary biology was centrally concerned with organic transformation (though evolution had previously referred to embryological development). **Evolution** by natural selection, the preeminent achievement of the century's life sciences, was independently formulated by Darwin and **Alfred Russel Wallace** (1823–1913) and then ably defended and explored by **T. H. Huxley** (1825–1895), Hooker, Asa Gray (1810–1888), and a host of others.

In broad terms, biology might be seen as a protracted reaction against the earlier preoccupation of natural historians with cataloguing animals, plants, and minerals. More substantively, biology was organized around topics such as "life," "cell theory," "vitalism," and "evolution." These topics themselves offered the space in which biologists readdressed or subverted problems which had occupied the minds of their eighteenth-century predecessors.

Purely empirical classifications played a minor role during the nineteenth century; instead historical and reproductive relations of organisms came to be stressed. Introducing a temporal dimension into the structure of biological classification had far-reaching consequences. Most famously, Darwin demonstrated that the key to the natural system was genealogical descent. Relations of historical ancestry would henceforth provide the principle of group subordination and the differential weighting of characters. Darwin's conclusions concerning the phylogenetic basis of classification were enthusiastically endorsed by many of his British disciples after midcentury, but most effectively by Ernst Haeckel (1834–1919) in Germany, who initiated the practice of constructing "family trees" to represent taxonomic relationships of organic groups.

As conceived by Lamarck, the new biology was to be concerned with the phenomena of life. Although knowledge of the variety, distribution, and ordering of beings had improved over the period 1760–1820, the nature of living processes remained clouded in myth and mystery. With the emergence of "life" as a concept fruitful avenues of research were opened. Such research was prompted and sustained by the growing conviction that the essential nature of plants and animals was the same, and this belief, in turn, was powerfully reinforced from the late 1830s by the development of cell theory. This theory, which identified the cell as the fundamental unit of structure and function in both plants and animals, was introduced by Theodor Schwann (1810–1882) and was one of the greatest synthesizing conceptions of the period. Moreover, announced in the course of investigations at the microscope, the theory gave a great boost to the prestige and use of that instrument. Important technical improvements to the microscope in the 1830s made possible a whole range of new explanations. The observation of nature's minutiae became a popular pastime, but observation, then as now, was not a neutral activity and was never able to guarantee the privilege of the cell as a unit. Huxley, for one, emphasized the properties of the protoplasm rather than the individuality of the cell; by 1900, notions such as "germ plasm" had emerged, linking cytology with the beginnings of modern genetics.

The cell theory was successful in reinforcing belief that animal-plant similarity was manifest at the level of internal organization rather than visible structure. Researchers also looked for common properties of living things that distinguished them from inanimate objects. In so doing, they fueled a debate of metaphysical as well as scientific proportions between mechanism and vitalism. Could life be explained in purely mechanical (physical and chemical) terms, or was some special "vital" principle at work? Great diversity of opinion existed, even within each camp, but most biologists in the early part of the century held nonmechanist views. Part of the explanation for this lay in the continuing presence in British intellectual soil of natural theological modes of thought.

Natural theology was the study of the existence and attributes of God manifested to human reason through the works of nature. The study paralleled science's stress on the unity and order of the natural world and many notable scientists explored those parallels in the Bridgewater treatises in the 1830s. This tradition was severely undermined by Darwinian evolution which insisted that the apparent design of nature was the result not of a presiding creative Mind, but of random variation and struggle. Like cell theory, vitalism, and indeed "biology" itself, evolution set in motion important new research programs. These were gradually articulated through institutions, teaching, specialist journals, and professional bodies. "Biology" had been an obscure term buried in a footnote in a German periodical of 1800. A century later, it was a vigorous and powerful reality: an autonomous, disciplined science with a future of yet more stunning progress ahead.

MICHAEL SHORTLAND

Bibliography

Allen, David E. *The Naturalist in Britain: A Social History.* 1976.

Coleman, William. *Biology in the Nineteenth Century: Problems of Form, Function and Transformation.* 1971.

Mayr, Ernst. *The Growth of Biological Thought: Diversity, Evolution and Inheritance.* 1982.

Mendelsohn, Everett. "The Biological Sciences in the Nineteenth Century: Some Problems and Sources." *History of Science,* vol. 3, pp. 39–59.

Nordenskiold, Erik. *The History of Biology: A Survey.* 1928.

Oppenheimer, Jane M. *Essays in the History of Embryology and Biology.* 1967.

Thomson, John A. *The Science of Life: An Outline of the History of Biology and Its Recent Advances.* 1899.

. . . . .

BIRD, ISABELLA
(1831-1904)

The celebrated Victorian traveler Isabella Bird (Bishop) wrote several popular accounts of her journeys. Her titles reveal a preference for remote areas: *The Englishwoman in America* (1856); *The Hawaiian Archipelago* (1875); *A Lady's Life in the Rocky Mountains* (1879); *Unbeaten Tracks in Japan* (1880); *The Golden Chersonese and the Way Thither* (1883); *Journeys in Persia and Kurdistan* (1891); *Among the Tibetans* (1894); *Korea and Her Neighbours* (1898); and *The Yangtze Valley and Beyond* (1899). A talent for photography yielded *Chinese Pictures* in 1900.

Bird's clergyman father died in 1858. Two years later, her family moved from Huntingdonshire to Edinburgh. Ill health sent her abroad in 1872 on the first significant journey of her restless travel career. When the loss of her adored sister Henrietta in 1880 deprived Bird of her immediate family, she married the physician John Bishop.

Bird's active social and religious conscience inspired her early writings on the miserable living conditions of Scotland's poor. An advocate of medical missions, she financed the establishment of several Asian hospitals. This sympathetic reforming spirit made her unusually responsive to foreign peoples.

Bird legitimized the role of the Victorian woman traveler. She was recognized by the Royal Scottish Geographical Society, and in 1892, the RGS in London made her its first woman fellow. Adventurous, practical, and energetic, she set the standard for her type.

JOAN CORWIN

Bibliography

Allen, Alexandra. *Travelling Ladies.* 1980.

Barr, Pat. *A Curious Life for a Lady: The Story of Isabella Bird.* 1970.

Havely, Cicely Palser, ed. *This Grand Beyond: The Travels of Isabella Bird Bishop.* 1985.

Middleton, Dorothy. *Victorian Lady Travellers.* 1965.

Stoddart, Anna. *The Life of Isabella Bird.* 1906.

· · · · ·

BIRTH CONTROL

A term coined in the twentieth century by Margaret Sanger, birth control includes contraception (the use of techniques and appliances to prevent conception), **abortion**, and **infanticide**. As a result of birth control—practiced first by the upper classes, then by the middle classes, and finally by the working classes—family size declined from 6.16 children in 1861-1869 to under three at the end of the century. Despite technological advances (such as the vulcanization of rubber, which made the modern diaphragm and condom possible), this decline resulted less from improved contraceptives than from improved communication and an awareness of traditional methods of fertility control, primarily prolonged periods of abstinence and coitus interruptus.

Nineteenth-century interest in birth control was initiated by two groups. The first, dominated by people concerned about overall population growth, began with Thomas Malthus (1766-1834), who published *An Essay on the Principle of Population as It Affects the Future Improvement of Society* (1798). Malthus, who was not interested in artificial means of birth control, believed that individuals should practice restraint. The second group, dominated by people who believed that individuals had the right to control their fertility, was more interested in birth control techniques and appliances.

Like many other medical self-help movements during the early part of the nineteenth century, the birth control movement was largely in the hands of amateurs—in this case quacks, retailers of rubber goods, and midwives. Folklore about sexuality, led by *Aristotle's Works* (1684), continued to dominate the field. In addition, the condom was still associated, as it had been in the eighteenth century, with the prevention of **venereal disease**. As a result, most Victorian doctors, who were trained to treat disease rather than to prevent it, were reluctant to discuss birth control. Moreover, because many physicians confused abortion and contraception and believed that artificial methods of contraception were injurious to health, the medical community did not openly support the birth control movement. Recognizing that repeated pregnancies often injured women's health, however, physicians encouraged women to space their children and recommended three forms of natural birth control: prolonged nursing, the rhythm method, and abstinence.

Others tried to overcome this conspiracy of silence. In 1823 **Francis Place** (1771-1854), a radical tailor and political figure, distributed pamphlets in working-class districts which contained information on the sponge, the condom, and withdrawal. Richard Carlile (1790-1843) reprinted Place's pamphlet in the *Register* (1825) and printed his own work on the subject, *Every Woman's Book* (1826).

The first scientific work on artificial methods of birth control, *Fruits of Philosophy or, the Private Companion of Young Married People* (1832), was written by American physician Charles Knowlton (1800-1850). While the information contained in Knowlton's book is reliable, the book was not widely read until **Charles Bradlaugh** (1833-1891) and **Annie Besant** (1847-1933) decided to make it a test case. Bradlaugh and Besant published the work and told police that they planned to sell it. Arrested for publishing an obscene work, they were prosecuted and found guilty. The trial greatly stimulated sales of *Fruits of Philosophy* (125,000 copies were sold during the trial) and provided a public forum for the defendants to discuss the advantages of family limitation. Because of public interest in fertility control, Besant wrote her own pamphlet during the trial, *The Law of Population: Its Consequences and Its Bearing Upon Human Conduct and Morals* (1877), which sold 175,000 copies before she withdrew it in 1891.

Public interest in fertility control also led to the creation of the Malthusian League (1877), an organization established to demonstrate the validity of Malthus's arguments about the danger of overpopulation. The Malthusian League rejected Malthus's recommendation of moral restraint and advocated the practice of birth control within marriage. However, it offered no clinical instruction in the use of birth control until 1881, when a medical branch was opened; and most of its efforts were involved in the communication of tried and true methods rather than in scientific research.

Although it is tempting to look for a connection between the birth control movement and the feminist movement or the labor movement, both groups generally left decisions about birth control to individuals. Leaders of the feminist movement, insistent that husbands be as pure as their wives, were pointedly silent about artificial methods of contraception and argued instead for the wife's right to demand periods of abstinence from her husband. Even without the support of larger groups, however, it is apparent that the majority of the population was practicing some form of birth control by the end of Victoria's reign.

CAROL A. SENF

Bibliography

Banks, Joseph A. *Prosperity and Parenthood.* 1954.

──── . *Victorian Values: Secularism and the Size of Families.* 1981.

Banks, Joseph A. and Olive Banks. *Feminism and Family Planning in Victorian England.* 1964.

Chandrasekhar, S. *"A Dirty, Filthy Book": The Writings of Charles Knowlton and Annie Besant on Reproductive Physiology and Birth Control and an Account of the Bradlaugh-Besant Trial.* 1981.

Fryer, Peter. *The Birth Controllers.* 1965.

Ledbetter, Rosanna. *A History of the Malthusian League.* 1976.

McLaren, Angus. *Birth Control in Nineteenth-Century England.* 1978.

Soloway, Richard Allen. *Birth Control and the Population Question in England, 1877-1930.* 1982.

See also POPULATION AND DEMOGRAPHICS; SEX EDUCATION

· · · · ·

BIRTH RATE see POPULATION AND DEMOGRAPHICS

· · · · ·

BISHOP, HENRY ROWLEY (1786-1855)

Henry Rowley Bishop's most durable composition is the ballad "Home, Sweet Home" from his opera *Clari* (1823), but in the first half of the nineteenth century he was preeminent as a composer, opera conductor, and lecturer. He was the first musician to receive knighthood from the sovereign in person (1842).

The son of a London shopkeeper, Bishop studied under Francesco Bianchi (c. 1752–1810). His first big success was the opera *The Circassian Bride* (1809). Of more than one hundred stage works to which he contributed music, some of the most famous were *The Maniac* (1810), *The Miller and His Men* (1813), *Cortez* (1823), and *Aladdin* (1826). He also set several Shakespeare "operas" and adapted operas by Mozart, Rossini, and others. He was musical director at Covent Garden or Drury Lane from 1810 to 1840. Subsequently he directed the Concert of Ancient Music (1840–1848) and became professor of music at Edinburgh (1841–1843) and Oxford (1848–1855).

Bishop was a proficient composer, particularly good at descriptive music, and wrote some charming songs and glees. The theatrical conventions of his day seem to have placed his stage works beyond revival.

NICHOLAS TEMPERLEY

Bibliography

Carr, Bruce. "Theatre Music, 1800-1834." In *The Athlone History of Music in Britain*, vol. 5. 1981.

Northcott, Richard. *The Life of Sir Henry R. Bishop.* 1920.
. . . . .

BLACK, CLEMENTINA (1853-1922)

As an activist for women's political and economic rights, Clementina Black is best known for her leadership of the Women's Industrial Council and her role in the Anti-Sweating League (organized in 1906). She wrote novels—the first, *A Sussex Idyll*, was published in 1877—was a literary critic, and translated French and German works into English. Her social commentary includes articles on women's work, a book on the minimum wage (1907), and a book on married women's work which she edited in 1915. An active suffragist, she held office in the London Society for Women's Suffrage.

Born in Brighton, Black was the eldest daughter in a family of eight children and was educated primarily at home. Shortly after her first novel was published, she moved to London where she spent several years studying at the British Museum. In the mid-1880s, she began to organize women workers into **trade unions** through the Women's Trade Union League and subsequently the Women's Trade Union Association. When the association disbanded in favor of the Women's Industrial Council in 1894, Black became one of the council's founders and eventually its president.

Black was a social feminist because she looked to social reform as a method of achieving women's economic rights. From the 1880s, she realized that low pay was "at the root of most of the wrongs and sufferings of working women in this country." This belief shaped her work with the Women's Industrial Council and the Anti-Sweating League. She helped guide the council in its investigative and propagandistic work to improve the economic position of working women. In 1913 Black was awarded a civil list pension in recognition of her work.

ELLEN F. MAPPEN

Bibliography

Black, Clementina, ed. *Married Women's Work.* 1915; rpt. with intro. by Ellen F. Mappen. 1983.

Glage, Liselotte. *Clementina Black: A Study in Social History and Literature.* 1981.

Mappen, Ellen F. "Strategists for Change: Social Feminist Approaches to the Problems of Women's Work." In Angela V. John, ed., *Unequal Opportunities: Women's Employment in England, 1800-1918.* 1986.

See also SOCIAL FEMINISM; SWEATSHOPS
. . . . .

BLACKBURN, HELEN
(1842-1903)

A pioneer and leader in the women's suffrage movement, Helen Blackburn was editor for thirteen years of the *Englishwoman's Review*.

Blackburn was born at Knightstown, Valencia Island, County Kerry, the only surviving daughter of Bewicke Blackburn and his wife Isabella Lamb. She emigrated to London with her family in 1859. Her father was a noted inventor of early motor cars and two- and three-wheel bicycles.

Blackburn became involved with the woman's suffrage movement in the late 1860s. She served as secretary of the National Women's Suffrage Society from 1874 to 1895 and also of the Bristol and West of England Suffrage Society from 1880 to 1895. In these capacities she joined other women in speaking for the suffrage movement throughout England. From 1890 to 1903 Blackburn served as editor of the *Englishwoman's Review*, which during her tenure returned to quarterly (rather than monthly) publication.

Blackburn's history of the suffrage movement, *Women's Suffrage: A Record of the Movement in the British Isles* (1902) still appears in bibliographies as a definitive source for the early years. Other publications include: *A Handbook for Women Engaged in Social and Political Work* (1881), *Because: Reasons Why Parliamentary Franchise Should Be No Longer Denied to Women* (1888), *The Conditions of Working Women* (with J. Boucherett, 1896), *Words of a Leader* (1897), and *Women Under the Factory Acts* (with N. Vynne, 1903).

ROSEMARY T. VAN ARSDEL

· · · · ·

BLACKMORE, RICHARD DODDRIDGE
(1825-1900)

An historical and regional novelist, author of the classic *Lorna Doone* (1869), R. D. Blackmore was the second surviving son of a country curate, John Blackmore, and Anne Bassett Knight Blackmore, who died three months after her son's birth. Handicapped by epilepsy, he was raised in Wales and near Oxford by his mother's sister. He received a B.A. in 1847 from Exeter College, Oxford, did legal work, married Lucy Maguire in 1853, published *Poems by Melanter* (1854), and briefly taught classics at a Twickenham school. In 1857 an inheritance allowed him to purchase land in Teddington where he worked as an avid gardener, especially of fruit trees, for the rest of his life. He wrote fiction mainly to supplement his income and remained, even as a celebrity, a shy and reserved but kindly man, with a gift for humor and picturesque speech.

Blackmore's novels were well received by readers and critics who overlooked his superficial historical understanding and appreciated his well-drawn, likeable characters and his convincing evocation of the scenery, life, and dialects of rural regions in southern England. *Lorna Doone* owed its appeal to a special combination of qualities: its description of the wild, romantic setting of seventeenth-century Exmoor; the contrast between its respectable farmers and the noble but savage outlaw Doones; its admirable heroes, in the charming Lorna, captive of the outlaws, and the brave but gentle John Ridd, who overcomes many obstacles to win her; its dramatic events, from a snowstorm and a historical battle to the shooting of the young bride at her wedding; and the picturesque style in which the rustic Ridd narrates his own adventures.

Never again as successful, Blackmore preferred among his later novels *The Maid of Sker* (1872), whose narrator is a roguish late eighteenth-century Welsh fisherman. In *Alice Lorraine* (1875) and more ambitiously in *Springhaven* (1887), he described southern England at the time of the Napoleonic Wars; and in *Perlycross* (1894), set in his father's East Devon parish, he imitated the early Thomas Hardy.

Profiting from a new vogue for romantic historical fiction by Robert Louis Stevenson and Rudyard Kipling, which some critics believe Blackmore's novels helped create, *Lorna Doone* achieved its greatest popularity in the 1890s, when a single edition sold over 100,000 copies. The novel continues to charm all who appreciate romantic characters, exotic locales, and a strong story line.

MONIKA BROWN

Bibliography

Budd, Kenneth. *The Last Victorian: R. D. Blackmore and His Novels.* 1960.

Dunn, Waldo Hilary. *R. D. Blackmore: The Author of "Lorna Doone."* 1956.

Sutton, Max Keith. *R. D. Blackmore.* 1979.

. . . . .

BLACKWELL, ELIZABETH (1821–1901)

In both the United States and England, Elizabeth Blackwell was the first woman to become a fully accredited physician. Blackwell was born in England but her family emigrated to the United States when she was eleven. Admitted to medical school after a long struggle, she received her M.D. from Geneva College, New York, in 1849. She then studied abroad for two years before returning to America, where she successfully practiced medicine for the next eighteen years. In 1869 she settled permanently in England.

Blackwell's campaign to open the British medical profession to women began in 1858–1859, when she applied for British certification and made a lecture tour encouraging women to study medicine. She succeeded in getting her name placed on the British medical register (1859), and although the larger battle to certify women physicians in Britain was not won until 1875, her lectures fired others to work for reform. Among those Blackwell inspired was **Elizabeth Garrett Anderson**, who in 1869 became the second woman placed on the British medical register. By 1881 there were twenty-one registered women doctors in England, and by 1895, 264.

Blackwell helped establish the London School of Medicine for Women, where she became professor of gynecology in the late 1870s. She was a founder of the National Health Society (1871) and was one of the few women physicians to participate in feminist protests against the Contagious Diseases Acts. Other issues on which she took stands include artificial birth control, vaccination, and animal experimentation, all of which she opposed. An active lecturer and writer, Blackwell published extensively on women, health, and morality.

SUZANNE GRAVER

Bibliography

Bell, E. Moberly. *Storming the Citadel: The Rise of the Woman Doctor.* 1953.

Blackwell, Elizabeth. *Pioneer Work in Opening the Medical Profession to Women: Autobiographical Sketches.* 1895.

Hays, Elinor Rice. *Those Extraordinary Blackwells.* 1967.

Monteiro, Lois A. "On Separate Roads: Florence Nightingale and Elizabeth Blackwell." *Signs,* vol. 9, pp. 520–533.

Morantz, Regina Markell. "Feminism, Professionalism, and Germs: The Thought of Mary Putnam Jacobi and Elizabeth Blackwell." *American Quarterly,* vol. 34, pp. 459–478.

Ross, Ishbel. *Child of Destiny: The Life Story of the First Woman Doctor.* 1949.

Wilson, Dorothy Clarke. *Lone Woman: The Story of Elizabeth Blackwell, the First Woman Doctor.* 1970.

. . . . .

BLAVATSKY, MADAME (1831–1891)

Helena Petrovna Blavatsky, spiritualist and cofounder of the Theosophical Society, promoted its philosophical and religious system in works including *Iris Unveiled* (1877), *The Secret Doctrine* (1888), *The Key to Theosophy* (1889), and *The Voice of the Silence* (1889).

Blavatsky's claim to have spent seven years in inaccessible Tibet studying under Hindu mahatmas is now disputed. Claiming enlightenment by revelations from esoteric Eastern cults, she began developing a Theosophical movement in Russia in 1858. In 1875 she and Colonel Henry Steel Olcott cofounded the Theosophical Society in New York, later establishing a temple at Adyar near Madras, India, as the society's center of operation. She edited the *Theosophist* journal from 1879 to 1888 and in later years organized an Esoteric

Section of the Theosophical Society for the advanced study of occult sciences.

In 1884 Blavatsky was accused by the Indian press of fictitious spiritualist phenomena, and in 1885 was declared a fraud by the London **Society for Psychical Research**. Protesting her innocence, Blavatsky believed that **Theosophy** enabled the select to evolve into perfect balance by self-realization through karma (the force which perpetuates successive reincarnations and deaths), finding liberation from bodily existence and peace in celestial Nirvana, home of intelligence and soul.

MARIAN R. FISHER

Bibliography

DeZirkoff, Boris. *Rebirth of the Occult Tradition.* 1977.

Hanson, Virginia. *H. P. Blavatsky and The Secret Doctrine.* 1971.

Leonard, Maurice. *Madame Blavatsky: Medium, Mystic, and Magician.* 1977.

Meade, Marion. *Madame Blavatsky: The Woman Behind the Myth.* 1980.

Ryan, Charles J. *H. P. Blavatsky and the Theosophical Movement.* 1975.

See also SPIRITUALISM

· · · · ·

BLIND, MATHILDE (1841-1896)

Mathilde Blind was a poet whose experiences as a political refugee and world traveler marked her work with romantic idealism and democratic vision. She was born in Germany, but raised an Englishwoman. She traveled throughout the Continent, to Egypt and to India, and had firsthand acquaintance with political outcasts like Garibaldi, Ledu-Rollin, and particularly Mazzini. She lived for a time with **Ford Maddox Brown** and his wife.

Blind published *Poems* (1867) under the pseudonym Claude Lake. Then under her own name came two long poems, *The Prophecy of St. Oran* (1881), a moonlit tale of temptation and godlessness, and *The Heather*

on Fire (1886). She also wrote an unremarkable prose romance, *Tarantella* (1885); did biographies of George Eliot (1883) and Madame Roland (1886) for the Eminent Women series; translated *The Journal of Marie Bashkirtseff* (1890); and published *Dramas in Miniature* (1891), *Songs and Sonnets* (1893), and *Birds of Passage* (1895).

Blind's most ambitious work was *Ascent of Man* (1888; reprinted with an introduction by Dr. Alfred Wallace in 1899), an epic tracing Darwinian **evolution**. Sorrow guides Man through chaos to the "infinite goodness of God" and love. Blind dedicated the work to **Elizabeth Barrett Browning** whose *Aurora Leigh* had served as a revelation of female possibility. The epic contains much social comment on impoverished women and children, concerns that also characterized much of Blind's other work. On her death she willed a small fortune to Newnham College to support the education of women.

SHELLEY J. CRISP

Bibliography

Miles, Alfred Henry. *The Poets and the Poetry of the Nineteenth Century.* 1905-1907.

Symons, Arthur, ed. *The Poetical Works of Mathilde Blind.* 1900.

· · · · ·

BLOODY SUNDAY (November 13, 1887)

Socialist propaganda emerged on the streets of London and in provincial cities with the formation in the early 1880s of Marxist and non-Marxist socialist groups: the Democratic Federation (later the Social Democratic Federation), the Socialist League, and the Fabian Society. In the middle years of the decade the groups' agitation led to a struggle with the police over the use of public streets and footpaths for political meetings and demonstrations. The "Dod Street affair" of September 20, 1885 was succeeded by riots on "Black Sunday" (February 8, 1886), when free traders and the unemployed held competing demonstrations in Trafalgar Square. In 1887 a new Tory government intent on law and order took office; a military officer was named chief commissioner of police. Late in the year various groups took to the streets in large numbers: the unemployed protested against the system of poor relief, socialist and anarchist groups against the imminent executions of the Chicago anarchists, and radicals and Irish nationalists against the arrest and treatment in prison of William O'Brien, M.P.

On November 8, 1887 the commissioner of police, Charles Warren, banned public meetings in Trafalgar Square. Socialist groups, the Metropolitan Radical Clubs, and the Irish National League, with the active support of W. T. Stead, editor of the *Pall Mall Gazette*, determined to defy the order. On the following Sunday, November 13, four main columns of marchers approached the square from the north, south, east, and west. Contingents of police, using batons, met and dispersed each procession well short of the square, in sharp engagements opposite the Haymarket Theatre, at Seven Dials, on Parliament Street near Westminster Bridge, and on the Strand at Wellington Street. When the remaining marchers straggled to Trafalgar Square, they found it guarded by 1,500 foot police and 300 mounted constables ready to break up any incipient gathering. At 4:00 p.m.—with an estimated crowd of 20,000 around the square—300 mounted Life Guards started patrolling the perimeter, and shortly thereafter 300 Grenadier Guards marched to the front of the National Gallery and formed ranks, with bayonets fixed, while a magistrate read the Riot Act. The day's activities led to some 150 arrests, and 200 injuries were treated at Charing Cross, Guy's, St. Thomas's, and Westminster hospitals. Alfred Linnell, the one fatality clearly resulting from the conflict over the square, was injured in the crowds of onlookers charged by mounted police on the following Sunday, November 20, and died several weeks later.

Meetings were effectively prohibited from the square; and on several subsequent Sundays thousands of volunteer constables were deployed there and in suburban centers. In the aftermath of the demonstration, individual organizers—**William Morris**, Stead, **George Bernard Shaw**, H. M. Hyndman, John Burns, **Annie Besant**, **Eleanor Marx-Aveling**, and **R. B. Cunningham Graham**—and their groups combined to form the Law and Liberty League, with a journal, the *Link*, to collect funds for the legal defense of those arrested and to pursue legal redress against the government.

EUGENE D. LeMIRE

Bibliography

Morris, William. "London in a State of Siege." *The Commonweal*, November 20, 1887.

The Pall Mall Gazette, November 14, 1887.

Thompson, E. P. *William Morris: Romantic to Revolutionary.* 1955.

The Times, November 14, 1887.

· · · · ·

BOARD AND TABLE GAMES

Organized competition in games began in England in the latter half of the nineteenth century. Clubs, leagues, championships, trophies, and all manner of record-keeping brought elements of formality, and the names of the best players began to be widely known.

Chess had been known in England since the tenth century, but the first chess club was formed in 1810 and the first formal competition organized in 1881. Impetus was provided by the Exhibition of 1851, which brought foreigners to London in huge numbers. Since chess was played by slightly different rules in various parts of Europe, a congress of chessplayers to write a uniform code was organized and a tournament to determine the best player among the conferees was held at the St. George's Club. The chief organizer of the event was Howard Staunton (1810–1874), chess columnist of the *Illustrated London News*, who wrote a book of the games called *The Chess Tournament* (1852).

The idea of tournaments, however, was slow to take hold, and chess was mostly played informally, as a casual diversion in country houses and in a very different atmosphere in coffeehouses and divans, where games were played for small stakes. Various Continental troubles brought exiles to England who earned precarious livelihoods through chess and made London the leading European chess center for much of the period. A lively account of the London chess scene can be found in Charles Dickens's *Dictionary of London* (1879).

Whist, the most popular Victorian card game, was also played competitively in the latter nineteenth century. The eighteenth century had thought of whist primarily as a form of gambling, played in coffeehouses and gaming clubs, often for large stakes. By the end of the Regency, however, it had become respectable, and a common after-dinner diversion among upper and middle classes. In 1857, as a result of a recurring argument over whether success at whist was a consequence of skill or luck, Henry Jones, a leading writer on the game (under his pseudonym of "Cavendish"), invented duplicate whist, a contest in which the players hold cards identical to those held by their competitors at different tables. Whist and its offspring, bridge, did not develop into successful tournament games until after the Victorian age.

DAVID DANIELS

Bibliography

Daniels, David. *The Golden Age of Contract Bridge.* 1980.

Golombek, Harry, ed. *Golombek's Encyclopedia of Chess.* 1977.

See also TOYS AND GAMES

· · · · ·

BODICHON, BARBARA LEIGH SMITH (1827–1891)

Barbara Leigh Smith Bodichon inaugurated organized British feminism during the third quarter of the nineteenth century. When she reached her majority in 1848, the women's movement in Great Britain was still only a series of fragmented efforts. She activated feminism through the publication of *A Brief Summary in Plain Language of the Most Important Laws Concerning Women* (1854) and the organization of the **Married Women's Property** Committee in 1855. An organizer first and foremost, Bodichon was a catalyst for the women's movement. She created the first women's network in Britain and led the **Langham Place Circle**, the most important group of feminists active between 1858 and 1865.

She was the eldest daughter of Radical M. P. Benjamin Leigh Smith and his common-law wife, Anne Longden. Several generations of Smiths had devoted their energies to political campaigns to remove social and religious inequalities from English law, abolish slavery, and extend education and the franchise. Raised in the Smith family tradition of rationalism, religious toleration, and social responsibility, Bodichon became the center of an upper middle-class circle of women whose families were intimately associated with every major social and political reform effort of the 1860s and 1870s. Her career epitomized a radicalism which might best be described as progressive conservatism, a social philosophy that resulted in societal changes built on middle-class reform movements.

The feminist circle that developed around Bodichon in the 1850s undertook the first concrete actions by women on their own behalf. Following the unsuccessful married women's property campaign, Bodichon and the members of her committee worked to expand women's employment opportunities. Despite her marriage in 1857, which meant that half her year was spent in Algiers, Bodichon remained dominant in feminist efforts. She wrote *Women and Work* in 1857 and was instrumental in founding the **English Woman's Journal** in 1858 and the Society for the Promotion of the Employment of Women in 1859. Bodichon was, in addition, the first writer to attribute an economic value to the tasks of wife and mother.

In 1865 Bodichon formed the first major women's suffrage committee, which worked first to gather signatures for petitions which J. S. Mill presented to Parliament in 1866. After internal divisions led to the dissolution of the committee in 1867, Bodichon left formal suffrage work to join with Emily Davies in the founding of Girton College, Cambridge. She devoted the remainder of her life to that project.

By the time that Barbara Ayrton Gould, daughter of scientist Hertha Ayrton, a Girton student who was Bodichon's protégée, became a member of Parliament in 1945 almost one hundred years had lapsed since Bodichon's coming of age. During that time feminism had emerged as a major factor in societal reform in Great Britain. Looking back, it is apparent that the Married Women's Property Committee was its first formal structure and Barbara Bodichon its earliest organizing agent.

SHEILA R. HERSTEIN

Bibliography

Herstein, Sheila R. *A Mid-Victorian Feminist, Barbara Leigh Smith Bodichon.* 1985.

Matthews, Jacquie. "Barbara Bodichon: Integrity in Diversity." In Dale Spender, ed., *Feminist Theorists.* 1983.

· · · · ·

BOER WAR
(1899-1902)

The Anglo-Boer War, the last of the Victorian imperial wars, was the largest in scope and cost, damaged the image of British colonial invincibility, and demonstrated England's diplomatic isolation in the days before World War I. After a preliminary skirmish in 1881, in which the British government allowed the Afrikaners independent republic status, tensions again developed in South Africa between the British authorities and the Boer republics. The gold and diamond fields, which were of such interest to the British, mattered much less to the theocratic, agrarian Boers. They were concerned about the increasing flow of *uitlanders* (outsiders) into the Boer republics, and Boer treatment of *uitlanders* occupied British attention.

The Jameson raid of 1895–1896—a failed conspiracy of **Cecil Rhodes** and others to overthrow the Transvaal government—was followed by a series of incidents between the Boer authorities and the predominantly British *uitlanders* who mined for gold and diamonds in the Boer republics. Several rounds of talks were held in an attempt to solve differences, although critics of British policy in South Africa have charged that neither British Colonial Secretary **Joseph Chamberlain** nor his high commissioner in South Africa, **Alfred**

Milner, tried very hard to prevent military action. Milner, in particular, is seen as an obstacle to peace. After political negotiations failed, the Boers invaded British Natal in October 1899.

Initial Boer military successes in December were characterized in Britain as "Black Week." General Methuen was bested at Magersfontein, General Gatacre was repulsed at Stormberg, and Commanding General Redvers Buller was forced to retreat from Ladysmith. The Boers were able to sustain an offensive against the British and besiege the strategically significant towns of Ladysmith, Kimberley, and Mafeking. The scale of these disasters led to the dismissal of Buller and his replacement with General Frederick "Bobs" Roberts, Lord Roberts of Kandahar.

The British ultimately reinforced their troops and turned the military tide, but even though they were able to relieve all of their forces, lift all three sieges, go on the offensive, and capture both Boer capitals by June 1900, fighting continued for two more years. In the expectation of immediate victory, Lord Roberts was recalled and General **Horatio Kitchener** was left to mop up the remaining Boer resistance. Parliamentary elections in 1900 centered around the issue of war. "Pro-Boer" Liberals such as David Lloyd George attacked government policy, while the Tory government wrapped itself in the flag. The "Khaki" election was a resounding endorsement for Tory policy and the war effort seemed vindicated.

The Boers abandoned full-scale encounters against the British and turned to guerrilla tactics conducted by small "commando" units. Britain proved to be friendless in Europe; the European press jeered the inability of the British army to defeat an enemy it outnumbered twenty to one. Finally Kitchener resorted to a scorched-earth policy, erecting miles of barbed wire with corner blockhouses. Boer women and children were herded into concentration camps where many died of disease. Britain was criticized around the world, while opposition leaders at home characterized government policy as "barbarism."

By the spring of 1902 peace talks were begun, centering around the questions of Boer independence and white sovereignty. In the peace agreement of Vereeniging (May 31, 1902), the Boers gained a degree of political autonomy while attaining complete racial supremacy. Britain also agreed to help rebuild Boer territories by granting interest-free loans. The war had cost about 22,000 British lives, while Boer military deaths exceeded 7,000. In addition, perhaps as many as 20,000 Boer women and children died in concentration camps. Rudyard Kipling, the poet of empire, expressed the attitude of many:

> Let us admit it fairly,
>   as a business people should.
> We have had no end of a lesson:
>   it will do us no end of good.

NEWELL D. BOYD

Bibliography

Farwell, Byron. *The Great Boer War.* 1977.

Kruger, Rayne. *Good-bye Dolly Gray: The Story of the Boer War.* 1959

Pakenham, Thomas. *The Boer War.* 1979.

Warwick, Peter, ed. *The South African War: The Anglo-Boer War, 1899-1902.* 1980.

See also JAMESON, LEANDER STARR; SOUTH AFRICA

· · · · ·

BOOLE, GEORGE
(1815-1864)

Called the father of modern **logic**, George Boole developed the analogy between the operations of logic and ordinary algebra, so that logical analysis depends not on the interpretation of symbols but on the laws of their combination. Subsequent systems based on similar axiomatic approaches to set theory are today designated Boolean algebras.

Born in Lincoln, the self-taught Boole studied mathematics only after becoming a schoolmaster at age sixteen. *The Mathematical Analysis of Logic* (1847) established algebraic methods for logical analysis. *An Investigation of the Laws of Thought* (1854) is sometimes considered his masterwork and reached a wider audience, but added little to the ideas of the original pamphlet. Boole was professor of mathematics at Queen's College in Cork, Ireland, from 1849 until his untimely

death from pneumonia. He married Mary Everest, who was much his junior, and had five daughters; the youngest was the novelist **Ethel Voynich**. Four early cameos by his wife provide pleasant insight into his genius; however, her later articles attributed his inspiration to mystical sources. Boole was a part-time Unitarian.

Boole's symbolic logic is a rigorous method of formal logic that achieves validity within itself. Freed from epistemological or linguistic ambiguities, this logic can encompass more than traditional methods hampered by language. Two important results of Boole's work are truth tables and the bivalued (1,0) techniques needed for computer design and switching theory. His other texts were on differential equations and finite differences. At the end of his life he was working on a philosophical unification of logical signs and the constitution of the intellect, but most commentators conclude that it was fortunate that it was never published unamended. Boole's concepts have been greatly modified and expanded, but remain the cornerstone of modern logic.

JOEL ATHEY

Bibliography

Barry, P. D., ed. *George Boole, A Miscellany.* 1969.

Kneale, W. "Boole and the Revival of Logic." *Mind,* vol. 57, pp. 149-175.

Laita, L. M. "Boolean Algebra and Its Extra-Logical Sources: The Testimony of Mary Everest Boole." *History and Philosophy of Logic.* vol. 1, pp. 37-60.

MacHale, Desmond. *George Boole, His Life and Work.* 1985.

Smith. G. C., ed. *The Boole-DeMorgan Correspondence 1842-1864.* 1982.

See also LOGIC

· · · · ·

BOOTH, CHARLES
(1840-1916)

Charles Booth was a highly successful businessman and shipowner who financed and directed a monumental survey of the conditions and occupations of the people of London at the turn of the century. Results were published in *Life and Labour of the People in London* (1891–1903). In the course of his career Booth rose from obscurity to become a privy councillor, fellow of the Royal Society, and honorary doctor of Liverpool, Oxford, and Cambridge universities.

Born and educated in Liverpool, Booth found work in a shipowner's office upon leaving school and in 1865 opened his own company in partnership with his brother. In 1871 he married Mary Macaulay, niece of Thomas Babington Macaulay and cousin of Beatrice Webb.

Booth was the product of a politically and religiously liberal background and actively participated in social controversies from the time he was a youth. Not long after moving to London to set up a branch of his business, he became deeply involved in the debates then raging over poverty's causes and its effects on the moral and intellectual state of the city's residents. Booth determined to conduct a survey to provide meaningful data on the conditions under which the various classes in the city actually lived and the occupations of the wage earners in the families studied.

In 1886 Booth organized his team of investigators and began the "wholesale interviewing" that was designed to provide the volume of information he felt was needed. The approach enabled him to combine the advantages of quantitative and qualitative analysis by correlating census findings with those derived from personal inquiries into the everyday lives of the survey's subjects. Booth's survey was responsible for destroying many of the myths commonly associated with the lower classes (drunkenness, dishonesty, etc.). In 1887 he read a paper on the "Conditions and Occupations of the People of the Tower Hamlets, 1886–1867" before the Royal Statistical Society. In 1889 he published his preliminary findings in *Labour and Life of the People*. The definitive version of *Life and Labour of the People in London* eventually grew to seventeen volumes, four on "Poverty," five on "Industry," seven on "Religious Influences," and one entitled "Notes on Social Influences and Conclusion."

Booth was widely respected as both social scientist and social reformer. Political and religious leaders recognized him as an authority on urban affairs and consulted him regularly on matters pertaining to London's poor. He was a prime mover in the passing of the Old Age Pensions Act (1908). His methodological approach to the social survey clearly marks him as a precursor of the modern sociologist.

SHEILA MONNET

Bibliography

Booth, Mary. *Charles Booth: A Memoir*. 1918.

Fried, Albert and Richard Elman, eds. *Charles Booth's London*. 1969.

Norman-Butler, Belinda. *Victorian Aspirations: The Life and Labour of Charles and Mary Booth*. 1972.

Simey, Thomas S. and M. B. Simey. *Charles Booth: Social Scientist*. 1960.

· · · · ·

BOUCICAULT, DION (1820–1890)

Victorian England's most prolific dramatist, adapter, and play doctor was born Dionysius Lardner Bourcicault in Dublin, probably in 1820. His parents were Anne Darley and Samuel Boursiquot, a wine merchant of Huguenot descent. After attending a variety of schools in Ireland and England, he was, by 1838, acting under the name of Lee Moreton in Bristol. His career as dramatist was securely launched at an astoundingly early age when Charles Mathews and Madame Vestris staged his *London Assurance* at Covent Garden in 1841. For almost fifty years thereafter Boucicault worked and lived hard, earning three fortunes and marrying three wives. He died in New York in 1890, having achieved great fame as playwright, actor, manager, and focus of gossip.

London Assurance seemed to assure Boucicault's future as a writer in the great tradition of English stage comedy, a prospect furthered by *Old Heads and Young Hearts* (1844). But the economics of Victorian theater (with its tyranny by managers and lack of royalties for authors) and the taste of audiences condemned Boucicault to translating, adapting, and concocting **melodramas**, a drudgery which produced almost two hundred works attributable to him.

In melodrama, Boucicault became a master of staging and construction. His version of *The Corsican Brothers* (1852) with Charles Kean as the telepathic twins was an instant success, luring Queen Victoria to see it five times, and establishing the Corsican "gliding" trap as a widely used piece of stage machinery. It also gave Henry Irving one of his most effective vehicles.

While touring with his second wife, actress Agnes Robertson, whom he had followed over from England in 1853, Boucicault established himself as successfully in America as he had done in England. His fame no doubt helped him, together with R. M. Bird and G. H. Boker, to get a copyright law through Congress in 1856. *The Poor of New York* (1857) used topical financial crashes and the spectacle of flaming tenements to pull in audiences. The success of *The Octoroon* (1859) was ensured by the controversy over abolition, the brilliant slave auction scene, the exploding river boat, and the up-to-the-minute device of using photography to solve a crime.

Boucicault's record of success was capped with *The Colleen Bawn* (1860), which had an unprecedented run of 278 performances at the Adelphi in London. *The Colleen Bawn* and Boucicault's other Irish plays, *Arragh-na-Pogue* (1864), *The Shaughraun* (1874), and *Robert Emmet* (1884) reveal not only his mastery of comic and sensational melodrama, but also his affection for Ireland and understanding of the love-hate relationship that plagues the Anglo-Irish situation. The plays also gave Boucicault two great comic roles: Saun the Post, and Conn.

Although Boucicault's success dwindled as tastes changed in the 1880s, he was the cleverest, raciest, and most theatrically inventive playwright of his age. He is remembered for his contributions to English, Irish, and American theater and as an influence on such later dramatists as Sean O'Casey and even George Bernard Shaw.

ANDREW PARKIN

Bibliography

Fawkes, Richard. *Dion Boucicault.* 1979.

Hogan, Robert. *Dion Boucicault.* 1969.

Krause, David. *The Dolmen Boucicault.* 1964.

Molin, Sven E. and R. Goodefellowe, eds. *Dion Boucicault, the Saughraun.* 1979.

Parkin, Andrew, ed. *Selected Plays of Dion Boucicault.* 1987.

. . . . .

BRADDON, MARY ELIZABETH (1835–1915)

Unmasking a fair-haired angel of the house as bigamist, child deserter, and murderess, Mary Elizabeth Braddon made her fortune with *Lady Audley's Secret* (1862), a sensational novel whipped up to launch John Maxwell's *Robin Goodfellow*. She took her lead from Wilkie Collins's *The Woman in White* (1860) and uncovered more unsavory secrets and crimes in such successes as *Aurora Floyd* (1863), *The Doctor's Wife* (1864), and *Charlotte's Inheritance* (1868). Besides eighty novels, she produced poems, plays, anonymous tales for penny dreadfuls, and edited *Belgravia* and *Temple Bar*.

Braddon was born in London, the daughter of a failed solicitor. To support her adored Irish mother, she went on the stage before she took up writing. She wrote sensation stories "because I think the shilling can only be extracted by strong measures." Braving Victorian censure, she lived out of wedlock with John Maxwell until his insane wife died in 1874 and they married. She raised five stepchildren plus her own five.

Well-read, she learned from Balzac, Flaubert, and Zola, as well as from Bulwer-Lytton, Dickens, and Collins. Fellow writers like Thackeray, Stevenson, and James admired her theatrical flair, narrative ease and invention, and eye for realistic detail. She ferreted out the reality behind the appearance and had a Pirandellian grasp of the many selves concealed in every individual. Braddon's novels never warranted the moral outrage that first greeted them, but they do show flashes of sharp social criticism and an underlying feminism. They are also enriched by her courage and wisdom, won by facing up to harsh realities. "We are on the verge of a precipice," she once wrote, "and nothing but a bold grapple with our difficulties can save us." Braddon transcends the **sensation novel** in mature work, such as *Joshua Haggard's Daughter* (1876), *Ishmael* (1884), *The Rose of Life* (1905), and *The Green Curtain* (1911).

TAMIE WATTERS

Bibliography

Wolff, Robert Lee. *Sensational Victorian.* 1979.

. . . . .

BRADLAUGH, CHARLES (1833-1891)

Charles Bradlaugh, radical working-class lecturer, debater, and publisher, is best known for winning the right to sit in Parliament as an atheist. Through leadership in the National Secular Society (1866), the *National Reformer* (1860-1891), and the Freethought Publishing Company, Bradlaugh articulated and disseminated the concerns of **freethought**.

Bradlaugh's rise from working-class, orthodox origins figured significantly in his lifelong commitment to social and political reform and his conviction that disestablishment of the Anglican church was essential to achieve a just society. Although his wife was incapacitated by alcoholism, Bradlaugh's two daughters joined him in lecturing, writing, and publishing on the virtues of freethought and the evils of orthodoxy.

Bradlaugh's work from 1850 to 1880 was primarily antitheological; writings include *The Bible: What It Is* (1859); *The Free-thinker's Textbook* (1876); and *A Plea for Atheism* (1864). Among freethinkers, Bradlaugh distinguished himself by arguing that Christianity must be destroyed both as dogma and as political power before any new world view could take its place. He preferred to be known as an atheist, with its "negativist" connotation, rather than as a secularist, and often signed his articles "Iconoclast."

The Investigator (1854-1859) and the *National Reformer* also raised such issues as suffrage reform, republicanism, international liberal revolution, Malthusianism, temperance, and abolition of oaths. Bradlaugh be-

came notorious in 1877 when he and **Annie Besant** were prosecuted for publishing the Malthusian book *The Fruits of Philosophy*. In the 1880s Bradlaugh achieved his greatest success when, after a five-year struggle to substitute an affirmation for the usual oath, he took his seat in Parliament as an atheist.

For the rest of his life Bradlaugh pursued his interests primarily in political rather than theological terms. He continued to reject socialism as an answer to the plight of English workers, and late in life espoused the infant cause of Indian independence.

SHIRLEY A. MULLEN

Bibliography

Arnstein, Walter. *The Bradlaugh Case: A Study in Late Victorian Opinion and Politics.* 1965.

Bonner, Hypatia Bradlaugh. *Charles Bradlaugh: A Record of His Life and Work.* 1894. 2 vols.

Saville, John, ed. *A Selection of the Political Pamphlets of Charles Bradlaugh.* 1970.

Tribe, David. *President Charles Bradlaugh, M.P.* 1971.

. . . . .

BREWERIES AND PUBLIC HOUSES

Railway transport combined with changes in taxation and licensing to accelerate trends already evident in the brewing industry. Brewing had established itself as a specialized trade in London in the seventeenth century. In the second half of the eighteenth the use of stationary steam engines, thermometers, hydrometers, and some other early devices for scientific brewing provided important economies of scale. The principal beer of the time, porter, lent itself to production in large batches. By 1800 the London market was dominated by twelve large brewers. They had already introduced the tied house system, mainly through lending money to publicans in return for exclusive sale of the brewer's product. By 1817 nearly half of the pubs in London were tied, and publicans who brewed their own beer were declining rapidly.

The railways after 1830 reduced the cost of

moving beer in barrels, and in particular, facilitated the shipment of the pale ales of Burton-upon-Trent to London. Although London brewers increasingly shifted from porter to pale ales, Burton became a major national brewing center, with thirty-one breweries by 1886. The Midland Railway built a beer depot into the lower floor of its St. Pancras Station in 1867 to transfer beer from Burton to London pubs.

Wellington's Beer House Act of 1830 provided for issuance of licenses (at two guineas per year) for pubs serving only beer. In 1830 the excise on beer was dropped in favor of lesser taxes on malt and hops. Both measures were intended to encourage a shift from gin and other spirits to beer, which was considered a beverage of moderation and a major source of nutrients. The ease of gaining licenses also attacked the tied house system. Within a decade about 40,000 beer houses were established. Regulation of hours began in 1838 with a requirement that London pubs close from midnight Saturday to noon Sunday. Later legislation was more general and restrictive.

The questionable efficacy of ease in licensing as a temperance device caused licensure to be returned to magistrates by the Wine and Beer House Act of 1869. Upon passage of the act there were about 9,000 fully licensed public houses and 49,000 beer houses, of which about 31,000 remained by 1894. Gladstone's Free Mash Tun Act of 1880 repealed the tax on malt in favor of an excise on beer based on the specific gravity of the wort, which effectively reduced the strength of beer. Beginning with Guiness in 1886, the major breweries began converting themselves into publicly held limited liability companies and consolidating through mergers. Increasingly, the larger breweries owned public houses which were either leased by publicans or run by paid managers. By 1900 about 90 percent of pubs were tied. Rivalry between the brewers produced an architectural golden age of pubs in the 1890s.

Output of beer grew from about 14 million barrels in 1830 to 20 in 1860, 32 in 1890, and 37 in 1900. Consumption rose more than proportionately to income until 1880, but thereafter the **temperance movement**, competition from other beverages, and expanded amusement opportunities tended to reduce beer sales relative to income and population growth. Output declined absolutely after 1900. Bottled beer was available during the nineteenth century, but was not popular, mainly because bottling added about 7 percent to the price. Publican-brewers were approaching extinction by the end of the century.

It is notable that Britain continued to consume top-fermented ales while the rest of the world, including British overseas dominions, converted between 1840 and 1880 to bottom-fermented lagers of Austrian, Czech, and German types. A lager brewery was founded at Wrexham in 1882, but it mainly served British transatlantic liners. Britain did not begin this conversion until nearly a century later.

GEORGE W. HILTON

Bibliography

Baker, Julian L. *The Brewing Industry*. 1905.

Corran, H. S. *A History of Brewing*. 1975.

Girouard, Mark. *Victorian Pubs*. 1975.

Hawkins, Kevin H. and C. L. Pass. *The Brewing Industry*. 1979.

Monckton, Herbert A. *A History of English Ale and Beer*. 1966.

Vaizey, John. *The Brewing Industry, 1886-1951*. 1960.

. . . . .

BRIDGES, ROBERT (1844-1930)

Robert Bridges was named **poet laureate** in 1913. His reputation rests on his early lyric verse. The best collection is *The Shorter Poems* (1890). He also wrote several long poems, including *Prometheus the Firegiver* (1883) and *Eros and Psyche* (1885), and did critical studies of Milton (1893) and Keats (1895).

Bridges was born in Kent, educated at Eton and Corpus Christi College, Oxford, and went to London as a medical student in 1869. Interest in poetry, however, challenged his commitment to medicine. He published several pamphlets of verse in the 1870s, and in *The*

Growth of Love (1876), a collection of sonnets, expressed his resolve to remain faithful to the poet's calling even though it went against the scientific tendencies of the age. Bridges retired from the medical profession in 1881 and devoted the rest of his life to poetry, music, and typography.

At the end of the Victorian era, Bridges was highly acclaimed by leading literary figures. He was sometimes compared to the Elizabethan poets, especially Edmund Spenser, or to his friend Gerard Manley Hopkins who, like Bridges, wrote poems in stress meter. In 1913, when Alfred Austin died, Rudyard Kipling was the popular choice to succeed him as poet laureate, but the appointment went to Bridges, who was at the time generally unknown to the wider public. Popularity and fame came with the anthology *The Spirit of Man* (1916) and the long philosophical poem *The Testament of Beauty* (1929).

Bridges's major contribution to Victorian literature is in such short lyric poems as "London Snow" and "On a Dead Child." His main theme was the poet's sensitivity to beauty, grief, and nature. In the final analysis he was more of a traditionalist than an innovator.

NORBERT J. GOSSMAN

Bibliography

Berg, Mary Gretchen. *Prosodic Structure of Robert Bridges' Neo-Miltonic Syllabics.* 1962.

Guerard, Albert, Jr. *Robert Bridges: A Study of Traditionalism.* 1941.

Ritz, Jean Georges. *Robert Bridges and Gerard Hopkins, 1863-1889: A Literary Friendship.* 1960.

Stanford, Donald E. *In the Classic Mode: The Achievement of Robert Bridges.* 1978.

· · · · ·

BRIGHT, JOHN
(1811-1889)

John Bright, a champion of reform causes, was a middle-class manufacturer and Quaker from Rochdale who opposed monopoly in all its manifestations and who symbolized the **Manchester School** of economic thought. He was an unyielding advocate of **free trade** and a leader and spokesman for the **Anti-Corn-Law League** (1838-1846). To oppose aristocratic misrule, Bright advocated the extension of suffrage, the secret ballot, and redistribution of parliamentary representation. He opposed landlordism by supporting tenant rights, compensation for improvements, and opportunities for peasant proprietorship. As a Dissenter, he also opposed Anglican church establishment.

Bright entered public life in 1834 as an opponent of church rates and first came to national prominence as a lecturer for the Anti-Corn-Law League. He entered Parliament in 1843 when he stood as the free trade candidate in by-elections at Durham. In Parliament, Bright campaigned against the **Game Laws,** resisted factory legislation as an infringement upon freedom of contract, and opposed the Maynooth Grant as tantamount to establishment of another denomination in Ireland. In 1847 Bright was returned as M.P. for Manchester.

Despite considerable public support for the **Crimean War** (1854-1856), Bright opposed British war policy, questioning the sacrifice of so much blood and treasure. In the 1857 elections Bright and other "Cobdenite" noninterventionists were defeated, but Bright was soon returned as Liberal M.P. for Birmingham (1857-1889).

In the 1860s Bright continued to advocate extension of the franchise to all ratepayers and pressed for decentralization of the Indian administration. He joined the first Gladstone ministry (1868-1874) as president of the Board of Trade and pushed for disestablishment of the Church of Ireland and the Irish Land Act of 1870, though he did not support **Home Rule** for Ireland in 1886. Bright served in the second Gladstone ministry (1880-1884) but resigned from the cabinet in 1882 in protest over British bombardment of Alexandria. Disappointed that Gladstone's 1884 Reform Act did not provide for redistribution of seats, Bright insisted on a Redistribution Act which was adopted the following year.

RICHARD FRANCIS SPALL, JR.

Bibliography

Read, Donald. *Cobden and Bright: A Victorian Political Partnership.* 1967.

Robbins, Keith. *John Bright*. 1979.

Trevelyan, George M. *The Life of John Bright*. 1913.

. . . . .

BRIGHT, URSULA MELLOR (1830?–1915)

Ursula Mellor Bright, the daughter of a Liverpool merchant, was a leader of the British feminist movement between 1867 and 1890. In 1855 she married Jacob Bright (1821–1899), a Rochdale manufacturer and member of Parliament for Manchester who was for several years the feminists' chief representative in the House of Commons. The Brights had one daughter, Esther.

Ursula and Jacob Bright were founder members of the Manchester Society for Women's Suffrage (1867). Ursula Bright was a skilled lobbyist, and was connected by marriage to several members of Parliament: her husband; his brother, **John Bright**, M.P. for Birmingham; and his sister Priscilla's husband, Duncan McLaren, M.P. for Edinburgh. Bright was a founder member of the Ladies' National Association for the Repeal of the Contagious Diseases Acts (1870). Her greatest contribution was her work as treasurer of the **Married Women's Property** Committee (MWPC) from 1874 until the passage of the Married Women's Property Act of 1882; she and **Elizabeth Wolstenholme Elmy**, secretary of the MWPC, were largely responsible for its passage.

Along with Wolstenholme Elmy, Richard Pankhurst, and others, the Brights broke with the Manchester Society for Women's Suffrage in 1889 when it endorsed a suffrage bill which would have enfranchised only widows and spinsters. They formed the Women's Franchise League which advocated not only married women's suffrage but also equality for women in divorce, inheritance, and child custody laws. Due largely to Ursula Bright's work, the Local Government Act of 1894 guaranteed the local franchise to married women.

Through her daughter, a friend of Annie Besant, Bright became interested in **Theosophy** during the 1890s. Less well known than many of her contemporaries, Bright was a significant figure in the nineteenth-century feminist movement.

MARY LYNDON SHANLEY

Bibliography

Annual Reports of the Committee for Promoting the Married Women's Property Bill. 1869–1882.

Banks, Olive. *The Biographical Dictionary of British Feminists*. Vol. 1: 1800–1930. 1985.

Holcombe, Lee. *Wives and Property: Reform of the Married Women's Property Law in Nineteenth-Century England*. 1983.

. . . . .

BROAD CHURCH

Broad Church is a term, popularized in an *Edinburgh Review* article in 1853, for the movement in the **Church of England** that deemphasized the doctrinal and ecclesiastical issues that separated its major parties, **High Church** and **Evangelical**. It stressed the national and inclusive character of the church and was open to advances in modern thought, particularly **biblical criticism**.

The main sources of Broad Church thought were the later writings of Samuel Taylor Coleridge (1772–1834) and the historical thinking of **Thomas Arnold** (1795–1842), headmaster of Rugby. The Broad Church was never a large movement, notwithstanding the eminence of its leaders; it was hardly an organized movement at all, but rather a collection of individuals and small groups who manifested some common tendencies. These ranged from the history and philology of Connop Thirlwall (1797–1875, later bishop of St. David's) and Archdeacon Julius Hare (1795–1855), to the **Christian Socialism** (1848–1854) of **Frederick Denison Maurice** (1805–1872) and **Charles Kingsley** (1819–1875), to Maurice's idiosyncratic but prophetic preaching and theology, to the historical studies and tolerant openness of A. P. Stanley (1815–1881, later dean of Westminster) and the biblical scholarship of **Benjamin Jowett** (1817–1893, later master of Balliol College).

The movement culminated with an attack on biblical literalism, *Essays and Reviews*

(1860), among whose contributors were Jowett, **Mark Pattison** (1813–1884), and the future archbishop Frederick Temple (1821–1902). Denounced by its "orthodox" opponents as rationalist, latitudinarian, and "neologist," the Broad Church movement virtually ceased to exist after the *Essays and Reviews* controversy, the theological counterpart to the contemporary controversy over Darwinism. Yet the Broad Church had managed to keep alive some links between religious and secular intellectuals, and many of its ideals would become commonplace in the twentieth century.

JOSEF L. ALTHOLZ

Bibliography

Chadwick, Owen. *The Victorian Church.* 1966–1970. 2 vols.

Cockshut, A. O. J. *Anglican Attitudes: A Study of Victorian Religious Controversies.* 1959.

Sanders, Charles R. *Coleridge and the Broad Church Movement.* 1942.

· · · · ·

BROADSIDES AND CHAPBOOKS

The two chief kinds of cheap publication that had been available to poor and working-class readers since the sixteenth century flourished with the urbanization and increased literacy of the early nineteenth century but had virtually disappeared by its end. The terms "broadside," "broadsheet," and "street ballad" are sometimes distinguished from one another but at other times used interchangeably. These publications were printed on a single sheet of paper and sold on the streets or at fairs and markets at prices ranging from a farthing to a penny by hawkers who aroused interest by singing the song or shouting out teasing details. Chapbooks were printed on a single sheet folded into sixteen or thirty-two small pages, and sold for a penny or two.

In the eighteenth century, chapbooks had been the major form of reading for the poor, printing such traditional peasant lore as folktales, prophecies, riddles, dream interpretations, ballad romances, and hero tales. By the early nineteenth century chapbooks were primarily for children, illustrated with woodcuts and featuring English fairy tales such as "Jack the Giant-Killer." (Middle-class parents generally disapproved of chapbooks, though memoirs reveal that middle-class children read them, perhaps through the agency of servants.) Early in the century there were also longer chapbooks with heavily condensed Gothic novels or other sensational literature, but these largely disappeared with the penny serials and other cheap fiction of the 1830s and 1840s.

Ballads and broadsides were both newspaper and entertainment for poor people until the rise of the cheap press in the 1850s. Produced by hundreds of printers in London and around the country, they used stock woodcuts, a variety of typefaces, short lines, and rhymes that made easy reading for the barely literate. Anonymous writers turned out a constant stream of verse and prose about events, disasters, political figures, crimes, comic topics, and imagined rows between members of the royal family. The language and subjects of some broadsides foreshadow the class-conscious culture developing in industrial areas that would later make the ballad a vehicle for radical protest.

The most salable subjects, however, were sensation, romance, and crime. A dozen purportedly accurate versions of a murder—particularly a crime of passion—would be on the streets within hours. Accounts of a criminal's "confession" and "last dying words" were sold to the crowds at a public execution even before the trap had dropped, and peddled in enormous numbers over the next few days: in 1849 a broadsheet on the execution of F. G. Manning and his wife Marie sold 2,500,000 copies.

The most famous publisher of ballads and chapbooks was James Catnach (1791–1841), who set up his printing press in Seven Dials in 1813. The business was carried on by his sister, Anne Ryle, and then by W. S. Fortey before closing down in 1883. By that time improved education, cheap newspapers, and popular magazines had taken over the role once filled by street literature and begun the process of creating a mass culture rather than the class culture represented by broadsides and chapbooks.

SALLY MITCHELL

Bibliography

Collison, Robert L. W. *The Story of Street Literature.* 1973.

Henderson, William, ed. *Victorian Street Ballads.* 1937.

Hindley, Charles. *Curiosities of Street Literature.* 1871; rpt. 1966.

James, Louis. *English Popular Literature, 1819–1851.* 1976.

Neuberg, Victor E. *Chapbooks: A Bibliography.* New ed., 1972.

———. "The Literature of the Streets." In H. J. Dyos and Michael Wolff, eds., *The Victorian City: Images and Realities*, vol. 1. 1973.

Shepard, Leslie. *The History of Street Literature.* 1973.

Vicinus, Martha. *The Industrial Muse.* 1974.

Watt, William Whyte. *Shilling Shockers of the Gothic School.* 1932.

Weiss, Harry B. *A Book About Chap-Books.* 1942; rpt. 1969.

· · · · ·

BRONTË, ANNE
(1820-1849)

Anne Brontë, the youngest sister of Charlotte and Emily Brontë, left a literary canon of two novels and fifty-nine poems. *Agnes Grey* (1847) (originally entitled *Passages in the Life of an Individual*) was begun as an autobiography in 1842 while Brontë was a governess at Thorp Green Hall. It was first published under her pseudonym of Acton Bell as the third volume with E. Brontë's two-volume *Wuthering Heights. The Tenant of Wildfell Hall* (1848) was considered controversial.

Brontë was the sixth and youngest child of Maria Branwell Brontë and Patrick Brontë. Soon after her birth, the family moved to Thornton, Yorkshire, where her father was perpetual curate of Haworth. Brontë was greatly affected by death: her mother died of internal cancer before she was two years old; her sisters Maria and Elizabeth died when she was five; her brother Branwell and sister Emily predeceased her.

Some of Brontë's poems, published in *Poems by Currer, Ellis, and Acton Bell* (1846), grew out of the Gondal and Angrian fantasies which the Brontë children wrote. Less well known than her sisters Charlotte and Emily, Brontë is nevertheless a writer of some significance in her emphasis on the plight of individual women. C. Brontë said that *Agnes Grey* is "the mirror of the mind of the writer." In *The Tenant of Wildfell Hall*, Brontë paints the portrait of Helen Graham, one of the first fictional women to become financially independent of her husband by her artistic labors.

JOANNA STEPHENS MINK

Bibliography

Allott, Miriam, ed. *The Brontës: The Critical Heritage.* 1974.

Chitham, Edward, ed. *The Poems of Anne Brontë: A New Text and Commentary.* 1979.

Ewbank, Inga Stina. *Their Proper Sphere: A Study of the Brontë Sisters as Early-Victorian Female Novelists.* 1966.

Gerin, Winifred. *Anne Brontë.* 1976.

Gilbert, Sandra M. and Susan Gubar. *The Madwoman in the Attic: The Woman Writer and the Nineteenth-Century Literary Imagination.* 1979.

Scott, P. J. M. *Anne Brontë: A New Critical Assessment.* 1983.

Wise, Thomas J. and J. Alexander Symington, eds. *The Brontës: Their Lives, Friendships and Correspondence.* 1933. 4 vols.

· · · · ·

BRONTË, CHARLOTTE
(1816-1855)

Sister of Anne and Emily, Charlotte Brontë was the only member of the family to achieve fame in her lifetime. Best known for *Jane Eyre* (1847), a work criticized for its violence and Gothic overtones, she gained respect for the more realistic *Shirley* (1849) and *Villette* (1853). She has also received attention for her interest in women's issues and influence on other women writers.

More gregarious than her sisters, Brontë was also more familiar with the outside world.

From August 1824 to June 1825, she attended the Clergy Daughters' School at Cowan Bridge, where her sisters Maria and Elizabeth died. Although the experience was traumatic, she later fictionalized it in *Jane Eyre*. Moreover, the experience convinced her father to educate his children at home. The result was that the sisters and their brother Branwell (1817–1848) collaborated on one of the most impressive bodies of juvenilia ever written, an effort that gave Brontë her first experience as a writer.

In 1831–1832, Brontë went to school at Roe Head and later served as a teacher there, then as a governess, and finally as a teacher at the Pensionnat Heger in Brussels. Despite her wish for independence and her realization that teaching was one of the few ways for a woman to achieve it, she was never happy as a teacher. Returning home in 1844, Brontë hoped to establish a school with her sisters. At this time, she discovered Emily's poems and proposed the publication of a joint volume. The result was *Poems by Currer, Ellis, and Acton Bell* (1846), the sisters choosing names that, while not definitely masculine, might prevent them from encountering prejudice as women writers.

Charlotte's contributions to *Poems* are inferior to those of her sisters, but it is significant that she initiated their efforts to publish. Even before *Poems* was in print, she sent *The Professor* (1857) to numerous publishers along with Emily's *Wuthering Heights* and Anne's *Agnes Grey*. Although *The Professor* was not published during her lifetime, Brontë achieved fame with *Jane Eyre*, a novel that combined the imagination of her juvenilia with a realistic setting and a concern with social issues, especially the treatment of governesses and women's limited opportunities.

Shirley, more realistic still, combines two love stories with historical material about the Luddite riots (1811–1812). *Shirley* also memorializes Brontë's sisters in Shirley Keeldar and Caroline Helstone. *Villette*, though less topical than *Shirley*, combines Brontë's interest in independence for women, realistic characters and settings derived from her Brussels experience, and flights of imagination. Though it lacks the passion of *Jane Eyre*, it is considered Brontë's masterpiece.

Brontë's contributions to the novel include combining a Gothic interest in passion with realistic settings and characters, and an emphasis on women's needs. As a result, she was misunderstood during her lifetime. Her letters are incomplete because her primary correspondent, Ellen Nussey, destroyed the most passionate; and contemporary reviews often singled out her anger and passion as inappropriate for a woman writer.

CAROL A. SENF

Bibliography

Alexander, Christine, ed. *An Edition of the Early Writings of Charlotte Brontë, 1826–1832.* 1987.

Crump, R. W. *Charlotte and Emily Brontë: A Reference Guide.* 1982.

Gerin, Winifred. *Charlotte Brontë: The Evolution of Genius.* 1967.

Gilbert, Sandra M. and Susan Gubar. *The Madwoman in the Attic: The Woman Writer and the Nineteenth-Century Literary Imagination.* 1979.

Neufeldt, Victor A. *The Poems of Charlotte Brontë: A New Text and Commentary.* 1985.

Passel, Anne. *Charlotte and Emily Brontë: An Annotated Bibliography.* 1979.

Ratchford, Fannie E. *Legends of Angria.* 1933.

Showalter, Elaine. *A Literature of Their Own: British Women Novelists from Brontë to Lessing.* 1977.

Wise, Thomas J. and J. Alexander Symington, eds. *The Brontës: Their Lives, Friendships, and Correspondence,* 1933. 4 vols.

· · · · ·

BRONTË, EMILY JANE (1818–1849)

Emily Brontë published *Poems by Currer, Ellis, and Acton Bell* (1846) with her sisters, Charlotte and Anne. Her novel *Wuthering Heights* (1847) was published with Anne's *Agnes Grey.*

The Brontë sisters are remarkable for the quality of their writing, although readers are often most fascinated by their lives. The six Brontë children were raised in isolated Haworth parsonage; their mother died in 1821, and the children became virtual recluses. In

1831 Anne and Emily began writing the Gondal manuscripts about a violent land ruled by strong women and intense weather, a work they continued throughout most of their lives; many Gondolan effects are central to *Wuthering Heights*.

Brontë's earliest dated poem is from 1836; between 1838 and 1842 over half of her surviving poems were written. The poems remained secret until 1845, when Charlotte read them and convinced her sisters to collaborate on the volume published in 1846. Brontë began *Wuthering Heights* in December of 1845 and sent the manuscript out the following July. Many readers assumed that Acton, Ellis, and Currer Bell were all one man, possibly Branwell Brontë, the brother. In 1850 Charlotte wrote introductions to her sisters' reissued novels that attempted to clarify their identities and differentiate their works, calling Emily "stronger than a man, simpler than a child" and *Wuthering Heights* "a rude and strange production."

Wuthering Heights defies categorization: a Gothic ghost story, a revenge tragedy, a social commentary, a romance, a Victorian fairy tale, and a local history told by a family servant who chronicles the gentry's financial and moral decay. The novel's narrative layers and fantastic characterization make it unique among Victorian novels, and critics today are often as befuddled as were the original readers. First filmed in 1920, and many times subsequently, the novel was popularized by a highly romantic 1939 movie starring Merle Oberon and Laurence Olivier; Heathcliff remains, along with Charlotte Brontë's Rochester, a model for the romantic antihero.

Although Brontë published only one novel and her poetry is just beginning to be appreciated, her use of local parish histories, landscape, old ballads, and the influence of Scott and Byron give her work a power that expands the range of Victorian literature.

SUSAN JARET MCKINSTRY

Bibliography

Eagleton, Terry. *Myths of Power: A Marxist Study of the Brontës*. 1975.

Gerin, Winifred. *Emily Brontë*. 1971.

Hatfield, Charles W. *The Complete Poems of Emily Jane Brontë*. 1941.

Ratchford, Fanny Elizabeth. *The Brontës' Web of Childhood*. 1941.

Vogler, Thomas, ed. *Twentieth-Century Interpretations of Wuthering Heights*. 1968.

· · · · ·

BROUGHTON, RHODA (1840–1920)

To mid-Victorian England the novelist Rhoda Broughton epitomized daring, a reputation owing as much to her bold wit as to the ardor and outspokenness of her lovesick young heroines. Following up the success of *Cometh Up as a Flower* (1867) and *Not Wisely, but Too Well* (1867) with *Red as a Rose Is She* (1870) and *Nancy* (1873), she reigned queen of the circulating libraries until the failure of *Alas!* (1890), tenth of her twenty-five novels. Turning from three-deckers to astringent one-volumes, she produced such amusing and satirical novels as *Mrs. Bligh* (1892), *Dear Faustina* (1897), *Foes in Law* (1899), *A Waif's Progress* (1905), and the autobiographical *A Fool in Her Folly* (1920).

Of old gentry stock, Broughton was educated by her father, Delves Broughton, squire and parson of Broughton Hall in Staffordshire. Her uncle **Sheridan Le Fanu** ran her first novels in his *Dublin University Magazine*. Unmarried, she lived with a sister and, after her death, with a cousin. Knowledgeable and original, she drew the eminent to her hospitable doors in Oxford and Chelsea, where she sojourned in later life. Her war against Oxford surfaces in *Belinda* (1883), notorious for its caricature of **Mark Pattison**.

Keatsian in her sensuous response, she was also a keen detector of character, of the absurd and ironic, and of social change as it affected country gentry life and ways. Broughton set her stamp on the novel with her sensitive portrayal of women and fresh observations and dialogue. But carelessness and passionate stances prevented her from becoming the Victorian Jane Austen some proclaimed her to be. She made an art of friendship. Those of her devoted circle like Anne Ritchie, Henry James, and Howard Sturgis declared that she wrote nothing so good as herself.

TAMIE WATTERS

Bibliography

Sadleir, Michael. *Things Past.* 1944.

Terry, Reginald Charles. *Victorian Popular Fiction, 1860-1880.* 1983.

Watters, Tamie. "An Oxford Provocation and Caricature." *Encounter,* vol. 36, pp. 34–42.

· · · · ·

BROWN, FORD MADOX (1821-1893)

Ford Madox Brown was an important painter associated with the **Pre-Raphaelite Brotherhood**, though not one of its founding members. From 1861 to 1874 he was also a member of the firm of Morris, Marshall, Faulkner and Co., for which he did decorative designs in several media.

Brown was born in Calais in 1821 and received his early artistic education at Ghent, Bruges, and (in 1837–1839) the Antwerp Academy, where he studied under Gustave, Baron Wappers, an academic master. In 1840–1843 he studied in Paris, paying particular attention to the work of Rembrandt, the Spanish realists, and contemporaries such as Delacroix and Delaroche. He moved to London in 1844, but returned to the Continent in 1845–1846, where he was particularly moved by the art of Holbein and of the German Nazarenes and Italian masters in Rome.

On his return to England Brown became acquainted with Dante Gabriel Rossetti and witnessed the formation of the Pre-Raphaelite Brotherhood in 1848. The combination of Pre-Raphaelite and Continental influences determined the essential features of Brown's mature style—firmness of line, clarity of light, vibrancy of color, immediacy of effect, an element of contemporaneity, and a heightened sense of dramatic narrative, to which Brown added a distinctive emotional force and expression.

Brown was sympathetic to the socialist cause and offered his home to those in need of refuge. The social criticism of Thomas Carlyle influenced two of his greatest paintings, *The Last of England* (1852-1855) and *Work* (1852-1865). The former, with its forceful composition tightly compressed into an oval frame and its stunning observation of marine light, is a poignant tribute to the contemporary problem of emigration; at one point Brown contemplated emigrating to India as a way of improving his own dire financial state. *Work,* with its accompanying sonnet of 1865, is Brown's allegory of Victorian labor, exhibiting the hard but honest toil of a group of navvies, the life of the mind signified by Carlyle and Frederick Denison Maurice, and the various degrees of parasitism, indulgence, and injustice elsewhere represented in minutest detail. Brown's work also encompassed religion (*Christ Washing Peter's Feet,* 1851–1856), literary illustration (*Lear and Cordelia,* 1849), history (*The Execution of Mary Queen of Scots,* 1842), landscape (*Windermere,* 1855), portraiture (*James Leathart,* 1864), and narrative realism (*Stages of Cruelty,* 1856; 1887–1890).

In 1878 Brown received one of the major public commissions of nineteenth-century England—to do twelve wall paintings for the Manchester Town Hall depicting scenes from the city's history. As a decorative artist, Brown is believed to have designed some furniture; and after joining the Morris firm he made at least one hundred designs for stained glass.

LARRY D. LUTCHMANSINGH

Bibliography

Hueffer, Ford M. *Ford Madox Brown: A Record of his Life and Work.* 1896.

Surtees, Virginia, ed. *The Diary of Ford Madox Brown.* 1981.

Walker Art Gallery. *Ford Madox Brown, 1821-1893.* 1964.

Watkinson, Raymond. *Pre-Raphaelite Art and Design.* 1970.

· · · · ·

BROWNE, HABLOT KNIGHT (1815-1882)

Famous as "Phiz," Hablot Knight Browne is known chiefly for his highly skillful, clever, and humorous book illustrations. He adopted the pseudonym "Phiz" to complement

First appearance of Mr. Samuel Weller.
Etching for Pickwick Papers, *1836.*
(*Browne used the signature N.E.M.O. for his first two* Pickwick *assignments.*)
Reproduced courtesy of Chapin Library, Williams College.

Charles Dickens's "Boz," and the two worked together throughout their careers. Browne also illustrated periodicals, children's books, and novels by Charles Lever, **Harrison Ainsworth**, and others.

The ninth son in a family of fifteen children, Browne (whose father died when he was nine) was apprenticed early to the prominent steel engravers, Finden's, where he received his only formal artistic education. He disliked, however, the laborious methods of steel engraving, preferring the freer processes of etching, drawing, painting, and wood engraving. Upon winning an important prize in 1833 from the Society of Arts for *John Gilpin*, an etching for a poem by Cowper, Browne left Finden's to work on his own. In 1836 he was commissioned to illustrate Dickens's *The Pickwick Papers*, succeeding Robert Seymour and R. W. Buss, both prominent artists, and winning out over Thackeray, who had also applied for the job. He hit the mark at once with "First appearance of Mr. Samuel Weller." Browne was twenty at the time and Dickens was twenty-four.

Critics disagree about whether Browne's illustrations, in addition to expressing the author's intentions, offer independent interpretations. His great skill as an illustrator, however, is beyond dispute. Particularly notable are his strong characterizations and striking tonalities, and his use of emblematic details, grotesquerie, and visual parallelism of structures. His work was highly sought by publishers until 1867, when he had a stroke. In 1878 he was awarded an annuity by the Royal Academy.

SUZANNE GRAVER

Bibliography

Harvey, John R. *Victorian Novelists and Their Illustrators.* 1970.

Leavis, Q. D. "The Dickens Illustrations: Their Function." In F. R. Leavis and Q. D. Leavis, *Dickens: The Novelist.* 1970.

Steig, Michael. *Dickens and Phiz.* 1978.

Thomson, David Croal. *Life and Labours of Hablot Knight Brown, "Phiz."* 1884.

· · · · ·

BROWNING, ELIZABETH BARRETT
(1806–1861)

Elizabeth Barrett Browning was a significant Victorian poet whose work was marked by bold thematic range, stylistic innovation, and empathy for victims of social injustice.

The eldest of eleven children in a wealthy landed family, Elizabeth Barrett lived until she was twenty at the family's country estate in Herfordshire. A vigorous autodidact, she taught herself Greek, composed poems at eight, and at thirteen wrote "The Battle of Marathon," a privately printed Homeric epic in four books. *An Essay on Mind, with Other Poems* appeared anonymously in 1826. A riding accident injured her spine when she was fifteen, and a ruptured blood vessel further limited her activities at twenty-two. The family suffered financial reversals after 1832, and moved first to Sidmouth and then to London. In 1833 Barrett published a translation of *Prometheus Bound*, and in 1838 *The Seraphim and Other Poems*, her first signed volume and a popular success. *The Seraphim* resembles Tennyson's 1832 *Poems* in its fluid versification, exotic settings, and high valuation of the poet's social role. Its rewriting of Christian myth and the celebration of the love of mother for child ("The Virgin Mary to the Child Jesus," "Isobel's Child") anticipate aspects of her later work.

Barrett's 1844 *Poems* established her among the foremost poets of her generation. Its opening work, "A Drama of Exile," inverts biblical and Miltonic accounts of the Fall, and casts Eve as a redemptress whose noble spirit and future motherhood foreshadow later human salvation. The 1844 *Poems* also included several ballads, among them "Lady Geraldine's Courtship"; a tribute to George Sand; and "The Cry of the Children," a denunciation of child labor.

Her correspondence with Robert Browning began the next year; she was then almost forty, and he was an impecunious thirty-three-year-old author of three little-read volumes of poetry. In defiance of her father, she secretly married Browning and eloped to Florence, Italy, where they lived for the next fifteen years. She bore a son, Robert Weidemann, in 1849.

Her next volume of *Poems*, which appeared in 1850, included "The Runaway Slave at Pilgrim's Point," a painfully empathetic inversion of her favorite theme of mother love, and the better-known *Sonnets from the Portuguese*, written during her courtship. Her chronicle of the healing effects of growing love influenced several later Victorian sonnet sequences, including Dante Gabriel Rossetti's "The House of Life" and Christina Rossetti's "Monna Innominata."

Barrett Browning's social sympathies deepened in *Casa Guidi Windows* (1851), which mourns the repression of Italian Nationalism by Pope Pius IX and Grand Duke Leopold of Tuscany, and more strikingly in *Aurora Leigh* (1857), which she considered "the most mature of my works, and the one into which my highest convictions upon Life and Art have entered." In this verse novel, she mixed her characteristic idealism with wit, sarcasm, and incisive social analysis, qualities rare in early Victorian poetry. *Aurora Leigh* is remarkable for its analysis of female archetypes, scathing critique of bourgeois marriage and heedless wealth, sympathetic portrayal of the servant Miriam, and direct examination of the facts of prostitution and rape. Above all, however, it is distinguished by its final celebration of an explicitly egalitarian marriage. Despite its apparent iconoclasm, *Aurora Leigh* was widely read and admired, and went through nineteen editions by 1885.

Barrett Browning's last works were *Poems Before Congress* (1860) and the posthumous *Last Poems* (1862). These include poetic treatments of slavery ("A Curse for a Nation"), seduction ("Lord Walter's Wife), art ("A Musical Instrument"), and bereavement ("Mother and Poet").

After a period of critical neglect, the lyricism, iconoclasm, and stylistic innovation of Elizabeth Barrett Browning's poetry have begun to regain some of the serious attention they amply merit.

FLORENCE BOOS

Bibliography

Barnes, Warner. *A Bibliography of Elizabeth Barrett Browning*. 1968.

Blake, Kathleen. "Elizabeth Barrett Browning and Wordsworth: The Romantic Poet as a Woman." *Victorian Poetry*, vol. 24, pp. 387-398.

Hayter, Althea. *Mrs. Browning: A Poet's Work and Its Setting*. 1962.

Kintner, Elvan, ed. *The Letters of Robert Browning and Elizabeth Barrett Browning, 1845-1846*. 1969.

Leighton, Angela. *Elizabeth Barrett Browning*. 1986.

Radley, Virginia L. *Elizabeth Barrett Browning*. 1972.

Rosenblum, Dolores. "Face to Face: Elizabeth Barrett Browning's 'Aurora Leigh' and Nineteenth-Century Poetry." *Victorian Studies*, vol. 26, pp. 321-338.

Taplin, Gardner B. *The Life of Elizabeth Barrett Browning*. 1957.

. . . . .

BROWNING, ROBERT
(1812-1889)

Robert Browning's poetic achievement is the dramatic monologue, as in *Men and Women* (1855). Less popular than Tennyson, he gained distinction as a sage with *The Ring and the Book* (1868-1869). By liberating language from conventional stuffiness, anchoring images in everyday reality, and experimenting with new poetic forms, he anticipated and influenced modern movements in the poetry of Hardy, Yeats, Pound, Eliot, Stevens, and Frost.

Born in Camberwell, south of London, Browning learned Latin and Greek from his bibliophile father and piety, love of nature, and music from his Nonconformist mother; both encouraged his poetry. He read his name in Elizabeth Barrett's *Poems* (1844) and first wrote to her on January 10, 1845, declaring "I do . . . love these books with all my heart—and I love you too." He saw her in May; they were clandestinely married on September 12, 1846 and a week later eloped, eventually settling in Florence. After her death in 1861, Browning returned to England where he gradually reentered society.

The anonymous *Pauline* (1833) sold not a copy; *Paracelsus* (1835) and the notoriously difficult *Sordello* (1840) fared a little better. Six plays (1837-1846) failed, but gradually Browning found his medium in the miniature dramatic scene, first brilliantly in *Pippa Passes* (1841). *Dramatic Lyrics* (1842) contained fourteen poems; eight are still standard favorites, including "My Last Duchess" (originally "Italy"), presenting sensational incidents in sharp detail as smouldering passions strain beneath the verse. Browning praised Elizabeth Barrett's directness in his second letter to her: "You speak out, *you*—I only make men & women speak—give you truth broken into prismatic hues." The fifty speaking portraits of *Men and Women* (1855) show mutual and defective lovers, Renaissance artists ("Fra Lippo Lippi" and "Andrea del Sarto"), musicians and religious thinkers who invite the reader to share their worlds and moral crises while also judging them. So in *Dramatis Personae* (1864) exotic locales and arcane learning mask contemporary controversies about Darwinism, biblical criticism, and mesmerism.

From 1860 Browning pondered the implications of a seventeenth-century Roman murder trial, recounted in an "Old Yellow Book." His bold plan interlocked twelve books of *The Ring and the Book* (1868–1869) in a multiple narrative, whose complex, ironic characters undermine conventional views of fiction, fact, and truth. Recognized on appearance as his masterpiece, sustained and demanding, it combines Browning's interests in psychology, philosophical and theological speculation, base action, and elevated thought and expression.

The long poems of the 1870s experimented with Greek dramatic sources and contemporary events and figures. In his last decade, Browning returned to shorter lyrics, except for the *Parleyings* (1887), conversations with obscure writers who influenced his ideas.

Browning has become a focus for editorial controversy: the "Ohio Browning" *Complete Works* (1969–) has been much challenged, especially by John Pettigrew and Thomas Collins who edited *The Poems* (2 vols., 1981).

Browning and Tennyson were the century's preeminent poets. Hailed at the end of his life as a Christian optimist, Browning habitually reflects on the integrity of his own art: questioning the grounds of truth, needing doubt to keep life human, quickening dead facts with fancy's power, and rejecting the efficacy of language while spinning magic words.

WILLIAM WHITLA

Bibliography

DeVane, William C. *A Browning Handbook*. 1955.

Irvine, William and Park Honan. *The Book, the Ring, and the Poet*. 1974.

Litzinger, Boyd and Donald Smalley, eds. *Browning: The Critical Heritage*. 1970.

Peterson, William S. *Robert and Elizabeth Barrett Browning: An Annotated Bibliography, 1951–1970*. 1974.

· · · · ·

BRUNEL, ISAMBARD KINGDOM (1806–1859)

Isambard Kingdom Brunel was the leading engineer of the century. Son of Marc Brunel, he was educated in England and France and by his father on the Thames tunnel project.

Brunel's greatest project was the broad-gauge Great Western Railway (opened 1838). He designed all aspects of the railway, including tunnels (Box), bridges (Maidenhead, Wharncliffe, Royal Albert at Saltash), locomotives (with Daniel Gooch), stations (Paddington, Bath, Bristol Temple Meads), and Swindon Village (with Matthew Digby Wyatt). The railway was the best engineered and fastest of its day. It captured popular imagination and was depicted in J. M. W. Turner's *Rain, Steam, and Speed.*

Brunel designed three steamships: the *Great Western* (1837), *Great Britain* (1843) and *Great Eastern* (1858). They incorporated advanced technology and were the largest ships ever built. The latter was the prototype of subsequent ocean liners and has been restored at Bristol.

Brunel was known for his attention to detail, charisma, energy, grandiose projects, and vision. Many of his works are extant. There is a museum to the Brunels at Rotherhithe.

WILSON J. HOFFMAN

Bibliography

Beckett, Derrick. *Brunel's Britain*. 1980.

Hay, Peter. *Brunel: Engineering Giant*. 1985.

Rolt, L. T. C. *Isambard Kingdom Brunel*. 1970.

See also RAILWAYS

· · · · ·

BULWER-LYTTON, EDWARD GEORGE EARLE LYTTON, FIRST LORD LYTTON (1803–1873)

A best-selling popular novelist, friend of Benjamin Disraeli and Charles Dickens, and author of over sixty books, Edward Bulwer-Lytton is now chiefly remembered for *Pelham* (1828), *Eugene Aram* (1832), and *The Last Days of Pompeii* (1834).

Pelham, the story of a dandy, is a novel of high life. Bulwer was described in *Fraser's Magazine* as "a silver fork polisher" and the label stuck; thereafter, novels of aristocratic life was referred to as belonging to the **silver-fork** school. The character of the hero's mother, Lady Frances, is justly admired: her letters of worldly advice to her son derive from those of Lord Chesterfield and are presented with a satirical edge that recalls Jane Austen's satire on heartless snobbery in *Persuasion*. Lady Frances's preference for black evening coats for men as against the then-popular blue set the style then and ever since. Bulwer was quickly identified with Henry Pelham, wit and dandy. Bulwer wrote in his diary, "There is a poetry in dress," and *Pelham* is remarkable for its portrait of Beau Brummell in old age, under the name "Mr. Russelton," whose conversation is convincingly absurd and delightful. But *Pelham* does not sustain the sparkling malice of its opening: it becomes by turns an embryo political novel, a picaresque novel showing the hero triumphant among thieves and sharpers in the manner of Smollett, a novel of ideas, and finally a murder mystery spiced with rape and insanity.

Bulwer's aristocratic style was combined, at least in youth, with radical sympathies: this, and his success, aroused envy and resentment. He was thought of as like Henry Pelham, self-centered, self-seeking, and a ruthless exploiter of inherited advantage. Pelham himself says, "Callous and worldly as I may seem . . . I have a conscience." Like his creator, Pelham conceals ambition and industry beneath an affected frivolity.

Eugene Aram is based on the true story of a self-educated scholar who committed a murder and was hanged in Knaresborough

Castle. *The Last Days of Pompeii* remained popular well into the twentieth century. Bulwer's historical work derives from Walter Scott's but, unlike Scott, he never found an authentic style of his own. Much of his writing is false and inflated, though when his interest in cultural change is engaged he can be shrewd and original. *The Last Days of Pompeii* is at its best in its analysis of marginal figures, people alienated and dispossessed: Nydia, the blind slave girl; Arbaces, Egyptian priest and villain. The psychology of these gloomy exiles, resentful vassals to the power of Rome, constantly brooding and manipulating when they can, has more vitality than the story of the insipid hero Glaucus and the heroine Ione, who escape by sea from the city's destruction and become Christians. Lytton's knowledge of Pompeiian art and history is, however, impressive.

VALERIE GROSVENOR MYER

Bibliography

Christensen, Allan Conrad. *Edward Bulwer-Lytton: The Fiction of New Regions.* 1976.

. . . . .

BURDETT-COUTTS, ANGELA GEORGINA (1814–1906)

Born to a life of privilege and heir to one of the century's greatest fortunes, Angela Burdett-Coutts devoted her time and energy as well as her money to **philanthropy** and social reform. A tireless worker, she had the vision to create impressive schemes for the betterment of women, children, and the working classes and the pragmatism to personally oversee practical details. Interested in science and a friend of physicist Michael Faraday, she became a member of the Royal Society under his sponsorship in 1847. In 1871 Burdett-Coutts was the first woman to be made a peer in recognition of her accomplishments. As Baroness Burdett-Coutts, she was also the first woman freeman of the City of London (1872) and of Edinburgh (1874).

The youngest of six daughters of Francis Burdett (1770–1844), a member of Parliament for the borough of Westminster who championed causes such as Catholic emancipation, prison reform, and free speech, she became independent in 1837. Her maternal grandfather, Thomas Coutts (1735–1822), founder of a London bank whose clients included George III, had bequeathed the bulk of his assets, including his partnership in the bank, to his second wife, the actress Harriot Mellon (d. 1837), and had left to her judgment the choice of a successor. Upon being named heir and adding her grandfather's name to her own, Burdett-Coutts moved with her governess, Hannah Meredith, into a house she had inherited, took part in the active management of the bank, and rejected proposals from fortune hunters. (It is said that Disraeli considered marrying her, and that she is the model for Adriana in his 1880 novel *Endymion*.)

Burdett-Coutts's first philanthropic efforts concentrated on improving the condition of young people of the poorest class. She established **ragged schools**, an orphanage, a reformatory school for boys, and a system of practical instruction in housework and skilled trades; she also helped families emigrate to colonies where work might be found. In 1846 she startled the respectable by taking an interest in prostitutes; Urania Cottage, founded in 1847 with the assistance of Charles Dickens, was a reformatory designed to teach practical skills to women who sought to leave the streets and then assist them in emigrating.

In undertaking philanthropic activities, Burdett-Coutts depended on her own investigation and her practical understanding. Dickens said that her conversations were the origin of his attack on useless education in *Hard Times* (1854). During the Crimean War, she not only supported soldiers' wives and children in England but also personally designed a machine for drying hospital linen and sent it to Florence Nightingale. In London's East End, Burdett-Coutts built model apartments, established social clubs for young people, instituted a series of night classes that eventually grew into the Westminster Technical College—and she also sent a lawyer to help costermongers preserve their right to street trading and wrote *A Summary Account of Prizes for Common Things* (1856), a practical guide giving poor women information about first aid, budgets, and recipes for cheap meals. Distrusting the centralization that imposed uniform reforms which might not be suited to people's own needs and desires, she established (for example) a traveling schoolmaster program in Torquay so that the dame schools, which had traditionally provided child care and early education for the working poor, could be preserved and improved instead of being shut down.

Burdett-Coutts had the vision and wealth to do things on a grand scale. She built two churches, one of them (St. Stephen's, Westminster) to the memory of her father. She not only supplied passage money for individual emigrants but also provided the endowments to establish bishoprics in Adelaide (1847), Cape Town (1847), and Victoria, on Vancouver Island (1857). She made spectacular donations to rehabilitate Irish fishing, agriculture, and industry, funded Livingstone's 1858 expedition to Zanzibar, and founded a college at the Cape to educate the sons of African chiefs. One of the first people to support cancer research, she began in 1850 to subsidize the building and work of the Brompton Cancer (now the Royal Marsden) Hospital. She organized the mass aid during the cholera epidemic of 1867. In 1870 she became president of the Ladies' Committee of the Royal Society for the Prevention of Cruelty to Animals—and held in her drawing room the meeting that gave rise to its offshoot, the Royal Society for the prevention of Cruelty to Children.

Hannah Meredith Brown, Burdett-Coutts's former governess, shared her life and home until she died in 1878. In 1881 Burdett-Coutts married William Ashmead Bartlett (1851–1921), who obtained a royal license to assume her surname and, in Parliament, pressed through reform of the army's medical services. Burdett-Coutts's tireless industry and clear understanding made her an extraordinary example of grand and practical philanthropy.

SALLY MITCHELL

Bibliography

Burdett-Coutts, Angela, ed. *Woman's Mission.* 1893.

Jonson, Edgar, ed. *Letters from Charles Dickens to Angela Burdett-Coutts, 1841–1865.* 1953.

Healey, Edna. *Lady Unknown: The Life of Angela Burdett-Coutts*. 1978.

Patterson, Clara B. *Angela Burdett-Coutts and the Victorians*. 1953.

· · · · ·

BURNE-JONES, EDWARD (1833–1898)

Edward Burne-Jones was an associate, though not an original member, of the **Pre-Raphaelite Brotherhood**; his painting and design established him as one of the outstanding British artists of the later nineteenth century. His career as an artist-craftsman who produced designs for stained glass, tapestry, tiles, book illustrations, and the decoration of furniture and musical instruments embodied the ideal of the **arts and crafts movement**.

Burne-Jones was born Edward Jones in Birmingham in 1833 at a time when the city was experiencing the problems of expansion and industrialization. Early exposure and continuing sensitivity to those problems led him to define his artistic concerns in imaginative and visionary terms, and in large part accounts for the retrospective and (later) aestheticizing character of his artistic style.

After attending King Edward's School in Birmingham, Burne-Jones entered Exeter College, Oxford, intent upon a career in the Church. But a variety of forces, such as the rebellious spirit of some like-minded companions (including William Morris), the reading of authors such as Scott, Carlyle, Ruskin, and Kingsley, and the study of medieval monuments, led to a change of purpose. Influenced by Pre-Raphaelite paintings and by the medieval art and architecture he saw in northern France during 1855, he determined to become an artist and left Oxford without graduating.

Moving to London in 1856, Burne-Jones studied with **Dante Gabriel Rossetti**, who exerted the single strongest influence upon his artistic development. This influence was, however, modified, and sometimes opposed, by that of several Italian Renaissance masters, notably Botticelli, Filippino Lippi, Mantegna, Leonardo da Vinci, and Michelangelo. His mature style is thus marked by a simplified but strong design, a linear elegance, and a sumptuous color that can be seen to great effect in such paintings as *Laus Veneris* (1873–1875), *The Golden Stairs* (1876–1880), the two *Briar Rose* series (1870–1873, 1889–1890), and *Love and the Pilgrim* (1897). *King Cophetua and the Beggar Maid* (1884) makes an oblique reference to the social consciousness which he usually held in check.

As early as 1857 Burne-Jones made designs for stained glass, but in 1861 he became chief designer in that medium for the firm of Morris, Marshall, Faulkner and Co., of which he had become a member. The "Resurrection" (All Hallows Church, Allerton, Lancs., 1885–1886) and "Last Judgement" (St. Philip's Cathedral, Birmingham, 1896) windows establish Burne-Jones as a preeminent modern practitioner in the medium. A comparable achievement is visible in some of his tapestry designs, such as *The Adoration of the Magi* (1890) and the several series on the *Quest of the Holy Grail* (1891 to 1896, one set completed posthumously). His other great decorative achievement was in book illustration, especially the eighty-seven designs for the Kelmscott Chaucer, collaboratively done with **William Morris** in 1893–1895. He also designed mosaic decorations for St. Paul's American Church, Rome (begun 1881, completed posthumously).

LARRY D. LUTCHMANSINGH

Bibliography

Arts Council of Great Britain. *Burne-Jones*. 1975.

Bell, Malcolm. *Edward Burne-Jones: A Record and Review*. 1892.

Burne-Jones, Lady Georgiana. *Memorials of Edward Burne-Jones*. 1904. 2 vols.

de Lisle, Fortunée. *Burne-Jones*. 1904.

Harrison, Martin and Bill Waters. *Burne-Jones*. 1973.

Lago, Mary, ed. *Burne-Jones Talking: His Conversations, 1895–1898, Preserved by His Studio Assistant Thomas Rooke*. 1982.

Sewter, A. Charles. *The Stained Glass of William Morris and His Circle*. 1974. 2 vols.

· · · · ·

BURTON, RICHARD FRANCIS
(1821-1890)

Anglo-Irish soldier, explorer, diplomat, linguist, pioneer anthropologist, and prolific writer, Richard Burton was born in Hertfordshire, and educated privately in Europe and at Trinity College, Oxford (1840-1841). He achieved the rank of captain in the service of the East India Company Army (1842-1861), and held minor diplomatic posts in the British consular service (1861-1890). He died at Trieste.

Among the first non-Muslim Europeans to gain entry to Mecca (1853), Burton led an expedition the following year to explore Somaliland (1854), and became the first white man to visit the forbidden city of Harar. Sponsored by the Royal Geographical Society, he led an expedition with John Hanning Speke in search of the sources of the Nile (1857-1859). Burton discovered Lake Tanganyika, which he mistook as the Nile's main source. While Burton lay ill, Speke discovered and named Lake Victoria. Burton bitterly disputed Speke's correct declaration of the Victoria Nyanza as the source of the Nile. Burton traveled widely in Canada and America (1860), and, while serving as British consul on the island of Fernando Po (1861-1864), traveled on the West African coast, ascended the Congo River to the Yellala Falls, and visited the much-feared King Gelele of Dahomey. While consul in Santos, Brazil (1866-1869), he traveled throughout South America. While serving as consul in Damascus (1869-1871), he traveled to Palmyra and Baalbek. As consul at Trieste (1872-1890), he found ample time to explore Etruscan and Roman antiquities in Italy, to lead an expedition sponsored by the Khedive of Egypt to Midian (1877-1878), and another to the Gold Coast of West Africa (1881-1882).

Burton was unusual among nonmissionary explorers in seeking to learn the languages of the peoples among whom he traveled, and was such a careful observer that he usually cast new illumination even upon ground already well trod by Europeans. His travels are exceedingly well documented, for he produced a profusion of books and articles covering virtually every episode.

Burton's main occupations were exploration and writing, and he wore his official duties lightly. Indeed, his flamboyance harmed his official careers. His report on the homosexual brothels of Karachi caused a scandal in the Indian government, while his failure at diplomatic intriguing led to his recall from Damascus and his reassignment to a picturesque exile in Trieste.

In his travel books Burton's lurid detailing of primitive customs appeared to shock his readers by design. Similarly, when later he turned to literary pursuits, he translated erotic oriental works such as *The Kama Sutra, The Perfumed Garden,* and *The Thousand Nights and a Night,* and appended elaborate notes on the sexual customs of other cultures. Burton shared this taste for the erotic with friends, such as **Monckton Milnes** and **A. C. Swinburne,** but not with his pious Catholic wife, Isabel Arundell.

Burton has attracted many biographers. However, his widow burned his diaries and unpublished translations, and published a bowdlerized portrait in her two-volume official life, which must be used with care.

N. MERRILL DISTAD

Bibliography

Brodie, Fawn M. *The Devil Drives: A Life of Sir Richard Burton.* 1967.

Burton, Isabel. *The Life of Captain Sir Richard F. Burton.* 1893. 2 vols.

Farwell, Byron. *Burton: A Biography of Sir Richard Francis Burton.* 1963.

Penzer, N. M. *An Annotated Bibliography of Sir Richard Francis Burton.* 1923.

Sisted, Georgiana M. *The True Life of Captain Sir Richard F. Burton . . . by His Niece.* 1896.

· · · · ·

BUSS, FRANCES MARY
(1827-1894)

A pioneer of women's education, Frances Mary Buss was the founder and first headmistress (1850-1894) of the North London Collegiate School for Girls, a secondary day school that transformed education by serving as a model for subsequent widespread reform.

Buss's father was an engraver and her mother a schoolmistress. When Frances Eastwood Buss opened a school in 1845, her daughter, who had begun teaching at fourteen, took charge of the older pupils. Three years later, she was among the first to attend the new Queen's College.

Buss made girls' education intellectually rigorous at North London Collegiate. Believing that educational standards for women should be the same as for men, she encouraged her students to take the Cambridge Local Examinations when the university experimentally opened these standardized tests to women in 1863. Buss's innovative curriculum included gymnastics and sports. In 1871 she added the Camden Lower School to North London Collegiate. Both began as reasonably priced private schools and became endowed public schools in 1875.

Like many Victorian educational reformers, Buss challenged prevailing assumptions concerning woman's mind and sphere but insisted on ladylike behavior. Some of her principles were class bound, but others were strikingly democratic. Her contributions to education were extensive. She helped to found the Association of Head Mistresses (1874), the Maria Grey Training College (1877), and The Teachers' Guild (1883). By 1900 nearly every town had a school modeled on the prototype created by Buss.

SUZANNE GRAVER

Bibliography

Burstall, Sara. *Frances Mary Buss: An Educational Pioneer.* 1938.

Kamm, Josephine. *How Different from Us: A Biography of Miss Buss and Miss Beale.* 1958.

Ridley, Annie E. *Frances Mary Buss and Her Work for Education.* 1895.

Scrimgeour, R. M., ed. *The North London Collegiate School: 1850-1950.* 1950.

· · · · ·

BUTLER, ELIZABETH THOMPSON (1843/6-1933)

Elizabeth Thompson Butler produced large **history paintings** on military subjects. Her most famous works, *The Roll Call* (1874), *Quartre Bras* (1875), and *Balaclava* (1876) were reproduced and distributed worldwide. Queen Victoria insisted on acquiring *Roll Call* from its original owner, a Manchester manufacturer, guaranteeing Butler's financial success. Her works soon sold for thousands of pounds.

Butler studied drawing and painting at the South Kensington School and in Italy. Affluent parents provided opportunities and encouraged Elizabeth and her sister Alice (later **Alice Meynell**, poet) to paint and write. The 1874 Royal Academy exhibition made her famous overnight. The hanging committee liked *The Roll Call* well enough to place it "on the line" (extremely rare for an unknown painter) and the public response required a policeman to control the crowds.

Butler's paintings are painstakingly worked on eight-foot canvases. She chose famous military moments, had uniforms made in correct shades of red, and interviewed dozens of witnesses. The popularity of her work made military authorities eager to cooperate. In later years her husband, Colonel William Francis Butler (1838-1910), whom she married in 1877, staged battles and parades to help her. War filled Butler's artistic imagination, and her striving for absolute veracity led her to present painful, touching scenes. Her best-known paintings focus on soldiers, not officers. *Balaclava* (1876) shows the exhausted survivors staggering back from the charge of the Light Brigade, and *The Roll Call* portrays a battalion mustering after battle while a sergeant tallies the casualties in his book.

After the Boer War, when Butler's painting had fallen out of favor, she wrote three books illustrated with her sketches: *Letters from the Holy Land* (1903), *From Sketch Book and Diary* (1909), and *An Autobiography* (1923).

JULIA M. GERGITS

Bibliography

Butler, Elizabeth Thompson. *An Autobiography.* 1923.

Lalumia, Matthew. *Realism and Politics in Victorian Art of the Crimean War.* 1984.

Ruskin, John. "Academy Notes (1875)." In E. T. Cook and A. Wedderburn, eds., *The Works of John Ruskin,* vol. 14, 1904.

· · · · ·

BUTLER, JOSEPHINE GREY (1828-1906)

Social reformer Josephine Butler is best known for her campaign against the Contagious Diseases Acts and her attack on the double standard of Victorian morality that justified male access to "impure" women.

Born in Northumberland, she was the seventh child of John and Hannah (Annett) Grey. Her father, an improving agriculturalist, inspired her commitment to liberal reform causes while her mother sparked an attachment to evangelical Christianity. Her husband, educator and Anglican clergyman George Butler, enthusiastically supported her public activism. The accidental death of their daughter Eva in 1864 was a turning point in Butler's life. Searching for "some pain keener than my own," she worked among prostitutes in Liverpool workhouses and in 1866 opened the House of Rest as a refuge for destitute women. From 1867-1873 she served as president of the North of England Council for Promoting the Higher Education of Women, convinced that better employment and educational opportunities were essential to eradicate **prostitution**.

In 1869 Butler assumed leadership of the Ladies' National Association for the Repeal of the Contagious Diseases Acts. The CDA (1864, 1866, 1869) were part of a wider reform of the British armed forces, which aimed to improve the health of soldiers and sailors. Effective in select port and army towns, they made it obligatory for any woman merely suspected of being a prostitute to report to a police station to be inspected for venereal disease. Butler condemned the acts as a blatant example of class and sex discrimination. Not only did they officially sanction male vice, but they deprived poor women of their constitutional rights and degraded them by forcing submission to an internal examination. Leading the repeal campaign from 1869-1874, Butler strove to inform the public about the circumstances that drove women to prostitution. Despite physical and verbal abuse, she and her followers lectured throughout England and successfully lobbied for the defeat of antirepeal candidates in by-election campaigns. In 1874 she undertook a Continental tour to seek international support for the cause, forming the International Society Against State Regulated Vice. So integral were her efforts to the ultimate revocation of the acts (1886) that the repeal movement has commonly been labeled "Josephine Butler's campaign."

Butler was also involved in other areas of the **social purity** crusade. In 1885 she assisted journalist W. H. Stead, editor of the London *Pall Mall Gazette*, with an investigation into West End prostitution and **white slave traffic**. In her last years, she edited *The Dawn* and *The Storm-Bell* and joined the public outcry over the sale of women to soldiers in India. Her most important works include *Personal Reminiscences of a Great Crusade* (1896) and *An Autobiographical Memoir* (1909).

Like many other feminists of the period, Butler insisted that it was the peculiar mission of women to defend home, family, and a single standard of sexual morality. Thus, she only partially challenged basic Victorian assumptions about sex roles and women's separate sphere of influence. Her particular achievements were to identify poverty, not "sin," as the principal cause of prostitution and to link moral reform to the wider goals of female emancipation. She was always convinced of the urgency of suffrage success to achieve her ends.

MARIE MARMO MULLANEY

Bibliography

Boyd, Nancy. *Josephine Butler, Octavia Hill, Florence Nightingale: Three Victorian Women Who Changed Their World.* 1982.

Butler, A. S. G. *Portrait of Josephine Butler.* 1954.

Forster, Margaret. *Significant Sisters: The Grassroots of Active Feminism, 1839-1939.* 1985.

Petrie, Glen. *A Singular Iniquity: The Campaigns of Josephine Butler.* 1971.

Stead, William T. *Josephine Butler: A Life Sketch.* 1888.

Walkowitz, Judith R. *Prostitution and Victorian Society: Women, Class, and the State.* 1980.

. . . . .

BUTLER, SAMUEL (1835-1902)

Samuel Butler, when asked for a personal designation to distinguish himself from several other writers of the same name in the British Museum catalogue, decided on "philosophical writer," an apt summation of his conscious approach to any subject. He was, by turn, a travel writer, novelist, essayist, poet, scientific writer, composer, translator, and painter, although he is most often remembered for *Erewhon* (1872), a satirical novel, and *The Way of All Flesh* (1903), an autobiographical fiction.

Butler was a child of the rectory, a detailed and unflattering description of which is presented in *The Way of All Flesh*; attended Shrewsbury School, where his grandfather had distinguished himself as headmaster; and graduated with some distinction from St. John's College, Cambridge. He emigrated to New Zealand in 1859 with 4,000 pounds, doubled his money in four years raising sheep, and described the experience in provocative detail in *A First Year in the Canterbury Settlement* (1863). Butler returned to England in 1864, established himself in Clifford's Inn, London, and, supported by a modest income (augumented considerably on the death of his father in 1886), pursued research in natural history, the origins of the *Odyssey*, Shakespeare's sonnets, music, and painting. Butler never married, although he maintained a close platonic relationship with Eliza Mary Savage until her death in 1885.

Butler's refusal to accept received opinion on most subjects and his stubborn tenacity in pursuing arguments give most of his books an iconoclastic ring. With mocking irony he pseudonymously attacked church orthodoxy in *The Fair Haven* (1873) and had the satisfaction of being taken literally by some reviewers. He questioned the theory of natural selection and, most particularly, the work of Charles Darwin in four long argumentative books: *Life and Habit* (1878), *Evolution, Old and New* (1879), *Unconscious Memory* (1880), and *Luck or Cunning?* (1887). His researches into the Homeric writings convinced him that the *Odyssey* had been composed by a Sicilian woman, a thesis presented in *The Authoress of the Odyssey* (1897).

Butler's work was not widely appreciated in his own time. His reputation as an important and original thinker had to await the clamorous initiative of George Bernard Shaw and the collected edition of his works (1923). He can now be seen as a clever, articulate, and consistent critic of Victorian society whose two great books (*Erewhon* and *The Way of All Flesh*) contribute effectively to the literary heritage of the age.

RICHARD LANDON

Bibliography

Harkness, Stanley B. *The Career of Samuel Butler, 1835-1902: A Bibliography.* 1955.

Jones, Henry Festing. *Samuel Butler, Author of Erewhon: A Memoir.* 1919. 2 vols.

Silver, Arnold, ed. *The Family Letters of Samuel Butler, 1841-1886.* 1962.

. . . . .

CABINET

By the accession of Queen Victoria the cabinet had established itself as the most important element in the British constitution, a fact confirmed by the political crisis of 1834-1835. During Victoria's reign the cabinet became increasingly dominant, as the influence of the monarchy declined and the cabinet increased its control over the business of **Parliament**. The Victorian period is often described as the golden age of cabinet government, for by the end of the nineteenth century the growing scale of government activity no longer made it possible for the cabinet to effectively debate the full range of affairs. As a result, there was a growing tendency to devolve responsibility to committees of the cabinet, such as the Committee of Imperial Defence established in 1902.

The cabinet had two primary roles in the Victorian era. The first was to provide coherence in the administration of the various departments of state, and the second was to supply political leadership in Parliament. To fulfill these functions the cabinet acquired an increasing degree of control, so that by the 1880s it had concentrated the power of initiative in its own hands. In the first half of Victoria's reign this process was mainly at the expense of the monarchy; in the second half, at the expense of the back-bench members of Parliament. In the Bedchamber Crisis (1839) **Robert Peel** (1788–1850) still felt it impossible to form a government without a majority in the House of Commons unless he had clear signs of royal approval, which the queen denied him. However, when the 1841 general election returned a Conservative majority in the Commons, Queen Victoria could not avoid inviting Peel to form a ministry. The growing independence of the cabinet from the personal views of the monarch was closely related to the development of the party system. The increased coherence of parties after the Second Reform Act (1867) gave the cabinet effective leadership over the House of Commons. Cabinets had been made and unmade several times during many of the parliaments of the 1840s and 1850s, but after 1867 the electorate felt that M.P.'s were elected to support a particular cabinet, either Liberal or Conservative. This combined with party partisanship to enable cabinets to rely upon support in the House of Commons, though after the 1880s Liberal cabinets always had the problem of being the minority in the House of Lords.

The cabinet was bound together by the doctrine of collective responsibility. This meant that while debate within the cabinet was unfettered, once a decision was arrived at all the members of the cabinet had either to give it their full public support or, if they felt unable to do so, resign. Cabinet discussion was therefore confidential and no records of cabinet meetings were kept. Collective responsibility ensured coherence among the leaders of a government, and tended to produce compromise on the important issues of the day. Resignation was a serious step, and although sometimes threatened as a tactic during cabinet debate, it was rarely carried out. In the mid-Victorian period, when the construction of cabinets was often a delicate task, even one resignation could bring about a government's collapse. After the 1870s this was less likely, but the withdrawal of any cabinet minister was a blow to a government's confidence and prestige. Another way in which the cabinet acted as the forum for settling disputed questions results from the belief that a cabinet should be balanced to reflect the main strands of opinion within a party or coalition and include the most able politicians.

These major political figures held the principal offices of state. Some involved the headship of large departments; the cabinet always included the chancellor of the exchequer, the lord chancellor, the foreign secretary, home secretary, secretaries of state for India, the colonies, and war, and the first lord of the Admiralty. Other offices did not always carry the privilege of cabinet rank. For most of the Victorian period cabinets averaged fourteen members, with the smallest being twelve. In the last two decades of the reign new offices were created, such as the secretary for Scotland. Together with the increased volume of business in other areas, such as the Local Government Board, this caused cabinet membership to rise to an average of nineteen. A further consequence of the greater workload was the growing predominance of the House of Commons members. In midcentury an equal division of peers and commoners was considered ideal, but by the 1890s the role of the former had declined, although the foreign secretaryship was the one major post still frequently held by a peer. The cabinet met once a week in the parliamentary session to plan business and tactics for the coming week. Up to the 1880s, meetings were held on Saturdays, often at the Foreign Office. By 1900 the customary day had become Wednesdays, in the cabinet room of 10 Downing Street, with the members seated round a table.

By the end of Victoria's reign the relationship between cabinet and **prime minister** was shifting in favor of the latter. This was caused by the concentration of public attention on the party leader and the control that prime ministers who were also party leaders had at their disposal through the party organization. Nevertheless, the prime minister still needed cabinet sanction for every important decision. Even in the 1890s it was still possible for a prime minister to be defeated in argument in the cabinet, and overruled. The predominance of the cabinet had been diminished, but it still remained at the heart of the British political system.

STUART BALL

Bibliography

Cooke, Alistair B. and John Vincent. *The Governing Passion: Cabinet Government and Party Politics in Britain, 1885–1886.* 1974.

Le May, G. H. L. *The Victorian Constitution.* 1979.

Mackintosh, John P. *The British Cabinet.* 3rd ed., 1977.

Ramm, Agatha. "The Parliamentary Context of Cabinet Government, 1868–1874." *English Historical Review,* vol. 99, pp. 739–769.

See also PARTY SYSTEM

. . . . .

CAIRD, EDWARD
(1835–1908)

Philosopher, essayist, critic, administrator, and teacher, Edward Caird was an important Scottish Hegelian of the later nineteenth century, and, indeed, one of the most important philosophers in the British Isles. He gained a reputation as a philosophical synthesizer whose work incorporated and harmonized German, French, and British ideas in metaphysics and ethics.

After a distinguished academic career in Scotland and at Balliol College, Oxford, Caird was elected to the chair of moral philosophy at the University of Glasgow in 1866. He regarded the election as the fulfillment of a life's ambition. Caird held the chair until 1893 when he was elected to succeed Benjamin Jowett as master of Balliol, the position he occupied until declining health forced his resignation in 1907. As a teacher and master of a college, Caird exercised a subtle but profound influence on a generation and more of undergraduate students in Scotland and England. The noted philosophers Henry Jones and J. H. Muirhead both counted themselves his disciples. Many of Caird's Glasgow students subsequently entered the ministry of the Scottish Kirk, and frequently they noted his influence on their vocation and the general liberalizing effect of his teachings.

As a philosopher Caird is now best known as a proponent of German philosophical conceptions, particularly of Kantian and Hegelian doctrines. As with many young men of his generation, he came to his study of German thought through reading **Thomas Carlyle**, and regarded his fellow Scot as the most important intellectual influence on him. Caird conceived the philosopher's vocation in the nineteenth century as the resuscitation of the ideas of continuity and unity in spiritual life. He accomplished his task by joining the Kantian analytic with an Hegelian notion of the underlying spiritual unity of reality, all of which he clothed in the language of modified Darwinian evolution. Caird was a Gifford lecturer twice, first in 1891–1892 and again in 1900. From these lectures came two of his most important works, *The Evolution of Religion* (1893) and *The Evolution of Theology in the Greek Philosophers* (2 vols., 1904).

In an extremely busy life, Caird found time and energy to support the work of Toynbee Hall, London, and Ruskin College for working men in Oxford. At Glasgow he was an outspoken advocate of education for women and was also the first member of an Oxford college to move in council that the university grant women degrees.

A gifted though not flamboyant teacher, Caird was an important influence in philosophy and on his students. With T. H. Green, Bernard Bosanquet, and F. H. Bradley, he helped to make philosophy once again an important discipline in British universities.

GEORGE MARIZ

Bibliography

Jones, Henry and J. H. Muirhead. *The Life and Philosophy of Edward Caird.* 1921.

. . . . .

CAIRD, MONA ALISON
(1858–1932)

Mona Caird was a feminist journalist, novelist, and antivivisectionist. Her feminist essays are collected in *The Morality of Marriage* (1897); her antivivisection writings include *A Sentimental View of Vivisection* (1893) and *Some Truths About Vivisection* (1894). Among her novels are *The Wing of Azrael* (1889) and *The Daughters of Danaus* (1894), both focusing on women's rights.

Although convinced of the necessity of monogamy, Caird attacked the institution of **marriage**, equating it with prostitution and slavery. She saw the intentional denial of women's freedom, access to education, and economic independence as oppression injurious to women and to society. In response to antifeminist **Eliza Lynn Linton**'s 1891 attack on the "wild women" (suffrage agitators), Caird analyzed the power imbalance structuring relations between men and women, denying that women's fight for political rights was an attempt to imitate men. Although she demanded that women be allowed access to jobs, Caird hoped, however, that they would be permitted to remain in the home to influence men and temper the greed and competition of the marketplace.

Both *The Wing of Azrael* and *The Daughters of Danaus* make it clear that individual feminist rebellion cannot succeed, since circumstance is more powerful than will or character. These novels critique the cultural expectation that women may be sacrificed for the good (and greed) of their families, and condemn the sheltered existence that makes it impossible for young women to make an informed choice in marriage.

LAURA STEMPEL MUMFORD

See also FEMINIST WRITING

· · · · ·

CALDECOTT, RANDOLPH (1846–1886)

Considered by some to be the father of the modern children's picture book, Randolph Caldecott provided innovative illustrations that breathed movement and spontaneity into children's books. Caldecott's pictures always extended the text, giving young children scenes which augmented the stories being read to them.

Caldecott published his first illustration in the *Illustrated London News* in 1861 at age fifteen. Henry Blackburn of *London Society* encouraged him to become an illustrator and eventually he gave up his job as a bank clerk at Whitchurch. His illustrations for *Old Christmas: From the Sketch Book of Washington Irving* (1875) were an immediate success. He produced sixteen highly successful picture books with engraver Edmund Evans, beginning with *John Gilpin* (1878) which sold 60,000 copies in six months. Most were based on nursery rhymes such as *The House that Jack Built* (1878) and *Three Jovial Huntsmen* (1880). He illustrated three books for **Juliana Ewing**, the best known of which is *Jackanapes* (1884). In 1880 he married Marian Brind who, like Caldecott, suffered from delicate health. They wintered in France or Italy and finally traveled to Florida where Caldecott died and was buried in 1886.

Caldecott's picture books were usually published in mustard-colored covers, with colored illustrations alternating with brown ink drawings. Often the mention of the figure in the text would be prefigured in a preceding drawing so a child viewer could anticipate what was going to happen. The drawings were always lively, image enriching image. As Maurice Sendak stated, "the word quicken, I think best suggests the genuine spirit of Caldecott's animation, the breathing of life, the surging swing of action that I consider an essential quality in pictures for children's books." As a tribute to Caldecott's work, the American Library Association has awarded since 1938 the Caldecott Medal for the best picture book published in America.

LOUISA SMITH

Bibliography

Alderson, Brian. *Sing a Song for Sixpence: The English Picture Book Tradition and Randolph Caldecott.* 1986.

Billington, Elizabeth T., ed. *The Randolph Caldecott Treasury.* 1978.

Hutchins, Michael, ed. *Yours Pictorially: Illustrated Letters of Randolph Caldecott.* 1976.

See also CHILDREN'S ILLUSTRATED BOOKS

· · · · ·

CAMBRIDGE UNIVERSITY

During the Victorian period Cambridge University was transformed from the small, cloistered center of learning that it had been since the Middle Ages into a modern educational institution that retained many of its traditional ties to the past. Although reforms were often slowed by the conservative temper of the college communities, Victorian Cambridge made numerous contributions to developments in the sciences, the liberal arts, and education for women.

As late as the mid-nineteenth century, mathematics was still the primary subject of study at Cambridge, and all members of the colleges were required to pass stringent religious tests. Education was a generally disorganized affair. Undergraduates were criticized for self-indulgence and idleness, and the role of tutors was often vague at best. Statutes that controlled the organization of the university had been in effect since the sixteenth century. In the early 1850s, soon after Prince Albert had been installed as chancellor of the university, a royal commission recommended a variety of reforms in the educational systems at Cambridge and **Oxford**. Tripos exams in natural and moral sciences were added in 1851, in law (1859), and in history (1870). Yearly admissions more than doubled between the 1820s and the 1890s. The first intercollegiate lectures were held in 1868, allowing for a degree of interaction between the colleges that had not previously existed.

Education for women at Cambridge began in 1869, when **Emily Davies** set up a house in Hitchin where university dons lectured to female students. This arrangement resulted in the founding of Girton College in 1873. Meanwhile Henry Sidgwick and **Anne Jemima Clough**, sister of the poet, were embarked on a similar project that led to the establishment of Newnham College in 1875. Sidgwick Hall was added in 1880. Women were not, however, allowed to take exams until 1881. These years also saw the beginnings of efforts to make a university education available to a larger number of middle-class students. All religious tests had been abolished in 1871, allowing non-Anglicans to teach and study at Cambridge for the first time. The sciences flourished after the opening of the Cavendish Laboratory in the 1870s, with **James Clerk Maxwell** as the first professor of experimental physics. Scholarships in the sciences also became available. Emphasis on professional education increased as the traditional study of mathematics and the classics gave way to courses in the applied sciences, law, medicine, and engineering. The decade of the 1870s also saw the establishment of joint Oxford-Cambridge entrance exams which allowed students from throughout Britain and the empire to compete for places at university. Other Victorian developments at Cambridge included the founding and growth of the Fitzwilliam Museum (1837), the expansion of the Cambridge University Press into the Pitt building, and the establishment of Selwyn College (1882) and Fitzwilliam Hall (1893).

Numerous figures in Victorian intellectual history had important connections to Cambridge. The Cambridge Conversazione Society—better known as the Cambridge Apostles—formed in the early years of the century and proceeded to bring together a group of remarkably distinguished undergraduates: Alfred Tennyson, A. H. Hallam, Richard Monckton Milnes, Frederick Denison Maurice, J. M. Kemble, and R. C. Trench. Leaders of the **Broad Church** movement emerged at Cambridge, as did reformers like Adam Sedgwick and William Whewell, both of whom entered into the evolutionary debate and helped to form a characteristic Victorian outlook. Charles Darwin himself had been a student at Christ's College, although he said that his time there had been "sadly wasted." Darwin returned to Cambridge as a fellow commoner to write up his notes after his voyage on the *Beagle*. Charles Kingsley likewise complained that he had been involved in more sport than study as an undergraduate; he nevertheless was named professor of modern history in 1860 and became tutor to the Prince of Wales, later Edward VII. William Makepeace Thackeray, Edward Fitzgerald, and John McTaggart all had connections to Victorian Cambridge. Before the century ended, G. E. Moore, Bertrand Russell, and J. M. Keynes had begun their associations with the university, forming alliances and developing ideas that would influence not only the Bloomsbury group but also the intellectual currents of the next century. Cambridge thus emerged from the nineteenth century as a modern research institution with many of its scholarly traditions intact.

ASHTON NICHOLS

Bibliography

Allen, Peter. *The Cambridge Apostles.* 1978.

Garland, Martha McMackin. *Cambridge Before Darwin.* 1960.

McWilliams-Tullberg, Rita. *Women at Cambridge.* 1975.

Reeve, F. A. *Cambridge.* 1976.

Rothblatt, Sheldon. *The Revolution of the Dons.* 1981.

Winstanley, D. A. *Early Victorian Cambridge.* 1940.

———. *Later Victorian Cambridge.* 1947.

· · · · ·

CAMERON, JULIA MARGARET
(1815–1879)

Portraits of famous authors and artists and poetic posings of women and children in vaguely Renaissance costumes characterize the photography of Julia Margaret Cameron. An amateur who had limited concern for technical considerations, Cameron's great interest was in expressive imagery.

Born Julia Margaret Pattle in Calcutta to an East India Company official and his French wife, she was educated in France, returned to Calcutta, and married jurist Charles Hay Cameron in 1838. Social and philanthropic work and translating books occupied her until 1848, when her husband retired to England.

In 1863 Cameron's daughter and son-in-law gave her a camera. At first her photographs were made only for recreation, or as gifts to friends such as Alfred Tennyson, John Herschel, or George Frederick Watts. Very quickly, however, Cameron received honors in Berlin (1865, 1866) and Paris (1867) exhibitions. She sold work through Colnaghi's in London and exhibited there and at London's German Gallery (1868). In 1874 and 1875 she published illustrations to Tennyson's *Idylls of the King, and Other Poems.* Her autobiographical *Annals of My Glass House* (the title refers to her chicken house studio) was begun in 1874 but never completed; Helmut Gernsheim's modern biography reprints what exists.

Cameron's work is best compared to **Pre-Raphaelite** imagery. Her female subjects— usually modeled by grandnieces or neighborhood girls—are slim and graceful, with delicate features and long hair. Her portraits focus on the features, with nearer elements in focus and farther parts less distinct. Because of her success in emphasizing photography's expressive qualities, Cameron is considered important in the rise of the new technique as an art form.

FLOYD W. MARTIN

Bibliography

Gernsheim, Helmut. *Julia Margaret Cameron: Her Life and Photographic Work.* 1975.

Harker, Margaret. *Julia Margaret Cameron.* 1983.

Hill, Brian. *Julia Margaret Cameron: A Victorian Family Portrait.* 1973.

Ovenden, Graham, ed. *A Victorian Album: Julia Margaret Cameron and Her Circle.* 1975.

Weaver, Mike. *Julia Margaret Cameron, 1815–1879.* 1984.

· · · · ·

CAMPBELL, MRS. PATRICK
(1865–1940)

Affectionately known as "Mrs. Pat" and indisputably one of the most magnetic actresses of her generation, Campbell made her stage debut in Liverpool in 1888. Her new species of beauty combined with her wit, unpredictable personality, and considerable talent to make her a powerful presence in the drawing room as well as onstage.

Born Beatrice Stella Tanner, she was the youngest daughter of Maria Luigia Giovanna, whose family were Italian political exiles, and her husband John Tanner. After a childhood of genteel poverty and brief study at the Guildhall School of Music, she met her future husband, Patrick Campbell, became pregnant, and married quietly in June 1884. By the summer of 1889 she had given birth to a son Beo (killed in action in 1917) and a daughter Stella (who also became an actress). Patrick Campbell disappeared to pursue a fortune in South Africa (where he was killed in 1900), leaving her to secure a job touring with Ben Greet's Woodland Players.

Although she won her first London success as Astrea in *The Trumpet Call* by George Sims and Robert Buchanan at the Adelphi in

1891, it was her Paula in Pinero's *The Second Mrs. Tanqueray* (1893) that brought her fame. She produced and performed in Bjørnson's *Beyond Human Powers* at the Royalty Theatre in 1901, played Ibsen and Maeterlinck, and performed Mélisande to both Forbes Robertson's Pélléas in 1898 and Sarah Bernhardt's Pélléas in 1904. In Shakespeare she had great success as Juliet and Ophelia (both with Forbes Robertson). Her title role in Sudermann's *Magda* prompted Matheson Lang to deem her superior to Duse. In a letter to his father in 1906 Yeats described her style as "a kind of magnificent hysteria." She played the title role in Yeats's *Deirdre* at the Abbey Theatre, Dublin, in 1908. Shaw created the role of Eliza Doolittle for her in *Pygmalion* (1914).

Jerome Kilty's adaptation of Campbell's correspondence with Shaw, *Dear Liar* (1960), confirms her fascination as one of the powerful theatrical forces of her generation, with an influence that extended beyond her Victorian and Edwardian heyday.

ANDREW PARKIN

Bibliography

Campbell, Mrs. Patrick. *My Life and Some Letters.* 1922.

Dent, Alan, ed. *Bernard Shaw and Mrs. Patrick Campbell. Their Correspondence.* 1952.

Dent, Alan. *Mrs. Patrick Campbell.* 1961.

Peters, Margot. *Mrs. Pat: The Life of Mrs. Patrick Campbell.* 1984.

· · · · ·

CANADA

Canada was a major colony of the British empire in Victoria's reign, during which the two cornerstones of British imperial policy—responsible government and dominion status—were instituted. Although the colonization of Canada dated from the old empire, long before Victoria, it made momentous strides during her reign. By the death of Victoria, Canada had evolved almost into an independent sovereign nation.

At the beginning of Victoria's reign Canada was in turmoil. The British had divided their possessions in Canada into Upper and Lower Canada, the former including Ontario and the latter Quebec. In 1837 both were in rebellion. Upper Canada was chafing under a system of virtually oligarchical rule by a few Anglican upper-class families known as the "family compact." Lower Canada was even more embroiled in conflict over nationalism. The French majority hated the bigoted English ruling group known as the *chateau clique*. Troops were sent and both rebellions were easily quelled, but Whitehall surmised that a serious problem existed. Fearful of a wider Canadian rebellion on the scale of that by the thirteen American colonies in the previous century, the Whig government understood the need to identify the problems and devise a solution.

In 1838 the prime minister, Lord Melbourne, decided to send to Canada a strong representative with extensive powers and selected John Lambton, first earl of **Durham**. Durham spent about five months in North America and published his report in February 1839. The Durham report has become one of the key documents in British imperial history. The pivotal concept endorsed by the report was the adoption of responsible government: that is, a government in which the ministers of state (in Canada's case the governor's executive council) were "responsible" to a popularly elected assembly. Adoption of the Durham report meant that Britain would allow a colony almost complete autonomy in domestic matters. In the future a colonial prime minister could act almost as his British counterpart, selecting his advisers so that they always had the confidence of the colonial assembly. By the mid-1850s, all five segments of British North America—Upper Canada, Lower Canada, Nova Scotia, Prince Edward Island, and New Brunswick—had obtained responsible government. (Newfoundland did not enter the federation until the mid-twentieth century.)

The second cornerstone of British imperial policy adopted first in Canada was the development of dominion status. In 1860 the Duke of Newcastle as head of the Colonial Office accompanied the Prince of Wales on a fact-finding trip to Canada. Newcastle reported that Canada would become "a strong and self-reliant Colony," and was in favor of a Canadian federation. The Colonial Office received a formal resolution from Canada in November 1864. Momentum for federation grew after the American Civil War, when Canada was no longer being used for fifth-column activity by Northern and Southern agents. In December 1866 delegates from the Canadian colonies met in London with representatives from the imperial government to frame what became the British North American Act.

The British North American Act was passed and officially proclaimed on July 1, 1867. Canada had achieved dominion status, the term coming from the reference to the queen as sovereign of all the "dominions across the sea." The Canadian prime minister was, therefore, to have dominion "from sea to sea." By the next year imperial troops were being removed from Canada, and by 1871 the full implications of responsible government had been realized. A precedent was established by what transpired in Canada, and in 1872 responsible government was inaugurated in the Cape Colony of South Africa.

Politically, Victorian Canada was dominated by the figure of John A. Macdonald. After becoming Canada's first prime minister, he remained in office, except for a short break from 1873 to 1878, until his death in 1891. He led the Conservative party to seven victories, and it was only in his declining years that the Liberal party, under French-Canadian leader Wilfrid Laurier, was able to challenge. Upon Macdonald's death, Laurier emerged as Canada's leading politician and served as prime minister from 1896–1911.

During the period 1867 to 1901 Canada completed the process of expanding from "sea to sea." The original dominion annexed additional territories in both east and west, adding provinces such as Rupert's Land (from the Hudson's Bay Company), Prince Edward Island, Manitoba, and British Columbia. By 1880 the imperial government had extended its dominion to an area of approximately 3.7 million miles. A transcontinental railroad was needed to facilitate westward expansion. In 1871 Macdonald pledged to have one built within the decade, but the last spike was not driven until 1885. Extensive government subsidy was used to encourage railway expansion: loans totaling over 27 million dollars as well as the distribution of over 25 million acres of land.

The completion of the railroad, in turn, helped in the settlement of the western territories, completing the Canadian "drive to the sea." Public land acts encouraged migration from eastern Canada, the United States, and much of Europe. An act of 1872 allowed homesteads of 160 acres from the public domain. Additional grants ranging up to 640 acres could be obtained by legitimate settlers. By the end of the century Canadian population totaled about 5.3 million; of these 4.6 million were Canadian born. The discovery of gold fields in Canada shortly before the end of Victoria's reign led to the prospect of considerable expansion in the following years. The close of the Victorian era found Canada in the early stages of immigrant, railway, and economic booms.

Canada in Victorian times, therefore, became the model for progressive British imperial policy. Rudyard Kipling aptly described the Canadian position relative to Britain: "Daughter am I in my mother's house, / But mistress in my own." In later years, long after the reign of Victoria, the events in Canada became a beacon for imperial administrators, the noble goal of a worldwide collection of commonwealth nations, a panoply of peoples and nations linked by their common imperial heritage.

NEWELL D. BOYD

Bibliography

Burroughs, Peter. *The Canadian Crisis and British Colonial Policy.* 1972.

Eldridge, C. C. *Victorian Imperialism.* 1978.

Martin, G., ed. *The Durham Report and British Policy.* 1972.

McNaught, Kenneth. *The Pelican History of Canada.* 1969.

Ward, John. *Colonial Self-Government.* 1976.

∙ ∙ ∙ ∙ ∙

CAPITAL PUNISHMENT see LAW ENFORCEMENT

∙ ∙ ∙ ∙ ∙

CARDIGAN, SEVENTH EARL (JAMES THOMAS BRUDENELL) (1797–1868)

The earl of Cardigan led the charge of a light brigade of cavalry at the battle of Balaclava on October 25, 1854, during the **Crimean War**. The charge, although a disaster, was immortalized by **Alfred Tennyson** in his poem, "The Charge of the Light Brigade."

Beginning in 1824, Cardigan purchased a number of military commissions (a normal practice at the time) culminating in 1835 when he became lieutenant-colonel of the 11th Light Dragoons, Prince Albert's favorite. A rigid disciplinarian in an age when military discipline was notoriously lax, Cardigan often quarreled with his fellow officers, driving some of them to insubordination, and was criticized for his ostentatious dress and living. His men, however, generally respected and liked him.

Cardigan was posted to the Crimea in the spring of 1854. In June he led a patrol toward the Danube with inadequate provisions. After scouting an area of about 1,000 square miles, this "sore back reconnaissance" returned to camp and Cardigan was both praised and vilified for the rigor with which he had carried out his orders.

On October 25 the Russian general, Liprandi, had 25,000 artillery stationed at the eastern end of the valley of Balaclava. The western end, a mile and a half distant, was in British hands. The hills on the northern side were in Russian hands. Earlier that morning the Russians had forced three Turkish redoubts to retreat from the Causeway Heights on the southern side. About midmorning the British commander in chief, **Lord Raglan**, from his position on the Chersonese Plateau at the western end, could see the Russians towing away the guns abandoned earlier by the Turks. He ordered the cavalry to advance in order to prevent the enemy from getting those guns.

Raglan's order was carried to Lord Lucan in the valley below by Captain Lewis Edward Nolan. Lucan could see guns only at the eastern end of the valley and, although he questioned Nolan, he handed the order on to Cardigan to be carried out. Cardigan too questioned Nolan, who did not perceive the necessity of clarifying which guns were to be seized. Cardigan protested that he would never be able to bring a single man back but, like Lucan, believing that he was ordered to ride the full length of the valley and attack, led his Light Brigade straight into Liprandi's artillery. They were fired upon from both sides and those who reached the Russian position at the eastern end were further decimated. Of the 673 officers and men who began the charge only 195, including the slightly wounded Cardigan, survived.

Cardigan returned home in January 1855. There were later attempts to discredit him, including Alexander William Kinglake's *The Invasion of the Crimea* (1863), which castigated all the officers involved in the charge and especially Cardigan. In the popular mind, however, he remained a hero.

JOAN MICKELSON GAUGHAN

Bibliography

Compton, Piers. *Cardigan of Balaclava.* 1972.

Thomas, Donald. *Cardigan.* 1974.

. . . . .

CAREY, ROSA NOUCHETTE (1840–1909)

Author of some forty-five novels, Rosa Nouchette Carey earned considerable popularity but no enduring reputation. Pleasantly descriptive and delicate in feeling, her works focus not on dramatic incident but on domestic relationships. As in *At the Moorings* (1904), they celebrate unselfishness in lives complicated by financial stress and ill health. Carey also wrote short stories serialized in the *Girl's Own Paper*, as well as *Twelve Notable Good Women of the Nineteenth Century* (1899), which includes biographical appreciations of Queen Victoria and Florence Nightingale.

Carey's first novel, *Nellie's Memories* (1868), a simple story of English home life, quickly enjoyed a popularity not matched by her second, *Wee Wifie* (1869), which she later revised after subsequent works had established her reputation. The widely read *Not Like Other Girls* (1884), about three impoverished but plucky sisters who become successful dressmakers, illustrates her favorite theme of young women reared as ladies who must work to survive or (as in *Uncle Max*, 1887) to feel useful. These resourceful protagonists defiantly undertake jobs deemed beneath their station, as in *Merle's Crusade* (1900), where the heroine becomes a children's nurse. Carey often interjects poignant digressions on spinsterhood and champions spirited, impetuous young women, even those who must learn self-control (e.g., *Wooed and Married*, 1875).

Although Carey's novels do not radically challenge the class system or prevailing notions of gentility, they remain interesting in that they tentatively explore how a gentlewoman could "shake off the prejudices of caste and declare herself free" (*Merle's Crusade*).

BEVERLY TAYLOR

Bibliography

Black, Helen C. *Notable Women Authors of the Day.* 1893.

. . . . .

CARICATURE

The popular humorous art known as caricature changed rapidly during the Victorian era because of shifts in public tastes, the growth of magazines and newspapers, innovations in printing, and the rising literacy rate. Caricature evolved into numerous forms—the social manners scene, the comic strip, the weekly periodical political commentary, and the daily newspaper political cartoon—and eventually became a generic term interchangeable with cartoons, comic art, and the comics. At the beginning of the Victorian era, however, English caricatures were more strictly defined.

Victorian caricatures stood in sharp contrast to the etchings of the late Georgian period which were, by Victorian standards, vul-

gar and obscene. The Georgian caricatures had emerged out of the Italian classical caricature style which originated in Bologna during the late sixteenth century at the studios of the Carracci brothers. In the mid-eighteenth century the Italian caricature style, a humorous but gentle depiction of the victim's personality and idiosyncrasies, was introduced in England by Arthur Pond, an engraver and print dealer. George, fourth viscount and first marquis Townshend, attacked his political enemies through his satirical and devastating sketches. James Gillray and his contemporaries transformed the Italian style into distorted human forms and crowded the print with images, symbols, and speeches alluding to topical political, social, and personal issues. The single-sheet engraved and colored caricatures were sold in print shops or hawked on street corners and circulated in private homes to entertain and to provoke conversations.

By the 1830s, however, English caricatures had begun to revert in their composition and form to the Italian models. John Doyle or "HB" set the new tone and style in his *Political Sketches*. His caricatures possessed a mildly amusing likeness to the subject and were simplified in design and uncluttered in composition. These black-and-white lithographs were bound and sold in series. While they expressed opinions on political and social issues, the caricatures seldom angered or incensed the viewer.

Doyle, along with William Heath ("Paul Pry"), Richard Dighton, and others, laid the foundations of the Victorian caricature which ultimately evolved into the political cartoon and the comic strip. During the 1830s these caricatures began to appear in magazines and, after 1841, when *Punch* was founded, they became a regular feature in numerous periodicals. *Punch* broadened the interpretation and changed the meaning of the word "caricature" in 1843. John Leech, the chief caricaturist for *Punch*, ridiculed the cartoons or designs submitted by England's most prominent artists who were competing to paint the frescoes in the new House of Commons. Hereafter, the word "cartoon" came to mean a comic design, and the classical Italian caricature and comic drawings or cartoons were fused together in the public mind.

A Novelist (Anthony Trollope).
by Leslie Ward,
Vanity Fair, *5 April 1873.*

While cartoons and caricatures became synonymous and encompassed varieties of comic art, some artists, especially those working for *Vanity Fair, Punch, Mayfair,* and similar magazines, continued to differentiate between a caricature and a humorous cartoon. But such classifications were difficult to maintain because of the developments in printing and journalism prompted by the inventions and innovations in the industry, the widening reading audience, the impact of changes in transportation and communication, and the emergence of specific stereotyped images, symbols, and models in the popular press. Of particular interest were the types of cartoons and comic art forms evolving in the weekly magazines and daily newspapers. *Punch* set the standards with its political commentaries by Richard Doyle, John Leech and, later, **John Tenniel**, who greatly influenced the late generation of Victorian caricaturists. **George du Maurier**'s social manners drawings for

Punch were especially effective in catching the essence of proper Victorian society.

At the other end of the socioeconomic spectrum was Ally Sloper, perfected through the pen of William G. Baxter. Ally Sloper first appeared in *Judy* and later *Ally Sloper's Half Holiday,* the penny comic weekly. This perennial outsider and gate crasher personified the little man who poked fun at his "betters." Ally Sloper's success inspired other cartoonists to draw illustrated stories depicting a wide variety of comic characters. These serialized escapades evolved into comic strips by the end of the Victorian period. Meanwhile, the political and social observations of Leech and Tenniel were copied by their successors at *Punch,* Bernard Partridge, Edward Lynley Sambourne, and Harry Furniss. These caricaturists at *Punch* and other publications produced scores of cartoons each week. They were laying the foundations for the daily newspaper political cartoons which became a popular feature by the end of the nineteenth century.

Caricature, at the beginning of the Victorian period, was a well defined but limited humorous art style, but by the close of the era its original meaning was drastically altered. Like so many of the artistic and cultural phenomena of the age, caricature was transformed by the political, economic, social, and educational forces into a popular and democratized art form that reflected the shifting values and tastes of Victorian England.

ROY T. MATTHEWS

Bibliography

Ashbee, Charles R. *Caricature.* 1928.

Gombrich, Ernst and Ernst Kris. *Caricature.* 1940.

Hillier, Bevis. *Cartoons and Caricatures.* 1970.

Hofmann, Werner. *Caricature from Leonardo to Picasso.* 1957.

Houfe, Simon. *The Dictionary of British Book Illustrators and Caricaturists, 1800-1914.* 1978.

Low, David. *British Cartoonists, Caricaturists and Comic Artists.* 1942.

Spielman, Marion H. *The History of "Punch."* 1895.

See also PERIODICALS: COMIC; RADICAL CARTOONS

. . . . .

CARLETON, WILLIAM (1794-1869)

William Carleton was the most powerful and perplexing of early nineteenth-century Irish writers. His major works, *Traits and Stories of the Irish Peasantry* (1830), *Valentine M'Clutchy* (1845), and *The Black Prophet* (1847), provide vivid portraits of the Gaelic world which was lost in the great famine. Yet for complex reasons both personal and financial, all of Carleton's work is riven by a vacillation between affection and contempt for his subject.

The son of poor Ulster farmers, Carleton was sporadically educated by itinerant masters in impromptu schoolrooms. He had hoped for the prestige and education of the priesthood, but spent his youth as a wandering storyteller and schoolmaster. In Dublin, he quickly achieved fame as a writer of short stories and novels, although his large family and improvident habits kept him impoverished throughout his life. Consequently, he wrote for periodicals which ranged from the hysterically anti-Catholic to the radically nationalist. Fantasy, comedy, and folk tale enrich *Traits and Stories* and his serial fiction, while his best novels chronicle in harrowing detail the effects of landlordism and famine.

Carleton's work embodied the terrifying contradictions of Irish rural life in the early 1800s. It thereby dignified characters who hitherto had been only comic stereotypes and revealed a subtle beauty within native speech. For these achievements, W. B. Yeats and others of the Irish literary revival were openly indebted to his model.

ELIZABETH GRUBGELD

Bibliography

Flanagan, Thomas. *The Irish Novelist, 1800-1850.* 1959.

Kiely, Benedict. *Poor Scholar.* 1947.

See also IRISH LITERATURE

. . . . .

CARLYLE, THOMAS (1795-1881)

An essayist and historian, social critic and moral teacher, Thomas Carlyle possessed one of the most influential minds of his era. His secularized alternatives to religious orthodoxy eased many Victorians through their crises of faith, even as his indictments of materialism, democracy, and laissez faire stung their consciences. His highly original genius shaped nonfictional prose into a genre of major artistic and intellectual importance. The Chelsea home of Thomas and Jane Welsh Carlyle (whom he married in 1826) served as a crossroads for the leading minds of their time.

Carlyle was born into a strict Scottish Calvinist family and attended Edinburgh University (1809-1814) with the intention of entering the ministry. By his mid-twenties, however, he was already seeking replacements for orthodox Christianity. He found partial answers in the work of Goethe and other German romantics, some of whom he introduced to English audiences through critical essays and translations. The autobiographical fiction, *Sartor Resartus* ("The Tailor Retailored," 1833-1834), portrayed his struggle with metaphysical despair and formulated the "Natural Supernaturalism" that finally vanquished it: his affirmation of the divine reality immanent in the changing "clothing" of human life and visible to the eye disciplined by duty, self-denial, and reverence.

Sartor's highly idiosyncratic style baffled more readers than it pleased, and only the publication of *The French Revolution* (1837) secured Carlyle literary success. He read in the French Revolution the vengeance of an angry god on a sham aristocracy, a destruction of decayed values necessary to their rebirth in new forms. In France's example Carlyle found a warning for England, where true leadership had seemingly abdicated to democracy and laissez faire, abandoning the country to economic and social chaos. *Chartism* (1839) first attacked these problems. *On Heroes, Hero-Worship, and the Heroic in History* (1841) provided examples of men whose insight into divine reality had enabled them to focus the religious, political, or artistic energies of their societies. *Past and Present* (1843) contrasted the medieval past, with its coherent faith and ordered social hierarchies, to the modern spectacle of scepticism, alienation, and a democracy that meant to Carlyle "despair of finding any heroes to govern you." He called on factory owners to become "captains of industry" who would restore paternalistic order between men and masters.

Carlyle's frustration over his society's intransigence found expression in *Latter-Day Pamphlets* (1850), his jeremiad against the inadequacies of democracy, bureaucracy, and philanthropy. Believing anarchy to be the only alternative to moral reform, he saw England's only hope in leaders strong enough to force society to reorder itself in divinely sanctioned ways. He thought that Frederick II of Prussia would exemplify such a leader, but experienced great difficulty in turning this cynical and sceptical pragmatist into a hero in his massive *Frederick the Great* (1858–1865). Among Carlyle's last significant works, "Shooting Niagra, and After?" (1867) reiterated familiar criticisms of the second Reform Bill, and *The Early Kings of Norway* (1875) continued his search for heroes. **James Anthony Froude**, Carlyle's literary executor and later his controversial biographer, published Carlyle's *Reminiscences* (1881) shortly after his death.

Carlyle showed the Victorians how they could salvage the stern ethic of evangelical Protestantism from its discredited doctrinal forms. His unfaltering faith in transcendent moral absolutes accessible to intuition alone both comforted and baffled this age of increasing relativism and rationality. Even many who disagreed with his controversial messages valued Carlyle as the definitive "Victorian sage": a courageous thinker who spoke with incomparable eloquence to the hearts and imaginations of his age.

ROSEMARY JANN

Bibliography

Froude, James Anthony. *Thomas Carlyle: A History of the First Forty Years of His Life, 1795–1835.* 1892.

——. *Thomas Carlyle: A History of His Life in London, 1834–1881.* 1884.

Holloway, John. *The Victorian Sage.* 1953.

Kaplan, Fred. *Thomas Carlyle: A Biography.* 1983.

LaValley, Albert J. *Carlyle and the Idea of the Modern.* 1968.

Levine, George. *The Boundaries of Fiction: Carlyle, Macaulay, Newman.* 1968.

Sanders, George R. and K. J. Fielding, eds. *The Collected Letters of Thomas and Jane Welsh Carlyle.* 1970–1983. 12 vols.

Rosenberg, John D. *Carlyle and the Burden of History.* 1985.

Tennyson, G. B. *"Sartor" Called "Resartus."* 1966.

——. "Thomas Carlyle." In David J. DeLaura, ed., *Victorian Prose: A Guide to Research.* 1973.

Traill, H. D., ed. *The Works of Thomas Carlyle.* 1896–1901. 30 vols.

Willey, Basil. *Nineteenth Century Studies.* 1949.

· · · · ·

CARPENTER, EDWARD (1844–1929)

Socialist, sexual prophet, eccentric at large, Edward Carpenter championed nearly every one of the bohemian movements that flourished in late Victorian Britain. He studied at Trinity Hall, Cambridge, won a clerical fellowship, and served as a curate under the Christian socialist **F. D. Maurice**. Religious doubts forced him to relinquish orders in 1874, and he redirected his spiritual energies into leftist politics.

He went on pilgrimages to Walt Whitman in Camden, New Jersey, and to India and Ceylon. From Whitman and the *Bhagavad Gita* Carpenter derived his belief that all individual souls are spiritually connected—"the doctrine of the Universal Self." That idea was the basis of Carpenter's faith in socialism and comradeship, and it found expression in his poem *Towards Democracy* (1883), written in the style of *Leaves of Grass*.

In that all-embracing spirit, Carpenter became a thoroughly ecumenical radical. He was a critic of the penal system, vivisection, and the Boer War, a partisan of feminism, sexual freedom, vegetarianism, antipollution legislation, land reform, progressive education, and "such degree of Nudity as we can reasonably attain to." Dedicated to "the Simplification of Life," he used his permanent income to set up a small farm at Millthorpe, near Sheffield, where he worked in the fields and made sandals. He supported H. M. Hyndman's Social Democratic Federation, William Morris's Socialist League, the Fellowship of the New Life, the **Fabian Society**, the Independent Labour Party, and the anarchist and syndicalist movements.

Carpenter is best known for his pamphlet *Homogenic Love* (1895), which defended **homosexuality** as a natural preference. He argued that love between men of different classes would break down class barriers: he himself lived with a Sheffield workingman named George Merrill (1869?–1928). As a homosexual advocate, Carpenter followed the lead of J. A. Symonds and, in turn, inspired **Havelock Ellis**, E. M. Forster, and Siegfried Sassoon.

JONATHAN ROSE

Bibliography

Tsuzuki, Chushichi. *Edward Carpenter, 1844–1929: Prophet of Human Fellowship.* 1980.

· · · · ·

CARPENTER, MARY
(1807–1877)

Mary Carpenter was a pioneer in the effort to provide schooling for poor and neglected children and an influential advocate of special treatment for juvenile offenders. Through the example of several schools and reformatory homes that she founded and ran, but even more through her writing, testimony, and personal impact on officials and social reformers, she was responsible for profound changes in social attitudes toward outcast children.

The eldest of six children, Carpenter was educated by her father, a Bristol Unitarian minister. He exerted a deep moral and spiritual influence on her, as did a family friend, Dr. Joseph Tuckerman, Boston abolitionist and social reformer. Highly intelligent, intensely self-critical, and driven by a keen sense of religious duty, she set aside her desire to pursue scientific studies and helped to support the family by teaching in schools run by her parents. Her father's death in 1839 was

both deeply traumatic and emancipating for Carpenter. As she cast about for an occupation worthy of his ideal, her attention was drawn to the plight of Bristol's children of the streets. In 1846 she opened her first "ragged school" (a term Carpenter disliked), thus initiating her life's work.

Horrified at the squalor and brutality of mid-Victorian prisons, which provided no specialized facilities for child inmates, Carpenter began to research and write on the need for residential care and training for wayward, abandoned, or criminal children. She recommended a three-tiered system of schools for the poor: ragged schools for the youngest children, industrial schools for noncriminal adolescents, and reformatory schools for all offenders under the age of fourteen. Carpenter opened a reformatory school for boys in 1852, followed by the famous Red Lodge school for girls in 1854. Her efforts were hampered by lack of money, ill health, the difficulty of finding competent staff, her own limited understanding of the culture of poverty, and the hostility of civil and clerical authorities suspicious of her independent, nonpunitive, and nonsectarian approach to rehabilitation. But her determination, plus some limited practical success, prevailed, and she gained influential admirers, among them **Frances Power Cobbe**, Lady Byron, and Matthew Davenport Hill.

The publication of Carpenter's *Ragged Schools* (1850), *Reformatory Schools for the Children of the Perishing and Dangerous Classes* (1851), and *Juvenile Delinquents: Conditions and Treatment* (1853) led to an invitation to testify before a parliamentary committee, and ultimately contributed to shaping the Youthful Offenders Act of 1854 and the Industrial Schools Act of 1857. She argued forcefully for a homelike environment, provision for recreation, firm but compassionate discipline, and moral and vocational training. Her national reputation was further enhanced by the annual papers she delivered before the National Society for the Promotion of Social Science.

Carpenter's fame spread internationally, and in the late 1860s she paid three long visits to India, where she undertook to advise the authorities on prison reform, education, and the status of women. Triumphal lecture and study tours of Germany and North America followed.

Like her colleague and rival, Florence Nightingale, Carpenter advanced the cause of women's emancipation more by example than by argument. Conservative in her views on "women's sphere" and hesitant to endorse feminist demands, Carpenter idealized marriage and motherhood, and at first shrank from public activity. But her work drew her more and more into the limelight and emboldened her. Toward the end of her life she participated in the campaigns for suffrage, social purity, and the professional education of women.

GAIL MALMGREEN

Bibliography

Carpenter, J. Estlin. *The Life and Work of Mary Carpenter.* 1879.

Manton, Jo. *Mary Carpenter and the Children of the Streets.* 1976.

May, Margaret. "Innocence and Experience: The Evolution of the Concept of Juvenile Delinquency in the Mid-Nineteenth Century." *Victorian Studies,* vol. 18, pp. 7–29.

Saywell, Ruby J. *Mary Carpenter of Bristol.* 1964.

Schupf, Harriet Warm. "Single Women and Social Reform in Mid-Nineteenth Century England: The Case of Mary Carpenter." *Victorian Studies,* vol. 17, pp. 301–317.

See also JUVENILE CRIME; RAGGED SCHOOLS

· · · · ·

CARROLL, LEWIS
(1832–1898)

Charles Lutwidge Dodgson, a little-known professor of mathematics at Oxford University, became world famous as the pseudonymous Lewis Carroll, author of several classics of **children's literature**.

Born in Daresbury, Cheshire, Carroll grew up in a large family, the members of which served as the captive audience for such early nonsense writings as *The Rectory Umbrella* and *Mischmasch*. Ordained deacon in 1861, Carroll spent practically all of his bachelor life at Oxford. Among his scholarly writings are *Euclid and His Modern Rivals* (1879) and *Curiosa Mathematica* (1888).

Carroll's greatest and most enduring achievements, however, are those unique works of fantasy, *Alice's Adventures in Wonderland* (1865) and its sequel *Through the Looking-Glass* (1872), both illustrated by **John Tenniel**. Carroll developed these stories from ones he told to Alice, Lorina, and Edith Liddell during a boat trip on July 4, 1862. Characters such as the Cheshire Cat, the Mad Hatter, the March Hare, the Red Queen, and the White Rabbit have become known the world over. Carroll's Alice books have won the admiration of a diversity of readers, from Queen Victoria to James Joyce. The books have been illustrated by numerous artists (including Salvador Dali), translated into practically every language in the world, and analyzed by literary, religious, psychoanalytical, social, and linguistic critics. They have been dramatized and made into motion pictures, have inspired ballets and musical compositions, and have influenced numerous works of literature. Furthermore, they have given rise to countless commercial products ranging from biscuit tins to postage stamps.

Carroll also wrote many humorous verses, the most popular being *The Hunting of the Snark* (1876). His best poems, however, are embedded within the two Alice books and include "The Jabberwocky" and "The Walrus and the Carpenter." His interest in spiritualism helped motivate him to write a bizarre novel entitled *Sylvie and Bruno* (1889) and its sequel *Sylvie and Bruno Concluded* (1893). The stories attempt to show what might happen if fairies actually existed and interacted with human beings.

Frustrated by his inability to draw, Carroll took up photography in 1856, when cameras had been available to the public for only a few years. His avocation quickly turned into a passionate devotion that lasted for nearly twenty years, during which time Carroll developed into one of the most skillful portrait photographers of the period. Obsessed with the theme of lost **childhood**, he was able to freeze youthful innocence through hundreds of photographs of young girls. He also sought out and photographed many eminent men and women, including Dante Gabriel Rossetti, Ellen Terry, and Alfred Tennyson.

Although most critics agree that Carroll's Alice books are complex works more suited to adults than to children, the fact remains that the works themselves are obsessed with the idea of the girl child. Carroll, who never liked little boys, sees the prepubescent girl as the embodiment of innocence and spirituality. Even his photographs of nude little girls exhibit a remarkable angelic chastity. Alice's fantastic voyages into Wonderland and Looking-Glass Land reveal Carroll's keen understanding of human dreamwork, anticipating the symbolic landscape of twentieth-century absurdism. Within Alice's world are masterpieces of satire, wit, and startling, exotic logic. In Wonderland time stands still: it is always six o'clock, tea time, and Alice can never grow old in that dream world. Deep beneath the rational world, Wonderland has its own logic, best expressed by the Cheshire Cat: "we're all mad."

Carroll was a most fastidious man who dedicated himself to imposing order and form upon the chaos of experience. Mathematics and logic were thus enormous comforts, which provided him with an immaculate, regulated world. His fascination with puzzles was an extension of this concern, for puzzles allowed answers to even the most complex questions. Behind all of Carroll's creations is his sense of life as an enormous puzzle, one to be worked out to the end and perhaps never completely solved. He could, however, create his own universe, complex but controlled, puzzling but rational. James Joyce thus appropriately addressed Carroll in *Finnegans Wake* as "Dodgfather, Dodgson and Coo," Dodgson as Father, Son, and Holy Spirit.

RICHARD KELLY

Bibliography

Cohen, Morton N., ed. *The Letters of Lewis Carroll.* 1979.

Gardner, Martin, ed. *The Annotated Alice.* 1960.

———, ed. *The Annotated Snark.* 1962.

Green, Roger Lancelyn, ed. *The Diaries of Lewis Carroll.* 1953–1954.

Greenacre, Phyllis. *Swift and Carroll: A Psychoanalytic Study of Two Lives.* 1955.

Guiliano, Edward, ed. *Lewis Carroll: A Celebration.* 1982.

Hudson, Derek. *Lewis Carroll.* 1976.

Kelly, Richard. *Lewis Carroll.* 1977.

Lennon, Florence Becker. *The Life of Lewis Carroll.* 1962.

Phillips, Robert, ed. *Aspects of Alice.* 1974.

· · · · ·

CARTE, RICHARD D'OYLY (1844–1901)

The leading impresario of English **operetta**, Richard D'Oyly Carte was the indispensable third partner of W. S. Gilbert and **Arthur Sullivan**. He efficiently produced all but one of their collaborations, never interfering with their artistic decisions.

Carte studied at University College, London, and then worked for his father's firm of musical instrument makers. He also composed operettas, including *Dr. Ambrosias* (1868) and *Marie* (1871).

In 1870 Carte became a concert and lecture agent. His clients included the Italian tenor Mario, Adelina Patti, Charles Gounod, Archibald Forbes, Henry Morton Stanley, Matthew Arnold, and Oscar Wilde. In 1874 he introduced Charles Lecocq's *Giroflé-Girofla* to London and commissioned Jacques Offenbach to compose *Dick Wittington and His Cat.*

In 1875 Carte, as manager of the Royalty Theatre, needed a short operetta to accompany Offenbach's *La Périchole.* He accepted Gilbert's libretto of *Trial by Jury,* on the condition that Sullivan write the music.

The success of *Trial by Jury* spurred Carte to launch the Comedy Opera Company, a syndicate of music publishers and businessmen. His production of *H.M.S. Pinafore* (1878) ran for 700 performances, breaking all records for London operetta. Carte dissolved the Comedy Opera Company in 1879, after quarreling with the directors. He formed a new partnership with Gilbert and Sullivan, under which the three agreed to divide their profits equally.

In the absence of international copyright agreements, many American producers had staged pirated versions of *Pinafore*. Carte defeated these plagiarists by premiering *The Pirates of Penzance* (1880) in New York. He eventually had as many as five touring companies in America, with another five working the provincial circuit in Britain.

In 1881 Carte shrewdly booked Oscar Wilde for a lecture tour in the United States. *Patience*, Gilbert and Sullivan's spoof of aestheticism, was playing there at the time; the operetta and the aesthete generated excellent publicity for each other.

On October 10, 1881 Carte opened the Savoy Theatre, which he had built specifically to stage Gilbert and Sullivan's operettas. It was the first London theater lit entirely by electricity. Carte also introduced the practice of having his patrons queue (rather than scramble) for unreserved seats. He generally raised the standards of British theatrical architecture, costuming, scenery, and refreshment stalls. In 1889 he opened the Savoy Hotel, which offered another Cartesian invention, the after-theater dinner.

In 1890 the Savoy triumvirate broke up over the notorious "carpet quarrel." Gilbert charged that Carte had run up excessive bills for staging *The Gondoliers*, including 500 pounds for new house carpets. No one profited from the subsequent lawsuit except the lawyers.

At the time, Carte was constructing the Royal English Opera House, where he planned to produce a new school of British **opera**. The house opened on January 31, 1891 with Sullivan's *Ivanhoe*, which exhausted its popularity after 160 performances. Having lost a reported 36,000 pounds, Carte sold the opera house.

Throughout his career, Carte was closely assisted by his secretary, Helen Lenoir (1852–1913), née Couper-Black. They were married in 1888. (Carte's first wife, Blanche Prowse, had died three years earlier.) After Carte's death, Helen managed his theatrical ventures and produced revivals of the Savoy Operas.

JONATHAN ROSE

See also AESTHETIC MOVEMENT; SAVOY OPERAS

. . . . .

CATHEDRAL MUSIC

Cathedral music may be defined as the music of the fully choral Anglican service as rendered by trained choirs of men and boys in cathedrals and other institutions (such as the chapels of the larger Oxford and Cambridge colleges) with choral foundations instituted for the purpose. The principal musical genres are the service (settings of certain fixed texts from the Prayer Book) and the anthem (settings of sacred texts that are not liturgically predetermined). During the Victorian period, elements of cathedral music became an increasingly frequent part of parochial worship.

At the period's beginning, English cathedral music was at its lowest ebb. Early Victorian cathedral foundations, with isolated exceptions, were noted for indifference regarding decorum in worship. **S. S. Wesley** (1810–1876) criticized these conditions in his tracts *A Few Words on Cathedral Music* (1849) and *Reply to the Inquiries of the Cathedral Commissioners* (1854).

An overall tendency of steady, even dramatic, improvement may be linked with the **High Church** revival that followed the Oxford Movement. The reanimation of cathedral music and worship emanated not from the cathedrals themselves, but from parochial and collegiate institutions, usually under the influence of devoted High Churchmen, clerical and lay. For example, cathedral-style choral services were introduced in 1841 at the Leeds Parish Church, in 1843 at the recently restored Temple Church, later in the 1840s at Radley College near Oxford and at King's College, London, and in the 1850s at Lincoln's Inn and Gray's Inn. The most remarkable establishment was the Church and College of St. Michael at Tenbury, founded in 1856 by the Reverend Frederick A. G. Ouseley (1825–1889) for the express purpose of maintaining daily choral worship in the highest standard of the cathedral tradition.

Cases such as these, together with the rising standard of volunteer parish choirs, sometimes proved embarrassing to the cathedrals, especially on the occasion of diocesan choral festivals of massed parish choirs, the first of which took place at Lichfield in 1865. Some cathedrals were virtually shamed into reform in the second half of the century. The appointment of noted High Church dignitaries to St. Paul's Cathedral laid the groundwork of support for the great musical improvements carried out by **John Stainer** (1840–1901), who was cathedral organist from 1872 to 1888. St. Paul's thus became a model and a challenge to other cathedrals, and Stainer's appointment a landmark in the course of general improvement.

In addition to Wesley, Ouseley, and Stainer, the chief Victorian cathedral composers include John Goss (1800–1880), T. A. Walmisley (1814–1856), Henry Smart (1813–1879), George J. Elvey (1816–1893), E. J. Hopkins (1818–1901), and Joseph Barnby (1838–1896). Their music is fundamentally conservative in style, preserving much from the past tradition. In the second half of the century, however, it is marked by increasing harmonic richness and expressive warmth. Discussion of individual Victorian composers and further stylistic commentary may be found in histories of English church music. Readers should beware of the severely antipathetic tone of many twentieth-century writers.

WILLIAM J. GATENS

Bibliography

Barrett, Philip. "English Cathedral Choirs in the Nineteenth Century." *Journal of Ecclesiastical History*, vol. 25, pp. 15–37.

Bumpus, John S. *A History of English Cathedral Music, 1549–1889.* 1908.

Fellowes, Edmund H. *English Cathedral Music.* Rev. ed., 1969.

Foster, Myles B. *Anthems and Anthem Composers.* 1901.

Gatens, William J. *Victorian Cathedral Music in Theory and Practice.* 1986.

Jebb, John, *The Choral Service.* 1843.

———. *Three Lectures on the Cathedral Service.* 2d ed., 1845.

Long, Kenneth R. *The Music of the English Church.* 1972.

Rainbow, Bernarr. *The Choral Revival in the Anglican Church 1839–1872.* 1970.

. . . . .

CATHOLIC CHURCH see ROMAN CATHOLIC CHURCH

. . . . .

CATHOLIC EMANCIPATION (1829)

Ireland entered the United Kingdom in 1801 with its large **Roman Catholic** majority excluded from first-class citizenship. Although some Catholics could vote, none could hold office or sit in Parliament. Representing the anti-Catholic essence of British nativism, the Lords and the monarchy resisted efforts to lift Catholic disabilities. In 1829 **Daniel O'Connell** directed an agitation that forced the government to emancipate Catholics.

O'Connell in 1823 took the lead in establishing the Catholic Association. Two years later he opened it to popular participation, enlisting priests as local recruiters and lieutenants. In 1826 they marched forty-shilling freeholders to the polls to vote for proemancipation parliamentary candidates, striking a blow at the landlord nucleus of Protestant ascendancy and British domination. Although he was religiously ineligible, O'Connell was voted to a seat in the Commons by Clare electors in 1828, forcing the prime minister, the duke of **Wellington**, and the home secretary, **Robert Peel**, to choose reform over potential revolution. They heeded O'Connell's warning that if the government did not surrender to constitutional agitation, his followers might resort to physical force.

The Catholic Relief Act was the first significant victory for liberalism in Metternich's Europe. And it advanced the causes of democracy and civil rights in the United Kingdom. The Catholic Association was a model for nineteenth-century British reform movements and for Irish political machines everywhere. As O'Connell intended, the agitation for Catholic emancipation launched modern **Irish nationalism**.

LAWRENCE J. McCAFFREY

Bibliography

Machin, G. I. T. *The Catholic Question in English Politics, 1820-1830*. 1964.

O'Faolain, Sean. *King of the Beggars*. 1938.

O'Ferrall, Fergus. *Catholic Emancipation*. 1985.

Reynolds, James A. *The Catholic Emancipation Crisis in Ireland, 1823-1829*. 1954.

. . . . .

CELTIC REVIVAL

In Victorian Ireland studies of Celtic literature, language, and antiquities became associated with cultural nationalism. Patriots and artists looked to pre-Norman Celtic Ireland and to contemporary Gaelic society for themes and symbols of Irishness.

The most significant accomplishments of the revival were literary. Eugene O'Curry (1796?-1862) and John O'Donovan (1809-1861) translated and edited scholarly versions of ancient Irish manuscripts, but it was not until Standish O'Grady's publication of *History of Ireland: The Heroic Period* (1878), a lively retelling of ancient legends in English, that the early literature was made accessible to nonscholars. Douglas Hyde's (1860-1949) translations of contemporary Gaelic folklore, stories, and poems, published in the 1890s, revealed the wealth of Gaelic oral lore still extant in Ireland. These works sparked the Irish literary renaissance: the creation of a new **Irish literature** written in English but using themes, topics, and characters from Irish legend and folklore. The most brilliant writer of the renaissance was poet **William Butler Yeats**.

Preservation of Celtic languages was another aspect of the revival. Decimation of native speakers by famine, emigration, and compulsory education in English alarmed those who felt that a nation was defined by its language. Hyde and others founded the Gaelic League in 1893 to promote use of the Irish language. Similar movements existed in Scotland; in Wales, the health of the language was indicated by an abundance of Welsh newspapers, periodicals, and books. The advocacy of **Home Rule** legislation in the English Parliament by Ireland, Scotland, and Wales at the end of the century was a political manifestation of the sense of cultural nationalism shared by these Celtic countries.

In the decorative arts, collections of magnificently crafted gold and silver work and illuminated manuscripts from the early Christian period popularized the use of Celtic ornament, characterized by elaborate interlace, filigree, zoomorphs, and flowing curvilinear design. The harp, shamrock, Irish wolfhound, round tower, and the female figure of Ireland became ubiquitous emblems of Irishness. Artists were prompted by Thomas Davis, leader of **Young Ireland**, to paint subjects from Irish history and legend as a means of raising a national consciousness; Daniel Maclise's *The Marriage of Strongbow and Eva* (1854) shows a strong nationalist sentiment.

NANCY MADDEN WALCZYK

Bibliography

Fallis, Richard. *The Irish Renaissance*. 1977.

Sheehy, Jeanne. *The Rediscovery of Ireland's Past: The Celtic Revival, 1830-1930*. 1980.

See also DUBLIN; GAELIC CULTURE; IRISH NATIONALISM; WALES AND WELSH NATIONALISM

. . . . .

CEMETERIES

As Britain became increasingly urbanized, the traditional place of burial—the parish churchyard—was no longer adequate, especially in densely populated city parishes. Even in the seventeenth century, central London churchyards were so crowded that repeated burials were made in the same grave; sometimes the uppermost would be only inches below the surface. Some parishes established separate burial grounds at the edge of the built-up area, but by the nineteenth century the city had expanded to surround these sites as well. Private speculators opened burial grounds and turned death into a profitable trade. Sometimes undertakers dressed as ministers conducted bogus funerals; bodies might be stolen after burial; coffins were reused. In

1824 the *Penny Magazine* began a campaign to establish public cemeteries, and by the early Victorian years sanitary reformers were urging that all city churchyards be closed and cleared.

In 1842 a Parliamentary Select Committee on the Health of Towns recommended that no further burials take place in urban churches or churchyards except in family vaults or in Westminster Abbey. Kesnal Green, the first large commercial cemetery built outside London's residential suburbs, opened in 1833 with 39 acres of ground consecrated by the Bishop of London and a further 15 acres reserved for Dissenters. Brompton Cemetery, originally also a private venture, was bought by the General Board of Health in 1852 and became the first major public cemetery. The largest cemetery to be created was Brookwood, in Surrey, about 30 miles from London, where thousands of bodies from London churchyards were reinterred. Other major cemeteries opened during the Victorian period include Norwood (1837) Highgate (1839), and the Jews' Cemetery in Willesden (1873).

The impressive design of the new cemeteries made them pleasant sites for afternoon excursions—and the grand monuments erected by Victorians freed from the restrictions imposed by parish churchyards gave visitors something to look at. The Ralli family's Doric mortuary chapel at Norwood represents a Greek temple; Richard Burton's tomb at Mortlake is in the form of an Arab tent; and the Beer mausoleum at Highgate was based on the tomb of Mausolus at Halicarnassus. Both monuments and inscriptions offered free reign to sentimentality. At St. Pancras and Islington, a large dog (paid for by public subscription) guards the grave of William French, who, as the inscription reports, "lost his life on July 13th 1896 while saving a dog from drowning." Highgate Cemetery, with its splendid views over London, was a popular tourist attraction. Among those buried at Highgate are Michael Faraday, Ellen Price Wood, Christina Rossetti, Herbert Spencer, George Eliot, and Karl Marx.

DAVID E. ANSELL

Bibliography

Curl, James Stevens. *The Victorian Celebration of Death*. 1972.

Meller, Hugh. *London Cemeteries: An Illustrated Guide and Gazetteer*. 1981.

See also DEATH AND FUNERALS

· · · · ·

CHADWICK, EDWIN (1800–1890)

Edwin Chadwick's belief that central government should administer the country's social services was not accepted by most of his contemporaries. His work as secretary of the Poor Law Commission (1834–1842) and commissioner for the Board of Health (1848–1854) was impaired by his inability to compromise with other views or see the limitations of his own theories. But his reports, particularly the *Report on the Sanitary Condition of the Labouring Population* (1842), were so thoroughly researched that they generated public enthusiasm for reform and profoundly affected social legislation, especially the **Poor Law** of 1834 and the **Public Health** Act of 1848, but also the Factory Act of 1833 and the Police Act of 1839. He was knighted in 1889.

Trained as a barrister, Chadwick turned to journalism, wrote for the *Westminster Review*, and was subeditor of the *Examiner*. His article on life insurance brought him to the notice of Jeremy Bentham, whose utilitarian ideas he tried to put into practice during his government service. Chadwick also admired French centralized government and the theories of laissez-faire economist David Ricardo. Zealous work left him little time for personal life, but he did marry Rachel Kennedy when he was thirty-nine. They had two children, Osbert and Marion.

Chadwick was the chief architect of the New Poor Law. It abolished "outdoor relief"—the widespread practice of supplementing wages out of the parish rates, based on the Speenhamland system that linked subsidies to the price of bread. Under the New Poor Law (at least in theory), people would have to be so poor that they were willing to live in the intentionally uncomfortable workhouse if they wanted to get any help at all. The poor would therefore be more industrious in order to stay outside, and employers would have to pay a living wage. However, unemployment kept wages low and local magnates resented the Poor Law Commission's intrusion. Bitter opposition led to compromise, ignoring of inspectors' reports, and Chadwick's removal from secretarial duties.

Deflected onto sanitation, he reported so comprehensively on foul living conditions that he became a commissioner on the first General Board of Health in 1848. His promotion of centrally administered pure water supplies, interconnecting systems of drains, and cemeteries outside cities united many London interests against him. He was forced to resign in 1854. Progress was piecemeal until surveys done by John Simon in the 1860s and improvement in Birmingham showed the benefits of unified systems.

Chadwick continued writing on education and civil service reform. Irascible and autocratic, he had made enemies. Events proved some of his enthusiasms misplaced—the use of sewage as fertilizer, the miasmatic theory of infection. But central administration, adapted to the British preference for cooperation among semiautonomous bodies, now used his mechanisms of independent inspection (first employed in the Factory Act of 1833), annual reports, and auditing to insure the proper functioning of government.

SIDNEY JOHNSON

Bibliography

Chadwick, Edwin C. *The Health of Nations*. 1887.

Finer, Samuel E. *The Life and Times of Sir Edwin Chadwick*. 1952.

Percival, Janet, comp. *The Papers of Sir Edwin Chadwick: A Handlist*. 1978.

Watson, Peter. *Edwin Chadwick, Poor Law, and Public Health*. 1969.

· · · · ·

CHAMBERLAIN, JOSEPH (1836–1914)

Joseph Chamberlain, perhaps the most important Victorian statesman who never became prime minister, was born in London the son of a master shoemaker with Unitarian religious views. At the age of eighteen he was sent to Birmingham to represent his father's interests in a screw manufacturing firm. Retiring with a comfortable income after twenty successful years in business, Chamberlain turned his attention to social engineering. By 1873 he had been elected mayor of Birmingham, and was reelected in 1874 and 1875.

While mayor of Birmingham, Chamberlain established a reputation as a radical; he endeavored in particular to improve housing conditions and public education. In 1876 he entered Parliament as Liberal member from Birmingham and in 1880 was invited by Prime Minister **W. E. Gladstone** to serve in the cabinet as president of the Board of Trade. Although Chamberlain held radical views on social reform, he was a traditionalist on questions of empire. When Gladstone introduced an Irish **Home Rule** plan in 1886, Chamberlain resigned from the cabinet rather than support the government's policy. He then founded the National Liberal Federation, which he hoped would become a national party.

In 1895 the marquis of **Salisbury** invited Chamberlain and his followers to participate in a Conservative ministry. Chamberlain, who could have named practically any cabinet position for himself, chose the Colonial Office. He maintained two objectives: cementing ties between Great Britain and the colonies, and increasing trade within the empire. Scholars have debated Chamberlain's role in fomenting the Anglo-Boer war of 1899–1902. Antiwar critics such as Lloyd George characterized it as "Joe's war."

Following the war, Chamberlain resigned from the Conservative government over the question of tariff barriers for members of the empire. He spent the remainder of his public life campaigning for his plan of "imperial preference," designed to create a commercial union to solidify the empire.

NEWELL D. BOYD

Bibliography

Amery, Julius and James L. Garvin. *The Life of Joseph Chamberlain*. 1932–1969. 6 vols.

Fraser, Peter. *Joseph Chamberlain: Radicalism and Empire, 1868–1914*. 1966.

Jay, Richard. *Joseph Chamberlain: A Political Study.* 1981.

See also BOER WAR; SOUTH AFRICA

· · · · ·

CHAMBERS, ROBERT (1802–1871)

Scottish publisher, antiquarian, biographer, historian, and amateur scientist, Robert Chambers was author of the controversial *Vestiges of the Natural History of Creation* (1844), which played a major role in introducing the British reading public to the concept of **evolution**. Chambers left school at sixteen to set up a small bookstall in Edinburgh. With his brother William (1800–1883), he founded the publishing firm W. and R. Chambers. *Chambers's Edinburgh Journal,* a lively potpourri of science, literature, history, and self-help, first appeared in 1832 and sold 20,000 copies on the first day. A series of immensely popular serial publications followed. The Chambers brothers made cheap journalism respectable and claimed to offer everything requisite for the education of the shopkeeper or artisan who aspired to self-improvement.

During the 1830s Chambers began to study **geology** and espoused the would-be scientific psychology of **phrenology**. *Vestiges*, which was published anonymously, went through four editions in six months, and ten in a decade. Speculation on its author's identity was rampant: William Thackeray, Charles Lyell, phrenologist George Combe, and even Prince Albert were targeted by the press.

In the 1850s Chambers came to believe in **spiritualism**, but this caused no conflict with his continuing scientific enthusiasms. His final work, *The Book of Days* (2 vols., 1862–1864), a miscellany of popular antiquities in connection with the calendar, remains a standard work on reference shelves.

Chambers's role as a synthesizer and popularizer of broad realms of knowledge is reflected in the *Vestiges* as well as in his publishing ventures. Although the book is often called a precursor of Charles Darwin's *The Origin of Species* (1859), Chambers's theorizing has more in common with the system-making monism of Auguste Comte or Herbert Spencer. In his useful *Explanations* (1845), Chambers explained that his object was not to establish a theory of life's origin, but rather to show that all creation—the solar system, the natural world, and mind and morals—is equally subject to universal laws, ordained by a rational Creator whose plan is linear evolutionary progress. Much of Chambers's argument is harmonious with eighteenth-century deistic natural theology. Its originality lies in his conceptual unification of contemporary theories of astronomy, geology, natural history, and moral science. Religious believers were shocked by Chambers's materialism, scientists by his credulous employment of dubious theories of transmutation and spontaneous generation. But the general public found the book compelling. Liberated from the narrow horizons of the professional scientist, Chambers shaped a broad cosmology that resonated sympathetically with the Victorian frame of mind.

DIANA POSTLETHWAITE

Bibliography

Altick, Richard D. *The English Common Reader.* 1957.

Chambers, William. *Memoir of William and Robert Chambers.* 1872.

Glass, Bentley, *et al. Forerunners of Darwin: 1745–1859.* 1959.

Hodge, M. J. S. "The Universal Gestation of Nature: Chambers' *Vestiges* and *Explanations*." *Journal of the History of Biology*, vol. 5, pp. 127–152.

Millhauser, Milton. *Just Before Darwin: Robert Chambers and "Vestiges."* 1959.

Postlethwaite, Diana. *Making It Whole: A Victorian Circle and the Shape of Their World.* 1984.

Yeo, Richard. "Science and Intellectual Authority in Mid-Nineteenth-Century Britain: Robert Chambers and 'Vestiges of the Natural History of Creation.'" *Victorian Studies*, vol. 28, pp. 5–31.

· · · · ·

CHANCERY AND DOCTORS' COMMONS

Both Chancery and Doctors' Commons were civil courts with specialized functions which had survived from an earlier time and were, in the Victorian period, under heavy attack. Both ultimately fell victim to **law reforms** which were intended to abolish legal anachronisms and establish uniform standards and practices.

The Court of Chancery originated in the later Middle Ages as the administrator of equity, a system of jurisprudence designed to provide remedies where the common law failed to do so. Cases—largely concerning contracts, trusts, and disputes to which no specific body of law could be applied—were traditionally decided on principles that had their origin in conscience or the law of nature. In practice, the system became burdened by heavy reliance on precedents, and in Victorian Britain Chancery had acquired among the general public a reputation that illustrated popular dissatisfaction with the legal system as a whole. There were repeated complaints about the length and cost of the legal process.

Despite conservatism on procedural matters, however, Chancery still provided relief in creative ways to doctrinal problems beyond the scope of common law. In 1842 and 1852 the abolition of ancient offices helped streamline procedure and reduce the fees. The Common Law Procedure Act of 1854 eliminated many of the lengthy delays. In theory the Judicature Acts of 1873 and 1875 merged common law and equity, providing that where legal rules conflicted, the principles of equity should prevail. In fact, however, the two bodies of law did not synthesize, and they retained their separate identities until the end of the Victorian period.

Doctors' Commons was the College of Advocates, or doctors of civil law, who handled ecclesiastical and admiralty cases. Of primary importance was their monopoly of jurisdiction over matrimonial cases, which derived from the understanding that marriage was primarily a religious sacrament (rather than a civil contract). Complaints about the expense and length of legal proceedings and nepotism in court personnel abounded in the early Vic-

torian period. Doctors' Commons fell victim to demands for utility in legal affairs, and the Matrimonial Causes Act (1857) proved a fatal blow by removing its primary jurisdiction and creating divorce courts. Doctors' Commons dissolved in 1858, held its last meeting in 1865, and its last member died in 1912.

RICHARD A. COSGROVE

Bibliography

Holdsworth, William. *A History of English Law*, vols. 15, 16. 1965, 1966.

Squibb, G. D. *Doctor's Commons: A History of the College of Advocates and Doctors of Law.* 1977.

See also JUDICIAL SYSTEM

CHARTISM

Chartism is the name applied to a variety of protest movements in the 1830s and 1840s that collectively aimed at eliminating social and economic injustices through political reform. Chartism should thus be seen more as a political movement than as an economic or social phenomenon. Chartists were so named because they formulated their political demands in a six-point petition, or People's Charter, which they hoped would be made law, to benefit the laboring classes. The goals included: annual parliaments, universal manhood suffrage, the abolition of the property qualification for members of the House of Commons, a secret ballot, equal electoral districts, and salaries for members of Parliament. Chartism was the first independent working-class movement in the world and had a greater mass following than any other reform movement in the nineteenth century, save socialism toward the end of the century.

The immediate impetus for Chartism lay in political and social disappointments and in the economic hardships felt acutely by the working classes in the 1830s and 1840s. The Reform Bill of 1832, for which workingmen had agitated, denied them the vote. In the north, a struggle started by Richard Oastler (1789–1861) aimed at achieving a ten-hour workday. The Factory Act passed by the Whigs in 1833, however, reduced hours in textile factories, but only for children. Trade union activity and the failure of strikes turned some labor leaders toward Chartism; the New Poor Law of 1834 and the introduction of work-houses into manufacturing areas were bitterly resented and added fuel to the movement.

Chartism was also tied to the trade cycles between 1836 and 1851, and to bad harvests and high food prices. By 1837 business fail-ures put some 50,000 out of work in Manches-ter. The first peak of Chartist activity corres-ponded with the trade depression in 1839. In 1842 mass unemployment resulted in an-other burst of Chartist activity in northern towns. The last great expression of Chartism came in 1848 following a winter's recession and the revolutions in Europe. In periods of relative prosperity Chartism lost its mass sup-port.

The organizational roots of Chartism were primarily two. In Birmingham Thomas At-twood (1783-1856) revived the Birmingham Political Union, which called for a general strike for 1839. In London, William Lovett (1800-1877), a former cabinetmaker, and Henry Hetherington (1792-1849) founded the London Working Men's Association (LWMA) that drafted the charter and its six points in 1838 for presentation to the House of Commons. It was the fiery but erratic **Feargus O'Connor** (1794-1855) who more than anyone "nationalized" Chartism, and by force of his bombastic oratory and editorship of the Chartist paper the *Northern Star*, gave the movement some semblance of unity.

All over the country meetings were held to elect representatives to a giant convention to prepare a petition that would accompany the charter to Parliament. Some wanted to turn the convention into a permanent "anti-Parlia-ment" if Parliament rejected the People's Charter. Others called for a general strike (a "national holiday"); others like Bronterre O'Brien (1805-1864), George Julian Harney (1817-1897), and O'Connor hinted at physi-cal force. The charter was introduced to the House of Commons in July 1839, bearing 1,280,000 signatures. The House rejected it by a vote of 235 to 46, after which time the convention broke up in confusion.

The movement floundered for lack of direc-tion. The failure of the People's Charter was a blow to the more moderate moral force ele-ments. Meanwhile the so-called physical force men like Harney and O'Connor gained con-trol of the convention and moved it to Bir-mingham to be closer to the base of popular support. They proclaimed a general strike for August 1839, but many of the workers had no employer to strike against, and support was lukewarm. The strike was canceled and in September the convention was dissolved. That winter there were riots in various parts of the country, and some 500 Chartist leaders were arrested, including Lovett and O'Con-nor. In November there was a small uprising in Newport, Wales, in which a group of 100 armed men rebelled. It was quickly sup-pressed. The government's response to the sporadic disorders was to assign troops to var-ious points in northern England, but there were no serious clashes.

When the economy took a downward turn in 1841-1842 Chartism was revived. This time there was greater unity, with O'Connor firmly in charge. In May 1842 another petition bear-ing 3,300,000 names was presented to Parlia-ment, only to be rejected by 287 to 59. A number of strikes ensued, and many Chartist leaders went to jail. In the public mind Char-tism was associated with violence.

The last major expression of Chartism came in 1848, fueled by excitement from revolu-tions in Europe and by high unemployment at home. In March serious rioting occurred in Glasgow, then in other cities. Finally another convention met in London on April 4 to pre-sent a huge petition for the charter. This one was said to contain five million names. In the face of what seemed like a serious threat to public order, if not revolution, the govern-ment massed considerable force in London, including some 200,000 citizens who volun-teered as special constables. The demonstra-tion was peaceful, but Parliament rejected the latest charter. Although the specter of Chart-ism remained, in substance the movement was dead, and nothing came of another con-vention that was summoned for April 1851.

Chartism had its greatest appeal to the rem-nants of the older decaying domestic and handicraft skills. The handloom weavers in Lancashire and Yorkshire, the nail makers in the Black Country near Birmingham, frame-work knitters in the Midlands, and miners in northern England and Wales were more the victims than the beneficiaries of the industrial revolution. It was strongest in the outworking villages and 'in medium-sized industrial towns like Bolton, Bradford, and Stockport. There wages had sunk to nearly starvation levels. In areas like Lancashire and the West Riding of Yorkshire Chartists were more militant and more attracted to physical force.

Chartism was also important in London, Birmingham, and Leeds, where there were large numbers of artisans following preindustrial skills like shoemaking, printing, cabinet-making, coachbuilding, and tailoring. In Leeds and Sheffield in the 1840s Chartists elected their own candidates to local offices, and their concern reflected the interests of the lower middle-class tradesmen from whose ranks they came. In Scotland, where the New Poor Law did not apply, and where some of the most underpaid jobs were filled by the Irish, moral force Chartism prevailed; in addition, the metallurgical industries had experienced a boom which helped the Scottish economy.

The Chartist movement was weak or nonexistent in rural villages and market towns, and in some of the newer small industrial towns like Crewe, Glossop, and St. Helens. They had benefited from rudimentary urban planning and were more modern, less crowded, and without the hordes of outworking weavers and framework knitters. Many trade unionists, machine makers, and new craftsmen avoided Chartism. In this sense Chartism was weaker in certain forms of modern industry.

Although there was no single Chartist doctrine of class, Chartism was intensely class conscious, and it was in these years that the terms "working class" or "middle class"—used frequently in the singular—denoted a sharper class identity. To Chartists, it was both the middle classes and the aristocracy who were seen as the enemies of the common people. The working-class identity of Chartism was so strong that attempts to ally it with middle-class radicals and with the Anti-Corn-Law League failed.

Chartism was weakened because it did not attract upper-class support and because it could not solidify its own ranks. It was not a national movement with its headquarters in London, but rather a mosaic of local and regional movements reflecting diverse experiences, traditions, and personalities, as recent scholarship has tended to underline.

If Chartism failed by 1848, it still had two profound results. First, it created an atmosphere favorable to reform. Within three-quarters of a century all but one of the six points of the charter had been enacted into law: the exception was annual parliaments. The working-class men who won the vote and the secret ballot in 1867, 1872, and 1884 owed much to Chartism. A more enlightened social policy and a retreat from laissez faire resulted in grants to education, a ten-hour day, the Public Health Act, and more generous Poor Law practices.

Another important effect was that Chartism fostered a political consciousness among the working classes and helped train them to participate in public life. By giving a direction and even some discipline to working-class protests, Chartist meetings could be seen as a safety valve for discontents that might have erupted in random violence and property destruction. The charter thus helped concentrate discontents toward common goals, while maintaining a relatively high degree of public order.

Chartism left traditions that influenced later British **socialism**, although it could not be considered a socialist organization. It was, as Thomas Carlyle put it, a "knife-and-fork question," unconcerned with the dialectics of Marxian socialist philosophy. Its impact on the later **Labour party** must be considered indirect. Chartism is best viewed as a British phenomenon, a product of its time, rather than as a forerunner of British socialism.

PHILLIP THURMOND SMITH

Bibliography

Carlyle, Thomas. *Chartism.* 1839.

Briggs, Asa, ed. *Chartist Studies.* 1959.

Epstein, James, and Dorothy Thompson, eds. *The Chartist Experience. Studies in Working-Class Radicalism and Culture, 1830–1860.* 1982.

Gammage, R. G. *History of the Chartist Movement.* 1854.

Hovell, Mark. *The Chartist Movement.* 1918.

Jones, D. *Chartism and the Chartists.* 1975.

Jones, Gareth Stedman. "Rethinking Chartism." In *Language of Class. Studies in English Working Class History, 1832–1982.* 1983.

Mather, F. C. *Chartism*. 1968.

Saville, John. *Ernest Jones: Chartist*. 1952.

Schoyen, A. R. *The Chartist Challenge: A Portrait of George Julian Harney*. 1958.

Thompson, Dorothy. *The Chartists. Popular Politics in the Industrial Revolution*. 1984.

Ward, J. T. *Chartism*. 1973.

See also COOPER, THOMAS; PLACE, FRANCIS; RIOTS AND DEMONSTRATIONS; STRIKES

• • • • •

CHEMISTRY

In the early nineteenth century, Britain made important contributions to chemistry through the work of men such as John Dalton, Humphry Davy, and **Michael Faraday**. But this achievement was not maintained, chiefly due to deficiencies in British chemical education. Instruction was available at medical schools, academies, universities (particularly in Scotland), and at mechanics' institutes, but research training was inadequate. The "decline of science" debate focused on chemistry.

Nevertheless, an emerging chemical profession was marked by the establishment of the Chemical Society (1841), the Pharmaceutical Society (1841), the School of Pharmacy (1842), the Royal College of Chemistry (1845), the (Royal) Institute of Chemistry (1877), and the societies of Scientific Industry (1874), Public Analysts (1874), and Chemical Industry (1881). Journals were established: *The Chemist* (1840-1858); *Journal of the Chemical Society* (1841-); *Chemical Gazette* (1842/3-1859); *Chemical News* (1859-1932); *The Analyst* (1876-); and the *Journal of the Society of Chemical Industry* (1882-). Chemistry was taught in the new universities; it entered the honors curriculum at Oxford (1850) and Cambridge (1851); it was taught in evening classes examined by the Department of Science and Arts with "payment by results" (1859-1897); and it was increasingly taught in secondary schools during the second half of the nineteenth century. Technological chemistry was examined by the Society of Arts (1873) and City and Guilds (1879). Notable teachers

were the German, A. W. Hofmann (Royal College); H. E. Roscoe (Manchester); and H. E. Armstrong (Central Technical College, London). However, much chemical instruction was theoretical or through lecture demonstrations. Practical work was chiefly restricted to inorganic analysis.

In theoretical chemistry, the chief contributions were in atomic theory and chemical combination (valency theory). To obtain atomic weights certain formulae must be known. Dalton had made some "educated guesses," but these were mostly mistaken. The Swedish chemist J. J. Berzelius had more success, but a valid method for determining simple formulae, and hence atomic weights, was only published by the Italian chemist S. Cannizzaro in 1858. Nevertheless, even before 1858, chemists calculated formulae and perceived patterns, despite some systematic errors. Certain groups of atoms (radicals) recurred in different compounds and could be substituted one for another; and according to a "theory of types" of J. B. Dumas and others (from 1839) there were certain chemical "types" with regularities of composition that displayed analogous properties. It became recognized that "radicals" could be substituted in types.

In 1852 E. Frankland of Owens College, Manchester (and later Hofmann's successor at the Royal College) referred to certain formulae (some erroneous) which suggested that each element had a particular "combining power" for atoms of other elements. In the theory of types and Frankland's suggestions lay the beginnings of valency theory.

The idea of the linking of carbon atoms in different combinations came to the German chemist F. A. Kekulé in 1854, while working in London. On returning to Germany, he proposed the idea of a "marsh-gas type," and eventually the notion of quadrivalent carbon. Independently, A. Scott Couper of Edinburgh announced the linking of carbon atoms (1858) and used dotted lines to represent valency bonds. Edinburgh professor A. Crum Brown wrote structural formulae with dotted lines for bonds (1861) and published several graphic formulae, including double bonds (1864). In 1865 Hofmann lectured using "ball-and-stick" models. In 1866 Frankland used Crum Brown's graphic formulae in lectures at the Royal School of Mines. Some chemists still thought the new formulae were unreliable and eschewed the atomic theory. Oxford professor B. C. Brodie offered a positivistic chemistry based on volume and weight relationships and symbolized chemical operations. However, the atomic theory, allowing an easier comprehension of phenomena, found general favor.

After Cannizzaro, correct atomic weight tables became available and chemists looked for patterns therein. Paralleling the investigations of the Russian D. R. Mendeléef, J. H. R. Newlands, chemist to the Royal Agricultural Society, noted (1865) a recurrence of properties at every eighth element (arranged in ascending atomic weight order) which he called the "Law of Octaves." A rudimentary periodic table was prepared by A. W. Williamson (1864) and a considerable advance on this by W. Odling (1865).

W. Crookes, student of Hofmann, independent London chemist and editor of *Chemical News*, investigated atomic spectra, discovering the spectrum of a new element, thallium (1861). Following Faraday, he also studied the passage of electricity through gases at low pressures, investigating cathode rays (1879), which he regarded as a "fourth state of matter." At the Cavendish Laboratory, Cambridge, J. J. Thomson interpreted cathode rays as negatively charged electrified particles, which could be deflected both magnetically and electrically, thus making possible the determination of their charge/mass ratio (1897). The particles were termed electrons, and finding them emitted from diverse substances, he regarded them as a common constituent of all atoms. In 1904 he pictured the atom as a ring of electrons in a sphere of positive electricity. He calculated that for atoms with many electrons these would be arranged in concentric rings, and he suggested relationships between these geometrical relationships and chemical valencies.

In 1892 W. Ramsay, Williamson's successor at University College, noticed density differences between chemically prepared nitrogen and that extracted from air. Collaborating with Lord Rayleigh, his work led to recognition of the inert gases of the atmosphere: argon's characteristic blue spectral line was announced in 1894. (N. Lockyer had noticed the spectrum of the inert gas helium from sunlight in 1868). The discovery of a group of inert elements of zero valency helped complete the periodic table and contributed to subsequent theories of atomic structure and valency.

Advances in chemistry led to innovations in industry, especially those based on coal and salt. Coal gas was used for lighting and coal tar provided the raw material for many dyestuffs. Cheshire salt deposits formed the basis of soda, caustic soda, chlorine, and bleaching powder manufacture. Old chemical processing methods, like the Leblanc soda process, were chemically inefficient, and grievously harmful to the environment and to workers' health. Disputes occurred between manufacturers and adjacent landowners, and from the 1860s efforts were made to control manufacturers' activities. Factory inspectors were appointed and prosecutions undertaken, but environmental problems were not fully overcome. The Leblanc process, however, succumbed to the technically superior Solvay process, introduced to Britain by the German chemist L. Mond who, with J. Brunner, began manufacture near Northwich in 1874. Thus "craft" chemical technology could not compete with the more scientifically based chemical industry.

Nineteenth-century advances in chemistry had their greatest industrial effect on dyestuffs used in the textile industry. The first coal tar dye, "aniline purple," was patented by Hofmann's student W. H. Perkin (1856). Hofmann showed how to prepare aniline and other materials needed for coal tar dyes from the benzene in coal tar. But after his move to Berlin (1856) British research was overtaken by German investigations, which yielded profits chiefly to German industry.

In the Victorian period, most British chemists of distinction received training in Germany. Industry lacked scientifically trained personnel, and its practices were inferior, both technically and socially, to those observed on the Continent. Reform of technical education was urged, particularly by L. Playfair of Edinburgh University and subsequently the Royal School of Mines, and improvements were made from the 1870s. Nevertheless, the long-term effects of laissez faire in education were adverse, and Britain's twentieth-century trade and power suffered accordingly.

DAVID OLDROYD

Bibliography

Bud, Robert and Gerrylynn K. Roberts. *Science Versus Practice: Chemistry in Victorian Britain.* 1984.

Haber, Ludwig F. *The Chemical Industry During the Nineteenth Century.* 1958.

Partington, James R. *The History of Chemistry*, vol. 4. 1964.

Russell, Colin A. et al. *Chemists by Profession: The Origins and Rise of the Royal Institute of Chemistry.* 1977.

. . . . .

CHILD LABOR

Children have always had a place in the employment pattern of British society, most noticeably in the domestic and agricultural spheres. The particular features that characterized Victorian child labor were the vast numbers involved, the poor working conditions, and the predominance of factory employment. Large numbers of children were still utilized on the land, either working as part of a family group or hired out. Rural girls might opt for domestic service because of the rough character of **agricultural labor** or might be more or less forced into domestic work, either to retain farming jobs for boys or to bolster the inadequate income that the family, as a whole, derived from agricultural labor.

The burgeoning of child employment stemmed from industrial and economic considerations. Children were ideally suited to particular industrial processes; with little ability to resist they could be made to work long hours, and their small stature allowed them access to regions of machinery too tiny to admit adults. Children were cheap to employ and their numbers seemed, for a time, limitless, particularly with the large supplies of orphaned or pauper children available from parish guardians. In addition, the rising middle classes demanded more children (and adults) as domestic **servants** to emphasize their growing wealth as feminine leisure came to be the hallmark of middle-class Victorian and Edwardian society.

Many personal accounts of Victorian childhood describe an idyllic existence for the working child, in both rural and urban settings. Such biographies usually stress a close, caring, family unit or an unusually sympathetic employer. However, the consensus is that conditions generally for the working-class child were, at best, poor.

The industrial revolution produced a vast range of new processes, notably in the textile trade. Steam-powered mills working around the clock came to be the dominant feature of the landscape of the north of England, particularly in Lancashire and Yorkshire. Within these mills children as young as four years worked shifts of twelve hours or longer beside their parents, as employees in their own right, or as subcontracted labor to overseers. Work might be initially restricted to cleaning in the environs of working looms until the child's strength and dexterity allowed promotion to the manufacturing process. Pay commenced at two to three shillings a week and accidents, mutilations, industrial disease, and death were commonplace. Further, a child would endure beatings and pay deductions for inattentiveness. By the end of a shift or during a weekend break (Saturday afternoon and all day Sunday), children generally had only enough strength and motivation to eat meals of bread and beef "dripping." Play and attention to personal hygiene came within the realm of luxury, adding to the debilitating effect of work. Child laborers who survived to adulthood often carried the scars of their early exploitation. (In towns like Oldham and Rochdale during the 1960s and 1970s significant numbers of old people with crooked legs or humped backs and generally short stature could still be seen. The hospitals treated lung disease acquired in poorly ventilated mills, long-term skin diseases, and the cancers induced by industrial pollutants.)

The Lancashire mills, from 1830 onwards, employed some 30,000 children a year. Children employed in the **mining** industry suffered even greater degradation. Work might be above ground—sorting coal, for example—or below ground—either assisting at the coal face or dragging wagons full of coal. The tasks were dangerous, mine safety was a low priority, and the heat induced workers to discard clothing, thus opening the way to illicit sexual activity. Work space was restricted and the labyrinthine nature of mining operations could result in children being lost for days at a time in total darkness.

In London the pattern of child employment was somewhat different in that many occupations were relatively free of mechanization. Nevertheless, the same general conditions prevailed: long hours, meager pay, few breaks, monotonous tasks, injury, and abuse. Girls were particularly exploited in the clothing and furniture trades. The most noticeable child occupation, however, was that of street hawker. In London at least 10,000 children worked the streets, providing all manner of goods and services. Crossing sweepers and the "little match girl" provided a sentimental photographic image for many more fortunate Victorian households. A street existence was precarious. Relative security could be achieved by being apprenticed, for example, as a chimney sweep's boy; but again conditions were harsh and unhealthy.

As the century advanced the demand for boys, in preference to adults, became striking, as they provided a cheaper (and healthier) workforce. Adults sacked to make way for the boys resented the fact, but in their turn the young boys would become dispensable adults.

Children also worked as prostitutes. Both sexes became involved, often to help out a hard-pressed family, and parents might openly condone involvement. Young girls were highly prized and not all were unwilling partners; some locked up or sedated the younger siblings entrusted to their care when parents went to work in order to solicit on the streets.

Domestic service was another large provider of work, especially for girls. The 1851 census indicated one million women and girls in service. About a tenth of these were children, and 500—employed as "nurses"—were between the ages of five and nine. Girls in domestic service were more isolated than factory workers: they were often virtual prisoners, with little recreational time and only a short annual vacation. Conditions varied but were often harsh. A dismissal for "poor work" was frequently masked punishment for a child's refusal to participate in illicit sexual activity.

Reformers in the child labor field appeared early, and by midcentury a growing body of opinion was instrumental in paving the way for a series of acts of Parliament that regulated or curtailed child labor practices. John

Fielden pamphleteered by calling child labor "The Curse of the Factory System"; women novelists such as **Frances Trollope** used the emotional power of fiction to bring children's sufferings to the attention of middle-class readers; Richard Oastler adopted antislavery tactics; Lord **Shaftesbury** attacked conditions in mines; and **Henry Mayhew**'s accounts of London's poor drew attention to the child **street traders**. The legislation was profuse and was sometimes concealed within instruments of broader legal range, but its effectiveness was tempered by economic considerations. Families that depended on children's wages, as well as employers who benefited from cheap labor, found ways to circumvent legislation. In the long run, it was not the legal moves against industry that provided the major instrument of reform but rather efforts to improve the educational standard of the workforce.

Although educational provision had been a feature of the workhouse, and **Sunday schools**—intended to educate working children on their one free day—proliferated during the century, W. E. Forster's Education Act (1870) made the first great move toward compulsory education and the exemption of children from paid employment. Still, parents might keep children away from school—at harvest time, for example—and as late as the 1920s rural schools arranged summer vacations to coincide with harvest.

W. JOHN SMITH

Bibliography

Burnett, John, ed. *Destiny Obscure: Autobiographies of Childhood. Education and Family from the 1820s to the 1920s.* 1982.

Lewis, Jane, ed. *Labour and Love: Women's Experience of Home and Family, 1850–1940.* 1986.

Simeral, Isabel. *Reform Movements in Behalf of Children in England of the Early Nineteenth Century.* 1916.

Walvin, James. *A Child's World: A Social History of English Childhood, 1800–1914.* 1982.

See also DOMESTIC INDUSTRY; FACTORY ACTS; JUVENILE CRIME; MINING AND MINERS

· · · · ·

CHILD SAVING

Prior to the advent of social welfare legislation, efforts to help unfortunate children (both in the workplace and on the street) were undertaken by individuals and organizations. During the Victorian era members of the leisured classes developed increased social awareness of the conditions in which children lived and worked. Lord **Shaftesbury** (1801–1885), who best personifies the Victorian child saver, narrowed his earlier varied philanthropies to concentrate on children. Homeless, jobless vagrants and the children of the chronically poor were seen as the crucial challenge. The first goal was to remove such children from the streets before they became irremediably sick or criminal. Shaftesbury, **Thomas Barnardo**, **Mary Carpenter**, and others promoted "**ragged schools**" where (lured by the promise of food and shelter) the "street arabs" were given instruction in reading, writing, and religion. Carpenter also proposed industrial schools which offered the foundations of a trade; others supported Barnardo's efforts to provide homes for orphans.

The unique feature of the Victorian period, however, was the unanimity of child savers in promoting the **emigration** of destitute children to Greater Britain overseas. State-aided emigration, it was argued, was the only practical remedy for the problem of vagrant youth. The mid-to-late Victorian social reformers were persuaded by the prevailing psychology that the abject poverty and evil habits of the "dangerous classes" were not inheritable traits (as had been previously believed) but were products of environment. This philosophical change stimulated reformers to improve the quality of living for the poor and particularly favored the idea of transplanting to the colonies those who were yet young enough to be dramatically improved by a new environment.

In practice, evangelical and imperialistic impulses mixed equally with social theory. The earliest attempt to place children in employment overseas was made by Edward Brenton's Children's Friend Society, which settled 300 boys and girls in the Cape of Good Hope (1830–1834) where, critics charged, they replaced laborers that had been lost when slavery was abolished. Beginning in the early 1850s, the Philanthropic Society's reform school sent formerly delinquent youths to the colonies and also to the United States. **Maria Rye**, Annie Macpherson, Thomas Barnardo, Kingsley Fairbridge, the **Salvation Army**, and both Catholic and Protestant churches were prominent in the work.

Between 1869, when group emigration of children on a large scale was begun in earnest by Maria Rye, and 1948, when the movement was legislatively discontinued, over 100,000 children were sent abroad. Criticized as indenture (as indeed it often was in the early days) and plagued by abuse, child saving through emigration must yet be weighed against the idealistic motives of its proponents and the life-threatening conditions under which children lived in English slums.

TREVOR J. PHILLIPS

Bibliography

Battiscombe, Georgina. *Shaftesbury: The Great Reformer.* 1975.

Bradlow, Edna. "The Children's Friend Society at the Cape of Good Hope." *Victorian Studies.* vol. 27, pp. 155–179.

Heasman, Kathleen. *Evangelicals in Action.* 1962.

Parr, Joy. *Labouring Children: British Immigrant Apprentices to Canada, 1869–1924.* 1980.

Pinchbeck, Ivy and Margaret Hewitt. *Children in English Society.* 1973.

· · · · ·

CHILDBIRTH

At the beginning of the nineteenth century, childbirth was a female-focused, decentralized, home-based event. By the end of the century it had become a male-controlled, centralized, scientific, professionalized social act. This shift changed childbearing from a socioeconomic physical function to a cultural construct which both shaped and was shaped by the nineteenth-century idealization of woman.

As late as 1800 most childbirths still occurred at home and were assisted by self-trained female **midwives** (often inaccurately characterized even in modern accounts as "ignorant" because they were denied the opportunity for the formal training male midwives received). The first lying-in hospital in Great Britain was established at Edinburgh in 1736, but by 1800 there were still only eight in England. These were primarily teaching clinics serving the poor. At the beginning of the nineteenth century, the mortality rate for London home births was 0.2 percent and for hospital births 2.9 percent; but by the 1840s hospital mortality rates averaged 12–26 percent. The most common cause of death in lying-in hospitals was puerperal fever. Nevertheless, hospital births increased throughout the century.

Three major factors influenced the nineteenth-century medicalization of childbirth: instrumentation, medicines, and lying-in hospitals. The world's single most important obstetrical instrument, the forceps, were invented by the Chamberlen family around 1616, were selectively available to medical men (but not to midwives) by 1726, and came into widespread use around 1800. The speculum, known since the early Christian era, came into common use at the beginning of the nineteenth century in a form developed by French midwife Anne Boivin. In 1832 John Mackenzie devised rods to dilate the cervix manually; James Young Simpson (1811–1870), Britain's leading obstetrician and the popularizer of chloroform, in 1843 adapted the sound for uterine examination; and in 1846 Joseph Recamier redesigned the curette for evacuating the womb. Such instruments instituted an intervention model, requiring special training and equipment, which came to form the ideal of childbearing for the middle class, whose access to social status through money led to the choice of a medical doctor with an array of equipment rather than the traditional midwife, whose skilled hands and knowledge of natural processes were her main tools.

The second factor in the medicalization of childbirth was chemical. Ether was first used in childbirth in America in 1842, but it was widely opposed on religious grounds, pain in childbirth having been divinely ordained and therefore necessary. Then in April 1853, Queen Victoria used chloroform, an ether substitute developed by Simpson in 1846, for the birth of her eighth child. Victoria's use of chloroform initiated an immediate public fervor in Britain for painless childbirth. The licensing of drug dispensing placed chloro-

form, ether, and other drugs (including the ergot and belladonna used by midwives for centuries) almost exclusively in physicians' hands.

The third factor in the medicalization of childbirth was a shift in its location. By 1900 more than half of all infants were born in **hospitals** and delivered by (usually male) doctors. As science gained in precision and status, it lent its authority to the men who controlled instruments, drugs, and hospitals and dealt a deathblow to the traditional model of female-centered childbirth.

The most prominent example of how childbirth became a social construct is the history of puerperal fever. Rare in earlier centuries and virtually unknown in midwife-assisted home births, puerperal fever became epidemic in Britain and on the Continent by the 1840s, as childbirth became a hospital function for middle-class women. In 1843 Oliver Wendell Holmes (1809–1894) first publicized the apparently contagious nature of the disease, and in 1846 Ignaz Semmelweis (1818–1865) discovered its etiology: that it was spread when doctors who had previously touched corpses or patients' decomposing tissues subsequently examined women who were giving birth. Physicians resisted Semmelweis's theory for years, refusing to believe that they could be carriers of infection. Although chlorine washing was known to be related to a decline in puerperal fever as early as 1822, Semmelweis had difficulty convincing his colleagues to use it even three decades later. In 1865 **Joseph Lister** (1786–1869) finally introduced carbolic acid to create an antiseptic context for childbirth, but it was not until 1879 that Louis Pasteur (1822–1895) isolated the organisms causing puerperal fever. In spite of high mortality rates and incontrovertible evidence, doctors sacrificed patients, the truth, and scientific progress in order to maintain the image of infallibility which gave them control over childbirth.

The medicalization of childbirth resulted in the definition of the nineteenth-century woman through her childbearing. Maternal "normality" became a medically defined term, and childbirth became pathological (i.e., an abnormal state in need of medical intervention). "Normal" childbirth required a short labor (hence more frequent need for forceps), and appropriate limitation of pain (enough to motivate the mother to expel the child rapidly, but not enough to cause the doctor serious trouble), and submission to medically advised practices (most readily accomplished in a hospital setting).

Because childbirth in the nineteenth century was as much a social as a medical construct, a number of nonmedical dicta about women borrowed the authority of medical support. Highly sexed or lustful women were thought to bear large numbers of children who would be abnormal or diseased. Puerperal fever was often blamed on the mother's poverty. The belief in Lamarck's theory of the inheritability of acquired characteristics controlled women's behavior by the threat of passing on "evil" to their children. Even the sex of the child was often seen as a result of the mother's behavior: "feminists" and other women of high vitality and decided opinions were believed to give birth largely to daughters, while appropriately feminine women were more likely to bear sons who would carry on the family line. In all these ways, the medical model of childbirth developed through the particular scientific advances pursued in the nineteenth century created and enforced a construct of woman that produced the Angel in the House.

LORALEE MACPIKE

Bibliography

Cutter, Irving S. and Henry Viets. *A Short History of Midwifery.* 1964.

Dally, Ann. *Inventing Motherhood: The Consequences of an Ideal.* 1982.

Donnison, Jean. *Midwives and Medical Men: A History of Inter-Professional Rivalries and Women's Rights.* 1977.

Flack, Isaac. *Eternal Eve: The History of Gynaecology and Obstetrics.* 1951.

MacPike, Loralee. *Childbirth as a Metaphor in the Nineteenth-Century Novel.* (Forthcoming.)

Oakley, Ann. *Women Confined: Towards a Sociology of Childbirth.* 1980.

Parry, Noel and José Parry. *The Rise of the Medical Profession.* 1976.

Shorter, Edward. *A History of Women's Bodies.* 1982.

Shryock, Richard Harrison. *The Development of Modern Medicine.* 1936.

See also ANESTHESIA

· · · · ·

CHILDHOOD

A mythology of childhood was central to Victorian attitudes. The Victorian adulation of childhood, however, is not easily described; it is characterized by the conflicting doctrines of original sin and original innocence, the competing ideologies of Rousseauists, evangelicals, and utilitarians, and the stark contrast between sentimental notions of childhood and the brute realities of industrialization and poverty.

The Victorian exaltation of childhood was rooted in eighteenth-century theology and philosophy. John Locke's *Essay Concerning Human Understanding* (1689), with its emphasis upon reason and its suggestion that the mind of a newborn is a tabula rasa, did much to promote new interest in educating children and to counter the Puritan emphasis on original sin. His immediate followers, the rational moralists, urged rigorous training to quicken the child's reasoning abilities. From this group evolved nineteenth-century utilitarians, guided by Jeremy Bentham (1748–1832) and James Mill (1773–1836). Utilitarians subjected children to an exacting curriculum of natural science, political economy, philosophy, and mathematics in order to shape the reasoning mind. Locke also influenced another group of serious-minded educators, the evangelicals. Sarah Kirby Trimmer (1741–1810) and Hannah More (1745–1833) deplored Locke's "godless" influence on young minds, but like the rational moralists stressed early and vigorous training to develop religious sentiments. Utilitarians and evangelicals in early Victorian Britain were decidedly unsentimental in their appraisal of childhood.

The work most crucial to understanding Victorian sentiments on childhood is *Emile* (1762) by the French philosopher Jean-Jacques Rousseau (1712-1778). Rousseau, like his evangelical contemporaries, denounced the primacy of reason and distrusted the sophistications of society. Yet his theories were even more disturbing to evangelicals than Locke's. Rousseau opposed the doctrine of original sin with his own claims of childhood's original innocence. Rousseau and his Victorian followers delighted in childhood, infusing it with all the glories of a vanished Eden or golden age. According to this view, the vivacity, joy, and freedom of childhood revitalize all they touch; the child allowed to grow unstunted by earnest schooling is guided by natural, and therefore moral, instincts and feelings; the child's instinctive innocence serves as a model for adulthood; and in this way, one's childhood becomes a spiritual touchstone in one's later years. *Emile's* provocative doctrine of original innocence appealed enormously to those dissatisfied with a stern religion and a heartless utilitarianism.

Victorians tried to come to terms with these opposing ideologies of childhood, to synthesize the disparate beliefs of the preceding generation. In the early years, however, evangelical and utilitarian notions of childhood predominated. From infancy religious training reminded children of their sinfulness, of God's magnanimity in offering them salvation, of the certainty of immortality if they would subject themselves to his will. Parents scrutinized even the youngest children for a sign of growing religious sensibilities. Parents took children to deathbeds, to prisons, to executions to impress upon the young the high stakes involved when duty to God was shirked. Tract fiction, written primarily for children, presented idealized children who accept the seriousness of salvation. These exemplary children dramatize the evangelical ideology of original sin and stringent duty to God, usually dying to afford others grace. An evangelical childhood, then, offered little diversion or entertainment that was not directly linked to religion. Frivolous fiction seldom found its way into early Victorian evangelical homes.

Some middle-class children faced rigorous training in the classics and in modern sciences, languages, and mathematics to prepare for life in an increasingly complex and industrialized world. James Mill educated his son, John Stuart Mill (1806–1873), to read Greek and Latin as a child, and to be well versed in the problems of philosophy, economics, and mathematics. The resulting enervation of such a driven childhood is memorably described by J. S. Mill in his *Autobiography* (1873). Though J. S. Mill's earnest childhood occurred in the early nineteenth century, it epitomizes the utilitarian model of childhood that achieved great influence in Victorian Britain. Charles Dickens's satiric look at "Gradgrindism," in *Hard Times* (1854), documents the continuing sway of Bentham and Mill at midcentury.

Indeed, complaints that childhood was a fettered thing, bound by a strident evangelism on the one hand and by a serious-minded utilitarianism on the other, began to appear in prominent journals in the 1830s. To concerned minds, childhood was under assault by the ugliness of industrialization, the degradation of poverty, and the narrowness of Puritanism. From the 1830s onward, writers articulated a romantic protest against the corruption of innocence. Rousseau's exaltation of childhood took root; joy and imagination, essential terms of romantic writers like William Blake and William Wordsworth, won new acceptance; and a revaluation of childhood occurred. Childhood itself became a potent and poignant symbol. From the publication of *Oliver Twist* (1837–1839), **Charles Dickens** did more than any other Victorian writer to redefine childhood for his age. The Dickens child is often preternaturally innocent, a spiritual orphan confronted by a corrupt society yet somehow able to resist its evil. When childhood is perverted in Dickens's novels, the result is tragic. Dickens's juxtaposition of innocent childhood and cruel experience took on an archetypal significance. Dickens is also central in any discussion of Victorian childhood for his vociferous protests against evangelical and utilitarian excesses; his children are informed by a romantic benevolence and a gentle Christianity. His fictive renderings of society's sins against childhood wrenched the Victorian consciousness in a way that no parliamentary commission could equal. Dickens insisted upon the uniqueness, the joyousness, the spontaneity of childhood, and in this way helped foster the cult of childhood that flourished from the 1860s on.

Increasingly, then, Victorians sentimentalized childhood. Children as natural, spiritual beings proliferated in the pages of magazines and novels. Even naughtiness, the mainstay of evangelical moral tales, lost its horror. Child protagonists no longer faced death and damnation for breaking rules; indeed, naughtiness was viewed as healthy, a necessary way for children to learn right from wrong and compassion for others. The energy of childhood was more tolerated in mid- and late-century literature. Adventure novels and magazines like the *Boy's Own Paper* glorified manly, active boys, and school novels idealized the playing fields of childhood. The emergence of a strong market for children's books bespeaks the special place childhood had in Victorian Britain. Indeed, by the last quarter of Victoria's reign, childhood seemed enshrined in its own glorious, secret garden. Yet serious writers for and about childhood tried to square its idealized portrayal with the realities of their times. Childhood mortality remained high, despite improved sanitation and lower birth rates after 1870. Poor children faced wretched living conditions, illiteracy, back-breaking employment, and the temptations of drink. Even in the sanctity of the middle-class home, children faced a confusing blend of affection and stern discipline. Moreover, William Acton's (1813–1875) and Sigmund Freud's studies of childhood sexuality clearly documented the underside of Victorian childhood. Childhood, then, became a rallying point for significant social change. The passage of the Factory Act of 1847 and the Elementary Education Act of 1870, the popularity and effectiveness of Dickens's child protagonists, and the emergence of a golden age of children's books all attest to the Victorian public's growing sensitivity to and tenderness for childhood.

SUSAN NARAMORE MAHER

Bibliography

Aries, Philippe. *Centuries of Childhood.* 1962. Trans. R. Baldick.

Avery, Gillian. *Childhood's Pattern.* 1975.

Bratton, J. S. *The Impact of Victorian Children's Fiction.* 1981.

Carpenter, Humphrey. *Secret Gardens.* 1985.

Coveney, Peter. *The Image of Childhood.* 1967.

Pollack, Linda A. *Forgotten Children.* 1983.

Roe, F. Gordon. *The Victorian Child.* 1959.

Walvin, James. *A Child's World.* 1982.

See also CHILDREN'S LITERATURE; EDUCATION; INFANT MORTALITY

· · · · ·

CHILDREN

Three topics are particularly important to the study of Victorian children: their numbers, their legal status, and the role of **family** in their lives. Children "were everywhere" and yet they were indistinguishable from adults in the criminal courts. On the other hand, hundreds of extant photographs proclaim the pride parents had in their progeny. For many children life was harsh, but, in general terms, its quality improved over the course of the century.

Between 1841 and 1911 the British population more than doubled (from 15,914,000 to 36,070,000) and children formed a significant proportion of the total. In 1841, 36 percent of the population was under fourteen years of age; in 1900 the figure was 32 percent. Infant and child mortality remained high throughout the century and in some areas markedly increased; in Glasgow in 1821 one child in 75 died, rising to one in 48 by 1861. **Infant mortality** in 1899 was still high (although far below most other European countries), particularly in the poorer classes. In Liverpool, the 1899 figures show that 136 children per thousand born in the better suburbs died in their first year, while in the city's poorest quarters the figure was 509 per thousand. Illegitimate babies had half the survival rate of legitimate infants and many deaths went unrecorded, as it was common practice not to baptize infants who died within a month of birth.

Infants were subject to hazards from disease, dirt, neglect, and misguided treatment. Opiates such as Godfrey's Cordial were used to quiet fretful babies; little was known about the sanitary precautions needed when infants were given food from any source other than the breast. Infections spread easily in poorer neighborhoods, where (even late in the century) toilet facilities were primitive, water difficult to obtain, and beds might be shared by several children and adults.

Disease, however, knew no social distinction. Innoculation almost eradicated smallpox (there was one epidemic late in the century) but whooping cough accounted for two-fifths of all deaths under five years of age. From five to eight, scarlet fever was the leading cause of child mortality. Measles regularly killed 7,000 people a year; tuberculosis was common; and in the 1860s and 1870s diphtheria became a major killer of children under thirteen.

As adult mortality rates decreased so that fewer marriages were terminated by death, the middle-class family became increasingly long lasting and intimate. Few children were fostered or apprenticed out, although boys were increasingly sent to boarding school as the century progressed. Schooling for girls had relatively low priority, although the lower middle classes began to see **education** for a profession such as teaching or nursing as one way of reducing the burden on paternal resources as a girl got older. The central aspects of life were focused within the boundary of the nuclear family, generating a mixture of repression and of intense concern for emotional, moral, and religious welfare.

By late in the century many among the working classes sought to emulate the middle-class lifestyle. For the first two-thirds of the century, however, evidence suggests that for the poor the family unit provided little moral and emotional support, as well as offering a poor physical environment. In contrast to the pattern in the middle classes, lower-class boys were apt to stay at home while the girls were sent away, often entering domestic service at as young as nine or ten years of age.

Children's status before the law became defined over the course of the century. As late as 1814 execution for petty crimes was a possibility. Imprisonment, flogging, and transportation to the colonies remained acceptable punishments for children as well as adults. In 1838 Parkhurst Prison became the first separate correction center for juveniles. Reform schools were established from midcentury, but not until the Children's Act (1908) were offenders under fourteen kept from prison. Flogging declined in the family as a chastisement, but remained a legal and educational corrective.

Legislation to improve the social and welfare conditions of children blossomed in the second half of the century from the seed of voluntary work sown in the first half. Such improvement as did occur was far-reaching, although it is symptomatic of British priorities that the Royal Society for the Prevention of Cruelty to Animals was founded in 1824 and the National Society for the Prevention of Cruelty to Children did not appear until sixty years later.

Specialized pediatric medicine may be said to begin with the opening of London's Great Ormond Street Hospital (1852). Health visitor schemes (dating from 1862 in Manchester and Salford) combined with the increased training of midwives to improve the chances of childhood survival. Other significant dates in childhood welfare provisions include: the compulsory registration of births in 1837; the 1846 act making it illegal to insure the lives of children under six (in the belief that insurance benefits encouraged neglect, which led to early death); a series of employment acts beginning in 1847 that addressed **child labor**; and the Prevention of Cruelty to Children Act (1889), which gave authorities the right to remove a child from its home if cruelty were suspected.

With the Education Act of 1870 and the subsequent refinements that made at least a few years of education both free and compulsory, children were for some part of every day removed from the family and working world into a separate culture. **Toys and games** were plentiful, literature for children flourished, and fashion catalogues displayed styles designed specifically for the young. If childhood is accepted as approximating the age range from birth to fourteen years, then by the end of Victoria's reign children had become a focal point of social interest.

W. JOHN SMITH

Bibliography

Behlmer, G. K. *Child Abuse and Moral Reform in England, 1870–1908.* 1982.

Burnett, John, ed. *Destiny Obscure: Autobiographies of Childhood, Education and Family from the 1820s to the 1920s.* 1982.

———."The History of Childhood." *History Today,* vol. 33, pp. 30–31.

Coveney, Peter. *The Image of Childhood.* 1967.

Ewing, Elizabeth. *Youth and History: Tradition and Change in European Age Relations, 1770-Present.* 1974.

Maill, Antony and Peter Maill. *The Victorian Nursery Book.* 1980.

Springhall, John. *Youth, Empire and Society: British Youth Movements, 1883-1940.* 1977.

Walvin, James. *A Child's World: A Social History of English Childhood, 1800-1914.* 1982.

Wohl, Anthony S. *The Victorian Family.* 1978.

See also INFANT FEEDING; JUVENILE CRIME; SEXUAL VIOLENCE

. . . . .

CHILDREN'S ILLUSTRATED BOOKS

The golden age of children's literature which began in Great Britain in the 1860s was also a golden age of design and illustration in children's books. The integration of text and pictures reached heights of aesthetic achievement made possible by new printing techniques, a renewed interest in education, the arts and crafts movement, and economic feasibility. The landmark year of 1865 saw the publication of both Lewis Carroll's *Alice in Wonderland* with **John Tenniel**'s illustrations, carefully executed under the author's supervision, and **Walter Crane's** "Toy Books" for Routledge, printed by Edmund Evans.

Precedents for illustrated children's books had been set by adult illustrated books and by the commercial success of John Newbery in the eighteenth century. Newbery's tradition was carried on by John Harris, who published *The Comic Adventures of Mother Hubbard and Her Dog* (1805) and *The Butterfly's Ball* (1807), the latter illustrated by William Mulready. The English publication of the Grimms' *German Popular Stories* (1823, 1826) established the appeal of fairy tales, which provided a vehicle for creative and imaginative illustrations. **George Cruikshank**, whose etchings accompanied the first Grimm collection, introduced his Fairy Library in 1853, and Richard Doyle turned to illustrating fairy tales fol-

lowing his resignation from *Punch* in 1850. In Edward Lear's *Book of Nonsense*, issued in two volumes in 1846, the lithographs were fully as important as the verses—and children's right to books whose main purpose was to entertain was firmly established. Lear's book was reissued by Routledge, Warne in 1861 with wood engravings by the Dalziel brothers, whose work dominated illustrated books.

Before the 1830s, color was applied by hand, making colored illustrations costly. Chromolithography and tinted wood engraving, invented in the mid-1830s, also proved expensive. In addition, they encouraged careless engraving and resulted in heavily colored works with an oily appearance. The wood block printing technique was, however, refined by printer Edmund Evans (1826–1905), who pioneered the application of photographic processes to the blocks and garnered the loyalty of artists by developing tints and inks that more closely approximated the original artwork. Evans printed Walter Crane's *The Baby's Opera* (1877) and his numerous toy books for the Routledge publishing firm. The latter—a series of inexpensive books in which text and illustration were thoroughly integrated—demonstrated the commercial rewards made possible when a very large press run could absorb the initial expenses of good reproduction.

When Routledge disagreed with Crane over royalty payments, Evans recruited **Randolph Caldecott** as a new toy book illustrator. Caldecott produced two toy books a year, based on traditional rhymes such as *The House that Jack Built* and *The Three Jovial Huntsmen*, from 1878 until his death in 1886. His light, deft, animated line was particularly suited to Evans's printing techniques. **Kate Greenaway**, an Evans find, completed the triumvirate of golden age illustrators. Although she was not so accomplished an artist as the other two, the naiveté and composition of Greenaway's work had lasting appeal for adults. One of Evans's final efforts was printing the work of **Beatrix Potter**, which was in the Caldecott tradition of strong line with an imaginative overlay of color and whimsy.

With the proliferation of illustrated magazines, the desire of parents to provide reading material for their children, and the application of photographic techniques to printing, the latter decades of the nineteenth century provided an abundance of illustrated works for children. Firms such as Macmillan reissued classics with illustrations; vast numbers of fairy books (including Andrew Lang's) appeared. There were many new illustrators, especially those of the black-and-white school such as the Brock brothers, Hugh Thompson, Arthur Rackham, H. R. Millar, and Heath and Charles Robinson. Illustrated children's books reached a height which, in the eyes of many, has not since been equaled.

LOUISA SMITH

Bibliography

Alderson, Brian. *Sing a Song for Sixpence*. 1986.

Barr, John. *Illustrated Children's Books*. 1986.

Houfe, Simon. *The Dictionary of British Book Illustrators and Caricaturists, 1800–1914*. 1978.

McLean, Ruari. *Victorian Book Design and Colour Printing*. 1963.

See also ILLUSTRATION; WOOD ENGRAVING

· · · · ·

CHILDREN'S LITERATURE

At the beginning of the nineteenth century children's literature was primarily morally improving and didactic. Developments in Victorian society such as increased literacy and the improved technology of the printing industry encouraged the evolution of a wealth of varied, and frequently light-hearted, writing for children. Fairy tales achieved respectability, new fiction genres were created, nonsense verse was firmly established and, by the second half of the century, periodicals were thriving.

Fairy tales had long been accessible to children through oral tradition and chapbooks. Pre-Victorian parents and educators viewed them as unsuitable for a number of reasons. In the 1840s **Henry Cole**, under the pseudonym Felix Summerly, edited the Home Treasury series (1843–1847), a selection of mostly traditional material, illustrated by such prominent artists as Henry Corbould and J. C.

Horsley, and published by Joseph Cundall in an attractive format designed to overcome the prejudices of middle-class parents. Its success opened the door for innumerable pretty and readable books of fairy tales, legends, rhymes and fantasy. A few collections had appeared before Cole's, notably the first English translation of *German Popular Stories* (1823) by the Brothers Grimm (with illustrations by **George Cruikshank**). In 1846 Hans Christian Andersen's tales were first translated into English (by **Mary Howitt**) under the title *Wonderful Stories for Children*. Three other translations appeared in the same year. Drawn from **folklore**, Andersen's stories were distinguished by a more intense and dramatic morality than that of wholly traditional tales.

By the late 1850s, several general folktale collections had been published, as well as some individual English tales, including "The Three Bears", which first appeared in print in Robert Southey's *The Doctor* (1837). With the publication of James Orchard Halliwell's collection of rhymes and tales, *Nursery Rhymes of England* (1842), the respectability of this traditional material increased. **John Ruskin's** arguments, presented in his preface to the 1869 edition of *German Popular Stories* and embodied in his own *King of the Golden River* (1851), did much to secure the position of fairy tales. This was confirmed by the work of the eminent folklorists Joseph Jacobs and **Andrew Lang**. Jacobs's collections of English, Celtic, Indian and other tales were published in the 1890s with scholarly notes, while Lang's beautifully bound but moderately priced Fairy Books (1889–1910) made a broad international selection of tales available to a wide audience of children.

This growing interest furthered the development of fantasy, though many of the early created fairy tales retained a strong moral flavor. Early examples include F. E. Paget's *Hope of the Katzekopfs* (1844), Thackeray's *Rose and the Ring* (1855) and Francis Browne's *Granny's Wonderful Chair* (1856). Inspired by Bunyan, many authors incorporated allegory into their work and wrote fairy tales designed to inculcate religious or moral messages. **Charlotte Tucker**, a convert to evangelicalism who wrote extensively and well under the pseudonym A.L.O.E. (A Lady of England), blended allegory with what were almost pure tract tales.

With increased respectability, fairy tales also became vehicles for propaganda. In 1847 **George Cruikshank** was converted to the cause of temperance and altered four traditional tales to convey his arguments. Although the series, George Cruikshank's Fairy Library (1853–1864), contained some of his best drawings, it was not a commercial success. **Charles Kingsley's** *Water Babies* (1863) was both a charming fantasy and a damning social commentary on the condition of chimney sweeps' climbing boys. **George MacDonald's** *Princess and the Goblin* (1872) and his other fairy-tale fantasies were heavily imbued with Christian allegory. *Alice's Adventures in Wonderland* was the first fantasy entirely free of moralizing. **Lewis Carroll** upended the moral tale, parodying it with nonsensical characters and absurd lessons. **M. L. Molesworth**, writing from the 1870s, and **E. Nesbit**, whose best work appeared from 1899, further developed the genre.

The moral tale of the eighteenth century had been moderated in the work of such 1830s authors as **Harriet Martineau**, Agnes Strickland, **Frederick Marryat** and William and Mary Howitt. **Catherine Sinclair's** *Holiday House* (1839) was the first work of fiction to break away from this pattern, and, despite an orthodox conclusion, depicted chronically mischievous children.

Also important in the evolution of children's fiction were the evangelical publishers, especially the Religious Tract Society (est. 1799). Their earliest publications, directed at a general semiliterate audience but easily read by children, presented religious conversion stories as factual accounts. With time, the stigma attached to fiction lessened, and by mid-century such firms had developed the more middle-class genres of juvenile adventure and school, family and "street arab" fiction. This last arose principally in imitation of philanthropist **Hesba Stretton's** stories and remained overtly evangelical. The charitable motives of Amy Catherine Walton, Mrs. G. Castle Smith, and others are readily apparent, but their formula tales in melodramatic prose about innocent, abused, and starving children lacked the freshness and immediacy of Stretton's work. **Anna Sewell's** *Black Beauty* (1877), on the other hand, made an informed and effective use of pathos to plead its cause—the prevention of cruelty to animals. While many books advocated active philanthropy, some of the periodicals organized activities for their readers. *Aunt Judy's Magazine* (1866–1885), for example, maintained cots in the Great Ormond Street Hospital for Sick Children.

From the 1860s, writers and publishers directed very different messages at male and female children. R. M. Ballantyne, W. H. G. Kingston and others wrote wholesome tales of high adventure in which the manly Christian hero performed feats of daring for the glory of God and, as the century progressed, Empire. Placed on a desert island, at sea, in a tropical jungle or arctic waste or in the British army, this figure became a staple of boys' fiction until World War I. The evangelical message, already secondary to the portrayal of the manly hero, had almost disappeared by the 1880s and 1890s, when the extremely popular **G. A. Henty** was writing. Equally strong on adventure but considerably weaker in moral purpose were the "penny dreadfuls" and the novels less specifically geared to a juvenile market. Their heroes drank, smoked and engaged in adventure for personal glory and gain. Better writers such as the popular French author, Jules Verne, had already added the appeal of popular scientific knowledge. **Robert Louis Stevenson** and **H. Rider Haggard** broke away from previous patterns to create plausible romantic adventures with realistic characters.

The first "school story" was **Thomas Hughes's** famous novel about Thomas Arnold's newly reformed Rugby, *Tom Brown's School Days* (1857). Equally popular, though ridiculed by later generations for its extreme sentimentality and naiveté, was F. W. Farrar's *Eric, or Little by Little* (1858). As the public schools evolved according to Thomas Arnold's principles, an audience for the school story was created. Numerous novels and serial stories by such well-loved minor writers as Talbot Baines Reed developed and confirmed the formula, even after the character of the school hero was tarnished with the publication of **Rudyard Kipling's** *Stalky & Co.* (1899). Girls' school stories only developed after the appearance of large schools for middle-class girls. L. T. Meade, a diverse and prolific writer and editor of the periodical *Atalanta* (1887–1898), produced a much-imitated formula for the girls' school story. Like

Henty's hero, her model heroine reflected a popular mythology of contemporary youth. The High Church response to evangelical fiction was exemplified in the girls' stories of **Charlotte Mary Yonge** and Cardinal Newman's sister, **Harriet Mozley**, who painted quiet family scenes in which the absence of colorful incident served to emphasize the home as the appropriate background for humble faith and charity. Yonge edited the *Monthly Packet* (1851-1898), the first girls' periodical and one which clearly reflected her High Church views. Girls were also likely to read the literature of an earlier generation— Jane Austen, Fanny Burney or Walter Scott. Cheap romances, frowned upon by parents and critics, were the girls' equivalent of penny dreadfuls.

Juvenile periodicals, a thriving institution from the 1860s, evolved partly in imitation of developments in the adult and family markets, including the spread of literacy. Religious periodicals, largely geared to the Sunday school market, predominated in the first half of the century. Of over forty such publications, two of the most successful were the *Child's Companion or Sunday Scholar's Reward* (Religious Tract Society, 1824-1932) and the *Children's Friend* (1824-1930). The latter was edited by Baptist minister William Carus Wilson, the model for Charlotte Brontë's Mr. Brocklehurst. Many of these were acceptable Sunday reading in all but the strictest households, in which only *Pilgrim's Progress* and the Bible were approved reading.

Prompted by an increase in the number of secular periodicals and penny dreadfuls, the Religious Tract Society and others began to publish less overtly didactic but still highly religious magazines. *Sunday at Home* (1854-1940), the juvenile and adolescent offshoot of *Leisure Hour*, contained the work of Hesba Stretton and G. E. Sargent. The Religious Tract Society made a further concession and created the *Boy's Own Paper* (1879-1967), consisting of suitable adventure stories and improving activities.

Periodicals outstanding for their literary merit also appeared. *Aunt Judy's Magazine* was established and edited by **Margaret Gatty** to provide a forum for the lively writings of her daughter, **Juliana Horatia Ewing**, and numbered Carroll and Andersen among its contributors. *Good Words for the Young* (1868-

1872) was edited by George MacDonald and included his work and Kingsley's. Stevenson's *Treasure Island* (1883) first appeared in *Young Folks* (1876-1897) and his *Catriona* (1893) in *Atalanta*.

The squat, heavily informative volumes of *Peter Parley's Annual* (1840-1892) were in a different vein. The name of Peter Parley, initially the pseudonym of American author Samuel Griswold Goodrich, was adopted by several English authors and publishers, among them William Martin, who edited the *Annual* for many years. The inculcation of as many facts as possible and the strict avoidance of any imaginative literature were the hallmarks of this school of writing, particularly popular in the 1830s and 1840s. It was parodied by Charles Dickens in *Hard Times* (1854), and Cole's Home Treasury series was intended as an attack on this earnest fact-peddling.

More domestic in nature were the practical girls' periodicals, chiefly the *Girl's Own Paper* (1880-1956), which offered information and advice on such subjects as housekeeping, fine sewing, music, health, careers and marriage. It was, in fact, the most consistently profitable of the Religious Tract Society's publications, although it does not seem to have had the same influence as the *Boy's Own Paper*, which molded the attitudes and beliefs of its readers.

In poetry, as with the classics of adult fiction, children read some works of major poets such as Blake and Wordsworth. The satirical humor of Goldsmith and Cowper was later annexed by children through Randolph Caldecott's picture-books. Lewis Carroll's parody of "How doth the little busy bee" in *Alice's Adventures in Wonderland* (1865) demonstrates the continuing popularity of the joyful hymns of eighteenth-century nonconformist Isaac Watts.

Edward Lear's collection of limericks, *Book of Nonsense* (1846), firmly established the genre of nonsense verse. Heinrich Hoffmann's *Struwwelpeter*, published in Germany in 1845 and translated into English in 1848, was the first comprehensive attempt to parody the "awful warnings" of earlier moral verse and encouraged a rash of imitations. By the end of the century, Hoffmann's blatant parodies had been transformed into the gentler satire of Hilaire Belloc's cautionary verses. Most often parodied, and itself reprinted frequently throughout the century, was Ann Taylor Gilbert's "My Mother", first published in 1804 but in spirit quintessentially Victorian.

In a different tradition, *Poetry for Children*, by Charles and Mary Lamb, published in 1809 and remaining popular throughout the century, heralded the cheerful, friendly verse of the Howitts, William Brighty Rands and the American, Eugene Field. **Christina Rossetti**'s *Sing-Song* (1872), intended for young children, was illustrated by **Arthur Hughes**.

Rossetti's *Goblin Market and Other Poems* (1862) contained two designs by Dante Gabriel Rossetti, and the 1893 edition was illustrated by Laurence Housman. With the evolution of the picture book came the fashion for separate publication of illustrated nursery rhymes and poems. In 1888, for example, Robert Browning's *Pied Piper of Hamelin* (1855) appeared with drawings by Kate Greenaway. One of the most delightful collections of verse to come out of the Victorian age was Robert Louis Stevenson's *A Child's Garden of Verses* (1885).

New technologies in printing and book illustration were vital to the development of Victorian juvenile literature. To the new breed of large commercial publishers looking for an area in which to specialize, children's literature had vast market potential. Dean and Son, for example, was known for its novelty books and George Routledge produced large numbers of toy books as well as reprints of juvenile classics. Institutional publishers such as the Religious Tract Society and the Society for the Propagation of Christian Knowledge, and commercial publishers with evangelical leanings such as James Nisbet and Thomas Nelson, published morally improving tracts, books and periodicals, including work by major children's authors. These and other firms used reward books—distributed by schools and Sunday schools for good conduct or proficiency—as a stable source of income.

In the late eighteenth century Thomas Bewick's innovative technique of wood engraving and the invention of lithography by Alois Senefelder had encouraged the use of illustration. Lithography was not commonly used in children's books until the 1840s, with chromolithography becoming increasingly popular by the 1860s, which also saw a revival of **wood engraving**. Many of the early *Punch*

artists, including **John Tenniel**, Charles Bennett, Richard Doyle and Ernest Griset, illustrated children's books, some by fellow staff members such as Mark Lemon and Henry Mayhew.

Children's book publishers were particularly interested in color work. From the 1850s engraver Edmund Evans worked to improve the quality of illustration and color reproduction. He printed for both Routledge and Warne and encouraged prominent illustrators, including the "nursery triumvirate" of **Walter Crane**, **Randolph Caldecott** and **Kate Greenaway**, who were responsible for the form of the modern picture book with its interdependence of illustration and text.

Artistic and literary critics were becoming increasingly aware of children's literature. In 1844 Lady Eastlake wrote a critical survey for the *Quarterly Review*, and in 1887 C. M. Yonge published *What Books To Lend and What To Give*. Edward Salmon's *Juvenile Literature As It Is* (1888) is of interest as much for its study of children's taste as for contemporary critical attitudes. Children's periodicals frequently included reviews, and a special issue of the fine arts journal, the *Studio* (1897–1898), was devoted to *Children's Books and Their Illustrators*.

Another development was the study of historical children's literature. Yonge wrote three articles on "Children's Literature of the Last Century" for *Macmillan's Magazine* in 1869. E. M. Field's *The Child and His Book* (1891) was also a historical account and Andrew Tuer's massive *History of the Horn-Book* (1896) included facsimiles. Charles Welsh published a biography of John Newbery (an early juvenile publisher) and was responsible for a series of facsimiles of late eighteenth- and early nineteenth-century juvenile classics. This rise in critical and historical interest reflects the maturity of an independent literature for children. The increasing separation of work and play contributed to the creation of books written to give pleasure and judged on literary merit rather than social message.

JILL SHEFRIN

Bibliography

Avery, Gillian. *Childhood's Pattern: A Study of the Heroes and Heroines of Children's Fiction, 1770–1950.* 1975.

Bratton, J. S. *The Impact of Victorian Children's Fiction.* 1981.

Darton, F. J. Harvey. *Children's Books in England: Five Centuries of Social Life.* 1982.

Demers, Patricia, ed. *A Garland from the Golden Age: An Anthology of Children's Literature from 1850 to 1900.* 1983.

Muir, Percy. *English Children's Books: 1600 to 1900.* 1954.

Rahn, Suzanne. *Children's Literature: An Annotated Bibliography of the History and Criticism.* 1981.

Salway, Lance. *A Peculiar Gift: Nineteenth-Century Writings on Books for Children.* 1976.

Thwaite, M. F. *From Primer to Pleasure: An Introduction to the History of Children's Books in England, from the Invention of Printing to 1900.* 1963.

Toronto Public Library. *The Osborne Collection of Early Children's Books: A Catalogue.* 1958, 1975. 2 vols.

See also CHILDHOOD

· · · · ·

CHOLERA

A disease caused by the microorganism *Vibrio cholerae*, cholera is transmitted through water or food contaminated by the feces of others who have contracted the disease. Violent diarrhea, vomiting, and purging of bodily fluid led to rapid dehydration and death in roughly half of nineteenth-century cases. Effective treatment for cholera was not developed until the twentieth century.

Cholera spread from Bengal through Asia and Europe, reaching Britain for the first time in the autumn of 1831. Four epidemics in Britain (1831–1832, 1848–1849, 1853–1854, and 1866) killed a total of 140,000 or more. Mortality was concentrated in poorer districts, where contamination of water supplies was greatest.

Prior to the discovery of *Vibrio cholerae* in 1883 and acceptance of the germ theory of cholera in the 1890s, British doctors differed over the nature of the disease and the manner of its transmission. During the first epidemic, doctors tended toward either a "contagionist" explanation that cholera was transmitted from person to person, or a "miasmatist" explanation that the disease was produced by noxious exhalations arising from sewage and the like. By midcentury, the promotion of miasmatism by **Edwin Chadwick** (1800–1890) and other **public health** reformers made it the dominant theory. In 1849 and 1854 John Snow (1813–1858) in London attempted to demonstrate that cholera was a "poison" transmitted by water. Scientifically plausible refutations of Snow's theory put forth by the miasmatists meant that it was accepted only by a minority of doctors by 1866.

In 1831–1832 the Privy Council created a temporary arrangement of local boards of health guided by a Central Board of Health in London for the prevention and treatment of cholera. These authorities encountered opposition from political radicals who suspected that "cholera" was a sham perpetrated by the government to serve the interests of the medical profession and sometimes violent resistance from the poor, who often believed that cholera was introduced into their neighborhoods to provide victims for dissection by the anatomists. During the later epidemics local management of cholera was left to the regular local authorities and, in 1853–1854 and 1866, to the new permanent boards of health established by a number of communities. The heightened social tension characteristic of the first epidemic was largely absent in later outbreaks.

HOWARD C. BAKER

Bibliography

Morris, Robert J. *Cholera, 1832.* 1976.

See also BACTERIOLOGY; EPIDEMIC DISEASES; MEDICAL SCIENCE

· · · · ·

CHOLMONDELEY, MARY (1859–1925)

Mary Cholmondeley awoke to fame upon the publication of *Red Pottage* (1899), a novel more admired for its delicious satire on religiosity in Middleshire than for its sensational but also sensitive love story. Promoted by **Rhoda Broughton**, Cholmondeley published *The Danvers Jewels* (1887), the first of nine novels which include *Diana Tempest* (1893), *Moth and Rust* (1902), *Notwithstanding* (1913), and *The Romance of His Life* (1921). Her *Under One Roof: A Family Record* (1918) contains the history of her remarkable sister Hester, model for the ill-fated novelist in *Red Pottage*.

Eldest daughter in the large family of the cultured vicar of Hodnet, Shropshire, she was early put in charge of the household, as her mother was often ill. Loyal and affectionate, she confided to her journal the frustration of being isolated in the country, "maimed with illness" and "without any outlet to thought in the way of conversation." Reading Emerson heartened her, and with her father's move to London in 1896, she eventually became part of the circle which included Henry James, Anne Ritchie, Howard Sturgis, and Rhoda Broughton. Her recognition of the salutary bond between women derived from her closeness to her sisters with whom she continued to live in London and in the summers at Ufford, Suffolk.

The inner tensions that Cholmondeley confesses prompted her to write are manifest in violent narrative scenes and eruptions in her witty Jane Austen style. Modern in her awareness of women's need for self-identification in love and work, she was, in her use of the enclosed world of the big country house and the heir's duty to it, a morally earnest Victorian, in the mold of her mentor George Eliot.

TAMIE WATTERS

Bibliography

Crisp, Jane. *Mary Cholmondeley 1859–1925: A Bibliography.* 1981.

Lubbock, Percy. *Mary Cholmondeley.* 1928.
. . . . .

CHORAL MUSIC

Choral singing played a great part in the religious revivals of both evangelicals and Tractarians, and in a secular context was valued as both an innocent recreation and a moral education.

In the early nineteenth century, music in cathedrals as well as in parish churches was in a sorry state. However, under the influence of the Oxford Movement (1833) and the Cambridge Camden (later Ecclesiastical) Society (1839) reform of the services of worship began. The Society for Improving Church Music (1846) and many diocesan choral associations were founded to improve the singing of both choir and congregation. Influential in this reform was **Samuel Sebastian Wesley** (1810–1876), whose 1849 manifesto (*A Few Words on Cathedral Music*), music, and practice set a new standard. Not everyone, however, wished to improve the choir's performance at the cost of denying participation to the people.

Certainly, people wanted to sing. Earlier in the century, secular singing classes were begun in some schools and through such organizations as the mechanics' institutes (1823); others were organized deliberately to raise the standard of congregational singing. Such was the motive of Sarah Glover (1786–1867), whose method of teaching children's choirs was adapted and popularized by the Reverend John Curwen (1816–1880). Expounded in *Singing for Schools and Congregations* (1843) and articles in Cassell's *Popular Educator* (1852), his tonic solfa movement had some 20,000 pupils in singing classes by 1856, and his choirs were giving public performances.

Curwen's method fought for acceptance with *Wilhem's Method of Teaching Singing* (1841) by John Hullah (1812–1884). Hullah, like Glover and Curwen, used the gamut (*do, re, mi*) developed on the Continent, but Curwen's system had the advantage of a moveable *do*, whereas Hullah's singers were restricted to C major. Both systems were widely used in schools, but Curwen's came to predominate, even when Hullah was made government inspector for music in schools (1872).

Choral singing was recommended not only for schoolchildren but also for the working classes, as an innocent recreation promoting temperance and cooperation. This emphasis on the moral excellence of singing, together with the musical limitations of any solfa system, meant that the vast quantity of music published in solfa notation tended to the sentimental and unexceptionable. Nevertheless, the widespread enthusiasm for choral singing supported two characteristic developments—choral festivals and "monster" choirs. Church choir festivals, popular in the eighteenth century, had been neglected in the early nineteenth but were revived in the 1880s. Competitive choir festivals also became popular at about the same time. Monster choirs were huge groups assembled for public performances, usually of oratorios. In 1862, the Sacred Harmonic Society mustered 3,625 voices for a performance at the Crystal Palace.

In such an event, choral music symbolizes several Victorian aspirations: in the massed voices raised in sacred music under the glass and iron canopy might be heard an exuberant sense of achievement and a longing for social harmony and moral certainty.

SUSAN DRAIN

Bibliography

Hutchings, Arthur. *Church Music in the Nineteenth Century.* 1967.

Mackerness, E. D. *A Social History of English Music.* 1964.

Pearsall, Ronald. *Victorian Popular Music.* 1973.

Rainbow, Bernarr. *The Choral Revival in the Anglican Church 1839-1872.* 1970.

———. *The Land Without Music: Musical Education in England 1800-1860.* 1967.

Scholes, Percy. *The Mirror of Music 1844-1944,* vol. 1. 1947.

Young, Percy. *The Choral Tradition: An Historical and Analytical Survey.* Rev. ed., 1981.

See also CATHEDRAL MUSIC;
MUSIC EDUCATION

· · · · ·

CHRISTIAN SOCIALISM

Christian socialism influenced British working-class politics between 1848 and 1854. Although its immediate impetus was the Chartist failure of 1848, it was the product of a number of forces which came together at midcentury, including the working-class movements of the "hungry forties"; the failure of **Owenite so**cialism; **Frederick Denison Maurice**'s liberal theology; fear that the French Revolution of 1848 would spread to Britain; and French socialism as transmitted through John Malcolm Ludlow.

The group that came to be known after 1850 as Christian socialists began forming in London on April 10, 1848. They produced a series of tracts and two periodicals, inspired **Charles Kingsley** to write his novels *Yeast* and *Alton Locke*, sponsored a series of workingmen's associations, and founded the Working Men's College in London. A later revival of Christian socialism (1877-1914) worked with more precisely defined political understandings of **socialism** than did the movement's founders.

The original impulse came from meetings among Frederick Denison Maurice (1805-1872), John Malcolm Ludlow (1821-1911), and Charles Kingsley (1819-1875) to observe the presentation of the People's Charter and determine how, in the face of the Chartists' failure, they could help avert revolution while assuring the working classes that their grievances were being addressed. Other important members included Charles Mansfield (1819-1855), F. J. Furnivall (1825-1910), **Thomas Hughes** (1822-1896), Walter Cooper (b. 1814), Lloyd Jones (1811-1886), Jules St. André le Chevalier, and Edward Vansittart Neale (1810-1892).

The theological basis for Christian socialism is found in Maurice's *The Kingdom of Christ* (1838). Maurice asserts that the kingdom of Christ is an existing reality in which people already live. Politics and religion are inseparable. The divine order exists, and the church is responsible for making that order manifest by addressing social questions. In essence, Maurice shifted the emphasis of Christianity from individual salvation to social salvation. Maurice rejected individualism and with it competition and selfishness, thereby opposing the prevailing doctrines of political economy and especially the principle of laissez faire.

Maurice and his followers were also at odds with prevailing views of socialism. The upper and middle classes were at best suspicious of socialism, tending to place it indiscriminately with communism, collectivism, and general immorality. Further, they thought that socialism was incompatible with if not antagonistic to Christianity. But Maurice believed that the socialist movement expressed the workers' desire for fellowship, thus bearing witness to a vital social principle at the center of Christ's kingdom. Following his lead, Christian socialists did not advocate collectivism under state ownership. In place of laissez faire, competition, and other materialist elements of the prevailing theories of political economy, they proposed cooperation, copartnership and profit sharing as ways to improve the personal status of the working classes and produce a just, Christian society.

If Maurice was the group's principal intellectual force, Ludlow may have been its prime mover and organizer. A barrister who had been born in India and reared and educated in France, Ludlow early came to dislike political and social privilege. In France he had known Louis Meyer, founder of the Société des Amis des Pauvres, whose members were supposed to devote their lives to the service of the poor. Ludlow's knowledge of Meyer's group suggested the concept of a brotherhood that would deal with social problems.

Initially, the group that began to form around Maurice and Ludlow in 1848 undertook educational and journalistic endeavors. They met for a series of weekly Bible readings with Maurice and founded a night school in Little Ormond Yard near Maurice's residence. Their journalistic efforts began with Kingsley's placard "Workmen of England," which he signed with the pseudonym "Parson Lot." In May, they began the short-lived periodical *Politics for the People*, edited by Ludlow and containing Kingsley's series of "Letters to Chartists" under the name "Parson Lot." At the end of July, however, the newspaper ceased publication.

In 1849, the group met Jules St. André le Chevalier, a French refugee who stayed for a time with Ludlow. Through le Chevalier and Ludlow as well as through their own reading, the British Christian socialists became acquainted with the teaching of Saint-Simon and Charles Fourier. Fourier's criticism of competitive systems governing production and consumption impressed them. In 1850, with the idea of providing joint work and shared profits, they founded a Working Association for Tailors with Walter Cooper as manager. Within six months after instituting a Society for Promoting Working Men's Associations with a governing Council of Promoters, the group founded

eight workers' associations. To explain their intentions, they issued *Tracts on Christian Socialism*—a title chosen in accord with Maurice's advice that they confront the issue of socialism directly. The first tract, written by Maurice, emphasized their effort to Christianize socialism and distinguished Christian socialism from other forms by emphasizing that fellowship expressed the principles of God's universe. The journal *The Christian Socialist* (Nov. 2, 1850–June 25, 1851) continued the tracts' effort to explain the movement and give it publicity.

Even by 1850, however, conflicts began to emerge. Edward Vansittart Neale and Lloyd Jones, whose orientation was essentially Owenite, pressed for extending the idea of association by sponsoring consumers' cooperatives. Supported by Neale and Thomas Hughes—but against the judgment of Maurice and Ludlow—the London Cooperative Stores opened in 1850. This action divided those who wished to concentrate on producers' cooperatives from those who advocated consumers' cooperatives as well. It also further alienated Maurice, who regarded associations as "machinery" and a misdirection of Christian socialist principles. When the Council of Promoters approved a Central Cooperative Agency to link the consumers' cooperatives, Ludlow resigned from the Council of Promoters. He believed that Neale and his supporters were losing sight of the principles of their organization. He also resigned from *The Christian Socialist*, which then changed its title to *A Journal of Association*, eliminated political commentary, and restricted its content to associative news.

In 1852, le Chevalier withdrew from the Central Cooperative Agency in a dispute, the *Journal of Association* failed for lack of funds, and Ludlow rejoined the Council of Promoters. But the Christian socialists' days as a coherent organization were clearly numbered. In 1853 they reorganized under a new constitution, dividing their work between the Association for Promoting Industrial and Provident Societies and the Industrial and Provident Societies' Union. Partly because of troubles at King's College (which eventually cost him his chair in 1853) and partly because he believed that the Christian socialists were becoming too attentive to "machinery," Maurice began to withdraw from their associative activities and concentrate on the attempt to found a college. In 1854 the Working Men's College opened in London, on a model provided by the People's College in Sheffield, and Maurice became its principal. Shortly thereafter the group disbanded. From the mid-1850s to the late 1870s the Christian socialist movement was inactive in Britain.

By the 1880s and 1890s and continuing into the first year of World War I, however, Christian socialists were again active and working in organized propaganda groups. For example, there was a Swedenborgian Socialist Society in London in the late 1890s, a Socialist Quaker Society begun in 1898, and Roman Catholic socialist societies in Glasgow and Leeds. Following Maurice's theological if not Ludlow's economic lead, Stewart Headlam (1847–1924) founded the Guild of St. Matthew, and B. F. Westcott (1825–1901) was eventually president of the Christian Social Union.

Christian socialism represents an attempt on the part of socially conscious people from the upper and middle classes to come to terms with the plight of workers in an industrial age and make the church responsive to that plight by showing Christianity and socialism to be compatible. Its theological substructure is but one aspect of the liberalizing thought of its most distinguished thinker, Frederick Denison Maurice.

LARRY K. UFFELMAN

Bibliography

Christensen, Torben. *Origin and History of Christian Socialism 1848–1854.* 1962.

Hartley, Allan John. *The Novels of Charles Kingsley: A Christian Social Interpretation.* 1977.

Jones, Peter d'Alroy. *The Christian Socialist Revival, 1877–1914: Religion, Class, and Social Conscience in Late-Victorian England.* 1968.

Ludlow, John Malcolm Forbes and Lloyd Jones. *Progress of the Working Class, 1832–1867.* 1867; rpt. 1973.

Masterman, N. C. *J. M. Ludlow: Builder of Christian Socialism.* 1913.

Maurice, Frederick, ed. *The Life of Frederick Denison Maurice, Chiefly Told in His Own Letters.* 1884.

Maurice, Frederick Denison. *The Kingdom of Christ.* 1838.

Ramsey, Arthur M. *F. D. Maurice and the Conflicts of Modern Theology.* 1951.

Raven, Charles Earle. *Christian Socialism, 1848–1854.* 1920.

Reckitt, Maurice B. *Maurice to Temple: A Century of the Social Movement in the Church of England.* 1947.

Wood, Herbert G. *Frederick Denison Maurice.* 1950.

See also CHARTISM; COOPERATIVE MOVEMENT

. . . . .

CHRISTMAS

Victorian Christmas combined a love of the past with a delight in innovation. Victorian traditions hearkened back to medieval times when the celebration of the winter solstice and of Jesus's birth united pagan and Christian rites. The Victorians enjoyed such medieval traditions as the yule log, the wassail bowl, and mummers' plays, and added new traditions like the Christmas tree and the Christmas card.

Prince Albert introduced the German tradition of the Christmas tree to England where middle-class families, fond of imitating the queen's household, quickly incorporated the decorated tree into their celebrations. Improvements in the postal service and the Victorian love of letter writing brought the Christmas card, the first of which was commissioned by John Calcott Horsley in 1843. Early Christmas cards generally represent the festivities of the season; very few depict religious scenes.

Christmas was a particularly important holiday for the middle class, which generally took to heart the religious significance of the day. A typical Christmas eve included dinner with family and friends, followed by gift opening, carols, and pantomimes, the latter reflecting the Victorian enjoyment of home theatricals. Christmas day began with matins, and often, in the spirit of the season, included visits of charity to those less fortunate. In the middle class especially, Christmas was also a celebra-

Engaging Children for the Christmas Pantomime at Drury Lane Theatre.
Illustrated London News, *7 December 1867. Library Company of Philadelphia.*

tion of the home and **family**. These were the aspects of Christmas that Charles Dickens in *A Christmas Carol* (1843) and Louisa May Alcott in *Little Women* (1868) chose to emphasize.

During the latter half of the nineteenth century, the greater availability of goods contributed to an increased commercialization of Christmas. Abundance at Christmastime, particularly in England, was a reflection of greater prosperity and boosted national pride. In many ways, Victorian Christmas reflects characteristic nineteenth-century traits such as nostalgia for the past and excitement about the future. Christmas also offered an opportunity for celebrating God, the home, and the nation at the same time.

MARTHA GOFF-STONER

Bibliography

Coffin, Tristram. *The Book of Christmas Folkore.* 1973.

Hervey, Thomas. *The Book of Christmas.* 1888.

Miall, Antony and Peter Miall. *The Victorian Christmas Book.* 1978.

Samuelson, Sue. *Christmas: An Annotated Bibliography.* 1982.

· · · · ·

CHURCH OF ENGLAND

The Church of England was and remained the official established church of the nation, but the meaning of "establishment" changed during the nineteenth century. With the admission of Protestant Dissenters and Roman Catholics to Parliament in 1828 and 1829 and the reform of Parliament in 1832, the old assumption of an alliance or identity of interest of church and state could no longer be made. The church had to find its place within the pluralism of English religion and the growing religious indifference of the masses.

The Anglican church had perhaps been too comfortably established in the eighteenth century. Supported not by taxes but by endowments of tithes and land, the clergy as a class was wealthy and interlocked with the gentry in dominating the countryside. 'This wealth was, however, unequally distributed, and most of the lower clergy were poor incumbents or underpaid curates, while the system of patronage ensured that social and political connection rather than devotion or talent generally determined who would get the better posts. Abuses such as nonresidence and pluralities were common. A structure of parishes, developed in the Middle Ages, no longer fitted the needs of an urbanizing and industrializing society. Nor was the teaching of the church such as to arouse the devotion of the people; scorning "enthusiasm," clergymen preached cool rationalistic sermons of latitudinarian theology and prudential morality. Reform did not come until the 1830s, but a religious revival—the **evangelical movement**—developed in the later eighteenth century. Although this produced Methodism and a revived Dissent, it also produced an Evangelical party within the established church, whose merits were increasingly appreciated after the French Revolution showed the danger to the old social order to which the church was so intimately attached. Slowly the standard of devotion was raised.

There remained for the church the problem of definition, especially after Anglicans lost their monopoly of public office and nonconformist groups came to have as many communicants as the establishment. The Anglican communion had been designed to be as comprehensive as possible; the word "Anglican" means simply English, that is, incapable of precise definition. The Thirty-Nine Articles (the doctrinal formulary) and the Book of Common Prayer were sufficiently imprecise to allow a variety of thought and practice ranging from Calvinism to Catholicism (not Roman). But this indefiniteness might make it difficult for Anglicans to make meaningful religious affirmations in an age of growing secularization. The evangelical movement was intended to obviate this danger by reviving the religious life of the nation, and the Anglican Evangelicals became a strong reforming party within the church; but the evangelical emphasis on individual faith provided little basis for improving the church as an institution. Some

Broad Churchmen, such as **Thomas Arnold** (1795–1842), gloried in doctrinal indefiniteness, stressing the national character of the church, open to all without preconditions; but this view was not widely shared. The most explicit response to the problem was that of the Oxford Movement, which was stimulated by the threat of political liberalism to advance a case for the independent authority of the church based on the apostolic succession. This gave a new sense of identity to the clergy; but the national phobia against clericalism and whatever smacked of popery ensured that High Churchmanship would be resisted at least as strongly as it was advocated. Other denominations had schisms and secessions; Anglicanism maintained an outward unity but produced movements and parties whose struggles, sincere but not always seemly, lasted through the century and interfered with the mission of the church to the people.

The danger that the reformed Parliament would legislate for the church was real. One of its first acts was to reform the Anglican Church of Ireland (united with the English church since 1800), abolishing ten dioceses and many useless dignities and parishes and redistributing the revenue. This was the act that sparked the Oxford Movement. Further danger was headed off by Conservative leader Robert Peel (1788–1850), who set up an Ecclesiastical Commission to propose reforms, which were enacted into legislation. An act of 1836 reshaped some dioceses and distributed bishops' incomes more equitably; later, additional bishoprics were created to respond to shifts in population. Other acts abolished sinecures, limited the number of cathedral dignitaries, and corrected pluralism and nonresidence among the clergy. The revenues of the suppressed positions were made a fund under the Ecclesiastical Commissioners (mostly bishops) to raise the incomes of the poorer clergy. Tithes were commuted to a reasonable money payment. These reforms actually strengthened the church and made it better able to resist demands for more substantial change.

Such demands were forthcoming from Nonconformists. They were aggrieved by having to pay the church rate (a small local property tax for the upkeep of parish churches) and fought bitterly until it was abolished in

1868. They opposed the efforts of Anglicans, through the voluntary National Society, to provide and control the primary education of the poor, and this opposition prevented the development of a national system of schooling until 1870. The more radical demanded the entire **disestablishment** and disendowment of the national church. This was accomplished (with Irish assistance) for Ireland in 1869; but the English church proved tougher than anyone (including its fearful clergy) expected. Partly because the Liberals, whom Nonconformists supported, were led by so devoted a churchman as William Ewart Gladstone (1809–1898), partly due to confusion among Nonconformists themselves, and possibly also because of sheer exhaustion, the issue of disestablishment died down, except in Wales, where Dissenters were a local majority and made it a nationalist cause; the church in Wales was disestablished in 1920.

Meanwhile the church had to reconstruct itself to meet the needs of a growing and industrializing population, a spontaneous work of clergy and laity almost entirely supported by voluntary contributions. Legislation facilitated the creation of new parishes, but their churches (mostly Victorian Gothic) were built by private donations, and exceedingly many were built. The National Society was the largest provider of elementary education until 1870. A network of philanthropic organizations was developed. A more numerous and energetic clergy mastered and expanded the techniques of parish work. Bishops followed the example of Samuel Wilberforce (1805–1873) of Oxford in organizing and managing their dioceses, however unpopular "Soapy Sam" may have been. The clergy, better trained and paid (until the agricultural depression after 1879), felt a new sense of professionalism. The meetings of convocation, suspended since 1717, were resumed in the 1850s, and resolutions began to be passed which, though not legislation, expressed the common mind of the church. Mechanisms were developed for some participation by communicant laity. Except for the royal nomination of bishops and the legislative power of Parliament, the established church seemed to be taking on many of the characteristics of a voluntary denomination, financially supported by its members (especially after the value of landed endowments fell) and competing in a pluralistic society.

How effectively did it compete? The only religious census, in 1851, showed that non-Anglicans had more chapels and active members than the establishment. The effect of the expanding activities of the church was that it had held its own with an expanding population. More ominous was the figure of 42 percent who attended no church at all. These, generally from the lowest classes, were the special mission of a national church; but the new churches were often empty. Heroic efforts by **Christian socialist** movements and slum priests had little effect. The fact was that the lower classes had developed a lifestyle which, though not hostile to religion, did not include participation in it. The church did not lose the working class; it never had it. By the 1880s the nonattenders were a majority, which grew thereafter. Anglicanism, no less than dissent, was largely a middle-class phenomenon, except in the villages, and the villages were declining. The intellectual failures of the church to deal with modern science and criticism were less important, though they led to defections among the intellectual middle classes.

The Church of England survived attacks, escaped disestablishment, revived and reorganized itself, produced rich new schools of thought and lively debates, struggled heroically to keep up with an expanding and changing population, and shared in the vigor of religious life during most of the Victorian period and the common decline of religion at its end. It was the only denomination that sought to serve the nation as a whole; its divisions and its class basis limited its success.

JOSEF L. ALTHOLZ

Bibliography

Bowen, Desmond. *The Idea of the Victorian Church.* 1968.

Brose, Olive. *Church and Parliament.* 1959.

Carpenter, Spencer C. *Church and People, 1789–1889.* 1933.

Chadwick, Owen. *The Victorian Church.* 1966–1970. 2 vols.

Elliott-Binns, Leonard, E. *Religion in the Victorian Era.* 2d ed., 1964.

Machin, G. I. T. *Politics and the Churches in Great Britain, 1832 to 1868.* 1977.

———. *Politics and the Churches in Great Britain, 1869 to 1921.* 1987.

Warre-Cornish, Francis. *The English Church in the Nineteenth Century.* 1910. 2 vols.

See also BROAD CHURCH; HIGH CHURCH; NONCONFORMITY; RITUALISM AND ANTI-RITUALISM; THEOLOGY
. . . . .

CHURCH OF ENGLAND PARISH LIFE

The local rhythm of Victorian life often still moved to the customs and rituals of the Anglican church, although much less so at the end than at the beginning of the nineteenth century. Realistically, no parish was "typical," and the church's influence varied from north to south, from village to city, even from parish to parish. Broadly speaking, however, the church's social functions receded as its religious functions gained primacy throughout the century.

The popular image of the typical Victorian parish, though long discredited, remains that of an agricultural village dominated by a resident squire and peopled primarily by agricultural tenants of the squire and domestics in his household. The two nodes of influence in such a village would be the manor and the church, where the parson, often a relative or friend of the squire (and sometimes the squire himself), would dispense religion, morality, and charity to a religious and harmonious community.

The actual position of the Church of England on the local level was complicated. The church was more likely to be influential in the agricultural village than in the industrial village or in the city, but by the end of the century England was much more an urban and industrial society than a rural and agricultural one. And where from one point of view the alliance between squire and parson resulted in a unified and religious parish, from another perspective it allied the church with

forces of oppression. Some evidence exists that churchgoing was highest in rural areas with a resident squire, lower in parishes where the squire was nonresident or parishes made up of small freeholders, and lowest of all in the working-class districts of the cities. Certainly, however, the social functions of the church in both village and town declined as more and more aspects of everyday life (e.g., education; the registration of births, deaths, and marriages) came into the province of the state.

Often the tone of parish life was set by the local parson. The advowson, the right to appoint the parson to the living or benefice, rested most often with private individuals, and occasionally with the bishop, with a college of Oxford or Cambridge, or with a lay corporation. Once appointed, the parson held the benefice for life, and early in the nineteenth century many clergy held more than one living. The incumbent's title was "vicar" in parishes where the tithes on major crops were impropriated, that is, annexed to a lay corporation or individual. Where the tithes were annexed to the parson himself, he was termed "rector." Early in the period a "curate" commonly was a clergyman serving in a parish whose incumbent was not resident. He was appointed and often poorly paid by the incumbent, and he could be removed at any time. By the middle of the nineteenth century, after reforms had reduced the incidence of multiple livings, the curate was more likely to be an assistant serving under a resident parson. Attached to the living was the "glebe," a piece of land which might be farmed by the parson himself or leased out. In rapidly growing towns and cities additional churches needed to be built within existing parishes. Clergy assigned to these might be "perpetual curates"; and often, in the absence of glebe or tithes, they were paid out of fees, pew rents, and occasional collections.

At the beginning of the nineteenth century, the parson, usually a graduate of Oxford or Cambridge, found his duties defined rather loosely. He would conduct Sunday services, visit his parishioners more or less zealously, and perform baptisms, marriages, and funerals (of which he was the official government registrar as well as the religious celebrant). But he would also be deeply involved in the broader social life of the parish, often serving as a magistrate, socializing with the local gentry (even perhaps hunting or dancing, although these activities came under fire early in the period), and possibly, as one of the only educated people in the parish, pursuing some amateur scholarly project. It was this group that Samuel Taylor Coleridge, in *On the Constitution of Church and State* (1829), envisioned as a "national clerisy," which would distribute throughout the nation all those spiritual, cultural, and educational influences that he thought essential to preventing social dissolution. By the last quarter of the century, however, the declining social, educational, and financial position of the clergy, as well as the nation's increasingly urban and industrial character, exposed the nostalgia of such a dream.

The parish life, particularly of small agricultural villages, revolved around the Sunday services and other occasional activities which served as rites of passage (baptism, marriage, burial). The prayer book called for two services on Sunday (although two or more services were much more common by the middle of the century than at the beginning). The morning service usually began at 10:00 a.m. and consisted of morning prayer, Litany, Holy Communion (early in the period normally without the actual consecration and distribution of the elements), and sermon. The second service often began as early as 3:00 p.m. (although in the towns it was more likely to be in the evening and many town parishes had both afternoon and evening services) and consisted of evening prayer and a sermon. If the parish was without a resident clergyman, the time and frequency of the service would vary depending upon the parson's arrival. Daily morning and evening prayer was enjoined by the prayer book and became more common during the century, especially among High Church devotees. The gradual diffusion of both evangelical and Tractarian fervor throughout the century altered the form and the appearance of Sunday services. For example, celebration of Holy Communion increased, and hymn singing gradually replaced the reciting of metrical psalms led by the parish clerk. Marriages and funerals, traditionally performed on Sundays between services, were moved to weekdays. Large enclosed pews lost favor, although seating in many churches still mirrored social standing: the squire's and parson's family pews nearest

the front, the "free" seats in the back. The traditional church band and choir seated in the west gallery were displaced by the harmonium or organ and often a children's choir located in or near the chancel.

Visitation of the sick had always been a priestly duty, and most of the pastoral handbooks of the period urged parish visiting in general. In a small rural village, the parson might know everyone in his parish, but the influx of people into the urban parishes, many of whom either had no connection or did not retain their connection with the church, hastened the acceptance of lay "district visitors." During the first half of the century the church was largely responsible for both the secular and the religious education of the parish. **Sunday schools**, begun in the eighteenth century, became widespread in the nineteenth, often imparting secular as well as religious education, although their secular functions declined in the last half of the century. Many Anglican parishes also ran officially sanctioned and often state-supported day schools (a source of irritation to many non-Anglicans), until the Education Act of 1870 set forth the concept of secular "board schools" in districts where no Anglican school was present or where it refused to allow state inspection. Paradoxically, even as the state began to take over social functions heretofore reserved to the church, by the end of the century both Anglicans and Nonconformists were more deeply committed to providing a range of charitable and educational services. Innumerable church organizations flourished in the last half of the century: Mothers' Unions, provident societies, clothing clubs, coal clubs, boys' and girls' clubs, and the like.

By the end of the century the Church of England was still a powerful force on the parish level, but clearly more so in some regions than in others. Although even its own leaders sensed that its influence was declining, it never completely lost its tenacious hold on the English imagination.

MARK S. LOOKER

Bibliography

Addleshaw, G. W. O. and Frederick Etchells. *The Architectural Setting of Anglican Worship.* 1947.

Chadwick, Owen. *The Victorian Church*, vol. 2. 1970.

Gilbert, Alan D. *Religion and Society in Industrial England: Church, Chapel, and Social Change.* 1976.

Haig, Alan. *The Victorian Clergy.* 1984.

Heeney, Brian. *A Different Kind of Gentleman: Parish Clergy as Professional Men in Early and Mid-Victorian England.* 1976.

Inglis, K. S. *The Churches and the Working Classes in Victorian England.* 1963.

. . . . .

CHURCH OF SCOTLAND

The Church of Scotland in the nineteenth century was, and has remained, the Christian ecclesiastical body established by law in Scotland. As such, it has understood itself historically to be the catholic church within Scotland: national, endowed, presbyterian, and reformed.

King William sponsored the final enactment of presbyterianism in the Church of Scotland in 1690. This action ended 130 years of chaotic political fluctuation between presbyterianism and episcopacy. The presbyterians recognized two orders of ministry: presbyters or elders (including ministers and lay elders) and deacons. Further, the Church of Scotland was and remains governed by graded, representative assemblies or courts of ministers and lay elders. These are, in order of ascending jurisdiction, local kirk sessions, presbyteries, synods, and the General Assembly.

Since the union of the English and Scottish parliaments in 1707, the General Assembly of the Church of Scotland has served as Scotland's only national legislative assembly. It normally has met in Edinburgh each May. Matters regularly coming before Victorian General Assemblies included disciplinary cases forwarded from lower church courts and overtures or appeals from the same bodies concerning doctrine, church organization and extension, ministerial training, foreign missions, national education, and poor relief. The assembly was also an arena of confrontation between the two main parties in the church. The first of these, the Moderates, were self-conscious heirs of the Enlightenment—cultured, philosophical, educated gentlemen who valued the church's connection with the state and were stable to the point of dryness. Evangelicals, on the other hand, were fervid revivers of the Calvinism that had been allowed to lapse during the eighteenth century. They opposed the Moderates not only because many Evangelicals felt the moderate position to be wrong, but also because the Moderates had not experienced an evangelical conversion.

The moderator, who presided over the General Assembly, was elected annually by the presbyter delegates. After adjournment, the moderator functioned for one year as the Church of Scotland's official representative and chief dignitary, and was traditionally referred to as The Very Reverend. In 1901 the General Assembly embraced seventeen synods, eighty-seven presbyteries, and a host of congregations abroad, and listed a total national church membership of approximately 662,000 persons. These statistics reflect the Church of Scotland's continuing status as the country's largest religious body. Its leading competitors included the **Free Church of Scotland** (288,000 members in 1901), the United Presbyterian Church (194,000), the Scottish Episcopal Church (47,000), and a smaller number of Baptists and Methodists. To these were added a growing number of Roman Catholics, composed mainly of Irish immigrants concentrated in industrial centers such as Glasgow.

Established in 1560 with many of its ancient endowments intact, the Church of Scotland was supported also by teinds or tithes, a church tax principal landowners were obliged to pay on their crops to the parish in which their property lay. This obligation held whether the landowners were members of the Church of Scotland or not, and so was seen by many as unfair. In the 1870s and 1880s those who wished to see the Church of Scotland disestablished, such as supporters of W. E. Gladstone's Liberal party–Nonconformist political alliance, complained of teinds.

Patronage was another controversial legal aspect of establishment. Between its imposition by Parliament in 1712 and its repeal in 1874, patronage in the Church of Scotland provoked three major secessions from the national church. Patronage meant that vacant parish incumbencies were to be filled by ministers chosen by legally recognized patrons. These might be the Crown, town councils, colleges, or principal landowners called heritors. Again, there was no assurance that such patrons would be members of the Church of Scotland or have the church's interests at heart.

Thomas Chalmers (1780–1847) and other Evangelical ministers argued that patronage was an intolerable infringement by the state on the church's spiritual freedom to choose its own ministers. An Evangelical majority enabled the General Assembly to pass the Veto Act in 1834, which allowed the vote of a majority of male heads of households within a congregation to refuse a patron's nominee. During the ensuing decade, as this ruling came to be tested, the civil Court of Session persistently refused to uphold it. Thus occurred the dramatic disruption of the church. On May 18, 1843, 474 out of a total of 1,203 ministers and most of their church members left the established church to form the Free Protesting Church of Scotland, later known simply as the **Free Church of Scotland**. While the Church of Scotland recovered quickly from this institutional trauma, the schism was not healed until the next century, with the union of the Free Church and the United Presbyterian Church in 1900 to form the United Free Church, and the subsequent union of the United Free Church with the Church of Scotland in 1929.

The nineteenth century was a period of reassessment and self-criticism for the Church of Scotland. The patronage controversy and the disestablishment campaigns forced a rethinking of its relation to the state. But it had also to rethink its creed. The doctrinal traditions of the Church of Scotland are rooted in the Swiss Reformation and the Puritanism embodied in the Westminster Confession of Faith (1646), to which ministers and elders are required to subscribe. The General Assembly, however, relaxed the stringency of the form of this subscription for elders in 1889 and for ministers in 1893. (The latter was confirmed by Parliament in 1905.) These actions were partly a result of the influence of progressive historical-critical theologians like John Caird and John Tulloch.

Concurrently with this theological movement away from Puritan scholasticism, church historians and liturgical reformers such as R. H. Story, G. W. Sprott, A. K. H. Boyd, and James Cooper were urging a transformation of the worship of the Scottish church by bringing popular attention to neglected aspects of its own native Reformed tradition. By the end of the century organs, choirs, and a liturgy of common prayer were no longer unusual in many of the larger congregations of the Church of Scotland. In addition to its experience of rapid change in attitudes to the Westminster Confession and to worship, the national church underwent, along with other churches, the crisis of faith that accompanied first public exposure to the historical-critical study of the Bible, and the challenge of ministering to the rapidly multiplying urban masses, for whom the old rural parish system could not adequately provide.

DAVID R. BOONE

Bibliography

Brown, Stewart J. *Thomas Chalmers and the Godly Commonwealth in Scotland.* 1982.

Cheyne, A. C. *The Transforming of the Kirk: Victorian Scotland's Religious Revolution.* 1983.

Drummond, Andrew L. and James Bulloch. *The Church in Late Victorian Scotland, 1874–1900.* 1978.

———. *The Church in Victorian Scotland, 1843–1874.* 1975.

———. *The Scottish Church, 1688–1843: The Age of the Moderates.* 1973.

Story, Robert Herbert, ed. *The Church of Scotland, Past and Present.* 1890. 5 vols.

· · · · ·

CHURCHILL, LORD RANDOLPH HENRY SPENCER (1849–1895)

Lord Randolph Churchill, the father of Winston Churchill, was an ambitious and influential Tory political figure in the 1880s. He rose meteorically to become the **Conservative party**'s leader in the House of Commons in

1886 and rapidly lost influence following his miscalculated resignation in the same year.

Third son of the seventh duke of Marlborough, Churchill had an undistinguished career at Eton and Merton College, Oxford. In 1874 he married Jennie Jerome, the daughter of a New York entrepreneur, whose beauty was more tangible than her dowry, and was elected to the Commons for the family borough of Woodstock (over which his father had decisive influence).

During the 1880s, Churchill became the leader of a small group of maverick Conservative and radical M.P.'s nicknamed the "Fourth party." They gained visibility by opposing the seating of atheist Charles Bradlaugh. The "Fourth party" also opportunistically espoused a program of Tory Democracy designed to encourage mass support and helped found (in 1883) the Primrose League, the Conservative party's nearest approximation of a mass organization. Churchill attempted to undermine the authority of Stafford Northcote, the party's ineffective and failing leader in the Commons, and by using the press and hard-hitting platform oratory to establish a power base in the National Union of Conservative Associations, of which he became chairman in 1884.

After the fall of Gladstone's second ministry in June 1885, Lord **Salisbury** included Churchill in his cabinet as secretary of state for India. Churchill's administration was noteworthy principally for the annexation of Upper Burma (1886), although he had earlier attacked Gladstone for British expansion in Egypt. During Gladstone's third ministry (1886), Churchill strongly opposed **Home Rule** for Ireland and rallied opposition under the slogan "Ulster will fight; Ulster will be right."

When Gladstone's Home Rule bill was defeated and the Conservatives carried the subsequent general election, Salisbury was obliged to make Churchill, at thirty-seven, chancellor of the exchequer and the government's leader in the House of Commons. Churchill, however, made enemies by meddling in the departmental affairs of his cabinet colleagues. His impatient and erratic course is difficult to explain except on grounds of health; he was almost certainly suffering by this time from the degenerative syphilis to which he ultimately succumbed.

On December 20, 1886, Churchill resigned from the cabinet, ostensibly because the Admiralty and the War Office objected to the reduced defense appropriations his budget proposed. In all likelihood, he was bidding for leadership of the party, but Salisbury called his bluff and accepted his resignation. Exiled to the political wilderness, Churchill rapidly faded as a major political figure. Winston Churchill's two-volume biography, although written with filial piety, unsuccessfully attempted to show consistency and principle in his father's political career.

ROBERT S. FRASER

Bibliography

Churchill, Peregrine and Julian Mitchell. *Jennie, Lady Randolph Churchill: A Portrait with Letters.* 1974.

Churchill, Winston S. *Lord Randolph Churchill.* 1906. 2 vols.

Foster, R. F. *Lord Randolph Churchill: A Political Life.* 1981.

James, Robert Rhodes. *Lord Randolph Churchill.* 1959.

Martin, Ralph G. *Lady Randolph Churchill: A Biography,* vol. 1. 1969.

Primrose, A. P., Earl of Rosebery. *Lord Randolph Churchill.* 1906.

See also PARTY SYSTEM

· · · · ·

CIRCUS

Circuses (and **pantomime** shows) were a staple of Yuletide entertainment in cities. Outside this festive season, the spectacle—with sideshows—toured the provinces, pitching a week here, a week there in the marketplace or on common land. The local populace was bidden to "Roll up! Roll up for the fun of the fair!" Fun for various ages and tastes was to be found amid booths and stalls, on musical rides, at hoopla and skittles clustered around the circus tent. Some spectacles that now appear cruel, including the exhibition of armless women or other grotesques, did not offend the standards of the time. Fairgrounds operated subject to no regulations except those that the local constabulary might enforce.

The circus itself, which originated in the amphitheaters of ancient Rome, developed its definitive form by the end of the nineteenth century. Performing animals and certain acrobatic acts were staple entertainments at fairs from at least the Middle Ages. In the second half of the eighteenth century, Philip Astley began performing riding acts in a ring so that centrifugal force could help the rider maintain balance. Fixed amphitheaters for indoor performances—sometimes given the name "circus"—were built in the late eighteenth and early nineteenth century, but were not as popular in England as on the Continent. During the 1840s the circus tent was introduced from America and, as road surfaces were macadamized, the Big Top went on the move.

Mobility—and the sideshows—formed an integral element of popular appeal. Within the circus tent, the program came to feature a standard assemblage of acts: acrobats, aerialists (both high-wire and trapeze), trick riders, clowns, and animal trainers. Performing bears, common in medieval Europe, were rare in Britain until, like elephants, camels, and caged wild beasts, they were imported from Queen Victoria's expanding dominions.

Transatlantic influence was responsible for the introduction of impresarios into Britain's developing leisure industry. While Phineas T. Barnum (1810–1891) filled London's new exhibition hall at Olympia in the 1880s, two homebred showmen moved midstage upon the national arena. The Sanger brothers, John (1816–1889) and George (1825–1911) were household names, self-styled "Lords" in the tradition of sawdust ennoblement who turned Sanger's Circus into a family business. John's professionalism is immortalized by a ringmaster's long whips carved upon his tomb, and in an adjoining plot of St. John's Cemetery, Thanet, Kent, "Lord" George Sanger has three family clowns for eternal companionship.

SALLY MITCHELL

Bibliography

Coxe, Antony Hippisley. *A Seat at the Circus.* Rev. ed., 1980.

Fitzsimons, Raymund. *Barnum in London.* 1970.

Sanger, George. *Seventy Years a Showman.* 1926.

Speaight, George. *A History of the Circus.* 1980.

Wykes, Alan. *Circus!* 1977.

· · · · ·

CITIES

"Our age is preeminently the age of great cities," declared the historian Robert Vaughan in 1843. The growth of cities in Victoria's reign was so rapid that by 1851 more than half the population were living in towns of 10,000 or more, making Britain the first modern urbanized society. By 1901 more than three-quarters were classified by the census as urban, as compared to one-fifth in 1801.

Victorian cities grew chiefly by migration from the country rather than by natural increase. The need for a large, nonseasonal workforce and the greater efficiency of concentrating factories around power sources and transportation centers drew workers and manufacturers from rural areas. Transformed by the cotton boom of the 1770s and 1780s, the **Manchester**-Salford area quadrupled in size from 1801 to 1851, from 84,000 to 367,000. During the same period other industrial centers such as Liverpool, Birmingham, Leeds, and Sheffield showed similarly high rates of growth.

Although **London**'s rapid development was due less to its industry than to its position as the administrative and commercial capital, it followed the same pattern. At the 1861 census fewer than half of the males living in the city had been born there, and between 1841 and 1901 the number of inhabitants more than tripled from just under 1.9 million to 6.6 million.

The expansion of cities at the peripheries was often accompanied by a decreasing population in city centers. The development of underground and commuter railway lines speeded the redistribution of the urban population, making "suburbia," a term used in the modern sense as early as the 1790s, a widespread reality by the third quarter of the nineteenth century. When the first London underground train began operation in 1863 there were already over fifteen other railways serving commuters in the capital district.

The rush of indiscriminate demolition and new building in a jumble of architectural styles transformed many cities into a brick-and-mortar analogue of laissez-faire capitalism. Railway cuttings sliced into medieval town centers and whole districts were leveled to make way for terminals and railyards. The devastation was memorably described by Charles Dickens in *Dombey and Son* (1848): "The first shock of a great earthquake had . . . rent the whole neighbourhood to its centre." But in months new communities sprang up to replace the old. Midcentury was an era of great "Improvements," as they were called, such as the London Metropolitan Drainage System (1858–1875) and the Thames Embankment (1862–1874), as well as architectural testimonies to national and civic pride: the new Houses of Parliament (1837–1867), the neoclassical "Forum" of Liverpool (1841–1902), and the monumental Victorian Gothic edifice of the Manchester Town Hall (1868–1877).

The new means of rapid transport helped create specialized sectors for finance, industry, shipping, trade, and residence, the last almost infinitely subdivided by class, occupation, and economic level. Impoverished East London and the well-to-do West End offered physical evidence of what Benjamin Disraeli called "Two Nations," a Britain divided by an unbridgeable gulf between rich and poor. Stratification intensified as middle- and upper-class residents moved out of inner cities to more spacious suburbs, such as North London's "Metroland." In his classic study of the degradation of the urban poor, *The Condition of the Working Class in England* (1845), Friedrich Engels noted the "hypocritical town planning . . . common to all big cities," where the well-kept facades of the main thoroughfares insulated the "tender susceptibilities" of middle-class commuters from the sight and smell of back-street slums.

The social cost of urbanization was often high. Thousands of workers annually moved into cities that had no adequate facilities for them. Jerrybuilding and the subdivision of existing dwellings quickly produced overcrowding, and by 1841 unsanitary conditions and disease brought life expectancy among working people in Manchester down to about twenty years—half what it was in the country. The "Blue Books" of the 1840s, factory inspectors' reports on working conditions, shocked the public with their revelations. In its vast profitability and polluted squalor, Manchester was a lurid symbol of technological progress and its dehumanizing price. In *Coningsby* (1844) Disraeli observed ironically that, "Rightly understood, Manchester is as great a human exploit as Athens." Industrial novels about the "hungry forties," including *Hard Times* (1854) by Dickens, and *Mary Barton* (1848) and *North and South* (1855) by Elizabeth Gaskell, sympathetically described the plight of laborers in northern factory towns.

In the 1880s and 1890s "the discovery of poverty" in the East End focused public attention on London as it had on Manchester in the 1840s. Anticipated by the fieldwork of Henry Mayhew (*London Labour and the London Poor*, 1861–1862), the efforts of reformers and writers such as General William Booth (*In Darkest England and the Way Out*, 1890), Andrew Mearns (*The Bitter Cry of Outcast London*, 1883), Arthur Morrison (*Tales of Mean Streets*, 1894), and George Gissing (*The Nether World*, 1889) revealed that "darkest London" harbored a populace as exotic to West Enders and as needy as any African tribe. **Charles Booth** reported in his monumental study *Life and Labour of the People in London* (1891–1903) that a third of London's population were living in poverty, and concern with their situation played a crucial part in the development of modern social work and sociology.

If at the start of the nineteenth century "urban" still meant "urbane" and major cities were regarded with pride as centers of civilization, during Victoria's reign they also came to be seen as breeding grounds of depravity, radicalism, and atheism. London was estimated to shelter over 10,000 prostitutes, the urban crime rate was thought to be twice that of rural areas, and Chartist and socialist agitations were concentrated in cities. Religious observance was another urban casualty: in 1851 fewer than one resident in ten of Birmingham, Manchester, Sheffield, and Newcastle attended church or chapel.

Victorian art and poetry illustrate ambivalent, sometimes even hostile, attitudes toward the city. Paintings such as Dante Gabriel Rossetti's *Found* (1853–1882) and Augustus

Egg's *Past and Present* (1858) focus on the fallen woman, frequently depicted as a product and a symbol of the decadent modern Babylon. An overwhelming sense of what Matthew Arnold called the "unpoetrylessness" of modern life led many poets to avoid the city or deal with it only indirectly; thus Alfred Tennyson's *Idylls of the King* (1859–1885) substitutes legendary Camelot for nineteenth-century London in its analysis of contemporary society. While for Walt Whitman or Charles Baudelaire the city meant exciting new artistic possibilities, the Victorian repulsion from the city is exemplified by James Thomson's nightmare vision of urban monotony and solitude, *The City of Dreadful Night* (1874). In Arthur Hugh Clough's poem *Dipsychus* (1869) the alienating size, anonymity, and sexuality of the city constitute a frightening assault on personal identity.

Most city dwellers, having grown up in the country, felt a profound nostalgia for nature. Not until the 1870s and 1880s did artists of the aesthetic movement praise the city for the very quality that most Victorians had condemned—its artificiality. James McNeill Whistler painted atmospheric scenes of night-time London in his series of "Nocturnes," and in 1892 Richard LeGallienne summed up the new pleasures of the gaslit city being discovered by poets of the 1890s: "Ah, London! London! our delight, / Great flower that opens but at night."

But if painters and poets only belatedly learned to appreciate the city, Dickens, in novels such as *Bleak House* (1852–1853), *Little Dorrit* (1855–1857), and *Our Mutual Friend* (1864–1865), had already realized its fantastic energy and multiplicity. An anonymous reviewer in 1861 justly called Dickens "the epic poet of city life," and his popularity was due in part to the fact that, in Britain, modern life had become urban life.

WILLIAM CHAPMAN SHARPE

Bibliography

Briggs, Asa. *Victorian Cities.* 1963.

Coleman, Bruce I., ed. *The Idea of the City in Nineteenth-Century Britain.* 1973.

Doré, Gustave and Blanchard Jerrold. *London: A Pilgrimage.* 1872.

Dyos, H. J. and Michael Wolff, eds. *The Victorian City: Images and Realities.* 1973. 2 vols.

Mumford, Lewis. *The City in History.* 1961.

Nadel, Ira Bruce and F. S. Schwarzbach, eds. *Victorian Artists and the City: A Collection of Critical Essays.* 1980.

Olsen, Donald J. *The Growth of Victorian London.* 1976.

Sheppard, Francis. *London, 1808–1870: The Infernal Wen.* 1971.

Vaughan, Robert. *The Age of Great Cities.* 1843.

Walvin, James. *English Urban Life, 1776–1851.* 1984.

Weber, Adna F. *The Growth of Cities in the Nineteenth Century: A Study in Statistics.* 1899.

Williams, Raymond. *The Country and the City.* 1973.

See also HOUSING; PUBLIC HEALTH; SUBURBS AND PLANNED COMMUNITIES; TRANSPORTATION, URBAN

· · · · ·

CIVIL SERVICE

During the nineteenth century civil service reform constituted a key aspect of the construction of a modern state. The growth and elaboration of a bureaucratic apparatus characterized a Victorian "revolution in government." Two pivotal events mark the course of this development: the Northcote-Trevelyan Report of 1853 and the 1870 order-in-council that mandated the recruitment of civil servants by open, competitive examination.

In 1853 William Gladstone appointed Charles Trevelyan (formerly of the Indian Civil Service and assistant secretary of the Treasury from 1840 until 1859) and Stafford Northcote (who had begun his career as Gladstone's private secretary at the Board of Trade) to investigate the question of civil service reform. Their report, completed within the year, criticized the inefficiency of a civil service recruited by patronage appointment and called for recruitment by competitive, open examination, promotion based on merit, and the creation of a unified civil service that would embrace all departments and would separate questions of policy and administration from routine record keeping, thus distinguishing between "intellectual and mechanical work."

These recommendations received a warm welcome from the Administrative Reform Association and Victorian opinion makers such as J. S. Mill, himself a senior civil servant at the **East India Company**, and Charles Dickens, who pilloried government bureaucracy with his creation of the Circumlocution Office in *Little Dorrit* (1857). Approval was by no means unanimous, however. Many civil servants resented the attack on their competence implicit in the report. Anthony Trollope, who had risen to a position of responsibility at the post office under the old system, expressed his suspicions of reform in *The Three Clerks* (1858). Party managers, worried about how they would reward the faithful, strongly resisted any inroads on patronage. An 1855 order-in-council created the Civil Service Commission to certify the qualifications of all entrants to the civil service. This established the principle of meritocratic recruitment and technically brought patronage to an end, but in practice little actually changed.

Reform might have stopped with this modest adjustment but for the scandals of the Crimean War. The long-term success of civil service reform, however, derived in part from contemporary changes in education. Educational leaders at both the universities and the **public schools** perceived the opportunities created for the growing supply of classically trained young men they produced. The appeal to the principle of merit proved decisive within government circles. Gladstone implemented the most important item of Trevelyan's agenda, open competition examination, with an 1870 order-in-council.

This act significantly altered the character of the English civil service. Recruitment by examination severed the personal link of dependence forged by patronage appointment and thereby helped to create a body of men whose chief loyalty lay with the state rather than with a particular party, individual, or policy. This small but powerful elite remained

exclusively masculine until after World War I, although women took on the increasing volume of clerical work (subject to the Treasury requirement that female staff had to resign upon marriage), and some departments employed women as inspectors to deal with issues such as girls' education or women's work.

At the departmental level changes were slow and irregular. The Foreign Office opted out of open competition recruitment, as did the Scottish and Irish offices. Both the new Board of Agriculture (1889) and the new Board of Education (1899) preferred their own methods of recruitment to open competition. Nevertheless the principle held sway for the bulk of the home civil service by the end of the century, and Trevelyan's goals had largely been accomplished by 1919.

Industrialization, urbanization, and the expansion of empire all placed unprecedented demands on English government. The need to meet these demands created an impetus for civil service reform that appealed to a number of different constituencies. Tory radicals and Benthamites could unite in a denunciation of jobbery and inefficiency, while the enlargement of the political nation to include the middle class automatically called aristocratic patronage into question. Civil service reform did not, however, constitute a democratization of English government. Meritocratic recruitment by competitive examination favored the products of the public schools and the universities. The growing middle class had already permeated these institutions, but in so doing they had taken on many aspects of the aristocratic ethos, including the responsibility of public service. The English gentleman still ruled in England.

GAIL L. SAVAGE

Bibliography

Fry, Geoffrey K. *Statesmen in Disguise.* 1969.

Hanham, H. J. ed. *The Nineteenth-Century Constitution, 1815–1914: Documents and Commentary.* 1969.

Holcombe, Lee. *Victorian Ladies at Work.* 1973.

Martindale, Hilda. *Women Servants of the State, 1870–1938: A History of Women in the Civil Service.* 1938.

Mommsen, W. J., ed. *The Emergence of the Welfare State in Britain and Germany, 1850–1950.* 1981.

Pellew, Jill. *The Home Office, 1848–1914.* 1982.

Roseveare, Henry. *The Treasury: The Evolution of a British Institution.* 1969.

Stansky, Peter, ed. *The Victorian Revolution: Government and Society in Victoria's Britain.* 1973.

Sutherland, Gillian. *Studies in the Growth of Nineteenth-Century Government.* 1972.

See also GOVERNMENT: COLONIES AND EMPIRE

. . . . .

CIVIL WAR, UNITED STATES

At the beginning of the American Civil War both the Union and the Confederacy expected British sympathy and support. British commercial interests that anticipated vast profits from free markets in an independent South favored the Confederacy. Most British intellectuals supported the North. The British government determined on a policy of neutrality.

Britain's sale of the commerce raiders *Florida* and *Alabama* to the Confederacy seriously damaged Union shipping. When the Confederates then attempted to obtain ironclad rams with revolving gun turrets, the United States minister to Britain protested that the sale would violate British neutrality. It was eventually halted.

So long as the Lincoln government maintained that the war was being fought only to preserve the Union, Confederate propaganda could paint the North as an invading aggressor in a war over a purely constitutional issue. At the end of 1862 the Emancipation Proclamation made clear that preserving the Union and ending slavery were one cause. Union and emancipation societies in Britain distributed pamphlets and organized meetings, while Richard Cobden and John Bright labored in the House of Commons; Bright's oratory on June 30, 1863 defeated a motion that urged Britain to negotiate with other European powers for recognition of the Confederacy.

The Union blockade of the South caused serious distress in the textile districts of the north of England; the cotton famine of 1862–1864 forced mills to close and threw thousands of women, children, and men out of work. Textile workers, nevertheless, largely supported the Union cause; they grasped immediately that slavery was the real issue and saw the emancipation struggle as parallel to their own battle for political recognition and human dignity.

Although most British public figures favored the North, the press was cool or even hostile. **William Howard Russell**, sent by the *Times* to America in 1861, wrote a vivid description of the route of Northern troops at Bull Run, and was subsequently barred from accompanying McClellan in the campaign of 1862. Frank Vizetelly of the *Illustrated London News* often sent back sketches from the Confederate front lines.

Garnett Wolseley, later commander in chief of the British army, enormously admired Robert E. Lee and Stonewall Jackson. His postwar writings helped promulgate the vision of the South as a land of noble warriors defeated solely by superior fire power. A British nobleman offered Lee a residence and life pension, which he declined, but Jefferson Davis lived in England for fourteen months after his release from prison. A strong Confederate colony centered in London after the war. One of its members, Judah P. Benjamin, who had been Confederate secretary of war and subsequently of state, was admitted to the British bar in 1866, became a Queen's Counsel, and established himself as the preeminent authority on the British law of contracts.

BARBARA J. DUNLAP

Bibliography

Foner, Philip S. *British Labor and the American Civil War.* 1981.

Jenkins, Brian. *Britain and the War for the Union.* 1973.

Shaw, Frederick. J. *Anglo-American Relations, 1861–1865.* 1920.

. . . . .

CLARENDON, FOURTH EARL (GEORGE VILLIERS) (1800-1870)

The fourth earl of Clarendon was notable for his long career in government service. He served as an attaché at the British embassy in St. Petersburg (1820-1823), commissioner of customs with service in England, Ireland, and France (1823-1833), minister to Spain (1833-1839), and in the cabinet as lord privy seal (1840-1841), chancellor of the duchy of Lancaster (1840-1841; 1864-1865), president of the Board of Trade (1846-1847), and foreign secretary (1853-1858; 1865-1866; 1868-1870). Until he succeeded to his title (1839), he was known simply as George Villiers.

Objectivity and moderation were traits Clarendon consistently exhibited. In public life he concentrated most of his energy on foreign affairs, and headed the foreign office with first-hand knowledge of the international community, although he acted with uncharacteristic rashness in deciding to send the fleet into the Black Sea before the Crimean War. At the end of the war he led the British delegation at the Congress of Paris (1856) where he advocated stiff peace terms for Russia.

During Clarendon's last term as foreign secretary he attempted to get Prussia and France to disarm. Prince Otto von Bismarck predictably refused. Clarendon was also aware of possible repercussions from a Hohenzollern candidacy for the Spanish throne, but he miscalculated in not foreseeing the outbreak of war between France and Prussia in 1870. He died at a critical moment in European history, and Bismarck later told Clarendon's daughter that had her father lived there would have been no war. Clarendon had worked hard to keep the peace in Europe, but Britain was unprepared to intervene to prevent war.

LYLE A. McGEOCH

Bibliography

Maxwell, Herbert E. *The Life and Letters of George William Frederick, Fourth Earl of Clarendon.* 1913. 2 vols.

Millman, Richard. *British Foreign Policy and the Coming of the Franco-Prussian War.* 1965.

Villiers, George. *A Vanished Victorian: Being the Life of G. Villiers, Fourth Earl of Clarendon, 1800-1870.* 1938.

· · · · ·

CLASS

In early Victorian Britain class distinctions were relatively clear-cut, but as population and national wealth increased the structure of society began to change. Although class consciousness remained, the formerly rigid class divisions became more flexible and there was greater freedom of movement between classes. Changes in the religious and cultural realm were equally significant: a widespread cult of pious respectability together with better housing, education, public health, and welfare provision narrowed the obvious differences between people of various classes. With the advance toward an increasingly democratic political system, a variety of elites tended to become more significantly divisive than the old class structure based on birth.

Writing of England at Queen Victoria's accession (1837), **Benjamin Disraeli** criticized a "mortgaged" aristocracy, a middle class only just struggling into existence, a peasantry too numerous to support itself, and a rootless urban working class which was economically and culturally degraded. A society so stratified was in desperate need of leadership and reform, which Disraeli believed could be supplied only by a dedicated aristocracy.

No more than thirty years later, two other influential writers, Walter Bagehot and **Matthew Arnold**, emphasized the newly won political power of the middle class and analyzed (in Arnold's case very unfavorably) the character and beliefs of that class. Bagehot was most impressed by its deferential attitude to the aristocracy, Arnold by its complacent self-satisfaction. But both held that the era of aristocratic supremacy was drawing to an end; that the future lay with the emerging middle class; and that patronage and leadership for the poor, as the lowest class was generally and indeed accurately described, would be slowly transferred from the Barbarians (Arnold's name for the aristocracy) to the Philistines (his term for the middle class). He saw the members of the middle class as ignorant, narrow, and prejudiced. Their strength lay in ambition and energy, which gave them economic control of their own lives and thus the prospect of eventually establishing a new social order, under their leadership, which would be open to all who emerged from the populace with similar determination and values. Democracy, a buoyant economy, and open access to education were to be the means of breaking down obsolete class barriers and transforming England.

That sort of process, however, required time. Before it had gone far, the aristocracy had recovered its balance, abandoned some of its grosser practices, and grown several new limbs. Lawyers, bankers, and even business and professional men acquired titles or produced offspring whom the aristocracy was happy to embrace. (The most prominent nineteenth-century statesmen, Gladstone and Disraeli, fell into this category.) It was now in the main a working aristocracy, active in central and local government, favoring popular sports carried out in the public eye and to the public's satisfaction, such as horse racing, fox hunting, and cricket. In the major provincial cities a local elite arose, principally composed of businessmen who were generally nonconformist in religion and sometimes mildly radical. But the central core of the upper class was still the hereditary nobility and the landed gentry.

The mid-Victorian evolution of the middle class was complicated. Neither Disraeli nor Arnold used the term "**gentleman**" in their description of class structure. Soon, however, subtle distinctions within the middle class and the working class became more relevant to people's lives than crude classification on outdated models. As perceived by the middle class, the status of gentleman was arbitrary and uncertain, yet socially of vital importance. If the gentry represented a social elite, than ladies and gentlemen (collectively "gentlefolk") were those acceptable to that elite at a given time and place. There were also moral and behavioral criteria on which such judgments could depend. Even so, it was hard for gentlefolk who lacked sufficient income to maintain the appropriate standard of life.

Many, especially in the towns, were middle class on the basis of occupation, income, and respectability but did not aspire to be of the gentry. A clerk on an income of 200 pounds a year was unlikely to be regarded as a gentleman, but might see himself as a pillar of the middle class. In the social life of a small town, as described in Anthony Trollope's *The American Senator* (1877), the attorney is respected because he is in the confidence of the gentry; indeed, during his first marriage to the daughter of a clergyman, he had been accepted as a gentleman in the fullest sense of the term. By his second marriage to a relatively uneducated daughter of an ironmonger he lost that status in the eyes of many, but whether or not he was universally counted as a gentleman mattered little in practice; in the indigenous society of the little town, he was unmistakably one of the elite.

The idea of the elite was no less visible among workingmen. A *Punch* cartoon of 1865 shows three varieties of working-class elitism. One picture depicts a craftsman of the highest moral virtue sprouting angel's wings and drinking a glass of water; the second an intellectual, like Hardy's *Jude the Obscure* (1895), poring over his books by candlelight; the third an ardent radical republican vigorously trying to subvert the social order. The fourth picture in *Punch's* gallery was the common workingman stereotype, well known to *Punch's* middle-class readers, with his bovine face glazed over and a tankard of ale at his side.

Late Victorian society was hierarchical. Most people accepted the delegation of authority to select groups. The gentlemanly ideal served as a social cement within the upper section of the middle class and linked it structurally with the aristocracy. This process was reinforced by the rapid development of the **public schools**, for which of course fees were charged. The less affluent section of the middle class had to wait until the twentieth century before a national system of secondary education on the lines of the public school could develop.

As Victoria's reign drew to an end, the main division within the middle class was between those men who had attended a public school and entered one of the professions and those who had not. The clearest division within the working class was, as G. B. Shaw put it in *Pygmalion* (1912), between the deserving and the undeserving poor. No longer a class-ridden society in the old sense, England remained a society stratified on the basis of its elites.

DAVID HOPKINSON

Bibliography

Bagehot, Walter. *The British Constitution.* 2d ed., 1872.

Best, Geoffrey. *Mid-Victorian Britain, 1851–1875.* 1971.

Burn, W. L. *The Age of Equipoise.* 1964.

Clark, G. Kitson. *The Making of Victorian England.* 1962.

Phillips, K. C. *Language and Class in Victorian England.* 1984.

Reader, W. J. *Life in Victorian England.* 1964.

See also ARISTOCRACY AND GENTRY

· · · · ·

CLASSICAL SCHOLARSHIP

From Lord Elgin's sighting of the Acropolis (1800) to the establishment of the British School at Rome (1901), every field important to the Victorians was influenced by classical art and thought; and every category of contemporary interest was imposed upon the ideas and monuments of antiquity. Greek and Roman cultures provided sources, models, and inspiration; the Hellenic and Roman past was read typologically, foreshadowing the Christian present. Many Victorians were precocious classicists from childhood, reared on Greek and Latin in schools and universities, and devoted to quasi-professional classical studies.

Tennyson memorized Horace before going to school at the age of six (1815), and at fifteen wrote Greek and Latin meters easily. Arnold and Clough learned Greek at Rugby under Dr. Thomas Arnold; Connop Thirlwall read Latin at three, Greek at four; John Conington did textual comparisons of the *Aeneid* at eight, anticipating his edition of Virgil (1858–1871); J. S. Mill learned Greek at three, postponing Latin until eight. Froude

read through the *Iliad* and *Odyssey* twice before going to Westminster School at eleven, and Browning was reading Homer well by twelve, taught by his father. At the **public schools** and universities the classics formed what has been described as a rite of passage to manhood (or, more properly, gentlemanhood), although often the teaching depended on rote learning of a few set texts. Greek was required for university entrance until after World War I. Some curricular revision resulted from the royal commission which attacked low standards at **Oxford** and **Cambridge** in 1850, but in the Oxford University Act (1854) the emphasis in the classical syllabus remained on philology rather than on broader cultural and historical contexts.

New ideas arrived with the influence of German scholars (especially Müller's *History of the Literature of Ancient Greece,* 1840). Julius Hare (1795–1855) and Connop Thirlwall (1797–1875) at Cambridge collaborated in translating Niebuhr's *History of Rome* into English (1828–1842), which inspired Macaulay's *Lays of Ancient Rome* (1842). **Thomas Arnold**'s *History of the Peloponnesian War by Thucydides* (3 vols., 1830–1835) won him the professorship of modern history at Oxford and, with Thirlwall's *History of Greece* (8 vols., 1835–1844) initiated a liberal Anglican historiography. Plato's *Republic* was first lectured on at Oxford in the 1830s by William Sewell; **Benjamin Jowett** (1817–1893) initiated undergraduate lectures on Plato, Homer, Sophocles, and Aristophanes from 1847. Debate on the Homeric question had been sparked by Wolf's *Prolegomena to Homer* (1795), which denied the existence of Homer and argued that compilers had imposed poetic unity. **John Keble** in the 1830s and William Gladstone in the 1850s emerged as Homer's champions, with Thomas Carlyle as an opponent. The controversy continued to rage even to **Samuel Butler**'s *Authoress of the "Odyssey"* (1897).

The paintings of Leighton and Alma-Tadema depict Londoners in classical garb and settings: London is the Athens of Pericles, the Rome of Augustus. London's state buildings were erected by **Charles Barry** and other classical revivalist architects. **Thomas Babington Macaulay** modeled his history on the ancients; liberal political philosophy was reanimated by Athenian democracy. Ethics and theology drew heavily on Aristotle and Plato. Conflicting interpretations of Socrates raised hermeneutic problems about Jesus; theologians like Jowett also translated Plato; and higher criticism was applied equally to the Bible and Homer, with controversial effect.

Classical education also affected public life: prime ministers were authorities on Homer (Gladstone issued seven volumes and many articles on Homer betweeen 1847 and 1892) and George Grote, a philosophical radical in the Commons (1837), became the major historian of Greece (*History of Greece,* 12 vols, 1845–1856). Generations of classically trained civil servants held posts in Whitehall and knew Homer and Livy better than Chaucer or Hume. The English toured archaeological sites in Rome and Pompeii. Although major poets translated ancient epics (Morris, Clough, Browning), for most of the century the classical outpouring was a leisure pastime of amateurs, rather than a specialty of eminent scholars.

Of Cambridge's four professors of Greek during Victoria's reign, only the last, R. C. Jebb (1841–1905) had an international reputation. Oxford had only three in almost one hundred years: Gaisford, Jowett, and Ingram Bywater. Oxford's first Latin professor (1854) was John Conington (1825–1869); Cambridge (1869) appointed H. A. J. Munro (1819–1885). Oxford's chair in classical archaeology was established in 1885. Major classical tools appeared, such as Liddell and Scott's *A Greek-English Lexicon* (1843) and *A Dictionary of Greek and Roman Antiquities* (1842) by William Smith. New German ideas had little impact, despite the efforts of Thirlwall and **Mark Pattison**, until later in the century, with the establishment of new professorships and journals (*The Journal of Hellenic Studies,* 1880; *Classical Review,* 1887) and the British School at Athens (1883).

WILLIAM WHITLA

Bibliography

Brink, Charles O. *English Classical Scholarship.* 1986.

Clarke, M. L. *Classical Education in Britain, 1500–1900.* 1959.

Jenkyns, Richard. *The Victorians and Ancient Greece.* 1980.

Lloyd-Jones, Hugh. *Blood for the Ghosts.* 1982.

Sandys, John E. *A History of Classical Scholarship.* 1908; rpt. 1967. 3 vols.

Turner, Frank M. *The Greek Heritage in Victorian Britain.* 1981.

Wilamowitz-Moellendorff, Ulrich von. *History of Classical Scholarship.* 1982. Trans. Alan Harris; ed. Hugh Lloyd-Jones.

See also HARRISON, JANE ELLEN

· · · · ·

CLERKS AND CLERICAL WORK

Early Victorian clerks were a small but distinctive class of men employed in offices in nonmanual labor. They were responsible for maintaining the records, accounts, and correspondence of business and government, and they stood above the working class in both social and economic terms. Around midcentury the clerical workforce, which in 1851 was less than 1 percent of the working population, began to grow; it also became feminized and younger. These trends developed at an accelerating rate, especially after 1870, and continued well into the twentieth century, ultimately producing a "white-collar" clerical work force that is predominantly female, makes up over 15 percent of the working population, and occupies an ambiguous social and economic position often not distinguishable from that of the working class.

The primary qualifications for early Victorian clerks were the abilities to write and calculate quickly and legibly. Possession of these skills set clerks above the working class. Beyond basic literacy and computational skills, the clerk could be expected to have at least a superficial secondary education which included some acquaintance with Latin, history, and literature. Other knowledge or skills might enhance a clerk's value, but most important to employers were basic skills, judgment, and experience. Clerks were therefore trained on the job through apprenticeships lasting three to five years. Apprentices were paid subsistence wages at best while they performed routine tasks under the guidance of senior clerks. Young men destined by birth or connection for ownership or management often served apprenticeships to "learn the business." Their presence in offices provoked resentment and depressed apprentices' wages but also strengthened the bonds between employers and clerks and reinforced the clerks' hopes for social and economic advancement.

The early Victorian clerk's belief in self-improvement was not unfounded. Until late in the period, it was not uncommon for the ablest and most ambitious to advance to management or even partnership in a business, although for the majority of clerks, promotion came only in the form of salary increases and perhaps a position as "senior clerk" after years of service to the same employer. Through the 1860s, clerical workers generally achieved at least lower middle-class economic status. The youngest and less well paid had incomes comparable to skilled workers' wages. Salaries in commercial and mercantile firms varied widely depending on the size and prosperity of the business. Clerks in law offices were among the lowest paid; the best-paid clerks were employed in banking, insurance, and the **civil service**.

Working conditions, like salaries, varied widely. The typical Victorian office employed two to four clerks who divided work on the basis of personality and experience. A senior clerk's functions in such an office would be considered "managerial" in the twentieth century. Work schedules were irregular, and the ten- to twelve-hour day was common through the end of the century except in banking and the civil service. Moreover, clerks frequently complained about cramped quarters, poor light, bad air, and a lack of sanitary facilities. The clerical unions that emerged in the 1890s took up these complaints, but they were weak and, since they were unable to secure the application of the factory acts to offices, clerical work remained unregulated throughout the period.

Complaints notwithstanding, Victorian clerks enjoyed, at least through the middle decades of the period, a social and economic position which set them above the working class. Their salaries were generally higher than skilled workers' wages and they enjoyed much greater security of employment. Moreover, clerks had reasonable hopes for economic and social advancement and fre-

quently could expect some modest retirement compensation after years of service to the same employer.

Around midcentury, however, the number of clerks began to grow and their circumstances changed. Between 1851 and 1911 the clerical work force increased from less than 1 percent to over 4 percent of the working population, while becoming more rapidly feminized than virtually any other occupation. The number of female clerks was negligible in 1851, but by 1911 approximately 19 percent of all clerks were young middle-class women. Most of the increased number of clerks, however, were young men and boys.

The late Victorian increase in the number of young and female clerks was the result both of growth in the scale of business and of increased educational opportunities. The middle-class male clerk lost his monopoly on the essential clerical skills with the spread of popular elementary education and the general availability of commercial courses by the turn of the century. The new generation of young male and female clerks often possessing only minimal skills had one primary virtue for employers: they worked more cheaply. As a result salaries were depressed to working-class levels, and the National Union of Clerks was forced to campaign in the years before World War I for a minimum wage of 35 shillings per week in the hope of eliminating the "pound-a-week" clerk.

Clerical work in the late Victorian period became increasingly routinized. Larger-scale offices and more clerks allowed for a division of labor into categories such as "ledger clerk" or "billing clerk." Two new skills, typing and shorthand, were also introduced and created new clerical specialties. Shorthand was first employed in business offices in the 1850s and typewriters became generally available in the 1880s. By the end of the century nearly every office employed typing and shorthand clerks. Most of the shorthand writers and virtually all of the typists were women.

By the beginning of the twentieth century, there had emerged a rapidly growing clerical work force which was younger and increasingly female and whose pay scale was being eroded to working-class levels. These clerks had not abandoned middle-class aspirations or pretensions but would find them increasingly difficult to maintain intellectually or materially. This ambiguity in the clerical worker's class and status, which developed in the late Victorian era, only increased in the twentieth century.

FREDERICK E. LAURENZO

Bibliography

Anderson, Gregory. *Victorian Clerks*. 1976.

Crompton, Rosemary and Gareth Jones. *White-Collar Proletariat: Deskilling and Gender in Clerical Work*. 1984.

Crossick, Geoffrey, ed. *The Lower Middle Class in Britain. 1870-1914*. 1977.

Holcombe, Lee. *Victorian Ladies at Work: Middle-Class Working Women in England and Wales. 1850-1914*. 1973.

Lockwood, David. *The Blackcoated Worker: A Study in Class Consciousness*. 1966.

· · · · ·

CLIVE, CAROLINE (1801-1873)

Under the pseudonym "V" Caroline Clive won some celebrity as a poet, contributing prolifically to *Blackwood's Magazine* and publishing *IX Poems by V* (1840) and other books of verse. Her novel *Paul Ferroll* (1855), often regarded as the first "**sensation novel**," caused a considerable stir.

An heiress, crippled since infancy, Caroline Meysey-Wigley married the Reverend Archer Clive in 1840, nine years after she first fell in love with him. About eighteen months before the marriage, Archer had proposed to Georgiana Duff Gordon, and it has been argued that Georgiana was the model for Anne Gordon, first wife of the eponymous hero of *Paul Ferroll*. Paul's callous, seemingly unmotivated murder of Anne constitutes one of the novel's two sensational episodes; the other is his gunning down of a riotous workingman. In a sequel, *Why Paul Ferroll Killed His Wife* (1860), the novelist reveals that Paul had killed Anne (now renamed Laura) because she had tricked him into believing that the woman he really loved and had planned to marry was false to him. Similar ingredients in other stories and poems suggest that the de-

sire to "kill" her real-life rival and to punish the real-life lover who had temporarily turned away from her was Clive's major source of imaginative inspiration.

Paul Ferroll shows the influence of William Godwin and of Balzac, whom Clive began reading in the late 1830s. Clive's verse can best be characterized as a blend of genteel Gothic and diluted Elizabeth Barrett.

P. D. EDWARDS

Bibliography

Clive, Mary, ed. *Caroline Clive: From the Diary and Family Papers of Mrs. Archer Clive*. 1949.

Partridge, Eric. Introduction to *IX Poems by V*, by Caroline Clive. 1928.

———. Introduction to *Paul Ferroll*, by Caroline Clive. 1929.

· · · · ·

CLOTHING AND FASHION

The functions dress fulfills are myriad. Clothing, for example, protects the naked body from climate and the infringements of modesty. In a country noted for its inclement weather and in a society noted for its prudery these are not unimportant functions. Beyond these two basic functions lies a more complex one, that of identification of gender and **class**. Clothing functions to place the wearer in his or her proper place and defines the role the wearer is to play.

The Victorians were very aware of this function of dress. To nineteenth-century writers, the phrase, "clothes make the man," was no empty cliché, but a profound truth about the workings of society. "Lives there a man," the Victorian sage Thomas Carlyle asked in *Sartor Resartus*, "who can figure a naked Duke of Windlestraw addressing a naked House of Lords?" Clothing is not merely protective or aesthetic, he explained, but symbolizes the spirit of the individual and the hierarchical structure of society. Lady Eastlake, writing in the *Quarterly Review* of 1847, asserted that "dress becomes a sort of symbolic language—a kind of personal glossary—a species of body phrenology, the study of which it would be madness to neglect." Nineteenth-

Ludovicus Rex by William Makepeace Thackeray. From the Paris Sketch Book, *1840. Thackeray illustrates the transforming power of dress by demonstrating how his royal regalia changes a "little lean, shrivelled paunchy old man" into the glorious Sun King.*

century memoirs, novels, and magazines reveal how deeply the Victorians believed that dress provided clues to character and could even transform the personality. William Makepeace Thackeray pictured the extreme transformation wrought by dress in his *Paris Sketch Book* of 1840. He demonstrated how a "little lean, shrivelled paunchy old man of five feet two" could become the splendid impressive "Sun King," in Hyacinthe Rigaud's portrait of Louis XIV. His magnificent regalia dazzled his court but, Thackeray asked, was the wearer not affected as well?" "Did he not believe, as he stood there, on his high heels, under his ambrosial periwig, that there was something in him more than man—something above Fate?" The power of dress works two ways, transforming the wearer and the beholder. "Thus," Thackeray commented, "do barbers and cobblers make the gods we worship."

A vast army of barbers, cobblers, tailors, dressmakers, **seamstresses**, milliners, mantua makers, hatters, importers, shop girls, weavers, dyers, and textile workers were engaged in the process of transforming English descendants of Adam and Eve into elegant aristocratic lords and ladies, prosperous members of the bourgeoisie, genteel poor, and the many other layers of a hierarchical society.

The complexity of Victorian garments, in their number, their form, their construction, their nomenclature, their materials, and their decorations, can hardly be exaggerated. Simple dress can protect from weather and rude gazes, but complexity in dress is needed to provide an ample vocabulary for its symbolic language. This complexity Victorian dress achieved in abundance.

The basic form of male dress changed little during the Victorian period. The standard garments—trousers, shirts, jackets, and overcoats—remained relatively constant; complexity occurred in the details of collars, cuffs, lapels, hats, cravats or neckties, and hair, including facial hair. The numerous male garments designed for specific occupations and activities added to the complexity.

Female dress, on the other hand, exhibited enormous variety in its form, veering from wide crinolines to narrow hobble skirts, tight

Fashionable Dress of 1885. From the Geszler Collection, Fine Arts Library, Fogg Art Museum, Harvard University.

sleeves to broad leg-of-mutton sleeves, form fitting cuirasses to protuberant bustles. Women also developed a large number of garments for special activities, including the various stages of mourning, and an even larger variety of accessories, decorations, and hair styles. The names of garments include many still in use: boa, bodice, bolero, knickers, peplum or shawl; others are forgotten or dimly remembered: bertha, chatelaine, corsage, fanchon, pardessus, plastron, and redingote, to name a few. The French names reflect that for women, although not for men, Paris was the source of high fashion throughout the nineteenth century.

Underneath this array of garments women wore a number of basic undergarments: bustles, corsets, crinolines, and petticoats, each with their own variety of forms, materials, fasteners, and nomenclature, and each changing the configuration of the fashionable silhouette.

The **sewing machine** allowed for a revolutionary change in the construction of garments. Although it was invented in the United States in the 1840s, its use was not widespread in England until the late 1850s. By 1865 both chain stitch and lock stitch machines had become common and hand sewing was confined to a few operations and to expensive garments. Paper patterns were developed and distributed at about the same time. Although the sewing machine allowed for mass ready-made garments to be sold off the rack, intricacies of high fashion and the difficulties of achieving a well-fitting garment forbade reliance on ready-made garments or amateur home sewing. Dressmakers and tailors were still the main production unit, but with the use of the sewing machine they became more efficient. Instead of eliminating the seamstresses, the sewing machine allowed the proliferation of ruffles and banded decoration which characterized women's dress in the 1860s.

Victorian dressmakers had over four hundred different fabrics from which to choose, ranging from delicate cotton nainsook to thick corded coteline, from sheer silk chiffon to stiff Muscovite, from soft woolen beche-cashmere to the coarse basin de l'aine. Some fabrics were woven on the busy looms of Manchester, Leeds, Macclesfield, and Bradford, and others were imported from the Continent or the British Empire. Analine dyes in the 1860s added a whole new spectrum of colors.

The greater complexity and elaborateness of women's clothing dated from the French Revolution. Before, men's dress was as costly and decorated as women's; during the revolutionary years both sexes wore relatively simple clothing. Afterwards, women's dress again became lavish in its decoration while men's dress remained plain and sober. The reason for this difference must be sought in the nature of society and the definition of gender and class roles. The economist Thorstein Veblen, in *The Theory of the Leisure Classes* (1899), explained that in the process of changing from an aristocratic feudal society to a capitalistic bourgeois society, women's role had been reduced to that of a "conspicuously unproductive expenditure" whose function is to "put in evidence her economic unit's ability to pay." Women must display conspicuous consumption, conspicuous leisure, and conspicuous waste. To fulfill the needs of conspicuous consumption, dress must look very costly, be made from rich fabrics, and have expensive decorations. A rapidly changing fashion fulfills the dictates of conspicuous waste, for garments must be discarded as out of fashion long before they are worn out. Conspicuous leisure may be demonstrated by wearing garments that preclude physical labor and necessitate the help of servants in dressing and maintaining a wardrobe. Garments such as very wide skirts or tight skirts, tightly laced corsets, or high-heeled shoes prohibit a woman from moving easily and freely. Fragile fabrics and delicate colors also are inappropriate to a working woman. A woman who is an effective symbol of conspicuous consumption must also show taste and refinement in her dress and etiquette. She must reflect those generations endowed with leisure and money that produce good breeding and cultivation. In becoming an expensive

and accomplished decorative object, she functions as an advertisement for her husband's (or father's or lover's) economic potency and privileged position.

No single theory can explain a phenomenon as involved and evolving as dress. Society has its claims, as Veblen's theory indicates, but so do the individual and even the internal logic of design. A woman may signal her sexual availability through her dress, and even her erotic preferences. Some Victorians, however, eschewed the signs of eroticism, hierarchy, and aesthetics to embrace the plain, even homely, clothing of the dress reformers. Other Victorians, mainly those in artistic circles, adopted a form of dress called "aesthetic" with its exotic, uncorseted, vaguely medieval look. Many of the lower, middle, and working classes had not the time or money to engage in these subtle splendors of dress. They were concerned with keeping up respectable appearances. Novels often contain poignant episodes of characters trying to make an old black serge a little less shiny or hoping a new ribbon will brighten up a dress hopelessly worn and out of fashion. The really poor wore what was given them or what could be purchased from second-hand clothiers. At the bottom of the economic scale, their clothing choices were reduced to the basic needs of modesty and warmth. At the other end of the social and economic scale clothing reached heights of complexity, signaling the intricacy and variety of the Victorian age.

HELENE ROBERTS

Bibliography

La Belle Assemblée, or Bell's Court and Fashionable Magazine. 1806–1868.

Buck, Anne. *Victorian Costume and Costume Accessories.* 1961.

Byrde, Penelope. *The Male Image: Men's Fashion in Britain, 1300–1970.* 1979.

Costume: The Journal of the Costume Society. 1967–.

Cunnington, C. Willett. *English Women's Clothing in the Nineteenth Century.* 1937.

Englishwoman's Domestic Magazine. 1852–1879.

Gernsheim, Alison. *Fashion and Reality: 1840–1914.* 1963.

Ginsburg, Madeleine. *Victorian Dress in Photographs.* 1983.

Ladies' Cabinet of Fashion. 1832–1870.

Laver, James. *Dress: How and Why Fashions in Men's and Women's Clothes Have Changed During the Past Two Hundred Years.* 1957.

Moers, Ellen. *The Dandy.* 1960.

Myra's Journal of Dress and Fashion. 1875–1893.

Newton, Stella Mary. *Health, Art and Reason: Dress Reformers of the Nineteenth Century.* 1974.

The Queen. 1861–.

Steele, Valerie. *Fashion and Eroticism: Ideals of Feminine Beauty from the Victorian Era to the Jazz Age.* 1985.

Sylvia's Home Journal. 1878–1894.

Walkley, Christina and Vanda Foster. *Crinolines and Crimping Irons: Victorian Clothes: How They Were Cleaned and Cared For.* 1978.

World of Fashion. 1824–1891.

See also AESTHETIC MOVEMENT; SOCIAL SEASON *(illus.)*

· · · · ·

CLOUGH, ANNE JEMIMA (1820-1892)

Anne Jemima Clough—the first principal of Newnham College, Cambridge—devoted herself to the education of girls of all ages and classes, and to the training of their teachers, so that women could lead fuller lives. She was the sister of the poet **Arthur Hugh Clough**, whom she called her "best fiend and advisor."

Born in Liverpool, the daughter of a cotton merchant of Welsh gentry origin, Clough grew up in Charleston, South Carolina, where she was educated by her mother. Living again in Liverpool, 1836–1852, she taught Sunday school and in the Welsh national school, gave private classes, and briefly had a school; then for ten years she ran Eller How School in Ambleside, where Mary Arnold (Mrs. Humphrey Ward) was a boarder. After her brother Arthur's death in 1861, she lived with his

widow (formerly Blanche Smith) until 1871 when, at Henry Sidgwick's request, she took charge of a house for five women students in Cambridge, a venture that led to the founding of Newnham College in 1880.

It was through her sister-in-law Blanche that Clough met the educationalists **Barbara Bodichon**, **Frances Mary Buss**, and **Emily Davies** and became seriously involved in the reform of women's education, recommending the establishment of the London School Mistresses Association with its Teachers' Library. She formed a similar association in Liverpool and also served on the North of England Council which organized University extension lectures for girls over eighteen in northern cities. Her successes at **Cambridge** stemmed from her character—kind, persevering, and uncannily perceptive.

TAMIE WATTERS

Bibliography

Clough, Blanche Athena. *A Memoir of Anne Jemima Clough.* 1897.

See also EDUCATION, WOMEN'S

· · · · ·

CLOUGH, ARTHUR HUGH (1819-1861)

The author of such poems as "Say Not the Struggle Nought Availeth" and "The Bothie of Tober-na-Vuolich," Arthur Hugh Clough is most famous as the subject of Matthew Arnold's elegy "Thyrsis." Clough's own poems appeared in *Ambarvalia* (1849), *Amours de Voyage* (1849), *Dipsychus* (1850), and *Mari Magno or Tales on Board* (1861).

Educated at Rugby and Balliol College, Oxford, Clough became a fellow of Oriel and then principal of University Hall, London. Later he was an examiner of the Education Office. In the 1850s Clough was an important voice on matters of religious and intellectual unrest. Like Arnold, Clough is companionable, charming, a stoic spectator of the human condition. Fine lyrics, such as the group in *Dipsychus* entitled "Songs in Absence," capably analyze states of consciousness. But Clough's most characteristic voice is found in seriocomic hexameter verses, such as "The Bothis" and *Amours*, a narrative about an English lover who is disillusioned with Italian romance and patriotism.

Clough rejected the fashion of romantic subjectivity in exchange for dramatized narration and satire. His genius for social observation and poised skepticism reveal him to be an important link between such figures as John Dryden and Lord Byron and the modernists such as Ezra Pound, W. H. Auden, and Louis MacNeice.

SANDRA PARKER

Bibliography

Chorley, Lady Katharine. *Arthur Hugh Clough: The Uncommitted Mind.* 1962.

Houghton, Walter E. *The Poetry of Clough.* 1962.

Mulhauser, Frederick L., ed. *The Poems of Arthur Hugh Clough.* 1974.

. . . . .

CLUBS, GENTLEMEN'S

Gentlemen's clubs reached their apogee in Victorian England, although two of the most exclusive, White's and Brooks's, originated in the eighteenth century as centers of extravagant conviviality and gambling. They, as their names suggest, were proprietary clubs. The nineteenth century saw the rise of the member-owned club—the first being the Union (1805)—whose object was economy through collectivized luxury. As one observer remarked "the clubs of London show how the principle of combination may be applied to the increase of luxury. Palaces are reared containing comforts for a large body of men which they could not have individually or separately." Indeed the Italian Renaissance palazzo was the favored architectural model for the clubs which increasingly monopolized Pall Mall and St. James's Street, the twin axes of clubland.

The advantages of club membership were both psychological and material. An entrance

The Military, Naval, and County Service Club, St. James's Street—Principal Drawing Room. Illustrated London News, *12 January 1850. Library Company of Philadelphia.*

fee of 20 to 30 pounds and an annual subscription of 5 to 10 pounds entitled members to swagger with a proprietorial air through a building grander than many ducal residences, command numerous servants, and have a good address for mail; one could also eat cheaply and well in a country where **restaurants** were expensive and few, have the finest wine practically at cost, not have to tip anyone, and then retire to an excellent library (particularly important for literary men and journalists). The archetypal clubman could center his whole public existence on the club, only retiring at the day's end to inexpensive rooms adequate for sleeping. In his diary A. J. Munby lovingly describes the amenities of the United University Club, adding "somehow one feels hardly worthy of all this: feels, also, that it might lead to selfish indulgence, to morose bachelor habits." Why trade such serene, economical luxury for the responsibilities and expenses of marriage? Some observers indeed argued that the attractions of club life were deterring middle-class men from matrimony, thereby further exacerbating the "surplus women" problem.

But such benefits were not for everyone. Exclusion was part of the point—the clubman derived satisfaction from "pilling" the unwanted. At times this could reach unhealthy levels, as when Brooks's split into factions over the Home Rule issue and a war of blackballs was waged. Most of the major clubs were formed with a certain constituency in view. There were numerous military clubs led by the United Services (senior officers only) and the Army and Navy; political clubs, notably the Carlton (conservative) and Reform (liberal); clubs artistic like the Garrick, intellectual like the Athenaeum, or sporting like the Turf. Many clubmen had multiple memberships: Thackeray belonged to the Garrick, Reform, and Athenaeum but never made it into the more snobbish Travellers'. New clubs mushroomed in the later Victorian period, some of them "Juniors" for disappointed aspirants to top clubs. Long waiting lists and the cachet of club membership encouraged entrepreneurs to launch new proprietary clubs. Although most clubs barred ladies entirely, a few allowed them to dine as guests and a couple elected members of both sexes. Of these the best known was the Albemarle,

famous as the club where the marquess of Queensberry left his card for Oscar Wilde.

CHRISTOPHER KENT

Bibliography

Escott, Thomas H. S. *Club Makers and Club Members.* 1914.

Kent, Christopher. "The Whittington Club: A Bohemian Experiment in Middle Class Social Reform." *Victorian Studies*, vol. 18, pp. 31–55.

Nevill, Ralph. *London Clubs.* 1911.

· · · · ·

COBBE, FRANCES POWER (1822–1904)

Philanthropist, journalist, feminist, and moralist, Frances Power Cobbe founded the Victoria Street Society for the Protection of Animals from Vivisection (renamed in 1875 as the National Anti-Vivisection Society) and served as joint secretary until 1884, when she left to form the British Union for the Abolition of Vivisection, a group that sought to abolish vivisection through a single legislative act.

The only daughter of a Dublin landowner, Cobbe was educated first at home and later in a school in Brighton. She remained at home until her father's death in 1857 freed her to pursue her own interests. Her first of numerous trips to Italy (1857) provided her with experiences that she would later use as Italian correspondent for the *Echo* (1868–1875).

The following year began her association with **Mary Carpenter** on the Red Lodge reformatory and **ragged schools** and the beginnings of her public attention to feminist causes. During the 1860s and 1870s, she threw herself wholeheartedly into the feminist movement, writing and lobbying for women's university education, suffrage, and entry into the professions, and for married women's legal protection. Far from radical in her feminist views, she supported the popular Victorian ideal that women were naturally more moral than men and argued that this greater morality was the primary reason they should be given a greater voice in public affairs. Her essays on women's causes appeared in many periodicals, and both her essays and lectures were later published in book form. Her investigation into physical abuse of wives influenced the 1878 Matrimonial Causes Act.

Cobbe also wrote on religious issues, publishing *Religious Duty* in 1864 and editing the works of Theodore Parker (1863–1871). Her autobiography, *The Life of Frances Power Cobbe* (1894), details her progress from Evangelical Christianity to **agnosticism** to theism.

During the last four decades of her life, Cobbe was one of the leaders of the antivivisection movement. In addition to founding two of the movement's chief organizations, she edited the *Zoophilist*, lectured, and wrote numerous pamphlets and books on the subject. Interested in both moral and rational arguments against vivisection, she attempted to maintain a firm distance from the more emotional and hysterical members of the movement, though her distrust of science was certainly fueled by hostility to the medical profession.

CAROL A. SENF

Bibliography

Bauer, Carol and Lawrence Ritt. "'A Husband Is a Beating Animal'—Frances Power Cobbe Confronts the Wife-Abuse Problem in Victorian England." *International Journal of Women's Studies*, vol. 6, pp. 99–118.

French, Richard D. *Antivivisection and Medical Science in Victorian England.* 1975.

Lansbury, Coral. *The Old Brown Dog.* 1985.

See also ANIMAL PROTECTION

· · · · ·

COBDEN, RICHARD
(1804–1865)

Richard Cobden was the champion of free trade in Victorian Britain. He was a leader of the **Anti–Corn-Law League** (1838–1846) which agitated for the repeal of the Corn and Provision Laws. Cobden was a middle-class manufacturer and M.P. who advocated **free trade**, nonintervention in foreign affairs, an end to aristocratic misrule, and a variety of radical political reforms including suffrage extension and the ballot.

Cobden became interested in the Manchester Anti–Corn-Law Association in 1838 and helped to transform it into the National Anti-Corn-Law League. With other leaguers Cobden stumped the country for free trade, lobbied Parliament for repeal of the **Corn Laws**, and helped the league organize its electoral activities. League agitations created the political climate which made repeal of the Corn Laws irresistible in 1846 as the famine in Ireland made immediate action imperative.

Cobden entered Parliament in 1841 when he was elected for Stockport. In 1847 he was returned for the West Riding of Yorkshire, and worked for international arbitration, financial reform, and arms reductions. Cobden opposed the conduct of the Crimean War (1854–1856) and was among several proponents of "Cobdenism" in foreign policy to be defeated in 1857. He returned to Parliament in 1859 as M.P. for Rochdale.

In 1860 Cobden negotiated significant reciprocal tariff reductions with France for the Palmerston government. He hoped that the Cobden-Chevalier Treaty would not only stimulate trade and industry in both nations but also improve the strained relations between them.

RICHARD FRANCIS SPALL, JR.

Bibliography

Cobden, Richard. *The Political Writings of Richard Cobden.* 1867; rpt. 1969.

Edsall, Nicholas C. *Richard Cobden, Independent Radical.* 1986.

Hinde, Wendy. *Richard Cobden: A Victorian Outsider.* 1987.

Morley, John. *Life of Richard Cobden.* 1881.

Read, Donald. *Cobden and Bright: A Victorian Political Partnership.* 1968.

· · · · ·

COCKERELL, CHARLES ROBERT
(1788–1863)

Charles Robert Cockerell was one of the last architects to specialize in the classical style amid the Victorian popularity of neo-Gothic. The Greco-Roman character of his work—derived in part from his own archaeological work in Greece, Italy, and Asia Minor—was particularly appropriate for museums and educational institutions that were themselves dominated by the classics.

Cockerell's father, the architect Samuel Pepys Cockerell (1754–1827), was related on his mother's side to the diarist Samuel Pepys. Educated briefly at Westminster School, Cockerell entered his father's offices and served as assistant to Robert Smirke (1781–1867), designer of the British Museum.

In 1819, after beginning his own practice, Cockerell became surveyor of St. Paul's Cathedral. He was responsible for replacing the ball and cross at the top of the dome in 1821. The bulk of his work, however, was secular and institutional. In 1833 he became architect to the Bank of England, and made his reputation building branch banks in large industrial cities (including Bristol, Plymouth, Manchester, and Liverpool). He also designed the head offices for several insurance companies, among them the Sun Fire and Life Assurance offices in Threadneedle Street (1840–1842). The best of his surviving works are the Fitzwilliam Museum, Cambridge (1845–1847) and the Ashmolean Museum and Taylorian Institute, Oxford (1841–1845).

JOHN REYNOLDS

Bibliography

Hitchcock, Henry-Russell. *Early Victorian Architecture in Britain.* 1954. 2 vols.

Watkin, David. *The Life and Work of C. R. Cockerell.* 1974.

· · · · ·

mission in 1823–1835, and from 1838 to 1852 he was an assistant keeper. In 1843 he assumed the nom de plume Felix Summerly, under which he wrote children's stories and gallery catalogues, and in 1846 he launched "Felix Summerly's Manufactures" after winning a Society of Arts silver medal for a tea service. Cole sought to achieve a reconciliation of high art and commercial manufacture, and his firm employed a number of well-known artists. To this end too he founded the *Journal of Design and Manufactures* in 1849.

Also in 1849 Cole became involved in the plan for an international exhibition, which was realized in 1851. His appointment to secretaryship of the Schools of Design and government acquisition of a number of examples from the Great Exhibition led to his involvement with the reform of design education, and eventually to the foundation of the South Kensington Museum. Cole was also involved in the foundation of the Royal Albert Hall and the Royal College of Music, and in postal and sanitation reform.

LARRY D. LUTCHMANSINGH

Bibliography

Boe, Alf. *From Gothic Revival to Functional Form.* 1957.

Bonython, Elizabeth. *King Cole: A Picture Portrait of Sir Henry Cole, KCB 1808–1882.* Rpt. 1982.

Cole, Henry. *Fifty Years of Public Work.* 1884. 2 vols.

Naylor, Gillian. *The Arts and Crafts Movement.* 1971.

See also EXHIBITION OF 1851

· · · · ·

COLE, HENRY
(1808–1882)

Henry Cole was an art administrator, critic, and designer who achieved prominence through association with the Exhibition of 1851 and as founder of the South Kensington (later Victoria and Albert) Museum.

After his early education at Christ's Hospital, Cole was employed at the Record Com-

COLERIDGE, MARY ELIZABETH
(1861–1907)

Mary Elizabeth Coleridge, poet, essayist, and novelist, wrote for *Merry England, Cornhill,* the *Monthly Review,* and the *Times Literary Supplement.* Her first novel, *The Seven Sleepers of Ephesus* (1893), was an adventure praised by Robert Louis Stevenson. *The King with Two Faces* (1897), a historical romance, established her reputation. Other novels followed. In 1900 *Non Sequitur* (essays) was published. Coleridge published two poetry volumes under the pseudonym "Anodos": *Fancy's Following* (1896) and *Fancy's Guerdon* (1897). Posthumous volumes were *Poems, Old and New* (1907) and *Collected Poems of Mary Coleridge* (1954).

Living within an intimate circle of family, friends, and literary acquaintances, Coleridge attended King's College and taught at the Working Women's College. Her prose impressed popular audiences for a time, but she was not well known as a poet. After her death many poems were discovered "in notebooks and in letters in odd corners here, there, and everywhere" (*Gathered Leaves*, 27). Her lyricism demonstrated classical simplicity but was considered obscure. She wrote symbolist as well as Greek revivalist verse in the genteel tradition. A typical theme is language's inability to represent numinous moments, hence enigma and obscurity.

Coleridge's best work combines late Victorian romanticism with female images to define creative woman, as in "The Witch," "The Wedding in the Snow," and "The Other Side of the Mirror." Coleridge celebrates female imagination in "A Day-Dream" and "White Women." Coleridge recharged the depleted forms and suggestive imagery of fin de siècle and early Edwardian poetry with woman's search for poetic voice.

SHELLEY J. CRISP

Bibliography

Coleridge, Mary E. *Gathered Leaves from the Prose of Mary E. Coleridge. With a Memoir by Edith Sichel.* 1910.

Whistler, Theresa, ed. *The Collected Poems of Mary Coleridge.* 1954.

. . . . .

COLLINS, WILKIE
(1824-1889)

William Wilkie Collins is acknowledged to be a master of the "**sensation novel**," a melo-dramatic form of fiction with the thrills and coincidences of the Gothic novel placed in a contemporary setting and given the abundant detail of realism. Although Collins had learned from Charles Dickens to infuse his intricately woven plots with comedy and sentiment, his narrative skill is thought to have influenced Dickens's control of structure in his later novels.

Collins, the son of the painter William Collins, refused an opportunity for university study but later trained for the law. Although he became a barrister, he never practised, preferring to make his living as a writer. He became a frequent contributor to Dickens's magazine *Household Words* in the 1850s and was appointed assistant editor in 1856. Although Collins's first novel *Antonia* had been a historical romance set in ancient Rome, his next two books *Basil* (1852) and *Hide and Seek* (1854) were novels of mystery and suspense in a setting of Victorian middle-class life. *After Dark* (1856) and *The Queen of Hearts* (1859) were collections of stories, most of which had appeared in *Household Words*.

One night in the 1850s, a woman dressed in white ran screaming across the path of Collins and a friend. When Collins pursued and rescued her, he learned the story of how she had been kidnapped and imprisoned. From this bizarre incident plus the details of a French criminal case, Collins developed the work which established his reputation as a master storyteller, *The Woman in White* (1860). The character of the courageous Marian Halcombe is one of the most admired in Victorian fiction, while that of the scheming Count Fosco is recognized as a model of the grotesque but attractive villain. *No Name* (1862) presented another brave woman, Magdalen Vanstone, in her determined struggle to retrieve a lost fortune. *Armadale* (1865), a story of a frightening dream that comes true, continued to display Collins's narrative ingenuity. With *The Moonstone* (1868) Collins established the genre of the detective novel, which was to prove so popular in subsequent decades: his coldly logical but eccentric Sergeant Cuff is one of the early models for Conan Doyle's Sherlock Holmes, and the street urchin, Gooseberry, is the forerunner of the Baker Street Irregulars. In *The Moonstone* Collins reached the height of his literary achievement, chiefly because of his skill in handling multiple points of view through reports, diaries, letters, and journals. As his friendship with Dickens became closer, the two collaborated on plays and on fictional works for the Christmas numbers of *All the Year Round*, the most notable of which was *No Thoroughfare* (1867).

After the death of Dickens in 1870, Collins's career underwent a change, and his later novels are either overly sensational or overly didactic. This decline has been variously attributed to his increased use of laudanum in order to combat fits of gout; to the pressure of reviewers who demanded moral uplift in his novels; and to the influence of Charles Reade, whose sensation novels always carried a social message. Even so, Collins holds a place in English literature through his two masterworks, *The Woman in White* and *The Moonstone*, and he continues to entertain the readers of *No Name*, *Armadale*, and his short tales. In his best work his talent for intricate structure and melodramatic incident is accompanied by psychological insight and traditional Victorian breadth of scene, a combination outmatched only by his mentor Dickens.

RICHARD S. KENNEDY

Bibliography

Beetz, Kirk H. *Wilkie Collins: An Annotated Bibliography*. 1978.

Davis, Nuel Pharr. *The Life of Wilkie Collins*. 1956.

Marshall, William. *Wilkie Collins*. 1970.

Page, Norman. *Wilkie Collins: The Critical Heritage*. 1974.

Petersen, Audrey. *Victorian Masters of Mystery: From Wilkie Collins to Conan Doyle*. 1984.

Phillips, Walter Clarke. *Dickens, Reade, and Collins, Sensation Novelists*. 1919.

Robinson, Kenneth. *Wilkie Collins, A Biography*. 1952.

· · · · ·

COMEDY

Victorian comedy is best characterized by its emphasis on social concerns and political issues. In contrast to their eighteenth-century predecessors, Victorian authors relied less on exaggerated or surreal characters, and instead focused humorous social commentary on realistic ones; their comedy was based on the relationship between this realism and the rising middle class. No longer was sentimentality or burlesque always necessary to provoke laughter. George Meredith wrote in the prelude to *The Egoist* (1879) that "Comedy is a game played to throw reflections upon social life. . . ."

Aristotle defined comedy as "written about persons of minor importance whom their faults rendered ridiculous," a conception that generally held through the eighteenth century. Early nineteenth-century comedy had its origins in Steele's sentimental comedy; Jane Austen examined social issues while at the same time modifying eighteenth-century sentimentality. The **silver-fork novels** of the 1820s, which used gentrified dandies, contrived language, clever expression, and trite plot lines, never really situated themselves in the comic realm; instead they alternated between wit and morality. Earlier Regency literature, such as Thomas Love Peacock's "comedy of ideas," attempted to create humor from philosophical notions. Peacock's genre never really developed, but the concept of intellectualizing comedy stayed on throughout the century.

The period between 1820 and 1870 was comedy's real transition time, although critics disagree on the specifics of its development. Charles Dickens, W. M. Thackeray, and Anthony Trollope used comedy to explore social situations. There was a shift from sentimental to intellectual humor, a decreasing dependence on blasphemy, ridicule, parody, mimicry, or exaggeration, a growing preoccupation with elaboration, art, and play.

The Victorian period was also an age of "light" humor. Writers such as Lewis Carroll, with his nonsense and riddles, Edward Lear, and W. S. Gilbert flourished in comic magazines which were becoming increasingly popular in midcentury. By late in the century the sophistication of comedy as an art form established a more polished, involuted wit and humor, combining comedy with social commentary. Writers such as Max Beerbohm, Oscar Wilde, and G. B. Shaw utilized techniques such as paradox, transmutation, and parody. Even so, a work such as *The Importance of Being Earnest* (1894) exploited the modes of the older, sentimental, "well-made" play for its comic expression.

Victorian comedy led the way to the twentieth century's comedy of incongruity through its sense of the absurd in social life, its recourse to earlier modes, and its combination of middle-class consciousness with intellectualized wit.

ELISABETH HIRSCHHORN

Bibliography

Henkle, Roger B. *Comedy and Culture: England 1820-1900.* 1981.

Knoepflmacher, U. C. *Laughter and Despair.* 1971.

Martin, Robert Bernard. *The Triumph of Wit: A Study of Victorian Comic Theory.* 1974.

Meredith, George. *On the Idea of Comedy and the Uses of the Comic Spirit.* 1877.

Polhemus, Robert M. *Comic Faith: The Great Tradition from Austen to Joyce.* 1980.

See also FARCE; PERIODICALS: COMIC

. . . . .

COMMON LAW

By 1837 the common law had already undergone more than six centuries of evolution. Much of the common law, originally expressed in judicial decisions and guided by precedent, had become by the start of the Victorian era embodied in statutes. The great social changes of industrialization and urbanization provided a major challenge to the common law. The pace of change was reflected in the constant demand for reform that characterized most of the reign.

Initial popular dissatisfaction with the common law arose from the cost and length of litigation. In general, therefore, advocates of **law reform** stressed rationalization of procedure by abolishing ancient forms of action, lowering the expense of proceedings by ending sinecures, and improving the efficiency of the **judicial system**. These demands affected all three courts of common law. Although jurisdictional battles had complicated the court system

immeasurably, the general proposition that the Queen's Bench handled criminal matters, the Common Pleas settled civil disputes, and the Exchequer heard financial cases still held.

The common law had focused historically on matters of property. In Victorian times, liberty of contract became the legal ideal that permeated popular values to the greatest extent. The right of individuals to enter into contractual obligations constituted the fullest expression of liberty, especially with regard to conditions of employment. Stress on the reform of property rights had an important impact, for example, in the issues surrounding women's rights. The **Married Women's Property** Act (1882), which ended the common law of coverture, did not arise from concerns of theoretical equality for women; the statute did reflect the realization that the logic of private property doctrines demanded protection for the property of wives. The campaign for the statute's passage illustrated well the connection between law and public opinion that existed throughout the Victorian period.

The common law met the challenge of social transformation effectively in three different areas. First, traditional doctrines such as in the law of contract were radically changed; new areas of law generated by industrialization appeared, as in the law of torts or in commercial law; legal specialties were redefined, as with conflict of laws. In each of these fields, as in many others, new legal principles were enunciated to cope with the changing circumstances of domestic life, the economy, the workplace, and international relations. The legal doctrines of 1837 were scarcely recognizable by 1901.

Second, the educational basis of Victorian common law underwent a significant reform. While the Inns of Court remained the backbone of training for barristers, the university teaching of the common law became more definitive. One important result of this innovation was the legal treatise, a compilation of principles for a particular field abstracted from the vast number of reported cases. By the 1880s this new legal literature had created a greater precision in the articulation of legal doctrine and had pioneered new concepts in some branches. The university teaching of the common law complemented the traditional training afforded by the Inns of Court, though the relationship was not always harmonious.

Finally, the jurisprudential underpinnings of Victorian common law profited from attempts to place it on a scientific basis. Analytic jurisprudence, the legacy of Jeremy Bentham (1748-1832) and John Austin (1790-1859), reacted strongly against the intellectual complacency associated with William Blackstone and Lord Eldon. While the attempt at comprehensive codification failed, nevertheless the demands for a science of law gave to the common law a more rational structure. Analytic jurisprudence did little to influence the development of the common law itself, but did contribute greatly to the understanding of how the legal system operated. Central to this venture was the distinction between law and morality, the necessity to separate the law as it was from the law as it ought to be. Many Victorian jurists accepted the distinction as a starting point for jurisprudence even if they did not apply the formula rigorously. Analytic jurisprudence represented the foremost intellectual movement within the Victorian common law.

If by 1901 the common law still did not suit every individual or interest group, it had acquired a more secure place in the opinion of a majority of its constituents. Given the challenges of the Victorian era, this has remained a significant achievement.

RICHARD A. COSGROVE

Bibliography

Austin, John. *The Province of Jurisprudence Determined.* 1832.

Bagehot, Walter. *The English Constitution.* 1867.

Dicey, Albert V. *Lectures Introductory to the Study of the Law of the Constitution.* 1885.

Holcombe, Lee. *Wives and Property: Reform of the Married Women's Property Law in Nineteenth-Century England.* 1983.

Holdsworth, William S. *A History of English Law.* 1903.

Lawson, F. H. *The Oxford Law School, 1850-1965.* 1968.

Rumble, Wilfrid E. *The Thought of John Austin: Jurisprudence, Colonial Reform, and the British Constitution.* 1985.

See also **LEGAL PROFESSION**

· · · · ·

COMMONS AND OPEN SPACES

Common land stands central to the history of open space preservation in Victorian Britain. The Commons Preservation Society (CPS) was founded in 1865 to promote acceptance by the courts of a new legal interpretation preserving public access to commons. People drawn into the fight for preserving commons influenced other open space organizations and campaigns which resulted, with continued CPS support, in retaining substantial open space for public enjoyment.

Common land, a legal anomaly, had a recognized owner, but other individuals—commoners—possessed various rights to its use, most importantly the right to graze cattle. The owner, prohibited from interfering with the rights of commoners, did not have unrestricted use of his land. Enclosure, usually accomplished, physically, by fencing the land, was the action landowners took to extinguish common rights. Enclosure was legal in the early Victorian era when authorized by an act of Parliament or undertaken under provisions of the Statute of Merton (1235), which allowed enclosure of part of a common provided that the remainder sufficed to provide for the rights of commoners. Enclosure accomplished under the Statute of Merton could be reversed by judicial action initiated when a commoner asked the court to determine whether, in fact, sufficient land had been left unenclosed. The law assumed a medieval clash between the owner's agricultural pursuits and the commoners' grazing rights, whereas in the nineteenth century the conflict was usually between the owner's wish to sell the land for residential development and the desire of commoners, and of the wider community, to keep it open for recreation.

During the eighteenth century governmental policy encouraged enclosure. By the 1830s, however, the value of commons near rapidly growing cities for recreation and as reservoirs of fresh air was recognized. An act of 1845 established that Parliament must weigh recreational against agricultural needs when authorizing enclosure.

In 1864 an effort to enclose Wimbledon Common in south London proved pivotal. Four consequences ensued. First, a select committee report in 1865 emphasized the recreational potential of commons and suggested that enclosure could be prevented by utilizing in the courts the conflict of legal interests inherent in the law of commons. Second, to promote application of the select committee's suggestion, Philip Lawrence (1822-1895) and George John Shaw-Lefevre (1831-1928) founded the Commons Preservation Society. Third, the Metropolitan Commons Act (1866) forbade parliamentary enclosure within the Metropolitan Police District. Fourth, during the next decade, the owners of many commons challenged the new legal interpretation by initiating enclosure under authority of the Statute of Merton, but in notable test cases skillful legal work by Lawrence and by Robert Hunter (1844-1913), solicitors of the CPS, reversed enclosures attempted at Berkhamsted, Wimbledon, Hampstead, and Epping Forest. In the process, a new body of case law was constructed supporting the CPS contention that enclosure necessarily abridged rights of commoners and was therefore illegal. Upon urging by Henry Fawcett (1833-1884) the CPS in 1869 expanded its interest from the metropolis to England as a whole, with the result that all attempts to enclose rural commons were delayed from 1869 to 1876, when a new Commons Act, shaped largely by the CPS, virtually ended further enclosures by mandating consideration of the interests of all segments of society, not merely commoners and owners. Effective repeal (1893) of the Statute of Merton was primarily of symbolic importance because judicial acceptance of the CPS position had made its invocation useless.

As a result of these actions, thousands of acres of common land which otherwise would have been built upon were preserved as open spaces. In London much of this land came to be managed by the Metropolitan Board of Works and, after 1888, by the London County Council (LCC). The LCC, under the guidance of Lord Brabazon (Lord Meath after 1887) (1841-1929), first chairman of its Parks Committee, also launched an active program to purchase additional areas as permanent open spaces. In his private capacity as founder of the Metropolitan Public Gardens Association (1882), Meath directed an organization responsible for providing other open spaces in London, especially the conversion of disused burial grounds into pleasantly developed

neighborhood parks. Similar work was pursued by the Open Spaces Committee of **Octavia Hill's** (1838-1912) Kyrle Society (1876). Hill was an important publicist in various late Victorian efforts to gather money from both public and private sources for purchase of open land threatened with development. Urban commons saved beyond London included those at Bristol, Harrogate, Preston, and Tunbridge Wells, and important public parks established after **Joseph Paxton's** (1803-1865) pioneering design at Birkenhead (1843) were at Bradford, Glasgow, Halifax, Hull, Leeds, Manchester, Middlesbrough, and Sheffield.

The National Trust (1895), founded by Hill, Hunter, and Canon Hardwicke Rawnsley (1851-1920), a preserver of Lake District scenery, sought acquisition (by purchase or gift) and preservation of open spaces. Attempts to maintain access to undeveloped terrain in northern England and Scotland began with sponsorship in 1884 by James Bryce (1838-1922) of the Access to Mountains bill. Although Access to Mountains legislation was not passed until 1939, frequent discussion in Parliament made familiar the concept of public responsibility for assuring access to open spaces.

JOHN RANLETT

Bibliography

Eversley, Lord. *Commons, Forests and Footpaths.* 1910.

Hoskins, W. G. and L. Dudley Stamp. *The Common Lands of England and Wales.* 1963.

Malchow, H. L. "Public Gardens and Social Action in Late Victorian London." *Victorian Studies,* vol. 29, pp. 97-124.

See also GARDENS AND PARKS

· · · · ·

CONDUCTORS

The role of orchestral conductor emerged, during the early nineteenth century, from combining the duties of the concertmaster (called "leader" in Britain) and the continuo player. Well into early Victorian times, there was still a musician "presiding at the pianoforte" in many orchestral concerts. This was the method of direction habitually adopted by George Smart (1776-1867) and **Henry Bishop** (1786-1855).

Baton conducting, introduced by Continental visitors such as Louis Spohr and Felix Mendelssohn, brought immediate benefit in the form of improved ensemble and discipline. In 1844 the **Philharmonic Society** invited the Italian Michael Costa (1808-1884) to be the first regular conductor of its concerts, and accepted his terms, which included suppression of the leader as a rival authority. According to his obituary, "under Costa's rule the orchestra became a model of punctuality and serious work." After Costa resigned in 1854, Richard Wagner conducted for one memorable Philharmonic Society season, followed by William Sterndale Bennett (1856-1866) and William George Cusins (1867-1883).

The glamour associated with conducting was established by a Frenchman, Louis Antoine Jullien (1812-1860), whose ostentatious gimmicks tended to monopolize the audience's attention. Primarily a conductor of popular music, Jullien tried to elevate the taste of his public by including the classics in his programs; when he was to conduct Beethoven, he had a pair of clean kid gloves and a jeweled baton handed to him on a silver salver.

The greatest Victorian conductors were German born. August Manns (1825-1907) established Britain's first permanent orchestra, the Crystal Palace Orchestra, in 1855. He performed orchestral music daily, with special series of classical music on Saturdays in which many major composers, including Schubert, were first introduced to the Victorian music lover. Charles Hallé (originally Carl Halle, 1819-1895), first known as a pianist, in 1857 founded the Manchester orchestra that still bears his name, and conducted it for more than thirty years: its high standard was renowned, and it gave annual tours. Hans Richter (1843-1916) came to London in 1877 as a champion of Wagner's music, but stayed to direct an important series, known as the Richter Concerts, from 1879 to 1897; he then took over the Hallé Orchestra at Manchester. Richter familiarized the Victorians with the late romantic German school, but also gave valuable support to Elgar and other native composers.

In the 1890s two English-born conductors began to make their way to prominence. Henry Wood (1869-1944) in 1895 began his famous Promenade Concerts of popular classics at the newly built Queen's Hall, a series that has continued in unbroken succession to the present. At Bournemouth a similar series was started by Dan Godfrey (1868-1939).

Like much else in music, the art of conducting came to the Victorians from abroad. It was highly appreciated: Costa, Manns, and Hallé all achieved knighthood. In the twentieth century British conductors were able to equal or even surpass their Continental models.

NICHOLAS TEMPERLEY

Bibliography

Carse, Adam. *The Orchestra from Beethoven to Berlioz.* 1948

Foster, Myles. *The History of the Philharmonic Society of London, 1813-1912.* 1912.

Hallé, Charles. *Life and Letters.* 1896.

See also ORCHESTRAS

. . . . .

CONGREGATIONAL CHURCH

The Congregational church of the Victorian era traced its roots to the separatist movement of the late sixteenth century and to the Independents in the English Civil War. Holding that the authentic form of the church was the individual congregation of believers and that the church must be organized on the voluntary system, its members consistently opposed external structures and the principle of religious establishment. In the late eighteenth century a few county and district associations of churches were organized, and the spirit of the evangelical revival encouraged many individual members to join societies created for missionary purposes at home and abroad. This gradually led to an interest in greater cooperation.

The Congregational Union of England and Wales was established in May 1831 and the

Declaration of Faith, Church Order, and Discipline approved two years later. Conceived as a supplement to local congregations and associations, rather than a higher authority, the union soon was composed of thirty-seven county and district associations; by 1839, twelve more had joined. Fears that the union would intrude on congregational independence or become dominated by ministers made many suspicious of its increasing activities, and contributions toward the support of its work were minimal for most of this period.

Although precise statistics were not available until the end of the century, it is clear that the Congregational churches grew considerably over this period. Estimates suggest that the number of Congregationalists in England and Wales more than tripled between 1800 and 1838, when figures were put at 127,000 for England and 43,000 for Wales. By 1900 the total number of British Congregationalists was just over 435,000, with 59 percent in England and 34 percent in Wales. Although rates of growth declined over the century, numerical totals did not begin to decline until after 1906. In the union itself, during the tenure of Alexander Hannay as its secretary from 1870 to 1890, the number of participating churches grew from 2,923 to 4,423 and the number of ministers from 1,958 to 2,732.

The denomination's organizational life was represented in the annual *Congregational Year Book*, first published in 1846. A number of independent journals edited by Congregational ministers influenced religious and theological opinion and offered literary and cultural commentary; chief among these were the *Congregational Magazine*, *Eclectic Review*, *British Quarterly Review*, and *Congregationalist*. Congregationalists historically had valued an educated ministry, and in the nineteenth century they took the lead among Nonconformists in developing theological colleges out of the older Dissenting academies. By 1871 there were sixteen such Congregational institutions. Mansfield College, established in Oxford in 1886, was the first Nonconformist institution to be brought to the ancient universities; A. M. Fairbairn, originally from Scotland and a leading theologian, became its first principal. Other religious and theological leadership was provided in the denomination during the Victorian era by J. A.

James, Thomas Binney, Robert Vaughan, Henry Allon, R. W. Dale, and J. Guiness Rogers. Two Congregationalist members of Parliament, Edward Baines and Edward Miall, were particularly active in representing Nonconformist views on political issues.

DALE A. JOHNSON

Bibliography

Currie, Robert, Alan Gilbert, and Lee Horsley. *Churches and Churchgoers: Patterns of Church Growth in the British Isles Since 1700.* 1977.

Dale, Robert W. *History of English Congregationalism.* 1907.

Jones, Robert Tudur. *Congregationalism in England, 1662-1962.* 1962.

Peel, Albert. *These Hundred Years: A History of the Congregational Union of England and Wales, 1831-1931.* 1931.

· · · · ·

CONRAD, JOSEPH
(1857-1924)

In the two decades between 1895 and 1915, Joseph Conrad established himself as one of England's most important novelists despite the fact that he did not begin learning English until he was twenty-one years of age. His works such as *Lord Jim* (1900), *Heart of Darkness* (1902), *Nostromo* (1904), and *Victory* (1915) have a taken place among the lasting masterworks of British literature.

Józef Teodor Konrad Korzeniowski was born in Berdyczów, Poland. His father, Apollo, was a Polish aristocrat of moderate means; a romantic intellectual who wrote poetry and translated Hugo, Vigny, Dickens, Shakespeare, and others; and a patriot committed to Polish nationalism. With his wife, Ewa, and his son, Apollo was sentenced to exile in northern Russia in 1862 for his support of a peasant insurrection. Ewa Korzeniowska died of tuberculosis in 1867; Apollo died in 1869. The orphaned twelve-year-old was left in the care of his maternal uncle, Tadeusz Bobrowski.

Conrad left Poland in 1874 to join the

French merchant service in Marseilles. He sailed on his first English ship in 1878, and in 1886 became a British subject and passed the examination for master in the British merchant marine. He left his last position as a seaman in 1894, the same year that he finished his first novel after five years of writing; with the publication of *Almayer's Folly* (1895), the thirty-eight-year-old Korzeniowski adopted the anglicized pen name Joseph Conrad. In 1896 he married Jessie George and published his second novel, *An Outcast of the Islands.*

The earliest works were autobiographical in subject and setting, dealing with exotic places and interesting characters Conrad had known as a seaman. *Heart of Darkness*, completed in 1899, details a journey down the Congo by the British master Marlow and draws heavily on Conrad's own experiences in the Belgian Congo in 1890. *Lord Jim* stresses Conrad's most insistent themes—the importance of fidelity, duty, and honor in a modern world bereft of traditional faith—while its narrative, presented principally by Marlow as a series of memories and discoveries, violates traditional chronological form in favor of associational development. *Nostromo*, generally considered his greatest novel, creates the imaginary land of Costaguana in South America as the setting for a complex, impressionistic narrative that deals in both private morality and public ethics and reveals Conrad at his best in synthesizing plot, structure, language, and themes. *Chance* (1913) was Conrad's first work to achieve anything approaching popular success, despite the fact that in it he uses one of his most complex narrative techniques—filtering the story through five levels of narration. *Victory*, a symbolic novel that reiterates Conrad's insistence upon human action rather than a safe detachment, is his last great achievement, though he continued to write until his death.

From the success of *Chance* in 1913 to his death in 1924, Joseph Conrad was the most discussed living British novelist. In his subordination of conventional chronology and plot structure to larger, overall artistic purposes he helped to broaden the horizons of the English novel; in his alter ego and model seaman Marlow, he created one of the great characters of English fiction; and in his focus upon struggles, rather than upon victories or defeats, Conrad learned to penetrate deeper meanings hidden beneath the surface of traditional narrative.

W. CRAIG TURNER

Bibliography

Baines, Jocelyn. *Joseph Conrad: A Critical Biography.* 1960.

Ehrsam, Theodore G. *A Bibliography of Joseph Conrad.* 1969.

Guérard, Albert. *Conrad the Novelist.* 1958.

Hewitt, Douglas. *Conrad: A Reassessment.* 1952.

Jean-Aubry, G. *Joseph Conrad: Life and Letters.* 1927.

Karl, Frederick. *A Reader's Guide to Joseph Conrad.* 1960.

Leavis. F. R. *The Great Tradition.* 1948.

Najder, Zdzislaw. *Joseph Conrad: A Chronicle.* 1983. Trans. Holina Carroll-Najder.

Sherry, Norman, ed. *Conrad: The Critical Heritage.* 1973.

Teets, Bruce E. and Helmut E. Gerber. *Joseph Conrad: An Annotated Bibliography of Writings About Him.* 1971.

Watt, Ian. *Conrad in the Nineteenth Century.* 1980.

. . . . .

CONSERVATIVE PARTY

Conservatism is an essentially pragmatic political outlook concerned with preserving what is valued in the existing order. It is sceptical about general theoretical principles. Thus it is difficult to define a fixed body of Conservative doctrine, particularly as English Conservatism proved more pliant than its Continental counterparts. Nevertheless certain notions influenced most Conservative thought during the Victorian period: first, the importance of community and the belief that individual political significance is defined largely in social terms that prescribe duties as well as rights; second, historically derived institutions constitute the authentic structure of government; and third, there exist limits to political action beyond which other considerations, most often religious, preside.

The Conservative party had its origins in the legacy of William Pitt (1759–1806), the writings of Edmund Burke (1729–1797), and the political practice of Lord Liverpool (1770–1828), George Canning (1770–1827), and William Huskisson (1770–1830). This inheritance stressed the importance of defending property, the inspiring nature of tradition, and the dangers of late eighteenth-century revolutionary ideologies. In his "Tamworth Manifesto" of December 1834, **Robert Peel** (1788–1850) defined Conservative policy as the careful review of institutions, combining the protection of established rights with the correction of proven abuses. Peel's minority ministry from December 1834 to April 1835 gave birth to the Conservative party. The Carlton Club, founded in 1832, provided a social base for the parliamentary party, which initially consisted of about 275 members of Parliament. By 1837 about forty M.P.'s who had been Whig reformers in 1832 crossed over to the Conservatives. At the same time an extra-parliamentary organization was established by the party agent F. R. Bonham (1785–1863).

Although the Conservative party's victory in the 1841 general election gave Peel a Commons majority of 76, his repeal of the **Corn Laws** in 1846 split the party and precipitated his resignation in June 1846. Some 112 Conservatives adopted the designation Peelites, but after Peel's death in 1850 they ceased to be a cohesive parliamentary group. Some returned to the Conservative party; others, most notably **William Gladstone** (1809–1898), eventually joined the **Liberal party**.

Those Conservatives who opposed Corn Law repeal, including **Benjamin Disraeli**, temporarily adopted the designation Protectionists. Lord Stanley (1799–1868), who succeeded his father as fourteenth earl of Derby in 1851, formed minority governments in February 1852 and February 1858. Disraeli served as government leader in the Commons and as chancellor of the Exchequer in both ministries. The first relinquished protectionism as Conservative policy. The second suffered a major defeat over its parliamentary reform bill in March 1859. Derby formed a third minority government in June 1866.

In 1867 Derby's cabinet introduced a reform bill that became the subject of intense political maneuvering. Many clauses were changed by amendments, producing what Derby described as "a leap in the dark." The 1867 Reform Act almost doubled the electorate; 36 percent of adult males became eligible to vote. Its passage revealed Disraeli's strategic genius, but suggestions that the measure encapsulated Disraeli's vision of a "Tory Democracy" are misleading.

After 1867 the party underwent organizational changes in response to the broadening electorate. A National Union of Conservative and Constitution Associations was formed in 1867, which had a central office in London and worked through the chief whip at Westminster to coordinate central and local activity. Disraeli's May 1872 speech at the Crystal Palace redefined Conservative policy in terms of imperial commitment and social reform. This complemented his "One Nation" doctrine, suggesting a unity of interest between the aristocracy and the working class to counter the socially divisive impact of modern capitalism.

Following the general election of February 1874, Disraeli formed a Conservative government which, for the first time since 1841, enjoyed a majority in the Commons. Social reform measures passed in 1875 included the Public Health Act, the Artisan's Dwelling Act, and the Food and Drug Act. Peaceful picketing was legalized. Disraeli also pulled off a diplomatic coup by persuading the government to purchase a majority of shares in the Suez Canal Company. In 1876 Disraeli created the title Empress of India for Queen Victoria, and was himself elevated to the House of Lords as earl of Beaconsfield.

The 1880 election, however, was a devastating defeat for the Conservatives, and in April 1881 Beaconsfield died. Party leadership was shared between Stafford Northcote (1818–1887) in the Commons and the **marquess of Salisbury** (1830–1903) in the Lords, an unsatisfactory arrangement that encouraged **Lord Randolph Churchill** (1849–1894) to form the "Fourth party" in 1880. The **Home Rule** crisis of 1885–1886 affirmed Salisbury's leadership and identified the Conservatives as a staunchly Unionist, anti–Home Rule party. Salisbury led an interim Conservative government from June 1885 to January 1886. In July 1886 he formed a Conservative ministry and, except between August 1892 and June 1895, remained premier until July 1902.

In domestic affairs Salisbury retained a truly conservative scepticism about democracy, perceiving the party's role to be a holding action against the movement of the age. He was, however, a master of parliamentary management and created an extraparliamentary organization under the auspices of the Conservative party agent R. W. E. Middleton (1845–1905) which, along with the Primrose League, became the model for the more democratic Conservative party of the new century. In foreign affairs Salisbury stressed the importance of empire and the balance of power in Europe. Salisbury's nephew **A. J. Balfour** (1848–1930) succeeded his uncle as both prime minister and party leader in July 1902.

ANGUS HAWKINS

Bibliography

Blake, Robert. *The Conservative Party from Peel to Thatcher.* 1985.

Feuchtwanger, Edgar J. *Disraeli, Democracy and the Tory Party.* 1968.

Gash, Norman, ed. *The Conservatives: A History from their Origins to 1965.* 1977.

Pugh, Martin. *The Tories and the People: 1880–1935.* 1985.

Southgate, Donald, ed. *The Conservative Leadership. 1832–1932.* 1974.

Stewart, Robert. *The Foundation of the Conservative Party. 1830–1867.* 1978.

· · · · ·

CONTAGIOUS DISEASES ACTS see PROSTITUTION

· · · · ·

COOK, ELIZA
(1818–1889)

By age twenty Eliza Cook had gained considerable reputation for the simple, unpretentious, and moral verse that she regularly contributed to London periodicals, especially the *Weekly Dispatch*. The titles of her most famous poems reflect their domesticity and unaffected sentiment: "The Old Arm Chair," "The Old Farm Gate," "The Last Good-Bye." Besides compiling volumes of her poetry (*Lays of a Wild Harp*, 1835; *Melaia and Other Poems*, 1838; *Poems, Second Series*, 1845; *New Echoes, and Other Poems*, 1864; and collected editions), Cook edited and wrote much of a biweekly periodical, *Eliza Cook's Journal* (1849–1854). From it she later collected brief essays of general interest in *Jottings from My Journal* (1860).

Eliza Cook's Journal focused primarily on social issues as they concerned women and children. It also included short stories, biographical sketches, inspirational essays, book reviews, poetry by Cook and others, and a regular column of aphorisms she later collected in *Diamond Dust* (1865). The topics indexed for one year of the journal range from "Australian salt mines" to "modern yachting."

As a poet Cook evoked the commonplace in simple forms—iambic tetrameter couplets, unadorned blank verse. Her favorite subjects included the dignity of humble life and the insignificance of rank and money; the worth of the downtrodden—poor laborers, blacks, American Indians; the virtue of honesty and the power of love. Sometimes humorous, usually sentimental but not mawkish, her work is consistently humane. Reviews occasionally characterized her "unfashionably democratic" humanitarianism and social conscience as "gipsy lawlessness," but defended her emancipation of woman's mind from "the trifling, minute, and evanescent affairs of life." Although she aimed at uncultured tastes through inexpensive volumes, she sometimes deserved a more sophisticated audience.

BEVERLY TAYLOR

· · · · ·

COOPER, THOMAS
(1805–1892)

In the history of **Chartism** few individuals are as enigmatic as Thomas Cooper. Born to working-class parents in Leicester, Cooper enjoyed a reputation in the 1820s and 1830s as a self-taught schoolteacher, journalist, and lecturer before enthusiastically embracing the Chartist cause in 1840. Five years later his stormy career as a Chartist ended and Cooper turned to poetry, Baptist preaching, and the education of the working class.

Cooper became a Chartist after covering one of their meetings for the *Leicestershire Mercury* in 1840. Assuming control of the local radical paper, the *Midland Counties Illuminator*, he gained a reputation for organizing one of the most active physical force groups of Chartists in the country. He wrote several Chartist songs and spoke at various demonstrations. As an advocate of mass strike activity, he was arrested for sedition in 1842, serving two years in jail. There he rejected violence. Later, in *The Life of Thomas Cooper, Written by Himself* (1872), an excellent—if biased—account of the movement, he downplayed his role as a physical force Chartist. In 1845 he broke with **Feargus O'Connor** (1794–1855) over the Chartist Land Plan and was expelled from the movement.

In jail he wrote *The Purgatory of Suicides* (1845), a lengthy poem which earned him the respect of literary critics. **Charles Kingsley** (1819–1875) modeled his Chartist hero in *Alton Locke* (1850) on him. In 1849 Cooper launched the *Plain Speaker* and in 1850 *Cooper's Journal*, two popular papers through which he attempted to convert the working class to his gospel of radical politics, knowledge, temperance, and self-help. Later in life he became a Baptist, lecturing extensively about the need for class reconciliation, religious faith, and self-improvement.

For all his commitment to the working class, Cooper remained intellectually aloof from the masses. He was, first and foremost, an autodidact. In his later years he lamented the decline of the autodidact tradition, believing that the working class had "gone back, intellectually and morally."

CHRIS WATERS

Bibliography

Cole, G. D. H. *Chartist Portraits.* 1941.

Conklin, Robert J. *Thomas Cooper, the Chartist (1805–1892).* 1935.

Cooper, Thomas. *The Life of Thomas Cooper, Written by Himself.* 1872; rpt. 1971.

———. *The Poetical Works of Thomas Cooper.* 1877.

Harrison, J. F. C. "Chartism in Leicester." In Asa Briggs, ed., *Chartist Studies.* 1959.

———, and Dorothy Thompson. *Bibliography of the Chartist Movement, 1837–1976.* 1978.

· · · · ·

THE COOPERATIVE MOVEMENT

Cooperation, which seeks the equitable division of profits among managers, workers (producers), and consumers, arose simultaneously with trade unionism and the reform movement. Its chief advocate, the socialist Robert Owen (1771–1858), believed that given the proper program of education this alternative to competitive capitalism could effect a complete reformation of society based on harmony, equity, and self-help.

Owen planned to create self-supporting "Villages of Cooperation" that would reduce welfare, replace competition with cooperation, and eliminate economic rivalries. Though never the national success he hoped, this larger vision did spawn numerous Owenite societies that planted the cooperative seed. The first, founded by the printer George Mudie in London in 1821, was followed by many others, including the London Cooperative Society (1824), founded by the working-class activists James Watson and William Lovett. *Co-operative Magazine* (1826) was founded to promote the movement, and in 1827 the philanthropist Dr. William King founded the Brighton Cooperative Society and its journal, *The Co-operator* (1828), which encouraged local application of Owen's ideas. The British Association for the Promotion of Cooperative Knowledge (1829) was one early attempt to centralize the over three hundred cooperative societies that soon appeared. Most were consumer societies that established cooperative stores, run by workers, to sell goods to members. Originally a small part of Owen's scheme, these became the most familiar manifestations of it. One especially notable success was the society founded in 1844 by the Rochdale Equitable Pioneers, textile workers in the town of Rochdale. Their sound financial policies initiated the modern cooperative movement.

Early attempts to create producers' societies and to consolidate the forces of trade unionism and cooperation were unsuccessful. Untimely strikes, sectional rivalries, and swift, severe punitive measures by the Whig government also doomed Owen's plan to form a national union to link cooperative societies with trade unions, Friendly Societies, and other benevolent societies. But when **Christian socialists** founded the Society for Promoting Working Men's Associations (1849), cooperatively run factories were again advocated, this time with greater success. Meanwhile, the Industrial and Provident Societies Acts (1852, 1855, 1862) gave legal status to cooperatives, and resumed agitation for a national union of cooperatives led some Rochdale leaders to establish, in 1863, the Cooperative Wholesale Society. Through its wholesale activities with member societies, the large and diverse CWS in effect created a cooperative network and soon expanded into production. The movement's first true central body, the Cooperative Union, was established in 1869 by the first annual Cooperative Congress, which thereafter met regularly.

Expanding steadily, the cooperative movement enjoyed the support of women, spread to the Continent, and eventually entered politics to safeguard its position. The movement claimed 600,000 members in 1880, and had nearly tripled by 1900. Many women, first attracted by the movement's emphasis on consumerism and thrift, soon saw cooperation much as it was originally intended, as an agency for social reform. Growing to maturity in the 1890s, the Women's Cooperative Guild supplied numerous influential leaders for the movement. Alice Acland (1849–1935) and Catherine Webb (1859–1947) were notable forces of cooperative propaganda and education, and Margaret Llewelyn Davies (1861–1944), a remarkable leader of great influence, helped direct the movement toward reform at home and expansion on the Continent. There cooperation had already taken hold, in part from earlier efforts by the secularist **G. J. Holyoake** (1817–1906) to spread its principles. British and French leaders formed cooperative alliances in the 1890s, and a search for direct parliamentary representation for cooperative interests led the move-

ment, healthy and well established, into the twentieth century.

Though not effecting the complete reformation Owen intended, the cooperative movement did improve working-class life and encourage labor consolidation at a time of great industrial turmoil.

STEVEN N. CRAIG

Bibliography

Bailey, Jack. *The British Cooperative Movement.* 1974.

Cole, G. D. H. *A Short History of the British Working-Class Movement: 1789–1947.* 1948.

Gaffin, Jean. "Women and Cooperation." In Lucy Middleton, ed., *Women in the Labour Movement: The British Experience.* 1977.

See also OWENITE SOCIALISM

· · · · ·

COPYRIGHT

By the nineteenth century, statutory copyright meant the protection of published literary property for a stated period of time, after which anyone was free to reprint and sell a given work. Unpublished compositions and letters enjoyed perpetual protection. The Copyright Acts of 1709, 1814, and 1842 increased the duration of protection from fourteen, to twenty-eight, to forty-two years respectively. These were minimal guarantees and in fact an author's copyright remained valid throughout his or her life plus seven years. The principle of linking copyright and lifespan was further extended to an author's lifetime plus fifty years in 1911.

The eighteenth- and nineteenth-century statutes broadened the scope of copyright to include engravings and printed reproductions, and dramatic and musical compositions and their corresponding live performances. In 1862 paintings, drawings, and photographs also received protection. Excerpting material for book reviews or inclusion in an encyclopedia or anthology remained ambiguous until 1911 when the doctrine of fair usage was instituted.

Although the rights of domestic authors and artists were generally understood in the Victorian age, those applying to foreigners were obscure. The law clearly forbade the importation of piracies: reprints of works by British authors, composers, and engravers published outside of Great Britain. This guarantee also covered foreign authors living on British soil at the time that their work first appeared. In *Routledge vs. Low*, 1868, the House of Lords broadened the meaning of "British soil" to include the entire empire, but could not agree whether publication in Britain protected a nonresident foreign author.

Reciprocal copyright treaties with other nations were authorized by statute in 1838 and 1844. The Berne Convention of 1886 greatly simplified the process, yet numerous unauthorized American reprints continued to appear until 1891 when the United States agreed to discontinue sanctioning the practice of literary piracy.

JAMES J. BARNES
PATIENCE P. BARNES

Bibliography

Ladas, Stephen P. *The International Protection of Literary and Artistic Property.* 1938. 2 vols.

Myers, Robin. *The British Book Trade from Caxton to the Present Day: A Bibliographical Guide.* 1973.

See also MUSIC PUBLISHING

· · · · ·

CORELLI, MARIE (1855–1924)

Defying the trends toward materialism and determinism, Marie Corelli's exotic first novel, *A Romance of Two Worlds* (1886), captured the public imagination with its view of a Christian universe bound by a benevolent electrical force. Her thirty books include the popular *Vendetta* (1886), *Thelma* (1887), *The Soul of Lilith* (1892), *Barabbas* (1893), *The Sorrows of Satan* (1895)—the best seller of the entire century—*The Mighty Atom* (1896), and *The Master Christian* (1900). Bane of the critics for her effusiveness and

simplistic division of the world into good and bad, she was idolized by the public and admired by Gladstone, Queen Victoria, the Prince of Wales, and Oscar Wilde.

Raised Minnie Mackay at Box Hill, Dorking, as the adopted daughter of the balladeer Charles Mackay, she was actually his love child, perhaps by a Venetian mother. Billed as Signorina Marie Corelli in a London pianoforte improvisation in 1884, she launched herself as a novelist under this name. In 1899 she and her lifelong friend Bertha Vyver settled in Stratford-upon-Avon, where she kept a gondola and maddened officialdom with her self-proclaimed guardianship of Shakespeare's memory. Patriotic journalism in support of World War I revived her faded popularity and offset the hurt of her unreciprocated love for the sculptor Arthur Severn, an affair fictionalized in the posthumous *Open Confession* (1925).

Corelli's success as the best-paid, most read, and most talked about novelist at the fin de siècle stemmed from her championship of crumbling but cherished values and beliefs and, more importantly, from her powerful imagination, which swept readers to exotic landscapes, even to outer space, and held them in a state of excitement with bizarre characters and situations. She wrote under the influence of the romantic poets and the hypnotic Ouida, and in reaction to Zola, Ibsen, the New Woman novelists, and the agnosticism of Mary Ward's best seller, *Robert Elsmere* (1888). She is still in print and was admired by Henry Miller despite her inaccuracies, prolixity, humorlessness, tirades, and incredible self-promotion.

TAMIE WATTERS

Bibliography

Bigland, Eileen. *Marie Corelli, the Woman and the Legend: A Biography.* 1953.

Masters, Brian. *Now Barabbas Was a Rotter.* 1978.

Vyver, Bertha. *Memoirs of Marie Corelli.* 1930.

· · · · ·

CORN LAWS

The Corn Laws regulated the importation of all cereal grains into Britain. Though they had long been a feature of British commercial policy, the Corn Laws were suspended during the Napoleonic Wars to ensure an adequate supply of food. In 1815, Parliament, dominated by landed interests, reimposed the Corn Laws in the form of a fixed duty in order to protect domestic agriculture, reduce dependence upon foreign supplies of grain, prevent wild fluctuations in price, and enhance government revenues. The manufacturing interests opposed the Corn Laws as protectionist class legislation which served to retard British economic growth and progress.

In 1828 William Huskisson, president of the Board of Trade, proposed an amendment to the Corn Laws which established a sliding scale in which the duty was inversely proportional to the price of grain. It was this law that was opposed by the **Anti–Corn-Law League**. When Ireland faced famine in 1846 the Peel ministry (1841–1846) enacted the immediate temporary suspension of the Corn Laws, which drove **Robert Peel** from office and split his Conservative party. For all practical purposes the Corn Laws were permanently abolished in 1849.

RICHARD FRANCIS SPALL, JR.

Bibliography

Barnes, Donald G. *A History of the English Corn Laws from 1660–1846.* 1930.

See also AGRICULTURE; ELLIOTT, EBENEZER; FREE TRADE

· · · · ·

COST OF LIVING

The falling cost of living created the Victorian period. The first stages of the industrial revolution did not benefit the working classes, whose standard of living failed to improve during the period 1815 to 1842. In many cases the lives of the working classes may have gotten worse, while the middle class gained great wealth and the aristocracy retained its property and position. Chartism and other forms of protest expressed the workers' discontent and generated forebodings among the middle class and the aristocracy. Only in the second half of the 1800s did the calm thought to be characteristic of Victorian Britain settle on

society because of a rising standard of living for the working classes. That relative serenity was produced by a declining cost of living rather than by an intentional increase in wages. In other words, after 1842 the higher classes unintentionally redistributed some of the nation's wealth to the workers through lower prices for food and other necessities of life.

Victorian economic history is divided into the boom (1842–1873) and the great depression (1873–1896). Those labels obscure the course of events because they are misleading. The boom benefited the middle class and some workers, but most of the population did not share in rising profits during the boom. Labor constituted almost 90 percent of the population and only portions of the labor force shared in the new wealth. The aristocracy of labor with skilled trades increased their **wages** as did many factory hands, but handloom weavers and agricultural workers did not. More important, prices remained relatively stable; for example, a four-pound loaf of bread in London fluctuated from 7½ pence in 1850 to 8½ pence in 1872. On the whole workers held their own during the boom, but the cost of living remained almost constant until the great depression.

The depression was only of prices, profits, and interest rates. The working classes benefited enormously, especially because the great depression saw a decline in food prices. The four-pound London loaf fell to 5½ pence in 1890. As a result of the decline, workers consumed more food in greater variety than ever before. Fruit, meat, cheese, and sugar became common fare; in 1860, for example, per capita consumption of sugar was 35 pounds, but in 1900 it exceeded 80 pounds. At the other end of the consumption spectrum, opium use per head went down as the poor needed it less to relieve their suffering. Cheap goods lowered the price of existence and even made life enjoyable. Ready-made clothes and factory-made boots provided better apparel. Fish and chips shops appeared and provided the luxury of dining out. Even durable goods became common. **Bicycles** created affordable transportation and **sewing machines** made some working-class fashion possible. Cheap newspapers enlarged the reading public. Music halls sprouted to entertain, and professional soccer began in 1885. Also, new state services lowered the cost of living, in a sense. The 1870 Education Act set up schools, and factory acts lowered the hours of the work week. Health regulations and municipal baths were incalculable improvements, making a clean life possible on a working-class budget.

The middle-class standard of living improved also, but in a different pattern. The boom was its golden age. High profits and cheap labor seemed to insure a lifestyle that could match or at least mirror that of the aristocracy, but the depression was named by the middle class to describe its lot after 1873. A far smaller portion of middle-class income was spent for food, so declining food prices helped them little. In some cases depressed profits and interest lowered income. Generally the cost of living rose for the middle class as it declined for the working class. The most obvious change was in the keeping of **servants**. Servants were considered a necessity because middle-class status meant having servants. Individuals with as little as 100 pounds per year often kept a servant, but this became more of a financial burden as domestic servants' wages rose substantially. As a result, male servants gradually disappeared from all but the largest households. The cost of other middle-class expenses such as **public schools** rose also. In an effort to fight the higher costs of middle-class living, the middle class turned to **birth control** in the 1870s. As the upper middle-class limited their numbers to cope, the aspiring **clerks** and poor white-collar workers saw the symbols of middle-class life slipping from them. Servants became too expensive for the lower middle class, and workers asserted their independence by refusing domestic service whenever possible. Some of the working class grew to afford a lifestyle comparable to that of the lower middle class in many instances.

If the declining cost of living began to blur that class line, the aristocracy continued to enjoy a standard of living that ignored the mundane costs of life. Although some of the upper class suffered from the agricultural depression, others adjusted with new crops, while yet others made fortunes from urban real estate and coal.

At the other end of the social pyramid, the poor failed to notice many of the improvements created by the declining cost of living: 25 to 30 percent of the population lived in **poverty**. Nearly 10 percent of all families could not keep their members in good health. The other 15 to 20 percent lived on the edge of want with unemployment and old age destroying the margin of comfort. A national old age pension did not come until 1908, which meant that the improved working-class life disappeared for many of those who lived past their productive years. So while the decline in living costs among the majority of the population created the Victorian period it failed to include the whole society, and created expectations that were not fulfilled. The Victorian period ended in the early 1900s when the cost of living began to rise again and destroyed the general confidence in an ever-improving standard of living.

DENNIS J. MITCHELL

Bibliography

Burnett, John. *A History of the Cost of Living.* 1969.

———.*Plenty and Want. A Social History of Diet in England from 1815 to the Present Day.* 1968.

———.*The Annals of Labour.* 1974.

Clapham, J. H. *An Economic History of Modern Britain.* 1967.

Crouzet, François. *The Victorian Economy.* 1982.

Hobsbawm, E. J. *Industry and Empire.* 1968.

Tames, Richard. *Economy and Society in Nineteenth-Century Britain.* 1972.

· · · · ·

COTTON FAMINE see CIVIL WAR, UNITED STATES

· · · · ·

COUNTRY SOCIETY

To our minds, country society would seem to include everyone living outside of cities: landowners, tenant farmers, landless agricultural laborers, craft and professional people, and merchants in market towns. To Victorians, the term referred only to those with whom it was proper for a person of gentle birth, who did not have to work for a living, to mix socially.

The parliamentary enclosures of the eighteenth and early nineteenth centuries resulted in a three-tier system of responsibility for the land. The owner of an estate usually took an interest in its efficient running and, at the least, employed an agent to supervise improvements such as hedging, draining, and animal husbandry. He might also reduce rents or delay them during bad harvests, or invest in a tenant farmer's improvements. He was motivated by paternal interest in his tenants—and by the difficulty of replacing tenants who failed.

Some independent yeoman farmers still worked holdings of from less than one hundred to several hundred acres. Most farmers, however, were tenants of the larger landowners. The farmer usually held a lease, either for twenty-one years or for three lifetimes. If the latter, farmers had a strong interest in improvements, and might put their own capital into the farm, though major works had to be done by the landowner.

Landless laborers lived in cottages provided by the farmer and spent their days in such toil that they had little time for anything else. They might stay in one location all their lives, but they could seek better employment at seasonal hiring fairs, as could domestic servants.

The well born had subtly defined rankings and tried to stay within them. The activities of "society" were determined as much by the need to exercise business and political influence and to find suitable marriage partners as by natural desires for company and entertainment.

Because social life centered in London during the season, the country house was cared for by servants during much of the year. There were certain annual county events, such as the assize ball. But the main pleasures of landed families during summer and autumn were house parties, often organized for hunting, coursing, or shooting. Railways made these gatherings more simple to manage for weekends, so the importance of the London season dwindled as the ease of visiting grew.

Liberal hospitality and the maintenance of appearances suitable to one's rank were important duties of the upper classes. Impressive display at family celebrations was expected.

Serious attention went into house renovation and planning gardens and parks. Separate servants' quarters, smoking rooms for gentlemen and withdrawing rooms for ladies, corridors for privacy, and better drainage were frequent additions. Libraries, music rooms, and conservatories reflected not only the position but also the taste of the owner.

The leisured class did pursue serious interests, such as holding unpaid local government posts (until the creation of county councils in 1888 removed the need) or engaging in national politics. Some were philanthropists and social reformers. Many had highly developed intellectual occupations, collected rare books and works of art, and supported concerts and literature. All but a few radical thinkers among them believed that their fulfillment of the duties of their class entitled them to the deference of the lower orders.

SIDNEY JOHNSON

Bibliography

Girouard, Mark. *The Victorian Country House.* 1971.

Stone, Lawrence and Jeanne C. Stone. *An Open Elite? England, 1540–1880.* 1984.

Thompson, F. M. L. *English Landed Society in the Nineteenth Century.* 1963.

See also ARISTOCRACY AND GENTRY; CHURCH OF ENGLAND PARISH LIFE; SOCIAL SEASON; SOCIETY, ETIQUETTE AND CUSTOMS OF

. . . . .

COUNTRY SPORTS

Hunting and shooting were preeminently the sports of aristocrats and gentry with country estates. By the opening of the Victorian period both sports were informally governed by codes of etiquette and gentlemanly behavior which arose in the eighteenth century and were firmly established by the end of the Napoleonic Wars.

Hunting—the pursuit of animals by hounds—had come by the nineteenth century to mean primarily fox hunting; riders follow the hunt on horseback to watch the pack of hounds pursue and kill the fox. By the century's second quarter the sport was mythologized as an institution that encouraged manliness and preserved rural society by inducing the gentry to winter in the country rather than in London. England was informally divided into "countries" with clearly understood boundaries for each hunt. The pack of hounds was generally maintained by subscription, although a few men kept up packs at their own expense. In 1835, ninety-one packs were formally recognized, with as many as one hundred riders following each.

The master of foxhounds was responsible for overseeing the pack, establishing hunt days, and maintaining good relations with farmers whose land the hunt would cover. It was a position that required—and supplied—a great deal of social prestige. The huntsman, who actually performed the work of training and hunting the hounds, might be either a gentleman or a professional; in either case, most of the actual work was done by various hunt servants, whose pay also came from the subscription. Hunting was by tradition open to all comers, but most regular hunters were drawn from the rural gentry who had leisure for weekday hunting and the wherewithal to maintain good horses. Farmers also hunted but did not generally wear scarlet. By the latter part of the century, with good rail transportation, middle-class townsmen with time and money increasingly joined subscription hunts.

Over the course of the century, hunting became the center of an elaborate social life of balls, breakfasts, dinners, and races sponsored by the hunt or by hunt clubs. The balls were generally attended only by gentry, although farmers were more often included at all-male dinners. Women did not usually ride to the hounds until after midcentury, but by the 1860s, when hunting was unquestionably the most fashionable winter recreation, increasing numbers of women were seen in the field.

Shooting was an even more exclusive pastime. Even with the liberalization of game laws in 1831, game could be legally killed only by property owners. Shooting parties were arranged by landowners to provide sport for houseguests. In the eighteenth century, with muzzleloading guns, it was usual to shoot at game flying away. As weapons improved

the conventions changed; drivers flushed the birds and drove them toward the guns, making the shot more difficult and more sporting. Nevertheless, the success of the shoot was measured in the size of the day's bag—which, on large estates, could run into the thousands.

Landowners who valued shooting took great pains to preserve suitable breeding grounds, prevent poaching, and observe seasons. The result was a certain amount of conflict between hunters and gamekeepers, since the latter tended to kill foxes and object to the incursion of horses and hounds. The Prince of Wales turned Sandringham into one of the finest shoots in Europe. Shooting was most exclusive in Scotland, and the annual opening of the grouse season on August 12 provided the date by which Parliament finished its business for the session.

Deer stalking was far less common in the Victorian period than it had been earlier, except in Scotland and on some very large English estates. Deer hunters, referred to as "the guns," took up their positions before dawn and spent much of the day motionless in thickets until a stag came within range. Women participated only as distant observers; an engraving of the period shows Queen Victoria seated sidesaddle upon a pony led across gorse-covered moorland by a kilted retainer. The sparsely populated areas of the Scottish Highlands were ideal stalking country. The sport was therefore open only to the few; legitimate guns were likely to be equaled in number by poachers.

Fishing was a less exclusive country sport; indeed, cheap rail fares made coarse fishing more popular during the period. Fly-fishing, however, became more expensive, and landowners increasingly preserved the choice locations on their own property. The very rich, once more, went to Scotland for their sport. The old lower-class country sports, such as cockfighting, dog fighting, and bull baiting, were suppressed by statute in 1835, though the first two were never completely eradicated.

SALLY MITCHELL

Bibliography

Blaine, Delabere P. *An Encyclopedia of Rural Sports*. 1840.

Carr, Raymond. "Country Sports." In G. E. Mingay, ed., *The Victorian Countryside*, vol. 2. 1981.

———. *English Foxhunting: A History.* 1976.

Greville, Violet, ed. *Ladies in the Field.* 1894.

Itzkowitz, David C. *Peculiar Privilege: A Social History of English Foxhunting, 1753–1885.* 1977.

See also ANIMAL PROTECTION; GAME LAWS; SPORTING LITERATURE

. . . . .

COURTS, CRIMINAL *see* JUDICIAL SYSTEM

. . . . .

CRAIK, DINAH MARIA MULOCK (1826–1887)

A popular novelist best known for *John Halifax, Gentleman* (1856), as well as a journalist, poet, and children's writer, Dinah Mulock Craik wove through her life's work a concern for women's experiences, emotions, and need for independence. Born in Stoke-on-Trent, she was the eldest child of Dinah Mellard Mulock and the preacher and pamphleteer Thomas Mulock, who moved the family to London in 1839 and abandoned his children after their mother died in 1845. Dinah Mulock supported herself by miscellaneous magazine writing and published her first novel, *The Ogilvies*, in 1849. In 1865 she married a man eleven years her junior, the nephew and namesake of historian George Lillie Craik. They adopted a daughter, Dorothy, in 1869.

Dinah Mulock secured her reputation among contemporaries at the age of thirty with her fifth novel. By following from 1794 to 1834 the life of a virtuous young man whose kindness and hard work bring him, through many difficulties, from low-level worker to responsible capitalist and from orphaned child to loving husband and father, *John Halifax, Gentleman* made concrete the ideals of the mid-Victorian liberal, religious middle class. Charles Kingsley praised it in a sermon on "Heroism"; to an American editor it was a

modern *Pilgrim's Progress*, showing how to imitate Christ in an industrial age. Twentieth-century critics recognize in the novel both a historical allegory about the transfer of economic power from the aristocracy to the productive workers and a projection of the author's ideas about how independent women might function in the world.

Her next publication, *A Woman's Thoughts About Women* (1858), offered practical advice to self-supporting single women while encouraging in women of all classes self-reliance, mutual support and empathy, and sympathy for the "fallen." Such themes, together with an ideal of marriage based on equality and respect, pervade Craik's writings. Besides *John Halifax*, her better novels include *Olive* (1850), an interesting variation on Charlotte Brontë's *Jane Eyre* (1847); *A Life for a Life* (1859), which parallels the gradual reformation of a man who has committed murder and a woman who has borne an illegitimate child; and *Mistress and Maid* (serialized in 1862), about the daily lives and problems of four single women. Her children's classic, *The Little Lame Prince and His Travelling Cloak* (1875), charms young girls by creating sympathy for its dispossessed hero and has been read by adults as an allegory of the artist's or the woman's triumph through imagination over handicaps. Her poetry reached a wide public in collected editions (1859, 1880, 1888) and anthologies.

Taken seriously enough by her contemporaries to appear in critical essays alongside Charlotte Brontë, Elizabeth Gaskell, and George Eliot, Craik has enjoyed, in the second half of the twentieth century, a well-deserved place in studies of women's fiction. Because she wrote naturally and felt deeply, understood her social context, and engages the reader's sympathy, her best fiction remains interesting, readable, and deserving of critical study.

MONIKA BROWN

Bibliography

Foster, Shirley. *Victorian Women's Fiction: Marriage, Freedom and the Individual.* 1985.

Mitchell, Sally. *Dinah Mulock Craik.* 1983.

Showalter, Elaine. "Dinah Mulock Craik and the Tactics of Sentiment: A Case Study in Victorian

Female Authorship." *Feminist Studies*. vol. 2., pp. 5-23.

—— . *A Literature of Their Own: British Women Novelists from Brontë to Lessing*. 1977.

. . . . .

CRANE, WALTER (1845-1915)

Illustrator Walter Crane heralded the advent of quality design in children's books during the later Victorian period. Preceding Randolph Caldecott and Kate Greenaway in developing color printing with Edmund Evans, Crane insisted on line and organic design in books.

Trained as an engraver under W. J. Linton, Crane joined with Evans to produce a series of sixpenny toy books published by Warne in 1863. These books proved so popular that George Routledge issued his own series, *Sixpenny Toybooks* (1867), also illustrated by Crane and displaying his distinct flattening of form, influenced by the Japanese.

Crane's work for toybooks was unprofitable but his decorative style attracted offers to design friezes and Morris wallpapers for the nursery, which did make money. In 1875 he illustrated the first of sixteen books for **Mary Louisa Molesworth**, *Tell Me a Story*. His own book, *The Baby's Opera* (1877), was rejected by the book trade because of its advanced design but sold over 40,000 copies. Other landmark books with illustrations by Crane include Oscar Wilde's *The Happy Prince and Other Tales* (1888), Nathaniel Hawthorne's *A Wonderbook for Girls and Boys* (1892), William Morris's *The Story of the Glittering Plain* (1894), and Crane's own *Flora's Feast: A Masque of Flowers* (1889).

Associated with **William Morris** and the **arts and crafts movement**, Crane served as president of the Arts Workers' Guild in 1884. Several of his books reflect Socialist League and **Fabian Society** concerns for the working poor and their living environment.

Crane believed that art should ornament as well as illustrate. He designed a book as an organic whole, integrating text and illustration across a two-page spread. From 1884-1907, Crane was also an innovator in educa-tion. Believing that reading should be taught by associating words with pictures, he produced *The Golden Primer* with J. M. D. Meiklejohn in 1884 and the *Walter Crane Reader* with Nellie Dale in 1899.

LOUISA SMITH

Bibliography

Crane, Walter. *Of the Decorative Illustration of Books Old and New*. 1921.

Engen, Rodney K. *Walter Crane as a Book Illustrator*. 1975.

. . . . .

CRICKET

In an age dominated by the cult of athleticism, the Victorians exalted sports in general but still reserved a special place for cricket, which they regarded as a unique national symbol and by far the purest form of all manly recreations. The game therefore became an essential feature of the curriculum in public schools and universities. Hundreds of cricket clubs were founded and sustained by wealthy patrons who considered them as vital to the community as literature and the arts.

During the midcentury, touring professional cricketers did most to popularize the game, but they were gradually superseded in the 1860s by the emerging county clubs, numbering thirty-seven altogether. Of these, sixteen eventually became designated as first class in 1895. The county championship, which is still being held, was regularized after 1873. Gloucestershire did extremely well during the 1870s when the mighty Graces were at their peak. Thereafter, the competition became dominated by Nottinghamshire and Surrey with their galaxy of professional stars. At the turn of the century, Yorkshire, ably led by Lord Hawke, became dominant.

Professional cricketers left Britain to coach in the colonies and encourage the development of international competition. By the 1880s Anglo-Australian cricket rivalry had already become extremely keen. South Africa also began to play Test cricket in 1889, but the game inexplicably languished in North America, although the first English cricket tour abroad, undertaken in 1859, had been to

Canada and the United States.

The Marylebone Cricket Club emerged as the game's leading authority and was especially responsible for codifying and amending its laws. Among the most notable decisions reached by the MCC during the nineteenth century were the legalizing of round-arm bowling in 1835 and of over-arm bowling in 1864.

KEITH A. P. SANDIFORD

Bibliography

Altham, Harry S. and E. W. Swanton. *A History of Cricket.* 1948.

Brookes, Christopher. *English Cricket: The Game and Its Players Through the Ages.* 1978.

Midwinter, Eric. *W. G. Grace: His Life and Times.* 1981.

Patterson, William S. *Sixty Years of Uppingham Cricket.* 1909.

Swanton, Ernest W., ed. *Barclay's World of Cricket.* 1986.

See also GRACE, WILLIAM GILBERT

. . . . .

CRIME

The nineteenth century brought not only a threefold growth in population and changes wrought by urbanization and the industrial revolution, but also major alterations in the law and the establishment of modern police forces. By the 1830s the criminal law had been overhauled, redefining offenses and penalties and drastically reducing capital punishment. By that time the London Metropolitan Police had been created (1829) and the borough and county police forces were either established or improved, so that maintaining order and preventing crime were firmly entrenched as a public, not a private, responsibility.

The principal sources for the study of crime in the nineteenth century are often sparse and unsystematic, or simply inaccurate, particularly before 1856. Furthermore, changes in police practice, in the courts, and in public opinion could have a marked effect on crime rates in a given locality.

Victorian crimes fit into either indictable (felony) or summary (misdemeanor) categories. The more serious offenses for which an indictment would be returned, resulting in a jury trial, included murder, armed robbery, burglary, larceny, fraud, rape, violations of public order such as rioting or assaults on police, and an assortment of other crimes. Summary offenses (dealt with summarily before a magistrate) included certain offenses against property, vagrancy, drunkenness, **prostitution**, minor larceny, and minor offenses against the person. The categorization of crimes could vary in different localities. In addition, changes in the law during the 1850s allowed some indictable offenses to be included within summary jurisdiction.

In discussing crime trends, historians further classify offenses into crimes against property and crimes against the person, since the trends differ somewhat. To these might be added crimes against morality and custom, and crimes against public order. Prosecution of crimes against morality was often haphazard, and depended greatly on the zeal of the police and magistrates in a given locality. Public order offenses such as rioting, assaults on police, and unlawful assembly were usually dealt with summarily unless they were particularly serious.

Historians generally agree that crime in Victorian England was lower than in previous centuries, and was decreasing. High levels of both violent crimes and property crimes persisted after the Napoleonic Wars and to the 1840s, followed by a long decline until the 1930s. It appears that crime steadily became less violent from roughly the middle of the century. For example, recorded homicides declined by about 53 percent between the early 1870s and World War I. Robbery (theft with violence) declined by a factor of seven from its recorded peak in 1857 to the end of the century. The decrease in violence possibly reflects a growing humanitarian outlook in all classes (as evidenced, for example, by the abolition of blood sports and public executions), a greater willingness to prosecute acts of violence, and the various controls exerted at all levels within a more orderly and policed society.

Property crime without violence made up 90 percent of all indictable offenses, with larceny by far the most common property offense. Until the early nineteenth century, indictments for property crime varied with changes in food prices; as food prices went up, leading to consumer distress, so did property crime. By the Victorian period, when industrial capitalism had developed, the harvest cycle was being superseded by swings in the trade and investment cycles, resulting in a positive correlation between depression, food prices, unemployment, and property crime. In good economic times such crimes declined. On the other hand, crimes of personal violence (such as assault and other offenses triggered by drunkenness) dropped in times of depression but increased in times of prosperity, most notably in the early 1870s when alcohol consumption reached a peak. This suggests that prosperity resulted in increased alcohol consumption and, in its turn, drink-related violence.

By the 1880s the old correlations between hardship and theft seemed to have reversed, so that peaks in property crimes coincided with peaks of prosperity. This relationship lasted until the beginning of the new century and the economic difficulties of the Edwardian period. In the 1830s and 1840s (1842 was possibly the high point for Victorian crime) there was an unfortunate coincidence of economic depression, high unemployment, and high food prices—a situation that was especially acute in the industrial cloth industries. This combination of problems occurred again in the Edwardian years, which saw inflation, falling real wages, and industrial stagnation. In both periods distress apparently caused more people to steal. The crime figures for the industrial county of Lancashire throughout the Victorian age were about double those in the rest of England, although they followed the national trends.

London crime trends also followed national patterns, although short-term fluctuations deviated considerably. The years from 1820 to 1850 marked the peak of a crime wave that began after the Napoleonic Wars. Indictable thefts then fell by a ratio of three to one between the 1840s and the early 1870s and continued downward through the 1920s (though a reversal occurred between 1899 and 1908).

One offense that did not decline was burglary, which seemingly replaced robbery as the preferred method of theft. Robbery was particularly rare, resulting in only 150 arrests

per year in London in the 1890s. Also in London the rates of convictions for murder, manslaughter, attempted murder, and grievous assault were at their highest recorded levels in the 1840s. In that decade there were perhaps five times as many of those crimes, relative to population, as in the 1920s. In fact, after 1890, London, with a population of more than six million, had only around 20 murders and 40 manslaughters a year. Nationally the reported murder and manslaughter figures were in the 250 to 350 range between 1890 and 1914.

If Victorian England enjoyed an overall drop in crime, the reasons can only be surmised. The establishment and improvement of police forces undoubtedly had some effect. As the cost of prosecution fell and laws and their enforcement improved, more people were willing to participate in legal processes, as indicated by the public's growing toleration of a more intrusive police presence. An improving socioeconomic system; better public health, street lighting, and other urban amenities; more consumer goods and services; the absorption of potentially riotous and criminal elements into the full-time labor market; the education of children; political democratization; the moralizing messages of temperance, religious, and other reformers—all of these factors helped suppress crime. Far from creating crime, as many contemporaries believed, the urban industrial age brought a battery of social disciplines that put a premium on regularity, punctuality, sobriety, cleanliness, and orderly behavior. Victorians of all classes were accommodating themselves to the prevailing social order and its mores, to the rule of law, and to the necessary restraints called for by an industrial and urban world.

PHILLIP THURMOND SMITH

Bibliography

Emsley, Clive. *Crime and Society in England, 1750–1900.* 1987.

Gatrell, V. A. C. "The Decline of Theft and Violence in Victorian and Edwardian England." In V. A. C. Gatrell, Bruce Lenman, and Geoffrey Parker, *Crime and the Law.* 1980.

Lane, Roger. "Crime and the Industrial Revolution: British and American Views." *Journal of Social History,* vol. 7, pp. 287–303.

Philips, David. *Crime and Authority in Victorian England.* 1977.

Rudé, George. *Criminal and Victim: Crime and Society in Early Nineteenth-Century England.* 1985.

Smith, Phillip Thurmond. *Policing Victorian London: Political Policing, Public Order and the London Metropolitan Police.* 1985.

Tobias, John Jacob. *Crime and Industrial Society in the Nineteenth Century.* 1967.

———. *Crime and Police in England, 1700–1900.* 1979.

See also GAME LAWS; JACK THE RIPPER; JUDICIAL SYSTEM; JUVENILE CRIME; LAW ENFORCEMENT; LAW REFORM; PRISONS AND PRISON REFORM; SMUGGLING

. . . . .

CRIMEAN WAR

After nearly forty years of peace in Europe, Great Britain as an ally of France and the Ottoman Empire (Turkey) declared war on Russia on March 28, 1854. The Crimean War, the only major European war fought by Great Britain during the Victorian age, is often described as unnecessary and remembered for logistical defects and military blunders. Nevertheless, the Allied victory after two years of fighting temporarily preserved the Ottoman Empire and briefly checked Russian expansion in the Balkans.

The Eastern Crisis began in the summer of 1853 when Emperor Nicholas I of Russia dispatched troops to occupy Moldavia and Wallachia on the condition that Turkey fulfill its treaty obligations by establishing a Russian protectorate over the Orthodox Christians in the Ottoman Empire. The occupation forced England, France, Austria, and Prussia to react. Diplomacy failed to resolve the dispute and Turkey, strengthened by Anglo-French support, declared war on Russia (October 4, 1853).

The British cabinet was divided over the best means of preventing war. Prime Minister Lord Aberdeen advocated renewed negotiations, while Lord Palmerston pressed for increased naval presence in the Black Sea. With the opening of hostilities between Turkey and Russia, the ministers discarded the latest Russian overtures, the Olmutz Proposals (which seem to have been sincerely offered as a peaceful solution) and adopted a more militant policy. The drift to war was accelerated when the Russians sank several Turkish ships anchored in Sinope Harbor (November 30, 1853). Although a justifiable act of war, the incident aroused war fever in England. The cabinet sent a joint ultimatum with the French late in February 1854 demanding evacuation of the principalities. Receiving no answer, Great Britain, followed by France, declared war on Russia.

Lord Raglan was named commander of the British expeditionary force of 25,000. Arriving in Turkey, the army took up positions to defend Constantinople and the Dardanelles. In June 1854 most of the Allied troops were advanced to Varna in Bulgaria to support the besieged Turks at Silistria. When the Russians raised the siege and withdrew across the Danube, the British and French governments instructed their commanders to invade the Crimea and attack Sebastopol. Reluctantly, the Allied commanders gave in to the ministers in Paris and London, who held that it was essential to capture Sebastopol and destroy the Russian fleet.

After being delayed by the ravages of cholera, the Allies landed in mid-September at Calamita Bay north of Sebastopol. The Russians offered little resistance until the Allied armies (62,000 strong) reached the river Alma in their march southward. There under Prince Menschikoff the Russian force of nearly 40,000 made a stand. With the British troops bearing the brunt of the fighting (at a cost of 2,000 casualties), the Russians were defeated and forced back upon Sebastopol. Failing to exploit their victory, the Allied commanders made a controversial decision to forgo an immediate assault on Sebastopol from the north in favor of a systematic siege from the south. (Lord Raglan was inclined to immediate attack, but, for the sake of the alliance, deferred to Marshall St. Arnaud, the French commander.) The Allies took up positions south of Sebastopol where, for the next twelve months, the British army would be committed to defending the land flank of the Allied armies from Russian attack and laying siege to Sebastopol.

Lord Raglan decided to use the village of Balaclava as the British supply base. Because Balaclava had an inadequate harbor and was badly situated for maintaining communications with the plateau where troops were positioned, the decision brought near-disaster. The Russians were repulsed in the costly battles of Balaclava (October 25, 1854), during which the light brigade under the earl of **Cardigan** made its senseless and suicidal charge and the heavy brigade its equally heroic charge to save the day, and Inkerman (November 5, 1854), the bloodiest, most fiercely contested, and decisive battle of the Crimean War. Although the British saved their position before Sebastopol, they lost the Causeway Heights and its very important Woronzov road, which linked Balaclava to the camps and siege works. The British were destined to spend the winter without adequate provisions in the small corner of the Crimea that they occupied.

The critical situation magnified the military weaknesses caused by parliamentary and administrative neglect since Waterloo, but the immediate causes of the winter's suffering were the inadequate harbor and the lack of a surfaced road to the camps. After a storm on November 14 wrecked several ships and destroyed the supplies they carried, the British faced severe shortages of food, clothing, ammunition, and medicines. The lack of fodder and the breakup of the unpaved road contributed to a complete failure of land transport. The troops, already overextended in the trenches, were faced with short rations and the task of bringing up themselves what supplies they could from Balaclava.

Daily accounts of the misfortunes reached the British public from **William H. Russell**, war correspondent for the *Times*, and others who fed the English newspapers with livid stories. The ensuing public outrage turned against Lord Raglan. The ministers lost confidence in their commander but stopped short of recalling him. In late January 1855, parliamentary adoption of John Arthur Roebuck's motion to appoint a committee of inquiry into the conduct of the war brought down the Aberdeen government. By this time, however, the government had already begun to correct the system's worst faults. The establishment of a land transport corps, the creation of a military board, the reorganization of the War Office, and the reform of the Medical Department and the hospitals (associated with **Florence Nightingale**) were the first results of the public demand for military and administrative reforms unleashed by the bitter Crimean experience. During the first months of 1855, food, clothing, hutting materials, medical supplies, and ammunition poured through Balaclava to troops in the Crimea, and by April the army was again in good condition.

Sebastopol did not fall until September 1855, ten weeks after Raglan had died from cholera. Although inclined to continue and enlarge the war, Lord Palmerston, Aberdeen's successor, bowed to French pressure, and the war was concluded in March 1856 by the Peace of Paris. The treaty terms were unpopular in England and were not of lasting importance. In 1871 the Russian emperor began to refortify Sebastopol and rebuild a Black Sea fleet, again raising a sense of the futility of the Crimean War, which cost more than 21,000 British lives, 16,000 of whom had perished from disease. Its long-term significance, however, lay not in the terms of peace but in the revival of British naval and military strength produced by the introduction of modern weapons and the enactment of reforms.

F. DARRELL MUNSELL

Bibliography

Anderson, Olive. *A Liberal State at War.* 1967.

Bentley, N., ed. *Russell's Dispatches from the Crimea, 1854–1856.* 1966.

Collins, H. P. "The Crimea: The Fateful Weeks." *Army Quarterly,* vol. 71, pp. 86–96.

Gibbs, Peter. *Crimean Blunder.* 1960.

Gooch, Brison. "The Crimean War in Selected Documents and Secondary Works Since 1940." *Victorian Studies,* vol. 1, pp. 271–279.

Hamley, Sir Edward. *The War in the Crimea.* 1890.

Hibbert, Christopher. *The Destruction of Lord Raglan.* 1963.

Kinglake, A. W. *The Invasion of the Crimea.* 1877–1879. 6th ed. 9 vols.

MacMunn, Sir George. *The Crimea in Perspective.* 1935.

Munsell, F. Darrell. *The Unfortunate Duke: Henry Pelham, Fifth Duke of Newcastle, 1811-1864.* 1985.

Palmer, Alan. *The Banner of Battle.* 1987.

Russell, William H. *The War from the Landing in Gallipoli to the Death of Lord Raglan.* 1855.

· · · · ·

CROSS, RICHARD ASSHETON (1823-1914)

As home secretary (1874-1880), Richard Assheton Cross legalized labor unions with the Employers and Workmen Act (1875), enabled municipalities to clear slums and build public housing with the Artisan's Dwelling Act (1875), and brought in measures that improved public health, factory conditions, and prison government. The only active reformer in **Benjamin Disraeli**'s cabinet, Cross turned Disraeli's vague promises of Tory Democracy into legislation.

Cross grew up near Preston where his family had moved over the generations from tannery works into the law and the Anglican church. Heavily influenced by a sense of Christian duty, Cross entered politics dedicated to preserving the established church and the existing political structure through reforms that would bring them into harmony with industrial society.

Cross made his political career by defeating William Gladstone in a parliamentary election in Lancashire (1868). In 1874, Disraeli gambled on Cross by appointing him, untried, to the Home Office. Cross's reform legislation contributed much to the success of the government; and during the Eastern Crisis (1876-1878) Cross emerged also as a significant spokesman on foreign policy. He reached the peak of his political power by defeating the Liberals and Derby's influence in the election of 1880.

Later elevated to a peerage, Cross served in Lord Salisbury's cabinet at the India Office (1886-1892). Lacking strong interest in India, Cross left the bureaucracy largely undirected. To combat an Indian "home rule" movement, he passed the Indian Councils Act (1892), which led to Indian representation in the colonial government.

During his early career, Cross was the practical architect of Tory Democracy who attempted to reshape government to the needs of an industrial society. His creed was based on Christian principles and practical experience in Lancashire. His intention was to prevent the development of democracy by having the propertied classes govern wisely and well.

DENNIS J. MITCHELL

Bibliography

Cross, Richard Assheton. *Family History.* 1903.

Feuchtwanger, E. J. *Disraeli, Democracy and the Tory Party: Conservative Leadership and Organization After the Second Reform Bill.* 1968.

Smith, Paul. *Disraelian Conservatism and Social Reform.* 1967.

· · · · ·

CROWE, CATHERINE STEVENS (1800?-1876)

Though Catherine Stevens Crowe would write successfully such domestic novels as *Susan Hopley, or the Adventures of a Maidservant* (1841) and *The Story of Lily Dawson* (1847), her publications in defense of the instinctual life and of the supernatural were her most important contribution to the Victorian era. *The Night Side of Nature, or Ghosts and Ghost Seers* (1848), Crowe's most ambitious work on supernaturalism, is of interest not only as literature but also as psychology and science.

Born around 1800 at Borough Green, Kent, Catherine Stevens was married in 1822 to Lieutenant-Colonel Crowe; she had one child. She lived in Edinburgh and in 1859 experienced a brief bout of insanity. Her career as a writer began with the anonymously published drama *Aristodemus* (1838). Domestic works like *Susan Hopley, Lily Dawson,* and

Linny Lockwood (1854) dealt with the prosaic, daylight side of life. *Lily Dawson*, for instance, advanced ideas about the need for educational reform for women.

In such works as Justinius Kerner's *Die Seherin Von Prevorst*, which Crowe translated in 1845, *The Night Side of Nature, Ghosts and Family Legends* (1859), and *Spiritualism and the Age We Live In* (1859), Crowe crusaded for the spiritual and the supernatural. In *Night Side*, she gathered data about every kind of unusual phenomenon—from clairvoyance to wraiths to doppelgangers to ghosts—and called for serious philosophical and scientific investigation of these occurrences. In these works Crowe reveals that Victorian sensibility which rode the crest of scientific and technological advances while fondly clinging to the mysterious. Crowe's writings on the supernatural are not only an outgrowth but also a recording of this ambivalent facet of the period.

VANESSA D. DICKERSON

Bibliography

Crawford, Anne, ed. *The Europa Biographical Dictionary of British Women*. 1983.

Sergeant, Adeline. "Mrs. Crowe." In Margaret Oliphant, ed., *Women Novelists of Queen Victoria's Reign*. 1897.

See also SUPERNATURAL FICTION

· · · · ·

CRUIKSHANK, GEORGE (1792-1878)

George Cruikshank gained early recognition as a spirited political cartoonist. Illustrating Pierce Egan's *Life in London* (1821) brought him fame. Abandoning cartooning for book illustration, he created his best-known plates for Charles Dickens's *Oliver Twist* (1838). Cruikshank's illustrations were an integral part of the serial novel and vital to its success. His serial pictures *The Bottle* (1847) and its sequel *The Drunkard's Children* (1848) reflect this reformed drinker's preoccupation with the **temperance movement**. His books of drawings include *George*

Cruikshank's Omnibus (1841) and *The Comic Almanack* (1835-1853).

Cruikshank was born into a family of London artists. William Hogarth's realistic satires and the grotesques of Thomas Rowlandson and James Gillray influenced his artwork. In the 1830s he applied the technique of copperplate etching to steel plate, which became the accepted medium of published illustration. Leading book publisher John Macrone secured the celebrated artist's talents to back the works of two relatively unknown writers, William Harrison Ainsworth and Dickens, whose pseudonym, Boz, Cruikshank retained from their first collaboration, *Sketches By Boz* (1836). *Oliver Twist* inspired Cruikshank's most famous plates. "Oliver Asking for More" demonstrates his skillful shadow play, fine detail, and caricature.

Struggles over authority ended Cruikshank's collaborations with Dickens (1841) and Ainsworth (1844). He enjoyed brief success with *The Bottle* and *The Drunkard's Children*, but failed in trying to revive Regency styles in his own books of drawings. His career ended in controversy over his exaggerated claims that his illustrations altered Dickens's original concept of *Oliver Twist* and inspired Ainsworth's *The Miser's Daughter* (1842) and *The Tower of London* (1840).

Ranked foremost among etchers by leading art critic John Ruskin, Cruikshank died all but forgotten. His style, modeled most notably by Hablot Knight Browne (Phiz), kept British illustration distinct from Continental styles. His contributions to Victorian fiction, recently reappraised, show illustration and text working together as one expressive art form.

CATHERINE J. GOLDEN

Bibliography

Buchanan-Brown, John. *The Book Illustrations of George Cruikshank*. 1980.

Cruikshank, George. *The Artist and the Author*. 1870.

See also CARICATURE; TEMPERANCE MOVEMENT *(illus.)*

· · · · ·

Oliver Asks for More
(*illustration from first installment of* Oliver Twist)
Bentley's Miscellany, *February 1837.*
Reproduced from Graphic Works of George Cruikshank, *ed. Richard A. Vogler,*
Dover Publications Inc.

CRYSTAL PALACE see EXHIBITION OF 1851

· · · · ·

DANCE AND BALLET

Britain has never been as prominent as Continental Europe in the art of dance. During the nineteenth century, however, there were significant developments in three primary categories: theatrical, ballroom, and folk dancing.

Traditional folk dances, which had been falling into decline, were consciously revived as a part of the general antiquarian interest in folk traditions. The ceremonial forms of sword dance and the morris dance were done only by men. The country dance (also known as the contra dance), performed by both men and women, became a popular ballroom dance in the eighteenth and early nineteenth centuries. Mayday dances—both round and processional—which also have ritual significance, gave rise to "club walks," seasonal processions which sometimes culminate in dance.

Europe also converted folk dances into ballroom dances, which in the early nineteenth century began to supplant the popular English country dance. The waltz, for example, was derived from the German *Landler* and the quadrille from the French *Cotillon*, a four-couple figure dance similar to the English country dance. The quadrille, first introduced in 1816, was rapidly accepted by the British. The intricacies of its steps were simplified with much use until it could merely be walked through. The waltz, also introduced to England early in the nineteenth century, made slower headway because of the moral outrage it provoked among people not accustomed to the closeness of the dancers to one another. Its status, however, was given a considerable boost when Queen Victoria and Prince Albert danced it at the coronation ball. Two other folk dances translated to the ballroom were introduced somewhat later: the polka, imported from Czechoslovakia in the 1840s, and the mazurka.

Ballet, which had been growing in popularity since the turn of the century, blossomed during the 1840s and 1850s. Jules Perrot (1810-1892), a notable choreographer, projected a dreamlike, otherworldly quality in his romantic ballets. Some of Perrot's most famous ballets, staged while he was ballet master at Her Majesty's Theatre, include *Ondine* (1843), *La Esmerelda* (1844), and *Pas de Quatre* (1845). *Pas de Quatre* had the distinction of showcasing Europe's four leading dancers—Marie Taglioni (1804-1884), Fanny Cerrito (1817-1909), Carlotta Grisi (1819-1899), and Lucile Grahn (1819-1907)—in a single performance. One of the best-known ballets performed at Her Majesty's was *Giselle*. Conceived for Grisi by French critic Theophile Gautier (1811-1872), it was choreographed by Perrot and Jean Coralli (1779-1854) and debuted in Paris in 1841. Opening in London on March 12, 1842, it was an overwhelming popular and critical success.

As opera began to compete for national attention, interest in ballet fell off. The opera offered steadily diminishing roles for dancers, and no national ballet company had taken root. While some English dancers, including Clara Webster (1821-1844), showed considerable promise and talent, they were overshadowed by Europeans. Most were discouraged from seeking ballet careers in England. In a more popular form, however, two music-hall theaters—the Alhambra (opened in 1872) and the Empire (1884)—featured ballet, though it was not given the critical recognition of earlier ballet and the dancers were less technically sophisticated.

DIANE McMANUS

Bibliography

Guest, Ivor. *The Romantic Ballet in England: Its Development. Fulfillment and Decline.* 1972.

Kennedy, Douglas. *England's Dances: Folk-Dancing To-Day and Yesterday.* 1950.

Leeper, Janet. *English Ballet.* 1944.

Sharp, Cecil J. and A. P. Oppe. *The Dance: An Historical Survey of Dancing in Europe.* 1924; rpt. 1972.

Walker, Katherine Sorley. "British Ballet." In Anatole Chujoy and P. W. Manchester, eds., *The Dance Encyclopedia.* 1967.

· · · · ·

DANCE MUSIC

Dancing was a popular recreation for Victorians of all social classes, except those whose religion proscribed it. Music for dancing, particularly the waltz, was a strong influence on music of other kinds.

In centers of high fashion, such as Almack's and the court, the older English country dances were gradually ousted by the waltz and quadrille from about 1815, to be joined later by the galop (1829) and polka (1844). For royal state balls no further innovations were permitted for the rest of the reign. Military bands were sometimes used at large balls, but the ordinary band was a medium-sized orchestra of woodwinds, brass, strings, and percussion.

A second layer of dance halls and clubs existed for wealthy businessmen and their families. In 1845 the "tea dance" (*thé dansant*) was introduced for the newly genteel. A small band of strings and piano was normally engaged, and new dances were eagerly taken up: the mazurka, polonaise, redowa, and schottische from the Continent; and, toward the end of the century, the barn dance, Washington Post, and cake walk from the United States. One country dance, the Sir Roger de Coverley, survived as the traditional wind-up at the end of a ball.

Among working people, dancing took place in barns, taverns, warehouses, and the open air. The country dance lasted longer, as we learn from Dickens's description of Mrs. Fezziwig's ball (accompanied by a lone fiddler) and from Hardy's novels.

The sensuous waltz, in which partners clasped one another in unaccustomed intimacy, was greeted successively with disapproval, excitement, enthusiasm, and finally widespread acceptance. Promenade concerts, introduced from Paris, arrived in London in 1838, with the waltz as their staple fare. They were soon imitated at all the leading resort towns, generally on the pier or seafront pavilion.

Waltz songs abounded in stage works from opera and ballet to music hall, and were transcribed for piano, harmonium, and street organ: songs like "Oh where, oh where has my little dog gone" (1847), "I'm called Little Buttercup" from *H.M.S. Pinafore* (1878) and "Daisy, Daisy" (1892) were as broad in their appeal as any music of the time. Leading composers and arrangers of dance music were the Weippert family; Charles d'Albert (1809–1886); and Dan Godfrey senior (1831–1903), composer of the popular Mabel Waltz (1863).

NICHOLAS TEMPERLEY

Bibliography

Pearsall, Ronald. *Victorian Popular Music.* 1973.

Temperley, Nicholas. "Ballroom and Drawing-Room Music." In *The Athlone History of Music in Britain*, vol. 5. 1981.

· · · · ·

DARWIN, CHARLES ROBERT (1809–1882)

Author of books on geology, natural history, botany, and **evolution**, Charles Darwin's *On the Origin of Species by Means of Natural Selection, or the Preservation of Favoured Races in the Struggle for Life* (1859) first definitively established the reality of organic evolution and then proposed the theory of natural selection—Darwinism, strictly speaking—to explain how evolution had occurred. By 1876 Darwinism had altered the views of many scientists and effected a revolution in most areas of thought.

Darwin was born into a family of wealth, intelligence, and intellectual interests. While studying medicine at Edinburgh and then divinity at Cambridge, he pursued self-education in natural history and thus qualified for the position of naturalist on H. M. S. *Beagle.* During the five years of the *Beagle* voyage (December 1831–October 1836) he explored the coasts of South America and the Atlantic and Pacific islands, geologizing and collecting animals and plants. After the voyage he settled in London and became active in the London Geological Society. **Geology** was then a burgeoning science, and the Geological Society was the outstanding center of scientific activity in England. Darwin published his *Journal of Researches into the Geology and Natural History of the Various Countries Visited by H. M. S. Beagle* (1839), *The Struc-*

ture and Distribution of Coral Reefs (1842)—which enunciated a new theory for the origin of coral reefs—and books on the geology of the volcanic islands visited by the *Beagle* (1844) and on the geology of South America (1846).

In the meantime, in the years 1837–1838, he had first come to believe in evolution after noting the spatial and temporal relationships between some of the animals he had collected on the *Beagle*. Then, after about fifteen months of intensive study of facts about the life and death of species, he read Malthus's *Essay on the Principle of Population* and was stimulated to originate the theory of natural selection and to begin collecting evidences for this theory. Soon afterwards he married, and in 1842 moved to a country house at Down where he lived for the remaining forty years of his life.

During his first fourteen years at Down, in addition to publishing accounts of all living and then all fossil barnacles, he corresponded with leading scientists, breeders of plants and animals, and other informants, accumulating thousands of observations in most of the areas of science that pertained to his evolutionary theory. He began writing a big book on his theory in 1856. In 1858—after **Alfred Wallace** independently discovered natural selection— Darwin stopped working on the big book, condensed his accumulated information, and wrote *The Origin of Species*.

In the thirteen years (1859–1872) following the appearance of the *Origin*, Darwin responded to the opinions of supporters and critics and made revisions in five successive editions. In three other books—*The Variation of Animals and Plants Under Domestication* (1868), *The Descent of Man, and Selection in Relation to Sex* (1871), and *The Expression of the Emotions in Man and Animals* (1872)—he expanded on aspects of the *Origin*: he advanced a theory of pangenesis to explain phenomena of heredity, proposed a theory of sexual selection to explain the origin of certain attributes (mostly in primates) which were not explained by natural selection, and assembled evidence demonstrating human descent from primates. In the last decade of his life he published a succession of botanical books showing how plants supplied evidence for natural selection.

Darwin was an affectionate husband and father (four of his sons had distinguished careers in science) and a steadfast friend to several eminent scientists, including the geologist Charles Lyell, botanist Joseph Hooker, and biologist Thomas Huxley. For most of his adult life he suffered from a fluctuating stomach illness which sometimes gravely curtailed his work, and which was probably caused in large part by anxieties over the difficulties in proving his evolutionary theory.

Almost 150 years have passed since Darwin first conceived of the theory of evolution by natural selection. Many scientists believe that the theory remains valid and that it can be successfully adapted to changes in knowledge: to advances in biology, molecular biology, statistics, and genetics, and to new concepts of evolution such as cladistics and punctuated equilibrium.

RALPH COLP, JR.

Bibliography

Allan, Mea. *Darwin and His Flowers: The Key to Natural Selection.* 1977.

Barlow, Nora, ed. *The Autobiography of Charles Darwin, 1809–1882: With Original Omissions Restored.* 1958.

Barrett, Paul, ed. *The Collected Papers of Charles Darwin.* 1977.

Berry, R. J., ed. *Charles Darwin. A Commemoration, 1882–1982: Happy Is the Man That Findeth Wisdom.* 1982.

Brent, Peter. *Charles Darwin: "A Man of Enlarged Curiosity."* 1981.

Burkhardt, Frederick et al., eds. *A Calendar of the Correspondence of Charles Darwin, 1821–1882.* 1985.

———— eds. *The Correspondence of Charles Darwin.* 1985-.

Colp, Ralph, Jr. *To Be an Invalid: The Illness of Charles Darwin.* 1977.

De Beer, Sir Gavin. *Charles Darwin: Evolution by Natural Selection.* 1964.

Freeman, Richard B. *The Works of Charles Darwin: An Annotated Bibliography Handlist.* 1977.

Ghiselin, Michael T. *The Triumph of the Darwinian Method.* 1984.

Himmelfarb, Gertrude. *Darwin and the Darwinian Revolution.* 1962.

Kohn, David, ed. *The Darwinian Heritage.* 1985.

. . . . .

DAVIES, EMILY
(1830-1921)

Emily Davies founded Girton College in 1869, convinced that higher education offered women the best way to achieve equality. In *The Higher Education of Women* (1866) she rejected theories of woman's nature as factually unfounded and presented an educational philosophy based on similarities between the sexes. Instead of "womanly" education, Davies adopted the curriculum and examination standards of the men's universities.

Daughter of Mary Hopkinson and her husband, Evangelical clergyman and author John Davies, Sarah Emily Davies became interested in feminism through her brother, a supporter of F. D. Maurice, and her friend **Barbara Bodichon**. Shrewd strategist and indefatigable letter writer, Davies organized a women's employment society; assisted **Elizabeth Garrett Anderson** in her struggle to become a doctor; edited *The Englishwoman's Journal* (1862) and *Victoria Magazine* (1864); and delivered the first women's suffrage petition to John Stuart Mill (1866). Davies persuaded the Schools Inquiry Commission to include girls' secondary schools in its 1864 study, and negotiated the admission of girls to the Cambridge Local Examinations (1865). Founder and secretary of the London School Mistresses' Association (1866–1888), she was elected to the London School Board in 1870. *Thoughts on Some Questions Relating to Women, 1860–1908* (1910) contains her essays on education, employment, and suffrage.

Davies worked more than forty years for Girton—soliciting funds, finding students, setting policy. Her recently microfilmed papers indicate that she was strict, decorous, and single-minded. To escape the distractions of home and society, Davies located her college in the country; to ensure privacy, she gave each student rooms of her own—despite extremely limited funds. Using Cambridge faculty, the college opened with 6 students and grew to include 101 by 1897. As a women's community committed to the rigorous study of the classics and mathematics, Girton generated considerable controversy. However, as Girton students passed the demanding Cambridge examinations and embarked on teaching careers, they demonstrated women's ability to succeed in the university system.

ROBIN SHEETS

Bibliography

McWilliams-Tullberg, Rita. *Women at Cambridge: A Men's University—Though of a Mixed Type.* 1975.

Murray, Janet Horowitz, ed. *Strong-Minded Women and Other Lost Voices from Nineteenth-Century England.* 1982.

Stephen, Barbara. *Emily Davies and Girton College.* 1927.

Vicinus, Martha. *Independent Women: Work and Community for Single Women, 1850–1920.* 1985.

See also CAMBRIDGE UNIVERSITY; EDUCATION, WOMEN'S

. . . . .

DAY NURSERIES

Charitable institutions that provided care for the young children of working mothers were founded in London and other British cities in the late 1860s and 1870s. They were often operated by philanthropic women, such as Marie Hilton who ran a well-known day nursery in the East End. Day nurseries were intended to help prevent infant mortality and child neglect by providing care for the children of poor working mothers, who often left their infants with older siblings, elderly relatives, or hired childminders. These caretakers, it was charged, fed their charges improperly and used laudanum or gin to keep them quiet. Most day nurseries accepted only the children of respectable parents and charged a small fee, sometimes based on the parents' ability to pay.

Late in the century, some medical men and child welfare workers urged the establishment of more such nurseries, modeled on the French crèche system, but little was done to implement the proposals. The opposition to day nurseries stemmed from concern that providing too much assistance to the poor would encourage them to rely on state aid, and from the growing emphasis on removing women from the workplace rather than providing safe child care that would permit mothers to do waged work.

ANN R. HIGGINBOTHAM

Bibliography

Hewitt, Margaret. *Wives and Mothers in Victorian Industry.* 1958.

Weir, Alexander M. "The Sanitary and Moral Influence of the Crèche." *Sanitary Record.* vol. 1, pp. 1–5.

See also BABY FARMING

· · · · ·

DEATH AND FUNERALS

The Victorians were preoccupied with death and the rituals surrounding it: they decorated their homes with reminders of it, planned elaborate funerals, and observed a strict period of mourning. They were concerned about the disposal of the body and the destination of the soul. Moreover, concern with social status made an elaborate funeral the expected response to a death in the family.

Reminders of death were inescapable, especially for the poor. Inadequate sanitation and overcrowding caused constant outbreaks of disease. In 1849 a cholera epidemic killed 16,000 in London alone. In towns, one in every two children died before the age of five. Both to soften and reflect this reality, Victorian homes were filled with funeral tea sets, samplers, china ornaments, and photographs commemorating the dead and attesting to belief in reunion in heaven.

More than a chance to show respect for the dead, elaborate funerals allowed a display of wealth as well. The very poor were put into paupers' graves and buried by the parish, but anyone able to pay for a funeral had a great range of prices and symbols from which to choose. The simplest funeral could cost as little as 4 pounds; a funeral for an aristocrat might cost 1,500 (in a time when a middle class family of four could live on 300 pounds a year). Elegant middle-class funerals cost around 50 pounds and included mourning coaches decked with ostrich feathers and draped in black velvet, and a horse-drawn hearse carrying a cambric-lined coffin decorated with brass hardware and covered by a silk pall. The funeral procession was attended by pages and coachmen in appropriate mourning clothes and hired mourners, called mutes. The desire for a "respectable" funeral was so strong that a widow might spend the rest of her life paying off the debts incurred. The poor might delay a funeral for weeks until they could afford a proper ceremony.

Belief in the resurrection of the body made its disposal important. Lively debates were carried on between those who thought cremation with urn burial would be more convenient, hygienic, and aesthetically pleasing and those who believed that the resurrection of the body could take place only if the body were interred intact. The great **cemeteries** were established in London after 1830 when churchyards had become overcrowded; burial in a cemetery soon became a mark of affluence.

Grief was symbolized by dress and strict mourning etiquette. Men's clothes required little alteration: a crepe hatband, black gloves, and a dark suit were sufficient; women's clothes, however, were precisely prescribed. Only certain materials were appropriate for the first and most intense period of mourning; black crepe, an expensive fabric, was preferred. Mourning jewelry was made of jet and the hair of the deceased. Restrictions fell most heavily on widows: they wore crepe and a widow's bonnet for one year; after twelve months, custom allowed a widow to "slight" her mourning by wearing plain black; after two years, she could go into "half mourning," which would allow her to wear lavender, black, gray, and white. For the first year, she could accept no invitations, and after that her return to society had to be gradual.

Each family relationship had its required period of mourning: twelve months for a parent or child, nine for grandparents, six for brothers and sisters. "Complimentary mourning" was sometimes worn in sympathy with those who grieved. Children often wore white for mourning, while family servants were given black mourning clothes to wear. Mourning stationery and envelopes were trimmed in black, the width of the trim dictated by the nearness of the relation.

Victoria's long and ostentatious widowhood kept elaborate funerals and mourning popular until her death (she wore "widow's weeds" from Albert's death in 1861 until her own death forty years later), but as the lower social classes planned funerals that imitated the sumptuousness of those of the rich, the custom of elaborate funerals and strict mourning died out.

CYNTHIA CARLTON-FORD

Bibliography

Morely, John. *Death, Heaven, and the Victorians.* 1971.

Reed, John R. *Victorian Conventions.* 1975.

Stewart, Garrett. *Death Sentences: Styles of Dying in British Fiction.* 1984.

See also *SUICIDE*

. . . . .

DEBT, IMPRISONMENT FOR

Until 1869, persons unwilling or unable to pay their debts could be arrested at the suit of any person to whom money was owed. In London, there were three prisons to which debtors could be sent: Marshalsea, Queen's Bench Prison, and the Fleet. Debtors, however, enjoyed advantages other prisoners did not have. They could be accompanied by their families, bring in things that prisoners confined for criminal offenses could not (such as tobacco), and have visitors. Those imprisoned at the Queen's Bench could even have their mail addressed to "No. 1, Belvedere Place, London."

Early in the century, debtors could be arrested for even the smallest amounts. The Imprisonment for Debt Act of 1827 allowed summary arrest only if the debt were larger than 20 pounds and the creditor swore on affidavit that the money was owed. The arrest was made by sheriff's officers called bailiffs. Debtor's prison was not considered punishment for the offender but rather security for the creditors: the debtor was released as soon as money had been raised to pay the person who brought suit. Once someone had been arrested for one debt, however, other creditors generally rushed to swear out their own affidavits and ensure that the debtor remained safely in prison until their bills were also paid. People "with the bailiffs at their heels" had a tendency to skip out on all their debts by leaving the country.

For England and Wales, sentences of imprisonment for insolvent debtors were abolished by the Debtor's Act (1869). Defaulting trustees could still be imprisoned, as could those able—but unwilling—to pay their debts. In 1870 the Absconding Debtors' Act gave authorities the power to arrest insolvent debtors in order to stop them from going abroad. Scottish law provided for a Small Debt Court to handle claims under 12 pounds, and abolished imprisonment for debt in 1880.

JOHN REYNOLDS

See also *BANKRUPTCY*

. . . . .

DECADENCE (1890-1900)

Decadence, the term most often used to describe the **fin de siècle** atmosphere of the 1890s, came to England from France, especially from such influences as Théophile Gautier (1811-1872), Charles Baudelaire (1821-1867), Paul Verlaine (1844-1896), and Joris-Karl Huysmans (1848-1907), whose *A Rebours* or *Against the Grain* (1884) the decadents considered a touchstone work. The French stressed form, nuance rather than rhetoric, and artificiality—jewels, cosmetics, the music halls of the city—as opposed to the natural. Gautier defended **art for art's sake**, but that doctrine came more immediately to the decadents from the aestheticism of the 1880s, particularly from the "Conclusion" to *Studies in the History of the Renaissance* (1873) by Walter Pater (1839-1894). Pater's cultivated prose, his image of life as a series of fleeting impressions, his notion of art as a means of concentrating and quickening the consciousness of those impressions, until the mind burns with a "hard, gemlike flame," greatly influenced the decadents.

Lists of decadent artists vary among critics, but the following are usually included within the movement: John Barlas (1860-1914), **Aubrey Beardsley** (1872-1898), Olive Custance (1874-1944), Lord Alfred Douglas (1870-1945), Ernest Dowson (1867-1900), John Gray (1866-1934), Lionel Johnson (1867-1902), Richard Le Gallienne (1866-1947), **George Moore** (1852-1933), **Algernon Charles Swinburne** (1837-1909), Arthur Symons (1865-1945), **Oscar Wilde** (1854-1900), and Theodore Wratislaw (1871-1933). Decadence was also associated with various little magazines that flourished in the 1890s, particularly with the *Yellow Book*, although much of its material was not decadent, and with the *Savoy*, which was edited by Symons and Beardsley.

In "The Decadent Movement in Literature" (1893), Symons identifies decadent qualities as "an intense self-consciousness, a restless curiosity in research, an over-subtilizing refinement upon refinement, a spiritual and moral perversity." It is the expression of a civilization grown overluxurious and overinquiring, of a culture that has reached its end and exhausted its energies—hence the decadent emphasis on artifice. Decadence also stresses parts rather than the whole, individual words or sentences rather than the corporate poem or narrative—narrative itself, rather than following a continuous story line, tends to break down into a series of motifs or elaborate descriptions, as in *Against the Grain* or Wilde's *The Picture of Dorian Gray* (1891), in which a chapter is devoted to the artifacts that Dorian accumulates.

The cult of the artificial appears in the poems of Symons's *London Nights* (1895), in which nature is called unreal and life is compared to a music hall. Decadents also emphasized artifice in their language by the use of arcane or learned terms ("the fulvous Nile") and exotic metaphors.

Sexual explicitness and daring also characterize the decadents. Casual sexual encounters punctuate the poems of *London Nights*. In Wilde's *Salomé* (1894), the young dancer expresses a frankly erotic desire for Jokanaan, while Herod lusts for her. In *The Sphinx* (1894) Wilde imagines every sexual possibility—with human, animal, and mythical partners. In Swinburne's "Dolores" (1866), which gave the decadents a prototype of the dangerous woman, sexuality is a "pleasure that winces and stings," and it leads to the search for new passions and undiscovered sins. **Homosexuality**, or "the love that dare not speak its name," appears in Douglas's "Two Loves." But perhaps the most sexually explicit art of the decadents was Beardsley's, both in his drawings—the illustrations for *Salomé* and the *Lysistrata*—and in his elaborately detailed, erotic mock epic, *The Story of Venus and Tannhäuser* (1907).

The decadents' thirst for new, forbidden sensations was complicated, however, by a longing for lost innocence and spiritual renewal. Beardsley, Douglas, Dowson, Gray, Johnson, and Wilde became Roman Catholics, and express such religious themes as the need to worship and the meaning of Christ in the modern world. Dowson, in "Benedictio Domini" (1896), calls the service in an old church "The one true solace of man's fallen plight." Other poems, like Gray's "Le Voyage à Cythère" (1893) and Johnson's "The Dark Angel" (1894), are indictments of sensuality and worldly pleasure. *Against the Grain* ends with the decadent hero, Des Esseintes, praying for pity "on the sceptic who would fain believe." Among the lovers in Symons's *London Nights* is the young woman who wakens his regret for her lost innocence, so that he "would fain call back the child that's gone."

Thus decadence, though it rebelled against much that Victorians had held sacred, was itself, like the Victorian age, wandering between two (or perhaps many) worlds. Its complexity is undoubtedly why critics still are not agreed on exactly what decadence was or who the decadents were; but for the same reason it remains an important and illuminating focus upon the end of the Victorian age.

RICHARD BENVENUTO

Bibliography

Beckson, Karl, ed. *Aesthetes and Decadents of the 1890s: An Anthology of British Poetry and Prose.* 1981.

Dowling, Linda C. *Aestheticism and Decadence: A Selective Annotated Bibliography.* 1977.

———. *Language and Decadence in the Victorian Fin de Siècle.* 1986.

Ellmann, Richard, ed. *Edwardians and Late Victorians: English Institute Essays.* 1960.

Fletcher, Ian, ed. *Decadence and the 1890s.* 1979.

Jackson, Holbrook. *The Eighteen Nineties.* 1913.

Munro, John M. *The Decadent Poetry of the Eighteen-Nineties.* 1970.

Reed, John R. *Decadent Style.* 1985.

Stanford, Derek, ed. *Poets of the 'Nineties: A Biographical Anthology.* 1965.

Temple, Ruth Z. "Truth in Labelling: Pre-Raphaelitism, Aestheticism, Decadence, Fin de Siècle." *English Literature in Transition*, vol. 17, pp. 201–222.

Thornton, R. K. R. *The Decadent Dilemma.* 1983.

See also AESTHETIC MOVEMENT

· · · · ·

DE MORGAN, WILLIAM
(1839–1917)

William De Morgan was a designer associated with William Morris and the **arts and crafts movement**, noted especially for his innovations in ceramics and, later in his life, for his novels.

De Morgan's early artistic training was acquired at the Royal Academy Schools. After meeting Morris and some members of the **Pre-Raphaelite Brotherhood**, he abandoned his artistic ambition to work as a designer in stained glass and pottery for the firm of Morris and Co. His interest in traditional craft techniques and in color led De Morgan to experiment in glazing processes and to rediscover a traditional type of luster glazing which became a distinctive feature of his pottery decoration. Despite the excellent qualities of his tiles and pottery, however, De Morgan enjoyed little financial success.

In 1885 De Morgan married the artist Edith Pickering, and from 1892 he spent part of his time in Florence. In his last years, he achieved considerable fame as a novelist.

LARRY D. LUTCHMANSINGH

Bibliography

Stirling, Anna M. W. *William De Morgan and His Wife.* 1922.

Victoria and Albert Museum. *Catalogue of Works by William De Morgan.* 1921.

· · · · ·

DIALECT WRITING

Dialect writing may be loosely defined as the use of nonstandard forms of written English to signify a localized form of speech. Until the beginning of the nineteenth century, virtually the only use of dialect in general literature was for comic or low-life characters, yet by the middle of the Victorian period it was established as a significant language tool for serious as well as comic matters. Major figures such as Dickens, the Brontës, Gaskell, Kingsley, and Eliot in fiction; Barnes and Tennyson in poetry; and Boucicault in popular drama proved its range and gave it respectability.

This change marked a literary response to the growing awareness of varied regional, social, and industrial lifestyles. New reading audiences came from new sociolinguistic communities. The provincial or working-class hero and heroine in the novel of social realism epitomize this change. A complementary factor was the example of national dialects in Scottish and Irish literature. Scotland had a long-established written tradition, but the enormous popularity of Walter Scott and the general acceptance of writers such as John Galt (1779–1839) and Susan Ferrier (1782–1854) consolidated the practice. Among Irish novelists Samuel Lover (1797–1868) and Charles Lever (1806–1872) were widely popular. Both literatures used native speakers as characters to create a sympathetic awareness of national life and national problems, although also taking advantage of the comic tradition by fusing it with more serious elements.

Support for the respectability of regional dialects came also from scholarly and general interest in language, which culminated in the *English Dialect Dictionary* (*EDD*) (1898–1905). A chauvinistic pride in the Anglo-Saxon language reflected luster on dialects as preservers of much "pure" Old English. This view, coupled with a revived interest in **folklore**, led to the publication of many dialect anthologies. Local dialect societies, old and new, flourished. In 1873 the English Dialect Society was formed. (One of its first publications was a study of George Eliot's dialect use.) The list of publications used as sources by the *EDD* is a guide to dialect activity in the period. Cockney requires a separate comment. Originally a social as much as a linguistic term, its literary conventions were established in the fiction of Dickens and others. Aspects were then appropriated for low-life, uneducated, or criminal characters in general. "Dialects" of affected gentility also appeared; sensitivity to class distinctions produced sensitivity to the social implications of language.

Writing in dialect for the general reader had to be a compromise between readability and accuracy. Charles Dickens experimented widely in *Nicholas Nickleby* (1839) with cockney, northern, and class dialects, but attempted realism really begins with Emily Brontë's *Wuthering Heights* (1847). Charlotte Brontë discussed its usage in her preface to the second edition (1850), having used regional and class dialect herself in *Shirley* (1849). Elizabeth Gaskell in *Mary Barton* (1848) produced the first major novel to deal with the factory workers of Lancashire, while Charles Kingsley in *Westward Ho!* (1855) added Devon sailors to the London types he had portrayed in earlier works. George Eliot, with the success of *Adam Bede* (1859) and *The Mill on the Floss* (1860), consolidated the prestige of dialect use in fiction. The scholarly Dorset poet William Barnes (1801–1886) gave status to contemporary dialect poetry, to which Tennyson later contributed, and was a direct influence on Thomas Hardy (1840–1928). In *Barrack-Room Ballads* (1892), Rudyard Kipling (1865–1936) gave cockney a serious role in poetry, while his stories ranged with authority across the dialects of class and many countries.

EDGAR WRIGHT

Bibliography

Blake, N. F. *Non-Standard Language in English Literature.* 1981.

Brooks, George L. *English Dialects.* 1963.

Phillips, K. C. *Language and Class in Victorian England.* 1984.

Wakelin, Martyn F. *English Dialects.* 1972.

Wright, Joseph. *The English Dialect Dictionary.* 1898–1905. 6 vols.

See also BARRIE, J. M.; WORKING-CLASS NOVELISTS; WORKING-CLASS POETS

· · · · ·

DIARIES AND DIARISTS

Diary writing was immensely popular during the Victorian era. Bringing together such disparate items as the price of a railway ticket and speculations about the nature of God, the beauty of midsummer's eve and the pathos of a loved one dying of cholera in India, the latest riddles and the technological wonders of the Great Exhibition, diaries capture the flux of Victorian Britain, yet place it within manageable limits. An activity available to all who could write and afford to buy paper, diary writing allowed the famous as well as the obscure to construct a record of the texture of lived experience.

Although a given diary may be written for a specific purpose, such as to evaluate the writer's spiritual progress or to capture the political climate, diaries generally contain comments about the weather, important social and cultural events, and death. Diarists tend to organize their works around personally significant events such as birthdays, the end or beginning of the year, and the anniversaries of births and deaths of significant others. These recurring markers provide the diary with a form that is cyclical as well as linear.

Although men's and women's diaries were similar in form, the subject matter tended to differ. Men's diaries were often more outwardly directed, dealing with the social, political, and economic world as it influenced the life of the writer. Male diarists often discussed war, politics, the ramifications of professional life, and the pursuit of sport and money. Women diarists also considered the political arena, but their entries usually focused on the familial context. This difference between men's and women's diaries exemplifies the concept of separate spheres and also suggests the disparate uses scholars make of their records. Women diarists often serve as family chroniclers; hence their diaries can fill in gaps in our knowledge of childbirth, marriage, relations between the sexes, and the role of service in women's lives.

An important consideration for the scholar is the distinction between published and manuscript works. Because the diary encompasses a wide variety of forms, it is essential to know the genesis of an individual journal. Most published diaries have been severely edited; many combine several forms such as the letter, memoir, travelogue, and account book. Manuscript diaries may be recorded in a printed diary format or one created by the diarist. They may graphically illustrate an individual's imprint in the dots, dashes, additions, and deletions which are generally removed or regularized when a diary is published. Both manuscript and published diaries require attention to the question of audience. Victorian diaries were not ordinarily composed simply for the writer, but created with the diarist's family or a larger reading public in mind.

The existence and location of both manuscript and published diaries are treated in a number of bibliographies. The work of William Matthews is the largest single tool for locating diaries and their contents.

Among noted diarists, the Reverend Francis Kilvert (1840–1879) created a portrait of country life that is treasured for its literary quality. Diaries by **Arthur Munby** (1828–1910) and Hannah Cullwick (1833–1909) detail the relationship between servant and master. Caroline Fox (1819–1871) delineates the conversation of her father's friends, who included John Stuart Mill, the Carlyles, and Wordsworth. Better-known figures such as William Gladstone and Queen Victoria kept lengthy diaries, yet their accounts paint a slimmer portrait of Victorian life. Still, the publication of Queen Victoria's journals served to popularize diary writing as a means of expression for the average Victorian, whose impulse to capture the impact of the age stands as a testament to the genre and its practitioners.

CYNTHIA HUFF

Bibliography

Batts, John Stuart. *British Manuscript Diaries of the Nineteenth Century: An Annotated Listing.* 1976.

Fothergill, Robert A. *Private Chronicles: A Study of English Diaries.* 1974.

Huff, Cynthia. *British Women's Diaries: A Descriptive Bibliography of Selected Nineteenth-Century Women's Manuscript Diaries.* 1985.

Matthews, William. *British Diaries: An Annotated Bibliography of British Diaries Written Between 1442 and 1942.* 1950.

O'Brien, Kate. *English Diaries and Journals.* 1943.

Ponsonby, Arthur. *English Diaries: A Review of English Diaries from the Sixteenth to the Twentieth Century with an Introduction on Diary Writing.* 1922.

. . . . .

DICKENS, CHARLES (1812–1870)

Charles Dickens is the single most important figure in Victorian literature. His bustling presence as a popular novelist, magazine editor, journalist, and social reformer dominates and helps to characterize this period of extremes. No other English novelist can compare to Dickens in the extravagant variety of his characters and narratives or the rich, powerful exploitation of all of the resources of language and symbol that he managed to achieve.

Dickens's own fairy tale life provided the stuff of which his fiction was made, especially the closely autobiographical *David Copperfield* (1849). David's struggle to rise from the boyhood misery of the infamous blacking warehouse to a position of wealth and renown as a novelist parallels his creator's own experiences. After a few false starts in acting and parliamentary reporting, Dickens's career took off with the publication of *Sketches by Boz* (1836). The subtitle of this volume proclaimed them "Illustrative of Everyday Life and Everyday People," an apt description both of these stories and of much of Dickens's work. The *Sketches* were not, however,

Charles Dickens.
Illustrated London News, *18 June 1870. Library Company of Philadelphia.*

merely lively journalistic pieces about common events or familiar types of London humanity; they were sparked by the uncommon insight into personality, close observation of social interaction, and amazing verbal felicity that would become known as "Dickensian."

Success followed success for Dickens. *Pickwick Papers* (1836) began the fashion for monthly serial publication. This format, though onerous for many slower-working novelists, was congenial to the energetic, exuberant creative temperament of Dickens. He always worked at dazzling speed, with intense concentration, seldom making serious artistic compromises. A phenomenal best seller, *Pickwick Papers* was eagerly passed from hand to hand, read aloud by parents to their families and by hired readers to illiterates in pubs. Dickens found himself in young manhood more than an established writer: he was an international celebrity.

Dickens's literary work falls into three distinct periods. The first extends through *Oliver Twist* (1837), *Nicholas Nickleby* (1838), *The Old Curiosity Shop* (1840), and *Barnaby Rudge* (1841). These brilliant early achievements are already marked by such recurrent features in Dickens's art as the sympathetic treatment of thieves, prostitutes, and other outcasts, indignation at all forms of hypocrisy, compassion for the afflicted, and profound empathy with the feelings of sensitive, unprotected children. Satire, sentiment, and sensation coexist harmoniously within a framework of bursting abundance, ranging through the whole of England from Fagin's foul urban den in *Oliver Twist* to Squeers's brutal boarding school in *Nicholas Nickleby.*

Dickens's triumphant speaking tour of the United States inaugurated his middle period. He formed a poor opinion of the country, which he satirizes for boorishness in the American section of *Martin Chuzzlewit* (1843). In the same year that Dickens began the serialization of this uneven novel, he also published his first "Christmas book," *A Christmas Carol.* This work, arguably the first product of Dickens's maturity as an artist, is regarded by many as his most representative and by some as his best. In his treatment of the unloved boy who becomes the loveless elderly miser Scrooge, he achieved perhaps the most memorable dramatization of the central Dickensian theme, which could be called "the death of the heart." Dickens was fascinated by the forces in childhood and society that distort healthy human development. When Scrooge finally saves Tiny Tim, he also restores the innocent child within himself. This "resurrectionist" theme runs throughout all of Dickens's later fiction, becoming perhaps most pervasive in *A Tale of Two Cities* (1859).

Of the numerous works closely following *A Christmas Carol*, *Dombey and Son* (1846) is the most impressive. This novel, with the masterful psychological plausibility of the "poor little rich girl" Florence, demonstrated Dickens's ability to portray believable female characters other than grotesques and empty-headed ingenues. The serialization of *David Copperfield* (1849) ended this creative decade to great acclaim.

The next twenty years produced the amazing string of classics for which Dickens is perhaps chiefly known: *Bleak House* (1852), *Hard Times* (1854), *Little Dorrit* (1855), *A Tale of Two Cities* (1859), *Great Expectations* (1861), *Our Mutual Friend* (1864), and *The Mystery of Edwin Drood* (1870). These gripping later novels, all partially plotted within the new mystery genre, are distinguished by a deepening engagement with issues of social injustice, a more probing exploration of the enigma of differences among family members, and darker philosophical vision. Dickens had moved from the sunniness of Mr. Pickwick's picnics to the chilling opium den fantasies of John Jasper.

Dickens died suddenly at his Gad's Hill home in 1870, literally in midsentence, leaving the half-finished *Edwin Drood* an exciting puzzle to challenge his readers forevermore. His death at the peak of his powers made front page news throughout the English-speaking world and for weeks mourners lined up to pay their final respects at Dickens's grave in Westminster Abbey. The most unforgettable dimension of his legacy, to many Dickensians, resides in the extraordinary characters that he created. They have become not only a part of our language but also of our way of perceiving. To say of a devious man that he is "a regular Uriah Heep," for example, is to render a devastating caricature. The people in Dickens form an indispensable element of our sensibility.

In addition to his literary achievements, Dickens's tireless contributions to social reform helped to change the child labor laws and the educational system that he deplored in the form of Gradgrind's "school of facts" in *Hard Times.* That children today are commonly regarded, in literature and in life, as beings with imaginations and feelings to be carefully nurtured, is perhaps more to Dickens's credit than it is to Freud's. One could reasonably maintain that the period of "High Victorianism" ended with the death of Dickens in 1870, to be followed by an age of transition essentially premodern in nature. With his keen psychological examination of the divided aims of the human mind in the last novels, Dickens prefigured the introspective period in which we now live.

NANCY ENGBRETSEN SCHAUMBURGER

Bibliography

Dexter, Walter, ed. *The Letters of Charles Dickens.* 1938.

Ford, George H. *Dickens and His Readers.* 1955.

Forster, John. *The Life of Charles Dickens.* 1872.

Garis, Robert. *The Dickens Theatre.* 1965.

Johnson, Edgar. *Charles Dickens: His Tragedy and Triumph.* 1952.

Marcus, Steven. *Dickens: From "Pickwick" to "Dombey."* 1965.

Miller, J. Hillis. *Charles Dickens: The World of His Novels.* 1958.

Orwell, George. "Charles Dickens." In George Orwell, *A Collection of Essays.* 1954.

Partlow, Robert, ed. *Dickens the Craftsman.* 1970.

Stone, Harry. *Dickens and the Invisible World.* 1979.

Wilson, Angus. *The World of Charles Dickens.* 1970.

Wilson, Edmund. "Dickens: The Two Scrooges." In Edmund Wilson, *The Wound and the Bow.* 1952.

See also BROWNE, HABLOT K. (*illus.*); CHILDHOOD; CRUIKSHANK, GEORGE (*illus.*)

· · · · ·

DICTIONARY OF NATIONAL BIOGRAPHY

A multivolume collection of biographies of notable British men and women, the *Dictionary of National Biography* is the product of the vision and financial backing of George Smith, publisher, entrepreneur, and proprietor of the *Cornhill Magazine* and *Pall Mall Gazette.* Having formed the plan in 1882, Smith engaged **Leslie Stephen** to edit

the *DNB.* As editor, Stephen's goal was to create accurate, readable, scholarly volumes, published punctually every quarter. Stephen set up the editorial machinery that produced the original edition of sixty-three volumes, containing 29,120 lives, in fifteen years (1885–1900). When possible, he obtained specialists to write the biographies. In all, 653 contributors wrote entries, although a handful, 34, contributed half the total. Stephen himself produced 378; Sidney Lee, his successor as editor, 820. As editor and contributor, Stephen established the *DNB*'s style— condensed and precise. When poor health forced Stephen's retirement in 1891, Sidney Lee, who had served as his assistant editor since 1883 and coeditor since 1890, completed the original edition and edited the first two supplements as well. In 1917 copyright passed to Oxford University Press, which has continued the series for twentieth-century figures. The *DNB* remains a monument of Victorian publishing enterprise and intellectual energy.

MARK REGER

Bibliography

Annan, Noel. *Leslie Stephen: The Godless Victorian.* 1984.

Lee, Sidney. "The *Dictionary of National Biography:* A Statistical Account." In Sidney Lee, ed., *Dictionary of National Biography*, vol. 1, pp. v–xxii. 1900.

· · · · ·

DINOSAURS

Dinosaurs, a now-discarded biological classification comprising two distinct families of terrestrial prehistoric reptiles (while excluding pterosaurs, ichthyosaurs, and plesiosaurs, among others), were first discovered and reconstructed in nineteenth-century England. Georges Cuvier, the great French comparative anatomist, visited Oxford in 1818 and while there identified some gigantic fossil bones found nearby as reptilian. Gideon Mantell (1790–1852) described others from Tigate Forest (near Cuckfield, Sussex) in 1822. A brief reconstruction by James Parkinson that year and a paper by William Buckland in 1824 then established *Megalosaurus* as the first of the great saurians.

In 1825 Mantell announced his discovery of *Iguanodon*, the first herbivorous dinosaur (and all the more remarkable because no present-day plant-eating reptiles were then known). He followed with *Hylaeosaurus*, the first armored dinosaur, in 1832 and would later add *Regnosaurus* and *Pelorosaurus* as well. In 1841, at a meeting of the British Association for the Advancement of Science, the comparative anatomist Richard Owen proposed to group *Megalosaurus*, *Iguanodon*, and *Hylaeosaurus* into a single order of reptiles, which he called dinosaurs. The name was not immediately acceptable, however, as Mantell and others continued to prefer "saurians."

Mid-Victorians did not know the dinosaurs most familiar to us; *Brontosaurus*, *Stegosaurus*, and *Tyrannosaurus* were all late nineteenth-century discoveries from America. Nor did they conceive of *Megalosaurus*, *Iguanodon*, and *Hylaeosaurus* as we do. The most famous Victorian dinosaur reconstructions are those created by Benjamin Waterhouse for the Exhibition of 1851; they may still be seen at Syndenham. He imagined both *Megalosaurus* and *Iguanodon* as quadrupeds. John Martin's painting, "The Country of the Iguanodon," extant now only as the frontispiece to Mantell's *The Wonders of Geology* (1838), is an important predecessor. Conspicuous literary references appear in Tennyson's *In Memoriam* (1850) and *Maud* (1852), Dickens's *Bleak House* (1852), Disraeli's *Lothair* (1870), Bulwer-Lytton's *The Coming Race* (1871), H. G. Wells's *A Vision of the Past* (1887), and Hardy's *A Group of Noble Dames* (1891). Arthur Conan Doyle's *The Lost World* appeared belatedly in 1912. But all of these sensationalized depictions caricature more sophisticated scientific understanding.

DENNIS R. DEAN

Bibliography

Charig, Alan J. *A New Look at Dinosaurs.* 1979.

Dean, Dennis R. *Gideon Mantell, Discoverer of Dinosaurs.* (Forthcoming.)

· · · · ·

DISESTABLISHMENT

The legal position of the established church in Great Britain evolved through an accumulation of statute and precedent. It included aspects of state control over the church (e.g., the appointment of bishops and deans, the right to define doctrine and regulate forms of worship, and final judicial review in cases involving the church) as well as legal privileges held by the church (e.g., bishops held seats in the House of Lords; property owners were required to pay tithes and church rates to the parish). Disestablishment of the **Church of England** was one of the most heated political and religious questions of the Victorian era, especially between the years 1826–1852 and 1868–1886.

Britain's transformation from a Christian commonwealth to a pluralistic society is seen in the debate over establishment. The question of church-state relationships functioned on two levels: first, of ideas, and second, of political and social developments. By the Victorian era the model of the Christian commonwealth—that the constituencies of church and state were the same and that the state had a duty to uphold religious truth—was increasingly at odds with social and religious realities. There were larger and more visible religious alternatives to Anglicanism (especially Methodism, Roman Catholicism, and a revived Protestant Nonconformity). Gradual elimination of religious disabilities in politics made it impossible to count on Parliament being Protestant (after 1829), Christian (after 1858), or even religious (with the Bradlaugh case in the 1880s). The state took over the registration of vital statistics. The religious test for attendance at Oxford and Cambridge was removed. A vigorous secularist perspective grew hostile to the special status of the Church of England. Was it any longer the church of the nation?

Such a question led eventually to the disestablishment of the Anglican church in Ireland (1869) and Wales (1914). Scotland continued with a somewhat loose Presbyterian establishment, but the church there was independent of the state in terms of its own operations. Critics of the Church of England sought similar redress in England. Debate often took place within and without the church under the larger theme of "church reform." Many continued to defend the idea of a "national church" which establishment symbolized, among them S. T. Coleridge and Thomas Arnold, at the beginning, and Bishop Mandell Creighton and Samuel Barnett at the end of the period.

Nonconformist agitation for disestablishment was led by the Liberation Society, founded in 1844 as the British Anti-State Church Association, which published pamphlets and organized speaking tours on behalf of religious equality. Edward Miall (1809–1881), M.P. for Rochdale from 1852, was its moving spirit and the chief parliamentary advocate for disestablishment. A number of Anglican ritualist priests, among them A. H. Mackonochie (1825–1887), took up the cause in the 1870s as a way of freeing the Church of England from state control. One major sticking point was whether disendowment would have to accompany disestablishment. The Church Defence Institution, founded in opposition to the Liberation Society, promoted the principle of establishment.

W. E. Gladstone was the most important single figure in the controversy. He led the Liberal party to victory in the 1868 general elections, which prepared the way for passage of the Irish disestablishment bill in the following year. His own views had changed as he came to recognize that the principle of popular self-government had become the basis of political constitutions and that Christendom had dissolved from one into many communions. He believed, however, that the issue of establishment should be decided by a practical rather than a theoretical test. In Ireland, with the people predominantly Catholic, an Anglican establishment could not meet that test. But by the same token, the Church of England still qualified.

Nonconformists and secular critics felt betrayed when Gladstone refused to pursue disestablishment in England. The split in the Liberal party over Irish Home Rule in the 1880s marked the end of serious parliamentary discussion of the question, but the resolution of most of the religious disabilities and the emergence of a state education system after 1870 had also reduced the number of grievances. By the twentieth century disestablishment became largely an internal Anglican issue.

DALE A. JOHNSON

Bibliography

Bell, Philip M. H. *Disestablishment in Ireland and Wales.* 1969.

Mackintosh, William H. *Disestablishment and Liberation.* 1972.

Nicholls, David, ed. *Church and State in Britain Since 1820.* 1967.

Vidler, Alexander R. *The Orb and the Cross.* 1945.

See also FREETHOUGHT; NONCONFORMITY

· · · · ·

DISRAELI, BENJAMIN (1804–1881)

Benjamin Disraeli's enduring fame is the result of his extraordinary career in politics. He was twice prime minister (1868, 1874–1880) and gained the status of a Conservative statesman through his conduct of foreign affairs during the period of England's greatest prestige as a world power. But he is also justly remembered for his novels, particularly the trilogy of the 1840s, *Coningsby* (1844), *Sybil* (1845), and *Tancred* (1847).

Disraeli was born in London into a Jewish family of moderate, independent means. All of the children were baptized into the Church of England in 1817. Disraeli received his primary education at minor private schools before being permitted to turn to the resources of his father's library.

As a youth of Byronic sensibility, Disraeli attempted to penetrate London's fashionable society, and through extravagant dandyism and unwise speculations he soon contracted large debts. His first novel, *Vivian Grey* (1826–1827), based loosely on events in John Murray's circle, gained a reputation for scandalous indiscretions. A second novel in the **silver-fork** style, *The Young Duke* (1831), was completed just before Disraeli set out on a Mediterranean tour in which he deliberately followed Byron's earlier footsteps as far as Greece, but then went on to Palestine and Egypt.

Between 1832 and 1837 Disraeli was deeply engaged in writing pamphlets and political journalism. *A Vindication of the English Constitution in a Letter to a Noble and Learned Lord* (1835) and "The Letters of 'Runnymede'" (1836), which appeared in the *Times*, did much to establish his reputation as an advocate of Conservative views and showed clearly the nature of his intellectual debts to the political ideas of Viscount Bolingbroke (1678–1751). In these years Disraeli twice attempted to write dramatic poetry and he continued to try to earn money by writing novels. *Henrietta Temple, A Love Story* (1837) is a psychological romance reflecting both the central ambivalence of Disraeli's personality and, in disguised form, the significance of his recent love affair with Lady Henrietta Sykes.

In 1837 Disraeli was elected to the House of Commons as a member for Maidstone and two years later he married his constituency colleague's widow, Mary Anne Wyndham-Lewis. By 1841 Disraeli anticipated a seat in Robert Peel's cabinet. Alienated by Peel's neglect, he formed an opposition group within the **Conservative party** and for the next several years gained considerable fame and notoriety as the promoter of Young England's nostalgic paternalism. *Coningsby; or, The New Generation* (1844) was widely seen as a political manifesto; it clearly reflects the Tory ideology Disraeli espoused in the 1830s, especially the desire to regenerate the natural leadership of the aristocracy. *Sybil; or, The Two Nations* (1845) continues this theme in an allegorical treatment of the unifying power of religious piety wedded to secular political leadership.

Peel's conversion to the repeal of the Corn Laws in 1845 brought Disraeli into open opposition to government policy. His savage and witty attacks on Peel did much to incite the Protectionists' revolt that ultimately brought down the Conservative administration. The third novel of the political "trilogy," *Tancred; or The New Crusade* (1847), appears at first to be a continuation of the **Young England** motifs of religious piety and noble political leadership. But the implausible romance plot seems equally concerned with the issues of trust and sincerity raised by public perceptions of the expediency of Disraeli's attacks on Peel.

In 1852 Disraeli became chancellor of the exchequer in Lord Derby's government and in the same year published *Lord George Bentinck: A Political Biography*, which is both a tribute to his deceased friend and an autobiographical account of the years 1845–1850. He was chancellor again in the second short Derby government of 1858–1859 and for a third time in the Tory revival of 1866–1867. Throughout these years Disraeli was the most important Conservative member in the Commons, but his position as heir to the party leadership was not secure until 1867, when his dexterous management of the second Reform Bill made his succession to Lord Derby all but inevitable.

Disraeli first became prime minister in 1868, but the government was in a minority position, and the Conservatives themselves were soon divided by Gladstone's motions to disestablish the Irish church. In the ensuing election the Liberals won a clear majority and Disraeli resigned the government before Parliament met. In his most popular novel, *Lothair* (1870), his vision of patrician society is informed by satirical wit.

In 1874 Disraeli became prime minister with a decisive majority and held office until 1880. The years of this second Disraeli administration were marked both by extensive domestic legislation for social reform (largely initiated by members of the cabinet, particularly the home secretary, **Richard Cross**) and by dramatic events in the conduct of foreign affairs, including the purchase of the **Suez Canal**, the Royal Titles Act (1876), the Turkish atrocities, the Eastern Question, the Congress of Berlin (1878), and the Afghan and Zulu wars. These years are also the climax of the great antagonism between Disraeli and Gladstone which had continuously intensified since the mid-1840s, although after Disraeli's elevation to the peerage as earl of Beaconsfield in 1876 the personal battle shifted from debates in the Commons to the wider realms of public opinion. In the same years, Disraeli's great tact and sensitivity in his relations with Queen Victoria made him her favorite prime minister.

In the election of 1880 the Conservatives were again defeated. Later the same year Disraeli published his last completed novel, *Endymion* (1880). Longmans offered him the remarkable sum of 10,000 pounds for the rights to it without having read the manuscript. The novel's central theme is the powerful influence of women on the political careers of men they love or admire. The work's charm, however, derives from the genial and lightly satirical retrospective glance Disraeli casts over the political society of the previous fifty years.

Disraeli's greatest fame deservedly arises from his distinguished political career, based as it was upon extraordinary personal qualities that amounted to imaginative genius. His speeches are among the most readable examples of Victorian prose, and from them it is clear that he was able to dramatize political issues to an extent unusual even for his times. His role in extending British influence in European and imperial matters and his vision of a natural alliance of the working classes and the aristocracy within the Conservative party are now seen as his greatest achievements.

ROBERT O'KELL

Bibliography

Blake, Robert. *Disraeli*. 1966.

Braun, Thom. *Disraeli the Novelist*. 1981.

Feuchtwanger, E. J. *Disraeli, Democracy and the Tory Party*. 1968.

Gunn, J. A. W. et al., eds. *Benjamin Disraeli Letters*. 1982–.

Jerman, B. R. *The Young Disraeli*. 1960.

Kebbel, Thomas E., ed. *Selected Speeches of the Late Right Honourable the Earl of Beaconsfield*. 1882. 2 vols.

Levine, Richard A. *Benjamin Disraeli*. 1968.

Monypenny, William F. and G. E. Buckle. *The Life of Benjamin Disraeli, Earl of Beaconsfield*. 1910–1920. 6 vols.

O'Kell, Robert. "The Autobiographical Nature of Disraeli's Early Fiction." *Nineteenth-Century Fiction*, vol. 31, pp. 253–284.

Smith, Paul. *Disraelian Conservatism and Social Reform*. 1967.

Stewart, Robert. *Benjamin Disraeli: A List of Writings by Him, and Writings About Him, with Notes*. 1972.

· · · · ·

DIVORCE

Until 1857 jurisdiction in divorce cases lay with the ecclesiastical courts. The only way to obtain a civil divorce was by a private act of Parliament, which was prohibitively expensive for most people. The ecclesiastical courts issued two kinds of divorce decrees. A divorce *a mensa et thoro* (from bed and board) was granted for adultery, extreme cruelty, or desertion; it allowed neither party to remarry. Divorce *a vinculo* (from the bonds of marriage) was a nullification of marriage, and was granted only when the marriage was invalid due to age, mental incompetence, sexual impotence, or fraud.

To obtain a parliamentary divorce required that the plaintiff first obtain a divorce *a mensa et thoro* from the ecclesiastical court, and then win a civil suit for damages for "criminal conversation" against the spouse's lover. After 1800 some ten divorce bills passed Parliament each year; only three were ever awarded to women, all for adultery combined with bigamy or incest.

The Divorce and Matrimonial Causes Act of 1857 created a civil divorce court in London, with authority to grant judicial separations and divorce decrees. Under the act the grounds for divorce were a wife's adultery, and a husband's adultery if it was aggravated by cruelty, incest, bigamy, or bestiality. The grounds for judicial separation were adultery, cruelty, or desertion for two years.

The act also provided that a wife deserted by her husband could apply to a local magistrate's court for a protection order, which would have the effect of a judicial separation and give her *feme sole* rights over her property. The Matrimonial Causes Act of 1878 authorized magistrates' courts to grant protection orders to wives whose husbands had been convicted of aggravated assault; the Maintenance of Wives (Desertion) Act of 1886 empowered magistrates to order a husband to maintain his wife; and the Summary Jurisdiction (Married Women) Act of 1895 allowed magistrates to issue a protection order to a woman who was driven from her home by her husband's cruelty or failure to maintain her and her children. Protection orders, like judicial separations from the divorce court, did not allow either spouse to remarry.

In the decade after 1859, the divorce court granted an average of 148 divorces each year. By the beginning of the twentieth century, the divorce court issued some 600 divorce decrees and 80 judicial separations each year, while the magistrates' courts dispensed about 8,000 protection orders (judicial separations).

Criticism of the divorce law centered mainly on the expense of the proceeding, which had to be conducted in London; on the sexual double standard which allowed men to divorce their wives for simple adultery but forbade divorce to the wife of an adulterer unless he also committed bigamy, incest, cruelty, or bestial acts; and on the narrow grounds for divorce. No changes were made in the grounds for divorce until the Matrimonial Causes Act of 1923, which equalized the grounds of divorce by allowing a woman to sue an adulterous husband for divorce. The Matrimonial Causes Act of 1937 added desertion, cruelty, and insanity as justifications for divorce.

MARY LYNDON SHANLEY

Bibliography

Graveson, Ronald H. and F. R. Crane. *A Century of Family Law, 1857-1957.* 1957.

Horstman, Allen, *Victorian Divorce.* 1985.

Macgregor, Oliver. *Divorce in England.* 1957.

Stetson, Dorothy. *A Woman's Issue.* 1982.

See also MARRIAGE LAW; SCOTS LAW

. . . . .

DOGS AND DOG SHOWS

The Victorians' relationship with their dogs reflects the contradictory and complex nature of their society. The surreptitious and illegal practice of dog fighting and bull baiting contrasts with the concern for animal welfare reflected in the establishment of the Society for the Prevention of Cruelty to Animals as a royal society in 1840. The anthropomorphic paintings of **Edwin Landseer** (1802-1873) and the application of Darwinian science to dog breeding indicate further connections between dogs and Victorian life.

Dog shows, established at Newcastle in 1859, grew out of fanciers' concern with evaluating their sporting stock. The mutilation of dogs for show was greatly curtailed when the Kennel Club, founded in 1877 as the registry for purebred dogs, prevented the exhibition of maimed canines. When Charles Crufts, who established the most renowned of British dog shows in 1866, offered a class for stuffed dogs, he responded to the affection of the English for their dogs and to their recognition of the connections between their own and their pets' mortality.

Edwin Landseer's *Laying Down the Law* (1840) features a white standard poodle surrounded by a variety of other breeds to satirize the judge and courtroom scene, while *The Old Shepherd's Chief Mourner* (1837) emphasizes the human-dog bond, important both realistically and symbolically in Victorian England. This bond cut across class boundaries. The poachers who used their lurchers to get meat and the Lancashire miners whose racing whippets might double their weekly earnings formed as long-lasting a bond with their dogs as did the aristocracy and gentry whose hounds, setters, and spaniels hunted the fox or pheasant. The Victorians' realization of dogs' multifaceted use resulted in the creation of many new breeds as well as the importation of others. Queen Victoria was instrumental in securing and popularizing exotic breeds, such as the chow and pekingese. The reverence and exploitation of dogs represented the Victorian fusion of feeling and reason, sentimentality and utility, aesthetics and science.

CYNTHIA HUFF

Bibliography

Ritchie, Carson I. A. *The British Dog: Its History from Earliest Times.* 1981.

Shaw, Vero. *The Illustrated Book of the Dog.* 1881.

Turner, James. *Reckoning with the Beast: Animals, Pain, and Humanity in the Victorian Mind.* 1980.

Walsh, John Henry. *The Dogs of the British Islands.* 1878.

See also ANIMAL PROTECTION

. . . . .

DOMESTIC INDUSTRY

Domestic industry in nineteenth-century Britain was largely a casualty of industrialization, beginning in the 1820s with the demise of the handloom weavers, whose plight became for many later Victorians a symbol of the evils of industrialism. A few industries remained largely domestic until late in the century: framework knitting of woolens, bootmaking and gloving, nail and chain making, straw-plaiting and lacemaking, tailoring and dressmaking. Local brewing of beer continued, despite competition from station pubs serving beer brought in by rail. Most remaining domestic workers were women and children, particularly once the **Factory Acts** regulated the ages and working conditions of factory children. The passing of domestic industry particularly harmed the rural lower classes and hastened large-scale migration to cities, where factory work was available.

Industrialization created and later destroyed the occupation of handloom weaving. Richard Arkwright (1732–1792) developed a water frame capable of making cotton thread strong enough to be woven into all-cotton cloth; putting domestic spinners out of business, it created a demand for weavers. Until power looms were perfected in the 1820s, handloom weaving paid relatively well and attracted many workers. The tragedy of the weavers' obsolescence may have been that there was no alternate domestic industry available for them, as handloom weaving had been for displaced spinners and fustian weavers.

Framework knitters, found mostly in the Midlands, endured longer because entrepreneurs used a piecework system to their advantage. Woolen hosiery was knitted by domestic outworkers hired by retailers who provided knitting frames and marketed the finished products. Though some mass production of woolens was possible early in the century, the fluctuating demand for hosiery made a domestic system attractive: committing little capital by using domestic workers and renting out frames, entrepreneurs minimized their economic risk. The introduction of the wide frame, on which lengths of woolen material were produced and later cut and seamed into stockings, genderized the industry; eventually men knitted on wide frames in factories and women seamed at home for lower piecework

wages. With the abolition of frame renting (1874), framework knitting ceased to be a large-scale domestic industry; rural knitters were hardest hit by its demise.

Rural families suffered most from the decline in domestic industry, which coincided with several agricultural failures and dropping prices for farm products. Just as domestic industry became essential for many households to survive, the opportunities and remuneration declined. Those occupations that remained were laborious and poorly paid: the most common were straw-plaiting for hats and trim, and lacemaking. Children worked from the age of three on, and many attended plaiting and lacemaking "schools" where fourteen-hour workdays were nominally mitigated by occasional Bible reading. Plaiting was less onerous than lacemaking, as it could be done while talking or socializing. As the century progressed, factory-made lace and changes in fashion lessened the demand for these products as well.

The later Victorians romanticized domestic industry, perhaps because of their dismay over the industrialized world that surrounded them. John Ruskin and William Morris wrote regretfully of the loss of meaningful work, self-determination, and integrated work and family life. Nonetheless, evidence suggests that domestic industry was grueling, dispiriting, and poorly paid; only through long hours of tediously repetitive labor could a worker eke out a living, becoming essentially a human machine.

LAURA NOVO

Bibliography

Bythell, Duncan. *The Handloom Weavers: A Study in the English Cotton Industry During the Industrial Revolution.* 1969.

Perkin, Harold. *The Origins of Modern English Society: 1780–1880.* 1969.

Perry, P. J. *A Geography of Nineteenth Century Britain.* 1975.

Pinchbeck, Ivy and Margaret Hewitt. *Children in English Society*, vol. 2. 1973.

See also LACEMAKERS;
SWEATSHOPS

. . . . .

DOWRY

Dowry in nineteenth-century England conformed to a pattern found with variations throughout Eurasia, where women could inherit the property of men. The custom had social and economic as well as legal implications.

Dowry consisted of the contribution by the bride's family toward a fund intended to support and benefit the couple while alive and the bride when widowed, and to provide for their children. It could consist of her entire inheritance, given at marriage, or, in the case of an heiress, a "settlement" might be made in addition which entailed her future estate. The bride's family contribution was matched by a commitment on the part of the groom to provide her with an income ("jointure") after his death, and an allowance ("pin money") during his life.

Dowries were a sensitive measure of the relative social status of bride and groom and thus a matter of honor to both families. Anthony Trollope in *Phineas Finn* (1869) delicately suggests that the delay in payment of Lady Laura's dowry enabled her rich but common-born husband to dominate her and embarrassed her aristocratic father and brother.

Among aristocratic equals, dowries of 10,000 to 30,000 pounds were usual, and the bride could expect a jointure of 10 percent. If a woman did not marry, her "portion" or inheritance was used to support her after her father's death. Money that supported single women—widows or heiresses—was usually held for them by trustees in conservative investments such as government securities. Normally, returns on investments, other than highly speculative ones, ran around 5 percent, so the jointure represented a good return, and was an encumbrance on the husband's estate when he died. The pin money of an upper-class wife amounted to about 1 percent of her dowry—less than normal return on an investment—but it was supposed to be for her free use, over and above her maintenance. In reality, the exact purpose of pin money was unclear, and more than one well-dowered wife was reduced to maintaining herself and her children on her pin money when her husband ran through her fortune.

In common law all of a married woman's goods and chattels belonged to her husband; her freehold property, though remaining hers, was under his control during the marriage. The situation was gradually modified in the case of the wealthy by the development of a rule in equity that property could be given to trustees to hold for the wife's benefit; her husband then had power only over the income. From 1870 a series of **Married Women's Property** Acts at last extended to all women some of the protection of separate property that had previously been reserved to the rich.

DOROTHY STEIN

Bibliography

Goody, Jack and S. J. Tambiah. *Bridewealth and Dowry*. 1973.

Keeton, George W. *An Introduction to Equity*. 1965.

Thompson, F. M. L. *English Landed Society in the Nineteenth Century*. 1963.

· · · · ·

DOYLE, ARTHUR CONAN (1859–1930)

Born in Edinburgh to Roman Catholic parents, Arthur Conan Doyle became one of the most popular and prolific writers of the Victorian and Edwardian periods. Educated at Jesuit schools in England, Doyle was an athletic youth, more interested in sports and the outdoors than in academics. He returned to Edinburgh to study medicine, settling down to private practice in Portsmouth in 1884. Waiting for the patients he hoped would produce a flourishing practice, Doyle whiled away time writing fiction. His published efforts drew little attention until *A Study in Scarlet* appeared in *Beeton's Christmas Annual* (1887); from then on his medical practice became secondary to his literary career.

Doyle did not seek to produce high art; instead he felt comfortable turning out adventure and action stories that pleased his reading public. Writing primarily for popular magazines, he used recurring characters such as

Brigadier Gerard, a French soldier fighting for Napoleon, and Professor George Challenger, an irascible scientist, to create several series of stories and serialized novels. He also wrote historical novels such as *Micah Clarke* (1889), *The White Company* (1891), and *Sir Nigel* (1906), which reflect his national pride and patriotism as well as his allegiance to a chivalric code of honor and virtue.

Doyle's most famous literary creation, however, was the series of four novels and fifty-six short stories comprising the adventures of Sherlock Holmes. The Holmes stories were published in magazines over a forty-year period and collected regularly: *The Adventures of Sherlock Holmes* (1892), *The Memoirs of Sherlock Holmes* (1894), *The Return of Sherlock Holmes* (1905), *His Last Bow* (1917), and *The Case-Book of Sherlock Holmes* (1927). Except for *The Hound of the Baskervilles* (1902), the Holmes novels—*A Study in Scarlet* (1887), *The Sign of Four* (1890), *The Valley of Fear* (1915)—are generally less satisfactory than the short stories, perhaps reflecting Doyle's inability to sustain an extended suspenseful plot.

Doyle actively participated in the Boer War as a physician, and subsequently published defenses of British involvement—*The Great Boer War* (1900), *The War in South Africa* (1902)—for which he was knighted in 1902. His inability to accept the loss of several relatives in World War I caused him to turn to the spiritualist movement during his later years. *The History of Spiritualism* (1926) is well researched, but Doyle's other books about the occult, such as *The New Revelation* (1918), *The Vital Message* (1919), and *The Coming of the Fairies* (1922), made him the object of some ridicule. To the end, however, Doyle perpetuated in his life and writing the Victorian values of hard work, virtue, and absolute integrity, standards he hoped also to inculcate in his readers.

DON RICHARD COX

Bibliography

Carr, John Dickson. *The Life of Sir Arthur Conan Doyle.* 1949.

Doyle, Arthur Conan. *Memories and Adventures.* 1924.

Green, Richard Lancelyn and John Michael Gibson. *A Bibliography of A. Conan Doyle.* 1983.

Nordon, Pierre. *Conan Doyle.* 1966. trans. Frances Partridge.

See also MYSTERY AND DETECTIVE FICTION

· · · · ·

DRAMA CRITICISM

Every nineteenth-century periodical of consequence devoted space to dramatic criticism. Following traditions established by earlier writers—Lamb, Hazlitt, Leigh Hunt—Victorian journalists evolved idiomatic prose styles which struck a balance between straightforward reporting and casual impressionism. After 1840 the increasing number of theaters brought a plethora of new plays, adaptations, and revivals. Responsible commentators therefore attempted to alert the public to the bugbear of substandard stage entertainment. Some critics, like **G. H. Lewes** (1817–1878), studied performances by individual actors in order to discern the "artistic truth" of their interpretations; some, like Henry Morley (1822–1894), showed greater interest in the nature of specific productions, while others, such as **William Archer** (1856–1924), dwelt on the apparent discrepancy between "Life" as portrayed on the stage and life as commonly experienced.

Henry James took the view (*Galaxy*, May 1877) that an English audience was "intellectually much less appreciative" than its Parisian counterpart. But Victorian critics in general came down heavily on the dramatist or actor who underestimated the intelligence of the average playgoer. The sentimental and melodramatic tendencies of much midcentury drama, and the artificiality still present in the plays of Tom Taylor (1817–1880) and T. W. Robertson (1829–1871) prompted critics to demand a plausible stage realism; eventually even the "well-made" plays imported from France forfeited their earlier ascendency.

The "Renascence of the English Drama" for which **Henry Arthur Jones** (1851–1929) pleaded did not take place overnight; but public discussions of the techniques adopted by Ibsen and other "modernists" helped to induce a more enlightened attitude toward dramatic art. Why could not dramatists, the critics asked, mediate a mature view of human affairs such as was found in the work of major novelists? Of A. W. Pinero's (1855–1934) tragic masterpiece, William Archer wrote (May 31, 1893): "There is no illogical compromise in *Mrs. Tanqueray*, nothing impossible, nothing flagrantly improbable. . . . " That could hardly have been said of any play by a contemporary English author twenty or even ten years earlier.

George Bernard Shaw's and Archer's championing of the drama of ideas was, however, not universally followed. In the long battle of words over "Ibsenism," Clement Scott (1841–1904) took violent exception to the Norwegian playwright's "repulsive" subject matter. Other controversies of the period concerned the legitimacy of censorship, the status of contemporary drama "as literature," and the extent to which the state should subsidize the theater.

E. D. MACKERNESS

Bibliography

Archer, William. *About the Theatre*. 1886.

Kaminsky, Alice R. *George Henry Lewes as Literary Critic*. 1968.

Morley, Henry. *The Journal of a London Playgoer*. 1974. Ed. Michael R. Booth.

Nagler, A. M., ed. *A Source Book in Theatrical History*. 1959.

Rowell, George, ed. *Victorian Dramatic Criticism*. 1971.

Schoonderwoerd, N. H. G. *J. T. Grein: Ambassador of the Theatre. 1862–1935*. 1963.

Shaw, George Bernard. *Our Theatres in the Nineties*. 1895; rpt. 1932.

· · · · ·

DRESSMAKERS see SEAMSTRESSES

· · · · ·

DRUGS AND PATENT MEDICINES

Until 1868 the sale of drugs was unrestricted, and they were freely available from a number of sources like any other commodity. There was, for example, a vigorous trade in **opium**-based preparations, which were used as home remedies for a variety of medical problems and also put to uses which were not strictly medical, such as quieting fractious babies. A large number of other drugs, many of them potentially dangerous, were easily obtainable either in their pure state (for making home remedies), compounded according to a recipe in the chemist's shop, or as proprietary medicines patented by their manufacturer.

Chemists and druggists were probably the largest source of supply for patent medicines. Although the function of chemists and druggists was theoretically to make up prescriptions written by qualified medical practitioners and to supply drugs to the public, they also gave medical advice to many people who could not afford doctors' fees, especially among the urban proletariat. The right of chemists and druggists to buy, compound, dispense, and sell drugs and medicines wholesale or retail had been established, both in practice and by act of Parliament, early in the nineteenth century. Their number increased substantially during the century. The Pharmaceutical Society of Great Britain was established in 1841. In 1852 the society compiled a register of chemists and druggists, associates, and students and was given the power to examine persons for registration.

Despite this move towards the professionalization of pharmacy, a great variety of drugs and patent medicines were available over the counter from other retail outlets. National and local newspapers, periodicals, billboards, and trade directories all carried advertisements for various remedies. Many of these nostrums (which often had alcohol as their chief ingredient) claimed to cure an astonishing variety of ills. For example, the Chartist newspaper the *Northern Star* published an advertisement in January 1851: "*Holloways Pills* for ague, asthma . . . Dysantary . . . Female irregularities . . . Scrofula . . . Venereal affections etc. etc. . . . @ 1/1, 2/9, 11/-, 22/- & 33/- each box."

The efficacy of Holloways Pills and similar remedies was at best dubious, at worst dangerous—although it should be remembered that the same could be said of orthodox medicine. Self-medication was widely practiced in all classes, but especially by the poor. Many patent remedies could also be obtained by mail, a method particularly favored by purchasers in search of an abortifacient ("female irregularity" was generally understood as a code for "delayed menstrual period") or a "cure" for venereal disease.

PHILIP SWAN

Bibliography

Berridge, Virginia and Griffith Edwards. *Opium and the People: Opiate Use in Nineteenth-Century England.* 1981.

Bynum, W. F. and Roy Porter, eds. *Medical Fringe and Medical Orthodoxy.* 1987.

Marland, H. "The Medical Activities of Mid-Nineteenth-Century Chemists and Druggists." In *Medical History*, vol. 31, pp. 415–439.

Matthews, Leslie G. *History of Pharmacy in Britain.* 1962.

Trease, George E. *Pharmacy in History.* 1964.

· · · · ·

DUBLIN

The Irish literary renaissance of the late nineteenth and early twentieth century immortalized Dublin as a dynamic cultural center. The Easter 1916 Rebellion, the first anticolonial revolt of the twentieth century, ignited revolutionary imaginations. Throughout the Victorian era, however, the first city of Ireland was stagnant, decaying, and slum ridden.

Located in the middle of the eastern coast of **Ireland** on the Irish sea, Dublin was founded about 841 by Danes who saw the Liffey estuary as a potential trading center. In 1170 the Normans captured the city and held it in the name of Henry II. Dublin Castle, built in the early thirteenth century, remained the bastion of English rule in Ireland for seven hundred years. The religious wars of 1640 and 1690 left Dublin in a state of decay. But in the

eighteenth century it grew in population, trade, and manufacturing, and became the seat of an independent Parliament. By the end of the century Dublin had seen a remarkable renaissance. Public buildings, fine houses, broad streets, and parks were built in elegant Georgian style and Dublin became a thriving cultural city.

The Act of Union (1800) which established the United Kingdom marked the beginning of Dublin's decline. Once political power and influence had moved to Westminster, the city lost attraction for many among the aristocracy and gentry. About 100 peers and 300 commoners from the Irish Parliament left, along with their families and supporters and the tradespeople and shopkeepers who catered to their needs. They were replaced to a degree by a professional class of barristers and bureaucrats who carried out Dublin Castle's governmental and administrative duties, but the city was unable to recover from the exodus.

Dublin was slow to enter the industrial age. Alien rule, penal legislation, racial and religious conflict, and more than a century of trade restrictions on native Irish industry hindered economic development. A disastrous land tenure system and poverty-stricken peasantry made it impossible for the city to profit from the hinterland. So while most Victorian cities were experiencing rapid industrial growth and increasing population, Dublin was undergoing industrial decline and demographic stagnation. Without leadership and capital, Irish woolens, silk, linen, and other industries were unable to compete. The general social and political unrest that was always present to varying degrees in Ireland also discouraged English capitalists.

By the mid-nineteenth century Dublin had acquired the characteristics that distinguished it during the Victorian period: low employment, overcrowding, unsanitary housing, and widespread poverty. The employment opportunities that did exist were largely for unskilled laborers, especially with steamship companies, building contractors, coal merchants, and the railways. The most distinguished business in Dublin was the Guiness brewing company, which claimed the largest output of any brewery in the world and employed at least 2,000 workers. Other avenues of employment were in distilling, printing, the clothing trades, and domestic service. The severe lack of industry and skilled labor made the workforce extremely vulnerable to victimization by employers. Men and women suffered long hours and low wages; the loss of a job meant emigration or the workhouse.

Whether organized or not, the working class of the Irish capital had little bargaining power. Yet throughout the nineteenth and early twentieth centuries many workers continued to press for better working conditions and trade union rights. However, it was not until James Larkin founded the Irish Transport and General Workers Union in 1911 that Dublin workers became disciplined and militant.

Low employment and depressed wages meant that most Dubliners lived in the worst slums in Europe. The task of civic improvement fell to the Dublin Corporation, which acted as the city's municipal council. Its local powers came from the Municipal Corporations Act (1840) and the Dublin Improvement Act (1849). Despite extensive jurisdiction the Dublin Corporation faced enormous obstacles. Most of the well-to-do had moved to the suburbs, leaving Dublin with a diminished rate base. The Corporation was also considered by many to be the only representative Irish institution and thus often became bogged down in nationalistic controversies. By the end of the century there had been only very modest improvements in streets, lighting, and sewers. Perhaps the single advantage of Dublin's lack of industrial progress was that its eighteenth-century public buildings and houses were spared from a building craze. The city entered the twentieth century with Georgian grace, although a bit tattered.

Although Dublin lacked all the conventional features of a leading city, it still acted as the headquarters for nationalist organizations from **Daniel O'Connell**'s Catholic Association to Patrick Pearse's Easter 1916 rebels. It was also the center for the literary movement which included such artists as **William Butler Yeats**, James Joyce, John M. Synge, Sean O'Casey, A. E. (George Russell), and Lady Augusta Gregory, and was home to the Abbey Theatre, which was founded in 1899. Life in Dublin's slums lives on in the plays of O'Casey, and the character of its society has been forever captured in Joyce's *Dubliners* (1914). Robert in Joyce's play *Exiles* (1918)

sums up the history of Victorian Dublin when he classified its public statues: those with folded arms are pondering "How shall I get down?" and those with right arms outstretched seem to say "In my time the dunghill was so high."

EILEEN McMAHON

Bibliography

Daly, Mary E. *Dublin: The Deposed Capital: A Social and Economic History, 1860-1914.* 1984.

Harvey, John Hooper. *Dublin: A Study of Environment.* 1949.

Kain, Richard M. *Dublin in the Age of William Butler Yeats and James Joyce.* 1972.

O'Brien, Joseph V. *"Dear, Dirty Dublin": A City in Distress, 1899-1916.* 1982.

Somerville-Large, Peter. *Dublin.* 1979.

· · · · ·

DU MAURIER, GEORGE (1834-1897)

George Du Maurier was an artist, illustrator for *Punch*, minor novelist, and personality. Of French and English extraction, he was educated in England and studied painting on the Continent. Eye trouble forced him to turn to illustrating in black and white.

For years, Du Maurier was one of the leading contributors to *Punch*; his sketches were **caricatures** of fashionable London society. As a novelist, Du Maurier reflects his French background but also the influence of his adopted English world. *Peter Ibbetson* (1891) combined social satire with fantasy; Du Maurier presented it as the autobiography of an insane criminal. *Trilby* (1894), his greatest success, gave the reader a romantic version of the Latin Quarter in Paris and the figure of Svengali, now used as a type name. *The Martian* (1898), which deals with the dream of a Martian as he visits earth, suggests the kind of fiction characterized by H. G. Wells.

Du Maurier was part of the literary and artistic circles of London and knew Thackeray, Eliot, Whistler, and many others. He was the father of actor Gerald Du Maurier and grand-father of novelist Daphne Du Maurier.

DENNIS GOLDSBERRY

Bibliography

Du Maurier, Daphne. *The Du Mauriers*. 1937.

Wood, T. Martin. *George Du Maurier*. 1913.

· · · · ·

DURHAM, EARL OF (1792–1840)

Born John George Lambton, the first earl of Durham was one of the major architects of the Reform Act of 1832. He was also author of the Durham *Report* which called for a measure of colonial self-government in British North America.

Lambton's father died when he was only five. His inheritance was truly magnificent—over 30,000 coal-rich acres in the north of England. Elected to the House of Commons in 1813, he sat for his home county of Durham until he entered the House of Lords upon being created a peer in 1828. He was associated with the Whig group centered around the second Earl Grey, whose daughter he married in 1816, a year after his first wife had died of tuberculosis. At this time his proposals for a wide extension of the franchise and other radical measures earned him the nickname "Radical Jack."

Durham joined Lord Grey's cabinet in November, 1830, as lord privy seal. As its most radical member, he served on a committee with **Lord John Russell** and two others which drafted the unsuccessful reform bill of 1831. A modified version was enacted as the Reform Act of 1832, though it did not include the secret ballot Durham advocated.

After revolts in Lower **Canada** (Quebec) and Upper Canada (Ontario) in 1837, Durham reluctantly accepted appointment as high commissioner and governor-general of the British provinces in North America with a view to solving the problems that had given rise to the revolts. Arriving in Quebec in May 1838, he resigned five months later, returned to England, and composed the *Report on the*

Affairs of British North America (1839), which called for the union of Upper and Lower Canada as a means of ending the strife and assimilating the French Canadians into a wholly British North America. He also recommended responsible government, a measure of self-government requiring that in internal affairs the governor general act on the recommendations of colonial representatives.

Though union was effected in 1840, and responsible government came within the next decade, Durham's direct influence has been questioned. By the time his *Report* was presented to Parliament, Durham was mortally ill; he succumbed to the tuberculosis that had already decimated his family in July 1840.

ROBERT S. FRASER

Bibliography

Cooper, Leonard. *Radical Jack: The Life of John George Lambton, First Earl of Durham*. 1959.

Coupland, R., ed. *The Durham Report: An Abridged Version with an Introduction and Notes*. 1945.

Martin, Ged. *The Durham Report and British Policy: A Critical Essay*. 1972.

New, Chester W. *Lord Durham: A Biography of John George Lambton. First Earl of Durham*. 1929.

Reid, Stuart J. *Life and Letters of the First Earl of Durham, 1792–1840*. 1906. 2 vols.

· · · · ·

EARLY ENGLISH SCHOLARSHIP AND CRITICISM

The nineteenth-century renaissance of Early English scholarship and criticism dates from the foundation of the Roxburghe Club (1812) and flourished in the works of Frederick James Furnivall (1825–1910) and Richard Morris (1833–1894), who founded the Early English Text Society (1864). This society supported the production of scholarly and critical editions of Early English works. Henry Sweet (1845–1912) produced *An Anglo-Saxon*

Reader (1876) and The Oldest English Texts (1885), and Walter W. Skeat (1835–1912) founded the English Dialect Society (1873) and produced An Etymological Dictionary (1882). Under Furnivall's editorship these scholars, joined by scores of others, produced 247 volumes of critical editions for the Early English Text Society between 1864 and Furnivall's death in 1910.

JOHN J. CONLON

Bibliography

Greenfield, Stanley. A Critical History of Old English Literature. 1965.

Heusinkveld, Arthur. A Bibliographical Guide to Old English. 1931.

Wrenn, Charles L. A Study of Old English Literature. 1967.

· · · · ·

EAST AFRICA

East Africa contained the British colonies Kenya, Uganda, Tanganyika (modern Tanzania), and Zanzibar.

Although Louis Leakey discovered the first traces of human life in the Olduvai gorge in Tanzania, little is known of the history of East Africa. The area is hot, semidesert in some places and dense jungles in others. The result has been thinly spread, often migrant populations.

Modern British interest in east Africa initially centered on the search for the source of the Nile. **Richard Burton**, John Henning Speke, and the Scots missionary, **David Livingstone**, explored the area around Victoria Falls. Burton and Speke "discovered" Lake Tanganyika and Speke returned to discover Lake Victoria. Then, with James Grant in 1862, he became the first white man to set eyes on the source of the Nile, which he named Ripon Falls. Twelve years later **Henry Stanley** circumnavigated Victoria Falls and then explored the Congo.

Trade, strategic and imperial interests, and the desire to "civilize" Africa all played a role in drawing the interests of European powers to Africa. It was the Congress of Berlin (1884–1885), however, which opened the "scramble

for Africa." King Leopold of Belgium had persuaded Stanley to return to the Congo to open the area to trade. Leopold's claim was disputed by France, Germany (which had claims in west, southwest, and east Africa), Britain, and Portugal. The Berlin Congress awarded the Congo to Leopold and divided east Africa between German and British spheres of influence. Italy, encouraged by the British (who feared French expansion from Algeria and Morocco), declared a protectorate over the Eritrean coast; France established a protectorate in the Jibuli area; and Britain proclaimed a protectorate over the Somaliland in the area around Berbera. In 1889, the Treaty of Uccialli gave Ethiopia to Italy. The treaty, however, was disputed by the Ethiopian emperor, Menelik II, who in 1896 defeated an Italian force at the battle of Adawa. Protocols in 1891 and 1894 settled the boundaries between Italian and British spheres of influence in the Somalis and in 1896 Menelik II signed a treaty with Britain recognizing those boundaries.

In central east Africa an Anglo-German agreement in 1886 divided their spheres of influence along a line from south of Mombasa, then north of Kilimanjaro to a point on the eastern shore of Lake Victoria. A British East Africa Association, created in 1887 to compete with the German East Africa Company, was transformed in 1888 into the Imperial British East Africa Company (IBEAC). The rivalry between the two companies resulted in an Anglo-German agreement in 1890. Zanzibar became a British protectorate and the Germans recognized British claims to the headwaters of the Nile. Britain thus maintained the area crucial for **Cecil Rhodes**'s dream of a British-controlled route from the Cape to Cairo.

In the early 1890s, the IBEAC's caravan leaders were diverted to Buganda because of an attempted coup against the Buganda ruler, Mwanga, in 1888. Frederick (later Lord) Lubard and his successors interposed themselves between the Muslim and Christian factions in the conflict and were thus able to establish control over the most powerful African regime in the interior. Then, when the IBEAC was forced by impending bankruptcy to withdraw, a British imperial protectorate was established in 1894 over "Uganda." Since it would have been manifestly impossible for the Uganda commissioner to exercise control

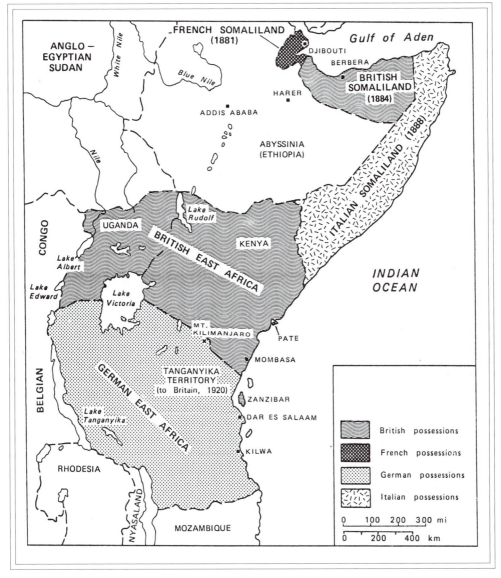

FRENCH SOMALILAND (1881)

ANGLO-EGYPTIAN SUDAN

Gulf of Aden

DJIBOUTI
BERBERA

BRITISH SOMALILAND (1884)

HARER

ADDIS ABABA

ABYSSINIA (ETHIOPIA)

ITALIAN SOMALILAND (1888)

CONGO

UGANDA

Lake Rudolf

BRITISH EAST AFRICA

KENYA

INDIAN OCEAN

Lake Albert

Lake Edward

Lake Victoria

MT. KILIMANJARO

PATE

MOMBASA

BELGIAN

GERMAN EAST AFRICA

TANGANYIKA TERRITORY (to Britain, 1920)

ZANZIBAR

DAR ES SALAAM

Lake Tanganyika

KILWA

RHODESIA

NYASALAND

MOZAMBIQUE

British possessions
French possessions
German possessions
Italian possessions

0   100   200   300 mi
0   200   400   km

British Possessions in East Africa.

over the coast, a boundary was drawn along the Rift Valley to separate Uganda from the British East African Protectorate. That line eventually became the boundary between Kenya and Uganda. Zanzibar became a direct protectorate in 1890. After World War I (in 1921), German East Africa became a British mandate as Tanganyika.

Some African peoples welcomed their European rulers from the outset, seeing them as allies who could help them defend or even enlarge their interests against their rivals. More often, however, the Europeans encountered violent opposition, frequently couched in religious terms. In an attempt to quell that resistance, British policy was to rule indirectly through indigenous chiefs as far as possible. The **slave trade** was ended, and the expansion of education, health services, and communications created a native elite which spearheaded the movements for independence following World War II.

JOAN MICKELSON GAUGHAN

Bibliography

Bennett, George. *Kenya: A Political History*. 1963.

Bennett, Norman. *Arab Versus European: Diplomacy and War in Nineteenth-Century East Central Africa*. 1986.

Flint, John E., ed. *The Cambridge History of Africa*, vol. 5. 1976.

Haight, Mabel V. *European Powers and South-East Africa*. Rev. ed., 1967.

Marsh, Zoe and G. W. Kingsnorth. *A History of East Africa: An Introductory Survey*. 4th ed., 1972.

Ogot, Bethwell A. *Zamani: A Survey of East African History*. New ed., 1974.

. . . . .

EAST INDIA COMPANY

Chartered by Queen Elizabeth I on December 31, 1600, as the Governor and Company of Merchants of London trading with the East Indies, the company was initially formed to share in the East Indian spice trade, then a monopoly of the Dutch and Portuguese. In the mid-eighteenth and nineteenth centuries, however, "John Company" served as the agent of British imperialism in India and became active in the Persian Gulf, Southeast Asia, and China.

Beginning in 1612 the company's servants were granted general permission by the Mogul emperors to establish factories (enclaves containing warehouses and residences), first at Surat (moved to Bombay in 1668) and then at Madras and Calcutta. The bulk of its trade was in indigo, saltpeter, spices, cotton, silk, and tea.

Following Robert Clive's defeat of the French-backed nawab of Bengal at the battle of Plessey in 1757, the company governed Bengal. The Regulating Act (1773) and William Pitt's India Act (1784) established parliamentary control over Indian policy through a governor-general and a Board of Control responsible to Parliament.

In 1813 the company's monopoly on Eastern trade was ended but it remained the agent for the British government of India until the Sepoy Mutiny in 1857. The British India Act of 1858 deprived the company of all remaining political power, and the company itself was dissolved in 1873.

JOAN MICKELSON GAUGHAN

Bibliography

Brown, Hilton. *The Sahibs*. 1948.

Edwardes, Michael. *British India, 1772-1947*. 1967.

Spear, Thomas G. P. *India: A Modern History*. 1972.

See also INDIA; INDIAN MUTINY

. . . . .

EASTLAKE, ELIZABETH RIGBY
(1809-1893)

The daughter and sister of obstetric physicians, Elizabeth Rigby lived in Edinburgh, traveled in Germany, and lived for two years in Russia with a married sister. In 1841 she published *A Residence on the Shores of The Baltic* and from 1842 became the sole female contributor to the *Quarterly Review*. In 1849, she married the painter Charles Lock Eastlake, keeper and then director of the National Gallery (1843-1847, 1855-1865) and president of the Royal Academy (1855-1865). She translated and edited several histories and surveys of art and was herself an amateur painter.

She is best known as a writer, however, for a single article in *Quarterly Review*, "Vanity Fair . . . Jane Eyre . . . Governesses" (December 1848), which censures Charlotte Brontë's novel for its "coarseness" and "laxity of tone," and calls it "pre-eminently an anti-Christian composition," and its heroine "the personification of an unregenerate and undisciplined spirit."

Her other signal role in Victorian England was as confidante to Effie Gray Ruskin during her separation from **John Ruskin** in 1854. She had met the Ruskins in 1850 and, soon after, Effie Ruskin is supposed to have disclosed to Lady Eastlake that her marriage to John Ruskin in 1848 had never been consummated. Lady Eastlake encouraged and reassured Effie Ruskin through visits and letters during the Ruskins's separation, the annulment of their marriage, and Effie's subsequent marriage to painter John Millais. The contrast between her conventional piety and shock at Jane Eyre's boldness and the liberalism of her views on Effie Ruskin's unhappy marital condition and romance with Millais is a felicitous example of Victorian duality.

ZELDA AUSTEN

Bibliography

Lutyens, Mary. *The Ruskins and the Grays.* 1972.

Smith, Charles Eastlake, ed. *Journals and Correspondence of Lady Eastlake.* 1895.

· · · · ·

ECONOMICS

The Victorian era, with its adulation of "progress," was a fertile period in the history of economic thought. **John Stuart Mill**'s *Principles of Political Economy* (1848) remained the basic textbook in both British and American universities until 1900. Mill's orthodoxy was criticized, most obviously by Karl Marx (1818–1883). The first volume of *Capital* (1867) was, however, not translated into English until 1887, and remained peripheral to mainstream British economics. W. S. Jevons's *Theory of Political Economy* (1871) introduced concepts—labeled revolutionary by some—that have come to dominate modern economics. Alfred Marshall (1842–1924) intended his long-awaited *Principles of Economics* (1890) to be a synthesis of Mill's classical and Jevons's neoclassical economics.

Mill united Malthusian population doctrine, the **Utilitarian** philosophy derived from Jeremy Bentham (1748–1832), a belief in the virtues of the free market and free trade, and a solid faith in a well-managed gold standard with the recognition that although laws of production are bound by the state of technology, laws of distribution—how much of the product is to be consumed and by whom—can be determined by society's laws and customs. Despite the implications of parodies of political economy, such as Dickens's *Hard Times* (1854) with its "Gradgrind School," Mill was a reformer. For example, he saw the Malthusian claim that food supplies must necessarily grow at a slower rate than population as a warning that, properly heeded, could ensure a less disastrous future for the working classes. To this end, he was arrested at seventeen for distributing birth control information—an action consistent with Mill's view that "political economy" should be part of a compulsory education, supported but not provided by the state.

Mill supported the trade union movement. He urged the revision of inheritance laws, and claimed that, if adopted, his proposals would eliminate all large fortunes in two generations. The "Ten Hours Bill" (1847), which Mill did not support, was an instance where Mill the feminist and Mill the humanitarian came into conflict. Limiting hours of work was in the public interest, but since the bill excluded women from factories it implied that women, unlike men, were not "free agents." Mill was sympathetic to the socialist ideas of Saint-Simon (1760–1825) and Fourier (1772–1837), but traced the social costs of capitalism to inadequate safeguards against abuse of property rights rather than to private property in itself. Mill was always conscious of the potential costs of eliminating financial incentives. He retained his faith in the market, claiming that laissez faire should be the general rule, with proposals for government interference considered on an individual basis. His opposition to the Corn Laws (repealed in 1846) stands as evidence.

The demise of classical economics is usually dated from Mill's recantation of the "wages-fund" doctrine in response to W. T. Thornton's *On Labour* (1869). This doctrine, in its simplest form, states that there exists a fund of money capital available for the wages of labor. Since labor is to be fully employed (a feature of classical thought known as Say's Law), the average wage can be calculated by dividing the "fund" by the number of workers. This stringent formulation leaves no room for unemployment, trade unions, or social intervention in the distribution of income. Mill's version was always more flexible. Nevertheless, his formal recantation was seen as undermining a pillar of orthodoxy, and it thereby opened the gate for innovations known collectively as the "Marginal Revolution."

Jevons's *Theory* (1871) presented ideas similar to those advocated by Carl Menger

(1840-1921) in Austria and Leon Walras (1834-1910) in Switzerland. Neoclassical economics focused on pricing and resource allocation with fixed supplies of labor, land, and capital, rather than on changes in the quantity and quality (and remuneration) of these factors of production over time. Capitalists, workers, and rentiers disappeared from the analysis, and were replaced by "economic agents" with the common goal of maximizing the "utility" or satisfaction they derived from the choices they made. Commodity prices were determined not simply by costs of production (as they ultimately were for Mill), but by the demand which depended upon subjective value consumers placed on one particular good relative to their alternative choices.

By the late 1880s Marxism (and Fabianism) began to animate the British labor union movement. Although the *Communist Manifesto* (1848) was published the same year as Mill's *Principles*, and *Capital* in 1867, neither Jevons nor Mill nor Marshall explicitly wrote in response to Marx's work. Marx did challenge orthodox economists, some of whom eventually read *Capital*, but it was a later generation of neoclassical writers rather than his close contemporaries who responded to his work.

Marx's economics, like Mill's, focused on the long-run declining rate of profit and the immiserization of the working classes. Unlike Mill, he rejected Malthusianism, and his cost-of-production theory of pricing was linked to a strict "labor theory of value" which was intended to show that the total amount of value produced by an economy was equal to the value of the labor used to produce it. The difference between the value produced by labor and the "value of labor time" which workers received as wages was "surplus value"—the source of the profit that accrued to capitalists. The greatest difference between Mill and Marx was that, according to Mill, the intelligent management of social institutions would preserve capitalism. According to Marx, the evolution of capitalism would cause increasing antagonism between the classes and worsening economic crises, ultimately bringing about its collapse. But Marx's economics was only one aspect of a much larger intellectual project, and he remained marginal to orthodox economics.

The Victorian era ended with the emergence of Marshall, whose greatest achievement was his explicit consideration of the time period. This made it possible for him to integrate classical and neoclassical thought, and to claim (contrary to Jevons) that there was nothing "revolutionary" about the latter. Jevons's short-run theory of pricing was compatible, according to Marshall, with long-run prices determined by costs of production, as Mill claimed.

Whether or not the transformation in economic thought during the 1870s was a "revolution" is a debate that has preoccupied historians of economics for decades, and it is still raging. Whatever the ultimate verdict, it cannot be denied that the Victorian period, and its policy issues, encouraged the rapid development of economic theory.

E. L. FORGET

Bibliography

Blaug, Mark. *Economic Theory in Retrospect.* 1985.

Hollander, Samuel. *The Economics of John Stuart Mill.* 1985. 2 vols.

Schumpeter, Joseph A. *History of Economic Analysis.* 1954.

· · · · ·

EDEN, EMILY (1797-1869)

Emily Eden wrote two society novels, *The Semi-Detached House* (1858) and *The Semi-Attached Couple* (1860), and the two-volume *Up the Country* (1866) based on her travels in India. Her *Portraits of the Princes and People of India* (1844) is a collection of watercolor sketches.

The Edens were neighbors and friends of William Pitt for whom Emily's father, William Eden, undertook several diplomatic missions. In 1818, Emily and her sister Fanny went to live in London with their brother George. In 1835 George, now Lord Auckland, was appointed governor-general of India. Emily, Fanny, and a nephew accompanied Auckland to Calcutta where, as they had in London, the sisters presided over Auckland's social obligations. In October 1837 the Edens and a vast entourage embarked on a diplomatic tour of India's northwest provinces which lasted until March 1840. Throughout the tour, in her letters and in her journal, Eden recorded her impressions of Indian people and places. This journal became *Up the Country*. Her *Portraits of the Princes and People of India* was also done on the tour. The Edens returned to London (and Auckland to the Admiralty) in 1842. His death in 1848 and Fanny's four months later deprived Emily of her two dearest friends. None of the three had ever married.

Her two novels give an unrivaled picture of early nineteenth-century Whig family life. Her style is easy, graceful, witty, and bears some resemblance, perhaps consciously, to Jane Austen's novels, especially *Pride and Prejudice*.

JOAN MICKELSON GAUGHAN

Bibliography

Dunbar, Janet. *Golden Interlude*. 1955.

· · · · ·

EDINBURGH

The capital of Scotland, "the modern Athens," Edinburgh, which is described as a "pre-eminently romantic" city, is built on a series of hills close to the Firth of Forth and dominated by Edinburgh Castle, dating from the twelfth century. Other notable features of the city include Calton Hill, site of the Royal and City Observatories and the Napoleonic War memorial; the Old Town ("seemingly lawless picturesqueness"), containing St. Giles Church, Parliament House, and the University; the New Town, of formal Georgian design and originally separated from the Old Town by a loch, now filled in as the Prince Street Gardens containing the Scott memorial; and Arthur's Seat, a basaltic crag dominating the city and lying above the Royal Palace of Holyrood. As a former capital reduced in stature and prestige, Edinburgh was a center of Scottish nationalist sentiment.

Edinburgh grew greatly in the Victorian era, from approximately one square mile in 1856, to more than seventeen in 1901, as the suburbs expanded and the Old and New Towns incorporated the surrounding land and the seaport of Leith. The population (as judged by the parliamentary district) grew from 138,000 in 1841 to 197,000 in 1871 and 316,000 in 1901.

By an act of Parliament in the wake of the Reform Bill, the city was governed from 1833 by a town council consisting of thirty-one members (increased to fifty in 1885) elected by parliamentary electors, to which were added a deacon of trades (elected by the trades councils) and a dean of guild (elected from the brethren of the guilds). The councilors elected from their number a lord provost and four bailies (later increased to six and then to seven). The council's responsibilities extended beyond the usual provision of municipal services to an active role in the administration of Edinburgh University (most of the professorships were in the power of the council), the City Observatory, the Edinburgh High School, the city churches of the **Church of Scotland**, and various cultural and educational organizations. A city police existed from 1805, supplanting an ineffective town guard dating from the sixteenth century. The most important increase in the town establishment came in 1862, with the appointment of the first medical officer for health in Scotland.

Side by side with the civic structure were remnants of the ancient national government. Joined with England to form the United Kingdom by the Act of Union of 1707, Scotland lost its Parliament but retained its judiciary. The supreme court, or Courts of Justice (dating from 1532), met in the Old Parliament House across the High Street from St. Giles Cathedral. The presence of a law school at the University, the administrative structure of the city and county, and the court system of the nation insured a good number of lawyers for Edinburgh, then as now. The Advocates' Library, one of the libraries of copyright deposit for Britain, was the best one in Scotland and the basis of the National Library.

In the nineteenth century, Edinburgh became the second city of Scotland in terms of population and economic activity, due to the rise of manufacturing in Glasgow. It nevertheless retained its position as the administrative, legal, medical, religious, cultural, and intellectual capital of Scotland, and was a strong financial center, the home office of the Bank of Scotland. Yet Victorian Edinburgh lived in the cultural shadow of the golden age of Enlightenment and Romantic Scotland, when that land was one of the great literary, philosophical, and scientific centers of the world. From the circle of poet Allan Ramsay in the early eighteenth century to the times of the *Edinburgh Review* and Walter Scott in the early nineteenth, Edinburgh's culture was unparalleled in Britain and the equal of any other country. Victorian Edinburgh felt itself an age of brass. Scott's death in 1832 put the seal on the previous age; eminent writers of Edinburgh would leave the city, rather than write about it.

The three greatest writers associated with Edinburgh in the Victorian era were Robert Louis Stevenson (1850-1894), James Barrie (1860-1937), and Arthur Conan Doyle (1859-1930). The first made Edinburgh more a home than the others, although it was the low life of Edinburgh that he wove into his fiction, rather than the prim bourgeois Edinburgh into which he was born. Alone of the three, Stevenson produced a book on the city, *Edinburgh, Picturesque Notes* (1879); like the others, he eventually left the city for good.

Edinburgh publishing remained brisk throughout the nineteenth century, especially in the house of William (1800-1883; lord provost of the city, 1865-1869) and **Robert Chambers** (1802-1871). The emphasis, however, turned to educational, reference, and especially medical books, rather than literature. Publishing was closely tied to the university, which had an international reputation, especially in philosophy, physics, and medicine. *The Scotsman* was the preeminent Victorian newspaper of the city, its influence felt throughout Scotland.

In Victorian times, the city's most striking feature was its suburban development. The suburbs leapfrogged into the surrounding countryside, following the train lines out from the city. Of interest among the many revival architectural styles of the suburban villa was the Scottish baronial style, looking back to castle architecture of the Scottish Middle Ages.

While the central city's look had been set by the slow development of Old Town, the Georgian planning of New Town, and the garden separating the two—all substantially complete by 1830—several downtown buildings date to the Victorian period. The National Gallery, National Portrait Gallery, and Antiquarian Museum were newly quartered in the nineteenth century. Assembly Hall, the meeting place of the General Assembly of the (Presbyterian) Church of Scotland, was also used as a church. Erected in 1843, it embodied the Gothic revival in the city. The other religious groups followed suit. New College, the seminary and college of the Free Church of Scotland, was founded in 1843 and built in Gothic revival style. St. Mary's Cathedral (1879), designed in early Gothic, carried the style to Scottish episcopacy. The Walter Scott memorial, finished in 1846, likewise used the Gothic, in a magnificent spire that dominates the central garden of the city. Other revival styles predominated in other settings. The Medical School was separated from the rest of the university and housed in new Italian Renaissance style buildings. Edinburgh also saw the construction of a number of large hospitals in the nineteenth century, notably the Royal Infirmary.

In the late nineteenth century, Edinburgh tastes often ran to renovation of older structures, hearkening back to an earlier era of greater power and prestige. One of the major projects was St. Giles Cathedral (restored in 1873-1883, at the urging of William Chambers), the closest thing that existed to a national church, tradition ascribing to it the beginning of the Protestant Reformation in Scotland.

Tenements were a constant feature of Edinburgh, predating the industrial revolution. Edwin Chadwick (1800-1890), the Victorian health reformer, characterized the slums of Edinburgh and Glasgow as "the most wretched account of the stationary population" that he had found. The poorer residents of the city lived in one- or two-room houses or apartments carved out of large, poorly lit, and poorly ventilated buildings. The collapse of a seven-story tenement on the Edinburgh High Street on November 24, 1861 caused a public outcry. In 1862, the town council appointed Dr. Henry Duncan Littlejohn (1828-1914) as the medical officer for health. Littlejohn had extensive powers to promote the public health of the city, wider than any provided by other British cities. Working in conjunction with Lord Provost William Chambers, Littlejohn cleared great numbers of slum tenements. The tenements proved persistent, however. In the later nineteenth century, they followed the spread of the suburbs, pressing against the garden communities of the outskirts, while freeing up the congested parts of the very center of the city.

PAUL THEERMAN

Bibliography

Best, G. F. A. "Another Part of the Island." In H. J. Dyos and Michael Wolff, eds., *The Victorian City: Images and Reality*. 1973.

Catford, Edwin Francis. *Edinburgh: The Story of a City*. 1975.

Gifford, John, et al. *Edinburgh*. 1984.

McLaren, Moray. *Stevenson and Edinburgh: A Centenary Study*. 1950.

Minto, Charles Sinclair. *Victorian and Edwardian Edinburgh from Old Photographs*. 1973.

Royle, Trevor. *Precipitous City: The Story of Literary Edinburgh*. 1980.

. . . . .

EDUCATING THE DEAF AND BLIND

Systematic education for children with handicaps began at the end of the eighteenth century and continued to develop, under the influence of private philanthropy, through the nineteenth century. Toward the end of the Victorian period specialized education became a state responsibility. An 1889 royal commission report pragmatically pointed out that adequate education would ease the expense of supporting handicapped adults in the workhouse, and an act of 1893–1894 made education compulsory for deaf and blind children between the ages of seven and sixteen.

The first British schools for the blind were opened in Liverpool (1791) and London (1799). The Victorian period was marked by debates over the content of specialized education and the competing claims of various methodologies. The system developed by Louis Braille was adopted in some schools from about midcentury, while others preferred the

raised alphabet based on simplified roman letters that was invented by Englishman William Moon (1818–1894). Moon also founded the London Home Teaching Society (1873), which brought instruction to blind children in their homes. Some institutions emphasized vocational skills (including the traditional brushmaking and piano tuning), while others promoted adequate aids so that blind adults could engage in intellectual professions. There was also debate over whether blind children should or should not have sighted teachers. A Royal Normal College for the Blind was in operation by the last quarter of the century, and S. S. Forster became principal of a college at Worcester where three out of four staff were blind. Between 1866–1896 students from Forster's college went on to achieve four firsts and seven honours degrees at universities.

Education of the deaf made somewhat slower progress, since it took a long time to recognize that the speechlessness of children born without hearing was not a sign of mental retardation but rather a consequence of their inability to learn language through imitating sounds and words. A systematic sign language was developed in France during the eighteenth century and toward the end of the century Thomas Braidwood (1715–1806) opened the first school for the deaf in Great Britain. By 1870 there were fourteen residential schools for deaf children and a fully developed debate over teaching through the oral method (emphasizing lip reading and the production of speech) or the sign and manual method, which allows earlier communication but impairs interactions between deaf people and those who do not share their language. Midcentury schools generally used a mixture of the two methods. After the baroness M. A. de Rothschild and others founded the Association for the Oral Instruction of the Deaf and Dumb (1871), teaching through lip reading gradually became the accepted method of instruction in the United Kingdom. Vocational training for the deaf tended to emphasize draftsmanship for boys and, for girls, laundry work (which was notoriously ill paid and physically demanding).

After the Elementary Education (Blind and Deaf) Act (1893–1894) made education compulsory for deaf and blind children, additional residential and day schools were founded, and those that had previously been supported by philanthropy generally became part of the state system.

JOHN REYNOLDS

· · · · ·

EDUCATION, ADULT

Self-help, evangelical religion, radical movements, and the generally well-intentioned (if sometimes self-serving) middle-class desire to impose order and create a work force suited to a more complex society led to the establishment of Bible study groups, Owenite "Halls of Science," **mechanics' institutes**, adult night schools, working men's and working women's colleges, and a great variety of other educational projects including, toward the end of the century, university extension classes.

Among the working classes most of those adults who could read had no more than two or three years' schooling; even in 1880, when elementary education became compulsory, attendance was required only from ages seven to ten. Those who had not learned to read were served, early in the century, in self-help groups organized by radical workers and in adult Sunday schools run by Nonconformists who valued private reading of the Scriptures. By midcentury there were also evening schools; the 1851 census counted 1,545 of them in England and Wales, with 39,783 students. Evening schools generally charged a penny a week and provided instruction in arithmetic and perhaps geography and history as well as reading and writing.

Throughout the period there was a tension between radical, reforming, or workers' self-improvement groups and the middle class that provided most organized adult education. The middle class often saw education as a moral good in itself, while workers tended to want practical skills. Like the mechanics' institutes, adult schools often hoped to reach manual laborers but found that most students came from the artisan and lower middle classes. The London Working Men's College was founded in 1854, largely through the efforts of Christian socialists, with F. D. Maurice as principal. It was open to all men over sixteen who were competent in reading, writing,

and basic arithmetic, and the founders intended to provide a liberal education in the broadest tradition; the name "college" was deliberately chosen to imply a community of teachers and students. In the early years the teachers—all volunteers—included F. J. Furnival (who taught English grammar), John Ruskin, D. G. Rossetti, Charles Kingsley, George Grove, Leslie Stephen, and Frederic Harrison. Thomas Hughes supervised the boxing class. About half of the students, however, were small craftsmen, and the rest were clerks and shopworkers; and the college found it necessary to add both an elementary class (for basic literacy) and, later, commercial and technical subjects. The College for Working Women, established in 1874 by a women's committee headed by Frances Martin, included practical subjects from the outset; shop assistants, domestic servants, milliners, and other working women were encouraged to improve their skills and seek better employment.

In the latter part of the century the university extension movement provided courses for adults in a number of towns and cities. The idea was originally suggested by **Anne Jemima Clough** to the royal commission investigating secondary schooling in 1866. In the following year Clough and Josephine Butler persuaded a fellow of Trinity College, Cambridge, to give lecture courses in four cities. Although open to any adult able to pay the fees, the courses were primarily attended by schoolteachers and other ambitious young women for whom no adequate secondary or higher education was available. The movement gained official recognition and support from Cambridge in 1873 and Oxford in 1878.

SALLY MITCHELL

Bibliography

Harrison, John F. C. *Living and Learning, 1790–1960.* 1961.

Kelly, Thomas. *A History of Adult Education in Great Britain.* 1962.

———. *A Select Bibliography of Adult Education in Great Britain.* 1952.

· · · · ·

EDUCATION, ELEMENTARY

Until 1870, England and Wales had no national system of education. Elementary education was provided primarily by religiously affiliated educational societies and paid for by parents and charitable subscribers. England lagged behind other European countries partly because of the British reluctance to compel parents to send children to school but mostly because prolonged political squabbles over the role of religious education stalled parliamentary attempts to establish a national system.

It was clear long before 1870 that state-supported education was inevitable. Utilitarians supported mass education as a means of inculcating middle-class values in the working class, thus ensuring social order. British industry increasingly required a literate, numerate work force. Humanitarians argued that some degree of formal education should be a British birthright.

British education at the beginning of the century was uncentralized. Local authorities, usually parishes, provided for the destitute with workhouses and industrial schools. **Ragged schools**, begun by philanthropists and organized in the Ragged School Union (1844) continued to provide charitable education until the 1870s. Rural areas often boasted craft "dame" schools, where children worked at cottage industries like straw-plaiting and lacemaking and listened to the occasional perfunctory reading of the Bible; children who attended these schools contributed some of their earnings to its upkeep. The **Sunday School** Society (founded 1785) flourished, providing the poor with reading and sometimes writing instruction well into the century; by 1851, over two million students were enrolled. Middle-class children attended private schools and paid fees, while most upper-class children were educated at home, boys only until they were old enough for boarding school.

Two religiously affiliated societies, the National Society for Promoting the Education of the Poor in the Principles of the Church of England (1811) and the British and Foreign Schools Society (1808), took on the bulk of the task of educating working-class children for most of the nineteenth century. They

could afford to run large-scale programs because they used the new monitorial system of teaching, developed originally by Andrew Bell in India. This system posited a school where students were grouped by ability; the top group would learn from a teacher, then divide to teach the lesson to students in lower classes. The National Society used Bell's method, while the British Society adopted a version especially modified for English students by Joseph Lancaster. The system was cheap because one teacher could instruct large numbers of students, and the mechanical, oppressive quality of learning was not thought to be a disadvantage, as it taught children orderliness and respect, qualities desirable in the working-class adults they were to become.

By 1833, the government had begun giving small grants to aid the societies in building schools and later in training teachers. In 1839, the first government agency for education was established, the Educational Committee of the Privy Council Office, with **James Kay-Shuttleworth** (1804–1877) as its secretary. The most important government figure of the century in English education, Kay-Shuttleworth instituted government inspection of schools that received grants and in 1846 started the pupil-teacher program to counteract the shortage and poor quality of elementary teachers. Pupil-teachers were promising students who stayed on in their elementary schools to teach and were themselves tutored by the senior teachers; eventually they competed for places in training colleges to become full-fledged teachers.

Meanwhile, the educational societies struggled for dominance. The National Society had the support of Anglicans and Conservatives, while the British Society appealed to Nonconformists and Radicals. The Wesleyans had schools of their own and in 1847 the Catholic Poor School Society was formed. The question of how much educational autonomy should be relinquished in return for government grants became a primary concern. The Voluntaryist movement (1843) successfully raised money for schools that accepted neither government money nor controls until it foundered in 1867.

The difficulty over government controls centered on religious education. Though many areas contained several schools of different affiliations, others had only a single school. If a child's religious background differed from that of the school, the government wanted to ensure the child's right to refuse sectarian religious training as a matter of conscience. The scheme adopted in 1831 by the British government for Irish elementary education had combined non-sectarian religious training for the school as a whole, with optional sectarian instruction given by clergy to those students who desired it. The government hoped that such a system might be instituted in England, but the National Society refused to acknowledge that religious instruction might be separated from any other educational activity, and the other societies feared that the National Society's influence would induce Parliament to promote Anglican instruction over other religious training.

There was also the question of what curriculum was most beneficial to the working-class child. The Newcastle Commission argued in 1861 that the government should advance the teaching of rudimentary skills in the basic subjects of reading, writing, and arithmetic. Accordingly, in 1862, Robert Lowe introduced the Revised Code, which tied government grants to annual examination results in these three areas. The system, popularly known as "payment by results," standardized previously varied elementary curricula, as schools that had stressed crafts, domestic subjects, drawing, applied science, and other academic subjects deemphasized them to concentrate more on those that produced revenue. Other organizations soon offered grants for some additional subjects; the Department of Science and Art, for instance, increased the amount of its support for the study of science. Though the Revised Code was universally disliked, it was not wholly dismantled until 1895.

The advances in pedagogic theory of the nineteenth century, with the exception of the sublimely pragmatic monitorial system, were centered mostly on infant schools. The theories of Johann Pestalozzi, a Swiss teacher, were particularly influential. He believed that education should be developmental, drawing out the inherent abilities of children by means of contact with the concrete sensory environment; he pioneered the object lesson, in which students acquired information by asking and answering questions about an object

presented by the teacher. Object lessons were popular in England, but undersupplied teachers all too often had to make do with describing an object rather than producing it for the class, negating the effect Pestalozzi had intended. Robert Owen and Samuel Wilderspin, among others, extended Pestalozzian theories in their own English infant schools. Later in the century, Friedrich Froebel's German kindergartens were emulated. The New Code of 1871 raised the age of children undergoing examination for grants to seven, so infant schools maintained innovative curricula after many elementary schools abandoned them.

Education for middle- and upper-class children also became more standardized as the century progressed. Increased competition for places in public and grammar schools, due largely to rising middle-class expectations and to educational reforms at these schools, produced more preparatory schools and made it less common for children to be educated at home. Girls' education became more substantial as socioeconomic conditions changed; no longer was early marriage a near-certainty, and women had to consider finding employment, whether for support or occupation. Greater opportunities in higher education for women produced more high schools, often staffed by university women, and thus more feeder schools for girls at the elementary level. Though domestic subjects and "accomplishments" were still stressed, academic subjects at a high level were increasingly available. Coeducation was common in Scottish parochial schools and in working-class schools, but grammar and preparatory schools remained largely single-sex. Infant schools were coeducational as a matter of course.

From 1870, the Elementary Education Act, sponsored by **W. E. Forster**, provided national elementary education in England and Wales. The demand for such education had increased steadily through the century, particularly as government limits on child labor minimized the economic value of a child kept out of school. Voluntary schools were not always adequately distributed, and before 1870 the government had no authority to set up schools of its own where they were needed. Repeated efforts to pass educational acts foundered on two issues: the conscience clause and the process by which rates would finance schools, for if schools were supported by local rates, local boards would insist on controls unacceptable to many voluntary schools. When the act was finally passed, it substituted local rate aid for the private charitable contributions that had filled out the voluntary schools' budgets in the past and established local school boards; schools that chose to remain voluntary were excluded from rate aid, but continued to receive grant money. In 1880 education was made compulsory until the age of ten.

In many cases, poorer children attended the recently created board schools while more affluent children continued to patronize denominational schools. Better distribution of educational resources was possible once the government had the power to create or close schools. Some curricular innovation took place, particularly in higher-grade voluntary schools, where students sometimes stayed until the age of fourteen or fifteen and studied subjects similar to those found in grammar schools. In general, the school-leaving age rose. As the century ended, British attention shifted to secondary education, which was to be made universally accessible in England with the Balfour Act of 1902.

LAURA NOVO

Bibliography

Ball, Nancy. *Educating the People.* 1983.

Blyth, W. A. L. *English Primary Education: A Sociological Description.* 1965. 2 vols.

Digby, Anne and Peter Searby. *Children, School and Society in Nineteenth Century England.* 1981.

Gardner, Philip W. *The Lost Elementary Schools of Victorian England: The People's Education.* 1984.

Horn, Pamela. *Education in Rural England 1800–1914.* 1978.

Hurt, J. S. *Elementary Schooling and the Working Classes, 1860–1918.* 1979.

Murphy, James. *The Education Act, 1870: Text and Commentary.* 1972.

Sutherland, Gillian. *Policy-Making in Elementary Education 1870–1895.* 1973.

See also NONCONFORMITY; TEACHERS' EDUCATION AND TRAINING
. . . . .

EDUCATION, HIGHER

The nineteenth century witnessed the transformation of British higher education. A number of new institutions joined **Oxford**, **Cambridge**, and the Scottish universities. The curriculum became more modern with an increasing emphasis on science and modern languages. Especially at the ancient universities, the system of governance experienced considerable change. Finally, a number of nonuniversity educational institutions, notably the **mechanics' institutes**, also grew up in the second half of the century.

Until the period after the Napoleonic Wars, the ancient universities in England (Oxford and Cambridge) and the institutions of higher education in Scotland enjoyed an uncontested reign. Their monopoly ended in 1826 when Lord Brougham and several of his Whig allies in Parliament established the University of London. In fact, the "university" lacked a true charter and could not confer degrees. However, it provided the metropolis with university-level instruction at considerably lower cost than any other institution and required no religious tests. The Tories, led by the duke of Wellington, established a similar Tory-inclined institution in 1829. The educational anomaly achieved completion in 1836 when the king granted a royal charter to a new University of London which could examine students and award degrees, but which lacked any teaching faculty. Thus began the practice of awarding so-called "external degrees" that characterized the university for most of the nineteenth century. External degrees capped the educations of those who received instruction through night classes, correspondence courses, and the colleges that proliferated in the nineteenth-century metropolis until 1889 when an act of Parliament authorized the University of London to amalgamate several colleges and medical schools into a single body and to offer instruction.

The foundation of the University of London as an examining institution and the interests of many industrialists and civic officials in higher education spurred the creation of a number of so-called university colleges. These institutions offered instruction to students while the University of London conferred the degrees. The curricular model for most university colleges was the Scottish universities; and in addition to the traditional subjects such as classical languages, philosophy, and literature, they offered instruction in mathematics, sciences, and modern languages. Frequently these burgeoning universities amalgamated with already existing local medical colleges.

Owens College, Manchester, was the most illustrious of the university colleges. The Manchester merchant and philanthropist, John Owens (1790-1846) left an endowment of 100,000 pounds for the foundation of a college, and Owens College admitted its first class in 1851. It emphasized the sciences as well as more traditional disciplines in its curriculum, and did not require religious tests for admission. In 1871 an act of Parliament incorporated Owens College with the local Royal School of Medicine. By the late 1870s many Owens professors desired to escape from the restraints that the University of London's external degree requirements placed on their curriculum, and urged the college to seek full university status. Owens joined its efforts to those of several nearby institutions, and by a series of acts in the 1880s and 1890s, Parliament joined Owens College with university colleges in Liverpool, Leeds, and Sheffield to create Victoria University with degree-granting status. By 1904 the latter three institutions had become independent, and the title Victoria University attached solely to Manchester. Together with the Cavendish Laboratories at Cambridge, Manchester played a leading role in basic scientific research, especially in the epochal work on atomic structure.

A number of other university colleges appeared in the second half of the nineteenth century. The mother institution of the University of Bristol opened in 1876. The philanthropist Josiah Mason endowed Mason College of Science, the forerunner of the University of Birmingham, in 1880. University colleges were established also in Hull, Southhampton, Reading, Nottingham, Exeter, and Leicester.

The nineteenth century also witnessed the introduction of new subjects into the curriculum and the reform of university governance, especially at Oxford and Cambridge. At Cambridge examinations in classics, law, history, and the natural sciences supplemented the traditional tripos in mathematics. The Honours Schools at Oxford, which examined all students, began in 1800. Parliament intervened in the administration and internal governance of both institutions in 1854, 1856, and again in 1877. The abolition of religious tests opened the universities to students regardless of their faith. Likewise, most institutions opened scholarships and exhibitions to competition, allowing able students with meager financial resources to obtain a university education. A greater emphasis on science and engineering became evident in the last three decades of the nineteenth century as fear spread among politicians and in the industrial and business communities that Britain was losing ground to Germany and France.

As the century progressed women played an increasingly important role in higher education. Lectures for ladies at King's College in 1847 grew into Queen's College in 1848, and Bedford College for Women was established in 1849. Lady Margaret Hall, the first Oxford women's college, offered its first class in 1878, and Somerville (1879), St. Hugh's (1886), and St. Hilda's (1893) followed. At Cambridge, Girton (1869) and Newnham (1871) led the way, though women could not receive fully accredited degrees at Cambridge until after World War II. In the newer universities women achieved equality much earlier. Owens College removed all disabilities for women in 1871, and the University of London did likewise in 1878. Leeds admitted women on the same basis as men from its inception in 1874.

Nonuniversity institutions of higher education had an uneven history. Some, such as the old Dissenting Academies dating from the Restoration, entered a period of serious decline. After the universities eliminated religious tests, their raison d'être died. On the other hand, both the mechanics' institutes and university extension classes prospered. The former provided practical instruction for workers and artisans in subjects ranging from philosophy and history to economics and chemistry. Many of the most able young Oxford and Cambridge men made their ways in the cities in whole or in part through teaching for the university extension movement, which provided instruction for a diverse clientele.

Higher education spread in both quantity and quality during the nineteenth century, and Britain once again achieved a position of educational eminence in the sciences, especially in biology, physics, history, and philology. However, in technical and applied fields ground was lost to the Continent.

GEORGE MARIZ

Bibliography

Armytage, W. H. G. *The Civic Universities*. 1955.

Flexner, Abraham. *Universities: American, English, German*. 1930.

Kneller, George F. *Higher Learning in Britain*. 1955.

Mountford, Sir James. *British Universities*. 1966.

Truscot, Bruce. *Red Brick University*. 1943.

See also LEGAL PROFESSION; MEDICAL EDUCATION

. . . . .

EDUCATION, SECONDARY

In the first half of Queen Victoria's reign, the state began to encourage and regulate the education of young children. Little, however, was undertaken in the zone lying between elementary schools and universities until late in the century. Most secondary schools were in private hands, unregulated, and available only to those whose parents could pay fairly substantial fees.

Beginning in the Middle Ages, guilds and pious philanthropists had established and endowed grammar schools intended to provide a free education in classical languages for local boys. By the beginning of the nineteenth century most endowed grammar schools were in a sorry state; inflation had lowered the endowment's value and the curriculum was often limited to Greek and Latin—many schools did not teach writing or English or even mathematics. Other endowed grammar schools had ensured their survival by taking sons of the aristocracy and gentry as fee-paying boarders. By the opening of the nine-

teenth century a few (including Eton, Winchester, and Rugby) had become national institutions and were being referred to as "the great **public schools**."

Even in the best schools, however, the teaching and the living conditions were so inadequate that many families preferred private schooling for boys who intended to enter the universities. Those who could afford it hired a resident tutor. Anglican clergymen often supplemented their income by giving private lessons to one or two local boys or taking a few boarders into their household.

In addition, there were hundreds of private schools and academies. Some had been founded by Dissenters for the religious and secular education of their own children. The majority, however, were proprietary—that is, schools run for profit by an individual proprietor. Proprietary schools were free to introduce science and other curricular innovations, and some prepared boys for particular occupations. Most, however, were small, short-lived, and stunted by lack of funds and vision. Even in the best boarding schools, boys suffered under fagging, flogging, and scanty food; the worst are represented with (not undue) exaggeration in Dickens's *Nicholas Nickleby*. The few schools available for girls were almost all proprietary. Small boarding schools—often in fashionable neighborhoods—offered drawing, music, French, and other "accomplishments" to girls of the upper middle class; a limited number of day schools taught girls up to the age of fourteen or so, but generally the curriculum could be described as elementary rather than secondary. Most girls who were educated at all were taught by **governesses** or by parents.

Over the middle years of the century, the public schools gradually reformed themselves. Although retaining their emphasis on Greek and Latin, they added other subjects, organized boys to govern themselves through house systems and prefects, emphasized sports to absorb free time and adolescent energy, and established their preeminence as the schools of choice for those with the money and social background to gain admission. Enrollment pressures caused new "public" schools to be established, some of which made curricular innovations and taught modern subjects such as science and mathematics that provided a more suitable vocational preparation for many middle-class boys. Preparatory boarding schools for boys under the public school entry age of thirteen were also established. Initially they catered to parents who lived abroad due to service in the army, colonial government, and Britain's expanding commercial empire; but as the preparatory schools developed their own prestige, a boy destined for public school often learned from a governess (who also taught his sisters) until the age of eight or nine, after which he became a boarder at a prep school.

Local grammar schools were revived following the Endowed Schools Act (1869), which freed them from strict adherence to the terms of their charters (often dating from the Middle Ages) and allowed them to add instruction in such subjects as English, history, geography, and modern languages. Most provided a few free places for the "poor local boys" they were originally intended to educate but became, by and large, fee-paying day schools for the middle class.

By 1860, awareness of the need for a populace educated beyond rudimentary literacy and pressures from the middle class encouraged the state to look into secondary education, and various royal commissions were established. Religious contention and other concerns caused them to tread cautiously, and their recommendations were seldom carried out in full. The Taunton Commission (1864–1868) recommended establishing a national system of secondary education in schools of three grades. The first would have the same objective as the public schools: to prepare boys for entry to the university or to a professional training at the age of eighteen. The second grade school would provide for those leaving at age sixteen; a suitable target might be found in the local examinations in various subjects conducted under the auspices of Oxford and Cambridge universities, and the curriculum would include a sound training in mathematics, science, and modern studies. The third grade school would serve the needs of the lower middle class and skilled artisans, who could not afford to keep their children at school beyond the age of fourteen but wanted them to have a thorough knowledge of English and arithmetic (often called a "clerk's education") and some instruction in technical and practical subjects.

The Taunton Commission also took testi-mony from Francis Mary Buss and Dorothea Beale, and found only thirteen girls' schools in the country offering an education that could be described as secondary. The commission's report paid considerable attention to the need for schools that would provide secondary education to middle-class girls and helped establish a climate favorable to female education. In twenty-five years the number of endowed secondary schools for girls had increased to eighty-six, and a few mixed grammar schools were also in operation.

The other recommendations of the Taunton Commission were not implemented. Efficient schools of the second grade were manifestly insufficient and schools of the third grade were virtually nonexistent. Writing in 1885 after his retirement from public service, Matthew Arnold described the situation of English secondary education as a "chaos when her Majesty's reign began and a chaos still." Arnold advocated a national system in which secondary education to age sixteen could be followed by the alternative of classical and commercial high schools to age eighteen or nineteen, and, parallel with these, technical and special schools for those who required them.

The landmark Education Act of 1870 opened the way to a free and compulsory elementary education for every child in the land, and thus—although no provision for secondary education was made—increased the demand for continued schooling suited to a changing economic climate. The government's Science and Art Department, reorganized in 1874, offered grants to all types of schools able to teach science and present successful candidates for the examinations that it conducted. By 1882, with 68,000 candidates entered, the department had clearly contributed to modernizing concepts of what a secondary curriculum should include.

In 1880 county and borough councils were established as the principal authority for education in every local area, entrusted with the provision of practical instruction and technical education, and provided with an unexpected windfall through a fund originally set aside for compensating former licencees of public houses. This "whiskey money" was largely channeled to the cause of secondary education. An act of 1876 had granted three additional years of free education to children who passed a standard examination at the age of ten, which produced better school attendance and an extended school life, thus leading in turn to an enriched curriculum, particularly in those towns where progressive school boards provided a secondary style of education by creating "select classes" in elementary schools or organizing a central school for those wishing to stay at school to the age of fifteen.

There was by 1890 a widespread conviction that a democratic political system in a modern industrial and trading society must be backed by a much better-educated people. Scottish secondary education had long been held superior to English, and a Scotsman, James Bryce, was chosen to head a royal commission set up in 1895. The Bryce Commission recommended creating a central authority to define the nature and purposes of secondary education and to encourage and supervise local education authorities. Political rivalries arose among the various bodies that had some powers over education and controversies over instruction in religion resurfaced. In 1899, however, the Board of Education was created; its president was, in effect, the national minister for all education up to, but not including, the universities. At the same time, the school-leaving age was raised to twelve.

Finally, in 1902, Parliament passed a major education act which made secondary education the responsibility of counties and county boroughs in consultation with the Board of Education. It was to be their duty "to supply or aid the supply of education other than elementary and to provide and to promote the general co-ordination of all forms of education." Although progress toward the ideal of secondary education for all was slow, and many felt that technical education was slighted and the traditional academic approach of the grammar schools overvalued, the act of 1902 enabled the creation of secondary day schools, provided scholarships for able elementary children to attend local endowed grammar schools, and formed the basis of subsequent developments in British secondary education.

DAVID HOPKINSON

Bibliography

Archer, R. L. *Secondary Education in the Nineteenth Century*. 1921.

Banks, Olive. *Parity and Prestige in English Secondary Education*. 1955.

Bishop, A. S. *The Rise of a Central Authority for English Education*. 1971.

Evans, Keith. *The Development and Structure of the English School System*. 1985.

Lownders, G. A. N. *The Silent Social Revolution*. 1969.

Roach, John. *Public Examinations in England, 1850–1900*. 1971.

See also EDUCATION, TECHNICAL; OXFORD AND CAMBRIDGE LOCAL EXAMINATIONS

. . . . .

EDUCATION, TECHNICAL

Technical education—the training of laborers in skills and crafts—suffered (like nineteenth-century English education in general) from poor organization and misguided planning. It was impeded by the low level of primary education, the state's unwillingness to intervene in education, and the class attitudes that rendered technical education unsuitable for the middle classes.

The emergence of technical education in England can be traced to the founding of the Society of Arts in 1755 and the Royal Institution in 1810. Both were concerned with the dissemination of "useful knowledge" and the improvements of "arts and manufactures." On a more informal basis mechanics' institutes conducted regular courses and special lectures and published mechanics' magazines. Strictly speaking, the objective of these early institutions was to provide education in the scientific principles behind manufacturing techniques, crafts, and natural phenomena. This theoretical approach, which persisted until late in the century, was suited more to middle-class audiences than to the working classes. Working men's colleges, established first in Sheffield (1842) and later in London (1854), addressed the workers' need for basic education as well as issues of social and economic importance. The Society for the Diffusion of Useful Knowledge, established in 1825, published cheap tracts and pamphlets that added to the growing body of popular scientific and technical literature.

Government assistance was provided toward a central school of design in 1838 and to local schools established on the same pattern in manufacturing districts. By 1859 state grants were being allocated by the Science and Arts Department to support evening classes, and these were later supplemented by private and philanthropic groups. Support from the department, which primarily covered teachers' wages, was contingent on the ability of committees to raise money for books, equipment, facilities, and administering examinations. Local committees were encouraged to "impose as high a scale of fees" as possible, although the state did subsidize the fees of artisans in select subject areas.

The Livery Companies of London established the City and Guilds London Institute under the direction of Philip Magnus, which took over the technological examinations from the Royal Society of Arts and in 1883, with Magnus as principal, opened the Finsbury Technical Institute, the first college for technological studies. The direction taken by the City and Guilds London Institute, the London Artisan's Club (1868), the Trade Guilds of Learning (1873) and the Artisans' Institute (1874) represented an ideological shift toward the value of training workers in skills.

At the Paris Exhibition of 1867 it became clear that British industry was lagging behind its European counterpart. Subsequent committee investigations (1868 and 1871–1875) advocated improvements in scientific and technical education but failed to receive government support. In 1884 the Samuelson Commission, headed by Bernhard Samuelson, surveyed scientific and technical education in Europe and produced a comprehensive report that finally attracted attention. A royal commission under R. A. Cross pointed to the importance of primary education for scientific and technical learning and tried to strike a compromise between principle and practice. In 1889 pressure from the recently founded National Association for the Promotion of Technical Education helped pass the Technical Instruction Act, which allowed local authorities to use taxes for technical instruction. Though the revenue provided was small, it was later supplemented by a tax on

liquor ("whiskey money") for the assistance of technical instruction as well as secondary education. In 1895 the Royal Commission on Secondary Education proposed a strong central education authority which emerged in the Education Act of 1902. By that time, according to many, the lack of a systematic education program and the misunderstanding of technical education's role had resulted in a serious decline in British industry and technology.

ALAN RAUCH

Bibliography

Armytage, W. H. G. *The Rise of the Technocrats*. 1965.

Cotgrove, Stephen F. *Technical Education and Social Change*. 1958.

Macleod, Roy. "Scientific and Technical Education." In Gillian Sutherland, ed., *Education in Britain*. 1977.

Millis, Charles T. *Technical Education: Its Development and Aims*. 1925.

Roderick, Gordon W. and Michael D. Stephens. *Scientific and Technical Education in Nineteenth-Century England*. 1972.

Women's Industrial Council. *Technical Education for Girls*. 1897.

. . . . .

EDUCATION, WOMEN'S

The nineteenth century saw important changes in girls' and women's education: the establishment of academic day and boarding schools for girls, the beginnings of college and university education, and, most important, the grudging acceptance that women had an equal capacity with men for intellectual activity.

In the eighteenth century, the growing middle classes began to express concern over the superficiality of women's education. By the nineteenth century, feminists, evangelicals, and reformers of all shades agreed that female education was unsystematic and disorganized, merely teaching accomplishment in music, conversation, and trivial pastimes suitable for ornamental young ladies whose careers lay in marriage. Girls from the middle and upper classes were generally taught at home by their mothers or by **governesses**. Masters were sometimes employed for lessons in special subjects (such as music), and girls might be sent to school for a year or two in their early or mid-teens. Most governesses were themselves ill educated, and the schools for girls that existed were privately run by ladies who emphasized the homelike atmosphere, taking in thirty to fifty girls at the most and sometimes only seven or eight. Teaching usually consisted of hearing "lessons" learned by rote. The women teachers and governesses, working in isolation with a few pupils, had no educational guidelines except those of gentility.

Critics of such education argued that the superficiality and idleness for which women were trained was inadequate preparation for their role as good wives and mothers, responsible for their children's moral welfare and for providing husbands with a haven from the world's pressures. Feminists like **Emily Davies**, **Maria Grey**, and **Josephine Butler** further pointed to the futility of decorative idleness; middle-class women needed to be educated, like men, to make a positive contribution to society and to earn a living if they remained unmarried. Both feminists and conservatives set up institutions for reforming women's education.

New varieties of secondary schools for girls began to be founded in the 1840s. Queen's College, London, began in 1848 to offer lectures and examinations that would improve the training of governesses and provide certificates of their proficiency. Because the students' academic preparation was so weak, it was soon found necessary to establish a preparatory division for younger girls. Reformers such as **Frances Buss** and **Dorothea Beale** established secondary day and boarding schools on new plans. Unlike the older private schools that were the sole property of the headmistress, the new schools were trusts or companies for which shares were issued; they were, that is, fee-paying public schools for girls. They had boards of governors that included women, and the fees were kept reasonable; the schools were aimed at the middle classes, not the gentry and aristocracy. Day schools, such as the North London Collegiate School founded in 1850 by Frances Buss,

overcame the objections to sending girls away from home and also reduced the costs. By late in the century some had developed into municipal or endowed "high schools" with very modest fees. Other schools, following the example of Dorothea Beale at Cheltenham Ladies' College, developed into large boarding schools similar to the boys' public schools.

In 1863 girls were provisionally admitted to the Cambridge Local Examinations. (Admission was regularly allowed from 1865.) Outside examinations certified a girl's achievement so that governesses and girls' schools could aim at a recognized standard of attainment. Some of the pioneer girls' public schools worked toward the level required for university entrance. Provincial associations of schoolmistresses and other interested people were formed. These pressure groups became instrumental in establishing schools, providing examinations for governesses and teachers, and creating lecture courses. Feminist pressure led to the inclusion of girls' schools in the inquiries of the Taunton Commission (1864). Orchestrated by Emily Davies, sympathizers gave evidence to the commission. Its report, published in 1868–1869, was a blueprint for many later developments; and the official sanction of reform brought publicity and support to the movement.

Wide support for reform, however, meant a diversity of opinions. Some argued merely that girls required a more serious systematic education and others that women's education should be comparable to men's. Guided by the latter belief, a group of women and men led by Emily Davies founded Girton College, Cambridge (1869), financed through public subscriptions. In all essentials a Cambridge college, with a mistress as female equivalent of the master of a men's college, Girton was denied official status by the university. Women undergraduates were taught separately by sympathetic dons and allowed to take degree examinations on an informal basis, some obtaining first-class results, but women were not granted degrees at Cambridge until the twentieth century.

Newnham College, on the other hand, was established at Cambridge in 1871 but did not insist that women should complete the degree syllabus. Two women's colleges were opened in Oxford in 1879: Lady Margaret Hall (founded on Church of England principles) and Somerville, which was nondenominational. As the successful women's colleges at Oxford and Cambridge demonstrated that women could study the same subjects at the same level as men, without ill effects on their health or social status, the Scottish and the new provincial universities began to admit and grant degrees to women: Manchester New College in 1876, St. Andrew's in 1877, London University in 1878.

A process of feedback operated throughout the development of women's education: pioneers opened the doors and gradually the system expanded. By the latter part of the century, growing numbers of university-educated women were important in opening some professions to women and in providing qualified teachers for the girls' schools that were founded in increasing numbers. Some schools were financed through the Endowed Schools Act (1869), some were the result of local pressure groups, and some, like the Girls' Public Day School Company and the Church Schools Company, resulted from wider national organization. The variety of day and boarding schools and fees reflected the social class system; day schools were in general less socially selective than boarding schools. Whether founded directly as a result of feminist principles or less directly as a result of reforms already achieved, the new girls' schools had in common a view of the potentialities of girls very different from that prevailing early in the century. In addition to accepting that some middle-class women needed to earn a living, all schools stressed the importance of academic education coupled with healthy physical exercise, thus dispelling the myth that education would harm women's delicate biological balance and fitness for motherhood.

Pioneer headmistresses continued to provide teacher-training facilities in their schools, while others supported the training colleges that had been founded by the state to provide teachers for the elementary schools. But the lower social class of elementary school teachers and their pupils meant that training colleges were unpopular with university-educated women.

The major changes in women's education in the nineteenth century were motivated by middle-class concerns and resulted in the provision of quality secondary education for mid-dle- and upper-class girls. Elementary schools, provided and controlled by the state, were intended primarily for the working classes and the poor, and attendance did not become compulsory until 1880. Girls and boys followed the same basic curriculum, though generally in separate classrooms, and with some differences in vocational training; needlework, for example, was compulsory for all girls. Feminist school board members attempted to alter the sexual discrimination that existed, but the major factor affecting the education of working-class girls continued to be the assumption that they needed domestic skills in order to be satisfactory servants and, eventually, the "mothers of Englishmen." When schooling became compulsory, absentee rates were higher among girls, who were often kept at home to help with the family.

By the twentieth century, the establishment of schools and colleges for women and the provision of educated women teachers for girls had begun to alter the view of women as physically weak and intellectually inferior creatures. However, sufficient Victorianism remained at almost all levels to prevent coeducation. A policy of "separate but equal" facilities operated, and chaperones existed for undergraduate women into the twentieth century.

ROSAMUND BILLINGTON

Bibliography

Beale, Dorothea. "Girls' Schools, Past and Present." *Nineteenth Century*, vol. 23, pp. 541–554.

Burstyn, Joan. *Victorian Education and the Ideal of Womanhood.* 1980.

Delamont, Sara and Lorna Duffin, eds. *The Nineteenth Century Woman: Her Cultural and Physical World.* 1978.

Dyhouse, Carol. *Girls Growing Up in Late Victorian and Edwardian England.* 1981.

Holcombe, Lee. *Victorian Ladies at Work.* 1973.

Kamm, Josephine. *Hope Deferred: Girls' Education in English History.* 1972.

———. *Indicative Past: A Hundred Years of the Girls' Public Day School Trust.* 1971.

Spender, Dale, ed. *The Education Papers: Women's Quest for Equality in Britain, 1850–1912.* 1987.

Widdowson, Frances. *Going Up Into the Next Class: Women and Elementary Teacher Training, 1840–1914.* 1980.

Zimmern, Alice. *The Renaissance of Girls' Education in England: A Record of Fifty Years' Progress.* 1898.

See also CLOUGH, ANNE JEMIMA; EDUCATION, HIGHER; EDUCATION, SECONDARY; ELMY, ELIZABETH WOLSTENHOLME; MEDICAL EDUCATION; OXFORD AND CAMBRIDGE LOCAL EXAMINATIONS; SEWELL, ELIZABETH MISSING; SHIRREFF, EMILY

.　.　.　.　.

EGAN, PIERCE
(1814–1880)

The son of the well-known sporting journalist, the younger Pierce Egan was trained as an artist. His early work (in the style of George Cruikshank, but blander) includes etchings for his father's *The Pilgrims of the Thames in Search of the National* (1838). By the early 1840s, Egan had concentrated his energies on authorship. His early works are lurid historical romances: *Wat Tyler* (1841), *Robin Hood* (1840), whose installments sold in the 100,000s and started a fad for the subject, and *Quintin Matsys, the Blacksmith of Antwerp* (1839) were among the best received. Later Egan produced novels in other styles. For the *London Journal* (which was, along with *Reynolds's Miscellany*, to which Egan also contributed, the great midcentury outlet for working-class fiction) he supplied twenty-five serials in twenty years, many of them illustrated by John Gilbert. Most of these stories are domestic with sensational touches: the virtuous country is opposed to the corrupt city, social classes are set against yet entangled with one another, and there is an emphasis on romantic love. In 1859 the *London Journal* tried to replace Egan's work with reprints of novels by Walter Scott, but this effort to raise the tone of the magazine failed and Egan was rehired. He continued writing for the *Journal* until his death.

Well liked by both colleagues and readers, Egan worked hard. While his novels are still readable, none has an outstanding place even in the history of fiction for the lower classes. Egan is significant for his benign literary opportunism. *The Waits* (1857) is urban melodrama in **G. W. M. Reynolds**'s style set within the frame of a Dickensian Christmas story, and *Wat Tyler*—fictionalized Chartism—culminates in an account of London disorders created by a radical movement, a subject it shares with the contemporaneous *Barnaby Rudge* and *Old Saint Paul's* but treats more sympathetically.

RICHARD MAXWELL

Bibliography

James, Louis. *Fiction for the Working Man, 1830–1850.* 1963.

Reid, John C. *Bucks and Bruisers: Pierce Egan and Regency England.* 1971.

.　.　.　.　.

EGERTON, GEORGE (MARY CHAVELITA DUNNE BRIGHT)
(1859–1945)

George Egerton was a short story writer, novelist, and playwright most famous for her **New Woman** story collections, *Keynotes* (1893) and *Discords* (1894).

Though some have male protagonists, most of Egerton's short stories explore brief episodes in women's lives, often focusing on dependence and suppressed emotion. They are remarkable for their acknowledgement of women's sexuality, and, more obliquely, of antagonism between women and men. Yet, as Elaine Showalter points out, such antagonism is neither directly confronted nor resolved, and while it can be marginally characterized as feminist, Egerton's work offers no political analysis. Her characters are isolated and introspective, and she was heavily influenced by the

Scandinavian realists, some of whose works she translated. In "A Keynote to *Keynotes*" (1932) she claimed that her "life as a woman" took precedence over her art, and that it would be a long time before women writers could meet the best male writers "on equal terms."

Her other works include *Symphonies* (1897) and *Fantasias* (1898), collections of short stories; the semiautobiographical novel *The Wheel of God* (1898); *Rosa Amorosa* (1901), fictional love letters based on her relationship with a Norwegian lover; several plays and adaptations; and a translation of Knut Hamsun's *Hunger*. The memoir by Egerton's cousin, Terence de Vere White, is often patronizing, but includes many of her letters.

LAURA STEMPEL MUMFORD

Bibliography

Showalter, Elaine. *A Literature of Their Own.* 1977.

White, Terence de Vere. *A Leaf from the Yellow Book: The Correspondence of George Egerton.* 1958.

. . . . .

EGG, AUGUSTUS LEOPOLD (1816–1863)

A painter of literary scenes, history pictures, and contemporary life, Augustus Leopold Egg was born in London. He entered the Royal Academy schools in 1836 and began exhibiting paintings of young girls in opera dress or Spanish costume, young lovers, and comic scenes from Le Sage, Cervantes, Shakespeare, Byron, Moore, and Scott. In the 1840s Egg was painting comic scenes from history, usually from historical novels. A more serious treatment marks his carefully researched diploma picture for election to the Royal Academy, *Queen Elizabeth Discovers She Is No Longer Young* (1848), and *The Night Before Naseby* (1859), depicting Cromwell in prayer before battle. *The Life and Death of Buckingham* (1855) and *Past and Present* (1858) show Egg's debt to the moral series of Hogarth. The influence of the Pre-Raphaelites, especially William Holman Hunt, whom Egg

befriended, is evident in the moral earnestness of *Past and Present* and the meticulously painted costumes and landscape of *The Travelling Companions* (1862), Egg's last picture.

Egg was a friend of Wilkie Collins and acted in Charles Dickens's amateur theatrical company. He married in 1860. He died in Algiers on March 25, 1863 from chronic respiratory disease. The definitive catalogue and biography is Hilarie Faberman's 1983 Yale dissertation.

MICHAEL COHEN

Bibliography

Faberman, Hilarie. "Augustus Leopold Egg, R. A. (1816–1863)." Ph.D. dissertation, Yale University, 1983.

See also ACADEMIC PAINTING
. . . . .

EGYPT

The story of British relations with Egypt in the nineteenth century divides neatly into two parts: the period before the British takeover in 1882, and the years of occupation that followed. The first period is marked by three major events: the completion of the **Suez Canal** in 1869, the gradual bankruptcy of Egypt under the Khedive Ismail who ruled the nation from 1863 to 1879 as a semi-independent viceroy of the sultan of Turkey, and the Arabi revolt of 1881–1882 that prompted the British takeover.

Even though Britain had thwarted French attempts in 1798 to conquer Egypt and endanger British interests in India, France's success in opening the Suez Canal forced Britain once again to focus its attention on Egypt, especially since Britain soon came to use the canal heavily. Unfortunately for both Egypt and Britain, Ismail weakened his country by borrowing recklessly from European moneylenders, contracting crushing debts connected with the building of the canal, and spending extravagantly. Consequently, Ismail became vulnerable in the 1870s to Egyptian nationalists and Islamic reformers such as Jamal al-Din al-Afghani. These elements combined with dissidents in the government and military, and a revolutionary movement coalesced around army colonel Ahmad Arabi. The situation worsened rapidly: Ismail's son, Tawfiq, replaced him in 1879; famine in 1878 and 1879 exacerbated the discontent of the exploited and overtaxed peasantry; and in 1882 Britain had to wrest control of the country from Ahmad Arabi and occupy Cairo. From 1882 until the end of World War I, British influence in Egypt was intense.

Although the need to safeguard European financial interests in Egypt was obviously strong, Britain was not eager to occupy Egypt and did so finally because of its interest in the Suez Canal. Britain appointed Lord Cromer (Evelyn Baring) consul-general in Egypt in 1883, a post he held until 1907. Cromer had been an exceptionally successful administrator in India, and his severe but efficient rule stabilized Egypt's finances by the end of the century.

Cromer, furthermore, promoted great advances in agriculture, particularly through a program of canals and irrigation culminating in 1902 in a large dam at Aswan. As a result of this extensive irrigation, cotton production grew rapidly. A necessary accompaniment to these improvements was a major expansion of transportation facilities: a better harbor at Alexandria and many more miles of railroads. In sum, Cromer's administration was effective despite his inattention to education and government reform, and despite a personality that led to his being called "Over-Baring" by some.

An important consequence of the British occupation of Egypt was a need to protect the upstream Nile regions from predation by Italy, Germany, and France. Thus in the 1890s the British prime minister, Lord Salisbury, directed a series of military and diplomatic maneuvers to keep the Sudan under British control. The chief hero in securing the Sudan was Herbert Kitchener, who won a decisive victory over Muslim forces at Karari and faced down the French at Fashoda. The conclusion to Britain's efforts to maintain its influence in the area was the establishment in 1899 of the condominium, Cromer's arrangement for separate political status for the Sudan under the joint sovereignty of Egypt and Britain. Thus the nineteenth century closed with a comparatively stable situation for the British up and down the Nile.

FRANK DAY

Bibliography

Collins, Robert O. and Robert L. Tignor. *Egypt and the Sudan.* 1967.

Mansfield, Peter. *The British in Egypt.* 1971.

Robinson, Ronald, John Gallagher, and Alice Denny. *Africa and the Victorians: The Climax of Imperialism.* 1961.

· · · · ·

ELECTIONS AND THE FRANCHISE

Five years before Victoria ascended the throne, the government of Lord Grey had secured the passage, not without difficulty, of the Reform Act of 1832. Grey and his Whig colleagues understood that the stability of English government and the authority of aristocratic leadership required that the legitimate grievances of the middle classes be removed through a measure of parliamentary reform.

The 1832 Reform Act conferred votes on propertied adult males. That property could assume a variety of forms. In the county constituencies the qualification before 1832 had been the ownership of freehold property valued at no less than 40 shillings per year. The legislation of 1832 retained this qualification and also made eligible for the vote those adult males possessing a copyhold or long-term leasehold worth at least 10 pounds per annum, and those who rented land worth 50 pounds per annum or more. In the borough constituencies, adult males who owned or occupied property worth at least 10 pounds per year were entitled to the vote if they had paid all taxes charged on the property, met the one-year residential qualification, and had not received poor relief in the preceding twelve months. In addition, individuals who had exercised the vote before 1832 on any one of the ancient franchises then extant retained their vote.

The act's impact on the size of the electorate can not be stated with precision (there was no registry of voters before 1832), but the increase was substantial without being dramatic. In 1831 approximately 366,000 adult males in England and Wales (11 percent of all adult males) had the vote; in 1833 there were nearly 653,000 eligible electors (18 percent of the adult male population). Separate reform acts were passed for Scotland and Ireland. In Scotland the electorate was transformed—from 4,000 electors in 1831 to 64,000 in 1832. In Ireland the increase was more modest—from 39,000 to 93,000.

The 1832 Reform Act also extinguished many boroughs in which the representation had been controlled by a single individual ("proprietary" or "pocket" boroughs), created new parliamentary boroughs in previously unrepresented urban communities (primarily in the industrial north), and drew new electoral boundaries. The redistribution made the 658-member House of Commons more representative of important social and economic interests, but it was not intended to create electoral districts based on population. The 1832 act diminished somewhat the electoral influence of the south in relation to the north, the rural in relation to the urban, the landed classes in relation to the middle classes. But it did not substitute middle-class political rule for that of the aristocracy. The system continued to be heavily weighted in favor of traditional interests.

Another feature of the 1832 settlement established a registration system, which inhibited some eligible electors from becoming actual voters. The complexity of the franchises, the apathy of many who could have qualified had they taken the trouble, and the manipulation of the register by interested parties choked off some of the potential growth in the size of the electorate.

Heightened party conflict and the persistence of bribery and treating (plying electors with food and drink) meant that the cost of contesting elections remained high. These features of the electoral system, in conjunction with the unpaid character of parliamentary service and middle-class deference to the landed elite, ensured that government by the aristocracy continued to thrive during the early and mid-Victorian years.

Parliamentary reform returned to the center of the political stage in 1866–1867. The defeat of the Liberal government's moderate Reform Bill in 1866 led to the resignation of Lord Russell and William Gladstone. A minority Conservative government was formed under Lord Derby and Benjamin Disraeli. The

bill they presented in 1867 was greatly altered by a complex amendment process (although John Stuart Mill's motion to substitute the word "person" for "man" was defeated by a vote of 196 to 73). The resulting measure enfranchised far more adult males than even the most advanced parliamentary politicians would have thought possible in 1866. In the boroughs the vote was given to all male householders who satisfied a one-year residential qualification. In the counties the vote was extended to occupiers of property rated at 12 pounds or more annually. The electorate of England and Wales was nearly doubled, rising from just over one million in 1866 to almost two million in 1868. Once again Scotland and Ireland were treated separately, the electorate of the former increasing from approximately 105,000 to 240,000 and that of the latter from 197,000 to 225,000. The redistribution scheme that accompanied the suffrage reform of 1867 was not ambitious. So long as so much else remained virtually unchanged, the addition of substantial numbers of working-class voters in the boroughs did not represent a serious threat to the ascendancy of the established governing class.

The electoral reforms introduced between the Reform Acts of 1867 and 1884 concentrated on cleaning up the system. A Corrupt Practices Act of 1868 transferred jurisdiction for the trial of election petitions (filed by defeated candidates claiming their opponents had corrupted electors) from a committee of the House of Commons to judges of the superior courts at Westminster. In 1872 Gladstone's government secured the adoption of the secret ballot, which was designed to protect voters against intimidation. Although the ballot did not entirely extinguish undue influence, it reduced the din and disorder of elections. The Corrupt Practices Act of 1883 imposed strict limitations on electoral expenditures. Instances of bribery and treating declined significantly after 1883, as did the cost of contesting elections.

In 1884 the Gladstone government presented to Parliament a county household suffrage bill. The redistribution scheme of 1884–1885 was radical by comparison with its predecessors. Two-member boroughs whose population was less than 15,000 were eliminated; those between 15,000 and 50,000 lost one of their two members. Only twenty-four boroughs returned two members after 1885. For electoral purposes the country was carved up into single-member constituencies, some consideration being given to establishing a rough equality in their numerical size.

It would be wrong to conclude that the reform package of 1884-1885, the last of Victoria's reign, completed the transition from an aristocratic to a democratic electoral system. The Third Reform Act, which applied the principle of household suffrage across the board and throughout the United Kingdom, brought onto the rolls an additional two and a half million voters. But as late as 1911 just under 60 percent of all adult males were registered to vote; women were excluded entirely; some voters enjoyed more than one vote; and electoral districts, although more equal in relation to population than before 1885, were nothing like uniform in size.

Nevertheless, the reforms of the nineteenth century had set Britain firmly and irrevocably on the path toward electoral democracy. In response to irreversible social and economic change, the aristocracy sponsored alteration of the electoral structure to provide the middle classes and then the working classes with a slice of the political pie. The traditional governing classes used their leverage (and until the 1880s it was considerable) to keep as much for themselves as possible while accommodating the aspirations of other classes. The pace and character of electoral reform was generally consistent with the needs and expectations of the nation.

BRUCE L. KINZER

Bibliography

Brock, Michael. *The Great Reform Act.* 1973.

Cowling, Maurice. *1867: Disraeli, Gladstone and Revolution: The Passing of the Second Reform Bill.* 1967.

Gash, Norman. *Politics in the Age of Peel: A Study in the Technique of Parliamentary Representation. 1830-1850.* 1953.

Hanham, Harold J. *Elections and Party Management: Politics in the Time of Disraeli and Gladstone.* 1959.

Hayes, William A. *The Background and Passage of the Third Reform Act.* 1982.

Hoppen, K. T. *Elections, Politics, and Society in Ireland, 1832-1885.* 1984.

Kinzer, Bruce L. *The Ballot Question in Nineteenth-Century English Politics.* 1982.

Moore, David C. *The Politics of Deference: A Study of the Mid-Nineteenth-Century English Political System.* 1976.

O'Leary, Cornelius. *The Elimination of Corrupt Practices in British Elections, 1868-1911.* 1962.

Pelling, Henry. *Social Geography of British Elections, 1885-1910.* 1967.

Seymour, Charles. *Electoral Reform in England and Wales: The Development and Operation of the Parliamentary Franchise, 1832-1885.* 1915; rpt. 1970.

Smith, Francis B. *The Making of the Second Reform Bill.* 1966.

See also SUFFRAGE, WOMEN'S
· · · · ·

ELECTRICITY

Victorian Britain produced the basic theories that explained the phenomenon of electricity: **Michael Faraday**'s discovery of electromagnetic induction in 1831; **James Clerk Maxwell**'s publication in 1873 of a coherent field theory which explained electricity, magnetism, and optics in a series of equations; and Joseph Thomson's discovery of the electron in 1897. Despite this scientific leadership, Britain by 1914 lagged behind the United States and the Continent in the generation and application of electric power.

Except for the **telegraph** and a few lighthouses, electricity made no impact on everyday life until the independent invention in 1878-1879 of the carbon-filament incandescent lamp by American Thomas A. Edison and Englishman Joseph W. Swann. Thereafter the demand for electric power grew rapidly. Independent generating and **lighting** systems were immediately installed in large public buildings such as St. Enochs Station, Glasgow (1879) and the British Museum (1880). The first public power stations were put into operation in London and New York in January and September 1882. Regulation of the new industry began with Electric Lighting Acts in 1882 and 1888 which respectively gave local authorities the right to purchase plants after twenty-one and forty-two years.

Through the 1880s British electric supply and lighting systems remained small and localized while elsewhere the major experiments and developments were begun in the long-distance, large-scale transmission of power. From the mid-1880s Britain began to lag behind the European and American competition in adopting electric power. Development was retarded by the availability of and investment in gas and steam power for lighting and manufacturing along with competition between public authorities and private enterprise. A British engineer, Charles Parsons, invented in 1897 the steam turbine which provided the vital connection between coal and electricity and became the twentieth century's power source. But in 1900 Britain still thought of electricity primarily in terms of lighting. Despite the introduction of electric power into such areas as shipbuilding and light manufacturing, Britain in 1914 was behind in the electrification of most industries including mining and chemicals.

FREDERICK E. LAURENZO

Bibliography

Bynum, I. C. R. *The British Electrical Industry, 1875-1914.* 1979.

Crowther, James Gerald. *British Scientists of the Nineteenth Century.* 1936.

Hannah, Leslie. *Electricity Before Nationalisation.* 1979.

Maclaren, Malcolm. *The Rise of the Electrical Industry During the Nineteenth Century.* 1943.

· · · · ·

ELGAR, EDWARD (1857-1934)

Edward Elgar, composer, is considered the most significant English musician between Henry Purcell and Benjamin Britten. Although Elgar composed in all musical forms except opera, his reputation rests chiefly on three works: *Variations on an Original Theme*, also known as the *Enigma Variations* (1899); *The Dream of Gerontius* (1900); and the first *Pomp and Circumstance* march (1901).

Elgar's training and early career, including activities as organist, violinist, and conductor, took place around his home in Worcester. There, in 1883, his first major orchestral composition, *Intermezzo: Sérénade mauresque*, was premiered.

After his marriage (1889) and a brief, unsuccessful period in London (1890-1891) Elgar settled in Malvern, where he spent the next thirteen years. During the 1890s Elgar became well known chiefly through his cantatas. His concentration on vocal forms culminated with *The Dream of Gerontius*, an oratorio which is considered his masterpiece.

In 1900 Elgar's *Enigma Variations* premiered in London, and within the year the University of Cambridge conferred an honorary doctorate upon him in recognition of this work. Shortly thereafter he composed the first *Pomp and Circumstance* march, which became internationally famous in connection with the coronation of Edward VII (1902). Elgar was knighted in 1904.

The aesthetic of Elgar's music may be described as "functional romanticism." He had an abundant melodic gift, and his formal and harmonic procedures are clear and precise. Although his musical output extended well beyond the Victorian era, his musical style remained firmly rooted in the nineteenth century.

MICHAEL FINK

Bibliography

Kennedy, Michael. *Portrait of Elgar.* 1982.

Knowles, John. *Elgar's Interpreters on Record: An Elgar Discography.* 1977.

McVeagh, Diana M. *Edward Elgar: His Life and Music.* 1955.

Moore, Jerrold N. *Edward Elgar: A Creative Life.* 1984.

Newman, Ernest. *Elgar.* 1906.

Pirie, Peter J. *The English Musical Renaissance.* 1979.

Reed, William H. *Elgar as I Knew Him.* 1936.

Shaw, George Bernard. "Sir Edward Elgar." In Dan
H. Lawrence, ed., *Shaw's Music*, vol. 3. 1981.

· · · · ·

ELIOT, GEORGE
(1819–1880)

George Eliot was the pen name of Mary
Anne (also spelled Mary Ann and Marian)
Evans. Although she did not begin to write
fiction until she was thirty-seven, the three
long stories of *Scenes of Clerical Life* (1858)
were well received, and the publication of her
first novel, *Adam Bede* (1859), made "George
Eliot" instantly famous. Six novels followed:
The Mill on the Floss (1860), *Silas Marner*
(1861), *Romola* (1863), *Felix Holt, the Radical* (1866), *Middlemarch* (1871–1872), and
Daniel Deronda (1876). She also published
verse, reviews, and essays. Despite shifts in her
reputation and in the assessment of particular
works, her achievement in fiction places her
among the greatest novelists. Indeed, the
critic F. R. Leavis, praising her moral sensibility and luminous intelligence, argued that she
"is not as transcendently great as Tolstoy, but
she *is* great, and great in the same way."

Mary Anne Evans was raised in Warwickshire on the Arbury estates, which her father
managed. In her childhood, she was particularly close to her brother, Isaac, who would
later play Tom to her Maggie in *The Mill on
the Floss*. Her schooling made her a convert
to Evangelicalism, but it was in other respects
quite ordinary and ended when she was sixteen. After her mother died in 1836, she kept
house for her father until his death in 1849.
During those years, she avidly studied on her
own music, theology, philosophy, literature,
and foreign languages (German, Italian,
French, Latin, and Greek).

At twenty-two, she moved with her father to
Coventry, where she became friends with a
group of freethinking intellectuals, whose rationalist inquiries intensified her own growing
doubts about her earlier devout Evangelicalism. This led to her rejection of all religious
orthodoxies and to a rift with her father over
her refusal to attend church. It led also to her
translating David Friedrich Strauss's *Life of
Jesus, Critically Examined* (1846) and Ludwig Feuerbach's *Essence of Christianity*

(1854), both heterodox works which reject the
divinity of Christ and of the Gospels and propose instead a religion of humanity. The only
published work on which Marian Evans's
name appears is her translation of Feuerbach,
whose views she claimed to be very much in
harmony with her own. The belief they shared
in a morality based on human love, sympathy,
and tolerance, and on the sacredness of the
everyday, became vital to her literary aesthetic, helping to shape her concept of realism. She also translated, but never published,
Spinoza's *Tractatus Theologico-Politicus*
(1849) and *Ethics* (1854).

After her father's death, she changed the
spelling of her name to Marian and went to
London, where she became a distinguished
essayist and served as anonymous editor of
the influential *Westminster Review* (1851–
1854). In 1854 she began living with **George
Henry Lewes** in a union they could not legal-
ize because of his prior marriage, but one they
regarded as totally binding. She adopted the
name Marian E. Lewes, and they lived together until his death in 1878. Their relation
was vital to both her professional and personal
life, although it did estrange her from her
brother Isaac. It was Lewes who suggested that
she try writing fiction, and his care and encouragement sustained her throughout her
career. In the last year of her life she married
John W. Cross, who was nearly twenty years
her junior.

In contrast to the exceptional and rebellious quality of her own life, Eliot's fiction was
devoted to exploring and dramatizing the inescapable pressures and limits that social conditions and psychological disposition exert on
common human needs and aspirations. Her
aesthetic of realism fuses together individual
and social history in such a way as to capture
both the particularity of individual lives and
the typicality of the predicaments her characters suffer. Vital to her aesthetic was the moral
imperative of presenting "mixed human
beings in such a way as to call forth tolerant
judgment, pity, and sympathy" (*Letters*
2:299). Eliot's dense social contexts, together
with her penetrating psychological portraits,
create the complex moral explorations that
are at the center of her fiction.

But however conventional her moral aesthetic may appear on the surface, it has its
own unorthodoxies, for it consecrates the

commonplace, replaces the divine with the human, and rewrites history by celebrating unhistoric lives. Her novels so disguise her heterodoxy that relatively few Victorian readers suspected her subterfuge, while many came to revere her as a sibyl or seer. In the post-Victorian revolt of the 1890s–1940s, Eliot's very reputation as a portentous moralist damaged her standing, and her work was criticized for dissociating art and morality, imagined life and intellectual analysis.

After World War II, however, Eliot's mind and art were reassessed. She continues to be admired for her large social observations, for the intellectual and emotional power of her fiction, and for the range and depth of her characterizations, narrative voices, social analysis, and wry humor. At the same time, formal studies of her work, particularly of her analogical imagination, metaphorical brilliance, and organic structure, have greatly increased the appreciation of her artistry. While Eliot's preoccupation with moral problems continues to fascinate readers, she is now admired not for her moral surety but for her presentation and understanding of complex moral dilemmas.

Victorian readers tended to view Eliot's work as divided between the pastoral mode of *Adam Bede* and *Silas Marner* and the highly analytic and often critical mode of parts of *The Mill on the Floss* and the later novels. Although her contemporary readers thought *Middlemarch* a masterpiece, they often expressed a preference for the charm of the earlier novels, in part because they were unsettled by the ironic and critical tone, which in the later works coexisted with the sympathetic voice they loved. Modern readers favor a probing, skeptical and self-divided George Eliot. Eliot's realism, though it strives to locate the ideal in the real and discover the poetic in the commonplace, exhibits great tensions between the two. The organic form of her fiction brilliantly uncovers dysfunction in the social organism. Her much-disputed feminism places in conflict what it strives also to reconcile: self-development with selfless devotion to others, independence with connection. But while oppositions such as these pervade her work, Eliot's very struggle and ultimate refusal to resolve persistent tensions in individual and social life contribute vitally to her abiding power.

SUZANNE GRAVER

Bibliography

Beer, Gillian. *George Eliot.* 1986.

Carroll, David, ed. *George Eliot: The Critical Heritage.* 1971.

Gilbert, Sandra M. and Susan Gubar. *The Madwoman in the Attic: The Woman Writer and the Nineteenth-Century Literary Imagination.* 1979.

Graver, Suzanne. *George Eliot and Community: A Study in Social Theory and Fictional Form.* 1984.

Haight, Gordon S. *George Eliot: A Biography.* 1968.

———. ed. *The George Eliot Letters.* 1954–1978. 9 vols.

Hardy, Barbara. *The Novels of Geroge Eliot: A Study in Form.* 1959.

Harvey, William J. *The Art of George Eliot.* 1962.

Knoepflmacher, U. C. *George Eliot's Early Novels: The Limits of Realism.* 1968.

Leavis, F. R. *The Great Tradition: George Eliot, Henry James, Joseph Conrad.* 1948.

Redinger, Ruby. *George Eliot: The Emergent Self.* 1975.

Showalter, Elaine. "The Greening of Sister George." *Nineteenth-Century Fiction,* vol. 35, pp. 292–311.

See also SIMCOX, EDITH

· · · · ·

ELLIOTT, EBENEZER (1781–1849)

"The Corn-Law Rhymer" was Ebenezer Elliott's proudest title, but a slightly misleading one. His poetry—*The Village Patriarch* (1829), *Corn Law Rhymes* (1830), *The Splendid Village* (1833)—is not only topical and political (and therefore condemned to obscurity once the issues had faded); it is also a social document—poetry of and for the urban poor, by a writer who had shared their experience.

Acclaimed as a laborer-poet, Elliott was not actually a foundry worker but a foundry owner, though he had labored, wageless, in his father's workshop and known poverty when his own first business failed. Nevertheless, he recovered his fortunes sufficiently to retire to the country in 1842 and indulge in pastoral verse. His radicalism was, in fact, strictly limited: he did not disapprove of wealth in general, only of the landowners whose wealth derived from the bread tax; he abhorred socialism and communism, and even broke from the Chartists because their demands for reform went beyond calling for the repeal of the **Corn Laws**. These, to his mind, were the cause of all the economic and social ills of England, and his poetry pathetically depicts those ills, and rudely attacks their cause.

He wrote for a working-class audience, and familiar song tunes were often suggested for his shorter rhymes. A few—the most famous of which is "When wilt thou save the people?"—found their way into Unitarian hymnbooks. These shorter pieces are powerful; the longer poems, showing the influence of Crabbe, have a wider range, by turns descriptive, sentimental, and harsh. Both his faults and his strengths derive from his genuine concern and his impatience for improvement. Although now little more than a footnote to the Corn Laws, Elliott's voice is still curiously strong, despite its limited themes.

SUSAN DRAIN

Bibliography

Briggs, Asa. "Ebenezer Elliott, the Corn Law Rhymer." *Cambridge Journal*, vol. 3, pp. 686–695.

Carlyle, Thomas. "Corn Law Rhymes." In Thomas Carlyle, *Critical and Miscellaneous Essays*, vol. 4. 1890.

Eaglestone, Arthur A. *Ebenezer Elliott: A Commemorative Brochure*. 1949.

Odom, William. *Two Sheffield Poets: James Montgomery and Ebenezer Elliott*. 1929.

Watkins, John. *The Life, Poetry and Letters of Ebenezer Elliott*. 1850.

Wilson, John. "Poetry of Ebenezer Elliott." *Blackwood's Magazine*, vol. 35, pp. 815–835.

. . . . .

ELLIS, HENRY HAVELOCK
(1859–1939)

Havelock Ellis wrote more than fifty books on medicine, eugenics, genius, criminal law, literature, travel, men and women, love, marriage, and sex. His most important work, *Studies in the Psychology of Sex* (1897–1928) became the most comprehensive account of human sexual behavior in English, and influenced the English and Americans to regard sex more tolerantly and with more enthusiasm than previously.

Ellis came from an intelligent, respectable, and conventional Victorian family. When he was sixteen he resolved to devote his life to studying sex—an area then little known and much misunderstood—believing that sex was the "central problem of life," and that it could be understood by the Darwinian method of collecting and reasoning from facts. After graduating from medical school he supported himself by writing on literary and social topics. In 1894 he published *Man and Woman—* an account of secondary sexual characteristics—and from 1897–1910 six volumes of *Studies in the Psychology of Sex*. The seventh and final volume appeared in 1928.

Ellis based *Studies* on case histories of individuals—some of whom were his acquaintances—and on previously published accounts. He tried to report all that was known about sex and to identify it in areas (such as childhood, religion, and art) where it was not outwardly apparent. Some of his assertions about sexual behavior were as follows: **homosexuality** and sexual deviations (such as fetishism, exhibitionism, bestiality, uralognia, and corprolagnia) were neither diseases nor crimes—as some believed—but congenitally acquired and part of normal sexual life; sexual intercourse was essential for the fullest human development and sexual abstinence was unhealthy; female sexuality was more diffuse, massive, and passive than male sexuality; and the ideal condition for sexual development was a sustained monogamous relationship.

Ellis was married to an English author, Edith Leese, and after her death he lived with a Frenchwoman, Françoise Delisle. He also formed close friendships with Olive Schreiner, Margaret Sanger, and other intellectual women. However, he appears to have been unable to achieve full sexual intercourse with a woman; and he was erotically attracted by what he described as "the act of urination in a beloved person." Yet he was deeply loved by most of the women who knew him, and after his death his male and female acquaintances remembered him as "a radiance who touched their lives." His autobiography, *My Life* (1939), is notable for its candor and self-awareness.

Studies in the Psychology of Sex has now been superseded as a source of facts about human sexuality. Its case histories, judged by the standards of contemporary sexology, are too few in number to permit generalizations, lack many essential biographical facts, and lack the psychological insights that Freud brought to his case histories. Yet the attitudes of tolerance and enthusiasm that Ellis brought to the subject of sex cleared the way for acceptance of the work of Freud, Kinsey, and Masters and Johnson.

RALPH COLP, JR.

Bibliography

Brecher, Edward. *The Sex Researchers.* 1969.

Brome, Vincent. *Havelock Ellis: Philosopher of Sex.* 1979.

Calder-Marshall, Arthur. *The Sage of Sex: A Life of Havelock Ellis.* 1959.

Grosskurth, Phyllis. *Havelock Ellis: A Biography.* 1980.

Marcus, Steven. *Freud and the Culture of Psychoanalysis.* 1984.

Robinson, Paul. *The Modernization of Sex: Havelock Ellis, Alfred Kinsey, William Masters and Virginia Johnson.* 1976.

See also SEX EDUCATION

· · · · ·

ELLIS, SARAH STICKNEY (1799-1882)

Sarah Stickney Ellis is best known for writing *The Women of England* (1838) and other advice books. She learned "woman's duty" by nursing her dying sisters, serving as their children's adopted mother, and managing her husband's household. Her writing—fiction, poetry, books on education and etiquette—was intended to do good and make money. Despite public success and the encouragement of her husband, missionary and author William Ellis (1794–1872), she came to resent the "odious inkpots" and to find more enjoyment in educational projects for young women.

The preface to her first collection of tales, *Pictures of Private Life* (1833–1837), rejects romance in favor of domestic realism—ordinary settings described in detail, characters with common feelings and frailties, probable plots—and defends fiction as "a key" to open "minds that would be closed against a sermon." Later novels, such as *The Brewer's Family* (1863), warn against drinking or parental neglect. *Home, or The Iron Rule* (1836) criticizes tyrannical fathers; *The Mother's Mistake* (1856) admonishes mothers who misunderstand their children's characters.

The Women of England and its sequels were perhaps the century's most popular conduct manuals for middle-class women. To promote domestic happiness in a newly industrialized competitive society, Ellis advocates acceptance of one's sphere, accommodation to the needs of others, and obliteration of self. Women are the "secret spring" of the social machine, but it is in their interest to deny their feelings, conceal their talents, and maintain men's superiority. In her personal life, Ellis often disregarded her own advice; in public she remained staunchly conservative. When other writers urged women to participate in major reform movements, Ellis continued to limit her reader to "the particular minutiae of practical duty" within her own home.

ROBIN SHEETS

Bibliography

Colby, Vineta. *Yesterday's Woman: Domestic Realism in the English Novel.* 1974.

The Home Life and Letters of Mrs. Ellis Compiled by Her Nieces. 1893.

See also WOMANHOOD

· · · · ·

ELMY, ELIZABETH WOLSTENHOLME (1834-1918)

Elizabeth Clarke Wolstenholme Elmy was a forceful advocate of women's rights throughout her life. Her father was a Methodist minister from Eccles; she was orphaned at fourteen, at which time her formal education ended.

Elizabeth Wolstenholme established a girls' boarding school in Congleton, Cheshire, near Manchester and began her work in women's causes by pressing for educational opportunities. She testified before the Schools Inquiry Commission in 1866, established the Manchester Board of School Mistresses, and in 1867 helped found the North of England Council on Higher Education for Women with **Anne Jemima Clough** and **Josephine Butler**. In 1867 she was one of the founding members of the Manchester Women's Suffrage Society. With **Ursula Mellor Bright** she headed the **Married Women's Property** Committee from its founding in 1868 until passage of the Married Women's Property Act of 1882.

In 1875 Elizabeth Wolstenholme married Ben Elmy, a crepe manufacturer of Congleton, and thereafter called herself "Mrs. Wolstenholme Elmy."

Wolstenholme Elmy was almost single-handedly responsible for persuading Parliament to pass the Infant Custody Act of 1886. She also helped to found the Women's Freedom League (1889-1890) and the Women's Emancipation Union (1891-1899), which pressed for the vote for all women, married or single.

After 1890 Wolstenholme Elmy and Ben Elmy, both singly and together, used the pen name "Ellis Ethelmer" to publish feminist articles and tracts. Among these were books of sex education for children—*The Human Flower* (1894), *Baby Buds* (1895)—and poems and essays about the evolution of human society on feminist principles: *Woman Free* (1893), *Life to Woman* (1896), and *Phases of Love* (1897). Using the pen name "Ignota," Wolstenholme Elmy also wrote more than twenty-five articles on women's rights for the *Westminster Review* between 1897 and 1906.

MARY LYNDON SHANLEY

Bibliography

Ethelmer, Ellis. "A Woman Emancipator." *Westminster Review*, vol. 145, pp. 424-428.

Pankhurst, Estelle Sylvia. *The Suffragette Movement*. 1931.

· · · · ·

EMBROIDERY

Embroidery, the art of sewing patterns or designs on material, was popular throughout the nineteenth century. After the invention of elaborate sewing and weaving machines, lower-class women could no longer rely upon embroidery for income, but many women, from private servants through titled ladies, practiced "fancywork." Mass-produced patterns and new materials made embroidery work easier. The Pre-Raphaelites, particularly **William Morris** (1834-1896), revived embroidery as an art form, reinstating it as "the sister art" of painting.

Although embroidery remained a familiar addition to clothing, it was not nearly as common as it had been. Most embroidery work was simply decorative: scenes for framing, fire screens, pillow covers, chair coverings, purses, and, occasionally, children's clothing. Girls demonstrated their sewing abilities in imaginative samplers. Energetic needlewomen copied famous paintings, tapestries, prints from books, and patterns from popular journals, such as the *Englishwoman's Domestic Magazine*. They preferred realistic scenes, landscapes, still lifes, or naturalistic designs (repeating tendrils of vines, leaves, or flowers).

Victorians particularly favored white-on-white embroidery and Berlin wools—brightly colored, soft wools. They also used English worsted, silk, gold and silver threads, chenille, braid, and union cord. Often designs would incorporate beads, straw, nacre (from mother-of-pearl), ribbon, polished steel, or colored foil. The underlying material varied according to purpose and budget, but was usually some kind of linen or canvas.

Berlin wools and printed patterns greatly simplified embroidery. Brightly colored Berlin wools appeared in the 1830s, followed in the 1840s by colored designs: squared patterns indicated each step, allowing the sewer to count the squares and cover coarse canvas with thick wools. George Edmund Street (1824–1881), an eminent architect and friend of Morris, attacked foreign wools on the grounds that they deteriorated the fine art of English embroidery.

William Morris began a revival of artistic embroidery in 1857, when he had Jane Morris, Elizabeth Burden (her sister), and Burne-Jones's sister embroider his patterns. He not only created new designs, but he also dyed his own wools. Although these works were not tapestries (tapestry is woven, not sewn), they were often wall hangings and furniture covers. The art needlework movement began to study historic examples of needlework, and in 1872 the Royal School of Art Needlework was established.

JULIA M. GERGITS

Bibliography

Day, Lewis F. and Mary Buckle. *Art in Needlework: A Book About Embroidery.* 1900.

Jones, Mary Eirwen. *British Samplers.* 1948.

Jourdain, Margaret. *The History of English Secular Embroidery.* 1910.

Parry, Linda. *William Morris Textiles.* 1983.

Sebba, Anne. *Samplers: Five Centuries of a Gentle Craft.* 1979.

See also NEEDLECRAFTS

· · · · ·

EMIGRATION

Between 1815 and 1914 more than 20 million persons emigrated from the United Kingdom. The sheer scale of this movement, particularly when viewed alongside a domestic population increase of 26.5 million to a 1911 total of 35.4 million, suggests its profound impact on British society. Late Victorian imperialists like Cecil Rhodes saw emigration as the only alternative to revolution, and several generations of historians have described it as a "safety valve" which protected Britain from the serious social and political dislocations common in Europe.

The study of emigration has been dominated by economic historians, who, through sophisticated econometric analyses, have built on inadequate and incomplete statistical data to provide useful explanations for various phases of population movement. The earliest studies made simple associations between population pressure, social distress, and emigration, particularly during the early nineteenth century when Malthusian population theories, the **Poor Law**, and rural unemployment were under frequent discussion. The first half of the nineteenth century saw innumerable projects to relieve distress by shipping large numbers of predominantly rural laborers to the colonies. Historians, struck by these obvious connections and intent on showing that emigrants were motivated more by the "push" of economic hardship than by the "pull" of superior overseas opportunities, concluded that economic distress was the central cause of early Victorian emigration, and, moreover, that the bulk of emigrants came from rural backgrounds.

This interpretation, however, took no account of the great majority of emigrants who were not given public or private assistance and traveled independently to the United States rather than to the colonies. Out of 20 million emigrants in the century preceding 1914, 13 million went to the United States. In the 1950s Brinley Thomas developed a model of the "Atlantic economy," in which emigration was related to business cycles in Britain and America. This shifted the focus to the majority of emigrants, introduced "pull" factors into the explanation, and attempted to relate emigration to internal British rural-urban migration. But the fundamental determinant remained economic and the belief persisted that most emigrants had rural origins. More recent work by Charlotte Erickson and Dudley Baines has cast doubt on these traditional interpretations of the causes of emigration. Baines demonstrates that most emigrants had urban backgrounds and that the primary determinant was information provided by friends and relatives who preceded them. "Chain" migration of townspeople stimulated by emigrants' letters and returned migrants thus exceeded the "stage" migration (about 30 percent) of rural people who moved initially to the towns, and later overseas. Only "crisis" emigration, like that provoked by the Highland clearances and the **Irish famine** from 1845, can be shown to have been a mass movement of dispossessed rural dwellers. Baines shows that "pull" and "push" factors in motivating emigrants cannot easily be separated and that internal migration and emigration were complementary rather than alternative. The finding that most emigrants were established town dwellers rather than the urban or rural poor is particularly important, since it demands reassessment of the traditional "safety valve" theory of emigration.

For social historians these causal explanations provide a starting point rather than a conclusion, and stimulate questions that are only now beginning to be explored. Erickson's focus on emigrants' letters shifts emphasis away from economic causes to the social meaning of emigration, both for individual emigrants and for Victorian society. Women, for example, while invariably a minority in annual emigration counts, emigrated in substantial numbers from all social classes, both independently and within families and larger social groupings; their experience offers a fruitful vehicle for the study of other aspects of Victorian society. The same can be said of **Dr. Barnardo**'s child migration and the movements of other national, regional, and local groups. Periods of intense interest in emigration, such as the "craze" of the early 1850s (which attracted comment by writers like Charles Dickens in *David Copperfield*) can offer valuable insights into the preoccupations and aspirations of Victorians quite apart from the statistical aggregates.

Students of Victorian emigration will still find it rewarding to begin by examining demographic sources, and thanks to economic historians like Baines, the inadequacy of the raw statistical data no longer constitutes the serious handicap that it once did. But the more challenging method will attempt to integrate demographic and social information, so that such sources as emigrants' letters, emigration propaganda, and philanthropic records will shed light on issues such as gender, class, and family as well as on emigration history.

A. JAMES HAMMERTON

Bibliography

Baines, Dudley. *Migration in a Mature Economy: Emigration and Internal Migration in England and Wales, 1861-1900.* 1985.

Brander, Michael. *The Emigrant Scots.* 1982.

Carrier, Norman H. and J. R. Jeffery. *External Migration: A Study of the Available Statistics, 1815-1950.* 1953.

Carrothers, William A. *Emigration from the British Isles.* 1929.

Erickson, Charlotte. *Invisible Immigrants: The Adaptation of English and Scottish Immigrants in Nineteenth-Century America.* 1972.

Fitzpatrick, D. *Irish Emigration, 1801-1921.* 1984.

Hammerton, A. James. *Emigrant Gentlewomen: Genteel Poverty and Female Emigration, 1830-1914.* 1979.

Johnson, Stanley C. *A History of Emigration from the United Kingdom to North America, 1763-1912.* 1913.

Thomas, Brinley. *Migration and Economic Growth: A Study of Great Britain and the Atlantic Economy.* 2d ed., 1973.

Wagner, Gillian. *Children of the Empire.* 1982.

See also CHILD SAVING; POPULATION AND DEMOGRAPHICS

. . . . .

EMPIRE AND IMPERIALISM

At the end of the nineteenth century the British Empire covered one-fourth of the earth's land and included a quarter of its population. Emerging after the loss of the thirteen American colonies in 1783, the second empire grew haphazardly. In addition, the British dominated international shipping and communications, provided the capital and engineering for rail networks on every continent, and recreated a distinctive pattern of life and values wherever they settled. In early Victorian times the empire had little meaning for most Britons, but by the century's closing decades the country was swept by a wave of "new imperialism" that climaxed with Queen Victoria's Diamond Jubilee in 1897. British superiority seemed unassailable and unquestionable; and popular enthusiasm for the empire did much to paper over the rifts of nationalism and class division both at home and abroad.

Although the British Empire grew steadily throughout the century, there was no deliberate plan of expansion. Its primary components were India, the colonies of white settlement, and an assortment of dependent territories. Remnants of the first empire remained from the seventeenth- and eighteenth-century European expansion into thinly populated sections of the globe. Other colonies were acquired as the outcome of wars (e.g., French Canada) or "claimed" by explorers and adventurers. Shipping and trading interests established ports (Singapore, Hong Kong) and penetrated new territories in search of markets. After 1857, the **East India Company** was disbanded and Britain took over direct rule of India; and in India, as elsewhere, new territories were subdued in order to protect the borders of existing colonies or make trade routes secure. Around the world, islands and coastal enclaves provided coaling stations for naval and merchant ships. During the last quarter of the century, Britain added many parts of Africa for purely imperial motives: to prevent them from being claimed by other European powers.

During Victoria's reign, eighteen major territories and a host of minor possessions were added, at a pace that increased from the 1870s. The British Empire of 1897 included **India**, **Canada**, **New Zealand**, and the states of **Australia**; Ashanti, Basutoland, Bechuanaland, British **East Africa**, Cape Province, Gambia, the Gold Coast, Natal, Nigeria, Nyasaland, Rhodesia, Sierra Leone, Somaliland, Uganda, and Zanzibar in Africa; Aden, Brunei, Ceylon, Hong Kong, Labuan, the Malay Federated States, North Borneo, Papua, Sarawak, and Singapore in Asia; the Bahamas, Barbados, British Guinea, British Honduras, the Virgin Islands, the Falkland Islands, Jamaica, the Leeward Islands, Newfoundland, Tobago, Trinidad, Turks and Caicos Islands, and the Windward Islands in America; the Channel Islands, Gibraltar, the Isle of Man, and Malta in Europe; and dozens of other islands scattered about the oceans of the world, including Ascension, Bermuda, St. Helena, Tristan da Cunha, Mauritius, the Seychelles, Ellice, Gilbert, Southern Solomon, Fiji, Pitcairn, and Tasmania.

The empire had no constitutional basis or regularized central government; the sole unifying factor was allegiance to the Crown. During Victoria's reign the principal colonies of white settlement (Australia, New Zealand, Canada) achieved virtual self-government; other components of the empire were administered by mechanisms that ranged from the extensive and well-organized Indian Civil Service to the lonely commissioner in an isolated protectorate. Subject peoples were not required to provide troops for imperial defense. About half of the British army, at any given moment, was overseas. Regular infantry battalions were garrisoned in India, Ireland, Malta, South Africa, Gibralter, **Egypt**, Mauritius, Canada, the **West Indies**, Singapore, Bermuda, Ceylon, and Hong Kong. The Indian army, composed largely of native troops but with an entirely British officer corps (generally career soldiers drawn from the middle class, not the aristocrats and gentry who commanded the regular army), was also available for defense, for maintaining internal order—and for territorial expansion on the Indian frontier.

The empire's administrators were largely middle-class men; educated at **public schools** (but not at Eton), they found, in the colonies, a degree of power and a standard of living that only aristocrats could enjoy at home. Although by late in the century Canada and Australia offered assisted passage to qualified workers and artisans, British emigrants in most parts of the empire were principally business and professional people who continued to consider Britain "home." Wherever they settled they tended to form an isolated British community with its own Anglican church, bank, club, and residences. As transportation improved and attitudes changed, social interchange and intermarriage with the local residents became less common; the liaisons that had produced a significant Eurasian population in parts of India and the Far East were largely an earlier phenomenon.

The sense of the empire as an entity, which grew so strong by the century's end, was made possible largely by the technological revolution in communication and transportation. More than half of the world's merchant shipping carried the British flag, and with the coming of efficient steam vessels the passage to

India was shortened to seventeen days. Australia could be reached in four weeks. Complicated express routings combined rail and ship to move mail and parcel post at an even speedier rate. By the 1890s, almost all British possessions could be reached instantly over the networks of telegraph lines and submarine cables. The empire's primary bequest to its heirs, in fact, may have been the technological infrastructure that it developed for its own commerce and administration; just as the Romans left behind the roads of Europe, the British Victorians strung wires and relay stations across some of the world's most desolate territory and invested both capital and engineering skills to create rail lines, spectacular bridges, and deep-water ports.

The causes and consequences of British imperialism in the nineteenth century continue to be a subject of investigation and debate among historians. Commercial interests, the search for markets, and the classic pattern of colonialism (in which the subject territory serves as a source of raw materials and an outlet for manufactured goods) were certainly important, as were national interests and the sheer adventure of exploring. There were also humanitarian and ideological components. Some territories were acquired as part of the effort to suppress the **slave trade**. Queen Victoria defined the imperial mission as "to protect the poor natives and advance civilization."

The spirit of empire, at the end of the century, occupied a key role in the British imagination. It was a hallmark of the nation's commercial strength and world position, a source of pride, and the subject of endless stories in boys' and girls' magazines and the popular journalism of Alfred Harmsworth's *Daily Mail*. The anti-imperialist sentiment that had also persisted throughout the century was muted, though it remained alive among Gladstonian Liberals and found new form in the voices of a few from the working class, who perceived that the benefits of empire failed to trickle down very far. Nationalist movements among subject peoples were as yet barely visible; and few foresaw the disappearance—or doubted the rightness—of the vast swathes on the world's map that were colored British red.

SALLY MITCHELL
JAMES D. STARTT

Bibliography

Benians, Ernest A. et al. *The Cambridge History of the British Empire.* 1929–1959.

Cain, Peter J. *Economic Foundations of the British Overseas Expansion 1815–1914.* 1980.

Eldridge, Colin G., ed. *British Imperialism in the Nineteenth Century.* 1984.

Flint, John E. *Books on the British Empire and Commonwealth.* 1968.

Hyam, Ronald E. *Britain's Imperial Century 1815–1914: A Study of Empire and Expansion.* 1976.

MacInnes, Charles Malcolm. *An Introduction to the Economic History of the British Empire.* 1935.

Morris, James. *Pax Britannica.* 1968.

Porter, Bernard. *The Lion's Share: A Short History of British Imperialism, 1850–1970.* 1975.

Thornton, A. P. *The Imperial Idea and Its Enemies: A Study in British Power.* 1959.

Winks, Robin W., ed. *The Historiography of the British Empire-Commonwealth: Trends, Interpretations and Resources.* 1966.

See also FAR EAST; GOVERNMENT: COLONIES AND EMPIRE; MISSIONARIES; SOUTH AFRICA; WEST AFRICA; WEST INDIES

. . . . .

ENGINEERING

The engineering profession emerged in Britain in the eighteenth century, when John Smeaton (1724-1792) and others began to describe themselves as "civil engineers" as distinct from military engineers, and to join together to form professional associations. Of course, engineering itself as the art of making and building things goes back to antiquity, when "ingenious" men were employed to build roads and earthworks and to construct simple machines. But the men employed in these operations were traditionally artisans or craftsmen who practiced their trade without any sense of professional identity, and it was only with the onset of rapid industrialization in Britain in the eighteenth century that constructional projects of a substantial and continuing nature began to require the specialized expertise that made possible the awakening of professional self-consciousness. Civil engineers developed rapidly in numbers and organization, particularly in response to the demand for railways, and became one of the most colorful and highly esteemed of the new professions that rose to prominence in Victorian Britain.

The first successful professional organization among engineers was the Institution of Civil Engineers, founded in 1818. Thomas Telford (1757–1834), an outstanding builder of roads, bridges, and canals, agreed to become its first president in 1820, and held the post until his death in 1834. The institution, which received its royal charter in 1828, continued to represent the whole of the engineering profession until the boom in railway construction caused a sharp increase in the demand for engineers and led some who were involved in railway work to feel that the Institution of Civil Engineers was not paying sufficient attention to their interests. The result was the foundation of the Institution of Mechanical Engineers in 1847. George Stephenson, doyen of railway builders, became the first president, and after his death in 1848 was succeeded by his son Robert Stephenson. The new institution, initially based in Birmingham, encouraged a proliferation of organizations, both national and regional.

The body of engineers composing the engineering profession in Britain rose from about 1,000 in 1850 to around 40,000 in 1914. By 1914, moreover, there were seventeen major national institutions reflecting increasing specialization, with separate organizations for mining engineers, marine engineers, water engineers, electrical engineers, and so on. In continental Europe, however, the pattern was somewhat different because engineers relied more on university degrees for their social status than on the "clubability" and mutual improvement provided by the British institutions.

The professional engineering institutions incorporated much of the self-help ethos popularized by **Samuel Smiles**, who had chosen many engineers as embodiments of his ideal type of character (*Self-Help* was published in 1859 and his *Lives of the Engineers* followed in 1862). By providing regular programs of papers, discussions, and publications, the engineering societies enabled members to keep up to date on scientific and technical developments in their specialized fields.

Victorian engineers were prominently involved in all the major constructional events of the period. The creation of the **railway** network engaged many civil engineers, and the provision of locomotives, rolling stock, and signaling gave continuing employment to large numbers of mechanical engineers engaged in the railways' workshops. Naval architects and marine engineers took a prominent part in transforming the traditional wooden sailing ship into the iron or steel-hulled steamship, which operated in all the navies and on all the trade routes of the world by the end of the nineteenth century. I. K. Brunel's last great steamship, the paddle- and screw-propelled *Great Eastern*, was launched in 1859 and remained the largest ship built in the century. Although not a commercial success, it was used very effectively to lay the first Atlantic telegraph cable, and the steady expansion of telegraphic links around the world was another important field of engineering activity.

Victorian engineers also played an outstanding part in transforming town life through the provision of piped water, gas, drains, paving, and sewage disposal. A comprehensive scheme for improving London's drainage and waste removal was carried out by Joseph Bazalgette for the Metropolitan Board of Works between 1855 and 1875. The scheme involved northern and southern trunk sewers running from west to east on opposite sides of the Thames, intersecting all the older sewers which had drained directly into the river and carrying the waste to outfall points placed well down the tidal estuary. Large pumping engines maintained the flow in these sewers, and the Victoria Embankment in central London was constructed as part of work on the northern trunk. Similar but smaller schemes were adopted by towns all over the country.

Great reservoirs were built in the upland districts to impound fresh water which was then piped to the urban centers. By the end of the century, electrical engineers were providing electric light, electric tramway services, and other facilities from large-scale power-generating stations. Sebastian Ferranti built the first large London power station at Deptford in 1888. In bridge building, civil engineers learned important lessons from the collapse of the Tay railway bridge in 1879, and incorporated these in the great cantilever railway bridge over the Forth, opened in 1890. The Tower Bridge of 1894, although Gothic in appearance, made use of advanced hydraulic equipment to raise the lifting sections.

Meanwhile, the increase in productivity which was such a striking characteristic of Victorian industrialization was being achieved by engineers in all the leading industries, from coal mining to the iron and steel industry, from machine tool manufacture to the production of chemicals and the provision of telephone systems. Engineering performed a vital animating function in the Victorian economy. More than any other group in the community, the professional engineers provided the means whereby industrial output was increased and the mass of the population began to enjoy an improved standard of living.

Despite all of these very considerable achievements, engineering lost something of its excitement in the second half of the century. There were many more engineers doing much more work than hitherto, but they became increasingly anonymous. The heroic age of engineering in Britain came to be identified with the men whom Smiles had immortalized, and their contemporaries: Smeaton and Brindley, Telford and Rennie, the Stephensons and the Brunels. When both Robert Stephenson and I. K. Brunel died in 1859, the nation mourned, and posterity has remembered them. Their successors, although eminently successful professional men, achieved only a fraction of the public fame enjoyed by the earlier engineers, and were virtually forgotten by posterity. To a great extent, this loss of individual color was the price that the engineering profession had to pay for successful specialization and institutionalization. But it did mark a decline in public awareness and thus anticipated some of the problems that the profession has faced in the twentieth century.

R. A. BUCHANAN

Bibliography

Armytage, W. H. G. *A Social History of Engineering.* 1961.

Briggs, Asa. *Victorian Cities.* 1970.

Buchanan, R. A. *Industrial Archaeology in Britain.* 2d ed., 1982.

Burstall, Aubrey F. *A History of Mechanical Engineering.* 1963.

Dunsheath, Percy. *A History of Electrical Engineering.* 1962.

Rolt, L. T. C. *George and Robert Stephenson: The Railway Revolution.* 1960.

———. *Isambard Kingdom Brunel: A Biography.* 1957.

———. *Thomas Telford.* 1958.

———. *Victorian Engineering.* 1970.

Smiles, Samuel. *The Lives of the Engineers.* 1862; rpt. in 3 vols., 1968.

See also ATLANTIC CABLE; STEAM ENGINE; TECHNOLOGY AND INVENTION

. . . . .

ENGLISH WOMAN'S JOURNAL, ENGLISHWOMAN'S REVIEW

The *English Woman's Journal,* a monthly magazine established in 1858, and the employment register that grew up around it were instrumental in providing opportunities for women to enter new professions. After the *Journal* ceased publication in 1864, the *Englishwoman's Review* filled its role as center of the network of communications linking feminists, and may be considered virtually the journal of record for the women's movement until the expansion of social feminism, trade union activity, and militant suffragism in the century's final years.

The *English Woman's Journal* originated with the women of the **Langham Place Circle.** Organized by **Bessie Raynor Parkes** and

Barbara Leigh Smith Bodichon, it was the first periodical in England devoted specifically to women's affairs. The first issue declared the magazine's interest in describing existing employment for women, both intellectual and manual, exploring the best methods for expanding that employment, and promoting reform of laws affecting the property and condition of the sexes. Edited for a time by **Emily Davies** (who later founded Girton College), the *Journal* reprinted speeches on women's issues, waged campaigns to improve the condition of governesses and provide physical education for girls, and closely followed legal questions. Its premises also housed the Society for Promoting the Employment of Women and a Ladies Institute that provided a reading room, place to receive mail, and lunchroom for women who were in search of employment.

The *English Woman's Journal*, however, never managed to become financially viable. In 1864 it was merged with a new monthly, the *Alexandra Magazine*. The editor, Bessie Raynor Parkes, tried to broaden the circulation by adding some lighter material. In 1865 the *Alexandra Magazine* also ceased publication. In the following year Jessie Boucherett (1825-1905) revived the *English Woman's Journal* under the title *Englishwoman's Review of Social and Industrial Questions* (1866-1910). Although she served as titular editor for only four years, Boucherett remained involved with the journal until her death. Succeeding editors were Caroline Ashurst Biggs (1870-1889), **Helen Blackburn** (1890-1903), and Antoinette Mackenzie. *The Englishwoman's Review* was published quarterly except for the period 1875-1890, when it appeared monthly.

The *Englishwoman's Review* supported women's causes in various articles and news stories, but its most important function was, as the editors wrote in 1890, to record "women's progress in social and industrial questions in all parts of the world." Thus it summarized political debates, with lists of M.P.'s who voted for or against important bills; printed the deliberations of philanthropic organizations; published election results in boroughs where women ran as Poor Law guardians or for the school board; reported court proceedings; and provided lists of the names, degrees, and honors of women students. The articles, summaries, and lists in the *Englishwoman's Review* therefore provide a matchless primary resource for the study of legal questions, suffrage, and women's progress in education, medicine, and employment, although researchers should note the editors' class bias and their "hands-off" policy toward sensitive issues such as the campaign against the Contagious Diseases Acts.

SHEILA R. HERSTEIN

Bibliography

Herstein, Sheila R. "The *English Woman's Journal* and the Langham Place Circle: A Feminist Forum and Its Women Editors." In Joel Wiener, ed., *Innovators and Preachers: The Role of the Editor in Victorian England*. 1985.

Murray, Janet Horowitz. "Class vs. Gender Identification in the Englishwoman's Review of the 1880s." *Victorian Periodicals Review*, vol. 18, pp. 138-142.

—— and Myra Stark. Introduction to *The Englishwoman's Review of Social and Industrial Questions: An Index*, compiled by Janet Horowitz Murray and Anna K. Clark. 1985.

· · · · ·

ENVIRONMENTAL POLLUTION

As pioneer in the industrial revolution, Britain was also the first country to confront the concomitant problems of environmental pollution. Water and air pollution received most of the attention, but visual pollution caused by obtrusive outdoor advertising and noise pollution also created concern.

Water pollution arose from the almost universal feeling that streams and rivers were drains supplied by nature for carrying away both household and industrial wastes. The problem was amplified from the 1840s as growing commitment to public health brought improved town drainage and greater use of water closets. The "great stink" of 1858, when the Thames became so foul that the proceedings of Parliament were interrupted, dramatized the problem. Most mechanical solutions merely changed the focus of pollution. With the completion (1868) of Joseph William Bazalgette's (1819-1891) main drainage system, London's sewage was still released into the Thames, although at Barking rather than upstream. Eventually most sewage found its way to the ocean, and by 1900 illnesses contracted from contaminated shellfish indicated that even the seas were not immune to pollution. Inland cities found no obvious remedies; one, Birmingham, was faced for years with contradictory court orders on discharging, or not discharging, its sewage.

No satisfactory legislative solution was found. In theory, the common law of nuisance could be applied to water pollution, but the expense of the procedure and the virtual impossibility of fixing individual blame made that route impracticable. The Royal Commission on the Prevention of Pollution of Rivers (1864-1873) was unable to establish explicit standards for defining inadmissible pollution, and the Rivers Pollution Prevention Act (1876) ruled out antipollution steps that might injure industry. Only toward the end of the century, when the Mersey and Irwell Joint Committee (1891), the Ribble Joint Committee (1891), and the West Riding of Yorkshire Rivers Board (1893) were created with power to manage pollution reduction for entire drainage areas, did a feasible solution appear to be forthcoming.

Smoke pollution, originating in medieval England with the burning of coal for domestic heating, was intensified by the industrial revolution. The consequences—dirt, reduced visibility, respiratory complications—became especially obvious with the great London fogs, really combinations of fog and smoke, or smog (a word coined in 1905), which increasingly marked the late Victorian era. Although romanticized by Charles Dickens as "London particulars," and in Arthur Conan Doyle's Sherlock Holmes stories, the fogs could be deadly; that of the winter of 1879-1880 caused 2,400 fatalities. Since smoke pollution resulted from imperfect combustion caused by badly designed grates and furnaces and careless stoking, more efficient equipment properly operated would virtually end smoke pollution and prevent waste of coal. But despite obvious economic incentives, smoke pollution continued, partially because it was popularly associated with employment,

prosperity, and progress; everyone knew that bustling cities were smoky, while pure air suggested rural decadence.

Repeated attempts to reduce atmospheric smoke met with little success. Manchester, Leeds, Bradford, and other northern industrial cities applied in the 1840s for local acts limiting smoke production. Major smoke reduction acts for London were passed in 1853 and 1891, and public health acts of 1866 and 1875 contained clauses mandating the reduction of industrial smoke outside London. But legislative attempts were largely ineffective. It was difficult to define "smoke" with legal exactitude, and industries of major economic importance tended to be exempted. Arguments that further reduction of smoke was not "practicable" given available technology were accepted as defense. There was, additionally, a general disinclination to prosecute (especially where magistrates were also factory owners). Domestic smoke, estimated to constitute up to 95 percent of the whole, was excluded from the ordinances. Parliamentary hearings in 1843 publicized industrial furnaces designed to consume their own smoke, as did the Smoke Abatement Exhibitions organized by **Octavia Hill** (1838-1912) and Ernest Hart (1835-1898) which were held in 1881-1882 at South Kensington and Manchester. Founded to publicize smoke reduction methods and agitate for better enforcement of existing antismoke legislation were the National Smoke Abatement Institution, which existed for several years in the mid-1880s, and the Coal Smoke Abatement Society (1898), convened by William Blake Richmond (1842-1921).

Also polluting the air were "noxious vapours" produced by the chemical industry. The Alkali Act (1863), passed at the insistence of Lord Derby (1799-1869), whose estate at Knowsley was assaulted by destructive fumes emanating from chemical works at St. Helens and Widnes, created a measurable standard of permissible emission and established a professional inspectorate which rapidly achieved compliance. Notable was the close cooperation between the alkali inspectorate, headed first by Robert Angus Smith (1817-1884), and the chemical industry, which became allies in efforts to convert polluting waste products into salable commodities. Amending acts, suggested by the inspectorate, substantially tightened standards while simultaneously extending the range of processes the acts governed, but growth of the chemical industry outran provisions of legislation, so that the hope of achieving pure air in chemical manufacturing areas was never realized.

Outdoor advertising struck some Victorians as visual pollution, especially after the saturation campaigns promoting Beecham's Pills and Lipton's Tea became models for other advertisers. In 1893 Richardson Evans (1850–1931), a newspaper leader writer, established the Society for Checking the Abuses of Public Advertising, generally known by its acronym, SCAPA. SCAPA contacted its natural adversaries, the United Billposters' Association and the London Billposters' Protective Association, and in concert with them drafted legislation adopted by Parliament as the Advertisements Regulation Act (1907), which permitted local authorities to make bylaws limiting excesses in outdoor advertising.

Noise bothered some Victorians, perhaps most famously Thomas Carlyle, whose elaborately constructed soundproof study in Chelsea proved a failure. William Morris's *News from Nowhere* (1891) envisaged a world devoid of the "sound of riveting and hammering," but to most Victorians such sounds were inevitable signs of progressive activity. Memoirs of the mid-Victorian period recall the deafening sound of carriage wheels rolling over stone paving blocks, a roar audible even in the middle of Regent's Park. In the north of England, it was customary for families of the ill to reduce traffic noises by covering the cobblestones with thick bark. Wooden pavement blocks impregnated with oil, widely used late in the century, reduced noise substantially, but the rubber tire and the automobile were eagerly anticipated as the ultimate solution to the problem of urban traffic noise. In the late 1890s an Association for the Suppression of Street Noises was in existence, but accomplished little. Noise of all sorts remained a problem not only unsolved, but even largely unrecognized.

JOHN RANLETT

Bibliography

Brimblecombe, Peter. *The Big Smoke: A History of Air Pollution in London Since Medieval Times.* 1987.

Evans, Richardson. *An Account of the Scapa Society.* 1926.

Flick, Carlos. "The Movement for Smoke Abatement in Nineteenth-Century Britain." *Technology and Culture*, vol. 21, pp. 29–50.

MacLeod, Roy M. "The Alkali Acts Administration, 1863–84: The Emergence of the Civil Scientist." *Victorian Studies*, vol. 9, pp. 85–112.

Wohl, Anthony S. *Endangered Lives: Public Health in Victorian Britain.* 1983.

See also PLUMBING; PUBLIC HEALTH

. . . . .

EPIDEMIC DISEASES

The concentration of the urban poor in squalid conditions made epidemics inevitable. In the late 1840s—when smallpox, typhus, Asiatic cholera, and scarlet fever struck at once—the fatalities provided the impetus for sanitary reform. More accurate statistical methods, surveys, and record keeping, together with the eventual isolation of the bacterial causes of many diseases, led to an understanding of how diseases were transmitted and to more hygienic practices.

Until 1850, when William Jenner distinguished between typhoid and typhus, they were confused. Relapsing and other "continued" fevers were sometimes mistaken for them. Typhoid is an intestinal disease spread by infected water or milk, whereas typhus is a blood disease carried by lice, as is relapsing fever. Major epidemics of typhus occurred from 1837–1839, 1847–1848, and 1862–1865, but not all epidemics of this or any other disease affected the whole country. Typhoid increased toward the end of the century, probably because it was difficult to trace sources of pollution, whereas typhus declined with better washing facilities.

Asiatic **cholera** first came to Britain in 1831. Three more waves followed, in 1848–1849, 1853–1854, and 1865–1866. The ravages of this disease spurred civic bodies and medical officers to improve the health of towns. The **Public Health** Act of 1848 encouraged drainage installation on a national scale.

Improvement was piecemeal because of conflicting private interests and theories about the cause of disease. Was it a miasma emanating from filth or contagion from contact with a physical or chemical source? Not until late in the century did bacteriological evidence come in, with the 1880s being the watershed decade.

A close atmosphere and careless practices facilitated contact with chest and throat disease bacteria. **Tuberculosis** spread insidiously and increased over a long period from 1750 to 1840. It did not really start to decline until 1880, but it was not an obvious epidemic because of its slow-killing nature.

Scarlet fever, or scarletina, went in waves between 1830 and 1890 and increased in virulence during that period. It was often confused with diphtheria until the great diphtheria pandemic in 1855–1856 distinguished the two beyond doubt. Whooping cough and measles were always present and killed children who had little resistance.

Smallpox was the one disease for which prevention was available. Edward Jenner's **vaccination** had mixed success but was promoted by the Vaccination Acts after the epidemics of 1837–1840, 1848–1849, and 1870–1873.

Modern social science methods applied to historical records are leading to a much deeper understanding of the complexity of social, environmental, and medical factors that led to the improvement of health at the end of the century.

SIDNEY JOHNSON

Bibliography

Rosen, George. "Disease, Debility, and Death." In Harold Dyos and Michael Wolff, eds., *The Victorian City*. 1973.

Woods, Robert and John Woodward, eds. *Urban Disease and Mortality in Nineteenth-Century England*. 1984.

Wrigley, E. A. and R. S. Schofield. *The Population History of England, 1541–1871: A Reconstruction*. 1981.

See also BACTERIOLOGY

. . . . .

ETHNOLOGY

Ethnology, or the history of human races, was the historical predecessor of modern day **anthropology**. Under the evolutionary synthesis of the 1860s it became a specialized subdiscipline of the latter. The object of ethnological study was to trace the geographical distributions of, and relations between, the peoples or races that constituted the human species. Their physical or racial characteristics, moral beliefs, social customs, material cultures, and historical records were analyzed for evidence relating to the broad chronology of human history since the creation. Ethnography was ethnology's descriptive counterpart and synthesized data collected by travelers, explorers, and missionaries to create descriptive catalogues of the physical and cultural characteristics of primitive peoples.

"Ethnology" came into common use in the 1840s. James Cowles Prichard (1786–1848) used the term in his 1843 *Natural History of Man* to refer to the study of the history of "nations." The word was further popularized by its adoption into the titles of numerous societies, such as the Ethnological Society of London (1843), formed at this time to promote study of the different races or varieties of humankind. Ethnologists, working within a Mosaic time frame, sought to document the history of humanity since the creation. As a whole ethnologists believed in the unity (monogenesis) of the human species and sought to document that unity through the ethnographic data that ever-increasing trade, travel, missionary work, and empire made readily available.

The ethnology of the 1840s and 1850s sought to establish historical links between races through a comparative study of their languages. The success of contemporary philologists in identifying genealogically linked families of languages motivated ethnologists to use philology as a tool for establishing historical connections between different racial groups. They hoped to use language as a means of charting the migration of peoples through space and time.

By the 1860s increased interest in racial morphology led many investigators to shift attention from the linguistic similarities among racial groups to their physical differences. The significance of language as a sign of historical linkage was deemphasized and new weight was placed upon the extent and origin of racial variation. The discovery of human antiquity also disproved all chronologies based upon the biblical record. Ethnology was relegated to a contributory role in an expanded anthropological science which treated the entirety of the human record in evolutionary terms.

DAVID K. VAN KEUREN

Bibliography

Stocking, George W. *Victorian Anthropology*. 1987.

See also RACE

. . . . .

ETIQUETTE see SOCIETY, ETIQUETTE AND CUSTOMS OF

EUGENICS

Although the ideas of eugenics, the "science" of better breeding, can be traced back to the writings of Plato, the modern movement was founded in 1865 by **Francis Galton**. Galton, convinced that various physical and behavioral characteristics were inherited, believed that social ills could be cured by controlling the reproduction of "undesirables" (negative eugenics) and encouraging the breeding of superior individuals (positive eugenics) to the end of breeding a better race.

Fueled by the rediscovery of Mendel's laws in 1900, the movement gained a nationalistic fervor and enjoyed widespread support among professionals and academics such as Karl Pearson, Caleb William Saleeby, Major Leonard Darwin, Montague Crackanthorpe, William Chapple, Arnold White, Ferdinand Schiller, William Inge, and William and Catherine Whetham. In 1904 Galton founded a research fellowship at the University of London which eventually became the Galton Laboratory of Eugenics. In 1907, the Eugenics Education Society was founded and attracted

a substantial number of biologists, sociologists, psychologists, and religious leaders.

Many eugenists believed that every human characteristic from feeblemindedness to musical ability was determined by simple genes inherited in typical Mendelian fashion.

The idea that the "undesirable" classes were out-producing the "desirable" classes and would lead to race suicide became an integral part of the movement. The differential birth rate and the changing social character of Britain became primary foci. Marriage certificate laws, tax rebates for dependent children (only the middle and upper classes paid taxes), and the Mental Deficiency Act of 1914, which provided for the detention and segregation of the feebleminded, were passed.

CHARLES L. VIGUE

Bibliography

Blacker, C. P. *Eugenics: Galton and After*. 1952.

Greer, Germaine. *Sex and Destiny: The Politics of Human Fertility*. 1984.

Kevles, Daniel J. *In the Name of Eugenics: Genetics and the Uses of Human Heredity*. 1985.

Searle, Geoffrey Russell. *Eugenics and Politics in Britain, 1900-1914*. 1976.

Soloway, Richard Allen. *Birth Control and the Population Question in England, 1877-1930*. 1982.

Webb, Sidney. *Eugenics and the Poor Law*. 1909.

See also SOCIAL DARWINISM

. . . . .

EVANGELICAL MOVEMENT

The term "evangelical" is used in two senses in reference to Victorian England. In its more general sense, it refers to the complex of movements and denominations that grew out of the evangelical revival of the eighteenth century. In a narrower sense, it denotes one part of that movement, the Evangelical party within the **Church of England**. In both senses, evangelicalism represents an emphasis on the spiritual transformation of the individual by conversion and the "serious" Christian life resulting therefrom. This is the religious base of what is called "Victorian" morality.

The roots of evangelicalism lay in the Puritanism of the seventeenth century, and its revival was a reaction to the cold moralistic rationalism that had supplanted it in the eighteenth. The new element was the emphasis on personal experience rather than formal doctrines or institutions, the experience of conversion: consciousness of sin, awakening to grace and commitment to Christ. That experience, akin to a new birth, is best described in the words of John Wesley (1703–1791): "I felt my heart strangely warmed. I felt I did trust in Christ, Christ alone, for salvation; and an assurance was given me that he had taken away my sins, even mine, and saved me from the law of sin and death." Evangelical Protestantism is characterized by moral earnestness, rigorous standards of conduct, frequent examination of conscience, Bible reading, family prayers, and lay activity.

Wesley's conversion in 1738 is regarded as the beginning of the evangelical movement, although others were also at work. Responding to a spiritual hunger among the lower classes, Wesley found himself hindered by the structure of the established church and excluded from most pulpits. He was driven to preach out of doors, to set up religious groups, and eventually to develop an organization of his own. After his death, the Wesleyan Methodist "connection" became a new nonconformist denomination; secessions from it spawned still more denominations. There were also non-Wesleyan Methodists, notably the Welsh Calvinistic Methodists.

Methodism was not the only product of the evangelical revival. It found an echo in some of the older nonconformist bodies, especially the **Baptists** and **Congregationalists**, into whom it breathed new life. It also stimulated a revival in one section of the Church of England. Through these groups, evangelicalism was able to reach (and become the religious expression of) the middle classes and to influence even the upper class. Crossing denominational lines, evangelicals often worked together in the voluntary societies characteristic of the nineteenth century—Bible societies, religious tract societies, missionary and philanthropic societies—meeting in May at Exeter Hall in London.

Evangelicalism found a home within one wing of the established Anglican church, sometimes called the "Low Church," and this gave evangelical influences their widest diffusion. One center of this movement was at Cambridge University, where Charles Simeon (1759–1836) encouraged the training and careers of Evangelical clergymen. Another center was the London suburb of Clapham, where a number of influential upper middle-class lay figures settled. The most prominent member of this "Clapham sect" was William Wilberforce (1759–1833), a Tory member of Parliament who led the successful campaign against slavery. This was the most famous of the causes that the Claphamites advocated. Their primary interest was in the moral improvement of the lower classes, sometimes patronizingly, with a view to deflecting revolutionary tendencies, but sometimes out of a genuine humanitarianism which, along with their moralism, was diffused generally beyond strictly evangelical circles.

The evangelicals infused a distinctive seriousness and moralism into the life of Victorian England. They had largely accomplished this before Victoria came to the throne, by which time the evangelical movement was beginning to lose its original force and direction. The quality and effectiveness of Anglican Evangelicals fell off after the first generation. Their only great figure after 1830 was Lord Ashley, later the seventh earl of **Shaftesbury** (1801–1885), the reformer of the conditions of factory labor. Evangelicalism, forming a strong faction within the church, hardened into the narrowness of a party, with exclusive tenets and a special cant. Its theology, both Bible centered and Bible limited, was inadequate to meet new intellectual challenges and tended to be expressed in quasi-Calvinistic language which repelled many by its harshness. Its chief newspaper, the *Record*, was noted for vitriolic denunciations of the **High Church** and **Broad Church** parties and for strident no-popery and Sabbatarianism. Meanwhile, non-Anglican evangelicals had become absorbed in the great nonconformist causes such as disestablishment and temperance. In becoming politicized, they lost sight of their original demand for individual regeneration.

In religion, nothing fails like success. Evangelicalism had moralized Victorian England and promoted a diffused humanitarianism which eventually could not be contained within specifically evangelical movements.

JOSEF L. ALTHOLZ

Bibliography

Balleine, George R. *A History of the Evangelical Party in the Church of England.* New ed., 1951.

Bradley, Ian. *The Call to Seriousness.* 1976.

Brown, Ford K. *Fathers of the Victorians.* 1961.

Finlayson, Geoffrey B. A. M. *The Seventh Earl of Shaftesbury 1801–1885.* 1981.

Heasman, Kathleen. *Evangelicals in Action.* 1962.

Meacham, Standish. "The Evangelical Inheritance." *Journal of British Studies,* vol. 3, pp. 88–104.

See also NONCONFORMITY

· · · · ·

EVOLUTION

Before 1859, when **Charles Darwin's** (1809–1882) *The Origin of Species* was published, the predominant view of living organisms was that they were products of God's creation and had not appreciably changed in form and function since Genesis. However, from antiquity to Victorian times, naturalists and philosophers had regarded creation theory as an inadequate explanation for such phenomena as the diversity of life and the fossil record. They considered the concept of organic evolution, i.e., the process of continuous, gradual change in the structure and function of living things, an alternative to creationism.

Aristotle utilized the concept of evolution when making observations about the natural world. Post-Renaissance naturalists such as John Ray (1627–1705), Pierre de Maupertuis (1698–1759), Comte de Buffon (1707–1788), and Darwin's grandfather, Erasmus Darwin (1731–1802), found evolution an attractive alternative to the view that living species were immutable. They did not offer enough evidence to overturn the popular view of creation, nor did they construct a satisfactory mechanism that could account for evolutionary change, although Erasmus Darwin's poem, *The Temple of Nature,* posthumously published in 1803, included an evolutionary scheme.

The French naturalist, Jean Baptiste de Lamarck (1744–1829), developed a theory describing how all living things had evolved from more primitive forms. His most important work, *Philosophie zoologique* (1809) explained that the environment helped shape an organism's traits by inducing in them certain body movements and habits which ultimately led to the formation of new organs. For example, the giraffe developed its long neck by stretching to reach the leafy vegetation at the top of trees. To Lamarck, environmentally induced changes were inherited by an organism's offspring and, if enough modifications accumulated, a new species would be formed. However, Lamarck selected poor examples to support his theory and he did not provide a mechanism adequate enough to show how new species developed.

Robert Chambers (1802–1871), a journalist and amateur scientist, created a stir when he wrote and anonymously published *The Vestiges of the Natural History of Creation* in 1844. Chambers's work was rejected by the scientific community, including **Thomas Henry Huxley** (1825–1895), later a staunch defender of Darwin's evolutionary theory. Like Lamarck's, Chambers's theory lacked sufficient evidence and failed to provide a plausible mechanism for evolution. The theory blended some elements of Lamarck's theory with vitalism, i.e., the belief that evolution was not determined by mechanical causes alone but by an overall design or purpose in nature. He seriously damaged his theory's credibility when he accepted spontaneous generation, the discredited belief that nonliving matter could spontaneously produce living things.

Fifteen years later, Darwin proposed his theory of evolution based upon the concept of adaptation, i.e., useful characteristics which improve an organism's viability. Darwin suggested that natural selection allowed individuals with favorable characteristics to be preserved, and it excluded those with non-adaptive traits, a process quite similar to artificial selection when horses or dogs with more desirable characteristics are selected for breeding. In Darwin's view, organisms with such adaptations produced many descendants, while forms without them produced fewer offspring, and nature thereby was selecting the more adaptive traits.

How was Darwin able to develop an evolutionary theory that could survive the attacks and ridicule that plagued his predecessors? The previous decade's debate about Chambers's theory had made thought and discussion about evolution more respectable by 1859. Also, Darwin was fortunate in being able to travel to distant and exotic lands, with their enormous variety of living things and environments. Darwin cited the influence of Thomas Robert Malthus (1766-1834), whose *Essay on Population* (1798) he had read in 1838, as crucial in developing the theory of natural selection. In the *Essay*, Malthus illustrated how food supply and living space and conditions limited the growth of human populations. In the *Origin*, Darwin utilized Malthus's ideas of environmental restraints on population growth to explain evolution in all living things except humans.

At the same time and independent of Darwin, another naturalist, **Alfred Russel Wallace** (1823-1913), discovered natural selection. Wallace also attributed his success in finding the natural selection principle to reading Malthus's *Essay*. Darwin received much greater acclaim for his work, despite the coincidental discoveries, because he had worked considerably longer on the problem of evolution and already had a substantial reputation in the scientific world. His position also was enhanced by his skillful use of massive evidence in support of a coherent theory. The priority granted Darwin for proposing the theory of natural selection was never disputed by either Darwin or Wallace.

Although there was a more receptive climate to evolutionary theories in 1859 than previously, Darwin's ideas in the *Origin* were opposed by virtually all humanists, philosophers, and scientists, excluding biologists. Adam Sedgwick (1785-1873), Darwin's geology professor at Cambridge University, had predicted a brilliant scientific future for Darwin, but by 1860 was deeply disturbed by the conflict between Darwinian theory and Scripture. Philosopher William Whewell (1794-1866) found the *Origin* to be a mass of conjecture and voiced the objection of other philosophers when he argued that Darwin had not been able to prove his hypotheses. Lord Kelvin (William Thomson, 1824-1907) and other physicists estimated the age of the earth and found that the measurement did not allow time for the slow changes suggested in

Darwin's theory. Kelvin's calculations later proved to be badly underestimated, but they created problems for evolutionists when they were first proposed.

There was a good deal of division among supporters of evolution. In the latter part of the nineteenth century, many biologists accepted the idea of evolution but rejected natural selection as its prime force. Darwin's cousin, **Francis Galton** (1822-1911), favored a method by which new types of organisms arose suddenly, i.e., evolution by saltations. Philosopher **Herbert Spencer** (1820-1903) embraced some of Lamarck's ideas, while including the Darwinian principle that the fittest types survived competition and thrived. He stated that competition did not, as the Darwinians maintained, eliminate the unfit, but instead forced poorly adapted organisms to develop more useful traits and become fit.

Among the evolutionists who upheld the principle of natural selection, there was also disagreement. Darwin and Wallace differed sharply over human evolution. In his *Descent of Man* (1871) Darwin maintained that natural selection helped shape the development of humans. Wallace, however, believed that if evolutionary change such as the development of the human mind could not be demonstrated to be the result of natural selection, it must be due to extranatural forces. Wallace was influenced by his view of human beings as unique creatures, and his strong religious convictions (he was a spiritualist) allowed him to state that "providence" played an important role in the development of the human brain.

Although Darwin regarded natural selection as the main force in determining evolution, he recognized that the occasional and sudden appearance of traits might have resulted from other factors. To explain why female birds or insects selected males with bright coloration, and why brightly colored traits were transmitted to future generations and dull-colored males' characteristics were rejected, he suggested sexual selection.

After Darwin's death in 1882, his position was upheld by such naturalists as George John Romanes (1848-1894), E. Ray Lankester (1847-1929), Henry Walter Bates (1825-1892), and Edward Bagnall Poulton (1856-1943). However, no consensus was reached until well into the twentieth century, when

Darwinian evolution was successfully joined to the modern discoveries in genetics.

Evolution influenced every aspect of nineteenth-century intellectual activity because it helped shatter the Victorians' faith in their society's immutability. Now the historian studied the past as a living organism, the critic examined the evolution of "types" in literature, and the lawyer treated law as an evolving institution. Social Darwinists such as Spencer employed evolutionary ideas in support of the popular laissez-faire attitudes of the day. They advocated no government help for the poor because they felt such assistance would be fruitless. Spencer, particularly, suggested instead that if natural forces were left alone, the strong would prosper and increase in number, and the weak would either become stronger or disappear. Thus, the discussion and eventual acceptance of evolution helped strengthen the century's deeply held confidence in inevitable progress.

JOEL S. SCHWARTZ

Bibliography

Bowler, Peter J. *The Eclipse of Darwinism: Anti-Darwinian Evolution Theories in the Decades Around 1900.* 1983.

Eisen, Sydney and Bernard V. Lightman. *Victorian Science and Religion: A Bibliography.* 1984.

Greene, John C. *The Death of Adam: Evolution and Its Impact on Western Thought.* 1959.

Moore, James R. *The Post-Darwinian Controversies: A Study of the Protestant Struggle to Come to Terms with Darwin in Great Britain and America, 1870–1900.* 1979.

Schwartz, Joel S. "Darwin, Wallace, and the Descent of Man." *Journal of the History of Biology,* vol. 17, pp. 271–289.

Vorzimmer, Peter J. *The Origin of Species and Its Critics, 1859–1882.* 1970.

. . . . .

Her mother **Margaret Scott Gatty** eked out their income by writing children's tales and works of natural history, but Juliana (nicknamed "Aunt Judy") was the family storyteller. When Margaret Gatty was asked to edit a children's periodical, she called it *Aunt Judy's Magazine* and first serialized most of Juliana Gatty's works.

In 1867 she married Major Alexander Ewing. He was posted to Fredericton, New Brunswick, and there, for *Aunt Judy's*, she wrote her first full-length novel, *Mrs. Overtheway's Remembrances* (1869). Though interrupted by ill health and the constant moves of army life, Ewing entered an extremely productive period. She wrote readily for boys or girls or both (her only attempt to write for adults was a failure) and among professionals (thus excluding Lewis Carroll) none did it better.

Ewing generally avoided sentimentality. Her great strength was that she did not write down to children, nor did she produce sermons: her message, moral or patriotic, was clear but not obtrusive. She sometimes, as in *Jackanapes* (1883), probably her best-known book, forgot that she was a clergyman's daughter; she never forgot that she was a soldier's wife. The staunchly Victorian values probably account for the current neglect of her work.

ELLIOT ROSE

Bibliography

Avery, Gillian. *Mrs. Ewing.* 1961.

Blom, Margaret Howard and Thomas E. Blom, eds. *Canada Home: Juliana Horatia Ewing's Fredericton Letters, 1867–1869.* 1983.

Eden, Horatia K. *Juliana Horatia Ewing and Her Books.* 1896; rpt. 1969.

Maxwell, Cristabel. *Mrs. Gatty and Mrs. Ewing.* 1949.

. . . . .

EWING, JULIANA GATTY (1841–1885)

Juliana Horatia Gatty was one of the numerous children of a Yorkshire clergyman.

EXHIBITION OF 1851

The Great Exhibition of the Works of Industry of All Nations, commonly referred to as the Great Exhibition of 1851 or the Crystal Palace Exhibition, was the first true world's

The Great Exhibition Building. Harper's New Monthly Magazine, *April 1851.*
Library Company of Philadelphia.

fair. It opened May 1, 1851 and closed five months later, having accommodated some six million visitors. It is often taken as a symbol of the mid-Victorian age and of Britain's role as the workshop of the world. The exhibition organizers, who included **Prince Albert** and **Henry Cole**, intended for it not only to demonstrate British industrial supremacy, but also to be a running commentary on the gospel of free trade, peace, and the virtues of democracy and the British constitution. Its central building was the Crystal Palace, a gigantic greenhouse three times the length of St. Paul's Cathedral; it was erected in Hyde Park at the location just south of the Serpentine.

Designed by **Joseph Paxton**, whose plan was selected from 254 submitted, the Crystal Palace was the one purely functional building of any size in the Victorian period and was the world's first large edifice built out of metal and glass. It was a prefabricated structure and was based on large greenhouses Paxton had designed for the duke of Devonshire. The building covered 18 acres and was 1,848 feet long, 404 feet wide, and 66 feet high, except in the transepts, which were 108 feet high. All the material used was interchangeable: the 2,300 girders, the 3,300 columns, the gutters, and the sash bars were identical throughout the whole structure. The main supports were hollow cast-iron columns which acted as rainwater conduits. Some 900,000 square feet of glass, made into the largest panes ever produced, were applied to the weblike structure. The color scheme was bright, with blue predominant on the columns and girders. There were touches of yellow and large expanses of red behind the balconies, which made a dramatic backdrop for the exhibits.

There were over 13,000 exhibitors, and more than half the area was occupied by British and colonial exhibits. Of the many foreign nations represented, France and Germany were the most important. The objects were divided into four groups: raw materials, machinery, manufactures, and fine arts. The machinery gallery was the noisiest and most popular, where visitors could see huge marine engines, locomotives, hydraulic presses, reapers, and the like. An electric **telegraph** was installed inside, which was connected with Edinburgh and Manchester. In the eastern nave there was exhibited the 186-carat Koh-i-Noor diamond from India.

A triumph of Paxton's design was the ability to take apart and reassemble the building. The Crystal Palace was reerected to a modified design in Sydenham between 1851 and 1854. Surrounded by gardens and fountains, the structure served as a pleasure garden and cultural center for South London until it was destroyed by fire in 1936.

PHILLIP THURMOND SMITH

Bibliography

Briggs, Asa. "The Crystal Palace and the Men of 1851." In Asa Briggs, *Victorian People: A Reassessment of Persons and Themes, 1851–1867.* 1970.

DeMaré, Eric. *London 1851: The Year of the Great Exhibition.* 1973.

Dixon, Roger and Stefan Muthesius. *Victorian Architecture.* 1978.

Fay, Charles R. *Palace of Industry, 1851: A Study of the Great Exhibition and Its Fruits.* 1951.

Gibbs-Smith, Charles H. *The Great Exhibition of 1851.* 1981.

Hobhouse, Christopher. *1851 and the Crystal Palace.* 1950.

· · · · ·

EYRE, EDWARD JOHN (1815-1901)

Colonial administrator Edward John Eyre's harsh suppression in 1865 of a native insurrection while governor of Jamaica created a furor in England. The public debate, known as the Governor Eyre Controversy, centered around governmental use of martial law to control colonial populations. It reflected middle- and upper-class fears over working-class agitation for suffrage and concern about maintaining the empire.

Born in Yorkshire, Eyre emigrated to Australia in 1832. Appointed resident magistrate (1836), he was markedly humanitarian, earning him the title "Protector of the Aborigine." He was sent to St. Vincent, West Indies as acting governor in 1854 and was appointed acting governor of Jamaica in 1862. Eyre's administration engendered difficulties with the white planters and the Assembly. Nonetheless, two years later the Colonial Office approved his appointment to governor.

Eyre's lengthy imposition of martial law to subdue a black uprising, and accounts of numerous executions and floggings, forced his recall and a governmental inquiry in 1865. Eyre's supporters, including Charles Dickens, Thomas Carlyle, and John Ruskin, feared similar domestic agitations and formed the Eyre Defence and Aid Fund.

John Stuart Mill's Jamaica Committee, concerned with British policies of martial law in the colonies, sought to prosecute Eyre for murder. The efforts to indict Eyre failed. He was granted a second-class pension, dying after the martial law controversy resurfaced during the Boer War.

CHERYL M. CASSIDY

Bibliography

Semmel, Bernard. *Jamaican Blood and Victorian Conscience.* 1963.

· · · · ·

FABIAN SOCIETY

A select group of intellectual socialists, the Fabian Society was committed to a strategy of incremental reform rather than revolution, research rather than mass agitation. Its members were mainly middle-class professionals: journalists, educators, clerks, civil servants, and clergymen.

Though the Fabians sincerely wanted to abolish poverty, many of them felt that the laboring class should not be entrusted with too much political power. Following Plato and Auguste Comte, they looked forward to a managerial state governed by enlightened experts and bureaucrats. Before 1910, none of the leading Fabians advocated equality of incomes: they were less concerned with egalitarianism than with administrative efficiency. Generally, they disliked anarchism, Marxism, and any form of determinist or materialist philosophy. Carlyle, Ruskin, Henry George, Samuel Butler, and the marginal-utility economics of William Stanley Jevons were far more important than Karl Marx in shaping Fabian ideology.

To a large extent, Fabianism was a substitute for religion. The early Fabians were mainly former Anglican Evangelicals who had gravitated to the Fellowship of the New Life, a small spiritual sect gathered around the Scottish mystic Thomas Davidson. In 1884 nine members of the fellowship, led by Edward Pease (1857-1955) and Frank Podmore (1855-1910), broke away to form the Fabian Society. (Podmore invented the name, a historically doubtful allusion to the delaying tactics of the Roman general Fabius Cunctator.)

By 1886 the Fabians had been joined by **George Bernard Shaw** (1856-1950), **Sidney Webb** (1859-1947), **Annie Besant** (1847-1933), Graham Wallas (1858-1932), and James Ramsay MacDonald (1866-1937). Membership rose to about 150 in 1890 and more than 800 in 1899.

The society was governed by an elected executive, which could reject applicants for membership. Beginning in 1890, daily business was carried on by a paid secretary; Edward Pease held that office until 1913. The monthly *Fabian News* was launched in 1891.

At first Fabian activities were limited largely to lectures and discussions. No dogma was imposed, no clear program for combatting poverty was agreed on. Occasional tracts were published, but most of them represented the opinions of the authors, not of the society as a whole.

On November 1, 1887—"**Bloody Sunday**"—radical and socialist demonstrators converging on Trafalgar Square were routed by soldiers and London police. For many socialists, that fiasco demonstrated the futility of revolutionary agitation in Britain, especially as the Fabians went on to score some notable victories using more moderate tactics. In 1888 Annie Besant, assisted by several other Fabians, organized a successful strike of girl workers at the Bryant and May match factory. *Fabian Essays in Socialism*, edited by Shaw, was published by the society in 1889 and sold unexpectedly well.

In March 1892, Sidney Webb and five other Fabians were elected to the London County Council, where they worked for "municipal socialism"—public ownership of utilities and tramlines, health and housing regulations, better wages for city workers, and improved education and technical training. Webb's campaign was financed by Beatrice Potter

(1858-1943), a recent Fabian convert, whom he married the following July.

By 1892 there were thirty provincial Fabian groups in addition to the London organization, and the society began to attract some working-class socialists, including **Keir Hardie** (1856-1915), Will Crooks (1852-1921), and Ben Tillett (1860-1943). Based in Manchester, Robert Blatchford (1851-1943) reached a large proletarian audience with his socialist weekly the *Clarion* and his utopian tract *Merrie England* (1893).

The provincial Fabians brought an unaccustomed, almost religious fervor to the society, and many of them soon gravitated to the new Independent Labour party. Shaw and Sidney Webb flirted with the ILP, and they denounced Gladstone's last government in "To Your Tents, O Israel!" published in the *Fortnightly Review* (November 1, 1893). By and large, however, the Fabians preferred the tactic of "permeation," working discreetly within the **Liberal party** to convert its leaders to socialistic policies.

In 1894 the Henry Hutchinson bequest left the Fabian Society 10,000 pounds for "propaganda and other purposes." On the initiative of Sidney Webb, the money was used to found the London School of Economics. Although the LSE trained many socialists and social scientists, it was also Britain's first business college, offering courses in insurance and railway management. It is significant that the Fabians used their windfall, not for socialist agitation, but for the education of a new class of administrators, who would serve capitalist as well as state enterprises.

That new class, the Fabians hoped, would bring efficient government not only to England but to the whole British empire. The founding Fabians had been passionately anti-imperialist, but the society grew more sympathetic to colonialism toward the end of the century. Shaw argued that imperialism was a step in the direction of a world socialist state: it would create larger and more cost-effective units of government, bringing scientific Fabian administration to backward peoples. In 1899 the society followed the advice of Shaw and Sidney Webb and voted, 259 to 217, not to take a position on the Boer War. Ramsay MacDonald and sixteen other members resigned in protest. Thereafter, the Fabians frequently used imperialism as an argument for welfare legislation: they contended that decent wages, housing, education, health measures, and sewers were needed to produce healthy soldiers and productive workers for the empire.

JONATHAN ROSE

Bibliography

Britain, Ian. *Fabianism and Culture.* 1982.

Hobsbawm, E. J. "The Fabians Reconsidered." In E. J. Hobsbawm, *Labouring Men.* 1964.

McBriar, A. M. *Fabian Socialism and English Politics, 1884–1918.* 1966.

MacKenzie, Norman, and Jeanne MacKenzie. *The Fabians.* 1977.

Wolfe, Willard. *From Radicalism to Socialism: Men and Ideas in the Formation of Fabian Socialist Doctrines, 1881–1889.* 1975.

See also LABOUR PARTY; MATCHWORKERS; SOCIALISM

· · · · ·

FACTORIES

Modern factories arose in late eighteenth-century Britain. Beginning in the cotton and iron industries, factories slowly spread to other industries and replaced the decentralized domestic method of manufacturing. Within a century, most industries operated by the factory system, though examples of domestic manufacturing remained.

The factory is regarded as the heart of the first industrial revolution. A factory or mill is a centralized place of production under one roof, utilizing large-scale units of operation, laborsaving machinery, and regimented labor.

The crucial years for the rise of factory production in cotton were between 1770 and 1785. **Inventions**, especially Arkwright's water frame, made the factory the only feasible mode of production. Boulton and Watt **steam engines** provided a central and independent source of power. By 1785 all elements of the factory system were present in the industry.

The iron industry was likewise transformed throughout the eighteenth century by discoveries and inventions. Abraham Darby discovered coke for smelting, Henry Cort and Peter Onions patented the puddling and rolling process, and the application of the steam engine provided increased power for blowing the blast furnace and mechanical power for forging. The sick industry of earlier years became a leading industry by 1800.

The conversion of cotton and iron to the factory system was conspicuously successful. By 1812 cotton outstripped the traditional woollen industry in importance and by 1815 cotton textiles were 40 percent of the value of British exports. Pig iron production quadrupled between 1788 and 1806, and by 1810 the iron industry accounted for 6 percent of the national income. Most industries operated by the factory system by 1850, and Britain was known as "the Workshop of the World."

The factory system produced social as well as economic changes. The middle class—factory owners, merchants, shopkeepers, and professionals—grew in numbers and influence. The proletariat, created by factories, was class conscious by 1820, though it never numbered more than 50 percent of the workforce. The traditional agricultural workers declined in number, and landed artistocrats were challenged by the other classes. Bitter class tensions characterized the social structure of the nineteenth century.

Historians have differed in recent decades about the living and working conditions of the proletariat. Contemporary literary views by writers such as Charles Dickens, though skewed by the depressions in which they wrote, still prevail today. Undoubtedly there was much suffering, especially during the transition years between the domestic and factory systems. Workers who never became part of the factory system suffered the most, and factory workers who had no benefits suffered immensely during cyclical depressions. Some workers, known as Luddites, burned factories because of inferior machine goods, and in hard times mass protests and violence were common.

Revisionist historians take a different view. Factories did not create long hours, low wages, job insecurity, and child and female labor. Such conditions existed in the domestic system. Workers did not complain about these conditions but about discipline and reg-

The Pen-Grinding Room. Illustrated London News, *22 February 1851.*
Library Company of Philadelphia.

imentation which had not prevailed before. Workers' organizations, such as the **Chartists**, demanded political rather than economic reform.

The concentration of workers in factories made reform of bad working conditions possible. In 1784 Manchester magistrates limited working hours for children. In 1802 and 1819 Parliament passed factory acts, although neither was enforceable. In 1832 Michael Sadler's Parliamentary Committee to Inquire into Child Labor in Factories set the precedent for subsequent parliamentary investigations into working conditions. It resulted in passage of the Factory Act of 1833, the first effective act. Though limited to child labor in cotton mills, the act established the principles of government regulation and enforcement by creating factory inspectors. A series of later **factory acts** extended reforms to adults, safety, sanitation, and all other industries, including domestic workshops.

The effect that factories had upon workers' families has also been debated since the early nineteenth century. Parliamentary reformers thought factories had disastrous consequences upon female workers' morals and the home life of the proletariat. Workers hotly denied these allegations, and modern studies tend to support their view. The number of married working women was relatively small,

and their morals were those of their class, not of the mill. There is evidence that the emancipation movement for women began among factory operatives in the 1850s.

The factory system revolutionized production in Britain and was an integral part of the industrial revolution. By the mid-nineteenth century Britain was the foremost industrial power of the world. Mass production reduced the cost of goods and increased the material standards of living for most people. The standard of living for factory workers, except for periods of depression, improved as the factory system came to be almost universally adopted. By 1914 workers were protected against the worst aspects of the system, and the eight-hour day was not far in the future.

WILSON J. HOFFMAN

Bibliography

Checkland, S. G. *The Rise of Industrial Society in England, 1815–1885.* 1964.

Dean, Phyllis. *The First Industrial Revolution.* 1965.

Mantoux, Philip. *The Industrial Revolution of the Eighteenth Century.* 1961.

Mathias, Peter. *The First Industrial Nation: An Economic History of Britain, 1700–1914.* 1969.

Perkin, Harold. *The Origins of Modern English Society.* 1969.

Pinchbeck, Ivy. *Women Workers and the Industrial Revolution, 1750–1850.* 1969.

Thomson, E. P. *The Making of the English Working Class.* 1963.

See also CHILD LABOR; DOMESTIC INDUSTRY; TEXTILE INDUSTRY

· · · · ·

FACTORY ACTS

The factory acts were a series of laws passed to regulate the new working conditions created by the industrial revolution. The acts began tentatively in the Poor Law tradition and progressed slowly in the face of laissez-faire ideology, which was actively hostile to regulation.

The 1802 Health and Morals of Apprentices Act, the first factory act, was an extension of the Elizabethan Poor Laws. Applying only to pauper children apprenticed under the Poor Law, it limited their factory work to twelve hours a day, required education, and regulated working conditions. Justices of the peace were responsible for enforcing the law, but they proved lax and inefficient.

Between 1819 and 1833 a series of acts sought to set hours and ages for children employed in cotton mills. None of the acts was effective, but Parliament gradually learned how to create industrial legislation. The major breakthrough came in 1833 when, in the tradition of Tory paternalism, **Lord Shaftesbury** passed a factory act that provided for professional inspectors armed with the power to enter factories, examine the premises, and assess fines. The 1833 factory act prohibited the employment of children under the age of nine in textile mills and limited the work of children under twelve to forty-eight hours per week.

Regulation was extended to the coal mines in 1842 after a royal commission exposed horrible working conditions. A pattern was established: information on industrial abuses required legislative action, but the legislation was limited to protecting women and children. Workmen began to agitate for a ten-hour day. Although unwilling to abandon the theory that men (unlike women and children) were free agents, Parliament passed the Ten Hours Act in 1847. Even though men were excluded from the act, shortening the day for women and children, whose work was essential to factory production, effectively limited the hours of labor in the mills for everyone.

Over the next two decades, smaller workshops and more industries were added to the list of inspected factories. By the late 1860s a tacit public consensus had emerged that factory acts were necessary and that laissez-faire theory could be set aside.

During Benjamin Disraeli's administration the Home Office culminated three-quarters of a century's experience with a consolidation act bringing the patchwork of laws and inspectors into one act. The 1878 act enabled factory inspectors to enforce the law widely. Subsequent acts added to the list of dangerous industries, established specific regulations, and permitted the appointment of women as factory inspectors. Finally, a factory act in 1901 absolutely forbade employment of children under twelve in any factory or workshop.

DENNIS J. MITCHELL

Bibliography

Hutchins, B. L. and Amy Harrison. *A History of Factory Legislation.* 1903.

Ludlow, John Malcolm Forbes. *Progress of the Working Class, 1832–1867.* 1867; rpt. 1973.

Woodward, Ernest Llewellyn. *The Age of Reform, 1815–1870.* 1938.

See also CHILD LABOR; LABOR LAWS; WORKING HOURS

· · · · ·

FAIRY LORE

The Victorian fascination with fairies, partially inherited from the romantic era, manifested itself in the collection of native fairy lore and the use of this material in literature, painting, and drama. Increased speculation on the origin and nature of fairies and their lore was spurred first by nationalism and the threats of industrialism, urbanism, and materialism. Later, stimulated by interest in the occult, Darwinism, and advances in the social sciences, Victorians accumulated and analyzed fairy lore, providing most of the materials available today.

Interest in fairy lore and legends or *Sagen* (half-believed tales of elfin activity) was revived by romantic antiquarians, including Walter Scott. To influential romantic collections like Thomas Keightley's *Fairy Mythology* (1828), Victorians added new information, as in J. F. Campbell's *Popular Tales of the West Highlands* (1860–1862), William Henderson's *Folk Lore of the Northern Counties of England* (1862), and John Rhŷs's *Celtic Folklore, Welsh and Manx* (1901).

Fairy lore permeates Victorian literature; it pervades the novels of Charles Dickens and Charlotte and Emily Brontë as well as the poetry of Tennyson, Christina Rossetti, William Morris, William Allingham, and William Butler Yeats. It influences fairy tales and fantasies—including those of Charles Kingsley, Lewis Carroll, and George MacDonald. Its popularity contributes to the rise, in the 1840s, of a new genre: fairy painting. Noteworthy examples include Richard Dadd's *Fairy Feller's Master Stroke* (1855–1864), Joseph Noël Paton's *Fairy Raid* (1867), and Richard Doyle's illustrations to *In Fairy Land* (1870). Fairy lore also infiltrates **pantomime** and legitimate theater through fairy plays like James Barrie's *Peter Pan* (1904).

By the 1880s increasing interest in occultism led some to assert the reality of fairies. Yeats and Robert Louis Stevenson were among those who provided *memorats* (personal accounts of supernatural experiences). Arthur Conan Doyle defended the authenticity of the controversial Cottingley fairy photographs (1917)—pictures of fairies taken by two young girls. Meanwhile, eminent anthropologists and folklorists—including Edward Burnett Tylor, **Andrew Lang**, and David MacRitchie—were investigating the origins of fairies and fairy lore. Their major theories included: the "mythological" theory (lore is the detritus of ancient myth or the distortion of ancient language); the "pygmy" theory (fairies and their lore grew from folk memories of dwarflike Mongol invaders later conquered by the Celts); and the "survival" theory (lore preserves vestiges of the "savage" stage of prehistoric culture).

CAROLE SILVER

Bibliography

Briggs, Katharine M. *The Fairies in English Tradition and Literature*. 1967.

Doyle, Sir Arthur Conan. *The Coming of the Fairies*. 1922.

Evans-Wentz, Walter Yeeling. *The Fairy-Faith in Celtic Countries*. 1911.

Hartland, Edwin Sidney. *The Science of Fairy Tales: An Inquiry Into Fairy Mythology*. 1891.

MacRitchie, David. *The Testimony of Tradition*. 1890.

Silver, Carole. "On the Origin of Fairies: Victorians, Romantics, and Folk Belief." *Browning Institute Studies*, vol. 14, pp. 141–156.

See also FOLKLORE

· · · · ·

FAIRY TALES

Although the term "fairy tale" suggests their presence, fairies are absent in the great majority of stories so labeled. Fairy tales may be defined as narratives of various length with a mortal protagonist which involve the marvelous. *Märchen* are traditional fairy tales that have been transmitted orally for generations and recorded by a collector; *Kunstmärchen*, or literary fairy tales, can be attributed to a specific author.

The English term "fairy tale" is derived from the French "contes des fees." Of the collections created for the court of Louis XIV, the best known are Madame D'Aulnoy's *Contes des fees* (1697) and Charles Perrault's *Histoires, ou contes du temps passé* (1697), which were translated respectively as *Tales of Mother Bunch* and *Tales of Mother Goose* and circulated in England as chapbooks. At the beginning of the nineteenth century, such fairy tales were considered a secondary form of literature for unsophisticated readers such as children and peasants.

Many pious parents felt that tales of elves, fairies, and sprites came dangerously close to witchcraft. Authors such as Maria Edgeworth, Sarah Trimmer, and Mary Sherwood, under the influence of the educational philosophies of John Locke and Jean-Jacques Rousseau, argued that **children's literature** should be strictly factual. The battle over the suitability of fairy tales for children continued until the 1840s.

Edgar Taylor's translation of the collections that Jacob and Wilhelm Grimm published in 1812 and 1815 did much to introduce fairy tales into the Victorian nursery. Unlike the Grimms' first edition, Taylor's *German Popular Stories* (1823, 1826) was specifically intended for children and had delightful illustrations by **George Cruikshank**. Its success encouraged **Henry Cole**, under the pseudonym of Felix Summerly, to initiate his Home Treasury series in 1842 and Francis Edward Paget to begin his Juvenile Englishman's Library in 1844. Both made a wide variety of traditional fairy tales available to children. The literary fairy tales of Hans Christian Andersen, which appeared in three different English translations in 1846, also contributed to the popularity of fairy tales as acceptable reading for children.

Although the Grimms' work inspired the publication of national collections in most European countries, English Puritanism had silenced many native fairy tales before folklorists had the opportunity to collect them. During the 1850s, London publishers turned to the **folklore** of other European nations, and overseas collectors compiled tales of Asia and Africa under the aegis of the British Empire. The international approach culminated in **Andrew Lang**'s Coloured Fairy Book series, beginning with *The Blue Fairy Book* (1889) and Joseph Jacobs's "Fairy Tales of Many Lands" series, initiated with *English Fairy Tales* (1890).

The British also created literary fairy tales, which became virtually a fad between 1840 and 1875. Beginning with **Catherine Sinclair**'s "Uncle David's Nonsensical Story About Giants and Fairies" in her novel *Holiday House* (1839) and Edward Francis Paget's book-length *The Hope of the Katzekopfs* (1844), these modern fairy tales borrowed from the French fairy court and the German folk tale but dealt with the social concerns of the middle class.

Well-known contributions such as John Ruskin's *The King of the Golden River* (1851), William Thackeray's *The Rose and the Ring* (1855), and Frances Browne's *Granny's Wonderful Chair* (1857) were also stimulated by the growing market for children's books. The genre allowed the merging of imaginative and didactic impulses; the domestic nature of the tales, the themes of family and material success, and the happy endings made them popular among parents who bought books for their children on the assumption that they would be entertaining but also essentially edifying. Although Victorian fairy tales are less heavy-handed than the children's literature of the previous generation, texts such as Charles Kingsley's *The Water-Babies* (1863) and George MacDonald's *Dealing with the Fairies* (1867) retained a pervasive moral tone.

Fairy tales also became popular on stage, replacing classical mythology as the source of plots for the Christmas **pantomimes** produced by Henry James Byron and James Robinson Planché during the 1840s and 1850s. Lewis Carroll's *Alice's Adventures in Wonderland* (1865) and *Through the Looking-Glass* (1872), strongly influenced by the pantomimes, inspired a host of other literary fairy tales including Jean Ingelow's *Mopsa the Fairy* (1869), Christina Rossetti's *Speaking Likenesses* (1869), and Alice Corkran's *Down the Snow Stairs* (1887).

By 1875 there was a gradual shift to an adult audience for literary fairy tales. Although books such as Lucy Clifford's *Anyhow Stories* (1882) and Andrew Lang's *Prince Pringo* (1889) and *Prince Ricardo* (1893) continued to be written for children, more frequently the literary fairy tales, such as Oscar Wilde's *The Happy Prince and Other Stories* (1888), Laurence Houseman's *A Farm in Fairyland* (1894), and Max Beerbohm's *Happy Hypocrite* (1897), were written by fin de siècle authors for an adult audience.

As the fields of anthropology and folklore developed during the final quarter of the century, the audience for traditional tales also became more adult. Members of the English Folk-Lore Society (including Andrew Lang, Edwin Sidney Hartland, and Joseph Jacobs) began serious research on fairy tales through their scholarly publications and editions. By the end of the century, both literary and traditional fairy tales had slowly made their way out of the nursery and into the library and study.

JAN SUSINA

Bibliography

Avery, Gillian and Angela Bull. *Nineteenth Century Children: Heroes and Heroines in English Children's Stories, 1780–1900.* 1965.

Darton, F. J. *Children's Books in England: Five Centuries of Social Life.* 1932.

Dorson, Richard. *The British Folklorists: A History.* 1968.

Kotzin, Michael. "The Fairy Tale in England, 1800–1870." *Journal of Popular Culture,* vol. 4, pp. 130–154.

Quayle, Eric. *Early Children's Books: A Collector's Guide.* 1983.

Salway, Lance, ed. *A Peculiar Gift: Nineteenth Century Writing on Books for Children.* 1976.

See also FANTASY LITERATURE

· · · · ·

FAITHFULL, EMILY (1835–1895)

Emily Faithfull, a member of the **Langham Place Circle** of feminists led by **Barbara Bodichon** and **Bessie Parkes**, founded the Victoria Press (1860) in order to give women the opportunity to work in the printing trade. Although her family was of sufficiently high status that she was presented at court—the traditional debut in society for young women of a certain rank—Faithfull devoted most of her life to opening opportunities for women to work in skilled trades.

In 1859 the Society for the Promotion of the Employment of Women was formed and affiliated with the **National Association for the Promotion of Social Science** (NAPSS). Convinced that women could be trained as compositors, Faithfull coupled her own resources with financial backing from G. W. Hastings of the NAPSS to establish the Victoria Press. She recognized that the heavier work involved in carrying type and lifting iron chases would be difficult for women and therefore concentrated her efforts on training them as compositors. She solved the problem of fatigue by introducing three-legged stools. The publishing trade was hostile to the new press and the unions refused to admit women.

The Victoria Press, however, became printer for the **English Woman's Journal** and for the *Transactions* of the NAPSS and also did contract work for other organizations. Eventually the press gained Queen Victoria's approval, and Faithfull was appointed Printer and Publisher in Ordinary to Her Majesty.

In 1863 Faithfull founded the *Victoria Magazine,* an interesting attempt to combine serious articles on women's issues with the fiction and lighter material that would appeal to a broader readership. After withdrawing from the Victoria Press in 1867, she engaged in a variety of activities designed to further women's causes. The *West London Express,* which she started in 1877, again provided employment for many women typesetters. She was an early member of the Women's Trade Union League and the Women's Printing Society.

Faithfull published two novels, *Change Upon Change* (1868) and *A Reed Shaken with the Wind* (1873), made successful lecture tours in the United States, and wrote a number of articles and pamphlets. Although also a supporter of women's suffrage and higher education, Faithfull is important chiefly for her work in improving women's employment opportunities.

SHEILA R. HERSTEIN

Bibliography

Banks, Olive. *The Biographical Dictionary of British Feminists,* vol. 1. 1985.

Fredeman, William E. "Emily Faithfull and the Victoria Press: An Experiment in Sociological Bibliography." *The Library,* vol. 29 (series 5) pp. 139–164.

Kamm, Josephine. *Rapiers and Battleaxes.* 1966.

Strachey, Ray. *The Cause.* 1928; rpt. 1978.

· · · · ·

FAMILY

The institution of the family assumed new emotional importance in the nineteenth century as a retreat from the stress and turmoil of the industrial world. In a society rapidly transformed by industrialization and urbanization, the family was idealized, especially by the middle classes, as a center of stability amidst instability and uncertainty. The pleasures and virtues of home life were exalted and constituted a major theme in Victorian art and literature.

The sharp demarcation between the private domestic sphere and the outside world emerged as factories replaced home workshops. The household, no longer functioning as a productive unit, was viewed as separate from the world of work, grounded in values in opposition to those of industrial capitalism. Whereas the public sphere honored competition, rationality, and self-interest, the family, in its idealized form, fostered love, cooperation, and peace. This separation of work and home included the differentiation of sexual spheres. Men left the home to go to work, and therefore the public sphere was identified as the man's world. Married women, even among the working classes, usually stayed in the home, which became their domain, and they the guardians and exemplars of domestic values.

The middle-class family structure was primarily nuclear. In preindustrial England, nuclear families were also the norm, but households often included apprentices, clerks, and servants who were not sharply differentiated by class from their employers. By the early nineteenth century, it was less common for nonfamily members to live in the household, except for **servants** who were socially separated from the family by the rigid class divisions that emerged with industrialization. The word "family" took on a new meaning as a reflection of this social change, and came to signify "blood ties" rather than "household." The middle-class nuclear family was also more isolated from its larger kinship network, although unmarried women, a sizable group in the nineteenth century, often lived with married siblings, and family firms commonly employed relatives from the extended family. Aristocratic families were more open to the outside world, and kinship ties beyond the nuclear core remained of primary significance. Working-class families were also less privatized, for they often housed lodgers within the home, and their extended family relationships were important for mutual support in times of dislocation and crisis.

In contrast to preindustrial society, when marriages were commonly based on economic calculation and arranged by parents,

the pattern in the nineteenth century was the companionate **marriage**, with participants exercising free choice based on mutual love, subject only to parental veto. The choice of marriage partner was, however, narrowed in 1835 by Lord Lyndhurst's Act, which made marriages of affinity as well as consanguinity absolutely void rather than merely voidable. Repeated attempts to modify this act by allowing marriage with a deceased wife's sister were not successful until 1907. Cousins were not within the prohibited degrees, and the preindustrial aristocratic pattern of cousin marriage continued among all classes of Victorian society until its decline in the late nineteenth century, when the writings of Darwin and other scientists created concern about the dangers of consanguinity.

Families were rarely broken by **divorce**, even after the Matrimonial Causes Act of 1857 made divorce accessible through the courts. Death continued to be the primary dissolver of marriage. Since mortality rates were still high among young adults, multiple remarriages and the resulting complex nuclear families, with stepparents and step- and half-siblings, were common. Legal adoption of children was not possible until 1926.

Because the birth rate remained high until the 1870s and infant mortality declined except among the urban working classes, Victorian families typically included a large number of children, who lived at home until a later age than in preindustrial times. There was great emphasis on children's welfare and training, and therefore the role of the mother, who was freed from productive work within the household, expanded to include new duties. Maternal breastfeeding replaced wetnursing as accepted practice, and mothers had the responsibility of educating their small children and guarding them from moral corruption. The familial closeness of the child-centered household was particularly characteristic of the middle classes. In very wealthy families, there was more physical distance between parents and children, with nurseries in separate wings of the house supervised by nannies and maidservants. Poorer working-class mothers who worked outside the home were also separated from their children; often they had to send their infants to baby farms, a practice first regulated by the Infant Life Protection Act of 1871.

Despite the emphasis on conjugal love and the feminization of the domestic sphere, the family structure remained patriarchal. The common law of coverture, depriving a married woman of her legal personality, was only partially amended by the **Married Women's Property** Acts of 1870, 1882, and 1893. Until the courts ruled otherwise in the 1891 case of *Regina* vs. *Jackson*, a husband could use physical force to confine his wife within the home. The mother's role was honored, but it was the father who had authority over the children, up to age twenty-one. In case of separation or divorce, the husband, until 1839, had exclusive guardianship of the children. The Infant Custody Act of 1839 gave courts the discretion to grant the mother custody of children under seven years of age, provided she was not proved guilty of adultery. In 1873 the law was extended to allow the possibility of maternal custody of children up to age sixteen, even if adultery had been proved. An unmarried mother always had complete control of her children.

The legal authority of the paterfamilias was reinforced by evangelicalism; the father assumed the role of God's viceroy within the home, typically leading the family in daily prayers and Bible reading. There was strong resistance to legislation that impinged on the father's rights, such as child labor laws or compulsory education. Other legislative restrictions included the Poor Law Amendment Act of 1868, which made it an offense for a parent to neglect children under fourteen years of age, and the Prevention of Cruelty to, and Protection of Children Act of 1889, which provided for the removal of children neglected or abused in their own homes. Despite evidence that crowded working-class housing fostered widespread familial sexual abuse of children, there was no law against incest until 1908, in part because of the fear of governmental interference in private family life.

The privatized, emotionally bonded family, a middle-class model which, by the end of the nineteenth century, characterized all levels of society, engendered strong feelings of both love and rage. The love took the form of intense lifelong familial attachments, which in many cases precluded adult extrafamilial relationships. The rage, particularly against patriarchal authority, was often manifested as religious rebellion, or, especially among women, in the popularity, in the 1860s and thereafter, of the **sensation novels** of familial murder and escape. The family, therefore, idealized as a sanctuary from a stressful world, was in reality often a source of tension and disquiet. The image of the family, however, remained of central importance in Victorian consciousness, and, with its social isolation and child-centeredness, it was the primary institution in the formation of the Victorian personality and values.

NANCY FIX ANDERSON

Bibliography

Anderson, Michael. *Approaches to the History of the Western Family, 1500-1914.* 1980.

——. *Family Structure in Nineteenth Century Lancashire.* 1971.

Anderson, Nancy Fix. "Cousin Marriage in Victorian England." *Journal of Family History,* vol. 11, pp. 285-301.

Gay, Peter. *The Bourgeois Experience: Victoria to Freud.* 1984-1986. 2 vols.

Gillis, John R. *For Better, For Worse: British Marriages, 1600 to the Present.* 1985.

Mintz, Steven. *A Prison of Expectations: The Family in Victorian Culture.* 1985.

Tilly, Louise A. and Joan W. Scott. *Women, Work, and Family.* 1978.

Wohl, Anthony, ed. *The Victorian Family.* 1978.

See also CHILDHOOD; NURSERY AND NANNY; WOMANHOOD

· · · · ·

FANE, VIOLET (1843-1905)

Mary Montgomerie Lamb Singleton, later Lady Currie, chose to publish under the name "Violet Fane"—taken from Disraeli's novel *Vivian Grey* (1826-1827)—because her aristocratic family disapproved of her aspirations as a writer. Despite their reservations, Fane contributed numerous poems, stories, and essays to various nineteenth-century journals and magazines. She also published several novels and books of verse, one play, and an eight-volume translation of the *Memoirs of Marguerite de Valois*, with introduction and notes (1892).

Fane came from a distinguished literary family of French and English heritage. She married Henry Singleton in 1864, gave birth to four children, and became well known in fashionable London social circles. Singleton died in 1893. In 1894 Fane married Philip Currie, the newly appointed British ambassador to Turkey; the couple lived in Constantinople from 1894–1898 and in Rome from 1898–1903 before retiring to England. Upon her husband's elevation to the peerage in 1898, Fane became Lady Currie.

Fane's chief works include her poems, collected in 1880 and 1892, her verse novel *Denzil Place* (1875), her prose essays, collected in 1902, and her miscellaneous articles on social subjects which appeared in the *Nineteenth Century, Blackwood's,* and *Littell's Living Age* between 1902 and 1905; the latter are uncollected. A frequent subject of Fane's poetry and fiction was marriage, which she characteristically criticized. For example, *Denzil Place,* written in the manner of Elizabeth Barrett Browning's verse novel *Aurora Leigh* (1857), implicates the Victorian marriage market in the adultery and death of its heroine. Overall, Fane's work is original, sympathetic, and humane—far less sentimental than most of the popular literature of her day.

KATHLEEN HICKOK
· · · · ·

FANTASY LITERATURE

Though the Victorian period is often acclaimed as the age that brought narrative realism to its maturity, the period's more original accomplishment was the development of literary fantasy. Literary fantasy began around midcentury with works often, though by no means always, written for children, and grew into a tradition of astonishing range and complexity. It is not surprising that this development should take place in the age of George Eliot and Thomas Hardy, for fantasy literature is in a sense the alter ego of the realistic tradition, addressing subjects and using techniques that the realists, because of their very

assumptions, were incapable of attempting.

Victorian fantasy emerged through a coalescence of sources bequeathed by earlier periods. The most important was certainly the traditional folk or fairy tale. The nineteenth century saw both a prodigious effort to record the traditional tales, until then preserved only orally, and an interest in writing original tales *Kunstmärchen* in imitation of the popular material. The Grimm brothers' collection of German popular tales was translated into English in 1823, and by midcentury the folktales of Ireland, Scotland, England, and Norway were becoming available. The precedent for original *Kunstmärchen* was also foreign, the two most important influences being E. T. A. Hoffman in Germany and Hans Christian Andersen in Denmark. The latter's tales especially, first translated into English in 1846, seemed to prompt the beginnings of a Victorian tradition, highlighted by John Ruskin's *The King of the Golden River* (1851), George MacDonald's *Dealings with the Fairies* (1867), and Oscar Wilde's *The Happy Prince and Other Tales* (1888). Another important folk tale influence was *The Arabian Nights,* which had retained its popularity since its first appearance in English early in the eighteenth century, instilling a taste for exotic settings and magical plots, perhaps most clearly seen in George Meredith's fantasy *The Shaving of Shagpat* (1856).

A second major source for Victorian fantasy was the romantic movement, with its emphasis on the power of the imagination and the centrality of feeling and intuition in intellectual life. To a mind attuned to these serious concerns, fantasy supplied an opportunity for imaginative speculation and psychological self-exploration. While the appeal of fairy tales lay in the remote setting, giving the impression of a world quite disengaged from our own and running by its own rules, several Victorian authors created a more complex effect by exploring the tenuous borderline between familiar and fantastic experience. Notable fantasies of this type include Lewis Carroll's *Alice's Adventures in Wonderland* (1865) and *Through the Looking-Glass* (1871), MacDonald's *Phantastes* (1858) and *At the Back of the North Wind* (1869), and Charles Kingsley's *The Water-Babies* (1863). The last title defuses the common charge that fantasy is irrelevant, for it successfully focused public attention on the suffering of chimney sweeps, leading directly to the government's first attempt, in 1864, to regulate such labor. The sheer complexity of Carroll's and MacDonald's fantasies, on the other hand, shows that such works are not limited to children.

The third major source of Victorian fantasy was the **Gothic** tradition, which flourished in England in the romantic period. Though pure Gothic is not common in Victorian literature, certain of its features—its staginess, its villains, its use of horror and the supernatural—became quite pervasive. At the crudest level the result was the "penny dreadful" or popular thriller, of which *Varney, the Vampyre or, The Feast of Blood* (1847, attributed to J. M. Rymer and T. P. Prest) is surely the most extreme example, running to about 870,000 words of gaudy prose. In serious literary hands, however, the thriller could become an effective experiment in the psychology of horror. The best works of this tradition are Sheridan LeFanu's *In a Glass Darkly* (1872), Robert Louis Stevenson's *The Strange Case of Dr. Jekyll and Mr. Hyde* (1886), Wilde's *The Picture of Dorian Gray* (1891), and Bram Stoker's *Dracula* (1897). The last three titles especially created primal images of enduring fascination.

The wealth and variety of fantasy produced near the end of the Victorian period indicates its continued ability to thrive in a number of guises: a subtly elusive ghost story in Henry James's *The Turn of the Screw* (1898), a troubling metaphysical journey in MacDonald's *Lilith* (1895), utopian fantasies such as Samuel Butler's *Erewhon* (1872) and William Morris's *News from Nowhere* (1891), animal fantasies such as Rudyard Kipling's *The Jungle Book* (1894), recreations of mythic material in Richard Garnett's *Twilight of the Gods* (1888) and Arthur Machen's *The Great God Pan* (1894), and the beginnings of **science fiction** with H. G. Wells's early work.

DOUGLAS THORPE

Bibliography

Cott, Jonathan, ed. *Beyond the Looking Glass: Extraordinary Works of Fairy Tale and Fantasy.* 1973.

Hume, Kathryn. *Fantasy and Mimesis: Responses to Reality in Western Literature.* 1984.

Jackson, Rosemary. *Fantasy: The Literature of Subversion.* 1981.

Kiely, Robert. *The Romantic Novel in England.* 1972.

Manlove, Colin. *The Impulse of Fantasy Literature.* 1983.

———. *Modern Fantasy: Five Studies.* 1975.

Prickett, Stephen. *Victorian Fantasy.* 1979.

Schlobin, Roger C., ed. *The Aesthetics of Fantasy Literature and Art.* 1982.

Sewell, Elizabeth. *The Field of Nonsense.* 1952.

Tymn, Marshall B., et al., eds. *Fantasy Literature: A Core Collection and Reference Guide.* 1979.

See also *FAIRY TALES; SUPERNATURAL FICTION; UTOPIAN FICTION*

· · · · ·

FAR EAST

British interest in the Far East, apart from **India**, centered on trade, primarily in Burma, Malaysia, Ceylon, China, and Siam. Various concessions and special arrangements were forced or negotiated, but there were relatively few colonial possessions under actual British administration.

After it had reconquered Arakan and Assam in the mid-eighteenth century, Burma occupied a position on the frontier of British India. Forced to sue for peace, Burma lost both provinces. Following the Second Anglo-Burmese War (1852), Lower Burma was placed under the government of India. The Third Anglo-Burmese War (1885) resulted in the removal of Burma's last king, Thibaw (1878–1885); the entire kingdom became a province of India. As an Indian province, Burma changed from a barter to a money economy. The Irawaddy Delta was put to the highly profitable cultivation of rice, but the Indians, British, and Chinese, not the Burmese, reaped the benefits.

British interests in Malaysia began when the **East India Company**, looking for a source of goods to be sold in China, acquired Penang Island from the Dutch in 1786. Malacca was captured in 1796, and in 1819 Stamford Raffles established a settlement on Singapore Island. Rivalries among various nationalities, however, created administrative problems. Chinese immigrants began the development of tin mining and manufacture, and the industry remained in Chinese hands throughout the nineteenth century. Racial clashes in the tin fields of Perak brought British intervention. In 1867 Malacca, Singapore, and Penang were brought directly under the control of the British Colonial Office. In 1896 the four states of Perak, Selangor, Negro Sembilan, and Pahang were brought together as a federation with Kuala Lumpur as the capital. Rubber, introduced with indifferent success in the 1870s, became Malaysia's second major industry in the late 1890s. Acreage was allotted to individual Malay and Chinese smallholders, but it was primarily south Indians who worked rubber plantations.

In China, the East India Company's importation of opium from India, especially after 1819, brought the company into conflict with the crumbling Manchu dynasty. The Opium War (1841) was followed by the Treaty of Nanking which ceded Hong Kong and five other ports to Britain. Chinese opposition to the Manchus was often couched in anti-Western, anti-Christian terms. The Taiping Rebellion (1850-1864), which involved Charles G. "Chinese" Gordon, and the Boxer Rebellion (1900), in which the legations in Peking were beseiged, were antiforeign as well as anti-Manchu.

Siamese kings received British traders and diplomats politely and signed limited treaties with them beginning in 1826. Western influences—carefully controlled by King Mongkut—brought in printing, vaccination, technicians, and teachers, including Anna Leonowen, who wrote an account of Mongkut's reign. Although westernization continued under Mongkut's son Chulalongkorn, Siam successfully retained its independence and its share in the profits of international trade.

Ceylon was known for its spices—especially cinnamon and pepper—which brought first Portuguese and then Dutch penetration. Britain seized Ceylon from the Dutch in 1796 and reduced the previously independent kingdom of Kandy in 1818. Under British colonial rule, cinnamon, pepper, sugarcane, cotton, and coffee were cultivated for export. In the 1870s tea replaced coffee as the dominant product in Ceylon's economy.

JOAN MICKELSON GAUGHAN

Bibliography

Costin, William C. *Britain and China, 1833-1860.* 1937.

Greenberg, Michael. *British Trade and the Opening of China, 1800-1842.* 1951.

Harvey, Godfrey E. *British Rule in Burma, 1824-1942.* 1946; rpt. 1974.

Thio, Eunice. *British Policy in the Malay Peninsula, 1880-1910.* 1969.

Vella, Walter F. *The Impact of the West on Government in Thailand.* 1955.

· · · · ·

FARADAY, MICHAEL (1791-1867)

A leading English chemist and physicist, Michael Faraday's most famous achievement was the discovery of electromagnetic induction in 1851, a phenomenon with wide-scale applications in the electric motor and dynamo, the telephone, and the transformer. Faraday was born into great poverty and began work for a bookbinder at the age of twelve. His interest in experimentation led to his engagement as Humphry Davy's assistant at the Royal Institution in 1813. Here he remained for fifty-four years, being appointed director of its laboratory in 1825 and Fullerian Professor of Chemistry in 1833.

Faraday began work on electromagnetism in 1821 by detailed and careful experimentation which he recorded meticulously in numbered paragraphs. A decade later he started the first section of his *Experimental Researches in Electricity* (3 vols., 1839-1855) with his discovery of electromagnetic induction. This showed that one current could generate another, and with his development of the dynamo he linked up mechanical motion and magnetism with the production of electricity. A series of profound findings followed, including specific inductive capacity, the Faraday effect, the laws of electrochemistry and the foundations of classical field theory. Faraday knew little mathematics and therefore conceived the theoretical explanations of his discoveries in graphic notions of lines of force. It was left to **James Clerk Maxwell** to develop a mathematical treatment of electromagnetic theory.

In addition to many technical works of **physics**, Faraday made important contributions to **chemistry** (his treatise on *Chemical Manipulation*, 1827, remains a useful reference source) and was able to popularize even the most abstruse subjects. His Christmas lectures at the Royal Institution and his *Chemical History of a Candle* (1861) reached large, appreciative audiences. Faraday was a member of the Sandemanians, a fundamentalist Protestant sect which stressed love and community. One aspect of Sandemanian doctrine was its emphasis on the unity of natural laws in the universe; this seems to have had a profound effect on Faraday's scientific work.

MICHAEL SHORTLAND

Bibliography

Grooding, David and Frank A. J. L. James, eds. *Faraday Rediscovered.* 1985.

Jones, H. Bence. *The Life and Letters of Faraday.* 1870. 2 vols.

Martin, Thomas, ed. *Faraday's Diary, Being the Various Philosophical Notes of Experimental Investigation Made by Michael Faraday.* 1932–1936. 7 vols.

Williams, L. Pearce. *Michael Faraday: A Biography.* 1965.

————, ed. *The Selected Correspondence of Michael Faraday.* 1971. 2 vols.

See also ELECTRICITY

· · · · ·

FARCE

Farce, a species of comedy highly popular in Victorian Britain, was presented most commonly as a one- or two-act play with a stylized, swift-moving comic plot and stereotypical characters. Farcical humor ranges from slapstick comedy to absurdist, black humor.

Farces throughout the period incorporated features essential to the genre: misunderstandings, secrets, and surprise revelations; coincidences in unrealistically rapid succession; and eccentric, unselfconscious characters too rigid by nature to develop in the course of the play. There were, however, two significant shifts of focus in nineteenth-century farce. Early Victorian farces (1830s–early 1840s), like those by John Baldwin Buckstone (1802–1879) that critics dubbed "Adelphi screamers," presented versions of the tangled love intrigues among upper-class characters common in eighteenth-century farce. After the Theatre Regulation Act of 1843 and the opening of many new theaters, the subject matter of farce changed to reflect the interests of the numerous middle- and working-class people in the audience. Both physical clowning (some say violence) and sentimentalism in the treatment of marriage and domesticity increased with the new attention to bourgeois life. *Box and Cox* (1847) by John Maddison Morton (1811–1891) and *How to Settle Accounts with Your Laundress* (1847) by Joseph Stirling Coyne (1803–1868) were typical of this period.

The second shift of focus in Victorian farce took place in the 1870s–1890s, when the long-established practice of adapting French plays and writing in the style of those plays brought about changes in the subject matter and technique of British farce. Sex, in and out of marriage, became the primary subject of farce, and "bedroom farce" grew to be synonymous with "farce." To various degrees, British playwrights also adopted the techniques of French "well-made plays," carefully composing their works so as to maintain suspense and keep action moving at high speed. The manifest design in these plays implies a fatalistic or absurd universe: the plot's clockwork operation traps individuals in situations which they may have initiated but can neither understand nor control. Late-century farces such as *Tom Cobb, or Fortune's Toy* (1875) by William Schwenck Gilbert (1836–1911) feature black humor and a dark, threatening tone.

Critics disagree about whether Victorian farce is a rebellious or a conservative genre. While farce's overriding purpose is to ridicule the social and physical laws that limit human potential, the plays also expose the absurd futility—immorality, as some British playwrights would have it—of attempts to transcend those limits. George Bernard Shaw (1856–1950) despised farce for what he saw as ideological irresponsibility. But farce, especially as Victorian authors from Buckstone to **Oscar Wilde** (1854–1900) and **Arthur Wing Pinero** (1855–1934) treated it, is a genre of contradictions: it both is and is not a philosophical art form. Ideas in farce are bound up in its portrayal of the unresolvable paradox of the human condition and in its ability to provoke laughter in the face of this paradox.

ELIZABETH J. DEIS

Bibliography

Bentley, Eric. "The Psychology of Farce." In Eric Bentley, ed., *"Let's Get a Divorce!" and Other Plays.* 1958.

Bermel, Albert. *The Comprehensive and Definitive Account of Farce: One of the World's Funniest Art Forms.* 1982.

Booth, Michael R., ed. *English Plays of the Nineteenth Century,* vol. 4. 1973.

Davis, Jessica Milner. *Farce.* 1978.

Reynolds, Ernest. *Early Victorian Drama, 1830–1870.* 1936.

Sypher, Wylie, ed. *Comedy: "An Essay on Comedy,"* by George Meredith and *"Laughter,"* by Henri Bergson. 1956.

Taylor, John Russell. *The Rise and Fall of the Well-Made Play.* 1967.

. . . . .

FARJEON, BENJAMIN (1838–1903)

A prolific minor novelist, Anglo-Jewish Benjamin Farjeon wrote over fifty novels, of which *At the Sign of the Silver Flagon* (1875), *Solomon Isaacs* (1877), *Aaron the Jew* (1894), and *Pride of Race* (1900) examine Jewish life. Although they were not as widely read as *Grif* (1868) and *Blade-O-Grass* (1871), Farjeon's novels about Jews refuted the traditional stereotypes of the gibberish-speaking Jew and the vulgar, unscrupulous Jewish businessman, as seen in the work of Thackeray, Trollope, Reade, and others.

Raised as an Orthodox Jew, Farjeon married an American Protestant and assimilated to English life. Nonetheless, he was the first novelist to explore contemporary Anglo-Jewish problems, both with the larger society (including English bigotry and appeals to convert) and within the community (especially intermarriage and nonreligious Jews). He met the challenge of bigotry with characters' stoic silence, and of appeals to convert with the quasi-scientific view that religion is an inherited instinct. He showed that difficulties raised by intermarriage could be solved by patience, but that nothing positive could be achieved by an individual's merely nominal adherence to Judaism.

Farjeon rebutted negative stereotypes with idealized Jewish characters but, unlike earlier Anglo-Jewish novelists who wrote carefully for an audience of both Christians and Jews, he was not afraid of offending non-Jewish readers. The first to depict various types of contemporary Jews and Jewish problems, Farjeon created the genre of the **Anglo-Jewish novel**.

LINDA GERTNER ZATLIN

Bibliography

Zatlin, Linda Gertner. *The Nineteenth-Century Anglo-Jewish Novel.* 1981.

. . . . .

FARMING see AGRICULTURE

. . . . .

FARR, FLORENCE (1860?–1917)

Florence Farr (Mrs. Edward Emery) began her career as an actress in the 1880s in William Morris's entertainments at the Bedford Park Theatre. Soon involved in avant-garde theater, she directed the English premiere of Ibsen's *Rosmersholm* in 1891, playing Rebecca, and appeared as Blanche in the Independent Theatre Society's production of Shaw's *Widowers' Houses* (1892). In 1894, financed by Annie Horniman, Farr mounted

Yeats's *Land of Heart's Desire* and Shaw's *Arms and the Man.*

With Yeats, Farr worked out a method of verse speaking to a psaltery designed to suit her voice. She used this "cantillation" at recitals of Yeats's poems; it also influenced her playing of Aleel in his *The Countess Cathleen* (1899) in Dublin. Farr arranged music and choruses for the Barker-Vedrenne productions of *The Trojan Women* (1905) and *Hippolytus* (1906). She published *The Music of Speech* (1909).

Farr's book *Modern Woman, Her Intentions* (1910) shows her as a conscious **New Woman**. Her interest in the occult is reflected in her 1905 production of Yeats's *The Shadowy Waters* for Theosophists at the Court Theatre and her publication of several occult books. She also wrote fiction, including *The Dancing Faun* (1894).

A promising actress, independent spirit, and senior member of the Order of the Golden Dawn, Farr went to Ceylon in 1912 and died there of cancer five years later.

ANDREW PARKIN

Bibliography

Bax, Clifford, ed. *Florence Farr, Bernard Shaw, W. B. Yeats: Letters.* 1942.

Johnson, Josephine. *Florence Farr: Bernard Shaw's "New Woman."* 1975.

· · · · ·

FASHION see CLOTHING AND FASHION

· · · · ·

FAWCETT, MILLICENT GARRETT
(1847–1929)

Millicent Garrett Fawcett served as president of the National Union of Women's Suffrage Societies (NUWSS) from 1897 to 1919. A political economist and writer, she dedicated herself to the "constitutional" struggle to enfranchise women, and was among the most prominent suffragists in Britain.

Taught from childhood the importance of women's independence, she was heavily influenced by the efforts of her sister, **Elizabeth Garrett Anderson** (1836–1917), to become a doctor. The impact of John Stuart Mill and other radicals was also strong, and her husband Henry Fawcett (1833–1884), a Cambridge professor and Liberal M.P., always encouraged her work. She joined the Women's Suffrage Committee in 1867 and began speaking and writing on the issue in 1868. A quiet supporter of Josephine Butler's campaign against the Contagious Diseases Acts and an active participant in the development of Newnham College (where her daughter Philippa, a brilliant mathematician, became in 1890 the first woman student to place above Cambridge's senior wrangler), Fawcett began her active lobbying for the vote in 1870 and soon emerged as a movement leader.

Although her political involvement was never limited to the suffrage fight, it was the main focus of her life's work. As president of the NUWSS, Fawcett maintained an essentially liberal position, emphasizing equal opportunity and insisting on constitutional methods of protest and demonstration. The emergence of the "militants" in 1905 and the tensions aroused by World War I created major divisions within the movement, but it was the union's advocacy of family allowances and mothers' pensions that eventually led to her resignation.

Fawcett received the O.B.E. in 1924. Among her many books are a novel, *Janet Doncaster* (1875); *Political Economy for Beginners* (1870); *Essays and Lectures on Social and Political Subjects* (with Henry Fawcett, 1872); *Women's Suffrage* (1912); *The Women's Victory—and After* (1920); several biographies, including *Josephine Butler* (with E. M. Turner, 1927); and her autobiography *What I Remember* (1924).

LAURA STEMPEL MUMFORD

Bibliography

Fawcett, Millicent Garrett. *What I Remember.* 1924.

Strachey, Ray. *The Cause.* 1928; rpt. 1978.

———. *Millicent Garrett Fawcett.* 1931.

· · · · ·

FEMINISM

Victorian feminism was a wide-ranging movement involving women and men of all classes, and encompassing all aspects of women's lives. Although the movement eventually focused on suffrage, it began with women's frustration over legal disabilities and the lack of opportunities for employment and education, growing over the latter half of the century to include the struggle against the Contagious Diseases Acts; the effort to establish colleges for women; the campaign for changes in marital property and divorce laws; the opening of new employment arenas; the expansion of the franchise at the municipal and national levels; and some alterations in conceptions of "femininity" and women's role.

The term "feminism" did not come into use in Britain until about 1895, but British interest in the "woman question" can be traced back at least to Mary Wollstonecraft's *Vindication of the Rights of Woman* (1792). Although not identified with a separate organized cause, individual women and men—particularly those involved in the Owenite socialist and St. Simonian movements—argued for radical changes in women's position. In the 1820s and 1830s journals like the *Westminster Review* and *Monthly Repository* championed the cause, as protective legislation limited women's jobs and working hours and major laws in the 1830s for the first time explicitly excluded women from the franchise and other government activities. **Anna Jameson**'s *Characteristics of Women* (1832) and **Harriet Martineau**'s *Society in America* (1835) were among the first important books arguing for an expansion of women's rights, and **Caroline Norton**'s campaign in the late 1830s for access to her children and control of her earnings was a first step in bringing about major changes in women's legal position.

By the early 1850s, the solidification of the **Langham Place circle** marked the beginning of organized feminism in Britain. While the movement always addressed many issues, activism in the 1850s and 1860s focused on increasing women's access to paid labor and the training required for it. Through a variety of activities, the Langham Place circle and others promoted the ideal of women's eco-nomic independence, partially in response to the problem of "superfluous" women, and in harmony with the Victorian view of work as inherently virtuous.

As the movement grew it attracted the interest of people outside its original circle of radicals, Unitarians, and Quakers. Although **Harriet Taylor Mill**'s *Enfranchisement of Women* appeared in 1851, the idea of women's suffrage began to gain real support only in the 1860s, and in 1866 **John Stuart Mill** introduced the first parliamentary motion to expand the franchise. Throughout this period feminists also worked for changes in marital property laws and for the establishment of colleges for women. While the founding of Queen's College (1848) and Bedford College (1849) were a beginning, higher education continued to be a major issue for feminists into the twentieth century. Changes in property laws also came slowly, with married women unable to control their own earnings until 1870.

In the early 1870s, Josephine Butler's campaign to repeal the Contagious Diseases Acts began to shatter the Victorian ideal of women's public silence and total ignorance of sexual matters. Along with feminist efforts to overcome the taboo on women's public speaking, Butler's shocking campaign forced people to confront deeply held views on women's proper behavior, and paved the way for greater changes in women's position. The position of prostitutes also became a major metaphor for women's situation, feminists arguing that **prostitution** resulted from limited employment opportunities and insisting that "fallen" women deserved sympathetic public attention.

Because the premises of Victorian feminism generally tallied with prevailing ideas about women's nature and sphere, politically shrewd feminists used these very premises to expand women's public role. Taking advantage of the assumption that women were more pious, altruistic, and self-sacrificing than men, feminists agitated for women's increased public **philanthropy**, and women were gradually permitted to vote in municipal elections (1869) and to serve as Poor Law guardians and school board members (1870). The notions of separate male and female spheres and of women's greater altruism and innate pacifism underlay most feminist campaigns. Midcentury activists took great pains not to offend convention, largely avoiding discussions of **birth control** or women's sexuality, demanding a single standard of sexual chastity, and often softening their rhetoric in order not to be perceived as antimarriage or antifamily. From John Stuart Mill's *Subjection of Women* (1867) to the writing of feminists like **Mona Caird** (1858-1932) at the turn of the century, few openly challenged the ideal of heterosexual marriage, and many even couched the argument for women's education in terms of making women better wives and mothers. But the dramatic increase in the population of "superfluous" women allowed feminists to demand independence for them, opening the way to married women's rights as well.

Despite their caution, conservatism, and focus on the rights of **single women**, feminists were inevitably seen as strong-minded, threatening to the social order and violating decorum. Efforts to gain access to **medical education** were especially offensive to prevailing mores.

By the late 1880s women's suffrage had become the central issue, although most feminists continued to work in other areas as well, and there was a split between those who saw the vote as primary and those who continued to emphasize education and employment. The suffrage movement aroused even more hostility than earlier campaigns, and some who had long supported the feminist cause—like **Mary Ward** (1851-1920)—organized in opposition. The vote (not gained until 1918) shaped the feminist struggle for the rest of the century.

LAURA STEMPEL MUMFORD

Bibliography

Banks, J. A. and Olive Banks. *Feminism and Family Planning in Victorian England.* 1964.

Bauer, Carol and Lawrence Ritt. *Free and Ennobled: Source Readings in the Development of Victorian Feminism.* 1979.

Holcombe, Lee. *Wives and Property: Reform of the Married Women's Property Law in Nineteenth-Century England.* 1983.

Liddington, Jill and Jill Norris. *One Hand Tied Behind Us: The Rise of the Women's Suffrage Movement.* 1978.

Strachey, Ray. *The Cause.* 1928; rpt. 1978.

Taylor, Barbara. *Eve and the New Jerusalem: Socialism and Feminism in the Nineteenth Century.* 1983.

Vicinus, Martha. *Independent Women: Work and Community for Single Women, 1850-1920.* 1985.

See also EDUCATION, WOMEN'S; ELECTIONS AND THE FRANCHISE; MARRIED WOMEN'S PROPERTY; SUFFRAGE, WOMEN'S; WOMEN'S EMPLOYMENT

. . . . .

FEMINIST WRITING

Victorian feminist writing encompassed all genres and addressed the entire spectrum of issues important to the feminist movement of the time. Because discussion of the woman question was ubiquitous, it informed a wide range of literature. In addition to the essays that played a central role in the growing debate over women's rights, writers of fiction, poetry, and drama used literature to express their ideas about women's role and often to agitate for political and social change.

Feminist writing can be roughly divided into those works that explicitly advocate change and those that embody a feminist impulse in their treatment of particular themes. Among the overtly feminist are political essays by women like **Anna Jameson** (1794-1860) and **Harriet Martineau** (1802-1876), who argued in the 1830s for an expansion of women's rights. **Harriet Taylor (Mill)**'s *Enfranchisement of Women* (1851) and **John Stuart Mill**'s *Subjection of Women* (1867) were among the most important midcentury essays promoting women's rights, and feminist journals like the *Englishwoman's Review* (1866-1906) published arguments advocating fundamental changes in women's status, as well as feminist poems and short stories. Victorian feminists also began to develop a form of feminist literary criticism, as in Anna Jameson's *Characters of Women or Shakespeare's Heroines* (1832).

Many prominent Victorian literary figures were identified with the feminist cause to different degrees, and their writing reflected this. One of the most important feminist literary works of the period is **Elizabeth Barrett Browning**'s 1857 verse novel *Aurora Leigh*, which describes a woman writer's struggle between art and marriage and critiques conventional notions of women's education and sphere. Among the most influential novelists was **Olive Schreiner** (1855-1920), whose best-selling *Story of an African Farm* (1883) features an openly feminist protagonist who makes lengthy speeches in favor of women's rights. Others, like **Mona Caird** (1858-1932), depicted the dangerous effects of women's dependent position or, like **Sarah Grand** (1854-1943), focused on the sexual double standard.

Given the strictness of Victorian literary convention, departures from traditional views of women often implied a feminist perspective. Novels that focused on "fallen" women who were sympathetically portrayed (rather than directly punished for their sexual activity), such as **Elizabeth Gaskell**'s *Ruth* (1853), presented an open challenge to convention. So did those that, like **George Eliot**'s *Mill on the Floss* (1860) and *Middlemarch* (1872), demonstrated women's dissatisfaction with their access to education or the difficulty of making a meaningful contribution to society. Eliot and Gaskell are typical of the implicitly feminist writers of the period, for while their works may lack clearly identifiable feminist protagonists and polemical passages on women's rights, they present women struggling with their traditional position and chafing against conventional restrictions on their activities. Such novels analyze and critique the conditions that shape women's lives, although Eliot's despairing conclusions do not offer much hope for feminist change.

A feminist impulse can also be seen in Victorian novels by women not easily identified as feminists. Gilbert and Gubar, for example, read **Charlotte Brontë**'s *Jane Eyre* (1847) and *Villette* (1853) as covert expressions of feminist anger, and *Jane Eyre* in particular was perceived by Victorian readers as expressing female passion in an unseemly way. Such refusals to portray women as asexual and pacific contributed to the feminist challenge and confronted the prescriptive nature of standard literature about women.

Feminist poets incorporated their political ideas into powerful and often moving works.

Augusta Webster's long poem "A Castaway" (1870) was seen by many as the century's most effective treatment of prostitution, and her poetry often criticized the idealized conceptions of maternal love and marriage that constrained women. Other poets, like **Adelaide Anne Proctor** (1825-1860), questioned the Victorian notion of self-sacrifice, and **Mary Coleridge**'s "The White Women" (1900) is a feminist utopia. As Hickok points out, a feminist impulse is present in much Victorian poetry by women, both in overt criticism of women's traditional position and in the poets' attempts to portray women's lives honestly, regardless of literary convention.

Drama was also touched by feminism, as in Elizabeth Robins and Lady Florence Bell's controversial play *Alan's Wife* (1893), which acknowledges women's sexual passion and questions conventional assumptions about motherhood. Most influential, however, were the English-language productions of plays by Henrik Ibsen, first mounted in the 1890s.

"New Woman" writers participated in the feminist debate, but their work cannot be easily characterized as feminist because it tends to depict changes in women's status superficially. Some male writers, like **George Gissing** in *The Odd Women* (1893), demonstrated the efforts feminists were making to increase women's opportunities to live autonomously, although Gissing's portrait of feminist Rhoda Nunn is extremely ambiguous. Other New Woman novels, like **Grant Allen**'s *The Woman Who Did* (1895), entertained the possibility of change, but clearly reinforced prevailing ideas about the impropriety of women's departure from standard morality.

Antifeminist writers like **Eliza Lynn Linton** (1822-1898) also used essays and literature to further their political position. Among the most famous efforts is **Coventry Patmore**'s "The Angel in the House" (1854-1856), which remained a symbol of antifeminist thought into the twentieth century. It is important, however, to distinguish between those works that were explicitly antifeminist (like Linton's essays) and those that (like **Ellen Price Wood**'s *East Lynne*, 1861) merely followed Victorian literary and social conventions. And many works that dealt with the woman question were ambiguous. Typical is **Alfred Tennyson**'s "The Princess" (1847), which may have been intended as a serious argument in favor of women's higher education, but which is easily read as a trivialization of that goal.

Feminism altered the course of Victorian literature by challenging the literary conventions that governed the portrayal of women and women's experience. More important, writing by feminists and those influenced by their ideas formed part of the movement that led to expanded opportunities, increased independence, and fundamental shifts in attitudes towards women, and ultimately changed women's lives.

LAURA STEMPEL MUMFORD

Bibliography

Gilbert, Sandra and Susan Gubar. *The Madwoman in the Attic: The Woman Writer and the Nineteenth-Century Literary Imagination.* 1979.

Hickok, Kathleen. *Representations of Women: Nineteenth-Century British Women's Poetry.* 1984.

Showalter, Elaine. *A Literature of Their Own: British Women Novelists from Brontë to Lessing.* 1977.

· · · · ·

FICTION SYNDICATION

Fiction syndication, the simultaneous serial publication of novels and stories in several newspapers and magazines, usually arranged by literary agencies, originated in France early in the nineteenth century but was a late development in both England and America. Despite some newspaper appearances of serialized novels (Harrison Ainsworth's *Old Saint Pauls* first appeared in the *Sunday Times* from January–December 1841), the practice did not become common until the late Victorian period with the expansion of weeklies and dailies.

The pioneer in syndication in England was the newspaper firm of William Tillotson and Sons. In 1868 they began to serialize novels in their *Bolton Weekly Journal*, primarily as a means to draw more subscribers. In 1873 they inaugurated Tillotson's Fiction Bureau as an agency to syndicate fiction in six provincial newspapers, and soon extended their operation to newspapers throughout the country. The first English novel syndicated in England

was Mary Elizabeth Braddon's *Lucius Davoren*. Braddon was followed by such popular writers as Walter Besant, Rhoda Broughton, Hall Caine, Marie Corelli, G. Manville Fenn, H. Rider Haggard, and Ouida. Among "classic" writers, Thomas Hardy and Robert Louis Stevenson first reached a wide readership through their connection with the Tillotsons.

Inevitably, as the financial rewards of syndication became known, Tillotson's did not long enjoy their monopoly. Among later enterprises was the National Press Agency, whose most famous client was Anthony Trollope. There is evidence, as with Mayne Reid, that authors occasionally arranged their own syndication. A. P. Watt, the first commercial literary agent in England, was quick to seize on this outlet.

A bold, but ultimately unsuccessful, attempt to undercut Tillotson's and the commercial literary agencies was made by the Author's Syndicate, inaugurated in 1890 by a literary lawyer, William Morris Colles. Colles offered writers direct contact with editors and publishers at half the commission charged by other agents. Colles was closely associated with Walter Besant as legal counsel to the Society of Authors, founded by Besant in 1884. During its first years the syndicate was housed in the headquarters of the Society of Authors as a kind of writers' cooperative. *The Author*, organ of the society, carried the advertisements of the syndicate and regularly reported on its activities until early in 1898, when Colles broke off the connection, apparently finding it impractical to carry on at the minimal fees required by the society. Colles continued to manage the Authors' Syndicate as a commercial literary agency until his death in 1926.

The Tillotson firm sold its syndicate operation to Newspaper Features Ltd. on the eve of World War II. Their records are on deposit in the archives of the John Rylands Library, Manchester.

ROBERT A. COLBY

Bibliography

The Author. 1890–1898.

Colby, Robert A. "Tale Bearing in the 1890s: *The Author* and Fiction Syndication." *Victorian Periodicals Review,* vol. 18, pp. 2–16.

Jones, Aled. "Tillotson's Fiction Bureau: The Manchester Manuscripts." *Victorian Periodicals Review*, vol. 17, pp. 43–48.

Singleton, Frank. *Tillotson's, 1850–1950: Centenary of a Family Business.* 1950.

Turner, Michael. "Tillotson's Fiction Bureau." In
*Studies in the Book Trade in Honour of Gra-
ham Pollard.* 1975.

See also SERIAL LITERATURE

· · · · ·

occasional effort to locate the writings of Michael Field within the aesthetic movement.

SUZANNE GRAVER

Bibliography

Moore, T. Sturge, and D. C. Sturge Moore, eds.
*Works and Days, from the Journal of Michael
Field.* 1933.

Sturgeon, Mary. *Michael Field.* 1922.

——. and T. Sturge Moore, eds. *A Selection from
the Poems of Michael Field.* 1923.

· · · · ·

FIELD, MICHAEL

Michael Field is a pen name for Katherine
Harris Bradley (1846–1914) and her niece,
Edith Emma Cooper (1862–1913), who coauthored twenty-seven poetic dramas and eight
volumes of lyrics.

Katherine Bradley lived in the Cooper
household and helped to raise Edith, whose
mother was an invalid. Both aunt and niece
came from prosperous and cultured merchant families. Bradley attended Newnham
College, Cambridge, and the Collège de
France while Cooper was growing up. In 1878
the two women moved to Bristol and studied
at University College. They lived together as
devoted companions from then on.

The Michael Field pseudonym came into
existence in 1884 with the publication of
Callirrhoë. Bradley had published a volume
of lyrics in 1875, and she and Cooper a poetic
drama in 1881, both of which went unnoticed. As Michael Field, however, they made
a brilliant debut: some critics thought
Callirrhoë Shakespearian. The play was classical in theme, as were several of their subsequent dramas, though the majority were
grounded in English and Scottish history. So
close was their collaboration that they were
often unable to disentangle their respective
contributions. They became known to one
another and to their intimate friends as Michael (Bradley) and Henry (Cooper).

Although a number of writers admired the
work of Bradley and Cooper, among them
Browning, Meredith, Swinburne, and Wilde,
the early praise was for the most part replaced
by indifference and neglect. Their work remains virtually unknown today except for an

FIN DE SIÈCLE

Literally "end of the century," the term "fin
de siècle" encompasses various attitudes that
filtered into the late Victorian consciousness.
Including a preference for the artificial over
the natural and a sense of decline and disillu-
sion, these attitudes logically followed the earlier **aesthetic movement** and an increased national identification with ancient Greece and
Rome. Moreover, such feelings were intensified by the coincidence of the century's end
with the final years of Victoria's long reign.

Characteristic literature of the period, as
written by poets Lionel Johnson (1867–
1902), Ernest Dowson (1867–1900), and Arthur Symons (1865–1945), dealt with exotic,
highly self-conscious psychic helplessness.
However, social reformers like G. B. Shaw
(1856–1950) were also part of the fin de siècle
sensibility. Since the popular theme of decay
implied dynamism and possible renewal, it
could produce conclusions as different as despair and political progressivism (often with
considerable overlap). Magazines such as the
Yellow Book (1894) and the *Savoy* (1896)
explored the contradictions.

In graphic arts, the illustrations of Aubrey
Beardsley (1872–1898) combined the delicate and the grotesque to suggest moral
decadence. However, symbolist art and the
emerging **art nouveau** also contained many
elements of the unofficial fin de siècle credo,
notably an organic lushness suggesting the
inevitable decay to follow. Artists like William
Morris (1834–1896), Edward Burne-Jones
(1833–1898), and Walter Crane (1845–1915)

either anticipated or helped shape the fin de siècle mood.

CYNTHIA J. NOWAK

Bibliography

Fletcher, Ian, ed. *Decadence and the 1890s.* 1980.

Jackson, Holbrook. *The Eighteen Nineties.* 1913.

Thornton R. K. R. *The Decadent Dilemma.* 1983.

· · · · ·

FIREARMS

In 1801 firearms had been unchanged for generations, yet by 1901 modern small arms had been largely perfected. Many late Victorian models remained in production until the mid-twentieth century. Arms makers innovated incessantly, and reflected several central trends of the industrial revolution. This gave the industrial nations a massive superiority in firepower, with far-reaching military and political consequences.

Metallurgy and manufacturing techniques were well advanced when Eli Whitney employed mass production and interchangeable parts while making muskets in 1798. This did not immediately eliminate handmade guns, but a progressive series of innovations soon altered their nature. First, the old flintlock system, in which sparks ignited gunpowder, was slowly displaced by the copper percussion cap, usually filled with fulminate of mercury. Both systems employed muzzle-loaded powder charges and projectiles, which yielded a slow rate of fire. Uniting projectile, powder charge, and percussion primer in a self-contained, metallic cartridge promoted the switch from muzzle to breech loading. Breech loading, in turn, promoted the use of rifled barrels, which were more accurate than smooth bores. By the end of the century smokeless powder, or cordite, both reduced corrosion and left shooters better concealed.

During the 1830s Samuel Colt perfected a multishot pistol with a revolving cylinder for a magazine. His genius extended to marketing, and his guns, later adapted to take metallic cartridges, dominated the marketplace despite many competitors, most notably Smith and Wesson, Remington, and—in Britain—

Adams, and Webley. Colt revolvers were ubiquitous and synonymous with the pistol, as a cheap, reliable arm.

Repeating rifles also soon appeared, and the sliding bolt action and hinged lever action emerged as the preferred mechanisms for handling the new cartridges. Designers sought to combine the principle of rapid fire with larger magazines, but then had to eliminate overheating. The most successful of these early "machine guns," Richard Gatling's (patented 1862), employed multiple barrels revolving around a central axis when turned by a crank. By the end of the century Hiram Maxim's machine gun encased a single barrel in a cooling water jacket, and sustained fire mechanically from the expanding gases of its own discharges. This achieved such a great saving in weight and size that two men could easily carry and operate the weapon. Gas-operated reloading was also applied to pistols by gunmakers such as Borchardt, Mauser, and Browning in the 1890s, and thus the semi-automatic pistol was added to the world's arsenal of small arms.

N. MERRILL DISTAD

Bibliography

Pollard, Major Hugh B. C. *A History of Firearms.* 1926.

Rosa, Joseph G. *Colonel Colt, London: The History of Colt's London Firearms, 1851–1857.* 1976.

Taylerson, A. W. F. *The Revolver, 1889–1914.* 1970.

———, R. A. N. Andrews, and J. Frith. *The Revolver, 1818–1865.* 1968.

Wahl, Paul and Donald Toppel. *The Gatling Gun.* 1965.

· · · · ·

FIREFIGHTING

British firefighting efforts were locally controlled and generally disorganized until the twentieth century; during the Victorian period, firefighting units might be controlled by a town, insurance company, or police force and might be staffed by industrial personnel, country house servants, or volunteer, paid, or

The London Fire Brigade at Practice on the Thames Embankment.
Illustrated London News, *14 March 1868. Library Company of Philadelphia.*

partly paid firefighters. High-risk metropolitan areas were the first to organize. Edinburgh established a professional department in 1824 under the supervision of James Braidwood (1800–1861). In London insurance companies that had previously supported inefficient and competitive fire units moved to amalgamate those units in 1832 when they established the London Fire Engine Establishment. In 1866 this became the Metropolitan Fire Brigade and, taken under public control, was made responsible to the Metropolitan Board of Works; in 1888 the unit was renamed the London Fire Brigade and placed under the control of the newly organized London County Council.

When the London Fire Engine Establishment was formed in 1832, Braidwood was brought from Edinburgh to serve as superintendent. At that time the brigade had five foremen, nine engineers, sixty-six firemen, fourteen hand pumpers, one oar-propelled float with hand pumps, and five reserve engines. In 1833 the establishment answered 592 fire calls and other alarms; by 1850 these had increased to 1,038 and included fires at

the Houses of Parliament (1834), the Cornhill Royal Exchange (1838), and the Tower of London (1841). There was, however, little effort to share fire safety information and encourage fire-safe construction until 1858 when insurance companies established the Fire Offices Committee for that purpose. In the following year, the brigade acquired its first steam fire engine.

Braidwood was killed by a falling wall at the Tooley Street fire of 1861, the greatest London wharfside fire of the century. He had become a popular hero; his mile-and-a-half funeral procession included men of title as well as more than 1,000 policemen and 700 members of the London Rifle Brigade, while the churchbells of London tolled slowly throughout the day. Braidwood was succeeded by another larger-than-life figure, Captain Eyre Massey Shaw (1830–1908), a graduate of Trinity College, Dublin, and a former superintendent of the Belfast Police and Fire Brigade. A fashionable figure mentioned by Gilbert and Sullivan in *Iolanthe*, Shaw was a friend of the Prince of Wales, himself an enthusiastic amateur fireman.

Under Shaw the number of London firefighters, all former sailors, increased to 576 in 1882 and 706 in 1891, the year of his retirement. In 1891 the brigade had thirty-three miles of fire hose; it had only four when Shaw took office. Fire stations (fifty-nine by 1891) were linked by electric telegraph, and the central station was moved from Watling Street to Southwark Bridge Road, where it remained until 1937. Shaw became first president of the National Fire Brigades Union; it provided a massive demonstration of men and equipment in 1887 at Oxford in honor of the Queen's Jubilee. International fire exhibitions were held in 1893 and 1896 at the Royal Agricultural Hall, London. The culmination of Shaw's career came with the review of his men before the Prince of Wales and emperor of Germany at the Crystal Palace in 1891. Shaw resigned shortly afterwards and was succeeded by J. Sexton Simonds, who was asked to resign in 1896, and then by Lionel de Lantour Wells, who served until 1903.

BETTY RICHARDSON

Bibliography

Hardwick, Arthur. *Memorable Fires in London Past and Present.* 1926.

Insurance Institute of London. *The Work of the Insurance Companies in Combating and Preventing Fires.* 1966.

Roetter, Charles. *Fire Is Their Enemy.* 1962.

White, Jack. *Fifty Years of Fire Fighting in London.* 1931.

· · · · ·

FITZGERALD, EDWARD (1809–1883)

Poet and translator Edward Fitzgerald might be considered a major minor figure of the Victorian period. His works and translations are: *Euphranor: A Dialogue on Youth* (1851), *Polonius: A Collection of Wise Saws and Modern Instances* (1852), *Six Dramas of Calderon* (1853), the *Rubaiyat of Omar Khayyam* (1859), and *Readings on Crabbe* (1879).

Fitzgerald was born in Bredfield, Suffolk, and graduated from Trinity College, Cambridge in 1830. He married Lucy Barton but separated from her within a year of the marriage. Most of his later years were spent as a semirecluse in Suffolk.

Fitzgerald's version of the *Rubaiyat of Omar Khayyam,* best considered an adaptation and translation, became one of the most popular poems of the period. Captured in the rhythmic beauty of Fitzgerald's quatrains, Khayyam's epigrammatic attitudes and his fatalism and hedonism could be easily incorporated into certain Victorian views of life. The Pre-Raphaelite discovery of Fitzgerald's version of *The Rubaiyat* reveals the manner in which the poem represents the shifts in taste and attitude that occurred in the middle decades of the Victorian period.

DENNIS GOLDSBERRY

Bibliography

Bentham, George, ed. *The Variorum and Definitive Edition of the Poetical and Prose Writings of Edward Fitzgerald.* 1902.

Jewett, Iran B. Hassani. *Edward Fitzgerald.* 1977.

Terhune, Alfred McKinley. *The Life of Edward Fitzgerald.* 1947.

Wright, William Aldis, ed. *Letters of Edward Fitzgerald.* 1901.

· · · · ·

FLOWERS, LANGUAGE OF

In the nineteenth century, the language of flowers was understood to be a symbolic one. Books explaining the floral language were very popular. There was, however, no one official language of flowers; individual writers chose whatever plants and meanings they wished.

While flowers have been given various meanings throughout history, the language of flowers first appeared in France early in the century. Since it is the language of the love affair, most of the flower meanings are suitable only for romance. *Le Langage des Fleurs* by "Charlotte de Latour" (probably a pseudonym for Louise Cortambert), first published in December 1819, began the fashion for the language of flowers in England and America.

From the 1820s to the 1860s, explanatory books padded with poetry, illustrations and sentimental descriptions of nature were published in great numbers. Besides *Le Langage*, the most important were Henry Phillips's *Floral Emblems* (1825), Frederic Shoberl's translation of Latour, *The Language of Flowers with Illustrative Poetry* (1834), and the American Elizabeth Gamble Wirt's *Flora's Dictionary* (1829). The concept was burlesqued in Frederick Marryat's *The Floral Telegraph* (1836) and Taxile DeLord's *Les Fleurs Animées* (1847).

The language of flowers was popularized in the Victorian period by publishers catering to the gift annual trade, the books being frequently used as New Year's gifts. It is not certain that it was much used by Victorians in their everyday lives and still less certain that it influenced artists and writers. Much of the recent interpretation of the language of flowers has been inaccurate.

BEVERLY SEATON

Bibliography

Seaton, Beverly. "The Flower Language Books of the Nineteenth Century." *The Morton Arboretum Quarterly*, vol. 16, pp. 1-11.

· · · · ·

FOLK MUSIC

What is today referred to as folk music—the music chiefly of a rural populace transmitted through oral tradition—was more often called by other names in the Victorian era: "country song," "old English song," "traditional ballad airs," "English county songs," "traditional tunes," "national music," or simply "popular music." The word "folksong," a translation of the German *Volkslied*, began to appear in the 1890s, was first used in a title by William Alexander Barrett in 1891, and was adopted in 1898 as the name of a new group of collectors—the English Folk Song Society—who were intent upon breaking away from the Victorian attitudes toward folksong evidenced in earlier collections.

The earlier Victorian attitudes, with a few exceptions, discounted music of the rural folk as rude and primitive, having artistic worth only when arranged with piano accompaniments and bowdlerized or completely rewritten texts. The collections of the Reverend Sabine Baring-Gould are a prime example; others—especially those of John Broadwood, Frank Kidson, J. Collingwood Bruce and John Stockoe, and Heywood Summer—are more faithful to the music as found and less condescending to its transmitters.

Although the great era for regional collecting came just after the turn of the century, over 600 folk songs and a good deal of dance music were published from the 1840s onward. Carl Engel's call for a "national music" in 1866 may have spurred efforts, but most of the collecting was done by those interested in "popular antiquities" and local history. They tended to concentrate on music associated with local rituals, such as morris dancing and various May rituals, and on religious music, especially Christmas carols. Work songs in the form of sea shanties and plow songs were also collected. The long narrative ballads and love lyrics that dominate twentieth-century collections were thoroughly balanced by other sorts of music.

Nineteenth-century collectors distinguished and argued over regional differences. One major issue had to do with the primacy of England, Ireland, Scotland, or Wales as the place of origin for particular tunes. Neither collectors nor singers differentiated between the strictly rural and traditional music and that of urban street singers, who were common not only in London but also in the provinces. The ballads hawked by such singers, as eloquently described by Henry Mayhew, were joined to well-known tunes, some of which were parlor or theater songs and others straight from the oral tradition. These tunes and texts also made their way back to the countryside. Thus, tune directions for singing street songs found in the enormous broadside collections of Baring-Gould, Kidson, and others now in the British Museum and other libraries are another valuable source of information about traditional song repertoire of the Victorian era.

ANNE DHU SHAPIRO

Bibliography

Baring-Gould, Sabine and H. Fleetwood Sheppard. *Songs and Ballads of the West.* 1889-1892. 4 vols.

Barrett, William Alexander. *English Folk-Songs.* 1891; rpt. 1973.

Broadwood, John. *Old English Songs.* 1843.

Chappell, William. *The Ballad Literature and Popular Music of the Olden Time.* 1859; rpt. 1965. 2 vols.

Glen, John. *Early Scottish Melodies.* 1900; rpt. 1976.

Harker, David. *Fakesong: The Manufacture of British "Folksong," 1700 to the Present Day.* 1985.

Henderson, W. *Victorian Street Ballads.* 1937.

Kidson, Frank. *Traditional Tunes: A Collection of Ballad Airs.* 1891.

Stokoe, John and J. Collingwood Bruce. *The Northumbrian Minstrelsy.* 1882; rpt. 1965.

Sumner, Heywood. *The Besom Maker and Other Country Songs.* 1888.

See also STREET MUSIC

• • • • •

FOLKLORE

As a field of study in Great Britain, folklore bloomed, reached its apex, and gradually faded during the Victorian period. The intellectual discipline of folklore grew out of the encyclopedic anthologies of customs and beliefs such as John Aubrey's *Miscellanies* (1696), Henry Ellis's edition of John Brand's *Observations on Popular Antiquities* (1813), and William Hone's *Every-Day Book* (1830), which were collected by antiquarians interested in recording the customs and physical remains of England's past.

Antiquarian William John Thomas (1803–1885), writing under the name Thoms-Merton, first used the term "Folk-Lore" to replace "popular antiquities" in a letter, published in the August 22, 1846, *Athenaeum*, which recommended establishing a column to publish such material. By "Folk-Lore" Thoms meant "the Lore of the People," in particular the manners, customs, observations, superstitions, ballads, and proverbs of the common people which had not previously been considered worthy of study. Interest in the new area was immediate and intense. In 1849 Thoms

founded *Notes & Queries,* which extensively covered folklore.

Differing theories about folklore's origins and distribution quickly developed. The two best known were Max Müller's mythological school, based on philology, and the anthropological school with origins in the evolutionary theories of Edward Burnet Tylor (1832–1917), which was promoted most vigorously by **Andrew Lang** (1844–1912). Müller (1823–1900), a noted Sanscrit scholar at Oxford, was influenced by Jacob Grimm's hypothesis that all Indo-European people belonged to a common Aryan stock, and argued that the key to all the mythologies could be found in the Veda. Using philology, Müller postulated a "mythopoetic age" in which language could not convey abstractions. Through the "disease of language" various versions of the same myth developed as the Aryans dispersed from India. From the 1856 appearance of his influential essay "Comparative Mythology," Müller championed the idea that all mythology could be reduced to the single myth of the sun conquering the night.

Tylor, the father of anthropology, built on Darwin's theories of biological evolution and suggested in *Primitive Culture* (1871) that all societies went through a unilinear, three-stage cultural development of savagery, barbarism, and civilization. The relics of primitive belief and custom, which Tylor termed "survivals," linked rural peasants with contemporary savages and could be used to reconstruct the earliest states of culture.

Lang, who popularized the anthropological school of folklore, was quick to find fault with comparative mythology. He enlarged Tylor's limited sense of European folklore to include oral traditions from around the world. Beginning with "Mythology of Fairy Tales," which appeared in the May 1873 *Fortnightly Review,* Lang rejected Müller's appeals to philology and argued for independent but uniform development of myths in all cultures during the savage state.

With the formation of the Folk-Lore Society in London in 1878, the so-called "great team" of British folklorists—Lang, George Laurence Gomme, Alfred Nutt, Edwin Sidney Hartland, Edward Clodd, and William Alexander Clouston—worked for the triumph of anthropological folklore over the claims of comparative mythology. While all six were amateur folklorists who relied on library rather than field research, they produced an enormous amount of competent scholarship. Gomme prepared *The Handbook of Folklore* (1890), a manual intended to encourage collections of English folklore. Nutt was interested in the appearance of fairy mythology in English literature and Celtic studies. Hartland promoted the practical value of folklore for understanding the customs of local populations and thus improving administration of the British Empire. Clodd, an outspoken agnostic, delighted in exposing superstition in Christian ritual. (His 1896 presidental address to the Folk-Lore Society provoked the resignation of one eminent member: former prime minister W. E. Gladstone, who felt that myths supplied evidence of divine revelation.) Clouston concentrated on making Persian and Arabic tales available to English readers.

Significant contributions came also from other members of the Folk-Lore Society. Joseph Jacobs (1854–1916), whose five-volume series, Fairy Tales of Many Lands, rivaled Lang's Coloured Fairy Book series in popularity, gradually convinced Lang that folktales migrated from culture to culture rather than developing independently. With the support of volumes such as Marian Cox's *Cinderella* (1893), a collection of 345 variants and the first comparative study of a complex tale, Jacob's diffusion theory eventually replaced the evolutionary theory of Tylor. Another member of the Folk-Lore Society was **George Frazer** (1854–1941). *The Golden Bough* (1890), although widely praised by folklorists, was atypical of their research, since Frazer's primary concern was primitive religion and his approach was more in the tradition of the Cambridge anthropologists than of the Folk-Lore Society.

The high-water mark of Victorian folklore came in 1891 when the Folk-Lore Society hosted the second International Folk-Lore Congress in London, which received extensive coverage in the popular press. The appeals of folklore in the last third of the nineteenth century were many. Amateur enthusiasts found the British Empire a fertile ground for collecting, whether from servants at home or natives in the colonies. The cultural dynamics of gathering folklore allowed middle-class collectors to view themselves as representatives of the most civilized stage in

Tylor's evolutionary theory. With the spiritual doubts brought on by Darwin and others, many who were unwilling to investigate geology or natural history could find solace in tracing religion and myth.

While anthropology was quickly accepted into the universities, however, folklore flourished in the circles of gifted but amateur enthusiasts. With the deaths of the members of the "great team" and the subsequent loss of many nonprofessional scholars in World War I, the golden age of folklore in Great Britain had passed.

JAN SUSINA

Bibliography

Dorson, Richard. *The British Folklorists: History*. 1968.

——. *Peasant Customs and Savage Myths: Selections from the British Folklorists*. 1968. 2 vols.

See also FAIRY LORE; FAIRY TALES; GAELIC CULTURE

· · · · ·

FOOD AND DIET

The variety, quantity, and quality of food in the nineteenth-century English diet varied enormously according to social class, income, and geography. Generalizations about diet have been controversial, such as in the long-running "standard-of-living debate," in which socialist and capitalist historians argue endlessly over whether industrialization improved the workers' lot. However, numerous identifiable trends transformed the diet of the English people by the end of the Victorian period.

In the eighteenth century, tea (first introduced to England in the 1650s) and white bread began to replace beer and dark bread as staples in the traditional diet, to the chagrin of social critics such as William Cobbett (1762–1835). This trend is reflected in the fall of per capita beer consumption by more than a third between 1800 and 1850, despite its wider availability after the beer licensing act of 1830. Moreover, the disappearance of commonly held lands through the enclosure movement left the rural population with no place to graze livestock or gather firewood, the shortage of which helped lead to the decline of such traditional practices as home brewing and baking. The old practice of agricultural laborers living in, or at least taking their meals with the farmers who employed them, also declined, imposing a costly burden of dietary self-reliance.

The processes of population growth, urbanization, and industrialization created concentrations of consumers with limited access to primary food production, and little time in which to provide for themselves. Food shortages during the Napoleonic Wars caused prices to rise much faster than wages, and the resulting distress was widespread among the working classes. With the coming of peace in 1815 Parliament passed the **Corn Laws**, a tariff on imported wheat, to protect grain production on marginal land that had begun during the war when prices were high. Thus, the domestic price remained artificially high through postwar cycles of depression and unemployment. This policy of taxing the workers' bread to benefit landowners was opposed by the industrialists of the Anti-Corn-Law League, whose interest lay in cheap food and low wages, but repeal of the hated Corn Laws came only in 1846, when the government was forced to respond to the famine in Ireland.

Thus, before 1850 much of the proletariat lived close to the edge of starvation, and even at the best of times their largely farinaceous diet was short on protein and fat, for meat, cheese, and other dairy products were occasional luxuries, not everyday fare. In the country the more enterprising might poach fish and game, but did so at some risk because the punitive **game laws** preserved game for the landowning class. Direct results of dietary inadequacy may be seen in high infant and child mortality rates, and in the stunted growth that rendered so many lower-class recruits unfit for military service. Many found solace in strong drink, for despite the decline in beer consumption, per capita annual expenditure on alcoholic beverages stood at a steady three pounds, although the annual family income of workers often failed to exceed fifty pounds. The waste and misery caused by alcohol abuse inspired the

temperance movement, one of the great social phenomena of the Victorian era.

Evidence about food consumption among different classes of English society is to be found in cookbooks, which were produced in large quantities and aimed at all social classes. However, one must bear in mind that these volumes were as often prescriptive as descriptive. Cobbett's *Cottage Economy* (1821) and Soyer's *Shilling Cookery for the People* (1855) exhorted the working classes to better and more economical nutrition, while Francatelli's *Modern Cook* (1846) and *Cook's Guide* (1862) divulged the secrets of the royal kitchens to an aspiring, if still largely middle-class audience. The two most successful cookery books of the Victorian period were Eliza Acton's *Modern Cookery for Private Families* (1845) and Isabel Beeton's *Book of Household Management* (1861). Both contain a wealth of recipes and menus, which may serve to give the flavor of the food and dishes prepared and served at upper- and middle-class tables.

Unlike the lower classes, the upper and middle classes were well fed on a wide variety of foodstuffs. However, vitamins were unknown and the science of nutrition in its infancy, so mere prosperity was no guarantee of good dietary habits. However, the enormous class of domestic servants—the largest single occupational group in the land—generally benefited from access to a superior diet in the homes in which they served. As with most fashions, those in eating were set by the court. Once the anti-French phobia of the Napoleonic period subsided, French chefs were commonly engaged to cook in the great houses of England, beginning with Antonin Carême (1784–1833), chef to the prince regent (later George IV) (1762–1830). Most famous of them all was Alexis Soyer (1809–1859), who came to England in 1830, and as chef of the Reform Club dazzled society with his culinary flamboyance. Soyer also possessed a social conscience. He ran soup kitchens for the poor, went to Ireland to help feed the starving, and turned his hand to the reform of military cooking both in the field and aboard ship during the Crimean War. In addition he wrote a series of best-selling cookbooks, food histories, and memoirs, and marketed his own brand of sauces and condiments.

With the "haute cuisine" of the French chefs

came *service à la française*. In contrast to the traditional English service, which presented all dishes at once, the French manner prescribed successive courses, each made up of a large number of dishes presented simultaneously; each food course required a number of different wines. In the grandest multicourse extravaganzas the diner's personal servant fetched the food. At midcentury the fashion for *service à la russe* began, in which servants circulated around the table each offering a different dish. There might be even more sequential courses, but this system did reduce the total number of dishes. It did not become general until the 1870s, though by century's end it was the universal practice.

The middle class tended to emulate the habits of the upper class, but were restricted by their means, and particularly by the availability of servants. Many households employed a single servant, usually described as a "cook, general," and thus barely fulfilled the commonest definition of middle class. Such cooks were a far cry from Carême, yet their employers deemed two courses the minimum for any respectable dinner.

The hours at which meals were served had long been in flux, and evolved through the nineteenth century in a way that emphasized class differences. The elaborate traditional English breakfast is proverbial, may have been a holdover from the early medieval practice of dining in the morning, and prompted Somerset Maugham to quip "If you would eat well in England, you must eat breakfast three times a day!" A smaller, secondary meal then followed in late afternoon. Midday meals grew out of the need to provide sustenance as business and fashion pushed dinner to a point later and later in the day. By the Victorian period both breakfast and luncheon had grown into hot meals, and the truly fashionable would not dine earlier than Queen Victoria herself, at 8:00 p.m. The working class, however, generally took their main meal at midday. The long-standing practice among ladies of serving cakes and wine in the afternoon evolved into "afternoon tea" as the nonalcoholic beverage gained universality. Among the working class, however, "tea" became synonymous with the third meal of the day, served in late afternoon or early evening.

One aspect of diet united all social classes for much of the nineteenth century: vulnerability to the widespread adulteration of food and drink, which had not been a problem until urbanization created a large, anonymous society of consumers uninvolved in the production of their own sustenance. Many common adulterants were merely dishonest fillers or substitutions to fatten profit margins. Beer was commonly watered, and then perhaps doctored with iron sulfate (known as "heading") so it would continue to foam. Alum was added to cheap grades of flour to produce pristinely white loaves of bread, which might be further expanded by the addition of potatoes or even ground chalk. Copper salts were used to color pickles and preserves; used tea leaves or other kinds of leaves would be passed off as fresh tea. Other kinds of adulteration occasionally proved fatal. The chemist Frederick Accum (1769–1838) was the first to denounce such practices in his *Treatise on Adulterations of Food and Culinary Poisons* (1820). Despite some public revulsion and outcry, adulteration continued unchecked. In 1850 the crusading editor of the *Lancet*, Dr. Thomas Wakley (1795–1862), commissioned a series of exposé articles by the physician and chemist Arthur Hill Hassall (1817–1894). Hassall's analyses showed that the poor were not the only victims of adulteration, for it was almost impossible to buy unadulterated food at any price. Many people were so accustomed to adulterated food that they expressed a preference for it, and disliked the taste of the pure and unadulterated versions. These revelations led to some measure of self-regulation in the food and drink industry, and Parliament belatedly passed a series of laws after 1860 which culminated in the Adulteration of Food, Drink, and Drugs Act of 1872.

Apart from widespread adulteration, the nineteenth century was an age of mostly beneficial innovations in the provision of food and drink. The transportation revolution, which produced canals, railways, steamships, and (after about 1870) mechanical refrigeration, improved the marketing of perishables, such as produce, dairy products, meat and fish, as well as heavy and bulky comestibles such as beer, which had hitherto suffered a severely restricted range of distribution. By the later nineteenth century, domestic agriculture was no longer able to feed the growing population, and England began importing vast quantities of American and Canadian wheat, Australian and New Zealand lamb, Argentine beef, and Danish bacon and butter. New processes in preservation included the canning of food, a process developed during the Napoleonic Wars to improve provisioning for the Royal Navy.

These developments led to the rise of national distribution, a shift from bulk to prepackaged sales of food, and trademarked brands. This packaging and marketing revolution made such names as Crosse & Blackwell and Huntley & Palmer familiar in every household. Thomas Lipton (1850–1931), who began with a single shop in Glasgow in 1876, built a pioneering chain of grocery stores, which did not at once replace speciality vendors but did eventually yield modern supermarket chains as the dominant food retailers. The nineteenth century also gave birth to the **restaurant**. Prepared food had traditionally only been available in certain inns, taverns, and private clubs as well as in cookshops, where one took one's own food to be cooked. By 1858 there were enough restaurants in the capital to prompt publication of a guide to dining out, *London at Dinner; or, Where to Dine*, and by the end of the century, when dining out became especially fashionable, London, at least, was home to such celebrated establishments as Kettner's, Simpson's in the Strand, and the Café Royale.

It was also an era in which new foods were popularized, such as formerly exotic imports like bananas, or the socially suspect potato, or entirely new products such as sweetened chocolate in the form of edible bars. In 1869 margarine was patented as a cheap butter substitute. New cooking techniques also appeared. Soyer pioneered cooking with gas, and had an all-gas kitchen installed at the Reform Club in 1837. By the century's end the now ubiquitous fish and chips shop had appeared and provided a new staple in the diet of the working class. While there was little or no nutritional benefit in innovations such as bleached white bread, margarine, orange marmalade, tea and cheap sweets, fish and chips supplemented the diet of the working class with much-needed protein and fat. Thus, all classes of society entered the new century

not only with their food altered greatly from former times, but with improved opportunities for enjoying a diet both satisfying and nutritionally sound.

N. MERRILL DISTAD

Bibliography

Burnet, John. *Plenty and Want: A Social History of Diet in England from 1815 to the Present Day*. 2d ed., 1979.

Davis, Dorothy. *Fairs, Shops, and Supermarkets: A History of English Shopping*. 1966.

Dodd, George. *The Food of London, a Sketch of the Chief Varieties of Source of Supply*. 1856.

Drummond, John C. and Anne Wilbraham. *The Englishman's Food: A History of Five Centuries of English Diet*. 2d ed., 1957.

Filby, Frederick Arthur. *A History of Food Adulteration and Analysis*. 1934.

Harrison, Brian. *Drink and the Victorians: The Temperance Question in England, 1815–1872*. 1971.

Mennell, Stephen. *All Manners of Food: Eating and Taste in England and France from the Middle Ages to the Present*. 1985.

Morris, Helen. *Portrait of a Chef, the Life of Alexis Soyer, Sometime Chef to the Reform Club*. 1938.

Palmer, Arnold. *Movable Feasts, a Reconnaisance of the Origins and Consequences of Fluctuations in Meal-Times, with Special Attention to the Introduction of Luncheon and Afternoon Tea*. 1952; rpt. 1984.

Read, Jan and Maite Manjón. *The Great British Breakfast*. 1981.

Salaman, Redcliffe N. *The History and Social Influence of the Potato*. 1949; rpt. 1971.

See also POVERTY; SHOPS AND SHOPPING; STREET TRADERS

· · · · ·

FOREIGN RELATIONS

For most of the nineteenth century Britain was the strongest force on the international stage, controlling some 35 percent of all the world's shipping and almost half its insurance. British commerce dwarfed that of all Europe combined up to 1850 or later. The official value of British imports was approximately 47 million pounds and exports about 70 million pounds in 1830. By 1900 these values had grown to 523 million and 355 million pounds respectively. These remarkable statistics provide the key to Victorian foreign relations. Napoleon's defeat had left Britain supreme everywhere, and her supremacy was based on unchallenged leadership in trade, credit, and manufacturing. Recognizing that maintaining this position depended on maritime activity, Britain seized as many ports, islands, and naval bases as she could in 1815. She thus profited enormously from the Treaty of Vienna and did her utmost to keep that settlement intact.

Britain's diplomacy focused on playing off the major European powers against each other in order to prevent any one of them from becoming too influential. This required keeping a constant vigil over the two most dangerous rivals, France and Russia. So long as these two states remained at odds over the Middle East and Poland, Britain could count on the friendly neutrality of at least one of them. This was perhaps the greatest diplomatic advantage enjoyed by the Victorians up to the **Crimean War**. The general European fear of France was another. The Bourbons had been so aggressive that all of Europe traditionally mistrusted them. Bonapartism confirmed these anti-French suspicions, which Britain put to good use in maintaining what her statesmen euphemistically called a "Balance of Power." A long sequence of foreign secretaries, including Castlereagh, Canning, Palmerston, and Salisbury, interpreted this principle to mean the limiting of French and/or Russian aims in such strategic zones as the Baltic, the Netherlands, the Levant, and the Balkans. They tried to preserve the Ottoman Empire largely to protect the British trade route to India, and they insisted on the integrity of the Netherlands, which were too close to Dover to be allowed to fall under French dominion.

It was relatively easy for the early Victorians to preserve this European balance because Britain was the most advanced industrial state and its manufactures were in universal demand. London had also become the world's financial capital, and most European governments wished to do business with British financial houses. As Britain, in addition, possessed by far the most powerful navy, it was everywhere understood that the value of British support, whether material or moral, was simply enormous.

These advantages were counterbalanced by concomitant responsibilities. Britain could protect her worldwide interests only by taking an active part in world affairs. An army was needed to defend the colonies, especially in India and Africa, and hundreds of ambassadors, representatives, consuls, and agents to supervise and administer British interests throughout every continent. British foreign relations became very complicated, requiring a complex bureaucratic structure at home to coordinate them. The Foreign and Colonial offices steadily expanded, gradually depriving the foreign and colonial secretaries of their independence. Diplomacy became dictated by permanent officials and professional experts rather than political leaders, which largely accounts for the semblance of continuity in Victorian foreign relations.

Britain's influence dominated international politics between 1790 and 1860. Thereafter the diplomatic balance gradually shifted. The Crimean War left Russia so distrustful of the western allies that Russian support could no longer be counted on in the resolution of diplomatic difficulties. This left the later Victorians too dependent on the unreliable French. Moreover, Prussia's rapid industrialization made the newly created Germany one of the world's leading manufacturing nations. While Britain remained fearful of France and Russia, Germany emerged as the greatest European force.

The British did not regard Germany as a threat but, rather, as a potential buffer against both French and Russian acquisitiveness. Germany and Britain, with the strongest military and naval forces, often acted in informal alliance to dictate terms to the rest of Europe during the age of Bismark. After Bismark's fall, however, German diplomacy became distinctly more aggressive, driving France and Russia into a formal agreement in 1894. This alarmed both Britain and Germany, but they could find no common ground for a similar treaty of their own. Britain became progressively more isolated towards the end of the century when all other nations were seeking shelter under binding treaties.

The nineteenth century is often called the age of Pax Britannica, since Britain participated in only one major Continental struggle during the period 1815–1914. The term is, however, misleading; during the Victorian age, British troops were almost continuously engaged in military or naval actions to consolidate or expand the empire. The Victorians fought twice against the Chinese and often against Indian and African states, while preferring to trade peacefully with Europeans and North Americans. Despite disputes over Venezuela and Oregon and very serious misunderstandings during the American Civil War, Britain remained generally on friendly terms with the United States, which was increasingly regarded as a valuable proponent of Anglo-Saxon values.

KEITH A. P. SANDIFORD

Bibliography

Bell, Herbert C. F. *Lord Palmerston.* 1936.

Bourne, Kenneth. *The Foreign Policy of Victorian England, 1830–1902.* 1970.

Imlah, Albert H. *Economic Elements in the Pax Britannica.* 1958.

Platt, D. C. M. *Finance, Trade, and Politics in British Foreign Policy, 1815–1914.* 1968.

Seton-Watson, R. W. *Britain in Europe, 1789–1914.* 1937.

Swartz, Marion. *The Politics of British Foreign Policy in the Era of Disraeli and Gladstone.* 1985.

Temperley, Harold W. and L. M. Penson. *Foundations of British Foreign Policy, 1792–1902.* 1938.

See also CIVIL WAR, UNITED STATES; EMPIRE AND IMPERIALISM; GOVERNMENT: COLONIES AND EMPIRE; WARS AND MILITARY ENGAGEMENTS

· · · · ·

FORSTER, WILLIAM EDWARD (1818–1886)

The nicknames given to this Quaker turned Anglican statesman illustrate the trends of his career. In Yorkshire his constituents and employees called him "Lond Forster" and "the working-men's friend," and in his government service he was dubbed "Education Forster" and "Buckshot Forster."

W. E. Forster was born in Bradpole, Dorsetshire, on July 11, 1818, son of William and Anna Buxton Forster, from whom he inherited Quaker reformism. He was expelled from the Society of Friends (1850) upon his marriage to Jane Martha Arnold, daughter of the Reverend Thomas Arnold of Rugby School. After a successful career in the wool business, he represented Bradford as an "advanced" Liberal in the House of Commons (1861–1886). He soon became, in effect, minister of education and formulated the first national system of elementary education in England, under what is often called the Forster Education Act (1870).

Moving to other reforms, Forster successfully guided passage of the Ballot Act (1872) and participated in **antislavery**, arbitration, and imperial causes. When the Gladstone government returned to power (1880) Forster, who had been passed over as party leader (1875) because his education reforms antagonized powerful political and religious elements, served as chief secretary for Ireland (1880–1882). Forster implemented a coercive policy—thus the nickname "Buckshot"—and became the object of assassination plots. He objected to a policy change toward reconciliation involving **Charles Stewart Parnell**, and resigned only days before his successor and another official were murdered in Phoenix Park, Dublin (1882). He maintained his imperial interests. It was Forster's persistent questioning (1876) which elicited Disraeli's disastrous attempt to explain the Bulgarian atrocities, and, later, Forster was instrumental in forming the Imperial Federation League (1884). He died on April 5, 1886 and, after a funeral in Westminster Abbey, was buried at Burley. There is a statue on the banks of the Thames near the location of the London School Board building.

Forster contributed to periodicals on subjects related to his interests. He was elected lord rector of the University of Aberdeen (1875). The standard biography is by Thomas Wemyss Reid, editor of the *Leeds Mercury*. Forster is best known for his efforts for reform in education, although a recent study by Phil Gardner laments the demise of traditional working-class private schooling, ("the people's schools"), under the state system that was Forster's creation. Forster has been described as an excellent representatitve of the English middle class in public office: patriotic, independent, incorruptible, and a brilliant organizer.

EUGENE L. RASOR

Bibliography

Gardner, Phil. *The Lost Elementary Schools of Victorian England*. 1984.

Reid, Thomas Wemyss. *Life of the Right Honourable William Edward Forster*. 1888; rpt. 1970. 2 vols.

Temmel, M. R. "Liberal vs. Liberal, 1874: W. E. Forster, Bradford, and Education." *Historical Journal*, vol. 18, pp. 611–622.

Times, April 6, 1886, p. 11.

See also EDUCATION, ELEMENTARY

. . . . .

FRAZER, JAMES GEORGE (1854-1941)

James George Frazer was a classical scholar, folklorist, and social anthropologist. His most important works were *The Golden Bough* (1890; expanded and reissued in twelve volumes, 1907-1915), *Totemism and Exogamy* (1910), and *Folk-Lore in the Old Testament* (1918). He was knighted in 1914.

Frazer became interested in **anthropology** when he was invited by his friend William Robertson Smith to contribute articles on "Taboo" and "Totemism" to the *Encyclopaedia Britannica* (9th ed.). Later he began *The Golden Bough* by focusing on the priest of the Arician grove of Diana near Rome. This specific inquiry led Frazer into detailed studies of magic, the role of kings, ritual prohibitions, seasonal cycles, and scapegoats as they manifested themselves in many different regions of the world. Under the influence of Darwin and other nineteenth-century scientists, Frazer assumed an evolutionary pattern in the development of cultures. He believed that people everywhere attempted to control their environments originally through magic, next through religion, and finally through science.

Frazer's scheme permitted him to organize and classify vast quantities of highly diverse data, but modern anthropology has discredited many of his theories. The ultimate value of Frazer's work is more literary then scientific. *The Golden Bough* remains a vivid account of exotic customs and has inspired writers as diverse as T. S. Eliot, D. H. Lawrence, and James Joyce.

ALBERT E. WILHELM

Bibliography

Besterman, Theodore. *A Bibliography of Sir James George Frazer*. 1940.

Downie, Robert. *James George Frazer: The Portrait of a Scholar*. 1940.

Lang, Andrew. *Magic and Religion*. 1901.

Malinowski, Bronislaw. "Sir James George Frazer: A Biographical Appreciation." In *A Scientific Theory of Culture*. 1944.

VIckery, John. *The Literary Impact of The Golden Bough*. 1973.

. . . . .

FREE CHURCH OF SCOTLAND

The Free Church of Scotland, which existed from the Disruption of 1843 until 1900 (when it joined the United Presbyterians to form the United Free Church), was the presbyterian body that seceded from the **Church of Scotland** on two related principles: the usefulness of national establishments of Christianity and the spiritual independence of the church. The secession of the Free Church from the established Church of Scotland was the culmination of a controversy over the right of lay patrons to name clergy without reference to the desires of a congregation. Constituent ministers and members of the Free Church seceded in 1843 to assert freedom from state control.

Patronage in the Church of Scotland had been abolished by the Union of 1707 that united Scotland and England. Parliament, however, restored it in 1712. Popular unwillingness to tolerate this form of secular control of the church had resulted in the departure of two groups of dissenting presbyterians during the eighteenth century: the Secession (1737) and Relief (1761) churches. These were to join in 1847 to form the United Presbyterian Church.

During the first third of the nineteenth century younger Church of Scotland ministers like Thomas Chalmers (1780–1847) who had experienced an evangelical awakening were replacing the older Moderate party that had dominated the establishment during the eighteenth century. Such evangelicals were often dogmatic Westminster Confession Calvinists zealous for the Crown Rights of the Redeemer, a seventeenth-century convenanting phrase which in nineteenth-century practice meant the popular rights of congregations to choose their own ministers.

In 1834 evangelicals for the first time had a majority in the Church of Scotland General Assembly. By passing the Chapels Act and Veto Act the 1834 assembly provided legal material for a decade of litigation in church and civil courts. These two acts represented the evangelicals' attempt to alter the legal basis of the national church. The Chapels Act helped ensure an evangelical majority in the assembly and the Veto Act attacked the patronage system by enabling a majority of male heads of households within a congregation to refuse a patron's nominee and demand that the patron nominate another person.

By 1843 it was clear that the civil Court of Session would uphold neither of these crucial 1834 General Assembly actions. Nor did Parliament care to address the situation. Evangelicals therefore hoped that with a continued majority in the 1843 assembly they could sever the Church of Scotland's connection with the state, thereby disestablishing and freeing themselves as a unified national church.

Evangelicals, however, did not carry a majority in the 1843 assembly and so felt that they had to sever themselves from what they considered a corrupt and enslaved establishment. The 470 ministers who left the established church to form the Free Church of Scotland on May 18, 1843 sacrificed stipends, church buildings and endowments, and manses. Because of their initial vision of themselves as the true free national church pledged to foster a godly commonwealth, Free Church leaders attempted to duplicate the legally established church not only in the building of local parish churches and manses, but also in programs of education, poor relief, and mission work.

The Free Church continued through the end of the Victorian period as the second largest presbyterian body in Scotland. Under the leadership of principal Robert Rainy (1826–1906) of New College, Edinburgh, the Free Church abandoned the establishment principle in the 1870s, allying itself with Gladstone's unsuccessful Scottish disestablishment campaign against the Church of Scotland and developing more cordial relations with the United Presbyterians. The 1900 merger of the Free Church with the United Presbyterian Church prefigured the reuniting of all three groups in a new Church of Scotland in 1929.

DAVID R. BOONE

Bibliography

Bayne, Peter. *The Free Church of Scotland: Her Origin, Founders, and Testimony.* 1893.

Brown, Stewart J. *Thomas Chalmers and the Godly Commonwealth in Scotland.* 1982.

Drummond, Andrew L. and James Bulloch. *The Church in Victorian Scotland, 1843–1874.* 1975.

Lyall, Francis. *Of Presbyters and Kings: Church and State in the Law of Scotland.* 1980.

Simpson, Patrick Carnegie. *The Life of Principal Rainy.* 1909. 2 vols.

Watt, Hugh, comp. *New College Edinburgh: A Centenary History.* 1946.

· · · · ·

FREE TRADE

The origins of the free trade movement may be traced to the reaction against mercantilism in the late eighteeenth century and the emerging predisposition in favor of laissez faire. Adam Smith's *Wealth of Nations* (1776) argued that unrestricted international trade would encourage all nations to exploit their natural economic advantages and maximize an efficient international division of labor. For Victorians, the term "free trade" denoted a fiscal policy designed to achieve this end through the absence of discrimination between domestic and foreign commodities and the elimination of barriers to free exchange. Though primarily associated with the abolition of protective tariffs, free trade did not require the removal of all duties; it was recognized that some might be retained for purposes of revenue.

Modest steps to liberalize trade policy in the 1780s were nullified by the French wars (1793–1815), which served to strengthen the mercantilist framework. The **Corn Laws** were added to existing restrictions on imports in 1815 to protect British agriculture by excluding foreign grain until domestic produce reached an optimum selling price. With sources of direct taxation limited after repeal of the wartime income tax (1816), revenue depended heavily on the yield from customs. The mercantilist tariff stood virtually intact in 1840, with duties chargeable at various rates on a total of 1146 imported articles. **Robert Peel's** first budget (1842), an imaginative response to the problem of deficit, moved decisively toward free trade. By reimposing income tax he was able to offset loss of revenue caused by a simplified three-tiered tariff on raw materials, semimanufactured goods, and manufactured goods. A healthy budget surplus in 1845 encouraged Peel to further reduce import duties on raw materials and to abolish all export duties.

Repeal of the Corn Laws (1846) has generally been viewed as the most significant triumph of the free trade campaign. Ineffective, in practice, as protection for agriculture, the Corn Laws were denounced as taxes on bread and as a levy in the form of high food prices exacted from the consumer by the landed interest. Repeal of the Navigation Acts (1849) and **W. E. Gladstone's** budgets (1853, 1860) completed the demolition of the mercantilist system. For the remainder of the Victorian period Britain was a free market open to the goods of all nations, maintaining only a low tariff for revenue on a narrow range of goods not produced at home.

Although economic historians are now less certain, few Victorians doubted the beneficial impact of free trade, especially as its arrival coincided with the "great Victorian boom" (1850–1873). Free trade, according to conventional wisdom, allowed the "workshop of the world" to buy its food and raw materials in the cheapest markets and to sell its manufactures in the most costly. Though **Richard Cobden's** ideal of free trade as an international movement was reinforced by the reciprocal tariff reductions ratified in his Anglo-French Treaty (1860), the ensuing trend to liberalization was short-lived. After 1870 new industrial powers, like Germany and the United States, led a return to tariffs, leaving Britain isolated in its attachment to free trade. Protectionist sentiment was revived, notably in the movements for "fair trade" after 1881 and "tariff reform" after 1903, and drew support from farmers and manufacturers hard pressed by foreign competitors. But free trade survived, buttressed by unswerving Liberal support and the electoral popularity of the cheap loaf.

DILWYN PORTER

Bibliography

Crouzet, Francois. *The Victorian Economy.* 1982. Trans. Anthony Forster.

Hirst, Francis. *From Adam Smith to Philip Snowden: A History of Free Trade in Great Britain.* 1925.

McCord, Norman, ed. *Free Trade: Theory and Practice from Adam Smith to Keynes.* 1970.

Semmell, Bernard. *The Rise of Free Trade Imperialism.* 1970.

See also MANCHESTER SCHOOL; TAXES AND TARIFFS

· · · · ·

FREETHOUGHT

"Freethought" and "freethinkers" describe an amorphous grouping of Victorian individuals and interests who shared three characteristics. First, they believed that established Christian orthodoxy was inimical to freedom and democracy, and especially to working-class progress. Second, they actively sought to eradicate the misbeliefs of orthodoxy and the social injustices perceived to arise from established religion's privileged status. Third, they pursued the construction of alternative (and superior) moral foundations and community institutions to replace those traditionally provided by the church. Though the movement continued into the twentieth century, its origins and diversity are best understood by studying the lives and works of such individuals as **George Jacob Holyoake** (1817–1906) and **Charles Bradlaugh** (1833–1891), the activities of the National Secular Society and Fleet Street House, and the periodicals *Oracle of Reason* (1842–1843), *Movement* (1843–1845), *Herald of Progress* (1845–1846), *Reasoner* (1846–1861, 1865–1872), *London Investigator* (1854–1859) and *National Reformer* (1860–1890).

Victorian freethinkers drew inspiration from the French Enlightenment, the deist tradition, **Owenite Socialism**, the English radical heritage, and the Protestant legacy of private judgment and zealous personal commitment to one's faith. The typical freethinker grew up in a Nonconformist family, rejected Christianity after exposure to Enlightenment thought, and came to freethought via Unitarianism or Owenite Socialism after perceiving an inextricable connection between a society's religious beliefs and its social and political progressiveness.

Above all, freethinkers sought to make the working classes more "respectable" and more free. Any project or agitation that contributed to those ends drew active freethought support. Such causes included **temperance, birth control**, the **cooperative movement**, the abolition of **taxes on knowledge**, the extension of suffrage, the disestablishment of education, the operation of public recreation and transportation on Sunday, and the abolition of the "oath" in court and in Parliament. Skills that would enable working people to rise in society were promoted in freethought periodicals and taught in the community centers set up by local freethought societies. These competencies included reading, writing, speaking, singing, dancing, and job skills such as carpentry.

What distinguished freethought among Victorian reform and self-help movements was the freethinkers' conviction that the ultimate success of these ventures depended on promoting appropriate moral, theological, and metaphysical thinking. Thus, in addition to education for political agitation and self-help, the freethinkers' lectures, debates, pamphlets, and periodicals proclaimed the moral and epistemological bankruptcy of orthodoxy and exposed the social injustice arising from the church's privileged position in English society. Many freethinkers cultivated an alternative belief system ("secularism") based on faith in science, morality, humanity, and progress. Secularists also published a secular hymnbook and printed appropriate rituals for marking such occasions as births, marriages, and deaths, in an effort to retain the socially functional and personally satisfying elements of religion.

Freethought increasingly lost its vitality after 1870. Though the movement peaked in membership at about 10,000 during the 1880s (at the time of Bradlaugh's efforts to enter Parliament as an atheist), internal tension among freethought leadership and the stimulus from public persecution—both of which had helped sustain the movement's creativity and sense of purpose—tapered off in the last quarter of the century. Major leaders like Bradlaugh and Holyoake diverted their attention to less abstract avenues of working-class reform—Bradlaugh through work in Parliament; Holyoake through the Manchester-centered cooperative movement. Rank-and-file freethinkers found their way into Positivist churches, the emerging labor movement, ethical societies, and other end-of-century groups promoting moral and social progress. Freethought was a peculiarly Victorian phenomenon, for it depended on the very principles it criticized; if orthodoxy is not to be taken seriously, neither can the promotion of heterodoxy.

SHIRLEY A. MULLEN

Bibliography

Budd, Susan. *Varieties of Unbelief: Atheists and Agnostics in English Society, 1850–1960.* 1977.

Robertson, John M. *A History of Freethought in the Nineteenth Century.* 1930.

Royle, Edward, ed. *The Infidel Tradition from Paine to Bradlaugh.* 1976.

———. *Radical Politics, 1790–1900: Religion and Unbelief.* 1971.

———. *Radicals, Secularists, and Republicans: Popular Freethought in Britain, 1866–1915.* 1980.

———. *Victorian Infidels: The Origins of the British Secularist Movement, 1791–1866.* 1974.

Tribe, David. *100 Years of Freethought.* 1967.

See also AGNOSTICISM

. . . . .

FRIENDS, SOCIETY OF

At the close of the Napoleonic Wars, the majority of British Quakers (numbering approximately 25,000) still adhered to the quietist tradition that had dominated their society for a hundred years. Early in the eighteenth century, Friends abandoned the vigorous proselytizing that had characterized Quaker founder George Fox (1624–1691) and his early disciples. Ostensibly to preserve the purity of their beliefs, Friends had eschewed all "creaturely" activity and embraced a distinctive lifestyle, including peculiarities of speech and dress, which isolated them from the general community. During the course of the nineteenth century, however, Friends shed many of their idiosyncrasies and briefly moved closer to the Protestant mainstream before finally assuming a stance that combined a refined version of traditional Quaker beliefs with advanced social and political views.

In 1806 Thomas Clarkson's *Portraiture of the Society of Friends* pictured a close-knit religious body largely untouched by the wave of evangelical enthusiasm then sweeping over Protestant Christianity. But several important Quaker leaders saw the evangelical revival as a God-sent means not only of rescuing their society from the lethargy into which it had sunk but also of combatting the rationalistic and deistic influences of the Enlightenment, which had tainted even Quakerism.

Very early in the nineteenth century, the anti-Unitarian tracts of Henry Tuke sounded the evangelical tone that would soon characterize nearly all Quaker devotional literature. By the mid-1820s, under the influence of the "fire and vision" ministry of Joseph John Gurney (1788–1847), the Society of Friends had moved a considerable way toward mainstream evangelical Protestantism.

This evangelical revival forced the Victorian Society of Friends out of its self-imposed exile and back into the rough-and-tumble of national life. By 1860 Friends had ceased to automatically disown those who "married out" and also abandoned the compulsory codes of speech and dress to which they had so tenaciously clung. Of more significance to the larger society was an unbridled Quaker penchant for social activism. Throughout the century, Friends, both individually and collectively, formed a ubiquitous presence in the Anti-Slavery Society, the prison reform movement, famine relief activities, adult schools, and every other sort of philanthropic enterprise. Quakers also took a leading role in the establishment of the Peace Society in 1816, a public and collaborative manifestation of their long-standing peace testimony. But if evangelical Friends were more ready and active in public ministry, the beliefs they espoused also helped to create serious and disruptive conflicts within their religious society.

Traditionally, the guiding principle of Quakerism had been its attachment to and exaltation of the universal and saving Light of Christ, inwardly revealed, without the necessity for priest or ritual, to all who would open themselves to it. This "Inward Light" might be guided or aided by scriptural revelation, but it was, finally, the spiritual authority to which each Friend must adhere. Evangelical Friends, by contrast, maintained that personal salvation was made possible only though the atoning sacrificial act of Jesus Christ, a doctrine justified and sustained by accepting the entire Bible as the literal and infallible word of God. For these Friends, then, the "outward" authority of Scripture replaced the "inward" authority of the saving Light.

The dispute about whether Scripture or the Inward Light was the ultimate source of spiritual authority led to a series of divisions or "separations" from which the evangelicals generally emerged with majority support. The most serious of these disputes, the Hickite

Separation of 1828–1829, occurred in the Philadelphia Yearly Meeting, but had profound repercussions in Britain. Quaker historians, however, have asserted that the evangelical influence, although broad, was "superficial" and that a conservative strain, resistant to biblically based doctrines, ran deep. John S. Rowntree's *Quakerism, Past and Present* (1858) pictured Friends not as a vigorous evangelical body but as a numerically declining sect, with neither an active ministry nor a distinctive creed.

The first serious challenge to the authority of a scripturally based theology was issued by a group of younger Manchester Friends led by David Duncan (1825–1872) and greatly influenced by works such as *Essays and Reviews* (1861). Although he was eventually disowned for Unitarian tendencies, Duncan was trailblazing pioneer for the liberal theology that gripped late-Victorian Quakerism with the same riveting force that had marked the evangelical revival three generations earlier.

With the anonymous publication of *A Reasonable Faith* in 1884 by three Friends (William E. Turner, Francis Frith, and William Pollard) and Edward Worsdell's *The Gospel of Divine Help* two years later, the Quaker renaissance was well underway. While such works were ignored or condemned by most elderly Friends, the younger and better educated received them with overwhelming enthusiasm. To a generation for whom higher **biblical criticism** and Darwinian evolution had made scriptural literalism impossible, the new theology's emphasis on "right living" as opposed to "right belief" was both comforting and illuminating. Makers of the Quaker renaissance pictured the Bible not as an infallible spiritual authority but as a progressively revealed spiritual guide, a powerful but not singular tool for helping to educate Friends to meet the challenges they would face in the twentieth century.

The first decisive triumph for the reformers was the rejection by the London Yearly Meeting in 1888 of the Richmond Declaration of Faith, an American-born, evangelically inspired credal statement intended to affirm the overarching authority of the Bible. Thereafter, the younger men and women who had led the fight against the Richmond Declaration began to move Friends in an entirely new direction. This movement culminated in 1895 at a special conference in Manchester where liberal-minded Friends finally succeeded in bringing their society to grips with modern secular and scientific ideas.

As evangelical influence declined, the "Inward Light" reemerged as the guiding principle of British Quakerism. As interpreted by modern thinkers, the Light allowed Friends both to adhere to "primitive" religious practice and to embrace progressive social and intellectual ideals. The invigorating impact of the Quaker renaissance was a major influence on the revitalization of the Friends' peace testimony. The Boer War (1899–1902) provided the ground for planting seeds of resistance which, after careful nurturing during the Edwardian years, blossomed into full-scale opposition to war and conscription from 1914 to 1918 and effectively shaped the pacifist image of twentieth-century Quakerism.

THOMAS C. KENNEDY

Bibliography

Brayshaw, Alfred Neave. *The Quakers: Their Story and Message.* 1921; rpt. 1982.

Grubb, Edward. *Authority and the Light Within.* 1908.

——. "The Evangelical Movement and Its Impact on the Society of Friends." *Friends Quarterly Examiner,* vol. 58, pp. 22–28.

Isichei, Elizabeth. *Victorian Quakers.* 1970.

Jones, Rufus M. *The Later Periods of Quakerism,* vol. 2. 1921.

Punshon, John. *Portrait in Grey: A Short History of the Quakers.* 1984.

Scott, Richenda C. "Authority or Experience. John Wilhelm Rowntree and the Dilemma of Nineteenth Century British Quakerism." *Journal of the Friends Historical Society,* vol. 49, pp. 75–95.

Wilson, Roger C. "Friends in the Nineteenth Century." *The Friends' Quarterly,* vol. 23, pp. 353–363, 405.

See also EVANGELICAL MOVEMENT; PRISONS AND PRISON REFORM

· · · · ·

FROUDE, JAMES ANTHONY (1818-1894)

James Anthony Froude distinguished himself as an historian and man of letters. His major historical works include *The History of England from the Fall of Wolsey to the Defeat of the Spanish Armada* (1856-1870) and *The English in Ireland in the Eighteenth Century* (1872-1874). He edited *Fraser's Magazine* (1861-1874), was **Thomas Carlyle**'s biographer, and served as Regius Professor of modern history at Oxford from 1892-1894.

Froude, a clergyman's son, went up to Oriel College, Oxford in 1836, following the death of his older brother Hurrell, prominent in the early Oxford Movement. To retain a fellowship he was ordained deacon in 1845, but his growing religious doubts surfaced in *The Nemesis of Faith* (1849). Controversy over this novel led Froude to leave Oxford and begin work on the *History of England*, which countered the Oxford Movement's Anglo-Catholic biases by vindicating the political and religious choices made by Henry VIII and Elizabeth. The book's brilliant style and controversial interpretations attracted criticism from scholars like Edward A. Freeman, intent upon advancing the claims of a professionalized historiography against so-called literary amateurs.

Froude's judgments about Ireland's incapacity for self-rule, expressed in American lectures (1872-1873) and in *The English in Ireland*, aroused further controversy. A staunch supporter of stronger ties to England's colonies, he was twice sent to South Africa by Lord Carnavon (1874-1875) to explore possibilities for confederation. After meeting Carlyle in 1849, he became a close disciple, and was entrusted with his letters and memoirs. Notwithstanding legal disputes over his right to Carlyle's papers and public controversy over his frankness about the Carlyles' private lives, Froude completed his four-volume biography of Carlyle (1882-1884). He also published biographical studies of *Becket* (1878), *Caesar* (1879), *Bunyan* (1880), *Luther* (1883), and *Lord Beaconsfield* (1890), and a follow-up to the *History, The Divorce of Catherine of Aragon* (1891).

Froude resolved a typical early Victorian struggle between orthodoxy and scepticism by adopting Carlyle's theories of hero worship, social change, and social order, although he informed these with a unique—and underrated—eloquence in his writings. He gave voice to the Victorians' patriotism, their Protestantism, and their uneasy dogmatism, and acted out their belief in the moralizing power of the historian, the intellectual, and the man of letters.

ROSEMARY JANN

Bibliography

Burrow, J. W. *A Liberal Descent: Victorian Historians and the English Past.* 1981.

Dunn, Waldo. *James Anthony Froude.* 1961.

Goetzman, Robert. *James Anthony Froude: A Bibliography of Studies.* 1977.

Jann, Rosemary. *The Art and Science of Victorian History.* 1985.

Paul, Herbert. *The Life of Froude.* 1905.

Willey, Basil. *More Nineteenth Century Studies: A Group of Honest Doubters.* 1963.

· · · · ·

FRY, ELIZABETH (1780-1845)

Elizabeth Fry was a Quaker philanthropist who crusaded to alleviate the plight of criminals and the insane. Inspired by the American Quakers William Savery and Stephen Grellet, she humanized the incarceration of women at Newgate and other prisons, becoming a legend in her lifetime. Her sanitized *Memoirs*, published in 1847, were culled by her daughters from forty-four manuscript volumes.

In 1818 Fry founded the Society for the Improvement of Prison Discipline (SIPD) and commenced her extensive mission. Between 1838 and 1841 she traveled as a celebrity throughout most of Europe. With support from royalty and such statesmen as William Wilberforce and Robert Peel (whose Prison Act was passed in 1823), she initiated these reforms: classification of criminals, segregation of sexes, female supervisors for women, religious and secular instruction, productive labor, and general hygiene. She was an activist rather than a theoretician; her approach to prison reform was similar to that of Jeremy Bentham.

Her rising fame outpaced her continuing impact on prison reform, for after 1825 many of her followers, particularly the members of the powerful SIPD, argued that criminals needed severer punishment, such as solitary confinement and hard labor. She thus had little influence on the Prison Act of 1835, which took as its model the harsh prison system of Philadelphia.

BRUCE A. WHITE

Bibliography

Cooper, Robert Alan. "Jeremy Bentham, Elizabeth Fry, and English Prison Reform." *Journal of the History of Ideas*, vol. 42, pp. 675–690.

Rose, June. *Elizabeth Fry.* 1981.

· · · · ·

FURNITURE see HOME FURNISHINGS

· · · · ·

GAELIC CULTURE

Gaelic culture was not only important to Irish nationalism but also helped form the basis for the Irish literary revival, which in turn had a significant effect on the development of literature in English.

The Gaelic language underwent a rapid decline in the nineteenth century. In 1801 about half of the Irish population was monolingually Gaelic speaking; by 1851 this proportion had fallen to a mere 5 percent with bilingual Gaelic speakers making up less than 25 percent of the Irish people. The decline was largely the result of deliberate choice by the Gaelic-speaking population, who associated the English language with the gentry, the wealthy, and the successful. After the introduction of the National School system in 1831, in which instruction was given through English, Gaelic-speaking parents encouraged schoolteachers to punish children for speaking their native tongue. Gaelic suffered a fur-

ther blow with the great famine, which was most severe along the western seaboard; most of the million famine deaths occurred in this largely Gaelic-speaking area. The dramatic increase in emigration to the United States and England reinforced the decline in the use of Gaelic. By 1901 only 0.5 percent of the population were monolingual speakers of Gaelic.

Those interested in preserving Gaelic culture before the formation of the Gaelic League in 1893 were mostly Protestant antiquarians, linguists, and poets, although the two greatest Gaelic scholars of this period, John O'Donovan (1809–1861) and Eugene O'Curry (1796–1862), were Catholics. One of the most important coteries of scholars devoted to preserving Gaelic culture met in the topographic and historical sections of the Ordnance Survey. George Petrie (1789–1866) produced several volumes on Irish architecture, antiquities, and ancient music. He and his assistants, O'Donovan and O'Curry, laid the foundations of modern scholarship in Gaelic through their cataloguing, transcription, and translation of the Gaelic manuscripts collected by the Ordnance Survey. O'Curry, who became professor of Irish history and archaeology at the Catholic University, published his valuable lectures in 1861. O'Donovan's most important work was his translation and editing of *The Annals of the Four Masters* (1848–1851).

The most influential force in the field of Gaelic language, folklore, and scholarship was the Gaelic League. Unlike earlier bodies such as the Royal Irish Academy (founded 1785), The Irish Ossianic Society (founded 1853) or the Society for the Preservation of the Irish Language (founded 1876), which were mainly antiquarian or preservationist, the Gaelic League set out not merely to preserve the Gaelic language but to establish it as the spoken tongue of Ireland; it wanted not simply to preserve old Gaelic writings but to promote a modern literature in Gaelic. The Gaelic League's first president, the Protestant Douglas Hyde (1860–1949), hoped to keep politics out of the league and to use Gaelic as a means of culturally uniting Protestants and Catholics; in this he was like earlier Protestant writers and promoters of Gaelic legend and folklore, Samuel Ferguson (1810–1886) and Standish O'Grady (1846–1928). However, nationalists—and especially the Irish Republican Brotherhood—eventually gained control of the league and charted it on a political course in 1915.

BRIAN GRIFFIN

Bibliography

Brown, Malcolm. *The Politics of Irish Literature: From Thomas Davis to W. B. Yeats*. 1972.

Byrne, Francis J. and F. X. Martin, eds. *The Scholar Revolutionary: Eoin MacNeill, 1867-1945, and the Making of the New Ireland*. 1973.

Daly, Dominic. *The Young Douglas Hyde: the Dawn of the Irish Revolution and Renaissance 1874-1893*. 1974.

Hogan, Robert et al., eds. *Dictionary of Irish Literature*. 1979.

Howarth, Herbert. *The Irish Writers: 1880-1940*. 1958.

MacDonagh, Oliver. *States of Mind: A Study of Anglo-Irish Conflict 1780-1980*. 1983.

O'Tuama, Sean, ed. *The Gaelic League Idea*. 1972.

Thompson, William. *The Imagination of an Insurrection*. 1968.

See also CELTIC REVIVAL; IRISH LITERATURE

. . . . .

GALTON, FRANCIS (1822-1911)

Francis Galton is known for his pioneering work in meteorology, fingerprinting, anthropology, biostatistics, human heredity, and **eugenics**. He coined the term "anticyclone"; demonstrated how fingerprints could be used for identification; derived the correlation coefficient; was the first to use twins in the study of human heredity; demonstrated the influence of heredity in determining mental characteristics; and developed eugenic thought. Galton's most noted works are *Hereditary Genius: An Inquiry Into Its Laws and Consequences* (1869) and *Inquiries into the Human Faculty and Its Development* (1883). He was elected to the Royal Society in 1856 and was knighted in 1909.

Galton was the cousin of Charles Darwin and the grandson of Erasmus Darwin. He began to study medicine, but his father's death made him independently wealthy and provided him with time to pursue his other interests, which in his later years focused on human heredity and eugenics. His study of human intelligence convinced him that heredity was more important than the environment in shaping one's mental characteristics and led to his development of eugenic thought. In his autobiography (*Memories of My Life*, 1908) he outlined his objectives of eugenics as the "checking of the birthrate of the unfit" and "the improvement of the race by fostering the productivity of the fit by early marriages and healthful rearing of their children."

Galton's eugenic ideas had profound influence on social thought throughout the world. After the rediscovery of Mendel's laws of heredity in 1900 Galton's ideas quickly gained popularity and led to the development of marriage and sterilization laws and immigration restriction.

CHARLES L. VIGUE

Bibliography

Fancher, Raymond E. *The Intelligence Men: Makers of the IQ Controversy*. 1985.

———. *Pioneers of Psychology*. 1979.

Forrest, Derek W. *Francis Galton: The Life and Work of a Victorian Genius*. 1974.

Galton, Francis. *Memories of My Life*. 1908.

Harre, R., ed. *Some Nineteenth Century British Scientists*. 1969.

Middleton, Dorothy, ed. *Francis Galton's Art of Travel*. 1971.

Pearson, Karl. *The Life, Letters, and Labours of Francis Galton*. 1914-1930. 3 vols.

See also NATURE VERSUS NURTURE

. . . . .

GAMBLING

Publicly the Victorians frowned on gambling and claimed to believe that heavy gambling was a thing of the past. In fact, the

Victorian period witnessed the birth and growth of the first commercialized mass betting industry in England, an industry centered largely around horse racing.

The major characteristics of this new kind of betting were the appearance of professional bookmakers who were willing to take bets, for as little as sixpence or one shilling, from all comers, and the fact that on-course betting was only a tiny fraction of the total. Most of those who bet probably never witnessed a race; they followed the sport in the racing newspapers which became an important feature of Victorian popular culture. The press was supplemented by an army of racing tipsters who offered to sell inside information. Both racing and betting were aided by the expansion of communications and transportation. Betting on horse racing (in contrast to the eighteenth-century mass betting on lotteries, in which the winners were determined by chance) stresses rational calculation of the chances of each horse, and thus particularly suited the Victorian spirit.

Other forms of Victorian gambling were less significant. People commonly bet informally on card games in their homes. Books of game rules, however, tended to omit information on betting until very late in the century, although information on betting had been a major feature of such books in the eighteenth century.

There were those who opposed all gambling, no matter how trivial. The National Anti-Gambling League, founded in 1890, worked to eliminate all forms of betting, including friendly card games, church raffles, and even some forms of dealing on the stock exchange.

The law refused to recognize gambling debts as legally collectable and made some forms of gambling criminal offenses. The major motive behind legislation on gambling was to protect the poor and to keep gambling from becoming a source of working-class social disorder. Victorian legislation tended to outlaw those forms of ready-money gambling that were most prevalent among the working class and to allow gambling on credit, which was only accessible to the middle and upper classes. Generally speaking, however, the laws against gambling were only sporadically enforced.

Late in the century there was a flurry of interest in high-stakes casino gaming, especially in the newly opened casino at Monte Carlo. Baccarat became the rage in some wealthy circles, and the game was brought to national notoriety as a result of the Tranby Croft cheating scandal of 1890–1891, which resulted in a sensational trial that marginally involved the Prince of Wales.

DAVID C. ITZKOWITZ

Bibliography

Bailey, Peter. *Leisure and Class in Victorian England: Rational Recreation and the Contest for Control, 1830–1885.* 1978.

McKibbin, Ross. "Working-Class Gambling in Britain, 1880–1939." *Past and Present,* no. 82, pp. 147–178.

Vamplew, Wray. *The Turf: A Social and Economic History of Horse Racing.* 1976.

See also RACING AND RACEHORSES

· · · · ·

GAME LAWS

When William Cobbett in 1823 said that one-third of all English prisoners were in jail because of the Game Laws, he was drawing attention to one of the major causes of social strife in the nineteenth century. Dating back to the Middle Ages, these laws restricted game hunting to the landed gentry. Unqualified persons who hunted, possessed snares or hunting dogs, or were found in possession of dead game, were liable to a fine of five pounds or three months in prison. Among the supplementary regulations the most severe were the Night Poaching Acts (1817), under which anyone found hunting armed at night might be transported for seven years.

These laws applied to pheasants, partridges, moor game, and hares. Fox hunting was open to all, while deer and rabbits were classed as private property and protected by much sterner laws. An unqualified farmer broke the law if he destroyed the hares that ate his turnips, as did the countryman who snared a grouse for his supper. Though the game trade was illegal, game was openly sold and eaten. By the 1820s, at the height of agricultural unrest, gang poaching to supply this market had almost reached the stage of open warfare.

In 1831, the game trade was legalized, and hunting was opened to all who purchased a license. Nevertheless, landowners might reserve the sporting rights over their tenants' farms; not until 1880 could all farmers legally kill hares and rabbits. The Night Poaching Act of 1828 remained in force, with stern penalties. And as hunting game on private property remained a trespass, poaching continued, as it does to this day.

JEAN O'GRADY

Bibliography

Chenevix Trench, Charles. *The Poacher and the Squire*. 1967.

Hopkins, Harry. *The Long Affray: The Poaching Wars in Britain, 1760–1914*. 1985.

Munsche, Peter. *Gentlemen and Poachers: The English Game Laws, 1671–1831*. 1981.

See also COUNTRY SPORTS

. . . . .

GARDENS AND PARKS

The history of gardening during the nineteenth century reflects the cultural, social, and scientific changes that were taking place in Victorian society. From the eighteenth century the Victorians had inherited a rich tradition of landscape gardening that was essentially rural and aristocratic in nature. They transformed that tradition, making it both urban and democratic. They also changed the aesthetic quality of the garden, largely through their interest in the developing sciences of botany and horticulture.

Eighteenth-century gardens such as Stowe or Stourhead had been planned to reflect the cultured taste of aristocratic owners rather than the skill of the horticulturalist. At Stowe one passes through the "Elysian Fields" to view the Temple of Ancient Virtue; at Stourhead a quotation from Virgil at the Temple of Flora warns the uninitiated: "Begone!" These gardens were also designed to appeal to an eye trained in the conventions of the picturesque. They provided a series of vistas that composed themselves like paintings, and the viewer was not to be distracted from the general spatial effects by the obtrusiveness of individual flowering plants. It was the Victorians who developed the flower garden and taught us to number the streaks of the tulip.

The way was prepared by Humphry Repton (1752–1818), who allowed flowers near the house. This practice was continued and developed by J. C. Loudon (1783–1843), who claimed in 1840 that the "picturesque" was giving way to the "gardenesque." The characteristic feature of the new style was that it displayed the beauty of individual plants. Such a display appealed to the Victorian love of detail, as reflected, for example, in Pre-Raphaelite painting. It also appealed to the new interest in botanical classification, which had been stimulated by the founding of the Royal Horticultural Society in 1804. Exotic plants had begun to reach England during the eighteenth century, encouraged by George III, who established a botanical collection at Kew. In 1841 Kew was opened to the public. The gardens were greatly extended and the Palm House (a handsome steel and glass structure, itself a monument to the new technology) was built to house exotic tropical flora. The addition of an herbarium and arboretum, the Museum of Scientific Botany, and a library made Kew a first-rate research facility. Moreover, its vast collection of plants from every corner of the globe no doubt served as a proud reminder of empire. On a more serious level, such collections were the botanical equivalent of the Victorian interest in comparative religion and mythology, and in historical and cultural relativism.

Kew was also designed to give pleasure to the nonscientist, and in this respect it resembled other royal London parks that were given to the people. But the new industrial cities had to create green spaces in the urban wasteland. Liverpool led the way with Birkenhead Park, laid out in 1843–1847 by **Joseph Paxton**, designer of the Crystal Palace. Birkenhead was to become typical of urban parks in its use of screened walks, shrubberies, and earth mounds to create semiprivate spaces. This was a direct reaction to the urban environment. Eighteenth-century gardeners had emphasized vistas because the distant view was rural and unspoilt. Paxton realized that the urban park needed to shut out its surroundings, and to provide seclusion for those escaping from overcrowded slums. The Victorian garden was to become a series of small enclosures, often richly decorated with flowers and shrubs. Hidcote Manor Garden (in the Cotswolds) is an outstanding example, although it was developed early in the twentieth century.

Another democratic development was the creation of the garden suburb. In 1838 Loudon published *The Suburban Gardener, and Villa Companion*, giving detailed plans for various classes of garden, ranging in size from one perch to ten acres or more. Even a garden of one acre might become a miniature country estate with its lawn, pleasure ground, and kitchen and flower gardens. If, in this world of small gardens, every man became his own gardener, the publication of Mrs. Loudon's *Gardening for Ladies* (1840) extended the invitation to women. Ladies were, however, advised to don clogs and thick leathern gloves before wielding spades or trundling wheelbarrows.

The size of the suburban garden imposed no limitations of style on its owner. The available space might be divided between an alpine rockery, a formal flower garden, a "wilderness," and a lawn just big enough to accommodate the ritual of afternoon tea. The Victorians had inherited two major gardening traditions: one formal, Latinate, or classical; the other informal, "English," or romantic. As the century progressed, however, the romantic garden became the more popular. This was largely owing to the work of William Robinson (1838-1935) whose *Wild Garden* (1870) laid down the principles of the "paradise" garden in which even exotic plants seemed to grow in natural, untutored profusion. His work was carried on by **Gertrude Jekyll** (1843-1932) and his influence may be seen in most modern English flower gardens, particularly in the lovely gardens at Sissinghurst Castle, created by Vita Sackville-West (1892-1962).

The great achievement of the Victorians was to bring the country into the city, creating secluded spaces where millions of urban dwellers could enjoy a "green thought in a green shade." Their gardens reflected a middle-class compromise between urban and country living, the continuing nostalgia for rural solitude, and the English passion for privacy. They made the English into a nation of gardeners,

and their finest creation, the "paradise" or "wild" garden, has never been surpassed.

PAULINE FLETCHER

Bibliography

Allan, Mea. *William Robinson, 1838-1935: Father of the English Flower Garden.* 1982.

Carter, Tom. *The Victorian Garden.* 1984.

Chadwick, George F. *The Park and the Town: Public Landscape in the Nineteenth and Twentieth Centuries.* 1966.

Clifford, Derek. *A History of Garden Design.* 1962.

Creese, Walter L. "Imagination in the Suburb." In U. C. Knoepflmacher and G. B. Tennyson, eds., *Nature and the Victorian Imagination.* 1977.

Hyams, Edward. *The English Garden.* 1964.

Massingham, Betty. *A Century of Gardeners.* 1982.

See also LANDSCAPE
ARCHITECTURE

· · · · ·

GASKELL, ELIZABETH CLEGHORN (1810-1865)

Elizabeth Cleghorn Gaskell is best known for her novels of social protest and for the psychological insights in her later novels. *Mary Barton* (1848), *Ruth* (1853), and *North and South* (1855) expose social problems during the height of the industrial revolution. *Cranford* (1851-1853) shows an interest in feminine lives and psychology, which Gaskell continues to examine in *The Life of Charlotte Brontë* (1857), *Sylvia's Lovers* (1863), and *Wives and Daughters* (1866).

Born Elizabeth Stevenson in 1810 in Chelsea, Gaskell was raised by her Aunt Lumb in Knutsford after her mother died when Gaskell was thirteen months old. Her marriage to Unitarian clergyman William Gaskell in 1832 brought her to Manchester where she lived for the rest of her life. She had four daughters; one son died in infancy.

Set in Manchester, *Mary Barton* exposes the squalid slum conditions in which the mill-workers were forced to live and the resulting conflict between the workers and the masters. John Barton's attempt and failure to obtain rights for the workers is a fictionalized account of Parliament's rejection of the People's Charter in the 1830s; and his emotional decline dramatizes the psychological effects of the workers' plight. Gaskell's sympathetic portrayal of the working class pleads for a moral solution through a recognition of the common humanity of all people.

In *Ruth*, Gaskell attacks the hypocrisy of a society that simultaneously keeps women ignorant of men and ostracizes these women if they are seduced. In the sympathetic delineation of Ruth Hilton's seduction and redemption, Gaskell's plea is again for societal awareness of common human dignity.

While *Cranford* departs from the pattern of the social problem novel in that it is a light comedy depicting the domestic lives of women in a society without men, *North and South* again focuses on the conflicts between workers and masters, but is sympathetic to both classes. Here, Gaskell portrays a strong female hero. Through Margaret Hale's struggles to sympathize with the masters as well as with the workers, the philosophies of each are explained and a reconciliation is reached.

Gaskell wrote *The Life of Charlotte Brontë* at the request of the Reverend Patrick Brontë, who knew of her friendship with and admiration of Charlotte. Gaskell shows both the influence of the sad and lonely existence at Haworth and Brontë's conflicts as a woman—her duty to her father and her duty to herself. In Gaskell's intimate portrayal of the woman and the writer, *The Life of Charlotte Brontë* is considered to be one of the best biographies ever written.

In showing the influence of background on character in the *Life*, Gaskell had written her first psychological "novel." The force of *Sylvia's Lovers* is in Gaskell's insight into Philip Hepburn's obsession with Sylvia Robson and the resulting emotional destruction, which provide the tragedy for what she called "the saddest story I ever wrote."

Wives and Daughters is considered to be Gaskell's masterpiece because of her analysis of family relationships. While the depiction of the droll Mrs. Kirkpatrick is delightfully humorous, the brilliance in *Wives and Daughters* is in Gaskell's study of parents' influence on their daughters' emotional development. Because of her mother's indifference to her as a child, Cynthia Kirkpatrick depends on men for approval and identity. She hides her vulnerability behind a shield of coquetry. Molly's problems arise because of her relationship with her affectionate but emotionally distant father. Because of her mother's early death, she idealizes him (and thus all men) and fails to recognize her own strengths. Endowed with an innate sense of integrity, however, and a network of surrogate mothers, Molly achieves a self-awareness that Cynthia can never acquire.

While Gaskell was popular in her own time, after her death attention to her work waned. Until the second half of the twentieth century, *Wives and Daughters* and *Cranford* were the only novels given consideration because they were thought best suited to her "woman's hand" in their depiction of women's lives. Contemporary criticism praises the insight and empathy the "woman's hand" created in all of her novels. Gaskell pleads for the dignity of all individuals as a moral solution to the social problems that resulted from rapid industrial advance; and her psychological analyses of relationships and particularly of women's lives led her to speak for the best humanistic interests of both her time and ours.

LAURIE E. BUCHANAN

Bibliography

Chapple, J. A. V. and Arthur Pollard, eds. *The Letters of Mrs. Gaskell.* 1967.

Gérin, Winifred. *Elizabeth Gaskell: A Biography.* 1976.

Lansbury, Coral. *Elizabeth Gaskell: The Novel of Social Crisis.* 1975.

Pollard, Arthur. *Mrs. Gaskell: Novelist and Biographer.* 1966.

Rubenius, Aina. *The Woman Question in Mrs. Gaskell's Life and Works.* 1950.

Selig, Robert L. *Elizabeth Gaskell: A Reference Guide.* 1977.

Wright, Edgar. *Mrs. Gaskell: The Basis for Reassessment.* 1965.

See also SOCIAL PROBLEM NOVEL

. . . . .

GATTY, MARGARET (1809-1873)

Margaret Gatty, a naturalist and writer for children, is now almost forgotten. Her short tales for children are of less significance than her work as founding editor of *Aunt Judy's Magazine* (1866-1885); her greatest source of contemporary fame was her widely admired *Parables from Nature* (5 vols., 1855-1871).

The daughter and the wife of Anglican clergymen, Gatty spent her life in the service of the church, churchmen, and family. Despite youthful literary enthusiasms, she did not publish an original work until 1851 (*The Fairy Godmothers and Other Tales*), inspired by her own large family (four daughters and four sons survived infancy) and prompted by the need for additional income. *Parables from Nature*, her second book, contained heavily moralized tales of birds, beasts, and botany, serving to demonstrate the unity of natural and moral law. Over the next sixteen years, additional series of *Parables* and numerous reprints alternated with collections of fairy and domestic tales (e.g., *Aunt Judy's Tales*, 1859; *Aunt Judy's Letters*, 1862). Her editorship of *Aunt Judy's Magazine* allowed her to publish the stories of her more famous daughter **Juliana Horatia Ewing** (1841-1885) and those of Lewis Carroll and C. S. Calverley. In addition, Gatty was an amateur algae specialist and wrote an authoritative nontechnical guide, *British Sea-Weeds* (1863).

In her own writing for children, Gatty epitomizes the "nature-and-morality" school, which has since become unfashionable, but she appreciated and encouraged, as editor and mother, the flowering of more realistic and less didactic writing.

SUSAN DRAIN

Bibliography

Ewing, Juliana H. G. "In Memoriam, Margaret Gatty." In Lance Salway, ed., *A Peculiar Gift.* 1976.

Maxwell, Christabel. *Mrs. Gatty and Mrs. Ewing.* 1949.

. . . . .

GENRE PAINTING

Genre painting—scenes of everyday life—dominated the sale rooms and exhibition halls of Victorian Britain. Often combining a storytelling component with a moral message, Victorian genre paintings have conjured up negative images of sentimentality and banal anecdote for many modern viewers. However, a more sympathetic appreciation of these works reveals their documentary value as well as their frequently high level of technical expertise.

The audience for genre painting increased after the 1840s with the development of more sophisticated methods of engraving; large editions of inexpensive prints could be reproduced from the most popular paintings. In addition, the themes of domesticity and childhood so prominent in Victorian genre paintings appealed to the taste and values of an increasingly affluent middle class.

The roots of Victorian genre painting can be found in seventeenth-century Dutch examples—scenes of peasant life and urban conviviality which entered English collections in large numbers in the eighteenth century; in the moralistic genre of the French painter Jean Baptiste Greuze (1725-1808), whose work was well known from engravings; and in the art of William Hogarth (1697-1764), with its sequential narrative series like *Marriage À-la-Mode* (1743-1745).

One of the most influential nineteenth-century genre painters was the Scottish artist, David Wilkie (1785-1841). Many of his scenes of rural life such as *Pitlessie Fair* (1804) and *The Penny Wedding* (1818) were done before the Victorian era had begun. Reproductions of his work brought him an international reputation, and his success assured the popularity of genre painting through the end of the century. One of his followers, William Mulready (1786-1863), who specialized in scenes from childhood, was an important teacher at the Royal Academy. The vibrancy of his colors and his practice of painting on a white ground were admired by the Pre-Raphaelites, who adopted some of his technical methods for their own purposes.

Another genre painter who concentrated on themes of childhood was Thomas Webster (1800-1886), the pivotal figure of a group of artists known as the Cranbrook Colony,

Thomas Webster R.A. The Village Choir, 1847.
By courtesy of the Board of Trustees of the Victoria and Albert Museum.

named for the village in Kent, England, where they settled. Composed of friends and relatives, among them Frederick Daniel Hardy (1826–1911) and George Bernard O'Neill (1828–1917), the Cranbrook Colony continued the traditions of Wilkie with their rustic genre scenes set in cottage interiors.

A recurrent genre theme was the role of women in Victorian life; examples covered a vast spectrum of images such as the dutiful wife in George Elgar Hicks's *Woman's Mission* (1863) and the "fallen" woman in **William Holman Hunt**'s *The Awakening Conscience* (1854). One of the most successful painters of the lives of his fellow Victorians was William Powell Frith (1819–1909). A member of a group known as The Clique, a sketching society that included the genre painters **Augustus Leopold Egg** (1816–1863) and Henry Nelson O'Neil (1817–1880), Frith painted literary themes at the outset of his career but turned to subjects from modern life after a summer holiday at the seashore. His *Life at the Seaside (Ramsgate Sands)* (1854) was purchased by Queen Victoria, and brought the artist immense acclaim. Equally celebrated were his other two panoramic scenes of Victorian life, *Derby Day* (1858)

and *The Railway Station* (1862), which, with their microcosmic realism, were visual parallels to the novels of Charles Dickens.

While the Pre-Raphaelites also tackled genre subjects, works such as **John Everett Millais**'s *Autumn Leaves* (1856) and *The Blind Girl* (1856), with their complex symbolism and ambiguous meaning, transcend the more purely anecdotal quality of most Victorian genre painting. **Ford Madox Brown** (1821–1893), who was associated with the **Pre-Raphaelite Brotherhood** though not one of the founding members, painted two genre scenes, *Work* (1852–1865) and *The Last of England* (1855), with the colorism and painstaking detail typical of their art. Both pictures treat an aspect of contemporary Victorian life (manual labor in the one, and emigration in the other) with a heroic dignity and poignancy that impart a forceful social message.

By the 1870s, a growing awareness of social neglect manifested itself in such paintings as *Applicants for Admission to a Casual Ward* (1874), a scene of the homeless seeking a night's shelter, by Luke Fildes (1843–1927); and *Eventide—A Scene in the Westminster Union* (1878), which portrayed old women in a workhouse, by **Hubert von Herkomer**

(1849-1914). These had been worked up by the artists from their illustrations in the *Graphic* magazine, a weekly founded by William Luson Thomas, which concentrated on the burning social issues of the day.

Both Fildes and Herkomer were influenced by **Frederick Walker** (1840-1875). An artist with an immense following, Walker was a member of the St. John's Wood Clique, an informal group of genre painters who lived near one another and whose members included Henry Stacy Marks (1820-1898), Philip Hermogenes Calderon (1833-1898), and William Frederick Yeames (1835-1918). While their genre subject matter covered a wide range and included historical, literary, and modern life themes, their penchant for practical jokes rather than any single artistic pursuit was their principal unifying bond.

A counterpoint to the images of poverty that appeared in the 1870s was the glittering society world depicted in the genre paintings of James Tissot (1836-1902), a French-born artist who lived in London from 1871 to 1882. His sometimes satirical portrayal of the Victorian nouveau riche in such works as *The Ball on Shipboard* (c. 1874) and *Too Early* (1863) have an ambiguous narrative. Another artist in this vein was William Quiller Orchardson (1832-1910), who tackled the tensions of a disintegrating aristocratic marriage in *Mariage de Convenance* (1883) and *The First Cloud* (1887).

Genre painting went into a decline in the last two decades of the nineteenth century as artists downgraded narrative and became more concerned with the process of making art for its own sake. Nevertheless, a group of French-trained painters who settled in the Cornwall village of Newlyn in the 1880s carried on the genre tradition, at the same time employing the modern *plein-air* techniques of their Continental training. **Newlyn School** artists Frank Bramley (1857-1915), with *A Hopeless Dawn* (1888), and Stanhope Forbes (1857-1947), with *The Health of the Bride* (1889), created two masterpieces of later Victorian genre painting.

LEE M. EDWARDS

Bibliography

Bendiner, Kenneth. *An Introduction to Victorian Painting.* 1985.

Lambourne, Lionel. *An Introduction to "Victorian" Genre Painting.* 1982.

Maas, Jeremy. *Victorian Painters.* 1969.

Reynolds, Graham. *Victorian Painting.* 1966.

Wood, Christopher. *Victorian Panorama: Paintings of Victorian Life.* 1976.

See also ACADEMIC PAINTING

· · · · ·

GENTLEMAN

During the nineteenth century the gentleman stood as the foremost ideal of manliness. The Victorian conception of gentlemanliness derived from older traditions reshaped to accommodate social change. The resulting complex of values and norms exhibited great power and resilience, resonating through English culture into the twentieth century.

The nineteenth century saw England utterly transformed. In one hundred years a rural and agricultural nation ruled by an aristocracy which drew its wealth and status from hereditary land ownership became an urban and industrial nation served by clerical, white-collar, and professional occupations. All this took place within a social and political continuity; aristocrats added corporate directorships to their broad acres, and the middle classes used their newfound resources to acquire the requisites of gentility. A revitalized conception of the gentleman fused these groups together into a coherent and effective elite.

The figure of the gentleman has its roots in the chivalric ideal. Essentially a warrior's creed, the ethics of chivalry enjoined bravery and loyalty upon a brotherhood that established itself as hereditary. Chivalry, however, developed complexities that gave it an imaginative life of its own. Both Christianity and courtly love provided knighthood with larger and nobler ends to serve. The definition of gentlemanliness underwent further elaboration during the Renaissance to include the attributes of courtesy, wit, and education. But for eight hundred years gentlemanly conduct, however understood, remained an obligation of rank and did not by itself define or identify rank.

This cultural heritage served as an arena for the Victorian definition of manliness. The romantic impulse sparked a taste for the medieval, which in turn generated a self-conscious revival of the chivalric ideals. Applying chivalry to nineteenth-century life required imaginative reinterpretation. Charlotte M. Yonge's enormously popular *The Heir of Redclyffe* (1853) featured a hero endowed with a distinct and charming personality, a family, and Tractarian moral seriousness. From these ingredients, Yonge created a character that embodied the attributes of a "true knight" in modern dress—the Christian gentleman. In a medieval tale for children, *The Little Duke* (1854), Yonge underlined her message. When the hero laments the disappearance of the dragons that had tested the brave in legend and saga, his nurse reassures him that "there be dragons of wrong here and everywhere."

Dragons, in whatever form, constitute a challenge. Victorian men girded themselves to meet that challenge. "Muscular Christianity" put a premium on action and physical prowess. The phrase described the characteristics praised by Charles Kingsley in his sermons and stories and by Thomas Hughes in *Tom Brown's School Days* (1857). **Sport** had always been a gentlemanly prerogative, but Kingsley and Hughes provided an additional rationale for the Victorian mania for games and exercise. Both sanctified masculine vigor by the ends it served and warned of the temptation and danger in mere mindless activity.

The **public schools** took on the task of directing the native energy of English youth toward right conduct. Squire Brown sent his son, Tom, to Rugby so that he could become "a brave, helpful, truth-telling Englishman and a gentleman and a Christian." (In 1908 Robert Baden-Powell drew upon the same tradition when founding the Boy Scout movement.) Building character became the key element of the Arnoldian regeneration of the public schools. Their proliferation in the second half of the nineteenth century provided the means to turn larger numbers of young boys into gentlemen. Thus a hierarchical social structure could retain its traditional authority while also absorbing the upwardly mobile.

If birth no longer adequately functioned as the sole criterion for status, character could

be pressed into service. Gentlemanliness, as reworked by the Victorians, was readily assimilable by the professions, old (doctors, lawyers) and new (civil servants, even engineers). It proved adaptable to the demands of imperialism as well. However, the entrepreneurs and businessmen applauded by American culture as "Captains of Industry" found that the quest for material gain was by definition ungentlemanly. (Anthony Trollope's novels provide a fine delineation of these distinctions.)

The figure of the Victorian gentleman bound together the aristocracy, the gentry, and the professional middle class, but separated that elite from its source of wealth. Women played only a peripheral role in this complex of values, serving either to inspire men toward or tempt them from the path of duty. A paternalistic concern for the underdog and fair play could generate social reform, but did not so easily accommodate the direct participation of workers in the political process. The gentlemanly ideal thus underwrote deep divisions of **class** and gender, but nevertheless retained a powerful hold on English hearts and minds not loosened until the Battle of the Somme cruelly exposed its limitations.

GAIL L. SAVAGE

Bibliography

Chandos, John. *Boys Together: English Public Schools, 1800–1864.* 1984.

Girouard, Mark. *The Return to Camelot: Chivalry and the English Gentleman.* 1981.

Letwin, Shirley Robin. *The Gentleman in Trollope: Individuality and Moral Conduct.* 1982.

Mason, Philip. *The English Gentleman: The Rise and Fall of an Ideal.* 1982.

Newsome, David. *Godliness and Good Learning.* 1961.

Perkin, Harold. *The Origins of Modern English Society, 1780–1880.* 1969.

Vance, Norman. *The Sinews of the Spirit: The Ideal of Christian Manliness in Victorian Literature and Religious Thought.* 1985.

Wiener, Martin J. *English Culture and the Decline of the Industrial Spirit, 1850–1980.* 1981.

See also ARISTOCRACY AND
GENTRY; MEDIEVALISM;
WOMANHOOD

· · · · ·

GENTRY see ARISTOCRACY AND GENTRY

· · · · ·

GEOLOGY

Geology emerged from late eighteenth-century investigations in **natural history**; it was loosely prompted by industry's needs for improved techniques of mineral prospecting and may be seen as a product of the increasing secularization of nature associated with the Enlightenment. Great practical and theoretical conquests marked its progress during the nineteenth century, nowhere more spectacularly than in stratigraphy and **paleontology**. Relatively little has happened during the 1900s to impel any drastic revision of the geological principles established in the nineteenth century.

The most significant advances were made from about 1790 to 1840, a period dubbed the "heroic age of geology." During these decades, geology became an independent science, it became an established science, and it became a popular science. The Geological Society of London was founded in 1807; chairs in geology were inaugurated in Cambridge (1818), Oxford (1819), and London (1832); and textbooks such as **Charles Lyell's** *Elements of Geology* (1838), Henry De la Beche's *A Geological Manual* (1831), and John Phillips's *A Guide to Geology* (1834) were widely diffused. Geology, particularly fieldwork, became a fashionable pastime; by the 1830s, wrote Harriet Martineau, the middle classes were buying five times as many books of geology as they were novels. Amateur geologists made substantial contributions to the science, at least until midcentury; after that geology seems to have become too technical to retain wide appeal. Nevertheless,

for a solid portion of the Victorian era geology remained a powerful stimulus in the realms of science, religion, art, and literature. Few remained unaware of the alterations geology had brought to conceptions of change, time, and history.

Early in the century, debate within the field concerned which major agency of geological change was most significant. The Neptunists, influenced by Abraham Werner (1749–1817) and his pupil Robert Jameson's *Elements of Geognosy* (1808), postulated the overwhelming causative power of water and conceived the earth's rocks to be precipitations from a primal ocean. They postulated a cataclysmic global history and identified the Mosaic deluge as only the last of many great aqueous revolutions. The Vulcanists, on the other hand, saw the major geological agency as igneous and described the earth's history in terms of cycles caused mainly by its central heat. As enunciated in James Hutton's tediously wordy *Theory of the Earth* (1795) and rendered readable by his colleague John Playfair in *Illustrations of the Huttonian Theory of the Earth* (1802), Vulcanism (or Plutonism) rejects a scenario of unruly, earth-shattering upheavals in favor of regular rules of nature.

Those who accepted Hutton's description of nature's steady operations were able to devise a scale to measure rates of change and time. The evidence revealed the remarkable slowness of that change and the consequent vastness of time since the earth's formation. Time was the great theme of geology in the nineteenth century, and by its early decades all serious geologists may be said to have broken its bounds. Traditional Christian opinion, derived from the genealogy of figures in the Old Testament, put the creation no further back than 6,000 years. Imaginative readings of the Bible were therefore required for geologists such as the Reverend William Buckland (1784–1856) and the Reverend Adam Sedgwick (1785–1873) to reconcile Genesis and geology. Gradually, however, paleontological and mineralogical evidence demonstrated the earth's enormous age. The now-familiar Paleozoic, Mesozoic, and Cenozoic eras were established and further subdivided into the Cambrian, Ordovician, Silurian, and other periods. To some, a world with "no vestige of a beginning,—no prospect of an end" (Hutton) brought trauma; to others, like evolutionists, it brought joy by bolstering the claims for a slow and gradual progression of life forms over time. **Charles Darwin** said that his books seemed to come "half out of Sir Charles Lyell's brain."

Lyell is the most imposing figure of nineteenth-century geology, particularly for his brilliant application of Huttonian ideas in *Principles of Geology* (1830-1833). Here Lyell put forward the doctrine of uniformitarianism, stating that throughout earth history the same terrestrial forces now operating have always been active, at about the same intensity, and that these forces are adequate, given ample time, to account for all the earth's features. Actualism, a form of uniformitarianism, was expressed in the work of George P. Scrope (1797-1876) and John Fleming (1785-1857). Actualism argued that certain causes had ceased to operate and that others did so to a lesser degree than formerly. **Robert Chambers** (1802-1871) showed in *Vestiges of the Natural History of Creation* (1844) that actualism could combine with evolutionary speculation to spectacular and controversial effect. All shades of uniformitarian opinion emphasized the rule of law and attacked the catastrophism of Buckland and Georges Cuvier (1769-1832) as an antiquated science prone to resort to miraculous rather than natural explanations of change.

In stratigraphy, marked progress was achieved once the orderliness of the strata column became accepted in the late eighteenth century. Stratified rocks and their faults had long excited geological curiosity; now, they engendered two kinds of geological activity. First, the occurrence and outcropping of particular strata were plotted on a large scale with the establishment of the Geological Survey in 1835 headed by De la Beche and then by Roderick Impey Murchison (1792-1871). Stratigraphical maps were produced and widely used, starting with the wonderfully accurate and detailed work of William Smith (1769-1839). Second, separate formations were identified, each of which represented a distinct period of the earth's history. The focus of debate shifted from the cause of change to the identification of various strata.

In paleontology, the century opened on the brilliant systematic descriptions of vertebrate fossils by Cuvier and of marine fossil shells by Jean Baptiste Lamarck (1744-1829). Such work inspired decades of extraordinary activity and creativity; regularities in the horizontal and vertical distribution of particular fossils in specific stratal formations suggested that fossils might serve as indicators of these formations wherever they might occur on the globe. Smith's *Strata Identified by Organized Fossils* (1816-1819) was the first of many such texts. On the vertical scale, fossils became valuable and versatile indicators of time: they showed not only that life had a history (and thus was not created in one brief moment) but also what that history might be. Furthermore, the fossil record revealed that for some unfortunate beasts, life also had an end—extinction was a reality, as the recovered and reconstructed remnants of the mammoth and ichthyosaur amply demonstrated.

Here, as in many other aspects of nineteenth-century geology, the surprising, spectacular, and far-reaching came together to grand effect. There were many more prosaic and practical achievements—in petrology, geomorphology, and coastal geology, for example—and to the historian of science these are undoubtedly important. But the enormous impact of geology on the Victorian mind was in the way that previous conceptions of time, history, and the origins of life on earth were altered—often shattered and recast—by a discipline which, during its heroic age at least, was at the cutting edge of all science.

MICHAEL SHORTLAND

Bibliography

Allen, David E. *The Naturalist in Britain: A Social History*. 1976.

Bowler, Peter J. *Fossils and Progress: Palaeontology and the Idea of Progressive Evolution in the Nineteenth Century*. 1976.

Dean, Dennis R. "'Through Science to Despair': Geology and the Victorians." In James Paradis and Thomas Postlethwait, eds., *Victorian Science and Victorian Values: Literary Perspectives*. 1981.

Geikie, Archibald. *The Founders of Geology*. 1897.

Gillispie, Charles C. *Genesis and Geology: A Study in the Relations of Scientific Thought, Natural*

Theology, and Social Opinion in Great Britain, 1790–1850. 1959.

Jordanova, L. J. and Roy S. Porter, eds. *Images of the Earth: Essays in the History of the Environmental Sciences.* 1979.

Moore, Ruth. *The Earth We Live On.* 1957.

Porter, Roy. *The Earth Sciences: An Annotated Bibliography.* 1983.

Rudwick, M. J. S. *The Great Devonian Controversy: The Shaping of Scientific Knowledge Among Gentlemanly Specialists.* 1985.

Rupke, Nicolaas A. *The Great Chain of History: William Buckland and the English School of Geology (1814–1849).* 1983.

Wendt, Herbert. *Before the Deluge: The Story of Palaeontology.* 1968.

· · · · ·

GILBERT AND SULLIVAN see SAVOY OPERAS

· · · · ·

GILBERT, JOHN
(1817–1897)

A prolific illustrator and painter of large-scale historical and literary subjects, John Gilbert was among the most successful Victorian artists. He began showing his work at the Royal Society of British Artists in 1836, then at the British Institution the next year and the Royal Academy in 1838. He became president of the Royal Society of Painters in Water-Colours (1871), was knighted (1872) and elected to the Royal Academy (1877), and left a fortune reportedly worth over 200,000 pounds at his death.

The most productive illustrator of Victorian periodicals, Gilbert was said to have contributed about 30,000 drawings to the *Illustrated London News* alone, with *Punch* and the *London Journal* also providing frequent outlets. The most prolific book illustrator of the 1850s, he prepared volumes ranging from William Harrison Ainsworth's ballads and Robert Southey's poems to a famous edition

of Henry Wadsworth Longfellow. His finest illustrating is probably the 1856–1858 Routledge *Shakespeare.*

Gilbert's output in painting was similarly prodigious; between 1852 and his death he exhibited at least 270 works at the Gallery of the Old Water Colour Society alone, most of them marked by his characteristic large style, massive coloration, broad chiaroscuro, and vigorous designs. Noted for big, powerful oils on historical subjects, for which he rarely used models, he also painted murals in national buildings.

Gilbert's grand scale frequently achieves dignity and grandeur despite the post-Victorian declining taste for heroic evocations of British history. As an illustrator, he remains among the most noted in the art's greatest age.

BEVERLY TAYLOR

Bibliography

Reid, Forrest. *Illustrators of the Sixties.* 1928.

See also HISTORY PAINTING; ILLUSTRATION

· · · · ·

GIRLS' SCHOOLS see EDUCATION, WOMEN'S

· · · · ·

GISSING, GEORGE
(1857–1903)

In the twenty-four years of his working life, George Gissing produced twenty-three novels, over one hundred short stories, and assorted nonfiction including *Charles Dickens: A Critical Study* (1898), the first book-length critical work on Dickens. Gissing wrote about major concerns of the century's last two decades: the urban working classes in *Workers in the Dawn* (1880), *Demos* (1886), *The Nether World* (1889), and other novels of his first period; the woman question in *The Odd Women* (1893), *In the Year of Jubilee* (1894), and *The Whirlpool* (1897). Only *New Grub*

Street (1891) and *The Private Papers of Henry Ryecroft* (1903), however, achieved wide sales. Gissing's bleak picture of urban life, his misogyny and social conservatism, and his unsparing dissection of human character make his novels more respected than enjoyed.

Gissing's father was proprietor of a chemist's shop. After his death Gissing earned a scholarship to Owens College, Manchester, and seemed destined for a brilliant academic career. Then in 1876 he was caught stealing money from fellow students, stripped of his prizes, sent to jail for a month, and burdened with a guilty secret that he apparently believed barred him forever from the company of ladies and gentlemen. His first wife was Nell Harrison, the prostitute he had once dreamed of reforming. After her death he married a respectable London working-class woman, Edith Underwood. In his final years he separated from Edith and went through a form of marriage in France wtih Gabrielle Fleury.

The central themes of Gissing's novels are class, money, and sex. The protagonist is generally an outsider, often a person of intellectual tastes forced through poverty to live among unsympathetic people. During the 1880s, when many intellectuals were turning to socialism or settlement work, Gissing's portrait of slum life was bleak and without optimism. *Workers in the Dawn* details the misery that grows from Arthur Golding's inability to reform the alcoholic, promiscuous lower-class girl whom he marries out of pity and idealism. *Demos* analyzes the failures of socialist leader Richard Mutimer by demonstrating how the culture of poverty corrupts the poor. *The Nether World* is an unrelieved picture of hopeless misery and of slum dwellers' drunkenness, dishonesty, and cruelty. Valuable for their painstaking observation and accumulation of detail, these and other early novels show an idealist turned sour; Gissing denounces poverty but increasingly dislikes the poor.

More than any other Victorian novelist, Gissing drew material from his own life. Astoundingly, the bitter conclusion of *Workers in the Dawn* was written before—not after—he married Nell Harrison. Godwin Peake, the protagonist of *Born in Exile* (1892), shares Gissing's early life with one significant alteration—a social humiliation, rather than the "lower-class" crime of theft, forces him to leave college. Gissing's painful and penetrating self-examination makes him merciless to his characters as well as their society. *New Grub Street*, generally considered his masterpiece, protests the commercialism that degrades literature and prevents the novelist from fulfilling his artistic genius. Each of the central characters is to some extent a Gissing persona: Edwin Reardon, a classical scholar frustrated by the need to produce work that will sell; Biffin, with his grubby realism and his desire to take down verbatim the speech of grocers; and Alfred Yule, who marries a woman too inferior to be seen in public and thus destroys his chance to make the social contacts that would win him an editorship.

Gissing's reputation as a feminist is problematic. *The Odd Women* is a fascinating study of independent new women in contrast to helpless traditional women who fall victim to poverty, genteel alcoholism, and desperately unhappy marriage. Other books expose the ways in which marriage traps both women and men, but Gissing also seems to believe that women's education destroys good housekeeping. *In the Year of Jubilee* details the snobbery and shams of suburban life; *The Whirlpool* pillories a woman who neglects her family to pursue a career as violinist. Yet despite Gissing's exasperating tendency to alternate between idealization and condescension, female characters are important in most of his books, and they are often as complex and flawed as his male characters.

Gissing filtered some personal reminiscences and opinions through the mask of a serene old man in *The Private Papers of Henry Ryecroft*. Morley Roberts, who had been Gissing's friend since Owens College days, produced an imaginative fictionalized biography in *The Private Life of Henry Maitland* (1912). Several volumes of letters, journals, and uncollected writings have been brought into print since the revival of interest in Gissing's work which began during the 1960s.

SALLY MITCHELL

Bibliography

Collie, Michael. *George Gissing: A Bibliography.* 1975.

Coustillas, Pierre and Colin Partridge, eds. *Gissing: The Critical Heritage.* 1972.

Coustillas, Pierre, ed. *London and the Life of Literature in Late Victorian England: The Diary of George Gissing, Novelist.* 1978.

Halperin, John. *Gissing: A Life in Books.* 1982.

Korg, Jacob. *George Gissing: A Critical Biography.* 1963.

Michaux, J. P. *George Gissing: Critical Essays.* 1981.

Tindall, Gillian. *The Born Exile: George Gissing.* 1974.

Wolff, Joseph J. *George Gissing: An Annotated Bibliography of Writings About Him.* 1974.

· · · · ·

GLADSTONE, WILLIAM EWART
(1809-1898)

One of the great political figures of the age, William Ewart Gladstone was leader of the **Liberal party** from 1868 to 1875 and from 1880 to his retirement in 1894. He served as prime minister in four Liberal governments (1868-1874, 1880-1885, 1886, 1892-1894).

The fourth son of John and Anne Gladstone, the former a Liverpool merchant with extensive interests in shipping and in West Indian plantations, Gladstone attended Eton and entered Christ Church, Oxford, in 1828. In 1830 he was elected president of the Oxford Union and in the following year took a "double first" in classics and mathematics, an academic achievement of considerable distinction. In 1839 he married Catherine Glynne.

Throughout his long political career, stretching from 1832 to 1894, Gladstone's powerful intelligence, high administrative ability, moralistic fervor, and driving political ambition made him a formidable force. Elected to Parliament as a Conservative in 1832, Gladstone assigned himself the duty of fostering the ideal of an Anglican confessional state, an ideal treated in his first book, *The State in Its Relations with the Church* (1838). Experience in office under **Robert Peel** in the early 1840s led Gladstone to recognize the untenable features of this vision in a pluralistic society and showed him the importance of financial and commercial questions in government policy and social well-being. Standing by Peel and free trade in the Conservative split over the Corn Laws, Gladstone was estranged from most of his former Tory colleagues in the Commons.

Between 1846 and 1859 Gladstone sought to locate a viable political position within a confusing parliamentary environment. He participated in the Whig-Peelite Aberdeen Coalition of 1852-1855, producing his first great budget in 1853. By 1859 he had reluctantly concluded that the path back to office and usefulness lay in association with Lord Palmerston, in whose Liberal ministry Gladstone served as chancellor of the exchequer from 1859 to 1865.

Following Palmerston's death Gladstone joined with Lord John Russell in bringing forth a moderate Reform Bill in 1866, believing that the more respectable of the working classes had shown themselves worthy of the franchise. Although the bill was defeated and the government resigned, Gladstone succeeded to the Liberal party leadership at the end of 1867. With disestablishment of the Irish Church as his battle cry, he led the Liberals to a resounding victory at the 1868 general election.

Gladstone's active and constructive government of 1868-1874 was committed to justice for Ireland, administrative efficiency, and international law. Some of its policies, however, antagonized important interests, including the Nonconformists (who formed a major part of the Liberal constituency). After the Liberal defeat in the 1874 general election, Gladstone announced his retirement in January 1875, but soon returned to protest against the Turkish atrocities in Bulgaria and the Near Eastern policy of the Beaconsfield administration. His emotion-charged Midlothian campaigns of 1879 and 1880 carried him back to the premiership in the latter year.

Gladstone's second ministry could claim credit for valuable legislation concerning the Irish land question, corrupt electoral practices, and franchise extension. Nonetheless, Gladstone and his colleagues failed to satisfy the public on a number of matters. In the aftermath of the 1885 election—the outcome of which left in doubt which party would form a government—Gladstone's conversion to Irish **Home Rule** became known. His initiative split the Liberal party. After the defeat of the

1886 Home Rule Bill, a general election put the Conservatives in office. An election in 1892 brought about the formation of Gladstone's last ministry, but his 1893 Home Rule Bill, passed by a House of Commons understandably impressed by the performance of the eighty-three-year-old prime minister, was overwhelmingly rejected in the House of Lords. Gladstone resigned in early 1894, bringing to a close a remarkable political career of over sixty years.

There was nothing very unusual about Gladstone's political views, which on most issues were neither reactionary nor radical. His influence and power resided less in his opinions than in his capacity for conveying to his audience a seriousness of purpose and a moral integrity that had great purchase in the political culture of which he was a part. His education, Anglicanism, and regard for aristocratic leadership made him acceptable to the established governing classes; his Liverpool background and command of commercial subjects recommended him to the middle classes; his impassioned moralism won the sympathy and support of Dissenters; his respect for the dignity of labor and deeply felt endorsement of personal independence and responsibility attracted the leaders of the working classes and a goodly portion of the rank and file. Singularity of personality, a mind of uncommon strength and capaciousness, prodigious energy, and great rhetorical power enabled Gladstone to convert his embodiment of so much that was representative of his age into a political eminence unsurpassed during the reign of Victoria.

BRUCE L. KINZER

Bibliography

Butler, Perry. *Gladstone: Church, State and Tractarianism.* 1982.

Feuchtwanger, E. J. *Gladstone.* 1975.

Foot, M. R. D. and H. C. G. Matthew, eds. *The Gladstone Diaries.* 1968–. 9 vols.

Gladstone, W. E. *Gleanings of Past Years.* 1879. 7 vols.

Matthew, H. G. C. *Gladstone, 1809–1874.* 1986.

Morley, John. *The Life of William Ewart Gladstone.* 1903. 3 vols.

Parry, J. P. *Democracy and Religion: Gladstone and the Liberal Party, 1867–1875.* 1986.

Ramm, Agatha, ed. *The Political Correspondence of Mr. Gladstone and Lord Granville, 1868–1886.* 1952, 1962. 2 vols.

Shannon, R. T. *Gladstone, 1809–1965.* 1982.

Vincent, John. *The Formation of the Liberal Party, 1857–1868.* 1966.

· · · · ·

GONNE, MAUD
(1866–1953)

Maud Gonne was a speaker and organizer for Irish independence and political prisoners. She was the subject of many poems by **William Butler Yeats** (1865–1939), who fell in love with her in 1889. Though sometimes called the Irish Joan of Arc, Gonne was born in Surrey, England, of English parents, and accompanied her father to Dublin when he was assigned there as an officer in the British garrison.

In the 1890s she became known in Ireland for her famine relief work in the western counties and as a supporter of the Land League and cohort of James Connolly (1868–1916). In 1897 she organized protests against Queen Victoria's Jubilee visit to Ireland. Barred from the all-male revolutionary societies, Gonne in 1900 organized Inghinidhe na hEireann (Daughters of Erin) a women's group allied with the revolutionary Sinn Fein. In 1902 she played the title role in *Cathleen ni Houlihan,* the play Yeats wrote for her.

Gonne's controversial life included a brief marriage (1903–1905) to Major John MacBride, the Irish revolutionary hero executed for his role in the Easter 1916 Rebellion. After MacBride's death, she returned to Ireland from France, where she had lived after their legal separation, and resumed her activities under the name of "Madame MacBride." In later years she was active in the Women's Prisoners Defense League and was herself jailed on several occasions. Gonne is best known as the romantic interest of Yeats's life. He characterized her in his poetry as a great beauty who combined personal gentleness with a violent rhetoric of revolution. Her autobiography, *A Servant of the Queen* (1938) is a vivid but often inaccurate account of her life.

LINDA RAY PRATT

Bibliography

Cardozo, Nancy. *Lucky Eyes and a High Heart: The Life of Maud Gonne.* 1978.

Gonne, Maud. *A Servant of the Queen.* 1938.

Yeats, William Butler. *Memoirs.* 1972. Ed. Denis Donoghue.

See also IRISH NATIONALISM

· · · · ·

GORDON, CHARLES GEORGE
(1833–1885)

Charles George Gordon was a great hero of late Victorian England. He is linked with three historical episodes. First, he fought against the Taiping Rebellion in China, which earned him the nickname of "Chinese Gordon." Second, he governed the Sudan and tried to eliminate the slave trade. Last, and most famously, he became involved in a desperate siege at Khartoum against the powerful Mahdi. Gordon was killed and became an instant martyr—a cult figure.

Gordon was born in 1833 at Woolwich. His father, of Scottish ancestry, later became lieutenant general in the Royal Artillery. After attending Fullands School, Taunton, Gordon entered the Royal Military Academy, Woolwich. Commissioned into the Royal Engineers in 1852, he fought bravely and recklessly in the Crimean War.

Gordon's career in China began in 1860, when he took part in the Second Opium War and the capture of Peking. Later he was commissioned by the Chinese emperor to head the "Ever Victorious Army," a multinational force that helped dissolve the Taiping Rebellion. Though incorrect, the impression was created in English newspapers that "Chinese Gordon" almost single-handedly defeated the rebels.

In 1865 Gordon was appointed to supervise

fort construction at Gravesend. Ironically, he was never given command of British troops in any outpost of the empire. Perhaps he was considered too unconventional. He developed a deeply religious character, tinged with mysticism, and hated the social conventions of Victorian England.

In the 1870s Gordon accepted a position as the Egyptian Khedive's governor of the equatorial provinces of the Sudan, then became governor-general of the whole Sudan. He undertook exploration and survey work, but considered his major task to wage a crusade against the slave trade. Success was limited, but Gordon was admired more for what he stood for than for what he accomplished. His stock as a Victorian soldier-saint continued to rise.

Gordon resigned his Sudanese position in 1879 and could not settle to anything. In quick succession, he accepted posts in India, Mauritius, South Africa, and the Congo. But, in 1884, the British government persuaded him to return to the Sudan. His mission was to evacuate Khartoum in the face of a religiously inspired revolt organized by the Mahdi. It is clear that Gordon was not the man to carry out a retreat. Instead he adopted a policy of resistance. After almost a year under siege conditions Gordon was killed and several thousands massacred. A small relief force arrived two days late. Gladstone and the Liberal government were heavily criticized for failing to save General Gordon.

In 1898 the British public considered Gordon avenged when Kitchener defeated the followers of the deceased Mahdi at the Battle of Omdurman. The Sudan was ruled as an Anglo-Egyptian condominium until independence in the 1950s.

OLWYN M. BLOUET

Bibliography

MacGregor-Hastie, Roy. *Never To Be Taken Alive: A Biography of General Gordon.* 1985.

Nutting, Anthony. *Gordon, Martyr and Misfit.* 1966.

Chenevis Trench, Charles. *Charley Gordon: An Eminent Victorian Reassessed.* 1978.

· · · · ·

GOTHIC FICTION

Unlike the mainstream of Victorian fiction, which tends to depict domestic and social conflicts resolved through self-sacrifice and duty in a realistic manner, the Gothic novelist works unrealistically to arouse the reader's imagination and emotions, especially fear. Fear is central to the Gothic: common phobias like fear of darkness, of falling, of injury and death; more complex moral and psychological paranoias, like fear of the devil, of mental instability and insanity, of self and self-knowledge; and even collective social threats particular to a given time, like the implications of Darwin for the Victorians and nuclear warfare for twentieth-century readers. Although Gothic writers in general did not stand out during the first half of the Victorian period because they imitated their romantic forbearers, the second half culminated in an extremely productive decade of Gothic fiction, the 1890s, when legends still powerful for the modern audience were created.

The fifty-year popularity of Gothic romances had peaked by 1830; Ann Radcliffe and Matthew Lewis were clearly the important influences on later writers of the genre, along with Mary Shelley's *Frankenstein* (1818), Charles Robert Maturin's *Melmoth the Wanderer* (1820), and Walter Scott's historical Gothic novels. The Victorian Gothicists during the 1830s and 1840s perpetuated the same devices to arouse suspense and terror: remote, dark, often medieval settings; real or explained supernatural phenomena; melodramatic plots involving innocent maidens threatened by diabolical villains; sensational scenes and descriptions. The names of these writers have slipped into oblivion except for Gothic enthusiasts and scholars of popular culture: Captain **Frederick Marryat** (1792–1848), **Edward Bulwer-Lytton** (1803–1873), G. P. R. James (1801?–1860), and **William Harrison Ainsworth** (1805–1882), all of whom captured a wide Victorian audience. The same conventions embellished the fiction of writers not usually labeled as pure "Gothic," like **Emily Brontë** (*Wuthering Heights*, 1847), **Charles Dickens**, and **Wilkie Collins**, who integrated mystery, suspense, and supernatural suggestion into larger literary objectives. At the other end of the scale were the totally sensational penny dreadfuls or "bloods" like *Varney, the Vampyre, or The Feast of Blood* (1847), geared toward and devoured by lower-class Victorians.

Though **Sheridan LeFanu** (1814–1873) could be regarded as continuing Radcliffean traditions, the complexity of his protagonists and point of view in works like *Uncle Silas* (1864) and "Carmilla" (1872) anticipate the psychological ambiguity of modern Gothicism and separate LeFanu from lesser-known contemporaries. Fear of the present and future rather than the past also distinguishes the most significant Gothics of the period: **Robert Louis Stevenson**'s *Dr. Jekyll and Mr. Hyde* (1886), **Oscar Wilde**'s *The Picture of Dorian Gray* (1891), **H. G. Wells**'s *The Island of Dr. Moreau* (1896), and **Bram Stoker**'s *Dracula* (1897). Analyzed in view of late Victorian cultural phenomena—sexual repression, loss of religious faith and moral absolutes, scientific and psychological research, and imperialism—these novels demonstrate the power of Gothic fiction to address the shifting anxieties of readers coping with the changes, uncertainties, and dangers of both Victorian and modern worlds.

BETTE B. ROBERTS

Bibliography

Bleiler, E. F. Introduction to *Five Victorian Ghost Novels*. 1971.

King, Stephen. *Danse Macabre*.

Lovecraft, Howard Phillips. *Supernatural Horror in Literature*. 1945.

Punter, David. *The Literature of Terror: A History of Gothic Fictions from 1765 to the Present Day*. 1980.

See also SUPERNATURAL FICTION

. . . . .

GOTHIC REVIVAL

Most widespread of the many stylistic revivals in Victorian **architecture**, the Gothic revival had its roots in the late eighteenth century when the craggy irregularity and romantic mystery of medieval structures titillated a public grown weary of serenely rational neoclassicism. During the Victorian period,

Gothic Revived for Secular Use: Entrance to Assize Courts, Manchester,
Alfred Waterhouse Architect (1859).
From Charles L. Eastlake, A History of the Gothic Revival, *1872.*

however, Gothic ceased being merely a picturesque alternative mode of building; the revival took an exclusionary moral turn that transformed the rationale for the style and justified it with a new vocabulary. Although the movement produced many apologists, several representative influences may be singled out.

First were the ecclesiological organizations seeking to revive Anglican ritual, who needed churches in which it could be properly performed. Most important of these groups was the Cambridge Camden Society (after 1846 the Ecclesiological Society), founded at Cambridge University in 1839. In their influential journal the *Ecclesiologist* (1841–1868), read by scholars, architects, and patrons, they extolled the Gothic as the only fitting style for religious uses and insisted on rigorous archaeological correctness, which became a major standard in the revival's early phase.

The architect **Augustus Welby Northmore Pugin** (1812–1852) most energetically defended the Gothic's appropriateness for secular purposes by demonstrating that applying the style's inherent constructional principles rather than just correctly imitating its forms was essential to universal revival. In *The True Principles of Pointed or Christian Architecture* (1841), an early statement of architectural functionalism, he enunciated "two great principles of design": that all a building's features should be justified by "convenience, construction, or propriety," and that its ornament should serve solely to enhance basic construction. Only the Gothic architects, he maintained, had consistently carried out these standards, in natural response to a northern climate and materials. But beyond the refreshingly practical character of these principles, Pugin stressed their moral bearing, both in his vocabulary of charged terms like "honesty" and "truthfulness" and in his assertion that the Gothic was an organic expression of medieval religious values. An impassioned Roman Catholic convert, Pugin unabashedly declared that the ultimate means of reviving the Gothic in England was to restore the Roman Catholic church that had inspired it—a subversive position that limited popular acceptance of his ideas in a stoutly Protestant nation.

The revival's most famous exponent, even if he detested its results, was the critic **John Ruskin** (1819–1900). His eloquent celebration of Gothic beauty in *The Seven Lamps of Architecture* (1849), *The Stones of Venice* (1851–1853), and *Lectures on Architecture and Painting* (1854) reached a wider, less specialized audience than either the ecclesiologists or Pugin did. Like Pugin, whose influence he insistently denied, Ruskin applauded Gothic functionalism and exalted the style as the morally admirable product of a spiritually unified society, but argued further that such a society respected and incorporated into its buildings *individuals'* creativity, however imperfect. This interpretation proceeded from Ruskin's fervent Protestantism, which permeated his early work. Thus his most immediate service to the revival was, as Kenneth Clark claims, to "disinfect" Gothic architecture, making it acceptable to an audience wary of its ritualist and Catholic associations.

An array of structures erected throughout Victorian England attests to the revival's success. Beginning with the earliest landmark, **Charles Barry**'s and Pugin's Houses of Parliament (1837–1867), many neo-Gothic institutional buildings were constructed, such as the University Museum, Oxford (1855–1860) by Thomas Deane and Benjamin Woodward; **Alfred Waterhouse**'s Manchester Town Hall (1868–1877); and **George Edmund Street**'s New Law Courts in the Strand, London (1874–1882). Important churches ranged from William Butterfield's All Saints', Margaret Street, in London (1850–1859), which the ecclesiologists commissioned, to John Loughborough Pearson's Truro Cathedral (1880–1910) in Cornwall. Major commercial buildings like **George Gilbert Scott**'s Midland Grand Hotel (1868–1874) at London's St. Pancras Station appeared in the Gothic style; so did provincial pubs and milliners' shops. Great country houses underwent Gothicizing (such as Scarisbrick Hall in Lancashire, remodeled by Pugin between 1837 and 1845); lancet windows punctuated urban terraces, suburban villas, and rural parsonages.

But the revival inevitably declined with the rise of modern materials like plate glass, steel, and ferroconcrete that dictated both new construction principles and a new aesthetic; nor could the costly, deliberate Gothic building process, dependent on dying craft traditions, satisfy the contemporary demand for cheap, rapid production. The revival's justification of functionalism, however, as well as its insistence that architecture expresses a society's ethos and is thus worthy of serious criticism, constituted a significant theoretical legacy, while its surviving monuments remain a distinctive aspect of British cities and towns.

KRISTINE OTTESEN GARRIGAN

Bibliography

Bright, Michael. *Cities Built to Music: Aesthetic Theories of the Victorian Gothic Revival.* 1984.

Clark, Kenneth. *The Gothic Revival: An Essay in the History of Taste.* 3d ed., 1962.

Eastlake, Charles L. *A History of the Gothic Revival.* 1872.

Hersey, George L. *High Victorian Gothic. A Study in Associationism.* 1972.

Macaulay, James. *The Gothic Revival, 1745–1845.* 1975.

Thompson, Paul. *William Butterfield.* 1971.

White, James F. *The Cambridge Movement: The Ecclesiologists and the Gothic Revival.* 1962.

See also MEDIEVALISM

．．．．．

GOVERNESSES

The governess was a female teacher of middle- and upper-class children. The term referred to a teacher in a school as well as to a woman employed in the home, either on a daily basis (the "daily governess") or living with the family. Toward the end of the century the word came more usually to mean only the teacher who lived in the home.

The governess was expected to be of "gentle" birth, meaning that she was a "lady," not a member of the lower classes. Thus, she was theoretically of equal social status to her employers. Her gentle birth meant that she was competent to instruct the young ladies of the household in proper behavior and manners as well as in academic subjects. Her status in the household might vary widely. In some she was treated as a virtual member of the family; in others she was despised and given less consideration than the lower servants.

Poverty arising from, for example, the death or bankruptcy of her father or brother might drive an unmarried lady to become a governess. It has been estimated that in 1850 there were over 20,000 in the ranks of the profession, and there may have been others who went uncounted. Their salaries ranged from 15 to 100 pounds per year, with the average probably around 35 pounds. This included room and board, but not clothing, laundry, medical, or other incidental expenses. Furthermore, governesses could not expect any permanency or pension. They could be fired at the whim of the mistress and had nothing but their own savings to depend upon while they were unemployed. The low wages reflect the oversupply of would-be governesses. One reason for the superfluity of needy ladies was that many single men and younger sons emigrated to the colonies in search of fortune, or postponed marriage until their financial prospects improved.

Daughters of the clergy often became governesses; they supposedly had learned meekness of spirit at home. Daughters of army or naval officers were also acceptable, and a well-born daughter of any member of the gentry would bring prestige to her employers. If she could overcome homesickness and illness, a lady might seek a position abroad. There was snob appeal in having an English governess, and there are accounts of Russian, Austrian, Italian, French, and even Eastern and Moslem families employing English governesses for their children. It was an adventurous life, and although often in danger, few apparently came to any harm.

Once a lady became a governess, she had little chance of leaving the profession. Unless her family fortunes unexpectedly changed, it was rare that she would marry; unlike most servants governesses were seldom permitted to have suitors. Most mistresses deliberately chose unattractive women to be their children's governess. Sometimes the governess would be expected to fill in the numbers at table, but her presence in the drawing room was always unwelcome. She was apt to have a lonely life. The governess taught English, arithmetic, drawing, sketching, painting, music, French (perhaps Latin and German, too), history, geography, and needlework. Had she herself been well educated, she might manage a few of these subjects, but it was unlikely that she knew them equally well. Not all employers were so demanding; some mothers wished merely to have their children taught the manners of gentility: an overly educated child, particularly a girl, would not fare well in the marriage market. Governesses also served as chaperones for their charges.

The position of governesses caused considerable comment in the periodical press and in literature. While the impudent Becky Sharp in Thackeray's *Vanity Fair* (1848) alarmed some people, novels like Charlotte Brontë's *Jane Eyre* (1847) or Anne Brontë's *Agnes Grey* (1847) created more sympathy for the governess. Later in the century, Charlotte Yonge's works emphasized a new concern for the professionalism of teaching. The Governesses' Benevolent Institution was established in 1843 to provide some relief from the stringent conditions faced by governesses. It conducted a registry for employment and later became a source of charity for the old and infirm. After the turn of the twentieth century, as schools for girls became more acceptable to the middle class, the profession of governess began to die out.

CYNTHIA F. BEHRMAN

Bibliography

Howe, Bea. *A Galaxy of Governesses*. 1954.

Peterson, M. Jeanne. "The Victorian Governess: Status Incongruence in Family and Society." In *Suffer and Be Still: Women in the Victorian Age*. Martha Vicinus, ed., 1972.

Pitcher, Harvey. *When Miss Emmie Was in Russia: English Governesses Before, During and After the October Revolution*. 1977.

See also EDUCATION, WOMEN'S

· · · · ·

GOVERNMENT: COLONIES AND EMPIRE

In Victorian times the British colonial empire was governed by several agencies in London that acted on behalf of Her Majesty's government. In earlier years Parliament had played a more direct role through committees such as the Board of Trade and Plantations. By mid-Victorian times, however, the Colonial Office, headed by a secretary of state, became the main channel of contact for the imperial government. British holdings in India, however, were considered so important that a separate India Office was created in 1858 with its own secretary of state.

The Colonial Office, established in 1854, was relatively small and was popular with civil servants. (For such a minor department, the Colonial Office paid well.) At its head was a cabinet minister titled secretary of state for colonial affairs. During Victoria's reign the office was held by men of varying abilities. Lord John Russell and William Gladstone subsequently became prime ministers; Joseph Chamberlain, Victoria's last colonial secretary, was a major force in the Salisbury government of 1895 and, during the Boer War, was considered almost the equal to Salisbury in government policy. Other colonial secretaries, such as Edward Cardwell, Lord Carnarvon, Earl Granville, and the earl of Kimberley, never rose to political prominence, yet all made positive contributions to colonial administration.

Below the colonial secretary labored the permanent staff. The senior functionaries were called first-class clerks. In Victoria's days there were only some twenty to forty clerks, many of them bachelors married to the office. They often had been at public school and university together, and usually remained at the office many years. Rather than being educated in subjects such as agriculture, civil engineering or ethnography, which would be useful to administering a vast empire, the clerks were normally classically trained "all-rounders." The bureaucratic leadership was notably good; under chief permanent secretaries such as James Stephen, Herman Merivale, and Frederick Rogers, internal management at the Colonial Office was unsurpassed by any office in the British government.

In atmosphere, the colonial office resembled a Pall Mall men's club relocated to Whitehall Street across from 10 Downing Street. Clerks normally arrived at noon and left at five-thirty. Two months' holiday per year was common, and additional time off easily obtained. Between mail days, when the tempo was slowest, a clerk once bet he could conduct the entire work of the office unaided. (There were no takers.) Many of the clerks dabbled in personal colonial specialties such as etymology, trees, currency, or whaling. A happy working atmosphere resulted and, except in unusual circumstances, the office allowed the colonies to run themselves.

The Colonial Office would, however, sometimes intervene to prevent colonial governments from making egregious blunders or would receive tribal leaders who were seeking to go over the head of the colonial governor. The Colonial Office served, in essence, as an embassy in London for the colonies. In contrast to the system developed by other colonial powers, Colonial Office officials seldom became governors of colonies; there was almost a complete divorce between bureaucrats in London and administrators in the field.

Of all the British colonies, India was considered special. From 1773 to 1858 it had been ruled by the private East India Company. Following the 1857 Mutiny, however, Britain ceased using the company as a Crown agent and began governing India directly. Parliament created a new government agency and a secretary of state for India. The India Office was far grander and more stately than the Colonial Office; instead of being clubby and warm, it was somber, despotic, and powerful. The India Office library, through the efforts of a succession of eastern scholars, held the greatest Sanskrit collection in the world, priceless manuscripts, and a statutory right to every book published in India in any language. Parliament, however, had little actual control over Indian affairs because it lacked the power of the pursestrings. The funds for administering India—even the cost of running the India Office in London—were extracted from Indian taxpayers.

The real power lay with the governor-general, later given the title of viceroy, who presided over the British *raj* (rule) in India. After the Mutiny of 1857, most viceroys considered the possibility of Indian self-government too remote to consider; the best that could be done would be to allow future generations of "brown Englishmen" to rise as high as their capacities allowed—with no expectation that they could ever really become independent. In Victorian times an illusion of permanence in India was therefore created.

During the ascendancy of the *raj*, the viceroy was assisted by provincial governors, district superintendents, and the famed Indian Civil Service. The ICS was a body of civil servants, never large, which ran the daily administration of India. It also became a barometer of prevailing British philosophy toward indigenous populations throughout the empire. The number of Indians allowed into the service usually indicated the government's level of tolerance at the moment.

The ICS, like British administrators throughout the empire were almost all public school men. They had gone at about age thirteen to one of the fifty or sixty prestigious private schools where "**gentlemen**" were trained by schoolmasters who strove to instill a creed commonly described as "muscular Christianity." Sports, a heavy dose of chapel, and a classical education were the main items of a curriculum from which boys emerged at the age of eighteen or nineteen to begin the job of conquering and administering far-flung empires.

The British Foreign Office impinged on the activities of both the Colonial Office and the India Office, since it had central responsibility for colonial defense and diplomacy. Britain had full rights to enter into treaties and make war and peace on behalf of the entire colonial system. Even the self-governing dominions such as **Canada, New Zealand, Australia,** and the South African Republic were bound by Foreign Office strictures. In the same fashion, colonial defense was determined by the Foreign Office rather than the individual colonies. Colonies contributed men and money to imperial defense but could not influence policy. The head of the British army was called "chief of the imperial general staff," denoting his authority over troops throughout the empire.

Wherever possible the British employed one of two systems that required minimal administrative presence. The self-governing colonies achieved dominion status during the Victorian years. The formula, later codified in the Statute of Westminster (1931), stated that dominions were "autonomous Communities within the British Empire, equal in status," independent to enact their own domestic legislation, "though united by a common allegiance to the Crown." Only in matters of diplomacy and defense did the imperial government have authority to impose upon dominions.

A second form of administration, utilized primarily in the Crown Colonies, was known as "indirect rule." It was frequently useful for the imperial government to leave intact the systems of rule created by indigenous peoples so long as they were not at variance with British decorum. Tribal chiefs, therefore, could maintain their traditional authority so long as they did not boil missionaries in large pots. The colonial service could send out a district officer, often an old public school boy, to check that there were no cooked missionaries. If there were irregularities, the "Great White Queen" would be displeased, and the local chief might find himself replaced. Thus, ruling through existing rulers was "indirect" rule.

Overall, British administration of its sprawling empire was loose, informal, even amateurish. Occasionally the fleet had to be sent, and there were interminable little colonial wars, but, on balance, the empire ran itself rather well during the reign of Victoria. At the end of her life, the Anglo-Boer confrontation led to a diminution of British military and imperial confidence. Mercifully, perhaps, Victoria did not live to see the empire unravel.

NEWELL D. BOYD

Bibliography

Benians, E. A. et al. *Cambridge History of the British Empire.* 1919–1963.

Cell, John W. *British Colonial Administration in the Mid-Nineteenth Century: The Policy-Making Process.* 1970.

Cross, Colin. *The Fall of the British Empire.*

Gordon, Donald C. *The Moment of Power: Britain's Imperial Epoch.* 1970.

Jeffries, Charles. *The Colonial Office.* 1956.

Ward, John M. *Colonial Self-Government: The British Experience.* 1976.

See also CIVIL SERVICE; EMPIRE AND IMPERIALISM

. . . . .

GOVERNMENT: LOCAL AND COUNTY

Victorian local government was made up of a variety of administrative units from the Boards of Guardians to justices of the peace in both rural and urban areas. Major legislative actions were undertaken in the Local Government Acts of 1888 and 1894. The changes in local government exemplify the Victorians' struggle to adapt traditional structures to the new realities of urban growth and democracy.

Before 1834–1835 there was no general "local government" but rather a patchwork of overlapping jurisdictions and services. Parish vestries oversaw various matters of welfare and civil order within each parish—with great unevenness, depending on the nature of the parish and the civic energy of its inhabitants. Magistrates, who did both judicial and administrative business, had to be owners of freehold land and members of the Church of England; in practice, outside of the largest towns, they were almost always either local squires or clergymen. There were also some municipal corporations and various ad hoc bodies set up for special purposes by act of Parliament.

Over the middle years of the century the size and nature of local governments began to change. As necessities expanded from the provision of basic services (roads, bridges, jails) to more encompassing measures for health and safety (sewage, smoke abatement), it became necessary to coordinate activities over larger areas. The Poor Law Amendment Act (1834) joined parishes into larger administrative units for purposes of providing relief, and the Municipal Corporations Act (1835) established governments elected by ratepayers in 178 towns.

The reform of county government in 1888 was based on the municipal reforms of 1835 and 1882. The 1888 Local Government Act established sixty-one county boroughs and forty-nine administrative counties in England. The Local Government Act of 1894 created urban and rural district councils to replace the patchwork of sanitary authorities and parish councils and thus completed the work of local government reform, although two important areas of local administration—education and poor relief—still remained under elected ad hoc authorities.

The reform of 1888, however, did not radically affect the structure of administration at the county level. Justices of the peace had previously administered the business of county government through a system of committees; the same pattern was adopted by the new county councils. The most radical aspect of the reform was that county leaders were elected rather than appointed. In fact, few seats were contested in the early county council elections, and many of the county councilors and aldermen were former justices of the peace.

Neither did the reform of 1894 require any radical change in the structure of district administration. Prior to 1894 the basic units of government at the district level were Poor Law Unions and rural and urban sanitary authorities. In rural areas the board of guardians elected for each Poor Law Union was usually designated to act also as highway and sanitary authority. In urban areas, the Borough Council Improvement Commissioners or local Board of Health functioned as sanitary authority and also as highway authority. The urban area elected representatives to the Board of Guardians for the union in which it was situated. School boards were separately elected authorities. In practice, then, there was one local authority for rural areas, the Board of Guardians; urban areas might have several separate authorities; and urban and rural representatives acted together on the Board of Guardians to administer the Poor Law. After 1894, sanitary authorities became district councils but the general administrative structure remained fundamentally unaltered. The major change was that urban and rural district councils were to be elected by a more democratic franchise than that previously in use. Women voted and were elected to various local government bodies in the 1890s.

Major issues in local government revolved around rural and urban differences and the competing claims of central and local authority. The Poor Law Unions established in 1834 were delineated on the basis of market towns and their surrounding area; town and countryside were seen as a functional unit. Between 1830 and 1870, rapidly expanding towns and cities encouraged the belief that urban problems were distinct and should be treated independently. In the process of redefining boundaries of county, borough, and district as required by the reforms of 1888 and 1894, the principle of functional urban-rural units was disregarded in favor of the "island principle" of distinct urban and rural areas introduced in the Public Health Acts (1848, 1872, 1875) and the Highway Act (1862).

The separation of urban and rural areas had the pragmatic political value of allowing the middle classes to exercise power in urban areas, while preserving the traditional authority of landed interests in rural areas. County councils brought together middle-class and landed interests in one administrative body, but the possibility of broad creative cooperation between urban and rural interests was vitiated by the autonomy of the largest cities and the guarantee of certain areas of autonomy for those smaller cities and towns that were nominally subordinate to the county councils.

Despite conflicts between urban and rural, and middle-class and landed interests, the rural justices of the peace and the borough councilors were united in resenting and opposing interference by central government. The Poor Law reform of 1834 was a victory for centralization and bureaucracy; the municipal reform of 1835 was a counterbalancing victory for local authority. With the establishment of the Local Government Board in 1871, the gradual expansion of the central government's role in local affairs became the dominant trend. Some analysts, however, see the exercise of control from London as an inherent weakness of the English local government system. Had the structure depended, instead, on local representatives of the central government, their personal knowledge and experience could have mediated between central and local governments.

PRUDENCE ANN MOYLAN

Bibliography

Chester, Daniel Norman. *The English Administrative System, 1780–1870.* 1981.

Fraser, Derek. *Urban Politics in Victorian England.* 1976.

Freeman, Thomas Walter. *Geography and Regional Administration in England and Wales: 1830–1868.* 1968.

Keith-Lucas, Bryan. *English Local Government Franchise.* 1952

———. *English Local Government in the Nineteenth and Twentieth Centuries.* 1977.

Lipman, Vivian David. *Local Government Areas, 1834–1945.* 1949.

Redlich, Josef and Francis W. Hirst. *The History of Local Government in England.* 2d ed., 1970. Ed. Bryan Keith-Lucas.

Robson, William Alexander. *The Development of Local Government.* 1948.

Smellie, Kingsley Bryce. *A History of Local Government.* 4th ed., 1968.

See also ARISTOCRACY AND
GENTRY; EDINBURGH

. . . . .

GRACE, WILLIAM GILBERT
(1848–1915)

Dr. William Gilbert Grace was born in Downend, near Bristol, on July 18, 1848. He was the son of Dr. Henry Mills Grace and a nephew of Alfred Pocock, both of whom had been excellent cricketers. Grace was thus raised in "the atmosphere of cricket," as he himself put it, and grew up to become one of the most famous sportsmen in English history.

W. G., as he is still commonly known, was the first cricketer to exploit all the orthodox strokes, scoring with equal facility off both the front foot and the back. His timing and hand-eye coordination were so keenly developed that, virtually single-handed, he killed off a whole generation of fast bowlers. Grace therefore did much to inspire the evolution of spin bowling after 1870. He is generally acknowledged as the father of modern **cricket**, having left it at his death, on October 23, 1915, in much the same shape in which it is still being played.

One of the most successful all-rounders in the game's history, Grace scored 54,896 runs, held 871 catches, and captured 2,876 wickets in first-class cricket, mainly for Gloucestershire. He had the distinction of scoring the first Test century for England—152 against Autralia at the Kennington Oval in September 1880.

KEITH A. P. SANDIFORD

Bibliography

Altham, Harry S. and E. W. Swanton. *A History of Cricket.* 1981.

Grace, William G. *Cricketing Reminiscences and Personal Recollections.* 1899.

Midwinter, Eric. *W. G. Grace: His Life and Times.* 1981.

Parker, Grahame. *Gloucestershire Road: A History of Gloucestershire County Cricket Club.* 1983.

. . . . .

GRAHAM, ROBERT B. CUNNINGHAME
(1852–1936)

Adventurer, author, aristocratic crusader, Robert Bontine Cunninghame Graham was often described by his contemporaries as a modern Don Quixote. Born into an old family of deeply indebted Scottish landowners, he was educated at Harrow. In the 1870s he lived and worked among the gauchos of South America. He married in 1878: his wife, generally known as Gabriela de la Balmondière, was in fact born Caroline Horsfall (1858–1906), a doctor's daughter.

Graham served as Liberal M.P. for North-West Lanark (1886–1892), the first avowed socialist in the House of Commons. He denounced imperialism, child labor, and capital punishment; he fought for Scottish miners, striking dockworkers, preservation of the countryside, home rule for Ireland and Scotland, free education, the eight-hour day, and nationalization of industries.

At the great Trafalgar Square demonstration of November 13, 1887 ("**Bloody Sunday**") Graham was assaulted by the police. After a dramatic trial, he served a month in prison. Graham was instrumental in launching the Scottish Labour Party and the political career of Keir Hardie. He campaigned for **socialism** at the side of Bernard Shaw, John Burns, Peter Kropotkin, William Morris, H. M. Hyndman, and Friedrich Engels.

Graham's literary forte was the travel tale. His finest book, *Mogreb-el-Acksa* (1898), describes his attempt to trek across Morocco disguised as an Arab sheikh. *A Vanished Arcadia* (1901) was the first of his several histories of the Spanish conquest of South America. Graham's writings provided much of the technical background for Bernard Shaw's *Captain Brassbound's Conversion* and Joseph Conrad's *Nostromo*.

JONATHAN ROSE

Bibliography

Watts, Cedric and Laurence Davies. *Cunninghame Graham: A Critical Biography.* 1979

. . . . .

GRAND, SARAH (FRANCES ELIZABETH CLARKE McFALL) (1854–1943)

Sarah Grand was a feminist novelist, short story writer, essayist, and suffrage activist. Influenced in her teens by the campaign against the Contagious Diseases Acts, she incorporated the theme of women's moral leadership into her novels, and is said to have coined the phrase "**New Woman**." She married at sixteen and traveled widely with her husband, an army doctor, but left him in 1890 to live independently and write.

The Heavenly Twins (1892) best expresses Grand's demand for female autonomy and her faith in women's refusal to countenance men's immorality. The portraits of the independent Evadne and Angelica contrast with the character of Edith, who contracts syphilis from her husband and dies mad. Evadne's refusal to consummate her marriage because of her husband's premarital affairs demonstrates Grand's contention that women must set moral standards, while Angelica's adventurous spirit epitomizes the New Woman's frustration at her limited opportunities, for she is far more clever than her twin brother Diavolo, who nevertheless has far greater freedom and access to education. These ideas and many of the characters recur in *Ideala* (1888) and the semiautobiographical *The Beth Book* (1897), both of which trace the development of women writers. In the latter, which follows the protagonist from infancy to adulthood, Grand emphasizes the points at which wider experience, better education, or more sympathetic response would have eased Beth's situation.

The men in Grand's novels are usually sexually promiscuous, insensitive, corrupt, and even tyrannical, and several are doctors like Grand's husband who operate lock hospitals, in which women were compulsorily confined for the treatment of venereal diseases. For Grand such places, mandated under the Contagious Diseases Acts, epitomize the degradation of women for the convenience of men, and she criticizes the sexual double standard harshly. Through her characters she argues instead for moral purity based on a full knowledge of life in place of the supposedly elevating influence of women's innocence. She also demonstrates through Evadne, Angelica, and Beth the power of a strong will and the ability of intelligent and sensitive women to overcome obstacles like the denial of education, and to triumph over the social conventions that restrict them.

Grand's other works from this period include *Our Manifold Nature* (1893), a short story collection, and the novels *Singularly Deluded* (1892) and *Babs the Impossible* (1901); among her many essays are *The Modern Man and the Maid* (1898) and *The Human Quest* (1900). Her later works include the novels *Adnam's Orchard* (1912), *The Winged Victory* (1916), and two more volumes of short stories. As a member of several suffrage organizations, including the Women Writers Suffrage League, and as president of a branch of the National Union of Women's Suffrage Societies, she campaigned actively for the enfranchisment of women from about 1898, and served as mayor of Bath from 1922 to 1929. Gillian Kersley's biography of Grand emphasizes the later years and her friendship with Gladys Singers-Bigger.

LAURA STEMPEL MUMFORD

Bibliography

Cunningham, Gail. *The New Woman and the Victorian Novel.* 1978.

Gorsky, Susan. "The Art of Politics: The Feminist Fiction of Sarah Grand." *Journal of Women's Studies in Literature,* vol. 1, pp. 286–300.

Huddleston, Joan, ed. *Sarah Grand (Mrs. Frances Elizabeth McFall, née Clarke), 1854–1943: A Bibliography.* 1979.

Kersley, Gillian. *Darling Madame: Sarah Grand and Devoted Friend.* 1983.

Showalter, Elaine. *A Literature of Their Own: British Women Novelists from Brontë to Lessing.* 1977.

See also PROSTITUTION

. . . . .

GRAPHIC ARTS

The Victorian graphic arts may be classified according to audience: lithography and woodblock printing provided an unprecedented mass audience with cheaply reproduced images; the middle classes favored steel engravings and other handsomely reproduced images of famous or popular paintings; and connoisseurs collected etchings and other prints in small editions. From the time of the pioneering Thomas Bewick (1753–1828) until the photomechanical techniques of the 1890s, the woodblock reigned as the only method of cheaply printing pictures with text in a single pressing, and woodblock printers, working from drawings by correspondents, were able to provide for a mass audience the immediacy of today's photojournalism. The *Illustrated London News*, beginning in 1842, pioneered the format of picture magazines. Most woodblock printing thus falls within the category of popular culture and journalism rather than the fine arts.

Steel engravings and colored lithographs were typically Victorian arts. Steel mezzotints first appeared in 1820, and between 1825 and 1845 they dominated the market, extinguishing the tradition of line engraving. Because of its hardness, steel was tedious to work, but gave greater detail and much larger editions; lithography allowed for the exact reproduction of a drawing, and the easier use of color. In the early Victorian period illustrated books and annuals such as *The Keepsake* enjoyed a vogue: at this time famous artists such as J. W. M. Turner supplied drawings to distinguished engravers such as Samuel Cousins (1801–1887), who was the first engraver elected a full member of the Royal Academy (1855).

Mid-Victorian interiors were filled with framed prints. Middle-class buyers purchased thousands of engravings of pets, seaside resorts, idealized beauties (such as the heroines of Shakespeare), portraits of celebrities (the queen permitted dozens to be made of her and her family), and sporting scenes. After 1836 the Art Unions helped distribute prints, and the Printsellers Association, founded in 1847, was a professional body that registered and controlled the publication of prints to ensure continued profits for all concerned. Prices were moderate to high (in 1844, "Fox Hunting," a colored lithograph, brought one pound one shilling, and a mezzotint after Landseer brought two pounds). The copyright for paintings by artists such as Edwin Landseer (1802–1873) and J. E. Millais (1829–1896) was often worth more than the original canvas. The popularity of engravings even dictated the working methods of some Victorian artists; the Pre-Raphaelite Holman Hunt (1827–1910) could agonize for years over a single painting because the profits from engraved versions of biblical subjects such as "The Light of the World" (1860) were so immense. (Some printmakers, such as George Baxter, devoted most of their energy to works disseminated by missionary societies.) The mass market for prints encouraged speculations and abuses; the industry was somewhat shocked when Pears soap purchased the copyright to Millais's "Bubbles" and used it for advertising. By the turn of the century the practice of smaller, numbered editions, followed by the destruction of the plates, was more common.

Etching on copper in the manner of Rembrandt and Goya was not popular in the first part of the century, though good work was done in isolation. The revival of etching in France after Charles Meryon (1821–1868) stimulated artists in England, notably Francis Haden (1818–1910) and J. A. M. Whistler (1834–1903), to etch in the fine art tradition. Whistler's fortunes as a painter, damaged in the Ruskin trial of 1878, were recouped by his etchings in the 1880s of Venice, commissioned by the Fine Arts Society. His work emphasized the impressionistic rather than reproductive possibilities of the medium, and a large school of late Victorian etchers followed in his wake.

Victorian graphic art encompasses hastily produced woodcuts of the Crimean War, grandiose mezzotints of Victoria's coronation, and delicately etched landscapes: in its totality it mirrors all realms of Victorian life, and reaches into all corners of society.

DAVID E. LATANÉ, JR.

Bibliography

Bridson, Gavin and Geoffrey Wakeman. *Printmaking and Picture Printing*. 1984.

Davenport, Cyril. *Mezzotints*. 1904.

De Maré, Eric. *The Victorian Woodblock Illustrators.* 1980.

Engen, Rodney K. *Dictionary of Victorian Engravers, Print Publishers and Their Works.* 1979.

———. *Victorian Engravings.* 1975.

Hind, Arthur M. *A History of Engraving and Etching.* Rev. ed., 1927.

Hunnisett, Basil. *Steel-Engraved Book Illustration in England.* 1980.

James, Philip. *English Book Illustration, 1800–1900.* 1947.

See also ILLUSTRATION; WOOD ENGRAVING

. . . . .

GREAT EXHIBITION see EXHIBITION OF 1851

. . . . .

GREEN, JOHN RICHARD (1837–1883)

John Richard Green's *Short History of the English People* (1874) was the most popular Victorian history of England.

Born in Oxford, Green graduated from the University of Oxford in 1859. He developed his characteristic approach to English history through familiarity with the streets and architecture of Oxford rather than in tutorials and libraries. Ordained in 1860, he served several London parishes while also writing essays, chiefly for the *Saturday Review.* He left the parish ministry in 1869, published the *Short History* in 1874, and in 1877 married Alice Stopford, with whom he studied, traveled, and published books on English history and geography. After his death in 1883 she saw his unpublished work through the press and revised the *Short History.*

As historian, Green integrated political, literary, and social events into a larger whole, "the English people," thereby giving his books vividness, concreteness, and organic unity. He wrote clearly and precisely, avoiding the Latinate style of university discourse, and enriched his library research with visits to places where the events he was describing had occurred. Called a Whig, for his progressive view of historical change, and the "father of twentieth-century social history" for extending the scope of his work to include social, intellectual, and literary matters as well as political events, he is best characterized as one who saw in English history a national unity of character, purpose, and aspiration that transcended circumstances of time and place. This stance also appealed to British imperialists who were trying to sustain and extend a worldwide empire.

PHILIP M. TEIGEN

Bibliography

Brundage, Anthony. "John Richard Green and the Church: The Making of a Social Historian," *Historian,* vol. 5, pp. 32–42.

Gooch, G. P. *History and Historians in the Nineteenth Century.* 1959.

Green, John Richard. *Letters.* 1901.

Kenyon, John. *The History Men: The Historical Profession in England Since the Renaissance.* 1984.

Schuyler, Robert L. "John Richard Green and His *Short History,*" *Political Science Quarterly,* vol. 64, pp. 321–354.

. . . . .

GREENAWAY, KATE (1846–1901)

Kate Greenaway's significance as an artist rests on her popular rendition of children in quaint clothing. She introduced a style that was immediately recognizable and definitively hers. As a children's book illustrator who provided a transition between the Pre-Raphaelite and aesthetic movements, her work was acclaimed by both critics and the reading public.

Her father, John Greenaway, a wood engraver for the *Illustrated London News,* provided Kate with art instruction at schools such as the National Art Training School. She won a national medallion for design in 1864 and had her first work published in 1867. Never married, she met John Ruskin after her acclaimed success with *Under the Window* (1878) when she was in her thirties, he in his sixties. He served as a barbed mentor and critical friend. As she followed his advice, however, her popularity declined.

Along with Randolph Caldecott and Walter Crane, Greenaway formed a rewarding association with Edmund Evans, whose engraving process allowed for her delicate lines, colors, and sparse backgrounds. *Under the Window* rapidly sold out the first 20,000 copies and a second edition of 70,000 was printed. Altogether, their association produced over 900,000 copies of her various works. In 1883 she designed a miniature, painstakingly drawn almanac for children. These almanacs appeared every year until 1897. Some of her other works included *A Apple Pie* (1886), an alphabet book, and *The Pied Piper of Hamelin* (1888).

The young women and girls of her illustrations were dressed in bonnets, empire waist dresses, and slippers; the boys in high waists and ankle-length trousers. The clothing became a vogue. She helped form the Victorian concept of beautiful and innocent children, and for that she was greatly admired.

A hundred years later, imitations of her illustrations, greeting cards, and clothes are still available. To underscore her contribution to children's book illustration, the British Library Association presents the Kate Greenaway Award for the year's best children's book illustration in Britain.

LOUISA SMITH

Bibliography

Engen, Rodney. *Kate Greenaway: A Biography.* 1981.

Spielmann, Marion H. and G. S. Layard. *Kate Greenaway.* 1905.

. . . . .

GREENWELL, DORA
(1821–1882)

Dora Greenwell, Jean Ingelow, and Christina Rossetti were hailed a triumvirate of Victorian women poets. Greenwell was also an essayist. Her early poetry was well received, though unremarkable, but *Poems* (1867), dedicated to Elizabeth Barrett Browning, distinguished her. *Carmina Crucis* (1869) emphasized faith in Christ as the culmination of life's trials. Her subsequent poetry addressed rebellion against, compliance with, and regeneration through Christian belief. Her prose included *A Present Heaven* (1855), *The Patience of Hope* (1860), *Two Friends* (1863), and *Colloquia Crucis* (1871). Greenwell's charitable work in jails, lunatic asylums, and poorhouses led to essays on social reform: "On Single Women" (*North British Review*, February 1862) and "On the Education of the Imbecile" (*North British Review*, September 1868).

Greenwell led an isolated life of poor health and poverty. Her small circle of friends included Josephine Butler, Ingelow, and Rossetti. (They once challenged each other to a sewing contest to prove that they possessed "useful" talents.) Greenwell's life gave way to grace and serenity in her work. Though her prose meditations were undistinguished, Greenwell's voice was inspired. Her spiritual content spilled into her poetry as composure and control, as in "Daria," where simplicity belies knowledgeable, profound respect for the human dilemma. In "The Singer" conflict and strife are the source of rapturous creativity, while "Poets" attributes artistic power to a gift from God. "The Sunflower" powerfully allegorizes devotion to Christ. "A Valentine" expresses a characteristic theme that lyricism and soul are failed by language. "Bring Me Word How Tall She Is"—Greenwell's reparation for the misogynous interpretation of the Fall—reveals her sympathy with woman's plight.

Greenwell's best work combines orthodox religion and human compassion in a singularly self-constituting acceptance of hardship. She wrote well beyond the conventional restraint of unquestioning piety to convey a deceptively humble, deeply tried Christian faith.

SHELLEY J. CRISP

Bibliography

Dorling, William, ed. *Poems by Dora Greenwell.* 1889.

Maynard, Constance. *Dora Greenwell: A Prophet for Our Own Times on the Battleground of Our Faith.* 1926.

. . . . .

GYPSIES

During the nineteenth century Britain's gypsy population came under increasing attack from those concerned about vagrancy and social order. In popular and serious fiction, however, the conventions that accumulated around the figure of the gypsy were expanded and transformed. By the end of the century gypsies and their lore and language had also attracted the attention of both amateur and professional scholars.

Gypsies had been present in England—and also persecuted under both vagrancy acts and special statutes—since at least the sixteenth century. In the nineteenth century they continued to have a reputation for petty theft, horse stealing, and confidence tricks associated with fortune telling. As industrialization increased the need for a disciplined workforce the gypsies' vagrant ways and lack of Christian religion left them open to growing harassment by rural police, and there were various proposals to use public health statutes against gypsy tents and wagons or compulsory education acts to "rescue" their children.

The reality of gypsy life, however, had little to do with the conventions of popular literature. In the century's early decades the gypsy lurked in Gothic novels and cheap serials as a dark outsider—tainted with the supernatural, feared for amorality, yet envied for freedom. Plots were fueled by gypsies who stole children, engaged in acts of lawless revenge, and pronounced prophecies and curses which could not be evaded. Popular works such as G. P. R. James's *The Gipsy* (1835) and Thomas Pecket Prest's *Ela the Outcast: Or the Gipsy of Rosemary Dell* (1838)—as well as dozens of stage melodramas—used titles that signal the theme's appeal. In a great many of these works, however, the hero was not actually a gypsy after all, but a tragic outcast of noble background who had found refuge with a gypsy band.

As the century progressed the gypsy figure grew increasingly romanticized and—in se-

rious works at least—less villainous. Urban intellectuals projected ideas of natural simplicity and ideal freedom onto gypsy figures, and works such as Matthew Arnold's "The Scholar-Gipsy" (1853) add a philosophical dimension to the subject. The lore of romantic curses and stolen children survived, however, in children's books and adult light reading; many forgotten popular novels from the century's last three decades have titles playing on the words "curse," "gipsy," and "queen."

Serious study of gypsies also originated with romantic fascination. George Borrow's *The Romany Rye* (1857) records gypsy customs but has been criticized for its many inaccuracies; probably the gypsy informants simply gave Borrow the colorful stories he obviously wanted to hear. In the 1870s and 1880s there were scholarly studies such as Charles G. Leland's *The English Gipsies and their Language* (1874), various collections of songs and folktales, and numerous articles on gypsies in publications such as the *Edinburgh Review, Dublin University Magazine*, and *Saturday Review*. The Gypsy Lore Society published a journal from 1888.

SALLY MITCHELL

Bibliography

Behlmer, George K. "The Gypsy Problem in Victorian England." *Victorian Studies*, vol. 28, pp. 231–253.

Reed, John R. *Victorian Conventions.* 1975.

Vesey-Fitzgerald, Brian. *Gypsies of Britain: An Introduction to Their History.* 1946.

. . . . .

HAGGARD, HENRY RIDER
(1856–1925)

Active in several aspects of public life, Henry Rider Haggard's principal achievement was as a novelist. Among his more enduring works are the African romances *King Solomon's Mines* (1885), *She* (1887), *Allan Quatermain* (1887) and *Ayesha* (1905).

After working as a civil servant in South Africa (1875–1877) and the newly annexed Transvaal (1877–1879), Haggard returned to England, briefly studied law and then turned to a career of writing and the study of agriculture. His agricultural writings, early African experience and civic-mindedness led to an appointment with the Colonial Office (1905), knighthood (1912), membership in the Dominions Royal Commission (1912–1917), the Royal Colonial Institute (1916), the Empire Settlement Committee (1918), and elevation to Knight of the British Empire (1919).

As a result of the growing literacy fostered by the Education Act (1870), a new novelistic phenomenon appeared in the 1880s, the "best seller." Haggard's strength as a storyteller, like that of his contemporaries, Robert Louis Stevenson (1850–1894), Anthony Hope (1863–1933), Arthur Conan Doyle (1859–1930) and Rudyard Kipling (1865–1936), ensured the popularity of his adventure stories. Haggard's formula involved fast-paced action based on motives of love and hate, greed, and wanderlust. The African adventures celebrate the beauty of the land, the virtues of the noble savage, the joy of adventure in daring quests and exploits, and the mysteries of the Dark Continent. As a creator of credible but limited characters in exotic settings and situations of high adventure, Haggard helped form a popular subgenre outside the mainstream of the Victorian novel.

JOHN J. CONLON

Bibliography

Cohen, Morton. *Rider Haggard: His Life and Works*. 1960.

Etherington, Norman. *Rider Haggard*. 1984.

Haggard, H. Rider. *The Days of My Life: An Autobiography*. 1926. Ed. C. J. Longman.

——. *The Private Diaries of Sir H. Rider Haggard*. 1980. Ed. D. S. Higgins.

Higgins, D. S. *Rider Haggard, The Great Storyteller*. 1981.

Scott, James E. *A Bibliography of the Works of Sir Henry Rider Haggard*. 1947.

· · · · ·

HALL, ANNA MARIA (1800–1881) and SAMUEL CARTER (1800–1889)

Anna Maria Fielding and Samuel Carter Hall, both Irish, married in 1824 and worked together in London. A prolific and industrious writer, she is chiefly famous for sketches of Irish rural life and character and for children's books, from *Chronicles of a School Room* (1830) to *Grandmamma's Pockets* (1880). He, as journalist and editor, pioneered the wide dissemination of art and its criticism and used his influence to establish the first commercial connection of art and manufacture.

Despite the financial vicissitudes of the periodical press, Samuel Carter Hall produced influential ventures such as *The Amulet, a Christian and Literary Remembrancer* (1826–1837) and was connected at times with the *New Monthly Magazine*, *The Watchman*, *John Bull*, and *Brittania*; he also recalls, in *Retrospect of a Long Life* (1883), writing a children's history of France for an editor "in a fix." His real achievement was to create a public demand for art with the *Art Journal* (1839–1912) and to satisfy it with many volumes of engravings.

Anna Hall's Irish sketches were an acknowledged imitation of Mary Russell Mitford's fashionable pastoral, *Our Village* (1824). She worked industriously for the cause of temperance and used her influence with periodical editors to find professional opportunities for many young women and men seeking to earn their living through literature. Conservative, patriotic, and philanthropic, the Halls were well attuned to contemporary aesthetic, social, and religious values. Apparently bourgeois in appeal, their work in fact reached nearly as wide a range of classes as that of Dickens.

SHELAGH HUNTER

Bibliography

Maginn, W. *A Gallery of Illustrious Literary Characters*. 1873. Ed. W. Bates.

Roberts, Helene. "Art Reviewing in the Early Nineteenth-Century Art Periodicals." *Victorian Periodicals Newsletter*, vol. 6, pp. 9–20.

· · · · ·

HAMILTON, WILLIAM
(1788-1856)

A Scottish philosopher and logician, William Hamilton developed a philosophy that dealt with the Absolute, and a **logic** that dealt with syllogistic forms. He was famous for great erudition and volatile polemics.

Born in Glasgow and educated at Oxford, Hamilton became professor of civil history at Edinburgh in 1821, and in 1836 professor of logic and metaphysics. His works appeared in the *Edinburgh Review* from 1829 on, and were compiled in *Discussions on Philosophy and Literature, Education and University Reform* (1852). The topics included: (1) The philosophy of the conditioned, which viewed thought as imposing conditions on its objects. The Absolute is unconditioned, therefore inconceivable, yet one of a pair of inconceivables must be true (e.g., either bounded or unbounded space). God is an Absolute that is unknowable but deserving of belief because of this feature. (2) Perception, which is immediate and direct (following Thomas Reid's "common sense" school) but also relative (following Kant). (3) Quantification of the predicate, which attempted to enlarge the applications of the syllogism (although this proved faulty). (4) Condemnation of English universities, which included naive statements denigrating mathematical studies as unproductive.

Hamilton's philosophy has been charged with vacillation and self-contradiction, and his style characterized as pedantic and combative. Assigned to the camp of the pious and conservative, his notions of intuitionism were battered by the empiricists, especially in Mill's *An Examination of Sir William Hamilton's Philosophy* (1865), and have since been ignored. In his day, however, Hamilton had many adherents and was considered an important contemporary philosopher.

JOEL ATHEY

Bibliography

Ryan, A. Introduction to *An Examination of Sir William Hamilton's Philosophy*. In J. M. Robson, ed., *Collected Works of John Stuart Mill*, vol. 9. 1979.

. . . . .

HARDIE, JAMES KEIR
(1856-1915)

A man of integrity, principle, and humble origins, James Keir Hardie became a legendary figure of the labor and socialist movements at the turn of the twentieth century. A founder of both the Independent Labour party and the **Labour party**, he helped shape the nature of mainstream British **socialism** as a broad alliance of diverse interests and ideas.

Hardie was born out of wedlock on August 15, 1856 in Legbsannock, Scotland, to Mary Keir, a farm servant, and William Aitkins, a miner. In 1859 his mother married David Hardie, a ship's carpenter, who raised James and two additional children in conditions of great poverty in and around Glasgow. These impoverished circumstances forced Hardie to begin his working life at age eight; by ten he was in the coal pits. Nevertheless, he attended evening school briefly, read voraciously, and by his early twenties embraced liberalism, evangelicalism, and temperance as his guiding principles. While the former would be modified by his later socialism, the latter two remained with him throughout life, reinforced by his marriage (1879) to Lillie Wilson, a collier's daughter and mother of his two children.

During the late 1870s Hardie became involved in mine union organizational work. Both the union work and a new career in journalism brought him out of the pits to settle permanently in modest circumstances in Cumnock, Ayrshire (1881). The next several years were crucial to Hardie's intellectual development, as he was buffeted between older liberal notions of self-help and class harmony and the miners' increasing union militancy. An exposure to socialist literature led Hardie to renounce his formal Liberal associations, assume an outspoken radical working-class posture, and run for Parliament as an independent labor candidate (1888). While he lost the race it brought him national prominence and support from a wide variety of left-wing advocates, and determined his subsequent path of political and organizational activity. This led to the founding of two newspapers, the *Miner* (1887) and the *Labour Leader* (1889), the establishment of the Scottish Labour party (1888), a successsful second race for Parliament (1892), and the organization of the socialist Independent Labour party

(1893). Hardie's 1892 appearance in the Commons was a singular moment in British history: the red-bearded miner with the cloth cap, red tie, and sharp tongue signalled the opening of a new era of social and political change. The capstone of his efforts was the role he played in forming the Labour Representation Committee (1900), the early name of the Labour party. A Labour M.P. from 1900 until his death in 1915, Hardie served as the Parliamentary Labour Party's first chairman (1906–1908). Abroad he sided with the moderates in the Second International, while his last years were preoccupied with opposition to World War I.

A radical, a trade unionist, a liberal in the broad sense of the term, and an evangelical Christian, Hardie steered a careful course between doctrinaire socialism and pragmatic reform. He thus helped mold the new Labour party into the open, democratic socialist force it became in twentieth-century Britain.

ALFRED COHEN

Bibliography

Hughes, Emrys. *Keir Hardie.* 1956.

McLean, Iain. *Keir Hardie.* 1975.

Morgan, Kenneth O. *Keir Hardie: Radical and Socialist.* 1975.

Reid, Fred. *Keir Hardie: The Making of a Socialist.* 1978.

Stewart, William. *J. Keir Hardie.* 1921.

· · · · ·

HARDY, THOMAS
(1840–1928)

Thomas Hardy, the last of the Victorians, lived well into the twentieth century in which he was acknowledged as both a major novelist and major poet. During his long career he developed his local area of Dorsetshire into an imaginative geographical district known as "Wessex."

Hardy, son of a master mason and a former maidservant, lived his early life in a thatch-roofed cottage in the hamlet of Upper Bockhampton, a beautiful rural area that he depicted with much charm in *Under the Green-*

wood Tree (1872) and with threatening fatalism in *The Return of the Native* (1878). Although he attended schools in nearby Dorchester, he was self-educated after his sixteenth year, when he became apprenticed to an architect. Since it was his early ambition to become an Anglican minister, he taught himself Latin and Greek and read widely in theological works. However, the reading of such works as Darwin's *The Origin of Species* and the biblical criticism of *Essays and Reviews* (1860) led to his abandoning religious belief.

Although he began his literary career by writing poetry, he turned to novels as a more certain way to publication. His first work, *Desperate Remedies* (1871) was a sensation novel, but more characteristic of his talent for peasant characterization and rural setting was his pastoral comedy, *Under the Greenwood Tree. A Pair of Blue Eyes* (1873), a love story with melodramatic episodes, caught the attention of Leslie Stephen, editor of *Cornhill Magazine*, who invited Hardy to contribute a fictional serial. For this novel, *Far from the Madding Crowd* (1874), Hardy created the first of his celebrated heroines, the headstrong, passionate landowner, Bathsheba Everdene, who captures the love of three suitors. The success of this work (many thought George Eliot was the author) allowed him to marry Emma Gifford, whose social pretensions caused Hardy grief and embarrassment as the years passed.

The Hand of Ethelberta (1876) makes it clear that Hardy was unable to write about higher social spheres, but *The Return of the Native*, set with brooding fatalism on Egdon Heath, shows that he could create genuine tragedy in the novel form. Clym Yeobright, drawn inexorably by the dark beauty of Eustacia Vye, marries her only to find that she had hoped to escape from his beloved heath. After episodes involving nighttime trysts on the heath, ill-directed love affairs, and accidental deaths, Clym is left nearly blind and overcome with guilt for the circumstantial disasters that have taken place. Neither *The Trumpet-Major* (1880), an historical novel set in the Napoleonic period, nor *A Laodicean* (1881), a melodramatic romance, nor *Two on a Tower* (1882), the story of an astronomer's conflicts between love and a scientific career, are among Hardy's successes.

His next works, however, exhibit full tragic power. *The Mayor of Casterbridge* (1886) presents the fall of Michael Henshard from his position as a wealthy grain dealer and mayor of the town when the results of an early act of drunken folly rise up to damage his life: he had sold his wife and child to a sailor at a fair. *The Woodlanders* (1887) tells the story of Giles Winterbourne and his love for Grace Melbury, whose social position sets her beyond his reach; of Grace's ill-judged marriage to a faithless young doctor; of Marty South, the peasant girl whose devotion to Winterbourne is never rewarded.

Tess of the d'Urbervilles (1891), Hardy's finest achievement, follows the pathetic career of Tess Durbeyfield who is seduced by her supposed cousin Alec d'Urberville. After her illegitimate child dies, Tess meets a young man of good family, Angel Clare, who finally persuades her to marry. When on the wedding night she tells him of her former lover, Clare leaves her, and Tess sinks into the life of a field laborer. Reunited by chance to Alec, she is discovered by Clare when he returns. Distraught, she kills Alec, and after flight with Clare, she is arrested and hanged. Hardy's comment that "The President of the Immortals . . . had ended his sport with Tess" drew widespread criticism, as did his subtitle "A Pure Woman Faithfully Presented."

The Well-Beloved, a potboiler appearing serially in 1892, preceded Hardy's naturalistic novel, *Jude the Obscure* (1895), which reflected his early struggles to educate himself. Jude Fawley, an orphaned villager, yearning to attend Christminster University teaches himself Latin and Greek, but his ambitions are blunted when he is trapped into marriage by the sensual hoyden Arabella Donn. When Arabella leaves him, he travels to Christminster, only to find that his class position blocks admission to study. His attraction to his cousin, Sue Bridehead, an impetuous feminist, leads him into a common-law marriage. Poverty and misunderstanding cause Jude's son to hang himself and the other children; Sue breaks down and returns to her elderly husband; Jude is reunited to the scheming Arabella but dies alone and neglected reciting Job's curse on the day he was born. Hardy bore such a fusillade of criticism in response to the unorthodox behavior of his characters and the horrors he arranged for their lives that he resolved never again to write fiction.

He returned to the poetry of his early years and drew together a collection of old and new work, *Wessex Poems* (1898). With this venture Hardy inaugurated a new career, during which he published seven volumes of lyrics and narratives, the most important of which were *Poems of the Past and the Present* (1901) and *Time's Laughingstocks* (1909). He developed a distinctive style that hovers between colloquial speech and overly formal archaic diction. His rhythms tend to be harsh and his syntax is sometimes stiff or awkward, but this style is not inappropriate for his view of life which shows the world to be full of sorrows, unfulfilled desires, chance disasters, lack of human communication, and griefs caused by sexual problems. Human life is seen as driven by powerful determining forces, both natural and social, but also crossed by mischance. The concept of God that appears in the poems is that of a being who has forgotten the world or who operates the universe as a blind automaton. Hardy's bleak outlook is most fully developed in his poetic masterwork, *The Dynasts* (1904–1908), an epic drama of the Napoleonic Wars. His autobiography was published posthumously under the name of his second wife Florence Hardy as *The Early Life of Thomas Hardy, 1840–1891* (1928), and *The Later Years of Thomas Hardy, 1892–1928* (1930).

RICHARD S. KENNEDY

Bibliography

Gittings, Robert. *Thomas Hardy's Later Years.* 1978.

———. *Young Thomas Hardy.* 1975.

Millgate, Michael. *Thomas Hardy: A Biography.* 1982.

———. *Thomas Hardy: His Career as a Novelist.* 1971.

Orel, Harold, ed. *Thomas Hardy's Personal Writings.* 1966.

Purdy, Richard L. and Michael Millgate, eds. *The Collected Letters of Thomas Hardy.* 1978–.

· · · · ·

HARE, JOHN
(1844-1921)

Actor and manager John Hare is principally identified with the plays of **T. W. Robertson** and the managements of the Court Theatre, the St. James's Theatre, and the Garrick Theatre.

Hare began an acting career in Liverpool in 1864. From 1865 to 1870 he appeared in the first performances of Robertson's best-known plays, most often as a comic character in older roles. As manager of the Court Theatre (1875–1879) his successes included C. F. Coghlan's *A Quiet Rubber* (1876), which provided Hare with the enduring role of Lord Kildare.

During his subsequent management of the St. James's Theatre (1879–1888), Hare championed Arthur Wing Pinero as a serious playwright with productions of *The Money Spinner* (1881), *The Hobby Horse* (1886), and *The Squire* (1887). At the Garrick Theatre (1889–1895) he continued to produce Pinero: *The Profligate* (1889) and *The Notorious Mrs. Ebbsmith* (1895), which featured Mrs. Patrick Campbell.

Hare's greatest success as an actor was in the role of Benjamin Goldfinch in Sydney Grundy's *A Pair of Spectacles* (1890). After he returned from his first United States tour in 1895, he produced the first performances of Pinero's *The Gay Lord Ouex* (1899) and J. M. Barrie's *Little Mary* (1903).

Hare popularized the tradition, started by the Bancrofts, of verisimilitude in acting through well-chosen details of characterization. His hallmark was light comedy based on the precise observation of human eccentricity.

VICTOR EMELJANOW

Bibliography

Bancroft, Squire and Marie Bancroft. *Mr. and Mrs. Bancroft On and Off the Stage.* 1891.

Pemberton, Thomas Edgar. *John Hare, Comedian, 1865–1895.* 1895.

Pope, Walter Macqueen. *St James's: Theatre of Distinction.* 1958.

• • • • •

HARKNESS, MARGARET ELISE
(1861-1923)

Margaret Elise Harkness, using the pseudonym John Law, published the novels *A City Girl* (1887), *Out of Work* (1888), *Captain Lobe* (1889; later edition entitled *In Darkest London*), *A Manchester Shirtmaker* (1890), and *George Eastmont: Wanderer* (1905). These novels offer a rare representation of slum life and political agitation during the depression of the 1880s and 1890s.

Little is known about Harkness's life. Of middle-class origins (she was second cousin to Beatrice Webb), Harkness sought to make her living by writing novels. Living in London's East End, she came to know the poor as well as well-known writers and labor leaders, among them Olive Schreiner, Eleanor Marx, and Friedrich Engels. Engels addressed one of his most famous letters on literary realism to Harkness.

Harkness's novels illuminate the daily lives of the poor, especially poor women, and so try to dismantle the prejudices of an ignorant middle-class reader. Although largely nondidactic and melodramatic, probably in order to help sales, the novels' margins wrestle with the possibilities of Christian socialism and political socialism as solutions to the East End. Too, the novels occasionally feature protofeminist voices. Werner Urlaub claims that Harkness's novels were more widely distributed than the early novels of George Gissing or other slum novels of the 1890s.

Harkness is not an undiscovered major novelist. Yet her novels are important for students of the slums, of politics, and of the position of the woman writer and should be read to counterbalance novels such as Gissing's *Nether World* or *Demos*.

EILEEN SYPHER

Bibliography

Goode, John. "Margaret Harkness and the Socialist Novel." In H. Gustav Klaus, ed., *The Socialist Novel in Britain.* 1982.

Sypher, Eileen. "The Novels of Margaret Harkness." *Turn-of-the-Century Women,* Winter 1984, pp. 12–26.

Urlaub, Werner G. *Der spatviktorianische Sozial-roman von 1880 bis 1890.* 1977.

· · · · ·

HARNEY, GEORGE JULIAN
(1817-1897)

George Julian Harney was a prominent member of the "physical force" wing of the Chartist movement. Born in Deptford, Kent, of poor parents, he received a desultory education which included a brief stint at sea. He early attached himself to radical agitators distributing copies of Henry Hetherington's *Poor Man's Guardian*, edited by Bronterre O'Brien. Such activities resulted in three short jail terms. In 1837 he founded the East London Democratic Association. In 1839 Harney took part in the People's Convention, attacking William Lovett for his moderate views. He founded the *London Democrat* and by 1842 had joined Fergus O'Connor in Leeds and edited the *Northern Star* (1845-1850). He unsuccessfully stood for Parliament in 1841, 1847, and 1852. By 1850 Harney broke with O'Connor, and he seems to have withdrawn from Chartist activities by 1853 and settled in Jersey (1855). He emigrated to the United States (1862) but returned in 1878 and settled permanently in Richmond.

Harney's revolutionary enthusiasm brought him into contact with many political exiles and groups, including Marx and Engels. The first English translation of the *Communist Manifesto* appeared in his *Red Republican* in 1850. He occasionally moderated his enthusiasm for revolution. Although described as the "first English Marxist," he was repudiated by Marx and Engels and broke with their Chartist disciple, Ernest Jones. Harney's radicalism was closer to that of the French Jacobins; he wanted to be the "English Marat."

WILLIAM STOCKDALE

Bibliography

Black, Frank and Renee Metivier Black, eds. *The Harney Papers.* 1969.

Cole, G. D. H. *Chartist Portraits.* 1965.

Gammage, Robert G. *The Chartist Movement, 1837-1854.* 1854; rpt. 1969.

Schoyen, Albert R. *The Chartist Challenge: A Portrait of George Julian Harney.* 1958.

See also CHARTISM

· · · · ·

HARRIS, FRANK
(1855-1931)

James Thomas "Frank" Harris gained renown as an author, editor, and adventurer. As editor, he sensationalized the *Evening News* during the 1880s, liberalized the *Fortnightly Review* (which he edited in 1886-1894), and revitalized the fading *Saturday Review*. He bought the latter in 1894, recruited a bright young staff including George Bernard Shaw, H. G. Wells, and Max Beerbohm, and profitably disposed of the magazine in 1898. In the United States, he bought *Pearson's Magazine* in 1914 as a forum for his socialist and anti-British propaganda during World War I. His major literary studies on Shakespeare, Oscar Wilde, and George Bernard Shaw remain remarkable documents.

Although Harris is a biased and unreliable biographer in his Contemporary Portraits series (1915-1924), he contributed to a new sort of literary criticism based on current psychological and analytical theory in *The Man Shakespeare* (1909). He also produced two works of more than passing interest in the play *Shakespeare and His Love* (1910) and the study *The Women of Shakespeare* (1911). His efforts in the *Saturday Review* were widely acclaimed as brilliant; he produced a first-class literary and political weekly magazine. Harris's place in the era was always at the center of literary and political controversy.

JOHN J. CONLON

Bibliography

Harris, Frank. *My Life and Loves.* 1925-1930. 3 vols. Abridged by Grant Richards as *Frank Harris, His Life and Adventures.* 1947.

Pearsall, Robert. *Frank Harris.* 1970.

Pullar, Philippa. *Frank Harris: A Biography.* 1975.

· · · · ·

HARRISON, FREDERIC
(1831–1923)

A prolific writer and the foremost English advocate of **positivism**, Frederic Harrison touched the Victorian age at nearly every point. His first important essay, "Neo-Christianity," in the *Westminster Review* in 1860, critiqued the controversial *Essays and Reviews*, published earlier that year. In 1865 he helped found the *Fortnightly Review*.

Harrison studied at King's College School and at Wadham College, Oxford. In 1858 he was called to the bar by Lincoln's Inn. Devoting much of his life to causes, Harrison participated in the Working Men's College founded by F. D. Maurice (1805–1872) and his Christian socialist followers, and was active on the Jamaica Committee (1866) opposing Governor John Eyre (1815–1901). From 1867–1869 he represented trades unions on the Royal Commission of Trades Unions; also in the late 1860s, he was secretary to the Royal Commission for Digesting the Law. Although he said his practice of law was never more than "desultory," he was professor of jurisprudence, constitutional, and international law for the Council of Legal Education (1877–1889). As a supporter of Home Rule he attempted to enter Parliament in 1886. In 1893 he founded the *Positivist Review*.

Harrison's interest in positivism was aroused at Oxford by Richard Congreve (1818–1899). In 1855 he met Auguste Comte (1798–1857), the father of positivism. Harrison believed that the scientific basis of positivism provided a synthesis for a disintegrating age. This belief culminated for him in the Religion of Humanity, a faith in mankind devoid of belief in the supernatural. His views were detailed in essays later collected in such volumes as *The Positive Evolution of Religion* (1913), *The Creed of a Layman* (1907), *De Senectute* (1923), *The Philosophy of Common Sense* (1907), and *Autobiographic Memoirs* (2 vols., 1911).

He produced literary studies collected as *Studies in Early Victorian Literature* (1895) and *Tennyson, Ruskin, Mill and Other Literary Estimates* (1899). His interest in history produced essays collected as *The Meaning of History and Other Historical Pieces* (1894). His love of Byzantium produced a historical novel, *Theophano: The Crusade of the Tenth Century* (1904), and a blank verse play, *Nicephorus: A Tragedy of New Rome* (1906).

Frederic Harrison was a Victorian polymath, a man of great energy and boundless interests who lived a long life and knew nearly everyone of importance during his lifetime. On the eve of his death at the age of ninety-one, he was correcting the proofs of his thirtieth book.

LARRY K. UFFELMAN

Bibliography

Harrison, Austin. *Frederic Harrison: Thoughts and Memories*. 1927.

Harrison, Frederic. *Autobiographic Memoirs*. 1911; rpt. 1977. 2 vols.

Kent, Christopher. *Brains and Numbers: Elitism, Comtism, and Democracy in Mid-Victorian England*. 1978.

Mill, John Stuart. *Auguste Comte and Positivism*. 1865.

Sullivan, Harry R. *Frederic Harrison*. 1983.

Vogeler, Martha S. *Frederic Harrison: The Vocations of a Positivist*. 1984.

· · · · ·

HARRISON, JANE ELLEN
(1850–1928)

Educated at Cheltenham and at Newnham College, Cambridge, where she later lectured in Greek, Jane Ellen Harrison revolutionized the field of classical studies by appropriating the methods of archaeology and anthropology to what had formerly been an almost purely literary discipline. Her influential writing on Greek art and religion advanced a theory of ritualistic origins of mythology endorsed by later anthropologists. Reviews of her first book, *Myths of the Odyssey in Art and Literature* (1882), established her stature: the *Athenaeum* judged that it outstripped the accomplishment of "any book produced by any man at either university" in furthering knowledge of ancient art.

The innovative character of Harrison's methodology is seen in her most important works: *Prolegomena to the Study of Greek*

Religion (1903) and *Themis: A Study in the Social Origins of the Greek Religion* (1912) approach Greek theogony through ritual and other anthropological evidence. *Epilegomena to the Study of Greek Religion* (1921) analyzes religious impulses in light of Freudian and Jungian psychology.

Harrison's early work included *Introductory Studies in Greek Art* (1885), *The Mythology and Monuments of Ancient Athens* (1890), and translations and expansions of French manuals on Greek art. Her contributions continued into the twentieth century with *Primitive Athens as Described by Thucydides* (1906), *Ancient Art and Ritual* (1913), *Mythology* (1924), and *Myths of Greece and Rome* (1927).

After World War I Harrison lectured on Russian at Newnham and collaborated on a translation of Russian tales, *The Book of the Bear* (1926). She supported women's suffrage in a pamphlet *Homo Sum* (1909) and demanded that Cambridge grant degrees to women. Though she wrote an autobiographical *Reminiscences of a Student's Life* (1925), the best record of Harrison's accomplishment remains in twentieth-century archaeological and classical studies which rely on her scholarship even when they question her interpretive conclusions.

BEVERLY TAYLOR

Bibliography

Murray, Gilbert A. *Jane Ellen Harrison.* 1928.

Stewart, Jessie. *Jane Ellen Harrison: A Portrait from Letters.* 1959.

. . . . .

HEALTH

Health in Victorian England is a complex subject. If defined as increased longevity and absence from disease, health steadily improved. Both medical advances and **public health** legislation contributed to this overall improvement. However, a close look at the upper, middle, and working classes reveals that the improvement was bestowed unevenly.

Scarlet fever, diphtheria, measles, smallpox, diarrhea, syphilis, gonorrhea, typhus, and tuberculosis took their toll relentlessly through-
out the nineteenth century. Disease was epidemic as well as endemic. From 1831 to 1833 there were two cholera epidemics and one of influenza. **Cholera** reappeared in 1848, 1856, and 1866, prompting social action in the form of public health measures. An impressive list of regulations about housing, sewerage, and water supply were enacted from 1848 onward. The statistical basis for this legislation was provided by social accountants such as Edwin Chadwick, Southwood Smith, and William Farr.

Before the 1860s, medical science had little to offer for improved health. Competing sects and quack practitioners flourished. From mid-century onward, however, physicians became more effective in treating disease as their education began to include the scientific concepts of physiology and bacterial etiology. Central registration of vital statistics under the aegis of William Farr, combined with his meticulous classification of specific diseases, facilitated a uniform method of diagnosis and, eventually, more effective treatment. By the end of the Victorian era antisepsis, the introduction of anesthesia, and advances in biology marked the emergence of vastly improved medical care.

Medical care, however, does not necessarily determine an individual's perception of health. Memoirs of Victorians are often preoccupied with details about physical complaints. In some circles, robust health seemed unladylike; and for other Victorian women it seems evident that various illnesses—perhaps psychosomatic in origin—provided a socially acceptable way to avoid the roles and duties imposed by family expectations. Disease attacked not only the soma but also the psyche. An impressive list of philosophers and authors complained of depression, anxiety, and various aches and pains. John Stuart Mill, Charles Darwin, Herbert Spencer, and George Henry Lewes all admitted to chronic debility. Knowledgeable about scientific advance, they viewed self-mastery of physiology as a means to overcome their distress. Not all among the middle class, however, were proponents of medical science. Some staunchly opposed medical advances as intrusions into nature's plan. Disease in this context was seen as a divine punishment; suffering was to be expected and even welcomed. Nevertheless, membership in the privileged classes carried the benefits of improved environment, diet, and medical care.

Many among the working classes and the poor existed in conditions that produced an undernourished and debilitated state. Laborers in many trades were considered too old to work at thirty-five or forty. Edwin Chadwick's report, *The Sanitary Condition of the Labouring Population of Great Britain* (1842), presented an exhaustive array of statistics based on William Farr's superb work describing class differences in housing, sanitation, the prevalence of disease, and the death rate. The average life span in 1840, for example, in the Whitechapel district of London, was forty-five years for gentlemen and persons engaged in professions, twenty-seven years for tradesmen, and twenty-two years for mechanics, servants, and laborers. Infant death rates were equally telling. Based on census returns for Bath in 1839, vital statistician Alexander Finlaison concluded that one-half of all children born to agricultural and other laborers, artisans, and servants died before reaching their fifth birthday, compared with one in eleven in the landed gentry.

Although overall death rates improved during the course of the century, the class differences remained. In Preston in the 1860s the death rate by age five among the upper classes was 180 in 1,000, among the middle classes 360 in 1,000, and among the industrial classes approximately 630 in 1,000. As late as 1899 the upper-class wards of Liverpool had an infant death rate of 136 per 1,000, while the poverty-stricken wards reported 274 per 1,000. A few streets had a rate as high as 509 per 1,000.

The reasons for such high rates in the face of medical and sanitary advances are a complex mix of social, economic, institutional, and political factors. The example of wet-nursing offers some insight into class differences in health. Although wet-nursing was not used as a matter of course in England as it was among the well-to-do of some Continental countries, infant feeding by artificial means was very likely to result in death until quite late in the century. If, therefore, a woman in comfortable circumstances died or became seriously ill from childbirth or was for some other reason unable to nurse her infant, the services of a wet-nurse would be obtained. The impoverished mother who undertook the role would be housed, fed, paid, and quite possibly saved from the postpartum complications that resulted from inadequate nutrition and sanitation. Her own child, however, was placed at enormous risk. In 1848–1849, for example, 347 infant deaths occurred in Westminster to mothers employed as wet-nurses.

Conditions in the factories and mills were another source of fatality and morbidity for working children and adults. Accident reports resulting from the Factory Act of 1844 give some indication of the hazards. Long hours exposed workers to fumes, dust, and poor ventilation, resulting in chronic and debilitating respiratory problems. Unguarded, unsafe equipment accounted for gruesome accidents, strained backs, blistered hands, and burned skin. Long walks to work in all weather left workers with wet feet and clothes.

Workers in seasonal trades were also subject to unpredictable environmental conditions. The men and women employed on East London docks were often required to be "on call" whether or not work materialized. Thus they had to live within walking distance, and the available housing was substandard, dark, and overcrowded. By the 1870s and 1880s street and railway building displaced many of these workers without providing satisfactory alternatives. Although middle-class housing and health were improved, the casual poor were driven to makeshift shelters which were in blatant violation of the public health acts.

Although health, defined along a number of parameters, solidly improved throughout Queen Victoria's reign, the improvement was not evenly distributed. The upper and middle classes championed both public health reforms and medical practices (such as compulsory vaccination against smallpox) meant to improve the lot of the working classes. Their motives were partially humanitarian—and also partly self-interested; sanitary reformers had taught them to see slums as reservoirs of disease which could erupt in epidemics that affected everyone. Thus the way in which they framed the reforms enhanced their own well-being, sometimes to the advantage of the poor but sometimes to their disadvantage.

ROSA LYNN B. PINKUS

Bibliography

Eyler, John M. *Victorian Social Medicine: The Ideas and Methods of William Farr.* 1979.

Haley, Bruce. *The Healthy Body and Victorian Culture.* 1971.

Jones, Gareth Steadman. *Outcast London.* 1971.

Morley, John. *Death, Heaven and the Victorians.* 1971.

Rosen, George. "Disease, Debility, and Death." In H. J. Dyos and Michael Wolff, eds., *The Victorian City: Images and Realities,* vol. 2. 1973.

Smith, F. B. *The People's Health.* 1979.

See also EPIDEMIC DISEASES; MEDICAL SCIENCE

· · · · ·

HEMYNG, BRACEBRIDGE (1841-1901)

Admired by his fellow hacks in the penny dreadful trade as a most prolific writer, Bracebridge Hemyng was the author of the successful Jack Harkaway adventure series for boys which first appeared in 1871 in Edwin J. Brett's *Boys of England.* A barrister of the Middle Temple, Hemyng preferred to make his living by churning out sensation fiction with titles like *Secrets of the Turf* (1868), *The Season at Brighton* (1870), or *Curious Crimes* (1871) and popular journalism such as the section on prostitution in the final volumes of Henry Mayhew's *London Labour and the London Poor* (1861).

Jack Harkaway's Schooldays, a rough-and-tumble imitation of Thomas Hughes's *Tom Brown's Schooldays* (1857), began the Harkaway series which traced the adventures of three generations of Jack Harkaways through eighteen volumes appearing in magazines as well as book format.

In addition to publication in *Boys of England* and the short-lived *Jack Harkaway's Journal for Boys* (1893), Harkaway appeared in Frank Leslie's *The Boys and Girls Weekly* after the publisher invited Hemyng in 1873 to break with Brett and come to the United States. Hemyng returned to England and Brett in 1877. The final volume in the series, *Jack Harkaway's War Scouts,* appeared in 1899, but it is uncertain whether Hemyng or another author actually wrote the final four volumes.

Harkaway is always a plucky fellow who enjoys the excitement of being in a scrape and the fun of getting out of it, but the series is marred by Jack's never-ending stream of cruel practical jokes, his aggressive imperialism, and his racist tendencies.

JAN SUSINA

Bibliography

Anglo, Michael. *Penny Dreadfuls and Other Victorian Horrors.* 1977.

Haining, Peter. *The Penny Dreadful.* 1975.

James, Louis. "Tom Brown's Imperialist Sons," *Victorian Studies,* vol. 17, pp. 89-99.

Johannsen, Albert. *The House of Beadle and Adams,* vol. 2. 1950.

Rollington, Ralph. *The Old Boy's Books: A History of the Old Time Journals for Boys.* 1913.

Turner, Ernest S. *Boys Will Be Boys.* 1948.

· · · · ·

HENLEY, WILLIAM ERNEST (1849-1903)

William Ernest Henley achieved prominence as a poet, critic, and dramatist. He collaborated with Robert Louis Stevenson on five dramas, including *Deacon Brodie* (1880). His critical work included editing over a dozen collections of poetry, drama, and prose as well as thirty-two volumes in the Tudor Translations series (1892-1903). His poetry, principally *A Book of Verses* (1888), *For England's Sake* (1900), and *A Song of Speed* (1903), was noted for both its traditional and novel qualities.

Like the chronically ill Robert Louis Stevenson, Henley was afflicted early in life with a form of tuberculosis. Stevenson and Henley met in Edinburgh in 1875 and began a period of collaboration as playwrights in the 1870s and 1880s. Henley also served as a model for Long John Silver in Stevenson's *Treasure Island* (1883).

Henley's poetry struck a new vein in *A Book of Verses,* which presented his own observations of hospital life with a combination of realism and sentimentalism. Yet compared to the decadence that was a growing literary force, Henley's poetry is also traditional. This is even more the case with *For England's Sake* which expresses utter chauvinism in the face of the Boer War (1899–1902). His *Song of Speed*, a work with more modern elements, celebrates a reckless ride in a Mercedes automobile. A minor but representative poet, Henley exemplifies the concerns of the mainstream middle class.

JOHN J. CONLON

Bibliography

Buckley, Jerome. *William Ernest Henley: A Study in the "Counter-Decadence" of the 'Nineties.* 1945; rpt. 1971.

Flora, Joseph. *William Ernest Henley.* 1970.

Robertson, John H. *W. E. Henley.* 1949.

· · · · ·

HENTY, GEORGE ALFRED (1832–1902)

George Alfred Henty's stories of war and empire enjoyed an enormous popularity among boys throughout the English-speaking world. Using plots based on both historical and current events, Henty produced several books annually during the last twenty-five years of his life. Schoolmasters and devoted aunts seized on Henty's books as suitable prizes and gifts, and his faithful readers marched along *With Roberts to Pretoria* (1902) and *With Lee in Virginia* (1890) or compared the English imperial system (*With Clive in India*, 1884) to the Spanish (*By Right of Conquest*, 1891) or the Roman (*Beric the Briton*, 1893). Although no exact figures exist, his sales probably totaled in the millions.

The eldest son of a stockbroker, Henty attended Westminster and Caius College, Cambridge. As a young man he served in the army's hospital commissariat during the Crimean War, managed coal mines in Wales and Sardinia, and, from 1865 until 1876, worked as a war correspondent for the London *Standard*. His health then forced him to settle down and trade real-life adventure for writing adventure tales for his "dear lads." Henty also edited several magazines for boys, including the *Union Jack*, Beeton's *Boys' Own Magazine* and *Camps and Quarters.* Henty's prolific and complex publication record continues to challenge bibliographers and collectors, but he left no private papers, thus precluding the possibility of a full-scale biography.

Henty's significance lies in his immense popularity and in the way his stories display one vein of the aggressive imperialism that characterized English public opinion during the last quarter of the nineteenth century. Henty's cheerily bellicose tales of empire exhibit none of the defensiveness, ambivalence, guilt, or fear found in the fiction of Kipling, Buchan, and Conrad. Economic necessity rather than duty motivates Henty's heroes, who reap the bounty of a world earmarked for the profit of white men. Plucky rather than sensitive, Henty's characters never trouble themselves with the moral burdens of this profit taking. Instead they regard the empire as a testing ground and a field of action during adolescence and young manhood. After passing the test and reaching maturity, his heroes return to England to enjoy the fruits of their labor in all the comforts of home. The popularity of Henty's vision of empire and the way it contrasts with other contemporary variations on the imperialist theme underscore the complexity of the imperial sentiment in late Victorian England.

GAIL L. SAVAGE

Bibliography

Arnold, Guy. *Held Fast for England: G. A. Henty, Imperialist Boys' Writer.* 1980.

Dartt, Robert L. *G. A. Henty: A Bibliography.* 1971.

Dunae, Patrick H. "Boys' Literature and the Idea of Empire, 1870–1914." *Victorian Studies,* vol. 24, pp. 105–221.

Fenn, G. Manville. *George Alfred Henty: The Story of an Active Life.* 1902.

Thompson, John Cargill. *The Boys' Dumas, G. A. Henty: Aspects of Victorian Publishing.* 1975.

· · · · ·

The Last Muster, 1875. Reproduced courtesy of National Museums and Galleries on Merseyside
(Lady Lever Art Gallery).

HERKOMER, HUBERT VON (1849-1914)

Hubert von Herkomer was one of the most successful and influential artists of the late Victorian age. His major **genre paintings** include *The Last Muster* (1875), *Eventide* (1878), *Hard Times* (1885), and *On Strike* (1891), all of which focus on a specific social problem. He was also an etcher and engraver, landscape painter, and brilliant portraitist, numbering among his subjects John Ruskin, Alfred Tennyson, and Lord Kitchener. In 1899 Herkomer was raised to the German nobility, thereafter adding the prefix "von" to his name. He was awarded a British knighthood in 1907.

Herkomer was born in Waal, Bavaria. His father was a woodcarver, his mother an accomplished pianist. The family emigrated to America in 1851, finally settling in Southampton, England in 1857. Herkomer attended the South Kensington Art Schools from 1867-1868 and briefly studied art in Munich. His work was influenced by **Frederick Walker** (1840-1875) and by contemporary German realism. In 1870 his illustrations, which often depicted scenes of poverty and distress, began to appear regularly in the *Graphic* magazine. Herkomer founded an art school in Bushey (1883-1904) and was Slade professor of fine arts at Oxford University (1885-1894). Additionally he was an author, composer, actor, playwright, and stage designer. From 1912-1914 he made and appeared in several films.

Herkomer's artistic achievement was fueled by his strong didactic impulse, willingness to experiment, and extraordinary energy. His work influenced Vincent van Gogh (1853-1890), younger-generation English artists such as George Clausen (1852-1944) and Stanhope Forbes (1857-1947), and the stagecraft of Edward Gordon Craig (1872-1966).

LEE M. EDWARDS

Bibliography

Baldry, Alfred L. *Hubert von Herkomer, R.A.: A Study and a Biography.* 1901.

Edwards, Lee M. "Hubert von Herkomer and the Modern Life Subject." Ph.D. dissertation, Columbia University, 1984.

Herkomer, Hubert von. *My School and My Gospel.* 1908.

——. *The Herkomers.* 1910-1911. 2 vols.

Mills, John Saxon. *Life and Letters of Sir Hubert Herkomer C.V.O., R.A.: A Study in Struggle and Success.* 1923.

· · · · ·

HERSCHEL, JOHN FREDERICK WILLIAM (1792-1871)

John Frederick William Herschel, the only son of noted astronomer William Herschel and Mary Pitt, took his B.A. and M.A. at Cambridge. He discontinued studies at Lincoln's Inn to concentrate on **astronomy**.

His study of double stars in northern skies produced catalogues (1824-1833) superior to his father's famous publications. His *Preliminary Discourse on the Study of Natural Philosophy* (1830) treated methodological and ethical aspects of physical science. His *Outlines of Astronomy* (1849), a paradigm of scientific exposition, had numerous editions and many translations. *Results of Astronomical Observations Made During the Years 1834-1838 at the Cape of Good Hope* (1847) was his most prestigious single publication.

An advocate of educational reform, Herschel collaborated, while at Cambridge, with George Peacock (1791-1858) to improve mathematical instruction at the university. At Capetown he proposed an inclusive system of state education for all regardless of race or creed. He served on the royal commission to investigate curricula at Cambridge and Oxford.

Herschel's contributions to **photography** include early experiments with sodium thiosulfate which produced a fixing agent superior to Louis Daguerre's (1787-1851) and William Henry Talbot's (1800-1877). He invented a photographic process independent of existing systems. His experiments with mercury chloride were used in the collodion process and his work with iron salts advanced blueprint processing. Herschel was among the earliest to use the term "photography" and he was the first to add "positive" and "negative" to the photographer's lexicon.

JOHN J. WOODS

Bibliography

Buttmann, Gunther. *The Shadow of the Telescope: A Biography of John Herschel.* 1970.

Clerke, Agnes M. *The Herschels and Modern Astronomy.* 1901.

Eder, Josef Maria. *The History of Photography.* 1978.

Evans, David S., ed. *Herschel at the Cape: Diaries and Correspondence of Sir John Herschel, 1834–1838.* 1969.

Ferguson, W. T. and R. F. M. Immelman. *Sir John Herschel and Education at the Cape, 1834–1840.* 1961.

Herschel, Sir John F. W. *Essays from the Edinburgh and Quarterly Reviews, with Addresses and Other Pieces.* 1857.

Schaaf, Larry. "Herschel, Talbot and Photography: Spring 1831 and Spring 1839." *History of Photography,* vol. 4, pp. 181–204.

———. "Sir John Herschel's 1839 Royal Society Paper on Photography." *History of Photography,* vol. 3, pp. 47–60.

· · · · ·

HIGH CHURCH

"High Church" is the most convenient and comprehensive label for one of the two great tendencies in the **Church of England**: the "Catholic" side of the church, emphasizing the role of tradition, sacraments, and authority. High Churchmen (or "Anglo-Catholics") held that the church was not the creature of the state but was instituted by God, part of one catholic and apostolic church, possessed of a divine commission and authority ordained by Christ and transmitted by the "apostolic succession" of bishops. In the nineteenth century this tendency produced a major party within the Anglican communion, the rival of the Evangelicals.

A High Church tendency had been present in Anglicanism since the days of Elizabeth, representing the alternative to Puritanism and producing a respectable body of divinity. In disfavor during the eighteenth century, some of this sober "old High Church" survived into the nineteenth (not to be confused with the "high and dry" element, concerned only with the privileges and wealth of the church). However, the movement had a virtual rebirth in the 1830s, centered at Oxford and known as the "Oxford Movement." The occasion was the admission of non-Anglicans to Parliament and advent of a Liberal government seemingly inclined to interfere in or despoil the church, which now had to assert its own authority, independent of the state. The first signal for such an assertion came from the saintly poet-clergyman **John Keble** (1792–1866), but the active leadership came from younger men: two fellows of Oriel College, **John Henry Newman** (1801–1890) and **Richard Hurrell Froude** (1803–1836), and later the Regius professor of Hebrew, **Edward Bouverie Pusey** (1800–1882), after whom the movement was sometimes called "Puseyite." Newman became the most effective propagandist through his writings, his sermons to university audiences, and especially his inspiration of the series of *Tracts for the Times* (1833–1841), which gave the name "Tractarian" to the Oxford phase of the movement. After some early success, especially among the clergy (whose office it magnified), the movement met opposition from the "low" side of the church, Evangelicals and others who saw in it an unwarranted clericalism tending to the dreaded "popery." Newman regarded the Church of England as representing a middle way (*via media*) between the extremes of Roman Catholicism and Protestantism; his opponents urged that any derogation from full-fledged Protestantism would inevitably lead to Romanism. For many, including Newman himself, it eventually did. Most of the bishops did not welcome the role in which the Tractarians cast them and condemned Newman's Tract 90 (1841), in which he argued that the Thirty-Nine Articles were not incompatible with many Roman doctrines. He submitted to Rome in 1845. Many (but not most) went with him, or converted later, when the movement received further shocks.

The Oxford or Tractarian phase ended in 1845, but not the movement. Many insisted on the rightful place of Anglo-Catholicism in the Church of England. Pusey assumed the leadership; but most of his followers were no longer at Oxford but in parishes. Oxford produced doctrines; parishes engaged in worship and the sacraments. In Anglo-Catholic hands this meant an emphasis on the element of ritual—solemn, fully vestmented, often elaborate, and sometimes imitative of Roman usages. Hence the later, parochial phase of the movement is often called "**ritualism**," which became the object of Low Church animosity, frequent lawsuits, and occasional legislation. Ritualistic priests refused to submit; persecution led to "martyrdoms" which engaged much sympathy. Eventually their place within the church had to be conceded. By the end of the century, Anglo-Catholicism was gaining support, at least among the clergy.

The Anglo-Catholic insight was the tri-polar nature of Christianity: as doctrine, as institution, and as worship, all serving toward the promotion of holiness, hence interpenetrated by the sacramental principle. Emphasizing the corporate and historical character of religion, the High Church revival was the counterpart of romanticism; but in the practical circumstances of a state church in an age of liberalism, it had to take on the character of an embattled party.

JOSEF L. ALTHOLZ

Bibliography

Brilioth, Yngve. *The Anglican Revival.* 1925.

Chadwick, Owen, ed. *The Mind of the Oxford Movement.* 1960.

——— *The Victorian Church.* 1966-1970. 2 vols.

Church, Richard W. *The Oxford Movement: Twelve Years, 1833-1845.* 1891.

Faber, Geoffrey. *Oxford Apostles: A Character Study of the Oxford Movement.* 1954.

Newsome, David. *The Parting of Friends: A Study of the Wilberforces and Henry Manning.* 1966.

See also EVANGELICAL MOVEMENT

. . . . .

HIGHER CRITICISM see BIBLICAL SCHOLARSHIP

. . . . .

HILL, OCTAVIA
(1838-1912)

Octavia Hill was a reformer and philanthropist who devised a housing management system for the poor. She was also a founder of the National Trust. Her writings include *Home of the London Poor* (1875) and *Our Common Land* (1877).

Hill came from a family of social reformers. When only fourteen, she was made supervisor of the children employed by the Ladies Cooperative Guild, a Christian Socialist enterprise managed by her mother. Through the guild, she met F. D. Maurice and John Ruskin. When Maurice added classes for women to his Working Men's College, Hill became administrative secretary and teacher (1855-1861). She also taught at a school for poor children started by her family (1861-1865).

This first-hand experience with the poor led to Hill's work in housing reform. In 1864, with financial backing from Ruskin, she purchased three houses, hoping to turn them into model lodgings for the unskilled laboring poor. She managed the buildings and worked closely with the tenants, urging self-reliance, self-respect, and communal responsibility. Her aim was to combine housing reform with reform of character. Viewing financial accountability as both a moral duty and a practical necessity, she demanded prompt payment of rent, but turned over all profits to improvements suggested by the tenants. Capital was acquired by managing the schemes as a five percent investment.

This plan proved so effective that it grew into a system involving thousands. Hill became a national figure. In 1869 she became adviser to the Charity Organization Society. The Artisans' Dwelling Act of 1875 reflects her work and concerns. In 1884 she testified before the Royal Commission on Housing and took charge of some 4,000 slum houses for the Ecclesiastical Commission. In 1905 she was appointed to the Royal Commission on the Poor Law. She also recruited and trained the many social workers required by her system of housing management.

While Hill's pioneer work in housing reform was highly regarded in Victorian Britain, her system of management was based on principles that later placed her outside the mainstream. A strong supporter of individual rights and limited government powers, Hill favored private initiative over state-supported socialism, and local reforms over large-scale subsidized housing. Central to her program for housing reform was her belief in the redeeming power of home life, which caused her also to favor a domestic role for women, though she herself was a public servant. Her ideal social worker was an educated woman, who fostered mutual sympathy between the classes by living and working among the poor as a voluntary professional. Hill's work in conservation has had clearer lasting effects, particularly the founding of the National Trust (1894), which continues to preserve for the common good the historic places, monuments, and countryside of Britain.

SUZANNE GRAVER

Bibliography

Bell, E. Moberly. *Octavia Hill: A Biography.* 1942.

Boyd, Nancy. *Three Victorian Women Who Changed Their World.* 1982.

Hill, William Thomson. *Octavia Hill: Pioneer of the National Trust and Housing Reformer.* 1956.

Maurice, C. Edmund, ed. *Life of Octavia Hill as Told in Her Letters.* 1913.

Owen, David. *English Philanthropy, 1660–1960.* 1964.

Wohl, A. S. "Octavia Hill and Homes of the London Poor." *Journal of British Studies*, vol. 10, pp. 105–31.

Woodroofe, Kathleen. *From Charity to Social Work in England and the United States.* 1974.

See also COMMONS AND OPEN SPACES

. . . . .

HILL, ROWLAND
(1795–1879)

An inventor, educator and political bureaucrat, Rowland Hill was the best known of a prominent family of Benthamite reformers. Among his reforms was the penny post, established in 1840. Awards, testimonials, honors, and some resentment followed.

Hill was born in Kidderminster, the third of five sons of Thomas Wright and Sarah Lea Hill, Birmingham Unitarian educators. The Hill family established several schools and were active radicals. Rowland Hill formulated an innovative system of school management and student governance. Trained in science, he invented scientific instruments, a printing press, and the adhesive postage stamp. In 1827 he married Caroline Pearson. He flirted with Owenism and developed interests in poor relief, colonization, and railroad management.

During the 1830s Hill funneled his energies into reform of the post office. He initiated a detailed investigation of a complicated and inefficient system and called for "A Penny Postage paid in advance for carrying half-an-ounce weight inland, from Post Town to Post Town, for any distance long or short." For a decade Hill worked from outside touting "laws of political economy" and finally prevailing over entrenched and obdurate officials. Then, through the next two decades (1846–1864), Hill ruled the post office as an insufferable tyrant. In his memoirs he depicts himself as "misunderstood prophet triumphing against adversity and ignorance." Whether or not the penny post worked is problematical. Critics complained of nepotism, disruption, and resistance to change. Nevertheless, the political and public authorities showered him with money, honors, and a knighthood. Hill died on August 27, 1879 and was buried in Westminster Abbey.

EUGENE L. RASOR

Bibliography

Daunton, Martin J. *Royal Mail: The History of the Post Office Since 1840.* 1985.

Hill, George Birkbeck. *The Life of Sir Rowland Hill.* 1880. 2 vols.

See also POSTAL SERVICES
. . . . .

HISTORICAL NOVEL

Writers, critics, and common readers continued to admire the historical novels of Walter Scott well into the Victorian period. However, they did not ignore Scott's defects; and the debasement of the historical novel wrought by Scott's immediate imitators—**Edward Bulwer-Lytton, Harrison Ainsworth,** and G. P. R. James—was recognized and deplored. The most interesting among the many Victorian historical novels are William Makepeace Thackeray's *The History of Henry Esmond, Esq. A Colonel in the Service of Her Majesty Q. Anne: Written by Himself* (1852); Charles Dickens's *A Tale of Two Cities* (1859); and George Eliot's *Romola* (1863). But most modern critics agree that the greatest historical novels after Scott's were produced by Continental writers rather than the English.

Writing in 1858, Walter Bagehot criticized Scott's failure to depict his characters' intellect and soul. Scott's use of external characterization serves him well for the anomalous characters and great historical figures of the Waverley novels, but proves unsatisfactory for his romantic heroines and heroes. Scott excels in presenting historical figures and their times just as the reader would expect them, and generally, in his realistic portrayal of human society. Bagehot particularly notes how effortlessly Scott's imagination passes from historical, martial scenes to the sentiments of his individual heroes and heroines.

But, Bagehot says, Scott's successors often have difficulty with these transitions; that may be symptomatic of the most prominent flaw in Victorian historical novels: the authors' failure to create a significant relationship between the history in the novel and its protagonist. Georg Lukács points out, for example, that both Scott and Thackeray (in *Henry Esmond*) deal with the Stuart restoration attempts of the eighteenth century. But in contrast to Scott's relatively broad, objective historical perspective, Thackeray presents through Esmond an intensely subjective one, limited to petty upper-class intrigues and aimed at exposing pseudogreatness while illuminating and exalting the virtues of Esmond. Here history serves as a screen on which the author's immediate concerns can be projected; to many critics, the concerns Thackeray expresses in *Henry Esmond* are quite personal, not intrinsically related to the historical setting, and the result is an intriguing bildungsroman but a mediocre historical novel.

Critics today fault the historical novels by Dickens and Eliot for much the same reason: lack of organic connection between the concerns and experiences of the protagonists and the historical aspects of the novels. They do admire Eliot's use of detail in *Romola* which conveys the cultural texture of Florence in the 1490s, as well as Dickens's use of grotesque characters and symbolism to recreate the French Revolution as nightmare in *A Tale of Two Cities*.

KENNETH A. ROBB

Bibliography

Bagehot, Walter. "The Waverley Novels." In Mrs. Russell Barrington, ed., *The Works and Life of Walter Bagehot*. 1915.

Fleishman, Avrom. *The English Historical Novel: Walter Scott to Virginia Woolf.* 1971.

Lukács, Georg. *The Historical Novel.* 1962. Trans. Hannah Mitchell and Stanley Mitchell.

Maynard, John. "Broad Canvas, Narrow Perspective: The Problem of the English Historical Novel in the Nineteenth Century." In Jerome H. Buckley, ed., *The Worlds of Victorian Fiction.* 1975.

Sanders, Andrew. *The Victorian Historical Novel, 1840–1880.* 1979.

Shaw, Harry E. *The Forms of Historical Fiction: Sir Walter Scott and His Successors.* 1983.

• • • • •

HISTORY AND HISTORIANS

History provided the Victorians with the dominant intellectual paradigm of their era. Appreciation of the principle that all life forms developed through time powerfully influenced Victorian science and social science; arguments for historical continuity were central to religious and political debate. The unprecedented acceleration of change sent the Victorians to the past for explanations, guidance, and authority. Influenced by both romanticism and rationalism, earlier Victorian historians strove to combine an historicist sympathy for recreating the past (inspired in part by Walter Scott) with a demonstration of the historical "laws"—both moral and political—that should shape the future. Continuing concern for making historical study more scientific in its methods led ultimately to its professionalization as a discipline.

The romantic reaction against rationalism and the quest for solutions to early Victorian political crises shaped the Liberal Anglican school of historians, the most prominent of whom were **Thomas Arnold** (1795-1842), Julius Hare (1795-1855), Connop Thirlwall (1797-1875), and Henry Milman (1791-1868). For the Utilitarians' linear and secular conception of progress they substituted a process of moral and intellectual development by which nations fulfilled God's purposes. Following Giambattista Vico (1668-1744) and Barthold Niebuhr (1776-1831), they theorized that nations, like individuals, went through the same stages of development, and that only nations at analogous stages of growth could be validly compared. **Thomas Carlyle** (1795-1881) similarly reacted against rationalism by adopting an organic and cyclical conception of change in which an abiding supernatural reality manifested itself in the changing "clothing" of human institutions and spoke through heroes necessary to the nation's social and moral health. In major historical works like *The French Revolution* (1837), *Past and Present* (1843), and *Frederick the Great* (1858-1865). Carlyle sought to recreate the multidimensionality of past experience and to identify object lessons for a society sorely in need of true faith and leadership. His disciple, **James Anthony Froude** (1818-1894), likewise hoped that his *History of England from the Fall of Wolsey to the Defeat of the Spanish Armada* (1856-1870) would provide religious and political correctives to the drift of Victorian society.

The rationalist tradition had been sustained in the work of the Scottish conjectural historians; their model of change, which established a linear and universal scale of progress and posited self-interest as the mechanism of advance, influenced later utilitarian and positivist histories like James Mill's *History of British India* (1818), George Grote's *History of Greece* (1846-1856), and Henry T. Buckle's *History of Civilization in England* (1857-1861). It also had some influence on the Whig view, which dominated Victorian historiography. From the seventeenth century the Whig interpretation sought historical authority for parliamentary limitations on the power of the monarch and tended to shape past events into a series of precedents for the political balance desired in the present. Henry Hallam's *Constitutional History of England* (1827) anticipated the Victorian generation of Whig histories, foremost of which was **Thomas Babington Macaulay's** *History of England* (1848-1855). By presenting England's revolutions as preservative of more ancient norms, Macaulay in effect made progress itself traditional and thus blunted the revolutionary potential of events like the Reform Bills. Despite his rationalist assumptions about human nature, Macaulay had an incomparable gift for imaginatively recreating past events and was responsible for establishing the importance of social history to the explanation of progress. This emphasis was continued in the work of **John Richard Green** (1837-1883) who, along with the other "Oxford school" medievalists, William Stubbs (1825-1901) and Edward Augustus Freeman (1832-1892), pushed the argument for political continuity back into England's earliest history.

Stubbs and Freeman also played a part in history's late Victorian transition from a branch of belles lettres to a professionalized discipline. They joined historians like Samuel R. Gardiner (1829-1902), **John Robert Seeley** (1834-1895), and Frederic Maitland (1850-1906) in putting scholarly demands for impartiality, thoroughness, and archival evidence above the public's desire for entertaining and uplifting narrative. University reform granted history new status as an academic discipline at Oxford and Cambridge. Because the professoriate was not successful in attaining the autonomy and authority it had under the German model, however, the study of history tended to remain subordinate to the aims of liberal education, despite the efforts of Regius professors like Stubbs, Charles Firth (1857-1936), John Bagnell Bury (1861-1927), and Lord Acton (1834-1902) to raise professional standards. Adolphous W. Ward (1837-1924) and Thomas F. Tout (1855-1929) had more success in shaping university study to professional needs at Owens College, Manchester. The move toward professionalization was facilitated by the founding of the Royal Historical Society in

1868, *The English Historical Review* in 1886, and the Historical Association in 1906.

ROSEMARY JANN

Bibliography

Brooks, Richard A. E. "The Development of the Historical Mind." In Joseph E. Baker, ed., *The Reinterpretation of Victorian Literature*. 1950.

Burrow, J. W. *A Liberal Descent: Victorian Historians and the English Past*. 1981.

Chandler, Alice. *A Dream of Order: The Medieval Ideal in Nineteenth-Century English Literature*. 1970.

Culler, A. Dwight. *The Victorian Mirror of History*. 1985.

Forbes, Duncan. *The Liberal Anglican Idea of History*. 1952.

Gooch, George Peabody. *History and Historians in the Nineteenth Century*. 1913; rpt. 1959.

Jann, Rosemary. *The Art and Science of Victorian History*. 1985.

Levine, Philipa. *The Amateur and the Professional: Antiquarians, Historians and Archaeologists in Victorian England, 1838–1886*. 1986.

Kenyon, John. *The History Men: The Historical Profession in England Since the Renaissance*. 1983.

· · · · ·

HISTORY PAINTING

History painting was defined by Leon Battista Alberti in *Della pittura* (1435) as a narrative subject employing the human figure. Seventeenth-century French theorist André Félibien des Avaux restricted the term to the monumental idealization of man's noblest actions in history or legend expressing universal truths. He ranked it as the supreme expression in painting. England adopted this theoretical primacy in the eighteenth century when Sir Joshua Reynolds promoted the "Grand Style" in his *Discourses* before the Royal Academy (1769–1790). Despite Reynolds's eloquent pleas for the universal over the specific, portraiture and historical anecdote were the more popular subjects in painting.

Artists including Benjamin Robert Haydon and Martin Archer Shee continued to promote the grand style into the 1830s. The opportunity to turn theory into practice came in 1841 when the interior walls of the new Palace at Westminster were designated for decoration. The Fine Arts Commission, with Prince Albert as president, collected data on history painting and heard testimony on Renaissance and modern European tradition. Although the commission sat for two decades, their formulation was presented in their *Report* of 1842. Monumental paintings in the palace would depict ennobling subjects drawn from national history and legend.

The frescoes in the House of Lords Chamber (1846–1848) painted by William Dyce, Daniel Maclise, C. W. Cope, and J. C. Horsley and the Arthurian frescoes in the Queen's Robing Room (1849–1864) by Dyce illustrate the theory. Virtues such as Generosity, Chivalry, and Justice are exemplified with a minimum of detail in austere, grand-scale representations. Later works, however, such as Maclise's *Meeting of Wellington and Blücher* (1859–1861) and *The Death of Nelson* (1864) in the Royal Gallery, mark a return to anecdotal specificity and narrative detail. Despite the critical reception for the works at the Palace at Westminster, and further efforts elsewhere by Frederick, Lord Leighton, Frank Dicksee, **G. F. Watts**, and others, true history painting was subsequently eclipsed by popular historical anecdote in the later Victorian era.

DEBRA N. MANCOFF

Bibliography

Boase, T. S. R. *English Art, 1800–1870*. 1959.

Mancoff, Debra N. "An Ancient Idea of Chivalric Greatness: The Arthurian Revival and Victorian History Painting." In *The Arthurian Tradition: Essays in Convergence*. 1988.

Redgrave, Richard and Samuel Redgrave. *A Century of Painters of the British School*. 1866.

Strong, Roy. *And When Did You Last See Your Father? The Victorian Painter and British History*. 1978.

See also ACADEMIC PAINTING

· · · · ·

HOBBES, JOHN OLIVER (PEARL RICHARDS CRAIGIE) (1867–1906)

The novelist and playwright who wrote as John Oliver Hobbes was born near Boston, Massachusetts. Her parents were Laura Arnold Richards and John Morgan Richards, a businessman, who moved his family to England in 1868. After schooling in Newbury, London, and Paris, Pearl Richards married in 1887 the aristocratic banker Reginald Walpole Craigie. Repelled by his dissolute life, she left him in 1891 after bearing a son, John Churchill Craigie. Influences on her writing, besides her difficult marriage and scandalous divorce, included an early friendship with classics professor Alfred Goodwin at University College; her 1892 conversion to Catholicism; her family's wealth and position, which provided a flamboyant social life among political and literary luminaries; her refusal to remarry; and, after 1898, her close friendship with a priest, Father William Francis Brown, to whom she wrote almost daily.

In her twelve novels, beginning with *Some Emotions and a Moral* (1891), John Oliver Hobbes blended social satire with abstract spirituality; moral themes like virtuous self-denial with sensation–novel plot devices; witty dialogue and flippant epigrams worthy of Oscar Wilde with serious insights into life. At her best, she revealed her religious values and her insights into relationships and mental suffering in the intelligent upper class. *Some Gods, Some Mortals, and Lord Wickenham* (1895), about the consequences of a man's unwise marriage, resembles Thomas Hardy's *Jude the Obscure*, written in the same year. *The School for Saints* (1897) and its sequel *Robert Orange* (1900), embraced by Catholic readers, follow a man's path to the priesthood, by way of conversion, novel writing, politics, and an idyllic second marriage renounced when it proves bigamous. Her last novel, *The Dream and the Business* (1906), reveals in its more realistic heroines her own personality. Among Hobbes's nine plays, only her Wildean comedy *The Ambassador* (1898) was a stage success.

If the writings of John Oliver Hobbes now seem uneven period pieces with a few quotable passages of wit and psychology, Pearl Craigie herself survives in her letters, her father's biography, and the works of others. Her lectures were parodied by Max Beerbohm and her behavior influenced Henry James's portrait of an American heiress in *The Wings of the Dove* (1902). George Moore, collaborator on her comedy *Journeys End in Lovers Meeting* (1894) and a spurned lover, drew on her sensual spirituality for *Evelyn Innes* (1898) and *Sister Teresa* (1901). Both Hardy and G. K. Chesterton commented on the bitterness she concealed under clever conversation and extravagant dress. In such paradoxes lay the contribution of John Oliver Hobbes and her works to fin de siècle life and culture.

MONIKA BROWN

Bibliography

Colby, Vineta. *The Singular Anomaly: Women Novelists of the Nineteenth Century*. 1970.

Maison, Margaret. *John Oliver Hobbes: Her Life and Work*. 1976.

Richards, John Morgan. *The Life of John Oliver Hobbes*. 1911.

. . . . .

HOLYOAKE, GEORGE JACOB (1817–1906)

A conspicuous working-class journalist, editor, and agitator for social reform for over five decades, George Jacob Holyoake is best known as a freethinker and founder of secularism and as an advocate and chronicler of the cooperative movement.

Born in Birmingham into a working-class family, Holyoake was an early supporter of Chartism and Owenite socialism, but a belief in nonviolence and a growing commitment to atheism led him to seek an alternative reform posture that eschewed both militancy and religion. Shortly after a brief imprisonment for blasphemy, Holyoake started the *Reasoner*, published weekly from 1846 to 1861, to promote socialist unity by advocating a rational, antireligious approach to reform. His writings became the philosophical platform of the Secular Society, founded in 1852. Secularism held that social harmony could be better achieved by eliminating religious irrationalism and by focusing instead on realistic efforts to improve social well-being. Holyoake also promoted cooperative trade unionism. His book *Self-Help by the People* (1858), an enormously popular history of one cooperative society, the Rochdale Pioneers, greatly enhanced his international reputation as a cooperative leader. Holyoake followed this with other histories of the movement, most notably *The History of Cooperation in England* (2 vols., 1875, 1879). A tireless editor, writer, and lecturer and an ardent supporter of Gladstone liberalism, Holyoake also encouraged labor emigration and helped raise support for the Italian patriot Garibaldi.

Holyoake's main role in the reform movement was not as an organizational leader, but as a persistent agitator for social renewal and as an informed and broadly respected spokesman for the working class.

STEVEN N. CRAIG

Bibliography

Grugel, Lee E. *George Jacob Holyoake: A Study in the Evolution of a Victorian Radical.* 1976.

See also COOPERATIVE MOVEMENT; FREETHOUGHT

. . . . .

HOME FURNISHINGS AND DECORATION

Victorians have been frequently accused of abandoning taste and common sense in their household furnishings. Until recently, their heavily carved mahogany furniture, overstuffed chairs, and endless knickknacks were excoriated as intolerable eyesores, the products of a bourgeois generation. However, Victorian decorations and furnishings have been reclaimed by antique aficionados—and by those seeking to understand the semiotics of a culture.

Victorian interiors reveal a highly stratified society: ladies lounged in drawing rooms and bedrooms furnished with plush flowered carpets, delicate furniture, and airy plants; gentlemen lurked in billiard rooms, smoking rooms, and libraries decorated in dark hues, with heavily carved furniture and dark paneling; and servants lived in small, poorly furnished, unheated rooms, often at the tops of houses, and worked in dark kitchens and food cellars, usually in basements.

Although fashions changed throughout the century, the middle classes were slow to adopt the less cluttered interiors advocated by artists like William Morris and Charles Eastlake. Interiors were crowded with as much furniture and paraphernalia as possible. Popular oracles of style, like Mrs. Haweis, argued for a casual arrangement of furniture and small tables, which in practice produced sitting rooms and parlors overflowing with randomly placed furniture. Victorian furnishings required massive effort to maintain even moderate cleanliness. An army of servants dusted, washed, brushed, and swept each room, every day. Clean clutter indicated a family's affluence.

Individual rooms were often furnished in a jumble of period styles, with little attention to historical correctness. Grecian, Elizabethan, and Gothic furnishings might adorn different rooms in a single home, with occasional Japanese or Middle Eastern accents. A. W. N. Pugin (1812–1852) helped popularize Gothic interiors in *Gothic Furniture*, and, with some help from John Ruskin, the Gothic was embraced as the most "British" style. Despite Eastlake's plea for simple, consistent home furnishing, most advisors recommended "eclectic" interiors.

Most Victorians bought ready-made furnishings, and furniture manufacturers were quick to publish pattern books, much like modern department store catalogues, to aid their customers. R. Charles's *The Compiler* assembled hundreds of detailed illustrations of furniture from all ages and countries. Although machines for cutting veneer and carving wood were used, furniture was essentially handmade, which produced sturdy pieces. Some patent inventions, like wound springs, became very popular and required fatter, rounder chairs and sofas. Many woods and metals were popular in chair and table design: mahogany, walnut, oak, kingwood, calamander, rosewood, zebrawood, satinwood, yew, elm; brass, tin, and even gold. Woods

Her Majesty's Private Drawing-Room in the Palace of Saint Cloud. Illustrated Times,
1 September 1855. Library Company of Philadelphia.

were stained, painted, and tinted to match more expensive materials. Upholsterers finished new furniture, often in the resplendent colors made possible by recently discovered dyes. Papier-mâché furniture was popular from 1835–1870. Made of pulped paper, glue, chalk, and sand, papier-mâché was pressed, molded, and baked into tea trays, chairs, letter racks, clock bodies, tables, cabinets, and card boxes. A surprisingly strong material, it was painted and sometimes inlaid with mother-of-pearl or gold leaf. Tunbridge mosaics, popularized by James and George Burrows, adorned many tabletops with geometric patterns, Berlin patterns, and naturalistic scenes.

Most rooms were stuffed with furniture, but it is possible to outline typical furnishings. An entry hall was usually more traditional, perhaps Gothic, in design, with the family's coat of arms, or other ancestral trappings, hanging on the walls, a dark wood floor, dark paneling, and heavy curtains. Less "English" in style, the slightly brighter drawing room was the ladies' domain, in which they displayed their

singing, sewing, and drawing skills. Most of all, the drawing room was an emblem of their "taste." This room was often furnished in a Renaissance or Continental style, cluttered with stuffed and round-backed chairs, sofas of every possible shape, footstools, heavily carved wood tables, bookshelves, a piano, whatnot tables, work desks, fire screens, embroidery frames, wax fruit, stuffed birds, plants, glass ornaments, and yards of Berlin-work **embroidery**. The drawing room often had a flowered or Oriental rug; sometimes a Landseer or landscape painting was reproduced on a carpet for the amazement of art lovers. Patterned wallpaper and paintings adorned the walls.

The dining room was often ponderously furnished in Gothic or "naturalistic" style, with dark woods and wall hangings, portraits of illustrious relatives, a long sideboard for serving dinners and a long, heavy table standing on curved, stout legs, surrounded by round- or straight-backed chairs. Bedrooms were more sparsely furnished and brightly colored. Particularly after about 1870, when Victorians began to worry about proper ventilation, brass and iron beds gradually replaced wood bedsteads buried in curtains. A small bedside cabinet, for the chamber pot, dressing table draped with cloth, mahogany wardrobe, chest of drawers, washstand with mirror, and toilet mirror with drapery completed the bedroom. As were the rooms in most homes, the bedroom would be heated by a small coal-burning fireplace and lit by candles (not gas).

The more functional rooms—bathroom, kitchen, and laundry rooms—were furnished simply. Bathrooms occasionally contained full-length bathtubs and even showers; many had waste water pipes and toilets. Most middle- and upper-class homeowners avoided entering the servants' domain, and therefore cared little whether kitchens, cellars, pantries, or laundry rooms were attractive. Some enterprising architects attempted to modernize kitchens and sculleries, but little progress was made until much later.

Middle- and upper-class Victorians had more money and time to spend on furnishing their homes, and women were primarily responsible for tastefully and sensibly selecting furnishings. Since no single style reigned and innumerable materials were available, many self-styled experts set out to dictate good taste. Furniture dealers furnished ideal rooms in their showrooms. Magazines like *The Lady*, *The Queen*, and *The Lady's Pictorial* arose to help dazzled housewives select patterns and materials. The experts' conflicting opinions appropriately matched the plethora of styles. Mrs. Haweis proclaimed that eclecticism was quite correct and that chairs should follow the body's shape. Charles Eastlake defended medieval furniture and simple, straight lines, and heartily attacked shaped dressers and side tables. Only much later, in the 1890s, did simpler styles and a more open arrangement of furniture become more popular.

JULIA M. GERGITS

Bibliography

Allsopp, Bruce. *Decoration and Furniture: The English Tradition*, vol. 1. 1952.

Barker, Lady. *The Bedroom and Boudoir*. 1878.

Charles, Richard. *The Compiler: Furniture and Decorations*. 1879.

Cooper, Nicholas. *The Opulent Eye: Late Victorian and Edwardian Taste in Interior Design*. 1976.

Eastlake, Charles. *Hints on Household Taste in Furniture, Upholstery, and Other Details*. 1877.

Girouard, Mark. *The Victorian Country House*. 1979.

Haweis, Mrs. H. R. *The Art of Decoration*. 1889.

Joy, Edward T. *English Furniture, 1800–1851*. 1977.

Yarwood, Doreen. *The English Home: A Thousand Years of Furnishing and Decoration*. 1956.

See also AESTHETIC MOVEMENT; HOUSEWORK AND DOMESTIC TECHNOLOGY; HOUSING

· · · · ·

HOME RULE

The term "Home Rule" came into widespread use in the 1860s to describe a moderate constitutional solution to England's Irish question or problem. This limited measure of self-government called for the restoration of a separate Irish Parliament whose existence had ended with the parliamentary union between Great Britain and Ireland in 1801. This Irish legislature, with an executive responsible to it, would have jurisdiction over domestic affairs but be subordinate to the United Kingdom Parliament at Westminster.

Home Rule was an expression of constitutional nationalism influenced by the examples of federalism or devolution in the United States, Australia, Canada, and Austria-Hungary. The movement was part of the majority tradition of **Irish nationalism** which used constitutional methods, in contrast to the minority tradition of the Fenians, the Irish Republican Brotherhood, and other groups that advocated physical force and sought a separate, independent Irish republic.

Isaac Butt (1813–1879), a Protestant barrister, formed a Home Government Association in 1870 (replaced by the Home Rule League in 1873) to advocate the cause. An Irish Parliamentary or Home Rule party grew from the league under Butt's leadership. The party won its first electoral success in the general election of 1874 when Irish voters, protected by the secret ballot introduced in 1872, elected a majority of Ireland's M.P.'s. After the broadening of the franchise in 1884, the Home Rule party never fell short of winning 80 percent of Ireland's parliamentary representation.

Charles Stewart Parnell (1846–1891), the party's leader in the 1880s, abandoned the conciliatory tactics of Butt and obstructed business in the Commons to gain British attention. Following **W. E. Gladstone's** conversion to Home Rule in 1885, Parnell and his highly disciplined Home Rulers sought to attain their goal in alliance with the **Liberal party**. Two Home Rule bills (1886 and 1893) were promoted by Liberal governments headed by Gladstone. The first was defeated in the Commons when the Liberal party split on the question; the second was overwhelmingly defeated in the Conservative-dominated House of Lords.

Three main lines of opposition explain the failure to achieve Home Rule for Ireland. Opponents of Home Rule argued that it would be dangerous and unjust to hand over Irish Protestant loyalists (concentrated in Ulster) to the mercy of a Parliament in Dublin dominated by Irish Catholics. Second, many feared that limited Irish self-government would inevitably lead to the total separation of Ireland from Great Britain and thus contribute to the dismemberment of the empire. Finally, it was widely believed in the remainder of the United Kingdom that the Irish were not to be trusted or were unsuited to rule themselves. These arguments were strong enough to defeat Home Rule, and by the time their strength had declined Irish nationalism would no longer be satisfied with the limited self-government in the Home Rule proposals.

ROBERT S. FRASER

Bibliography

Beckett, James C. *The Making of Modern Ireland.* 1966.

Curtis, Lewis P. *Coercion and Conciliation in Ireland, 1880–1892: A Study in Conservative Unionism.* 1963.

Hammond, John L. *Gladstone and the Irish Nation.* 1938.

Lyons, Francis S. L. *The Irish Parliamentary Party, 1890–1910.* 1910.

McCaffrey, Lawrence J. *The Irish Question, 1800–1922.* 1968.

Morton, Grenfell. *Home Rule and the Irish Question.* 1980.

O'Brien, Conor C. *Parnell and His Party, 1880–1890.* 1957.

Thornley, David. *Isaac Butt and Home Rule.* 1964.

· · · · ·

HOMOSEXUALITY

In the early nineteenth century there was no concept of "the homosexual" as a type of personage or state of being. The term was invented in 1869, entering the English language in the 1880s. Nor was there a concept of "the lesbian," a term largely unknown until the 1890s. Men have engaged in homosexual acts throughout history, but a homosexual identity is a uniquely modern construct. Likewise, while Victorian society condoned passionate friendships between women, a lesbian identity only began to take shape much later, despite the fact that as early as the seventeenth century women poets invoked Sappho as a source of their power.

Until 1885 British law did not define the male homosexual as a distinct entity. Rather, the law was directed against specific male-male sexual acts. Sodomy was a capital offense until 1861, and between 1800 and 1835 eighty men were hanged for this "crime against nature." In several treatises on the subject, Jeremy Bentham (1748–1832) explored the nature of the fears that bred such homophobia, urging greater tolerance of male homosexual activity.

Women were immune from the legal sanctions that prohibited two men from engaging in "sinful" sexual activity, an indication of the extent to which lesbianism and male homosexuality have vastly different histories. Under the "double standard" of Victorian sexuality, women were considered to be "passionless," although a class of prostitutes existed to cater to male lust. Moreover, "separate spheres" of male and female activity tended to segregate women of the middle and upper classes from their male counterparts. Given the existence of separate spheres and a sexual ideology that attributed little sexual passion to women of these classes, it was possible for them to engage in intense emotional and physical relationships with each other without any suspicion of impropriety. Later in the century many passionate relationships also occurred between young women in boarding schools. Nonetheless, women remained legally subordinate to men, and although physical excitement and eroticism could play a role in these relationships, men viewed them as sexually innocent and nonthreatening to the dominant heterosexual kinship system.

Intimate relationships between men were more restricted than were those between women. However, by midcentury public schools and other single-sex institutions fostered both the development of homoerotic attachments between men and male entry into a homosexual subculture, a secret world which offered meeting places and access to male prostitutes. *Teleny*, a semipornographic novel (1890s), in part attributed to Oscar Wilde (1854–1900), describes this underground world of **prostitution**, transvestism, and cross-class relations. By the 1890s public attention had been focused on this subculture through a series of police investigations. The exposure of a male brothel in the Cleveland Street scandal (1889) and the trials of Oscar Wilde (1895) led to the development of an image and label of the "male homosexual" and a typology of deviant behavior. Moreover, in 1885 the Labouchere amendment to the Criminal Law Amendment Act, under which Wilde was prosecuted, defined all acts of "gross indecency" between men, in public or private, as illegal.

Increased awareness and persecution of homosexual activity led writers to study the phenomenon. In *A Problem in Greek Ethics* (1883) and *A Problem in Modern Ethics* (1891), **John Addington Symonds** (1840–1893) suggested that man-boy love had been encouraged by the ancient Greeks and that since the homosexual condition was "congenital," "natural," and "ineradicable," it should be tolerated. In *The Intermediate Sex* (1908), **Edward Carpenter** (1844–1929) delineated the characteristics of a "third" or "intermediate" sex, challenging Victorian sexual ideology and viewing "comradeship" between men as an essential ingredient of a socialist society. **Havelock Ellis** (1859–1939) popularized the term "sexual inversion" in his book of

that title (1897). Piecing together literary, historical, and anthropological evidence of homosexuality, he distinguished between those who occasionally engaged in homosexual activity and the true "invert."

By classifying male homosexuality as a distinct "pathological condition," these sexologists paved the way for activists to argue for the decriminalization of homosexuality: if homosexuality was an innate characteristic of certain men, then those men should not be penalized. Women fared less well under the scrutiny of male sexologists. While no documented lesbian subculture existed in Victorian Britain, homoerotic friendships flourished until people who had encountered the work of sexologists began to view them with suspicion. Ellis, emphasizing the primacy and naturalness of the heterosexual drive, described in an unflattering light nongenital relationships between women as "lesbian." Others began to use the label to stigmatize women's friendships and feminist activity as aspects of "deviant" sexuality.

The existence in the nineteenth century of distinct gender roles and of women's legal subordination to men meant not only that the experience of same-sex intimacy had vastly different meanings for men and women, but also that the emergence of lesbian and male homosexual identities inevitably followed different paths.

CHRIS WATERS

Bibliography

Crompton, Louis. *Byron and Greek Love: Homophobia in Nineteenth-Century England.* 1985.

Faderman, Lilian. *Surpassing the Love of Men: Romantic Friendship and Love Between Women, from the Renaissance to the Present.* 1981.

Hyde, H. Montgomery. *The Other Love: An Historical and Contemporary Survey of Homosexuality in Britain.* 1970.

Jeffreys, Sheila. *The Spinster and Her Enemies: Feminism and Sexuality, 1880–1930.* 1985.

Plummer, Kenneth, ed. *The Making of the Modern Homosexual.* 1981.

Rowbotham, Sheila and Jeffrey Weeks. *Socialism and the New Life: The Personal and Sexual*

Politics of Edward Carpenter and Havelock Ellis. 1977.

Sedgwick, Eve Kosofsky. Between Men: English Literature and Male Homosocial Desire. 1985.

Vicinus, Martha. Independent Women: Work and Community for Single Women, 1850–1920. 1985.

Weeks, Jeffrey. Coming Out: Homosexual Politics in Britain, from the Nineteenth Century to the Present. 1977.

See also WOMEN'S FRIENDSHIPS
· · · · ·

HOOD, THOMAS (1799–1845)

Thomas Hood was a man of letters: poet, novelist, essayist, satirist, comic writer, humanitarian, editor, and engraver. He bridged the romantic and the Victorian ages; his comic verse entertained and his humanitarian poems roused his generation and its descendants.

Hood's accomplishments were remarkable not only for their variety but also for their triumph over the ill-health and financial crises that plagued his life. Perhaps his happy home life (he married Jane Reynolds in 1825 and had two children) buffered these misfortunes, even though he spent five years in financial exile in Germany and Belgium.

Hood's engraving career began to yield to literary pursuits when he joined the staff of the London Magazine in 1821, gradually becoming a "sort of sub-editor" and making the acquaintance of Hazlitt, Lamb, DeQuincey, and Wordsworth. Over the next six years he produced a range of publications: Odes and Addresses to Great People (with J. H. Reynolds, his brother-in-law, in 1825) and Whims and Oddities (1826 and 1827), both in the comic and satiric vein; National Tales (fiction) and The Plea of the Midsummer Fairies (poetry) in 1827, both serious works and both failures. Editing began to take more of his time, as he worked on The Athenaeum and his own Comic Annual (1830–1839, 1842), contributing his own pieces to both. The popularity of Hood's Own Magazine (1838) and his Ger-

man travel-sketches-cum-novel Up the Rhine (1840) did little to ease the financial crises brought on by quarrels with his publishers. Similar disputes ended his editorship of the New Monthly Magazine (1841–1843) and threatened Hood's Magazine and Comic Miscellany, begun 1844. Only the help of friends and his assistant editor kept Hood's going, until he succumbed to his illnesses in 1845.

Hood's early verse was derivatively Keatsian. The originality of his genius became manifest in his comic verse. He was a master of that undervalued device, the pun, and he showed an astonishing metrical skill. But his verse ranged beyond boisterous comic extravagance; it reveals a persistent fascination with the grotesque, the macabre, and the mysterious border between reality and dream. The humanitarian poems, among them "The Song of the Shirt" (1843) and "The Bridge of Sighs" (1844), crowned his career. Though his social concerns were anticipated in earlier poems, with these last works Hood, like his friend Dickens, stirred the social conscience of thousands and contributed greatly to early Victorian humanitarian fervor.

SUSAN DRAIN

Bibliography

Clubbe, John. Victorian Forerunner: The Later Career of Thomas Hood. 1968.

Henkle, Roger B. Comedy and Culture: England 1820–1900. 1980.

Jeffrey, Lloyd N. Thomas Hood. 1972.

Jerrold, Walter, ed. The Complete Poetical Works of Thomas Hood. 1906.

Morgan, Peter F., ed. The Letters of Thomas Hood. 1973.

Reid, John C. Thomas Hood. 1963.
· · · · ·

HOPKINS, GERARD MANLEY (1844–1889)

The English poet and Roman Catholic priest Gerard Manley Hopkins lived and died in relative obscurity, his collected poems not published until 1918. In the 1930s critics ranked Hopkins among the great poets of nature and religion.

Born into an affluent middle-class family, Hopkins was educated at Oxford, where acquaintance with the Tractarians influenced his conversion to Roman Catholicism in 1866. Upon entering the Society of Jesus in 1868, he gave up writing poetry until he felt sanctioned by his order to commemorate the deaths of five nuns shipwrecked at sea. This poem and those that followed were sent to Robert Bridges, who, along with Coventry Patmore and Anglican Canon Richard Watson Dixon, constituted Hopkins's sole audience during his lifetime. "The Wreck of the Deutschland" (1875–1876) was his first completed experiment with "sprung rhythm," Hopkins's metrical invention that gives priority to stresses rather than to the accentual-syllabic measures characteristic of modern English verse.

Hopkins's rhythms and theories of "inscape" and "instress" (pattern and energy, respectively, observed in nature and caught in his poetry) struck his friends as eccentric. But the lyrical power of poems like "The Windover" (1877), and the so-called "terrible sonnets" (1885–1889) recounting his spiritual sufferings, have earned him a reputation as a poet of great originality and technical virtuosity. In articulating his struggles with faith, Hopkins is characteristically Victorian.

ELIZABETH A. CAMPBELL

Bibliography

Abbot, Claude C., ed. *The Correspondence of Gerard Manley Hopkins to Richard Watson.* 1955.

———. *The Letters of Gerard Manley Hopkins to Robert Bridges.* 1955.

Devlin, Christopher, ed. *The Sermons and Devotional Writings of Gerard Manley Hopkins.* 1959.

Dunne, Tom. *Gerard Manley Hopkins: A Comprehensive Bibliography.* 1976.

Gardner, William H. *The Poems of Gerard Manley Hopkins.* 4th ed., 1970.

House, Humphry and Graham Storey, eds. *The Journals and Papers of Gerard Manley Hopkins.* 1959.

Storey, Graham. *A Preface to Hopkins.* 1981.

· · · · ·

HORNE, R. H.
(1803–1884)

R. H. Horne was an adventurer, editor, journalist, government official, poet, dramatist, and critic. He was acquainted with many well-known Victorian writers but his own quest to be a major literary figure was not fulfilled. His best-known poem is *Orion* (1843), and his plays include *Cosmo de Medici* (1837), *The Death of Marlowe* (1837), and *Gregory VII, A Tragedy* (1840). He is remembered chiefly as an editor of the *Monthly Repository* (1836–1837); as the editor of *A New Spirit of the Age* (1844), a collection of literary essays; and as a correspondent of Elizabeth Barrett Browning between 1839, when they first met, and 1846.

Horne served as a midshipman in the Mexican navy, fighting in the war for independence from Spain. After establishing his literary career in London, he voyaged with William Howitt to Australia in 1852. (He went to Australia as Richard Henry Horne but returned as Richard Hengist Horne—hence the subsequent confusion about his middle name.) There he held such positions as land commissioner for the gold fields (1853–1854) and territorial magistrate (1855–1869). He returned to England in 1869 and became a civil list pensioner in 1874.

Horne's life and myriad interests were similar to those of his contemporary, Leigh Hunt, for whom Horne wrote a compassionate obituary in the Australian *Southern Cross* (1859). Like Hunt, he had no genius in a particular genre; therefore he never received the recognition he apparently sought. The sheer variety of his exploits and interests, however—and the ease with which he moved from the military service to the literary life and finally to government service—make him a fascinating Victorian personality.

HANS OSTROM

Bibliography

Blainey, Ann. *The Farthing Poet: A Biography of Richard Hengist Horne.* 1968.

Forman, H. Buxton. "A Brief Account of Richard Henry Horne." In W. Robertson Nicoll and Thomas J. Wise, Eds., *Litery Anecdotes of the Nineteenth Century.* 1895

Howitt, Margaret, ed. *Mary Howitt: An Autobiography.* 1891.

Taplin, Gardner B. *The Life of Elizabeth Barrett Browning.* 1957.

Walker, R. B. "'Orion' Horne and the Bushranger Daniel Morgan." *Australian Literary Studies,* vol. 11, pp; 263-265.

· · · · ·

HORSES AND CARRIAGES

In spite of the railway's advent in 1825, at the end of Queen Victoria's reign there were still about four million horses in Great Britain, and the vast majority were working in harness. Horses hauled farm produce to market, transported commercial goods to and from railway stations, brought middle-class commuters to work, and, with fashionable carriages, provided the wealthy with public proof of social standing. Victorian horses frequently had a hard and short life, depending on the type of duty they served. The average life of a cab horse was only about two years due to stress, inclement weather, and accidents. **Anna Sewell's** *Black Beauty* (1877) shed public light on some of these difficulties.

The two most popular breeds for light harness work were the Cleveland bay and the hackney. Cleveland bays, originally established in Yorkshire in 1884, are strong, long-backed horses also useful as saddle mounts. Hackneys, developed in the eighteenth century, are noted for their stylish, high-stepping action. In addition to these were the Norfolk trotter, a large-sized trotting horse from which many racing trotter breeds are descended; the Welsh and Irish cobs, smaller but strong snd surefooted; and the Yorkshire coach horse, a cross between the Cleveland bay and the thoroughbred.

Heavier loads were pulled by one of several draft breeds: the Clydesdale (Scotland, 1877),

noted for its prominent white markings, long feathers (hair) on feet and legs, and high leg action; the Suffolk punch (1880), a compact, powerful, and docile horse; the Percheron (from France), a strong, short-legged, yet agile breed; and the Shire (1878), a huge, massive animal capable of moving enormous loads. Ponies were used as economical pack animals, for hauling coal in mines, and as saddle mounts for children.

In 1814 the number of carriages in England was about 60,000; this had increased to over 500,000 by 1901. Part of the increase was due to the spreading use of macadamized pavement, which allowed the relatively easy passage of iron-rimmed wooden carriage wheels. Most Victorian carriages were descended from the *coach,* which was a large, heavy, enclosed four-wheeled carriage with two inside seats, an elevated seat in front for the driver, and an additional seat or room for luggage at the rear. The *mail coach* carried paying passengers, mail on the top, and a guard at the rear. A *hackney coach* was any coach for hire. The *coach-and-four* (usually ceremonial) was drawn by four horses. Gradually, after the 1840s, the coach succumbed to the railway, although it was revived as a popular means of tourist excursions at the end of the nineteenth century. A privately owned coach used for leisure travel was known as a *drag.* A *diligence* was a large, compartmentalized coach which held up to sixteen people.

A popular means of public transport introduced in 1829 was the *omnibus,* which carried twelve passengers on longitudinal benches inside a cramped compartment, and ten outside on an upper deck reached by a ladder or narrow iron steps. The whole contraption including driver and conductor was drawn by two horses, usually Percherons. The first horse-drawn *tram* opened in 1858, but trams did not become widely used until electrified at the end of the nineteenth century.

Four-wheeled, two-horse, privately owned carriages included the *barouche* (or *calash*), an open carriage suspended on C-springs with two transverse facing seats; this was succeeded by the *landau,* which was a little more weatherproof. The *brougham,* first built in 1838, was one of the most popular middle-class substitutes for the coach. It was a light (one-horse) enclosed carriage, driven by a coachman, equally suited for town or country. A heavier version of the brougham used for hire was the *clarence*, better known as the "growler" cab because of the deafening noise it made on macadam roads. The *phaeton* was a high, open, doorless, four-wheeled, sporty conveyance most popular in 1790. This was replaced by the elegant *Victoria* in 1844, and the *wagonette* in 1843, a cheaper middle-class alternative to the brougham.

Lighter, sporty, two-wheeled conveyances were drawn by one horse. A very popular Victorian taxi was the *hansom*, originally designed in 1834 but modified in 1836. The distinctive feature of this low, snug, private, and stylish carriage was the elevated driver's seat at the rear. Doorless descendents of the French *chaise* included the *gig*, ancestor to the *cabriolet*, which had a folding top; and the *curricle*, a gig drawn by two horses and popular with men-about-town. A *dog cart*, originally designed to carry sporting dogs in the ventilated boot, became a popular all-purpose light vehicle for short errands.

SARA A. HELLER

Bibliography

Clabby, John. *The Natural History of the Horse.* 1976.

Dent, Anthony. *The Horse Through Fifty Centuries of Civilization.* 1974.

Goodall, Daphne Machin. *Horses of the World.* 1965.

Huggett, Frank E. *Carriages at Eight: Horse-Drawn Society in Victorian and Edwardian Times.* 1979.

Quennell, Marjorie and Charles Quennell. *A History of Everyday Things in England.* 6th ed., 1961.

See also RACING AND RACEHORSES; TRANSPORTATION, URBAN

· · · · ·

HOSPITALS

Voluntary hospitals were first founded in the eighteenth century and provided medical treatment for the sick poor unable to afford fees demanded by physicians and surgeons. Paupers, however, were to receive medical treatment from the parish under the Poor Law; thus there may have been more sick in the **workhouses** than in the hospitals in the early nineteenth century. In London between 1720 and 1760 were founded 5 general hospitals, 3 lying-in and 2 special hospitals. Three general hospitals and 11 special hospitals were added in the first four decades of the nineteenth century. In the provinces there were 38 hospitals by 1800, 114 by 1840. Voluntary hospitals in England and Wales held approximtely 4,000 available beds in 1800, 6,850 in 1836, and 11,848 in 1861.

It was, however, only in the second half of the nineteenth century with the advent of antiseptic and aseptic techniques and the development of a germ theory that hospitals could be truly effective and freer from the dangers of cross-infection. Yet with rapid population growth and urbanization there was increased demand for every kind of medical provision including that undertaken in hospitals.

Voluntary hospitals were usually founded on local initiative, often by local dignitaries, the clergy, the nobility, and others of the social elite. Funding came by means of a subscription list which entitled the subscriber to play a part in the administration of the hospital. Subscribers also had the right to nominate a certain number of patients to the hospital during the year, the number depending on the amount of money subscribed. The only way to enter a voluntary hospital was on the recommendation of a subscriber (except for urgent or accident cases). The hospitals also received donations and many undertook fund raising to supplement the subscription list.

The medical staff of the hospitals provided medical services generally without payment. An honorary appointment conferred prestige, and many practitioners built up their private practice on the strength of a reputation derived from their success in hospital work. Paid staff included the apothecary, hospitaler, and matron. Hospital nurses were more servants than medical attendants and were, until the 1850s, required to undertake cleaning duties.

The efficacy of the voluntary hospital system in the eighteenth and nineteenth centuries has been seen as minimal; indeed, the hospitals have been called "gateways to death." In the nineteenth century William

Farr and **Florence Nightingale** presented the view that hospitals killed more people than they cured, and often from an affliction other than that with which they were admitted. This viewpoint has, however, been qualified by research which suggests a relatively low rate of mortality, if only because the admission policy of hospitals often excluded those most at risk.

Admissions to voluntary hospitals were limited according to certain criteria. The hospitals were available only to the "deserving poor" who did not have access to any other medical provision. A prospective patient needed to be nominated by a subscriber and thereby certified as a suitable candidate for charity. Additional rules varied between hospitals. Hull General Infirmary, for example, required a deposit from patients of 10 shillings from which was deducted laundry costs. Caution money to defray the cost of a funeral in the event of death was demanded by some institutions. There were also restrictions to entry on medical grounds. The hospitals were reluctant to admit pregnant women, the chronically sick, and sufferers of infectious diseases. The rules of Liverpool Infirmary stated that no person who was dying, incurable, or suspected of having the smallpox or other infectious disease would be admitted as an inpatient, or if inadvertently admitted, be allowed to stay.

Lying-in hospitals developed separately and were created as specialist institutions in the same manner as hospitals for infectious diseases. The founding of lying-in hospitals largely relied on the initiative of doctors who had specialized in obstetrics. Other specialist hospitals developed in the nineteenth century to cover areas neglected by the general hospitals, including children's hospitals, of which the first was Liverpool Children's Hospital (1851), and eye hospitals. The end of the 1850s saw the spread of hospitals into rural areas in the form of "cottage hospitals."

The Poor Law workhouse provided medical treatment to paupers not eligible to enter the voluntary hospital and to those suffering from epilepsy, tuberculosis, and venereal disease. Conditions for care of the sick in the workhouse were generally worse than in voluntary hospitals and only improved when pressure was brought to bear in the second half of the nineteenth century by philanthropists, doc-

tors, and nurses. Pauper hospitals were established after revelations concerning workhouse conditions in the 1860s, and separate infirmaries were encouraged.

One impetus to the hospital movement of the nineteenth century was the need for hospitals as teaching and research centers. This development meant more money and prestige for those medical practitioners with hospital appointments who could now charge a fee for both teaching duties and medical services. It also led to a growing demarcation between the general practitioner and the consultant. Nursing care improved due to better training in schools, the most famous of which is that started by Florence Nightingale at St. Thomas's Hospital in 1860.

PHILIP SWAN

Bibliography

Abel-Smith, Brian. *The Hospitals, 1800–1948: A Study in Social Administration in England and Wales.* 1964.

Sigsworth, E. M. "Gateways to Death? Medicine, Hospitals and Mortality, 1700–1850." In Peter Mathias, ed., *Science and Society.* 1972.

Smith, Francis B. *The People's Health, 1830–1910.* 1979.

Waddington, Ivan. "The Role of the Hospital in the Development of Modern Medicine: A Sociological Analysis." *Sociology,* vol. 7, pp. 211–225.

Woodward, John. *To Do the Sick No Harm: A Study of the British Voluntary Hospital System to 1875.* 1974.

See also CHILDBIRTH; MEDICAL EDUCATION; MEDICAL PRACTICE; NURSING

. . . . .

HOUSEWORK AND DOMESTIC TECHNOLOGY

"Housework" meant far different things to women of different classes in Victorian England. Wives of wealthy men were responsible for overseeing as many as forty women

servants (menservants were usually the husband's responsibility), but a housekeeper would handle all accounts, hire and train servants, and supervise day-to-day activities. Middle-class women managed without a housekeeper and did their own accounts, menu planning, and light cleaning, although they generally had at least two servants. Poor women lived in subhuman housing, with every day a struggle for survival. For many of them, housework meant income, since many became "maids-of-all-work," the most common type of servant.

Because the industrial revolution was slow to reach the home, cleaning and cooking were physically demanding; it was perhaps because servants were such cheap labor that improved methods arose only late in the century. Households made their own cleaning supplies, for example. Books and magazines provided recipes for soaps, acids, and other solutions to supplement simple traditional recipes. Potatoes smashed into a pulp and mixed with water were used to clean curtains; vitriol (a mild form of sulfuric acid) and lemon juice removed stains from marble. Before a room was cleaned, the fireplace had to be swept, blacked, polished, and restocked with coal. After the coat dust settled, rugs were swept and taken outside for thorough beatings. Floors were dusted, washed, and polished; walls were periodically washed down; and furniture, knickknacks, and wall hangings were dusted. Candleholders were cleaned and replenished; tallow or kerosene lamps were refilled and new wicks added. In bedrooms, chamber pots and slop buckets were emptied; water was heated and carried up for washing. Housekeepers fought a continual battle with bedbugs and roaches. Sometimes maids seduced bugs with bowls of beer and other times slaughtered them with poisons mixed with oil.

Maintaining an orderly house was an arduous job. In London, there was a never-ending battle with "blacks" (small pieces of soot that flew in at all apertures), inadequate **plumbing**, and faulty ventilation. In the country, fresh air helped with ventilation and sanitation, but problems of supply arose—it was difficult to purchase a variety of vegetables and meats—and houses in the country were often older and less convenient buildings. Hannah Cullwick (1833–1909), a maid-of-all-work most of her life, notes in her diaries that

her work often began before 5:00 a.m. and continued until 11:00 p.m. On a typical day, she cleaned the stove flues, started the coal fire, scrubbed the front stoop, black-leaded the fire grates, cleaned the sitting room, set the dining-room table, and finally cooked breakfast—all before 8:00 a.m. While the family ate breakfast, she finished tidying the front hallway and parlor, cleaned the kitchen, and began collecting the slop water from the bedrooms. Although Cullwick was proud of her ability to work hard, her work load was not unusual.

Laundry disrupted the household routine and was therefore done as seldom as possible; one advantage of wealth was having enough clothing and linen so that washday could come only every six weeks. Servants might rise as early as 2:00 a.m. to begin heating large cauldrons of water; inefficient soaps made it necessary to beat and boil soiled clothing to get it clean; major physical effort was required to wring out sheets and other heavy items; and drying not only depended on the weather but also, in urban areas, might leave the newly washed clothes grey with soot from the outside air. In middle-class homes the housewife usually shared the work, at least to the extent of doing most household chores so the cook and other servants could give full time to washing; and the family probably ate cold meals or leftovers on washday.

Employers often demanded unrealistic devotion and perpetual work from servants. Few Victorian homes were clean by modern standards—it was simply impossible—but most servants worked nearly continuously, six days a week. In *A Woman's Thoughts About Women* (1861), Dinah Craik chastizes middle-class women for forgetting that their servants are sisters, to whom they owe respect and mercy. The technological innovation that accumulated so rapidly in other areas had little effect on housework until late in the century and even then spread slowly; laborsaving inventions were generally found only in wealthy homes at the end of the World War I.

The most dramatic change in household technology was the spread of domestic piped water. Until late in the century obtaining and transporting water from a stream, pump, or standpipe was an onerous daily task which, in poorer families, generally fell to older children. In more prosperous neighborhoods each house would have a cistern and contract with a waterman to fill it periodically from a water cart. When piped water arrived it provided the luxury of unlimited supplies for cleaning, washing, and sanitation.

Cooking in prosperous households was done on the closed iron range heated by coal or wood, which had been introduced early in the nineteenth century; the poor used a kettle or grill over an open fire. Almost all houses were heated by coal fires in open grates; despite the dirt and labor of coal fires, even the wealthy generally resisted such innovations as closed Franklin stoves or hot-water central heating. Gas and electricity would eventually save the labor of hauling coal, tending fires, and filling lamps, as well as improving comfort and cleanliness, but they were in very limited domestic use during Victoria's reign. Gas began to be installed for lighting in newly built homes during the 1880s and 1890s. Experimental gas cooking stoves were exhibited as early as the 1820s, but the innovation was rarely used in homes until the 1880s. **Electricity** was used for public and industrial purposes in the same era, but although there were demonstrations of electric cooking and ironing in the 1890s, the domestic use of electricity was restricted to a few wealthy tinkerers who had their own generating plants installed. As other kinds of waged work became more attractive to women and the number of servants began to fall, women in the middle and even upper classes took on more of the household labor; a gas range and hot-water heater in the kitchen could perhaps substitute for the scullery maid whose duty had been to assist the cook with the dirtiest and heaviest parts of her job.

JULIA M. GERGITS

Bibliography

Cullwick, Hannah. *The Diaries of Hannah Cullwick, Victorian Maidservant.* 1984. Ed. Liz Stanley.

Davidson, Caroline. *A Woman's Work Is Never Done: A History of Housework in the British Isles, 1650–1950.* 1982.

See also FOOD AND DIET; HOME FURNISHINGS AND DECORATION; LIGHTING

· · · · ·

HOUSING

While the Victorian country house has received a great deal of attention from scholars, most Victorians were accommodated in much less glamorous types of housing including cottages, cellars, rows, flats, and suburban developments. The Victorian age witnessed dramatic variations in the quantity and quality of housing available for the rural and urban working classes as well as for the middle classes.

Middle-class Victorian housing has not received the same degree of attention as the more highly visible slums of Britain's industrial cities. The Victorian middle class included a wide range of economic and social levels ranging from the great industrialists to the shopkeepers and clergy.

Many middle-class Victorians fled from the inner cities to housing estates and suburbs. The Victorian suburb was the result of the separation of the home from work and of improved public transportation. In their desire for space and privacy, Victorian middle-class families increasingly occupied detached houses. Many building developers catered to their middle-class patrons by providing attractive scenery, including parks and trees, by imposing restrictive convenants on buildings, and by insuring privacy with locked gates. In the Park Estate in Nottingham, the residential nature of the middle-class estate was ensured by the absence of churches, schools, pubs, etc. Middle-class housing stressed privacy and space with quiet and attractive neighborhoods.

An upper middle-class family might have a ten-room house with six bedrooms and a bathroom with a bath and piped water supply. Privacy and segregation were encouraged within the middle class houses; dining rooms, drawing rooms, libraries, etc. served specific functions. Middle-class houses were also designed to display the wealth and status of the owners.

Victorian housing reformers tended to contrast the idyllic housing of rural laborers in quaint thatched cottages with the squalor and filth of urban workers' row houses, but although scholars must depend upon contemporary descriptions by humanitarian and government inspectors, it seems likely that many rural laborers also lived in overcrowded and unsanitary conditions. A close look at the romanticized thatched cottage reveals inadequate space and sanitation facilities. One government survey found in 1851 an average of 4.4 persons per cottage; single-bedroom homes accommodated four persons per bedroom with each bedroom averaging 10 feet by 10 feet. Many Victorian observers made note of the possibilities for incest and immorality when whole families shared the same bedroom.

Because of the low wages paid to farm workers, most speculative builders found it uneconomical to build for the rural housing market. While some major landowners provided subsidized housing for the tenants of their estates, most rural landlords rented their housing from small builders and tradesmen in rural villages. While farm servants were generally housed on the farm or estate, many day laborers had to find accommodation in nearby villages, often at a considerable distance from the fields. Some farm workers were forced out of the "closed parishes," often dominated by a paternalistic landlord, to an "open parish" in a nearby village with overcrowded and unsanitary housing often owned by a small proprietor.

Evidence given by witnesses before several royal commissions in the 1880s and 1890s suggests that there had been some general improvement in the quality of rural housing by the end of the century. One or two bedrooms had increased to two or three bedrooms and a kitchen or scullery had been added to the living room along with an external water closet.

Census returns and reports of the registrar general make it quite evident that urban overcrowding was a statistical reality. Using a criterion of two or more persons per room, **Charles Booth** (1840–1916) calculated in his *Life and Labour of the People in London* series that in the 1880s 1,294,072 persons or 31.5 percent of the total population of London were living in overcrowded conditions.

There was little agreement among Victorian housing reformers regarding the causes and effects of urban overcrowding. Although most middle- and upper-class observers believed that overcrowding threatened the social order and social stability, there was little agreement regarding the other perceived effects: the threat to established institutions such as the church, marriage, and family; poor health and sanitation; the association of the working classes with criminals and paupers; social segregation; and excessive drinking and immorality. There was even less agreement about the causes of overcrowding. For many Victorians overcrowding was a function of low or irregular wages; the poor simply lacked the money to pay for adequate housing. For others, overcrowding reflected moral failure; the poor were themselves responsible for their own poverty. Other causes given for overcrowding included high rents, the migratory habits of the poor, railway demolition schemes, and street improvements.

Many reformers concentrated on the sensational and visibly overcrowded housing of the working classes who occupied cellars, common lodging houses, and tenements (houses that had been subdivided into separate rooms). Speculative builders began to build the back-to-back row houses; each house had windows and doors only on the front walls. The more skilled urban worker might live in a terraced house with two ground-floor rooms and two bedrooms above with a garden in the rear. Multistory tenement housing was provided for a small minority of the Victorian working classes by philanthropic societies like the Peabody Trust. The majority of the working-class housing in Victorian Britain was provided by the individual speculative builder.

The passage of the Public Health Act of 1875 and the adoption by local authorities of building by-laws saw general improvement in the physical construction of working-class housing, although by-laws were permissive and applied only to new construction. Late Victorian by-law housing often consisted of terraced houses with improved water and sanitary systems. A skilled worker might occupy a terraced house with three rooms downstairs and two to three rooms upstairs; the more respectable house would include a parlor. By the end of the Victorian age, the poorest of the working class still occupied one and two rooms in rows of back-to-backs.

The quantity and quality of housing for the majority of Victorians did show a gradual improvement by the end of the century. The middle classes along with the more prosperous working classes enjoyed an increasingly comfortable standard of housing; a large number of rural and urban poor were still badly housed as the age drew to an end.

NEIL KUNZE

Bibliography

Burnett, John. *A Social History of Housing 1815–1970.* 1978.

Daunton, M. J. *House and Home in the Victorian City: Working-Class Housing 1850–1914.* 1983.

Dyos, H. J. and Michael Wolff, eds. *The Victorian City: Images and Realities.* 1973. 2 vols.

Englander, David. *Landlord and Tenant in Urban Britain 1838–1918.* 1983.

Gauldie, Enid. *Cruel Habitations: A History of Working-Class Housing 1780–1918.* 1974.

Mingay, G. E., ed. *The Victorian Countryside.* 1981. 2 vols.

Muthesius, Stefan. *The English Terraced House.* 1982.

Quiney, Anthony. *House and Home: A History of the Small English House.* 1986.

Rubenstein, David. *Victorian Homes.* 1974.

Simpson, M. A. and T. H. Lloyd, eds. *Middle-Class Housing in Britain.* 1977.

Sutcliffe, Anthony, ed. *Multi-Storey Living: The British Working Class Experience.* 1974.

Wohl, Anthony S. *The Eternal Slum: Housing and Social Policy in Victorian London.* 1977.

See also SUBURBS AND PLANNED COMMUNITIES

. . . . .

HOUSMAN, ALFRED EDWARD
(1859–1936)

The author of *A Shropshire Lad* (1896), A. E. Housman also published *Last Poems* (1922) and, posthumously, *More Poems* (1936) and *Some Poems, Some Letters and a Personal Memoir* (1937). He also wrote *The Name and Nature of Poetry* (1933) and was a classical scholar who studied such figures as Juvenal, Aeschylus, Sophocles, and Euripides.

Housman, born near the Shropshire Hills, attended St. John's College, Oxford. In 1892 appointed to the chair of Latin at University College of London University and in 1911 named professor of Latin at Cambridge, Housman's fame was nonetheless earned as the author whose poems were composed between 1890 and 1895 in London while working at the British Patents Office. The lyric series *A Shropshire Lad* reveals focused craftsmanship and recurrent themes: mutability, nature, beauty, patriotism, pessimism. Exhibiting the townsman's bright nostalgia for the countryside, the poetry is tinged with a bracing melancholy as in "Loveliest of Trees, The Cherry Now"; or his unadorned precision may reveal a unique mixture of the colloquial and allusive as in his "Terence, This Is Stupid Stuff" where the persona stoically argues that poetry can immunize one against the pains of life.

Called a best-loved poet, Housman was personally taciturn. His critical reputation has undergone several reevaluations. Modest praise in youth was followed by Georgian worship; he influenced figures such as John Masefield and W. H. Auden. Accessible alike to common readers and critics, Housman's strengths are resonant pastoral fantasies, dramatic flair, sparse ornamentation, and irony.

SANDRA PARKER

Bibliography

Carter, John and John Sparrow. *A. E. Housman: A Bibliography.* Rev. ed., 1982.

Graves, Richard. *A. E. Housman: The Scholar Poet.* 1979.

Houseman, A. E. *Complete Poems.* Ed. Basil Davenport and Tom Burns Haber. 1959

Leggett, Bobby J. *The Poetic Art of A. E. Housman.* 1978.

. . . . .

HOWARD, ROSALIND, COUNTESS OF CARLISLE
(1845–1921)

Rosalind Howard, ninth countess of Carlisle, was a dedicated supporter of Home Rule for Ireland, a temperance reformer, and a fighter for women's suffrage. Daughter of the second baron Stanley, she married George

Howard in 1864; he succeeded to the title earl of Carlisle in 1889.

A radical Liberal, Rosalind Howard was a "Little Englander" and opposed the Boer War. Converted to teetotalism in 1881, she became president of the North of England Temperance League as well as a vice-president of the United Kingdom Alliance, a prohibitionist organization. In 1903 she was elected head of the National British Women's Temperance Association.

Rosalind Howard was also committed to the fight for women's suffrage. Opposing leading members of the Women's Liberal Federation, including its president, Mrs. Catherine Gladstone, she succeeded in 1893 in persuading the federation to adopt women's suffrage as a major objective. The following year she was elected president of the federation. In addition to her work for suffrage, she fought for women's equality in other spheres, including trade unions and public office.

LILIAN LEWIS SHIMAN

Bibliography

Henley, Lady Dorothy. *Rosalind Howard, Countess of Carlisle.* 1958.

Roberts, Charles H. *The Radical Countess: The History of the Life of Rosalind, Countess of Carlisle.* 1962.

See also TEMPERANCE MOVEMENT

. . . . .

HOWITT, MARY BOTHAM (1799–1888) AND HOWITT, WILLIAM (1792–1879)

William and Mary Howitt were writers, editors, and translators whose 180 full-length works and hundreds of articles are a register of Victorian thought about literature, art, religion, and social change.

The Howitts were both born to Quaker families and educated under Quaker tutelage, he at Ackworth and Tamworth and she at schools in Croyden and Sheffield, as well as at home in Uttoxeter, where they married on April 16,

1821. William Howitt briefly tried to make a living as a chemist before both turned to literature. His *Rural Life of England* (1838) and *Visits to Remarkable Places* (1840) helped arouse popular interest in English folk ways and rural life. Together they published their first works of poetry: *The Forest Minstrel* (1823) and *The Desolation of Eyam* (1827). Other joint productions include *The Literature and Romance of Northern Europe* (1852) and writing for and editing *Howitt's Journal* (January 2, 1847–June 24, 1848).

The Howitts' interest in religious matters is reflected in William's controversial *A Popular History of Priestcraft* (1833) and in their own spiritual journey from the Society of Friends to Unitarianism, spiritualism, and, for Mary Howitt, the Church of Rome. Mary Howitt introduced Swedish novelist Fredrika Bremer to English readers, translating *Neighbours* (1842) and other Bremer works. In 1852 William Howitt went with his two sons to search for gold in Australia; his experiences are recorded in *A Boy's Adventures in the Wilds of Australia* (1854), *Land, Labour, and Gold* (1855), and *Tallangetta* (1857). His other significant works include *Homes and Haunts of the Most Eminent British Poets* (1847) and *Woodburn Grange* (1867). Mary Howitt's other notable works, *Wood Leighton* (1836) and two children's books, *The Children's Year* (1847) and *Our Cousins in Ohio* (1849), incorporate much personal material, as does her *Autobiography* (1889), edited by her daughter Margaret.

Though few of their works are still read, the Howitts were important in their time as supporters of the romantic poets, the Pre-Raphaelites, electoral reform, women's rights, improved factory conditions, international copyright laws, and other significant Victorian movements.

CAROL A. MARTIN

Bibliography

Lee, Amice. *Laurels and Rosemary: The Life of William and Mary Howitt.* 1955.

Walker, Mary Howitt. *Come Wind, Come Weather: A Biography of Alfred Howitt.* 1971.

Woodring, Carl Ray. *Victorian Samplers: William and Mary Howitt.* 1952.

. . . . .

HUGHES, ARTHUR
(1832–1915)

Painter Arthur Hughes, although never a member of the brotherhood, was influenced by the Pre-Raphaelites, as evident in his meticulous attention to detail and his jewel-toned palette. He is best known for inventions upon themes from Tennyson and his interpretation of chivalric imagery.

Born in London in 1832, Hughes enrolled in the School of Design under the tutelage of Alfred Stevens in 1846. In the following year he transferred to the Royal Academy Schools and won a silver medal for antique drawing in 1849. A copy of the journal *The Germ* introduced him to the work of the **Pre-Raphaelite Brotherhood** in 1850, and their effect upon his style is seen in his evocative portrayal of *Ophelia* (Manchester City Art Gallery) exhibited at the Royal Academy in 1852. In subsequent years the influence of John Everett Millais would shape the colorism and poignant expression that distinguished his style.

Hughes earned praise from John Ruskin in 1856 with *April Love* (Tate Gallery, London), inspired by Tennyson's *The Miller's Daughter* and innovative for its daring juxtaposition of color. In 1857 he participated in Dante Gabriel Rossetti's ill-fated Oxford Union murals project, and chivalric subjects, including *The Knight of the Sun* (c. 1860; private collection), entered his repertoire. In 1858 Hughes retired to the suburbs with Tryphena Foord, his wife since 1855. He turned to sentimental subjects, such as *Home from the Sea* (1863; Ashmolean Museum, Oxford), and illustrated books, including editions of Tennyson's *Enoch Arden* (1866) and Christina Rossetti's *Sing Song* (1872). The late years of his career were marked by a diminution of activity, but his Pre-Raphaelite colorism and sensibility remained consistent until his death in Kew Green in 1915.

DEBRA N. MANCOFF

Bibliography

Gibson, Robin. "Arthur Hughes: Arthurian and Related Subjects of the Early 1860's." *Burlington Magazine*, vol. 112, pp. 451–456.

Wood, Christopher. *The Pre-Raphaelites*. 1981.

. . . . .

HUGHES, THOMAS
(1822–1896)

Famous as the author of *Tom Brown's School Days* (1857), Thomas Hughes is apt to be forgotten as the radical M.P., legal counsel, and parliamentary watchdog for the cooperative and trade union movements and for the United States. The gusto, exuberance, and simple virtues of Tom Brown reappear in the dedicated energies and frequent blunders of the statesman.

In *Tom Brown at Oxford* (1861), his only other book worth reading, the nice hearty youth evolves into a troubled Christian socialist. Hughes joined F. D. Maurice's group in 1848, when it was founded, and was called to the bar the same year. Although he was chiefly useful, as a boxer, for keeping order at public meetings, he was to become a more genuine and longer-lasting socialist than Maurice, concerned especially with cooperatives and the laws relating to them. From 1854 he ran Maurice's Working Men's College.

Tom Brown's School Days, which made Hughes a national figure, has colored the picture of the English **public school** from that day to this. No doubt his fame helped when, at Lambeth in 1865, he became the first person ever elected to Parliament with trade union endorsement. He secured reforms in labor law, but his real enthusiasm was for cooperatives for production (rather than consumption). The victory of the consumer side of the movement was the defeat of his greatest hope.

ELLIOT ROSE

Bibliography

Briggs, Asa. *Victorian People*. 1955.

Mack, Edward C. and W. H. G. Armytage. *Thomas Hughes*. 1952.

Worth, George J. *Thomas Hughes*. 1984.

See also CHRISTIAN SOCIALISM

. . . . .

HUNT, WILLIAM HOLMAN
(1827–1910)

Born in London of lower middle-class parents, William Holman Hunt was intended to follow a career in business like his father, who was a warehouse manager. Thus he was employed at the age of twelve as an office clerk. However, Hunt continued his artistic efforts on the side, and when he was sixteen he persuaded his father to let him apply to the Royal Academy. He was accepted by the school in 1844 after his third attempt to gain admittance.

Hunt's early pictures were portraits and copies done in the accepted conventions of the period; however, he was looking for more original techniques. In 1847 he made friends with John Everett Millais and Dante Gabriel Rossetti, two fellow academy students. He also was deeply influenced by the early volumes of John Ruskin's *Modern Painters* and Keats's poetry. Discussions with Millais and Rossetti led to the conviction that English art required a new style and iconography; thus, in 1848, the **Pre-Raphaelite Brotherhood** was formed.

Hunt's first painting bearing the "PRB" signature was *Rienzi* (1849), the subject taken from the novel of the same name by Edward Bulwer-Lytton. It was conceived as a revolutionary painting in its theme—sympathy for the oppressed—and in its rejection of conventional artistic practices, being painted outdoors rather than in the studio. His second painting, *A Converted British Family* (1850), employed so much ecclesiastical symbolism that suspicion was roused that the Pre-Raphaelites were a wing of the Oxford Movement.

Between 1850 and 1855 Hunt undertook some of his most famous works: *Valentine Rescuing Sylvia, The Hireling Shepherd, The Light of the World,* and *The Awakening Conscience,* all pictures that reveal his characteristic style of symbolic realism. In 1854 Hunt left England to visit the Holy Land, which inspired a series of major religious paintings, *The Finding of the Saviour in the Temple, The Shadow of Death, The Triumph of the Innocents,* and *The Scapegoat.*

Hunt returned home in 1857 and became infatuated with an illiterate model, Annie Miller, whom he kept as his mistress. The affair, which ended in 1859, also caused a break between him and Rossetti, who had designs on Annie. In 1865 Hunt married Fanny Waugh and embarked on his second trip to the Middle East. While en route, Fanny died in Florence, Italy, following a fever after childbirth. Hunt went on to Jerusalem and did not return to England until 1872. In 1875 he married his sister-in-law, Edith Waugh, against her family's wishes, marriage to the sister of a deceased wife being illegal in England at that time.

During the later stages of his career, Hunt enjoyed wealth and critical esteem. He took many portrait commissions and did *May Morning on Magdalen Tower* (1888–1891) and *The Lady of Shalott* (1886–1905). In 1892 he made his last visit to the Middle East, but undertook no new works because his eyesight was failing. In 1905 he completed his rather acidic memoirs in which he seemed to take more than his share of credit for the formation of the Pre-Raphaelite Brotherhood, while disallowing Rossetti's influence as the intellectual leader of the movement. Hunt saw himself as the true defender of the principles of Pre-Raphaelitism and regarded his old colleagues as backsliders who fell away from the faith. Hunt's last works, both visual and literary, were those of an aggrieved man. He was at odds with the times, himself, and his old friends. While his art is impressive for his dedication and seriousness of conception, there is also something unattractive and harsh about his style and choice of subjects. The morality is oppressive, and the aura of Victorian religiosity and sentiment hangs too heavily over his strongly realistic scenes. He died in 1910 embittered by the awareness that Rossetti and Ford Madox Brown were regarded as the originators of the Pre-Raphaelite movement and that the artistic creed that he had been the prophet of was losing adherents to the new influence of impressionism from France.

HALLMAN B. BRYANT

Bibliography

Hilton, Timothy. *The Pre-Raphaelites.* 1970.

Holman-Hunt, Diana. *My Grandfather, His Wives and Loves.* 1969.

Hunt, William Holman. *Pre-Raphaelitism and the Pre-Raphaelite Brotherhood.* 1905. 2 vols.

Tate Gallery Exhibition Catalogue. *The Pre-Raphaelites.* 1984.

Walker Art Gallery. *William Holman Hunt: An Exhibition.* 1969.

. . . . .

HUNTING see COUNTRY SPORTS

. . . . .

HUXLEY, THOMAS HENRY (1825-1895)

T. H. Huxley, pre-eminent among Victorians for his virtuoso performance as the dual man of science and letters, created a new cultural voice as spokesman for science and critic of contemporary society. He was the author of numerous textbooks, scientific papers, and volumes of essays; his chief works, including *Man's Place in Nature* (1863), *Lay Sermons, Addresses, and Reviews* (1870), *American Addresses* (1877), *Hume* (1878), *The Crayfish* (1880), *Science and Culture* (1881), *Essays on Some Controverted Questions* (1892), and *Evolution and Ethics* (1893), were masterpieces of prose exposition that ranged widely across Victorian intellectual and social terrain, promoting his philosophy of scientific naturalism. His fifty-year career as scientific researcher, educator, and administrator, mainly in London with the Government School of Mines (later to become the Imperial College of Science and Technology), traced the rise of science as a profession and university subject in England and America. Huxley served on ten royal commissions, including that on vivisection (1876), was president of the British Association for the Advancement of Science (1870-1871) and of the Royal Society (1883-1885), and was made privy councillor by Queen Victoria in 1892.

Born in the village of Ealing, a few miles west of London, Huxley was the seventh child of Rachel and George Huxley. With only two years of formal education at the Ealing School, where his father was mathematics master, Huxley pursued medical studies at Charing Cross Hospital in London (1842-1845) and secured appointment to the Royal Navy as assistant ship's surgeon aboard H.M.S. *Rattlesnake* on a mapping voyage to Australia and New Guinea (1846-1850). His shipboard study of ocean invertebrates led to key morphological papers that earned him election to the Royal Society in 1851 and the society's gold medal a year later. In 1855, he married Henrietta Heathorn, an Australian he had met in Sydney; their eldest son, Leonard (1860-1933), was the father of Julian Huxley (1887-1976) and Aldous Huxley (1894-1963).

Huxley made fundamental contributions to the fields of **physiology**, morphology, **paleontology**, and **ethnology**. He brought a rigorous new methodology to anatomy that incorporated German embryological studies of development with comparative anatomical analyses. Throughout his career, Huxley remained a strict empiricist in biological method. Hence, although he became famous for defending Charles Darwin's theory of **evolution** against Bishop Samuel Wilberforce at Oxford in 1860, he was unable to accept evolution as proven, without physiological evidence of acquired infertility between divergent species.

Huxley's emphasis on the laboratory extended to his conviction, expressed in *Hume*, that the forecourt of philosophy lay in the dissecting room. This view, which drew inspiration from the skepticism of David Hume and the *Logic* of John Stuart Mill, was the essence of his scientific naturalism, which made physical causation, as determined by scientific method, the criterion of knowledge. The same reticence was embodied in his famous coinage of the term "**agnosticism**." In his *Man's Place in Nature* (1863) and "The Physical Basis for Life" (1868), Huxley firmly located body and mind in the descriptive grid of physical process. His increasingly vigorous opposition to a priori methods led to his break with Herbert Spencer in the 1880s over Spencer's adoption of evolutionary competition as the dynamic of social progress.

As an essayist, Huxley was the unsurpassed Victorian commentator on science and its cultural implications. Dubbed the "prince of debaters" by his friend Matthew Arnold, Huxley engaged in literary warfare with a zest reminiscent of the Augustans, with whose prose his vigorous, abbreviated style bears many close literary resemblances. Although Huxley's values were distinctly humanist, his emphasis on science as a criticism of life was clearly against the grain of traditional humanist text-centered culture. His late views are found in his Romanes lecture, "Evolution and Ethics" (1893), in which he astonished his contemporaries, including John Dewey and Leslie Stephen, with the formulation that man, although of nature, was irretrievably at war with nature.

JAMES PARADIS

Bibliography

Bibby, Cyril. *Scientist Extraordinary: The Life and Scientific Work of Thomas Henry Huxley.* 1972.

Desmond, Adrian. *Archetypes and Ancestors: Paleontology in Victorian London, 1850–1875.* 1982.

Di Gregario, Mario. *T. H. Huxley's Place in Natural Science.* 1984.

Huxley, Leonard. *Life and Letters of Thomas Henry Huxley.* 1900; rpt. 1979. 2 vols.

Huxley, T. H. *Collected Essays.* 1893–1894; rpt. 1968. 9 vols.

——. *The Scientific Memoirs of Thomas Henry Huxley.* 1898–1903. Ed. Michael Foster and E. Ray Lankester. 4 vols. and supplement.

Irvine, William. *Apes, Angels, and Victorians: The Story of Darwin, Huxley, and Evolution.* 1955.

Paradis, James. *T. H. Huxley: Man's Place in Nature.* 1978.

. . . . .

HYMNS

A hymn is a sacred poem intended to be sung strophically—that is, with the same music repeated verse by verse. Hymns were the principal popular, collective expression of Protestant religion. As such, they had long been cultivated by Nonconformists and evangelical Anglicans; by midcentury they were also adopted by the High Church party, which had discovered the medieval and post-Tridentine liturgical hymns of the Catholic Church.

Hymns occupied an essential place in the worship of Baptists, Methodists, and Congregationalists. In the Church of England they were not part of the liturgy (with the sole exception of the ordination service), but had always been tolerated at certain points in the services. They were also cultivated in many devout homes, with piano or harmonium accompaniment. Outdoor hymn singing was a great attraction for revival meetings, which gained a new impetus with the tour of the American evangelists Dwight Moody and Ira Sankey in 1873–1875. The chief British revival movement was the Salvation Army, founded in 1865. Revival hymns generally included a catchy refrain, and the Salvation Army specialized in brass bands to encourage hymn singing on the streets.

The composition of both hymns and hymn tunes swelled to huge proportions in the Victorian period, reaching its peak in the 1860s. The mass production of hymn books, often attended by sharp commercial practice, was unbridled; most successful of all was *Hymns Ancient and Modern* (1861, expanded 1868, 1875, 1889) which sold more than half a million copies a year. It was originally a High Church book, but by the end of the century was used in some 90 percent of rural Anglican parishes and had deeply influenced Nonconformist hymnody as well. The leading free churches brought together their differing local traditions in such books as *The Methodist Hymn Book* (1877), *The Congregational Church Hymnal* (1887), and *The Baptist Church Hymnal* (1900); while the established Church of Scotland produced its official *Hymnary* in 1901.

Victorian hymnody became increasingly eclectic. Denominational traditions tended to merge; translations of Latin and German hymns played a large part. In new hymns, theology often gave way to social or emotional aspiration. New classes of hymns, such as those for missions and for children, flourished. Hymn tunes also were drawn from many periods and countries; but there was a distinctively Victorian style of tune which has proved durable in the face of critical attack. Its composers, wishing to make hymn singing a form of high art, treated the necessarily simple melodies with the full resources of romantic harmony. If one hymn must be chosen to represent the style, ethos, and sentiment of Victorian hymnody, it should probably be "Abide with me" by Henry Francis Lyte (1793–1847), with its tune "Eventide" by William Henry Monk (1823–1889), the musical editor of *Hymns Ancient and Modern.*

NICHOLAS TEMPERLEY

Bibliography

Benson, Louis F. *The English Hymn: Its Development and Use.* 1915.

Frost, Maurice. *Historical Companion to Hymns Ancient and Modern.* 1962.

Temperley, Nicholas. *The Music of the English Parish Church.* 1979.

See also ADAMS, SARAH FLOWER; PROCTOR, ADELAIDE ANNE

· · · · ·

ILLUSTRATION

Illustration occupied a central place in the books, newspapers, and especially periodicals that served as the Victorians' major sources of information about current events and provided much of their leisure-time entertainment. Illustration both increased visual interest and provided needed expansion of texts for a newly emerging class of readers whose habits of visualization had been conditioned by the iconography of graphic satire. Change in illustration occurred as more and more illustrators received formal art education, and as narrative or **genre painting**, with its greater emphasis on subjects from daily life and simpler, more concrete expressions of reality, became increasingly popular. Illustration was also influenced by innovations in **photography** and the photomechanical transfer of images.

The major impetus for illustration at the beginning of the Victorian period was the popularization, in the 1830s, of the serialized novel published in monthly parts. **George Cruikshank**, **Hablot K. Browne** ("Phiz"), John Leech, and Richard Doyle, the illustrators who helped establish illustration as an essential ingredient of the serial, were trained as etchers and caricaturists, rather than as artists in the academic tradition. Their techniques were heavily influenced by their knowledge and appreciation of the works of late eighteenth-century graphic satirists, primarily James Gillray, William Hogarth, and Thomas Rowlandson.

During the early Victorian period there was considerable interaction between illustrators and novelists. The collaborations of Charles Dickens, William Makepeace Thackeray, and Anthony Trollope with their illustrators have been well-documented, and there is considerable evidence that novelists were very conscious of readers' reliance on illustrations to expand their imaginative grasp of literature. Pictures that could be "read" were extremely popular with the reading public.

This interest in the visual elaboration or expansion of textual material coincided with important technical achievements in printing that dramatically increased the speed and efficiency of print production for the mass market. **Wood engraving**, though hardly a new graphic technique, became the most popular medium for illustration during the nineteenth century, primarily because it allowed both illustrations and textual matter to be printed together.

Such technical improvements, along with the abolition of the newspaper stamp tax in 1855 and the removal of duty on paper in 1861, fueled the rapid growth of periodicals during the mid-Victorian period. Illustrations had played an important role in some magazines since the early 1840s, when the *Illustrated London News* set a new standard for pictorial journalism, but the periodicals that appeared during the period 1855–1875, generally referred to as "the Sixties," attempted to give a particular form and place to visual matter.

Relying heavily on serialized fiction and poetry, such periodicals as *Once a Week*, *Cornhill Magazine*, *Good Words*, *London Society*, and the *Argosy* established illustration as an important staple of the popular magazine. The illustrators whose work achieved prominence during the Sixties differed from their predecessors in that almost all had received at least some formal artistic training at the Royal Academy or other art schools. Drawing on idealized classical models, rather than **caricature**, for their inspiration, Sixties illustrators created conventionally realistic, highly appealing images of Victorian life and society that accompanied fiction and poetry, travel literature, articles on current events, popular science, and many other subjects.

John Everett Millais was one of the best-known, most influential, and most successful

ILLUSTRATION   388

of the Sixties illustrators. Other important fig ures included Arthur Boyd Houghton, **George Du Maurier**, J. D. Watson, **Frederick Walker**, Charles Keene, Frederick Sandys, and William Small.

After 1875, change in illustration occurred largely as a result of continuing technical innovation in production and printing. Photomechanical techniques facilitated the rapid transfer of drawings onto wood and led to photoengraving, which made possible the easy enlargement or reduction of drawings. The commercial introduction of the halftone screen in the 1880s paved the way for photography to replace illustration as the primary visual medium of the popular magazine of the twentieth century.

During the late Victorian period, the **art nouveau** and **aesthetic movements** brought about a brief resurgence of interest in wood-engraved illustration in a self-consciously archaic style. Figures such as **Walter Crane**, **Randolph Caldecott**, and **Kate Greenaway** patterned their illustrations for children's literature on eighteenth-century models. **Aubrey Beardsley**, the last major illustrator to emerge during the Victorian period, was also influenced by eighteenth-century sources, but he preferred the newer photomechanical processes for producing his drawings.

STEPHEN ELWELL

Bibliography

Bland, David. *A History of Book Illustration: The Illuminated Manuscript and the Printed Book.* 2d ed., 1969.

Crane, Walter. *The Decorative Illustration of Books Old and New.* 1896; rpt. 1984.

Harvey, J. R. *Victorian Novelists and Their Illustrators.* 1971.

Ray, Gordon N. *The Illustrator and the Book in England from 1790 to 1914.* 1976.

Reid, Forrest. *Illustrators of the Sixties.* 1928; rpt. 1975.

Reynolds, Graham. *Victorian Painting.* 1966.

Wakeman, Geoffrey. *Victorian Book Illustration: The Technical Revolution.* 1973.

White, Gleeson. *English Illustration, "The Sixties": 1855-70.* 1897.

See also GIBSON, JOHN; GRAPHIC ARTS

. . . . .

INDIA

When Victoria came to the throne, India was a distant colonial possession, of mostly economic concern to only scattered portions of British society. The Indian Mutiny of 1857 brought India into the mainstream of British politics and public concern. By the end of the century India was the centerpiece of the British Empire, both a symbol and the linchpin of Britain's enormous imperial wealth and international influence.

Chief among those select groups with an early interest in India was the **East India Company** and its beneficiaries. The company was transformed from a trading corporation into a government proper during the period 1770–1857. As its power and territorial acquisitions expanded, so did its need for better-quality officials both in England and in India. It soon attracted the interest of aristocratic families seeking lucrative positions for younger sons, and of ambitious intellectuals. James Mill and Edward Strachey, for example, both found the nepotism of the company congenial for establishing family sinecures.

The company's control over Indian affairs was subject to parliamentary supervision in the form of the Board of Control, whose president held cabinet-level status. Political pressure was sometimes exerted on the company, largely by the **Manchester school**, led by John Bright, who wished to see India opened up to more economic penetration than the company cared to allow. To Bright and his followers, the company was a holdover from the age of mercantilism and an impediment to progress in free trade between India and England. The Manchester school was primarily interested in markets for British industrial goods. Under their pressure, the company began building railroads and digging canals to open up India's interior for British goods and for the extraction of raw materials such as cotton, indigo, and sugar.

India also interested liberal reformers. James Mill and the Benthamites were instrumental in creating a spirit of reform in the company's administration during the 1820s and 1840s. Evangelical interest was strongest before Victoria's reign, but continued in the form of missionary activity. The missionaries, the Utilitarians, and the Manchester industrialists were generally of the same opinion; that India was fertile ground for the expansion of Western civilization.

The **Indian Mutiny** of 1857 put an end to the company's rule and closed the era of liberal reform. Benjamin Disraeli and the Tories blamed the rebellion on the excesses of reform, thus joining the chorus of voices claiming that the company was unfit to rule. Direct Crown rule, through a secretary of state for India, was established.

The mutiny also brought India into the mainstream of Victorian popular consciousness. British newspapers and the popular press feasted on the "atrocities" of the rebels and gloated over British reprisals. Numerous books and pamphlets quickly appeared, some by old India hands and some by popular writers such as Harriet Martineau. The mutiny swept in an era of popular imperialism which both Disraeli and **Rudyard Kipling**, in their different ways, would come to symbolize.

The postmutiny period saw a resurgence of conservatism in India which paralleled the political spirit of late Victorian Britain. A new generation of India officials emerged. Gone was the liberal hope, enunciated best by J. S. Mill and T. B. Macauley, that Indians could be educated into European habits and culture. In its place was the sense that Indians were culturally, intellectually, and even racially inferior. Hence the British mission was not to uplift India through political, religious, or economic reform. Instead, argued a new generation of Anglo-Indian officials such as Fitzjames Stephen and John Strachey, the British were in India to give it law and order, to restrain the lawlessness and chaos which, in their view, characterized pre-British India.

The political tussle between Disraeli and Gladstone, and between conservatives and liberals in general, had its parallels in Indian policy. Disraeli cashed in on popular interest by making Victoria empress of India in 1877. Conservative policies followed; Disraeli's secretary of state, Lord Salisbury, restricted the press in India and pursued an aggressive, militaristic policy on the northwest frontier (because of fears of Russian expansion into Afghanistan). Gladstone reversed these policies after 1880, lifting the restrictions on the press and pursuing his antiexpansionist and antimilitaristic "Little England" policy. Salisbury's government saw a renewal of militarism and conservative indifference to the first stirrings of Indian nationalism, as well as a bitter struggle between Lords Curzon and Kitchener over the military role in Indian policymaking.

These political changes during the course of Victoria's reign obscured British economic exploitation of Indians. The era of naked extortion of large fortunes had already passed by the 1850s; Burke's famous tirades against Warren Hastings and the nabobs who returned incredibly rich after short tours of duty in India had sounded the death knell for quick riches and overt corruption. Still, India proved a constant and increasing source of wealth for Victorian officials, merchants, and intellectuals.

For the official class, India provided appropriately handsome incomes and pensions. William Bentinck, whose governor-generalship set the tone for liberal reformism, returned home in 1835—after seven years' service—with a savings of 70,000 pounds sterling, which he used to liquidate a series of large debts. The second son of the third duke of Portland, Bentinck typified the manner in which Indian taxpayers kept lesser sons of the British aristocracy in comfortable circumstances. Among the many others to enjoy this situation were Lords Salisbury, Lytton, and Curzon, and the young Winston Churchill.

India also held out lucrative opportunities for the middle classes. The company's slow response to the complaints of the Manchester school quickened in the 1850s, when Lord Dalhousie's administration opted for large-scale investment in railroads to open up India to economic penetration. The conjunction of government activity and trading interests bore increasing fruits: by the end of Victoria's reign India had been transformed from a self-sufficient, net exporter of cotton goods into a major market for British textiles. Tea merchants and indigo planters likewise found India an increasingly good place to do business because of favorable government policies.

Victorian intellectuals also enjoyed imperialism's economic fruits. The list of noted writers who drew a salary paid by Indian taxpayers includes Malthus, the Mills, Thomas Love Peacock, T. B. Macaulay, Charles Trevelyan, H. H. Wilson, Fitzjames Stephen, Henry Maine, Edward and Richard Strachey, and others. The substantial rewards often provided the leisure and comfort needed for sustained intellectual output. Macaulay retired after six years of India service, living comfortably on his company pension while writing his *History of England*. J. S. Mill wrote both *A System of Logic* and *Principles of Political Economy* at his India House desk; the work load was so light that he had most afternoons free to write or to entertain fellow intellectuals, such as Thomas Carlyle, at his office. Mill's most famous, mature works were all written while he drew a handsome pension after retiring in 1858.

India, furthermore, emerged as a source of inspiration for Victorian writers. Retired India hands had often written memoirs or novels about India; for instance, Matthew Arnold's brother William had early success with his novel *Oakfield* (1853). With the growth of popular imperialism late in the century India loomed even larger in Victorian literature. Rudyard Kipling was only the most famous and successful of the writers who took advantage of the popular thirst for imperial adventure.

Thus India was a changing object of interest to the Victorians. While its economic value—a place of lucrative employment and easy markets—remained a constant, only increasing as Victoria's reign wore on, its role in British consciousness altered considerably. India emerged as a symbol of Victorian imperial might and splendor, losing its psychological and intellectual distance even more quickly than steamships, telegraph wires, and the Suez Canal could eclipse its physical distance.

LYNN ZASTOUPIL

Bibliography

Chandra, Bipan. *The Rise and Growth of Economic Nationalism in India.* 1966.

Greenberger, Allen J. *The British Image of India: A Study in the Literature of Imperialism, 1880–1960.* 1969.

Hutchins, Francis G. *The Illusion of Permanence: British Imperialism in India.* 1967.

Metcalf, Thomas R. *The Aftermath of Revolt: India, 1857–1870.* 1964.

Stokes, Eric. *The English Utilitarians and India.* 1959.

See also ANGLO-INDIAN LITERATURE; GOVERNMENT: COLONIES AND EMPIRE; SUTTEE

· · · · ·

INDIAN MUTINY (1857)

The Indian Mutiny was a rebellion by north Indian people against the **East India Company**, which then ruled most of India. The rebellion was suppressed, but only with difficulty and considerable cruelty on both sides. It spelled the end of the East India Company and evoked the first manifestation of popular imperialist sentiments.

The rebellion began in Bengal among the company's Indian soldiers, called sepoys (hence the misnomer "mutiny"). It soon drew support from leading princes, including the Mughal emperor, and great landlords of north India. The causes were complex, and involved fears of Christian missionary activity, social and economic changes brought on by British rule, and political alterations, especially the company's annexations of numerous princely states in the 1850s. The rebellion was suppressed by 1859, but only with the aid of troops from China and Britain.

British repression of the rebellion was severe. The rebels had massacred some groups of British women and children, and British public opinion was outraged. Savage reprisals were effected, and received approbation at home, leading John Stuart Mill to complain of boasting about the reprisals "in a manner most disgustful to humanity." Arbitrary arrests, floggings, and summary executions were common. The sons of the Mughal emperor were executed by a British officer, and numerous key leaders were blown from cannons in the Indian fashion. The governor-general, Charles Canning, drew the nickname "Clemency" Canning from the British community in India because he advocated moderate reprisals.

The mutiny was a watershed in British-Indian relations. It meant the end of the East India Company, whose original charter was granted by Elizabeth. The company had been assailed for years by free-traders, such as John Bright, as an anachronism and an impediment to commercial progress. The events of 1857 convinced many others of the company's unfitness for ruling India. The company defended itself by having no less a personage than J. S. Mill (then a key administrator for the company) draft a lengthy pamphlet in defense of the company's rule. But the public cry for direct Crown administration was too great, and company rule ceased in September 1858.

The mutiny marked the first manifestation of popular imperialism in Victorian Britain. Before 1857 India was far removed from the interests of most British people. Occasional outbursts of parliamentary hearings were the work of select interest groups, such as the merchants who wanted entrance into the lucrative markets of India. But the mutiny captured the public imagination. Newspapers were filled with gory accounts of rebel outrages and appropriate reprisals. Numerous books and pamphlets on India quickly appeared to meet the sudden public interest.

The mutiny evoked debate along predictable political lines. Conservatives such as Disraeli argued that the company's reforms of the previous thirty years, accompanied by disrespect for Indian customs and institutions, were the cause of the revolt. Palmerston's ministry insisted that it was a purely military mutiny, unconnected with social and political reforms conducted by the company. The views of Disraeli won out, and British administration in India after the mutiny was considerably more conservative in tone. Aristocrats and princes were mollified, social reforms and missionary activity were curtailed, and a general spirit of caution and respect for established practices prevailed. This new conservatism paralleled the waning interest in reform and the revival of conservatism in late nineteenth-century Britain.

LYNN ZASTOUPIL

Bibliography

Hutchins, Francis G. *The Illusion of Permanence: British Imperialism in India.* 1967.

Metcalf, Thomas R. *The Aftermath of Revolt: India, 1857–1870.* 1964.

· · · · ·

INDUSTRY

From 1780 to 1870 the industrial revolution created an economic and social transformation in England paralleled in cultural significance only by such momentous events in human history as the discovery of fire or the domestication of animals. England was the pioneer industrial nation until the early 1870s, which mark the beginning of its decline as the workshop of the world. This century of industrial progress divides into two phases: the emergence of the cotton industry, preeminent until the 1830s, followed by the railway age and its climactic boom in the 1840s. In human terms, the cost of change and the attendant rearrangement of social relations was high. The historian and essayist Thomas Carlyle and the novelists Charles Dickens and Elizabeth Cleghorn Gaskell reminded their contemporaries of the price paid by the mass of working men, women, and children for whom the coming of the industrial age offered a questionable boon.

The cotton industry epitomizes the growth and change associated with the industrial revolution. The phenomenal example of Manchester is testimony to the dynamism inherent in the new and revolutionary industry. From 1760 to 1830 Manchester grew over ten times in size. Until passage of the Reform Bill of 1832, this center of the industrial north had no representation in Parliament.

In human costs, the evolution of the cotton industry illustrates the dislocations that technological change created both in its transitional phase and in its permanent accomplishment, the creation of the factory system. The lack of balance in the development of spinning and weaving machinery created unforseen misery for handloom weavers. Between 1760 and 1780, the invention of the "mule" speeded up the process of spinning, especially after the application of steam power. The number of handloom weavers grew to meet the demand. But when the power loom came into use after the Napoleonic Wars, the handloom weavers were made obsolete. From 1815 to 1840 the cotton industry increasingly did its weaving in factories rather than in the cottages of weavers. Following sixty years of evolution, the technology of cotton spinning and weaving was complete and in balance.

The factory system changed the lives of the working classes in a radical way by disrupting traditional family relations as well as time-honored habits of work. Nostalgia for the patriarchal family unit of a preindustrial era conjured a picture of the cottage weaver at his hand loom with his wife and children assisting in his effort. The power loom reversed these roles, making manual power irrelevant and enabling employers to use the former support personnel—women and children—as their principal workers in factories—workers who were more tractable and who could be paid less. As Benjamin Disraeli pointed out in his industrial novel *Sybil* (1845), an underemployed handloom weaver lost his authority over an employed daughter who chose to leave her home to set up house for herself with another young factory woman.

The agricultural laborer who left the farm for the factory also left behind age-old rhythms of work. In the fields, his hours of labor had been affected by weather and the changes in seasons, his tasks varying accordingly. But the factory clock dictated the hours of labor all year round, hours of unvaried, monotonous routine. Factory work meant discipline enforced by fines for tardiness and, according to Frances Trollope in her novel, *Michael Armstrong, the Factory Boy* (1840), physical abuse of children who fell asleep on the job. Factory work also meant a six-day week, and not until 1847 was the work of women and children limited to ten hours a day. Without leisure for holidays, the factory workers of Lancashire watched preindustrial pastimes—cockfighting, folksinging, rush bearing, and wrestling—die out after 1840.

The iron and coal industries had to wait for the railway age to reach their economic take-off point. Production trebled between 1830 and 1850 when 6,000 miles of railways were constructed in Britain. A glut of investment culminated in the "railway mania" of 1845-1847. In these two decades marked by work-ing-class protest in the form of the Chartist movement—the latter decade called the "hungry forties" after the catastrophic depression of 1841-1842—the middle and upper classes had accumulated a vast amount of capital which they sought to invest in anything but low-yielding public stocks. Disraeli caught the economic division of the 1840s when he subtitled his novel *Sybil* (1845) *The Two Nations*, defining the two as the rich and the poor. When Tennyson described his poem *Maud* (1856) as the "history of a morbid poetic soul" in a "recklessly speculative age," he had in mind no doubt the "railway mania" of the previous decade. In spite of the waste than accompanies a glut, by 1850 the **railways** achieved a level of performance that did not change appreciably until the end of the steam-powered train a century later.

The economic depression of the early 1840s, the worst in the nineteenth century, drew attention to the price paid in human terms, the result of the impersonal attitude of political economy as well as the inexorable march of technology. One of the leading interpreters of the signs of the times, Thomas Carlyle in his *Past and Present* (1843) made the ironic observation that "Cotton is conquered, but the 'bare backs'—are worse covered than ever." The factory system was perfected, but factory workers could not afford to purchase the goods that they produced. A subsistence-level wage for the worker was considered sufficient. Prevailing economic thought did not entertain the idea of worker as consumer: hence the periodic gluts in production with no home market for surplus goods. Carlyle also expected a greater sense of social responsibility from the modern captain of industry whose cash nexus relationship with his workers was antisocial. The employer's responsibility for the welfare of his employees needed to extend beyond the mere payment of wages. Capital and labor needed to be bound to one another by a sense of mutual obligation.

Charles Dickens's *Hard Times* (1854) captures the harshness of existence in the industrial society of his day better than any other novel with an industrial theme. Along with the smoke and grime of Coketown, Dickens attacked the "popular fictions" of the employers of labor who complained that they would be ruined if they set aside time for school for factory children or permitted factory inspectors to look in on their works or fenced their machinery or checked their smoke pollution. In addition to satirizing the myth that anyone can rise from rags to riches, Dickens decries the loss of freedom of the factory worker caught between the two tyrannies of employer and trades union.

The novelist of consequence who knew the industrial north at first hand was Elizabeth Gaskell. Writing from the Chartist working-man's point of view in *Mary Barton* (1848), Gaskell took up the themes of economic injustice, sexual exploitation, and arrogant pride as they related to a Manchester manufacturer and his family. In *North and South* (1855) Gaskell subdued the stridency of the earlier novel in her characterization of John Thornton, a millowner from the north who learns to appreciate the cultural and moral values of the agricultural south. Initially a believer in the principles of laissez faire, in the course of the novel Thornton sheds his ideas of economic individualism for experiments that facilitate personal relations between employer and employee.

For the most part, the efforts of literary men and women were conciliatory rather than divisive in this period of cultural upheaval. As England came to a crisis at the end of the first phase of the industrial revolution in the hungry forties, its literary figures contributed in no small measure to the era of social peace which began at midcentury.

The Great Exhibition of 1851 was a celebration of England's status as the workshop of the world. The worst evils of the industrial revolution were over. The repeal of the Corn Laws in 1846 meant cheaper foodstuffs. The inauguration of **free trade** in the same year signified that England was confident of markets. The **Factory Act** of 1847 restricted the hours of labor for women and children. The political revolution of 1848 which rocked the Continent manifested itself in a Chartist march on Parliament, which came to nothing. Despite the Preston strike of 1853 and the Sheffield labor outrages of 1866, labor strife subsided. For another twenty years, England continued supreme as the world's preeminent industrial power. Though not as severe as that of the 1840s or the 1930s, the period from 1873 to 1896 has been called the "great depression" by economic historians. England survived it but emerged the weakest of the three great industrial nations after having been surpassed in the 1890s by the United States and Germany.

IVAN MELADA

Bibliography

Hobsbaum, Eric. J. *Pelican Economic History of Britain. Vol. 3: Industry and Empire.* 1970.

Melada, Ivan. *The Captain of Industry in English Fiction, 1821–1871.* 1970.

Mantoux, Paul. *The Industrial Revolution in the Eighteenth Century: An Outline of the Beginnings of the Modern Factory System in England.* 1981.

See also CHILD LABOR; DOMESTIC INDUSTRY; FACTORIES
. . . . .

INFANT FEEDING

In 1800 four methods of infant feeding were practiced: suckling by the mother, suckling by a wet-nurse, the use of animal milks, and the use of pap (bread dissolved in water or milk) and panada (cereals cooked in broth). By the century's end wet-nursing had almost died out and paps and panadas were used only by the least informed.

While science recognized the value of colostrum (the high-protein, laxative substance secreted in the few days following delivery), many doctors regarded it as "unclean" milk and prohibited suckling in the first days. The infant, fed on water, wine, animal milk or gruel, could develop gastroenteritis. Until midcentury a woman of any means who did not suckle her infant would employ a wet-nurse. Sometimes the wet-nurse was available because her own baby had died or was weaned, but too often necessity forced her to commit her own infant to a "minder" or a **baby farm**.

Cow's milk was the usual alternative for artificial feeding. Until late in the century, no standards ensured cleanliness or purity. Cows were often kept in urban areas, where they stood deep in their own dung. Milk was highly adulterated, and furthermore had to be modified by water and a sweetener to be digestible. Poor sanitation and impure water supplies encouraged gastroenteritis and diarrhea. Soothing syrups laced with **opium** further compromised infant nutrition by narcotizing the baby so that it lost the inclination to suck.

Technological and scientific advances made artificial feeding far safer by 1900 than it had been at midcentury. The glass feeding bottle, first introduced in 1830, was easier to clean than the animal horns and cloth bags which had been in use for centuries. Teats made of vulcanized rubber improved rapidly after their introduction in 1856. The importance of sterilization was recognized as the implications of Pasteur's work became known.

In 1899 the first depot offering cheap sterilized milk was established. Artificial feeding, properly administered, had become safe enough for most doctors to prefer it to the moral and physical hazards of wet-nursing. Maternal suckling remained the ideal in both medical and popular treatises on infant care, but was no longer to be taken for granted.

BARBARA J. DUNLAP

Bibliography

Hardyment, Christina. *Dream Babies: Three Centuries of Good Advice on Child Care.* 1983.

Wickes, Ian. "A History of Infant Feeding: Parts 3, 4 and 5." *Archives of Disease in Childhood,* vol. 28, pp. 332–340, 416–422, 495–502.

Wohl, Anthony. *Endangered Lives: Public Health in Victorian Britain.* 1984.

· · · · ·

INFANT MORTALITY

Although the overall death rate declined in the second half of the nineteenth century, the infant mortality rate remained constant from 1840, when statistics first became available, until around 1900. Since civil registration of births and deaths was not mandatory until 1874, the official statistics must be viewed with caution; it is certain, for example, that midwives and physicians frequently failed to report stillbirths. The reported infant mortality rate for England and Wales in 1840 was 153/1,000 live births, nearly ten times as high as that in industrialized nations in the late twentieth century. Nonetheless, Victorian

Britain had the lowest infant mortality rate in Europe outside of Scandinavia.

The overall figure for infant deaths conceals wide variations. The central districts of industrial cities like Birmingham, Blackburn, Leicester, Liverpool, and Salford reported an infant mortality rate of 220 or higher in the 1890s. No reliable statistics on class differences exist for the country as a whole, but several studies of individual communities showed that children of the poor might die at twice the rate of children from the middle and upper classes. Illegitimate children had the lowest survival rate of all; depending on the parish, estimates of their death rate ranged from 53 percent to 93 percent.

Diarrheal diseases, prematurity, and respiratory infections accounted for most infant deaths. Gastrointestinal infections, particularly common in the hot summer months, were associated with the growing prevalence of bottle feeding; water and milk supplies were frequently contaminated and sanitary facilities grossly inadequate. The poor health of Britain's undernourished and overworked working-class women contributed to the large number of premature and low-birth-weight babies.

Victorian reformers fastened on other causes. In the 1860s and 1870s they blamed **baby farming** for many infant deaths; however, the Infant Life Protection Act of 1871, which regulated baby farming, had little effect on the infant mortality rate. In the 1890s reformers focused on the factory employment of women as a detriment to breastfeeding. The Factory Act of 1891 prohibited employers from knowingly employing the mother of an infant less than four weeks old, although the provision was not enforced. Beginning in the 1850s, those who considered the ignorance of mothers to be the primary cause of infant mortality organized campaigns to educate poor and working-class women through home visits and distributing tracts on prenatal and infant care. In the early 1900s efforts to prevent infant mortality centered on improving milk supplies through pasteurization, more systematic inspection of dairies, and the distribution of special formulas for babies.

It is very difficult to determine why the infant mortality rate fell rapidly between 1900 and 1914, but a decline in the birth rate, improvements in the milk supply and in domestic and municipal sanitation, and the instruction of mothers in the handling of milk all probably played a role.

ALISA KLAUS

Bibliography

McCleary, G. F. *Early History of the Infant Welfare Movement.* 1933.

Smith, F. B. *The People's Health, 1830–1910.* 1979.

Wohl, Anthony. *Endangered Lives: Public Health in Victorian Britian.* 1983.

See also CHILDREN; HEALTH; INFANT FEEDING

. . . . .

INFANTICIDE

The murder of infants under one year old, like other forms of murder, was a capital offense in the nineteenth century. Although the law did not define infanticide as a separate crime, Victorians commonly referred to it as a special form of murder. Some believed that infanticide explained the high levels of infant mortality. Working-class parents were accused of murdering their infants to collect burial insurance or remove an unwanted burden. The victims most frequently cited, however, were illegitimate infants, who were said to be in danger from baby farmers (childminders who would neglect and drug their charges) and from their mothers, who were anxious to avoid the burden and stigma of single motherhood.

Despite the perception that infanticide was widespread, few women were executed for or even convicted of infant murder. Only a handful of baby farmers were charged with the murder of nursed-out infants, and in the last half of the century no woman was executed for the murder of her own child under one year old. The few who were convicted had their sentences commuted. The low conviction rate may indicate that the extent of infanticide was exaggerated by observers who assumed that working-class parents had little feeling for their infants, whether legitimate or illegitimate. The Victorians, however, blamed

juries for their reluctance to convict women of capital crimes and their sympathy for unmarried mothers. The rules of evidence also created difficulties. To convict a mother of murder, the prosecution needed proof that the infant had been born alive and was fully separated from the mother before the crime occurred, but medical experts were seldom able to provide such complete assurances. Unmarried mothers suspected of murder were often charged with a lesser crime, concealment of birth, which carried a maximum sentence of two years in prison.

Members of the legal and medical professions concerned about the low conviction rates in cases of child murder called for changes in the law regarding evidence and for classifying infanticide as a separate crime with a lesser penalty. These proposals were considered by a parliamentary commission on capital punishment in 1866 but were not acted upon until the 1920s when a separate crime, not a capital offense, was created to cover the murder of infants by their mothers.

ANN R. HIGGINBOTHAM

Bibliography

Radzinowicz, Leon. *A History of English Criminal Law and Its Administration from 1750.* 1948– . 5 vols.

Rose, Lionel. *Massacre of the Innocents: Infanticide in Britain, 1800–1939.* 1986.

Ryan, William Burke. *Infanticide: Its Law, Prevalence, Prevention and History.* 1862.

Sauer, R. "Infanticide and Abortion in Nineteenth-Century Britain." *Population Studies,* vol. 32, pp. 81–93.

See also BABY FARMING

. . . . .

INGELOW, JEAN
(1820–1897)

Popular poet and writer of children's stories, Jean Ingelow is best known for her literary fairy tale, *Mopsa the Fairy* (1869). Born in Boston, Lincolnshire, Ingelow was educated at home by Evangelical parents who were unaware of her literary interests until they discovered poems she had written on the shutters of her bedroom.

Her earliest publications were stories contributed to *Youth's Magazine* under the pen name "Orris." *A Rhyming Chronicle of Incidents and Feelings* (1850) drew praise from both Tennyson and Fitzgerald. With the publication of *Poems* (1863), which went through thirty editions during her lifetime, Ingelow was celebrated as one of the major lyric poets of the period. Her ballads and lyrics, strongly influenced by Wordsworth and Tennyson, combine keen appreciation for nature, conventional religiosity, and a sentimental longing for the Lincolnshire of her childhood.

Christina Rossetti judged Ingelow her poetic equal and "a formidable rival to most men, and any woman." She was suggested as a candidate for poet laureate in 1892 upon the death of Tennyson. Few of the poems, however, have withstood the changes in literary taste. Her verse is artfully composed, pleasantly musical, conventionally moral, and ultimately second-rate.

Ingelow is best remembered for her children's books, especially *Mopsa the Fairy*, which was published four years after the appearance of *Alice in Wonderland*. While *Mopsa* owes its inspiration and plot to *Alice*, its dreamy, Pre-Raphaelite atmosphere is closer to the mystical tone of George MacDonald's tales. In *Mopsa the Fairy* Ingelow's talents in poetry and prose combine to achieve a mysterious and memorable narrative.

JAN SUSINA

Bibliography

Black, Helen. *Notable Women Authors of the Day.* 1893.

Green, Roger Lancelyn. *Tellers of Tales.* 1946.

Lewis, Naomi. "A Lost Pre-Rapnaelite." *TLS*, December 8, 1972, pp. 1487–1488.

Peters, Maureen. *Jean Ingelow: Victorian Poetess.* 1972.

Some Recollections of Jean Ingelow and Her Early Friends. 1901.

See also FAIRY TALES

· · · · ·

INHERITANCE

The transfer of possessions and responsibilities from one generation to succeeding generations is governed by inheritance customs and laws. In Victorian England, four different legal systems complicated inheritance problems.

Civil law, with origins in Roman law, governs private rather than criminal, political, or military matters. Common law, with origins in medieval England, is the "unwritten law" based on custom and court decision. Canon law is promulgated and administered through ecclesiastical councils and courts. Equity, originating in medieval England so lord chancellors could circumvent common law for the king, settles controversies using concepts of conscience or natural justice in Courts of Chancery. All four types of law, with their different systems of courts, procedures, and practitioners, governed inheritance.

Until their reform in the twentieth century, Oxford and Cambridge law faculties were concerned with civil law. Inns of Court developed during the Middle Ages for the practice and study of common law, an evolving system of precedents that focuses power in courts, judges, and lawyers. Ecclesiastical courts had jurisdiction over marriages and wills. Chancery, now a division of the High Court of Justice, had jurisdiction in matters of equity. Chancery, common, and canon procedure were different, but often different courts tried the same inheritance case through a series of preliminary discussions and delayed decisions.

Until 1926, real property and personal property were subject to different systems of law. Real property consists of lands and the titles thereto, buildings, crops, and mineral rights. Personal property consists of movables (called chattel), both incorporeal (as in stocks and bonds) and corporeal (as in furniture, jewels, and people). Medieval social and power structures were based on ownership of land distributed by the king. After 1066, the royal courts continued authority over personal property, but ecclesiastical courts gained power over personal property. The church discouraged primogeniture (the inheritance of undivided real property by the eldest son) and advocated multiple heirs for personal property so the church could inherit wealth. Inheritance controversies caused by this division had to be decided by the lord chancellor's court on the basis of equity.

Customarily, real property descended unpartitioned to one heir, even at the peasant level, in order to keep landholdings large enough to support a family. Undivided descent of land was especially beneficial to the nobility, because it concentrated social, political, and military power. In England, primogeniture continued as the rule of intestacy until 1925. The law of entail prevented owners of inherited real property from selling, mortgaging, giving, or willing away property. In 1882, when entail was restricted, land improvements and freer markets were possible.

The formalities of witnessed wills were frequently contested. Until 1857, the ecclesiastical courts had jurisdiction over wills, and controversies involving the inheritance of real and personal property could be considered under separate systems of laws and court procedures. These distinctions of procedures and property, as well as conflicts of church and state power, complicated inheritance during the nineteenth century.

DOROTHY ATKINS

Bibliography

Miller, William L. "Primogeniture, Entails, and Endowments in English Classical Economics." *History of Political Economy*, vol. 12, pp. 558–581.

. . . . .

INSANITY

The nineteenth century witnessed enormous changes in the public attitude toward the insane and initiated sweeping reforms in the treatment of insanity. The lunatic, madhouse, and mad-doctor of the eighteenth century were transformed into the mental patient, asylum, and alienist or specialist physician of the Victorian era.

Until the establishment of St. Luke's Hospital for Lunaticks (1751), the only official institution for the insane in England was Bethlehem Hospital. The notoriously brutal conditions at Bedlam, as it was popularly known, reflected the eighteenth-century abhorrence of the insane as irrational and consequently dehumanized creatures to be chained and confined like animals in unlit cells. After 1755, the public conscience was aroused and its attention drawn to the problems of diagnosing and treating insanity by a series of events including the first successful pleas of insanity in court trials; the rise of private madhouses; the publication of books like Thomas Arnold's *Observations on the Nature, Kinds, Causes and Prevention of Insanity* (1782), which suggested that madness was a peculiarly English affliction; and, most importantly, public revelations about the madness of King George III.

Public interest in insanity reached epidemic proportions during the nineteenth century. For the first time, journals and parliamentary select committees published in-depth clinical studies, statistics, and treatises on insanity. This new flood of information on a formerly ignored subject seemed to indicate that insanity was becoming more and more prevalent in England and Wales. Beginning in 1800 with the Criminal Lunatics Act, Parliament reinforced this fear in the public mind by authorizing a series of legislative investigations and reforms including the Lunacy Act (1808); the Insane Prisoners Act (1840), amended 1864; the Lunacy Act (1842); the Lunacy Act (1845), amended 1862; the Criminal Lunatics Asylum Act (1860); the Trial of Lunatics Act (1883); the Criminal Lunatics Act (1884); and the Lunacy Act (1890). Before 1839, no medical periodicals specialized in mental disorders; in the next sixty years ten periodicals specializing in psychology and neurology were founded. Medical books on the diagnosis and treatment of insanity became best sellers, while insanity became a staple feature in imaginative literature. The works of Charlotte Brontë, George Meredith, Charles Dickens, William Thackeray, Wilkie Collins, Charles Reade, Mary Elizabeth Braddon, Anthony Trollope, Edward Bulwer-Lytton, Robert Browning, and Alfred Tennyson reflect nineteenth-century England's obsession with madness.

National interest in the problems of madness led to the establishment of the Metropolitan Commission in Lunacy, which issued a series of reports between 1829 and 1844. Much of the medical debate throughout the century focused on the causes and diagnosis of insanity. Generally, the causes of insanity were categorized as physical or moral, with a further breakdown into predisposing and exciting causes within each category. These categories were not mutually exclusive. Physical predisposing causes included hereditary madness, irregular blood circulation, poor blood, old age, and female gender. Physical exciting causes included blows to the head, accidents, sunstroke, alcoholism, phases of the moon, and masturbation. Moral predisposing causes included dissipation, debauchery, and excesses of one kind or another. For example, both overindulgence and excessive asceticism could lead to madness. The Victorian public was warned about the especial dangers of gluttony and overindulgence in working, studying, and novel-reading. Moral exciting causes included nervous shocks, disappointments in love, rape, and masturbation.

Everybody agreed that there was an absolute difference between the sane person and the mad person, but there was considerable disagreement about where the line of difference should be drawn. Traditionally, insanity was classified as either mania or melancholia and as acute or chronic. As the century progressed, insanity generally was divided into four basic types that, physicians agreed, often merged in a variety of ways: melancholia or monomania; mania; partial insanity; and moral insanity. Melancholia was characterized by severe depression while monomania was marked by an obsessive preoccupation with some one thing. Mania was exemplified by the raving, violent lunatics that people used to pay a penny to see in Bedlam. Partial insanity was either periodic or partial and included hypochondria and hysteria. Moral insanity, a term coined in 1833 by Dr. James Cowles Prichard (commissioner in lunacy, 1844–1848), meant a perversion of the moral sense and was characterized by antisocial behavior and a lack of self-control.

The difficulties of differentiating between merely eccentric or atypical behavior and abnormal or mad behavior are obvious and led to abuse. Women who did not conform to the Victorian ideals of femininity could be and occasionally were diagnosed as insane. Rebellious daughters and recalcitrant wives could be readily brought to obedience by the very real threat of confinement since it was popu-larly accepted that the female reproductive system rendered women peculiarly susceptible to insanity. According to the medical profession, puberty, pregnancy, childbirth, lactation and menopause simply placed additional stress on a body and nervous system biologically undermined by the inescapable vulnerability of its female gender. However, men, too, could be subject to wrongful confinement, a situation exploited by Charles Reade in his best seller *Hard Cash* (1863). There were major parliamentary inquiries on the issue of wrongful confinement in 1858–1859 and 1876–1877; and the 1862 amendment to the Lunacy Act of 1845 tried to make more stringent the prohibitions against any medical man with interest in a private asylum signing a certificate for the admission of a patient into that house. Separate examinations by two physicians and the signature of a magistrate were required for the confinement of a mental patient, unless the patient were a pauper in which case only one medical certificate was required. Despite the characteristically Victorian emphasis on morals to be found in discussions of the causes and diagnosis of insanity, the nineteenth century moved quickly toward a general recognition that insanity could be authoritatively diagnosed, certified, and treated only by medical experts.

Recognition that insanity was primarily a medical, rather than a moral, problem is reflected in the important Lunacy Act of 1845, which established a permanent lunacy commission, required all counties to provide adequate asylum accommodation for pauper lunatics to separate them from the merely indigent or criminal, and made the medical inspection of all private asylums compulsory.

Whereas the private madhouses and charity asylums of the eighteenth century were designed to simply confine their inmates, nineteenth-century asylums were increasingly perceived as therapeutic in their primary function. There was a call for asylum architecture that featured cheerful interiors, sufficient grounds for healthy exercise, adequate separation of the inmates for individual treatment, and, in response to reports of female inmates abused by male keepers, a strict segregation of the sexes extending even to the kitchens and sometimes the mortuaries. The public also demanded the abandonment of such traditional treatment of the insane as whippings, forced feedings, haphazard drugging, and confinement in straitjackets, chains, and dark rooms. Much of the public's newfound awareness of alternate methods of treating the insane can be credited to Samuel Tuke's *Description of the Retreat* (1813), an account of the Quaker York Retreat, which was founded on the principles of moral management, and to John Conolly, whose tenure as physician superintendent of the Middlesex County Lunatic Asylum at Hanwell proved that even large lunatic populations could be managed without the use of force or restraint. Since moral managers believed that insanity could be combated by the cultivation of self-control, their asylums created a homelike environment in which the inmates were encouraged to develop self-respect, perseverance, and industry. Although moral management was challenged by the growing acceptance of insanity as a medical issue, the techniques of moral therapy continued to be popular and were frequently used to make patients more amenable to medical treatment. During the 1830s and 1840s, hydropathic establishments became popular as a humane and socially acceptable alternative to strict confinement and the common overuse of drugs, especially opium, to treat insanity. Besides submerging themselves in special baths for prolonged periods of time, patients undergoing the **water cure** abstained from tea, coffee, alcohol, and other stimulants. Such reactions against the use of physical coercion and mechanical restraints earned the English an international reputation for their humane treatment of the mentally disturbed.

However, the abolition of degrading and painful methods of treatment was more an ideal than an actuality for half of the century. The early 1900s even contributed two innovative ways to torture the insane: the tranquilizer chair, which completely immobilized the limbs, trunk, and head of the patient; and the rotary machine or swing, which consisted of a suspended chair that could be whirled faster and faster, inducing vomiting, loosened bowels, and unconsciousness. Physicians who believed insanity to be a disease of the blood continued to advocate leeching, cupping, purging, vomiting, and blistering while canvas gloves, hobbles, leg locks, wrist locks, and straitjackets were used in both private madhouses and public asylums until the 1850s.

Women were especially subject to inhumane treatment. As late as 1848, an article in the *London Medical Journal* recommended ice water in the rectum, ice in the vagina, and leeching of the labia and the cervix to treat suspected insanity in menopausal women. From 1850 to 1880 some physicians regularly performed clitoridectomies as a cure-all for all forms of female insanity.

During the last third of the nineteenth century, pessimism about the value of asylum treatment and the possibility of curing insanity encouraged a new emphasis on means of preventing insanity. This foreshadowed the beginning of the distinction between public (institutional) and private (office-based) psychiatric practice. The 1880s were marked by the controversial claims of the emerging specialty of neurology, which favored complete rest cures and treatments by machines that administered static electricity to the patient. Influenced by the work of Sigmund Freud, the medical profession by the end of the century had separated insanity into diseases of the mind to be treated by psychiatrists, and diseases of the brain to be treated by neurologists.

MARILYN J. KURATA

Bibliography

Hunter, Richard and Ida Macalpine, eds. *Three Hundred Years of Psychiatry, 1535–1860*. 1963.

Jones, Kathleen. *Lunacy, Law, and Conscience 1744–1845*. 1955.

Leigh, Denis. *The Historical Development of British Psychiatry*. 1961.

Scull, Andrew, ed. *Madhouses, Mad-Doctors and Madmen: The Social History of Psychiatry in the Victorian Era*. 1981.

———. *Museums of Madness: The Social Organization of Insanity in Nineteenth-Century England*. 1979.

Showalter, Elaine. *The Female Malady: Women, Madness, and English Culture, 1830–1980*. 1985.

Skultans, Vieda. *English Madness: Ideas on Insanity, 1580–1890*. 1979.

———. *Madness and Morals: Ideas on Insanity in the Nineteenth Century*. 1975.

Smith, Roger. *Trial by Medicine: Insanity and Responsibility in Victorian Trials.* 1981.

Walker, Nigel. *Crime and Insanity in England.* Vol. 1: *The Historical Perspective.* 1968.

· · · · ·

IRELAND

Near the end of the nineteenth century, Ireland underwent a vigorous revival of art and culture. Throughout most of Victoria's reign, however, the country suffered the effects of extreme poverty, agrarian disorder, and ineffectual political representation. The century was also characterized by an indefatigable nationalism, manifest in numerous constitutional reform movements, armed rebellions, and the influence of two parliamentary politicians, **Daniel O'Connell** (1775–1847) and **Charles Stewart Parnell** (1846–1891).

By 1837 Ireland was isolated and impotent. Since the 1800 Act of Union, which abolished the Dublin Parliament, many powerful families moved to England, where social and political opportunity were now centralized. Absentee landlordism was rampant, and subdivisions of farmland and new competition from England were leading toward agricultural chaos. The only real success had been O'Connell's campaign to allow Catholics to sit in Parliament and hold offices of state.

O'Connell and his followers dominated the first half of the century as Parnell dominated the latter half. Although as a Catholic O'Connell was unable to hold office, he was elected for County Clare in 1828, in the first demonstration of his remarkable organizational abilities. Only a year later, the Roman **Catholic Emancipation** Act passed, despite vehement opposition from George IV. O'Connell turned next to repeal of the Act of Union, and organized masses of people from every class into what were then known as "monster meetings." The Protestant and established churches, previously rivals, united in their reactionary panic. In 1843 O'Connell was arrested and his meetings were suppressed. He died four years later. Unlike previous rebellions, O'Connell's was genuinely broad-based and geared toward constitutional reform. His failure to secure repeal through constitutional methods may have been partially responsible for the decades of militaristic extremism that followed.

The **Irish famine** too aided in the decline of reformist movements, for much of the populace was concerned first with survival, and became convinced that England was unable to look after their interests. The Catholic west was most severely affected, although the famine reached all classes, regions, and sects. Historians are currently reassessing the famine's causes, but it has been thought that its origins lay in overpopulation and dependence upon a single crop. Subdivisions left the average farm in the west at less than five acres, and the potato was easily grown in a small space. The crop had intermittently failed throughout the 1820s and 1830s, and experts warned of imminent disaster. In September 1845 the first signs of widespread blight were reported. For the next two years, the entire crop failed and throughout the rest of the decade, only partial harvests were available. During the famine decade, Ireland lost 20 percent of its population through emigration, disease, and starvation. Governed by stern guidelines of laissez-faire economics, the English treasury secretary, Charles Trevelyan, provided only inadequate and inept relief, and finally England tossed the burden to private charities and local landlords.

The effects of the famine were numerous. Since cattle ranching brought more immediate financial reward, tillage converted to grazing, and the next fifty years saw the end of subdivision. Younger children had no alternative but to emigrate, and Ireland's population halved in the second part of the century. With large numbers of bitter, homesick Irish in the United States, America became a resource for nationalist rebels seeking financial and political support. Since the famine decimated the Gaelic-speaking population, the language and the customs it articulated gradually disappeared.

With the demise of Gaelic, Ireland lost a wealth of literature, only part of which was recorded or translated. Throughout the famine years, the powerful fiction of one of the century's finest Irish novelists, **William Carleton**, continued to depict this lost world. His stories remain one of the few records of Gaelic life before the famine.

Around the same time, a group who called themselves **Young Ireland** produced im-

Women at Field-Work in Roscommon.
Illustrated London News, *7 May 1870. Library Company of Philadelphia.*

mensely popular patriotic poetry and ballads. Originally composed of O'Connellites, the group attempted to bridge sectarian and class lines. The poet Thomas Davis founded a patriotic newspaper, *The Nation*, which enjoyed a remarkably wide circulation, considering that most of the country was in severe distress. After Davis's death in 1845, the more radical John Mitchel assumed leadership and addressed the controversial issue of land reform. Another Young Ireland leader, Charles Gavan Duffy, followed Mitchel's lead in forming the first Tenant Right League in 1850, and later the first independent Irish political party. Mitchel split off in 1848 to create the *United Irishman*, and after making numerous inflammatory remarks, was arrested and transported for treason. Although Young Ireland achieved no immediate reforms, it had a profound influence on later events. Its newspapers were the first of their kind to circulate in Ireland and exposed the impact that nationalist poetry, ballads, and essays could have among the general populace. Early, some members of the movement articulated the primary issues of the land reform movement of the 1870s, and Young Ireland in part inspired the numerous uprisings of the 1850s and 1860s.

In 1848 Young Ireland backed a violent but pathetically disorganized uprising which marked the start of several decades of paramilitary nationalism. Ten years later the newly created Irish Republican Brotherhood held similarly inept attempts at rebellion. The Fenian rebellions of the 1860s drew their strength and numbers from American Civil War veterans, but were continually undermined by unrealistic expectations and paid informants.

Typically, these rebels had their greatest effect as symbols of martyrdom. Throughout the last decades of the century, their names were repeatedly recalled by the constitutional reformers whose methods they would have despised. The dominant figure in the reform movement was Charles Stuart Parnell, whose own name was to be invoked in the next century.

Son of an old Protestant landholding family, Parnell early associated himself with tenant rights and land reform. At the end of the 1870s a new famine threatened rural Ireland. In response, Michael Davitt, son of an evicted Mayo farmer and Fenian prisoner, founded the Land League. Parnell, a member of the Home Rule party, was elected president. The league argued for an end to evictions, reduction of rates, and transfer of ownership to tenants. The Land League drew support—however surreptitiously—from peasant agrarian societies who practiced vigilante violence. Land reform had begun to seem inevitable, and Parliament passed two Land Acts by 1881. The Land Acts radically transformed the social, economic, and political structure of Ireland, effectively ending the centuries-old system of dominance by a few. Parnell's other cause, **Home Rule**, was not so successful.

By the 1880s many priests had altered their position on Home Rule and thrown their support behind Protestants like Parnell. Such ecumenism was unusual and promising. Parnell established a combative, yet cooperative relationship with Prime Minister Gladstone, who was generally sympathetic to Irish claims. However, the chief secretary for Ireland and his assistant were murdered in May 1882 by a group of nationalists who called themselves the Invincibles. English popular opinion linked the group with the Land League, and turned against Irish claims. Parnell had to drop his pressures for Home Rule until England's mood again became receptive. In 1886 a Home Rule Bill was introduced, and its relatively narrow defeat seemed to promise future passage.

However, in 1889 Captain William O'Shea sued for divorce and named as his wife's adulterous partner Charles Stewart Parnell. A humiliating public hearing resulted in Parnell's dismissal as party chief. Parnell's cooperative relationship with Gladstone collapsed and the Catholic church turned against Home Rule on moral grounds. Despite his attempts to regather his power, Parnell died defeated in 1891. His contemporaries interpreted his defeat as the symbolic defeat of nationalist aspirations, and nationalist expression tended to be artistic rather than political until the rising of 1916.

In the exuberance and subsequent despair of the last decades, Ireland blossomed in painting, printing, weaving, glasswork, and literature. Because literature most directly permitted association with causes, its influence was the most profound. The German linguists had made available translations of medieval Irish epic and poetry, and Irish Pre-Raphaelites like Samuel Ferguson (1810–1886) gave contemporary treatment to some of these native materials. Standish O'Grady (1846–1928) produced readable prose versions of the epic tales. Later the first president of the Republic of Ireland and founder of the Gaelic League, Douglas Hyde (1860–1949) collected folklore from the Gaelic Catholics of the remote western coast. Novelists like Edith **Somerville** (1858–1949) **and** "Martin Ross" (Violet Martin, 1862–1915) chronicled the demise of rural Irish aristocracy with seriousness rather than apologetic humor. Young writers like **W. B. Yeats** (1865–1939) and his circle drew stories, themes, and images almost exclusively from Irish sources.

Victoria's reign may have ended with no prospect of Home Rule. But the century-long movement for land reform transferred a rural, landless, and disenfranchised Catholic poor into more prosperous roles in an increasingly urbanized—if depopulated—nation. And in the face of such change, Irish artists drew from that traditional culture the materials from which they made Ireland at the beginning of the twentieth century one of the most original and productive artistic centers of the world.

ELIZABETH GRUBGELD

Bibliography

Fallis, Richard. *Irish Renaissance*. 1977.

Lee, Joseph. *The Modernisation of Irish Society, 1848–1918*. 1973.

Lyons, F. S. L. *Charles Stewart Parnell*. 1977.

———. *Ireland Since the Famine*. 1973.

MacDonagh, Oliver. *Ireland: The Union and Its Aftermath*. 1977.

O'Tuathaigh, Gearoid. *Ireland Before the Famine, 1798–1848*. 1972.

See also ANGLO-IRISH LITERATURE; ANGLO-IRISH LIFE AND SOCIETY; CELTIC REVIVAL;

DUBLIN; GAELIC CULTURE;
IRISH LITERATURE; IRISH
NATIONALISM; IRISH PARTY
· · · · ·

IRISH FAMINE

The partial failure of the potato crop in the late autumn of 1845 plunged Ireland into a catastrophic period. With three successive crop failures, more than 1,500,000 Irish people died from starvation or famine-related diseases and approximately an equal number emigrated from the troubled country during the four-year period of the famine. The crisis worsened the already strained relations between England and Ireland, united under the same government by the Act of Union in 1800, and served as a major watershed in Irish social and political history.

Phytophthora infestans, a fungus that spreads rapidly under wet conditions, caused the blight that destroyed the potato crops. The impact of the blight on rural Ireland was particularly harsh since the primitive Irish agrarian economy forced almost half of the population to depend on the potato for food. The extreme poverty of Ireland, caused primarily by the land system, made the famine devastating. Out of a population that had exceeded 8 million in 1841, 5.5 million were dependent on agriculture. These unfavorable conditions, coupled with the social and political disabilities under which Irish Catholics had long suffered, stifled industry and enterprise and encouraged the further subdivision of land, which had by 1841 already reduced 45 percent of all holdings to fewer than five acres. The potato blight turned an already desperate situation into a tragedy.

When reports of the potato failure reached London in late October 1845, Prime Minister Robert Peel ordered the purchase of 100,000 pounds worth of Indian corn from the United States and set in motion a program of public works to create employment so that the Irish people could purchase imported grain. But the Peel ministry resigned in June 1846 and was succeeded by a Whig administration under Lord John Russell that was committed even more stringently to the concepts of laissez faire. Not wishing to use the state to provide food and holding that Irish property must be made to support the Irish poor, the ministers in 1847 transferred the responsibility of famine relief to the Irish Poor Law. Consequently, the famine relief was inadequate. But the British government's greatest failure was its neglect of larger measures that would stimulate economic growth and reconstruct Irish society so as to remove the causes that made famine endemic. To the most fervent Irish nationalists, government policy during the famine was genocidal. Most Irish historians today, however, see British policy as either benign or malign neglect. In any case, the Irish famine stirred **Irish nationalism**, and out of the sufferings of that tragic episode emerged the strains of modern Ireland.

F. DARRELL MUNSELL

Bibliography

Edwards, R. Dudley and Desmond Williams, ed. *The Great Famine: Studies in Irish History, 1845-1852.* 1956.

Mokyr, Joel. *Why Ireland Starved: A Quantitative and Analytical History of the Irish Economy, 1800-1850.* 1983.

Woodham-Smith, Cecil. *The Great Hunger: Ireland 1845-1849.* 1962.

· · · · ·

IRISH LITERATURE

In both politics and literature, Victorian Ireland was concerned with the question of its national identity. By the Act of Union in 1800, the Irish Parliament had been absorbed into Westminster; loss of a distinct political entity prompted writers to examine what it meant to be "Irish." This identity crisis was reflected in Ireland's dual literary traditions: the literature of Gaelic Ireland, which had been in decline since the seventeenth century, and that of English-speaking or Anglo-Ireland. The merging of these two traditions to create a new literature, one that combined the English language with subjects from the Irish, was the dominant literary movement of the era, resulting in the Irish literary renaissance of the 1890s.

The foundation for the literary revival was laid early in the era by scholars such as Eugene O'Curry (1796–1862) and John O'Donovan (1809–1861), who provided scholarly translations of manuscripts that had lain abandoned for years in the libraries and museums of Ireland and Britain. O'Curry's *Lectures on the Manuscript Materials of Ancient Irish History* (published in 1861, 1873) and O'Donovan's *The Annals of the Four Masters* (1848–1851), along with the publication of tales from the early Irish cycles, proved that Gaelic Ireland did, indeed, have an ancient and respectable body of literature, a view that was given an additional support by Matthew Arnold's lectures *On the Study of Celtic Literature* (published in 1867).

But it took the urging of Thomas Davis (1814–1845), head of the **Young Ireland** movement, to inaugurate the deliberate creation of a national literature that would combine Irish themes and subjects with English literary forms. Davis, along with Charles Gavan Duffy and John Blake Dillon, founded *The Nation*, a sixpenny Saturday weekly dedicated to promoting both political and cultural nationalism. Davis believed that a common literature could help unify Gaelic and Anglo-Irish Ireland and would prefigure their political union. He urged writers, poets, painters, and balladeers to use Irish themes, himself contributing such stirring ballads, as "A Nation Once Again" to the cause. Unfortunately, the resulting work tended to have more patriotic sentiment than literary quality.

James Clarence Mangan (1803–1849) was the best of the poets published in *The Nation*. He knew little of the Irish language and used translations by others as the basis for re-creations of the original themes. He experimented with the Irish Gaelic syllabic style of rhythms and accents and introduced a wonderful lyrical quality into such intensely nationalistic poems as "Dark Rosaleen" and "O'Hussey's Ode to the Maguire."

Samuel Ferguson (1810–1886) was one of the first to attempt to re-create, in English, material from the early Irish bardic poetry and literary cycles. Ferguson favored the epic mode, and, in his *Lays of the Western Gael* (1865) and his long epic poem *Congal* (1872), he attempted to elevate the Irish epic to Homeric style.

The materials that Ferguson worked with were still so obscure to the general reading public that he had to add prefaces and explanatory notes. It was not until Standish James O'Grady (1846–1928) published *History of Ireland: The Heroic Period* (1878), a boldly imaginative prose retelling of the early Irish mythological and heroic cycles, that this material was popularized. His book ignited the imaginations of writers, introducing them for the first time to figures such as Deirdre, Cuchulainn, and Fionn MacCumhail, and earned for O'Grady the title "Father of the Irish Renaissance."

O'Grady may have fathered the revival, but it was **William Butler Yeats** who nurtured and reared it. When Yeats asked that he not "less be counted one / With Davis, Mangan and Ferguson" he was naming his poetic antecedents whose choice of subject and struggles with translations had begun to create the new Irish literature. Their experiments, although vital, rarely yielded first-rate poetry. Yeats's publication of *The Wanderings of Oisin and Other Poems* (1889) marked the beginning of the renaissance, which was characterized by the use of mythology, folk and fairy lore, and heroic and romantic legends gleaned from Irish Gaelic literature, but expressed in English.

As Gaelic manuscripts were being mined, the oral traditions were also collected and translated. Spurred in part by similar folklore movements in Europe and by a sense, after the famine, that the Gaelic language and culture were rapidly slipping away, attempts were made to preserve the living culture. Douglas Hyde (1860–1949) both translated poems from the Gaelic, as in his *Love Songs of Connacht* (1893), and wrote poetry in Gaelic under the pen name An Craoibhin Aoibhinn. George Sigerson's (1836–1925) *The Poets and Poetry of Munster* (1860) and *Bards of the Gael and Gall* (1897) were popular translations from the Irish. Popular fairy tale and folklore collections included Patrick W. Joyce's *Old Celtic Romances* (1879), Patrick Kennedy's *Legendary Fictions of the Irish Celt* (1866), and Samuel Lover's *Legends and Stories of Ireland* (1832, 1834). Yeats contributed collections of folk and fairy tales, one of which, *The Celtic Twilight* (1893), supplied a rather facetious title to the literary movement of the 1890s.

The writing of the Irish novel, although prolific, reached few achievements comparable with the Victorian novel in England. Writing primarily for an English and Anglo-Irish audience, Irish writers felt compelled to "explain" Ireland and to comment on its economic ills. As a result the novels tend to be overly didactic, sentimental, or patronizing.

William Carleton (1794–1869), the first writer from Gaelic-speaking Ireland to make a living with the pen, gave voice and identity to the people previously seen only as a nameless, vaguely threatening mob, existing beyond the pale of Anglo-Irish experience. *Traits and Stories of the Irish Peasantry* (1830–1833), his best-known work, shows the life of prefamine Ireland. His best novels, which gave him the title of "the peasant novelist," were written during the great famine. *Valentine M'Clutchy, the Irish Agent* (1845), *The Black Prophet* (1847), and *The Emigrants of Ahadarra* (1848) showed the disastrous effects of the imbalanced land ownership that produced the famine, and of the emigration that decimated the Irish-speaking population in Carleton's time.

Many other novelists wrote about land ownership, an issue that dominated the politics of the day. Charles Kickham's (1828–1882) *Knocknagow* (1879) describes the inequities from the point of view of a farmer. Charles Lever's (1806–1872) *The Martins of Cro' Martin* (1856) views the same problem from the landowners' vantage point as it traces the decline of one of the Big Houses into the Encumbered Estates Court.

Popular novelists of the period include Samuel Lover (1797–1868), whose title character in *Handy Andy* (1842) is an example of the "stage Irishman" translated to the novel, and **Joseph Sheridan LeFanu** (1814–1873), in whose **Gothic novels**, such as *Uncle Silas* (1864), elements of the mysterious and supernatural seem to evolve from the human subconscious. Dublin-born **Bram Stoker** gave the world *Dracula* in 1897.

At the end of the nineteenth century, the Irish novel began to mature. **Somerville and Ross's** *The Real Charlotte* (1894) and **George Moore's** *A Drama in Muslin* (1886) stand out for their realistic (and naturalistic) treatments of the decline of Anglo-Irish society; Moore's *Esther Waters* (1894) ranks among the best Victorian novels.

In drama, as in the novel, the Victorian period opened weakly; Ireland was little more than a provincial stage for English acting companies. Irish actor Tyrone Power strutted the boards in conventional stage Irishman roles (many created by Samuel Lover) portraying the imbibing, garrulous, merry, hot-tempered Irishman familiar from Elizabethan and Restoration plays. This character type was perpetuated by the most popular Irish dramatist of the Victorian period, **Dion Boucicault** (1820–1890), whose melodramas *The Colleen Bawn* (1860), *Arragh-na-Pogue* (1864), and *The Shaughraun* (1874) combined comedy, pathos, and sentiment. Lack of serious threater in Ireland led Dublin-born playwrights **Oscar Wilde** and **George Bernard Shaw** to seek their livelihoods in London. But Yeats and Lady Augusta Gregory (1852–1932) determined to expand their vision of literary nationalism into the drama. Despising the "stage Irish" of the commercial theater, their "Prospectus for the Irish Literary Theatre" (1898) declared their intent to "show that Ireland is not the home of buffoonery and of easy sentiment, but the home of ancient idealism." The theater debuted with Edward Martyn's *The Heather Field* and Yeats's *The Countess Cathleen* in 1899. In 1901 it presented the first play ever performed in the Irish language, Douglas Hyde's *Casadh an tSugain* (The Twisting of the Rope). No dramatic tradition existed in Irish until Hyde provided one by creating this play, based on an Irish tale. In 1902 the theater presented "the first masterpiece of Irish dramatic nationalism" in Yeats's *Cathleen ni Houlihan*. The end of the Victorian period saw the stage set for the full flowering of the Abbey Theatre, the powerful center of the renaissance in Irish drama.

NANCY MADDEN WALCZYK

Bibliography

Fallis, Richard. *The Irish Renaissance*. 1977.

Harmon, Maurice. *Modern Irish Literature 1800–1967: A Reader's Guide*. 1967.

McHugh, Roger and Maurice Harmon. *Short History of Anglo-Irish Literature: From Its Origins to the Present Day*. 1982.

See also ANGLO-IRISH LITERATURE; CELTIC REVIVAL; GAELIC CULTURE

. . . . .

IRISH NATIONALISM

Throughout the Victorian period the Irish national question polarized and, at times, dominated British politics. Born in earlier years, modern Irish nationalism developed and flourished in the nineteenth century to become the central focus of Irish public life.

Irish nationalism had various roots. Some went back to Ireland's centuries-old stormy relation to England. More immediately, the Act of Union, passed in 1800, abolished the Irish Parliament and merged it with the Parliament at Westminster. Nationalism was also an outgrowth of Ireland's Gaelic culture.

Many conditions in the nineteenth century nourished the growth of a nationalist persuasion. The Irish poor were lost in poverty. Troubles between tenants and landlords as well as questions about land, education, and economic development abounded. The failure of the British to respond adequately to the great famine of the late 1840s—one of the most profound natural calamities of modern times—encouraged anti-British feelings among the Irish masses. Religious faith blended with national consciousness and became a symbol of nationality for the majority of Irish people.

Nationalism is always a complex phenomenon. The mainstream of Irish nationalism, for instance, failed to embrace the Protestant majority living in the northeastern province of Ulster. Moreover, Irish nationalism assumed various forms: cultural, militant, political, or some mixture. Members of the **Young Ireland** movement of the 1840s, who staged an unsuccessful rebellion in 1848, were primarily cultural nationalists. Two decades later the Irish Republican Brotherhood, or Fenians, staged a second unsuccessful rebellion. Accepting Young Ireland's doctrine of a separate Irish nationality, they concentrated on a single aim, independence, and advocated physical force as the only way to achieve it. Other Irish nationalists worked within the existing political framework and tried to use legislative means to reach their goal.

This last group, exponents of political nationalism, were a major force in both Irish and British public life. Daniel O'Connell involved great numbers of Irish people as well as the Irish clergy in popular parliamentary politics. In 1829 he was successful in achieving Catholic emancipation, which gave Catholics access to Parliament and other offices. He failed, however, to achieve his other great goal, the repeal of the Act of Union. Toward the end of the century a second major figure, Charles Stewart Parnell, became leader of the Irish Home rule party (founded in 1874 by Isaac Butt) and forced **Home Rule** to the center of British politics. The Liberal prime minister, William Ewart Gladstone, introduced an Irish Home Rule Bill in the House of Commons in 1886. Dissident Liberals and Conservatives, however, united to defeat the measure.

When the century ended, Home Rule was still the national goal for the majority of Irish people. Hopes for its success, however, were slim. Meanwhile, Ulster Protestants intensified their century-long defense of the Act of Union, and a galaxy of new national movements appeared on the scene. Some, like the Anglo-Irish literary revival and the more popular Gaelic League, were cultural. Others, like the Sinn Fein and the Irish Socialist Republican party, were political, though quite different from the political nationalism embodied in the Home Rule movement. Also, the militant Fenians experienced a revival. Consequently, Irish nationalism faced an uncertain future as the century ended.

JAMES D. STARTT

Bibliography

Hurst, Michael. *Parnell and Irish Nationalism.* 1968.

Kee, Robert. *The Green Flag: A History of Irish Nationalism.* 1972.

McCaffrey, Lawrence J. *Irish Federalism in the 1870s: A Study in Conservative Nationalism.* 1962.

Ō Broin, Leōn. *Fenian Fever: An Anglo-American Dilemma.* 1971.

See also GAELIC CULTURE

· · · · ·

IRISH PARTY

The Act of Union (1800) gave Ireland a direct representation by 100 members of Parliament (increased to 105 by the 1832 Reform Act), with 32 peers added to the House of Lords. This constitutional arrangement replaced the Protestant Dublin legislature known as "Grattan's Parliament" and provided the setting for Irish nationalist M.P.'s for the next 120 years.

Following **Catholic emancipation** in 1829, **Daniel O'Connell** (1775-1847) headed a parliamentary Irish party that focused on the Irish tithe to the Anglican Church of Ireland and on repeal of the Act of Union. Before 1829 O'Connell had created a powerful extraparliamentary mass movement, the Catholic Association, but his parliamentary career was more equivocal. In the Lichfield House Compact of 1835, O'Connell allied the Irish party with Whigs and Radicals. The Whig's Tithe Act (1838) converted the tithe into a money payment fluctuating with the price of grain, but by 1843 O'Connell's campaign for the repeal of the Act of Union had failed.

Between 1850 and 1859 the short-lived Irish Brigade (known derogatorily as the "Pope's Brass Band") pledged themselves to the redress of Irish land grievances. But weak leadership, dwindling numbers, and differences with the Catholic Defence Association and the Tenant League (upon which the brigade depended for popular support) frustrated the brigade in its aims.

The Irish Home Rule League was founded in 1873, and in the following year fifty-nine **Home Rule** M.P.'s were elected. A Protestant lawyer, Isaac Butt (1813-1879), led the party. It was, however, the charismatic personality of **Charles Stewart Parnell** (1846-1891) that raised Irish parliamentary nationalism to its greatest effectiveness. Against a background of widespread rural agitation and violence in Ireland, sixty-one Home Rule M.P.'s were elected in 1880. Parnell became leader of the parliamentary Home Rule party while skillfully exploiting, but never committing himself to, agrarian violence and unconstitutional methods.

In 1885 the election of eighty-six Home Rule M.P.'s gave Parnell the balance of power between the Conservative and Liberal parties in the Commons. He then supported William Gladstone in his dramatic conversion to Home Rule (1885) and unsuccessful attempt to pass a Home Rule bill in 1886. Parnell's subsequent career, however, was marred by two public scandals. He emerged from the Pigott forgeries of 1887 proven innocent of involvement in acts of political violence, but the O'Shea divorce case of 1890, in which Parnell was cited as corespondent and found guilty of adultery, ended his career.

Following Parnell's death in 1891 the Home Rule party split in two, with John Redmond (1856-1918) leading the Parnellite faction and Justin McCarthy (1830-1912) and Tim Healy (1855-1931) the anti-Parnellite faction. The groups reunited under Redmond's leadership in 1900. After 1893, however, when Gladstone's second Home Rule bill passed the Commons but was defeated in the House of Lords, Ireland rather than Westminster became the primary arena for **Irish nationalism**.

ANGUS HAWKINS

Bibliography

Mansergh, Nicholas. *The Irish Question, 1849-1921.* 1975.

McCaffrey, Lawrence J. *The Irish Question, 1800-1922.* 1968.

O'Brien, Conor Cruise. *Parnell and His Party, 1880-1890.* 1964.

O'Day, Alan. *The English Face of Irish Nationalism.* 1977.

Whyte, John H. *The Independent Irish Party, 1850-59.* 1958.

· · · · ·

IRVING, HENRY
(1838-1905)

Actor and theater manager Henry Irving was the first actor to be knighted (1895). Remembered for his interpretations of Shakespeare, he was popular in his own day for melodramas full of mystery and the supernatural. His productions represent the triumph of romanticism in English theater and were distinguished by spectacle and by lavish sets and costumes.

Born John Henry Brodribb, he adopted the name Henry Irving to avoid embarrassing his

Methodist mother. After a ten-year apprenticeship with provincial companies, he made his London debut in 1866, joined the Lyceum Theatre in 1871, and took over as manager in 1878.

As manager, he engaged Ellen Terry as leading lady and commissioned artists such as Burne-Jones to design scenes and costumes. The Lyceum was successful in London and on tour until 1897, but dramatic tastes were changing. Undaunted, Irving made a comeback, and both his last American tour (1903–1904) and his last London season (1905) were successful. He died during a provincial tour and is buried in Westminster Abbey.

In addition to acting, Irving also published *English Actors* (1886) and *The Drama: Addresses by Henry Irving* (1892), wrote for the *Nineteenth Century*, and addressed numerous professional organizations.

Among his other credits, Irving staged Tennyson's *The Cup, Queen Mary*, and *Beckett*. It may be objected that his style was counter to the prevailing trend toward naturalism, realistic settings, and contemporary themes. Nevertheless, Irving was instrumental in securing the recognition of acting as a respectable profession.

CAROL A. SENF

Bibliography

Bingham, Madeleine. *Henry Irving: The Greatest Victorian Actor*. 1978.

Rowell, George. *Theatre in the Age of Irving*. 1981.

·····

JACK THE RIPPER

In the autumn of 1888 the murder of several prostitutes in London's East End galvanized the city. The killer, also known as the Whitechapel murderer, cut the throats of his victims, disemboweling and viciously mutilating the corpses. The savagery of the killings, as well as taunting notes sent to the police and signed "Jack the Ripper" (one accompanied by part of a victim's kidney) made the crimes a national scandal. Scotland Yard's inability to apprehend a killer added to the Ripper's legend, which became the subject of newspaper articles, songs, and stories.

Despite endless speculation about the Whitechapel murders, little is known about the killer or his motive. Although the popular imagination for years associated Jack the Ripper with any prostitute murders (as many as twenty killings have been attributed to him), Scotland Yard apparently believed that only five murders, committed over a ten-week period, were actually the Ripper's work. A secret Scotland Yard file (sealed until 1992) allegedly exists, although there is disagreement on what, if anything, that file will reveal.

One popular theory blames the Whitechapel murders on Russian anarchists; another suggests that there was a conspiracy to cover up the killer's identity because Queen Victoria's grandson, Prince Edward, duke of Clarence, was involved. According to this scenario, Prince Eddy, a somewhat unconventional member of the royal family, married and had a child by a lower-class shopgirl. In an effort to silence a blackmailer or put an end to scandalous rumors, some person or persons eliminated those who knew about Eddy's liaison. Several people have been popularly identified as either killers or conspirators; most of those suspected also had some ties with the duke of Clarence. Frequently named are Montague Druitt, J. K. Stephen, Frank Miles, Walter Sickert, George Chapman, Dr. Alexander Pedachenko, John Netley, and Sir William Gull.

DON RICHARD COX

Bibliography

Farson, Daniel. *Jack the Ripper*. 1972.

Howells, Martin and Keith Skinner. *The Ripper Legacy*. 1987.

Knight, Stephen. *Jack the Ripper: The Final Solution*. 1977.

Odell, Robin. *Jack the Ripper in Fact and Fiction*. 1965.

Walkowitz, Judith R. "Jack the Ripper and the Myth of Male Violence." *Feminist Studies*, vol. 8, pp. 543–574.

·····

JAMESON, ANNA BROWNELL MURPHY (1794–1860)

Writer, art historian, and social critic Anna Brownell Murphy Jameson was the daughter of a painter and worked as a governess in her early years. Her first work, *The Diary of an Ennuyée* (1826), was published with the encouragement of her husband, barrister Robert Jameson. She decided to live separately from him after the 1836 journey to Canada that she describes in her remarkable memoir, *Winter Studies and Summer Rambles in Canada* (1838).

Although Jameson wrote imaginatively about women in literature, especially in the study of Shakespeare's heroines entitled *Characteristics of Women* (1832), she was increasingly concerned with women's problems in a newly industrialized society. *Memoirs and Essays* (1846) includes articles on women's employment; *Sisters of Charity* (1855) calls for Protestant sisterhoods to train women in nursing and social service; *Communion of Labour* (1856) argues for extending maternal influence into society.

Jameson produced museum guidebooks; the influential *Memoirs of the Early Italian Painters* (1845); and several books on the symbolism of Christian art, including *Sacred and Legendary Art* (1848) and *Legends of the Madonna* (1852). Her work for women inspired younger feminists; and her essays on art formed popular taste, contributed to the historical study of art, and helped establish the specialized practice of art criticism.

ROBIN SHEETS

Bibliography

Holcomb, Adele M. "Anna Jameson: Sacred Art and Social Vision." In Claire Sherman and Adele Holcomb, eds., *Women as Interpreters of the Visual Arts.* 1981.

———. "Anna Jameson: The First Professional English Art Historian." *Art History,* vol. 6, pp. 171–187.

Thomas, Clara. *Love and Work Enough: The Life of Anna Jameson.* 1967.

· · · · ·

JAMESON, LEANDER STARR (1853–1917)

A physician and South African politician, Leander Starr Jameson was born in Edinburgh and educated in London. Not long after assuming a medical partnership in Kimberley, he established a close friendship with **Cecil Rhodes**. As Rhodes's devoted assistant, Jameson helped to secure the British South Africa (BSA) Company's control over Rhodesia (1891–1893). While serving as resident commissioner of the Bechuanaland border strip adjacent to the Boer Transvaal Republic, Jameson launched his ill-fated raid into the Transvaal in late December 1895.

Jameson precipitately invaded the Transvaal in hopes of taking advantage of non-Boer insurrection, but was surrounded and compelled to surrender to a Boer force on January 2, 1896. He was repatriated to England, tried, and sentenced to fifteen months imprisonment. Released after six months, he returned to Rhodesia to assist Rhodes in dealing with native uprisings. At the onset of the second **Boer War** in October 1899, Jameson left Rhodesia for Natal and was caught up in the Boer siege of Ladysmith. In 1900, he was elected to the Cape Parliament, but throughout 1901 attended to Rhodes until Rhodes's death in early 1902.

Jameson subsequently became leader of the Progressive party in the Cape Parliament and prime minister in 1904. Contrary to all expectations, he proved conciliatory toward the Boers and was responsible for much constructive legislation. He resigned as prime minister in 1908 but continued in Cape politics until for health reasons he left for England in 1912.

Knighted in 1911, Jameson became president of the BSA Company in 1913. During World War I he worked to succor British prisoners of war. A lifelong bachelor, he was buried beside Rhodes in South Africa. Jameson was an enigmatic personality who achieved notoriety for the raid fiasco and, later, considerable respect for his constructive role in South African politics.

J. O. BAYLEN

Bibliography

Butler, Jeffery E. *The Liberal Party and the Jameson Raid.* 1963.

Colvin, Ian D. *The Life of Jameson.* 1922. 2 vols.

Lockhart, John Gilbert and C. M. Woodhouse. *Rhodes.* 1963.

Pakenham, Elizabeth. *Jameson's Raid.* 1960.

van der Poel, Jean. *The Jameson Raid.* 1951.

· · · · ·

JEKYLL, GERTRUDE (1843–1932)

Gertrude Jekyll was in many ways comparable to the multitalented craftsman William Morris (1834–1896): educated both by the local traditions of her regional neighborhood and by travel, self-sufficient, a talented painter, a craftswoman in wood, and adroit in embroidery, Jekyll was, most notably, the preeminent gardener of the late Victorian and Edwardian periods. Her painter's eye created Jekyll plantings characterized by impressionistic floral groupings reflecting both the "wildness" called for by her contemporary, William Robinson (1838–1935), as well as a controlling order achieved through color harmonies and the structure of a more architectonic layout, this latter quality an influence from **Edwin Lutyens** (1869–1944) with whom she collaborated on over a hundred gardens.

Some of Jekyll's most successful plantings for Lutyens's houses include Chinthurst Hill (1893), her home Munstead Wood (1896), Orchards (1897–1899), Deanery Garden (1899–1901), Marshcourt (1901–1904), and Folly Farm (1901 on). Millmead (1904–1907) was built for Jekyll as a speculation and presents an intimate garden on a very small scale. The traditional materials and vernacular style of Lutyens's architecture, together with a return to more formal and architectonic devices of garden ornament, produced a synthesis of house and garden: a building linked by garden walls and paths with climbing plants and coordinated levels seemed to grow out of the ground, just as the courtyards, garden "rooms," and views were calculated extensions of the house itself.

Jekyll extended the herbaceous border to create tonal gardens in which sequences of coordinated plantings of one dominant color, then another, presented a tapestry of foliage and floral masses. Her concern for texture, color, and shapes joined her keen appreciation for native Surrey cottage gardens to create pictorial, painterly gardens, both natural and architectural, and designed to delight the eye.

ROBERT M. CRAIG

Bibliography

Brown, Jane. *Gardens of a Golden Afternoon: The Story of a Partnership: Edwin Lutyens and Gertrude Jekyll.* 1982.

Jekyll, Francis. *Gertrude Jekyll: A Memoir.* 1934.

Lewis, Cherry, ed. *The Making of a Garden, Gertrude Jekyll: An Anthology of Her Writings, Illustrated with Her Photographs and Drawings, and Watercolours by Contemporary Artists.* 1984.

Massingham, Betty. *Miss Jekyll: Portrait of a Great Gardener.* 1966.

Weaver, Lawrence. *Houses and Gardens by E. L. Lutyens.* 1913.

See also GARDENS AND PARKS; LANDSCAPE ARCHITECTURE AND DESIGN

· · · · ·

JERROLD, DOUGLAS (1803–1857)

As a dramatist, Douglas Jerrold played a key role in the development of popular English theater; as a journalist and humorist, particularly as "Mr. Punch," he satirized Victorian self-importance. His nautical melodrama, *Black-Eyed Susan* (1829), had a record first-year run of four hundred nights in six theaters. Jerrold's prolific output of short stories, sketches, and essays, of which the *Punch* serial, *Mrs. Caudle's Curtain Lectures* (1845) is the best known, and his efforts as founder and editor of other magazines and weekly newspapers make him a significant figure in the history of periodical literature.

Born into a theatrical family, Jerrold left home at the age of ten to join the navy, a life he would later celebrate in his nautical melodramas. One of Jerrold's goals as playwright was to restore native drama to the English stage in a period dominated by adaptations of French farces. After writing for the unlicensed theaters, he made his debut at Drury Lane with an original domestic melodrama, *The Rent Day* (1832), which featured stage tableaux and bore the seeds of social criticism.

While he continued to write melodramas, farces, and—with less success—comedies and tragedies, Jerrold's career as a journalist flourished. He published frequently in the *Athenaeum, Punch in London*, and *Blackwood's Magazine* in the 1830s, attacking game laws, war, governmental policies, dishonest lawyers, and religious hypocrisy. The pseudonym Barabbas Whitefeather was used for *The Handbook of Swindling* (1839), and the signature "Q" marked Jerrold's first contribution to *Punch* (1841). As editor of the *Illuminated Magazine* (1843), Jerrold experimented with the use of color illustration, and with *Douglas Jerrold's Shilling Magazine* (1845) he attempted to make monthly miscellanies, which usually sold for a half-crown, more accessible.

Many of Jerrold's works have yet to be collected and much of the "criticism" of his work is contained in glowing memories of his descendants; consequently, his contributions to Victorian drama and periodical literature and his influence upon such contemporaries as Wilkie Collins, Dickens, and Thackeray have yet to be fully explored.

CHRISTINE DEWAR

Bibliography

Jerrold, Walter. *Douglas Jerrold and "Punch."* 1910.

Kelly, Richard. *Douglas Jerrold.* 1972.

· · · · ·

JEWRY AND JUDAISM

In 1850 approximately 20,000 Jews resided in London and a smaller number in the provinces; 90 percent were native English people and the remainder immigrants from continental Europe. Two major currents brought this community under constant scrutiny: the successful struggle for full emancipation, and the mass immigration which began in the 1870s and had by 1914 profoundly transformed a community of over 300,000 Jews.

In 1829, with the grant of Catholic emancipation, Jews remained virtually the sole group in Britain that did not possess full civil and political rights. Because Jews did enjoy general freedom of occupation and residential mobility, few were directly affected by the partial denial of equality. Nevertheless, Jewish disabilities were considerable. Parliament remained closed to Jews, obstructing their capacity to play a role in political life. Similarly Jews were barred from the military, enjoyed only limited access to the bar, and could not matriculate at either Oxford or Cambridge.

In large measure, these disabilities were an outgrowth of church-state relations. Opponents of Jewish emancipation maintained that England was a Christian country. Full equality, in their view, should not be granted those who failed to intermarry with Christians, and whose primary loyalties, allegedly, were to Palestine. Proponents of Jewish emancipation agreed that Jews possessed objectionable characteristics but hoped that emancipation would improve their character.

In the end, emancipation arrived in stages. In 1858 Lionel de **Rothschild** was permitted to assume his seat in the Commons without taking the offensive oath, "by the true faith of a Christian." In 1870 Jews were permitted to matriculate at the universities. Emancipation was completed in 1890 when Jews were permitted to occupy the positions of lord chancellor or lord lieutenant for Ireland.

Jews regarded their emancipation as the "liberal compromise." Subsequently Jews would be regarded as "English people of the Jewish persuasion." Jewish values were understood to parallel British values, and Jews became eager to demonstrate their loyalty to Britain by, for example, loudly proclaiming their patriotism during the Boer War. In gratitude to the Liberals for spearheading the emancipation struggle, Jews, at least until the 1890s, generally inclined toward Liberal candidates.

It was no accident that during these years Jews should attract considerable comment, both favorable and unfavorable. One detects echoes of the emancipation debate in Victorian novels. Jewish characters are frequently depicted by exaggerated images. For instance, Dickens alternates between the monstrous Fagin of *Oliver Twist* (1837–1838) and the entirely virtuous Riah of *Our Mutual Friend* (1864–1865). George Eliot similarly portrays *Daniel Deronda* (1874–1876) as embodying all that is good and noble. **Benjamin Disraeli**, too, in *Alroy* (1833), *Tancred* (1847), and other novels idealized Jewish heroes as leaders in thought and philosophy. Conversely, Carlyle portrayed Jews as lacking a sense of humor and contributing nothing of a spiritual nature.

In many ways these authors perpetuated stereotyped images of Jews. Absent were realistic, authentic portraits. The best of the Jewish novelists sought to escape these extremes of disgust and adulation. **Israel Zangwill**, for instance, in *Children of the Ghetto* (1892), focused on the clash of Jewish heritage and Western culture in London's East End.

Zangwill's novel symbolized the major transformations, owing to mass eastern European immigration, that occurred at the close of the Victorian era. This immigration affected virtually all facets of Jewish communal, institutional, and religious life. Economically, Jews became a lower middle-class element with particularly heavy representation in the clothing industry, which employed a quarter of the Jewish work force.

More tellingly, the immigrants challenged existing religious and communal leadership. In 1870 the United Synagogue Act created a unified financial structure for member congregations under the supervision of the chief rabbi. Although the few sephardic and reform synagogues remained technically outside this structure, the chief rabbi became the authoritative spokesman of Judaism and ambassador to the outside world. The institution functioned as a cohesive force and as a centralized religious authority. Chief Rabbi **Nathan Adler** (succeeded in turn by his son Hermann Adler) lent personal coloring and prestige to the office. In 1855 Adler established Jews' College to train ministers along his model of Jewish ambassadors to British society.

Not all segments of the community accepted this claim. Reform Judaism had originally risen as a communal schism and a rejection of Orthodox leadership for being insufficiently active in the battle for emancipation. The sephardic Bevis Marks synagogue also remained outside the United synagogue, looking to its own *Haham* for religious leadership. Despite the communal ban Chief Rabbi Adler placed upon Reform Judaism, however, its actual practice differed but little from Orthodoxy. Only in the twentieth century did Reform Judaism in England sharply diverge from historical communal norms.

Immigration, however, did weaken the cohesiveness of the United Synagogue. The immigrants formed small synagogues outside the existing structure. Immigrant clergymen often rejected the authority of the chief rabbi. In particular many opposed the outspoken anti-Zionism of Hermann Adler.

Finally, immigration challenged the prevailing leadership institutions of Anglo-Jewry. The community had long been directed by a small number of elite families (commonly referred to as the cousinhood) known for their philanthropy and communal service, who expressed great satisfaction with Britain. The Rothschild, Montefiore, and Montagu clans dominated the cousinhood, frequently intermarrying with one another, and rotating communal offices among leading family members. The *Jewish Chronicle*, established in 1841, functioned as the mouthpiece of communal leadership and articulated the virtues of emancipation and the liberal compromise. The Board of Deputies of Anglo-Jews served as the communal watchdog, guarding the religious rights of the community. Together with the Anglo-Jewish Association, it established the Conjoint Foreign Committee to ameliorate the plight of beleaguered Jews abroad.

The immigrant community was by no means satisfied with this leadership. Challenges arose from the provinces, the Yiddish press, and the Zionist organizations. Edwardian Britain would, in turn, witness substantial shifts in Jewish communal life owing to the ongoing transformation of Anglo-Jewry.

STEVEN BAYME

Bibliography

Bermant, Chaim. *The Cousinhood.* 1971.

Burman, Rickie. "'She Looketh Well to the Ways of Her Household': The Changing Role of Jewish Women in Religious Life, c. 1880–1930." In Gail

Malmgren, ed., *Religion in the Lives of English Women, 1760–1930.* 1986.

Gartner, Lloyd. *The Jewish Immigrant in England.* 1973.

Lucien, Wolf. "The Queen's Jewry." In Lucien Wolf, *Essays in Jewish History.* 1934.

Namann, Anne. *Jews in the Victorian Novel.* 1980.

Newman, Aubrey. *The United Synagogue.* 1976.

Salbstein, M. C. N. *The Emancipation of the Jews in England.* 1982.

See also ABRAHAMS, ISRAEL; ANGLO-JEWISH NOVEL; MONTEFIORE, MOSES H.

. . . . .

JEWSBURY, GERALDINE ENDSOR (1812–1880)

A northern novelist and budding feminist, Geraldine Jewsbury scandalized even her friends with her advanced ideas and convention-defying heroines in *Zoe* (1845) and the superior but less-known *The Half-Sisters* (1848). She wrote the Lancashire novel *Marian Withers* (1851), the children's tale *The History of an Adopted Child* (1853), and reviews for the *Athenaeum*. Her admiration for Thomas Carlyle led to a stormy friendship with his wife Jane Welsh Carlyle and the correspondence later edited by Mrs. Alexander Ireland in *Selections from the Letters of Geraldine Endsor Jewsbury to Jane Welsh Carlyle* (1892).

Born in Measham, Derbyshire, and raised in Manchester, Jewsbury was early motherless and responsible for her merchant father's household after the marriage in 1832 of her talented sister Maria, to whom Wordsworth addressed "Liberty" (1829). In 1854 she moved to Chelsea near Jane Carlyle. Abounding in mental and nervous energy, she was a witty little woman with a circle of intellectual friends, including T. H. Huxley, Connop Thirwall, J. A. Froude, and W. E. Forster. As manuscript reader for Bentley and for Hurst and Blackett, she exercised influence over the popular fiction published in midcentury.

Zoe and *The Half-Sisters*, though tediously discursive and didactic, present broad panoramas against which the strong-minded heroines, both illegitimate offspring of Latin mothers, work out their destinies, proving themselves more resilient and self-fulfilling than their conventional English counterparts. These melodramatic novels have great scope and retain interest because of their uncanny perception of women's needs and future development.

TAMIE WATTERS

Bibliography

Fahnestock, Jeanne Rosenmayer. "Geraldine Jewsbury: The Power of the Publisher's Reader." *Nineteenth-Century Fiction*, vol. 28, pp. 253–272.

Howe, Susanne. *Geraldine Jewsbury.* 1935.

Woolf, Virginia. "Geraldine and Jane." *TLS*, February 28, 1929.

. . . . .

JEX-BLAKE, SOPHIA LOUISA (1840–1912)

Sophia Jex-Blake was the real pioneer of women's **medical education** in Britain. Both Elizabeth Blackwell and Elizabeth Garrett Anderson had their names placed on the medical register by using loopholes that were subsequently closed. Jex-Blake, however, succeeded in opening a path to licensed medical practice that other women could follow.

The youngest daughter of Thomas Jex-Blake (a proctor of Doctor's Commons) and his wife Maria Emily Cubitt, Jex-Blake enrolled at London's Queen's College for Women in 1858 and, between 1859 and 1861, tutored mathematics there. She also taught in Germany and visited coeducational colleges in America, where she became friends with Dr. Lucy Sewell of the New England Hospital for Women and Children and decided on a career in medicine.

Jex-Blake at first intended to train in America, but was called home in 1868 by the death of her father. Furthermore, the Medical Education Act (1858) refused to recognize foreign degrees (Blackwell had gained registered status because hers was earned before 1858). Jex-Blake turned her attention to establishing women's right to medical education in Britain. In 1869, after their first application had been denied, she and five other women were permitted to matriculate at Edinburgh University and pursue a special course of medical studies for women, although with increasing difficulties. In 1872 the university refused to graduate the women, offering instead to award "certificates of proficiency." (The certificate—without the degree—would not allow them to be placed on the medical register.)

Although no other medical school would admit them, Jex-Blake discovered a few sympathetic professors at various London teaching hospitals and persuaded them to give lectures at the London School of Medicine for Women which was established, through her efforts, in 1874. In 1877 the school finally secured cooperation from a hospital and was able to offer the requisite clinical training. Meanwhile, Jex-Blake had also secured allies in Parliament. She supplied the arguments and even the first draft of what became the Russell Gurney Enabling Act (1876), which granted all examining bodies the power to examine women. Jex-Blake, who had already been awarded an M.D. by the University of Berne, made use of the new act to secure certification from the Irish College of Physicians (1877) and became legally entitled to practice medicine in Great Britain.

Jex-Blake settled in Edinburgh in 1878, where she engaged in private practice. In 1885 she founded a women's hospital, and in 1886 a school of medicine for women. Ten years later when the University of Edinburgh finally agreed to grant the M.D. to women, much of the credit was due to Jex-Blake for her unremitting pressure.

Because of her ceaseless efforts to open medical education to other women, Jex-Blake may be regarded as a more significant pioneer than Elizabeth Garrett Anderson. Jex-Blake's publications include: *A Visit to Some American Schools and Colleges* (1867); *Medical Women* (1872); *The Care of Infants* (1884); and articles in *Fortnightly Review* (1875) and *Nineteenth Century* (1887, 1894).

ROSEMARY T. VAN ARSDEL

Bibliography

Todd, Margaret. *Life of Sophia Jex-Blake.* 1918.

· · · · ·

JONES, HENRY ARTHUR (1851–1929)

An important figure in the renascence of English drama and a tireless campaigner for the establishment of a national theater, Henry Arthur Jones first achieved fame as a contriver of sentimental comedies and melodramas. *The Silver King* (1882), produced by Wilson Barrett at the Princess's Theatre, was praised for raising popular drama once more to the plane of literature. The play's long run assured Jones a measure of financial independence. In pieces like *Saints and Sinners* (1884), *The Middleman* (1889), and *Judah* (1890) Jones attempted to deal with more complex social and moral issues, although his denouements still smacked of melodramatic contrivance.

During the 1890s Jones's popularity was at its height, and he wrote for many of London's leading impresarios. Herbert Beerbohm Tree produced *The Dancing Girl* (1891) and *The Tempter* (1893) at the Haymarket, and George Alexander *The Masqueraders* (1894) at the St. James's Theatre with a cast that included Mrs. Patrick Campbell. In 1896 Johnston Forbes-Robertson suffered one of Jones's few failures with *Michael and His Lost Angel*, a work the playwright continued to regard as among his best. It is, however, in the series of society dramas composed for Charles Wyndham between 1893 and 1900 that Jones found a unique and individual voice. The figure of the worldly-wise *raisonneur* who dominates *The Case of Rebellious Susan* (1894), *The Liars* (1897), and *Mrs. Dane's Defence* (1900) provided both author and actor with opportunities to extend their range.

In the early part of the twentieth century Jones's reputation suffered an eclipse from which it has yet to emerge. The playwright's last years were occupied by bitter (and largely one-sided) political disputes with George Bernard Shaw and H. G. Wells.

JOEL H. KAPLAN

Bibliography

Cordell, Richard A. *Henry Arthur Jones and the Modern Drama.* 1932.

Hamilton, Clayton, ed. *Representative Plays.* 1925. 4 vols.

Jackson, Russell, ed. *Plays by Henry Arthur Jones.* 1982.

Jones, Doris Arthur. *The Life and Letters of Henry Arthur Jones.* 1930.

Jones, Henry Arthur. *The Foundations of a National Drama.* 1913.

——. *The Renascence of the English Drama.* 1895.

　· · · · ·

JONES, OWEN (1809-1874)

Owen Jones was a prominent designer, architect, and writer of the midcentury who achieved a lasting reputation for his handbook, *The Grammar of Ornament* (1856).

Jones studied architecture under Lewis Vuillamy in 1825-1831, and art at the Royal Academy in 1829. He then traveled to the Middle East and Spain in 1832-1834 and 1837. One result was a study of the Alhambra, in which Jones first presented his views on decoration. This was followed by his designs of tiles and mosaics, in which he developed a Moorish style.

In 1850 Jones was appointed joint architect of the **Exhibition of 1851** and was responsible for its interior color scheme. But he was critical of most of the exhibits displayed, and so devoted much thought to the reform of design. His *Grammar of Ornament* (1856) incorporated designs from several regions of the globe. In 1852 he was appointed director of decorations for the Crystal Palace in Sydenham. He designed for a variety of media, including furniture, wallpaper, fabric, and carpets. His architecture featured the use of iron and glass, notably in St. James Hall (1858).

Jones was an early advocate of the use of new industrial materials in architecture and of the principle that decoration should follow function. He also promoted the abstraction of

nature in ornament. His most significant influence came through the compendium of design in the *Grammar.*

LARRY D. LUTCHMANSINGH

Bibliography

Boe, Alf. *From Gothic Revival to Functional Form.* 1957.

Jones, Owen. *Examples of Chinese Ornament.* 1867.

——. *The Grammar of Ornament.* 1856.

　· · · · ·

JOURNALISM AND JOURNALISTS

The history of journalism is the history of the Victorian age. Not just as a vivid contemporary record, but in its huge quantity and vast range, its penetration of all levels of society, and its close interaction with the realms of literature, philosophy, religion, and politics, the work of the journalists—the writers, editors, publishers, and sellers of periodicals—is of unprecedented and unequaled significance.

The political power of newspapers had been recognized in the taxes or stamp duties on every copy, which were intended to restrict their circulation among the working classes. Although the fourpenny tax was reduced to a penny in 1836, it was not until midcentury that a campaign promoting the educational power of the press succeeded in abolishing the **"taxes on knowledge."** Lower prices and increasing literacy broadened readership; technological advances in printing (faster presses, cheaper inks, wood pulp paper) and in communication (telegraphs to assemble and railways to distribute the news) enabled publishers to provide readers with a dozen London dailies and hundreds of provincial papers.

This "golden age" saw a gradual shift in the function of newspapers, from partisan political organs to avowedly commercial ventures. By the 1880s and 1890s the so-called new journalism catered frankly to its consumers. Influential editors such as W. T. Stead oversaw the transformation of Victorian into recognizably modern newspapers, with front-page news rather than advertisements, less commentary, more illustration and human interest, interviews, sports coverage, and typographical changes that improved readability and reflected the changing relationship between reader and newspaper.

By the end of the century, newspaper journalists had also changed: a newspaper's proprietor and manager were no longer likely to be its editor and chief writer as well. Attempts to achieve professional status through the Institute of Journalists (chartered in 1890) foundered in the conflict between owners and working journalists, so that the unionization of the latter followed naturally (1907). Writing journalism for a living was not a sufficiently exclusive occupation to become a profession like medicine or the law. Nevertheless, its reputation did improve over the century. In 1825 even editing a newspaper had been thought degrading for a gentleman, although journalism in non-newspaper periodicals was always somewhat more respectable.

The questionable status of journalists is linked with the practice of anonymity, which did not begin to break down until the 1860s. Anonymity lent the authority of the whole journal to its individual writers, but opponents attacked it as irresponsible and widely abused. Editors, however, were grateful for the flexibility it gave them. Furthermore, anonymity allowed writers to contribute to a variety of journals and helped unknowns and an increasing number of women to get into print. It also encouraged outsiders such as politicians or lawyers who did not want their contributions acknowledged. The shift to signatures meant an increasing reliance on big-name experts, to the detriment of the all-round journalist who would tackle any topic under cover of anonymity.

In fact, to speak of Victorian journalists is to speak of a wide variety of amateurs and professionals. The very number of periodicals (more than 50,000 titles between 1824 and 1900) meant that for the first time it was possible for many to earn a decent living with the pen. The 1871 census recorded over 2,100 "authors, editors, and journalists"; the 1901, 11,000. Though the new Grub Street had its shadowy back alleys, it was also a respectable thoroughfare traversed by nearly every literary aspirant. Nor was journalism just a literary career; it was a major part of intellectual activity in all areas. Historians, scientists, politicians, theologians, and critics all wrote for the periodicals. Recent scholarly work in identifying authorship is revealing the extent of this intellectual cross-fertilization.

In the world of the higher journalism, the great quarterly reviews—the *Edinburgh* (1802) and the *Quarterly* (1809)—were losing their preeminence to the monthlies such as the variously titled *Westminster Review* or the misleadingly titled *Fortnightly* (1865), which could respond more quickly to current issues. Even more flexible were the weeklies, among them the *Saturday Review* (1855) and the *Academy* (1869), which drew Oxford and Cambridge graduates and dons into journalism as reviewers and "revilers." The magazines that followed *Blackwood's* (1817)—including *Fraser's* (1830), *Macmillan's* (1859), and *Cornhill* (1860)—were miscellanies, not bound by the convention that every article was at least nominally a book review. They varied widely in aim and content, were generally lighter than the reviews, and were noted for their fiction. Those who wrote for and edited these publications took seriously their responsibilities as intellectual, moral, and cultural leaders, even in a popular family magazine like Dickens's *Household Words* (1850).

Other journalists had more specialized, sometimes less lofty, aims. There were hundreds of earnestly "improving" magazines, from the *Penny Magazine* (1832) of the Society for the Diffusion of Useful Knowledge, through countless religious titles, to *The Magdalen's Friend* (1860). Specialist periodicals met every conceivable professional or leisure interest and espoused every cause. Sensationalism such as that in *Lloyd's Penny Weekly* (1843) sold well even before the stamp tax was lifted; comic journals such as *Hood's Monthly Magazine and Comic Miscellany* (1844) flared and sputtered, while *Punch* (1841) proved that wit need not be ephemeral. *The Servant's Magazine* (1837), *Boy's Own Paper* (1879), *Girl's Own Paper* (1880), and the like were directed to particular readerships. Women's magazines of fashion, domesticity, and piety were perennially successful, while those with a broader vision of woman's role found fewer readers.

Journalism provides a context for the extraordinary, and Victorian journalism is itself an extraordinary achievement, recording and embodying the growth and diversity of its time. Its many voices are only now being identified, and their import and influence have yet to be fully appreciated.

SUSAN DRAIN

Bibliography

Bennett, Scott et al. *Victorian Periodicals: A Guide to Research*. 1978.

Brown, Lucy. *Victorian News and Newspapers*. 1985.

Cross, Nigel. *The Common Writer: Life in Nineteenth-Century Grub Street*. 1985.

Gross, John. *The Rise and Fall of the Man of Letters*. 1969.

Journal of Newspaper and Periodical History. 1984–.

Madden, Lionel and Diana Dixon. *The Nineteenth-Century Periodical Press in Britain. A Bibliography of Modern Studies, 1901–1971*. 1976.

Palmegiano, E. M. *Women and British Periodicals, 1832–1867. A Bibliography*. 1976.

Shattock, Joanne and Michael Wolff, eds. *The Victorian Periodical Press: Samplings and Soundings*. 1982.

Sullivan, Alvin, ed. *British Literary Magazines*. Vol. 3: *The Victorian and Edwardian Age, 1837–1913*. 1984.

Victorian Periodicals Newsletter. 1968–1978. Subsequently *Victorian Periodicals Review*. 1979–.

See also PERIODICALS; PRESS; RUSSELL, WILLIAM HOWARD

. . . . .

JOWETT, BENJAMIN (1817–1893)

Benjamin Jowett was a biblical critic and classical scholar; above all, he was an educator. At Oxford, as tutor (1842) and master (1870) of Balliol College, and as Regius professor of Greek (1855), he deeply influenced many able pupils whom he trained to be leaders of the nation.

Educated at St. Paul's School and Balliol,

Jowett became a fellow of his college in 1838 and was ordained in 1842, when he became a tutor. His early interest was in **biblical criticism**, in association with his friend A. P. Stanley; he was influenced by German scholarship. His commentary on St. Paul's epistles (1855) contained an essay on the atonement which attacked conventional views, producing an unsuccessful but humiliating opposition to his Greek professorship. He contributed an essay "On the Interpretation of Scripture" to *Essays and Reviews* (1860), saying that the Bible should be read "like any other book" and pleading eloquently for freedom of scholarship.

The hostile reaction to *Essays and Reviews* led Jowett to abandon biblical studies. Thereafter his publications consisted of classical translations and editions, notably his translation of Plato's dialogues (1871). His **classical scholarship** was often inaccurate, but no deeper mind has ever been applied to the subject. One of his pupils, Algernon Charles Swinburne, incorporated the classical spirit into English literature. Meanwhile Jowett was a successful teacher, as tutor and professor, building a body of pupils with whom he maintained close contact and to whose careers he was devoted. He was active in university reform. Balked of the mastership of Balliol in 1854, he obtained it in 1870, and in his day Balliol was the first college in Oxford. He was vice-chancellor of the university from 1882 to 1886. Jowett was a major scholar, but it was through his pupils, many of whom achieved eminence, that he influenced English history.

JOSEF L. ALTHOLZ

Bibliography

Abbott, Evelyn and Lewis Campbell. *The Life and Letters of Benjamin Jowett, M.A., Master of Balliol College, Oxford*. 1897. 2 vols.

Faber, Geoffrey. *Jowett: A Portrait with Background*. 1957.

. . . . .

JUDICIAL SYSTEM

At the outset of the Victorian era the judicial system encompassed two separate, though complementary, court hierarchies.

The lord chancellor presided over the entire structure by virtue of his position as chief legal officer of the Crown and his presiding over the Court of Chancery. **Chancery** administered equity law, the body of legal rules that had arisen in the later medieval period to provide remedies for problems unresolved by the common law courts. In 1837 the common-law courts—Queen's Bench, Common Pleas, and Exchequer—were substantially as they had been since the thirteenth century. The intervening centuries, however, had blurred jurisdictional boundaries, and **common law** and equity composed two parts of one judicial system. Less-important courts, because their business was limited, were the Prerogative Court of Canterbury and the Court of Admiralty. These courts relied primarily on civil law principles, and dealt with matrimonial and naval prize cases respectively.

Most courts served as a court of first instance, and an appeals procedure from original courts troubled the entire system. Throughout the Victorian period attempts were made to rationalize the traditions that made the system proverbial for delay and expense. Not until the Judicature Act of 1875, however, was a formal court of appeal established for the unified Supreme Court of Judicature. Despite controversy over its role, the House of Lords remained the court of final appeal, although ordinary members of the Lords could no longer hear appeals. The other court of appeal for the Victorian period was the Judicial Committee of the Privy Council, which functioned as the appeals court for the civil law courts and for appeals in colonial cases.

On the regional level the judicial system was organized into various circuits for the purpose of making Crown justice available on a regular basis. In these courts were heard both criminal and civil cases, almost always of a substantial nature. For the ordinary citizen encounters with the court system usually occurred, if at all, on the local level, where the presiding official would be either a magistrate or justice of the peace. Most litigation was decided in these local courts.

Throughout the evolution of the legal system the role of judge-made law had constituted a major strength of the common law. The judiciary, using precedent to create certainty in the law, nevertheless had little hesitation in rendering decisions that made new law. In this fashion judges blended tradition with change, permitting the law to alter in conformity with diverse social, economic, and political needs. The Victorian judiciary wrestled with the problem of whether court decisions should embody forthrightly personal policy choices. Reformers emphasized the need for the law to possess a scientific basis free from individual caprice. By the middle of the nineteenth century, sparked by the demands for scientific **law reform** associated with Jeremy Bentham (1748–1832), the theory of judicial decision-making had become a formal process. The assumption that the law existed in either case law or statutes, and waited only for discovery by the judge, became the prevalent judicial technique. Nevertheless, the fact remained that judges inevitably injected personal preferences into decisions.

The judiciary also shared in the Victorian emphasis on professionalization. The course of judicial reform reflected concern for rationalization of procedure, preservation of status, and discharge of duties in a competent, dignified atmosphere. Stress upon efficiency accorded well with the changing social values of Victorian Britain. Whereas the judiciary in the eighteenth century had originated primarily in the landed classes and expressed the norms of an agricultural society, the Victorian judiciary was increasingly drawn from the middle classes created by industrialization. Judicial legislation made it possible for the law to adapt to the changed social circumstances generated by urbanization and industrialization.

Perhaps the greatest change in the judicial system during the Victorian period came in public acceptance. In 1837 the court structure possessed a reputation for inefficiency and expense. By the end of the Victorian period, however, due to the incremental process of reform, the system had acquired a much stronger approval from the general public. The transformation of the court system, which would attract admiration from many quarters in the twentieth century, was a Victorian accomplishment. Thus the Victorian judicial system both initiated and reflected important social trends. To have done this, while gaining a greater dimension of public confidence, was no small feat. Whether viewed as a form of paternalistic social control or the expression of Victorian ideals, the judicial system played a major role in the modernization of Victorian society.

RICHARD A. COSGROVE

Bibliography

Duman, Daniel. *The Judicial Bench in England, 1727-1875: The Reshaping of a Professional Elite.* 1982.

Duncan, G. I. O. *The High Court of Delegates.* 1971.

Fifoot, Cecil H. S. *Judge and Jurist in the Reign of Victoria.* 1959.

Heuston, R. F. V. *Lives of the Lord Chancellors, 1885-1940.* 1964.

Howell, Peter A. *The Judicial Committee of the Privy Council, 1833-1876: Its Origins, Structure and Development.* 1979.

Stevens, Robert. *Law and Politics: The House of Lords as a Judicial Body, 1800-1976.* 1978.

See also INHERITANCE;
SCOTS LAW

· · · · ·

JUVENILE CRIME

In the years immediately after the Napoleonic Wars, Londoners began to express concern over the extreme youthfulness of many convicted criminals, and believed that there had been an alarming increase in the number of offenses committed by children and young people. No separate legal code or court system existed for juveniles; children over the age of seven were tried, imprisoned, and transported on the same grounds as adults. In the 1830s and 1840s, articles on juvenile delinquency appeared frequently in periodicals. (One essay competition used the term "juvenile depravity.") Reformers such as Mary Carpenter (1807-1877) and Lord Shaftesbury (1801-1885) proposed legal changes and new institutions intended to separate juveniles from hardened criminals and prevent children from becoming enmeshed in a life of crime. By the late 1850s, contemporaries sensed a decline in juvenile crime and a re-

duction in the floating population of young vagrants; by 1870 most agreed that hordes of hardened juveniles were no longer a frightening component of the urban scene.

In the absence of a separate legal code, the word "juvenile" was used loosely, but generally applied to those between about eight and eighteen to twenty years of age. Since there was no effective birth registration, however, courts depended on a culprit's own statement of age, and experienced offenders quickly learned to say whatever they thought would lead to the most favorable treatment. One reason for the increase in juvenile crime can be found in the demographic changes that accompanied industrialization; earlier marriage, rising birth rates, and the dislocations of urbanization created a society with a high proportion of children, and dramatically increased the drifting population of rootless teenagers who were orphaned, deserted, runaways, or simply on their own.

Such children were likely to be sentenced to prison for actions that might be considered only boyish mischief in other classes. Contemporaries, however, were greatly concerned by the existence of a "criminal class"—in which children simply followed their parents' trade—and by children's progress from minor to more serious offenses. Charles Dickens, Henry Mayhew, and others were both fascinated and appalled by the colorful and clannish nature of London's criminal subculture. There were, indeed, gangs of boys under adult direction as portrayed in *Oliver Twist* (1837-1839); they were trained as pickpockets, used as decoys to lure or distract victims of robbery, lifted through high windows to gain entry for burglary, posted as lookouts, and employed to pass bogus bills and coins. Fear and loyalty prevented gang members from giving evidence; and sometimes the leader successfully passed as an irate middle-class parent, promised swift punishment, and saved his young accomplice from arrest. Urban slums contained "rookeries" that were effectively controlled by criminals and almost impervious to police penetration. Common lodging houses served as schools where gang members could instruct one another. The midcentury reformers who tried to rescue prostitutes discovered that girls often slipped casually into sexual activity with the boys of a gang at age twelve or thirteen and were, soon afterwards, working the streets. Carefully veiled language in a few contemporary sources indicates that young boys also offered themselves as prostitutes.

In 1837, a report from the commissioners on criminal law recommended changes in the treatment of juvenile offenders. It was apparent that repeated short sentences (typically one to three months) for offences such as stealing food from a stall had little deterrent effect, accomplished nothing in the way of reformation, and placed children in prison with adults who could school them in crime. The Juvenile Offenders Act (1847) allowed magistrates to exercise summary disposition in cases of petty larceny committed by those under fourteen, and to discharge the offender without punishment if they thought it best. A further act in 1850 raised the age to sixteen. Informally, many magistrates simply handed such children over to someone who promised to look after them.

In another attempt to prevent children from beginning a criminal career, charitable reformers established "ragged schools" for those too poor and too "rough" to attend other schools. After 1850 pauper children were generally housed in schools separate from the general workhouse population; and the better unions made an effort to provide effective vocational training. Mary Carpenter and others began reformatory schools, intended to break the pattern of repeated short prison terms by confining children for two years or more in an institution that would provide both education and distance from former companions in crime. Carpenter's testimony had a major influence on the acts that gave legislative sanction to reformatory schools (1854) and industrial schools (1857). It subsequently became usual to send juveniles to a reformatory school on a second offence if the crime were one that could be punished by imprisonment. Industrial schools provided agricultural or other vocational training for children who had committed lesser crimes or even none at all if authorities believed that they lived in dangerous circumstances.

Although nineteenth-century criminal statistics are notoriously difficult to interpret, it is generally agreed that juvenile crime diminished markedly after about 1860. Most Victorians believed the decrease was a direct conse-quence of the institutional reforms of the 1850s. In addition, society became more stable as new generations of town dwellers succeeded those dislocated by the industrial revolution. Although areas of poverty remained, the general level of income rose. Improved policing made detection of crimes more likely and stolen property harder to dispose of. Although juvenile criminal gangs still existed in the more desperate slums at the end of the century, they had ceased to be a terrifying feature of ordinary urban life.

JOHN REYNOLDS

Bibliography

Chesney, Kellow. *The Victorian Underworld.* 1970.

Manton, Jo. *Mary Carpenter and the Children of the Streets.* 1976.

Mayhew, Henry. *London Labour and the London Poor*, vol. 4, 1861–1862; rpt. 1968.

Morrison, Arthur. *A Child of the Jago.* 1894.

Tobias, J. J. *Crime and Industrial Society in the Nineteenth Century.* 1967.

· · · · ·

KAVANAGH, JULIA (1824–1877)

Born in Ireland and raised in France, Julia Kavanagh, author of some fifteen novels and many short stories, became extremely popular through her representations of French provincial life. She collected her stories in *Seven Years, and Other Tales* (1860) and *Forget-Me-Nots* (1878) and published inspirational biographical works: *Woman in France During the Eighteenth Century* (1850), *Women of Christianity Exemplary for Acts of Piety and Charity* (1852), *French Women of Letters* (1862), and *English Women of Letters* (1862).

In *Madeleine* (1848), the first of the novels set in France that established Kavanagh's reputation, and *Rachel Gray* (1856), a novel commended by George Eliot for exploring the "every-day sorrows of our commonplace fellow-man," the heroines remain unmarried. More typically, Kavanagh's heroine overcomes adolescent pride and temper to win a fine but reserved older man who has become independent through professional diligence.

Two Lilies (1877) treats a male protagonist, but even here Kavanagh pursues her favorite topic of a lively girl eventually loved by a man who once viewed her as a child. Although *Daisy Burns* (1853) and *Beatrice* (1864) are set principally in England, Kavanagh characteristically prefers French landscape and manners and contrasts the insouciance and vitality of foreign heroines with English reserve and lifelessness.

Despite their spirited girls, Kavanaugh's novels endorse women's dependence on protective men. Their preponderantly domestic scenes are occasionally spiced with sensational material such as attempted murder (e.g., *Sibyl's Second Love*, 1867, and *Silvia*, 1870). *Rachel Gray* is distinguished among her works for its strong social criticism. But even though Kavanagh remained primarily concerned with suspense and what reviewers termed poetic feeling, her novels project a subtle pessimism through recurring themes of the triviality of polite society and the fickleness of the world's approbation.

BEVERLY TAYLOR

Bibliography

Macquoid, Katharine. "Julia Kavanagh, Amelia Blandford Edwards." In *Women Novelists of Queen Victoria's Reign*. 1897.

See also SOCIAL PROBLEM NOVEL

· · · · ·

KAY-SHUTTLEWORTH, JAMES PHILLIPS
(1804–1877)

James Kay-Shuttleworth was a social reformer who played a central role in the development of popular education in England. He believed that mass education could help cure social ills such as poverty and vice and assist social stability.

James Kay, the son of a cotton manufacturer, was born in Rochdale, Lancashire, in 1804. (He added his wife's name of Shuttle-

worth on his marriage in 1842). After working in his uncle's bank, he studied medicine at Edinburgh University (he received his M.D. in 1827). As a doctor he worked in a poor and unsanitary area of Manchester where he gathered information for his book *The Moral and Physical Condition of the Working Classes* (1832).

In 1835 he exchanged the career of doctor for public administrator, first as assistant Poor Law commissioner, then, between 1839 and 1849, as the first secretary of the newly created Committee of Council on Education. He helped design the foundations of a national system of education, which worked through religious denominational organizations. His scheme included the inspection of schools (1839), a government-supported pupil-teacher system (1846), and the certification of teachers (1846). Kay-Shuttleworth opened and initially ran the Battersea Teachers' Training College in 1840.

He was made a baronet in 1849, when he resigned his public office due to ill health. He wrote several novels and books, including *Four Periods of Public Education* (1862).

OLWYN M. BLOUET

Bibliography

Bloomfield, B. C. "Sir James Phillips Kay-Shuttleworth: A Trial Bibliography." *British Journal of Educational Studies*, vols. 9 and 10, pp. 155–177, 76–80.

Smith, Frank. *The Life and Work of Sir James Kay-Shuttleworth*. 1923.

See also EDUCATION, ELEMENTARY

· · · · ·

KEAN, CHARLES JOHN
(1811?–1868)

Son of the tragedian Edmund Kean, Charles Kean made his stage debut in 1827. Although he lacked his father's genius and was criticized for a weak voice and rigid movements, he was a reasonably successful actor, creating a niche for himself in a species of genteel romantic melodrama imported from France. He was praised in the double role of

Louis and Fabian dei Franchi in Dion Bouci-cault's adaptation of *The Corsican Brothers* (1852), for which production he had designed the sliding "Corsican trap," and for his perfor-mance in the title role of the same play-wright's *Louis XI* (1855).

Kean is best known, however, for his man-agement of The Princess's Theatre from 1851 to 1859 where with the help of his wife and leading lady Ellen Tree (1806–1880) he staged an important series of Shakespearean revivals characterized by their pageantry and attention to historical detail. Himself a fellow of the Society of Antiquaries, Kean strove in his productions to depict with archival accu-racy the sartorial, geographical, and architec-tural splendors of Shakespeare's fables. The plays were often severely cut to accommodate such material, a practice that earned for Kean the dubious tag of "Great Upholsterer." Ad-mirers of Kean's productions had particular praise for their handling of crowd scenes and their exploitation of the moving panorama.

SHEILA STOWELL

Bibliography

Cole, John William. *The Life and Theatrical Times of Charles Kean F.S.A.* 1859. 2 vols.

Odell, George C. D. *Shakespeare from Betterton to Irving.* 1920. 2 vols.

· · · · ·

KEBLE, JOHN
(1792–1866)

John Keble, Anglican priest, poet, and scholar, influenced the direction of the Victo-rian church as a founder of the Oxford Move-ment. His volume of devotional poetry, *The Christian Year* (1827), was one of the most widely read works of the nineteenth century.

Born and raised in his father's parish of Fairford, Gloucestershire, Keble distinguished himself at Corpus Christi, Oxford and at nine-teen was elected fellow of Oriel College. From 1831 to 1841 Keble lectured as professor of poetry at Oxford and, on July 14, 1833 at St. Mary's, Oxford, preached the assize ser-mon, "National Apostasy," which John Henry Newman later marked as the beginning of the Oxford Movement. With Newman and others Keble authored a number of the "Tracts for the Times" (1833–1841) which set forth High Church positions on the catholicity of the An-glican church. From 1835, the year of his marriage to Charlotte Clarke, until his death in 1866, Keble served as vicar of Hursley, near Winchester. In 1869 Keble College, Oxford was founded in his honor.

Keble's reputation as a poet rests on *The Christian Year*, whose verses correspond to the structure of the Book of Common Prayer. His poetry fuses a Wordsworthian love for na-ture with a deeply religious sense of natural objects as signs or veiled hints of God's crea-tive and redemptive nature. The volume went through scores of editions in the nineteenth century before critical and popular taste for it dulled.

As professor of poetry Keble delivered the "Praelectiones Academicae" (1831–1841, later issued as *Lectures on Poetry*), which claim an intimate connection between reli-gion and poetry. Central to Keble's poetics are: (1) expressiveness, whereby the poet dis-charges some overpowering emotion hitherto repressed, bringing relief to the mind so over-charged; (2) "reserve," in which the poet's deepest feelings thus unburdened are veiled by allegory and restrained by metrical regu-larity; and (3) "analogy," a concept Keble found in Bishop Butler's *The Analogy of Reli-gion* (1726), whereby the world of nature is seen to be a "symbolic language" of God.

Keble's writing influenced both Tractarians and a wider spectrum of religiously minded Victorians, but he was perhaps best known for his example of unassuming holiness and sim-plicity in life and service.

MARK S. LOOKER

Bibliography

Battiscombe, Georgina. *John Keble: A Study in Limitations.* 1963.

Martin, Brian. *John Keble: Priest, Professor, and Poet.* 1976.

Tennyson, G. B. *Victorian Devotional Poetry: The Tractarian Mode.* 1981.

· · · · ·

KEMBLE, FANNY (FRANCES ANNE KEMBLE) (1809–1893)

Niece of Sarah Siddons and daughter of Charles Kemble, Fanny Kemble made her debut as Juliet to her father's Mercutio at Covent Garden in 1829 and became famous for her interpretation of Shakespeare. She also wrote and translated plays and gave celebrated play readings. She was equally popular in America where she married the southern plantation owner Pierce Butler and recorded her abhorrence of slavery in *Journal of a Residence on a Georgian Plantation* (1863).

Born in London, carefully brought up, and educated in France, Kemble was intended for polite society by her actor parents, although she had literary ambitions. To help her father out of dire financial straits, she went on stage, later accompanied him to America, although it meant separation from her sister Adelaide Sartoris, and published—for the proceeds—her *Journal* (1835), with its mockery of American life, against the will of her new husband. Butler, unable to bear her outspokenness and independence, divorced her in 1849.

William Macready thought her acting affected because of her sonorous tones and grand manner; yet she had a passionate heart and probed her characters to their depths. Short, upright, with expressive eyes, she was not a great beauty but a commanding presence both on and off stage. In old age she was highly regarded in London circles for her formidable wit and her authorship of fascinating social history in *Records of a Girlhood* (1878), *Records of Later Life* (1882), and *Further Records* (1890). Henry James called her "the first woman of London."

TAMIE WATTERS

Bibliography

Marshall, Dorothy. *Fanny Kemble.* 1977.

Ransome, Eleanor, ed. *The Terrific Kemble: A Victorian Self-Portrait from the Writings of Fanny Kemble.* 1978.

· · · · ·

KINGSLEY, CHARLES (1819–1875)

A Broad Church clergyman and controversialist, Charles Kingsley is most often remembered as a "muscular Christian," the author of *The Water-Babies* (1863), and as John Henry Newman's antagonist in a dispute that prompted Newman to write his *Apologia Pro Vita Sua* (1864). Kingsley wrote more than sixty books, including seven novels, popular studies of geology and biology, a volume of poetry, *Andromeda and Other Poems* (1858), and a volume of essays, *Miscellanies* (1859).

Borne at Holne Vicarage, Devonshire, Kingsley attended school at Clifton, and later at Helston, where he was tutored by Derwent Coleridge. A degree from Cambridge in 1842 completed his education. In 1844 he became rector of Eversley Church, Hampshire, and married Frances Grenfell.

Influenced by the work of Samuel Taylor Coleridge, Thomas Carlyle, and most profoundly by Frederick Denison Maurice, who taught him that the Kingdom of God is to be discovered in the material world, Kingsley preached a socially conscious Christianity. From his own experience of marriage came his acknowledgment of the role of sexuality in human development and his consequent hostility to advocates of celibacy. These attitudes put him at odds with High Church Anglicans and with Roman Catholics.

Kingsley's espousal of **Christian socialism** found expression in two novels of social protest: *Yeast* (1848) and *Alton Locke* (1850). *Yeast* deals with conditions among agricultural laborers. The pamphlet *Cheap Clothes and Nasty* (1850) and *Alton Locke* attack conditions in the London tailors' trade. Kingsley returned to the question of the condition of England in *Two Years Ago* (1857), focusing on sanitation reform, the Crimean War, and the abolitionist movement in America.

Kingsley's belief that history reveals God's continuing revelation found expression in three novels set at times of crisis: *Hypatia* (1853), *Westward Ho!* (1855), and *Hereward the Wake* (1866). Set in fifth-century Alexandria, *Hypatia* presents a battle between Neoplatonism and the emerging medieval church for the souls of the young.

Kingsley believed that the event was mirrored in his own time by the appeal of Roman Catholicism and by what he called "Emersonian Anythingarianism." *Westward Ho!* presents England's sixteenth-century confrontation with Spain in terms applicable to the Crimean War, and *Hereward the Wake* tells the heroic story of the last Anglo-Saxon holdout against the Norman Conquest.

An amateur naturalist who readily accepted Charles Darwin's *The Origin of Species* (1859), Kingsley also wrote on scientific subjects: *Glaucus* (1855) and *Madam How and Lady Why* (1868), the latter for children. However, Kingsley's reputation as a writer for children rests on *The Heroes* (1856), a retelling of classical legends, and on *The Water-Babies*. In this tale of a child's moral rejuvenation in an underwater world, Kingsley imaginatively links theology and evolution.

The range of Kingsley's interests makes a study of his work an avenue into the mid-Victorian age. Although admittedly of the second rank, he remains a writer of considerable imaginative power.

LARRY K. UFFELMAN

Bibliography

Chitty, Susan. *The Beast and the Monk: A Life of Charles Kingsley.* 1975.

Colloms, Brenda. *Charles Kingsley: The Lion of Eversley.* 1975.

Harris, Styron. *Charles Kingsley: A Reference Guide.* 1981.

Hartley, Allan John. *The Novels of Charles Kingsley: A Christian Social Interpretation.* 1977.

Kingsley, Frances, ed. *Charles Kingsley: His Letters and Memories of His Life.* 1877. 2 vols.

Martin, Robert Bernard. *The Dust of Combat: A Life of Charles Kingsley.* 1959.

Uffelman, Larry K. *Charles Kingsley.* 1979.

Vance, Norman. *The Sinews of the Spirit: The Ideal of Christian Manliness in Victorian Literature and Religious Thought.* 1985.

· · · · ·

KINGSLEY, MARY
(1862–1900)

Mary Kingsley devoted her short professional life to exploring and describing the land and inhabitants of West Africa. Her researches generated three books: *Travels in West Africa* (1897), *West African Studies* (1899), and *The Story of West Africa* (1899).

Kingsley was the niece of the celebrated novelist **Charles Kingsley** and the daughter of George Kingsley, physician, sportsman, and travel writer. Having lost both parents in 1892, she made two trips to West Africa, in 1893 and 1894–1895, to collect fish specimens and study native culture.

Kingsley's books, articles, and lectures, composed in England from 1895 to 1899, constitute a vigorous defense of the African. She condemned missionary efforts to destroy native culture and criticized insensitive colonial policies, like the 1898 hut tax, which violated tribal custom. Instead, because she saw trade as a powerful civilizing force, she promoted the interests of men like George Goldie of the Royal Niger Company, and so came into conflict with the colonial secretary, Joseph Chamberlain.

Though opposed to women's suffrage, Kingsley successfully penetrated the male-dominated spheres of exploration, science, and politics. In 1898 she was elected a member of the Anthropological Society. Her *Travels in West Africa* endures as one of the most perceptive and best-written of English travel books.

JOAN CORWIN

Bibliography

Campbell, Olwen. *Mary Kingsley: A Victorian in the Jungle.* 1957.

Frank, Katherine. *A Voyager Out: The Life of Mary Kingsley.* 1986.

Gwynn, Stephen. *The Life of Mary Kingsley.* 2d ed., 1933.

Kingsley, Mary. "Memoir." In George Kingsley, *Notes on Sport and Travel.* 1900.

Stevenson, Catherine Barnes. *Victorian Women Travel Writers in Africa.* 1982.

· · · · ·

KIPLING, RUDYARD
(1865-1936)

Joseph Rudyard Kipling—poet, novelist, and short story writer—became in 1907 the first British author to be awarded the Nobel Prize for literature. He has proven to be one of the most controversial late Victorian writers, warmly regarded and highly praised by admirers, but thoroughly disdained by detractors.

Born in Bombay, Kipling was taken to live in a foster home in England in 1871, a traumatic five-year experience that he recorded in "Baa, Baa, Black Sheep" (1888), *The Light That Failed* (1891), and *Something of Myself* (1937). After four years at the United Services College, the basis for *Stalky & Co.* (1899), he returned to **India** in 1882 to assume the position of subeditor for the Lahore *Civil and Military Gazette* where many of his early works first appeared. Though a volume of poetry, *Departmental Ditties* (1886), was his first work to be reviewed in England, it was *Plain Tales from the Hills* (1888), a collection of short stories, that began to win him a reputation as the precocious successor to Dickens. He moved to England in 1889 where he met and in 1892 married an American, Carrie Balestier. The Kiplings settled in Vermont for five years before they returned to England.

During the American sojourn, Kipling published the two *Jungle Book* volumes (1894, 1895), a series of stories intended both as children's fables and adult myths that trace the adventures of Mowgli, a lost child raised by animals. He also began work on *Captains Courageous* (1897), a novel about a spoiled rich boy who learns duty and hard work after falling from a luxury liner and being rescued by a Yankee fishing boat. Kipling turned to his Indian background for his masterpiece, *Kim* (1901), a novel detailing the experiences of an Irish soldier's orphaned son who is taken from the streets of Lahore by a Tibetan lama and later trained as a British secret agent. Though he continued to write until his death, Kipling's later years were marred by personal tragedies and ill health, and as his writings grew less inspired and more polemical he became known as a defender of British imperialism.

Kipling's typical themes focus on duty and the importance of "the Law." At his best, Kipling, an intuitive rather than intellectual ar-

tist, tells simple, compelling stories characterized by great facility of language and close touch with life; at his worst, he can be brutal, crude, and patently propagandistic. Though he remains a controversial figure, his fiction continues to sell and to be read throughout the English-speaking world.

W. CRAIG TURNER

Bibliography

Carrington, Charles. *Rudyard Kipling: His Life and Work.* 1955.

Gilbert, Elliot L. *Kipling and the Critics.* 1965.

Lascelles, Mary. *The Story-Teller Retrieves the Past.* 1980.

Page, Norman, *A Kipling Companion.* 1984.

Stewart, J. McG. *Rudyard Kipling: A Bibliographical Catalogue.* 1959.

Tompkins, J. M. S. *The Art of Rudyard Kipling.* 1959.

Wilson, Angus. *The Strange Ride of Rudyard Kipling: His Life and Works.* 1977.

· · · · ·

KITCHENER, HORATIO HERBERT
(1850-1916)

Horatio Herbert Kitchener was a distinguished soldier and administrator in the British Empire. He served in Egypt, the Sudan, South Africa, and India. At the outbreak of World War I (1914), he was appointed secretary of state for war. Kitchener was a popular figure, fulfilling the role of national hero.

The son of a retired army officer, Kitchener was born in Ireland in 1850. After training at the Royal Military Academy, Woolwich, he was commissioned in the Royal Engineers in 1871. Following survey work in Palestine and Cyprus, he was appointed second in command of the Egyptian cavalry in 1882. He undertook intelligence work when General **Charles Gordon** was besieged and killed by the Mahdists in Khartoum.

Kitchener was rapidly promoted, being made commander in chief of the Egyptian army in 1892. He commanded the Anglo-Egyptian campaigns to reconquer the Sudan which culminated in the defeat of the Mahdists at the Battle of Omdurman (September 2, 1898). Kitchener gained national acclaim as the avenger of Gordon, and received a peerage. Between 1898 and 1900 Kitchener was ruler of the Sudan. He became popularly known as Kitchener of Khartoum (K. of K.).

After initial British setbacks in the **Boer War** (1899-1902), heroes were needed. Kitchener was sent to South Africa in 1900 as second in command to Lord Roberts. Some success followed and Kitchener was left in charge. But the war dragged on. Kitchener's policies, which included burning farms and placing civilians in camps, were criticized then and later, although the Boers eventually capitulated.

Between 1902 and 1909 Kitchener was commander in chief in India. A dispute over control of the military developed with the viceroy, Lord Curzon. Kitchener won when the British government accepted Curzon's resignation. Kitchener, who was extremely ambitious, coveted the viceroyalty of India, but was offered the consul-generalship of Egypt, where he developed agricultural and land reform.

When World War I began Kitchener was appointed secretary of state for war. He anticipated a long war and successfully raised a new voluntary army; his face became immortalized on recruiting posters. He died in 1916, en route to Russia, when H.M.S. *Hampshire* struck a mine.

Most authorities agree that Kitchener was shy, brusque, and autocratic. His strengths included thoroughness, drive, and the ability to get the best out of others.

OLWYN M. BLOUET

Bibliography

Arthur, Sir George. *Life of Lord Kitchener.* 1920. 3 vols.

Cassar, George H. *Kitchener: Architect of Victory.* 1977.

Magnus, Philip. *Kitchener: Portrait of an Imperialist.* 1958.

Warner, Philip. *Kitchener: The Man Behind the Legend.* 1985.

· · · · ·

LABOR LAWS

British labor organized and sought legal recognition in the face of strong opposition. The common law held labor organizations to be illegal conspiracies in restraint of trade and the predominant philosophy of the age was individual self-help. Combination Acts passed in 1799 and 1800 had specifically outlawed workers' organizations, but in the 1820s reformers found that these acts contravened the free market theory which allowed workers to sell their labor at the best price. In 1824 Parliament legalized peaceful persuasion in trade disputes. Following an outbreak of violent **strikes**, the next Parliament reenacted the common-law precept that labor combinations restrained trade, but recognized that unions could exist as long as they did not strike or threaten to strike.

When Victoria's reign began, unions existed in a legal twilight, tolerated but insecure. In the 1850s, through restraint and work, **trade unions** began to gain respectability. In 1855 they won the right to protect their funds by depositing their rules with the Registrar of Friendly Societies. In 1859 the Molestation of Workmen Act legalized severely limited forms of picketing.

Respectability, however, was not legal recognition. In 1866, when a boilermakers' union sued one of its local treasurers to recover embezzled funds, the courts held that union funds were unprotected because unions were illegal, although not criminal, organizations. Both the unions and Parliament responded quickly; urban workers were enfranchised in 1867, which provided motivation to attend to union demands. An 1868 act provided interim protection for union funds and postponed the larger questions. In 1871, Parliament passed the Masters and Servants Act, which again specifically legalized the existence of labor unions, but the Criminal Law Amendment Act set down lists of legal and illegal conduct governing picketing and strikers' behavior. In 1872 the courts ruled that the act had not adequately repealed the common law. London gasworkers who struck were convicted of conspiracy and sentenced to twelve months at hard labor. In another case, wives of striking **agricultural laborers** were convicted of "intimidating" strikebreakers. Workers continued to be imprisoned for breaking their labor contracts, while employers could only be sued for civil damages.

Organized labor pressed both political parties to act. Benjamin Disraeli and his home secretary, R. A. Cross, passed the Employers and Workmen Act (1875) and the Conspiracy and Protection of Property Act (1875). The first ended workers' criminal liability for breaching of employment contracts. The second gave unions immunity from prosecution for conspiracy as long as they were striking in a trade dispute. Labor considered itself emancipated.

In the 1870s and 1880s unions pressed for an act that would force employers to compensate workers injured at work. An 1880 effort was wrecked by the "common employment" rule, which allowed employers to shift responsibility to other employees. Until 1901, labor concentrated on such less-basic laws, but that year the courts again dealt a potentially fatal blow to unions. The Taff Vale railway, which had been struck by the Amalgamated Society of Railway Servants, sued the union for damages. The courts found the union liable and ordered it to pay the railway company for the losses caused by the strike. If the Taff Vale precedent had stood, unions could have been held liable for losses caused by any strike, which would have rendered them impotent.

Victoria's reign ended as it had begun, with the unions' legal position in doubt. Both the prevailing philosophy of individualism and the common law were hostile to unions. The restraints imposed by the common law and the prevailing economic philosophy were never totally overcome despite good-faith efforts by unions and both political parties.

DENNIS J. MITCHELL

Bibliography

Abrahams, Gerald. *Trade Unions and the Law.* 1968.

Brown, Kenneth D. "Trade Unions and the Law." In Chris Wrigley, ed., *A History of British Industrial Relations 1875-1910.* 1982.

Citrine, Norman Arthur. *Trade Union Law.* 1950.

Cole, G. D. H. *British Working Class Politics, 1838-1914.* 1941.

MacDonald, Donald F. *The State and the Trade Unions.* 1976.

· · · · ·

LABOR UNIONS see TRADE UNIONS

· · · · ·

LABOUR CHURCH

Growing up with the independent labor movement in the 1890s, the Labour church sought to serve working-class spiritual needs outside orthodox Christianity—"to set free the tremendous power of religious enthusiasm . . . pent up in the great labor movement." Eschewing creeds or set forms, it held only to a belief in essential human spirituality.

Founded in Manchester (October 1891) by John Trevor (1855-1929), a strict Calvinist in his youth and then a Unitarian associate of Philip Wicksteed (1844-1927), the Labour church shared much with the Independent Labour party in membership, speakers, and meetings. Services consisted of a hymn, a prayer, a "reading from some Religious or Democratic Book," and an address. The Labour Church Union (1893) provided the only central organization apart from Trevor's enthusiasm. While concentrated in Lancashire and Yorkshire and never numbering more than fifty-four at one time, Labour churches were scattered from Scotland to Wales. Trevor edited the journal *Labour Prophet* (1892-1902) and the *Labour Church Hymn Book* (1892), and with Wicksteed published *Labour Church Tracts* (1892-1896).

Before 1900 decline was evident and few churches survived World War I. Few were attracted to any distinctive Labour church faith and most saw it as just another means toward a united labor movement.

CARL W. CHEATHAM

Bibliography

Inglis, K. S. "The Labour Church Movement." *International Review of Social History*, vol. 3, pp. 445-460.

Labour Church Tracts. London, 1892-1896.

Labour Prophet (*Labour Church Record*). London, 1892-1902.

Trevor, John. *My Quest for God.* London, 1897.

· · · · ·

LABOUR PARTY

The origins of the Labour party are to be found in the late Victorian era. It developed not from the extension of the franchise to a substantial part of the urban working class in the Second Reform Act (1867), but from several factors in the 1880s and 1890s. The most important of these was the expansion of trade unions and the development of the "new unions," often of unskilled workers. Their successes in the late 1880s produced an employers' counteroffensive in the 1890s, during which a series of lawsuits, some decided only in the House of Lords, seemed to undermine the legal position established by the Trade Union Acts of 1871 and 1876. As the unions suffered reverses and lost membership, they increasingly felt the lack of representation in Parliament, then at the height of its popular reputation and prestige. The **trade unions** did not aim to create a governing party of their own, nor to replace the existing parties. They merely sought that labor, in parallel with other interest groups in society, should have a voice in the passage of legislation that affected working conditions, industrial relations, and the unions themselves.

Previously trade union leaders had looked to the **Liberal party**, but by the 1890s some felt that this strategy had failed. At the national level, the Liberal party was principally concerned with other issues, and both the 1886 and 1892–1895 Liberal ministries were barren from the labor viewpoint. At the local level, Liberal constituency associations proved reluctant to adopt working-class candidates. The reason lay only partially in the need to find the money to support them; Liberal activists, often from the middle class, did not want to see their own issues pushed to the background by a candidate claiming priority for the interests of labor. The Liberals were also hostile to "independent labour" candidatures which, by dividing the radical vote, could only benefit the Conservative party.

Such independent candidacies, though few in number and limited mainly to industrial urban districts in Yorkshire, Lancashire, Wales, and Scotland, occurred in the late 1880s and 1890s. The first of significance was by **Keir Hardie** (1856–1915) in the Mid-Lanark by-election (1888). Although he came bottom of the poll on this occasion, Hardie won West Ham South in the 1892 general election and became the first Independent Labour M.P. These candidatures were usually under the auspices of one of the small socialist societies which had been produced by the revival of interest in socialist ideas in the 1880s. The first was the Social Democratic Federation (SDF), founded by H. M. Hyndman (1842–1921) in 1881; the other important organization was the Independent Labour party (ILP), founded at a conference of all those interested in labor representation held in Bradford on January 13, 1893, in which Hardie was prominently involved. Both organizations formed branches in constituencies and encouraged or endorsed candidatures. The third important socialist society, which did neither of these things, was the **Fabian Society**, founded in 1884 and led by Annie Besant (1847–1933), George Bernard Shaw (1856–1950), and Sidney Webb (1859–1947). The Socialist League, in which William Morris (1834–1896) was the central figure, seceded from the SDF in 1884, partly in opposition to its parliamentary strategy.

The Trades Unions Congress of 1899, reacting to the establishment of the Employers Parliamentary Council (1898), resolved to summon a conference of trade unions, cooperative societies, and socialist societies to improve labor representation in Parliament. Meeting at the Memorial Hall, Farringdon, on February 27–28, 1900, the conference established the Labour Representation Committee (LRC). A number of "new" unions, together with the railway and boot and shoe workers, became affiliated and provided funds and an organizational framework. The ILP, the Fabians, and the SDF also joined, but the latter withdrew within a year. In the 1900 general election the LRC endorsed fifteen candidates, of whom two were elected. The Taff Vale judgment (1901) spurred further trade union affiliations to the LRC. Its growing strength was reflected in the pact negotiated in 1903 between its secretary, Ramsay MacDonald (1866–1937), and the Liberal chief whip, Herbert Gladstone (1854–1930), which was designed to avoid competing candidatures. As a result, the LRC were able in the 1906 general election to elect twenty-nine M.P.s, who on their arrival at Westminster adopted the name of Labour Party.

STUART BALL

Bibliography

Bealey, Frank and Henry M. Pelling. *Labour and Politics, 1900–1906.* 1958.

Hinton, James. *Labour and Socialism: A History of the British Labour Movement, 1867–1974.* 1983.

Howell, David. *British Workers and the Independent Labour Party, 1888–1906.* 1983.

Pelling, Henry M. *The Origins of the Labour Party, 1880–1900.* 2d ed., 1965.

Smith, Harold. *The British Labour Movement to 1970: A Bibliography.* 1981.

See also SOCIALISM

· · · · ·

LACEMAKERS

Industrialization hastened the gradual decline that the lacemaking trade experienced throughout the eighteenth century in all but the Midland counties, where lacemaking continued to be a thriving occupation. In the nineteenth century, the development of machinery for turning out inexpensive lace net robbed many skilled workers of employment. An increase in the purchasing power of wage-earning consumers fueled a demand for cheap laces of inferior quality, further reducing the need for expert lacemakers. Children were extensively hired to handle the simpler and more tedious tasks associated with machine-made lace, such as repairing broken threads or drawing fabric; not surprisingly, child labor caused wages to plummet throughout the trade.

Lacemaking, like other **domestic industries**, traditionally employed women and children almost exclusively since the work could be done at home. The term "outwork" refers to the domestic locale of the work; it was carried on outside of the workshop and factory. As with other outworkers, lacemakers frequently were married women supplementing their husband's earnings. Lacemakers' wages alone were usually inadequate, and undependable because of market fluctuations.

The lace dealers or manufacturers extracted the largest share of the profit from finished works. Dealers distributed the mate-

rials required for lacemaking to intermediary agents, or "mistresses," who in turn distributed them to the lace runners or embroiderers. It was not unusual for two or three mistresses to stand between the dealer and the runner, leaving very little profit for the laceworker. In 1840, Nottingham lace runners organized themselves into a group and staged a strike, appealing to dealers to set the percentages that mistresses could claim. Many dealers, however, withheld their support; the strike dissipated and conditions remained unimproved. The action is significant, however, because it reveals the willingness—and ability—of women outworkers to organize.

DONNA PRICE PAUL

Bibliography

Drake, Barbara. *Women in Trade Unions.* 1920.

Lewenhak, Sheila. *Women and Trade Unions: An Outline History of Women in the Trade Union Movement.* 1977.

Palliser, Mrs. Bury. *History of Lace.* 4th ed., 1911.

Pinchbeck, Ivy. *Women Workers and the Industrial Revolution, 1750–1850.* 1930.

· · · · ·

LANDOR, WALTER SAVAGE (1775–1864)

Combining romantic and Victorian sensibilities, Walter Savage Landor wrote voluminously, poetry and prose, in English, Latin, and Italian. His contemporaries rated most highly the 152 prose *Imaginary Conversations*, written primarily in the 1820s, but continuing even to his final year. Cast as dialogues between historical or legendary personages from the classical to the present age, they treat political and literary topics and vary in tone from satiric to idyllic. More widely read today are his finely wrought epigrams and brief lyrics such as those to Ianthe or "Rose Aylmer."

Having been withdrawn from Rugby and rusticated from Trinity College, Oxford, Landor in 1808 financed and led troops against Napoleon's Spanish incursions. From 1814 until his marital rupture in 1835, and again from 1858 until he died, he lived in Italy, driven from England first by debt and the second time by litigation. During Landor's final years in Florence, Robert Browning helped manage his strained economic and family relationships.

His ignored first collection of *Poems* (1795) included a volume in Latin and a piece in the stanza later used in Tennyson's *In Memoriam*. A long heroic romance, *Gebir* (1798), enthusiastically reviewed by Robert Southey, was romantic in its political radicalism and Oriental settings, but distinguished by austere language and classical influences. Landor translated *Gebir* into Latin, anticipating what became a frequent practice with his later verse. Throughout his career he wrote closet dramas (1812, 1839–1840, 1844). Pronounced classicism, especially in his epigrammatic skill, controlled rendering of feeling, and stylistic polish mark his later verse collections—*Hellenics* (1846, 1847), *Italics* (1848), *Last Fruit off an Old Tree* (1853), and *Heroic Idylls* (1863).

Admired exceedingly by fellow writers, Landor correctly anticipated an enduring but limited reputation: "I shall dine late but the room will be well-lighted and the guests few but select."

BEVERLY TAYLOR

Bibliography

Forster, John. *Walter Savage Landor.* 1869.

Pinsky, Robert. *Landor's Poetry.* 1968.

Super, R. H. *Walter Savage Landor.* 1954.

· · · · ·

LANDSCAPE ARCHITECTURE AND DESIGN

Certain pre-Victorian influences from William Chambers (1723–1796), Uvedale Price (1747–1829), and Humphry Repton (1752–1818) helped to shape the character of nineteenth-century landscape design. Landscaping and gardening during the Victorian age were influenced by internationalism, scientific interests, new technology and, finally, a reaction against all three. The prime molder of landscape was no longer the architect but the gardener; the character of work by the horticulturalist or botanist emerged from science rather than from poetry, philosophy, or painting, and the client shifted from the holder of a landed estate to the resident of a suburban villa or rural cottage. Stylistically, landscape developments paralleled those of architecture: from the picturesque romantic classicism of John Nash (1752–1835) and Repton, to the horticulture and technics of John Claudius Loudon (1783–1843) and **Joseph Paxton** (1801–1865), to the Continental eclecticism of **Charles Barry** (1795–1860), William Andrews Nesfield (1793–1881), and Reginald Blomfield (1856–1942), to the arts and crafts vernacular and nativism of William Robinson (1838–1935) and **Gertrude Jekyll** (1843–1932).

Some continuity from the eighteenth century tradition of Lancelot ("Capability") Brown (1715–1783) continued into the nineteenth century in the work of Humphry Repton, who softened the sweeping lawns and reduced their scale, framed the otherwise vaster "prospects," and composed a prettified picturesque which set the stage for the Victorian flower garden. Repton introduced prominent foreground elements to enframe or contrast with the picturesque middle ground: drives, balustraded terraces, flower beds with their color effects visible close up, and even fountains and other elements of Continental formality. This Repton picturesque helped create the sentimental Victorian gardens.

The rise of the scientific gardener is best evidenced in the careers of J. C. Loudon and Joseph Paxton. Loudon, through the *Gardener's Magazine* (founded in 1826), offered information about the enlarged range of available plants: new exotics brought to England from worldwide travels as well as new cultivars resulting from horticultural experiments. Gardening magazines and books helped the new breed of middle-class amateur gardeners engaged in their own plantings to enjoy success and variety. Among professional periodicals, the *Journal* of the Horticultural Society became the most important. The enthusiasm for foreign plants reflected the age's architectural eclecticism. Changing tastes promoted specialized garden areas within larger gardens, and the fashion for Japanese gardens echoed the availability of Oriental trees, shrubs, and plants.

Joseph Paxton, gardener to the Duke of Devonshire, planted exotic trees and plants at Chatsworth and built the "Great Stove" (1836–1840) where large collections of annuals could be amassed for bedding out. Paxton's reputation is based on his innovative greenhouse designs. Also from this period, Decimus Burton's (1800–1881) Palm House at Kew (1844–1848) remains perhaps the most graceful ever built, still used and admired at the Royal Botanical Gardens.

Italianate architecture and scientific gardening encouraged a new formality in landscape. Islands of flowers set in carpets of lawn were made possible by the development of hothouses, conservatories, and greenhouses (and the practice of bedding out) and the invention by Edwin Beard Budding (c. 1796–1846) in 1830 of the lawn mower. If carpet bedding's kaleidoscopic overlays on flat lawns represented low-style Victorian geometric formality, the high style was the neo-Italianate terraced garden of Charles Barry, as at Cliveden (1850–1851) in Buckinghamshire. William Andrews Nesfield was most responsible for the layout of avenue vistas at Kew: the Pagoda Vista, the Broad Way, and the Syon Vista. At the century's end, Reginald Blomfield sought to improve the excesses of the Victorian Italianate garden by returning to the simpler architectural models of the Renaissance and the seventeenth century. His publication in 1892 of *The Formal Garden in England* celebrated garden ideals very much in conflict with the vernacular revival already being promoted by William Robinson.

Robinson led the way to the rejection of formality with *The Wild Garden* (1870) and *The English Flower Garden* (1883). He argued that the form, foliage, and color of plants (rather than arbitrary geometry) should govern their placement in the garden. Coloristic and formal effects within the plantings themselves were further developed by Gertrude Jekyll, whose tonal gardens became impressionistic color poems comparable to those of her contemporary, Monet. Both Robinson and Jekyll found inspiration in the indigenous English countryside, and while Robinson was also eager to grow interesting plants from abroad, Jekyll may well have

developed, with **Edwin Lutyens** (1869–1944), the ideal synthesis of the geometric and natural garden.

ROBERT M. CRAIG

Bibliography

Clifford, Derek. *A History of Garden Design*. 1966.

Country Life. 1897–.

Fleming, Laurence and Alan Gore. *The English Garden*. 1979.

Garden History. 1972–.

Hadfield, Miles. *A History of British Gardening*. 1969.

Hyams, Edward. *The English Garden*. 1966.

Thacker, Christopher. *The History of Gardens*. 1979.

See also GARDENS AND PARKS

· · · · ·

LANDSCAPE PAINTERS

Despite earlier examples from Flanders, Holland, and Italy, landscape painting remained virtually unpracticed in Britain before the later seventeenth century. Over the next hundred years, however (and particularly after 1760), formal gardening, architecture, stagecraft, literature, painting, and changing travel habits all reflected an increasing awareness of and appreciation for the beauty, picturesqueness, and sublimity of landscape. Justifications for this interest were usually aesthetic, psychological, or theological, but science, history, economics, and broadened curiosity entered in as well.

After years of imports, fakes, and local imitations, a genuinely British school of landscape painting emerged in the later eighteenth century, with Richard Wilson (1714–1782) and Thomas Gainsborough (1727–1788) among its more notable contributors. A freely imagined, often theatrical alternative flourished for a time in works by Joseph Wright (1734–1797), Philip James De Loutherbourg (1740–1812), John Martin (1789–1854), and Francis Danby (1793–1861). John Linnell (1792–1882) and Samuel Palmer

(1805–1881), both followers of William Blake, created visionary landscapes. Victorian interest in fanciful scenes declined sharply after midcentury, however. A more factual tradition—though still heightened by romanticism, color, and emotion—then continued through such minor but well-received figures as the Orientalist David Roberts (1796–1864), the animal portraitist **Edwin Landseer** (1802–1873), and the roadside landscapist Myles Birket Foster (1825–1899), who was a popular book illustrator as well.

Two early nineteenth-century British painters later accorded significantly higher standing were John Constable (1776–1837) and **J. M. W. Turner** (1775–1851). Like Wordsworth, with whom he is often compared, the determinedly untheatrical Constable did not easily achieve lasting popularity. Similarly, Turner's distinct originality was not fully appreciated by the general public for some years. Attention focused on Turner during his final decade when the still undergraduate John Ruskin (1819–1900) championed his work in *Modern Painters* (1843ff.), a stirring, often impassioned, discussion of Victorian aesthetics. Under the influence of Roberts, Ruskin proposed "truth to nature" as the chief criterion of excellence in landscape painting.

Stimulated by Ruskin's insights, and later defended by his opinions, several painters associated with the **Pre-Raphaelite Brotherhood** devoted considerable attention to landscape. Among them, Ford Madox Brown (1821–1893), William Holman Hunt (1827–1910), John Everett Millais (1829–1896), John William Inchbold (1830–1888), and John Brett (1831–1902) became most productive. William Dyce (1806–1864), Edward Lear (1812–1888), and Ruskin himself were related figures of particular interest. During the latter third of the nineteenth century, a period of diminished creativity in landscape art, some British painters favored almost photographic standards of realism, as Ruskin and those he influenced (Inchbold, Brett) often did; others experimented with impressionist trends anticipated in part by Turner; a few retained the bold colors and enigmatic allusiveness of the Pre-Raphaelites; while numerous popular suppliers continued to market romantic topography or effete prettiness. James McNeill Whistler (1834–1903) became a final provocation.

Critical discussions of Victorian landscape painting attempt to evaluate its originality, its substance, its "accuracy," and its profundity or significance. The development of railroads, and later steamships, was central to the genre's increasing factuality. Prior to the impressionists, however, few landscapists actually painted out-of-doors. Most earlier artists worked only in the studio, relying entirely on sketchbooks and memories. When published, such works were often elaborated or distorted by engravers, general impressions being more important than reliable details. Later, as Victorian expectations of accuracy became strident, artists painted on location, with the desired prospect before them.

The development of photography (after 1840) also fundamentally changed British landscape painting. With such accurate and rapid—but far from instantaneous—memoranda available to all, general interest in the once-popular hobby of sketching quickly declined. (Ruskin himself eventually photographed the Alps.) In general, artists responded to photography by mimicking its particularity of detail (an almost microscopic realism) while emphasizing color (not yet available to photographers), exquisite composition, and perfected, anecdotal subjects. Alternatively, some artists deliberately exaggerated scenic wonders like the Alps, so as to recreate the actual experience of confronting them. Rebelling against the tyranny of fact, these post-Darwinians often rejected particularity. By the end of the nineteenth century, however, social, psychological, and political attention to the plight of individuals had reduced landscape painting in Britain to a relatively minor genre.

DENNIS R. DEAN

Bibliography

Carli, Enzo. *The Landscape in Art.* 1980.

Cummings, Frederick and Allen Staley. *Romantic Art in Britain: Paintings and Drawings, 1760–1860.* 1968.

Grigson, Geoffrey. *Britain Observed.* 1975.

Maas, Jeremy. *Victorian Painters.* 1984.

Stainton, Lindsay. *British Landscape Watercolours, 1600–1860.* 1985.

· · · · ·

LANDSEER, EDWIN
(1802-1873)

Born in London, Edwin Landseer was taught to draw at an early age by his father, a talented engraver. Something of a prodigy, he published his first work, an engraved picture of a St. Bernard, when he was 13. He also produced two other animal pictures at this time which were exhibited at the Royal Academy—*Portrait of a Mule* and *Portrait of a Pointer Bitch and Puppy* (1815). When he was 14, Landseer became a student at the Royal Academy, studying under Benjamin Haydon, who ingrained in him a sense of sound anatomy by having him dissect dead dogs.

Landseer's early work shows deft draftsmanship and concern with details, but his style changed in 1824 after a trip to the Scottish Highlands. Here he undertook the first of many hunting scenes, *Taking a Buck* (1825), which was done on a larger scale and in a looser manner. Other pictures of deer followed, among the most famous being *The Monarch of the Glen* (1851), *Stag at Bay* (1846), and *The Challenger* (1844). Each captures the energy of the subject and suggests the potential violence of nature, showing a feeling for the sublime in terrible scenes. His treatment of the elemental aspects of the natural world links him with the harsher European romanticism of Casper David Friedrich and Gericault. Landseer's images of great stags that defiantly face down their enemies against backdrops of misty crags or primeval lakes convey a moral meaning that is not deflected by sentimentality. Though the noble beasts show grace under pressure, nature is nevertheless "red in tooth and claw."

On the other hand, Landseer's anthropomorphic treatment of dogs no longer has the appeal it had for the Victorians, who loved Landseer's dog pictures because they epitomized domesticity, dependency, and fidelity. *The Old Shepherd's Chief Mourner* (1834) and *Dignity and Impudence* (1839) made him a celebrity and court favorite. These dewy-eyed dogs are mainly intended to arouse pathos, although they also satirize human behavior and show morality in the natural world—the good shepherd forgotten by all but his faithful collie or the upstart terrier admonished by the solemn decorum of the basset hound. Landseer's animals are made to imitate the better side of human nature—as if to indirectly support Darwin's view that life is a series of evolutionary steps up the scale of being.

Landseer painted other creatures as well—game birds, parrots, monkeys, cats, cows, and horses. He also painted people, including facile portraits of Prince Albert and Queen Victoria, but dogs and stags were his forte. An artist who enjoyed great renown and popularity in his lifetime, Landseer was elected to the Royal Academy in 1831 and honored with a knighthood in 1851. In 1865 he was offered the presidency of the Royal Academy, but declined it for reasons of failing mental health. Despite his deepening depressions, he completed the bronze lions that decorate the base of Nelson's column in Trafalgar Square in 1867. When he died in 1873, insane and alcoholic, a grieving nation paid homage with burial in St. Paul's and a monument bearing a copy in stone of his most famous painting, *The Old Shepherd's Chief Mourner.*

HALLMAN B. BRYANT

Bibliography

Arts Council of Great Britain. *Great Victorian Pictures.* 1978.

Hill, Ian B. *Landseer: An Illustrated Life.* 1973.

Maas, Jeremy. *Victorian Painters.* 1969.

Muther, Richard. "The Art of Landseer." In *Masters in Art: A Series of Illustrated Monographs,* vol. 5. 1904.

Ormand, Richard. *Sir Edwin Landseer.* 1981.

Stephens, Frederic G. *Sir Edwin Landseer.* 1880.

Woodward, John. *Sir Edwin Landseer.* 1961.

. . . . .

LANG, ANDREW
(1844-1912)

Andrew Lang was considered "the last of the generalists"—a man who could write something worth saying on any topic that interested him. He was a poet, novelist, classical scholar, and folklorist as well as one of the leading literary journalists of London from the 1870s through the 1890s. Even by Victorian standards, his output was enormous and includes 120 books or pamphlets, 150 volumes which he either edited or appeared in as contributor, and more than 5,000 essays, articles, and reviews.

Born in Selkirk, Scotland, Lang attended St. Andrews University and Balliol College, Oxford, where he showed promise as a classicist. Lang was a fellow at Merton College, Oxford, for seven years, but with his marriage in 1875 he moved to London to make his living as a journalist. As a critic, he showed a preference for romance and adventure, being one of the first to praise the work of Robert Louis Stevenson, Rudyard Kipling, and H. Rider Haggard.

Lang's most influential work was as a folklorist. While at Oxford, he was influenced by E. B. Tylor's pioneering work in anthropology. Lang enlarged Tylor's limited concept of **folklore** as European peasant tradition to incorporate oral tales and customs from around the world. In *Custom and Myth* (1884) and *Myth, Ritual and Religion* (1887), Lang successfully demolished the claims of Max Muller and other solar mythologists who had argued that all myths were part of a common Aryan inheritance. Lang maintained that the universality of folktales and customs was the result of all cultures undergoing the same cultural evolution rather than being derived from one original source.

Lang is best remembered for his Coloured Fairy Books, a series of twelve fairy tale collections intended for children, beginning with *The Blue Fairy Book* (1889). Lang emphasized that he was merely the guiding spirit of the series and not the author. Much of the translating and editing was done by his wife Leonora Alleyne Lang.

JAN SUSINA

Bibliography

Dorson, Richard M. *The British Folklorists: A History.* 1968.

Green, Roger Lancelyn. *Andrew Lang, A Critical Biography.* 1946.

———. *Andrew Lang.* 1962.

Jacobs, Joseph. "Andrew Lang as Man of Letters and Folk-Lorist." *Journal of American Folk-Lore,* vol. 26, pp. 367–372.

Langstaff, Eleanor De Selms. *Andrew Lang.* 1978.

Maurer, Oscar. "Andrew Lang and *Longman's Magazine.*" *University of Texas Studies in English*, vol. 24, pp. 152–178.

Weintraub, Joseph. "Andrew Lang: Critic of Romance." *English Literature in Transition*, vol. 18, pp. 5–15.

See also FAIRY TALES; MYTH

· · · · ·

LANGHAM PLACE CIRCLE

The Langham Place circle founded the middle-class women's rights movement in Britain. During the 1850s and 1860s, this small band of London activists organized campaigns to improve the legal, economic, and educational position of women, using the techniques of propaganda and voluntary association so characteristic of Victorian social reform.

The movement started in the mid-1850s when several young women from radical families began to agitate for changes in the married women's property laws. When that effort faltered, they established the **English Woman's Journal** (1858–1864). The *Journal* attracted women from less radical backgrounds, and its offices on Langham Place gave the group a name. Members of the circle organized the Victoria Press, the Female Middle-Class Emigration Society, and the Society for Promoting the Employment of Women. Led by **Bessie Parkes** (1829–1925), **Barbara Bodichon** (1827–1891), and **Emily Davies** (1831–1921), they participated in efforts to reform female education and initiated the women's suffrage campaign, persuading John Stuart Mill to raise the issue in Parliament. In addition to writing books, pamphlets, and articles on the woman question, various members of the circle launched the *Alexandra Magazine* (1864–1865), the *Victoria Magazine* (1863–1880), and the *Englishwoman's Review* (1866–1910), as well as the *Journal*.

By 1870 the circle had dissolved. Some members preferred to concentrate on a single aspect of the struggle. Others retired into private life. But, due to the efforts of these pioneers, there were many women willing to carry on the movement that the Langham Place circle had begun.

DIANE CHASE WORZALA

Bibliography

Lacey, Candida, ed. *Barbara Leigh Smith Bodichon and the Langham Place Group.* 1987.

Robson, A. P. W. "The Founding of the National Society for Women's Suffrage, 1866-1867." *Canadian Journal of History,* vol. 8, pp. 1-22.

Strachey, Ray. *The Cause: A Short History of the Women's Movement in Great Britain.* 1928; rpt. 1978.

Worzala, Diane. "The Langham Place Circle: The Beginnings of the Organized Women's Movement in England, 1854-1870." Ph.D. dissertation, University of Wisconsin, 1982.

See also FAITHFUL, EMILY

. . . . .

LANGTRY, LILLIE (1853-1929)

Emilie Charlotte Langtry was the only daughter of Emilie Martin and William Courbet Le Breton, dean of Jersey. She married Edward Langtry, son of a well-to-do shipping man, on March 9, 1874. She always hated her given names and throughout the rest of her life was known as Lillie Langtry. The marriage was not happy; according to Le Breton family legend, it was never consummated, although when she was ill with typhoid two years after her marriage, Langtry thought she might be pregnant.

In 1876 Langtry coerced her husband into moving to London and soon after was painted by John E. Millais. He coined the name "The Jersey Lily," which she used throughout her career. When her photographs by Frank Miles appeared in store windows, her ascent as a "professional beauty" began. In 1877 Langtry became the first publicly acknowledged mistress of Edward, Prince of Wales. She later became the mistress of Prince Louis of Battenberg; he was the father of her daughter Jeanne-Marie, born March 8, 1881. Edward Langtry, having retreated into his bottle

and obscurity, was apparently unaware when, years later, Lillie divorced him.

Partly to ease her financial difficulties, Langtry became an actress and was popular in both England and the United States. Her admirers included James Whistler, Prime Minister Gladstone, and Judge Roy Bean. She married Hugh de Bathe and, later, became Lady de Bathe. When she died in Monaco on February 12, 1929 she left an estate of almost 50,000 pounds.

JOANNA STEPHENS MINK

Bibliography

Brough, James. *The Prince and the Lily.* 1975.

Gerson, Noel B. *Because I Loved Him: The Life and Loves of Lillie Langtry.* 1971.

Langtry, Lillie. *The Days I Knew.* 1925.

Sichel, Pierre. *The Jersey Lily: The Story of the Fabulous Mrs. Langtry.* 1958.

. . . . .

LAW ENFORCEMENT

When young Queen Victoria ascended the throne, policemen were unfamiliar and unwelcome sights in London and rarely seen outside that city. For the first twenty years of her reign, reformers continued eighteenth-century efforts to establish and expand police forces, despite general public opposition. By 1856 the London Metropolitan Police system was demonstrably effective and was used as a model elsewhere in England and Wales. After that time, efforts focused on expansion, on increasing professionalism, and on new technological tools of crime detection.

The need for police was obvious even in the 1750s when writer Henry Fielding and his blind half-brother John Fielding, magistrates at Bow Street, had organized the Bow Street Runners. Teeming slums, unlit streets, cheap gin—these breeding grounds for crime had been created by the industrial urbanization of England and by its growing population. At that time, however, the Statute of Winchester (1285) still governed law enforcement; it remained the primary regulating act until the Metropolitan Police Act of 1829. Under the medieval statute, all citizens bore responsibility for policing their communities, although constables, sometimes aided by watchmen, had special duties including the presentation of criminals in court. All citizens were expected to do duty as constables, but, in reality, those who could afford to pay substitutes paid those who could not. Thus, constables and their watchmen generally came from the ranks of the insolvent, if not the senile and alcoholic. Although local systems varied widely, constables frequently reported to justices of the peace (magistrates), whose own powers had expanded enormously since first defined in 1361. Possessing both judicial and constabulary powers, justices might arrest suspects, examine them, serve as witnesses against them, and pass sentence upon them. The system invited corruption which, by the time of the Fieldings, was notorious.

Dubious outside London, the system was totally unworkable within it. Constables, such as they were, were confined to small districts; in some cases they were powerless to cross a street in order to halt a crime in progress on the other side. A rising crime rate drew public and parliamentary attention to the system's flaws, and increasing political turmoil complicated problems as the eighteenth century drew to an end. Military forces were called out for the Gordon ("no-popery") Riots of 1780, the Luddite working-class terrorism that followed, the anti–Corn-Law demonstrations that then ensued, and the Peterloo Massacre of 1819. The results were both bloody and chaotic.

Despite the sight of cavalrymen cutting down unarmed women and children, resistance to the establishment of police forces remained strong. Many feared that police would limit traditional freedoms or be used to control political dissidents, as in France. Taxpayers objected to the cost. Nonetheless, in 1792 the Middlesex Justices Bill resulted in the organization of metropolitan London, excluding the City of London, into seven districts, each with a police office staffed by three paid magistrates and by officers. This system temporarily coexisted with the Bow Street Runners, constables, watchmen, and City of London officers. Indeed, as late as 1842, the Parish Constables Act attempted to keep the constable system alive although it had long since proven generally unworkable.

Among the original twenty-one magistrates appointed in 1792 was Patrick Colquhoun (1745–1820), formerly lord provost of Glasgow. From 1797 to 1806 Colquhoun published revisions of his *Treatise on the Police of the Metropolis*, which argued for a preventive police force and for separation of police and judicial functions. By the final version, he recommended a central board of police commissioners, possessing wide-ranging powers and responsible to the Home Office. In the meantime, he worked with John Harriott (1745–1817) to develop a system of river police, implemented in 1798. A Marine Police Institution was headquartered at Wapping New Stairs with a permanent staff of eighty and a fleet of well-armed barges manned by river constables. The success of this experiment led to the 1800 Thames Police Bill, spearheaded by Colquhoun and by utilitarian reformer Jeremy Bentham (1748–1832).

A lengthy series of parliamentary inquiries and bills continued to address problems of law enforcement. Many were given impetus by **Robert Peel** (1788–1850). As home secretary in 1822, Peel saw to it that a head constable (inspector) was appointed to each police office and that uniformed patrols were begun. When he returned as home secretary under Arthur Wellesley, duke of Wellington (1769–1852) in 1828, he began efforts that led to the Metropolitan Police Act of 1829. As a result of this legislation, the metropolitan area was divided into seventeen districts, each headed by a superintendent overseeing four inspectors and sixteen sergeants. Each sergeant, in turn, had nine constables, eight patrolling beats and one in reserve in the station house. Charles Rowan (1782?–1852), a veteran of Waterloo, and Richard Mayne (1796–1868) were named commissioners of the metropolitan force. Recruiting of police began—although, of the original 2,800 men, 2,238 were quickly dismissed, many for drunkenness on duty.

One of the new districts was located in Great Scotland Yard, Whitehall, and had special responsibilities from the beginning. It housed the commissioners' staff, including clerks and accountants, as well as reserves that could be summoned by any district. Its superintendent made daily rounds of inspection to all districts and reported back to the commissioners.

This district was eventually to house the Criminal Investigation Division (CID), which began in 1842 as the Detective Department with two inspectors and eight sergeants. Despite renewed public hostility, as early as 1840 Inspector Nicholas Pearce was given a roving commission to investigate certain murders and other serious crimes and to watch the activities of habitual criminals. When the Detective Department was established, one of the original six detectives was Jonathan Whicher, famous as the investigator of the Constance Kent murder (1860) and as Sergeant Cuff of Wilkie Collins's *The Moonstone* (1877). He was soon joined by Charles Frederick Field, the Inspector Bucket of Charles Dickens's *Bleak House* (1853). By 1846 detectives were operating from each division with power to move among divisions.

Outside the metropolitan area development was slow and uneven. In 1835 Lord John Russell's (1792–1878) Municipal Corporations Bill enabled boroughs (towns) in England and Wales to establish police forces and to lay down principles of compensation for officers made seriously ill or injured in the line of duty. Additional enabling legislation in 1839 extended similar permission to counties. So necessary did police seem, by then, that Benthamite reformer Edwin Chadwick (1800–1890) urged one policeman for each 1,769 people or 4,403 acres in his *First Report of the Commissioners Appointed to Inquire as to the Best Means of Establishing an Efficient Constabulary Force in the Counties of England and Wales* (1839).

Resistance, however, remained high. In 1851, when the metropolitan force numbered 5,500 men, Liverpool had a force of 956, Manchester 554, Birmingham 350, and Bristol 301. Among the counties, Lancashire had 657, West Riding 487, and Gloucestershire 254. Many boroughs and counties simply retained or rehired ineffectual night watchmen, and even as late as 1856, thirteen boroughs continued to ignore the legislation completely. As a result, additional legislation in 1856 created the Home Office Inspector of Constabulary with power to enforce a uniform standard of police efficiency, based upon the metropolitan model, throughout the country. County forces, headed by a chief constable, were administered by a Standing Joint Committee of County Councils and Quarter Sessions; the chief constable, usually a member

of the gentry, was in effect head of the police forces. In the boroughs, constabularies were under the jurisdiction of Watch Committees, and the chief constable was no more than an executive officer for that committee.

In the meantime, in the metropolitan force, focus shifted to growth, professionalism, and advanced technology. The force increased at the rate of about 300 men a year under Edmund Henderson, who served as commissioner from 1868 to 1886, growing from about 8,500 to approximately 15,000 (statistics vary) in that period. The Turf Fraud Scandal of 1877, which deeply implicated certain Scotland Yard detectives, led to reorganization and a rigid rule of conduct that prohibited financial dealings between detectives and the public. Salaries remained low, however, and working conditions were severe. In the police strikes of 1872 and 1890 major issues were wages, assured pensions, the right to confer (organize), and, most tellingly, a weekly day off.

Henderson, who transformed the Detective Department into the CID in 1878, also began the Register of Habitual Criminals, later renamed the Criminal Record Office, in 1869. In 1867 telegraphs were installed in every metropolitan jurisdiction police station; in 1885 the metropolitan force was issued whistles to replace the traditional rattles. New Scotland Yard was built in 1890. Other developments included, in the early 1880s, the formation of the Special Irish Branch, later called the Special Branch, to respond to an outbreak of Fenian terrorism. The Black Museum, at first simply called the Museum, was established during that period, while in 1883 the *Police Gazette*—once Henry and John Fielding's *The Weekly, or Extraordinary Pursuit* and later *The Hue and Cry*—was moved from Bow Street to Scotland Yard.

In 1894 Scotland Yard adopted the anthropomorphic measurement system of Alphonse Bertillon (1853–1914) of the Paris police for identifying criminals, but soon replaced it with a fingerprint system developed by **Francis Galton** (1822–1911), whose *Fingerprint Directories* (1895) outlined the first system of digital classification to appear in print. Edward Richard Henry, who became CID commissioner in 1901, also developed a fingerprint system; it was adopted by the Indian government in 1897. Henry encouraged the introduction of other modern equipment, beginning with the telephone. Indeed, the Victorian age in one sense ended in 1910, when Dr. Hawley Harvey Crippen was arrested for the death of his wife. Escaping with his young mistress on a ship from London to Quebec, Crippen aroused the suspicions of the ship's captain who radioed back to shore. Scotland Yard Inspector Walter Dew, having caught a faster ship, was waiting to arrest Crippin at Quebec, and the age of modern law enforcement technology may be said to have begun.

BETTY RICHARDSON

Bibliography

Babington, Anthony. *A House in Bow Street: Crime and the Magistracy, London 1740-1881.* 1969.

Browne, Douglas. *The Rise of Scotland Yard: A History of the Metropolitan Police.* 1956.

Cobb, Belton. *The First Detectives and the Early Career of Richard Mayne, Commissioner of Police.* 1957.

Critchley, Thomas A. *A History of Police in England and Wales, 900-1966.* 1967.

Hart, J. M. *The British Police.* 1951.

Howe, Ronald. *The Story of Scotland Yard: A History of the C. I. D. from the Earliest Times to the Present Day.* 1965.

Mather, F. C. *Public Order in the Age of the Chartists.* 1959.

Radzinowicz, Leon. *A History of English Criminal Law and Its Administration from 1750.* 1948-1956. 3 vols.

See also CRIME; HOMOSEXUALITY; INFANTICIDE; JUVENILE CRIME; PRISONS AND PRISON REFORM

· · · · ·

LAW REFORM

During the nineteenth century the law of state and the machinery of government were overhauled and expanded to meet the needs of modern industrial society. Most crucial reforms were achieved by exercise of the legislative will of Parliament, spurred on by social reformers who wished to improve the conditions of the poor and unfortunate. In addition, major steps were taken to reform lawyers' law and improve the administration of justice.

Law reform, however, was not achieved by lawyers and judges. The innate conservatism of the legal profession had blocked reform for two centuries. Indeed, many of the changes eventually achieved in the Victorian era had been recommended, in vain, by the Hale Commission during the Cromwellian interregnum. Intellectually, Victorian law reform was the creature of Jeremy Bentham (1748–1832) and the Philosophical Radicals. Bentham had devoted his life to the study and reform of the law, with very few concrete results in his lifetime which, ironically, ended in the year of the first Reform Act. He abhorred the obfuscation of the common law so venerated by Blackstone and wanted the law to be codified so that it would be rational, simplified, and accessible to the general public.

Politically, the great impetus came from Henry Brougham, symbolized by his famous marathon speech in the House of Commons, which led to the appointment of a series of commissions and House of Commons committees to examine the operation of a court system that was riddled with extraordinary delays, widespread corruption, perplexing procedural anomalies, unintelligible legal language and, of course, injustice.

Much of the procedural and substantive English law had remained unchanged for five centuries. Those changes that had been effected made the law more technical and encrusted with legal fictions and procedural subterfuges. Antiquated procedural devices such as trial by battle, benefit of clergy, and *peine forte et dure*, though long disused, were not formally abolished until the 1820s. In the administration of criminal justice, the law had grown more stringent. By the early nineteenth century, over two hundred crimes were punishable by death. The pillory and the grisly ceremony of hanging, drawing, and quartering were still in existence when Queen Victoria began her reign. Transportation of convicts continued until midcentury. Prisons, as places of punishment, developed only during the nineteenth century.

Nor was the administration of justice necessarily as fair and just as is commonly believed. The accused were not allowed to give evidence on oath at their own trials until 1898. Defense counsel were not generally allowed until the nineteenth century, and then not universally permitted. The prosecution was perfunctorily performed by amateurs and the judge often doubled as an unofficial defense lawyer. Until 1843, persons "interested" in the accused's trial (such as spouses) were forbidden to give evidence. There was no regular criminal appeals court until the twentieth century.

But although the trial of the early nineteenth century was a very shallow affair, injustice was not inevitably the result. The judge and jury would often apply a form of "criminal equity" rather than expose the accused to an extraordinarily severe punishment (such as the death penalty for stealing an article worth five shillings). The judge might interpret the statute strictly to protect the accused or lean over backwards to discover procedural niceties leading to an acquittal. The jury might indulge in "pious perjury" by distorting the facts to rob the prosecution of a conviction.

By the end of Victoria's reign, criminal law had been revolutionized. The prosecution had become partly professionalized. Increasing numbers of the accused were represented by defense counsel. The law of evidence had taken on many more aspects of fairness (partly influenced by Bentham). Children charged with crime had been removed from adult courts and prisons and treated more humanely in juvenile courts and institutions. Probation had been instituted for first offenders. Advocates of codification, such as Thomas Babington Macaulay (1800-1859) and James Fitzjames Stephen (1829-1894), tried to rationalize the criminal law. They failed to persuade the English lawyers and judges to adopt a criminal code, although their efforts were rewarded with the adoption of codes in India, Jamaica, Canada, and some Australian states.

On the civil side, the court system was, if possible, even more chaotic. There were far too many courts with overlapping jurisdic-

tions. Many court officials and judges were paid on a piecework basis, and more processes meant more fees. The methods of initiating litigation were cumbersome; if an action were started in the wrong court or if an incorrect formula were used in the pleading, the litigant had to start again. Legal mumbo jumbo was omnipresent. Style took precedence over content. At common law, the formulary system dominated the law. This had two effects. First, the straitjacket of the forms of action stultified the law's creativity, failing to rectify wrongs that had no prescribed remedy. Second, the courts sometimes tried to circumvent the procedural rigidity by employing legal fictions, adding to obfuscation and impenetrable legalese.

The most notorious element of the court system was the Court of Chancery, so vividly exposed by Charles Dickens in *Bleak House* (1852-1853). **Chancery** dispensed equity, which was meant to provide a beneficent gloss on the common law by allowing the presiding lord chancellor, at his discretion, to alleviate injustices in individual cases. Ironically, the Court of Chancery became more rigid and corrupt than the conventional courts; instead of providing instinctive and summary justice, Chancery was synonymous with delay, exorbitant fees, bribery, and byzantine procedures.

These problems were solved by the Judicature Act of 1873, the procedural reform Magna Carta of the nineteenth century. The forms of action were abolished, which led to judicial creativity. The multiplicity of courts was reduced to a small group of specialized courts and the exclusivity of law and equity was abolished. Discretion was no longer limited to the old Court of Chancery.

GRAHAM PARKER

Bibliography

Dicey, A. V. *Law and Public Opinion in England.* 2d ed., 1914.

Holdsworth, William. *A History of English Law,* vols. 14, 15. 1964, 1965.

Radzinowitz, Leon. *A History of English Criminal Law.* 1948-1968. 4 vols.

See also JUDICIAL SYSTEM

· · · · ·

LAWS OF PUBLIC WORSHIP, SPEECH, AND THE PRESS

Although there had been no prepublication censorship in Britain since the licensing laws expired in 1694, speech in the Victorian era was notably unfree. Political comment was severely restricted, especially in the tumultuous early part of the century when revolution seemed imminent. Christianity was held to be not only a necessary guarantee of morality, but also part of the law of England; laws dating back to the Elizabethan settlement were still on the statute books that required assent to the doctrines of the established church and fined those who failed to attend it regularly. Although Toleration Acts of 1688 and 1812 had exempted Dissenters and Unitarians from these laws, they were not repealed until 1846. Even after the theory of uniform worship had been abandoned, irreligious and atheistic thought continued to be prosecuted as an attack on public order. The struggle for freedom of expression, which occupied much of the century, achieved success in all but sexual matters.

The laws restricting freedom of speech were directed mainly against public meetings associated with reform agitation. Common laws against blasphemy, seditious words, and seditious conspiracy were bolstered by temporary "gagging" acts at times of stress, notably in 1817 after Spa Fields and 1819 after Peterloo, which prohibited unlicensed lectures and speeches. The temporary measure passed during the Chartist unrest in 1848 was milder, and although freethinkers' and secularists' lectures continued to be harassed by the police, and as late as 1880 Charles Stewart Parnell was prosecuted for seditious conspiracy over his Home Rule meetings, public agitation generally became an accepted feature of political life.

The main instrument of control over the press, the law of criminal libel, should be distinguished from the civil libel or defamation of character still familiar. Criminal libel was defamation of such entities as the monarch, the constitution, or the church. Broadly, any writing that brought constituted authorities into disrespect and hence tended to provoke a breach of the peace might be considered libel-ous. Falsehood was not at issue: in fact it was held that "the greater the truth the greater the libel," since valid criticisms were the more disturbing. Criminal libels were of four types: seditious (political), defamatory (criticisms of high officials), blasphemous (religious), and obscene (sexual). All were misdemeanors in common law; the few statutes on the subject were not much invoked.

The law of seditious libel fell into disuse after a series of notable trials, particularly those of Thelwall, Wooler, John Hunt, and Burdett around the time of Peterloo and of Cobbett in 1831. The passing of the Reform Act (1832) was a sign that the constitution could be criticized and mildly adjusted, yet still survive. Blasphemous libel had a longer life. Though the bulk of the prosecutions occurred early in the century, G. W. Foote was convicted in 1883 for a blasphemous number of his *Freethinker*. Defamatory libel was modified in 1843 when Campbell's Libel Act allowed the truth of a comment on public officials to be taken into account in defense. The law of obscene libel, however, became increasingly restrictive. It was invoked against any sexual explicitness considered immoral, so that J. S. Mill in 1823 and Bradlaugh and Besant in 1877 were alike in trouble with the law for distributing information on birth control; and in 1888 Henry Vizetelly was fined for publishing Zola's *La Terre*, inaugurating a series of prosecutions of literary works that stretched well into the twentieth century.

Not only was the press restricted in what it might publish with impunity; it was also subject to stamp duties or **"taxes on knowledge"** which made newspapers too expensive to reach a lower-class audience. There were three duties, one on newspapers and pamphlets, one on paper, and one on advertisements. Imposed in 1711, they had increased until, by 1815, a newspaper generally cost sevenpence. An 1819 act suppressed "scurrilous" popular papers like Cobbett's *Weekly Political Register* by bringing all cheap, frequent papers of news and comment under the Stamp Acts and instituting a security system that required publishers to post bonds against possible prosecutions. In the 1830s a number of cheap radical papers defied the law by remaining "unstamped." After a spate of prosecutions, the stamp duty was lowered in 1836 but higher security deposits were demanded.

As a result, a wealthier, more law-abiding group was attracted to publishing and drove out the unstamped.

Finally, a campaign waged by the Association for Promoting the Repeal of the Taxes on Knowledge (1851) was gradually successful in bringing about the repeal of the duties on advertisements (1853), newspapers (1855), and paper (1861), and the end of the security system (1869). The association proved correct in its contention that the spread of information among the populace would not unleash anarchy.

JEAN O'GRADY

Bibliography

Collet, C. D. *History of the Taxes on Knowledge.* 1899.

Hollis, Patricia. *The Pauper Press.* 1970.

McCoy, Ralph E. *Freedom of the Press: An Annotated Bibliography.* 1968.

Stephen, James F. *A History of the Criminal Law of England*, vol. 2, 1883.

Wickwar, William H. *The Struggle for the Freedom of the Press, 1819-1832.* 1928.

See also FREETHOUGHT; PRESS, RADICAL AND UNSTAMPED

· · · · ·

LEAR, EDWARD
(1812-1888)

Edward Lear, the youngest surviving child in a family of twenty-one, was born at Holloway in 1812 and raised from an early age by his eldest sister. Although troubled throughout his life by emotional distance from his parents and by epilepsy, Lear showed early talent as an artist. His drawings of the parrots at the London zoo were published in 1831. In the same year Lord Stanley invited the young artist to his estate at Knowsley to illustrate the animals in his menagerie. Lear wrote the limericks for *A Book of Nonsense* (1846) for the Stanley grandchildren.

Asthma and a desire to study art led Lear, with Stanley's financial assistance, to Rome. He lived abroad for most of the rest of his life,

although he returned to England for three and a half years upon being accepted to the Royal Academy in 1850. As a landscape painter, Lear traveled from southern Europe to the Middle East and, later in life, to India and Ceylon. His paintings and travel journals were, however, only moderately successful. Lear's native talent was primarily as an illustrator. In 1846 he served as drawing instructor to the queen.

Although Lear enjoyed companionship, he found intimacy constricting. He feared his attraction to his closest male friend, and was too preoccupied by the possibility of marital discord to consider marriage. Lear's nonsense poems and limericks often echo the instability and alienation of his life, as well as his own sense of himself as an absurd character. The casually illustrated nonsense books lack the polished technique that distinguish Lear's landscape and natural history drawings. While his best-known poem is "The Owl and the Pussycat," his most telling is the autobiographical "How Pleasant to Know Mr. Lear."

ALAN RAUCH

Bibliography

Byrom, Thomas. *Nonsense and Wonder: The Poems and Cartoons of Edward Lear.* 1977.

Hark, Ina Rae. *Edward Lear.* 1982.

Jackson, Holbrook, ed. *The Complete Nonsense of Edward Lear.* 1947.

Noakes, Vivien. *Edward Lear: The Life of a Wanderer.* 1969.

· · · · ·

LEARNED SOCIETIES

Though they are unusually characteristic of the Victorian period, several important learned societies were founded earlier. The Royal Society of London (1660), whose *Transactions* dominated the eighteenth century, helped to foster modern science. Originally, all knowledge was its province, but specialized groups increasingly proved their worth. First to split off was the Society of Antiquaries (1718). The **Royal Academy of Arts** (1768) followed. Regional distinctions also became characteristic. The Royal Society of

Edinburgh (1783) grew out of a local philosophical society (common in the eighteenth century) which accepted papers on all topics and published some.

Differentiation continued among the scientifically inclined, in part because the Royal Society had become too diffuse and indiscriminate. Thus, the Linnaean Society (1788) restricted itself to natural history. Even more narrowly defined were the Royal Horticultural Society (1804), the Geological Society (1807), the Astronomical Society (1820), the Zoological Society (1826), the Geographical Society (1830), the Entomological Society (1833), the Statistical Society (1834), the Meteorological Society (1836), the Botanical Society (1838), the Microscopical Society (1839), the Chemical Society (1841), the Ethnological Society (1843), the Paleontographical Society (1847), and the Anthropological Society (1863). By the beginning of Victoria's reign, then, the Royal Society had to a considerable extent been supplanted by its own offspring.

Among those specialized derivatives, the Geological Society became most active, in part because (from 1824) open and sometimes fervent debates followed the presentation of papers. **Geology** itself, moreover, seemed more controversial than other sciences. Till midcentury at least, the ruling elites of the Royal and Geological societies significantly overlapped, and additional memberships in the Linnaean and Zoological societies were common. Women could not be admitted to any of these societies, though some were certainly deserving. Instead, they attended public lectures on the sciences, including those offered by the Royal Institution (1799) and the British Association for the Advancement of Science (1831), whose annual meetings and specialized sections became almost a parliament of Victorian science.

Britons in the 1840s manifested considerable alarm regarding the rapid deterioration of their traditional heritage. Thus, the English Historical Society (1838), the Oxford Society for Promoting the Study of Gothic Architecture (1839; later the Oxford Architectural and Historical Society), the Lincolnshire Society for the Encouragement of Ecclesiastical Antiquities (1844) and the Ecclesiastical Society (1846–1862) all arose, with **John Ruskin's** Arundel Society (1849–1897) for the preservation of Italian art as an international example. Promoted by Ruskin but founded by **William Morris**, the Society for the Protection of Ancient Buildings (1877) arrived a generation later.

The British Archaeological Association was founded in 1844. Over the next decade local archaeological societies arose in many counties. The Royal Historical Society appeared in 1868, the Oxford Historical Society in 1882, and the Scottish Historical Society in 1885.

There was also concern to recover and preserve the literary past. In the wake of the Camden Society (1837) came the Percy Society (1840), the Caxton Society (1844), and the Hakluyt Society (1846). Just as numerous scholarly editions of earlier English literature were beginning to appear, F. J. Furnivall founded, in turn, the Early English Text Society (1864), the Ballad Society (1868), the Chaucer Society (1868), the New Shakespeare Society (1873), and the Wiclif Society (1881). In such a milieu, the British Record Society (1889) and the London Bibliographical Society (1892) became almost inevitable.

Furnivall also founded the Browning (1881) and Shelley (1886) societies. Wordsworth, Ruskin, and FitzGerald all had their followers also, as did various alternative cultures, not to mention such devotees of reform as the **Fabian Society** (1884). As the Christian heritage became less meaningful there were such bold new directions as the famous Metaphysical Society (1869–1879), which included Tennyson, Ruskin, Huxley, Tyndall, Gladstone, and others as members. Even the **Society for Psychical Research** (1882) and its kindred were not immediately spurned.

In addition, artists, musicians, physicians, surgeons, lawyers, architects, engineers, and writers had societies of their own, though many did not publish transactions or promote research as such. There were literary and philosophical societies in many provincial centers, with natural history or field clubs equally abundant. The Athenaeum Club (1828) of London remained viable throughout the century as a generalist organization recognizing literary accomplishments of the broadest kind. **Mechanics' institutes**, a lower-class alternative, were also widely popular. Without attempting much research themselves, these groups often attracted prestigious speakers from those that did.

DENNIS R. DEAN

Bibliography

Hall, Marie Boas. *All Scientists Now: The Royal Society in the Nineteenth Century.* 1984.

Inkster, Ian and Jack Morrell, eds. *Metropolis and Provice: Science in British Culture, 1780-1850.* 1983.

McElroy, David D. *Scotland's Age of Improvement.* 1969.

. . . . .

LEE, VERNON (VIOLET PAGET) (1856-1935)

Vernon Lee has been described as a Victorian, puritan, aesthetician, romanticist, humanist, pacifist, and feminist. Her varied interests, literary versatility, progressive world view, and independent lifestyle are exemplary of the **New Woman**.

Lee (daughter of Matilda and Henry Ferguson Paget) was groomed from an early age to be a lady of leisure, breeding, and culture. She and her half-brother, the poet Eugene Lee-Hamilton, read voraciously and traveled widely. France, Germany, and Italy provided backdrops for Lee's writings in the romantic idyll (*Ottillie*, 1883), biography (*The Countess of Albany*, 1884), short story (*Hauntings*, 1890), drama (*Ariadne in Mantua*, 1903), and travel sketches (including *The Enchanted Woods*, 1905; *The Sentimental Traveller*, 1908; *The Golden Keys*, 1925). Lee's descriptive essays on the musical, visual, and literary arts reflect an extensive knowledge of Western civilization.

Reputed to be aloof, temperamental, and rebellious, Lee was at times criticized by mentors and detractors alike. Oscar Wilde and other aesthetes were offended by her satiric novel on the "art for art's sake" movement (*Miss Brown*, 1884). Henry James objected to her naive fictionalization of him in the story "Lady Tal" (1892). Bernard Berenson falsely accused Lee and her close friend Clementina (Kit) Anstruther-Thomson of plagiarism when they published their pioneering works on psychological aesthetics in art (*Beauty and Ugliness*, 1912; *The Beautiful*, 1913). Except for liberals like George Bernard Shaw, few supported her non-nationalistic stance on pacifism (*Satan the Waster*, 1920).

Despite loss of popularity, estranged relationships, bouts of depression and failing health, Lee had a long, vital, and productive career, publishing over forty volumes. Her correspondence (housed at Somerville College, Oxford, and Colby College, Maine) indicates that she had many devoted friends and admirers, including Ethyl Smyth, Maurice Baring, and Aldous Huxley. Vernon Lee was a woman in transition whose personal values and tastes were grounded in the near and distant past, but whose philosophical and social vision was clearly directed toward the future.

PHYLLIS E. WACHTER

Bibliography

Colby, Vineta. *The Singular Anomaly: Women Novelists of the Nineteenth Century.* 1970.

English Literature in Transition, vol. 26, pp. 231-312. (Issue on Vernon Lee.)

Gunn, Peter. *Vernon Lee: Violet Paget, 1856-1935.* 1964.

Mannocchi, Phyllis, "Vernon Lee and Kit Anstruther-Thomson: A Study of Love and Collaboration Between Romantic Friends." *Women's Studies*, vol. 12, pp. 129-148.

. . . . .

LEFANU, JOSEPH SHERIDAN (1814-1873)

With some thirty stories and fourteen novels to his credit, along with poems, verse plays and political pamphlets, Joseph Sheridan LeFanu is important for his contribution to **Gothic fiction**. Originally published in the collections *Ghost Stories and Tales of Mystery* (1851), *In a Glass Darkly* (1872), and *The Purcell Papers* (1880), all of his tales are now available in *Best Ghost Stories of J. S. LeFanu* (1964) and *Ghost Stories and Mysteries: J. S. LeFanu* (1975), both edited by E. F. Bleiler. Though he is not remembered for his historical romances and murder mysteries, his Gothic novels receive critical attention, especially *The House by the Church-*

yard (1863), *Wylder's Hand* (1864), *Uncle Silas* (1864), and *Haunted Lives* (1968).

A descendant of the dramatist Sheridan on his mother's side, LeFanu was born in Dublin. He graduated from Trinity College, studied law, and edited several newspapers and periodicals. Married in 1844, he became a recluse after the death of his wife in 1858. Scholars comment on his eccentric nocturnal writing habits and his death by a heart attack apparently caused by a nightmare similar to the horrors that tormented his protagonists. LeFanu's Gothicism shows innovation and variety, with tales like "The Ghost and the Bone-Setter" (1838) and "The Drunkard's Dream" (1838) based upon sportive humor and Irish folklore; the famous "Carmilla" (1872), based upon female vampirism; and "Green Tea" (1872) and "Mr. Justice Harbottle" (1872), based upon hallucination and supernaturalism.

Typically, his protagonists, like Maud Ruthvyn in *Uncle Silas*, are victimized by the visitations and torments of some inexplicable evil force. As Bleiler observes, LeFanu is unlike other popular Victorian writers of ghost stories, who continued to use supernatural elements in the Radcliffean tradition, because he infuses the unreal so deeply into the perception of his characters. In so doing, he anticipates the complex psychological reality of Henry James and modern Gothic writers.

BETTE B. ROBERTS

Bibliography

Begnal, Michael H. *Joseph Sheridan LeFanu.* 1971.

Browne, Nelson. *Sheridan LeFanu.* 1951.

Ellis, Stewart Marsh. *Wilkie Collins, LeFanu and Others.* 1951.

McCormack, W. J. *Sheridan LeFanu and Victorian Ireland.* 1980.

Sullivan, Jack. *Elegant Nightmares: The English Ghost Story from LeFanu to Blackwood.* 1978.

· · · · ·

LEGAL PROFESSION

The British legal profession during the reign of Victoria inherited from the remote past a division based on legal functions. In England barristers had a monopoly on practice before the common-law courts; advice on family matters, property transactions, and business in general was the preserve of attorneys, increasingly known as solicitors. Until 1857 advocates with doctorates in Roman and canon law from Oxford or Cambridge had exclusive rights to practice in the admiralty and ecclesiastical courts, while proctors functioned like solicitors in such cases. (The famous fictional firm of Spenlow and Jorkins, to which David Copperfield was articled, were proctors with offices in Doctors' Commons.) In Scotland, practice before the superior courts was the monopoly of advocates, while the other branch of the profession was reserved for "writers," also known as law agents or procurators and eventually as solicitors. Despite continued functional division, the British legal profession underwent profound changes in the Victorian era that broke with many traditions of prior centuries and established the modern legal profession.

Barristers, known collectively as the bar, generally enjoyed high social status. At the top, incomes reached aristocratic levels: in 1847, the year of the railway mania, Charles Austin (1799–1874) was rumored to have earned as much as 100,000 pounds. Then, as now, barristers could not practice in partnership, though they could share chambers. All barristers belonged to one of London's four historic Inns of Court—Lincoln's Inn, Gray's Inn, the Inner Temple, and the Middle Temple—which alone could call men to the bar. Until 1857 English advocates were regulated by a corporate body at Doctors' Commons. In Scotland the Faculty of Advocates played the role of the Inns of Court. Although in earlier centuries the centers of legal education, the inns had long ceased to function as universities of the law. The only remaining requirement for admission was that a candidate "keep" twelve terms at an inn, which meant no more than eating a few meals there each term. In 1852, in response to the report of a parliamentary select committee on legal education, the inns jointly established the Council of Legal Education which began to provide courses and in 1872 instituted bar examinations.

Judges of the common-law courts were chosen exclusively from the bar. Until 1875 only barristers who had been appointed serjeants-at-law were eligible. Forming the Order of the Coif, known for the headdress they wore, serjeants were never numerous: in the nineteenth century there were seldom more than forty at any one time. Ranking next after serjeants were Queen's Counsel. Because of their gowns, Queen's Counsel were known as "silks" and appointment to the rank as "taking silk." Queen's Counsel were "leading" counsel who could not appear in court unless accompanied by junior counsel whom they "led."

Unlike barristers, solicitors were not concentrated in London; instead they were located in every town. Also unlike barristers, solicitors could and frequently did form partnerships. A solicitor, usually intimate with the locally important family, was often referred to in contemporary documents as the family's "man of business." Solicitors performed many functions, some legal, such as serving as clerk of the peace assisting the justices of the peace at quarter sessions, some not, such as serving as election agents. The Law Society, established in 1825, came to regulate solicitors in England much as the Inns of Court regulated barristers. In Scotland the role was played by various bodies, principally by the Writers to the Signet, the Society of Solicitors in the Supreme Courts of Scotland, the Faculty of Procurators, and many local societies.

The most significant institutional development in the Victorian period, pregnant with permanent consequences for the legal profession, was the development of university education in English law. University College, London, offered law courses from its foundation in 1826; influential lectures on jurisprudence by John Austin (1790–1859), brother of the successful barrister, were delivered there from 1829 to 1832. As part of the midcentury reforms in legal education, both the historic universities established law schools: Oxford in 1850, and Cambridge in 1858. For a time both were linked with the history faculties but by the mid-1870s both were independent. Unlike American law schools, which followed Harvard's lead and became graduate professional schools, English law schools remained undergraduate faculties. In Scotland the development of modern legal education began when the commissioners, under the Universities (Scotland) Act (1858), created the degree of LL.B.; further progress came in 1874 when Scottish universities created the degree of B.L.

Law teaching produced a demand for textbooks, as well as academic lawyers with the time and objectivity necessary to supply them. In addition to practical treatises, academic lawyers produced scholarly studies that viewed law from new perspectives; the systematic study of jurisprudence, legal history, and comparative law dates from the late Victorian era.

Despite reformist elements, the Victorian legal profession was a broadly conservative force in society. Fees placed the services of the profession beyond the reach of most Britons. The English solicitor, W. P. Roberts (1806–1871), known as the "miners' attorney general," served militant trade unions, but most lawyers catered to the middle and upper classes. In Scotland the legal profession occupied a unique position. The Act of Union (1707) had deprived Scotland of its parliament but had left intact the nation's legal system, based on Roman rather than common law. Occupying the historic Parliament House in Edinburgh, the advocates helped preserve Scotland's rights and identity.

JOHN V. ORTH

Bibliography

Abel-Smith, Brian and Robert Stevens. *Lawyers and the Courts: A Sociological Study of the English Legal System, 1750–1965.* 1967.

Birks, Michael. *Gentlemen of the Law.* 1960.

Duman, Daniel. *The English and Colonial Bars in the Nineteenth Century.* 1983.

——. *The Judicial Bench in England, 1727–1875: The Reshaping of a Political Elite.* 1982.

Holdsworth, William S. *A History of English Law,* vols. 15, 16. 1965–1966.

Lawson, F. H. *The Oxford Law School, 1850–1965.* 1968.

Reader, W. J. *Professional Men: The Rise of the Professional Classes in Nineteenth-Century England.* 1966.

See also CHANCERY AND DOCTORS' COMMONS; JUDICIAL SYSTEM; SCOTS LAW

. . . . .

LEMON, MARK
(1809-1870)

First editor of *Punch* (1841–1870) and the author of approximately eighty plays, Mark Lemon was an influential comic voice in mid-Victorian letters. He enjoyed the respect and friendship of writers like **Wilkie Collins** and **Charles Dickens**.

Born to Martin and Alice Collis Lemon, he spent a middle-class childhood in London and the country. Employed in a brewery and a tavern in the 1830s, Lemon simultaneously wrote short sketches and verse. In 1837 his first farce *The P. L.; or, 30 Strand* was produced and in 1839 he married Nelly Romer. As his family grew to ten children, Lemon continued to write plays and novels, the finest of which are perhaps the dramas *Hearts are Trumps* (1849) and *Mind Your Own Business* (1852). With Edward Bulwer-Lytton, Collins, and others, Lemon collaborated with Dickens in the Strolling Players, performing amateur theatricals (1850s) to benefit impecunious artists through the Guild of Literature and Art. A talented actor, he became known for his version of *Falstaff* (1868). The Lemon and Dickens families frequently exchanged visits and shared vacations.

Although Lemon championed liberal causes, he was a cautious middle-class moralist. Wishing to protect his children from the corruptions of London, he removed them to Crawley, Sussex (1858), where he became a revered community figure. With his reputation for fairness and geniality, he was eloquently eulogized at his death.

LEONA W. FISHER

Bibliography

Adrian, Arthur A. *Mark Lemon: First Editor of "Punch."* 1966.

Dexter, Walter, ed. *The Unpublished Letters of Charles Dickens to Mark Lemon.* 1971.

Fowler, L. N. "Phrenological Description of Charles Dickens and Mark Lemon." *Human Nature,* vol. 4, pp. 366–369.

Hatton, Joseph. *With a Show in the North: Reminiscences of Mark Lemon.* 1871.

Price, Richard G. G. *A History of "Punch."* 1957.

Spielmann, Marion H. *The History of "Punch."* 1895.

———. "Mark Lemon." *Bookman,* vol. 37, pp. 77–86.

. . . . .

LEVY, AMY
(1861-1889)

Little is known about the Jewish poet and novelist Amy Levy. She was born in Lapham, lived in Brighton, and was educated at Newnham College, Cambridge, then became either a factory worker or teacher in London. She published three collections of poetry—*Xantippe and Other Verse* (1881), *A Minor Poet and Other Verse* (1884), *A London Plane-Tree, and Other Verse* (1889)—and one novel, *Reuben Sachs* (1888), a satirical exploration of Jewish culture. During the same year in which her novel won critical attention, she committed suicide by inhaling charcoal fumes.

Levy wrote as an anguished outsider. Her dramatic poems recount the damage that scorn and alienation cause the individual. "A Minor Poet" tells of the suicide of an artist with insufficient talent to exorcize his angst. "Medea" paints the famed villain as a victim. "Run to Death" is a poetic rendering of "A True Incident of Pre-Revolutionary French History" in which a gypsy and her baby provide the kill for an aristocrat's afternoon hunt. Levy's best poem is the dramatic monologue "Xantippe." On her deathbed, Socrates' wife explains her infamous acerbity: as a young woman, intelligent beyond propriety, she hoped for a responsive mate in the wise philosopher. He rebuffed her ideas because of her sex. This hypocrisy turns her hopes into "a sort of fierce acceptance of my fate," symbolized by the bitter expense of her life at the female task of spinning, where she "spun away / The soul from out my body, the high thoughts / From out my spirit." Levy's death, like Xantippe's fate, was a sure waste of undeveloped promise.

SHELLEY J. CRISP

. . . . .

LEWES, GEORGE HENRY (1817–1878)

George Henry Lewes was a critic, editor, biographer, dramatist, essayist, and common-law husband of **George Eliot**. His chief works are *Biographical History of Philosophy* (1845), *Life of Maximilien Robespierre* (1848), *The Life and Works of Goethe* (1855), *Sea-Side Studies* (1858), *The Physiology of Common Life* (1859), *Studies in Animal Life* (1862), *Problems of Life and Mind* (1874–1879); and the novels *Ranthorpe* (1847) and *Rose, Blanche, and Violet* (1848).

Lewes was born in London and had finished his formal education by the time he was sixteen. Married to Agnes Jervis, who later had children by Thornton Hunt, Lewes lived with George Eliot for over twenty years, and significantly encouraged and nurtured her as a writer.

Lewes's first novel, *Ranthorpe* (1845), is a direct descendant of Goethe's *Wilhelm Meister's Apprenticeship*. An uneven mixture of realism, autobiography, and melodrama, it traces a young protagonist's evolution to a fuller understanding of life. Both Edgar Allan Poe and Charlotte Brontë praised the novel. *Rose, Blanche, and Violet* (1848) was an attempt at a wholly realistic novel.

Lewes distinguished himself from most nineteenth-century critics by deriving his judgments from ideas rather than mere reactions. His reviews in various journals covered a range of subjects: English and American fiction, drama, and poetry. Lewes based his criticism on empiricism; truth and reality were important criteria. For example, in his well-known review of Charlotte Brontë's *Jane Eyre*, Lewes remarked that the action of the novel was plausible, and he singled out the conception of Jane Eyre's character as one based on reality, not fantasy. Lewes also insisted on psychological reality, a concept that involves the actual effect of phenomena on a character. With Thornton Hunt, Lewes was also coeditor of the *Leader* from 1850–1854. For this journal Lewes wrote both general articles with a liberal viewpoint and light, charming fillers under the pseudonym Vivian.

Lewes's biography of Goethe is an extension of his criticism. He approached Goethe's life through Goethe's own writings and provided translations of notable passages. Many of the prose translations were done by George Eliot. Indeed, Gordon S. Haight points out that the work is a collaboration, for Eliot reviewed and discussed the manuscript at great length. Lewes spent the last years of his life working on a mammoth study entitled *Problems of Life and Mind*, parts of which appeared periodically as books with the final two volumes, *The Study of Psychology*, published posthumously with George Eliot's assistance. In this project, Lewes attempted to relate the human mind to the workings of the body. Now dated, such a study was a pioneering effort in its time.

While Lewes's plays are of negligible importance, his two novels are historically significant for their subject matter. Lewes's greatest achievement is his critical advocacy of realism. His study of Goethe is still respected.

DENNIS GOLDSBERRY

Bibliography

Haight, Gordon S., ed. *The George Eliot Letters.* 1954–1978. 9 vols.

Hirshberg, Edgar W. *George Henry Lewes.* 1970.

Kaminsky, Alice R. *Literary Criticism of George Henry Lewes.* 1964.

Postlethwaite, Diana. *Making It Whole: A Victorian Circle and the Shape of Their World.* 1985.

Williams, David. *Mr. George Eliot.* 1983.

· · · · ·

LIBERAL PARTY

The Liberal party became one of the most important political and social movements of the Victorian period. The doctrine of Liberalism fused a Whig rhetorical tradition of political progress, English liberties and representative institutions; an evangelical movement that became associated with militant Nonconformity; **Manchester school** precepts of laissez-faire economics and foreign nonintervention; the utilitarian legacy of Philosophical Radicalism; and a body of philosophical thought exemplified in the writings of John Stuart Mill which encouraged individual self-determination and, at a governmental level, strengthened attitudes of disinterested equity. In political practice, Liberalism joined an elitist Whig administrative progressivism with a popular following that grew from the memory of Chartism and the Anti-Corn-Law League, the new cheap daily press, and organized labor. At the height of its power, from the 1860s to the 1890s, this powerful political alliance became personified in the administrative and moral zeal of **W. E. Gladstone**.

In June 1859, parliamentary Whigs, Liberals, Radicals, and Peelites, meeting in Willis's Rooms, united under the leadership of **Lord Palmerston**. Through the speeches of Gladstone and **John Bright**, this parliamentary association identified itself with militant Nonconformity, organized labor, and a cheap daily press beyond Westminster. In December 1868 Gladstone formed a Liberal government endorsed by a majority of the electorate that included not only the middle classes but also those large sections of the respectable working class enfranchised by the 1867 Reform Act.

Gladstone's government immediately launched itself into an ambitious program of reform. In 1869 it disestablished the Church of Ireland, and the following year passed an Irish Land Act entitling tenants to compensation for improvements to land they rented. The Education Act of 1870, associated with Home Secretary W. E. Forster, the Ballot Act of 1872, the Judicature Act of 1873, the army reforms of Edward Cardwell, the abolition of religious tests for university entrance, the introduction of competitive exams for entry into the civil service, the reform of local government, and a Licensing Act regulating the public sale of alcohol (a concession to Nonconformism) filled out the legislative achievement of Gladstone's first ministry.

The issues of education and religion, as well as Gladstone's noninterventionist foreign policy, however, fragmented Liberal support. Moreover, extensive legislative reform began to raise the doctrinal problem of reconciling individualist and collectivist principles. Following defeat in a general election the Liberal government resigned in February 1874, and Gladstone resigned party leadership a year later, differing with many Liberals over the role of denominational religion in elementary schools and over Church of England **disestablishment**.

In 1876, however, Gladstone came out of political retirement to campaign over the Bulgarian atrocities and Disraeli's cynical dismissal of the Turkish massacre of Christian populations. This campaign exemplified Gladstone's style of leadership as he united Liberals behind a single issue imbued with burning moral significance. In the Midlothian campaign (1879–1880) Gladstone brought the politics of conscience to a new intensity in a series of speeches indicting the policies of the Conservative government since 1874.

Following a Liberal victory at the 1880 election Gladstone resumed the party leadership and formed his second ministry, which included Whigs such as Lord Granville (1815–1891) and Lord Hartington (1833–1908) as well as the radical leaders **Joseph Chamberlain** (first president of the National Liberal Federation founded in 1877) and Charles Dilke (1843–1911). A second Irish Land Act (1881) extended tenants' rights and a third Reform Act (1884) established virtual household suffrage in both county and borough constituencies. At the beginning of 1885, Chamberlain, with earlier experience of municipal activism, proposed an "Unauthorised Programme" of social legislation.

Following the general election of November 1885 the Irish Home Rule party of Charles Stewart Parnell held the balance of power in the Commons. In December 1885 the dramatic revelation of Gladstone's conversion to Home Rule for Ireland, the "Hawarden Kite," fixed this question as the dominating Liberal issue of conscience. After Gladstone formed his third ministry in February 1886 Lord Hartington and Joseph Chamberlain broke away to form a **Liberal Unionist** party. The defeat of Gladstone's Home Rule bill in June brought down the government.

Thereafter, with its electoral strongholds reduced to the Celtic fringes of Wales, Scotland, and Ireland, the Liberal party maintained Home Rule at the top of its political agenda, although the "Newcastle Programme" of 1891 did put together a package of other reforms. Additional pressure was put on the party by the emergence of class-oriented political attitudes, which were antagonistic to Gladstone's notion of single-issue crusades that would traverse class divisions. Gladstone formed his fourth Liberal government in 1892. A second Home Rule bill (1893) passed the Commons but was defeated in the Lords, and as a result Gladstone added reform of the House of Lords to Irish Home Rule as the crucial questions of the day.

Gladstone's retirement in March 1894 left the Liberal party confused and demoralized. Party leadership was taken up by the earl of **Rosebery** (1824–1929), William Harcourt (1827–1904), the earl of Kimberley (1826–1902) and finally, in 1899, Henry Campbell-Bannerman (1836–1908). The instability confirmed the difficulties of the post-Gladstonian Liberal party. Liberal imperialists—largely younger, Anglican or Wesleyan, upper middle-class Liberals such as H. H. Asquith (1852–1928), R. B. Haldane (1856–1928), and Edward Grey (1862–1933) moved toward collectivist social reforms combined with an imperialist foreign policy. Another response, labeled "New Liberalism," merged collectivist reforms and social analysis couched in organic metaphors, as elaborated in the writings of J. A. Hobson (1858–1940) and L. T. Hobhouse (1864–1929), with anti-imperialist policies abroad. This "New Liberalism" established connections with Fabian socialists, the new Independent Labour party, and the popular press, dominating the resilience of Liberal thought in adapting to class politics, and facilitating the resurgence of the Liberal party after 1905.

ANGUS HAWKINS

Bibliography

Bradley, Ian C. *The Optimists: Themes and Personalities in Victorian Liberalism.* 1980.

Clarke, Peter. *Liberals and Social Democrats.* 1978.

Collini, Stefan. *Liberalism and Sociology.* 1979.

Emy, H. V. *Liberals, Radicals and Social Politics, 1892–1914.* 1973.

Freeden, Michael. *The New Liberalism: An Ideology of Social Reform.* 1978.

Hamer, David Allan. *Liberal Politics in the Age of Gladstone and Rosebery.* 1972.

Matthew, Henry C. G. *The Liberal Imperialists.* 1973.

Parry, Jonathan Philip. *Democracy and Religion: Gladstone and the Liberal Party, 1867–1875.* 1986.

Stansky, Peter. *Ambitions and Strategy: The Struggle for the Leadership of the Liberal Party in the 1890s.* 1964.

Vincent, John. *Formation of the British Liberal Party, 1857–1868.* 2d ed., 1976.

· · · · ·

LIBERAL UNIONISTS

The Irish Home Rule crisis of 1886 split the **Liberal party** in two, with ninety-three Liberal M.P.'s voting against the Home Rule bill of their party leader W. E. Gladstone (1809–1898), and thereby committing themselves to preservation of the union between Ireland and Great Britain. This schism created a parliamentary group known as the Liberal Unionists. Of the Liberals who opposed Gladstone's bill, forty-six were followers of the radical, **Joseph Chamberlain** (1836–1914). The radical elder statesman **John Bright** (1811–1889) also opposed the bill. The other forty-seven moderate Liberals and Whigs who opposed Home Rule looked to the marquess of Hartington (1833–1908) for leadership.

Gladstone called an immediate election on the issue of Home Rule, and both groups of Liberal Unionists formed extraparliamentary organizations. Chamberlain founded the National Radical Union; Hartington created the Liberal Unionist Association. Aided by electoral pacts with the Conservative party, seventy-nine Liberal Unionists, most of them supporters of Hartington, were returned in the July 1886 election. The Conservative government of 1886 to 1892 relied on Liberal Unionist support for its survival. Indeed, in January 1887 the Liberal Unionist G. J. Goschen (1831–1907) became chancellor of the Exchequer in Salisbury's Conservative cabinet. In 1887, efforts by Chamberlain and G. O. Trevelyan (1832–1908) to reunite their Unionist supporters with the Gladstonian Liberal party through a series of "round table" meetings failed.

In 1889 Chamberlain facilitated the merger of his supporters with Hartington's by renaming his organization the National Liberal Union. After Hartington succeeded to his title as eighth duke of Devonshire in 1891 and took his seat in the House of Lords, Chamberlain became Liberal Unionist leader in the Commons. In the 1892 election, forty-seven Liberal Unionist M.P.'s were returned. After 1893 and the failure of Gladstone's second Home Rule bill they moved toward closer collaboration with the Conservative party. In 1895, seventy Liberal Unionists were elected. Both Chamberlain and the duke of Devonshire joined Salisbury's Conservative cabinet in 1895. Thereafter, for most practical purposes, Liberal Unionists became absorbed into the Conservative party, although a distinct organization and political fund were maintained until 1912.

ANGUS HAWKINS

Bibliography

Fair, John D. "From Liberal to Conservative: The Flight of the Liberal Unionists After 1886." *Victorian Studies*, vol. 29, pp. 161–180.

Fraser, Peter. *Joseph Chamberlain: Radicalism and Empire, 1868–1914.* 1966.

———. "The Liberal Unionist Alliance: Chamberlain, Hartington and the Conservatives, 1886–1904." *English Historical Review*, vol. 77, pp. 53–78.

Jay, Richard. *Joseph Chamberlain, A Political Study.* 1981.

. . . . .

LIBRARIES AND LIBRARIANSHIP

During the first half of the nineteenth century, no publicly supported, national library system existed in England. Readers from the upper and middle classes and a few from the lower classes did have access to reading materials in libraries supported by religious and social organizations, in a few quasi-municipal libraries, and in subscription and circulating libraries whose membership was restricted to users able to pay fees.

Endowed libraries, cathedral and local parish libraries, and community and voluntary school libraries were supported by religious societies (representing both the Church of England and various dissenting sects) and by such groups as the Society for the Diffusion of Useful Knowledge. A few quasi-municipal libraries, such as the Chetham Library in Manchester, were open to the public without charge. Primarily because of irregular funding, however, services were usually inadequate; the collections were often sparse, and access was restricted.

Two types of fee-based libraries flourished. Subscription or proprietary libraries were owned by shareholders who paid entrance and annual subscription fees. The shareholders, often professionals with a common interest in science, social reform, or politics, selected books for the collections, which were usually restricted to works considered to have some permanent value. The London Library, founded in 1841 by Thomas Carlyle (1803–1855) and other prominent literary and political figures, was and still is one of the most successful proprietary libraries. A less formal variety of subscription library was the book club, patronized mainly by middle-class readers. Members paid entrance and subscription fees, but nonpermanent book collections were sold periodically to raise funds for new acquisitions.

The second type of fee-based library was the commercial circulating library such as Lane's Minerva Library, Booth's, and Mudie's. After paying an initial entrance fee, members were charged for each book borrowed. While circulating libraries offered some serious fiction and nonfiction, their huge success throughout much of the century was due to their sizable collections of current popular fiction, an emphasis that prompted their critics to attack them as "an evergreen tree of diabolical knowledge."

Research libraries were affiliated with learned societies such as the Royal Society of London or with universities and their colleges. Access was usually limited to members of the learned institution. The library housed within the British Museum was transformed during the nineteenth century from an underutilized, miscellaneous collection of rare curios to a research institution of international fame. The transformation was accomplished primarily through the vision and leadership of Anthony Panizzi (1797–1879), an Italian political exile, who started his career in the museum in 1831 as an assistant in the Department of Printed Books. In 1837 he was appointed keeper of the department and then in 1856 principal librarian, a position he held until his retirement in 1866.

Parliamentary investigations during the 1830s and 1840s concluded that the British Museum's Department of Printed Books and its reading room were inadequately funded; the investigations also called attention to overcrowding, inadequate staffing, and inefficient service. The collection, consisting largely of donated material from wealthy private libraries, was valuable but unbalanced. Panizzi redefined the library's mission and sought regular government funding. He wanted the library to become a world-renowned, national educational and research institution, open to scholars of all classes. Panizzi and his staff developed a collection policy that produced one of the largest and most representative research collections in the world. The collection was further augmented after 1850, when Panizzi received permission from Parliament to enforce the library's right of copyright, which it had held since 1757 but had never actively pursued. Panizzi improved access to the collection by developing a manuscript, alphabetical catalogue produced in accordance with a systematic cataloguing scheme based on the "Ninety-One Rules" formulated by Panizzi and four of his colleagues, John Winter Jones (1805–1881), Thomas Watts (1811–1869), Edward Edwards (1812–1886), and John Parry (1816–1880). In 1852, Panizzi drew up plans for the present-day reading room and its adjacent storage facilities, which opened in 1857.

Two types of nineteenth-century library tried to cater to working-class needs and interests: mechanics' institutes libraries, created principally during the first half of the century, and public libraries, created by the Public Library Act of 1850. For the most part, mechanics' institutes did not succeed in establishing operative working-class libraries. Depending heavily on middle-class donations, the book collections tended to be unbalanced, dull, and dated. Notably absent were politically or religiously controversial works, as well as newspapers and fiction—all were considered unsuitable for working-class readers.

The public library movement emerged in the 1830s and 1840s. A parliamentary committee was directed in 1849 to look into "the best means of extending the establishment of libraries freely open to the public, especially in large towns." After hearing testimony from British, European, and American libraries, the committee, whose members included William Ewart (1798–1869), Joseph Brotherton (1783–1857), Richard Monckton Milnes (1809–1885), and Benjamin Disraeli (1804–1881), concluded that library services throughout the United Kingdom were greatly inferior to those in other countries and should be improved and expanded.

In 1850, after heavy opposition in the House of Commons, a watered-down Public Libraries Act empowered municipal councils in towns with a population of more than 10,000 to levy a halfpenny tax in order to establish and maintain a museum and/or a library. The act also specified that books and museum pieces were to be obtained from donors, not through revenues. The Library Act of 1855 eliminated that restriction, allowing library funds to be used to buy books, and raised the maximum tax rate to one penny, an amount still grossly inadequate.

After an initial spurt of enthusiasm, during which large towns such as Norwich (1850), Winchester (1851), and Manchester (1852) adopted the act, progress slowed. By 1859, only eighteen towns had opened public libraries; in the next decade twelve were started; forty-eight more appeared in the 1870s.

Crippled by insufficient funds, the newly established public libraries were plagued by inadequate facilities, services, and staff. Patrons were drawn primarily from the lower middle class and upper working class. An unfortunate association with other charitable organizations such as soup kitchens made public or "free" libraries, as they were sometimes called, appear unsavory. Members of the lower working classes, particularly unskilled laborers, also made little use of free libraries, preferring to spend their limited leisure time in less educational pursuits.

Eventually, however, free libraries gained popularity. A number of factors such as the Education Act of 1870 and the Local Government Act of 1888 paved the way for a change in attitude that resulted in an accelerated growth during the century's last two decades. The greatest single impetus came from grants to public libraries from private benefactors such as John Passmore Edwards (1823–1911), Henry Tate (1819–1899) and, most notably, Andrew Carnegie (1835–1919). Generally, these grants freed libraries from the paralyzing constraints of the penny tax limitation by providing building funds.

During most of the nineteenth century, the concept of librarianship as a profession barely existed. Librarians were mainly underpaid custodians with little or no authority. In university libraries and the British Museum, many librarians were scholars in the teaching disciplines, whose understanding of the principles of librarianship developed only through their actual work in the library. The first generation of public librarians came from a variety of occupations; most had received only a rudimentary education and learned their skills on the job. Few university graduates were interested in public library positions since the salaries were meager, the hours long, and the working conditions often unhealthy. By the last quarter of the century, however, a sense of professionalism began to emerge among British librarians. The Library Association, founded in 1877, provided a forum for discussion through conferences and professional publications. The association also advocated specialized training in library science. During the 1880s it established a certification procedure based on a series of examinations, and in the 1890s it instituted specialized classes in library management.

ABIGAIL A. LOOMIS

Bibliography

Altick, Richard D. *The English Common Reader: A Social History of the Mass Reading Public, 1800–1890.* 1957.

Kaufman, Paul. *The Community Library: A Chapter in English Social History.* 1967.

Keeling, Dennis F., ed. *British Library History: Bibliography 1962–1968; 1969–1972; 1973–1976; 1977–1980.* 1972, 1975, 1978, 1983.

Kelly, Thomas. *A History of Public Libraries in Great Britain, 1845–1975.* Rev. ed., 1977.

Miller, Edward. *That Noble Cabinet: A History of the British Museum.* 1974.

Minto, John. *A History of the Public Library Movement in Great Britain and Ireland.* 1932.

Munford, W. A. *Penny Rate: Aspects of British Public Library History, 1850–1950.* 1951.

See also MUDIE, CHARLES EDWARD

· · · · ·

LIGHTING

New technology for illuminating streets and interiors brought enormous changes in the safety and comfort of life during the nineteenth century. At the beginning of Victoria's reign gas was as yet little used and electricity only a subject of curious experiments. By the end of the century municipal gasworks supplied the lighting for thousands of streets and houses, and electric lights were beginning to appear in wealthy homes.

The sources of lighting before the nineteenth century were inadequate and dangerous; they required constant tending and frequently led to fires. Massed candles and reflecting surfaces could brighten luxurious homes, but the poor depended on a single candle or used rushlights made by soaking rushes in household grease. In the 1840s the process of distilling kerosene or paraffin brought oil lamps within reach. Although they required cleaning, filling, and trimming, oil lamps were both safer and brighter than candles. After North American petroleum fields were tapped in the early 1860s, inexpensive oil lamps became the most common form of domestic light.

Westminster Bridge in London was lit by gas in 1813. The gas was produced by burning coal. Municipally owned gas works were established in Bristol (1816), Manchester (1817), Birmingham (1819), and other cities; and by midcentury hundreds of private suppliers also manufactured gas. During the 1840s gas lighting was installed in Buckingham Palace and the new Houses of Parliament. Gas illuminated most major thoroughfares; many people thought it was responsible for a reduction in crime. At least 380 lamplighters were employed in London in 1842.

Gas was chiefly used for public buildings, factories, shops, and streets. Early gaslights had a strong odor and consumed a great deal of oxygen, and were thus poorly suited to homes. The Welsbach incandescent mantle, which went on sale in 1887, improved combustion, used far less gas, and increased illumination; a single Welsbach mantle emitted up to 35 candlepower of light. Gas lighting became widespread in poorer and middle-class homes after the 1890s, and as late as 1937 as many as 40 percent of working-class homes in London were lit by gas.

Although experimental electric lights were exhibited at the Crystal Palace in 1851, the technology for generating and using **electricity** was not fully developed until late in the century. Early installations of electric lighting were in the machine rooms of the London *Times* (1878), the interior of the Royal Albert Hall (1879), and Victoria Station (1880). R. E. B. Crompton (1845–1940) began building small generators in the 1870s. Two of his carbon arc lamps replaced 180 gas jets at the General Post Office in Glasgow prior to 1882, when he made similar installations at the Mansion House in London. In the previous year, the town of Godalming (34 miles southwest of London) began to use electricity for public lighting.

Incandescent filament lamps were invented simultaneously by Thomas Alva Edison and Joseph Wilson Swan. An amalgamation of the two companies under the name of Ediswan opened the Holburn Viaduct generating station in 1882, and in 1884 Charles Parsons (1854–1931) invented the steam turbine, still generally used to generate Britain's electric power. Bristol was the first municipal authority to operate an electric power station of any size; the installation at St. Philips Bridge supplied electricity for offices, street lighting, the tramway system, and private homes. Electricity, however, remained more expensive than gas. At the end of Victoria's reign electric lights in houses were primarily a toy of the very rich, and the number of homes lit by electricity surpassed those lit by gas only in the late 1920s and early 1930s.

JOHN REYNOLDS

Bibliography

Rolt, L. T. C. *Victorian Engineering.* 1974.

Davidson, Caroline. *A Woman's Work Is Never Done: A History of Housework in the British Isles, 1650–1950.* 1982.

· · · · ·

LIND, JENNY
(1820–1887)

Noted for her rich coloratura voice, her vocal technique, and her emotive power, Jenny Lind, "the Swedish Nightingale," was the female singing sensation of the nineteenth century. Born out of wedlock, she was christened Johanna Marie and at the age of nine was enrolled in the Royal Opera School in Stockholm. At seventeen she starred in *Der Freischütz.* In 1852, on her American tour, she was married to the pianist and conductor Otto Goldschmidt (1829–1907) and became Jenny Lind-Goldschmidt.

From 1838 to 1849 Lind was primarily an opera star, first in Sweden, then in Germany and Austria, and finally in England. Among the operas that made her famous are *Norma, La Sonnambula, Robert de Normandie, La Figlia del Reggimento, Lucia di Lammermoor,* and *I Puritani.* After 1849 she was a concert singer, appearing in oratorios and recitals in England, Europe, and the United States. It is as a singer of oratorios that she is best remembered in England, where she first appeared at Her Majesty's Theatre in 1847 and where she settled in 1858. Felix Mendelssohn, a friend of Lind's, composed the soprano part in his oratorio *Elijah* for her.

In 1850 Phineas T. Barnum (1810–1891) brought Lind to the United States. The first world-class singer to appear there, she attracted crowds in the thousands. Generous with her money and time, Lind gave away substantial sums to charity and performed many benefit concerts. Her last public appearance was in 1883 at a recital on behalf of the Railway Servants' Benevolent Fund.

A court favorite in England, Germany, Sweden and Austria; a musical star with extraordinary mass appeal; and a singer whose artistry and dramatic intensity regularly moved her audiences to tears, Jenny Lind became a legend. In 1894 a plaque in her memory was unveiled just under the statue to Handel in the Poets' Corner in Westminster Abbey. She was the first woman so honored.

LARRY K. UFFELMAN

Bibliography

Bulman, Joan. *Jenny Lind: A Biography*. 1956.

Holland, Henry Scott and W. S. Rockstro. *Memoir of Madame Jenny Lind-Goldschmidt: Her Early Art-Life and Dramatic Career*. 1891. 2 vols.

Schultz, Gladys Denny. *Jenny Lind: The Swedish Nightingale*. 1962.

. . . . .

LINTON, ELIZA LYNN
(1822–1898)

Eliza Lynn Linton was a novelist and journalist best known for her virulent opposition to women's rights. Publishing under the name Eliza Lynn until her marriage to the Chartist engraver **William James Linton** (1812–1897) in 1858, when she styled herself E. Lynn Linton, she wrote twenty-two novels and contributed regularly to the major periodicals.

Linton, a dedicated opponent to women's emancipation, was herself an emancipated woman. The daughter of an Anglican clergyman, she left her family home in Keswick at age twenty-three to earn her living in London as a writer. She was the first Englishwoman to receive a regular salary as a journalist. An agnostic and in her youth a political radical, she earned notoriety for her iconoclastic attacks on Victorian respectability. *The True History of Joshua Davidson* (1872), a condemnation of modern Christianity, was her greatest literary success. Her brief marriage ended in separation, and she lived the rest of her life as an independent woman.

Linton made her reputation as a critic of women in a series of *Saturday Review* essays in the late 1860s and 1870s, most notably the sensational "The Girl of the Period" (1868). For the next thirty years she voiced her antifeminist views in periodicals and in such novels as *The Rebel of the Family* (1880) and *The One Too Many* (1894). Her thinly disguised fictional autobiography, *The Autobiography of Christopher Kirkland* (1885), in which she assumed the persona of a man, reveals the (unconscious) male identification that allowed her to deny to other women the freedom she claimed for herself.

Linton was an influential writer because she skillfully articulated the fears of social change shared by many of her contemporaries. By the 1890s, however, she had become so extreme that she was often satirized, and her last novels did not achieve the popularity of those of her middle years.

NANCY FIX ANDERSON

Bibliography

Anderson, Nancy Fix. *Woman against Women in Victorian England: A Life of Eliza Lynn Linton*. 1987.

Layard, George Somes. *Mrs. Lynn Linton: Her Life, Letters and Opinions*. 1901.

Van Thal, Herbert. *Eliza Lynn Linton: The Girl of the Period*. 1979.

. . . . .

LINTON, WILLIAM JAMES
(1812–1897)

Born in London in 1812, William James Linton was trained as a wood engraver, but became well known in several other fields, most notably as a journalist, translator, poet, anthologist, and Chartist. In 1866, he emigrated to the United States, where he achieved some financial success as an engraver and made the acquaintance of such eminences as William Page, Walt Whitman, and William Cullen Bryant.

Linton was apprenticed in 1828 to the wood engraver George Wilmot Bonner, in whose workshop he received a thorough training in the craft as well as exposure to the craftsmens' radical politics. He was employed by two other successful engravers: William Powis, from 1834 to 1836, and John Thompson, from 1836 to 1838. Linton soon developed his own radical ideas about wood engraving, proposing that the engraver should be seen as something more than a mechanical subordinate to the artist. To this end, he sought to develop his skill at white line engraving, in which the lines, rather than the spaces, are carved, thus, coming closer to the artist's original intent. Among Linton's outstanding engravings were those for *Thirty Pictures by Deceased British Artists* (1860); *Aldine*, an

American art magazine (1872); Bryant's *The Flood of Years* (1878) and *Thanatopsis* (1879); and his own *The Masters of Wood-Engraving* (1889), which Linton printed at his Appledore Press in Connecticut.

Linton combined craftsmanship with an active radical politics. In England he had been a Chartist and an associate of Mazzini and other European emigrés, and had written for several journals, including the *Red Republican* and the *English Republic*. He thereby became an influential example for a number of distinguished radical craftsmen of the later nineteenth century.

LARRY D. LUTCHMANSINGH

Bibliography

Gleckner, Robert F. "W. J. Linton, a Latter-Day Blake." *Bulletin of Research in the Humanities*, vol. 85, pp. 208-227.

Hanrick, Burton J. "William James Linton." *New England Magazine*, vol. 18 (n.s.), pp. 139-157.

Smith, Francis B. *Radical Artisan: William James Linton*. 1973.

See also LINTON, ELIZA LYNN; WOOD ENGRAVING

• • • • •

LISTER, JOSEPH
(1827-1912)

Founder of the antiseptic method, Joseph Lister was both a careful experimental scientist and a highly skilled surgeon. His work, together with the discovery of anesthesia, transformed the practice of surgery during the nineteenth century. He was elevated to the peerage as Baron Lister in 1897, the first medical man to be so honored.

Lister was born to a Yorkshire Quaker family and received his medical education at University College, London. As a student he witnessed the first surgical operation carried out on an anesthetized subject in Great Britain. After earning a medical degree in 1852 and qualifying as a fellow of the Royal College of Surgeons, he became assistant to James Syme, the eminent professor of surgery at Edinburgh. In 1856 Lister was married to the daughter of his mentor, Agnes Syme, who assisted in much of his work and kept the notebooks of his laboratory experiments.

Lister's early researches involved microscopic examination of muscular fibers. In 1860 he became professor of surgery at Glasgow, where his attention was occupied by the treatment of wounds and the repeated epidemics of hospital gangrene that swept Glasgow Infirmary. After reading Louis Pasteur's work, Lister carefully replicated his experiments and became convinced that putrefaction, like fermentation, was caused by the presence in the air of living organisms. He therefore theorized that infections could be prevented if germs already in a wound were destroyed by antiseptic agents, if all instruments and dressings were scrupulously clean, and if a method could be found to kill germs in the air. For the latter purpose he devised an apparatus that misted the operating field with a continuous spray of carbolic acid.

Lister's publications and presentations to the British Medical Association aroused great controversy. London surgeons were reluctant to accept innovations initiated elsewhere, and many resisted the germ theory. As Lister's dramatically lessened rates of infection became evident, however, the central features of his method were increasingly adopted. By 1887 Lister himself had abandoned the continuous carbolic spray and placed greater emphasis on additional aseptic techniques to maintain a sterile operating field.

In addition to his major work, Lister was responsible for other improvements in surgical treatment: he devised absorbable ligatures and drainage tubes, introduced the technique of elevating a limb to render it bloodless before applying a tourniquet, invented new instruments, and performed innovative operations. Most importantly, Lister's introduction of antiseptic techniques dramatically altered the risk of surgery and made possible its modern development.

SALLY MITCHELL

Bibliography

Fisher, Richard B. *Joseph Lister, 1827-1912*. 1977.

Godlee, Rickman John. *Lord Lister*. 1917.

Le Fanu, William R. *A List of the Original Writings of Joseph Lord Lister.* 1965.

Lister, Joseph. *The Collected Papers.* 1909. 2 vols.

Walker, Kenneth Macfarlane. *Joseph Lister.* 1956.

See also BACTERIOLOGY;
MEDICAL SCIENCE; SURGERY
AND SURGEONS

· · · · ·

LITERACY AND THE READING PUBLIC

Literacy and reading among the Victorians have been analyzed by contemporaries such as publisher Charles Knight and by modern literary and social historians, especially Richard D. Altick and Robert K. Webb. Several trends are well documented: increases in the number of people who could, at minimal levels, read and write; social and economic factors that promoted literacy and reading; diversity in reading habits of various groups; and the influence of readers and publishing on the writing of literature.

Literacy figures for Victorian Britain are less than reliable. Defining as "literate" people who can read a little or sign their names, historians have examined signatures on parish records, school attendance figures, school inspectors' reports, and navy recruitment lists. Findings suggest that in the Victorian age, building on improvements of the preceding half-century, minimal literacy steadily increased, with some regional variations. In 1837 a majority could read at least a little and half of adult males could minimally read and write. By the end of the century minimal literacy was almost universal.

Social and technological improvements, as well as expanded educational opportunities, furthered literacy and reading. Though interior lighting was poor, and crowded homes and long working hours burdened laborers, leisure time and exposure to print increased among two expanding groups: the professional and white-collar middle classes, and the new lower middle class of clerical, technical, and supervisory workers. Religious and utilitarian organizations, skeptical about light

reading, nevertheless supported libraries and reading for self-improvement and as harmless entertainment.

Though publishing data only suggests what people actually read, Victorian readers may probably be divided into two groups: "respectable" readers, ranging from the well-educated elite to ambitious working people, and the "mass" public. Moreover, the pattern of reading up to the mid-1870s differs from that of the last quarter of the century.

"Respectable" readers before the mid-1870s enjoyed both serious and light reading. They purchased religious pamphlets; the London *Times*; provincial newspapers; and many periodicals, from the small-circulation quarterly reviews to the monthly and weekly magazines such as Dickens's *Household Words*. Books were expensive, so subscription **libraries** flourished. Because they bought a large share of new books and quarterly reviews, the libraries influenced reading even after the late 1840s, when monthly serials and less expensive one-volume reprints from Bentley's and the Parlour Library appeared. Of 45,000 books published in Britain from 1816 to 1851, Knight identified 10,000 as religious and 4,900 as history and geography, compared with 3,500 works of fiction. Though the proportion of novels rose after 1850, Macaulay's *History of England* outsold any British book of fiction. A substantial intellectual elite, often self-educated, read widely in serious literature: the classics from Shakespeare to Scott, some foreign writing, and the better novels, poems, and nonfiction of the day.

The "mass" readership of this period—tradespeople, lower servants, and some factory, mine, and farm workers and their families—had a literature of its own. From street vendors they bought **broadsides** about current events and royal gossip, true crime stories, and chapbooks on history, humor, heroism, and crime. Newspapers, while highly taxed, circulated in public houses or sprang up as illegal publications. Cheap periodicals aimed at an aspiring working class were often conservative and serious. Inexpensive general magazines like *Chambers' Miscellany* sold up to 200,000 copies in the 1840s but declined as lower costs permitted specialty magazines for women's interests, sports, self-improvement, religion, sensational fiction, and entertainment. Neither one-volume novels nor

Dickens serials reached this market, which favored tales by writers like **Pierce Egan** and **G. W. M. Reynolds** which appeared in penny weekly parts or as serials in penny magazines.

In early and mid-Victorian Britain, the lower class of readers had little to do with the works traditionally defined as "literature." But the broad respectable reading public, together with publishing practices, had an unprecedented impact. The voices adopted by Victorian novelists and critics arose from their sense of a community of readers. General-interest periodicals started Carlyle in his critical career and sustained Arnold and Pater in theirs. Three-volume publication created novels of a distinctive length and texture, while serialization demanded a specialized kind of plotting and pacing, and also provided writers with feedback from the public while they were still in the process of composing subsequent installments.

The last quarter-century of Victoria's reign brought changes in the reading public and in literature. Among the respectable, there was a shift from general to specialized publications. Cheaper books made circulating libraries less influential. Increased leisure and spending money encouraged alternative entertainments such as travel, the theater, sports, and musical groups, which actually reduced reading. But the demise of a broad readership also freed authors to write more ambitious works for themselves and for a select audience. Meanwhile the mass reading public expanded to modern levels. By the late 1890s, *Pearson's Magazine* had a circulation of over a million. The large market attracted publishers and helped create a mass culture which blurred regional and class divisions. By 1901, British writers no longer found, even among the educated classes, a unified reading public.

MONIKA BROWN

Bibliography

Altick, Richard D. *The English Common Reader: A Social History of the Mass Reading Public.* 1957.

Cruse, Amy. *The Victorians and Their Reading.* 1935.

Knight, Charles. *The Old Printer and the Modern Press.* 1854.

Leavis, Queenie D. *Fiction and the Reading Public.* 1932.

Neuburg, Victor E. *Popular Literature: A History and Guide, from the Beginning of Printing to the Year 1897.* 1977.

Shattuck, Joanne and Michael Wolff, eds. *The Victorian Periodical Press: Samplings and Soundings.* 1982.

Webb, Robert K. *The British Working-Class Reader, 1790–1848: Literacy and Social Tension.* 1955.

———. "The Victorian Reading Public." In Boris Ford, ed., *The Pelican Guide to English Literature*, vol. 6. 1958.

West, E. G. "Literacy and the Industrial Revolution." *Economic History Review*, vol. 31 (second series), pp. 369–383.

See also NOVEL; PERIODICALS; PRESS; SERIAL LITERATURE; WORKING-CLASS LITERATURE
· · · · ·

LITERARY CRITICISM

Bridging romanticism and modernism, the Victorian period is notable less for critical works of original genius than for a large body of thoughtful literary criticism contributed by many of the best minds of the age. Victorian criticism, as practiced by such writers as **Thomas Carlyle**, **John Ruskin**, **Matthew Arnold**, and **Walter Pater**, both reflected and influenced the culture of its time. While examining new works and reevaluating classics, Victorian critics sought to define, for an increasingly scientific, materialistic, democratic, and literate age, suitable purposes and standards for art and literature. Ambitious, emotionally charged, and often eloquent, much Victorian criticism remains of value for its literary merit.

"Literature," though sometimes seen by Victorians as one of the arts, was more commonly treated as an equivalent to "humanities," incorporating history and philosophy as well as imaginative writing. As improved literacy, education, and library service combined with lowered publishing costs to promote the publication of much new and classic literature, readers turned to reviews and criticism for guidance. Besides books and the major quarterly reviews, critical forums included—in ever-increasing numbers—daily and weekly newspapers, weekly and monthly magazines, publications by scholarly societies, lecture halls at universities and in municipal buildings, and even poems and novels. Though attracting creative writers, university professors, politicans, preachers, and hack reviewers, the discipline of criticism was dominated by men and women of letters: journalists who wrote voluminously and intelligently on literature and other subjects. Until almost the end of Victoria's reign neither particular journals nor individual critics devoted themselves exclusively to literary topics.

Integrated within Victorian culture, literary criticism developed principles, standards, controversial issues, and analytic practices that survived for much of the century before gradually giving way to more modern approaches. The main concerns and practices were adapted in the 1820s and 1830s from an Enlightenment psychology of moral sympathy and from British and German romantic ideas of poetic inspiration and truth to nature. Victorian critics before the mid-1860s tended to agree neither with **Thomas Babington Macaulay**, whose "Milton" (1825) found the "magic lantern" of poetry to be fading, nor with **John Henry Newman**, who in "Poetry" (1829) favored a pure poetry of subjectivity and beauty, but with the Carlyle of *On Heroes and Hero Worship* (1840), for whom great literature not only expresses and sustains humanity's emotional, spiritual, and moral sides but also unifies a culture.

This view of literature suggested one primary standard of excellence, regardless of genre—broad appeal to readers' emotions, moral sympathy, and identification with other people and views—and several secondary ones, summarized by **George Henry Lewes** in "The Principles of Success in Literature" (1865-1866): effectively dramatized insight into life (its surface and its underlying truth); "sincerity," or freedom from distortions for effect; and a clear and moving style, unburdened by obscurity and eccentric imagery.

Agreeing on these standards and on the list of great writers—Dante, Shakespeare, Milton, Goethe, and Wordsworth—early Victorian crit-

ics debated a few specific issues. In identifying subjects that appealed to readers, classicists like **Coventry Patmore** and Archibald Alison (1792-1867) favored timeless, idealized emotions in poetry and historical topics in fiction. "Realists" like **Arthur Hugh Clough** and **William Makepeace Thackeray** argued for subjects from ordinary contemporary life. For poetry, subjectivity was another concern: should the best poetry express its author's own deepest feelings, as **John Stuart Mill** asserted, or should it strive for impersonality, as **John Keble** suggested? Ruskin, in the third volume of *Modern Painters* (1856) tried to resolve these issues, suggesting that "realism" and "idealism," the observation of nature and inner spiritual vision, are complementary in all great art.

Though by the 1860s England had produced a "scientific" theory of criticism in the *Poetics* of Eneas Sweetland Dallas (1828-1879) and some important literary biography and history, early Victorian criticism was dominated by review articles and essays. A typical article, anonymous and sermonlike in tone, would state principles, take positions on issues, pass judgments, make comparisons, and quote liberally. The interpretation and analysis of literary texts often focused on such extraliterary qualities as moral insight into life.

During the mid-1860s, which brought subject specialization, the early Victorian consensus divided. The dominant trend found its epitome and inspiration in Arnold. Like Carlyle, Arnold declared that literature can morally elevate readers, but his *Essays in Criticism* (1865, 1888) sometimes presented literature more as an escape than a guide and offered a new view of the critic's role: abandoning the general public of "Philistines," Arnold addressed a narrow audience, avoided reviewing inferior works, and proposed that criticism promote a new culture based on "the best that has been thought and known." Other promoters of cultural values were Richard Holt Hutton (1826-1897), **Leslie Stephen** and **John Morley**. Among Arnold's followers, anonymous judgments gradually gave way to acknowledged appreciation, and scholarly study expanded.

A second group of critics, inspired by Arnold's principles and by French literature and criticism, promoted literary beauty, reader pleasure, and the separation of art from life. Pater, the most prominent of the group, sympathized with aestheticism in his *Renaissance* (1873), although many of his critical writings support "noble" living, elevated subject matter, and permanent standards of artistic genius as embodied in Dante and Milton. Other syntheses of aesthetic and traditional values are found in **Algernon Swinburne's** commitment to both sensual beauty and serious classical themes, in **George Meredith's** notion of a detached **comedy** that reforms society, and in **William Morris's** optimism about transforming the working classes through new folk art.

Aestheticism, in separating literature as art from history and philosophy, helped shape the narrower role that writers and critics of literature would play in modern times. After the early 1880s, though literature's moral influence would concern the general public and writer-critics **George Bernard Shaw** and **Margaret Oliphant**, most critics shifted their attention from the reader to the writer and the text. Literary scholars narrowed their focus: Edmund Gosse (1849–1928) cultivated snobbery; literary historian George Saintsbury (1845–1933) valued fiction for its subjects and poetry for formal qualities; and specialists like **John Addington Symonds**, Austin Dobson (1840–1921), and Edward Dowden (1843–1913) paved the way for their modern discipline. Among the harbingers of literary modernism were critics who engaged in a lively debate about the novel as an art that balances plot and character, reality and artistic design. Engaging the critical talents of **Robert Louis Stevenson, Andrew Lang**, and **Vernon Lee**, this controversy about romance, realism, and naturalism inspired "The Art of Fiction" (1884) by Henry James (1843–1916) and **Joseph Conrad's** preface to *The Nigger of the Narcissus* (1897).

Even more important for modernism was a new aestheticism no longer encumbered by moral concerns. Although critical support for "decadence" did not long survive the fall of its best-known representative, **Oscar Wilde**, the movement's devotion to symbolism left its mark on critics of the next generation. As early as 1895, **William Butler Yeats** embraced a position prepared by late Victorian critics— that for the modern age, poetry would be not a "criticism of life" but "a revelation of a hidden life."

MONIKA BROWN

Bibliography

Armstrong, Isobel. *Victorian Scrutinies: Reviews of Poetry, 1830–1870.* 1972.

Buckley, Jerome H. *The Victorian Temper: A Study in Literary Culture.* 1951.

Graham, Kenneth. *English Criticism of the Novel. 1865–1900.* 1965.

Gross, John. *The Rise and Fall of the Man of Letters: Aspects of English Literary Life Since 1800.* 1969.

Olmstead, John Charles, ed. *A Victorian Art of Fiction: Essays on the Novel in British Periodicals.* 1979. 3 vols.

Orel, Harold. *Victorian Literary Critics.* 1984.

Parrinder, Patrick. *Authors and Authority: A Study of English Literary Criticism and Its Relation to Culture.* 1977

Stang, Richard. *The Theory of the Novel in England, 1850–1870.* 1959.

Tillotson, Geoffrey. *Criticism and the Nineteenth Century.* 1951.

Warren, Alba. *English Poetic Theory, 1825–1865.* 1950.

Wellek, René. *A History of Modern Criticism, 1750–1950,* vols. 3, 4. 1965.

Woolford, John. "Periodicals and the Practice of Literary Criticism, 1855–64." In Joanne Shattuck and Michael Woolf, eds., *The Victorian Periodical Press: Samplings and Soundings.* 1982.

See also AESTHETIC MOVEMENT; PERIODICALS

. . . . .

LITERARY PRIZES AND HONORS

Few national literary prizes existed until the end of Victoria's reign. School and university prizes indicated early promise; civil list pensions and state appointments recognized literary achievement.

Many eminent Victorians were distinguished prizewinners at the public schools (like Matthew Arnold at Rugby, 1840) and at

Oxford and Cambridge. Oxford's Newdigate Prize went to Arthur Stanley (1837), John Ruskin (1839), Matthew Arnold (1843), John Addington Symonds (1860), Oscar Wilde (1878), Laurence Binyon (1890), and John Buchan (1898). At Cambridge, the Chancellor's Gold Medal for English Poetry was won by Thomas Babington Macaulay (1819, 1821), Edward Bulwer-Lytton (1825), Alfred Tennyson (1829), F. W. Farrar (1852), and Lytton Strachey (1902). Cambridge's Seatonian Prize, offered from 1750 for an English poem on a sacred subject, was won three times by the Victorian hymn writer J. M. Neale (1842–1849).

A poet or critic (including John Keble, Matthew Arnold, and Francis Palgrave) could be elected to Oxford's professorship of poetry (established 1708). The universities also conferred honorary degrees on famous writers. Robert Browning was awarded an Oxford M.A. by diploma, the first since Dr. Johnson. Tennyson refused Cambridge honorary degrees four times. Universities also honored writers by election as rector (J. S. Mill at St. Andrews; Carlyle at Edinburgh).

Civil list pensions, established during Victoria's reign, honored "useful discoveries in science and attainments in literature and the arts." Tennyson received a civil list pension in 1845; others included George MacDonald, Matthew Arnold, and the surviving relatives of Charles Dickens, T. H. Huxley, Walter Pater, and Anthony Trollope.

The Victorian poets laureate were Southey, Wordsworth, Tennyson, and the forgotten Alfred Austin. Tennyson was also granted a peerage (1884). After death the nation conferred honor by burial in the Poet's Corner of Westminster Abbey, where Browning, Tennyson, Dickens, and Thomas Hardy lie.

WILLIAM WHITLA

Bibliography

Francis, John Collins. "Civil List Pensions." *Notes and Queries*, vol. 8 (9th series), pp. 1–10, 29–38, 57–60.

See also POET LAUREATE

· · · · ·

LIVINGSTONE, DAVID (1813–1873)

No other missionary or explorer captured the Victorian imagination like David Livingstone. He became a legend in his own lifetime, noted in three important respects: as a Christian missionary; as an antislavery crusader; and as a tenacious explorer who stirred interest in "discovering" the interior of Africa.

Livingstone was born in humble circumstances in a Scottish textile town. At age ten he worked long hours as a cotton piecer and taught himself Latin. Between 1833 and 1837 he studied medicine at Anderson's College and Greek at Glasgow University. After ordination by the London Missionary Society, Dr. Livingstone set out for southern Africa as a medical missionary in 1840.

Livingstone was unsuccessful as a missionary, but made several pioneering journeys into the African interior. In 1849 he discovered Lake Ngami and two years later the Zambesi River. He made a vast trek across Africa from the east to the west coasts, "discovering" and naming the Victoria Falls. After returning to England in 1856 he published a best seller entitled *Missionary Researches and Travels in South Africa* (1857).

In 1858 the British government appointed Livingstone as a consul for the east coast of Africa and leader of an expedition. In addition to exploration, the mission was to collect information about the **slave trade**, publicize its evils, and try to promote legitimate commerce. Exploration was difficult, partly because of the many rapids on the Zambesi river system, but several important discoveries were made, including Lake Nyasa. Livingstone returned to England in 1864 and was received as a celebrity.

He traveled again to Africa in 1865. This time the exploration project was partly funded by the Royal Geographical Society. The primary goal was to discover the sources of the Zambesi, Congo and, especially, Nile river systems. Livingstone journeyed long distances in central Africa and suffered from disease and food shortages. Several reports of his death led the owner of the *New York Herald* to send **Henry Morton Stanley** to search for Livingstone. The two men met in 1871, Stanley supposedly greeting Livingstone with the words "Dr. Livingstone, I presume." Livingstone could not be persuaded to return to England, and his health deteriorated. Having failed to locate the source of the Nile, he died in 1873. His body was painstakingly returned to England and buried in Westminster Abbey.

Livingstone's significance lies in his geographical discoveries and the way in which his adventures stimulated interest in Africa. His reports about the slave trade may have contributed to its demise. Tim Jeal, author of *Livingstone* (1973), concludes that Livingstone provided the moral basis for British imperial expansion into such areas as Uganda and Kenya. The British public viewed Livingstone as a saint.

OLWYN M. BLOUET

Bibliography

Clendennen, G. W. *David Livingstone: A Catalogue of Documents.* 1979.

Helly, Dorothy O. *Livingstone's Legacy: Horace Waller and Victorian Mythmaking.* 1987.

Huxley, Elspeth. *Livingstone and His African Journeys.* 1974.

Jeal, Tim. *Livingstone.* 1973.

Ransford, Oliver. *David Livingstone: The Dark Interior.* 1978.

. . . . .

LLOYD, MARIE
(1870–1922)

Marie Lloyd was one of the most successful music hall entertainers of the Edwardian era and was especially popular with London audiences.

Born in Hoxton of poor parents and baptized Matilda Alice Victoria Wood, she first appeared on stage in 1885. By 1886 she had adopted her stage name and was playing the best West End music halls. At her peak she earned 600 pounds a week.

Though not beautiful or of outstanding voice, she had charisma, flair, spirit, and the rare ability to establish rapport with audiences. She titillated audiences not with words but with well-timed suggestive motions (her wink was her trademark), though her reputation for lewdness was exaggerated. She never

lost the common touch, and she sang about what her audiences identified with—love, poverty, and the hard life. Her most famous songs were "The Boy in the Gallery," "Twiggy Vous," "One of the Ruins That Cromwell Knocked About a Bit," and "The Piccadilly Trot."

Unhappy in private life, Lloyd lived for her audiences. Collapsing on stage, she died at fifty-two. She was a consummate interpreter of the daily lives of the fans who referred to her as "Our Marie," and her songs reflect working-class morality and life.

WILSON J. HOFFMAN

Bibliography

Cheshire, David F. *Music Hall in Britain.* 1974.

Farson, Daniel N. *Marie Lloyd and Music Hall.* 1972.

Jacob, Naomi. *"Our Marie" (Marie Lloyd): A Biography.* 1936.

Lee, Edward. *Folksong and Music Hall.* 1982.

Macqueen-Pope, W. *The Melodies Linger on: The Story of the Music Hall.* 1950.

Mander, R. and Mitchenson, J. *British Music Hall.* 1974.

. . . . .

LOCAL GOVERNMENT see GOVERNMENT: LOCAL
. . . . .

LOCAL HISTORY

The study of local history became extremely popular in the nineteenth century. A romantic emphasis on the value of common life in the past spurred interest (particularly for remote areas such as Wales and the Scottish Highlands) while the fashion of seeking the picturesque brought the public to out-of-the-way landscapes by recently improved roads and, later in the century, by rail. Increased literacy created a demand for guidebooks and histories. People realized that the products of a preliterate society should be written down, as Walter Scott did with the ballads of the Scottish clans in *Minstrelsy of the Scottish Border* (1802). Work in geology, topography, and general **antiquarianism** was often intensified when layers of the past were exposed by the industrial revolution's effects on the landscape; and the nearly universal (if sometimes inchoate) sense that a landscape and way of life that had seemed timeless were about to be lost became perhaps the strongest incentive for people to study and record their regional past. The first national census, which took place in 1801, signaled a new attitude toward record keeping in a growing and increasingly mobile society; at the same time people became interested in protecting older parish and town records.

Local societies were formed to collect and publish documents and to support libraries and museums which often began with a nucleus of antiquities, not necessarily British, donated by a local wealthy collector and later enhanced by the field-archaeological finds of current enthusiasts. Sometimes these societies commissioned or collected subscriptions for local histories. Nineteenth-century Staffordshire, a typical example, produced topographical and commercial histories, gazetteers, biographies of notable personages such as Josiah Wedgwood, and parish and town histories; a subscription was taken in order to purchase for the county the library and records of the Salt family, members of the local aristocracy, and a library was established in 1872 to house them; and the Staffordshire Record Society was founded in 1879 to publish these records.

The actual writing of local history—accounts of towns, parishes, and especially counties—was originally, like so much Victorian scholarship, the lifework of dedicated amateurs, many of them rural and middle class. By the end of the century, however, much writing of local history was being done by committees and published by subscription.

The eighteenth-century guidebook for the student of the picturesque evolved into the documentary local history. The first substantial county history to attempt a thoroughly empirical, comprehensive survey of a region is probably Richard Colt Hoare's *The Ancient History of South and North Wiltshire* (1812–1821), which was exhaustively researched and illustrated with first-class maps. Technological advances in lithography and aquatint en-

hanced the value and appeal of illustrations in historical publications, and a high standard of topographical accuracy and artistic merit became expected. Between Colt Hoare's work and the establishment of the comprehensive and fairly uniform series Victoria History of the Counties of England (1899; first publication in 1900), local histories were published at an astounding rate.

The Victorians also took national steps to support the study of the past, particularly in making records accessible to historians. The Public Records Act (1838) established the first public records office and the Royal Commission on Historical Manuscripts (1869) was founded to publish privately owned manuscripts and records. The Victoria County Histories were a national project, though individual volumes were written by historians from the pertinent regions. This national attention to the priorities of local history simply reflected one feature of the British character: the British sense of identity was in the nineteenth century and remains today tied to regional affiliation.

LAURA NOVO

Bibliography

Piggott, Stuart. *Ruins in a Landscape: Essays in Antiquarianism.* 1976.

Simmons, Jack. *English County Historians.* 1978.

Trevor-Roper, Hugh. *The Romantic Movement and the Study of History.* 1976.

· · · · ·

LODER, EDWARD JAMES (1813–1865)

Edward James Loder was a talented composer who fell victim to the Victorians' indifference to native musicians. He composed *Raymond and Agnes* (1855), now regarded as the greatest Victorian opera before Sullivan.

Loder came from a Bath family of musicians, and studied in Germany with Ferdinand Ries (1784–1838). He began his career as a virtuoso pianist, and made his mark as an opera composer with *Nourjahad* (1834), which according to **George Macfarren** "was the inaugural work of the institution of modern English opera." As musical director of the Princess's Theatre, London, he brought out his best-known opera, *The Night Dancers*, in 1846. About 1850 he moved to Manchester as musical director of the Theatre Royal. *Raymond and Agnes* was produced there in 1855.

Loder lived near the poverty line, and was forced to produce quantities of popular music for publishers' profit. In later years he suffered from brain disease, and the last four years of his life were spent in coma.

Raymond and Agnes, long forgotten, was revived at the Arts Theatre, Cambridge, in 1966 and was acclaimed by critics for its surprising dramatic power, reminiscent of early Verdi. Loder also wrote some superb songs, a few of which are reprinted in *Musica Britannica*, vol. 43, and some attractive chamber music and piano pieces.

NICHOLAS TEMPERLEY

Bibliography

Temperley, Nicholas. "Raymond and Agnes." *The Musical Times*, vol. 107, pp. 307–310.

· · · · ·

LOGIC

After a protracted decline through the eighteenth and early nineteenth centuries, British logic entered one of its most fertile periods during the 1840s. The apex of philosophical logic, in **John Stuart Mill**'s *A System of Logic* (1843), was reached almost simultaneously with the birth of mathematical logic in **George Boole**'s *The Mathematical Analysis of Logic* (1847) and Augustus DeMorgan's *Formal Logic* (1847). These antithetical logics arose from two opposing traditions: antilogical British empiricism and sophisticated mathematical abstraction.

Mill's *Logic* promoted induction and a methodology for studying the natural and social sciences. The "logic" in this work is his systematic account of real propositions, or assertions of matters of fact; in other words, a logic of truth rather than a syllogistic logic of consistency. Mill included an important though subordinate role for the syllogism,

which was the subject of formal logic and had been repudiated by empiricists since John Locke (1632-1704). The traditional foundation of formal logic—that what can be said of a class can be said of its individual members—was rejected in favor of reasoning from particular events. Mill's logic of experience opposes the German a priori school. Even the "necessity" of mathematics is seen as an induction based on experience. This disposition denies necessitarianism and promotes political and social change. Mill's work has been praised as the brilliant completion of modern views on logic, but numerous commentators have pointed out its inconsistencies and lack of rigor.

Mathematical logic required a sophistication in axiomatics and number theory that was reached only in the nineteenth century. Standards of rigor in demonstration were based on Euclid, but a higher level of mathematical abstraction was achieved by the non-Euclidean geometries emerging after the 1820s. Algebra incorporated greater abstraction in works by Augustus DeMorgan (1806-1871) and others, and was able to furnish a model for a logical calculus.

Algebraic formulae to express logical relations were first used by Boole, who is thus called the father of modern logic, although Leibniz (1646-1716) had posited (but failed to methodize) quantification laws of logic. Boole based his calculus of logic on nonnumerical entities and on procedures that used some but not all of the laws of algebra. His detractors claim that so many discrepancies were later corrected by his followers, and such sweeping changes introduced into quantification theory by Gottlob Frege (1848-1925), that Boole's claim to preeminence is unfounded. Nonetheless, Boole freed logic from the domain of epistemology and created an independent science wherein logic is studied without reference to the processes of human minds; he associated logic with mathematics, not philosophy. The basis of symbolic logic is found in Boole's methods. Two results of his system are truth functions and decision procedures, which are the cornerstones, respectively, for later developments in logic and for electronic computing based on bivalues.

DeMorgan, a friend of Boole's, also saw the need for a systematic algebraicism of logic and provided some improved symbolism, although his principal contributions consisted of expanding the syllogistic and relating noun expressions that cannot be accommodated by the syllogism. He introduced the concept of the universe of discourse as used by Boole.

Subsequent refinements of the logical calculus were produced by John Venn (1834–1913), whose decision procedures are shown in Venn diagrams. The American C. S. Peirce (1839–1914) extended truth functions. William Stanley Jevons reduced Boole's bivalued methods to mechanics and in 1869 exhibited a logical machine at the Royal Society. All were admirers of Boole. While Boole showed logic to be part of mathematics, Frege's 1879 publication in Germany made arithmetic identical to logic; numbers are defined without reference to notions other than those in his calculus of logic. Mathematical logic thus broke the dominion of words and the grammar of ordinary language over our mental processes.

JOEL ATHEY

Bibliography

Copleston, Frederick. *A History of Philosophy*, vol. 8. 1967.

Hesse, Mary B. "Boole's Philosophy of Logic." *Annals of Science*, vol. 8, pp. 61–81.

Kneale, William and Martha Kneale. *The Development of Logic*. 1962.

McRae, R. F. Introduction to *A System of Logic*. In John M. Robson, ed., *Collected Works of John Stuart Mill*. Vol. 7. 1974.

Prior, A. N. "Logic, History of." In Paul Edwards, ed., *The Encyclopedia of Philosophy*, vol. 4. 1967.

Smith, G. C., ed. *The Boole-DeMorgan Correspondence 1842–1864*. 1982.

Van Evra, James W. "A Reassessment of George Boole's Theory of Logic." *Notre Dame Journal of Formal Logic*, vol. 18, pp. 363–377.

. . . . .

LONDON

During the nineteenth century, London's position as the commercial center of the world's most powerful nation was consolidated and a new factor appeared in the city's growth—industrialization. Commercial success was evident in dock construction; five were built east of the Tower of London between 1855 and 1886. Industry, however, never came to dominate London as it did the towns of the north of England. Commerce, rather than manufacture, was the lure for the tides of immigrants who flooded into the capital. The growing population called for new initiatives in local and central government and for expansion of the city limits. Generally, people became more affluent and expected improvements in personal and public environments. Paradoxically, the expanding population helped stem the growth of revolutionary activity.

In 1802 vast areas of London were still rural and Wordsworth's sonnet asked if "Earth has not anything to show more fair." By the 1860s the picture had soured; London had become Ruskin's "great foul city." The inner urban areas had a massive slum problem, though not all of the city was blighted—garden suburbs were increasingly a feature of the landscape. It all depends on what one considers "London." Three regions may be so described, beginning at the topographical heart with the City of London proper. A mere 668 acres, it gradually lost its inhabitants as the demand for office space converted it into the commercial heart of the metropolis. The population of 127,869 in 1851 had fallen to 26,923 by 1901.

Beyond the "City" is the city or inner London, an area composed of the metropolitan boroughs created in 1899 by the London Government Act. If the Cities of London and Westminster are included with this region, the whole showed a population increase from one million to five million during the course of the century. In addition, improvements in public transport allowed the development of a "greater London" conurbation which swallowed up parts of Middlesex, Essex, Surrey, and Kent. Thus by 1901 the total population within the sphere of London was almost seven million.

The various definitions of London reflect the multiplicity of nineteenth-century governing bodies. So complex was the capital's government that several different, often ill-defined, bodies might be responsible for the upkeep of one stretch of roadway. By midcentury overcrowding, poor health and sanitation, and adverse public opinion contributed to the process of change. An inquiry into public health (1845) was followed by legislation for a purer water supply (1852), and in 1855 the Metropolis Management Act created the Metropolitan Board of Works to oversee major public works such as drainage. In addition, the multiplicity of franchises was replaced by a system of voting for all male ratepayers. The board disappeared with the creation of the London County Council (1888), which in turn managed the creation of boroughs from older governing bodies, such as the seventy-eight vestries, which were rendered obsolete by the 1899 act.

London's poor social conditions were evident in the inner city. Unscrupulous landlords and a ghetto mentality among immigrants compounded a seemingly intractable **housing** problem. The slums were only partially swept away in the second half of the century by ambitious road and rail building programs. Railroad companies were legally compelled to replace demolished property, but frequently did not, or built houses that workers could not afford to rent.

Slum dwellers earned a living by any means available. The conditions were chronicled by Henry Mayhew in *London Labour and the London Poor* (1861–1862). Any service or commodity was available on the streets or in tiny back-street shops where the perpetual gloom in the polluted air required gas lights to burn all day, and where the customer could be entertained by a variety of buskers and other street entertainers: snake swallowers, acrobats, jugglers, and barrel organists. Thousands lived by scavenging off the streets, waterfront, sewers, and garbage dumps. Everything seemed to have a market, even dog dung—purchased by tanners in Bermondsey for purifying leather.

After work, music halls, gin palaces, public houses, opium parlors, and brothels all claimed devotees. **Prostitution** reached monumental proportions; girls under thirteen were forced into prostitution, often to help support the family. Reformers were thwarted in their attempts to collect reliable statistics by a police force whose officers were known to falsify figures.

Increasingly, the middle classes left central London areas to live in the new suburbs—largely thanks to the railroads, which were fast, cheap, and reliable. A rail line ran from London to Greenwich in 1836. The Doric splendor of Euston received the London and Birmingham Railway (1838) and the Great Western Railway reached Paddington in 1844. Throughout the middle and late century the capital was transformed by a network of track. Steam-powered subway trains appeared in 1863 (the Metropolitan Line), becoming electrified in 1890 (the first stretch being from King William Street to Stockwell). Speculative building followed the railroad lines but it did little to relieve inner-city overcrowding.

Railroads also established the city as a tourist attraction. The Exhibition of 1851 was a resounding financial success. (The profits purchased a site on which were built five colleges, four museums, the Royal Albert Hall, and the Albert Memorial.) The exhibition's grandeur and optimism mirrored the capital's growing wealth, seen also in the architectural enterprises that reshaped the face of the central areas: the Houses of Parliament (1840–1860), Big Ben (1858), Nelson's Column (1842), the Royal Opera House (1858), Westminster Bridge (1862), and Tower Bridge (1894). Queen Victoria established Buckingham Palace as the official London residence of the monarch. By the end of the century, tourist guides (e.g., *London, Past and Present*, 1880) and photographic collections (e.g., *Round London*, 1896) were displaying a city "on the whole well built," and much of the gloom and hardship had gone.

Lord Liverpool expressed fears to Chateaubriand that London was a potential source of popular unrest, and indeed three quite serious disturbances did occur (Corn Bill protests, 1815; Spa Fields riot, 1816; Queen Caroline disturbances, 1821). The capital was regarded as a Chartist center from 1842 to 1848. Significantly, however, the worst troubles predate the foundation of the Metropolitan Police Force (1829) and the bulk of the population explosion.

Variously described as the "Great Wen" and the "Great Babylon," London's physical and social structure was reshaped by the nineteenth century. Some problems were solved and some, like the slums, remained as a legacy well into the next century.

W. JOHN SMITH

Bibliography

Besant, Walter. *London in the Nineteenth Century.* 1909.

Dyos, H. J. *Victorian Suburb: A Study of the Growth of Camberwell.* 1961.

Goodway, David. *London Chartism, 1838-1848.* 1982.

Hibbert, Christopher. *London: The Biography of a City.* 1969.

Owen, David. *The Government of Victorian London, 1855-1889.* 1982.

Roebuck, Janet. *Urban Development in Nineteenth-Century London: Lambeth, Battersea and Wandsworth, 1838-1888.* 1979.

Sheppard, Francis. *London, 1808-1870: The Infernal Wen.* 1971.

Stamp, Gavin. *The Changing Metropolis: Earliest Photographs of London, 1839-1879.* 1984.

Young, Ken and Patricia L. Garside. *Metropolitan London: Politics and Urban Change, 1837-1981.* 1982.

See also GOVERNMENT: LOCAL AND COUNTY; TRANSPORTATION, URBAN

. . . . .

LOVELACE, ADA
(1815-1852)

Augusta Ada, countess of Lovelace, was an object of interest during her lifetime chiefly as the daughter of the poet Lord Byron (1788-1824). She was also a close friend of **Charles Babbage** (1791-1871), who from 1820 until his death experimented with mechanical calculating machines that were in theory capable of the functions of the modern computer. In 1843 she translated and published an article on Babbage's plans, to which she appended lengthy notes including several sketches for programs by which mathematical calculations could be performed. Consequently she has recently been (erroneously) hailed as the first computer programmer and as an accomplished mathematician. The "programs" as well as all the important ideas in the piece were in fact originated by Babbage himself, who wanted to use her article to promote additional government funding to build his "Analytical Engine." Lovelace's "notes" clearly reflected Babbage's already outdated philosophy of mathematics.

Lovelace's mathematical education began at age twenty-five, when she became a pupil of the logician Augustus DeMorgan (1806-1871), first professor of mathematics at University College. However, she made very halting progress, and in translating the article was forced to rely entirely on what Babbage told her. Thus she made exaggerated claims for the proposed engine—specifically that it would be capable of purely algebraic computations—that were not in fact true.

The collaboration effectively ended there. Lovelace turned to her more enduring scientific interest, assessing mesmeric phenomena, which were then thought to be the effects of a magnetic fluid on the nervous system, and which she feared were responsible for her frequent and severe attacks of mental and physical illness. In order to investigate the influence of electrical fields on nervous tissue she tried to become a pupil to Michael Faraday. When he refused, she turned to Andrew Crosse (1784-1855). Instead of learning laboratory technique, however, she came under the influence of Crosse's son John (1810-1880). Together they became involved in an elaborate set of horse-racing wagers that led to financial disaster just as the progress of uterine cancer destroyed her ability to act independently. Contrary to legend, there is no evidence that she attempted to construct a mathematical scheme to guide her betting, nor that she planned to use the money to finance Babbage's engine.

DOROTHY STEIN

Bibliography

Baum, Joan. *The Calculating Passion of Ada Byron.* 1986

Moore, Doris Langley. *Ada, Countess of Lovelace, Byron's Legitimate Daughter.* 1977.

"Sketch of the Analytical Engine invented by Charles Babbage, Esq. By L. F. Menabrea of Turin, Officer of the Military Engineers." Translated and with notes by A. A. L. In *Taylor's Scientific Memoirs,* 1843, vol. 3, pp. 666-731.

Republished, with numerous printer's errors corrected, in B. V. Bowden, *Faster Than Thought*, 1953; reprinted with errors uncorrected, in P. and E. Morrison, *Charles Babbage and His Calculating Engines*, 1961.

Stein, Dorothy. *Ada: A Life and a Legacy*. 1985.

· · · · ·

LUTYENS, EDWIN LANDSEER (1869–1944)

The leading British architect of the late-Victorian and Edwardian periods, Edwin Landseer Lutyens (knighted, 1918) designed domestic and public works of traditional style and brilliant sophistication. His best-known buildings include rural "vernacular styled" houses, many located in his native Surrey. Here, Lutyens developed a successful partnership with the gardener **Gertrude Jekyll** (1843–1932), and together they created the quintessential English image of the smaller "house in the country" (as opposed to the landscaped "stately country house") set in an English garden.

These Surrey houses—from Lutyens's first, Crooksbury (1889–1891), to Munstead Wood (1896–1897), built for Jekyll, to nearby Orchards (1897–1899)—epitomized the Lutyens architectural character: a concern for honesty of construction and materials and an interest in local traditions, forms, and techniques in building craft. These ideals derived in theory from A. W. N. Pugin and the Gothic revival and in practice from the arts and crafts movement and the works of Richard Norman Shaw and Philip Webb. Deanery Garden (1899–1903) was built inconspicuously into the fabric of the village of Sonning, Berkshire, for Edward Hudson, founder and editor of *Country Life* and an important promoter of Lutyens. Lutyens houses at Marshcourt (1901) and Folly Farm (1906) likewise displayed masterful gardens with Jekyll plantings, and Hestercombe (1901, 1906, 1912), where there is no Lutyens house, is one of his best and most architectonic gardens.

Among Lutyens's classically styled works are his "high-style Palladian" Heathcote (1906); the Cenotaph, Whitehall; his "Neo-

Georgian" house, The Salutation (1911); and his monumental Viceroy's House, New Delhi (1912–1930). Such works as these invite comparison with Christopher Wren. But it is in the "dream houses" of the period, through an architectural imagery still perceived as typically English, that Lutyens made his mark on the architectural landscape.

ROBERT M. CRAIG

Bibliography

Arts Council of Great Britain. *Lutyens*. 1981.

Brown, Jane. *Gardens of a Golden Afternoon: The Story of a Partnership: Edwin Lutyens and Gertrude Jekyll*. 1982.

Butler, A. S. G. *The Architecture of Sir Edwin Lutyens*. 1950. 3 vols.

Gradidge, Roderick. *Dream Houses: The Edwardian Ideal*. 1980.

———. *Edwin Lutyens: Architect Laureate*. 1981.

Hussey, Christopher. *The Life of Sir Edwin Lutyens*. 1950.

Inskip, Peter. *Edwin Lutyens*. 1979.

Irving, Robert G. *Indian Summer: Lutyens, Baker, and Imperial Delhi*. 1981.

Lutyens, Edwin. "What I Think of Modern Architecture." *Country Life*, vol. 69, pp. 775–777.

Lutyens, Mary. *Edwin Lutyens: A Memoir by His Daughter*. 1980.

O'Neill, Daniel. *Sir Edwin Lutyens: Country Houses*. 1980.

Weaver, Lawrence. *Houses and Gardens by E. L. Lutyens*. 1913.

· · · · ·

LYALL, EDNA (1857–1903)

Using the pseudonym Edna Lyall, Ada Ellen Bayly wrote some twenty highly popular novels. Her fiction supported such causes as Irish Home Rule (*Doreen*, 1894), the reform of divorce laws (*Wayfaring Men*, 1897), and opposition to the Boer War (her last book, *The Hinderers*, 1902). The novels defended the propriety of theatrical professions and depicted outspoken, independent career women who rejected social formulae and fought for humanitarian reforms.

After a first work of little distinction (*Won by Waiting*, 1879), Lyall in *Donovan* (1882) emphasized her recurring themes of Christian forgiveness and self-sacrifice. A sequel, *We Two* (1884), established her reputation and her continuing practice of connecting one novel to another by using characters from earlier works. *Doreen* rates among her best fiction for its suspense, vividness, large cast of engaging characters, and vibrant political and feminist concerns.

Lyall's plots follow a general pattern: the protagonists, usually orphaned and impoverished by misfortune or chicanery, must discover a useful vocation. Wrongly censured by society (a motif treated whimsically but bitingly in *The Autobiography of a Slander*, 1887), they eventually regain lost love and reputation. Though her works are usually set in the present, *In the Golden Days* (1885), *To Right the Wrong* (1893), *Hope the Hermit* (1898), and *In Spite of All* (1901) depict the seventeenth-century civil wars.

Lyall assessed Elizabeth Gaskell's accomplishment in *Women Novelists of Queen Victoria's Reign* (1897) and wrote an autobiographical account of childhood, *The Burges Letters* (1902). Admired by Gladstone and read by Ruskin on his deathbed, Lyall deserves to be remembered among late Victorian novelists for challenging traditional views in competent, sometimes engrossing tales.

BEVERLY TAYLOR

Bibliography

Black, Helen C. *Notable Women Authors of the Day.* 1893.

Escreet, Jesse M. *The Life of Edna Lyall.* 1904.

· · · · ·

LYELL, CHARLES
(1797–1875)

Victorian England's most influential geological writer, Charles Lyell is remembered primarily for his *Principles of Geology* (1830–1833, with subsequent editions—often impor-

tantly revised—through 1875). His other works include *Elements of Geology* (1838), *Travels in America* (1845), *A Second Visit to the United States of America* (1849), and *The Antiquity of Man* (1863), together with numerous scientific papers, periodical contributions, and lectures.

Born in Scotland, Lyell grew up in southern England and studied for the law at Oxford. Though qualified to practice, he soon realized that **geology** was his real interest. In both the Geological Society and the Royal Society of London, he quickly became known for calm professional argumentation. Opposing the common opinion that geological changes in the past had been primarily swift and catastrophic (like the fabled destruction of Atlantis), Lyell supposed them identical to those now operating, a position later termed uniformitarian. Lyell defended his uniformitarian beliefs at length in his *Principles* and elsewhere, though they did not achieve unqualified acceptance. He also traveled widely to describe relevant landforms at first hand. These discussions attracted the lay public to his works and popularized geological travel, observation, and reasoning.

Lyell emphasized the cumulative effects of earthquakes, volcanoes, marine erosion, uplift, and climate. He opposed theories attributing catastrophic origins to mountain chains and volcanic cones. For most of his career Lyell also attempted to refute the transformationist theories of Lamarck and others, even denying any kind of progression in the successive forms of terrestrial life. Under Darwin's influence, however, Lyell compromised his nonprogressionist view in *The Antiquity of Man* (1863) and reversed it altogether in the tenth edition of the *Principles of Geology* (1867).

Lyell contributed significantly to the rise of Victorian rationalism. A major aim in *Principles* was to dissociate geological theorizing from the Bible and see nature as the sole source of truth regarding the earth's history. Eventually nearly all major Anglo-American geologists accepted the extended view of geological time required by Lyell's uniformitarianism and Darwin's natural selection.

Lyell's insistence upon the uniformity of geological causes through time (as opposed to a more active younger earth), his emphasis upon marine (as opposed to subaerial) erosion, and his nonprogressionist biology were all challenged in his own time and have been discarded since. Nevertheless, Lyell remains the most significant geologist in Victorian England and one of the giants of the science.

DENNIS R. DEAN

Bibliography

Bailey, Edward. *Charles Lyell.* 1962.

Gillispie, Charles C. *Genesis and Geology.* 1951.

Lyell, K. M., ed. *Life, Letters, and Journals of Sir Charles Lyell.* 1881; rpt. 1983. 2 vols.

Wilson, Leonard. *Charles Lyell: The Years to 1841.* 1972.

· · · · ·

MACAULAY, THOMAS BABINGTON
(1800-1859)

As a member of Parliament, historian, essayist, and poet, Thomas Babington Macaulay was one of the most influential men and popular writers of his day. He became Baron Macaulay of Rothley in 1857.

Born into a prominent Clapham sect family, Macaulay went to Trinity College, Cambridge, in 1818, where he was elected a fellow in 1825. He published his first essay ("Milton") in the *Edinburgh Review* in 1824 and was called to the bar the following year. Elected to the House of Commons for Calne in 1830 and for Leeds in 1832, he distinguished himself in the debates on the Reform Bill, the abolition of slavery, and the renewal of the East India Company's charter.

Appointed to the Board of Control for India in 1832 and seated on the Supreme Council in 1833, Macaulay worked in India between 1834 and 1838, writing the Minute on Indian Education (1835) and composing a criminal code (1837) during his stay. In 1839 he was again elected to Parliament, served as minister at war (1839-1841) in Melbourne's cabinet, and began writing a history of England. He published *Lays of Ancient Rome* (1842) and, in 1849, the first two volumes of his *History of England*. The third and fourth volumes appeared in 1855 and the final volume was published posthumously in 1861.

Macaulay's histories made skillful use of manuscript sources and other primary evidence, but their great popularity was a consequence of his vigorous prose style, enthusiastic optimism, descriptive power, and ability to construct narrative. As a spokesman for the Whig viewpoint, Macaulay was an influential member of Parliament. His decisive work in shaping Indian policy remains controversial.

JOE LAW

Bibliography

Clive, John. *Macaulay: The Shaping of the Historian.* 1973.

———. and Thomas Finney. "Thomas Babington Macaulay." In David J. DeLaura, ed., *Victorian Prose: A Guide to Research.* 1973.

Hamburger, Joseph. *Macaulay and the Whig Tradition.* 1976.

Millgate, Jane. *Macaulay.* 1973.

Pinney, Thomas. *The Letters of Thomas Babington Macaulay.* 1974-1981.

Trevelyan, George Otto. *The Life and Letters of Lord Macaulay.* 1876.

· · · · ·

MACDONALD, GEORGE
(1824-1905)

A Scottish-born author, George MacDonald produced over fifty books of poetry, fiction, children's stories, sermons, and literary criticism. The titles now most commonly read are: *Phantastes* (1858), *At the Back of the North Wind* (1870), *The Princess and the Goblin* (1871), *The Wise Woman* (1875), *The Princess and Curdie* (1875), *The Gifts of the Child Christ* (1882), and *Lilith* (1895). The standard biography, by his son Greville, is highly subjective and prints inaccurate versions of MacDonald's letters.

MacDonald received his M.A. from Aberdeen and trained in the Congregational ministry at Highbury College, London, but was dismissed from his first parish for preaching the "heresy" of Universalism. Thereafter, he supported his wife and family with a steady stream of writing, lecturing, and guest preaching.

MacDonald's strength and originality derive from his blending of disparate sources, for he was an eclectic reader and fluent in eight languages. His otherworldliness, bred by Scottish folklore and a Calvinist education, was transmuted by his adult reading of mystics such as Boehme, Swedenborg, and Blake, and by his lifelong fascination with the German romantic *Kunstmärchen*. The texts resulting from this mix combine a lushness of surface with a sternness of theme and sentiment. Even in the more conventionally realistic novels—*Alec Forbes* (1865), *Wilfrid Cumbermede* (1871), *Sir Gibbie* (1879), etc.—MacDonald constantly infuses, even undermines, the fabric of everyday life with imaginative suggestion. MacDonald's richly symbolic romances *Phantastes* and *Lilith* carry this dissolving mode to an extreme and make difficult, though highly rewarding, reading.

These two romances are at the center of the revived interest in MacDonald spurred by C. S. Lewis and have had considerable influence on twentieth-century fantasy. MacDonald's children's stories, which show a brevity and humor often missing from his adult writing, have always been popular, though their complexity precludes reading by the very young. In his time, MacDonald was influential in liberalizing the stricter aspects of Calvinism by filtering them through the vividly spontaneous medium of his romantic sensibility.

DOUGLAS THORPE

Bibliography

Bulloch, J. M. "A Bibliography of George MacDonald." *Aberdeen University Library Bulletin*, vol. 5, pp. 679–747.

Hein, Rolland. *The Harmony Within: The Spiritual Vision of George MacDonald.* 1982.

Lewis, C. S., ed. *George MacDonald: An Anthology.* 1946.

MacDonald, Greville. *George MacDonald and His Wife.* 1924.

Prickett, Stephen. *Romanticism and Religion: The Tradition of Coleridge and Wordsworth in the Victorian Church.* 1976.

———. *Victorian Fantasy.* 1979.

Reis, Richard. *George MacDonald.* 1972.

Wolff, Robert Lee. *The Golden Key: A Study of the Fiction of George MacDonald.* 1961.

See also FANTASY LITERATURE

· · · · ·

MACFARREN, GEORGE ALEXANDER (1813–1887)

George Alexander Macfarren, in a long career, reached the heights of the musical profession, and was knighted in 1883. He composed successfully in every major branch of music, yet his works are today practically unknown.

His father George Macfarren (1788–1843) was a London fiddler and dramatic author. Macfarren entered the Royal Academy of Music in 1829. He had early trouble with his vision, and became totally blind by 1860. He taught at the academy for much his career, becoming principal in 1875, and also professor of music at Cambridge.

Macfarren was an active historian and scholar, particularly in the field of English music. He lectured widely, edited works of Purcell and Elizabethan composers, and arranged many folksongs. As a composer of opera, Macfarren was a nationalist. His best works were *King Charles II* (1849), *Robin Hood* (1860), and *Jessy Lea* (1863). Rejecting current Continental influences, Macfarren grounded his style on Mozart and colored it with English folksong.

Macfarren wrote as many as nine symphonies, despite the lack of public interest. His overture "Chevy Chace" (1836) was popular in Britain and Germany for many years. He was a prolific composer of chamber music, glees, songs, and piano music. A few of his songs have been reprinted in *Musica Britannica*, vol. 43, and one of his piano sonatas in *The London Pianoforte School*, vol. 16. In later life he concentrated chiefly on cantatas and oratorios.

NICHOLAS TEMPERLEY

Bibliography

Banister, Henry. *George Alexander Macfarren: His Life, Works, and Influence.* 1891.

Macfarren, George A. *Addresses and Lectures.* 1888.

Temperley, Nicholas. "Musical Nationalism in Victorian Opera." In Nicholas Temperley, ed., *The Lost Chord.* 1988.

. . . . .

Bibliography

Howes, Frank. *The English Musical Renaissance.* 1966.

Mackenzie, Alexander C. *A Musician's Narrative.* 1927.

. . . . .

MACKENZIE, ALEXANDER CAMPBELL (1847–1935)

Composer, teacher, and conducter, Alexander Campbell Mackenzie was principal of the Royal Academy of Music from 1888 to 1924. He was knighted in 1895 and made a K.C.V.O. in 1922.

Born into a prominent Edinburgh musical family, Mackenzie trained in Germany and at the Royal Academy of Music. He was active as a violinist, teacher, and conductor in Edinburgh from 1865 until 1879, when he moved to Florence to devote himself to composition. In 1885 he returned to London to become conductor of Novello's Oratorio Concerts. In addition to assuming duties as an educator, he became permanent conductor of the **Philharmonic Society** (1892–1899) and president of the International Music Society (1908–1912).

Among his more successful compositions were the cantata *The Bride* (1881), the opera *Colomba* (1883), and the oratorio *The Rose of Sharon* (1884). Much of his music, particularly the three orchestral Scottish Rhapsodies (1880, 1880, 1911) and Scottish Concerto for piano and orchestra (1897), has a nationalistic flavor. As a conductor, Mackenzie introduced British audiences to works by Dvorak, Liszt, Tchaikovsky, and Borodin. At the Royal Academy of Music, he improved the curriculum and instruction, moved the school into new quarters, established cordial relations with the Royal College of Music, and founded the Associated Board of the Royal Schools of Music in 1899. Although none of his music has proved lasting, Mackenzie was, with C. H. H. Parry and C. V. Stanford, one of the key figures in revitalizing British music in the latter part of the nineteenth century.

JOE K. LAW

MACKINTOSH, CHARLES RENNIE (1868–1928) and MARGARET MACDONALD (1864–1933)

At the eye of the progressive art movement that took late nineteenth-century Glasgow by storm were architect Charles Rennie Mackintosh and artist Margaret MacDonald Mackintosh. While "Toshie" concentrated on the design of buildings, interiors, and furniture, Margaret Mackintosh did book illustration and binding, needlework, metalwork, and gessowork, often executing decorative panels and details for her husband's interiors and furniture. Thus it was through the avenues of "acceptable" women's crafts that Margaret Mackintosh was able to enter the workforce as a commercial designer.

Though the Glasgow style had historicist roots in the Celtic and Scottish baronial past, the Mackintoshes stylized and invented new (often geometric) visual forms to produce a hybridized **art nouveau**, strikingly simple in comparison to the heavily embellished surfaces of a typical middle-class Victorian home.

The Glasgow School of Art was critical to the development of the Glasgow style. Charles Mackintosh and Margaret MacDonald met there as students in the early 1890s, where they were drawn together with other like-minded artists. The commission awarded to Charles Mackintosh in 1896 for the design of a new building to house the Glasgow School of Art launched his career. The building remains one of the quintessential examples of his talent.

By the end of the century the work of the Mackintoshes, spawned in the relative isolation of Glasgow, was known although not greatly admired throughout Britain. It won more enthusiastic acceptance on the Continent, and served as a major influence on the Vienna secessionists.

KEN CARLS

Bibliography

Billcliffe, Roger. *Charles Rennie Mackintosh: The Complete Furniture, Furniture Drawings, and Interior Designs.* 1979.

Callen, Anthea. *Women Artists of the Arts and Crafts Movement, 1870-1914.* 1979.

Doumato, Lamia. *Charles Rennie Mackintosh: Architect and Designer.* 1980.

Glasgow Museum and Art Galleries. *The Glasgow Style* (exhibition catalogue). 1984.

Howarth, Thomas. *Charles Rennie Mackintosh and the Modern Movement.* 1952.

Larner, Gerald and Celie Larner. *The Glasgow Style.* 1979.

MacLeod, Robert. *Charles Rennie Mackintosh: Architect and Artist.* Rev. ed., 1983.

Robertson, Pamela. *Margaret MacDonald Mackintosh, 1864-1933* (exhibition catalogue). 1983.

· · · · ·

MACKMURDO, ARTHUR HEYGATE
(1851-1942)

Arthur Mackmurdo, architect and designer, was associated with the arts and crafts movement. His notable achievements included the Century Guild, several influential buildings, and the art magazine *Hobby Horse*, which initiated a reform of book design.

Mackmurdo's early education included a brief architectural apprenticeship in London. He studied drawing (in Oxford) and Italian architecture (in Italy) with John Ruskin, whose influence was to shape many of his artistic and social ideas; Mackmurdo subsequently founded several Ruskin societies to further his mentor's teachings. He was also subject to the contrary influences of Herbert Spencer, T. H. Huxley, Walter Pater, and J. M. Whistler.

Soon after setting up his architectural prac-

tice in London in 1875, Mackmurdo built "Halycon House" at Enfield, Middlesex (after a design of 1872). Among the notable buildings that followed were two others at Enfield, the Savoy Hotel (1899), and perhaps his most remarkable design, 25 Cadogan Gardens, London (1899). Of related interest was an exhibition stand at the Liverpool International Exhibition of 1886, whose distinctive flat-topped finial became a hallmark of Mackmurdo's style.

His interest in the reform of craftsmanship led to his cofounding of the Century Guild in 1882. Outstanding among the guild's manufactures were furniture, wallpaper, and fabric, some of whose lively biomorphic patterns anticipate the art nouveau style.

Much of Mackmurdo's later life was devoted to matters of social and economic improvement, including an outline for "organic" townplanning and projects for currency reform and state socialism.

LARRY D. LUTCHMANSINGH

Bibliography

Lambourne, Lionel. *Utopian Craftsmen: The Arts and Crafts Movement from the Cotswalds to Chicago.* 1980.

Pevsner, Nikolaus. "A Pioneer Designer: Arthur Heygate Mackmurdo." *Architectural Review,* vol. 83, pp. 141-143.

Vallance, Aymer. "Mr. Arthur H. Mackmurdo and the Century Guild." *Studio,* vol. 16, pp. 183-192.

· · · · ·

MACREADY, WILLIAM CHARLES
(1793-1873)

Son of a manager of provincial theaters, William Charles Macready became the foremost tragedian of the early Victorian stage and an important influence on the development of acting in Britain. He debuted in London in 1816, and from 1823 to 1836 acted Shakespeare at Drury Lane. As manager at Covent Garden (1837-1839) and Drury Lane (1841-1843), he established a reputation for innovation and integrity. His close friendships with Dickens, Forster, and other Victorian worthies during these years are chronicled in his fascinating *Diaries.*

Macready thrice visited America to bolster his income. His last visit (1848–1849) was marred by a riot in New York outside a performance of Macbeth. Jingoistic supporters of the American actor Edwin Forrest instigated a confrontation with militia in which seventeen to twenty men were killed. Macready returned to England, and after a farewell tour of the provinces took his farewell as Macbeth at Drury Lane (February 3, 1851).

Macready is remembered for three contributions. His widely imitated style (marked by pauses and dynamic modulations) and his serious study of each part make him a forerunner of modern method acting. His managerial stints during periods in which spectacle reigned not only preserved the primacy of Shakespeare, but also helped return original versions to the stage (his *King Lear* in 1837 was the first in a century with the Fool). Finally, his cultivation of new plays by Knowles, Shiel, and Bulwer-Lytton, as well as his acting versions of Byron's tragedies, defined the theater-going experience in the first twenty years of the Queen's reign.

DAVID E. LATANÉ, JR.

Bibliography

Archer, William. *William Charles Macready.* 1890.

Downer, Alan S. *The Eminent Tragedian: William Charles Macready.* 1966.

Toynbee, William. *The Diaries of William Charles Macready, 1833–1857.* 1912. 2 vols.

· · · · ·

MAGAZINES see PERIODICALS

· · · · ·

MAGINN, WILLIAM (1793–1842)

A journalist, poet, writer of fiction, and critic whose facility for imitating several liter-

ary styles resulted in a failure to cultivate a memorable one himself, William Maginn launched his career in Ireland as a precocious classical scholar, graduating from Trinity College, Dublin in 1811. After a brief stint as a schoolmaster, he moved to Edinburgh, where he had established a connection with *Blackwood's Magazine,* and arrived in London in 1823. He wrote essays and reviews for several of the leading journals, founded *Fraser's Magazine* in 1830, and lived a life of vigorous dissipation as the leader of "the Fraserians." He died in penury at Walton-on-Thames in 1842.

Most of Maginn's writing is contained in articles published, often anonymously, in journals; only *Whitehall, or The Days of George IV* (1827) appeared separately during his lifetime. *Homeric Ballads* (1850), *Shakespeare Papers* (1859), and *Maxims of Sir Morgan O'Doherty, bart.* (1849)—his best-known pseudonym—further established his reputation as a wit and satirist. His *Miscellaneous Writings,* in five volumes, was edited by R. Shelton Mackenzie from 1855–1857. Maginn's masterpiece, however, was *A Gallery of Illustrious Literary Characters,* originally published in *Fraser's Magazine* in 1830, with portraits by Daniel Maclise. His trenchant, humorous descriptions of the best-known writers of the day are perfectly matched by Maclise's slightly caricatured images. A complete edition, edited by William Bates, was published in 1873.

RICHARD LANDON

Bibliography

Bates, William, ed. *A Gallery of Illustrious Literary Characters.* 1873.

Hall, Samuel Carter. *A Book of Memories of Great Men and Women of the Age.* 1871.

MacCarthy, B. G. "Centenary of Maginn." *Studies: An Irish Quarterly Review,* vol. 32, pp. 347–360.

Maginn, William. *The Fraserian Papers.* With a Life of the Author by R. Shelton Mackenzie. 1857.

Sadleir, Michael. *Bulwer: A Panorama. Edward and Rosina, 1803–1836.* 1931.

· · · · ·

MANCHESTER

A major industrial and commercial city 180 miles northwest of London, Manchester became a symbol of the bustling urban life that emerged in the British provinces during the industrial revolution. The title character of Benjamin Disraeli's *Coningsby* (1844) called it "the most wonderful city of modern times," and a few decades later it was being styled "the Capital of the North."

The name "Manchester" was commonly used in the Victorian period to refer both to Manchester and the adjoining city of Salford. After a tumultuous campaign for parliamentary representation, Manchester and Salford together obtained three parliamentary seats under the Reform Act of 1832. Further agitations led to the incorporation of Manchester (1838) and Salford (1844), giving each municipality a mayor and town council. Both were dominated by reforming Whigs and Liberals through the late 1860s.

Manchester, the site of momentous economic changes during the earliest phases of the industrial revolution, continued to be an industrial pioneer. It was linked by the newly developed steam railroads to Liverpool (1830), Leeds (1841), and Birmingham and London (1842), among other cities. Manchester contained over one hundred cotton factories at that time, with an increasing number being converted from water to steam power.

Cycles of economic distress continued to trouble the urban scene. The new municipal police force had to cope with the public disorders and high levels of crime which worsened during slumps. Chartist agitations seemed especially menacing in 1838–1839. Owenite socialism likewise struck deep roots in Manchester and provided a major challenge to capitalist ideologies and religious beliefs from the mid-1830s to the mid-1840s. Viewing these developments at first hand, Friedrich Engels concluded that "class warfare is so open and shameless that it has to be seen to be believed."

The **Anti–Corn-Law League** (1838–1846) represented a different type of movement. Established in Manchester, it attracted a national membership predominantly from the middle classes and sought (among other goals) to abolish restrictions on the grain trade for the mutual benefit of both capitalists and the working classes. The ideas represented by the Anti–Corn-Law League became enshrined in a school of thought known as the **Manchester school**, which helped to link laissez-faire ideology, social cooperation, and economic progress in the public mind.

The mid-Victorian period saw Manchester at the peak of its fame and influence. While its population grew at the prodigious annual rate of 2 to 3 percent in the 1830s and 1840s, growth slowed to around 1 percent per year during the next three decades. More moderate growth and relative prosperity helped government institutions to function more effectively. While economic downturns persisted, they were handled more effectively; indeed, the most severe downturn, the cotton famine of 1861–1865, provided an occasion for official and private relief on an unprecedented scale. Urban leaders were proud to point out that tens of thousands of individuals were aided during those years, helping to support the claim that social harmony was a growing aspect of urban society. Critics, meanwhile, continued to dispute this rosy view of social relations by pointing to such things as the violent "Manchester outrages" in the brickmaking trade and various local disturbances, by Irish Fenians.

The achievements of the Mancunian elite continued to be of primary importance in creating the image of mid-Victorian Manchester. Its accomplishments were exemplified by the founding of Owen's College (1851), a precursor of the University of Manchester; the Art Treasures Exhibition (1857), which attracted over a million visitors, including Victoria and Albert; the establishment of the Hallé Orchestra (1858), now the oldest in Britain; and the opening of parks, libraries, and museums for the benefit of all classes. There was also a distinctive shift in local architectural forms. Neo-Gothicism became the prevailing Mancunian style in the second half of the century, as seen in the Manchester Town Hall (1877), John Rylands Library (1899), and scores of churches and chapels built during the period.

By the late Victorian era population growth was slowing to less than .5 percent per annum. By 1880 most of Manchester's textile factories had moved out to surrounding towns, and the firms that remained suffered from increased international competition. These setbacks were only partially offset by the growth of engineering and chemical companies and of service-sector activities such as banking and food distribution. The most notable economic event of this period was the opening of the Manchester Ship Canal (1894), a 35-mile-long waterway which linked Manchester to the sea and made the city one of England's largest ports. Still, economic problems persisted and were increasingly represented in social developments. The rise of socialism in Manchester and the emergence of women's suffrage campaigns were among the most prominent new developments.

Manchester, Salford, and their adjacent townships composed one of the ten largest urban areas in the world during the Victorian age. Greater Manchester had transformed itself from the "shock city of the industrial revolution" into an urban center of great wealth, influence, and cultural attainment. Yet even the new economic ventures of the 1880s and 1890s could not reverse the pattern of relative decline which was to be its fate in the twentieth century, and which was already being glimpsed at the time of Victoria's death.

ROBERT GLEN

Bibliography

Ashton, T. S. *Economic and Social Investigations in Manchester, 1833-1933.* 1934.

Bergin, Tom, Dorothy N. Pearce, and Stanley Shaw, eds. *Salford: A City and Its Past.* 1975.

Bruton, F. A. *A Short History of Manchester and Salford.* 1927.

Frangopulo, N. J. and G. B. Hindle, eds. *Rich Inheritance: A Guide to the History of Manchester.* 1962.

Kidd, Alan J. and K. W. Roberts, eds. *City, Class and Culture: Studies of Social Policy and Cultural Production in Victorian Manchester.* 1985.

Messinger, Gary S. *Manchester in the Victorian Age.* 1985.

Ray, John Howson, ed. *Handbook and Guide to Manchester.* 1902.

Redford, Arthur and Ina Stafford Russell. *The History of Local Government in Manchester.* 1939. 2 vols.

See also TEXTILE INDUSTRY

· · · · ·

MANCHESTER SCHOOL

The Manchester school was a mid-nineteenth-century political movement whose leading figures were Manchester factory owners, merchants, and financiers. The movement's central concept was that any and all government interference in economic affairs must necessarily be harmful.

The main focus of the Manchester school was on the tariffs that the government placed on imported grain—the Corn Laws. The tariffs allowed British landowners (primarily the aristocracy) to sell grain raised on their land at prices higher than they would have received if the cost of competing foreign grain had not been artificially inflated by the tariffs. Since the price of bread sold to workers in Manchester and other cities was therefore higher than it would otherwise have been, the Corn Laws were seen to benefit the landowning aristocracy at the expense of both workers and the middle classes, to which belonged the manufacturers who were forced to pay workers wages high enough to purchase the bread that formed the staple of their diet.

Under the leadership of factory owner **Richard Cobden** (1804-1865) and **John Bright** (1811-1889), partner in a cotton mill, the **Anti–Corn-Law League** was founded in 1839 in Manchester and mounted a campaign of mass persuasion. Cobden, Bright, and others spoke to vast audiences of working people, arguing that **free trade** in grain and all other commodities would bring them a higher standard of living. In the House of Commons in February 1846, Disraeli gave the name "Manchester school" to the zealous advocates of free trade. Later that year Parliament repealed the Corn Laws.

While the Manchester school is known primarily for its campaign for free trade in grain, it also opposed other forms of government intervention. It opposed legislation to regulate the buying and selling of labor, in particular legislation regarding hours of employment and working conditions. Those associated with the Manchester school believed fervently that the free market in all things was one manifestation of the laws of nature that governed the universe. Even though they were Christians, they believed that compassion must be held in check.

The Manchester school also believed the British government should not interfere in the affairs of other countries. They opposed British participation in the Crimean War (1854–1856); in place of war, they urged the establishment of a system of international arbitration.

Cobden and Bright, the two leading spokesmen of the Manchester school, genuinely believed that free trade and noninterference, in foreign relations as well as in economic affairs, were the way to prosperity and peace. In attitudes toward the role of government there is a direct line of descent between the Manchester school and the conservative wing of the Republican party in the United States.

PAUL MARX

Bibliography

Grampp, William. *The Manchester School of Economics*. 1960.

· · · · ·

MANNING, ANNE
(1807–1879)

A prolific writer of short historical novels, Anne Manning was the oldest child of insurance broker William Oke Manning (1778–1859) and Joan Whatmore Manning. Educated by her mother in history, sciences, and languages, she won as a child a Royal Academy of Art medal for a painting after Murillo. Her memoirs, "Passages in an Authoress's Life," appeared in the magazine *Golden Hours* in 1872.

Manning's first novel, published anonymously, was *The Maiden and Married Life of Mary Powell, Afterwards Mistress Milton* (1849). Written as a diary in archaic diction and printed in antique type, *Mary Powell* was among the most popular works in a midcentury vogue for spurious antiques. Originating

with the *Lady Willoughby's Diary* books (1844, 1847) of Hannah Mary Rathbone (1798–1878), this vogue prompted Smith and Elder's mock-archaic printing of W. M. Thackeray's *Henry Esmond* (1852).

"The Author of *Mary Powell*" subsequently published about fifty one-volume historical tales in less than thirty years, including a sequel, *Deborah's Diary* (1859); *The Household of Sir Thomas More* (1851), narrated by More's daughter Margaret Roper; and *Cherry and Violet: A Tale of the Great Plague* (1853). Since they were cast as diaries or letters describing domestic life and religion, with historical figures in the background, Manning's tales avoided the drama and pedantry of historical novels by Edward Bulwer-Lytton or William Harrison Ainsworth. Nineteenth-century in spirit, they were praised by Cardinal Henry Manning for religious feeling and attention to historical detail.

Manning's novels had a small but faithful readership in England and America, and they paved the way for less archaic domestic historical fictions like *Chronicles of the Schoenberg-Cotta Family* (1863), a popular diary novel about Luther by Elizabeth Rundle Charles (1828–1896). But even *Mary Powell* and *The Household of Sir Thomas More*, republished as Everyman's books into the 1930s, are too stilted in diction to attract modern readers.

MONIKA BROWN

Bibliography

Simmons, James C. "Thackeray's *Henry Esmond* and Anne Manning's 'Spurious Antiques.'" *Victorian Newsletter*, no. 42, pp. 22–24.

Yonge, Charlotte M. "Anne Manning." In *Women Novelists of Queen Victoria's Reign*. 1897.

See also ANTIQUARIANISM
· · · · ·

MANNING, HENRY EDWARD
(1808–1892)

Appointed Archbishop of Westminster in 1865, Henry Edward Manning became the most important Roman Catholic leader in late Victorian England. As metropolitan of the English Catholic Church, he determined the main direction of church policies, had considerable influence at the Vatican, and was actively involved in major social issues. He was made a cardinal in 1875.

The son of a wealthy merchant and Tory M.P., Manning studied at Harrow and Oxford. Abandoning a plan for a political career, he was ordained in the Church of England and instituted rector of Lavington in 1833. By the late 1830s he became intensely interested in church policy, published a number of sermons and tracts, and rose rapidly in rank to archdeacon of Chichester in 1840. Although a leader of the **High Church** party, he was not clearly associated with the Oxford Movement. His fear of growing Erastianism within the established church led to his resignation in 1850. In the following year he was received into the Roman church.

Manning was soon ordained a Catholic priest and went to study theology in Rome. On his return to England he worked for eight years among London's poor. Although he lost influential Anglican friends by his defection, he made a favorable impression at the Vatican. In 1865, through the direct intervention of Rome, he was consecrated as the second archbishop of Westminster.

Manning's rapid rise within the Roman church evoked suspicion that he was overly ambitious, as depicted in Lytton Strachey's *Eminent Victorians* (1918). His austere manner and his ultramontane views also made for hostility in many intellectual and religious circles. No one, however, could doubt his devotion to duty nor his administrative success in both maintaining order within his clergy and keeping the allegiance of the Catholic working classes. The latter was achieved by aggressively expanding Catholic primary education and urging temperance and other measures to improve the moral and social environment. He was also sensitive to the Irish community, who formed a large element in urban congregations.

By the 1880s it was clear that Manning was interested in more than merely the Catholic poor. He became an outspoken advocate of social reform and (with the possible exception of women's rights) of the socially oppressed. He urged more government support for edu-cation and increased state intervention to correct social ills.

Manning particularly supported the labor movement, as in his published lecture, *The Dignity and Rights of Labour* (1874). He favored extending the franchise to all classes and strongly supported both urban and rural trade unionism. He was a major figure in settling the London dock strike of 1889.

Throughout his career as a Catholic leader, Manning was hostile to rationalism and criticized the more liberal theological attitudes of such respected figures as Cardinal Newman. Nonetheless, in his social concerns he was universally regarded as one of the nation's most progressive religious leaders.

PAUL T. PHILLIPS

Bibliography

Gray, Robert. *Cardinal Manning: A Biography.* 1985.

Leslie, Shane. *Henry Edward Manning. His Life and Labours.* 1921.

McClelland, Vincent Alan. *Cardinal Manning: His Public Life and Influence, 1865-1892.* 1962.

Norman, Edward. *The English Catholic Church in the Nineteenth Century.* 1984.

Purcell, Edmund S. *The Life of Cardinal Manning, Archbishop of Westminster.* 1895.

· · · · ·

MARRIAGE LAW

Matrimonial law underwent great changes during the nineteenth century. It became more secular, as Parliament created provisions for civil marriage and **divorce**. Married women achieved greater legal status, particularly with regard to their property, and fathers lost their exclusive right to custody of their children. Victorian jurists also tried to ease the plight of working-class women by allowing local magistrates' courts to issue judicial separations.

Civil marriage (as distinguished from marriage before a clergyman) became possible only in 1836. As in ecclesiastical law, in order to be valid an English marriage had to be publicized, solemnized in the presence of a minister or civil registrar, and be between persons outside the prohibited degrees of kinship, whether by birth or by marriage. (Marriage law differed in Scotland; an exchange of vows was sufficient to solemnize a marriage.) There were nearly annual efforts to abolish one of the prohibited degrees by authorizing marriage with a deceased wife's sister.

Ecclesiastical law also governed divorce proceedings prior to 1857. Until that year marriage was, for all intents and purposes, indissoluble, although the ecclesiastical courts could nullify marriages and grant separations. The ecclesiastical court also issued writs for the restitution of conjugal rights, which ordered a spouse to return to cohabitation or face ecclesiastical censure and imprisonment by the civil authorities.

In 1857 the Divorce and Matrimonial Causes Act created the Probate and Divorce Court in London which took over many functions of the ecclesiastical courts. A new provision allowed divorce for the adultery of a wife, or for a husband's adultery combined with cruelty, bigamy, incest, or bestiality. The act authorized local magistrates' courts to grant protection orders (judicial separations) to deserted wives too poor to apply to the Divorce Court, and subsequent acts created additional grounds for such separations.

Marriage significantly affected the legal status of women. Under the common-law doctrine of coverture, when a woman married she lost her independent legal personality as a *feme sole* and became a *feme couvert*. Her legal existence was subsumed in that of her husband. The rich avoided many of these legal disabilities by marriage settlements that gave women their "separate property" or "separate estate." Passage of the **Married Women's Property** Acts of 1870 and 1882 finally gave all married women the right to their own property.

A husband was obligated to support his wife, but this obligation was only enforceable if the wife entered the workhouse.

Under the common law a father's right to custody of his legitimate children was absolute. (Mothers had custody of children born out of wedlock.) By the Custody Act of 1839 a mother gained the right to petition the Court of Chancery for access to her minor children and custody of her children under seven years, which was raised to sixteen in 1878.

Only in 1886 did mothers gain the right to custody of their children upon the death of the father.

Despite substantial changes during the Victorian period, marriage law continued to grant more rights to men than to women at the turn of the century. The grievances most strongly voiced by legal reformers were the unequal grounds for divorce for men and women, and the fact that divorce was granted only for adultery and not for other marital faults.

MARY LYNDON SHANLEY

Bibliography

Bodichon, Barbara Leigh Smith. *A Brief Summary, in Plain Language, of the Most Important Laws of England Concerning Women.* 3d rev. ed. 1869.

Graveson, R. H. and F. R. Crane, eds. *A Century of Family Law, 1857–1957.* 1957.

Reiss, Erna. *The Rights and Duties of Englishwomen.* 1934.

Shanley, Mary Lyndon. *Feminism, Marriage and the Law in Victorian England 1850–1895.* 1989.

Waddilove, Alfred. *The Laws of Marriage, and the Laws of Divorce of England.* 1864.

See also SCOTS LAW

. . . . .

MARRIED WOMEN'S PROPERTY

The Married Women's Property Acts of 1870 and 1882 constituted a major change in women's rights under English law, giving every married woman for the first time the right to hold property in her own name.

Under the common law, when a woman married her legal status was absorbed in that of her husband. This suspension of the married woman's legal personality was known as "coverture." An unmarried woman was known in the law as a *feme sole* (a "single" woman), a married woman as a *feme couvert* (a "covered" woman). William Blackstone's *Commentaries on the Laws of England* gave the rationale for this rule: if husband and wife were "one body" before God, they were "one person" in the law, and that person was represented by the husband. This was sometimes referred to as the doctrine of spousal unity.

Under coverture, when a woman married her husband took possession of all her personal property (property other than land). This included any money she had saved before marriage and any wages she earned while married. A husband did not take absolute possession of his wife's real property (land); he could not sell it or leave it to anyone in his will. But he owned all rents or other income from it, and it was under his management.

Other consequences of coverture were that a married woman could not sue or be sued, could not sign contracts, and could not make a valid will unless her husband joined her in these actions.

Equity (another branch of English law) provided a way for rich women to avoid the consequences of coverture. They could establish trusts, which were known as a married woman's "separate property" or "separate estate." A wife with a separate estate could receive the income from her lands or investments, sue or be sued with respect to her separate estate, make her estate liable for her debts, and leave her estate to whomever she chose, just as if she were a *feme sole*. In the nineteenth century only about one in ten English wives had separate estates.

The first campaign to pass a law giving wives the same property rights as *feme soles* and men took place while Parliament was considering the Divorce Act of 1857. It was led by Barbara Leigh Smith (later Mme. Bodichon), and resulted in a clause being added to the Divorce Act authorizing magistrates to issue orders giving deserted wives *feme sole* rights over their property.

Repeated efforts from 1868 to 1882 were led by a Married Women's Property Committee headed by **Elizabeth Wolstenholme Elmy** (secretary) and **Ursula Mellor Bright** (treasurer). The Married Women's Property Act of 1870 was a partial measure which gave married women the right to possess the wages they earned after marriage, money invested in certain specified ways (including savings banks), and legacies of less than 200 pounds. All other property, however, still belonged to the husband. The Married Women's Property Act of 1882 gave a married woman possession of all the property she held before and after marriage as her "separate estate."

While they revolutionized the law of property, the Married Women's Property Acts did not abolish other aspects of coverture: a married woman could not have a legal residence apart from her husband, spouses could not sue one another for tort, and (since they were "one person") husband and wife could not be held to have conspired together. Nonetheless the Married Women's Property Acts were a major step in procuring equal legal rights for women.

MARY LYNDON SHANLEY

Bibliography

Holcombe, Lee. *Wives and Property: Reform of the Married Women's Property Law in Nineteenth-Century England.* 1983.

Reiss, Erna. *The Rights and Duties of English-women.* 1934.

Wharton, John J. S. *An Exposition of the Laws Relating to the Women of England.* 1853.

· · · · ·

MARRYAT, FLORENCE (1838-1899)

Popular writer and spiritualist Florence Marryat Church Lean was also an actress, operatic singer, playwright, entertainer, traveler, and the editor of *London Society* from 1872 to 1876. One of her specialties was the **sensation novel**, of which *Love's Conflict* (1865) was her first.

Marryat was the youngest of eleven children of author and naval officer **Frederick Marryat**. Omnivorous reading and a number of governesses supplied her education. She married twice: in 1878 she divorced Captain Ross Church (by whom she had eight children) to marry Colonel Francis Lean the following year.

Marryat produced fifty-seven novels and many volumes of journalistic work, short stories, poems, essays, lectures, plays, and ghost stories. Titles such as *Woman Against Woman* (1865), *"Gup": Sketches of Anglo-Indian Life and Character* (1868), *Her Lord* and Master (1871), *The Life and Letters of Captain Marryat* (1872), *A Little Stepson* (1878), *Her World Against a Lie* (1879), *Peeress and Player* (1883), *The Master Passion* (1886), *A Daughter of the Tropics* (1887), *A Scarlet Sin* (1890), and *How Like a Woman* (1891) indicate the range of her interests—interests weighted heavily toward women, passion, and marriage.

In *There Is No Death* (1891) and *The Spirit World* (1894), Marryat expounded her belief in **spiritualism** as a means of communication between the living and the dead. Helen Black, a contemporary, alleged that the power of *There Is No Death* showed "many people . . . the truth of spiritualism" and "won converts by the hundreds." Even scholars, scientists, and clergymen, in Black's phrase, "succumbed" to Marryat's "courageous assertions."

As a popular writer, Marryat's sensation novels expressed the New Woman's more aggressive and less angelic feelings about marriage and money; as a "queen" of the circulating libraries during the last quarter of the century, she touched a responsive chord in women who avidly read her works. In her writing on spiritualism, Marryat went beyond the merely fascinating rapping and tapping of the séance to describe a religion that provided a haven for the oppressed and a promise of future life.

VANESSA D. DICKERSON

Bibliography

Black, Helen. *Notable Women Authors of the Day.* 1893.

Furniss, Harry. *Some Victorian Women: Good, Bad, and Indifferent.* 1923.

Showalter, Elaine. *A Literature of Their Own: British Women Novelists from Brontë to Lessing.* 1977.

. . . . .

MARRYAT, FREDERICK
(1792-1848)

In 1830 Captain Frederick Marryat resigned from the navy, and drawing on twenty-four years of sea experience, turned to writing action-packed stories. Several appeared serially in the *Metropolitan Magazine*, which he edited (1832-1836), and the popularity of such sea stories as *Peter Simple* (1834) and *Mr. Midshipman Easy* (1836) survived into the twentieth century. Marryat's novels clearly show the influence of eighteenth-century novelists, especially Tobias Smollett; in turn, there are similarities between his works and those of his younger friend, Charles Dickens.

Although a prolific writer, Marryat barely supported his taste for fashionable living—and he was restless. *A Diary in America* (1839), based on a two-year journey there, proved financially disappointing and offended Americans, but his popular novels continued to appear. Retiring with his children to his Norfolk estate in 1843 (he and Charlotte Marryat had separated in 1839), Marryat wrote serious, didactic novels for juveniles, including *The Settlers in Canada* (1844) and *The Little Savage* (1848-1849). In eighteen years Marryat produced nonfiction and dramas along with almost two dozen novels.

Action is the core of the Marryat novel, though plots are often weak, but most memorable are his Dickensian caricatures, like Mr. Cophagus in *Japhet in Search of a Father* (1836) or Smallbones in *Snarleyyow, or the Dog Fiend* (1837). Though no masterpieces, his novels were justly praised by Virginia Woolf in 1935 for their craftsmanship, their style, and the sense of a real and ordinary world they conveyed. In the early Victorian period, Marryat vivified and modified some of the best literary qualities of his predecessors, Defoe, Smollett, and Fielding.

KENNETH A. ROBB

Bibliography

Marryat, Florence. *Life and Letters of Captain Marryat.* 1872.

Vann, J. Don. *Victorian Novels in Serial.* 1985.

Warner, Oliver. *Captain Marryat: A Rediscovery.* 1953.

Woolf, Virginia. "The Captain's Death Bed." In *Virginia Woolf, The Captain's Death Bed, and Other Essays.* 1950.

. . . . .

MARSH, ANNE
(1791–1874)

Anne Marsh was a domestic novelist best known for "The Admiral's Daughter" (1834) and *Emilia Wyndham* (1846).

Daughter of lawyer James Caldwell, wife of failed banker Arthur C. Marsh, and mother of seven children, Marsh published "The Admiral's Daughter" at the urging of Harriet Martineau. The story of a young woman's adultery, which was issued anonymously at her husband's insistence, became an immediate success. Marsh subsequently produced over twenty novels, stories, and translations. She became known as Anne Marsh-Caldwell in 1858 when she succeeded to the family property.

Marsh helped establish the respectability of the English novel. Her essay on domestic realism argues that the novel should be based on believable characters and on plots that connect causes and consequences. Rejecting romantic concepts of femininity and satiric stereotypes of the nagging wife, Marsh presents a womanly ideal emphasizing patience, gentleness, and perseverance. Instead of seeking adventure, heroines like the high-minded Emilia Wyndham must endure the wearisome struggles of daily existence. The suffering of the heroines often serves to criticize the way men could abuse their power within the domestic framework of the family. Marsh enjoyed considerable popularity, but her novels became increasingly conventional, and the promise of her early work was never fulfilled.

ROBIN SHEETS

Bibliography

Cruse, Amy. *The Victorians and Their Reading.* 1936.

Colby, Vineta. *Yesterday's Woman: Domestic Realism in the English Novel.* 1974.

Mitchell, Sally, *The Fallen Angel: Chastity, Class and Women's Reading, 1835–1880.* 1981.

Oliphant, Margaret. "Modern Novelists—Great and Small." *Blackwood's*, vol. 87, pp. 554–568.

$\cdot$ $\cdot$ $\cdot$ $\cdot$ $\cdot$

MARTINEAU, HARRIET
(1802–1876)

Among the most influential and prolific journalists of her time, Harriet Martineau proselytized for laissez-faire economics, the abolition of slavery, sexual equality, and universal education. Her writing also reveals the movement of a balanced and widely read mind from Unitarianism to necessarianism and ultimately to positivism. Her writing remains of value for its lucid, if opinionated, presentation of the ideas of her age and for its cameralike observations of the details of everyday life.

Born the sixth of eight children of a Norwich manufacturer, Martineau was early troubled by parental coldness and by increasing deafness; her experiences are recorded in *Household Education* (1849) and in her posthumously published *Autobiography* (written in 1855; published in 1877). Her childhood experiences and later ill health led her to theorize about child raising and the care of the sick and handicapped in the autobiographical works and in such others as "Letter to the Deaf" (1834) and *Life in the Sick-Room* (1844). The failure of her family's business forced Martineau to work and intensified her interest in the economic and educational disabilities of women, already evident in her earliest published essays, "On Female Education" and "Female Writers on Practical Divinity" (*The Monthly Repository*, 1822 and 1823).

Occasional invalidism and financial problems did not keep Martineau from extensive travel. She wrote most significantly about the United States in *Society in America* (1837) and *Retrospect of Western Travel* (1838). Travels in Egypt, Syria, and Palestine are recorded in *Eastern Life, Present and Past* (1848), which shocked contemporaries by its rejection of conventional religion. These books also bring commonplace Victorian activities vividly to life, as do "A Month at Sea" (*Penny Magazine*, 1837) and the three volumes she wrote for Charles Knight's *Guide to Service: The Maid of All Work* (1838), *The Lady's Maid* (1838), and *The Housemaid* (1839).

In her own time, however, these works were considered secondary to her twenty-five volume *Illustrations of Political Economy*

(1832–1834), the first source of her fame; *The History of England from the Commencement of the Nineteenth Century to the Crimean War* (completed work published 1864); and her translation of *The Positive Philosophy of Auguste Comte* (1853), which Comte himself had translated back into French to supersede existing editions.

Martineau was also known for prolific contribution to journals and newspapers including the *Daily News, Edinburgh Review, Household Words, Monthly Repository, People's Journal,* and *Westminster Review.* Her weakest writing appears in her novels: *Deerbrook* (1839) and *The Hour and the Man* (1841) suffer from expository and didactive weaknesses common to the lesser contemporaries of Jane Austen, upon whose fiction Martineau modeled her own.

BETTY RICHARDSON

Bibliography

Arbuckle, Elisabeth S., ed. *Harriet Martineau's Letters to Fanny Wedgwood.* 1983.

Pichanick, Valerie Kossew. *Harriet Martineau: The Woman and Her Work, 1802–76.* 1980.

Postlethwaite, Diana. *Making It Whole: A Victorian Circle and the Shape of Their World.* 1985.

Webb, Robert K. *Harriet Martineau: A Radical Victorian.* 1960.

. . . . .

MARTINEAU, JAMES
(1805–1900)

A Unitarian minister and religious philosopher thought by Gladstone to be the "greatest living English thinker," James Martineau brought English **Unitarianism** from Priestleyan rationalism and necessarianism to the verge of transcendentalism. *Types of Ethical Theory* (1885), *A Study of Religion* (1888), and *The Seat of Authority in Religion* (1890) are late summaries of a life's work which began with *A Rationale of Religious Inquiry* (1836) and developed through academic lectures and articles in the *Westminster Review,* the *Prospective Review,* and the *National Review.*

Born in Norwich, the son of a cloth manufacturer of Huguenot ancestry (and the brother of **Harriet Martineau**), he was educated by J. Lant Carpenter, disciple of Priestley and Hartley, and at Manchester College, of which he was later principal. Martineau taught that the Bible is an historical document and Christ the human manifestation of the Platonic ideality of God. He saw humankind as innately both scientific and religious, and worship as a natural function of the moral and aesthetic faculties.

While Martineau added nothing to the outstanding Unitarian record on social issues, Unitarianism, which he saw as one "dialect" in a universal religious language, was strengthened by his intellectual pluralism and emotional appeal. To many with Darwinian doubts it became (in Erasmus Darwin's words) "a featherbed for falling Christians."

SHELAGH HUNTER

Bibliography

Carpenter, J. Estlin. *James Martineau, Theologian and Teacher: A Study of his Life and Thought.* 1905.

Chadwick, Owen. *The Victorian Church,* vol. 1. 1966.

Drummond, James and C. B. Upton. *The Life and Letters of James Martineau.* 1902.

Holt, Raymond V. *The Unitarian Contribution to Social Progress in England.* 1938.

Howe, Daniel. *The Unitarian Conscience: Harvard Moral Philosophy 1805–1861.* 1970.

McLachlan, Herbert. *The Unitarian Movement in the Religious Life of England: Its Contribution to Thought and Learning, 1700–1900.* 1934.

. . . . .

MARX, ELEANOR
(1855–1898)

The youngest daughter of Karl Marx and his most politically conscious child, Eleanor Marx was active in the English labor movement in the years when it was first emerging to institutional maturity.

Following an abortive attempt at an acting

career, she embraced socialist politics at the time of her father's death in 1884, entering at the same time into a free-love union with the socialist, secularist, and freethinker Dr. Edward Aveling, who shared her political interests. With Aveling and others she founded the Socialist League, an organization that aimed at the "realization of complete revolutionary socialism" in England (1884). Turning from the league following its takeover by anarchists in the late 1880s, she devoted her efforts to the new unionism of the period. Convinced that unskilled workers needed broad-based unions with militant, class-conscious programs, she drafted the General Statement of Aims of the Gasworkers and General Labourers Union (1889). She formed the union's first women's branch, led a strike of women rubber workers in London's East End, and helped typists and tailoresses to organize. She organized the first English May Day celebration in 1890 and initiated agitation for the eight-hour day.

Eleanor Marx also edited several of her father's minor works and translated socialist and literary classics into English. With Aveling, she coauthored several books and essays on the labor movement in England and America. Their most important work was an early analysis of socialist feminism: *The Woman Question* (1886).

Unfortunately Eleanor Marx is most often remembered as European socialism's most famous tragic heroine rather than as a serious contributor. Her suicide on March 31, 1898 was directly attributable to her troubled personal life with Aveling, and became the basis for George Bernard Shaw's *The Doctor's Dilemma* (1906) as well as for more recent novels of which the researcher should be wary. Contemporaries and biographers have shared the sense that she did not live up to the promise of her birth.

MARIE MARMO MULLANEY

Bibliography

Ellis, Havelock. "Eleanor Marx." *Adelphi*, vol. 10, 11 (n.s.), pp. 342–352, 33–41.

———. "Eleanor Marx." *The Modern Monthly*, vol. 9, pp. 283–295.

Kapp, Yvonne. *Eleanor Marx.* 1972–1976. 2 vols.

Mullaney, Marie Marmo. *Revolutionary Women: Gender and the Socialist Revolutionary Role.* 1983.

Rosebury, Aaron. "Eleanor, Daughter of Karl Marx: Personal Reminiscences." *Monthly Review*, vol. 24, no. 8, pp. 29–49.

See also SOCIALISM
· · · · ·

MATCHWORKERS

In July 1888, 1,400 matchgirls employed by Bryant and May's London factory walked off the job. Their strike, led by the firebrand and socialist **Annie Besant**, provided employers across Britain, as well as the trade union movement, with a powerful example of the potential of organized women workers. The matchgirls' strike signaled the emergence of new unionism, a groundswell of labor activism by unskilled workers who had been ignored by the older unions.

Because the match-making industry was a major employer of women and because Bryant and May's factory offered a flagrant example of industry abuses, the matchgirls received special attention. In June 1888 Annie Besant, then editor of a leftist newspaper, the *Link*, launched an investigation and published her findings in a series of sensational articles. Public outrage ensued, as did the retaliatory firings of three matchgirls who had provided Besant with information.

The matchgirls' grievances resembled those of women in many other industries: inadequate wages, an elaborate system of punitive fines which further reduced their pay, and a dangerous work environment. In particular, the matchgirls complained of "phossy jaw" or necrosis, which resulted from phosphorous contamination and produced a deterioration of the jaw and the loss of teeth.

The matchgirls had previously struck in the autumn of 1885, but the attempt failed. Angered over the dismissal of their co-workers, approximately fifty of the women marched to the offices of the *Link* and asked for guidance. Besant helped them organize a union, raised contributions for its strike fund, aroused public sympathy, and negotiated a triumphant end to the strike.

Though phosphorous contamination remained a problem until Parliament prohibited its use twenty years later, the strike won higher wages, some improvement in working conditions, and assurance from the employers that no one would be punished for striking. The action by the women of Bryant and May's encouraged other unskilled workers to organize. New unionism, ushered in by the matchgirls, came of age the following year with dramatic and successful strikes by the London dock workers and gasworkers.

DONNA PRICE PAUL

Bibliography

Lewenhak, Sheila. *Women and Trade Unions: An Outline History of Women in the British Trade Union Movement.* 1977.

Nethercot, Arthur H. *The First Five Lives of Annie Besant.* 1960.

Stafford, Ann. *A Match to Fire the Thames.* 1961.

· · · · ·

MATHEMATICS

At the start of the Victorian period, British mathematics was emerging from a long spell of isolation from European developments and consequent stagnation. By the period's end mathematicians in England were contributing new work across the entire face of the discipline. In addition, the practice of mathematics passed in this period from the hands of amateurs into those of professionals who held academic positions.

Early in the century Britain was still bedeviled by overtones of the controversy between Newton and Leibniz concerning the creation of the calculus. It took energetic proselytizing by the Analytical Society at Cambridge, largely consisting of undergraduates, to pass beyond the question of historical justice to that of mathematical understanding. The members of the society did not admit Leibniz's claims to priority, but endorsed his notation as more transparent than Newton's. George Peacock (1791–1858), in particular, continued the work of the society in his later career and helped to raise the level of mathematical pedagogy.

Thanks to the society's efforts, the level of British mathematics was improving by the beginning of Victoria's reign. The work of Arthur Cayley (1821–1895) and James Joseph Sylvester (1814–1897) furnishes many examples. Cayley was placed in a category of his own by his college examiners, but left Cambridge over the issue of having to take holy orders. He was called to the bar and practiced for fourteen years, but nevertheless published over two hundred mathematical papers in that period. While practicing law, Cayley met Sylvester, who, because he was a Jew, had not been given a degree at Cambridge or been eligible to compete for the prestigious Smith's prizes. Although Sylvester was elected a fellow of the Royal Society at the age of twenty-five, he found it impossible to obtain a permanent position and, like Cayley, turned to the bar.

Ultimately both men found academic positions, Cayley as Sadlerian professor at Cambridge in 1863 and Sylvester at the Royal Military Academy in Woolwich. Even then, however, he was not the first choice of the electors and was superannuated at the early age of fifty-six. He then went to Johns Hopkins University, where he gave the nascent American mathematical community a figure of international reputation until he was lured back to England to become Savilian professor of geometry at the age of seventy.

Much of the work by Cayley and Sylvester opened up new areas of mathematics. Cayley remains one of the monuments of mathematical productivity, the author of 966 papers. In addition to working on the fashionable mathematical topics of the day, he founded the theory of abstract groups and is known for one of its basic theorems. Both he and Sylvester worked in the general areas known as graph theory and combinatorics; Cayley appears to have been the first mathematician to use the term "tree" in print technically, and Sylvester the first to use "graph" in the sense of graph theory. Both used and acknowledged the work of the French mathematician Camille Jordan, an indication that British mathematicians felt part of an international community as they had not during the previous generation.

Much of the influential British work in mathematics took place in algebra. William Rowan Hamilton (1805–1865) developed the theory of quaternions to generalize the behavior of complex numbers. **George Boole**

(1815–1864) took some of the ideas of Augustus DeMorgan (1806–1871) on logic and combined them with algebra as presented by Peacock to produce an algebra of logic of continued use. Both Cayley and Sylvester worked in the area of invariant theory, the study of polynomial expressions that are left unchanged by transformations. Although much of their work now seems to be the product of a misdirected enthusiasm for calculation, among its results are the theory of matrices and linear algebra. William Kingdom Clifford (1845–1879) had already made contributions to the study of noncommutative algebras by his early death.

The borderline between recreational mathematics and respectable topics had not yet been laid down in this period, and lawyers and clergymen took part in discussions with professional mathematicians. The *Educational Times* ran a column (starting in 1862) featuring mathematical problems, and contributions came in from all over the country. One of the best known of recreational mathematicians was Charles Lutwidge Dodgson (1832–1898), whose enthusiasm for puzzles peppers the Alice books. Although he wrote sparingly on the subject of electoral reform, his proposals suggest an understanding of the theory of voting procedures beyond that of his contemporaries. His technical works on the theory of determinants and geometry have more of the journeyman about them. The four-color conjecture (any map in the plane can be colored with at most four colors with the proviso that adjacent regions be colored differently) was a problem in recreational mathematics that grew into a focus of attention for the next century.

Before the Victorian period there was no distinction between mathematical and more general scientific or even literary societies. In 1864 the foundation of the London University Mathematical Society (changed the next year to the London Mathematical Society) offered the first forum for mathematical discussions alone. It began with a number of lawyers among its membership, but time brought an increasingly professional air to its ranks. The society's meetings and publications could be used as a medium for attacking some of the entrenched attitudes at Cambridge (the examination system, in particular), which were seen as standing in the way of further progress.

During the Victorian era British mathematics was rescued from the doldrums of the previous century and British mathematicians elevated to a level of international recognition unknown since Newton. This success was in some measure the result of looking for new areas of study rather than simply following European directions of research. The mathematical developments in Britain passed from the hands of amateurs to those of professionals, and the academic world found space for those whose work had gained an international reputation.

THOMAS L. DRUCKER

Bibliography

Ball, Walter William Rouse. *A History of the Study of Mathematics at Cambridge.* 1889.

Dauben, Joseph. *The History of Mathematics from Antiquity to the Present: A Selective Bibliography.* 1985.

Macfarlane, Alexander. *Lectures on Ten British Mathematicians of the Nineteenth Century.* 1916.

May, Kenneth O. *Bibliography and Research Manual of the History of Mathematics.* 1973.

Mehrtens, Herbert et al., eds. *Social History of Nineteenth-Century Mathematics.* 1981.

Young, Laurence. *Mathematicians and Their Times.* 1981.

See also BABBAGE, CHARLES; LOGIC; LOVELACE, ADA; SOMERVILLE, MARY

· · · · ·

MAURICE, FREDERICK DENISON (1805–1872)

Frederick Denison Maurice was a prominent clergyman, educator, and theologian during the mid-Victorian era. Associated in the popular mind with the **Broad Church** movement, Maurice denied that label and objected to all party divisions in the church. Most of his writing was theological, including

The Kingdom of Christ (1838; second edition, much revised, 1842), *Theological Essays* (1853), *What Is Revelation?* (1859), *Sequel to the Inquiry, What Is Revelation?* (1860), *The Claims of the Bible and of Science* (1863), *The Conscience* (1868), and *Social Morality* (1869). Organizations he founded include the Cambridge Apostles, the Christian socialist movement, Queen's College for women, and the Working Men's College. His literary associations included John Stuart Mill, Thomas Carlyle, and Alfred Tennyson. Charles Kingsley, John Malcolm Ludlow, and Thomas Hughes were among his disciples.

Raised in a family divided by religious difference, Maurice sought grounds for unity among all people. Unwilling to subscribe to Anglican doctrine after passing out in civil law at Cambridge, he left the university without a degree (1826), and after a difficult period in which he wrote his anonymous novel *Eustace Conway* (1828-1830; published 1834) and determined the future course of his life he entered Oxford (1830) to prepare for ordination in the Church of England. Following his ordination (1834) and a brief period in a rural parish, he moved to London (1836). He resided there until he returned to Cambridge as a professor (1866), where he died in 1872. In 1837 he married Anna Barton (1810-1845), the sister-in-law of John Sterling. Her early death left him to raise their two sons, John Frederick (1841-1912) and Edmund (1843-1926). In 1849 he married Georgiana Hare (1809-1890), the half-sister of Julius Hare.

Maurice's theology emphasized humanity's utter need for God and for recognition of a shared bond with all human beings, who perceive their fellows as threats from whom they are alienated rather than as creatures with whom they can identify as brothers and sisters. According to Maurice, human nature was misrepresented both by the Calvinists and utilitarians, who underrated it, and by the romantic idealists, who overrated it.

Maurice's public life was an ongoing attempt to convince others of his views by his actions as well as by his preaching and writing. As early as the publication of *The Kingdom of Christ* (1838), in which he sought to clarify common ground among all Christians, the conservative religious press began an attack that continued throughout the rest of his career. The attack intensified in 1848, when Maurice, Kingsley, and Ludlow founded the Christian socialist movement in an attempt to provide a safety valve for disappointed workers after the Chartist movement had failed. Maurice intended the movement to make Christians aware of their social responsibilities and socialists aware of values they shared with Christians. Elements of the religious press charged that Maurice was consorting with infidels and fomenting revolution.

Controversy erupted again with the publication of *Theological Essays* (1853), in which Maurice argued that the terms "eternal life" and "eternal death" in the New Testament referred to qualities of life, not to duration of time. Thus he held that the doctrine of unending torment for sinners had no basis in scripture. His adversaries, apparently in the belief that the working class would go berserk if unrestrained by fear of everlasting hell, had him dismissed from his professorship at King's College (1853). In the following year he founded the Working Men's College, one of his most successful undertakings, which made adult-level liberal education available to many otherwise deprived of it.

His remaining years in London were marked by controversies with Henry Longueville Mansel (in which Maurice argued against what he saw as Mansel's reduction of the Bible to a set of rules) and with Bishop John William Colenso. His last years, however, were largely free of controversy, and his appointment as Knightsbridge professor at Cambridge was widely approved.

While Maurice was one of the most controversial clerics of his time, he was also one of the most influential. Often misunderstood, he was much closer to the thinking of such literary figures as Mill, Carlyle, John Ruskin, Tennyson, and Matthew Arnold than were the Evangelicals or the Tractarians. Still relatively neglected by literary historians, he has been studied with much interest by theologians and church historians.

E. CLEVE WANT

Bibliography

Allen, Peter. *The Cambridge Apostles: The Early Years.* 1978.

Brose, Olive J. *Frederick Denison Maurice: Rebellious Conformist.* 1971.

Christensen, Torben. *The Divine Order: A Study in F. D. Maurice's Theology.* 1973.

———. *Origin and History of Christian Socialism 1848–54.* 1962.

Davies, W. Merlin. *An Introduction to F. D. Maurice's Theology.* 1964.

Maurice, Frederick, ed. *The Life of Frederick Denison Maurice Chiefly Told in His Own Letters.* 1884.

McClain, Frank Mauldin. *Maurice: Man and Moralist.* 1972.

Ramsey, Arthur Michael. *F. D. Maurice and the Conflicts of Modern Theology.* 1951.

Sanders, Charles Richard. *Coleridge and the Broad Church Movement: Studies in S. T. Coleridge, Dr. Arnold of Rugby, J. C. Hare, Thomas Carlyle and F. D. Maurice.* 1942.

Vidler, Alec R. *F. D. Maurice and Company: Nineteenth Century Studies.* 1966.

———. *The Theology of F. D. Maurice.* 1948.

Wood. H. G. *Frederick Denison Maurice.* 1950.

See also CHRISTIAN SOCIALISM; THEOLOGY

. . . . .

MAXWELL, JAMES CLERK (1831–1879)

The greatest theoretical physicist of the nineteenth century, James Clerk Maxwell made important contributions to many areas including the study of color vision, thermodynamics, electromagnetic field theory, and the statistical theory of gases. His most brilliant achievement was the *Treatise on Electricity and Magnetism* (1873), a landmark in the history of science.

Maxwell was born in Edinburgh in the year Michael Faraday announced his discovery of electromagnetic induction, and was educated there and at Cambridge. He was appointed professor at Aberdeen in 1856, at King's College, London in 1860, and in 1871 became the first professor of experimental physics at Cambridge, where he organized the Cavendish Laboratory and where he died at age forty-eight. In his *Treatise* Maxwell mathematically analyzed Faraday's theory of electrical and magnetic forces. Maxwell adopted the notion of an all-pervading ether as the carrier of electromagnetic waves. Noting that the speed of electric current in wires was roughly the same as that of light in empty space, he suggested that light is an electromagnetic vibration. This was later confirmed experimentally by Heinrich Hertz. Maxwell's investigation of the statistical theory of gas molecule motions led him to enunciate his "demon" paradox, expressing the statistical nature of molecular processes.

Maxwell's work was characterized by deep physical intuition combined with formidable mathematical capacity. He wrote four books (including an edition of Henry Cavendish's electrical papers) and more than one hundred papers (the first published when he was fifteen). He was also known for his joint editorship with T. H. Huxley of the scientific entries in the famous ninth edition of the *Encyclopaedia Britannica* in the 1870s. Maxwell's mark on Victorian science was immediate, and his influence on subsequent physics has been immense, but it is now recognized that he had an exceptional grasp of many other subjects, notably the history and philosophy of science.

MICHAEL SHORTLAND

Bibliography

Campbell, Lewis and W. Garnett. *The Life of James Clerk Maxwell.* 1882.

Everitt, C. W. F. *James Clerk Maxwell: Physicist and Natural Philosopher.* 1975.

Harman, P. M. *Energy, Force, and Matter: the Conceptual Development of Nineteenth-Century Physics.* 1982.

Niven, W. D., ed. *The Scientific Papers of James Clerk Maxwell.* 1890. 2 vols.

Tolstoy, Ivan. *James Clerk Maxwell: A Biography.* 1982.

See also PHYSICS

. . . . .

MAYHEW, HENRY
(1812-1887)

Popular journalist, novelist, and social historian, Henry Mayhew is best known for his interviews with London workers in the "Labour and the Poor" series for the *Morning Chronicle* (1849-1850) and his subsequent interviews with London street folk (1851-1852), published as *London Labour and the London Poor* (1861-1862). He is also credited with being one of the founders of *Punch* (1842).

One of seven sons of a well-to-do solicitor, Mayhew made a precarious living as a journalist in early Victorian London, writing whatever might pay—popular farces, comic novels, educational books, and travel accounts. An apparently indolent man, he left unfinished all his social surveys of London workers and street folk, as well as his later survey of *The Criminal Prisons of London* (1862).

After a bankruptcy in 1846, he was essentially cut out of his father's will and his financial insecurities led to ruptures with his friend Douglas Jerrold, whose daughter Jane had married Mayhew in 1844. In 1849, asked by the *Morning Chronicle* editors to be the metropolitan correspondent for the "Labour and the Poor" series, he displayed astonishing energy, imagination, and talent in interviewing hundreds of skilled and unskilled workers about their working and living conditions. The record of these interviews, though unfinished, repetitious, hastily brought to press and therefore subject to error in individual fact and figure, is as a whole one of the most powerful pictures of working-class life produced in Victorian England. This effect is partly due to the methods Mayhew devised for publishing his interviews: he eliminated his questions and published each interview as if it were an autobiographical statement in the "voice" of the worker. And partly it is due to Mayhew's open-ended questions and his empathy with his subjects.

Contemporary readers as well as modern ones have enjoyed the resulting text, though from the beginning some have worried about the accuracy of individual statements. Used as a whole, however, Mayhew's social surveys give an unparalleled glimpse into London lower-class life at midcentury.

ANNE HUMPHERYS

Bibliography

Humpherys, Anne. *Henry Mayhew*. 1984.

———. *Travels Into the Poor Man's Country.* 1977.

Thompson, E. P. and Eileen Yeo. *The Unknown Mayhew*. 1971.

. . . . .

MECHANICS' INSTITUTES

Mechanics' institutes were established throughout Britain from the 1820s until midcentury with the aim of offering educational opportunities to artisans and skilled workers. They had their origins in the agitation of the physician George Birkbeck (1776-1841) who, while teaching in Glasgow in 1800, developed a scheme to satisfy what he termed "the intelligent curiosity of the unwashed artificers." After some moderate success in Scotland and the establishment of some libraries and the *Mechanics' Magazine* (in 1823), Birkbeck launched the London Mechanics' Institution in 1824 for any man able and willing to pay the one guinea annual subscription. Within two years over one hundred similar institutions had appeared, eighteen in the London area, about forty in the industrial north, and nearly thirty in Scotland.

By and large, the institutes failed in the sense that the intended constituency remained largely untouched. The subscriptions were too high, the lectures often inappropriate, and the twelve-hour workday deterred all but the most strongly motivated from using their free time for education. Perhaps most importantly, the institutes disintegrated in the clash of class values. Philanthropic industrialists hoped to provide workers with skills and disciplined work attitudes. Political and religious disputation was prohibited, socialist speakers banned, and radical texts weeded out of the institute libraries. The result was the establishment of rival organizations, often Owenite Halls of Science. Women were not admitted and this too led to fierce struggles: in 1830, after a prolonged fight over democratization in which female membership was one of the reforms demanded, the Manchester Mechanics' Institution broke up in disarray. When the mechanics' institutes did finally admit women in midcentury, it was to groom them, as one feminist complained, "for the duties of wife and servant."

The mechanics' institutes did, however, provide a second chance for elementary education to thousands of working people. Many of the buildings that housed the institutes have disappeared or been converted to other uses; some developed into modern polytechnics (Leeds, Preston, Liverpool, Huddersfield) or into university institutions (Birkbeck College, London, and the University of Manchester Institute of Science and Technology).

MICHAEL SHORTLAND

Bibliography

Cardwell, Donald S. L., ed. *Artisan to Graduate: Essays to Commemorate the Foundation in 1824 of the Manchester Mechanics' Institution.* 1974.

Harrison, J. F. C. *Learning and Living, 1790–1960.* 1961.

Inkster, Ian. "The Social Context of an Educational Movement: A Revisionist Approach to the English Mechanics' Institutes, 1820–1850." *Oxford Review of Education.* vol. 2, pp. 277–307.

Kelly, Thomas. *George Birkbeck: Pioneer of Adult Education,* 1957.

Russell, Colin. *Science and Social Change, 1700–1900.* 1983.

Shapin, Steven and Barry Barnes. "Science, Nature and Control: Interpreting Mechanics' Institutes." *Social Studies of Science,* vol. 7, pp. 31–74.

Simon, Brian. *The Two Nations and the Educational Structure, 1780–1870.* 1974.

Tylecote, Mabel. *The Mechanics' Institutes of Lancashire and Yorkshire Before 1851.* 1957.

See also EDUCATION, ADULT

· · · · ·

MEDICAL EDUCATION

Medical education became increasingly formal during the nineteenth century. Apprenticeship gradually lost ground to hospital medical schools and, later, to reformed university degrees in medicine. Even at the century's end, however, a variety of routes could still yield the qualifications necessary for placement on the medical register.

Medical practitioners had traditionally been trained either through the indentured apprenticeship customary for skilled trades or, less formally, as a doctor's "paying pupil." The Society of Apothecaries required a five-year apprenticeship. Most surgeons were also apprenticed. The Royal College of Physicians, on the other hand, admitted only those who had a university degree; until 1830 their licensing examination was conducted in Latin. Oxford and Cambridge medical degrees, however, concentrated on classics and theory; the English universities offered no practical instruction in anatomy and no clinical training. Edinburgh University, by contrast, had used Edinburgh Royal Infirmary as a teaching hospital since the eighteenth century and was known for providing the best medical education in the United Kingdom.

During the second quarter of the century, apprenticeship was increasingly supplemented or replaced by instruction in private medical schools (which often taught only a single subject, such as anatomy), by "walking the wards" of a hospital, and by study with crammers who prepared pupils for the various licensing examinations. There was no recognized prior qualification for medical study. Pupils and apprentices were often boys in their middle teens, and had a reputation for drunkenness, indecency, and brutality. The most notorious abuse associated with medical education, however, was pre-Victorian. Until 1832 dissection could be legally practiced only on the bodies of felons who had been hung. As anatomical study became more important, doctors and students entered into a growing illegal trade with "resurrectionists" or "body-snatchers" who followed funerals and kept an eye on churchyards for fresh graves. After the 1827 trial of William Burke and William Hare for murdering destitute persons in order to sell their bodies for dissection, the Anatomy Act (1832) licensed schools of anatomy, gave them access to all unclaimed bodies, and required Christian burial of the remains.

The Apothecaries Act of 1815 required that candidates "walk the wards" of a recognized hospital for at least six months. The **hospitals** themselves did not supervise training; students arranged to visit wards with a medical man on the hospital's staff. London's first true teaching hospital was Charing Cross, founded in 1821 to provide medical education; the care of charity patients was a secondary mission. Westminster Hospital opened a school of medicine in 1834.

Over the middle decades of the century, a system of medical training approaching its modern form began to develop. The University of London offered degrees in medicine from 1838; and University College (like Edinburgh) acquired a teaching hospital. St. Bartholomew's established a residential college for medical students in 1842. As medicine became scientific, additional subjects were added. By 1858 all of the London hospitals that took medical students required medicine and surgery. Various hospitals offered botany, medical jurisprudence, pathology, histology, opthalmic and dental surgery, pharmacy, and public health. Clinical practice in midwifery was available only at Guy's, which, furthermore, began in 1849 to appoint three senior pupils who had passed the licensing examination as "resident obstetric clerks." Other hospitals also started to award clinical clerkships on the basis of seniority and merit.

Other routes of entry into the profession, however, remained open. Although the Medical Act of 1858 established the General Medical Council with authority to certify which degrees and diplomas qualified the holder to be enrolled on the general register, some nineteen separate licensing bodies still offered examinations. Furthermore, the Medical Act only covered those practitioners who sought official registration; unlicensed medical practitioners could not be penalized unless they claimed a qualification to which they were not entitled.

After 1858, medical education was increasingly designed to produce safe general practitioners who could be considered gentlemen. Medical schools developed a sequence of courses arranged in logical order and gave more examinations. By 1900 medical students generally had a four- or five-year curriculum after they had passed an entrance examination which required the equivalent of a public school or grammar school education. In 1869, **Sophia Jex-Blake** and four other women were matriculated as medical students at Edinburgh University, but after their first year of study (when four of the five had won honors in physiology and chemistry) legal barriers were erected that prevented them from taking required courses. Because no other British medical school would admit women, sympathetic professors from several London schools agreed to teach at the London School of Medicine for Women which Jex-Blake organized in 1874. In 1876 the school was recognized by the Irish College of Physicians, which agreed to admit women candidates to its licensing examinations. In 1878 the University of London opened all degrees, including medicine, to women.

Extended schooling helped contribute to changes in the social status of medical practitioners over the course of the century. When apothecaries were apprenticed young, many had been the sons of shopkeepers and tradespeople. Some studies suggest that nineteenth-century surgeons came (like university-educated physicians) from upper middle-class backgrounds. The apprentice to a surgeon in a leading London hospital might pay as much as 1,000 pounds for his indenture. Nevertheless, applicants paid only 30 guineas to take the examination of the Royal College of Surgeons in 1830, while the diploma fee for the Royal College of Physicians was over 100 pounds. And by the time medical education was opened to women its cost had become a serious impediment. The writer of a series of articles on professions for women in 1898 pointed out that a license to practice medicine required a good secondary education, an additional five years of study—during which nothing could be earned—and fees of at least 200 pounds a year; furthermore, no scholarships or clerkships of any material value were available to women medical students.

SALLY MITCHELL

Bibliography

Jex-Blake, Sophia. *Medical Women: A Thesis and a History.* 1886; rpt. 1970.

Newman, Charles. *The Evolution of Medical Education in the Nineteenth Century.* 1957.

Youngson, A. J. *The Scientific Revolution in Victorian Medicine.* 1979.

· · · · ·

MEDICAL PRACTICE

Medicine was practiced in a variety of settings, with a variety of licenses or none at all. Medical practice was often based upon social rather than professional criteria, and the profits varied widely. No woman had a license to practice medicine until 1865; fewer than twenty women were qualified by 1890.

Before 1858 a person might practice with qualifications from any of nineteen different medical corporations or universities or with no license at all. The Royal College of Physicians, the Royal College of Surgeons, and the Apothecaries' Society claimed to control practice, but their powers were limited. The Medical Reform Act (1858) created the General Medical Council and defined the legal terms of medical practice, but even after 1858 unlicensed practice was permitted. Registered qualifications were required for those signing death certificates or holding government appointments. The Medical Reform Act (1886) allowed for a consolidation of medical licensing examinations.

Two models defined style of practice. The general practitioner (sometimes called "surgeon," "apothecary," or "apothecary-surgeon") usually saw the patient in the first instance, and treatment took the form of drugs, diet, rest, or (relatively rarely) surgery. The general practitioner might call in a consultant (a physician—an internist, in contemporary American parlance—or consulting surgeon), who applied presumably superior skills and experience to the case. With or without a general practitioner's recommendation, a patient might see a specialist, one of the burgeoning group of practitioners who claimed (legitimately or not) special knowledge of a disease or physical system and labeled themselves accordingly (as ophthalmologists, gynecologists, laryngologists, etc.). Outside the boundaries of government control, men and women practiced midwifery, herbalism, bonesetting, homeopathy, and other forms of unlicensed medical practice.

Medicine was practiced in a variety of settings, depending on the patient's social class. Among the upper and middle ranks of society, the doctor came into the patient's home for consultation and treatment. More typically, a practitioner had rooms in his residence set aside for medical practice (usually called his "surgery"). Poorer patients saw the medical man or woman in a variety of institutional settings. Fraternal groups and workingmen's clubs contracted with a medical practitioner to treat all members who paid the subscription fee (typically sixpence to one shilling a quarter). Doctors on the staffs of charity **hospitals** provided in- and outpatient care to patients without charge. (After 1880 some hospitals had paying patients as well.) Paupers could get medical attention at the Poor Law Infirmaries provided by the government.

Fees were based upon the practitioner's status and the patient's ability to pay. Charity practice aside, fees ranged from threepence to sixpence for the poorest patient to hundreds of pounds (or more) for an operation on a wealthy client. The lowest-paid practitioner might earn from 10 to 50 pounds a year from a salaried appointment under the Poor Law or a workingmen's "sick club," or possibly even less in a marginal private practice. The wealthiest earned thousands of pounds a year.

Medical practice was secured on the basis of connections: medical school teachers served as patrons to place junior practitioners in hospital posts and introduce them to potential patients. Practitioners also relied on family connections, patronage, religious or ethnic ties, purchase or partnership in an existing practice, or salaried medical employment as links to patients. Women were excluded from most institutional posts but, from the 1880s, were sought by missionary societies for service in India, where women patients refused to be examined by male physicians. Other physicians without the connections to secure patronage also found emigration an attractive option.

Successful medical practice could lead to wealth: incomes of 10,000 pounds or more a year were not unknown in Victorian England—nor were they common. Moderate success might mean an income of 700 pounds a year in the mid-to-late Victorian years, but this was a standard most did not meet, for the profession was overcrowded. Although medical practice was not an avenue to wealth, the occupation was relatively open, and for many it served as the bottom rung of the ladder up to the ranks of gentlemen.

M. JEANNE PETERSON

Bibliography

Bell, E. Moberley. *Storming the Citadel: The Rise of the Woman Doctor.* 1953.

Brand, Jeanne L. *Doctors and the State: The British Medical Profession and Government Action in Public Health, 1870–1912.* 1965.

Carr-Saunders, Alexander M. and Paul A. Wilson. *The Professions.* 1933; rpt. 1964.

Crowther, M. A. "Paupers or Patients? Obstacles to Professionalization in the Poor Law Medical Service Before 1914." *Journal of the History of Medicine and Allied Sciences,* vol. 39, pp. 33–54.

Current Work in the History of Medicine (quarterly bibliography).

Donnison, Jean. *Midwives and Medical Men: A History of Inter-Professional Rivalries and Women's Rights.* 1977.

Peterson, M. Jeanne. *The Medical Profession in Mid-Victorian London.* 1978.

See also APOTHECARIES;
MIDWIVES; SURGERY AND
SURGEONS

. . . . .

MEDICAL SCIENCE

The Victorian era witnessed unprecedented advances in medical science, yet during the early decades of Victoria's reign these advances were met with competition and bias because of existing theories and beliefs. It took decades of steady accumulation of new facts before old ways of thinking could be replaced with new concepts.

At the start of Victoria's reign the "good" that a physician could do was virtually limited to keeping the patient comfortable while nature worked a cure. Indeed, basing their therapeutics on heroic methods of purging and dosing with harsh and dangerous drugs, physicians perhaps more often made patients worse. Over the middle years of the Victorian era three significant advances in medical science took place: the bacterial theory of disease was confirmed; anesthetics and the antiseptic method revolutionized the practice of **surgery**; and the experimental method turned medicine into a science. In combination, these three changes made physicians far more able to prevent disease and alleviate its discomfort.

Contemporaries were not, however, easily convinced. A conceptual revolution was needed to pave the way for scientific advance. The adoption of the germ theory of disease is a case in point. During most of Victoria's reign the miasma theory of disease was dominant. It was based on the belief that noxious odors caused disease in persons who were susceptible because of moral or physical weakness. Belief in the evils of atmospheric corruption was a mixed blessing. It supplied motivation for the public health campaign spearheaded by sanitarians Edwin Chadwick and Southwood Smith, which concentrated on ridding the environment of dirt by building sewers, clearing slum housing, regulating water supplies, and closing urban burial grounds. This environmental campaign dramatically improved overall health conditions. Based on a misinformed theory, however, it actually accelerated the spread of cholera in London in 1848 and 1864, for when the sewers were flushed to lessen their smell the cholera virus was washed into rivers that supplied drinking water.

The politicization of an incorrect medical theory at the hands of Chadwick and Smith retarded acceptance of the bacterial theory of disease. During the first decades of Victoria's reign at least three eminent scientists published work associating microorganisms with **cholera.** William Farr (1807–1883), compiler of abstracts at the registrar-general's office, examined correlations between the incidence of cholera and a variety of factors such as land elevation, poverty, and the composition and source of drinking water. Beginning in 1854 he repeatedly published findings, illustrated with detailed tables, that linked specific sources of drinking water to increased incidence of cholera. These findings appeared in the annual reports of the registrar-general.

Another contribution to early documentation of the germ theory was made by William Budd (1811–1880). In 1849 Budd was appointed to the Microscopical Subcommitttee of the Bristol Medico-Surgical Society. He carefully and definitively manipulated the evacuations associated with cholera patients and identified what he called a fungus, which he believed was the cause of cholera. For several months during 1849 the topic was debated in the medical and lay press. The conclusion of this debate was that Budd's findings were not reliable. Finally, a superb epidemiological study by John Snow (1813–1858) conducted in 1849 traced the incidence of cholera in South London to water supplied by the Broad Street pump. Yet despite these well-publicized efforts by respected professionals, belief in miasmas prevailed. Claims that a single "fungus" could cause a specific disease were, to some, quackery.

Joseph Lister's career, which innovatively applied Pasteur's work to the healing of surgical wounds, was also hindered by those who believed in miasmas. Pasteur had been well known since 1855 for his discoveries regarding the existence of microorganisms and fermentation. It took Lister's "prepared mind," however, to apply these findings to medical practice. He confirmed, through a series of experiments, the existence of microorganisms and their relation to wound infection. Unlike many of his contemporaries, however, he believed them to be live entities. After trial and error Lister reported success in the healing of a compound fracture with the use of a phenol-based substance called carbolic acid. This led to his 1867 publication in the *Lancet* of the principles of what was to be called the "antiseptic method." Not until Lister's retirement in 1893, however, did his method become commonplace.

Given Lister's carefully written reports of laboratory findings and his results, why were more than twenty years of constant and repeated explanation necessary before his ideas were accepted? The primary reason was that Lister's method proposed a totally new approach to surgery. If live microorganisms on dressings caused infection and slowed healing, could not these same "bugs" exist on hands, surgeons' clothes, instruments, and so forth? If so, entire operating rooms plus their personnel would have to become "antiseptic." The idea was preposterous, given the prevailing miasma theory of disease and infection, which incriminated multiple causal factors.

In addition, Lister offended hospital administrators with published accusations against established practice. The misuse of carbolic acid caused some surgeons to damage wound

tissue and thus impede healing. Many noted contemporaries failed to share Lister's belief in the existence and importance of live microorganisms. The renowned surgeon James Simpson typified Lister's opposition. A respected innovator himself, Simpson is best known for his contributions in applying chloroform anesthesia to surgery. These were, in and of themselves, major advances in medical science. Simpson nonetheless held staunchly to the miasma theory and used his professional stature to ridicule Lister's method as a hoax. Documenting that infections increased in hospitals, Simpson bluntly concluded that ventilating hospital operating rooms would solve the problem.

The dominance of the miasma theory also threatened to hinder the advance of experimental medicine. The introduction of anesthesia in 1846 enabled anatomists to perform vivisection of animals and thus learn about basic physiology. The French and Germans preceded the English in accepting experimental medicine, and it was not until 1870 that the new scientific method gained a foothold in established English medical circles. The influence of a small group of European-trained physiologists began to break down the conservative program of medical education at English universities. J. S. B Sanderson (1828–1905) accepted a full-time professorship of practical physiology and histology at University College, London, in 1870. E. A. Schafer (1836–1907) accepted a similar position as the first praelector of physiology at Trinity College in Cambridge. Also in 1870, the Royal College of Surgeons began reforms calling for more physiology requirements.

As experimental medicine gradually gained prominence, however, an antiscience attitude developed among sanitarians. They spoke of divine limitations on knowledge and asserted that scientists were infringing on these boundaries by experimenting on animals. Animal experimentation was attacked as inhumane in both the lay and medical press, which also carried "slippery slope" arguments predicting that hospitalized patients would be the next victims of the physician scientists.

These claims, diverse at first, were centralized in a powerful antivivisection movement which threatened to stop experimental medicine in Britain from 1870–1890. Between 1874 and 1877 royal commission reports investigated accusations about experimental medicine. Such incidents were not unique to Great Britain. David Ferrier (1843–1928), a distinguished French neurophysiologist, was taken to court for the animal experiments in which he localized sensory and motor functions within the cerebral cortex.

Despite these investigations and voluminous accusations published in the lay press, both the antivivisection movement and belief in the miasma theory gradually fell to the background. By 1890 the validity of the new science was secured. The pathogenic organisms for tuberculosis, anthrax, cholera, rabies, typhoid, and diphtheria were identified. Robert Koch (1843–1910) refined the microscope and provided scientists with the ability to isolate and separate microorganisms. No longer the sole domain of miasmists, preventive medicine had become integral to the program of scientific physicians. The spectacular growth of experimental medicine, along with the rise of hospitals, reforms in medical education, organized state support, and the political influence of the medical profession, created a context in which a new scientific paradigm flourished.

ROSA LYNN B. PINKUS

Bibliography

French, Richard D. *Antivivisection and Medical Science in Victorian Society*. 1975.

Kuhn, Thomas S. *The Structure of Scientific Revolutions*. 1967.

Pelling, Margaret. *Cholera, Fever and English Medicine*. 1978.

Shryock, Richard H. *The Development of Modern Medicine: An Interpretation of the Social and Scientific Factors Involved*. 1947.

Youngson, Alexander J. *The Scientific Revolution in Victorian Medicine*. 1979.

· · · · ·

MEDIEVALISM

The term "medievalism" refers to the Victorians' renewed interest in the ideas, art, literature, and architecture of the Middle Ages. Victorian medievalism usually presents an idealized view of the distant past. Its origins can be seen in the eighteenth and early nineteenth centuries. Richard Hurd's *Letters on Chivalry and Romance* (1762), Bishop Percy's *Reliques of Ancient English Poetry* (1765), Horace Walpole's Gothic romance *The Castle of Otranto* (1765) and his Gothic castle Strawberry Hill (constructed in 1748–1777) stand as testimony to the interest in the Middle Ages in the latter half of the eighteenth century. This interest continued in the early nineteenth century with Walter Scott's novels, Robert Southey's poetry, Augustus Charles Pugin's *Specimens of Gothic Architecture* (1821–1823), and Kenelm Digby's *The Broad Stone of Honor* (1822–1827). Medievalism, however, did not reach its apex until the Victorian period.

Much Victorian poetry employs medieval subjects and themes. Matthew Arnold's *Tristram and Iseult* (1852), Alfred Tennyson's serial poem *Idylls of the King* (1859–1885), Algernon Swinburne's *Tristam of Lyonesse* (1882) and *The Tale of Balen* (1896) are only a few of the major poetic narratives which rework medieval sources. In addition, D. G. Rossetti's ballads and Dantean love poems, as well as William Morris's Arthurian, Froissartian, and Icelandic verse give testimony to the diversity and widespread use of themes from the medieval past, as do Edward Bulwer-Lytton's novels *The Last of the Barons* (1843) and *Harold, The Last of the Saxon Kings* (1848).

Victorian prose writers argued that the medieval past afforded a superior economic, social, and spiritual life for the common people. Augustus Welby Pugin's *Contrasts* (1836), Thomas Carlyle's *Past and Present* (1843), John Ruskin's *Stones of Venice* (1851, 1853) and *Fors Clavigera* (1871–1884), and Morris's late prose romances such as *A Dream of John Ball* (1886) and *News From Nowhere* (1890) idealize medieval life and deprecate the present.

The Victorians also produced many editions and translations of medieval works. Three new editions of Malory appeared in the nineteenth century (1816, 1817, 1858), Lady Charlotte Guest's translation of *The Mabinogion* was published in 1838, and D. G. Rossetti's translation of *The Early Italian Poets* appeared in 1861. William Morris and Eirikr Magnusson translated medieval Icelandic sagas in the 1860s and 1870s.

The **Gothic revival** in architecture is one of the most opulent manifestations of medievalism. It was given credibility largely by the efforts of Ruskin, and by midcentury Gothic was the accepted architectural form in Victorian England. Three of the most popular architects were George Gilbert Scott (1811–1878), who designed the Albert Memorial; George Edmund Street (1824–1881), known for the Law Courts in London; and Alfred Waterhouse (1830–1905), who designed the Manchester Town Hall and the Natural History Museum. In addition, the founding of the Society for the Protection of Ancient Buildings (1877) signaled a renewed appreciation of medieval structures.

Other manifestations of medievalism can be seen in pictorial art, in politics, and in the revival of older religious rites and beliefs. The Pre-Raphaelite artists were especially enthusiastic about medieval subjects and themes: Rossetti, Morris, Edward Burne-Jones, Ford Madox Brown, and Millais are but a few painters who employed subjects from Dante, Chaucer, Boccaccio, Malory, and other medieval writers. In politics Benjamin Disraeli and the **Young England** movement espoused a paternalistic role for the state, and the Oxford Movement, although not a return to medieval Catholicism, emphasized a renewal of early church practices and beliefs.

Although medievalism was, like **romanticism**, in part a reaction against classicism, it sprang largely from the Victorians' desire to mitigate the rapid change, social instability, and moral uncertainty of their age. These problems grew from the industrial revolution, political unrest, and startling new scientific discoveries. Because of their dissatisfaction with the present, many Victorians came to view the Middle Ages as an ideal of social, moral, and religious stability, a time in which it was possible to achieve greater heroism, artistry, and love.

REBECCA COCHRAN

Bibliography

Chandler, Alice. *A Dream of Order: The Medieval Ideal in Nineteenth-Century English Literature.* 1970.

Clark, Kenneth. *The Gothic Revival: An Essay in the History of Taste.* 1974.

Dellheim, Charles. *The Face of the Past: The Preservation of the Medieval Inheritance in Victorian England.* 1982.

Ellis, Steve. *Dante and English Poetry: Shelley to T. S. Eliot.* 1983.

Girouard, Mark. *The Return to Camelot: Chivalry and the English Gentleman.* 1981.

Kaufman, Edward and Sharon Irish. *Medievalism: An Annotated Bibliography of Recent Research in the Architecture and Art of Britain and North America.* 1988.

Merriman, James Douglas. *The Flower of Kings: A Study of the Arthurian Legend in England Between 1485 and 1835.* 1973.

Reiss, Edmund et al. *Arthurian Legend and Literature: An Annotated Bibliography.* 1984.

See also ACADEMIC PAINTING; ARTHURIAN LEGEND; ARTS AND CRAFTS MOVEMENT; GENTLEMAN

. . . . .

MELBA, NELLIE
(1861–1931)

Coloratura soprano Nellie Melba graced Covent Garden and other international opera houses for almost thirty years. Born Helen Mitchell in Richmond, Australia, she made her first public appearance at the age of six at a Melbourne concert. Her father's objections to a stage career precluded voice instruction until after her marriage to Charles Porter Armstrong in 1882. Melba advanced rapidly under the tutelage of Pietro Cecchi, and later Madame Marchesi in Paris. Leaving her failed marriage behind her, she made a triumphant operatic debut in *Rigoletto* (1887) at the Théâtre de La Monnaie in Brussels, having adopted the stage name "Melba" the previous year.

Invited by impresario Augustus Harris to sing at Covent Garden, Melba appeared there in 1888 to great acclaim in *Lucia di Lammermoor.* Continuing to sing each season at Covent Garden, Melba also made many successful guest appearances on the Continent, including La Scala in Milan. In 1893 she made her American debut as Lucia at the Metropolitan Opera House; she subsequently made a series of transcontinental tours.

Blessed with a voice of extraordinary natural beauty and range, Melba excelled in coloratura roles such as Lucia, Violetta, and Lakmé. Not a gifted dramatic actress, her one failure was as Brünnhilde in *Siegfried* (1896). She retired from Covent Garden in 1926, her voice still superb, to become president of the Melbourne Conservatory.

LAUREN SMITH

Bibliography

Hetherington, John. *Melba*. 1967.

· · · · ·

MELBOURNE, SECOND VISCOUNT (WILLIAM LAMB) (1779-1848)

Whig statesman Lord Melbourne served as prime minister briefly in 1834 and then from 1835 to 1841. He helped smooth the path of monarchy for the young Queen Victoria and served as her chief mentor until her marriage in 1840.

Born nominally the second son of Sir Peniston Lamb, later first viscount Melbourne, he is believed by some authorities to have been the son of the third earl of Egremont. In addition to Lord Egremont, his mother, Elizabeth Milbanke, had as an admirer the Prince of Wales (later George IV) and as a confidante the poet, Lord Byron. Lamb was educated at Eton, Trinity College (Cambridge) and Glasgow University. In 1805, he abandoned a law career when the death of his elder brother made him heir to his father's peerages. In the same year he married Lady Caroline Ponsonby, better known under her married name as Lady Caroline Lamb. Their storm-tossed marriage was marked by the birth in 1807 of their retarded child, Augustus; by her affair with Byron (1812-1813); and by their separation in 1825 and her death in 1828. Melbourne was subsequently twice named in divorce cases.

Elected to the House of Commons in 1805, Lamb served until he succeeded to the peerage and the House of Lords in 1828, with a hiatus in 1812-1816, when he lost his seat due to his support of Catholic emancipation. He first held office as chief secretary for Ireland (1827-1828) and achieved cabinet office as home secretary in November 1830.

As home secretary, Melbourne placed the full weight of his authority behind the work of forcibly suppressing the agrarian disorders of the early 1830s and the conviction and sentence of the "Tolpuddle Martyrs" for union activity. A firm believer in a hierarchical society, he gave unenthusiastic support to the Reform Act of 1832 only because he recognized that it had become politically necessary.

Commissioned by William IV to form a ministry, Melbourne became prime minister in July 1834. The monarch, however, preferred Wellington and Peel and in November 1834 exercised for the last time the royal prerogative of dismissing a prime minister who still had the confidence of the House of Commons. Becoming prime minister again after Robert Peel's resignation in 1835, Melbourne's position was not strong. His ministry was supported by a minority in the House of Lords and by an unstable majority in the Commons, and its legislative accomplishments were limited, though it did adopt the act uniting Upper and Lower Canada (1840), and instituted the penny post (1840).

Melbourne's enjoyment of office was enhanced by the accession of the eighteen-year-old Queen Victoria in 1837. Combining political self-interest with fatherly affection, he became her constant companion and mentor. His initiation undoubtedly contributed to turning the young queen into a Whig partisan. In the "bedchamber crisis" the queen maneuvered Peel into declining to form a ministry after Melbourne resigned in May 1839. She misrepresented Peel's request that some of her Whig ladies of the bedchamber be replaced by Tories to Melbourne's cabinet as a demand to replace them all; the cabinet rallied to her support and the queen was able to retain the Melbourne ministry in office for another two years.

The weakened and increasingly unpopular Melbourne government was brought down in 1841. Melbourne had consistently supported the Corn Laws, which protected landed interests and inflated the price of food. In May 1841 the government was defeated (by one vote) on a vote of confidence. Instead of resigning, Melbourne chose to hold a general election, which was decisively won by supporters of Robert Peel. In the following year Melbourne suffered a stroke which effectively removed him from the center of political activity.

ROBERT S. FRASER

Bibliography

Cecil, David. *The Young Melbourne*. 1939.

———. *Lord M.* 1954.

Newman, Bertram. *Lord Melbourne*. 1930.

Sanders, Lloyd C., ed. *Lord Melbourne's Papers*. 1889; rpt. 1971.

Torrens, W. M. *Memoirs of the Right Honourable William Second Viscount Melbourne*. 1878. 2 vols.

Ziegler, William. *Melbourne: A Biography of William Lamb, 2nd Viscount Melbourne*. 1976.

See also NORTON, CAROLINE; WHIG PARTY

· · · · ·

MELODRAMA

Imported from the boulevard theaters of Paris during the last decade of the eighteenth century, melodrama in its various guises became the most popular form of stage fare in Victorian England. The first English play to call itself a "Melo-Drama" was Thomas Holcroft's *Tale of Mystery* (Covent Garden, 1802), a swift-paced story of a lost child, mysterious mute, and blackguard nobleman. The work presents in germinal form many of the genre's essential features: a rigid division of experience into opposing camps of good and bad, a set of emblematic stock characters (brave but inept hero, patient heroine, attitudinizing villain, comic couple), and the ulti-

mate triumph of virtue. Holcroft used theatrical practices associated with the form through much of the century: music to underscore emotional crises, tableaux to freeze characters into iconic confrontations, and a telegraphic paring down of language.

The romantic and domestic sensibilities that participate in Holcroft's work each spawned theatrical subgenres of immense appeal. The Gothic vogue of the early century made melodramatic villains of supernatural demons or brooding aristocrats. In *The Vampire* (English Opera House, 1820), **J. R. Planché** combined the two in Ruthven, earl of Marsden, the first in a long line of stage bloodsuckers—a half-century later the character could still be parodied in Gilbert and Sullivan's *Ruddigore* (Savoy, 1887). The 1820s also saw H. M. Milner's adaptation of *Frankenstein* (Coburg, 1823) and Edward Fitzball's *Flying Dutchman* (Adelphi, 1827) and *Devil's Elixir* (Covent Garden, 1829).

There was a longer vogue for pieces that presented the eternal struggle between light and darkness in more homely surroundings. Plays like J. B. Buckstone's *Luke the Labourer* (Adelphi, 1826), **Douglas Jerrold**'s *Rent Day* (Drury Lane, 1832), and John Walker's *Factory Lad* (Surrey, 1832) embody vice in a succession of squires, landlords, rent collectors, and greedy manufacturers who threaten eviction rather than evisceration—a fate of more immediate concern to the working-class audiences for whom these works were performed. Nautical melodrama—best represented by Jerrold's *Black-Eyed Susan* (Surrey, 1829)—celebrated Britain's naval glories in the person of the Jolly Jack Tar who rescues his heroine from pirates, shipwrecks, and scheming superior officers. Yet while their accidentals are altered, the worlds of these domestic plays with their humble cottages, manor houses, and dark Satanic mills remain idealized environments in which vice and virtue are distinguished with surreal clarity.

In midcentury melodrama acquired a specifically urban habitation, casting elegant confidence men as villains while entrusting virtue to a tribe of equally businesslike detectives. **Tom Taylor**'s *Ticket-of-Leave Man* (Olympic, 1863) sports a number of recognizable London haunts, a particularly dapper thief, and Jack Hawksure, progenitor of all later stage sleuths. Many of Taylor's innovations were freely appropriated by his contemporaries, especially **Dion Boucicault**, financially the most successful playwright of the period. Boucicault's *After Dark* (Princess's, 1868), a gritty drama of metropolitan intrigue, steers the genre in the direction of spectacle. At one point its hero is lashed to the tracks of the London underground while a locomotive bears down on him. The "sensation" plays produced at Drury Lane under the management of Augustus Harris catered to similar appetites; *Pluck* (1883) staged in rapid succession a snowstorm, a head-on railway collision, and a riot in which real windows were smashed by a rampaging mob.

Such devices were scorned by **Henry Arthur Jones**, whose *Silver King* (Princess's, 1882) attempted to raise melodramatic writing to the plane of "literature." The most popular (and profitable) of Victorian melodramas, Jones's tale of a man who clears his name, rescues his family, and apprehends a master criminal won the applause of Matthew Arnold and remained in active repertory for close to thirty years. In the society plays of the 1890s, Jones joined Arthur Wing Pinero and Oscar Wilde in recutting the fabric of melodrama for the more fashionable audiences of George Alexander's St. James's Theatre and the various playhouses managed by Charles Wyndham. In the early dramas of Bernard Shaw—especially *Widowers' Houses* (Royalty, 1892) and *Mrs. Warren's Profession* (1894; New Lyric Club, 1902)—the traditions of melodrama are effectively mustered to subvert its values and moral assumptions.

JOEL H. KAPLAN

Bibliography

Booth, Michael R. *English Melodrama*. 1965.

———, ed. *Hiss the Villain: Six English and American Melodramas*. 1964.

Rahill, Frank. *The World of Melodrama*. 1967.

Smith, James L. *Melodrama*. 1973.

———, ed. *Victorian Melodramas: Seven English, French and American Melodramas*. 1976.

Wischhusen, Stephen, ed. *The Hour of One: Six Gothic Melodramas*. 1975.

· · · · ·

MEREDITH, GEORGE (1828–1909)

Novelist, poet, journalist, and reader for major publishers, George Meredith is one of the major literary figures of late Victorian England in spite of the fact that his direct influence on contemporary literature was narrowly circumscribed. Meredith was the only son of Augustus Meredith, a naval outfitter, and Jane Eliza Macnamara. In 1849 he married Mary Ellen Peacock Nicolls, daughter of Thomas Love Peacock. The Merediths separated in 1857 after Mary Ellen had formed an alliance with Henry Wallis, a member of the Pre-Raphaelite group. She died in 1861, and in 1864 Meredith married Marie Vulliamy.

As a reader for Chapman and Hall, Meredith's judgments reflected artistic standards for style and substance that his own works sometimes failed to meet. Although his most famous rejection may be that of *East Lynne* by Ellen Price Wood, later a runaway best seller, Meredith also advised against the publication of Samuel Butler's *Erewhon* and G. B. Shaw's *Immaturity*.

Meredith's novels, with the partial exception of *Diana of the Crossways* (1885), were never widely popular, although he eventually attracted a select group of admirers that included Robert Louis Stevenson, William Earnest Henley, and Thomas Hardy. His reputation as a man of letters was not firmly established until the end of the century. Following Tennyson's death in 1892, Meredith was elected president of the Society of Authors, and in 1898 T. H. S. Escott called him "the foremost of English novelists now living." Meredith's status as a major writer was challenged by Ezra Pound in 1918 and denied outright by E. M. Forster in *Aspects of the Novel* (1927) and F. R. Leavis in *The Great Tradition* (1948).

Meredith's reputation has fluctuated since 1948 but has never regained the luster it enjoyed in the 1890s. Of his poetry, only "Modern Love" (1862) continues to elicit favorable comment. Of his numerous essays and reviews, "On the Idea of Comedy and the Uses of the Comic Spirit" (1877) is still mentioned regularly. Meredith's conception of the comic spirit receives its fullest elaboration in *The Egoist* (1879), acknowledged by many critics as his most successful novel.

Some recent studies have claimed Meredith

as an early feminist. Most of his heroines are denied a conventionally happy marriage, at least initially, and many are engaged in a struggle for self-actualization outside of marriage. The heroine of *Diana of the Crossways*, for example, supports herself as a writer. Meredith's repeated failure to pursue his insights into their struggles, however, ultimately disqualifies him as a feminist. His daring heroines may resist the restrictions of conventional female roles, but only briefly and always unsuccessfully. Meredith's tortured relationship with his first wife, the independent and intellectual Mary Ellen Nicolls, may be at issue; although Meredith was attracted to intelligent women, both in his life and in his fiction, he was also intimidated by them. He consistently created female characters of spirit and intellect who are eventually destroyed, like Mary Ellen, or are translated into shadows of the submissive and domestic Marie Vulliamy.

ELIZABETH BOYD THOMPSON

Bibliography

Bartlett, Phyllis B. *The Poems of George Meredith*. 1978.

Cline, Clarence L., ed. *Letters of George Meredith*. 1970. 3 vols.

Collie, Michael. *George Meredith: A Bibliography*. 1974.

Fletcher, Ian, ed. *Meredith Now: Some Critical Essays*. 1971.

Forman, Maurice Buxton. *A Bibliography of the Writings in Prose and Verse of George Meredith*. 1922.

———. *Meredithiana, Being a Supplement to the Bibliography of Meredith*. 1924.

Stevenson, Lionel. *The Ordeal of George Meredith*. 1953.

Williams, Joan, ed. *Meredith: The Critical Heritage*. 1971.

See also COMEDY

· · · · ·

MESMERISM

Mesmerism, or animal magnetism, was originated by Viennese physician Franz Anton Mesmer (1734–1815), who published his *Mémoire sur la Découverte du Magnétisme Animal* (1779) amid the heady radicalism of prerevolutionary Paris. Therein, Mesmer posited "a mutual influence between the Heavenly bodies, the Earth, and Animate Bodies which exists of a universally distributed and continuous fluid." The mesmerist could manipulate this fluid magnetic force to effect visionary and healing powers upon his subject.

Mesmerism proved a seductive combination of scientific rationalism and romantic mysticism. Like its cousin **spiritualism**, it offered a new faith to the Victorian whose God was disappearing. But mesmerism's leading English theorists came largely from the medical profession, and were led by Dr. John Elliotson (1791–1868), author of *Human Physiology* (1840). In 1843 Elliotson founded *The Zooist*, a journal of mesmerism and **phrenology**, materialistic and radical sciences which often shared an audience.

Despite its defeat by the scientific establishment, the mesmeric mania retained a widespread appeal throughout the 1840s and 1850s. The Brownings, Arnold, Clough, Collins, Thackeray, Trollope, George Eliot, and Herbert Spencer all took an interest; Dickens, Tennyson, and Harriet Martineau were themselves mesmeric practitioners. Scientist James Braid (1795?–1860) posited that although the mesmeric fluid was a physiological fiction, an intangible force of will did create a powerful relationship between mesmerizer and subject; Braid named this process "hypnosis."

DIANA POSTLETHWAITE

Bibliography

Darnton, Robert. *Mesmerism and the End of the Enlightenment in France*. 1968.

Fuller, Robert C. *Mesmerism and the American Cure of Souls*. 1982.

Kaplan, Fred. *Dickens and Mesmerism: The Hidden Springs of Fiction*. 1975.

Mesmer, Franz Anton. *Mesmerism: A Translation of the Original Scientific and Medical Writings of F. A. Mesmer*. 1980. Trans. George Bloch.

Parsinnen, Terry M. "Mesmeric Performers." *Victorian Studies*, vol. 21, pp. 87–105.

See also PSYCHOLOGY

· · · · ·

METHODISTS see PRIMITIVE METHODIST CHURCH; WESLEYAN METHODIST CHURCH

· · · · ·

MEYNELL, ALICE (1847-1926)

Alice Thompson Meynell's earliest volume of poems, *Preludes* (1875), was commended by Ruskin, Tennyson, and Aubrey de Vere, and contained the poem "Renouncement." Other collections were *Poems* (1892) and *Later Poems* (1901). Her essays in *The Scots Observer* were published in *Rhythm of Life* (1893); *The Colour of Life* (1896) contained selections from her *Pall Mall Gazette* column "The Wares of Autolycus." Essays on childhood appeared in *The Children* (1897).

Born Alice Christiana Thompson, she was the daughter of a prosperous family and sister of the painter **Elizabeth Thompson Butler**. She was educated at home and spent her childhood and early youth in Italy. After marrying **Wilfrid Meynell** in 1878 she was kept busy in the journalistic world by coediting, with him, *Merry England* and by contributing to the *Art Magazine*, the *Pall Mall Gazette*, the *Athenaeum*, and other major London periodicals. She was the friend to and was admired by Francis Thompson, Coventry Patmore, and George Meredith, among others.

Meynell's writing is marked by restraint and precision, for she selected not merely the rich experiences of life but the rarest. She has a subtle understanding of the sadness of day-to-day living, yet her poetry expresses confidence in her faith; like her husband, she was a convert to Roman Catholicism. She was considered for the position of poet laureate on the death of Alfred Austin, and was elected in 1914 to the Academic Committee of the Royal Society of Literature.

CHARMAZEL DUDT

Bibliography

Badeni, June. *The Slender Tree: A Life of Alice Meynell*. 1981.

Clark, Celia Tobin. *Alice Meynell: A Tribute*. 1923.

Meynell, Viola. *Alice Meynell: A Memoir*. 1929.

Tuell, Anne K. *Mrs. Meynell and Her Literary Generation*. 1923.

· · · · ·

MEYNELL, WILFRID (1852-1948)

A journalist, editor, and publisher, Wilfrid Meynell was founder, with his wife **Alice Meynell**, of *Merry England*, a liberal Roman Catholic journal in whose pages first appeared poets such as Francis Thompson and Hilaire Belloc, and essayists such as W. H. Hudson and Katharine Tynan. In 1881 Cardinal Manning bequeathed to him the management of the *Weekly Register* which Meynell edited, wrote for, and published for eighteen years. He conducted it according to a **Home Rule** and **Young England** policy in contrast to the Catholic Toryism of the *Tablet*. Around 1900 Meynell became managing director of the publishing house of Burnes and Oates where he did much to restore and influence the quality of typography. In this position he made popular the works of Robert Hugh Benson and Lionel Johnson, and published the works of Alice Meynell and Francis Thompson.

A convert to Roman Catholicism from Quakerism, Meynell descended from the family of the Tukes of York. He devoted his life to humanitarian concerns and the causes of the church.

Under the pseudonym of "John Oldcastle" he published *Journals and Journalism* (1880), the earliest guide for literary beginners. Other works include *Aunt Sarah and the War* (1914), an extremely popular novel during World War I; *Rhymes with Reasons* (1918) and *Verses and Reverses* (1910), volumes of occasional and whimsical verse; *Benjamin Disraeli: An Unconventional Biography* (1903); and journalistic contributions to the *Athenaeum*, *Pall Mall Gazette*, *Illustrated London News*, *Saturday Review*, and *Daily Chronicle*. In 1913 he retired to an estate in Greatham, Sussex where he and his wife maintained a literary salon visited by colleagues such as G. K. Chesterton, Wilfrid Blunt, Ezra Pound, J. L. Garvin, and W. E. Henley.

CHARMAZEL DUDT

Bibliography

Dudt, Charmazel. "Wilfrid Meynell: Editor, Publisher and Friend." *Victorian Periodicals Review*, vol. 16, pp. 104–108.

Meynell, Viola. *Francis Thompson and Wilfrid Meynell: A Memoir.* 1952.

Rogers, Cameron. "Wilfrid Meynell." *Thought*, vol. 3, pp. 479–490.

· · · · ·

MIDWIVES

During the nineteenth century midwives were regulated and supported by the governments of France and Germany but virtually eradicated by male practitioners in the United States. In Britain there was a prolonged battle over the midwife's scope, autonomy, training, and registration. A nonmedical folk craft with its own pharmacopoeia (ergot is reputed to have been discovered by early midwives) and techniques, midwifery was traditionally the province of women.

By the beginning of the nineteenth century, British doctors eager to establish their legitimacy wished to limit the activities of midwives without themselves having to perform the often tedious tasks associated with childbirth. Debate centered on the kind of midwifery women should do, on the nature of their training, and on the control of their licensing.

The simple solution of abolishing midwifery, advocated by a number of physicians, was not acceptable; low midwife fees could not induce male practitioners to attend the huge number of poor parturient women. One proposal was to place childbirth in the control of a body of expert midwives. At the turn of the eighteenth century, midwife Margaret Stephen taught women midwifery, including the use of forceps. In 1830 the newly established British Ladies' Lying-In Institution, headed by a female midwife, trained a few women. But the prospect of a large body of independent professional midwives was lessened when the medical establishment accepted a few women into regular medical training. Thereafter the most extensive training available for midwives was the three-month course required for the Obstetrical Society's diploma (established in 1872).

The second solution was to subsume midwifery training under nurses' training, keeping both subservient to the medical profession. But midwives and nurses alike resisted this solution; nurses because they feared a lack of professionalism from association with women trained for only three months, and midwives because they saw midwifery as a specialized function over which its practitioners should have authority.

The issue of training was inevitably linked to the issue of licensing. Various branches of the British Medical Association attempted to control midwifery. In 1851 the College of Surgeons set up a (male) midwifery license; and the Medical Act of 1858 established a system of (male) certification in midwifery by physicians. Only when Maria Firth's Obstetrical Association of Midwives (1872; precursor of the Midwives' Institute) threatened to create an autonomous body of women did the Obstetrical Society offer a diploma for female midwives. Licensing, however, was slow to gain acceptance among midwives; in 1890, only 140 a year were seeking licenses and not until 1900 did substantial numbers (754) accept this formal control by doctors.

In the last quarter of the century, the Midwives' Institute continued to seek authority for autonomous, well-trained midwives, while the British Medical Association wanted complete subordination of midwives to doctors. Six licensing bills were presented to Parliament between 1890 and 1900, but it took the Swanscombe incident of 1901 to convince the government to act. Three Swanscombe doctors refused to attend the labor of a poor woman whose husband could pay only half their fee. The woman died, and the resulting national outcry led to the Midwives' Act of 1902, which gave midwives a separate, if limited, area of operation and affirmed Britain's commitment to this form of childbirth care.

The act required new midwives to obtain the Obstetrical Society's diploma, thus maintaining doctors' right to examine midwives. However, midwives won the right to continue in unlicensed practice until 1910 and resisted the doctors' demand that they be relicensed annually. Licensing was assigned to the Midwives' Board, under the Privy Council, with a midwife representative to participate in the governance of her profession. Drawbacks of the act included the requirement of local registration, which could put some midwives at the mercy of local doctors; the act's minute requirements for dress, deportment, and duties; and the fact that doctors constituted a majority of the Midwives' Board.

Although far from perfect, the Midwives' Act of 1902 was clearly in the professional interests of midwives and the health interests of the nation: by 1905, 22,308 midwives were registered, half the births in Britain were attended by registered midwives, and the infant mortality rate dropped from 15.1 percent in 1901 to 10.6 percent in 1910. The century-long story of the British midwife's struggle for legitimacy parallels British women's attempts to gain legal rights, education, and employment as the angel moved out of the house.

LORALEE MacPIKE

Bibliography

Aveling, J. H. *English Midwives: Their History and Prospects.* 1872.

Donnison, Jean. *Midwives and Medical Men.* 1977.

Ehrenreich, Barbara and Dierdre English. *Witches, Midwives and Nurses: A History of Women Healers.* 1973.

Flack, Isaac Harvey. *Eternal Eve: The History of Gynaecology and Obstetrics.* 1951.

Forbes, Thomas R. *The Midwife and the Witch.* 1966.

Towler, Jean and Joan Bramall. *Midwives in History and Society.* 1986.

See also CHILDBIRTH

· · · · ·

MILL, HARRIET HARDY TAYLOR
(1807-1858)

Harriet Taylor Mill, author of "The Enfranchisement of Women," a provocative and influential article printed anonymously in the *Westminster Review* for July 1851, was the daughter of Thomas Hardy, a surgeon and male midwife, and Harriet Hurst. She seems to have been brought up in the Unitarian faith

and educated largely, if not entirely, at home. At the age of eighteen, she married (March 14, 1826) John Taylor, a wholesale druggist, by whom she had three children.

Both she and her husband had radical inclinations and by the early 1830s were associated with the advanced thinkers surrounding W. J. Fox, editor of the *Monthly Repository*, to which she contributed poems and reviews in 1831 and 1832. Here she met **John Stuart Mill** (1806-1873), who attributed to her his advanced socialist views and his full appreciation of the deleterious and widespread effects of the subordination of women to men. After Taylor's death in 1849, she married Mill (April 21, 1851).

"The Enfranchisement of Women" was reprinted by J. S. Mill in his *Dissertations and Discussions* (vol. 2, 1859) and issued as a pamphlet (1868) distributed by the National Union of Women's Suffrage Societies, of which John Stuart Mill was honorary president. Taylor Mill's influence was also exercised indirectly through her daughter, Helen Taylor, and through her contribution to the thought and action of John Stuart Mill, especially in his *Principles of Political Economy* (3rd ed., 1852), his amendment to the second Reform Bill (to include women), *The Subjection of Women* (1869), and the *Autobiography* (1873).

ANN ROBSON

Bibliography

Hayek, Friedrich A. *John Stuart Mill and Harriet Taylor.* 1951.

Mill, Harriet Taylor. Essays in appendices to *Essays on Equality, Law, and Education* in *Collected Works of John Stuart Mill*, vol. 21. 1984. Ed. J. M. Robson.

Packe, Michael St. J. *The Life of John Stuart Mill.* 1954.

· · · · ·

MILL, JOHN STUART
(1806-1873)

John Stuart Mill's reputation as the leading British philosopher of the nineteenth century is firmly based on his outstanding list of magisterial works. His two-volume *System of Logic* (1843), which pioneered the combination of deduction and induction, and his *Principles of Political Economy* (1848), a major work of synthesis which raised in a new fashion socialist issues such as distribution and the role of labor, both remained university textbooks through the century. He followed these with other writings that have maintained wide appeal, including *On Liberty* (1859), a discussion of central issues in social freedom; *Considerations on Representative Government* (1861), which centers on the tensions between efficient government and participatory democracy; *Utilitarianism* (1863), an examination of the dominant English ethical tradition; *The Subjection of Women* (1869), a strong indictment of sexual inequality; and the *Autobiography* (posthumous, 1873), which includes an intriguing subjective account of his upbringing and discovery of self-determination.

Born in north London, Mill was given an intensive education at home by his father, James Mill, known as "the Historian of British India." Beginning with Greek at the age of three, he was mastering calculus, political economy, and logic before entering his teens. He spent the year 1820–1821 in southern France with the family of General Sir Samuel Bentham, brother of Jeremy Bentham, the renowned legal and political reformer with whom James Mill was closely associated. While in France he attended university lectures at Montpellier, and learned to admire French social institutions and scenery; subsequently France was a second home to him, and French a second language. On his return to London he soon joined his father in the Examiner's Office of the East India Company, which he eventually headed, as his father had, retiring from it in 1858 when the Crown assumed full control of the company's affairs.

His early life was one of intense propagandism for the radical causes of the time, especially political and legal reform, Ricardian economics, and neo-Malthusianism. He was active as a journalist (his newspaper writings occupy four volumes of his *Collected Works*), and edited a radical quarterly, the *London and Westminster Review*, in the 1830s. Through these activities he knew and was known by many leading literary and public figures, but he followed a very private style of

life, particularly after 1830, when he met and became the intimate friend of Harriet Hardy Taylor, whom he married in 1851, two years after she had been widowed. With her he shared fully his intellectual life, and gave her credit as "joint author" of most of his writings subsequent to the *System of Logic*; much has been written about this assertion and his eulogies of her character and abilities, but while there is general agreement about the sincerity of his claims for her, few accept his judgment at face value.

After her death in 1858, Mill returned to an active publishing life, producing, in addition to the works mentioned above, *Dissertations and Discussions* (1859), a two-volume collection of his periodical essays (eventually enlarged to four volumes); these revealed even more of his range, containing substantial essays on historical writing and theory, on the classics, and on various aspects of equality, including racial. He also brought out *Auguste Comte and Positivism* (1865), an important index to the influence of the French sociologist, whose early writings had had an important part in determining the course of Mill's thought, and *An Examination of Sir William Hamilton's Philosophy* (1865), an intensely argued defense of the philosophy of experience and induction on which his practical as well as theoretical views were founded.

Partly as a result of the expanded notice given him by these works, as well as the frequent new editions of his principal writings, Mill's agreement was sought in 1865 to stand for Parliament. On election, he made a strong mark as a Liberal of radical disposition, making unpopular causes his special concern; his powerful speeches on women's suffrage (he moved an amendment to the Reform Bill of 1867 to replace the word "man" by the word "person"), proportional representation, parliamentary reform, and Irish affairs brought him into the center of controversy, as did some other causes, most notably his leading the campaign to bring to trial for murder ex-governor Eyre of Jamaica for his role in putting down the rebellion of 1866. Mill was defeated in the election of 1868, at least partly because he was seen as infected by an enthusiasm improper in one whose reputation was made as a sage. Spending much time in Avignon, where his wife had died (and where he also is buried), he pursued his writing, mainly of periodical essays and of his incomplete and posthumously published *Chapters on Socialism*, as well as continuing his avocation as an amateur botanist of distinction, finally dying of an infection incurred during a field trip.

Mill's *Collected Works* (University of Toronto Press), in thirty-one volumes, provides full evidence of his authorial career, with collated texts and specialized introductions to each title. It also includes previously unpublished works, journals, speeches, and correspondence. Of the many biographies, Michael St. J. Packe's is the fullest, though marred by undue romanticizing and inadequate accounts of Mill's writing.

JOHN M. ROBSON

Bibliography

Bain, Alexander. *John Stuart Mill.* 1882.

Berger, Fred. *Happiness, Justice, and Freedom.* 1984.

Garforth, F. W. *Educative Democracy: John Stuart Mill on Education in Society.* 1980.

Hamburger, Joseph. *Intellectuals in Politics.* 1965.

Laine, Michael. *Bibliography of Writings on John Stuart Mill.* 1982.

MacMinn, Ney et al. *Bibliography of the Published Writings of J. S. Mill.* 1945.

Mill News Letter.

Packe, Michael St. J. *The Life of John Stuart Mill.* 1954.

Robson, John M. *The Improvement of Mankind: The Social and Political Thought of J. S. Mill.* 1968.

Ryan, Alan. *John Stuart Mill.* 1970.

Sharpless, F. Parvin. *The Literary Criticism of John Stuart Mill.* 1967.

Thompson, Dennis. *John Stuart Mill and Representative Government.* 1976.

See also AUTOBIOGRAPHY; ECONOMICS; LOGIC; UTILITARIANISM

· · · · ·

MILLAIS, JOHN EVERETT (1829–1896)

John Everett Millais was one of the most naturally gifted and technically competent artists of the Victorian age. Proficient in oil painting, watercolor, and illustration, he is most famous as one of the cofounders of the **Pre-Raphaelite Brotherhood**, the first self-consciously avant-garde artistic movement in England.

Millais was born in Southampton of wealthy parents who supported his artistic talents. The family moved to London in 1838 to enroll their precocious son in Sass's famous drawing school. At the age of eleven, Millais was admitted to the Royal Academy as a pupil, the youngest student ever accepted. He completed the course at sixteen and exhibited his first picture, *Pizzaro Seizing the Inca of Peru* (1846), which was done in conventional academic style on a stock theme—the fall of empires. During the next year he became friends with **Holman Hunt** and **Dante Gabriel Rossetti**, fellow art students whose radical ideas excited his interest in a new way of painting. Stimulated by a mutual desire to reform English art, these three and four others (James Collinson, Thomas Woolner, Frederic Stephens, and William Rossetti) gathered in September 1848 at the Millais family house in 83 Gower Street to form the Pre-Raphaelite Brotherhood.

The Pre-Raphaelite program was to create pictures in a distinctive style. Millais's *Isabella* (1849) shows his adoption of Pre-Raphaelite techniques: small brushwork used over a white ground to make brighter, lighter pictures, attention to minute detail in the background as well as foreground, and subjects taken from English literature. While *Isabella* was well received by critics and the public (who dubbed it "The Kick"), such was not the case with Millais's next painting, *Christ in the House of His Parents* (1850). Millais was abused for his realistic representation of the holy family in a humble carpenter's shop. Undaunted, he tried another picture on a religious theme, *The Return of the Dove to the Ark* (1851). In the same year he took a subject from Tennyson's poem "Mariana" and here created his individual style of painting, in which languid mood and pathetic situation are combined with poetic subject matter and sharp detail. Also done in this period was *The Woodman's Daughter* (1851), the first Pre-Raphaelite treatment of a contemporary social problem—the sexual exploitation of working-class females.

In the 1850s Millais's popularity was somewhat revived by a series of narrative paintings, including *A Huguenot* (1852), *Ophelia* (1852), and *The Order of Release* (1853). At this point in his career, Millais became the protégé of critic John Ruskin, who had recently taken up the Pre-Raphaelite cause. During a vacation in Scotland, Millais and Ruskin's wife Effie fell in love and, after a scandalous divorce, they were married in 1855 and settled in Perth. Alienation from Ruskin and the need to make more money for his fast-growing family caused Millais to give up the meticulous Pre-Raphaelite method of painting. Later in the 1850s he turned to a more commercial style, although he painted a few more Pre-Raphaelite canvases: *Autumn Leaves* (1856), *The Blind Girl* (1856), *Sir Isumbras* (1857), and *The Vale of Rest* (1859), his last truly Pre-Raphaelite work. During the next decades Millais created popular paintings of lovers like *The Black Brunswicker* (1860), and cute children, as in *A Child's World* (1885), which came to be known as "Bubbles" after it was bought by Pears Ltd. as a soap advertisement.

In the last stage of his career, Millais acquired a reputation as a portrait painter; Carlyle, Tennyson, Gladstone, and Disraeli were among the important figures who sat to him. As Millais's fame grew so did his fortune, and he lived in the grand style, maintaining hunting and fishing lodges in Scotland and an imposing townhouse in London. In 1885 he was made a baronet, the first artist ever so honored. He died shortly after being elected president of the Royal Academy, and was buried in St. Paul's.

As one of the original Pre-Raphaelites, Millais's place in the history of British art is secure. He created numerous original works of art, and his early pictures influenced a whole generation of younger artists—Bowler, Hughes, Windus, and Wallis. Despite the current tendency to disparage his later work, it reveals great technical merit even if it lacks the inspiration of his Pre-Raphaelite period.

HALLMAN B. BRYANT

Bibliography

Bennett, Mary. *Millais Exhibition Catalogue*, Walker Art Gallery, Liverpool. 1967.

Bowness, Alan, et al. *The Pre-Raphaelites*. 1984.

Fish, Arthur. *John Everett Millais*. 1923.

Fredeman, William E. *Pre-Raphaelitism: A Bibliocritical Study*. 1965.

Lutyens, Mary. *Millais and the Ruskins*. 1967.

Millais, John Guille. *The Life and Letters of Sir John Everett Millais*. 1899. 2 vols.

Wood, Christopher. *The Pre-Raphaelites*. 1981.

· · · · ·

MILNER, ALFRED
(1854–1925)

Alfred Milner was a statesman and diplomat known especially for his imperial activities in South Africa during the second Anglo-Boer War (1899–1902). The son of an English businessman, he was born and lived for several years in Germany before studying at King's College, London, and Balliol College, Oxford. Although called to the bar in 1881, he felt compelled to a life of "public usefulness." For several years he worked as a journalist under John Morley and W. T. Stead. He was created a viscount in 1902.

In 1884, Milner began his public career as secretary to Viscount Goschen. In 1886 Goschen became chancellor of the Exchequer with Milner as his private secretary. In 1890 Goschen procured for Milner the position of director-general of accounts in Egypt, which led him to write *England in Egypt* (1892).

In 1897, at the request of colonial secretary Joseph Chamberlain, Milner became high commissioner for South Africa. He arrived in Africa in May 1899. Some scholars have concluded that Milner's intransigence helped lead to the war, which began on October 11, 1899. During the war, as British forces occupied much of the Boer territories, Milner was made administrator of the Orange Free State and the Transvaal.

Milner remained in South Africa until 1905 helping with its restoration. In his later years, he groomed a "kindergarten" of young men such as H. G. Wells, Edward Grey, Bernard Shaw, J. L. Garvin, and L. S. Amery, many of whom later became associated with British imperial administration. In 1916, Milner was selected by Lloyd George to serve as a member of the war cabinet. He was subsequently colonial secretary (1918–1921) and at his death had just been elected chancellor of Oxford University.

NEWELL D. BOYD

Bibliography

Crankshaw, Edward. *The Forsaken Idea: A Study of Lord Milner.* 1952.

Gollin, Alfred M. *Procounsul in Politics.* 1964.

Halperin, V. *Lord Milner and the Empire.* 1952.

O'Brien, Terence H. *Milner: Viscount Milner of St. James's and Cape Town, 1854–1925.* 1979.

Wrench, John E. L. *Alfred Lord Milner.* 1958.

See also BOER WAR

· · · · ·

MILNES, RICHARD MONCKTON (1809–1885)

"Dickie" Milnes, poet, politician, and bon vivant, was a dilettante who combined a private fortune and a gregarious nature into a singular talent for appearing to know everyone, go everywhere, and do everything.

Born to a Yorkshire family of textile merchants, Milnes attended Trinity College, Cambridge, where he excelled as a debater and as a member of the Apostles. He published his earliest verses in the *Athenaeum*, then run by the Apostles, and issued volumes of verse throughout his life.

Milnes entered Parliament in 1837 as Conservative member for Pontefract. After the wreck of the party over Corn Law repeal, he became a follower of Lord Palmerston and supported the extension of the franchise and other liberal causes. Although Milnes made little impact in politics, Palmerston elevated him to the peerage in 1863 as Baron Houghton of Great Houghton, West Yorkshire.

The balance of Milnes's time was dedicated to supporting worthy causes—his college, the Royal Society, the British Museum, the London Library, and the Royal Literary fund—and to indulging his taste for good living. A collector of books (including erotica), Milnes founded the Philobiblon Society, but his chief fame is as a collector and patron of interesting people. Milnes delighted in bringing together the most diverse talents and intellects, most of whom he enchanted with his charm, wit, and hospitality.

Greatly coveted were invitations to Milnes's dinners and breakfasts, where one was assured of a heterogeneous company so remarkable that it was said that Milnes earned his fame merely by having breakfast.

N. MERRILL DISTAD

Bibliography

Hennessy, James Pope. *Monckton Milnes: The Years of Promise, 1809–1851 and The Flight of Youth, 1851–1885.* 1951–1955. 2 vols.

Reid, Thomas Wemyss. *The Life, Letters, and Friendships of Richard Monckton Milnes, First Lord Houghton.* 1890. 2 vols.

· · · · ·

MINING AND MINERS

Coal warmed the houses and fueled the industrial development of nineteenth-century Great Britain. The production of coal rose from 10 million tons in 1810 to 100 million tons in 1865. Just ten years later 200 million tons were mined. There was a proportional increase in the number of coal miners, from 69,600 in 1801 to over 200,000 in 1850. In 1914 over 1.2 million miners worked 3,000 mines.

The work of miners throughout the century was arduous and dangerous. Improvements were made in mine ventilation, transport, safety, and pay, but the miners' work at the coal face in 1914 was done substantially in the same way and with the same tools as in 1800.

Mining was the most dangerous of all land occupations. Between 1850 and 1914 around 1,000 miners were killed annually in accidents. Isolated occurrences accounted for

Hydraulic Coal-Cutting Machine. Illustrated London News, *5 October 1867.*
Library Company of Philadelphia.

most of the deaths. There were, however, occasional disasters. In 1862 an accident in the single shaft of the Hartley Colliery killed the workers ascending in the cage and suffocated the 204 miners still underground. Another major accident took 269 lives at Ebbw Vale in 1878.

The ratio of nonfatal to fatal accidents ran at about 100 to one. Nearly 20 percent of underground mine workers were injured each year. Although accidents declined after mid-century, between 1869 and 1919 a miner was killed every six hours and one was seriously injured every two hours. The psychological stress was augmented by the absence, until the passage of the Workmen's Compensation Act of 1897, of any but local and voluntary employer compensation for the injured.

Work in the mines was strenuous, disagreeable, and ultimately debilitating. Miners labored virtually in the dark. Safety lamps (which replaced candles after 1815) prevented explosions but gave off only a fraction of the light of a candle. In the twenty years following the introduction of lamps, deaths increased rather than decreased; owners used the lamp as a defense against bad ventilation as they pushed workers into deeper and more dangerous seams. Though ventilation improved after 1839, the dust raised by hewing and transporting coal was choking. Rats were

omnipresent, and no provision was made for human waste at the pit ends.

Seams less than eighteen inches in height could be worked only with the greatest discomfort. Even in thicker seams, most hewers had to work on their knees. The putters or hurriers, who moved the coal in the mines, had to bend double to navigate passages which were generally less than three feet high and often partially filled with water. The laboring conditions sapped the vigor of miners before they were thirty. Premature old age and early death characterized the trade.

The employment of women underground was in decline by the nineteenth century. However, before Shaftesbury's Act of 1842, which outlawed underground work by women, girls, and boys under the age of ten, a number of women and girls still worked as putters. They sometimes wore wide leather belts around their waists with a chain passing between their legs, and crawled along on all fours dragging trucks of coal. In Scotland bearers were predominantly women. They carried over a hundredweight of coal through the passages and up ladders to the pit top. Young girls and boys were assigned to negotiate baskets through the narrowest seams. Children from five to eight years old were employed as trappers. Isolated and in pitch dark, their job was to open and shut the doors in the passages which controlled ventilation. Since the trappers were among the first to go down into the pits and the last to come up, these children were underground about fourteen hours a day.

Hewers were paid by piece rate, and their hours were not absolutely fixed. They had to mine an established minimum each shift, however, and were often tied to set periods for descending and ascending the shaft. A typical shift before 1850 was twelve hours, declining to ten by 1900.

Since hewers were paid according to the amount of clean coal they sent to the surface, there were continual disagreements concerning the tally. As a result of the Coal Mine Regulation Act of 1860, the hewers were entitled to pay men chosen by themselves to check the accuracy of the weighing and the fairness of deductions for excessive dirt and stone. These checkweights, as workers' representatives, became the focus for trade union activity. The Miners' Federation of Great Britain was established in 1889, and won its first great test in the strike of 1893, in which it successfully resisted a 25 percent cut in wages.

Miners, especially the hewers, were generally well paid in comparison to other workers. In addition to wages, they often received free housing or rent allowances, free coal, and even, in some locales, free beer. Miners' wages were, however, unpredictable. There were periods of forced unemployment and short-time work dictated by lack of demand.

Miners' wages were also affected by the truck system. During the first half of the century, it was not uncommon for miners to be paid monthly. Employers would give the miners advances on their next pay on condition that it be spent in a "tommy shop" run by the mine, which generally charged about 20 percent above the market price for goods. Although laws were passed against the truck system as early as 1831, the system persisted well into the 1870s.

Miners' disposable income grew significantly in the course of the century. Truck declined, fining became less severe, and the average earnings nearly tripled. During the boom of 1871 to 1874, Black Country hewers made around 5 shillings a day, but in depression times this fell to 12 shillings a week.

In periods of demand, when the piece rates were high, hewers worked less strenuously and took off "Saint Monday" after their pay. Miners tended to regard any earnings above their norm as a windfall, and their first inclination, motivated by self-defense against work conditions which wore men out prematurely, was toward leisure.

BERNARD A. COOK

Bibliography

Benson, John. *British Coalminers in the Nineteenth Century: A Social History.* 1980.

Fay, Charles R. *Life and Labour in the Nineteenth Century.* 1933.

Flinn, Michael. W. *The History of the British Coal Industry.* 1983.

Foster, John. *Class Struggle and the Industrial Revolution: Early Industrial Capitalism in Three English Towns.* 1974.

Holbrook-Jones, Mike. *Supremacy and Subordination of Labour: The Hierarchy of Work in the Early Labour Movement.* 1982.

Kirby, M. W. *The British Coalmining Industry, 1870–1946: A Political and Economic History.* 1977.

Mitchell, B. R. *Economic Development of the British Coal Industry, 1800–1914.* 1984.

Samuel, Raphael, ed. *Miners, Quarrymen and Saltworkers.* 1977.

· · · · ·

MISSIONARIES

Queen Victoria's reign was the heyday of British missionary enterprise overseas. It was part of a general European expansion, as Europe looked outwards to conquer and convert. Technological and economic developments associated with the industrial revolution enabled and encouraged a self-confident Britain to lead in imperial expansion. Trade, it was believed, followed the flag, but so too did missionaries, intent on spreading Christianity and Victorian culture. Christianization and "civilization" went hand in hand. Missionaries acted as agents of Westernization and imperial expansion.

Old missionary organizations, such as the Society for Promoting Christian Knowledge (1698/9) and the Society for the Propagation of the Gospel (1701), gained a new lease on life in the nineteenth century and spread their wings into exotic places. Relatively young groups, including the Baptist Missionary Society (1792), the nondenominational London Missionary Society (1795), and the Church Missionary Society (1799)—all products of the late eighteenth-century evangelical revival—became involved across the globe.

Christianity made a bid to become a world religion. Missionaries of all denominations increased their activities in the West Indies as the transition was made from slavery to freedom. The Christian community grew in India. China was forcibly opened to missionary endeavor after the Opium Wars (1839–1842). The China Inland Mission—one of the largest missions in the world—was founded in 1865 by James Hudson Taylor (1832–1905). Missionaries penetrated Africa in increasing numbers. The first non-European Anglican bishop was Samuel Adjai Crowther (c. 1806–1891), bishop of the Niger Territories (1864).

In true Victorian style missionary societies flourished as voluntary organizations, relying on charitable contributions. They reflected an increase in Christian energy and a feeling of material and moral superiority. Middle-class Victorians gave generously to missionary work. An outstanding example of a philanthropist was Robert Arthington (1823–1900), who bequeathed over one million pounds to the Baptist Missionary Society and London Missionary Society.

British missionaries made significant achievements. First, language barriers were cracked and the Bible was widely translated. Some languages were put into written form for the first time. William Carey (1761–1834), often viewed as the father of modern missionary work, was an active Baptist missionary in India, translating the Bible into Bengali, Sanskrit, and Marathi. Second, church and school went together as missionaries tried to develop education from elementary to college level. For example, Fourah Bay College was founded in West Africa in 1827 by the Church Missionary Society. Alexander Duff (1806–1878), missionary of the Church of Scotland, was influential in introducing Western education

into India. Third, missionaries aided the transference of ideas and technology. Many became involved in agricultural development. The mission farm was a common feature, especially in Africa. Fourth, the nineteenth century saw the development of medical missionary work. The most famous medical missionary/explorer was **David Livingstone**, son-in-law of another significant missionary figure, Robert Moffat (1795–1883). Livingstone was particularly motivated by the slave trade in Africa and wanted to destroy the evil by making "an open path for commerce and Christianity."

Missionary success should not be exaggerated. The number of converts was always relatively small in China and India. Christianity found it difficult to penetrate Islamic or Buddhist areas. In terms of geographical expansion, Christianity was most successful in the West Indies and Africa south of the Sahara. Missionaries inevitably became targets for anti-Western aggression. For instance, missionaries were victims in both the Indian Mutiny of 1857 and the Boxer Rebellion in China at the turn of the nineteenth century.

It is difficult to strike a balance between the "good" and "bad" effects of missionary enterprise. Missionaries may have contributed to the destabilization of some cultures by trying to introduce Western customs and standards. On the other hand, missionaries generally had a deep humanitarian concern and, in some cases, tried to defend local people from outside exploiters. Missionary work and politics became intertwined as European rivals sought to expand their influence on the international scene.

In the second half of the nineteenth century missionary activity took a number of new turns. Single women were accepted as missionaries in the field for the first time. New missionary groups, such as the Universities Mission to Central Africa (1859) and the Cambridge Mission to Delhi (1877) sprang up. In a broader context, student movements became involved in a mission to the underprivileged in British society, reflected by the work of such institutions as Toynbee Hall (1884) in the East End of London. The Salvation Army (1865) managed to combine a world missionary role with a mission to the British poor.

OLWYN M. BLOUET

Bibliography

Latourette, Kenneth Scott. *A History of the Expansion of Christianity.* 1937–1945. 7 vols.

Neill, Stephen Charles. *Christian Missions.* 1964.

———, Gerald Anderson, and John Goodwin. *Concise Dictionary of the Christian World Mission.* 1971.

· · · · ·

MOLESWORTH, MARY LOUISA (1838-1921)

The popular and prolific writer remembered for her children's books and supernatural fiction was born Mary Louisa Stewart and spent a comfortable childhood in Manchester where her father was in business. Married in 1861 to Richard Molesworth, a career military man, she found the union unhappy. They legally separated in 1879. Her literary work until 1877 was published under the pseudonym "Ennis Graham."

Molesworth's novels for adults—*Lover and Husband* (1870), *She Was Young and He Was Old* (1872), *Not Without Thorns* (1873), and *Cicely* (1874)—incorporate suspense and dissect married life, but have been overshadowed by her children's books. The first volume was *Tell Me a Story* (1875). *Carrots* (1876) and *The Cuckoo Clock* (1877) established her fame. Many of Molesworth's tales evolved from stories told by her grandmother, Margaret Wilson; others are remarkable for her memory—and her observation, as a mother—of childhood's looming terrors and seemingly insurmountable problems. She also contributed much to magazines and wrote some penetrating articles on children's literature.

Travel in Thuringen lay the groundwork for Molesworth's first supernatural tale, "The Unexplained," which appeared in *Macmillan's* (May 1885). It reappeared in *Four Ghost Stories* (1888). A second volume, *Uncanny Stories* (1896) followed. A. C. Swinburne, who admired both types of Molesworth's fiction, was but one among many devotees. Both ghost and children's stories are infused with senses of the unseen and a reaching into the infinite. Molesworth's large output makes for thin quality, but her best work merits reading.

BENJAMIN FRANKLIN FISHER, IV

Bibliography

Green, Roger Lancelyn. *Mrs. Molesworth.* 1961.

Laskhi, Marghanita. *Mrs. Ewing, Mrs. Molesworth, and Mrs. Hodgson Burnett.* 1950.

See also CHILDREN'S LITERATURE

· · · · ·

MONEY

Most Victorian money circulated in the form of coins. The gold sovereign (the pound) provided the standard form of exchange, supported by a variety of silver and copper coins. The pound equalled 20 shillings and the shilling was divided into 12 pence (written "d"). Thus there were 240 pence to the pound. The guinea (a gold coin worth 21 shillings) was no longer minted after 1813, although the word remained in use.

In descending order of value, the coins in circulation were: sovereign (20 shillings); half sovereign; crown (5 shillings); double florin (4 shillings); half crown; florin (2 shillings); shilling (12 pence); sixpence; groat (4 pence); threepence; twopence; penny; halfpenny; and farthing. Coins were called by a bewildering variety of slang terms. A pound was a quid, a bean, or, in less affluent society, a couter. A half crown was half-a-bull; sixpence could be a pig, half-a-grunter, or a sow's belly. A shilling was a bob.

Paper money, in the form of notes issued by a variety of individual banks, was used much less than coins. Since a banknote was only as good as the stability of the bank that issued it, only Bank of England notes were widely used as a medium of exchange. The five-pound note was the smallest in circulation. Notes were not legal tender in Scotland and Ireland, but in England Bank of England notes were legal tender and convertible on demand into gold coin. Thus, Britain operated on a strict gold standard. Checks first appeared in 1825 but were very slow to gain acceptance.

DENNIS J. MITCHELL

Bibliography

Capie, Forrest and Alan Webber. *A Monetary History of the United Kingdom, 1870–1982.* 1985.

Feavearyear, Albert. *The Pound Sterling: A History of English Money.* 1963.

McMurtry, Jo. *Victorian Life and Victorian Fiction: A Companion for the American Reader.* 1979.

See also BANKING

· · · · ·

MONTEFIORE, MOSES H. (1784–1885)

Moses Montefiore secured his fortune in business early in life and then retired to devote nearly sixty years to political and philanthropic concerns of world Jewry. An observant Jew, Montefiore became president of the Board of Deputies of Anglo-Jews, the defense agency created by Britain **Jewry** to protect Jews from both foreign and domestic foes. In this capacity Montefiore enlisted the support of the British government on behalf of persecuted Jews abroad, undertook numerous missions to impoverished or endangered Jewish communities, and initiated projects aimed at the renewal of Palestine. Within Anglo-Jewry he served as a staunch advocate for Orthodox Judaism in bitter opposition to the nascent currents of liberalization and Reform.

Essentially, Montefiore functioned as an international Jewish diplomat. Following the 1840 Damascus blood libel against the Jews of Syria, Montefiore enlisted the cooperation of Jewish leaders in other Western nations and secured the release from prison of the local Damascus Jews. In turn, he induced the local Moslem authorities to repudiate the blood libel. Twice he undertook missions to Russia (1846, and again in 1872) to persuade the czar to alleviate the conditions of Jews there. Seven times he visited **Palestine** in search of avenues to facilitate rebuilding of the Jewish homeland. These initiatives fostered the concept of an international Jewish community to which all Jews belonged and signified a change in the attitude toward Palestine from an object of charity to a potential site for Jewish renewal.

Montefiore's diplomacy was not always successful. He trusted overly in promises easily tendered and quickly forgotten. But his career symbolized the age of Jewish emancipation, in which Jews felt able to pursue Jewish communal interests within the liberal climate of Victorian Britain.

STEVEN BAYME

Bibliography

Goodman, Paul. *Moses Montefiore.* 1925.

Roth, Cecil. *Essays and Portraits in Anglo-Jewish History.* 1962.

· · · · ·

MOORE, GEORGE AUGUSTUS (1852–1933)

The autobiographies, fiction, plays, and conversation of George Moore incarnate most of the important currents of late Victorian and modern British letters.

Moore was born into a Catholic landholding family in rural Ireland. From youth, he rejected that life and assumed various social and literary identities: Parisian decadent, English naturalist, Gaelic enthusiast, "sage of Ebury Street." Following his father's death in 1870, Moore left Ireland to study art in London, then Paris. Realizing his insufficient talent, he turned instead to literature. Although during this period he produced only two volumes of derivative Baudelairian verse, he read voluminously and later met most of the important Parisian writers and painters, whose works and characters he sketched in his popular 1893 study, *Modern Painting.*

In 1880 rent strikes in Mayo cut short Moore's apprenticeship, and he returned to England to order his financial affairs and begin a life of self-disciplined authorship. During the 1880s he produced the naturalist *A Mummer's Wife* (1885), a study of an alcoholic actress, and *A Drama in Muslin* (1886), an indictment of the marriage market among genteel Irish society. When Mudie's Library suppressed his first novel, *A Modern Lover* (1883), Moore began his long battle with censorship. His story of an unwed mother, *Esther*

Waters (1894), became a great success despite Mudie's ban.

Moore returned to Ireland in 1901 as a participant in the Gaelic revival. His reacquaintance resulted in a volume of short fiction, *The Untilled Field* (1903)—a major influence upon Joyce's *Dubliners*—and *The Lake* (1905, 1921), a significant innovation in depicting the unconscious. His disenchantment produced one of the greatest modern autobiographies, *Hail and Farewell* (1911). In his later years, Moore refined his oral narrative style in retelling tales from biblical, Greek, and Gaelic traditions.

Because Moore was deliberately controversial and contradictory, evaluations of his life and work, especially by his contemporaries, must be taken cautiously. As a Victorian, Moore was too modern to be fully comprehended, and to the postwar generation, he was a peculiar, if intriguing, relic from a distant age. Although his life and works were widely read and vigorously debated during his lifetime, modern scholarship has only recently begun to appreciate his achievement.

ELIZABETH GRUBGELD

Bibliography

Cave, Richard. *A Study of the Novels of George Moore.* 1978.

Gilcher, Edwin. *A Bibliography of George Moore.* 1970.

Hone, Joseph. *The Life of George Moore.* 1936.

See also IRISH LITERATURE

. . . . .

MORLEY, JOHN
(1838-1923)

John Morley, statesman and man of letters, edited several important periodicals, wrote books on literature, history, and politics, and achieved prominence in public life. An elected member of Parliament (1883), he also served as chief secretary for Ireland (1886, 1892-1895) and for India (1905). As Viscount Morley of Blackburn (1908) he entered the House of Lords where he served as lord president of the council from 1910 until his resignation in 1914.

As an editor who opened the pages of the *Fortnightly Review*, the *Pall Mall Gazette*, and *Macmillan's Magazine* to such young and controversial writers as Algernon Charles Swinburne (1837-1909), Thomas H. Huxley (1825-1895), and Walter Pater (1839-1894), Morley helped spark a real change in late Victorian literary consciousness. His own works, including *Voltaire* (1871), and *Rousseau* (1873), expounded French rationalism and progress to a new generation already on the road to radical politics. The *Life of John Cobden* (1881), *Burke* (1889), and *Gladstone* (1903) continued to champion liberal views.

In addition to his active political life from 1883 until 1914, Morley formed the National Education League to oppose the Education Act (1870) and argued against the Irish Coercion Bill in 1882. His work for Ireland and India was characterized by sympathy and reform. An advocate of peace, he spoke out against the Boer War (1899-1902) and resigned from the Asquith cabinet in 1914 when the neutrality faction lost favor.

JOHN J. CONLON

Bibliography

Alexander, Edward. *John Morley.* 1972.

Das, M. N. *India Under Morley and Minto: Politics Behind Revolution, Repression, and Reforms.* 1964.

Gross, John. *The Rise and Fall of the Man of Letters.* 1969.

Hirst, F. W. *The Early Life and Letters of John Morley.* 1927.

Horner, D. A. *John Morley: Liberal Intellectual in Politics.* 1968.

Morley, John. *Recollections.* 1917.

———. *The Works of John Morley.* 1921.

. . . . .

MORRIS, WILLIAM
(1834-1896)

William Morris was a major Victorian poet, author of prose romances, pioneering designer, and leader of the early British socialist movement. He was also a cofounder of Morris and Co., founder of the Kelmscott Press and the Society for the Protection of Ancient Buildings, and writer of many essays on social issues, book design, and the decorative arts. His literary gifts, social compassion, and love of organic forms informed this immense range of accomplishments and activities.

Morris was the eldest son of Emma Shelton Morris and William Morris, a wealthy London broker who died when Morris was fourteen. He attended Marlborough College (1848–1851) and Exeter College, Oxford (1853–1856). At Exeter, he made several close friends, among them Edward Burne-Jones, and began the *Oxford and Cambridge Magazine* (1856), the first of many cooperative projects in which Morris took an active role. In 1856 he was apprenticed briefly to the Gothic revival architect G. B. Street.

In 1858 he published *The Defence of Guenevere*, a brilliantly innovative volume of lyric and dramatic verse. The following year he married Jane Burden, the daughter of an Oxford stableman, and commissioned his friend Philip Webb to design the neo-medieval Red House in Upton, Kent; Morris and his friends designed the furniture and decorations. In 1861 he and several friends founded "The Firm" (Morris, Marshall, Faulkner and Co.; after 1874 Morris and Co.). With his collaborators, Morris designed and produced furniture, wallpapers, textiles, glassware, stained glass, tapestries, and carpets, and made Morris and Co. the leading English decorating firm and supplier of stained-glass church windows.

In 1865 Morris moved to London with his wife and two daughters, Jane Alice ("Jenny," born 1861) and Mary ("May," born 1862). The success of *The Life and Death of Jason* (1867), a long narrative poem, encouraged him to complete *The Earthly Paradise* (1868–1870), a tapestry of twenty-four poetic narratives derived from classical and medieval tales. These swift-moving, lucid, and highly pictorial tales made Morris one of the most popular poets of his age.

In the early 1870s Morris wrote the intensely introspective poetic "masque" *Love Is Enough* (1873) and other poems later included in *Poems by the Way* (1891). He also cotranslated the *Volsunga Saga* with the Icelander Eirikur Magnusson, and published his *The Story of Sigurd the Volsung* (1876),

based on the saga. In 1877 he founded the Society for the Protection of Ancient Buildings, which preserved hundreds of English churches and other buildings from mutilation disguised as "restoration."

In 1883 Morris joined England's first socialist organization, H. M. Hyndeman's Democratic Federation, later renamed the Socialist Democratic Federation, and in 1884 he led a large faction which seceded to form the Socialist League. For the rest of the decade, Morris was a tireless activist for the cause; he met several times each week with his comrades and delivered hundreds of lectures. He suffered arrest in 1885, edited the *Commonweal* and wrote prolifically for its columns, and added to his canon a long series of socialist literary works, including the song collection *Chants for Socialists* (1884); a narrative poem, *The Pilgrims of Hope* (1885); the historical meditations *A Dream of John Ball* (1887); and his most influential work, *News from Nowhere* (1890), a pastoral utopian-communist vision of England in the twenty-first century as a truly "green and pleasant land."

Morris's health failed in 1890, and divisions between anarchists and socialists brought an end to his leadership of the Socialist League. He cofounded with Emery Walker in 1891 the Kelmscott Press, the first English fine art press. The press's great masterpiece was *The Canterbury Tales*, with inset drawings by Burne-Jones and ornamental designs by Morris.

Different aspects of Morris's extensive lifework have found favor in various literary and political climates since his death. In the early twentieth century, he was perhaps most widely known as the designer whose work inspired what came to be known as the **arts and crafts movement**. Smaller groups have always admired him as the foster-father of British **socialism**, foster-grandfather of the ecological movement, and perhaps the most significant English book designer since Caxton. His poetic reputation suffered for a time from the critical disparagement of romantic narrative poetry. In the end, perhaps, what is most impressive about Morris's lifework is the energy and skill with which he held in creative suspension tendencies that might seem dialectically opposed: literary romanticism and a Marxist view of history; tireless social activism and introspective art; zealous preservation of the environment and ancient buildings and influential innovation of modern design; the creation of complex forms of decorative art and simple evocation of natural emotion; blunt anger at human greed or inequity and faith in the redemptive value of communal effort; and a dreamlike talent at poetic fantasy and passionate belief in the pleasure and dignity of work.

FLORENCE BOOS

Bibliography

Aho, Gary L. *William Morris: A Reference Guide.* 1985.

Burne-Jones, Georgina. *Memorials of Burne-Jones.* 1904. 2 vols.

Calhoun, Blue. *The Pastoral Vision of William Morris.* 1975.

Faulkner, Peter, ed. *William Morris: The Critical Heritage.* 1973.

Goode, John. "William Morris and the Dream of Revolution." In John Lucas, ed., *Literature and Politics in the Nineteenth Century.* 1971.

Kelvin, Norman. *The Collected Letters of William Morris.* Vol. 1: 1848–1880. 1984.

Lindsay, Jack. *William Morris: His Life and Work.* 1975.

Mackail, J. W. *The Life of William Morris.* 1899; rpt. 1968.

Morris, May. *William Morris: Artist, Writer, Socialist.* 1936. 2 vols.

Silver, Carole. *The Romance of William Morris.* 1982.

Thompson, E. P. *William Morris: Romantic to Revolutionary.* 2d ed., 1976.

Thompson, Paul. *The Work of William Morris.* 1967.

. . . . .

MORRIS, ARTHUR
(1863–1945)

Arthur Morrison, journalist, author, and authority on Japanese art, was born of working-class parents near the East End of London, whose slums and people he vividly depicted in his fiction.

Little is known about Morrison's life. After working as a clerk in the People's Palace and publishing the supernatural stories of *The Shadows Around Us* (1891), he gained recognition with *Tales of Mean Streets* (1894), frank, discerning stories about the working classes. His best novel, *A Child of the Jago* (1896), starkly describes the imprisoning effects of crime and poverty on a young boy and his family, and demonstrates Morrison's intimate knowledge of the violent, brutalizing conditions of one of London's worst slums. Other working-class novels include *To London Town* (1899) and the more highly regarded *The Hole in the Wall* (1902), which is written, like Dickens's *Bleak House*, from both a first-person and an omniscient point of view. Morrison also wrote detective fiction in the 1890s, was one of the earliest and best imitators of Arthur Conan Doyle, and narrated the exploits of his serial detective, Martin Hewitt, with considerable skill and ingenuity of plot.

Once widely known and now unjustly neglected, Morrison at his best was an accurate, objective, and compassionate observer of the poor and working classes. His uncompromising vision and clear, uncluttered prose make *A Child of the Jago* one of the most noteworthy naturalistic novels written in England. By 1910, Morrison had virtually ceased writing fiction to devote himself to his collection of Japanese art.

RICHARD BENVENUTO

Bibliography

Bell, Jocelyn. "A Study of Arthur Morrison." In *Essays and Studies for the English Association.* 1952.

Calder, Robert. "Arthur Morrison: A Commentary with an Annotated Bibliography of Writings About Him." *English Literature in Transition,* vol. 28, pp. 276–297.

Frierson, William C. *The English Novel in Transition, 1885–1940.* 1942.

Keating, P. J. Biographical Study in *A Child of the Jago,* by Arthur Morrison. 1969.

Keating, P. J. *The Working Classes in Victorian Fiction.* 1971.

Krzak, Michel. Preface to *Tales of Mean Streets*, by Arthur Morrison. 1983.

See also WORKING-CLASS NOVEL

· · · · ·

MOZLEY, HARRIET NEWMAN (1803-1852)

The eldest sister of **John Henry Newman**, Harriet Mozley remained a staunch member of the Church of England and became estranged from Newman after his conversion to Roman Catholicism in 1845. She married Thomas Mozley (1806-1893), a Tractarian vicar and former pupil of Newman's at Oxford, in 1836.

Like her better-known contemporary, Charlotte Yonge (1823-1901), Mozley wrote juvenile fiction in order to advance and defend Anglican principles. Her most significant work, *The Fairy Bower* (1841), is notable for lively and realistic characterization despite a strong didactic purpose. The story, which explores the ramifications of a young girl's deception at a house party, satirizes permissive and romanticized approaches to education, which Mozley attributed to evangelical influence. A sequel, *The Lost Brooch* (1841), portrayed the same group of children as young adults; again, deception and manipulation were attributed to misguided evangelical fervor. Other works by Mozley include *Hymns for the Children of the Church of England* (c. 1841), an adult novel, *Louisa: Or, The Bride* (1842), *Bessie Gray: Or, the Dull Child* (1842), *The Old Bridge* (1842), and *Family Adventures* (1852).

ANITA C. WILSON

Bibliography

Avery, Gillian. *Nineteenth Century Children: Heroes and Heroines in English Children's Stories, 1780-1900*. 1965.

Bratton, J. S. *The Impact of Victorian Children's Fiction*. 1981.

Salway, Lance, ed. *A Peculiar Gift: Nineteenth Century Writings on Books for Children*. 1976.

Tillotson, Kathleen. *Novels of the Eighteen Forties*. 1954.

Ward, Maisie. *Young Mr. Newman*. 1948.

Yonge, Charlotte M. "Children's Literature: Part 3 Class Literature of the Last Thirty Years." *Macmillan's Magazine*, vol. 20, pp. 448-456.

· · · · ·

MUDIE, CHARLES EDWARD (1818-1890)

As proprietor of Victorian Britain's largest circulating library, Charles Edward Mudie influenced popular reading taste and the development of the three-volume novel as the period's dominant form.

In 1842 Mudie began lending books from his stationer's shop in Bloomsbury for a guinea a year; competitors charged from four to ten guineas. Mudie's Select Library moved to larger premises in New Oxford Street in 1852. Branches were established in the City of London, Birmingham, and Manchester, and books were sent by vans to provincial libraries and country houses.

Mudie bought large quantities of poetry, nonfiction prose, and novels (nearly half his stock). His moral bias was evident in his selection of novels—a strict Congregationalist, Mudie perpetuated the "young-girl standard": fiction should be suitable for family reading and should not offend the moral sensibilities of young ladies. Books Mudie considered objectionable were not circulated at all or were given token representation on his shelves and were excluded from advertised lists.

Ordinary readers who could not afford expensive three-volume novels borrowed them from circulating libraries. And publishers preferred large regular acquisitions by libraries to occasional individual purchases, so economic relations between publisher and librarian supported the three-volume form. But the extension of literacy and the growing popularity of serialized and cheap single-volume editions gradually undermined this system. In 1894 Mudie's library and its main competitor, W. H. Smith and Son, banned the triple-decker from their shelves, effectively ending the form's dominance. After Mudie's death his library operated, with declining success, until 1937.

SHARON LOCY

Bibliography

Altick, Richard D. *The English Common Reader: A Social History of the Mass Reading Public, 1800-1900.* 1957.

Cruse, Amy. *The Victorians and Their Books.* 1935.

Griest, Guinevere L. *Mudie's Circulating Library and the Victorian Novel.* 1970.

Irwin, Raymond. *The Origins of the English Library.* 1958.

Leavis, Q. D. *Fiction and the Reading Public.* 1932.

· · · · ·

and the Lamb (1820), *The Convalescent from Waterloo* (1822), *The Sonnet* (1839), *Crossing the Ford* (1842), and several paintings illustrative of *The Vicar of Wakefield* in the 1840s. While his works show the influences of both seventeenth-century Dutch models and such contemporaries as Wilkie, Mulready's scenes suggest the vulnerability and ambivalence of youth to a degree unusual for the period. In his use of brilliant color and his precise rendering of detail, he is a forerunner of the Pre-Raphaelites.

JOE K. LAW

Bibliography

Heleniak, Kathryn Moore. *William Mulready.* 1980.

Stephens, Frederic G. *Memorials of William Mulready, R. A.* 1890.

· · · · ·

MULREADY, WILLIAM (1786-1863)

William Mulready, best known for his popular anecdotal narrative paintings, was born in Ireland and brought up in London. He studied with the neoclassical sculptor Thomas Banks (1735-1803) in 1799, preparatory to entering the Royal Academy Schools in 1800. During these years Mulready helped support himself by illustrating children's books, including some for William Godwin (1756-1836). *The Looking Glass*, published by Godwin in 1805 under the pseudonym Theophilus Marcliffe, is based on Mulready's early life. In the Royal Academy, Mulready studied with John Varley (1782-1842), eventually becoming his assistant and in 1803 marrying his sister Elizabeth (1784-1864), from whom he was formally separated in 1810. Mulready became an associate of the Royal Academy in 1815 and a full member early in the following year. He was subsequently a teacher in the Royal Academy Schools.

Mulready's early works were principally landscapes, but after 1813 he turned increasingly to domestic genre paintings, particularly to scenes of childhood, young love, and literary themes. Among his best-known works are *The Fight Interrupted* (1816), *The Wolf*

MUNBY, ARTHUR JOSEPH (1828-1910) and HANNAH CULLWICK (1833-1909)

Arthur Joseph Munby was a civil servant, diarist, and minor poet, whose verse was admired during his lifetime for its celebration of country life and working-class women. He is now more famous for the diaries that record his friendships in London literary and artistic circles and reveal the extent of his obsession with working-class women.

The eldest son of a York solicitor, Munby took a degree at Cambridge and was called to the bar, but failed as a lawyer. He served as a bureaucrat in the office of the Ecclesiastical Commission (1858-1888), taught evening Latin classes at the Working Men's and Working Women's colleges, and published numerous volumes of verse. Munby's diaries and papers reveal an intense interest in working-class women, which prompted him to pursue, interview, record, and photograph them. This obsession had sexual overtones, and in 1873 he secretly married his maidservant, Hannah Cullwick (1833-1909), whom he personally educated and inspired to keep her own diary.

Their courtship was lengthy, and they lived together both as man and wife and as master and servant. During later years, however, they lived apart but visited and corresponded frequently.

Munby bequeathed his papers and diaries, together with Cullwick's, to Trinity College, Cambridge. Well-edited selections have been published. They represent an era that produced few first-class diarists, and provide sociological evidence about working women on a par with that of Henry Mayhew. They also record the tragic Victorian love story of two people who tried, but ultimately failed, to overcome the barriers of class.

N. MERRILL DISTAD

Bibliography

Cullwick, Hannah. *The Diaries of Hannah Cullwick, Victorian Maidservant.* Ed. Liz Stanley. 1984.

Davidoff, Leonore. "Class and Gender in Victorian England: The Diaries of Arthur J. Munby and Hannah Cullwick." In Judith L. Newton et al., eds. *Sex and Class in Women's History.* 1983.

Hudson, Derek. *Munby, Man of Two Worlds: The Life and Diaries of Arthur J. Munby, 1828–1910.* 1972.

See also HOUSEWORK AND
DOMESTIC TECHNOLOGY
. . . . .

MUSEUMS AND GALLERIES

The establishment of collections and exhibitions that were open to the general public and carefully arranged and catalogued to educate as well as provide viewing pleasure was a significant feature of the Victorian period. Important museums and galleries opened during the nineteenth century include the Victoria and Albert Museum, the National Gallery, the Tate Gallery, the National Portrait Gallery, the Dulwich College Picture Gallery, the Walker Art Gallery in Liverpool, the Birmingham Museum and Art Gallery, and the Manchester City Art Gallery. In addition, the British Museum (founded in 1753) flourished and grew during the Victorian era.

The Victoria and Albert Museum, begun under the guidance of Prince Albert and Henry Cole (1808–1882) after the Exhibition of 1851, was intended to demonstrate the close relationship between art and manufacture. Originally called the Museum of Ornamental Art, it opened in 1852 and moved in 1856 to an iron building in South Kensington which soon became known as the "Brompton Boilers." When this "Iron Museum" opened in 1857 it contained an educational museum, a museum of ornamental art under the direction of J. C. Robinson, and a museum of construction under Francis Fowkes. Other departments formed the basis of the Maritime Museum, the Science Museum, and several other museums of later years. In 1867 a large part of the "Iron Museum" relocated at Bethnal Green. New buildings subsequently arose at the original site; in 1889 Queen Victoria laid the foundation stone for the renamed Victoria and Albert Museum.

The **National Gallery** was founded in 1824, after Parliament approved the purchase and exhibition of the John Julius Angerstein collection. The first director was Charles Eastlake. From 1824 to 1834 the collection was exhibited at 100 Pall Mall. It moved to the present building, designed by William Wilkins, in 1838 and began to attract significant gifts and bequests, including Robert Vernon's collection of contemporary British painting (1847). In 1851 **J. W. M. Turner** bequeathed to the National Gallery all of the pictures remaining in his possession.

Many paintings from the National Gallery were eventually removed to the Tate Gallery, as were some collections of paintings from the Victoria and Albert. The Tate, officially opened in 1897 under Charles Holroyd as first keeper, housed the national collection of modern British art, limited to artists born after 1790.

The National Portrait Gallery was the achievement of Philip Henry, fifth earl of Stanhope. In 1856 Stanhope moved in the House of Lords to approve the founding of a "Gallery of the Portraits of the most eminent persons in British History." It was opened at 29 Great George Street in 1859.

The Dulwich College Picture Gallery, England's first public picture gallery, assumed major prominence in 1814 when it received four hundred paintings from the collection of art dealer Noel Desenfans. The Dulwich was the most important gallery in England in the early years of the nineteenth century, before the founding of the National Gallery.

Several other important galleries were founded in provincial cities during the Victorian period. The Brimingham Museum and Art Gallery originated after an exhibition in Birmingham in 1849 through the efforts of two citizens, J. T. Bunce and W. C. Aitlen, who believed the city needed an industrial museum. The Birmingham and Midland Institute opened in 1852 and provided classes for artisans, but it was not until 1870 that the city formed the Art Gallery Sub-Committee which instituted the Public Picture Gallery Fund the following year. H. Yeoville Thomason designed the gallery building. The city appointed George Wallis the keeper of the gallery in 1884 and officially opened the Birmingham Art Gallery in 1885.

In Manchester, the Institution for the Promotion of Literature, Science and the Arts was founded in 1823. Charles Barry designed its building, which was completed in 1834. In 1853 the south wing of the institution became the School of Design, which later developed into the Manchester School of Art. Under the Manchester Corporation Act of 1882, the institution became the City Gallery of Manchester.

The Walker Art Gallery in Liverpool had its origin in the collection of William Roscoe, which he sold in 1816. Part of this art collection went to the Liverpool Royal Institution, which eventually transferred it to the Walker, a gallery founded to house the annual autumn exhibition organized by the Liverpool Corporation Act in 1871.

In establishing galleries supported by state and municipal funds, the Victorians gave the stamp of official approval to certain artists and eventually made art available to a wide range of viewers, although the period was also marked by debates over free admission and Sunday openings, which were both necessary if working people were to have real (and not merely nominal) access to public institutions. The best sources of information are to be found in catalogues issued by the individual museums and galleries.

OWEN SCHUR

Bibliography

Altick, Richard. *The Shows of London*. 1978.

Boase, T. S. R. *English Art: 1800–1870*. 1959.

Catalogue of the National Portrait Gallery. 1949.

A Century of Collecting: 1882–1982: The Manchester City Art Galleries. 1983.

Darby, Michael et al. *The Victoria and Albert Museum*. 1983.

Davies, Stuart. *By the Gains of Industry: The Birmingham Museum and Art Gallery*. 1985.

Gaunt, William. *The Restless Century*. 1973.

The National Gallery Catalogue. 1955.

Pictures in the Walker Art Gallery. 1974.

The Tate Gallery. 1969.

See also ANTIQUARIANISM; NATURAL HISTORY; POPULAR SHOWS AND EXHIBITIONS

· · · · ·

MUSIC

Music was part of the fabric of Victorian life in all classes and in many contexts and situations, although the achievement of British composers was modest. Because music in performance is as evanescent as conversation, and most scores still await modern revival, knowledge of Victorian music today is less developed than knowledge of the other arts.

Germans, confident of their musical hegemony, often called Britain *Das Land ohne Musik*; there was even a German book with that title (about Britain in general), written by Oscar A. Schmitz and published in 1914. The notion that "the English are not a musical people" was widely held by the Victorians themselves, so much so that **George Alexander Macfarren** wrote a long article to refute it in the *Cornhill Magazine* (September 1868). It was founded on the undoubted fact that England for two hundred years failed to produce composers of the towering stature of Mozart, Beethoven, Berlioz, Chopin, Verdi, Wagner, or Tchaikovsky. No age was more inclined than the nineteenth century to measure the musical health of a culture in terms of individual genius.

Many cases of precocious musical talent are recorded among Victorian musicians—William Crotch (1775–1847), **William Sterndale Bennett** (1816–1875), and Frederick Ouseley (1825–1889) began with wonderful promise, but fell short of true greatness in their achievement. Even **Arthur Sullivan** (1842–1900) did not fulfill the hopes of his early admirers. The explanation must be sought in the climate in which composers had to work. Bennett wrote to his German publisher, Friedrich Kistner, in 1840: "You know what a dreadful place England is for music; and in London, I have nobody who I can talk to about good things, all the people are mad with Thalberg [a popular virtuoso pianist] and Strauss [the "waltz king"], and I have not heard a single Symphony or Overture in a concert [since] last June." This was a slight misrepresentation: symphonies and overtures were there for the hearing. But Bennett, who had recently returned from the stimulating musical life of Leipzig, spoke from the heart.

The inability of London to nurture and reinforce native composers was a negative aspect of that same middle-class leadership that was so positive and dynamic in other spheres. There was a long history of Puritan disapproval of church and theater music, and of indifference to domestic music; and, as many families now grew away from their Puritan heritage, the aristocratic model they adopted in its place fostered a new attitude, voiced in an earlier generation by the earl of Chesterfield: that music was an effeminate and ungentlemanly pursuit, which should be left mainly to the ladies, and even then only as a social accomplishment. As Mr. Brooke put it in *Middlemarch*, "there is a lightness about the feminine mind—a touch and go—music, the fine arts, that kind of thing, they should study those up to a certain point, women should, but in a light way, you know." Professional music making was better left to foreigners. Hence the serious native composer had to struggle against a strongly held presupposition that good music was German or Italian. If he was a man, he could not find, as Schubert did in Vienna, Berlioz in Paris, or Schumann in Leipzig, a circle of young male intellectuals who valued music highly as one of their serious interests. If she was a woman, it was

taken for granted that she was incapable of attaining anything important.

Despite these discouragements, some Victorian composers did produce fine work, and even an occasional masterpiece. Bennett and Macfarren themselves wrote much excellent orchestral and piano music and songs; Macfarren, **Michael Balfe**, William Wallace, **Edward Loder**, and others maintained a valid English school of **opera**, until in the 1870s Sullivan was able to raise it to decisive stature; in the indigenous field of **cathedral music** the Victorian period produced an undoubted genius, **Samuel Sebastian Wesley**, and a supporting set of talented composers. In the last two decades of the century a group headed by **C. H. H. Parry**, **C. V. Stanford**, and **Edward Elgar** generated a new boldness and excitement that some have termed an English musical renaissance. Even women composers like Maude Valérie White, Liza Lehmann, and Ethel Smyth began to win acclaim.

By any other yardstick than that of creative achievement, the Victorians were, indeed, a musical people. In rural areas throughout the United Kingdom there were flourishing traditions of folksong and fiddle dances, with, in Scotland and Ireland, the added cult of the bagpipe. Country wind and string bands played in English parish churches and dissenting chapels until ousted by barrel organ or harmonium, and still continued to adorn harvest festivals, morris dances, and weddings. The urban working class brought its **folk music** into the towns and factories; **broadsides** fitted the old tunes to new texts expressing the work ethic, hardship, or political aspiration. Mingled with the styles of art music, folksong formed the basis of both the hymn singing of open-air revivals and the commercial mass entertainment of the **music halls**. The brass band movement, a uniquely English development, provided recreation for tens of thousands of working-class people.

The wealth of the middle classes generated an explosion in the publication of sheet music and a burgeoning of concerts of all kinds, so that London's musical life at midcentury was at least as brilliant and varied as that of any European capital. As Bennett's remarks show, there was a growing split between the commercial **popular music** that appealed to everybody (the drawing-room **ballad**, waltz, and popular piano piece) and what was now called the "classical" music of high art; but the latter also had massive support, as is demonstrated by the huge number of orchestral, chamber music, and choral organizations in London and the provinces alike. Theater music, from **opera** and **ballet** to **musical comedy**, **pantomime** and burlesque, also flourished.

The Victorians loved **choral music**, which tended to unite all classes in amateur **oratorio** societies, and in great festivals at such towns as Birmingham, Leeds, Norwich, and the Three Choirs (Gloucester, Hereford, and Worcester). In these settings the ritual performance of Handel's *Messiah*, which Victorians thought of as the greatest religious masterpiece of all time and as a monument of Britain's greatness, was always the crowning event. The colossal performances staged at the Crystal Palace, and later at the Royal Albert Hall, had imperial overtones, and their decline in the 1960s coincided with that of the colonial empire.

NICHOLAS TEMPERLEY

Bibliography

Brown, James D. and S. S. Stratton. *British Musical Biography*. 1897.

Ehrlich, Cyril. *The Music Profession in Britain Since the Eighteenth Century: A Social History*. 1985.

Fuller-Maitland, John. *English Music in the XIXth Century*. 1902.

Gatens, William C. *Victorian Cathedral Music in Theory and Practice*. 1986.

Howes, Frank. *The English Musical Renaissance*. 1966.

Lloyd, Albert. *Folk-Song in England*. 1969.

Mackerness, Eric. *A Social History of English Music*. 1964.

Temperley, Nicholas, ed. *The Athlone History of Music in Britain*. Vol. 5: *The Romantic Age 1800–1914*. 1981.

———, ed. *The Lost Chord: Studies in Victorian Music*. 1988.

Vicinus, Martha. *The Industrial Muse*. 1974.

Weber, William. *Music and the Middle Class: The Social Structure of Concert Life in London, Paris and Vienna, Between 1830 and 1848*. 1975.

See also BANDS AND BAND MUSIC; DANCE MUSIC; HYMNS.

· · · · ·

MUSIC AND MORALS

Music and Morals was the title of a book by the London Broad Church clergyman Hugh Reginald Haweis (1838–1901). First published in 1871, it went through some sixteen editions during the author's lifetime, and continued to be printed well into the twentieth century. It was the most widely read work on its subject, and its premise was of continuing interest to Victorians, both earlier and later: namely, that the experience of music has a direct influence on the listener's moral character.

Haweis maintained that the experience of emotion leaves a lasting impression on one's moral character, and that music deliberately cultivates and manipulates emotional atmospheres. A more mystical view was advanced by Adolf Bernhard Marx (1795–1866), an English translation of whose *Allgemeine Musiklehre* (1839) was published by Novello in 1854, and partly serialized in the *Musical Times*. Marx claimed that music is an emanation from the profoundest reaches of the human spirit, but that it is susceptible to corruption into mere corporeal sensation and shallow virtuosity with deleterious moral consequences. John Ruskin, drawing on classical Greek sources, developed theories of music and morals, principally in his Robert Rede lecture (1867), *The Queen of the Air* (1869), *Fors Clavigera* 82 and 83 (1877), and the preface to *Rock Honeycomb* (1877). Edmund Gurney (1847–1888) in *The Power of Sound* (1880) denied the direct moral influence of music, but maintained that moral benefits can result as an indirect by-product of musical enjoyment.

The moral benefits of music were a chief foundation of the British singing class movement that began in the 1840s under the leadership of Joseph Mainzer (1801–1851), John Hullah (1812–1884), and John Curwen (1816–1880). It was part of the self-improvement ethos of the time and had links with the mechanics' institutes and the temperance movement. Mainzer's *Music and Education* (1848) developed a mystical theory of music and morals similar to that of A. B. Marx. There were also links between the singing class movement and the contemporaneous efforts by High Churchmen to revive choral worship in parish churches. Moral considerations, generally couched in spiritual and devotional terms, also played a part in the development of Victorian cathedral music.

WILLIAM J. GATENS

Bibliography

Gatens, William J. *Victorian Cathedral Music in Theory and Practice.* 1986.

Rainbow, Bernarr. *The Choral Revival in the Anglican Church 1839-1872.* 1970.

———. *The Land Without Music.* 1967.

Scholes, Percy A. *The Mirror of Music, 1844-1944.* 1947.

· · · · ·

MUSIC CRITICISM

Nineteenth-century musical criticism was frequently entrusted to journalists whose primary concern was drama. But with the emergence of a musical press, professional musicians began to contribute more specialized discussions of musical topics.

Perhaps the first Victorian music critic of consequence was Edward Holmes (1797-1859), a pupil of Vincent Novello (1781-1861), who wrote principally for the *Atlas* (1826-1852). Holmes's tastes were not, as his *Life of Mozart* (1845) might suggest, confined to the Viennese school: he also admired Berlioz and John Field, as well as Purcell, Bach, and the Elizabethans. Into the work of two midcentury critics, Henry Fothergill Chorley (1808-1872) and J. W. Davison (1813-1885), of the *Athenaeum* and the *Times* respectively, there enters a note of trenchant partisanship, the former championing Italian opera and the latter upholding the ethos of Mendelssohn in preference to that of Schumann, Liszt, and Wagner. Both these influential figures were

quick to condemn slovenly performances and to denounce the bugbear of complacent idolatry. A controversy over "The Music of the Future" preoccupied some writers until the end of the century.

Davison's successor on the *Times*, Francis Hueffer (1843-1889), was an enthusiastic Wagnerian, and Wagner also found adherents in men like Edward Dannreuther (1844-1905) and William Ashton Ellis (d. 1919), editor of the *Meister* (1888-1895). Before the turn of the century, Ernest Newman (1868-1959) had published important studies of Gluck and Wagner; but it was George Bernard Shaw (1856-1950) who offered, in *The Perfect Wagnerite* (1898), possibly the most plausible explication of Wagner's musico-dramatic objectives.

The verve and piquancy of Shaw's contributions to the *Star* and the *World* tend to obscure the fact that his judgments were distorted by his suspicions of academic composers and by his attempts to denigrate post-Handelian oratorio. Yet he did discredit the aridity that disfigured the purely technical discussions of music by men like George Macfarren (1813-1887), Frederick Gore Ouseley (1825-1889), and Ebenezer Prout (1835-1909).

The authoritative commentary found in the *Musical World* (1836-1891), the *Musical Times* (1844-), the *Tonic Sol-Fa Reporter* (1851-1920) and similar journals reflected a growing desire for enlightenment on subjects ranging from musical antiquarianism to the possibility of an English "nationalist" movement. Musical criticism of distinction is also to be found in the analytical notes supplied by John Ella (1802-1888) and George Grove (1820-1900) for programs sold at the Musical Union concerts and at the orchestral concerts given at the Crystal Palace.

E. D. MACKERNESS

Bibliography

Bennett, Joseph. *Forty Years of Music, 1865-1905.* 1908.

Chorley, H. F. *Thirty Years' Musical Recollections.* 1862.

Davison, Henry. *Music During the Victorian Era.* 1912.

Elgar, Edward. *A Future for English Music.* 1968. Ed. Percy M. Young.

Shaw, George Bernard. *Music in London.* 1932.

 . . . . .

MUSIC EDUCATION

The Victorian period saw the rise of music education in Britain: general, academic, and professional.

In the nation's elementary schools music was introduced on the recommendation of James Kay-Shuttleworth's Committee on Education, which believed that popular song was "an important means of forming an industrious, brave, loyal and religious people." Under the direction of John Pyke Hullah (1812–1884), schoolteachers from 1840 onward were trained in a new method of teaching singing, devised by Guillaume Wilhem for use in Paris schools. A superior method, adapted by the Congregationalist minister John Curwen (1816–1880) from an invention of the Norwich schoolteacher Sarah Anna Glover (1786–1867), gradually took over from Wilhem-Hullah and was established by the Education Act of 1870. Known as tonic sol-fa, it employed letters and a few other symbols, and allowed children to learn music easily without the complexities of conventional notation. At first they sang only religious and moralizing songs; later, Charles Stanford's *Class Singing for Schools* (1884) provided more attractive materials, making use of old English folksong.

In secondary education, which in Victorian times was confined to independent and endowed schools, music was slow to find a place other than as a traditional accomplishment for young ladies. The first music master at a boys' public school was a German, Paul David (1840–1932), appointed to Uppingham in 1865. The first organized university course on music, developed out of the requirements for the ancient degree of Bachelor of Music, was at Oxford, where the Reverend Sir Frederick Arthur Gore Ouseley, Bart. (1825–1889), professor of music from 1855, introduced written examinations in 1862. Cambridge followed suit under **William Sterndale Bennett** (1816–1875), professor from 1856; his predecessor Thomas Attwood Walmisley (1814–1856) had

given outstanding lectures on musical history. Courses of musical instruction were also introduced at Trinity College, Dublin (1871), London (1876), Edinburgh (1890), and Manchester (1891).

The first professional training school for musicians was the Royal Academy of Music, opened in 1823. Originally housing only ten boys and ten girls, it slowly grew, but remained financially precarious until the late Victorian period. From 1832 to 1859 the principal was the remarkable Philip Cipriani Hambly Potter (1792–1871), the first effective teacher of classical principles of composition; his pupils included Bennett, **George Macfarren**, and other leading composers.

The National Training School for Music, inspired by an idea of the prince consort, opened in 1876, and was reorganized as the Royal College of Music in 1883 with George Grove (1820–1900), the distinguished amateur musician and music historian, as its first director. Several independent conservatories, both in London and in provincial cities, arose between 1860 and 1900.

NICHOLAS TEMPERLEY

Bibliography

Corder, Frederick. *A History of the Royal Academy of Music from 1822 to 1922.* 1922.

Rainbow, Bernarr. *The Land Without Music: Musical Education in England, 1800–1860 and Its Continental Antecedents.* 1967.

———. "Music in Education." In Nicholas Temperley, ed., *The Athlone History of Music in Britain,* vol. 5. 1981.

See also CHORAL MUSIC

 . . . . .

MUSIC HALL

"Music hall" refers to both a popular form of miscellaneous entertainment and the institution that housed and promoted it; this form of entertainment grew from obscure origins in the 1830s and 1840s to dominate the commercialized popular culture of the late nineteenth century.

Created by the demands of an expanding urban population, the early halls were little more than adjuncts to the public house, where traditional amateur entertainments of song and dance were supplemented by other folk and theatrical forms and rapidly professionalized. From midcentury, publican-entrepreneurs operated larger, more elaborate, purpose-built premises with a direct admission charge. Drink sales continued to be important to the economy of the halls, but drew the fire of temperance reformers and compromised the promoters' claim to offer improved or rational recreation. By the 1870s music halls outnumbered theaters and were big business, though capital was still raised informally and management was as much a social as a market exercise.

The industry's aspirations to respectability, both to capture a wider audience and to defend itself against critics and hostile licensing authorities, contributed to the introduction of the deluxe hall or variety theatre in the mid-1880s which reproduced the house and stage design of legitimate theaters and facilitated more ambitious productions. Costs were compounded by tougher competition, stringent new safety regulations, and the inflation of stars' salaries. The music hall increasingly went public for its funds and though an undergrowth of pubs or "free halls" survived, particularly in the north, the independent owner-proprietor was mostly superseded by large national and regional combines under modern management, whose massive new "Empires" and "Palaces" dominated the big cities and their suburbs. Under oligopoly, the music hall became more acceptable to licensing authorities and respectable public opinion, but by 1914 its prosperity was threatened by overproduction, the rise of the cinema, and Americanized song and dance.

The music hall's most distinctive idiom was the comic song. Commercially produced, it told in naturalistic detail of the commonplace (mis)adventures of everyday life. Its apparent banalities were much enlivened by the performer's dynamic engagement with the audience and the use of parody and double entendre. The latter provoked charges of immorality and tighter managerial controls on performance, but despite the increased scale and pretension of variety theaters, the great comic stars of the later period, such as **Marie** **Lloyd** and Dan Leno, maintained a collusive and irreverent intimacy with their audience. Though its programs might include **ballet** and classical music as well as a wider range of specialty acts, borrowed and contrived, the music hall was forbidden to stage the legitimate drama by the 1843 Theatres Act, though its persistent challenge to the law won a concession for the dramatic interlude or sketch. Increased recruitment from the legitimate theater contributed to the creeping *embourgeoisement* of the variety profession.

Audiences were predominantly working class and lower middle class with a substantial proportion of the single young, male and female. Prostitutes attracted middle-class males on the prowl; only with its later respectability did the music hall attract a bourgeois family audience, though the middle-class home was long familiar with its songs through sheet music sales. The logistics of the classic music hall maintained the informal sociability of the pub, and a mobile and demonstrative crowd exercised certain customs of control over territory and performance as well as its ritual participation in chorus singing and exchanges with the performers. Fixed seating and the reduction of drinking in the auditorium produced a more stabilized and passive audience, and the combines' standardization of entertainment for a national market made the variety theater a powerful agent in the homogenization of popular taste.

Assailed in its day as degenerate, the music hall has since been idealized as an authentic people's art which despite its modern origins was yet "traditionally" English. Recent reassessments consider it more the product of an incipient mass culture whose ideology of petty consumerism and jingo patriotism contributed to working-class deradicalization. As a prototype modern entertainment industry, the music hall remains a major testing ground for the study of cultural production and use in a capitalist society.

PETER BAILEY

Bibliography

Bailey, Peter, ed. *Music Hall: The Business of Pleasure.* 1986.

Bratton, J. S., ed. *Music Hall: Performance and Style.* 1986.

Senelick, Laurence, David Cheshire and Ulrich Schneider. *British Music Hall, 1840–1923: A Bibliography and Guide to Sources*. 1981.

See also ACTORS AND THE ACTING PROFESSION

. . . . .

MUSIC, POPULAR see POPULAR SONGS AND MUSIC

. . . . .

MUSIC PUBLISHERS

Before the advent of the phonograph, sheet music was the principal means by which music was disseminated, and it brought profit to hundreds of publishers. The number of domestic copyright musical works received in one year by the British Museum rose from 151 in 1835 to 7,114 in 1900, but the total published may well have been five times that many.

British music publishing was overwhelmingly centered in London, the more so as communications improved. Printing was chiefly from engraved pewter plates or, after midcentury, by lithography. Some publishers went all out for the big profits, which were to be gained from popular piano music and ballads. Sales could be greatly increased by pictorial music covers, which became an important vehicle for illustrators. Ballads were often launched by famous singers who were paid royalties by the publisher. Other areas of mass consumption were choral music in tonic sol-fa notation (using letters instead of notes) and hymn books with tunes.

Naturally, it was in these areas that **copyright** was most important to publishers. An act of 1842 extended copyright coverage to performance as well as publication. Enforcement of the former was difficult until the establishment of the Performing Rights Society (1876), and even after that time there was a mounting flood of litigation until the passage of the Copyright Act of 1902.

Some publishers managed to combine profit with dignity and prestige by astute marketing of high art music. Novello and Co., founded by Vincent Novello (1781–1861), in the 1840s used new mass production techniques to market cheap octavo scores of Handel oratorios, and went on to provide series of anthems, partsongs, and cantatas for the large body of amateur choral societies. Wessel and Co. cornered the market for Chopin's piano music, much of which was published simultaneously in London, Paris, and Leipzig to reduce international pirating. Wessel added silly titles to the pieces, which greatly annoyed the composer, but may have spread the music to middlebrow consumers. British-born composers had less market appeal; but by the 1880s Boosey and Co. as well as Novello gave positive support to British composers. **Edward Elgar** gracefully acknowledged his debt to A. G. Jaeger, of Novello, by making him the subject of "Nimrod," one of his "*Enigma*" *Variations* (1899).

NICHOLAS TEMPERLEY

Bibliography

Coover, James. *Music Publishing, Copyright and Piracy in Victorian England*. 1985

Krummel, Donald. "Music Publishing." In Nicholas Temperley, ed., *The Athlone History of British Music*, vol. 5. 1981.

Novello, Ewer and Co. *A Short History of Cheap Music*. 1887.

. . . . .

MUSICAL COMEDY

With a few significant exceptions, Victorian composers did not excel in the sphere of "grand" opera. There were, however, many who were skilled at devising lighter pieces for the lyric stage. The bewildering variety of musical plays staged publicly from 1830 onward makes it hard to differentiate sharply between **operetta**, comic opera, and extravaganza. Since the ballad opera tradition ensured the popularity of dramas in which spoken words alternated with music, prototypes of modern musical comedy can be found early in the nineteenth century. But the kind of production usually known as musical comedy became especially common during the 1880s and 1890s.

The satirical edge of Gilbert's libretti makes it difficult to consider the **Savoy operas** as musical comedy in the sense applicable to *A Country Girl* (Lionel Monckton, 1902) or *The Belle of New York* (Gustav Kerker, 1897), though Sullivan occasionally adopted their conventions. The main features of this genre—loosely constructed plots, "romantic" situations, singable melodies, and exotic spectacle—suited a dramatic mode in which the darker side of life was largely ignored; *The Shop Girl* (Caryll, Monckton, and Ross, 1894), with its poignant story of integrity triumphing over duplicity, typifies this kind of production.

During the last quarter of the nineteenth century there existed a large public for whom the *opera seria* in a foreign tongue was too demanding, and who regarded the theater as merely a place for casual relaxation. To satisfy the taste for easygoing postprandial diversion, theatrical managers lavished huge sums on spectacular presentations in which an appeal to the eye was as important as aural gratification. As some of the titles suggest, musical comedy frequently placed attractive females at the center of the action, and this aspect of late Victorian theatrical life was made much of by impresarios like George Edwardes (1852–1917) at Daly's, the Prince of Wales's, and the Gaiety theaters. He and others made it possible for composers such as Leslie Stuart (1856–1928), Ivan Caryll (1861–1921), and Sidney Jones (1861–1946) to evolve a musical idiom—usually nostalgic, free from angst and always agreeable—which their Edwardian successors, now subjected to rivalry from American and central European competitors, were able to utilize with success. From the time of *A Gaiety Girl* (1893) to *Chu Chin Chow* (1916), a succession of musical comedies held the stage, occupying a median position between "highbrow" opera and the more risqué temptations of the **music hall**.

E. D. MACKERNESS

Bibliography

Gammond, Peter and Peter Clayton. *A Guide to Popular Music.* 1960.

Hughes, Gervase. *Composers of Operetta.* 1962.

Mackinlay, Malcolm Sterling. *Origin and Development of Light Opera.* 1927.

Maitland, J. A. Fuller, *English Music in the XIX*[th] *Century.* 1902.

Pope, W. Macqueen. *Gaiety: Theatre of Enchantment.* 1949.

· · · · ·

MUSICAL SCHOLARSHIP

Musicology as a formal discipline was a German invention of the 1880s. But the scholarly study of music (as distinct from the theory of music, which goes back to Aristotle) was pioneered by English scholars as an offshoot of romantic antiquarianism, and was well advanced by 1837.

Britain had already produced the first two general histories of music, those of Charles Burney (1776–1789) and John Hawkins (1776); the first historical concert series (the Concert of Ancient Music, 1771–1848); and the first scholarly anthology of early music, John Stafford Smith's *Musica Antiqua* (1812). In the Victorian era Britain again led the way with the earliest scholarly society devoted to music, the Musical Institute of London (1851), succeeded in 1867 by the Musical Association (made Royal in 1944); the first comprehensive study of a country's **folk music**, William Chappell's *Ballad Literature and Popular Music of the Olden Time* (1855, 1859); and the first critical edition of the works of a composer, the Handel Society's set of scores of Handel's oratorios (1843–1858), which, however, remained incomplete.

Later monuments of Victorian musical scholarship include the Purcell Society's complete edition of Henry Purcell's works (1878–1962); John Stainer's edition of *Dufay and His Contemporaries* (1898); and J. A. Fuller-Maitland and W. Barclay Squire's edition of the *Fitzwilliam Virginal Book* (1899). Scholarly books, articles, and lectures abounded. The amateur musician and scholar George Grove (1820–1900) summed up British scholarly achievements in his four-volume *Dictionary of Music and Musicians* (1879–1890).

Ancient, exotic, and folk music had first been prized for their romantic color. But the

Victorians developed a more thorough and realistic appreciation of historical styles. As the "classical" composers Haydn, Mozart, and Beethoven became increasingly isolated (in audience perceptions) from contemporary musicians who catered to popular and commercial forces, so there came a steady upward reevaluation of still earlier music, leading inexorably toward the comprehensive historicism of our own time.

Vincent Duckles has pointed out that the orientation of British musical scholarship, as opposed to German, was always toward music as a concrete experience rather than as a field for philosophical speculation. Hence the abundance of historical concerts reviving early music, and even, as early as 1889, the beginnings of authentic performance on restored early instruments, pioneered in London by Arnold Dolmetsch (1858–1940).

NICHOLAS TEMPERLEY

Bibliography

Duckles, Vincent. "Musicology." In Nicholas Temperley, ed., *The Athlone History of Music in Britain*, vol. 5. 1981.

Grove, George. *A Dictionary of Music and Musicians*. 1879–1890. 4 vols.

King, A. Hyatt. *Some British Collectors of Music.* 1963.

· · · · ·

MYSTERY AND DETECTIVE FICTION

Although it is generally acknowledged that detective fiction began in 1841 with Edgar Allan Poe's *The Murders in the Rue Morgue*, there are at least three important antecedents. The *Newgate Calendar* recorded (with some embellishments) factual accounts of criminals and their apprehension and punishment. Begun in 1773 and continued in various forms for about fifty years, the *Newgate Calendar* provided source material for several novels, including Dickens's *Oliver Twist* (1837–1838). In William Godwin's *Things as They Are; or, The Adventures of Caleb Williams* (1794) the young protagonist discovers that his employer murdered a neighboring squire and eventually elicits a confession. Al-

though the novel is more of a political statement than a murder mystery, it is notable because Godwin claimed to have begun with the last book and worked his way forward, a technique that later became standard in mystery writing. The *Memoires* (1828–1829) of Eugene Francois Vidocq (1775–1857), a French criminal who later became the chief of the Sûreté, were also influential: Vidocq relied upon careful observation, extensive disguises, and undercover work; his memoirs established the image of a detective as a powerful force who is sometimes above the law.

When the Metropolitan Police Force added the Detective Department in 1842, Charles Dickens went on expeditions through the London slums in the company of Inspector James T. Field and published accounts of their adventures in *Household Words*. Field, transformed into Inspector Bucket, became the first detective in English fiction in *Bleak House* (1853). Bucket is depicted as a friendly, observant man who easily wins the confidence of strangers and quietly gathers the facts before making his move. Dickens's unfinished final novel, *The Mystery of Edwin Drood* (1870), centers upon the disappearance of a young man who has evidently been murdered by his uncle, a choirmaster. The presence of Mr. Datchery, an elderly man apparently wearing a disguise, suggests that Dickens intended to use Datchery as an undercover detective who would apprehend the murderer.

Wilkie Collins's *The Woman in White* (1860), published by Dickens in *All the Year Round*, employs multiple narratives to tell the story of Sir Percival Glyde and his villainous friend Count Fosco who among other things, attempt to defraud a young woman of her inheritance by having her confined to an asylum. In *The Moonstone* (1868), which is generally considered to be the first detective novel in English, Collins also uses multiple narratives. His chief investigator, Sergeant Cuff, was based on an actual London police detective, Jonathan Whicher, who had arrested the notorious Constance Kent. Cuff's habit of making enigmatic remarks, his obvious eccentricities (demonstrated by his passion for roses), and his use of a young street urchin for assistance were features freely borrowed by creators of later detectives.

No surge of important detective fiction immediately followed *The Moonstone*, despite its popularity. Major writers did not seem interested in the genre, possibly because it was difficult to maintain suspense throughout a novel the length of those that were in vogue. Irish writer Sheridan LeFanu produced some minor works; his *Uncle Silas* (1864) and *Wylder's Hand* (1864) are the most notable. The best-selling mystery novel of the period was *The Mystery of a Hansom Cab* (1886) by the Anglo-Australian writer Fergus W. Hume, which was reported to have sold more than 500,000 copies. Hume went on to write over one hundred crime novels, but none equaled the success of his first, a rather pedestrian piece that apparently sold because of heavy advertising.

Arthur Conan Doyle brought detective fiction to maturity. *A Study in Scarlet* (1887) introduced Sherlock Holmes and Dr. Watson to the world. It was followed by *The Sign of Four* in 1890. Structurally, both novels are relatively weak, employing digressive flashbacks to expand what are esssentially long short stories. The Holmes adventures were better suited to a short format; when they began to appear monthly in *The Strand Magazine* their popularity soared. Doyle combined elements from earlier mystery writing to create the archetypal detective, observant and rational in exercising deductive analysis yet willing to don disguises or resort to minor theatrics when revealing his conclusions. Holmes calls himself a "private" consulting detective; he works apart from the police and engages in friendly competition with official detectives, who sometimes misinterpret clues or bungle their investigations. Holmes frequently refuses to divulge important information to the police and sometimes takes the law into his own hands to dispense justice.

Doyle's other significant contribution to the genre was the creation of Watson, an affable but plodding narrator whose perceptions serve as a counterpoint to the brilliance of Holmes—and also solve a great many technical difficulties by misdirecting the reader's attention. Doyle's narrative formula, as well as Sherlock Holmes's methods and his position outside official channels, became models for twentieth-century mystery writers.

DON RICHARD COX

Bibliography

Glover, Dorothy. *Victorian Detective Fiction.* 1966.

Hubin, Allen J. *The Bibliography of Crime Fiction. 1745-1975.* 1979.

Johnson, Timothy W. and Julia Johnson. *Crime Fiction Criticism: An Annotated Bibliography.* 1981.

Most, Glenn W. and William W. Stowe, eds. *The Poetics of Murder: Detective Fiction and Literary Theory.* 1983.

Ousby, Ian. *Bloodhounds of Heaven: The Detective in English Fiction from Godwin to Doyle.* 1976.

Symons, Julian. *Mortal Consequences: A History—from the Detective Story to the Crime Novel.* 1972.

See also MORRISON, ARTHUR

. . . . .

MYTH

The Victorian period saw an upsurge of interest in myth as a subject for scholarly research, popular essays, and verse. By "myth" Victorian scholars meant primarily classical mythology; as used by poets, myth also embraces the mythologies of other cultures (e.g., the Norse cycles) and other primitive narrative sources such as national heroic legends and folklore.

One of the major achievements of Victorian mythographers was raising mythography above the polemical level that had characterized previous work (the usual goal of which had been to demonstrate that pagan myth was a distortion of Christianity, or vice versa). Carl Ottfried Müller (1797–1840) was perhaps most influential in making myth a subject for legitimate scholarly study, arguing that myths are essentially distorted history. George Grote's *History of Greece* (1846) explained myth as the poetic expression of a culture's "prevalent emotion." Max Müller's widely read philological studies (*Comparative Mythology*, 1856) found a solar cult at the root of all myths; Müller's diagnosis of the variation among myths as owing to a fundamental "disease of language" anticipates contemporary linguistic theory. Charles Kingsley (*The Heroes*, 1855) and Thomas Bulfinch (*The Age of Fable*, 1855) offered bowdlerizations which, while contributing to a facile twentieth-century dismissal of Victorian mythography, attest by their enormous popularity to the widespread popular interest in the subject.

In the face of reviewers' demands for contemporary subjects, Victorian poets defended the value of myth for a contemporary audience on the grounds that myth embodied eternal verities no longer otherwise available. Poetic practice did not, however, always follow this appeal to the public good. Poems often figure myth as a place of retreat from an unpoetic age, as in Tennyson's "The Lotos-Eaters" or Arnold's "The Scholar-Gipsy." Perhaps the most interesting comment on myths' public utility is tacitly made in the almost universal avoidance of it by novelists, who seemed to find the subject antithetical to their realistic agenda.

Essayists frequently justified the use of myth in art, especially poetry, on the grounds that myth is essentially poetic. Ruskin, in *The Queen of the Air* (1869), argues that myth acquires its greatest, inherently moral, significance only after it has developed beyond primitive origins to become a consciously worked *objet*. John Addington Symonds, in *Studies of the Greek Poets* (1873), and Walter Pater, in "A Study of Dionysus" (*Fortnightly Review*, 1876), elaborate this aesthetic position.

A partial list of "essential" mythic poems from this period might include: Tennyson's *Idylls* (1859), seen as a retelling of a national myth; Arnold's *Empedocles on Etna* (1852), centrally concerned with mythopoeia; and Swinburne's *Atalanta in Calydon* (1865), perhaps the most successful mythic poem of the period. William Morris is the most prolific writer in this vein, departing from classical mythology to take up the Norse cycles in *Sigurd the Volsung* (1877) and recounting *The Life and Death of Jason* (1867); his *The Earthly Paradise* (1868–1870) is an extensive compendium of largely classic myths.

TERRENCE E. HOLT

Bibliography

Bush, Douglas. *Mythology and the Romantic Tradition in English Poetry.* 1937.

————. *Pagan Myth and Christian Tradition in English Poetry.* 1968.

Chase, Richard. *Quest for Myth.* 1949.

Feldman, Burton and Robert D. Richardson, eds. *The Rise of Modern Mythology, 1680–1860.* 1972.

Kissane, James "Victorian Mythology." *Victorian Studies*, vol. 6, pp. 5–28.

See also FOLKLORE; HARRISON, JANE ELLEN

· · · · ·

NADEN, CONSTANCE CAROLINE WOODHILL (1858–1889)

During her short life, Constance Naden was noted among women poets for dealing philosophically with "advanced" themes. Her *Songs and Sonnets of Springtime* (1881) expressed her early loss of faith in yearnings for erotic union with nature. In *The Modern Apostle . . . and Other Poems* (1887), which earned the praise of Oscar Wilde, Naden emerged as a **New Woman** in possession of a feminist cosmology. Thereafter she abandoned poetry for philosophy. Her last researches for a work on evolutionary ethics were published posthumously in the *Proceedings of the Aristotelian Society*.

Naden was born to middling prosperity and raised by her maternal grandparents after her mother died from obstetric complications. In 1876 Dr. Robert Lewins (1817–1895), a retired army surgeon and militant secularist, converted her from Calvinist Nonconformity to his personal synthesis of idealism and materialism, called "hylo-idealism," which posited the living motherhood of matter and the self-centeredness of perception.

From 1881 to 1887 Naden studied the sciences at Mason College in Birmingham and walked off with the best prizes. Meanwhile, under various pseudonyms, she promulgated hylo-idealism in letters, essays, and secularist pamphlets. The most important of these were collected after her death by Lewins and his disciples in *Induction and Deduction*

(1890) and *Further Reliques of Constance Naden* (1891).

In 1888, after an Oriental tour in which she studied Indian religions, Naden moved to London and worked in women's causes. Her health gave way a year later, an ovarian malignancy was diagnosed, and after surgery by Robert Lawson Tait (1845–1899), the leading Victorian ovariotomist, she rejoined "the unconscious Life, that waits for Birth," to use the words of her best-known poem, "The Pantheist's Song of Immortality." Herbert Spencer, who inspired Naden's work on evolutionary ethics, ranked her mental powers with George Eliot's.

JAMES R. MOORE

Bibliography

Dale, R. W. "Constance Naden." *Contemporary Review*. vol. 59, pp. 508–522.

Hughes, William R. *Constance Naden: A Memoir.* 1890.

Moore, James R. "The Erotics of Evolution: Constance Naden and Hylo-Idealism." In George Levine, ed., *One Culture: Essays in Science and Literature*, 1987.

. . . . .

NATIONAL ASSOCIATION FOR THE PROMOTION OF SOCIAL SCIENCE

The National Association for the Promotion of Social Science was one of the most important extraparliamentary agents influencing public policy in Victorian England between 1857 and 1885. An umbrella voluntary organization, associated with all forms of parliamentary and extraparliamentary reform, the association was also one of the leading institutions supporting the growth of organized feminism throughout the period.

The association began in the autumn of 1856 with an informal meeting at Lord Henry Brougham's home. Social workers, lawyers, educationists, economists, doctors, businessmen, and legislators gathered to discuss the founding of an organization for the collection and dissemination of information in the field

of social economics. Between 1857 and 1885 the association achieved nationally what earlier statistical societies had attempted locally. Its annual congresses were important civic occasions and resulted in volumes of *Transactions* which provide an invaluable documentary record of middle-class thought on social problems.

The association was the result of the combination of a number of groups, each concerned with a particular social issue. Its activities revolved around five main departments: jurisprudence and the amendment of the law, education, punishment and reformation, public health, and social economy. These issues brought a substantial body of influential people together. The General Committee alone had 139 members, including 9 peers or their sons (among them Lord Shaftesbury and Lord John Russell), 27 members of Parliament, 10 fellows of the Royal Society, and several eminent social theorists such as Edwin Chadwick, Charles Kingsley, John Stuart Mill, John Ruskin, James Kay-Shuttleworth, and John Simon.

The association provided the vehicle for a coalition between the wealthy manufacturing middle class and the evolving professionalism that reached its pinnacle in a highly trained civil service. Amateur reformers and the new professionals mingled in an attempt to create the science of society, which was their solution to the problems of industrialization and overpopulation. Results were uneven, and the *Transactions* contain as many platitudes as hard facts and statistical evidence. It cannot be denied, however, that the association created a new approach to social reform and embodied a new combination of the moral and scientific worlds.

SHEILA R. HERSTEIN

Bibliography

National Association for the Promotion of Social Science. *Transactions*. 1857–1885.

Rodgers, Brian. "The Social Science Association, 1857–1885." *Manchester School of Economic and Social Studies*. vol. 20, pp. 283–310.

See also PARKES, BESSIE RAYNOR

. . . . .

NATIONAL GALLERY

Founded in 1824, the National Gallery did not originate in a princely bequest, as was usual with such institutions, but rather in the government purchase (60,000 pounds) of a collection formed by John Julius Angerstein, the Lloyd's magnate. A permanent building was erected in Trafalgar Square between 1832 and 1838. Designed by William Wilkins, the new gallery was criticized from the start for its overextended facade and peculiar ornamentation: it was called the "National Cruet Stand." However, Ian Nairn has praised the portico for the way it helps to organize for the viewer the spaces and landmarks of central London. This elevated entryway is celebrated in James-Jacques-Joseph Tissot's painting *London Visitors* (1874, Toledo Museum of Art).

The National Gallery attracted controversy. During its first year 397,000 persons visited the new building, and 500,000 during its second. On "Saint Monday" especially, people of most ages and social classes mixed there—all suffering equally from the bad ventilation. In the mid-1850s Anthony Trollope argued that charging an admission fee two days a week would allow true connoisseurs to enjoy the collection in peace. Writing under Charles Dickens's editorship, Charles Collins claimed that most lower-class people visiting the gallery spent their time yawning. Collins also criticized the acquisition policies of Charles Eastlake (director of the gallery, 1855–1865); inretrospect Eastlake appears to have assembled a great collection, even if too narrowly focused on works of the Italian Renaissance.

RICHARD MAXWELL

Bibliography

Altick, Richard. *The Shows of London.* 1978.

Gould, Cecil. *Failure and Success: 150 Years of the National Gallery 1824-1974.* 1974.

Holmes, Sir Charles and C. H. Collins Baker. *The Making of the National Gallery, 1824-1924: An Historical Sketch.* 1924.

· · · · ·

NATURAL HISTORY

While **science** in Victorian Britain steadily evolved into a network of rigorously professional specialized fields, the older, broader field of natural history remained the glorious realm of the amateur and generalist. So great was the popularity of natural history, expressed in collections of natural objects and a vast appetite for books on the subject, that thousands of Britons of all classes and both sexes considered themselves avid naturalists. More importantly, Victorian natural history engendered metaphors for how to see the natural world—as composed of infinite material facts or particularities, as a vast museum, as a microcosm accessible to keen vision—metaphors that profoundly influenced Victorian culture, literature, and art.

Natural history had always been broad, descriptive, encyclopedic, the realm of untrained amateurs. In 1840 William Whewell (1794-1866) coined the term "scientist." Thereafter Thomas Henry Huxley and others sought to make the new sciences such as biology into formal bodies of knowledge, solidly based on experimental methods, and seeking to formulate general laws of nature. Rather than simply cataloguing and describing natural objects, the new Victorian sciences sought to link them together in grand conceptual schemes, the most famous of which is Darwin's theory of natural selection. Victorian science became the province of trained specialists: scientists.

But as scientific theories became complex and arcane, other people clung to the genial pleasures of natural history. Relaxed, acquisitive, eclectic, natural history in the traditional mold appealed to the layperson. Anyone with a keen eye could ramble across the countryside, making field observations of natural oddities. The favorite objects of the Victorian naturalist's attention—beetles, ferns, shells, fossils, and flowers—were studied not systematically, as **biology** and **geology** tried to do, but discursively, with pleasure and aesthetic appreciation. In fact, Victorian natural history can be thought of as aesthetic science. To the naturalist, natural objects, rather than being grist for scientific theories, were valuable in themselves, as distinct, beautiful, evocative "singularities."

Collecting was central to Victorian natural

history. By the 1820s low-cost achromatic microscopes were readily available, encouraging people to acquire and look closely at minute natural objects that previously they might have passed over. Individuals strove mightily to embellish their own private collections, artfully arranged in what were popularly called "cabinets of curiosities."

Natural history clubs flourished, serving as forums for shared collecting trips. Museums, popular in the eighteenth century, abounded in the nineteenth, led by the post-1840 growth of the Natural History Department of the British Museum. The opening of the Regent's Park Zoo in 1828, the popularity of the Wardian Case, or terrarium, from the 1840s on, and the proliferation of the aquarium (1850s) all fed the fervor for natural history.

The appetite for natural history was also whetted by the voyages of exploration undertaken with the help of Britain's strong navy. Accounts of the extravagant forms of tropical creatures testified to nature's variety. Many outstanding works of natural history were produced by explorer-naturalists, for example *Wanderings in South America* (1825), by Charles Waterton (1782-1865); *The Naturalist on the River Amazons* (1864), by Henry Walter Bates (1825-1892); *The Malay Archipelago* (1869), by Alfred Russel Wallace (1823-1913); and *The Naturalist in Nicaragua* (1874), by Thomas Belt (1832-1878). Charles Darwin, better known for his theoretical work in *On the Origin of Species* (1859), produced a sterling work of natural history in his earlier *Journal of Researches Into the Geology and Natural History of the Various Countries Visited by H.M.S. Beagle* (1839), popularly known as *The Voyage of the Beagle*.

Natural history became so popular because it neatly satisfied some of the Victorians' needs. In the post-romantic, post-Wordsworthian era, natural history satisfied the need to find beauty in nature. Because tramping in search of specimens was strenuous, naturalists could consider it done in the service of health; because the information gained thereby was educational, they could consider it done as a duty, and as valuable work. Even Samuel Smiles (1812-1904), whose *Self-Help* (1859) glorified dutiful industriousness, included two naturalists in his biographical gallery of admirably productive Victorians.

Natural history could also satisfy the religious impulse. After William Paley's (1743-1805) *Natural Theology; or, Evidences of the Existence and Attributes of the Deity, Collected from the Appearances of Nature* (1802), carefully scrutinized natural details easily could be marshalled as evidence for God's design and glory. Many of the most prominent nineteenth-century naturalists were quite religious, for example Philip Henry Gosse (1810-1888), whose *Omphalos: An Attempt to Untie the Geological Knot* (1857) disputed natural selection, and Hugh Miller (1802-1856), whose stance is amply displayed by the titles of two of his works, *Footprints of the Creator* (1849), and *The Testimony of the Rocks* (1857). In fact, the model for literary natural history was undoubtedly *The Natural History and Antiquities of Selborne* (1789), by the eighteenth-century country parson, Gilbert White (1720-1793)—indeed, the Victorian country parson/naturalist was so common as to be nearly a stereotype of the period.

P. H. Gosse was one of the best naturalists of his day. His observations were tireless, his descriptions copious and couched in appealing literary prose. Gosse, the stern father in Edmund Gosse's (1849-1928) *Father and Son* (1907), was adored by the reading public as the author of such books as *The Aquarium* (1854), which sparked a craze for keeping live marine specimens, *Seaside Pleasures* (1853), *Evenings at the Microscope* (1859), and *The Romance of Natural History* (1860). Other books that combined keen natural observation with poetic style, and thus fit into the distinct literary genre of natural history prose are *Glaucus: or, The Wonders of the Shore* (1855), by Gosse's novelist friend, Charles Kingsley (1819-1875), and *The Old Red Sandstone* (1841), by Hugh Miller.

The influential John Ruskin (1819-1900) brought many of the concerns of natural history to his writings about art, especially in *Modern Painters* (5 vols., 1843-1860). In emphasizing precise descriptions of nature and keenly observed particularities, Ruskin revealed his affinities both for natural history and for what has become known as the Pre-Raphaelite approach to art. It is important to note that many Pre-Raphaelite painters delineated infinitesimal natural details—blades of grass and drops of dew—with the same finicky exactitude that the naturalists displayed in both their written descriptions and in their art. Gosse, for example, produced exquisite paintings of specimens from nature, which his son Edmund found markedly similar in technique to Pre-Raphaelite paintings.

The profusion of natural history shaped literature as well. Portraits of naturalists abound in Victorian fiction. More importantly, verbal techniques of precise visual description link the writings of natural historians to better-known forms of Victorian literature, such as Pre-Raphaelite poetry and the poetry of Tennyson, Browning, and Hopkins. Like literary naturalists, many Victorian poets exploited the strengths of the natural history genre: scientific accuracy and visual acuity enlivened with subjective, evocative response.

Victorian natural history gave to both literature and art an emphasis on the particulars, the singularities, the minutely observed natural facts of the world. Natural history thus contributed a pleasant and positive materialism to the Victorian character, a real joy in what was optimistically perceived as the inexhaustible complexity of nature.

LYNN L. MERRILL

Bibliography

Allen, David Elliston. *The Naturalist in Britain: A Social History.* 1976.

———. *The Victorian Fern Craze: A History of Pteridomania.* 1969.

Ball, Patricia M. *The Science of Aspects: The Changing Role of Fact in the Work of Coleridge, Ruskin, and Hopkins.* 1971.

Barber, Lynn. *The Heyday of Natural History: 1820–1870.* 1980.

Christ, Carol T. *The Finer Optic: The Aesthetic of Particularity in Victorian Poetry.* 1975.

Knoepflmacher, U. C., and G. B. Tennyson, eds. *Nature and the Victorian Imagination.* 1977.

Merrill, Lynn L. *The Romance of Victorian Natural History.* 1989.

Scourse, Nicolette. *The Victorians and Their Flowers.* 1983.

See also GATTY, MARGARET; WOOD, JOHN G.

· · · · ·

NATURALISM

Literary naturalism in fiction and drama was a style of writing founded in realism and formulated by the French novelist Emile Zola (1840–1902), who applied the methods of nineteenth-century science to the writing of literature. A self-proclaimed "practical sociologist," Zola applied to his novels the determinist theories of Hippolyte Taine (1828–1893), Charles Darwin's (1809–1882) theories of natural selection and evolution, and contemporary hypotheses on heredity, psychology, physiology, and positivist philosophy. What Zola did in his fiction to complement his criticism especially *Le Roman experimental* (1880; *The Experimental Novel,* 1894) and *Les Romanciers naturalistes* (1881; *The Naturalist Novelists*) he was unable to do in drama to illustrate his *Le Naturalisme au theatre* (1881; *Naturalism on the Stage,* 1894). Henry Becque (1837–1899) did bring naturalist theory to life in the theater as he strove, unsuccessfully, to supplant the artificial, sentimental, and very popular melodrama of the age.

The principal agents for transmitting naturalism to England were the influential critic Walter Pater (1839–1894) and the novelist George Moore (1857–1933) in *A Mummer's Wife* (1885) and *Confessions of a Young Man* (1888). One principal English writer who developed a naturalist strain in his novels was Thomas Hardy (1840–1928), especially in *Jude the Obscure* (1895). Naturalism is also present to some extent in the work of Henry James (1848–1916).

Pater's defense of Zola's naturalism and Moore's imitation of Zola's fiction led several of Pater's disciples to join Moore as translators of Zola's work in the 1890s, among them Edmund Gosse (1849–1928), Arthur Symons (1865–1945), and Ernest Dowson (1867–1900). Moore's subject matter and technique in *A Mummer's Wife* were entirely naturalistic. He presents physical drives and psychological motivation relative to the harsh, sordid, and inexorable degeneration of an actor's wife. Hardy's brand of naturalism, surely founded upon Darwin's evolutionary thought and the sense of alienation in an impersonal universe ruled by chance, grew independently of Zola's but sprung from the same intellectual sources. A realist in his early novels,

Hardy produced a true naturalist masterpiece in *Jude the Obscure*, in which social convention, hereditary temperament, sex drives, the laws of nature, and blind chance conspire to destroy Jude.

As a force in late nineteenth-century thought naturalism was highly controversial. Since much naturalist literature dealt frankly with issues of sexuality, evolutionary determinism, and agnosticism or atheism, its creators were generally open to public censure. Henry Vizetelly, for example, was tried twice and jailed (1888) for publishing even bowdlerized translations of Zola's novels. The Victorian public were not, in general, favorably disposed toward naturalism.

JOHN J. CONLON

Bibliography

Brandes, George. *Naturalism in Nineteenth-Century English Literature.* 1957.

Conlon, John J. "Emile Zola." In F. N. Magill, ed., *Critical Survey of Long Fiction: Foreign Language Series.* 1984.

———. *Walter Pater and the French Tradition* 1982.

Powers, Lyall H. *Henry James and the Naturalist Movement.* 1971.

Schor, Naomi. *Breaking the Chain: Women, Theory, and French Realist Fiction.* 1985.

. . . . .

NATURE VERSUS NURTURE

Victorian interest in the comparative roles of environment and heredity in forming human personality reached its peak in the career of **Francis Galton** (1822–1911). Galton, best known for his studies in human inheritance and as the originator of **eugenics**, coined the phrase "nature versus nurture" in his *English Men of Science: Their Nature and Nurture* (1874). Under Galton's usage, nature signified that part of human personality stemming from physical inheritance, or what is now referred to as genetic constitution. Nurture included all aspects of personality induced by upbringing and environment.

In Galton's view nature and nurture were interdependent, and total personality was the result of both. Nevertheless, nature was the stronger of the two forces. Successful and productive individuals were the result of their natural inheritances. Talent, even in the face of compelling social disadvantages, would prevail. There existed a natural aristocracy of talent—such as that represented within the ranks of the Royal Society of London—which was central to the nation's intellectual productivity. One goal of Galton's eugenics was to promote the production of children by the intellectually gifted and discourage it by those judged to be genetically unfit.

Although Galton's theory of personality allowed a degree of influence from the effects of nurture, it was essentially hereditarian. Contrary to the thought of many of his contemporaries, however, Galton denied the possibility of the inheritance of acquired characteristics. Herbert Spencer (1820–1903) had proposed a theory of inheritance that allowed the environment to modify the physical units of heredity. Similarly, what Charles Darwin (1809–1882) identified as pangenes—the sources of inheritance—were open to modification from external influences. Galton's theory, based explicitly on his investigation and subsequent rejection of Darwin's hypothesis, denied any such influence of the environment upon the somatic unit.

In the later Victorian period, the emphasis on nature over nurture served as a defense of the status quo. Success in business and the professions was perceived to be the result of inherited talent. Failure was the outcome of insufficient talent, not the result of an unequal distribution of opportunity. Galton's hereditarian theory consequently became an integral part of the prevailing climate of **social Darwinism**.

DAVID K. VAN KEUREN

Bibliography

Forrest, Derek W. *Francis Galton: The Life and Work of a Victorian Genius.* 1974.

Jones, Greta. *Social Darwinism and English Thought: The Interaction Between Biological and Social Theory.* 1980.

. . . . .

NAVY

The navy during the Victorian era was seen on the one hand as "British and Best," a legendary force unchallenged and unassailable, and the supreme symbol of patriotism; and, on the other, as a "paper tiger," a "myth," and a backward, barbaric, "drowsy, inefficient, motheaten" service suffering from byzantine intrigues and disgraceful unreadiness. The navy was credited with saving the country and expanding the empire during the wars of the French Revolution and Napoleon (1793-1815) and seen as the first line of defense prior to World War I (1914-1918). In the interim, during the only real test, the navy blundered through the Baltic and Black Sea campaigns of the Crimean War (1853-1855); it emerged relatively untarnished, but its performance has been evaluated as muddled and confused. Although the British were the "Sailor Race" with "Hearts of Oak" and the naval leaders of the previous era were national heroes, the contemporary officers were superannuated and tyrannical, and conditions aboard ship were scandalously squalid.

Change is the theme of Victoria's reign: from sail to steam power, from smoothbore, muzzle-loading guns to those with rifled and breech-loading barrels, from barbaric conditions on the lower deck to a state of high morale and pride in service, and from divergent doctrines and archaic fighting instructions to an intellectual and practical analysis of sea power.

At the beginning of the long Victorian peace, the sailing ship of the line, of which the Royal Navy had over two hundred, dominated naval warfare as it had for two centuries. It was a sophisticated, complicated, costly juggernaut requiring 3,500 oak trees—900 acres of select forest—seasoned over twenty-five years, to build, and propelled by 50,000 square feet of sail. Lesser ships included frigates and corvettes.

By the end of the era, technological innovations transformed the capital warship into the dreadnought. It was constructed of iron and steel, displaced 20,000 tons, and was propelled by steam power. Enormous firepower came from rifled guns in turrets which projected high-explosive armor-piercing shells for a distance of twenty miles. Equally revolutionary changes created other types of war-

ships: the cruiser, battle cruiser, torpedo boat, torpedo boat destroyer, and submarine. These, together with mines, torpedoes, airships, airplanes, and oil-fired boilers transformed naval operations, tactics, and strategy—and also foreign policy.

Although no major naval war interrupted the Victorian peace, naval power was an instrument of foreign and colonial policies. The navy showed the flag, ubiquitously policed the seas, protected trade and commerce, provided humanitarian services, extended the imperial frontiers, and supported minor wars. Two creditable and significant contributions were navigational surveys and patrols against the Atlantic slave trade. In the former, the Hydrographic Department covered all navigable waters, and produced the best charts in the world, which were immediately made available to all. The latter required six decades (c.1810-1870) in which as much as one-fifth of the force, about fifty ships and 6,000 men, operating under unhealthy and dangerous circumstances, persisted until the slave trade was extinguished. These were tedious and thankless endeavors. The drudgery, boredom, danger, and misery were overlooked in the popular myths which stressed heroics and the long tradition of victories.

The naval organization included officers, enlisted men, the Royal Marines—always attached to the navy—and the shore establishment. Early in the century, success and global dominance had been achieved by an extraordinary series of outstanding leaders, including the admirals and lords St. Vincent, Nelson, and Collingwood, and by a large mobilized force. Demobilization after 1815 meant drastically reduced numbers of ships and personnel. A marked and formal dichotomy separated officers and enlisted men within the navy, and there was also a vast difference in supply and availability. Of enlisted men, whose abode was the lower deck, there was a dangerous shortage; of officers, symbolically placed on the quarterdeck, there was superfluity.

Officers of the Royal Navy came exclusively from the wealthy classes. Promotion was by seniority and there was no provision for retirement or purging. During times of peace and retrenchment, thousands of officers were asisgned to "half-pay," a kind of limbo status with no active duties. The result until late in

The Review at Spithead. Illustrated London News, *27 July 1867.*
Library Company of Philadelphia.

the century was large numbers of superannuated officers in the active ranks.

"Hire and discharge" was the equally archaic system of short-term service for enlisted men. Impressment, quotas, and bounty systems, all notorious, had been used to supplement numbers in the past and remained available if needed. These unsatisfactory methods of recruiting created serious difficulties. Stringent precautions were needed to retain seamen and prevent desertion. Naval ships became floating prisons; it became impossible to grant liberty or leave during a commission—a period of three to five years—because large numbers would abscond.

Reform of recruitment came in the 1850s. The continuous service system provided long-term service in ten-year intervals. After two consecutive engagements the seaman became eligible for a pension. The system attracted higher-quality and better-behaved seamen and created the career-oriented, professional naval rating.

Meantime, conditions on the lower deck were horrendous: berthing was overcrowded and squalid; food was scandalous; alcoholism was out of control; tyrannical officers abounded; and punishment practices, the foremost of which was flogging, were brutal, ruthless, severe, and extensive. Pay was grossly insufficient and often late. There were serious incidents in 1859 but no mutinies comparable to those of 1797 or 1931.

Urged on by public and parliamentary pressures, the authorities, beginning with the administration of the duke of Somerset as first lord of the Admiralty (1859–1866), made a series of humanitarian and administrative reforms. Leave was granted; pay was raised; educational and recreational opportunities were increased; the daily rum ration was reduced twice (from one-half to one-eighth of a pint); confinement replaced corporal punishment; and victualing and amenities improved. Health and medical arrangements "improved astonishingly," as documented by medical historians Christopher Lloyd and Jack Coulter. Naval medical officers, most of whom were trained in Scotland, enjoyed a high reputation. The dramatic incidence of venereal disease, however, created a civil issue. The naval bases of Malta, Portsmouth, and Plymouth were declared "infected areas." Parliament proposed to regulate **prostitution**

through the Contagious Diseases Acts of the 1860s, but after a persistent campaign led by feminist **Josephine Butler** and former naval lord James Stansfeld, the acts were repealed.

On large warships about one-quarter of the crew were Royal Marines whose functions included providing boarding and landing parties and maintaining internal security. The Royal Dockyards—the shore establishment—employed over 30,000 personnel by 1900. There were several domestic facilities, Portsmouth being most prominent, and significant expansion during the century at foreign bases such as Gibraltar, Malta, Bermuda, and Singapore. The Royal Dockyards were supplemented by a large private armaments and shipbuilding industry, primarily family businesses during the nineteenth century. Most dreadnoughts were built in private yards.

The executive authority of the Royal Navy was the Admiralty, situated opposite Trafalgar Square in London. In 1832 the Navy Board was abolished in a reform initiated by James Graham that was designed to consolidate control. The new Board of the Admiralty, consisting of five principal officers or sea lords, was made the responsible professional authority.

There were perennial debates over the navy's budget, usually in the spring when Parliament demanded retrenchment. Budgets decreased between 1815 and 1830 but then began to rise, due to more sophisticated materiel, higher personnel expenses, and occasional invasion scares. There was a plateau around 1870 because of uncertainty about design and a moderating international situation. After 1880 came a resumption of the upward trend as the classic arms race began.

The rhythm of budget changes was partly influenced by the identification of international competitors. The French, Spanish, Dutch, and Danish fleets had been neutralized in or before 1805, the year of the battle of Trafalgar. The last engagement of ships of the line was at Navarino (1827) where a British commander of an allied fleet defeated a Turko-Egyptian fleet. None of the naval operations during the Crimean War were creditable. Later in the century, fears of potential conflicts with France, Russia, Austria, and Italy stimulated development of a formal naval building policy. After 1900 cooperative arrangements, formal and informal, were concluded with Japan, France, and Russia.

Ultimately Germany emerged as the single hostile naval power confronting Great Britain.

Popular interest in the navy revived in the 1880s. The two Victorian Jubilees, the Golden (1887) and Diamond (1897), concentrated attention on the navy during major reviews. A powerful pressure group, the Navy League, was formed. Several influential newspaper editors, often with access to leaked confidential information, launched propaganda campaigns in support of naval policies. An extreme example was the "naval panic of 1909" when public opinion was mobilized and eight dreadnoughts were authorized.

Throughout the century the British Empire and enormous volumes of trade were maintained, protected, and expanded under the Royal Navy's operational initiatives and supervision. British naval mastery was directly linked to economic and imperial expansion. Naval theory and strategy, however, lagged. It was not until 1890 that an obscure American naval captain, Alfred Thayer Mahan, articulated a naval philosophy based on historical experience in *The Influence of Sea Power* (1890, 1892). Although Mahan cited Great Britain as the model for classical doctrines of naval strategy, British naval officers had shown little appreciation for such essentials as education, staff or war colleges, intelligence gathering, concepts of tactics, and war planning.

In the final decade of the century, remedial measures and institutions were developed. John Knox Laughton and Julian S. Corbett, among others, formulated strategic and intellectual debates to counter the materiel school which had been so dominant. The Navy Records Society was formed (1893) and published dozens of volumes. The *Naval Review* (1913) and the Royal United Service Institution popularized enquiry and debate. An articulate spokesman emerged from the lower deck. Lionel Yexley (actual name, James Woods), and created a journal and benefit societies. At the official level the Naval Intelligence Department and Committee of Imperial Defence were created.

Nevertheless, the lack of centralized staff coordination and war planning persisted. At a meeting of the Committee of Imperial Defence on August 23, 1911, during the Agadir crisis, Admiralty deficiencies were exposed and the army strategy of continental operations prevailed. New naval leadership, including Winston Churchill, was brought in to replace discredited and purged officials.

EUGENE L. RASOR

Bibliography

Bartlett, Christopher J. *Great Britain and Sea Power, 1815-1853.* 1963.

Baynham, Henry. *Before the Mast: Naval Ratings in the Nineteenth Century.* 1971.

Clowes, William L. *The Royal Navy, A History.* 1897-1903. 7 vols.

Higham, Robin, ed. *A Guide to the Sources of British Military History.* 1971.

Kennedy, Paul M. *The Rise and Fall of British Naval Mastery.* 1976.

Lavery, Brian. *The Ship of the Line.* 1983-1984. 2 vols.

Lloyd, Christopher and Jack Coulter. *Medicine and the Navy, 1200-1900.* 1957-1963. 4 vols.

Marder, Arthur J. *The Anatomy of British Sea Power.* 1940.

Rasor, Eugene L. *British Naval History, 1815-1985.* Military History Bibliography Series, vol. 30 (Forthcoming, 1989).

———. *Reform in the Royal Navy: A Social History of the Lower Deck.* 1976.

Rodger, N. A. M. *The Admiralty.* 1979.

Ward, William E. F. *The Royal Navy and the Slavers: The Suppression of the Atlantic Slave Trade.* 1969.

See also OCEANOGRAPHY; SHIPS AND SHIPBUILDING

· · · · ·

NEEDLECRAFTS

Needlecrafts of all kinds flourished throughout the nineteenth century, despite general lamentation about their decline. Although machines supplanted hand sewing and lacemaking, thereby destroying most **domestic industry**, needlecrafts remained modest sources of income for poor women. For the middle classes, proficiency at needlecrafts proved a woman's fitness for marriage and motherhood. The "true" Victorian woman embroidered, wove, and netted yards of both useful and truly useless items.

Although most poor women could no longer earn a living by sewing at home, some went into service as "sewing maids," where they had to sew and knit continually; for most other women servants, sewing was simply another chore among dozens. Even well-educated governesses were not exempt; Charlotte Brontë was expected to sew clothing by at least one family for whom she was a governess.

With the advent of machines for sewing, knitting, and bobbin lacemaking, needlework became an avocation, not a primary vocation, for most women. **Embroidery** was the most popular needlecraft because of its versatility. It was often compared to painting. Girls learned to sew as part of their basic education and embroidered samplers to demonstrate their facility. As adults, middle-class women covered nearly every inch of their homes with embroidered fire screens, pillow and chair covers, and wall hangings. Using silk or wool threaded on variously sized needles, they worked either on freestanding embroidery frames or on small lap frames. From the 1830s, Berlin wools—thick and brightly colored—flooded England. Easy-to-follow patterns were published in the *Englishwoman's Domestic Magazine, Bow Bells,* and many other women's and family periodicals.

Lace work was less popular than embroidery because it was more difficult and less versatile. Lace was used primarily for clothing. It was either woven with bobbins on a pillow or sewn with a needle over a parchment pattern. Bedfordshire, Buckinghamshire, and Northamptonshire were originally famous for their lace, but John Heathcoat's bobbin-net machine, invented in 1809, doomed most small craftworkers. During the 1830s, lace was used on evening gowns, morning caps, dress hats, capes, and aprons. In the 1840s, lace-covered skirts, lace shawls, and wedding veils became popular.

Crocheting and knitting were more practical needlecrafts. Machine-made knitwear had eliminated the need for large-scale knitting of stockings, underwear, or babies' clothing, but many women still preferred to make at least some of their family's personal garments.

Needles and hooks (much like the ones still in use) were made of ivory or smooth wood. Magazines like the *Englishwoman's Domestic Magazine* provided hundreds of innovative patterns for bonnets, slippers, shawls, and purses.

Ironically, as needlework became increasingly unnecessary, Victorians pushed for its revitalization. Needlecraft advocates made a simple correlation between the quantity of needlework women produced and their moral rectitude. John Ruskin and George Edmund Street argued that the popularity of simple patterns and Berlin wools degenerated British crafts and, therefore, damaged morality. Others went so far as to insist that poor women were depraved because they no longer sewed day and night. Middle-class women were judged on the quality and quantity of their embroidery, knitting, and lacemaking: the more they produced, the more upright they were, at least in theory.

JULIA M. GERGITS

Bibliography

Caulfeild, Sophia Frances Anne and Blanche C. Saward. *The Dictionary of Needlework.* 1882; rpt. 1972.

Day, Lewis F., and Mary Buckle. *Art in Needlework: A Book About Embroidery.* 1900.

Head, Mrs. R. E. *The Lace and Embroidery Collector: A Guide to Collectors of Old Lace and Embroidery.* 1922.

Sebba, Anne. *Samplers: Five Centuries of a Gentle Craft.* 1979.

· · · · ·

NESBIT, EDITH (1858–1924)

Edith Nesbit published poetry, novels, stories, and, most successfully, children's books under the signature "E. Nesbit." She was a **New Woman**, a socialist and an incipient feminist who lived most of her life in bohemian circles. In 1880 she married Hubert Bland; in 1884 she and her husband became charter members of the Fabian Society. Three years after Bland's death in 1914, Nesbit married a marine engineer named Thomas Terry Tucker.

Nesbit was seven months pregnant when she married Hubert Bland; the couple had three children, one of whom (Fabian) died at fifteen. In addition, Nesbit raised as her own two children born to Bland's mistress Alice Hoatson, who lived with them for more than thirty years. As a New Woman, Nesbit was unconventional in her dress, recreation, child-rearing methods, political opinions, and code of sexual morality.

Nesbit's poetry, written chiefly in the 1880s and 1890s, shows the influence of the Pre-Raphaelites and their followers. *Lays and Legends* (1886) includes "The Depths of the Sea," written to accompany Edward-Burne Jones's well-known painting. *Leaves of Life* (1888) features a study of a prostitute, "Refugium Peccatorum," reminiscent of Dante Rossetti's "Jenny" (1870). *Songs of Love and Empire* (1898), while showing the imperialist influence of Rudyard Kipling, also includes "The Ballad of the White Lady," one of several medieval romances on the theme of the femme fatale. *Ballads and Lyrics of Socialism* (1908) reveals Nesbit's continuing commitment to socialist ideas.

By the end of the century, Nesbit had essentially abandoned poetry to concentrate on fiction. Except for *The Red House* (1902) her novels were inconsequential. However, her books for children were excellent; the best and most popular were *The Treasure Seekers* (1899), *The Wouldbegoods* (1901), *The Railway Children* (1908), and *The Magic City* (1910). Many featured a likable family known as the Bastables, whose children were the brave and imaginative heroes of the stories. In the end, Nesbit made her most enduring contribution to literature as the author of more than thirty fine books for children.

KATHLEEN HICKOK

Bibliography

Moore, Doris L. *E. Nesbit: A Biography.* Rev. ed., 1967.

Streatfeild, Noel. *Magic and Magician: E. Nesbit and Her Children's Books.* 1958.

· · · · ·

NEWSPAPERS see PRESS

· · · · ·

NEW WOMAN

The term "New Woman," coined in 1894 by feminist novelist **Sarah Grand** (1854-1943), described a social and literary type that emerged in the 1880s. It referred to a woman who embodied many of the new ideas about female independence, but, while often equated with feminism, it defined a style of living rather than a political perspective. Although extremely popular as a literary figure and social category until World War I, few real women conformed to the image, and it was often used by antifeminists as a term of disapprobation.

The typical New Woman was middle class but worked for a living, often at a job newly opened to women. She insisted on sexual freedom and eschewed marriage as imprisoning, engaged in physical exercise, smoked and drank openly, advocated dress reform, and even wore men's clothes. To antifeminist critics this figure epitomized the horrors of emancipation in her forthright speech, unladylike behavior, and constant demands for independence; for feminists she often emblematized the freedom for which they were struggling, although some were alarmed at the emphasis on sexuality and her apparent promiscuity. But while opinions about the New Woman usually broke down along feminist/antifeminist lines, the term was so loosely applied and often so superficially related to real women's lives that its political significance is more a barometer of the user than a description of actual experience. The term was also used by feminists like **Olive Schreiner** (1885-1920) to contrast the traditional woman with both the free woman who agitated for change and the woman who would arise once emancipation was achieved, but the popular usage was less consciously tied to political struggle.

While many feminist writers created characters who conformed to some aspects of the stereotype, the most notable New Woman figures in literature came from novelists and short story writers not clearly committed to feminist change. Women writers like **George**

Egerton (1859–1945) became famous for portraits of independent women to whom sexual freedom and emotional autonomy were all-important, and many male writers, like **Grant Allen** in his best-selling *The Woman Who Did* (1895), traded on the popularity and shock value of the New Woman figure. Allen's novel is typical of the shallow and ambiguous use of the New Woman, for while the title character appears to live in an emancipated manner, her principles are superficially presented and most of her behavior is as traditionally feminine as any "old" woman's.

Far more sophisticated, if often equally ambiguous, portraits of the New Woman were created by serious male novelists like George Gissing, George Meredith, George Moore, and Thomas Hardy, and by playwrights like George Bernard Shaw and Henrik Ibsen. Influenced by realism and naturalism, the novelists incorporated into their work the contradictions and changes in women's lives, often emphasizing the apparently conflicting pressures of independence, sexuality, and love.

Hardy's portrait of Sue Bridehead in *Jude the Obscure* (1895) typifies serious treatments in many ways. Sue's insistence on autonomy, her disregard for social conventions, and her refusal to marry Jude reflect the New Woman's quest for independence, while her sexual coldness suggests the neurotic component many writers saw as central. Similarly, Gissing's Rhoda Nunn (*The Odd Women*, 1893) rejects traditional options and works actively to expand women's opportunities, but it is clear that few other women can live up to her standards, and her relationship with her lover rapidly degenerates into a power struggle. Like many New Woman writers, Gissing seems to reinforce traditional views of women even as he appears to challenge them.

The New Woman also figured prominently in magazine articles of the period, again usually characterized as either "advanced" or "fast" depending on the writer's perspective. As a composite social type, the New Woman was frequently the focus for opinions about changes in women's status, particularly changes in acceptable social behavior—hence the emphasis in many magazine portraits on bicycle riding, swearing, and smoking.

The notion of the New Woman differs from feminism largely in being less anchored in specific programs for political change and political analyses of women's position, and always remained more a literary and social concept than an accurate description of women's changing lives. Feminist writers and activists who made use of the type tended to tie their portrayals to particular social problems or political wrongs, as Sarah Grand did in *The Heavenly Twins* (1893). But the line is difficult to draw, and many critics closely connect the two impulses, partly because contemporary reviewers tended to identify any iconoclastic or independent female character of the period as a New Woman. Some recent critics see the New Woman figure as bound up with the transition from the Victorian to the modern novel, and for many it marks an important shift in the literary portrayal of women.

LAURA STEMPEL MUMFORD

Bibliography

Boumelha, Penny. *Thomas Hardy and Women: Sexual Ideology and Narrative Form.* 1982.

Cunningham, Gail. *The New Woman and the Victorian Novel.* 1978.

Fernando, Lloyd. *"New Women" in the Late Victorian Novel.* 1977.

Hickok, Kathleen. *Representations of Women: Nineteenth-Century British Women's Poetry.* 1984.

Showalter, Elaine. *A Literature of Their Own: British Women Novelists from Brontë to Lessing.* 1977.

. . . . .

NEW ZEALAND

From 1769, when it was first sighted by Captain James Cook, until 1836, New Zealand remained unexploited by European trade and settlement. The Bay of Islands was inhabited by sailors who had deserted from American and European whalers, escaped convicts from New South Wales (Australia), and the native Maoris (Polynesians), who were cannibals. Although New Zealand had been included in Captain Arthur Phillips's convict commission in Australia, the wildness of native and white inhabitants prompted Parliament to declare in 1817 that it was outside British jurisdiction, and it occupied an ambiguous position. In 1814, however, Reverend Samuel Marsden had come to New Zealand from Botany Bay, and his work prompted both the Church of England and the Wesley Missionary Societies to take it on as a mission field.

Missionary reports of anarchy and cannibalism finally forced government intervention. Edward Gibbon Wakefield, meantime, became interested in applying to New Zealand his plans for "systematic colonization" in which the government would offer land at a price high enough to dissuade the indigent. The profits would then be used to encourage further emigration. Wakefield and other philanthropists formed the New Zealand Association in 1837 to civilize the area and bring it under the British flag. The missionary societies, however, opposed white settlement on the grounds that it debased native cultures. Conflict with missionaries contributed to the dissolution of the New Zealand Association. Its successor, the New Zealand Company, proposed to make 2,000 pounds available for systematic colonization, but Lord Normanby of the Colonial Office opposed granting the company a charter for colonization. Wakefield's brother Arthur and several associates sailed in the ship *Tory* for New Zealand, arriving at Wellington in Cook's Strait in 1839 and thus forcing the government to annex New Zealand. Edward Wakefield came to Wellington in 1853.

Maori-white relations were particularly strained on the question of land. The Maoris held land in common and, in white views, used it wastefully. The New Zealand Company saw it all as Crown land to be sold to white settlers. The colonial governor, Captain William Hobson, concluded the Treaty of Waitangi with about fifty Maori chiefs on February 6, 1840. The chiefs ceded all rights of sovereignty while the government promised them undisputed possession of their lands. They became British subjects, enjoying the protection of the government. Meanwhile, however, Arthur Wakefield at Nelson concluded a treaty contrary to the intent of the Waitangi settlement, by which settlers acquired 20 million acres of land for 9,000 pounds, one-eleventh of which was reserved to the Maoris. In 1841 Arthur Wakefield and several other Europeans were killed while trying to arrest two Maori chiefs who resisted a British survey of land which the Maoris denied having sold. Following this "Wairau massacre" and several more skirmishes, George Gray arrived from South Australia in 1845, declared the Treaty of Waitangi in force, and by mid-1846 had restored peace.

Settlement of the South Island began in 1848 when Scots Presbyterians came to Otago. The Canterbury settlement of 1850 was a Church of England settlement and an example of systematic colonization at its best.

The New Zealand Company was dissolved in 1851, and in 1853 a central government was organized with an upper chamber nominated by a governor and an elected lower house. In 1856 New Zealand became essentially self-governing except for control of the armed forces and of native affairs—an exclusion designed to ensure protection for the Maoris. In 1865 the capital was moved from Auckland to Wellington.

Although some troubles persisted after 1856, the Maoris had been largely Christianized and cannibalism had died out. By the 1870s Maori resistance ended, and the Maoris entered New Zealand society with access to public office. With a parliamentary bill in 1893 which extended the vote to women, New Zealand became the first country in the world with universal adult suffrage.

JOAN MICKELSON GAUGHAN

Bibliography

Condliffe, John B. *New Zealand in the Making*. 1930.

Oliver, W.H., ed. *The Oxford History of New Zealand*. 1981.

Sinclair, Keith. *A History of New Zealand*. 1959.

· · · · ·

NEWGATE NOVEL

The rise of the Newgate or "rogue"novel accompanied reform in English criminal law during the 1830s. Edward Bulwer-Lytton's *Paul Clifford* (1830) specifically attacked the legal system as an instrument of class oppression. Although Newgate novelists differed in many respects, all featured criminals as sympathetic central characters.

Critics attacked Bulwer-Lytton, William Harrison Ainsworth, and Charles Dickens for violating morality by romanticizing criminals. William Makepeace Thackeray, for example, believed that criminals should be depicted as "downright scoundrels, leading scoundrelly lives"; he satirized the Newgate school in *Catherine* (1839–1840) and later in "George de Barnwell" (1847).

Nevertheless, Newgate novels were devoured by an avid reading public. Bulwer-Lytton's second rogue novel, *Eugene Aram* (1832), contained no theme of social reform. Instead, a romanticized hero is surrounded with a romantic plot. Aram is a highly regarded scholar, tempted to commit murder. Finally, after *Lucretia* (1846), a novel based on a contemporary poisoner, Bulwer-Lytton abandoned the genre, as Ainsworth and Dickens had already done.

Ainsworth's *Rookwood* (1834) featured a gentlemanly highwayman hero, Dick Turpin. A pleasant robber who sings and cavorts, Turpin is universally liked. Even the police admire his courage and prowess. *Jack Sheppard* (1839) portrayed the famous housebreaker and escape artist as a dandified, highly sentimentalized victim of the thief catcher, Jonathan Wild.

Although critics also condemned Dickens for sentimentalizing the prostitute Nancy in *Oliver Twist* (1838), he again dealt with Newgate materials in *Barnaby Rudge* (1841). Set during the Gordon riots, *Barnaby Rudge* included romantic elements but makes a serious statement on social problems and the pressing need for reform. Dickens depicted criminals as the harvest of "the wholesale growth of the seed sown by the law."

The Newgate novelists affected the portrayal of criminals in fiction. They depicted previously stereotyped villains as human beings with shades of guilt. Dickens continued to rework the theme of crime and criminality, particularly in *Bleak House* (1852–1853) and *Great Expectations* (1860–1861). Although the Newgate novel, strictly speaking, was in vogue for only a few years, it influenced the development of sensation fiction in the 1860s and left its mark on penny dreadfuls and detective fiction.

NATALIE SCHROEDER

Bibliography

Hollingsworth, Keith. *The Newgate Novel. 1830–1847: Bulwer, Ainsworth, Dickens, and Thackeray.* 1963.

· · · · ·

NEWLYN SCHOOL (1879–1895)

The term Newlyn school designates approximately twenty young European-trained English painters who constituted the core of an artist colony in the fishing village of Newlyn, Cornwall, from the early 1880s until the mid-1890s. The artists' exposure to popular Continental artistic ideas, in particular the French naturalist movement, resulted in their shared commitment to painting contemporary rural life on the spot in natural and varied light conditions. By the late 1880s they were instrumental in setting a higher standard for English painters of outdoor and genre subjects and in relaxing the Royal Academy's conservative and nationalistic attitude toward foreign training and influences.

The colony grew as individual members attracted friends from their student years in England, from the ateliers of Paris and Antwerp, and from summer holidays in the art colonies of Brittany and Venice. Long-term members included Stanhope Forbes (1857–1947), Frank Bramley (1857–1915), Walter Langley (1852–1922), T. C. Gotch (1854–1931), and Elizabeth Armstrong Forbes (1859–1912). While the Newlyners never stated a formal manifesto, they (and their critics) recognized the group's thematic and stylistic similarities.

The Newlyners gained popular approval because their subject matter fell into the traditional and still vital categories of Victorian **genre painting**. They also depicted the positive and nostalgic image of provincial life and the moral values their urban audience desired. Exterior scenes incorporating recognizable sites and local, nonprofessional models distinguished Newlyn work. Contemporaries felt that Forbes's *The Health of the Bride* (1889) and Bramley's *A Hopeless Dawn* (1888) exhibited superior technical skills and aesthetic sensibilities, and truthful but refined approches to nature and human emotions. The Royal Academy elected both associates, in 1892 and 1894 respectively.

Critics noted the Newlyners' Francophile leanings: a subdued palette, the diffused light of grey days, the contrasting effects of natural and artificial illumination, and the square brush technique for unifying figures with their environment. Often cited as followers of the popular French naturalist Bastien-Lepage, they did study and admire his *plein air* portraits of peasant life but also absorbed lessons from a wide range of their contemporaries, including Manet, Sargent, Whistler, the Hague school and the Impressionists. The Newlyn school was part of a pan-European artistic involvement with artist colonies, naturalism and its *plein air* component, tonalism, and nationalistic subjects.

BETSY COGGER REZELMAN

Bibliography

Birch, Mrs. Lionel. *Stanhope A. Forbes, A.R.A., and Elizabeth Stanhope Forbes, A.R.W.S.* 1906.

Fox, Caroline and Francis Greenacre. *Artists of the Newlyn School, 1880-1900.* 1979.

———. *Painting in Newlyn, 1880-1930.* 1985.

Meynell, Alice. "Newlyn." *Art Journal,* April 1889, pp. 97-102, 137-142.

Rezelman, Betsy Cogger. "The Newlyn Artists and Their Place in Late-Victorian Art." Ph.D. dissertation, Indiana University, 1984.

· · · · ·

NEWMAN, JOHN HENRY (1801-1890)

John Henry Newman was the greatest personality in the religious history of England in the nineteenth century. The leader of the Tractarian movement at Oxford, he shaped the **High Church** party in the Church of England, from which he himself seceded in 1845. As a Roman Catholic, he was the most prominent intellectual spokesman of his new faith, eventually becoming a cardinal.

After an evangelical upbringing, Newman went to Oxford University. As a fellow of Oriel College from 1822, he found himself in the most stimulating intellectual atmosphere in Oxford. He worked his way out of the prevailing religious liberalism to a High Church position in which he was joined by his colleague Richard Hurrell Froude (1803-1836). These young men were ready when the Oxford Movement commenced in 1833. Newman seized the leadership by originating the *Tracts for the Times*, to which he was the principal contributor. He built up the Tractarian party and, as vicar of the university church of St. Mary's, shaped the thought of a generation of students by his sermons. He was effective in two roles: privately, in intimate personal relationships, and publicly, as an apologist. He constructed a case for Anglo-Catholicism as a *via media*, or middle way between the extremes of Protestantism and Romanism.

Newman was soon challenged to prove that his *via media* was viable. His Tract Ninety in 1841, which attempted to show that the Thirty-Nine Articles were capable of a Catholic interpretation, was condemned by the bishops. He began to question whether the Anglican church was truly catholic. The chief difficulty in his slow acceptance of Roman Catholicism was the apparent changes in Roman practice from the days of the church fathers, a period on which he was the leading authority as a church historian. He worked out a theory of the development of doctrine which met this difficulty. Convinced that the Church of Rome was the only catholic and authoritative church, he converted in 1845; many followed him.

The Roman authorities were unsure what to do with this potential champion of their church, still feeble in England. Newman was reordained priest and made doctor of divinity, but he found a home for himself in a religious order, the Oratorians, building an Oratory, of which he was superior, in Birmingham. Occasionally he ventured forth to give series of controversial lectures. Invited to form a Catholic university in Dublin, he gave the lectures published as *The Idea of a University* (1852) and became its first rector in 1854, but the institution did not prosper and he returned to England. Ventures into periodicals, as the mentor of the young intellectuals who became the liberal Catholic movement, brought Newman "under a cloud" with church authorities. Newman was almost forgotten by the

English public when an incautious taunt by Charles Kingsley (1819-1875) gave him an occasion to write a history of his religious opinions, *Apologia pro Vita Sua* (1864), in which religious controversy was transformed into a classic of spiritual autobiography. The respect that this won for Newman among Protestants and Catholics alike vaulted him back into a leading position in English thought. He was emboldened to publish other works, notably his one major venture into philosophy, the *Grammar of Assent* (1870). He achieved the ultimate recognition of his church in his own lifetime, when the new pope, Leo XIII (1878-1903), awarded him the cardinalate in 1879. He had won a place, however precarious, for the free but disciplined intellect in the Roman Catholic Church. Newman died in 1890.

Newman's talents were multifarious. Above all a religious controversialist, he raised apologetics to the level of literature. In addition to works of theology and philosophy, his sermons, spoken or published, were of the highest order and he was a competent historian. He is a model of pure prose style, supple and persuasive but critics may find numerous ambiguities. Newman was also an excellent minor poet: "Lead, Kindly Light" (1833) and "The Dream of Gerontius" (1865) display his sense of the greater reality of the other world. His motto, *cor ad cor loquitur*, indicates the secret of his power: he was most effective, in his life and through his writings, when speaking as one heart to another.

The fascination of Newman's life and personality has tended to obscure the appreciation of his achievements. The ornament of two churches, though never entirely at ease in either, Newman was too great a man to be the exclusive property of any denomination.

JOSEF L. ALTHOLZ

Bibliography

Bouyer, Louis. *Newman: His Life and Spirituality.* 1958.

Chadwick, Owen. *The Victorian Church.* 1966-1970. 2 vols.

Church, Richard W. *The Oxford Movement: Twelve Years, 1833-1845.* Rev. ed., 1891.

Dessain, Charles Stephen. *John Henry Newman.* 1966.

——. et al., eds. *The Letters and Diaries of John Henry Newman.* 1961 ff.

Faber, Geoffrey. *Oxford Apostles.* 2d ed., 1936.

Trevor, Meriol. *Newman, Light in Winter.* 1962.

——. *Newman, the Pillar of the Cloud.* 1962.

Ward, Wilfrid. *The Life of John Henry Cardinal Newman.* 1912. 2 vols.

· · · · ·

NIGHTINGALE, FLORENCE (1820-1910)

The most famous woman—after Victoria—of the nineteenth century, Florence Nightingale was influential in a wide range of public reforms. Well known in aristocratic circles for her interest in nursing and hospitals, she superintended the first government-appointed women nurses sent to the British army during the Crimean War (1854-1856). Upon her return she lobbied successive governments for reform of the army medical and purveying systems, improved barracks and hospital architecture, medical training for army doctors, sanitation for military stations throughout the empire, and the permanent use of women nurses by the military. Funds donated in honor of her Crimean work were used to open in 1861 the first secular nursing school in England at St. Thomas's Hospital, London. By 1872, with the death or departure from politics of numerous political allies, she was "out of office," and turned her attention to public health. She devoted the remainder of her long life to encouraging women to become leaders of reformed nursing, publicizing the importance of home and public sanitation and cleanliness, encouraging schemes for district health visitors, and lobbying against the registration of nurses. In 1907 she was the first woman to be awarded the Order of Merit.

The younger daughter of the cultured and wealthy Fanny Smith and W. E. Nightingale, Nightingale received an exceptionally thorough education from her father; throughout her life she shared with him a taste for philosophical speculation. Both her mother and her sister, Parthenope, pinned their hopes for social success upon the brilliant Florence, but by her early twenties she disliked the rigid social round and sought to escape into social service. After a decade of quarreling, Nightingale's father gave her an income of 500 pounds per annum in 1853, and also his permission to head the Invalid Gentlewomen's Institution. This was to be her only direct nursing experience, aside from a brief sojourn in 1851 at the German Protestant Institution of Kaiserswerth. The misery of the years before 1853 is embodied in "Cassandra" (1928), her polemic against the prison life of upper-class women.

On October 15, 1854 Nightingale accepted the position of superintendent of nurses for the English General Military Hospitals in Turkey from her old friend, Sidney Herbert, then secretary-at-war for Lord Aberdeen's Liberal Government. The war correspondent William Howard Russell had revealed the wretched conditions of the hospitals in reports to the *Times*. To placate public opinion, the government sent out thirty-eight nurses under Nightingale and permitted her to use publicly raised funds to supply the sick with necessities. Both the military officers and the army doctors resented her intrusion upon an all-male enclave. Furthermore, her close ties with the government and her independent funds gave her a power that threatened their positions. Although she made some allies among the more progressive doctors, her entire stay was marked by discord, intransigence, and pettiness. Nevertheless, her strong leadership, insistence upon cleanliness and sanitation, and tight control of the nurses contributed to improved hospital conditions and secured recognition for women nurses.

Nightingale returned from the Crimea determined to vindicate "her" soldiers. The success of her coffeehouses, savings banks, and educational lectures had helped to change the prevailing image of the common soldier as a drunken ne'er-do-well. At her insistence a royal commission to investigate the health of the army was set up in 1857. Nightingale drafted the report, but the reforms it recommended were only slowly implemented by a resistant government. A second royal commission was formed at her instigation in 1859 to investigate military stations in India; again Nightingale wrote the majority of the report. Throughout her life sanitary conditions in India were a major concern.

Although Nightingale is chiefly remembered as the leader of reformed nursing, army sanitary reform was always her primary interest. She was, however, enormously influential because so many of her protégées from the Nightingale School of Nursing achieved positions of authority in key hospitals. In addition, hospital administrators repeatedly solicited her opinions on architecture, nurses' training, public health policies, ward reorganization, venereal disease, and sanitation.

For Nightingale cleanliness was both a moral and physical imperative. She never fully accepted the germ theory of disease, believing that medicine did not cure but merely removed the obstacles to nature's repair. Nurses had the unique task of caring for patients while they were mending. The connection between immorality and sickness made it imperative that the nurse be of exceptionally strong moral fiber. Nightingale pointed out "that it is the only case, queens not excepted, where a woman is really in charge of men."

Nightingale vigorously defended nursing as a respectable profession. To encourage ladies to become matrons, she recommended giving them complete authority over nurses, independent of the hospital hierarchy. But she never aligned herself with the feminist movement; she particularly disliked what she saw as feminists' reluctance to take on obvious social duties, and their personalizing of work. Only out of respect for John Stuart Mill did she agree to sign a petition for female suffrage. She refused to give public support to any cause because she believed that open use of her name would dilute her power to exercise influence behind the scenes.

Nightingale's acerbic style, her domineering personality, and post-Victorian changes in attitudes toward leadership made her an easy victim of Lytton Strachey's debunking in *Eminent Victorians* (1913). Suffering from hagiography during her lifetime, she has since been subjected to critical disparagement of her medical theories, reforming abilities, and leadership qualities. The unpublished evidence of some 14,000 extant letters and hundreds of personal papers is vast; to date, however, Edward Cook's monumental biography remains the standard work.

MARTHA VICINUS

Bibliography

Baly, Monica E. *Florence Nightingale and the Nursing Legacy.* 1986.

Bishop W. J. and Sue Goldie, eds. *A Bio-Bibliography of Florence Nightingale.* 1962.

Cook, Edward. *The Life of Florence Nightingale.* 1913. 2 vols.

Smith, Cecil Woodham. *Florence Nightingale. 1820–1910.* 1950.

Smith F. B. *Florence Nightingale: Reputation and Power.* 1982.

See also NURSING

· · · · ·

NONCONFORMITY

Nonconformity is the name given to that group of English Christians who are not members of the Church of England. Historically, it has reference to laws that gave special status to the Church of England and restricted the religious, political, and social opportunities of those outside it; while technically applying also to Roman Catholics, the label is normally reserved for the Protestant church bodies. In the first part of the nineteenth century Nonconformists (also referred to as Dissenters) were divided into two groups. "Old Dissent" describes those churches whose roots antedated the English Civil War—Presbyterians, Independents (later **Congregationalists**), and **Baptists**—plus Quakers (or the Religious **Society of Friends**). "New Dissent" was composed chiefly of Methodists who, because of their origin within the Church of England, did not have the same antipathy to religious establishment as did the older dissenting groups. "New Dissent" also included **Unitarians**, newly emerged from the eighteenth century's liberal and rational theologies to a separate denominational indentity. Over the course of the century a third form of dissent appeared in small sectarian groups such as the **Plymouth Brethren** or the **Salvation Army**, which owed their beginnings to one or more charismatic individuals or were organized on the basis of a distinctive founding principle. By the end of the Victorian era the major bodies had come to be identified as

"Free Churches," a label that emphasized positive rather than negative characteristics. It also reflected an increasingly cooperative spirit, since denominational identities had been established and institutional suspicions had generally been eroded.

The repeal of the Test and Corporation Acts in 1828 marked the beginning of a period of transition in Nonconformist attitudes to politics and societal questions. Prior to that date their primary concern had been for religious liberty, and thus Nonconformists had often been deferential to the religious establishment and willing to remain on the fringes of society in return for religious toleration. Repeal provided a ground for political involvement and made the continuing political, social, and educational disabilities more difficult to endure. A new goal of social equality emerged, one not fully achieved until the 1880s with the abolition of burial restrictions. The most controversial political activity was advocacy of **disestablishment** of the Church of England, first made concrete with the formation in 1844 of the Anti-State Church Association led by the Congregationalist minister, editor, and later M.P., Edward Miall.

The **Wesleyan Methodists**, the largest Nonconformist body in the early nineteenth century, were reluctant to identify with the older Nonconformist churches. They differed in organization (connectional, as opposed to congregational) and theological orientation (Arminian, as opposed to moderate Calvinist for many of the others); and their history was frequently punctuated by schism or internal controversy until the second half of the century. Congregationalists and Baptists followed Methodists in order of size; much of their vitality early in the century came from the impact of the **evangelical revival**. Two denominations whose influence was considerably greater than their relatively small size, due to the number of prominent individuals each produced, were Unitarians and Quakers. The latter group declined by almost 20 percent in the first half of the Victorian era, but recovered those losses in the second half so that by 1900 they numbered just over 17,000.

The nineteenth century was the great period of Nonconformist expansion in numbers and influence. Scotland and Ireland had their own distinctive religious configurations, which made Presbyterians dominant in the one and all of the Protestant Nonconformist churches negligible in the other. Nonconformists were well distributed throughout England and Wales; in Wales, they were clearly the majority. The religious census of 1851 for England showed total Nonconformist attendance very close to that of Anglicans; it outnumbered Anglican attendance in most of the chief manufacturing areas and was fairly represented in rural areas as well, becoming especially strong in locales where the influence of squire and parson was weak and where land ownership was divided. By the end of the century, even with a reduced rate of growth, the number of active Nonconformists exceeded that of active Anglicans.

The removal of disabilities and growing membership brought increasing involvement in politics and in the larger society. London University, chartered in 1828 with no religious tests for students, was one Nonconformist route to intellectual and academic respectability. Politically, the Nonconformist cause was linked closely to the **Liberal party** and its rise to power in Parliament under Gladstone's leadership. The party attracted Nonconformist support by advocating civil and religious liberty, opposing ancient privileges, working for reform, and supporting the principle of laissez faire. Gladstone's basic respect for Nonconformist religious integrity attracted significant loyalty from Nonconformist ranks, despite his own High Church convictions and his difference with them on several crucial issues.

The state's involvement in education and the place of religious instruction in the school system became prominent issues in this period. James Graham's 1843 bill for the education of factory children was defeated in Parliament in part because of strong Nonconformist opposition to the clause that would have given bishops the right to approve schoolmasters as competent to provide Anglican instruction. Most Nonconformists, afraid that Anglicans would dominate state-supported education, favored a totally voluntary school system. When the impetus for a national system grew, eventually supported by the Liberal party, Nonconformists were torn in two ways: between their view that the state should stay out of the business of education and their growing recognition of the failings of a voluntary system on one hand, and be-

tween their fear of Anglican control and their concern for religious instruction on the other. Many Nonconformists regarded the Education Act of 1870, with its support for denominational schools, as a betrayal by the Liberal party, despite the addition of a "conscience clause." Others defended the provision for religious (especially Bible) instruction in the schools.

This debate went on for some thirty years more, climaxing with the Education Act of 1902, which integrated denominational schools into the system and provided for their support from taxes. Since the Anglicans had the great majority of church schools, Nonconformists objected strenuously; some refused to pay the school taxes. It was, however, the last hurrah for Nonconformist crusading politics. With the Liberal party in decline after the Irish Home Rule split and with growing internal division over other political issues (e.g., the rise of the Labour party, the Boer War), Nonconformist political power came to an end.

Despite the moves toward Free Church unity and denominational consolidation (especially between Baptists and Methodists), the Nonconformist picture at the end of the century was one of great variety. In addition to political disputes, the century's challenge to theology—such as biblical and historical criticism, the rise of religious doubt, and the impact of the Tractarian movement—produced a number of conservative and liberal elements within most Nonconformist denominations. Denominational labels no longer clearly described theological views. Differences between small rural chapels and large urban churches together with economic and social class variables enlarged the variety, making the label "Nonconformist" more of a generic starting point than a particular identification of beliefs, attitudes, and understandings.

DALE A. JOHNSON

Bibliography

Binfield, Clyde. *So Down to Prayers: Studies in English Nonconformity, 1780–1920.* 1977.

Briggs, John and Ian Sellers, eds. *Victorian Nonconformity.* 1973.

Everitt, Alan. *The Pattern of Rural Dissent: The Nineteenth Century.* 1972.

Glover, Willis B. *Evangelical Nonconformists and Higher Criticism in the Nineteenth Century.* 1954.

Inglis, Kenneth S. *Churches and the Working Classes in Victorian England.* 1963.

Machin, G .I .T. *Politics and the Churches in Great Britain, 1832-1868.* 1977.

Sellers, Ian. *Nineteenth-Century Nonconformity.* 1977.

Thompson, David M. *Nonconformity in the Nineteenth Century.* 1972.

· · · · ·

NORTON, CAROLINE SHERIDAN (1808-1877)

Caroline Sheridan Norton is best known today for her campaigns to reform laws relating to women, but in her own day she was also famous for her literary writings, for her beauty, wit, and social and political influence, and for a difficult private life which sometimes brought her public notoriety. Norton was instrumental in achieving passage of the Infant Custody Act (1839) and the Divorce and Matrimonial Causes Act (1857). Her literature, although conforming in some ways to public taste, also contains elements of social criticism; she wrote one of the earliest factory reform poems, "A Voice from the Factories" (1836), and one of the most controversial "fallen woman" novels, *Lost and Saved* (1863).

Caroline Sheridan, granddaughter of Richard Brinsley Sheridan, married George Norton in 1827 and bore three sons. The marriage was marred from the first by financial difficulties and by intellectual, political, and emotional incompatibility. In 1836 George Norton sued William Lamb, Lord Melbourne, for damages for "criminal conversation" (adultery) with Caroline Norton, the necessary first step to obtaining a divorce by act of Parliament. The jury acquitted Melbourne without leaving their seats, but Norton's reputation had been damaged at the same time that her legal vindication made divorce im-

possible. Subsequently, George Norton took their three sons out of England and forbade Norton to see them; one child died, possibly from negligent treatment. Norton found that as a married woman her property, her children, and even her legal existence were in the hands of her husband. Thus began a series of campaigns to reform the laws.

Norton's literary works were more highly regarded in her time than they are today. Contemporary reviewers compared her favorably with Elizabeth Barrett Browning, and she was sometimes called the "Byron of Modern Poetesses." She considered *The Child of the Islands* (1845), written in honor of the Prince of Wales, to be the poem that best represented her interests. It warns the infant prince never to forget the poor who are exploited by a callous, privileged upper class.

Norton's three novels and two *novellas* combine popular melodramatic romance, autobiography, and social criticism. *Lost and Saved* was controversial because its heroine is an unwed mother who is "saved" by a happy marriage, and because it is relatively frank about sexual feeling.

Norton professed to believe that women are inferior to men by the will of God. Her introduction to *English Laws for Women in the Nineteenth Century* (1854) denies any intention to put forward an "absurd claim of equality"; all she asks, she writes, is legal protection for women similar to that recently provided for paupers, the insane, prisoners, and other helpless classes. However, her demands—for divorce, property, and child custody rights— seem to lead toward independence rather than protection. Norton benefited from the reforming pressures caused by the feminist movement, and the women's movement in turn benefited from Norton's considerable gifts as advocate. Bold, witty, and charming (though some thought her insincere), unconventional and extravagant, generous to friends and loving to children, Norton is a difficult figure to assess. George Meredith modeled his heroine in *Diana of the Crossways* (1885) after her. Upon George Norton's death (when she was sixty-nine), Norton married an old friend, William Stirling-Maxwell. She died three months later.

MICAEL M. CLARKE

Bibliography

Acland, Alice. *Caroline Norton*. 1948.

Hoge, James O. and Jane Marcus, eds. *Selected Writings of Caroline Norton*. 1978.

Hoge, James O and Clarke Olney, eds. *The Letters of Caroline Norton to Lord Melbourne*. 1974.

Perkins, Jane G. *The Life of Mrs. Norton*. 1909.

· · · · ·

NOVEL

Created by the new profession of "novelist," a group that now included women as well as men; printed quickly and inexpensively on the new steam-powered printing presses and distributed efficiently over the kingdom on the new railway system; welcomed as a source of moral and social instruction as well as of delight and entertainment by the newly expanded reading public, the novel stands as the central literary form of the Victorian era.

For the Victorians, the modern distinction between the literary novel and the popular best seller had not yet come into existence. The novels of Charlotte Brontë, Charles Dickens, George Eliot, Anthony Trollope, and Thomas Hardy were read not merely by a literary elite, but widely throughout the expanding middle class and, particularly in the case of Dickens, by the working class as well. This wide readership was aided by new methods of presentation and distribution. Early in the century, Dickens pioneered publication in inexpensive separate numbers with *Pickwick Papers* (1836-1837), and the practice was followed throughout the century with, for example, William Makepeace Thackeray's *Vanity Fair* (1847-1848) and Eliot's *Middlemarch* (1871-1872). Then, the novel usually appeared in a three-volume edition, a "three-decker," that readers borrowed from private lending libraries, of which the most famous was Mudie's. Eventually, the "three-deckers" were made available in less expensive form, "cheap editions" and "railway editions," the equivalents of modern paperbacks, distributed through national chains of booksellers, as well as in more expensive collected editions.

The dominance of the novel in this age of print emerged also from the intimate connection between the particular form of the Victorian novel, which can best be called "realism," with the desires, aspirations, and anxieties of its readers. For all their awareness of the contradictions involved in writing "realistic fiction" and their consciousness that language could not provide a transparent "objective" verisimilitude, novelists as realists still believed that language could represent the world beyond the text and convey a meaning outside of language, a nonverbal truth. Trollope shared with his audience the assumption that his Barsetshire novels, including *The Warden* (1855), *Barchester Towers* (1857), and *The Last Chronicle of Barset* (1867), could convey the social and emotional fabric of life in a cathedral community, as much as, for all its deconstruction of the possibility of a single reliable narrator, Eliot's masterpiece, *Middlemarch*, indicates the author's faith in the power to record the process of change in English provincial society.

Furthermore, realism, seen as a set of literary conventions, inscribes and presents as "natural" a specific version of reality, an equation of the "real" with the material life of a commercial, industrial society. The mode focuses on interpersonal relations and the desire for social status within a society that is, paradoxically, socially stratified yet open to class mobility. Characteristically, the "great expectations" of the protagonist in Dickens's novel of that name (1860-1861) are to rise to the higher social class of "gentleman" and to gain an independent income.

In a society that praised the virtue of individualism and lauded the "self-made" man, the making of the self and the reconciliation of this self to the society became a central issue and the Bildungsroman or novel of development a central fictional form. For male protagonists, the primary issue of the novel turned upon whether social aspiration within the class system could be reconciled with authentic desire and with moral feeling. This conflict in the lives of men, often with autobiographical reference, is played out in Dickens's *David Copperfield* (1849-1850), Thackeray's *Pendennis* (1848-1850), and Hardy's *Jude the Obscure* (1895).

Like all forms of Victorian fiction, the Bildungsroman must be classified by gender, for this was the age in which women were, for the first time, ranked equally with men as writers within a major genre. As women writing, they developed a specific language for female experience within a continuing tradition of women's literature. The female novel of development was central. The major issue for the female protagonist is the search for autonomy and selfhood in opposition to the social constraints placed upon the female, including the demand for marriage. This conflict, usually with autobiographical resonance and often framed in metaphors of imprisonment, is embodied in such novels as Charlotte Brontë's *Jane Eyre* (1847) and *Villette* (1853), Emily Brontë's *Wuthering Heights* (1847), and Eliot's *The Mill on the Floss* (1860).

As much as novelists were concerned with the development of the individual consciousness, they also sought to represent the transformations within their society—a world both urban and rural, commercial and traditional, fragmented yet coherent. Painting on a large canvas, writers shaped what might be called panoramic novels that move among the various classes and social settings. Dickens's *Bleak House* (1852–1853), for example, shifts from the estate of the highest aristocracy to the slums of London to represent the paradox of connectedness amid fragmentation. Rather than following the traditional plot/subplot structure, these fictions are "multiplot" with no one central figure and with manifold patterns of action. Here Thackeray's *Vanity Fair* (1847–1848) is exemplary, with its focus on the lives and interactions of many sets of characters in the years around Waterloo. Similarly, Eliot's *Middlemarch* is concerned less with the life of a single character than with the web that binds this provincial community. Trollope's Barsetshire novels represent the individual within a larger historical conflict between traditional institutions (such as the church) and new egalitarian, reformist impulses, as does his Palliser or political series which includes *Phineas Finn* (1869), *The Eustace Diamonds* (1873), *The Prime Minister* (1876), and *The Duke's Children* (1880).

The social transformations brought about by industrialism generated another popular form of realist fiction which flourished into the 1860s, the "industrial novel." Through protagonists drawn from many social classes,

these fictions present a variety of solutions to what was called the "condition of England"—how was the new urban proletariat to relate to the other new class, the factory owners, and how were these industrial classes to engage the power of the landowning aristocracy? Elizabeth Gaskell, writing with the authority of a resident of Manchester, in *Mary Barton* (1848) and *North and South* (1855); Dickens in *Hard Times* (1854), based on a strike in the north of England; Charlotte Brontë in *Shirley* (1849); Benjamin Disraeli in *Coningsby* (1844) and *Sybil* (1845); and Eliot in *Felix Holt* (1866) all sought to acclimate their readers to the new world of industrial capitalism and to present their varied imaginative visions of a just industrial society.

Within these representations of a shifting, fragmented society, coherence is often achieved through a narrative voice that comments upon the action and is unrelated to the consciousness of a single character. This often-misunderstood narrative method is appropriate to its subject, a society that a single participant cannot fully understand, and is employed with a complexity and multiplicity of functions—sometimes ominiscient and reliable; sometimes merely another character among multiple centers of consciousness; sometimes indeterminate and ironic; sometimes the voice of the community, the standard by which action may be judged and a guide to readers facing a new world which they, like the narrative voice, cannot fully comprehend.

HERBERT L. SUSSMAN

Bibliography

Beer, Gillian. *Darwin's Plots: Evolutionary Narrative in Darwin, George Eliot and Nineteenth-Century Fiction.* 1983.

Brown, Julia Prewitt. *A Reader's Guide to the Nineteenth-Century English Novel.* 1985.

Ermarth, Elizabeth. *Realism and Consensus in the English Novel.* 1983.

Gallagher, Katherine. *The Industrial Reformation of English Fiction: Social Discourse and Narrative Form 1832–1867.* 1985.

Garrett, Peter. *The Victorian Multi-Plot Novel: Studies in Dialogical Form.* 1980.

Gilbert, Sandra and Susan Gubar. *The Madwoman in the Attic: The Woman Writer and the Nineteenth-Century Literary Imagination.* 1979.

Levine, George. *The Realistic Imagination: English Fiction from Frankenstein to Lady Chatterley.* 1981.

Miller, D. A. *Narrative and Its Discontents: Problems of Closure in the Traditional Novel.* 1981.

Miller, J. Hillis. *The Form of Victorian Fiction.* 1968.

——. *Fiction and Repetition.* 1982.

Showalter, Elaine. *A Literature of Their Own: Women Novelists from Brontë to Lessing.* 1977.

Wheeler, Michael. *English Fiction of the Victorian Period 1830–1900.* 1985.

See also SERIAL LITERATURE; SOCIAL PROBLEM NOVEL

. . . . .

NOVELLO, CLARA (1818-1908)

The soprano Clara Novello was born into a family of well-known English musicians and publishers. After a year of study in Paris (1829), she became increasingly active in the Ancient Concerts in London. In 1832 she sang the soprano solo in a private performance of Beethoven's *Missa Solemnis*, the first in England. In 1837 she sang Mendelssohn's *St. Paul* under the direction of the composer, who invited her to concertize in Germany. In 1839 she studied in Milan and made her Italian operatic debut in Rossini's *Semiramide* in Bologna in 1841. Later that year Rossini invited her to sing in the first Italian performance of his *Stabat Mater*. She accepted a contract in Fermo, a small city in the papal states, in 1841, where she married Count Giovanni Baptista Gigliucci in 1843 and withdrew into private life. Active in the struggle for Italian independence, Gigliucci was exiled in 1849, and Novello soon resumed her singing career. Returning to England in 1851, she embarked upon a distinguished career as an oratorio singer. Praised for her seriousness and musicianship, she quickly became the leading soprano in this field. She regularly appeared at the Three Choirs Festival and sang before royalty on state occasions. After taking part in the Handel centenary celebrations in 1859, she retired in 1860 and returned with her husband to Italy in 1861.

JOE K. LAW

Bibliography

Gigliucci, Valeria, ed. *Clara Novello's Reminiscences.* 1910.

Mackenzie-Grieve, Averil. *Clara Novello, 1818–1908.* 1955.

. . . . .

NURSERY AND NANNY

The nursery, where middle- and upper-class Victorian children spent much of their time, consisted of a night nursery, where the children slept, and a day nursery, where they played. Furnished with leftovers not needed elsewhere, it could be a comfortable, easy, friendly area, with windows hygienically open top and bottom. Many children's stories describe the nursery in favorable terms from a child's point of view: shabby sofas, which could serve as ships or forts, worn carpeting, dollhouses, and toy cupboards. The nursery was attended by a nurserymaid, who brought coal, lit fires, and carried hot water and meals up and down stairs, sometimes three flights or more.

The nursery was the major focus of a child's life, presided over by the nanny, who appeared early, sometimes as soon as a month after birth. She might remain, if all went well, until the youngest of the family was old enough to graduate to governess, tutor or preparatory school. Sometimes nannies would stay on in the household as pensioners, no longer useful but too well loved to be turned out into the streets.

The nanny slept in the night nursery with her charges, easily available to comfort bad dreams or cope with midnight sickness. She dressed, washed, combed, tidied, fed, and amused the small ones, told them stories, filled them with good advice and cautionary tales. She was, in most respects, the parent figure in the child's life, although she was not expected to replace the mother. Children might see their parents briefly every day, but basically they spent life in the nursery, in sole charge of the nanny. Often the mother had little idea of the regime the nanny was imposing. So long as her children appeared in public healthy and well-mannered, she was content. Some nannies were arbitrary and tyrannical. Vivid Victorian memoirs tell of inhuman punishments such as sewing a child into a sack and leaving it in a dark cellar. But there are also many stories of nannies whose loving kindness and warmth was an island of security.

Nannies usually came from a working-class background, and thus Victorian children had more uniform moral and behavior codes than a strict class system might suggest. Most nannies learned their craft on an apprenticeship system, from their mothers, or as nursery-maids. In 1892, however, Mrs. Emily Ward started the Norland Nursing School to train girls to care for young children. Its success bred many imitators. In 1861 the national census counted 93,000 children's nurses, out of a total of 1,066,000 domestic servants. Although the census did not continue to detail categories of servanthood, by 1901 there were probably about 200,000 nannies in England and Wales.

CYNTHIA F. BEHRMAN

Bibliography

Gathorne-Hardy, Jonathan. *The Unnatural History of the Nanny.* 1973.

Howe, Bea. *A Galaxy of Governesses.* 1954.

King-Hall, Magdalen. *The Story of the Nursery.* 1958.

See also CHILDHOOD

· · · · ·

NURSING

Most nursing of the sick and invalids in the early nineteenth century was carried out in the home. When specialized services were needed, a local person practicing one of the forms of folk medicine might be called upon. A "wise woman," for example, might undertake midwifery, health care, and advice in times of illness. This form of community health care was necessary in the absence of cheap, accessible, and effective orthodox medical provision. From the early nineteenth century, however, the demand for medical services of all types increased as a consequence of industrialization, population growth, rapid urbanization, and improvements in medical science. As hospital provision increased, an expanded demand for nursing staff was accompanied by dissatisfaction with the structure of nursing and the lack of nurse training.

In the early part of the century, nurses were considered menials with a status equivalent to domestic servants; indeed, many of the nurse's duties were the same as a servant's tasks. **Florence Nightingale** observed that nursing was done by those "who were too old, too weak, too drunken, too dirty, too stolid, or too bad to do anything else." Her condemnation of all untrained nurses is now seen as an overstatement. The nurse in a voluntary hospital had no regular time off; she generally slept in a cot in or near her ward, made the patients' meals, did all of their personal care—and, through continued observation, might well understand the course of disease and the success of certain therapies more accurately than a physician whose training was largely theoretical. The pay—about a shilling a day in London—was relatively good for an unskilled woman. Those who entered into nursing were not necessarily required to have either training or experience, but some institutions were more demanding than others. Training for nursing staff tended to be informal, with no uniformity of approach between hospitals.

In the early part of the century, furthermore, the voluntary hospital was not a place the sick would normally choose to enter. The middle classes paid for and received health care at home, including perhaps the hiring of a "sick nurse." The working classes tended to use traditional forms of health care except in dire circumstances. Institutional medical provision was, however, available in voluntary hospitals or, as a final resort, in the workhouse. If nursing care in the voluntary hospitals was inadequate, that of the Poor Law (workhouse) hospitals was much worse. Most of the nursing in Poor Law hospitals was carried out by pauper inmates, and often the task was given to those least suited to the work. In both types of institution, the problem of inadequate and poor nursing care was related to the lack of systematic selection, training, and supervision of nurses, combined with low status, low remuneration, and bad working conditions, all of which created a barrier to improved nursing care.

Reforms during the second half of the nineteenth century brought new forms of systematic training and changes in recruitment, organization, and hospital administration. Much of the success of nursing reform has been attributed to Florence Nightingale, although recent historiography has tended to be more critical of her role. By midcentury, Anglican **sisterhoods** were emulating the Continental Roman Catholic and Lutheran orders in dedicating themselves to care of the sick poor. Nightingale's work in the Crimea highlighted the problems of nursing practice in a very dramatic way, created widespread public concern, and led to a public subscription to create a training establishment. The Nightingale training school was founded in 1860 at St. Thomas's Hospital. Suitable candidates for nurses' training, although not necessarily from the higher social classes, were those with some educational attainment and a high degree of moral behavior. Other training schools were also established, though not all achieved the high standards of the Nightingale school. The nursing reform movement was successful in bringing about the recruitment of what were considered to be suitable persons, and by the 1880s and 1890s nursing took a place alongside teaching as a respectable vocation for women.

Nursing reform must be considered in relation to other economic and social factors. Mid-nineteenth-century ideology held that nursing was "natural" for women; in *Notes on Nursing* (1859) Florence Nightingale wrote that at some point in her life "every woman is a nurse." The nurse's supportive role in relation to the doctor and patients was a direct corollary of the wife's role in relation to husband and family in the ideal middle-class marriage. Demographic factors led to a surplus of women over men at a time when the popular notion was that a woman's duty and fulfillment were to be found only in marriage. The necessity of career opportunities for unmarried women was, in turn, related to some

women's call for emancipation. Although the structure of nursing reflected many Victorian patriarchal values and assumptions, it also contributed to the widening of occupational opportunities for middle-class women. Furthermore, reform was intended to take the control of nursing out of the hands of male medical practitioners and hospital governors and give it instead to qualified matrons.

By the last quarter of the century, most voluntary hospital training schools admitted only candidates over the age of twenty-one. (To a certain extent this discouraged working-class entrants, who often had to become self-supporting by twelve or fourteen; it also meant that middle-class women who took up nursing had generally been in some other employment or had decided they were unlikely to marry.) In training the focus was on practical experience. Probationers worked on the wards for ten, twelve, or even fourteen hours a day, with classes and lectures sandwiched in at odd times. They lived in a residence provided by the hospital, under strict supervision. The discipline, the ideology of self-sacrifice, and the demand for skilled nurses created by rapid advances in medical knowledge and hospital care transformed the image of nursing. Although trained nurses who worked on the wards of public or voluntary hospitals continued to suffer from long hours, poor living conditions, and inadequate pay, other options were open: in private nursing, as district (public health) nurses, and in a multitude of senior supervisory and administrative positions created by the multiplication of health care institutions.

PHILIP SWAN

Bibliography

Abel-Smith, Brian. *A History of the Nursing Profession.* 1975.

Austin, Anne L. *History of Nursing Source Book.* 1957.

Baly, Monica E. *Florence Nightingale and the Nursing Legacy.* 1986.

Bullough, Vern L. and Bonnie Bullough. *Care of the Sick: The Emergence of Modern Nursing.* 1979.

Davies, Celia, ed. *Rewriting Nursing History.* 1980.

Holcombe, Lee. *Victorian Ladies at Work.* 1973.

Nightingale, Florence. *Notes on Nursing: What It Is, and What It Is Not.* 1859.

Vicinus, Martha. *Independent Women: Work and Community for Single Women, 1850-1920.* 1985.

. . . . .

OCEANOGRAPHY

The seas and oceans of the world have always been objects of wonder and curiosity. Scientists occasionally investigated marine phenomena in the seventeenth and eighteenth centuries, but only in the nineteenth century did oceanography, a term coined in the 1880s, emerge as an interdisciplinary science incorporating biological, chemical, physical, geological, and geophysical investigations.

Oceanography sprang from several sources. The British Admiralty began gathering hydrographic data in the eighteenth century, and under the direction of men such as Admiral Francis Beaufort (1774-1857), the Royal Navy's Hydrographic Service systematically mapped and charted much of the world's salt water. Major James Rennell (1742-1830), a surveyor of the East India Company, devoted years to studying winds and currents by analyzing ships' logs, which resulted in his posthumously published book *An Investigation of the Currents of the Atlantic Ocean* (1832).

Not to be outdone by the exploration efforts of others, the American government, after much political debate, commissioned a young naval officer, Charles Wilkes (1798-1877), to lead the great U.S. Exploring Expedition (1838-1842). Wilkes, who began with six vessels, roamed the seas and brought back enough material to fill more than the twenty volumes eventually published. The long tenure of Alexander Dallas Bache (1806-1867) as superintendent of the U.S. Coast Survey (1843-1867) ushered in major efforts to take soundings and chart American coastal waters. Meanwhile, Captain Matthew Fontaine Maury (1806-1873), Bache's great rival and head of the U.S. Navy's Depot of Charts and Instruments (1842-1861), applied himself to the study of winds and currents. Maury's book *The Physical Geography of the Sea* (1855),

an elegantly written exposition of technical data, became a best seller in several languages, and its publication marked a watershed in oceanography.

Further impetus to oceanographic research came from engineering projects, such as the laying of submarine telegraphic cables, beginning in the 1850s. Moreover, marine biology received boosts from Charles Darwin's many controversial publications and from European naturalists and governments concerned about the exploitation of fish stocks. Plankton studies had implications for the world's fishing fleets, while the study of deep-sea fauna and sediments held clues to the age of the earth and the origin of the oceans (and possibly of life). Answers to many oceanographic questions, such as the origin of the coral atolls, were slow in coming, though conflicting theories abounded. But answers required research and that required ships and money.

The U.S. Coast Survey supplied Alexander Agassiz (1835-1910) of Harvard with a vessel for an important series of cruises in the 1870s. Meanwhile, the British government and Royal Society dispatched an expedition aboard H.M.S. *Challenger* to investigate all aspects of the ocean depths. Under the leadership of Charles Wyville Thomson (1830-1882) and John Murray (1841-1914), the *Challenger* sailed 70,000 miles in three and one-half years. The expedition gathered material for a report that consumed nineteen further years of effort, and filled fifty volumes.

These later voyages marked oceanography's emergence as a mature science, which was confirmed before the end of the century by the establishment of the first permanent oceanographic research centers at Woods Hole in Massachusetts and the Scripps Institute in California. These centers depended upon philanthropists and universities, for money from governments was scarce. This, however, encouraged international cooperation. As early as 1853 a conference on maritime meteorology, organized by Maury, met at Brussels to promote cooperative collection of data. By 1899 the Scandinavians staged a major oceanographic conference, which gave birth, in turn, to the International Council for the Exploration of the Sea, founded in 1902, with its central bureau in Copenhagen.

N. MERRILL DISTAD

Bibliography

Day, Vice-Admiral Sir Archibald. *The Admiralty Hydrographic Service, 1795–1919.* 1967.

Deacon, Margaret. *Scientists and the Sea, 1650–1900: A Study of Marine Science.* 1971.

Herdman, Sir William A. *Founders of Oceanography and Their Work: An Introduction to the Science of the Sea.* 1923.

Linklater, Eric. *The Voyage of the Challenger.* 1972.

Ritchie, Rear-Admiral George Stephen. *The Admiralty Chart: British Naval Hydrography in the Nineteenth Century.* 1967.

Schlee, Susan. *A History of Oceanography: The Edge of an Unfamiliar World.* 1973.

. . . . .

O'CONNELL, DANIEL
(1775–1847)

As an Irish Catholic barrister Daniel O'Connell led campaigns for **Catholic emancipation** and for repeal of the union with Britain. O'Connell mobilized the Irish into a disciplined constitutional pressure group. In the process he created modern **Irish nationalism** and brought the Irish question into British politics.

Although born into the Catholic gentry in County Kerry, O'Connell was reared in a peasant cottage (as was the custom), where he learned the language and values of the common people. Because education was prohibited to Catholics, he left Ireland in 1791 to study in France and Belgium. In 1794 the French Revolution forced him to London where he studied law at Lincoln's Inn. He was called to the Irish bar in 1798.

O'Connell was converted to radicalism by reading William Godwin, Thomas Paine, Adam Smith, and Jeremy Bentham. The bloody Irish rebellion in 1798 convinced him that Irish violence would only lead to further oppression, and that change should be won by legal and constitutional means. The Act of Union with Great Britain (1800) brought O'Connell into politics. Out of a campaign for Catholic civil rights, O'Connell hoped to create an Irish nationalist movement which would ultimately lead to repeal of the union. He believed that only an Irish Parliament could adequately deal with Irish problems. As a member of the Catholic Committee, in 1815 O'Connell sabotaged governmental compromise that would have granted Catholic emancipation in exchange for a promise that the pope would not appoint anti-British bishops. He feared that the compromise would destroy Catholicism as the common bond of the Irish people by splitting the clergy and middle class from the peasants.

O'Connell ran for Parliament, although as a Catholic he could not take his seat, and in 1828 won a by-election in County Clare. Rather than face the threat of civil war, the duke of Wellington's government passed the Catholic Relief Act. O'Connell became known as "the Liberator."

In Parliament, O'Connell championed black and Jewish emancipation, prison and legal reforms, and other liberal causes. His primary objective, however, remained repeal of the Act of Union. Although he drew massive numbers of Irish Catholics to his meetings, repeal did not have supporters in Parliament or carry the same moral implications as emancipation. In 1843 Robert Peel called off a repeal meeting at Clontarf and had O'Connell arrested. He was tried and convicted for sedition and sentenced to one year in prison. (A legal technicality, however, allowed for his release.) Nearing seventy, O'Connell was too weary to resume mass agitation and was disheartened by the famine. He died at Genoa in 1847 while on a pilgrimage to Rome.

Besides winning civil rights for the Irish, O'Connell lifted them out of psychological serfdom and made Catholicism the distinguishing element in Irish nationalism. He also taught Irish Catholics to use the political institutions and values of the British parliamentary system, thus giving the Irish political skills which they used in both Great Britain and North America.

EILEEN McMAHON

Bibliography

Edwards, Robert Dudley. *Daniel O'Connell and His World.* 1975.

MacIntyre, Angus. *The Liberator: Daniel O'Connell and the Irish Party, 1830–47.* 1965.

McCaffrey, Lawrence J. *Daniel O'Connell and the Repeal Year.* 1966.

McCartney, Donal, ed. *The World of Daniel O'Connell.* 1980.

Nowlan, Kevin and Maurice O'Connell, eds. *Daniel O'Connell: Portrait of a Radical.* 1984.

O'Connell, Maurice, ed. *The Correspondence of Daniel O'Connell.* 1972–1980.

O'Faolain, Sean. *King of the Beggars.* 1938.

O'Ferrall, Fergus. *Catholic Emancipation.* 1985.

——. *Daniel O'Connell.* 1981.

· · · · ·

O'CONNOR, FEARGUS EDWARD (1794-1855)

The dynamic, controversial, and best-known Chartist leader Feargus Edward O'Connor was, perhaps, the most significant voice for working-class aspirations during the late 1830s and 1840s.

The son a radical nationalist whose family claimed descent from eleventh-century Irish kings, O'Connor was born in County Cork on July 18, 1794, attended Trinity College, Dublin, and was admitted to the bar. In 1820 he inherited a small estate that freed him to pursue political interests. Elected to Parliament in 1832, his earliest associations were with Daniel O'Connell and the Irish question, but bitter disputes led to a split with O'Connell and a shift in focus to social problems and the need for further parliamentary reform. After losing his seat in Parliament, O'Connor launched a successful weekly, the *Northern Star* (1837), which became the most effective organ of the newly organized Chartists (1839).

O'Connor's contributions to **Chartism** have always been controversial. Many thought his quarrelsome nature, emotional oratory, and seemingly inconsistent position between "moral" and "physical" force strategists ultimately hurt the cause. After a brief imprisonment (1840-1841) for inflammatory rhetoric, O'Connor emerged as the undisputed leader of Chartism during the 1840s; he pursued dis-

putes with the Anti-Corn-Law League as well as an impractical scheme for working-class land settlements. In 1848 he again played an uncertain role during the final attempt to implement the charter. A family history of mental illness and the failure of both Chartism and the land scheme contributed to O'Connor's final insanity (1852). Death followed in three years.

ALFRED COHEN

Bibliography

Epstein, James. *The Lion of Freedom: Feargus O'Connor and the Chartist Movement, 1832–1842.* 1982.

Read, Donald and Eric Glasgow. *Feargus O'Connor: Irishman and Chartist.* 1961.

Thompson, Dorothy. *The Chartists.* 1984.

· · · · ·

OLIPHANT, MARGARET OLIPHANT WILSON (1828-1897)

Margaret Oliphant was one of the most industrious and prolific writers of the Victorian age; her literary achievement, however, transcended mere bulk. In recent years, some of her novels have come back into print and her critical writings for *Blackwood's Magazine*, the *Spectator*, and other prominent journals, her biographies and travel writings, and most especially her deeply moving posthumously published *Autobiography and Letters* (1898) have found a small but appreciative readership.

Though she spent most of her life after the age of ten in southern England and in Europe, Oliphant retained a fierce loyalty to the Scotland of her birth and family background. From her earliest book, the novel *Passages in the Life of Mrs. Margaret Maitland of Sunnyside* (1849), to her last work, she drew on Scotland as her natural literary heritage. But the circumstances of her life and the richness of her imagination carried her far beyond its borders. She married her cousin Francis Wilson Oliphant in 1852. A gifted but impecunious artist, he became a kind of paradigm of the men who figured in both her life and fiction—charming, talented, good-natured, but feckless, financially irresponsible, and only too willing to depend on her industry.

When Francis Oliphant was striken with tuberculosis and obliged to seek a better climate, he took his wife to Italy where he died in 1859, leaving her virtually penniless with three small children to provide for. Writing fiction became a necessity and ultimately a burden as the demands of her family (parents, brothers, nieces, and nephews as well as her children) increased. Shrewdly recognizing the demands of the market, she produced novels in nearly every category of popular fiction—a sensation novel, *Salem Chapel* (1863), that briefly rivaled the popularity of Ellen Price Wood's *East Lynne* (1861); a series of novels of provincial clerical life collected as the Chronicles of Carlingford (the best of these are *Miss Marjoribanks*, 1866, and *Phoebe Junior*, 1876) much in the manner of Anthony Trollope's Barsetshire series; innumerable love stories and tales of family life; and stories of the supernatural (the best a novella, "A Beleaguered City," 1880, and the short stories "The Open Door," 1882, and "Old Lady Mary," 1885). Most of these, while conforming to popular taste and fashion, display a literary gift that redeems her from the stigma of hack writer—wit, sophistication, sharpness of observation, and objectivity balanced with compassion and warmth. Her writing is fluent and graceful, only rarely given to excesses of melodrama and sentimentality.

In Oliphant's later fiction, to be sure, the reader detects the effort and strain of writing under heavy financial and emotional burdens. As her *Autobiography* movingly records, the death of her only daughter at ten, the struggle to educate her sons at Eton and Oxford and their subsequent poor health and inability to make their own way (both predeceased her), and the never-ending need to earn money wearied her of novel writing.

Under happier circumstances, Oliphant confesses in her *Autobiography*, she would have preferred the more intellectually engaging work of history, literary criticism, and biography. Her biographies of Edward Irving, founder of the Apostolic Catholic church, and of a very distant relative, Laurence Oliphant; her *Literary History of England in the End of the Eighteenth and Beginning of the Nine-teenth Century* (3 vols., 1882); her *Historical Sketches of the Reign of George Second* (2 vols., 1869); as well as her periodical journalism and her solid history of William Blackwood and Sons (*Annals of a Publishing House*, 2 vols., 1897) suggest that she was a good judge of her talents.

VINETA COLBY

Bibliography

Colbey, Vineta and Robert Colby. *The Equivocal Virtue: Mrs. Oliphant and the Victorian Literary Market Place.* 1966.

Williams, Merryn. *Margaret Oliphant: A Critical Biography.* 1986.

Wolff, Robert L. *Gains and Losses: Novels of Faith and Doubt in Victorian England.* 1977.

• • • • •

OPERA

Opera has always been a costly and patrician entertainment. In Victorian times it was a glamorous feature of the London social season.

In London, as in most of Europe, Italian opera retained its dominant position through most of the nineteenth century. Her Majesty's (formerly the King's) Theatre lost its monopoly in the presentation of Italian opera in 1843, and the rival Royal Italian Opera House opened at Covent Garden in 1847; the prefix "Italian" was dropped only in 1892, while Her Majesty's closed finally as an opera house in 1887. Until that time German, French, and even English operas had to be translated into Italian (the first Wagner opera performed in London, "The Flying Dutchman," appeared as *L'Ollandese dannato* in 1870). A series of operas in Italian was seen as an essential part of the London season. They were generally imported from Continental houses. Among the few Italian operas premiered in London were **Michael William Balfe**'s *Falstaff* (1838) and Giuseppe Verdi's *I Masnadieri* (1847).

Opera in English occupied a distinctly lower position in social prestige. Nevertheless, many English composers, singers, and managers strove to overcome this prejudice. Efforts were made to promote a national company for serious opera: the English Opera, at the Lyceum Theatre (1834–1841); the Louisa Pyne and George Harrison company and its successor, the Royal English Opera (1856–1864); the Carl Rosa touring company (founded 1875); and Richard D'Oyly Carte's Royal English Opera (1891).

These were fragile undertakings. But the early success of John Barnett's *The Mountain Sylph* at the Lyceum in 1834 encouraged a substantial school of English romantic opera. The most successful composers were Michael William Balfe (1808–1870) and William Vincent Wallace (1812–1865); Balfe's *The Bohemian Girl* (1843) and Wallace's *Maritana* (1845) remained on the boards for nearly a hundred years. These operas usually had librettos by third-rate hacks who adapted French or German works that had already appeared on the English stage. The music is lyrical, often passionate, sometimes highly dramatic, but it tends to be episodic: spoken dialogue remained a feature. Its idiom was primarily based on Rossini and Weber, with some English elements such as the ballad and the glee.

The romantic school continued in the later Victorian period with such works as Julius Benedict's *The Lily of Killarney* (1862), Frederic Cowen's *Pauline* (1876), **Arthur Sullivan's** *Ivanhoe* (1891), and **Charles Stanford's** *Shamus O'Brien* (1896), their scores often colored by nationalistic or Wagnerian idioms. But the one enduring group of English operas from the nineteenth century is the set of thirteen collaborations between Sullivan and William Schwenck Gilbert, ranging from *Trial by Jury* (1875) to *The Grand Duke* (1896), known loosely as the "**Savoy operas.**" Both Gilbert and Sullivan were separately supported early in their dramatic careers by Thomas and Priscilla German Reed's entertainments at the Gallery of Illustration, Marylebone. These semidramatic productions virtually created a new public by providing respectable and innocuous pleasure in a building free of the disreputable associations of the theater. Gilbert and Sullivan continued this policy by setting themselves against the risqué humor of burlesque and French operetta. Sullivan nevertheless took much from the latter: the question-and-answer dialogues between singer and chorus, the patter songs, the limpid melodies over repeated chords.

Somewhat overshadowed by Sullivan were two other successful composers of light opera, Frederic Clay (1838–1889) and Alfred Cellier (1844–1891); Cellier's *Dorothy* (1886) enjoyed a phenomenal though not a lasting success. At that point opera begins to merge into **musical comedy**, which had its British heyday in the 1890s.

Provincial centers were chiefly dependent on touring companies for opera. During the brief life of an independent company at the Theatre Royal, Manchester, in the 1850s, an important English opera, **Edward Loder's** *Raymond and Agnes*, had its first performance (1855).

By the end of the nineteenth century opera in Britain had widened its audience and raised its intellectual level. But it had not ceased to be an essentially alien form, which Gilbert and Sullivan could anglicize only by demoting its high seriousness.

NICHOLAS TEMPERLEY

Bibliography

Burton, Nigel. "Opera 1865–1914." In Nicholas Temperley, ed., *The Athlone History of Music in Britain*, vol. 5. 1981.

Temperley, Nicholas. "The English Romantic Opera." *Victorian Studies*, vol. 9, pp. 293–301.

———. "Musical Nationalism in Victorian Opera." In Nicholas Temperley, ed., *The Lost Chord*. 1988.

White, Eric. *A History of English Opera*. 1983.

· · · · ·

OPERETTA

French operetta established a foothold in London in 1857, when Jacques Offenbach presented some of his one-acters at St. James's Theatre. *Orphée aux Enfers* followed in 1865, *Barbe-Bleue* and *La Belle Hélène* in 1866. An English mania for *opéra-bouffe* began with the 1867 production of *La Grande-Duchesse de Gérolstein*. Londoners would later enjoy *La Princesse de Trébizonde* (1870), *Geneviève de Brabant* (1871), *La Vie Parisienne* (1872), *Le Roi Carotte* (1872), *La jolie Parfumeuse* (1874), *La Périchole*

(1875), *Madame Favart* (1879), and *La Créole* (1886).

Beginning in 1874, English audiences also heard the works of Charles Lecocq: *Giroflé-Girofla*, *La Fille de Madame Agnot*, *Fleur-de-Thé*, *Les Prés Saint-Gervais*, *La petite Mariée*, *Le petit Duc*, and *Le Coeur et la Main*. In 1878 Robert Planquette's *Les Cloches de Corneville* began an astounding London run of 705 performances, under the title *The Chimes of Normandy*. Planquette also wrote *Rip van Winkle* (1882) and *Nell Gwynne* (1886) specifically for the English stage. The works of Edmond Audran were often more successful in London than in Paris: *Les Noces d'Olivette* (1880), *La Mascotte* (1881), *Le grand Mogol* (1884), and *La Cigale et la Fourmi* (1890). However, the first British production of Johann Strauss's *Die Fledermaus* (1876) was not a hit.

French operettas were usually bowdlerized and often translated badly by the hack writer Henry Brougham Farnie. Nevertheless, they prepared English audiences for W. S. Gilbert and Arthur Sullivan. *The Pirates of Penzance* (1880) owes much to Offenbach's *Les Brigands*, which Gilbert translated in 1871.

Gilbert and Sullivan created works as sharp and as tuneful as any French operetta, though less risqué. At first, working separately, they wrote several short pieces produced at Thomas German Reed's Gallery of Illustration. Sullivan's *Cox and Box* (composed in 1866) had a libretto by F. C. Burnand (1836–1917). Gilbert's most successful work for Reed was *Ages Ago* (1869), with music by Frederic Clay (1838–1889).

In the **Savoy operas**, written in collaboration with Sullivan, Gilbert brilliantly satirized the British legal system (*Trial by Jury*, 1875), the navy (*H.M.S. Pinafore*, 1878), the aesthetic movement (*Patience*, 1881), the House of Lords (*Iolanthe*, 1882), women's emancipation (*Princess Ida*, 1884), Gothic melodrama (*Ruddigore*, 1887), and republicanism (*The Gondoliers*, 1889). Sullivan was an equally clever musical caricaturist who spoofed everything from minstrel shows (*Utopia, Limited*, 1893) to Handel. He also drew on English folk music to produce some genuinely beautiful songs, especially in *The Yeomen of the Guard* (1888).

George Edwardes (1852–1915), former acting manager for **Richard D'Oyly Carte**, capi-talized on the success of Gilbert and Sullivan by producing still lighter operettas. *Dorothy* (1886) by Alfred Cellier (former musical director for D'Oyly Carte) outran every Savoy opera. The triumph of *The Mikado* (1885) inspired Sidney Jones (1869–1946) to compose Oriental operettas: *The Geisha* (1896) and *San Toy* (1899). Drawing on such tunesmiths as Jones, Ivan Caryll (1861–1921), and Lionel Monckton (1861–1924), Edwardes staged a succession of lucrative "girl" shows: *A Gaiety Girl* (1893), *The Shop Girl* (1894), *My Girl* (1896), *The Circus Girl* (1896), *A Runaway Girl* (1898), and *The Casino Girl* (1900). These confections marked the evolution of operetta into the fluffier genre of **musical comedy**.

JONATHAN ROSE

Bibliography

Hyman, Alan. *Sullivan and His Satellites: A Survey of English Operettas 1860–1914*. 1978.

Traubner, Richard. *Operetta: A Theatrical History*. 1983.

· · · · ·

OPIUM

During the 1800s physicians used opium to treat everything from tuberculosis to diarrhea, and the public employed it as a home remedy. There were no restrictions on its sale until the passage of the Pharmacy Act in 1868. Before that act, opium was sold in most shops and later with little restriction by pharmicists. It was mixed with alcohol to make a popular all-purpose medication called laudanum. Babies were regularly given the drug in Godfrey's Cordial and other patent medicines. In the 1850s the average yearly consumption was roughly two to three pounds per thousand persons. In the Fens consumption was higher because the local population sought relief from the fevers and diseases created by an unhealthy environment. On the whole, opium was not used for recreational purposes, but as a medicine by a population which usually treated its ills without formal medical attention. Although Great Britain fought Opium Wars with China to force that empire to accept Indian opium, most of the domestic market was supplied from Turkey.

Never before 1900 did the government accept the argument of reformers that the opium trade had to end. As late as 1895 a royal commission approved the continuation of the Indian trade with China.

But by the end of the 1800s attitudes toward the use of opium were changing. Doctors began to abandon it and home use declined as working-class living standards improved. The increasingly professional medical community discovered the potential for addiction to a derivative, morphine, which they had begun injecting with hypodermics. Crusaders against the Indian trade with China condemned opium as immoral and popular fiction played on racist sentiments by portraying opium smoking among the small Chinese community in the East End of London as an evil influence. For a combination of reasons, the habitual use of opium began to be considered a social evil, and a movement to control access to the drug began before 1900, but was not accomplished until the twentieth century.

DENNIS J. MITCHELL

Bibliography

Berridge, Virginia. "Victorian Opium Eating: Responses to Opiate Use in Nineteenth Century England." *Victorian Studies*, vol. 21, pp. 437–461.

Berridge, Virginia and Griffith Ewards. *Opium and the People: Opiate Use in Nineteenth-Century England*. 1981.

Hayter, Alethea. *Opium and the Romantic Imagination*. 1970.

Inglis, Brian. *The Forbidden Game: A Social History of Drugs*. 1975.

Latimer, Dean and Jeff Goldberg. *Flowers in the Blood: The Story of Opium*. 1981.

Parssinen, Terry. *Secret Passions, Secret Remedies: Narcotic Drugs in British Society, 1820–1930*. 1983.

Peters, Dolores. "The British Medical Response to Opiate Addiction in the Nineteenth Century." *The Journal of the History of Medicine and Allied Sciences*, vol. 36, pp. 455–488.

See also DRUGS AND PATENT MEDICINES

. . . . .

ORATORIO

The Victorian cult of the sacred oratorio was only in part a purely musical phenomenon. Public performances of works by Handel, Spohr, Mendelssohn, and Gounod amounted virtually to acts of communal devotion in a nonliturgical atmosphere, and ministered to the widespread enthusiasm for **choral music** fostered in the singing class movement promoted by John Hullah, John Curwen, and others. Oratorio enhanced biblical themes and characters through musical expression; it thus made a distinctive appeal to audiences who questioned the propriety of secular music-drama. Moreover, the diversified structure of oratorios allowed scope for vocal display, stirring choruses, and dramatic orchestral interludes. Over many decades choral works both sacred and secular figured prominently in the great provincial festivals held in cities like Bristol, Cardiff, Leeds, and Norwich. From the time of *Elijah* (Birmingham, 1846) these impressive gatherings did much to arouse a spirit of civic pride among musicians.

One consequence of the vogue for oratorio was that most serious Victorian composers aspired to excell in compositions bearing such titles as *Eli* (Michael Costa, 1855), *The Prodigal Son* (**Arthur Sullivan**, 1869) and *St. John the Baptist* (**G. A. Macfarren**, 1873). With the exception of **John Stainer**'s *Crucifixion* (1887)—a work especially designed to meet the needs and capacities of amateur choral societies—few of these are heard today. But they have their place in English musical history because they throw into relief the more substantial achievements of men like **C. V. Stanford** (*Eden*, 1891) and **C. H. Parry** (*Job*, 1892). Their efforts were, however, surpassed by those of **Edward Elgar**, whose major choral works display an unprecedented inventiveness. It is no exaggeration to say that *The Light of Life* (1896), *The Dream of Gerontius* (1900), *The Apostles* (1903), and *The Kingdom* (1906) are Wagnerian both in conception and execution.

E. D. MACKERNESS

Bibliography

Burton, Nigel. "Oratorios and Cantatas." In Nicholas Temperley, ed., *The Athlone History of Music in Britain*, vol. 5. 1981.

Dent, E. J. "Early Victorian Music." In G. M. Young,

ed., *Early Victorian England, 1830-1865.* 1934.

Howes, Frank. *The English Musical Renaissance.* 1966.

. . . . .

ORCHESTRAS

Permanent orchestras with full-time resident **conductors** were not a common feature of English musical life much before the middle of the nineteenth century. The formation of philharmonic societies in London (1813) and elsewhere was a step in this direction, though in some cases these organizations were not wholly professional. The usual practice was for concert promoters to engage instrumentalists on a temporary basis for single concerts or series of concerts. From the 1850s onward, commercial and artistic considerations led to the gradual adoption of contractual agreements similar to those that apply today.

When the Crystal Palace was removed to Sydenham after the Exhibition of 1851, an orchestra was established there as a result of efforts by George Grove and others. It gave Saturday afternoon concerts from 1855 to 1901 under the direction of August Manns (1825-1907). A North London rival to the Crystal Palace, the Alexandra Palace at Muswell Hill, likewise formed an orchestra of forty-two players conducted by Thomas Henry Weist-Hill (1828-1891). In Manchester Charles Hallé (1819-1895), who had already taken charge of the "Gentlemen's Concerts" in 1849, formed his own orchestra to provide music for the Manchester Art Treasures Exhibition (1857). The erection of large civic halls in such towns as Liverpool (1854) and Leeds (1858) encouraged music making on a grand scale by both choral and orchestral forces.

The uncertain conventions of engagement, however, made it difficult to curb the practice whereby (to the dismay of conductors) orchestral players would employ substitutes at rehearsals and concerts if more lucrative offers became available elsewhere. Some credit for introducing discipline must go to foreign conductors, among them Michael Costa (1808-1884) and Louis Jullien (1812-1860). Costa, an avowed enemy of the deputy system, also insisted that the responsibility for directing orchestral performances must rest entirely with the conductor and not, as formerly, be shared between the concert master and a pianist. Jullien's well-drilled body of players toured the United Kingdom, and achieved a standard of execution that was a revelation. His deliberately exhibitionistic manner on the podium, skillful deployment of soloists, and judicious programming of light music alongside serious works were particularly appropriate for the "promenade" style of concert, which enjoyed considerable popularity throughout Victoria's reign. Henry Wood (1869-1944) gave this type of event an enhanced significance, beginning with the Queen's Hall (London) Promenade Concerts in 1895. Wood improved on Jullien's sometimes flashy repertoire by including a higher proportion of first-rate symphonic masterpieces, and thus became a discreet popularizer of the best orchestral music.

At seaside resorts and inland watering places, where music-making had long been regarded as an essential amenity, the late nineteenth century witnessed—at such places as Scarborough, Harrogate, Bath, and Llandudno—a transition from military band concerts as the chief attraction to the provision by municipal authorities of full-size concert orchestras performing (with celebrated soloists) for a large part of the year. The record of Dan Godfrey (1868-1939) was outstanding in this connection. From modest beginnings in 1893, Godfrey built up the fine Bournemouth Municipal Orchestra, which was renowned for the adventurous nature of its programs and the versatility that ensured high-quality performances of both the standard classics and of modern works, in particular by composers such as Parry, Stanford, and Elgar, whose names are associated with the "English musical renaissance." The technical proficiency looked for by visiting Continental conductors was made possible by the expert tuition which became available at the newly established schools of music in London and the provinces; the aspiration to equal European orchestras in numerical strength and a rich sonority led to an increased sense of professionalism which in turn induced native composers to attempt more elaborate scoring.

Throughout the Victorian period the London opera orchestras attracted the best available metropolitan instrumental talent. Hardly less skillful were the theater orchestras found in all towns of consequence. These resourceful ensembles were expected to accompany the music-dramas put on by traveling opera companies which flourished up to 1914; but for most of the year they contributed incidental music for plays. Victorian conductors frequently gained practical experience in the theater before undertaking concert and festival engagements; they included such figures as William Cusins (1833–1893), Arthur Sullivan (1842–1900), Frederick Cowen (1852–1935), and Landon Ronald (1873–1938).

The most prestigious private orchestra of the Victorian age was that supported by the Queen herself, but other privately sponsored ensembles attained something more than amateur status. The all-female string orchestra conducted by Helen, Viscountess Folkestone (1846–1929) from 1881 to 1896 made many public appearances; an ambitious orchestral enterprise at Devonshire Park, Eastbourne, enjoyed the patronage of the seventh duke of Devonshire (1808–1891) and was the forerunner of the Eastbourne Municipal Orchestra. In the sphere of amateur music–making, the Royal Amateur Orchestral Society (1872) and the Strolling Players Amateurs Orchestral Society (1882) outlived the Victorian period. Such nonprofessional ventures played an important part in launching the "People's Concerts" undertaken in several large cities.

E. D. MACKERNESS

Bibliography

Bennett, Joseph. *Forty Years of Music, 1865–1905.* 1908.

Carse, Adam. *The Life of Jullien.* 1951.

Halle, Charles. *The Autobiography of Charles Hallé.* 1972. Ed. Michael Kennedy.

Nettel, Reginald. *The Orchestra in England: A Social History.* 1946.

Wood, Henry J. *My Life of Music.* 1938.

See also PHILHARMONIC SOCIETY

. . . . .

ORDNANCE SURVEY

During the nineteenth century the Ordnance Survey completed a national triangulation and topographical survey of the British Isles. Begun in the eighteenth century, the survey gathered momentum during the Victorian period and continues to the present day. The survey was formally established in 1791 under the Board of Ordnance. Originally, its work was designed for military needs, but later became important in the development of urban-industrial Britain.

Initially, southern England was surveyed at the scale of one inch to one mile. In 1824 six inches to the mile was used for the Irish survey. The Ordnance Survey Act of 1841 established authority for continued mapping activities, and tried to make boundary surveying and place name collection easier. By about 1850 the survey dominated map production in Britain.

The 1850s witnessed the "Battle of the Scales." Eventually, a royal commission report (1858) recommended the completion of the one-inch survey, and proposed mapping the whole country at six inches, with cultivated districts additionally mapped at twenty-five inches. The one-inch survey was finished in 1870; the six-inch survey in the 1890s.

Toward the end of the Victorian era one-inch maps were popular with bicyclists and early motorists. The maps provide an invaluable source for the study of the changing face of Victorian Britain.

OLWYN M. BLOUET

Bibliography

Harley, J. B., ed. *The Old Series Ordnance Survey Maps of England and Wales.* 1975.

———. *Ordnance Survey Maps: A Descriptive Manual.* 1975.

Seymour, W. A., ed. *A History of the Ordnance Survey.* 1980.

Smith, David. *Victorian Maps of the British Isles.* 1985.

. . . . .

OSLER, WILLIAM (1849–1919)

William Osler's publications in medicine, medical education, medical history, and public welfare reached an influential audience of Victorian readers and policymakers.

Although born on the edge of the Canadian wilderness, Osler received a superb preuniversity education. Aspiring first to the Anglican priesthood, he soon turned to natural history and then medicine, taking a medical degree in 1872 at McGill University, Montreal. After two years of advanced laboratory training in Europe, he returned and taught at McGill, the University of Pennsylvania, and Johns Hopkins until 1905 when he became Regius Professor of Medicine at Oxford University. Throughout these years he maintained a large network of correspondents in Great Britain and traveled there yearly lecturing, conducting research, and participating in all aspects of Victorian medical life. By the end of the century, he had become the leading statesman of the English-speaking medical world. Thus his call to Oxford was no surprise. There he assumed the role of public spokesman for an invigorated medical profession, for university reform in general, and for curricular reform at Oxford in particular. He was made a baronet in 1911 and died at Oxford in 1919.

Osler's life and career illustrate important Victorian cross-currents. His parents, moved by evangelical piety and missionary fervor, ventured from the center of the empire to its periphery in the Canadian wilderness. Osler, moved by similar but secularized motives, retraced their steps from the periphery to London and Oxford on behalf of the profession of medicine, which by the end of the Victorian era had become the dominant profession. By personal example, and with matchless persuasive skills, he played a key role in establishing that dominance, first by convincing physicians of the need for internal unity and peace and then by persuading Victorian society that it should privilege physicians for their noble ancestry, progressiveness, and singular beneficence.

PHILIP M. TEIGEN

Bibliography

Abbott, Maude, ed. *Classified and Annotated Bibliography of Sir William Osler's Publications.* 1939.

Cushing, Harvey. *The Life of Sir William Osler.* 1925.

Nation, Earl F., Charles G. Roland, and John P. McGovern, eds. *An Annotated Checklist of Osleriana.* 1976.

. . . . .

OUIDA (MARIE LOUISE DE LA RAMÉE) (1839-1908)

Under the pen name Ouida, Marie Louise de la Ramée swept to fame with spellbinding novels of high life: *Held in Bondage* (1863), *Strathmore* (1865), and *Under Two Flags* (1867), all featuring worldly guardsmen, wicked ladies, and stainless heroines. Author of more than forty novels, she championed the poor and oppressed in her poignant "A Dog of Flanders" (1872) and *In Maremma* (1882), one of several sympathetic portrayals of Italian peasants, and lashed out at high society in *Puck* (1870), *Folle-Farine* (1871), and the popular *Moths* (1880).

Born and bred in Bury St. Edmonds, Ouida moved to London in 1858 to further her writing. Her spirited French father had early triggered her imagination with stories of intrigue, and hints of secret missions and noble lineage—hence her expansion of the surname Ramé to de la Ramée. Attended always by her English mother, Ouida lavishly entertained guardsmen in London, picking their brains for her novels, and Italian aristocrats in Florence, where she moved in 1872. Arrogant and eccentric, she alienated would-be friends and the men she relentlessly pursued. She died impoverished in Viareggio tending a houseful of dogs.

Excessive, inaccurate, and fanciful, Ouida was nonetheless a powerful storyteller. *Under Two Flags* with its exotic setting among the French Legionnaires and the memorable "Cigarette" remains a page-turner. As G. K. Chesterton noted, "though it is impossible not to smile at Ouida, it is equally impossible not to read her." She had a genius for conjuring stories out of rapidly assimilated impressions and imbuing them with irresistible local color and romance. Accused of romanticism, she maintained the passionflower to be as real as the potato and more interesting. Moralists, outraged at her vaunted paganism and sophisticated repartee, failed to detect, beneath the worldly veneer, a mid-Victorian idealist. Her literary and political essays written in later life are as impassioned as the novels.

TAMIE WATTERS

Bibliography

Bigland, Eileen. *Ouida, the Passionate Victorian.* 1950.

Stirling, Monica. *The Fine and the Wicked: The Life and Times of Ouida.* 1958.

· · · · ·

OWENITE SOCIALISM

Both an ideology and an inspiration for numerous popular movements, Owenite socialism had a profound impact on attitudes toward British industrial capitalism from the 1820s to the 1840s. Its originator, Robert Owen (1771–1858), consequently ranks as a major voice in nineteenth-century socialist thought and as the most prominent English contributor to the "utopian socialist" tradition which influenced Karl Marx and his disciples.

Born in Newtown, Wales, of artisan-shopkeeper stock, Owen had only about five years of formal education. From the age of nine he worked in various towns. The seeds of his later ideas were probably sown during his years at Manchester (1787–1800). As proprietor of several cotton-spinning firms, he observed that urban problems (bad housing, drunkenness, crime, disease) seemed to be intensified by the spreading factory mode of production. Owen's proposed solutions drew on the ideas of French *philosophes* and British "enlightened" thinkers of the eighteenth century. While Owen was familiar with the utopian writings of Thomas Spence and others, William Godwin's *Enquiry Concerning Political Justice* (1793) perhaps influenced him most. Godwin extolled the virtues of reason and education, and criticized the extent to which corruption had permeated religion, politics, marriage, and the family—themes Owen was later to take up with the zeal of a religious crusader.

After marrying the daughter of a Scottish cotton manufacturer in 1799 and moving to the factory village of New Lanark, Owen had an opportunity to put his ideas into practice. The result was a highly structured (and financially profitable) model community in which progressive education, harmonious relations between employer and employees, and rational amusements successfully replaced drinking, fighting, and idleness in the lives of the workers and their children. This seemed to validate Owen's belief in environmental determinism, which became the theme of his first major work, *A New View of Society* (1813–14).

Owen was soon trying to exercise his benevolent paternalism on a wider stage by joining the factory reform movement, renouncing all existing religions as primary causes of suffering, and developing the concept of "villages of cooperation," which were first proposed to help the poor. In Owen's increasingly millennial thought, however, these villages were eventually depicted as small agricultural communes in which the "labor theory of value" would mandate that goods be exchanged on the basis of how much work went into their production. Communal settlements of this type, he believed, would be the perfect instruments to emancipate all social classes (not just workers) from competitive capitalism. He attempted to embody this dream at New Harmony, Indiana, in 1825, but disputes among the inhabitants led to its demise as a communal experiment within three years.

From about 1829 to 1834, Owen initiated various movements in Britain. His National Equitable Labour Exchange (1832–1834) was a producers' cooperative in which the labor theory of value was put into practice on a small scale in London and a few other cities. The Grand National Consolidated Trades' Union (1834) was intended to help realize a communalistic utopia by uniting all trades throughout Britain and using large-scale strikes. All of these initiatives, however, soon failed.

During the following decade, Owen was involved in his most fully developed movement. By using the Association of All Classes of All Nations and successor organizations, the widely circulated periodical *New Moral World* (1834–1845), and a number of highly publicized lecture tours, he promoted the establishment of scores of clubs devoted to spreading his views. By the early 1840s, Owenite adherents numbered in the thousands. But a community experiment, established in 1839 at Queenwood Farm, Hampshire, remained small and withered away after six years. More significant were the ideas Owen expressed in his *Lectures on the Marriages of the Priesthood of the Old Immoral World* (published in 1835), which examined the ways in which women were oppressed by British marriage laws and customs. This feminist tract, which went through many editions, was Owen's last major contribution to socialist thinking. In the final dozen years of his life, he drifted into spiritualism and unabashed millennialism.

Owenite socialism influenced many early socialists in Europe and North America. Among its most popular elements were the notions that social reform must be international, not merely national; that universal happiness requires changes not only in the ways people act but also in the ways they think; and that socialist reform must include significantly altered roles for women. Karl Marx, Friedrich Engels, and their nineteenth-century followers were among those who adopted these ideas, but they chose repeatedly to emphasize the differences between Owen's "utopian socialism" (as they denigrated it) and their own "scientific socialism." The Marxists especially disliked the ideal of class cooperation and the belief that isolated socialist communities could somehow induce widespread social change. Despite these undoubted differences, Owenite socialism deserves to be remembered as a major precursor to Marxist thought.

ROBERT GLEN

Bibliography

Garnett, Ronald G. *Co-operation and the Owenite Socialist Communities in Britain, 1825-45.* 1972.

Harrison, J. F. C. *Robert Owen and the Owenites in Britain and America.* 1969.

Owen, Robert. *The Book of the New Moral World.* 1836-1844.

———. *The Life of Robert Owen Written by Himself.* 1857-1858.

Pollard, Sidney and John Salt, eds. *Robert Owen, Prophet of the Poor.* 1971.

Taylor, Barbara. *Eve and the New Jerusalem.* 1983.

See also COOPERATIVE MOVEMENT; SOCIALISM; TRADE UNIONS

· · · · ·

OXFORD AND CAMBRIDGE LOCAL EXAMINATIONS

Local examinations, or locals, were a series of examinations administered to preuniversity students and instituted by the universities of Cambridge and Oxford after Parliament passed legislation reforming their governance in 1854. In part the examinations answered criticism from headmasters and administrators from the newer, middle-class schools whose candidates often failed to gain admission to the ancient universities. (For many years the examinations were known popularly in Oxford and Cambridge as middle-class examinations.) In addition, reformers hoped that locals would raise the standard of teaching at all secondary schools.

Oxford held its first locals in 1857, and Cambridge followed in 1858. In both universities examiners tested candidates in English language and literature, history, geography, mathematics, natural philosophy, French, German, and Latin. A test of "religious knowledge" was optional. After 1873 the two universities established a joint board to conduct the examinations. In 1865 Cambridge allowed women to sit for the locals (after an experimental trial negotiated by Emily Davies in 1863), though it was not until 1870 that Oxford began this practice. Likewise in 1868 Cambridge began to examine older students, especially women, to the end of awarding them certificates qualifying them to act as governesses.

Institution of the locals undoubtedly helped to bring the whole of the endowed school system closer to the universities and raised their standards of instruction. The achievement of certificates also aided students in the pursuit of a degree. By the 1870s successful examinees were exempted from part of the entrance examinations known as "responsions" or "Little Goes" at Oxford and "previous examinations" at Cambridge. Many professions came to waive qualifying examinations for candidates holding locals certificates. The significance of locals rapidly became apparent, and by 1887 more than 9,600 candidates sat for them.

Though less well known than the Oxford extension movement, the locals had a greater long-term effect on nineteenth-century British higher education, ranking second only to the great university reforms of 1854 in importance.

GEORGE MARIZ

See also EDUCATION, WOMEN'S

. . . . .

OXFORD ENGLISH DICTIONARY

The Oxford (or New) English Dictionary (OED or NED) is a monument to Victorian enthusiasm, scholarship, and cooperation, as well as a not-yet-superseded history of English from the twelfth century, detailing the changing forms and meanings of words, their pronunciation and etymology—all illustrated by more than 1.8 million quotations.

In 1878 James A. H. Murray undertook the dictionary originally proposed by the Philological Society twenty years earlier. He established its editing principles and designed its format; he also edited half the text himself, while coordinating a "small army" of volunteer readers (many of them women), subeditors, assistants, his own children, and eventually three independent coeditors (Henry Bradley, 1888; W. A. Craigie, 1901; C. T. Onions, 1914). The first section appeared in 1884, and the last of the 15,487 pages in 1928. It has since been corrected and supplemented, but only late twentieth century computer technology has permitted the revision of this invaluable word history.

SUSAN DRAIN

Bibliography

Aarsleff, Hans. "The Early History of the *Oxford English Dictionary*," *Bulletin of the New York Public Library*, vol. 66, pp. 417–439.

"Historical Introduction," *Oxford English Dictionary*. 1933.

Murray, Katharine M. Elisabeth. *Caught in the Web of Words: James A. H. Murray and the Oxford English Dictionary*. 1977.

. . . . .

OXFORD MOVEMENT see HIGH CHURCH

. . . . .

OXFORD NOVEL

The growing popularity of the university novel in the mid-to-late nineteenth century produced dozens of works set in the city of "dreaming spires." Most of them reflect nostalgia for a special place and time, and because they tend to be written by university graduates rather than established novelists, the literary quality is occasionally weak. As a social and critical index, however, the Oxford novel is important, covering a century of the university's—and students'—development.

Although earlier works use Oxford as a setting, it was not until *The Adventures of Mr. Verdant Green* (1853–1855) by "Cuthbert Bede" (the Reverend Edward Bradley) that the Oxford novel truly came into being. After spending one year at Oxford, Bradley always looked back on his college days with affection. In his novel's details of college life—with its boat races, town and gown rows, rambunctious students, dishonest scouts, and vague-minded elderly dons—Bradley set the standard for ensuing university fiction.

After the middle of the century, royal commissioners began to recommend certain reforms in Oxford's academic and social practices. The temptations of university life—most often in the form of drink, gambling, and sexual liaisons—appalled and fascinated novelists. From the 1860s until the turn of the century, the Oxford novel tended to fall into one of two camps. Moralists preached warnings to their readers in such tales as Frederic Farrar's *Julian Home: A Tale of College Life* (1859). Most famous of the stalwart fiction (many cuts above the general herd) is

Thomas Hughes's *Tom Brown at Oxford* (1861). Hughes's famous Rugby hero must resist the lures of his college's fast set and the local barmaid. *Liberty Hall* (1860) by William Winwood Reade (nephew of Charles Reade) argued for curricular revision; other reforming fictions include Harry John Wilmot Buxton's *The Mysteries of Isis* (1866) and Frederick Arnold's *Christ Church Days* (1867).

The late century's fascination with decadence and exoticism produced the second variety of Oxford fiction. Such works as C. Ranger-Gull's *The Hypocrite* (1898) and the Edwardian *Keddy* (1907), by Humphrey Neville Dickinson, show the downfall of the aesthete, even while the writers are attracted to the racy set's colorful hues. Of the satirical, sartorial novels that exaggerate the Oxonian pose, the best is Max Beerbohm's *Zuleika Dobson* (1911).

University novels focus on the student and the comradeship, for good or evil, of university life. Very little of the fiction actually deals with academics; more at stake is the formation—and defamation—of young men's characters. Women were finally admitted to Oxford in the 1870s (although they could not receive degrees until after World War I), and eventually a women's Oxford literature also developed.

ALLYSON F. McGILL

Bibliography

Green, Vivian Hubert Howard. *A History of Oxford University*. 1974.

Proctor, Mortimer. *College Life, an Exhibit of the English University Novel*. 1959.

——. *The English University Novel*. 1977.

Ward, William Reginald. *Victorian Oxford*. 1965.

· · · · ·

OXFORD UNIVERSITY

A quiet revolution transformed the University of Oxford during the last half of the nineteenth century. The reforms introduced during the period from 1850 to 1880 in particular brought the university into line with the needs of modern life.

The University of Oxford is a federation of residential colleges which have always had considerable independence. Three, University College (1249), Balliol College (1262), and Merton College (1264), have traced their histories to the very beginning. Members of the colleges have also always been members of the university, which alone has the power to confer degrees. Thus the university has never been simply the sum of its colleges. From the sixteenth century to the middle of the nineteenth century, however, the colleges dominated the university.

Oxford trained clergymen during the Middle Ages, when learning was confined to the church, and gentlemen during the Renaissance, when it was widely believed that every well-to-do young man ought to be educated. During the seventeenth century the Church of England established control over the university: the Act of Uniformity (1662) required students to sign the Thirty-Nine Articles at matriculation. Oxford thus developed into a finishing school for the privileged: churchmen, statesmen, and lawyers. Apologists for the system argued that the mental discipline of studying the classics prepared students to deal with any problems they might encounter, no matter what occupation they took up.

Dissatisfaction with this narrow system of higher education increased significantly during the first half of the nineteenth century. Many critics felt that the universities, which had been founded as public institutions, had been reorganized to promote private ends. Reformers like H. H. Vaughan, **Benjamin Jowett**, and **Mark Pattison** urged that Oxford again turn itself into a public institution. They argued that, on the basis of birth, religion, and wealth, Oxford denied a great many young people of ability a university education.

In 1801 the university introduced an examination that distinguished between pass and honors, but the reform movement proceeded very slowly. During the 1830s and 1840s, reform was interrupted by the Oxford Movement, which purported to revitalize the university's religious life. In fact, the movement opposed any attempt to alter the Anglican character of the university.

The first royal commission to examine the state of affairs at the ancient universities was set up in 1850. The commissioners recommended making university government more democratic by reducing the influence of the college heads; framing new constitutions to free the colleges from ties with families, places, and schools; reorganizing the professorial system; opening fellowships and scholarships to free competition; allowing Nonconformists to take the B.A.; and removing the obligation that fellows take holy orders. These recommendations formed the basis of the University of Oxford Act of 1854.

The Oxford extension movement (which got underway during the late 1850s) promoted the extension of university teaching. It inaugurated, for example, a system of examinations for schoolboys and a course of lectures for adults, especially women, in a number of large cities. Nevertheless, some Oxford liberals thought that the reforms had not gone far enough. The Universities' Tests Act (1871) abolished religious tests at both universities; all degrees except divinity were thrown open to Dissenters, and chapel attendance was no longer compulsory. Another royal commission, appointed in 1872, recommended establishing faculties of theology, law, arts, and sciences; providing new buildings, especially laboratories; abolishing life fellowships; establishing prize fellowships for research; allowing fellows to marry; and standardizing stipends. These recommendations formed the basis of the Oxford and Cambridge Act of 1877.

In 1878 an association for promoting the higher education of women at Oxford arranged for women's admission to college and university lectures. In 1879 two residential halls for women were founded: Lady Margaret and Somerville. Women, however, were not admitted to full membership of the university until 1920.

Thus the forces of liberalism that were at work in Oxford during this period revitalized the institution. For example, under Benjamin Jowett's mastership (1870-1893) Balliol College gained a reputation for producing statesmen and administrators. These reforms enabled the University of Oxford to play a vital role in shaping modern Britain.

ROBERT M. SEILER

Bibliography

Bill, Edward G. W. *University Reform in Nineteenth-Century Oxford: A Study of Henry Halford Vaughan.* 1973.

Brittain, Vera. *The Women at Oxford.* 1960.

Faber, Geoffrey. *Jowett: A Portrait with Background.* 1957.

Green, Vivian H. H. *Oxford Common Room: A Study of Lincoln College and Mark Pattison.* 1957.

Sanderson, Michael, ed. *The Universities in the Nineteenth Century.* 1975.

See also EDUCATION, HIGHER; EDUCATION, WOMEN'S

· · · · ·

PAGET, JAMES
(1814-1899)

James Paget was a surgeon, teacher of surgery, medical scientist, and administrator who presented definitive descriptions of several diseases and provided professional leadership for two-thirds of the nineteenth century.

Born in Yarmouth and the son of a businessman, Paget was educated locally and apprenticed to a local surgeon. With his brother's help he ventured to London where hard work and ability earned him the patronage of staff at the St. Bartholomew's Hospital and Medical School. In 1844 he married Lydia North, a cleric's daughter; they had two daughters and four sons.

From 1843 Paget held a series of posts on St. Bartholomew's teaching and surgical staff, offices (including the presidency) in the Royal College of Surgeons and, in 1860, the post of surgeon extraordinary to Queen Victoria. Other famous patients included the Prince and Princess of Wales and George Eliot. In 1871 the queen made him a baronet. Paget devoted time to a myriad of professional and government boards and commissions. From 1860 he served on London University's senate, and was vice-chancellor from 1883 to 1895. His success was measurable in financial terms as well; his estate at his death was worth almost 75,000 pounds, despite the burden of family debts.

Paget's scientific research led to publication of the first—and classic—description of *osteitis deformans* (Paget's disease of the bone) in 1876 as well as descriptions of other diseases. He published hundreds of articles ranging from technical pieces on anatomy and physiology to essays on topics such as professional education, drink, and science and religion. Many were reprinted in *Lectures in Surgical Pathology* (2 vols., 1853), *Clinical Lectures and Essays* (1875), and *Selected Essays and Addresses* (edited by Stephen Paget, 1902). Paget wrote with remarkable clarity and his views on controversial topics were moderate and measured. The volume of *Memoirs and Letters* (1901) edited by his son contains extensive quotations from Paget's correspondence but should be used with caution; his attitudes toward France as well as some details of family life and professional relations have been edited out.

As a medical scientist Paget bridges the gap between eighteenth-century theorizing and the new scientific methods of the late nineteenth and early twentieth centuries. His strength as a scientist was his skill as an observer and describer of natural structures and phenomena; it remained for the following generation of medical scientists to apply such disciplines as chemistry to anatomy and physiology. Like many of his professional colleagues, Paget was a man on the rise, but he was also scrupulously ethical and a serious scholar and teacher. Paget epitomized the social mobility and public success that could be attained in the Victorian medical profession.

M. JEANNE PETERSON

Bibliography

Paget, Stephen, ed. *Memoirs and Letters of Sir James Paget*. 1901.

Peterson, M. Jeanne. "Dr. Acton's Enemy: Medicine, Sex, and Society in Victorian England." *Victorian Studies*, vol. 29, pp. 569–590.

——. *The Medical Profession in Mid-Victorian London*. 1978.

Plarr's Lives of the Fellows of the Royal College of Surgeons of England. vol. 2. 1936.

Putnam, Helen C. *Sir James Paget in His Writings: Bibliography*. 1903.

· · · · ·

PALEONTOLOGY

Paleontology played an important role in the rise of Victorian science and particularly in the conflict between science and religion. Although few, if any, serious scientists adhered to Archbishop Usher's simplistic concept of a six-thousand-year-old earth, other doctrines, including the creation and the deluge, were very real matters for geologists and paleontologists. The central issues of the science centered around the manner in which the earth was formed, the way in which life appeared, and the manner of succession of life.

Collecting fossils was a common pastime, and many amateurs rose to prominence. Gideon Mantell, for example, was a physician whose *Wonders of Geology* (1838) helped establish him as a popular exponent of geology and paleontology. His discovery of Iguanodon, one of the more celebrated **dinosaurs** of the Victorian period, assured him a place in the history of the science. The debate that surrounded the features and structure of Iguanodon was typical of the debates that, even now, emerge from descriptive paleontology. Lectures on paleontology and **geology** were in great demand and, as a result, many controversies were a matter of public record.

From the late eighteenth century, geologists and minerologists had debated the earth's origin. In England James Hutton's "Plutonism" advanced volcanic activity as a primary shaping force. English "Wernerians," disciples of the German Abraham Werner, advanced Neptunism, which attributed the deposition of sediments to flood action. In France, Baron George Cuvier's Catastrophic Doctrine attributed changes in fauna and flora to catastrophes dating to the time between the creation and the flood; species, under this system, were the result of special creation and remained unchanged for their duration. Jean-Baptiste Lamarck's Transformist Doctrine, by contrast, postulated that modifications could occur within species.

William Smith, known as the father of English geology, played a major role in the close alliance of geology and paleontology. A surveyor, in an era when the economic importance of minerals and particularly coal was growing daily, Smith realized that the key to identification of mineral deposits was the fossils found within the strata. The method of systematically identifying strata became known as stratigraphical geology and was advanced by the distinguished geologist William Henry Fitton (1760–1861), among others.

The concept of stratigraphic paleontology was to develop systems based on the organic remains found in the strata. Little was known about the strata below the carboniferous (described by William Conybeare and William Phillips in 1822) and the description of the "greywacke" formations, as they were called, was extremely controversial. Roderick Impey Murchison, an established gentleman geologist, argued that the upper formations in the "greywacke" were part of a separate "Devonian" system. Murchison was also responsible for identifying the Silurian system, while Adam Sedgwick, Woodwardian professor of geology at Cambridge, identified the Cambrian. By 1873, Charles Lapworth had created the Ordovician system to fit neatly between the Silurian and Cambrian.

The diversity of fossil forms within the strata begged the question of the succession of life. Both Adam Sedgwick, at Cambridge, and William Buckland at Oxford subscribed to catastrophism. Among Buckland's students, however, was **Charles Lyell**, who rejected Buckland's use of geology in the service of scripture. Unhappy with the notion of catastrophic events that had no contemporary analogue, Lyell advanced "actualism," the use of present phenomena to interpret the past. Lyell expounded this steady state or uniformitarian theory in his influential and controversial *Principles of Geology* (1830–1833). The concept of uniformitarianism and the idea of a long history of the earth profoundly influenced Charles Darwin.

As a serious geologist, Darwin was concerned with the geological record but, more importantly, with the manner in which species emerged, diversified, and disappeared. His *The Origin of Species* (1859) shifted the focus of paleontology away from its descriptive foundations. Although paleontology itself continued to thrive, particularly in North America where fossil deposits were rich, Darwinian theory encouraged evolutionary biologists to investigate embryology. Richard Owen, who investigated fossil fishes and fossil amphibian reptiles from 1839 on, proposed an archetypal animal out of which a variety of

species might plausibly have evolved. Elsewhere, scientists like Ernst Haeckel and Karl Ernst von Baer, by investigating the developmental stages of animals, were also trying to arrive at an understanding of phylogeny via ontogeny. By the end of the century paleontology had become a sophisticated discipline within a larger group of related geological and biological sciences including anthropology.

ALAN RAUCH

Bibliography

Barber, Lynn. *The Heyday of Natural History, 1820–1870.* 1980.

Bowler, Peter. *Fossils and Progress: Paleontology and the Idea of Progressive Evolution in the Nineteenth Century.* 1976.

Desmond, Adrian. *Archetypes and Ancestral Paleontology in Victorian London. 1850–1875.* 1982.

Faul, Henry and Carol Faul. *It Began With a Stone.* 1983.

Rudwick, Martin J. S. *The Great Devonian Controversy: The Shaping of Scientific Knowledge Among Gentlemanly Specialists.* 1985.

———. *The Meaning of Fossils: Episodes in the History of Paleontology.* 2d ed., 1976.

· · · · ·

PALESTINE

Palestine's strategic location on Britain's route to India focused considerable British attention on it throughout the nineteenth century. Napoleon invaded Palestine in 1799 but was routed by British forces at Acre, and subsequent French efforts to gain dominance in the area failed. Russia waited eagerly for an opportunity to insert itself in the region as Turkish power weakened. By the close of the century the issues were richly complicated by the emergent Zionist movement.

Palmerston was successful in opening a British consulate in Jerusalem in 1839, with William Young as the first vice-consul. Young's formal instructions were to promote good will toward Great Britain and to develop a favorable climate for trade relations. The extent to which Palmerston sought a political protectorate over

Palestinian Jews as a deliberate scheme to advance British power in the region is open to debate. In his decision to open the consulate, Palmerston was undoubtedly influenced by the evangelical zeal of Anthony Ashley Cooper, the seventh earl of Shaftesbury, whose wife's mother married Palmerston as her second husband. Shaftesbury confided in his diary that God "gave me the influence to prevail with Palmerston." Although their role in the decision was less overt, the missionaries of the London Jewish Society exulted with Shaftesbury over the consulate's opening. In 1840, when Damascus Jews were accused of ritual murder in the slaying of a Franciscan friar, Palmerston promised Britain's help in protecting Jews in Palestine.

Two important figures in the history of British affairs in Palestine are James Finn and Samuel Gobat. Finn replaced Young as consul in 1845. His seventeen-year tenure was marked by keen devotion to the interests of the Jews; when he was recalled, the rabbis of Jerusalem petitioned to have him kept in his post. Gobat became the second Anglican bishop of Jerusalem when he succeeded Michael Solomon Alexander in 1846. (The bishopric, like the consulate, owed its establishment in 1842 to the influence of Shaftesbury, acting this time in concert with King Frederick William IV of Prussia, another proponent of the conversion of the Jews.) Gobat's proselytizing immediately embroiled him in disputes. On the whole, Finn seems to have worked constructively in the interests of both Britain and the Jews, whereas Gobat was disruptive in his pursuit of private aims.

Enthusiasm for restoring Palestine to the Jews intensified in 1865 when the Palestine Exploration Fund was established in London. Laurence Oliphant wrote *The Land of Gilead* (1880) and went to Haifa to promote the establishment of a Jewish agricultural settlement. The efforts of these sympathizers complemented work by the Hoveve Zion ("lovers of Zion") movement in England, culminating in the Fourth Zionist Congress held in London in 1900. The congress was marked by Theodor Herzl's praise of England's sympathy for Zionism and extraordinary attention from the British press. Support for the Zionist cause was also encouraged by Benjamin Disraeli's *Tancred* (1847) and George Eliot's *Daniel Deronda* (1876).

By the end of the century, the British public was well acquainted with Zionist aspirations, helped by such prominent figures as George Bernard Shaw. Herzl's invitation to address the Royal Commission on Alien Immigration legitimized the Zionist movement. British policy toward Palestine in the next two decades, concluding with the Balfour Declaration (1917), was shaped by a perception that British interests and Zionist goals were often compatible.

FRANK DAY

Bibliography

Esco Foundation for Palestine, Inc. *Palestine: A Study of Jewish, Arab, and British Policies.* 1947.

Hyamson, Albert M., ed. *The British Consulate in Jerusalem.* 1939.

Sokolow, Nahum. *History of Zionism, 1600–1918.* 1919.

Tibawi, Abdul L. *British Interests in Palestine, 1800–1901.* 1961.

Tuchman, Barbara W. *Bible and Sword: England and Palestine from the Bronze Age to Balfour.* 1956.

See also JEWS AND JEWRY

· · · · ·

PALGRAVE, FRANCIS TURNER
(1824–1897)

Francis Turner Palgrave, editor of the famous Victorian anthology *The Golden Treasury of the Best Songs and Lyrical Poems in the English Language* (1861) was also a greatly feared critic and a lesser poet of the "contemplative school" (which included Matthew Arnold and Arthur Hugh Clough). His best-selling volumes were *Hymns* (1867) and *The Visions of England* (1880). He was elected professor of poetry at Oxford for two terms (1885–1895). As an art critic he was best known for his defense of the Pre-Raphaelites, culminating in his *Handbook to the Fine Art Collections in the International Ex-*

hibition of 1862, which was withdrawn from circulation after only three weeks on the grounds that it libeled almost every non-Pre-Raphaelite artist exhibited.

But his greatest achievement is his *Golden Treasury*, which sprang from his desire to create an anthology that would foster a love of poetry in a general audience. His own taste for simplicity of language and subject combined with his love of romantic poetry (particularly that of Wordsworth) to present, in a unique thematically arranged format, an apparently complete history of the English lyric—the first such attempted, and one uniquely suited to the needs of the newly formed state education system which his work as a civil servant in the education ministry was helping to set up. The *Golden Treasury* was, for generations of students and general readers, their only exposure to lyric poetry, and it has formed the tastes of millions of readers.

MEGAN J. NELSON

Bibliography

Palgrave, Francis Turner. *Landscape in Poetry from Homer to Tennyson.* 1897.

Palgrave, Gwennllian F. *Francis Turner Palgrave: His Journals and Memories of His Life.* 1899.

. . . . .

PALMERSTON, LORD (HENRY JOHN TEMPLE) (1784-1865)

Holder of an Irish peerage which did not preclude his service in the House of Commons, Lord Palmerston had a parliamentary career of extraordinary length. He sat for fifty-eight years in the Commons and held political office for forty-eight of those years. Twice prime minister (1855-1858, 1859-1865), he also served for sixteen years as foreign secretary (1830-1834, 1835-1841, 1846-1851). Described as "the most English minister who ever governed England," he was an unashamed exponent of British national interests abroad.

Educated at Harrow School, Edinburgh University, and St. John's College, Cambridge, Palmerston became a Tory M.P. in 1807 and was named secretary-at-war in 1809. He served in this minor office (concerned with army administration rather than military policy) for nearly twenty years. During this period Palmerston played no prominent role in politics but did pursue the delights of London society; he was widely known as "Lord Cupid." In 1839 he married Emily Lamb, sister of Lord Melbourne and widow of Lord Cowper, who was probably one of his mistresses during this time.

In 1830 Palmerston joined Earl Grey's Whig-Canningite coalition government as secretary of state for foreign affairs. Although Palmerston supported the Reform Act of 1832, it broadened the franchise more than he wished. His constant opposition delayed the next installment of parliamentary reform until after his death in 1865.

As foreign secretary during the 1830s, Palmerston assertively defended British power and prestige abroad which, he believed, required preserving peace, maintaining a European balance of power, and sponsoring British-style constitutional liberalism on the Continent. He contributed to the creation of an independent Belgium, had temporary success in the establishment of constitutional regimes in Greece, Portugal, and Spain, and made some advances toward suppressing the international slave trade.

During his 1846-1851 tenure as foreign secretary, Palmerston gained wide public popularity by denouncing the repressive measures taken by Austria and Russia to suppress the revolutions of 1848. He became an even greater popular hero in 1850 by instituting a blockade to obtain compensation from the Greek government for a shady Gibralter-born moneylender whose house in Athens had been ransacked. In his famous dusk-to-dawn "civis Romanus sum" speech in the Commons, Palmerston advanced the proposition that a British subject anywhere had a right to the protection of his government.

Queen Victoria was alienated by Palmerston's policies and his withholding of dispatches from the palace, which left her ignorant of important transactions. Increasing pressure was put on Lord John Russell to remove Palmerston. He found the occasion in December 1851 when Palmerston gave approval to the coup d'etat by which Louis Napoleon (Napoleon III) overthrew the Constitution of the Second French Republic.

After refusing several invitations to join the minority government of the Conservative Lord Derby, Palmerston joined Lord Aberdeen's Whig-Peelite coalition as home secretary. This government took Britain into the Crimean War. Though as much responsible as the rest of the cabinet for the mistakes made during the war, Palmerston retained the nation's confidence and was named prime minister when Aberdeen resigned. After a narrow defeat in the Commons on the justification for Britain's 1857–1858 war with China in support of commercial interests, he appealed to the country. His victory in the 1857 general election was an unparalleled personal triumph. A year later, however, he suffered a defeat in the Commons and was briefly out of office.

Palmerston's strong second ministry, supported by a union of Peelites, Whigs, and Radicals, included Russell as foreign secretary and Gladstone as chancellor of the Exchequer, and marked the foundation of the modern **Liberal party**. As prime minister, Palmerston helped preserve Britain's neutrality in the American Civil War, supported Italian unification by recognizing the new Kingdom of Italy, and transferred the Ionian islands (which had been a British protectorate) to Greece. His understanding of the balance of power in international politics, however, faltered when he failed in his attempt to bluff Prussian Minister-President Otto von Bismark over the Schleswig-Holstein question.

Palmerston was a quintessential pragmatist: hardworking, cynical, tough, and sometimes unscrupulous. He exploited public opinion to gain his ends; he believed that the sole goal of a British foreign secretary was to further British interests and that, in pursuing that goal, Britain had "no eternal allies and no perpetual enemies. Our interests are eternal and those interests it is our duty to follow."

ROBERT S. FRASER

Bibliography

Bell, Herbert C. F. *Lord Palmerston.* 1936. 2 vols.

Bourne, Kenneth. *Palmerston: The Early Years, 1784–1841.* 1982.

Dalling, Lord and Evelyn Ashley. *The Life of Henry John Temple, Viscount Palmerston.* 1870–1876. 5 vols.

Judd, Denis. *Palmerston.* 1975.

Ridley, Jasper. *Lord Palmerston.* 1970.

Southgate, Donald. *"The Most English Minister . . .": The Policies and Politics of Palmerston.* 1966.

Webster, Charles. *The Foreign Policy of Palmerston, 1830–1841.* 1951. 2 vols.

See also FOREIGN RELATIONS

. . . . .

PANKHURST, EMMELINE GOULDEN (1858–1928)

Famous later as the sufragettes' leader, Emmeline Goulden Pankhurst was a radical feminist social reformer, growing up in a milieu of social and political reform involving world peace, the Anti-Corn-Law League, and anti-slavery. Her marriage (1879) to Richard Marsden Pankhurst, radical Liberal lawyer and founding member of the Manchester Women's Suffrage Society (1867), produced five children and widened her involvement in reform politics.

Pankhurst belonged to the minority of women suffragists dissenting from the policy of the National Society for Women's Suffrage led by Lydia Becker in Manchester and Millicent Garrett Fawcett in London, who sought to extend the franchise only to women property owners, therefore excluding married women. In 1889 she formed the Women's Franchise League in Manchester to demand the vote for women on equal terms with men and equal civil and political rights for all women.

Pankhurst was elected an Independent Labour party (ILP) candidate to the Chorlton Board of Guardians (1894) and the Manchester School Board (1900). She served her apprenticeship as political activist, organizer, and speaker through her work for the ILP, for the relief of the unemployed, as a Poor Law guardian, and (after being widowed in 1898) as a registrar of births and deaths. In 1896, with other ILP members, she was summonsed for "occasioning an annoyance"—addressing an open-air meeting. Although her case was dismissed, Pankhurst engaged in this activity aware of the likelihood of prosecution and watched by her daughters Christabel and Sylvia. Christabel Pankhurst later initiated similar tactics in the militant suffrage movement of which Emmeline Pankhurst became leader. Patronizingly dismissed by some as a "fanatic," Pankhurst's radical political activism and disillusionment with the failure of conventional politics to encompass women's interests came to be shared by thousands of women.

ROSAMUND BILLINGTON

Bibliography

Liddington, Jill and Jill Norris. *One Hand Tied Behind Us: The Rise of the Women's Suffrage Movement.* 1978.

Pankhurst, E. Sylvia. *The Suffragette Movement: An Intimate Account of Persons and Ideals.* 1931.

Pankhurst, Emmeline. *My Own Story.* 1914.

Rover, Constance. *Women's Suffrage and Party Politics in Britain, 1866–1914.* 1967.

· · · · ·

PANTOMIME, BURLESQUE, AND EXTRAVAGANZA

The pantomime, burlesque, and extravaganza were hybrid theatrical forms which combined fantasy with topical allusion and utilized song, dance, spectacle, and comic business. Traditionally associated with Christmas and Easter festivities, these genres were immensely popular during the Victorian period and drew large profits for the theaters, often subsidizing an entire season of plays.

Pantomime as inherited by the Victorians had its roots in the eighteenth century, but had attained a somewhat fixed structure early in the nineteenth with the career of its most loved and revered performer, the clown Joseph Grimaldi (1788–1837). Two distinct parts composed the pantomime. The "opening" presented a story derived from classical mythology, history, fairy tale, or other fantastic material, culminating in a "transformation scene" as the characters were converted to stock figures derived from the Italian commedia dell' arte. The lovers, Harlequin and Columbine, were then chased by the foolish Pantaloon and his agents (usually Clown and sometimes Lover) in the "harlequinade," which was characterized by broad, physical comedy largely in dumb show and by the sudden transformation of various objects as worked by Harlequin's magic bat. Edward Laman Blanchard (1820–1889) was the best known and most prolific of the Victorian pantomime authors (called "arrangers," as the production was actually built in conjunction with a theater's scenic artists and comedians), with over one hundred scripts to his credit. During the second half of the century, music hall acts were incorporated into the entertainment, and in London's West End theaters, the harlequinade was gradually abbreviated, the opening lengthened, and the use of spectacle increased, until, by the 1880s, Drury Lane pantomime included immense processions of splendidly costumed actors often completely extraneous to the story.

The distinctly Victorian form of extravaganza was firmly established in the 1830s by **James Robinson Planché** at the Olympic Theatre under the management of Madame Vestris. In *Recollections and Reflections* (1872), Planché defined the genre as "distinguishing the whimsical treatment of a poetical subject from the broad caricature of a tragedy or serious opera, which was correctly described as a burlesque." In practice, the terms "extravanganza" and "burlesque" were often used interchangeably to denote a comic piece with fantastic setting and characters, new lyrics written for familiar songs, and extensive word play (particularly puns). Planché popularized delicately humorous treatments of classical legends and fairy tales, as well as attempting to anglicize the French "revue," a loosely woven look at the past theatrical season. He was followed into the field by numerous authors, including Robert Brough (1828–1860), William Brough (1826–1870), Henry James Byron (1834–1884), and Francis Cowley Burnand (1836–1917). Increasingly lavish costumes and scenery characterized the form during the 1840s and 1850s, particularly at the Lyceum. By the next decade, a more boisterous version of burlesque (a specialty of the Strand Theatre), which reveled in profuse punning, energetic dancing, and revealing

Scene from the pantomime, "Harlequin and the Dragon of Wantley" at Sadler's Wells Theatre. Illustrated London News, *12 June 1850. Library Company of Philadelphia.*

costumes, had supplanted the earlier, more whimsical pieces, and the 1870s saw a decline in the genre's popularity.

While the holiday forms were eventually produced at both major and minor theaters, the theatrical licensing laws in effect until 1843, which restricted "regular" or spoken drama to the major theaters (Drury Lane and Covent Garden) undoubtedly influenced their development. Pantomime appealed to a heterogeneous audience. Extravaganza was aimed specifically at the middle class, but there was always much cross-fertilization between the genres. Most pieces were written in rhyming couplets; elaborate scenic transformations became standard in both the fairy extravaganza and the pantomime, and much reliance was placed upon the charms of the female performers. In particular, the transvestite role (called "principal boy" in pantomime from the 1870s) exploited the talents of an attractive actress cast as the young male hero. By the 1860s it was common practice for a male low comedian to play the "dame," or older woman. Noteworthy for their combination of fantasy and contemporary reality, these entertainments capitalized on a romantic interest in the remote and exotic, while functioning as an important theatri-

cal outlet for political and social comment. Their use of topical allusion and looseness of structure encouraged ad libs and last-minute additions which could evade the system of pre-censorship as administered by the lord chamberlain's office.

The holiday forms were an important component of the vast network of Victorian popular entertainment and now provide a valuable resource for studying certain aspects of that society. Burlesque-extravaganza was highly influential in the careers of W. S. Gilbert and George Bernard Shaw. Pantomime, in a modified form, survives in the modern British holiday theater.

KATHY FLETCHER

Bibliography

Booth, Michael R., ed. *English Plays of the Nineteenth Century.* Vol. 5: *Pantomimes, Extravaganzas, and Burlesques.* 1976.

Degan, John A. "A History of Burlesque-Extravaganza in Nineteenth-Century England." Ph.D. dissertation, Indiana University, 1977.

Mander, Raymond and Joe Mitchenson. *Pantomime: A Story in Pictures.* 1973.

Mayer, David, III. *Harlequin in His Element: The English Pantomime, 1806-1836.* 1969.

Meisel, Martin. "Political Extravaganza: A Phase of Nineteenth-Century British Theater." *Theatre Survey,* vol. 3, pp. 19-31.

Wilmeth, Don B. *American and English Popular Entertainment: A Guide to Information Sources.* 1980.

Wilson, Albert Edward. *King Panto: The Story of Pantomime.* 1935.

See also CHRISTMAS (illus.)

. . . . .

PARKES, BESSIE RAYNER (1829-1925)

Author, editor, and feminist activist, Bessie Rayner Parkes played a central role in organizing the mid-Victorian women's rights movement. During the 1850s and 1860s she served the women's cause in a number of capacities, most notably as propagandist. Her writings, especially her *Essays on Woman's Work* (1865), still provide an indispensable introduction to the activities, ideology, and atmosphere of the early years of the middle-class women's movement.

Daughter of Joseph Parkes, the radical politician, and Elizabeth Priestley, a member of the eminent Unitarian family, Bessie Parkes was born in Birmingham in 1829. She attended a progressive boarding school which encouraged its students to cultivate self-reliance and altruism. After leaving school, Parkes published two volumes of poetry, but finding no other outlet for her energy, she shared her discontent with several other young women who met regularly to discuss the woman question. These conversations inspired Parkes's *Remarks on the Education of Girls* (1854), which not only proposed reforms in education but also urged the right of self-determination for all women.

Involvement in the unsuccessful campaign to change the **married women's property** laws (1855-1857) convinced Parkes that women needed a periodical to publicize their concerns. With the assistance of Barbara Bodichon and others, Parkes founded the *English Woman's Journal* (1858-1864) as a public voice for the emerging women's movement. Coeditor and guiding spirit of the *Journal,* Parkes was also involved in **Langham Place circle** efforts to improve women's employment, education, and emigration. Seeking male allies, she became one of the first women to speak at meetings of the National Association for the Promotion of Social Science.

Over the years, Parkes grew increasingly doubtful about women's ability to compete with men, especially in the economic sphere. Her ambivalence was strengthened by her conversion to Roman Catholicism and by a growing disillusionment about women's capacity to work together without the sustaining bond of a common religion. After a serious illness in 1865, she began to widthdraw from active participation in the women's movement, although she did assist with the opening phase of the suffrage campaign (1866-1867).

Marriage to a Frenchman, Louis Belloc, in 1867 ended Parkes's public career. She did not abandon her writing, however, publishing occasional articles and several books during the remainder of her long life.

DIANE CHASE WORZALA

Bibliography

Lowndes, Marie Belloc. *I, Too, Have Lived in Arcadia: A Record of Love and Childhood.* 1942.

———. *Where Love and Friendship Dwelt.* 1943.

Strachey, Ray. *The Cause: A Short History of the Women's Movement in Great Britain.* 1928; rpt. 1978.

Worzala, Diane. "The Langham Place Circle: The Beginnings of the Organized Women's Movement in England, 1854-1870." Ph.D. dissertation, University of Wisconsin, 1982.

. . . . .

PARKS see GARDENS AND PARKS

. . . . .

PARLIAMENT

During the nineteenth century, power was transferred from the monarch to Parliament and from the House of Lords to a democratically elected House of Commons. Along with these changes came an expansion of the electorate, tighter party organization, and new methods of procedure that removed legislative initiative from private members and placed it firmly under government control.

The most pivotal change was the gradual transformation of the House of Commons into a popularly elected body. Although the Reform Act of 1832 did not result in a democratic Commons overnight, and Crown patronage had been diminishing prior to 1832, the Reform Act marked a clear turning point in British politics. With the abolition of rotten boroughs and the gradual establishment of uniform constituencies, the Crown no longer played a major role in determining the composition of the House of Commons and thus influencing the outcome of divisions. In its place was a system in which a free if limited electorate determined who sat in Parliament and, consequently, shaped the formation of ministries.

Despite reform, the Commons remained an exclusive club. Electoral expenses were heavy and members of Parliament received no salary. Thus parliamentary careers were effectively restricted to men of means. The early Victorian years were a period of shifting political allegiances and coalitions in the House of Commons; it was the golden age of the private member who had not yet come under party domination.

The need of ministries to secure stable majorities encouraged the growth of party organization. In the age of Robert Peel (1788–1850), a deferential society and a small electorate required only the incipient party structure in which club membership was a badge of party allegiance. With the extension of the franchise to urban working men in 1867 and to rural male householders in 1884, more definitive structures were needed. The Liberal and Conservative parties developed constituency organizations to select local candidates and register voters, and central networks— The National Liberal Federation (1877) and the National Union of Conservatives (1860)— to provide expertise and funding. The clubby atmosphere of the Commons gave way to a more heterogeneous membership and new strictures were placed on members to vote the party line. This trend was further encouraged by the removal of religious qualifications, thus allowing Jews (1858) and atheists (1888) to sit in Parliament. The formal abolition of property qualifications (1858) opened up parliamentary seats to men of all classes.

Legislation comprised only a minor part of the parliamentary schedule. Parliament maintained its traditional character as "the grand inquest of the nation," responsible for voicing grievances and scrutinizing the financial and administrative measures of the Crown. Parliament's primary duties were to provide for law and order and for national defense, and thus it was necessary to pass an annual budget with provisions to pay the national debt. The largest proportion of parilamentary time was spent in the work of investigating committees and in considering private members' bills.

Reform of Parliament encouraged the idea that goverment had a responsibility for the social welfare of British citizens. With the enactment of a great body of social legislation during the middle decades of the century, Parliament was transformed into a legislative body controlled by ministries in the interest of their party's program. Private members (i.e., those with no **cabinet** position) had a distinctly subordinate role. This development resulted in stricter rules of procedure and more rigid party discipline.

Changes in procedure were also necessitated by increased legislation; Parliament could no longer afford the luxury of devoting time to minor matters that had little hope of success. Old ways of consensus were breaking down. In 1881, the House of Commons was forced to introduce closure when a small number of Irish members deliberately kept the Commons in continuous session for over forty-one hours. Closure worked to the advantage of the government, as did other procedural changes. Certain days were reserved for ministerial business. The speaker's growing impartiality and the use of standing committees allowed governments to efficiently carry through a program of legislation. All bills except those dealing with finance, major legislation, and provisional orders were referred to a standing committee, which was more difficult to obstruct than the committee of the whole.

Despite the need for procedural changes, the years 1868–1885 have been seen as the high water mark of Parliament. The period was dominated by the alternating leadership of William Gladstone (1809–1898) and Benjamin Disraeli (1804–1881), whose differences dramatized the developing political ideologies and social issues that were played out on the floor of the House of Commons.

In the same manner that the monarchy lost power to Parliament, the position of the House of Lords declined relative to the House of Commons. Between 1832 and 1885 the Lords remained generally satisfied and challenged the Commons on matters of privilege rather than policy. The House of Lords had always represented stability; peerage titles were associated with landed property, and only the eldest son assumed a title. The Lords remained a fairly homogenous group. The bishops continued to provide a phalanx of support for the government. While most peers did not show up for sittings, the level of leadership remained high and peerages continued to be awarded for party services and as a mark of distinction.

The peerage gradually became more conservative, and thus when the House of Lords did become more active, trouble was created for the Liberals. Even before the Home Rule crisis of 1885, the Liberal leadership had difficulty securing votes in the Lords on crucial decisions. Over the middle years of the century the sense of difference between the two houses of Parliament was heightened. The Lords came to be viewed as representatives of property and the Commons of the popular will. The House of Lords was placed in a weakened position by its opposition to reforms that were widely seen as reasonable and necessary. The Conservative party's attempt to use the Lords to mutilate Liberal legislation eventually led to a clash that resulted in strict limitations of the Lords' veto power.

By Victoria's death, Parliament was dominated by two great parties, the Liberal and Conservative, and party politics played a central role in the formation of policy and legislation. Despite the noise of political battles, however, the nineteenth-century Parliament was innovative and responsive in meeting new conditions. Above all, Great Britain had the most stable government in Europe.

MARJORIE K. BERMAN

Bibliography

Butt, Ronald. *The Power of Parliament.* 1967.

Fraser, Peter. "The Growth of Ministerial Control in the Nineteenth Century House of Commons." *English Historical Review,* vol. 75, pp. 444–463.

Hanham, Harold John, ed. *The Nineteenth-Century Constitution: Documents and Commentary.* 1969.

Jennings, William Ivor. *Parliament.* 1939.

Le May, G. J. L. *The Victorian Constitution: Conventions, Usages and Contingencies.* 1979.

Mackintosh, Alexander. *From Gladstone to Lloyd George: Parliament in Peace and War.* 1921.

Redlich, Josef. *The Procedure of the House of Commons: A Study of Its History and Present Form.* 1908. 3 vols.

See also ELECTIONS AND THE FRANCHISE; PARTY SYSTEM

. . . . .

PARNELL, CHARLES STEWART (1846–1891

Charles Parnell was an Irish nationalist, the leader of the Irish Parliamentary party (1880–1891) and a major advocate of **Home Rule** for Ireland. His father was a moderately prosperous Anglo-Irish landlord but his American-born mother, daughter of a U.S. navy hero of the War of 1812, was outspokenly anti-English. Parnell was educated at English boarding schools and at Magdalene College, Cambridge, from which he was suspended before earning a degree.

In 1875 Parnell won election to the House of Commons as a member of the infant Home Rule party. Realizing that the moderate, conciliatory tactics of the party's leader, Isaac Butt, were ineffective, Parnell and others gained national prominence by using the filibuster: they obstructed legislation and hindered the business of the Commons in order to draw attention to Irish needs and force a hearing for Irish grievances. Although infuriating the House of Commons, political obstructionism gained widespread nationalist support for Parnell. In 1877 he was elected president of the Home Rule Confederation of Great Britain.

In 1879 Parnell became president of the Land League, which ex-Fenian Michael Davitt had founded to assist farmers threatened with eviction. Thus he became the central figure of a movement that combined revolutionary separatists, agrarian agitators, and constitutionalists in Parliament using obstructionist tactics in a common campaign for Home Rule and land reform. By the conclusion of a triumphant fund-raising tour of the United States and Canada in 1879-1880, Parnell was called "the uncrowned king of Ireland." In 1880, sixty-one committed Home Rulers were returned to the House of Commons and Parnell was elected party chairman, Ireland's first truly national leader since Daniel O'Connell. In the same year, however, he began his ten-year secret adulterous affair with Katherine O'Shea, during which he fathered three children.

Gladstone's Irish Land Act (1881), which provided for "dual ownership" of the land of Ireland and judicially determined rents, placed Parnell in a difficult situation. Although the act was a significant achievement, radicals were not satisfied. Parnell avoided a split in the movement by attacking Gladstone in violent language. He was arrested (probably in accordance with his wish) in October 1881 and the Land League was suppressed. Parnell gained his release in May 1882 by agreeing to rein in the agrarian agitation in return for additional legislative concessions for Irish tenant farmers. Within days of Parnell's release, nationalists murdered the Irish chief secretary and one of his senior officials in Dublin's Phoenix Park. Parnell publicly condemned the violence and, in October 1882, founded the more politically oriented National League to replace the Land League.

With the 1885 general election, the eighty-six elected representitives of the Irish Parliamentary party held the balance between Lord Salisbury's Conservatives and Gladstone's Liberals. When Gladstone announced his conversion to Home Rule, Parnell provided the support that permitted him to form a government. However, the Home Rule bill introduced in April 1886 split Gladstone's party and was narrowly defeated in the House of Commons.

Committed to his alliance with Gladstone, Parnell maintained and strengthened the Liberal–Home Rule alliance while keeping the agrarian agitation in Ireland as limited as possible. In 1887 the *Times* published a series, "Parnellism and Crime," which printed letters (allegedly in Parnell's handwriting) condon-

ing the Phoenix Park murders. A special commission investigation in 1888-1890 showed that the letters had been forged by Richard Pigott and cleared Parnell of most other charges made in the series. Parnell reached the height of his popularity in England and Home Rule seemed only a matter of time.

Then in December 1889, Captain O'Shea filed for divorce and named Parnell as correspondent. Neither Parnell nor Mrs. O'Shea offered any defense. They were subsequently married, in June 1891, but the moral climate was such that citation in a divorce court was a fatal blow to Parnell's public career. Gladstone announced that so long as Parnell remained leader there could be no Liberal alliance in support of Home Rule. The Irish Parliamentary party deposed Parnell from its leadership. The bitter speeches of Parnell's last year broke with the cautious constitutionalism that had characterized most of his political career, and which had enabled him to create an effective parliamentary party and, in Gladstone's phrase, "set the Home Rule argument on its legs."

ROBERT S. FRASER

Bibliography

Bew, Paul. *C. S. Parnell.* 1980.

Foster, Robert Fitzroy. *Charles Stewart Parnell: The Man and His Family.* 1976.

Larkin, Emmet. *The Roman Catholic Church in Ireland and the Fall of Parnell. 1888-1891.* 1979.

Lyons, F. S. L. *Charles Stewart Parnell.* 1977.

O'Brien, Conor Cruse. *Parnell and His Party, 1880-1890.* 1957.

See also IRISH PARTY

· · · · ·

PARRY, CHARLES HUBERT HASTINGS (1848-1918)

Composer, teacher, scholar, and principal of the Royal College of Music (1894-1918), C. H. H. Parry was knighted in 1898 and made a baronet in 1903.

After taking his Bachelor of Music degree while still at Eton, Parry studied at Oxford with Henry Hugo Pierson and later privately with Edward Dannreuther. Performances in 1880 of his piano concerto and *Scenes from Shelley's Prometheus Unbound* brought him wide acclaim. Joining the staff of the Royal College of Music when it opened in 1883, he followed George Grove as its principal in 1894. He also joined the faculty at Oxford in 1883 and became professor of music there (1900–1908).

Parry wrote much orchestral music (including four symphonies), twelve volumes of *English Lyrics*, organ music, and many choral works. Among the latter are his best-known works, "Blest pair of Sirens" (1887), the coronation anthem "I was glad" (1902), *Songs of Farewell* (1916), and "Jerusalem" (1918).

His most important scholarly works are *The Art of Music* (1893), in which he developed a Darwinian theory of music history, the volume on the seventeenth century for the *Oxford History of Music* (1902), a critical biography of Bach (1909), and *Style in Musical Art* (1911).

Parry's impact as both scholar and teacher was great, and recent years have also seen a resurgence of interest in his music. In his study of the music of the period, Frank Howes identifies Parry as the chief influence in revitalizing English music in the latter part of the nineteenth century.

JOE K. LAW

Bibliography

Fuller-Maitland, J. A. *The Music of Parry and Stanford.* 1934.

Graves, Charles L. *Hubert Parry.* 1926.

Howes, Frank. *The English Musical Renaissance.* 1966.

· · · · ·

PARTY SYSTEM

The party system in Parliament emerged in response to the inability of the monarchy to return a House of Commons predisposed to support ministers of the Crown. Increasingly, during the early nineteenth century, government survival became dependent upon predictable parliamentary support recognized in party allegiance. Although some of the rhetoric of earlier executive government survived into the 1840s, by 1835 M.P.'s represented a two-party alignment of political opinion. The **Conservative party** of Robert Peel (1788–1850) confronted a Whig-Radical-Irish alliance formed by the Lichfield House Compact of February 1835. The founding of the Carlton Club (1832) and the Reform Club (1836), the registration requirements of the 1832 Reform Act, and the work of F. R. Bonham (1785–1863) for the Conservatives and Joseph Parkes (1786–1865) for the **Whigs** began to project this configuration onto the extraparliamentary scene.

The Corn Law crisis of 1846 obscured distinct party alignment in Westminster, but faith in the virtue and necessity of party association survived. Confusion was prolonged, however, by domestic prosperity, Peelite aloofness, the rivalry between Lord Palmerston (1784–1865) and Lord John Russell (1792–1878), Conservative strategy in office and opposition, and the brief existence of the "Irish Brigade." The formation of the **Liberal party** in June 1859, embracing **radical** and former Peelite opinion, reestablished a relatively clear two-party alignment.

Events following the 1867 Reform Act transformed parliamentary parties into national parties, as popular and constituency organizations established close formal links between Westminster and the broadening electorate. (After 1867 approximately 36 percent of all adult males in England and Wales were enfranchised.) The National Union of Conservative and Constitution Associations (1867) and the National Liberal Federation (1877), for example, helped to engage the electorate in a two-party contest personified in the parliamentary confrontation between W. E. Gladstone and Benjamin Disraeli.

After 1886 the two-party system, further broadened by the 1884 Reform Act, was fractured by the issues of Ireland, the empire, and foreign policy, by the emergence of the Independent **Labour party**, **Liberal Unionists**, and class-oriented politics, and by ideological reappraisals of the state's responsibilities. Yet a constitutional orthodoxy had been established that saw in the party system the means by which, through elections, the interests and opinion of the enfranchised could determine the character of policies and government. This prepared the way for the democratic axioms of the next century.

ANGUS HAWKINS

Bibliography

Beattie, Alan, ed. *English Party Politics.* 1970. 2 vols.

Bulmer-Thomas, Ivor. *The Growth of the British Party System.* 1965. 2 vols.

Cowling, Maurice. *1867: Disraeli, Gladstone and Revolution.* 1967.

Gash, Norman. *Politics in the Age of Peel: A Study in the Technique of Parliamentary Representation, 1830-1850.* 2d ed., 1977.

———. *Reaction and Reconstruction in English Politics, 1832-1852.* 1965.

Hanham, Harold John. *Elections and Party Management: Politics in the Time of Disraeli and Gladstone.* 1959.

———. ed. *The Nineteenth Century Constitution, 1815-1914: Documents and Commentary.* 1969.

Jones, Andrew. *The Politics of Reform, 1884.* 1972.

Le May, G. H. L. *The Victorian Constitution.* 1979.

Pugh, Martin. *The Making of Modern British Politics, 1867-1939.* 1982.

Smith, Francis B. *The Making of the Second Reform Act.* 1966.

See also IRISH PARTY

. . . . .

PATENTS

The Victorian heritors of Britain's industrial revolution placed a high premium on continued technological innovation and sought to protect and foster it by legislative means. Chief among these means were a series of reforms in the nation's patent system during the second half of the nineteenth century and the signing of the International Patent Convention in 1884.

The English practice of granting patents for new inventions derived from a clause in the Statute of Monopolies (1624) exempting such grants from the general prohibition of monopolies. The purpose of this exemption was to encourage inventors to publish their discoveries by awarding them exclusive rights of manufacture, sale and distribution for fourteen years, after which time the invention became public property. Prior to the industrial revolution the number of patents applied for annually was relatively low, but the upsurge of applicants after 1760 strained the administrative capacities of the antiquated Stuart patent system and prompted calls for reform. A parliamentary inquiry was held in 1829 and the Patent Acts of 1835 and 1838 provided inventors with some relief, but significant reform came only with passage of the Patent Law Amendment Act of 1852. The act consolidated the previously separate patent systems of England and Wales, Scotland, and Ireland; halved patent fees; simplified application procedures; established a single, centrally located patent office in London; and appointed a number of commissioners of patents—most of whom were law officers of the Crown—to oversee its operations.

During the third quarter of the nineteenth century a campaign to abolish the patent laws was mounted by Robert Andrew Macfie, a Scottish sugar refiner who served as Liberal M.P. for Leithburgs from 1868 to 1874. Macfie's argument that patent protection was antithetical to free trade won him the editorial support of the *Times* and a limited following in business and scientific circles but failed to achieve its ultimate object. Parliamentary investigations into the working of the patent system were conducted in 1862-1864 and again in 1871-1872 and a series of abortive patent bills were introduced between 1875 and 1882. In 1883 a new Patent Act consolidated existing patent, designs copyright, and trademark legislation and placed the patent office under the jurisdiction of the Board of Trade. The following year Great Britain became one of fourteen signatories of the Paris Convention for the International Protection of Industrial Property, the first international patent agreement.

MOUREEN COULTER

Bibliography

Batzel, V. M. "Legal Monopoly in Liberal England: The Patent Controversy in the Mid-Nineteenth

Century." *Business History*, vol. 22, pp. 189–202.

Dutton, H. I. *The Patent System and Inventive Activity During the Industrial Revolution, 1750–1852.* 1984.

Machlup, Fritz and Edith Penrose. "The Patent Controversy in the Nineteenth Century." *Journal of Economic History* vol. 10, pp. 1–29.

· · · · ·

PATER, WALTER
(1839-1894)

Walter Pater, a fellow at Brasenose from 1865 until his death and noted lecturer on Plato and Platonics, wrote many works that contributed to the aesthetic and decadent movements. In his most influential work, *Studies in the History of the Renaissance* (1873), he coined the phrase which later became the aesthetes' slogan: "**art for art's sake**." And his historical novel, *Marius the Epicurean* (1885), presented an aesthete who cultivated not only his intellect but also his senses.

Pater was educated at King's School, Canterbury, and Queen's College, Oxford, where he considered becoming a clergyman but turned instead to the world of art. After receiving his fellowship, he established himself in rooms at Brasenose, although he shared a house with his two sisters, and devoted his time to his books and college duties.

His first book, *The Renaissance*, comprised articles earlier published in such reviews as the *Fortnightly* and the *Westminster*. In considering aspects of the Renaissance throughout the world, Pater took the scientific approach of seeking the essence of the movement and its contributors without attaching a moral significance to either. Placing art within the civilization that produced it, he rejected nothing that once engaged humanity's interest. His method was impressionistic, exemplified in his passage on da Vinci's "La Gioconda," and relativistic, caused by his acceptance of the isolation of individuals within their own consciousnesses.

Pater promoted the concept of nondoctrinal, nondiscursive, nonutilitarian art. He felt that literature should approach the condition of music, should fuse form and content. His own prose style was elaborate and highly wrought.

In the conclusion to *The Renaissance* (which was excised in the second edition but replaced in the third) Pater encouraged aesthetic experience. Accepting the scientists' notion of the world as flux, consisting only of unreflecting moments, Pater turned to art for its expansive, intensifying power; he believed that art recorded these moments and existed for these moments only. Art, thus, allowed the individual to burn always with a hard, gemlike flame. This essay exercised an unfortunate influence over young aesthetes and decadents who mistook this philosophy for a *carpe diem* injunction.

Pater also published *Imaginary Portraits* (1887); a collection of critical essays, *Appreciations* (1869); and *Miscellaneous Studies* (1895). "The Child in the House" (1894), a semiautobiographical tale, depicted his own aesthetic development and sensitive responses to life's pleasure and pain.

Pater encouraged in the aesthetes and decadents a posture of sensitivity and receptivity; also, he promoted nondoctrinal, nondiscursive aesthetic art. His work influenced such writers as Oscar Wilde and William Butler Yeats.

BONNIE JEAN ROBINSON

Bibliography

Benson, Arthur C. *Walter Pater.* 1968.

Cecil, Lord David. *Walter Pater.* 1955.

Child, Ruth C. *The Aesthetic of Walter Pater.* 1940.

Court, Franklin, ed. *Walter Pater: An Annotated Bibliography of Writing About Him.*

Crinkley, Richmond. *Walter Pater: Humanist.* 1970.

McGrath, Francis Charles. *The Sensible Spirit: Walter Pater and the Modernist Paradigm.* 1986.

Monsman, Gerald. *Walter Pater's Art of Autobiography.* 1980.

· · · · ·

PATERSON, EMMA SMITH
(1848-1886)

Emma Smith Paterson, a pioneer of women's trade unionism in England, was the only child of Henry and Emma Dockerill Smith. Her father was headmaster of various London schools for working-class children. She helped teach and was apprenticed to a bookbinder. Her father died when she was sixteen.

In 1866 Emma Smith became a secretary at the Working Men's Club and Institute Union, and in July 1867, at age nineteen, became assistant secretary of the union. The union's goal was to improve working-class men by keeping them from pubs and providing classes and reading rooms. After five years Emma Smith resigned to take up the post of secretary to the National Society for Women's Suffrage, which she held for a year. In 1873 she married Thomas Paterson, age thirty-nine, a cabinetmaker. They spent their honeymoon in the United States, where they studied sweated industries and trade unionism.

In April, 1874 Paterson published "The Position of Working Women, and How to Improve It" in *Labour News*, proposing the establishment of trade unions and a national benefit society for women. On July 8 a large public meeting was held and the Women's Protective and Provident League was formed. Paterson held the post of secretary of the WPPL until her death twelve years later.

Paterson helped to establish various women's unions in London: bookbinders, upholsteresses, shirtmakers, tailoresses, dressmakers, and others. In February 1876 she founded the monthly *Women's Union Journal*, which she edited, and established the Women's Printing Society to print it. Paterson and Edith Simcox served as the first women delegates to the Trades Unions Conference (TUC) congress in 1875. Paterson attended all subsequent TUC congresses until her death.

MARY LYNDON SHANLEY

Bibliography

Goldman, Harold. *Emma Paterson*. 1974.

Times, December 6, 1886, p. 9.

Englishwomen's Review, December 15, 1886, pp. 540–543.

. . . . .

PATMORE, COVENTRY KERSEY DIGHTON
(1823–1896)

A Roman Catholic poet, critic, and essayist, Coventry Patmore was author of *The Angel in the House* (1854–1856), *The Unknown Eros* (1877), *Amelia* (1878), and *The Rod, the Root and the Flower* (1895). He was closely connected with the Pre-Raphaelites and many literary personalities, and was a considerable influence on the Catholic literary revival.

The son of a professional critic and journalist, Patmore was educated privately, partly in Paris. His complex spiritual and aesthetic leanings were deeply affected by a visit to Rome in 1864 where he met his second wife, a wealthy Roman Catholic convert. Patmore was received into that faith before their marriage. Resigning his position under Anthony Panizzi in the printed book department of the British Museum, he retired into quiet private life, being married a third time in 1881. His final years included a close friendship with Alice Meynell.

Critical opinion has fluctuated widely as to the merit and place of Patmore's poetry. Influenced by study of the Catholic mystics and Swedenborg, Patmore's themes concern love, marriage, and the soul's relation to God; his treatment sometimes approaches the metaphysical. His work is characterized by experiments in meter and language, topics on which he corresponded with Gerard Manley Hopkins.

C. GORDON-CRAIG

Bibliography

Champneys, Basil. *Memoirs and Corrrespondence of Coventry Patmore*, 1900. 2 vols.

Page, Frederick, ed. *The Poems of Coventry Patmore*. 1949.

Reid, John C. *The Mind and Art of Coventry Patmore*. 1957.

. . . . .

PATTISON, MARK
(1813–1884)

Mark Pattison, rector of Lincoln College, was a major figure in Victorian Oxford, renowned for his learning, his radical views on religion and university reform, and his caustic tongue. Encyclopedic in his knowledge, he completed only a fragment of his life work on Joseph Scaliger (1540–1609) and published relatively little: a number of essays, including one in the reputedly heretical *Essays and*

Reviews (1860); editions of works by Pope and Milton; *Issac Casaubon* (1875); *Milton* (1879); and the posthumous *Memoirs* (1885), called by Gladstone "among the most tragic and memorable books of the 19th century."

Educated by his father, rector of Hauxwell in Yorkshire, Pattison studied classics at Oriel College, Oxford, and obtained in 1839 a fellowship at Lincoln, where he raised the reputation of the college by the excellence of his teaching. Though elected rector in 1861, he was so embittered by his failure to obtain the office a decade earlier that he largely ignored undergraduates and administrative duties and gave himself to study. The breakdown of his marriage to Emilia Francis Strong (1840–1904), a high-minded and clever woman twenty-seven years his junior, led to speculation that the Pattisons were part-models for Casaubon and Dorothea in George Eliot's *Middlemarch* (1872), a question still debated.

Scholarly in habit and visage, Pattison left an indelible impression on his contemporaries. Rhoda Broughton caricatured him as the pedant Professor Forth in *Belinda* (1883), and Mary Ward, formerly one of his many admiring young female disciples, modeled her misanthropic and scholarly Squire Wendover in *Robert Elsmere* (1888) after him. He curiously exemplified the age's religious upheavals by running the gamut from evangelical, to High Anglican, to Tractarian (almost following Newman to Rome), to agnostic. His argument that universities have other functions than educating youth, set forth in *Essays on the Endowment of Research* (1876), was farsighted.

TAMIE WATTERS

Bibliography

Green, Vivian. *Oxford Common Room.* 1957.

Sparrow, John. *Mark Pattison and the Idea of a University.* 1967.

. . . . .

PAWNSHOPS

Pawnshops—which lend money at interest on personal property which is deposited in the shop until redeemed—were the most accessible source of credit during the Victorian period. Middle- or upper-class borrowers who pledged jewelry or family heirlooms to meet an occasional debt or sudden emergency were served by "stylish" or "City" pawnshops, which generally had private compartments to protect the customers' identity. In working-class neighborhoods, pawnshops—like credit cards a century later—were an accepted means of gaining an advance on expected income; Sunday clothes were regularly pawned on Monday morning for cash to meet the week's expenses until payday, generally Saturday, when the clothes were redeemed.

Pawnshops were primarily an urban phenomenon. Their number more than doubled in the latter half of the nineteenth century. Despite their widespread reputation as cover for criminal activities such as receiving and fencing stolen goods, there is little evidence that most pawnbrokers engaged in such practices. The Pawnbrokers' Act (1872) set the maximum interest at a rate equivalent to 25 percent per year. Pawnshops were forbidden to accept military or naval equipment, clothing issued by the Guardians of the Poor, or goods belonging to others, such as a bundle of washing or unfinished clothing that a laundress or seamstress might pawn while waiting to be paid for her previous job. The latter provision, however, was largely ignored.

Pawnshops also fell under moral censure for contributing to drunkenness, shiftlessness, and thriftlessness. The government, however, recognized that the pawnshop was a boon to many working people. Notes and coins were pawned by those who did not have bank accounts; the pawnbroker's vault kept the money safe (and also beyond the reach of casual temptation). Buying good clothes and pawnable ornaments when their earnings were high allowed workers to have a cushion against slack times or illness. Artisans and street sellers used the pawnshop to raise working capital. By late in the century, when compulsory schooling helped spread middle-class values, some began to feel ashamed of using the pawnshop. When ill or unemployed, however, many preferred to pledge all they owned rather than go on poor relief.

SALLY MITCHELL

Bibliography

Ashley, W. J. *An Introduction to English Economic History and Theory.* 1893.

Chesney, Kellow. *The Victorian Underworld.* 1970.

Tebbut, Melanie. *Making Ends Meet: Pawnbroking and Working-Class Credit.* 1983.

Wilson, T. *A Discourse Upon Usury.* 1925.

· · · · ·

PAXTON, JOSEPH
(1803–1865)

Joseph Paxton, gardener and later manager at Chatsworth in Derbyshire, was knighted for his design of the Crystal Palace that housed the Exhibition of 1851. A horticulturalist, he edited *Paxton's Magazine of Botany and Flowering Plants* (1834–1849), wrote *A Pocket Botanical Dictionary* (1840), and co-founded the *Gardener's Chronicle* (1841). He also launched the *Daily News* (1846), was architect of two Rothschild mansions, Mentmore (1850–1855) in Buckinghamshire and Ferrieres (1853–1859) near Paris, was director of the Midland and other railways, and served as Liberal M.P. for Coventry (1854–1865).

Of farming stock, Paxton was born in Milton Bryan and attended the Woburn school. He married the enterprising Sarah Brown, who bore him eight children and managed Chatsworth in his absence. In 1826 the duke of Devonshire appointed him head gardener, and a remarkable friendship between the two men ensued as they contrived to reproduce at Chatsworth larger and finer specimens of rare plants discovered on their travels or collected by expeditions. Paxton also used his mechanical ingenuity to engineer at Chatsworth the Emperor Fountain (1844), at 267 feet the highest in Europe, the Grand Conservatory (1840) and Victoria Regia Lily House (1850), which made novel use of iron and glass construction and inspired the Crystal Palace.

All of Paxton's talents were brought to bear in his masterwork, the design and erection in less than nine months of the 1,851-foot-long Crystal Palace which housed the 100,000 exhibits of the Great Exhibition. The hall's pre-fabrication, its assembly-line construction, standardized parts, speedy erection, structural daring and vastness of interior space, and finally its adaptability (it was disassembled and reerected with additional wings in South London where it served as the centerpiece of Sydenham Gardens until destroyed by fire in 1936)—all of these argue for the building's precocious modernity and provide evidence of Paxton's extraordinary technical genius.

ROBERT M. CRAIG
TAMIE WATTERS

Bibliography

Anthony, J. *Joseph Paxton: An Illustrated Life, 1803-1865.* 1973.

Beaver, Patrick. *The Crystal Palace, 1851-1936: A Portrait of Victorian Enterprise.* 1970.

Chadwick, George F. *The Works of Sir Joseph Paxton.* 1961.

Markham, Violet. *Paxton and the Bachelor Duke.* 1935.

See also EXHIBITION OF *1851*
(illus.)

· · · · ·

PEEL, ROBERT
(1788–1850)

Twice British prime minister (1834–1835, 1841–1846), Robert Peel founded the **Conservative party** in the 1830s and was responsible for repeal of the Corn Laws (1846). The eldest son of a wealthy cotton textile manufacturer who was created a baronet in 1800, the younger Robert Peel was educated at Harrow School and in 1808 earned a double first in classics and mathematics at Christ Church, Oxford. He entered the House of Commons in 1809 as a Tory for an Irish constituency purchased for him by his father.

Serving as chief secretary for Ireland (1812–1818), Peel's administration suppressed the Catholic Board (Daniel O'Connell's organization to achieve Catholic emancipation), established a national police force (popularly known as the "Peelers"), and performed effective relief in the famine of 1817. Dubbed "Orange Peel" by O'Connell, Peel was the ablest parliamentary champion of the party that resisted Catholic emancipation.

Rejoining Lord Liverpool's administration as home secretary in 1822, Peel carried through wide-ranging reforms of the criminal law and the prison system, culminating with the Metropolitan Police Act (1829), which set up the first disciplined police force for the London area (hence the name "Bobbies").

In the ministry formed by the duke of Wellington in 1828, Peel was again home secretary. Daniel O'Connell's election to the House of Commons raised the prospect of civil war in Ireland if he were refused his seat, and led Wellington and Peel to carry through the Catholic Emancipation Act (1829). Peel was bitterly attacked for reversing his position and lost his seat for Oxford University, though he continued in the Commons for another constituency.

Out of office and in opposition from 1830–1834, Peel unsuccessfully resisted the Reform Act of 1832. When William IV unexpectedly dismissed the Melbourne ministry in November 1834, Peel was appointed prime minister. His first ministry lasted only one hundred days, but did much to restore his political prestige. In the general election of 1835, Peel issued a public statement known as the Tamworth Manifesto, proclaiming his support for moderate reforms "undertaken in a friendly temper, combining, with the firm maintenance of established rights, the correction of proven abuses and the redress of real grievances." It became essentially the unifying document around which the Conservative party took shape. Under Peel's leadership, the party grew steadily in both numbers and organization. In the 1841 general election, the Conservatives achieved a majority of about seventy.

Peel's second, talented, great, and last ministry (1841–1846) included six past or future prime ministers, including William Gladstone. Its goals included lowering the cost of living for the poorer classes, encouraging trade and industry, and promoting peace and security abroad. Peel's first budget reduced tariffs on many imports, ended duties on manufactured exports, and reintroduced the income tax (which had been abolished at the end of the Napoleonic Wars). These bold steps ended a run of deficits and provided a surplus which allowed further sweeping tariff reductions in 1845, moving the country closer to a free trade policy.

In foreign affairs, Peel pursued a firm but conciliatory policy which improved relations with France and the United States. The Bank Charter Act (1844) controlled the issue of paper money and fostered stability in banking and currency. Returning prosperity reduced the significance and violence of the Chartist movement. Peel also successfully opposed O'Connell's campaign to repeal the union with Ireland (halted in 1843) but—despite widespread opposition from his party—increased support for Maynooth College, which trained Roman Catholic clergy.

The failure of the Irish potato crop in 1845 crystallized Peel's decision to propose repeal of the Corn Laws. After savage attacks in Parliament (most notably by Benjamin Disraeli), Peel carried repeal in June 1846. The effort, however, split the Conservative party and brought about Peel's defeat and resignation. Out of office he continued to support free trade principles. His vision and diligence must be given a significant share of the credit for mid-Victorian Britain's prosperity and stability.

ROBERT S. FRASER

Bibliography

Clark, George Kitson. *Peel and the Conservative Party: A Study in Party Politics, 1832–1841.* 2d ed., 1964.

Gash, Norman. *Mr. Secretary Peel: The Life of Sir Robert Peel to 1830.* 1961.

———. *Sir Robert Peel: The Life of Sir Robert Peel After 1830.* 1972.

Mahan, Lord and Edward Cardwell, eds. *Memoirs by the Right Honourable Sir Robert Peel.* 1856–1857. 2 vols.

Parker, Charles S., ed. *Sir Robert Peel from his Private Papers.* 1891–1899. 3 vols.

Peel, George, ed. *The Private Letters of Sir Robert Peel.* 1920.

Ramsay, A. A. W. *Sir Robert Peel.* 1928.

· · · · ·

PENNY MAGAZINE
(1832-1846)

The *Penny Magazine* was the first mass-circulation magazine published in Britain. With an initial circulation of more than 150,000 copies, the *Penny Magazine* has commanded the attention of historians interested in literacy and the formation of class consciousness in early Victorian Britain.

The *Penny Magazine* first appeared in London on March 31, 1832 and continued weekly publication through June 19, 1846. The magazine used an eight-page format, printing general nonfiction and using high-quality woodblock illustrations extensively. News was not reported in the magazine, primarily to exempt it from the high costs imposed by stamp taxes. The magazine sold for onepence and was distributed widely throughout Britain.

The *Penny Magazine* was published by the Society for the Diffusion of Useful Knowledge (SDUK), an organization founded in 1826 by Henry Brougham (1778–1868) and other liberal members of the Whig party. In addition to the *Penny Magazine*, the society published a wide variety of nonfiction books, maps, music, almanacs, engraved portraits, and reference works. All observed high editorial standards and were published inexpensively. SDUK publications were meant to counter the "dangerous tendency" of other cheap publications that advocated radical change in political, economic, and social matters.

The *Penny Magazine* was printed by William Clowes (1779-1847), whose firm led the way in using steam power and high-speed presses in printing. The technical innovations in printing and illustration that made mass production possible are an important part of the history of the *Penny Magazine*. The journal was edited by Charles Knight (1791–1873). Knight became prominent in London publishing through his connection with the SDUK. As one of the society's publishers, and in his own right, Knight was a prolific author, editor, and publisher of inexpensive material aimed at a broad, national readership. His leadership in this market was partly entrepreneurial innovation, but was primarily the result of Knight's deeply held conviction that people with little to spend on reading matter were poorly served by the regular book trade.

The *Penny Magazine* has been important to understanding popular reading in early Victorian Britain. Originally, scholars saw the magazine and the SDUK as working against the revolutionary tenor of other cheap publications aimed at the working class. These and other press historians found little evidence that the *Penny Magazine* in fact played a significant role in the shaping of working-class consciousness. Recently, study of the commercial history of the *Penny Magazine* and of its unexampled success among massive numbers of readers has suggested the need to reconsider the link between journalism and readers' consciousness as members of a class or other community of interest.

SCOTT BENNETT

Bibliography

Altick, Richard. *The English Common Reader: A Social History of the Mass Reading Public, 1800–1900.* 1957.

Bennett, Scott. "The Editorial Character of *The Penny Magazine*: An Analysis." *Victorian Periodicals Review*, vol. 17, pp. 127–141.

———. "Revolutions in Thought: Serial Publication and the Mass Market for Reading." In Joanne Shattock and Michael Wolff, eds., *The Victorian Periodical Press: Samplings and Soundings.* 1982.

Knight, Charles. "The Commercial History of a Penny Magazine." *Penny Magazine*, vol. 2, pp. 377–384, 417–424, 465–472, 505–511.

———. *Passages of a Working Life.* 1864–1865.

Percival, Janet, ed. *The Society for the Diffusion of Useful Knowledge, 1826–1848: A Handlist of the Society's Correspondence and Papers.* University College (London) Library Occasional Publications No. 5, 1978.

Webb, R. K. *The British Working Class Reader, 1790–1848: Literacy and Social Tension.* 1955.

· · · · ·

PENNY THEATERS

In the 1830s London had eighty to one hundred penny theaters (or penny "gaffs"), an early form of urban entertainment for working-class youths. Their history offers insights into both working-class youth culture and middle-class strategies of social discipline.

Penny theaters enjoyed a precarious existence in converted shops, barns, and sheds in working-class districts. They seated, on average, two hundred spectators, mostly male and aged between eight and sixteen. Proprietors were often as impoverished as the audience, while actors came from the least-respectable stratum of an already outcast profession. Shows lasted approximately forty-five minutes and consisted of comic songs, pantomimes, burlesques, and melodramas. Actors seldom followed a written script, and considerable interaction took place between the performer and the audience.

The journalist James Grant (1802–1879), writing in *Sketches in London* (1839), claimed that penny theaters encouraged juvenile delinquency and sexual precocity. Like many other social investigators, he urged the provision of more "rational" recreation for working-class youths. The fear engendered by the "gaffs" was disproportionate to their actual influence in society, suggesting that the realities of early Victorian youth culture clashed with emerging middle-class ideals of **childhood**, respectability, and social order. Opposition to such places of entertainment was enormous, leading to a crackdown on penny theaters in the 1850s and 1860s. Nonetheless, the demise of the "gaffs" owes less to middle-class hostility than to the development of compulsory education and a mass leisure industry later in the century.

CHRIS WATERS

Bibliography

Sheridan, Paul. *Penny Theatres of Victorian London.* 1981.

Springhall, John. "Leisure and Victorian Youth: The Penny Theatre in London, 1830–1890." In John Hurt, ed., *Childhood, Youth and Education in the Late Nineteenth Century: Proceedings of the 1980 Annual Conference of the History of Education Society of Great Britain.* 1981.

· · · · ·

PERIODICALS: CHEAP AND POPULAR

The expansion of literacy and the growth of cheap and popular periodicals went hand in hand in the nineteenth century. Technological advances were also significant: steam-driven presses, railways for national distribution, stereotyping (which permitted the production of multiple copies with one setting of type) and, at the end of the century, the development of typesetting machines. Gradually the printing industry became one of the most successful examples of mechanized mass production with its consequent lowering of costs.

Following the Peterloo Massacre (1819), government acts aimed at undermining the radical reform movement impeded the growth of the cheap press and encouraged its initial development along nonpolitical lines. The fourpence tax on newspapers made them too expensive for most workers, but part issues of works previously published in book form and religious papers were exempt from the tax. This encouraged the serial publication of popular sensational tales, miscellanies compiled from books and other periodicals, and the didactic literature issued by the Religious Tract Society and the Society for the Propagation of Christian Knowledge (SPCK). In the early part of the century the cheap periodicals market was dominated by monthly magazines subsidized by religious denominations and by miscellanies.

As the taxes on knowledge disappeared or diminished toward the middle of the century, cheap periodicals rushed into the marketplace. In 1840, seventy-eight magazines costing twopence or less were issued in one week. Removal of the advertising duty in 1853 lessened publishers' dependence on party or denominational support. Although most working-class budgets could not stretch to the purchase of a daily newspaper, cheap Sunday or weekly papers with political news and opinion (usually radical), sporting news, and sensational accounts of crime and corruption became very popular. Often they were illustrated, which appealed to the semiliterate audience. Edward Lloyd's *Penny Sunday Times* (1841–1847) featured murders, kidnappings, and robberies. *Lloyd's Weekly Newspaper* (1842–1923) was a sensational imitation of the more decorous *Illustrated London News* (1842–). Other popular weekly papers included *Bell's Life in London* (1822–1886) and *Reynold's Weekly Newspaper* (1850–1924).

The SPCK and the Society for the Diffusion of Useful Knowledge (SDUK) were instrumental in bringing cheap periodical literature to the masses, although many of the intended audience preferred the racier sporting papers to their wholesome and utilitarian fare. In addition to numerous tracts and pamphlets, the two societies published miscellanies, the most successful being the SPCK's *Saturday Magazine* (1832–1844) and the SDUK's *Penny Magazine* (1832–1845), edited by Charles Knight. A more long-lived miscellany, independently published by William Chambers (1800–1883), was *Chambers' Edinburgh Journal* (1836–1956). Generally these patchworks of popular literature were numerous but short-lived. Their titles reflect the attempt to win over segments of the popular market: *Christians' Penny Magazine* (1832–1838), *Girls' and Boys' Penny Magazine* (1832–1833), *Penny Comic Magazine* (1832), *Penny Novelist* (1832–1934), etc.

By the 1850s there were popular magazines for nearly every taste. The *Family Herald* (1842–1939) and the *London Journal* (1845–1912) satisfied the appetite for sensational fiction, and journals such as Charles Dickens's *Household Words* (1850–1859) helped make cheap periodicals respectable in the eyes of the middle-class readers. Other family-oriented magazines included *Eliza Cook's Journal* (1849–1854), *Cottage Gardener* (1849–1861), *Family Friend* (1849–1921), and *Home Circle* (1849–1854). From the beginning periodicals had appealed to special interests; early cheap periodicals were subsidized by religious denominations or political organziations in order to propagandize readers. By the end of the century women of the working class were being intensively courted. The motto of *Woman* (1890–1912) was "Forward, but not too fast"—but the presence of a cheap periodical exclusively for women that was not devoted primarily to fiction or religion was a significant social barometer.

SHARON LOCY

Bibliography

Altick, Richard D. *The English Common Reader: A Social History of the Mass Reading Public.* 1957.

Ellegard, Alvar. *The Readership of the Periodical Press in Mid-Victorian Britain.* 1957.

James, Louis. *Fiction for the Working Man, 1830–1850.* 1973.

Mitchell, Sally. "The Forgotten Woman of the Period: Penny Weekly Family Magazine of the 1840s and 1850s." In Martha Vicinius, ed., *A Widening Sphere.* 1977.

Read, Donald. *England 1868–1914: The Age of Urban Democracy.* 1979.

Shattock, Joanne and Michael Wolff, eds. *The Victorian Periodical Press: Samplings and Soundings.* 1982.

Wolff, Michael et al. *The Waterloo Directory of Victorian Periodicals, 1824–1900.* 1977.

See also WORKING-CLASS LITERATURE

. . . . .

PERIODICALS: COMIC AND SATIRIC

Victorian comic and satiric periodicals reflected and distorted the politics, art, and culture of their age. These weekly, monthly, or annual publications combined puns, jokes, parodies, verse, familiar essays, and satire with political cartoons, comic illustrations, social sketches, and assorted doodlings to form loose collections of wit and humor.

Although many Victorian periodicals published humorous or satiric pieces, the witty radical papers and comic miscellanies that appeared during the early 1830s exerted the strongest influence on the form and tone of later comic periodicals. Foremost among the reform papers was *Figaro in London* (1831–1839), an unstamped weekly conducted first by Gilbert A'Beckett and then by Henry Mayhew. Early issues featured political **caricatures** by Robert Seymour, caustic paragraphs on politics and society, ridiculous extracts from other publications, puns or jokes aimed at prominent persons, and lengthy theater reviews. Many short-lived imitators appeared, with Douglas Jerrold's *Punch in London* (1832) the most substantial. The comic miscellany was primarily the creation of Thomas Hood, whose *Comic Annual* (1830–1898) continued long after his death. The larger number of pages and longer intervals between issues allowed for more elaborate parodies and essays; imitators included *The Comic Offering* (1831–1835) and A'Beckett's *The Comic Magazine* (1832–1834).

All of the writers mentioned above contributed to *Punch* (1841 to present), which brilliantly linked the weeklies' political satire to the polish and good humor of the miscellanies. Edited first by **Mark Lemon**, *Punch* provided a home for the work of such writers as William Makepeace Thackeray, and such artists as John Leech, Richard Doyle, John Tenniel, Charles Keene, and George Du Maurier.

Punch's full-page political cartoon, its small visual puns or joke illustrations, and its assortment of verbal jabs and short literary sketches profoundly influenced comic publications for the next fifty years, with *Puck* (1844), *The Great Gun* (1844–1845), *The Clown of London* (1845), *Joe Miller the Younger* (1845), *Mephystopheles* (1845–1846), two *Pasquins* (1847, 1850), *The Man in the Moon* (1847–1849), *The Puppet Show* (1848–1849), *The Penny Punch* (1849), *Diogenes* (1853–1855), *Punchinello* (1854–1855), and the inevitable *Judys* (1843, 1867–1907), and *Tobys* (1867, 1868, 1874, 1886–1889) among the most notable. Though humorous monthlies and annuals continued to appear—*Ainsworth's Magazine* (1842–1854), *The Illuminated Magazine* (1843), *The Comic Album* (1843) and various Christmas annuals—*Punch* towered over its rivals, both in its early radical days and in its later, prosperous life during the 1870s, 1880s and 1890s.

Apart from brief flurries of satiric publications responding to the second Reform Bill (1866–1867) and Irish Home Rule debates (1880s), comic periodicals generally followed *Punch* into a less political, more social humor. With its huge cartoons and sharp indictments of English social inequities, *The Tomahawk: A Saturday Journal of Satire* (1867–1870) was an impressive exception,

and *Fun, Punch*'s major rival, boasted the talents of W. S. Gilbert and H. J. Byron. But the growing trend was toward easy reading for hearths, schoolrooms, and trains. Cartoon, joke, and anecdote grab bags like *The Novelty* (1882–1885), *Funny Bits* (1883), *Nice Bits* (1884–1885), *Short Cuts* (1890), and far too many others became the fashion.

The 1880s and 1890s saw papers with even more cartoons, or "comic cuts," flooding the market. The king of these publications was *Ally Sloper's Half-Holiday* (1884–1923), "Being a Selection, Side Splitting, Sentimental, and Serious, for the Benefit of Old Boys, Young Boys, Odd Boys Generally, and Even Girls." Essentially an eight-page illustrated joke book, it led a pack of penny and halfpenny dreadfuls. *Ching Ching's Own* (1888–1893), *Comic Cuts* (b. 1890), *Funny Cuts* (b. 1890), *Illustrated Chips* (1890–1892), *The Joker* (1892–1897), *Nuggets* (1892–1895), *The World's Comic* (1892–1908), *Pictorial Comic Life* (1898–1928), and *The Coloured Comic* (1898–1906) were the hardiest.

Victorian comic and satiric periodicals thus changed with the times, adapting to new readers and conditions for reading, yet gesturing occasionally to the urbane security which only politely laughing *Punch* could provide.

CRAIG HOWES

Bibliography

Gray, Donald. "A List of Comic Periodicals Published in Great Britain, 1800–1900, with a Prefactory Essay." *Victorian Periodicals Newsletter*, no. 15, pp. 2–39.

Price, R. G. G. *A History of Punch.* 1957.

Savory, Jerold J. "An Uncommon Comic Collection: Humorous Victorian Periodicals in the Newberry Library." *Victorian Periodicals Newsletter*, vol. 17. pp. 94–102.

· · · · ·

PERIODICALS: MONTHLY MAGAZINES

The monthly magazines that provided entertainment and instruction for middle- and upper-class Victorians were miscellanies including fiction, poetry, and articles on subjects such as travel, current affairs, biography, and science, with the proportion of fiction increasing as the century aged. Individually, they had relatively small circulations, rarely more than 15,000; but as a group, they would eventually claim some 450,000 subscribers and a literary and cultural influence disproportionate to their share of the reading market. At their height, monthly magazines published the best writing of the era: the fiction of Dickens, Thackeray, Trollope, Eliot, Gaskell, Collins, Hardy, and Henry James; the poetry of Tennyson, the Brownings, Meredith, and Swinburne; and the essays of Arnold, Ruskin, Symonds, Leslie Stephen, and Pater.

Several popular general magazines were already generations old when Victoria took the throne. *The Gentleman's Magazine* (1731–1914) contained news, parliamentary reports, essays, and reviews. *The Lady's Magazine* (1770–1847) provided light fiction, needlework patterns, sheet music, advice columns, fashion, and society news. Most important for opinion and the arts at this time were magazines that had developed early in the century as alternatives to the more heavily intellectual reviews and quarterlies. *Blackwood's Edinburgh Magazine* (1817–1905), affectionately known as "Maga," dominated the scene. Providing outrageous and lively competition to the ruling *Edinburgh* and *Quarterly* reviews, it spoke for the Conservative party in Scotland during the reform era and consistently supported rural interests, particularly those of the landowning classes. While its failure to change made it seem old-fashioned in later years, *Blackwood's* exerted considerable influence on literature through its excellent poetry and fiction and the original criticism of many loyal contributors. It also translated foreign literature, particularly German, for British audiences.

Henry Colburn founded *The New Monthly Magazine* (1814–1884) to oppose the radical views of the *Monthly Magazine* (1796–1825) and to "puff" his company's publications; after 1821, it lessened its political emphasis and specialized in witty, enjoyable material. *Fraser's Magazine for Town and Country* (1830–1869), which set out to recreate the spirit of the early *Blackwood's*, was the most influential monthly of the 1830s. In its early years under **William Maginn**, "Regina" was Tory, anti-Catholic, and at times scurrilous in its attacks on individuals; its unusually varied materials included scholarly articles, satire, travel literature, and translations from ancient languages. Carlyle's *Sartor Resartus* first appeared there. After 1836, the magazine became more progressive in politics and more sober in tone, publishing excellent serious articles on politics, religion, and social conditions, as well as literature.

Tait's Edinburgh Magazine (1832–1861) was one of the first of the less-expensive monthlies; John Stuart Mill contributed to this radical organ, which included little fiction or poetry. University-educated converts to Roman Catholicism published another serious monthly of midcentury, *The Rambler* (1848–1862), which announced itself as a "journal of home and foreign literature, politics, science, music, and the fine arts"; its calls for church reform brought it under attack from more conservative Catholics. Several popular monthlies were edited by well-known fiction writers, whose reputations were used to draw readers and who, in turn, used the magazines to keep their names before the public. The *Metropolitan* (1831–1857) under Frederick Marryat and *Bentley's Miscellany* (1837–1868) under Dickens, for example, helped to popularize the serialized novel, which became the mainstay of many monthly magazines. As a major market for fiction, the monthlies would affect both technique and content in Victorian novels.

These earlier monthlies appealed to better-educated readers of the gentry and of the professional classes; at prices ranging from two shillings and sixpence to six shillings, they were beyond the reach of most middle-class readers. But the gradual removal of the taxes on knowledge by midcentury, together with improved printing technology, spurred the development of high-quality, inexpensive magazines for educated readers of modest means. At this time, the distinction between the review and the magazine began to break down. The first of these "shilling monthlies" was *Macmillan's* (1859–1907), from the publishing house of the same name. Though the magazine was used to promote the company's new fiction, serialized there before book publication, it was noted mostly for its serious articles on politics and religion. *Macmillan's* was one of the first magazines to publish only signed articles. Serving a similar readership, but with a greater emphasis on literature, was *The Cornhill Magazine* (1860-1975); its first issue, lavishly financed by publishers Smith, Elder and Co. and edited by Thackeray, sold a phenomenal 120,000 copies, raising the hope that a mass audience existed for beautiful illustrations and a high standard of literature. This hope ended when the *Cornhill* lost most of those readers to the many popular monthlies created in the wake of its success; catering to public demand for light and sensationalist fiction were magazines such as *Temple Bar* (1860-1906), *Argosy* (1866-1901), and *Belgravia* (1866-1899), each circulating about 20,000 copies in 1870. Such magazines assumed readers with a fairly low level of education and a lower tolerance for controversial or thought-provoking subjects. Generally, the influence and readership of the better literary magazines declined in the last decades of the century, as the glossily presented and increasingly inexpensive family magazines such as the *English Illustrated Magazine* (1884-1913) took over the field. Illustrated monthlies of the quality of *The Savoy* (January-December 1896), which published Yeats, Beardsley, Dowson, Beerbohm, and Ford Madox Ford, tended to be short-lived.

However important for making and breaking literary reputations and fortunes, the literary magazines were outnumbered by numerous nonliterary monthlies, the diversity of which can be only suggested by a sampling of titles. The *Art Journal* (1839-1912) and the *Magazine of Art* (1878-1904) reviewed art exhibitions, reported sales figures, and analyzed trends in marketing and display as well as artistic style. *The Theatre* (1877-1897) provided stories on actors, theaters, and the theater, as well as reviews of current plays in London and the provinces. The *British Controversialist and Impartial Inquirer* (1850-1872) was a debating forum for ambitious working-class men. Religious groups subsidized monthlies such as the *Christian Observer* (1802-1877), reviewing general and religious books for perhaps a thousand Evangelical clergymen; the *Servant's Magazine* (1837-1866), published by the Committee of the London Female Mission to provide moral instruction for women in domestic service; and the *Monthly Packet* (1851-1899), a magazine for middle-class girls and young women aged fifteen to twenty-four, edited by novelist

Charlotte Yonge. The *Boy's Own Paper* (1879-1900+), from the Religious Tract Society, contained adventure fiction, articles on science and sport, and puzzles, following the model of the Beetons' *Boy's Own Magazine* (1855-1874).

Samuel Beeton also established the first mass-circulation women's magazine, the *Englishwoman's Domestic Magazine* (1852-1881), which included needlework patterns and fiction as well as guidance on courtship, hygiene, nursing, and domestic economy. Changes in women's lives were reflected in such magazines as the *Woman's Gazette, or News About Work* (1875-1880), later titled *Work and Leisure* (1880-1893), which included information on job opportunities as well as fiction and other light reading. The vogue for science produced technical monthlies like the *Popular Science Review* (1861-1881). Other scientific magazines, begun for popular audiences, became more technical as their fields became professionalized; among them were the *Geological Magazine* (1864-) and the *Zoologist* (1843-1916). Specialized magazines targeting every conceivable readership were founded in the 1880s and 1890s, reflecting the increasing importance of magazine publishing as a marketing and advertising tool for reaching the mass buying public, and the heyday of the monthly magazine as a shaper of culture and opinion had ended.

NAOMI JACOBS

Bibliography

Madden, Lionel and Diana Dixon, eds. *The Nineteenth-Century Periodical Press in Britain: A Bibliography of Modern Studies, 1901-1971.* 1976.

Sullivan, Alvin, ed. *British Literary Magazines.* Vol. 3: *The Victorian and Edwardian Age, 1837-1913.* 1984.

Vann, J. Don and Rosemary T. VanArsdel, eds. *Victorian Periodicals: A Guide to Research.* 1978.

See also AINSWORTH, WILLIAM HARRISON; SERIAL LITERATURE

· · · · ·

PERIODICALS: REVIEWS AND QUARTERLIES

Periodicals of all sorts proliferated at an amazing rate throughout the nineteenth century, exerting a tremendous influence on an increasingly literate and education-hungry population. Even on the higher levels of literary culture, the reviews in periodicals were a major force in the development of taste. Most articles were unsigned, which lent them even greater authority.

The reviews and quarterlies of the Victorian era continued to imitate the tone and methods of the *Edinburgh Review* (1802–1929), which was phenomenally successful in its first few decades and remained important throughout the era. The *Edinburgh* printed powerful, impassioned—and unsigned—articles which ostensibly reviewed new books, but in fact often used the books as little more than pretext for an independent essay on an author, movement, public question, or other topic. Political bias was built into nearly all the *Edinburgh*'s opinions, and authors were generally praised or condemned on the basis of the extent to which their opinions fit in with the *Edinburgh*'s militant Whig views.

These traits—political slanting and anonymous review articles ranging far beyond the book in question—were quickly imitated because the *Edinburgh* attracted so much attention, was so widely read, and was so important in influencing public opinion. The Tory *Quarterly Review* (1809–1967) was founded specifically to counter the *Edinburgh*. Like its Whig model, the *Quarterly* enlisted many of the best writers of its day and maintained the policy of anonymity. Throughout most of the Victorian era these two quarterlies commanded the respect, if not the affection, of British authors and the British public. A third political stripe was represented by the radical *Westminster Review* (1824–1836, though it survived in one form or another with various name changes until 1914), presided over for a time by John Stuart Mill.

The political slant of these three quarterlies is readily apparent from a comparison of their contents during any given controversy. The *Edinburgh* typically favored reform, the *Quarterly* opposed it, and the *Westminster* used its Benthamite radical philosophy to argue for even deeper changes. Many reviews sprang up with even more narrowly sectarian purposes. The *London Quarterly Review* (1853–1931), for example, was founded to do much the same sort of reviewing as the *Edinburgh*, but from a Tory Methodist viewpoint. Indeed, it is a rare group in Victorian Britain that was not represented by some review.

An early journal that was intended to be not just intellectually compelling but also popular and even entertaining was *Blackwood's Edinburgh Magazine* (1817–1980). *Blackwood's* printed criticism at least as harsh as its competition's—the infamous review of Keats's poems is the best-known example—but it also published humorous articles, informal columns (notably the "Noctes Ambrosianae," a set of unbuttoned dialogues featuring thinly disguised, well-known Scottish contributors such as James Hogg and John Gibson Lockhart casually shredding the reputations of Whiggish authors), and even fiction. *Blackwood's* thus can be considered the first widely successful magazine (as opposed to review) in Britain. By midcentury the magazine approach became dominant and the circulations of the great quarterlies started to shrink.

Among the most successful of weekly reviews was the *Athenaeum* (1828–1921). Founded to compete with the quarterly reviews by being more timely and complete, it covered far more books on a wider range of subjects, and also offered records of the meetings of scientific societies and bibliographies of scientific works. The *Athenaeum* also attempted to be more moderate in its tone and criticism. Another powerful weekly, *The Spectator* (1828–1925), saw itself as a combination news magazine and review. *The Spectator* was politically Liberal, but moderate in most instances. A later, highly successful attempt to produce a weekly using both Liberal and Conservative writers was the *Saturday Review* (1855–1938). It saw itself as more serious and less news oriented than *The Spectator*, printing fewer but longer articles on a wide range of topics—its full title was *The Saturday Review of Politics, Literature, Science, and Art*. It maintained the *Edinburgh Review* traditions of anonymity and vituperative criticism. Politics, of course, were usually at the root of its judgments; it was, in the main, a moderate-conservative magazine.

The range of reviews and quarterlies published in the nineteenth century is enormous.

Since the late 1950s, scholars have come increasingly to realize what a wealth of material resides in the vast reservoirs of Victorian periodicals. Walter Houghton (1904–1983) undertook the mammoth task of trying to undo the vexed question of anonymous authorship. The results published in *The Wellesley Index to Victorian Periodicals, 1824–1900* have been invaluable to scholars.

RAYMOND N. MacKENZIE

Bibliography

Altick, Richard D. *The English Common Reader: A Social History of the Mass Reading Public, 1800–1900*. 1957.

Cox, R. G. "The Great Reviews." *Scrutiny*, vol. 6, pp. 2–20, 155–175.

Graham, Walter. *English Literary Periodicals*. 1930.

Gross, John. *The Rise and Fall of the Man of Letters*. 1969.

Houghton, Walter E., ed. *The Wellesley Index to Victorian Periodicals, 1824–1900*. 1966–. 5 vols.

Marchand, Leslie A. *The Athenaeum: A Mirror of Victorian Culture*. 1941.

Nesbitt, George L. *Benthamite Reviewing: The First Twelve Years of the "Westminster Review," 1824–1936*. 1934.

Sullivan, Alvin, ed. *British Literary Magazines*. Vol. 2: *The Romantic Age, 1789–1836*. 1983.

———. *British Literary Magazines*. Vol. 3: *The Victorian and Edwardian Age, 1837–1913*. 1984.

Vann, J. Donn and Rosemary T. VanArsdel, eds. *Victorian Periodicals: A Guide To Research*. 1978.

Wolff, Michael. "Victorian Reviewers and Cultural Responsibility." In Philip Appleman et al., eds., *1859: Entering an Age of Crisis*. 1959.

. . . . .

PERIODICALS: WOMEN'S

The proliferation of periodicals brought about by the nineteenth century's expanded literacy and cheapened publishing costs transformed the number and nature of magazines intended primarily for women. Early in the century the most important were the fashionable magazines such as *The Lady's Magazine* (1770–1837), *The Lady's Monthly Museum* (1798–1832), *La Belle Assemblée* (1806–1832), and *The World of Fashion* (1824–1851). Intended for readers whose class standing supplied leisure and some intellectual attainments, these magazines carried articles on literature, science, politics, and public affairs as well as descriptions—illustrated with both sketches and colored plates—of the latest London and Paris fashions.

Between 1832 and 1847 *The Lady's Magazine, La Belle Assemblée,* and *The Lady's Monthly Museum* merged. With the early Victorian years there was a greater emphasis on piety and domesticity. Characteristic magazines include *The British Mother's Magazine* (1845–1855), *The Mother's Friend* (1848–1859), and *The Christian Lady's Magazine* (1834–1849), edited by **Charlotte Elizabeth Tonna**. Tonna included moral instruction as well as entertainment, and she wrote both fiction and essays which she hoped would encourage readers to take an interest in factory and workshop conditions and other problems of the poor.

Samuel Beeton's *Englishwoman's Domestic Magazine,* begun in 1852, was the first inexpensive magazine of food, fashion, and fiction for middle-class women readers. It contained both fashion plates and diagrams for cutting and sewing; instructions and designs for many varieties of needlework; recipes; columns of advice on gardening, travel, and heatlh; a "Cupid's Letter Bag" feature that responded to readers' letters about problems in romance and courtship; and a serialized novel in addition to some poetry or other literature.

After midcentury there were also serious women's journals concerned with employment, education, and women's rights. *Eliza Cook's Journal* (1849–1854), an inexpensive weekly probably read chiefly by lower middle-class women, was ambivalent about overtly feminist issues but promoted self-help, emigration societies, education, and so forth. **The English Woman's Journal** (1858–1863), first edited by Bessie Parkes and Matilda Hays, was designed to promote women's employment. Of its two "offspring," Emily Faithfull's

Victoria Magazine (1863–1880) added literature and other features to attract a wider audience. *The Englishwoman's Review* (1866-1910) became virtually the magazine of record for the women's movement. By the end of the century, suffragists were also publishing periodicals. One of the most important was the *Woman's Signal* (1894-1899).

Throughout the century there were specialist periodicals published for those involved in a particular variety of charitable work or intended for a certain section of the reading public. Most of these were relatively short-lived, although the *Servants' Magazine* published by the London Female Mission ran from 1838 to 1869. Women of the poorer and working classes were more apt to read the penny weekly magazines that provided generous helpings of fiction. By the last decades of the century periodicals such as the *London Journal* (1845-1912) and the *Family Herald* (1842-1939), which had begun as "family magazines," were essentially women's magazines; they printed patterns and recipes and great dollops of romantic fiction. *Bow Bells* (1862-1893) was a similar periodical with a wide following.

The highly commercial women's magazines that were typical of the twentieth century began with the *Lady's Pictorial* in 1880. More than a dozen similar weeklies were founded during the 1880s and 1890s. Most were edited by men; they featured fashions, entertainments, weddings, and court news; and the profit was made from advertisements rather than sales.

OWEN SCHUR

Bibliography

Adburgham, Alison. *Women in Print: Writing Women and Women's Magazines from the Restoration to the Accession of Queen Victoria.* 1972.

Branca, Patricia. *Silent Sisterhood: Middle Class Women in the Victorian Home.* 1975.

Dalziel, Margaret. *Popular Fiction 100 Years Ago.* 1958.

Gorham, Deborah. *The Victorian Girl and the Feminine Ideal.* 1982.

Mitchell, Sally. *The Fallen Angel: Chastity, Class and Women's Reading, 1835-1880.* 1981.

Nestor, Pauline A. "A New Departure in Women's Publishing: *The English Woman's Journal* and *The Victoria Magazine.*" *Victorian Periodicals Review,* vol. 15, pp. 93-106.

Palmegiano, Eugenia M. "Women and British Periodicals, 1832-1867: A Bibliography." *Victorian Periodicals Newsletter,* vol. 9, pp. 3-36.

VanArsdel, Rosemary T. "Mrs. Florence Fenwick-Miller and *The Woman's Signal.*" *Victorian Periodicals Review,* vol. 15, pp. 107-118.

White, Cynthia L. *Women's Magazines: 1693-1968.* 1970.

See also COOK, ELIZA; FAITHFULL, EMILY

. . . . .

PHILANTHROPY

Victorian philanthropy confronted the vast social and moral problems of a rapidly industrializing society. Parish and private charity, which had been sufficient before the nineteenth century, proved unable to address the massive social dislocations caused by industrialization and urbanization. Eighteenth-century paternalism and the personal distribution of alms gave way to active involvement in the plight of the poor. Victorian charities were both prudent and humanitarian: they alleviated the worst miseries while also providing a mechanism to control the destitute and mitigate their unrest. Most philanthropic organizations reflected the sentimental and conservative characteristics of the middle class that organized and supported them.

Organizations devoted to moral and social reform multiplied throughout the century. Most philanthropies operated from a base in London with a network of provincial auxiliaries dotting the country. Generally using a committee structure, many boasted upper-class patronage and financial support, though the actual planning was done by the men who formed the directorates. The day-to-day operations often fell to women, who took an increasingly important role in philanthropy during the nineteenth century. Charities drew on the mercy, compassion, and leisure time that were women's special sphere. They also relied on women's willingness to perform the mundane tasks that keep a charity functioning. As philanthropic organizations multiplied, many people served on several, creating an interconnected army of middle-class humanitarians.

Evangelical Christianity provided a major impetus for Victorian charities. Religious philanthropies, concerned primarily with disseminating Christian manners and morals, included numerous Bible and tract societies, the Society for Promoting Christian Knowledge, and the Society for the Suppression of Public Lewdness. The influential Society for the Suppression of Vice, instituted by William Wilberforce in 1802, and the National Society for Promoting the Education of the Poor in the Principles of the Established Church were typical of Christian philanthropic organizations; showing little concern with fundamental reform of society, they were preoccupied with the morals of the poor.

Evangelical attitudes were indirectly expressed in hundreds of other philanthropic and missionary organizations. These societies reveal much about evangelical preoccupations: the Guardian Society for the Preservation of Public Morals by Providing Temporary Asylums for Prostitutes; the Ladies' Association for the Benefit of Gentlewomen of Good Family, Reduced in Fortunes Below the State of Comfort to Which They Have Been Accustomed; and the Friendly Female Society for the Relief of the Poor, Infirm, Aged Widows and Single Women, of Good Character Who Have Seen Better Days. These and similar philanthropies drew on the evangelical desire to save souls, while also imposing middle-class standards of behavior. The numerous "Female" and "Ladies'" societies, which generally took women and children as the object of their charity, provided, however, an incidental by-product: in doing charitable work, middle-class women learned to run meetings, raise money, keep books, secure publicity, and systematically inquire into the state of society.

Some philanthropies acted on the belief that public morality depended on private virtue and that society as a whole was threatened by private licentiousness. The Moral Reform Union, founded in 1882, typified the preoccupation with drunkenness and the sexual double standard. Other influential moral reform philanthropies included the Temperance Society, the Lord's Day Observance Society, and the Pure Literature Society.

Unlike the moral reforms, which addressed the outward manifestations of decay, social reforms sought to confront the deeper ills of British society. During the 1830s, major overhauls in factory legislation, education, and the Poor Laws reflected prevailing philanthropic ideals. Evangelical champions of the oppressed were led first by Richard Oastler and then by the earl of Shaftesbury. Though Shaftesbury sympathized more with the plight of the poor than with their aspirations, his patronage mobilized public opinion behind a range of charitable causes. Societies for educating and for bettering the condition of the poor operated throughout the century. Others assisted needlewomen, climbing boys, and "forlorn females." In times of national distress, such philanthropies served as an insurance against class revolt: charity alleviated the worst distress while inculcating socially approved attitudes among the poor.

The Charitable Organization Society (COS), founded in 1869, embodied the mid-Victorian attitude toward philanthropy. Formed to centralize the increasingly diffuse and inefficient system of private charities, the COS was the first important step toward collective action. However, its punitive approach in dividing the "deserving" from the "undeserving" poor and its equation of poverty with moral weakness demonstrated a limited conception of poverty's causes. The inclination to define social problems in moral terms and apply palliatives proved increasingly inadequate. **Ragged schools**, soup kitchens, and the London Truss Society for the Ruptured Poor did little to alleviate desperate living conditions. By the middle of the century, poverty was increasingly viewed as a public responsibility that required state intervention.

Victorian philanthropy, which had stepped into the void earlier in the century when private and local relief broke down, learned to promote a greater role for the state in providing social services. Private, voluntary charity was simply not enough; state funds and organization had to supplement individual benevolence. The disparity between the magnitude of the problem and the charitable resources available placed a greater burden on private charity than it could hope to discharge. Victorian philanthropy increasingly served to support and supplement the state in the process of improving social welfare. Women who had gained knowledge and experience in various charitable organizations took their place on the newly formed school boards and reorganized boards of parish guardians elected in the last decades of the century. Other volunteers ultimately originated the profession of social work; a statistical survey by Louisa Hubbard in 1893 suggested that half a million women in England were active in philanthropies and that 20,000 supported themselves as paid workers for charities.

KAREN I. HALBERSLEBEN

Bibliography

Briggs, Asa. *The Age of Improvement. 1783–1867.* 1959.

Burdett-Coutts, Angela, ed. *Woman's Mission.* 1893.

Houghton, Walter E. *The Victorian Frame of Mind, 1830–1870.* 1957.

Hunt, J. W. *Reaction and Reform, 1815–1841.* 1972.

Owen, David. *English Philanthropy, 1660–1960.* 1964.

Prochaska, F. K. *Women and Philanthropy in Nineteenth-Century England.* 1980.

See also BURDETT-COUTTS, ANGELA; EDUCATING THE DEAF AND BLIND; HILL, OCTAVIA; SETTLEMENT MOVEMENT

. . . . .

PHILATELY

The hobby of stamp collecting, or philately, began in Great Britain soon after the introduction of the postage stamp in May 1840. In 1841, the *Times* ran an advertisement from an anonymous woman soliciting donations of stamps to use as a wall covering. She is often considered the first collector, although Kasimir Bileski makes a case for Samuel Lord, Jr. (1823–1912), who in 1840 was writing literary notables and requesting their autographs. He mounted the autographs in an album together with the envelope, including stamp and postmark, in which it came. By 1842 collecting stamps had become enough of a fad to be satirized in a *Punch* poem.

In 1856, E. Stanley Gibbons (1840–1913) opened a stamp shop in a back room of his father's pharmacy in Plymouth. Catalogues and stamp albums were first seen in the early 1860s, and the first journal devoted to philately, the *Monthly Advertiser*, appeared in December 1862.

The Philatelic Society, London, was founded in 1869 by Edward L. Pemberton (1844–1879) and other prominent philatelists and inaugurated its own journal, the *London Philatelist*, in 1892. The growing sophistication of philately was indicated by the creation of the Philatelic Protection Association (1891) to guard against stamp forgeries and the Society for the Suppression of Speculative Stamps (1895) to protest the issuance of stamps attractive only to speculators.

Although the president of the Philatelic Society estimated in 1910 that there were 500,000 stamp collectors in Britain, the hobby took on a distinctly upper-class aura. The Duke of York (later King George V) accepted the presidency of the Philatelic Society in 1896, and the magnificent collection of the earl of Crawford (1837–1913) was bequeathed to the British Museum upon his death.

JOHN E. FINDLING

Bibliography

Bileski, Kasimir. *The First Philatelist?* 1973.

Boggs, Winthrop. *The Foundations of Philately.* 1955.

Kehr, Earnest A. *The Romance of Stamp Collecting.* 1947.

Sutton, R. J., comp. *The Stamp Collector's Encyclopedia.* 1966.

. . . . .

PHILHARMONIC SOCIETY

The Philharmonic Society, founded in 1813, was the first concert-giving organization controlled by its professional members with little dependence on aristocratic patronage. In Victorian times it played an essential if largely conservative role in London's musical life. The prefix "Royal" was conferred in 1912.

In its early decades the society had pioneered, and in some cases commissioned, works by leading contemporary composers such as Beethoven, Clementi, Cherubini, and Mendelssohn. Its eight concerts were the cornerstone of the musical season. Between 1836 and 1843 subscriptions declined (for reasons unknown), which compelled the directors to adopt a more cautious policy. The long programs of earlier times, mixing orchestral, chamber, and vocal music, gradually gave way to predominantly orchestral programs. Under Michael Costa as conductor (1844–1854) the orchestra became once more famous for the precision and verve of its playing. In 1869 the concerts were moved from the aristocratic Hanover Square Rooms to St. James's Hall (built in 1858), transferring to Queen's Hall in 1894.

In the later nineteenth century the programs relied more and more heavily on the "classics" of symphonic music—on Haydn, Mozart, Beethoven, and Mendelssohn, the last-named enjoying special favor with Victorians from the Queen downwards. Among a growing number of rivals, such as the New Philharmonic Society (1852–1879), the Crystal Palace Concerts (1855–1901), and the Richter Concerts (1879–1897), the Philharmonic maintained formal preeminence.

NICHOLAS TEMPERLEY

Bibliography

Foster, Myles. *The History of the Philharmonic Society of London 1813–1912.* 1912.

Nettel, Reginald. *The Orchestra in England: A Social History.* 1946.

· · · · ·

PHILOLOGY

Around 1830 the Danish interest in Anglo-Saxon language and literature spread to England. At this point English philology, or historical linguistics, acquired an organized existence. Instrumental in the early years were Benjamin Thorpe (1782–1870) and John Mitchell Kemble (1807–1857). Thorpe (1830)

published a translation into English of the Anglo-Saxon grammar by the Dane Rasmus Rask; a year later, he was busy usurping the plans of another Dane, N. F. S. Gruntvig, for the publication of early English texts. These plans went forward at a great rate over a period of two decades; meanwhile Kemble, who had been a student at Cambridge in the late 1820s, then a lecturer there, was carrying on a polemical battle against the older (and feebler) Anglo-Saxon scholarship in England—especially at Oxford. The controversy developed from presumably arcane matters, such as whether Anglo-Saxon texts should be printed in Saxon or Roman letters: Kemble favored the latter course as allowing greater accessibility. The larger issue was the claim of the new philology not only to greater accuracy but to scientific status.

The Philological Society of London was founded in 1842. In 1857–1858, three members of the society—Richard Chenevix Trench (1807–1886), Herbert Coleridge (1830–1861), and Frederick Furnivall (1825–1910, founder, in 1864, of the Early English Text Society)—hatched the great philological project of the period, the *New English Dictionary*, later the *Oxford English Dictionary*. The dictionary was to be based on a principle previously used by the *Greek-English Lexicon* (1843) of Henry George Liddell (1811–1898) and Robert Scott (1811–1887). Liddell and Scott aimed at comprehensiveness—comprehensiveness, moreover, on an historical principle. An entry devoted to a given word attempted to trace its origin and subsequent development. Negotiations with the Oxford University Press proving successful, the dictionary finally got off the ground in 1879, under the editorship of James Murray (1837–1915). Its 16,000 pages—9,000 more than originally planned—were completed fifty-four years later.

The Victorian philologists accomplished great things; but that does not explain their extraordinary popularity. Among the philologists best known to the public was Max Müller (1823–1900), professor at Oxford, whose lectures were attended by Victoria herself. Müller's books, along with the popular etymological essays of Trench, suggest the nonscientific—indeed the antiscientific—side of the new philology. Müller believed that words could be traced back to roots; the existence of these preformed roots implies the existence of God and the divine creation of language. Darwinian theories must therefore be nonsense. Detested by many professional philologists, Müller nonetheless influenced such powerful writers as Gerard Manley Hopkins—in whom the more dubious linguistic theories of the Victorian period take a poetic form. It has been argued (by Hans Aarsleff) that Victorian sages like Carlyle use a similar technique, tracing the histories of words as a way of eliciting wisdom from them. On occasion this approach could yield brilliant results, as it does in Ruskin's commentary on "Lycidas" (*Sesame and Lilies*, 1865).

RICHARD MAXWELL

Bibliography

Aarsleff, Hans. "Language and Victorian Ideology." *The American Scholar*, vol. 52, pp. 365-372.

———. *The Study of Language in England 1780-1860*. 1967.

Chaudhuri, Nirad. *Scholar Extraordinary: The Life and Profession of the Rt. Hon. Friedrich Max Müller, P.C.* 1974

Dowling, Linda. "Victorian Oxford and the Science of Language." *PMLA*, vol. 97, pp. 160-172.

See also DIALECT WRITING

. . . . .

PHOTOGRAPHY

The use of a camera to make and preserve images is a process that was developed in the early nineteenth century and quickly became accessible to many. The experiments and procedures of Louis Daguerre in France and **William Henry Fox Talbot** (1800-1877) in Great Britain became known in 1839. By the end of Victoria's reign, photography was well established both as an instrument of documentation and as an artistic process.

In one of history's remarkable coincidences, Daguerre and Talbot simultaneously developed, each without the other's knowledge, a means to preserve an image on paper. Talbot called his process "photogenic drawings": objects were placed on sensitized paper, then exposed to light, and then chemically "fixed" to preserve the image. Talbot's book *The Pencil of Nature* (1844) reveals his perception that photographs could be used to document, to educate, or as aesthetic objects.

Scottish painter David Octavius Hill (1802-1870) turned to photography and worked with Robert Adamson (1820-1848). Concentrating on portraits and genre scenes, Hill and Adamson helped make photography an accepted art form in its own right. **Julia Margaret Cameron** (1815-1879) also emphasized photography's artistic qualities. Her portraits of famous friends (Tennyson, Browning, Longfellow, Carlyle, Darwin, Hunt, Watts) and of family children in evocative costumes and poses were grounded in a concern for broad effect and refined beauty. Two other amateur photographers whose work has strong poetic qualities are Clementina, Lady Hawarden (1822-1865) and **Lewis Carroll** (1832-1898).

Other midcentury photographers emphasized the medium's documentary ability. Roger Fenton (1819-1869) was noted for pictures of the Crimean War. Antoine Francois Jean Claudet (1798-1867) established a "Temple to Photography" in London's Regent Street in 1851 to produce portrait calotypes. Francis Frith (1822-1898) sent back to England photographs of Egypt and the Near East; Samuel Bourne (1834-1912) photographed India beginning in 1861; and Philip Henry Delamotte (1821-1889) documented the reconstruction of the Crystal Palace in 1854.

Historic or literary themes interested William Lake Price (1810-1896), a watercolor artist who took up photography in 1854. His work signaled a rising interest in making photography as much as possible like painting. Two figures famous for composing such pictures (sometimes using as many as thirty negatives for one image) were Oscar Gustave Rejlander (1813-1875) and Henry Peach Robinson (1830-1901). Rejlander, a Swede who settled in England, produced *Two Ways of Life* in 1857. Nearly a yard long, it showed a youth contemplating a life of virtue on one side or of immorality on the other. Robinson's *Fading Away* (1858) showed the death of a young woman, with appropriate responses from her parents and a young man.

Peter Henry Emerson (1856-1936) furthered the sense that photography should have the aesthetic values of painting. He did not, however, support the practice of composing images from several negatives, but believed the artistic quality lay in the photographer's selection and shooting of a single image. Emerson published *Life and Landscape on the Norfolk Broads* (1886) and several other books on subjects taken from tidal or seacoast life. His *Naturalistic Photography* (1889) urged photographers to consider their craft as an art form.

Eadweard J. Muybridge (1830–1904), who emigrated from England to the United States around 1852, was particularly interested during the 1880s in using the camera to document motion. His use of photography to capture movements that could not be seen by the naked eye provides a contrast to its more poetic use by Emerson and others.

In 1892 one of Emerson's followers, George Davison (1856–1930) joined with others to form the Linked Ring, a group stressing photography's artistic potential. Davison, taking his subjects from farm life, was influenced by Impressionist painting and tried to capture depth and soft focus in his work. The Linked Ring also included Frederick H. Evans (1853–1943) and James Craig Annan (1864–1946). Evans, after retiring from bookselling in 1898, made photographs professionally, most notably of English cathedrals. Annan, represented in the American periodical *Camera Work* between 1901 and 1914, produced work with highly picturesque qualities and helped revive interest in earlier photographers such as Hill and Adamson.

Because it combines mechanical and aesthetic qualities, photography has from its beginnings been difficult to evaluate, though never unpopular. By the end of the century not only photographs but also cameras were affordable. Thus many works survive that have minimal artistic qualities but provide valuable information about society's concerns and interests, in addition to the photographs by both professionals and amateurs that have great aesthetic value.

FLOYD W. MARTIN

Bibliography

Bartram, Michael. *Pre-Raphaelite Photography.* 1983.

Coe, Brian. *The Birth of Photography.* 1977.

Flukinger, Roy. *The Formative Decades: Photography in Great Britain, 1839–1920.* 1985.

Gernsheim, Helmut. *Incunabula of British Photographic Literature: A Bibliography of British Photographic Literature, 1839–1875.* 1984.

——. and Alison Gernsheim. *The History of Photography: From the Camera Obscura to the Beginning of the Modern Era.* 1969.

Haworth-Booth, Mark. *The Golden Age of British Photography, 1839–1919.* 1980.

Mathews, Oliver. *Early Photographs and Early Photographers: A Survey in Dictionary Form.* 1973.

Newhall, Beaumont. *The History of Photography.* 5th ed., 1982.

Rosenblum, Naomi. *A World History of Photography.* 1984.

· · · · ·

PHRENOLOGY

A system of physiological psychology that enjoyed wide popularity in the first half of the nineteenth century, phrenology was brought to the British Isles by Johann Kaspar Spurzheim (1776–1832), the disciple of phrenology's founder Franz Joseph Gall (1758–1828); their *Recherches sur le système nerveux en général et sur celui du cerveau en particulier* (1809–1811) was the first textbook of the science. Scotsman George Combe (1788–1858) became phrenology's third apostle with his *Constitution of Man, Considered in Relation to External Objects* (2d ed., 1835).

Gall summarized the four chief tenets of phrenology: "The moral and intellectual dispositions are innate; their manifestation depends on organization; the brain is exclusively the organ of the mind; the brain is composed of as many particular and independent organs, as there are fundamental powers of the mind." It is the fourth that has been remembered as phrenology: "cranioscopy," bump-reading, the art of divining character by the contour of the skull. But the first three principles were equally radical: phrenology proposed that physiological dissection rather than philosophical reflection was the method by which to study the mind. As a materialist psychology, it was often allied with the equally controversial science of **mesmerism**.

Phrenology attracted not only credulous faddists, but also inquisitive intellectuals. Although repudiated by much of the scientific establishment, it significantly influenced Victorian thought: Auguste Comte used it as the foundation of a "positive psychology" in his *Cours de philosophie positive* (1830-1842); Robert Chambers saw it as an incarnation of natural law in the *Vestiges of the Natural History of Creation* (1844); it introduced Herbert Spencer and Alfred Russel Wallace to physiological psychology. Phrenologists also affected penal and educational reform.

DIANA POSTLETHWAITE

Bibliography

Cooter, Roger. *The Cultural Meaning of Popular Science: Phrenology and the Organization of Consent in Nineteenth-Century Britain.* 1984.

De Giustino, David. *Conquest of Mind: Phrenology and Victorian Social Thought.* 1975.

Postlethwaite, Diana. *Making It Whole: A Victorian Circle and the Shape of Their World.* 1984.

Young, Robert M. *Mind, Brain, and Adaptation in the Nineteenth Century: Cerebral Localization and Its Biological Context from Gall to Ferrier.* 1970.

See also PSYCHOLOGY

· · · · ·

PHYSICS

Physics was a Victorian invention. From natural philosophy and rational mechanics, two strands that were either overwhelmingly impressionistic and imprecise or rigidly mathematical, the physicists of the nineteenth century wove a new synthesis, applying sophisticated mathematical methods to the study of light, heat, sound, electricity, and magnetism. Victorian physicists worked out the conceptual approaches and the basic equations governing these realms.

The crowning achievement of Victorian physics was thermodynamics. The laws of the conservation of energy and increase of entropy were insights gained through the careful study of the relations between heat and mechanical work. Many scientists lay claim to discovering the law of the conservation of energy. In the 1840s experimental work by James Prescott Joule (1818-1889) was crucial. In one famous experiment, Joule heated water by means of friction from a paddle wheel. He found that the rise in temperature was proportional to the mechanical work expended, a correlation he called the mechanical equivalence of heat. Joule's work thus proposed a link between entities thought to be separately conserved but not rigorously joined: mechanical work and heat. A meeting betwen Joule and the young William Thomson (1824-1907; later Lord Kelvin) led to a seminal 1851 paper, "On the Dynamical Theory of Heat." Drawing also on work by W. J. Macquorn Rankine (1820-1872), the Frenchman Sadi Carnot (1796-1832), and the Germans Rudolf Clausius (1822-1888) and Hermann von Helmholtz (1821-1894), Thomson proposed the conservation of the combined quantity of heat and work, under the single name "energy." He also proposed the "dissipation of energy" as a law: the tendency of heat to flow from hot areas to cold, not the reverse (which was possible if the conservation law alone were true). These are now known as the first and second laws of thermodynamics.

Thomson fully realized the great importance of the discovery of the laws of "energetics." In the *Treatise on Natural Philosophy* (1867), written with Peter Guthrie Tait (1831-1901), Thomson reworked traditional Newtonian mechanics into "energetic" dynamics. Thomson and Tait had also hoped to extend the ideas to all branches of physics; this was left to other physicists, notably **James Clerk Maxwell** (1831-1879) in his *Theory of Heat* (1871) and *Treatise on Electricity and Magnetism* (1873), and John William Strutt (Lord Rayleigh; 1842-1919) in *The Theory of Sound* (2 vols., 1877-1878). Thomson himself applied the principles in geophysics and electrodynamics.

A rigorous investigation of the ether was a second defining characteristic of Victorian theoretical physics. The idea that a subtle continuous medium—an ether—was the source of the different physical forces of electricity, magnetism, heat, light, and even gravity, goes back at least to Newton. It was revived in the early nineteenth century, when the corpuscular or emission theory of light was replaced by the undulatory or wave theory, with its assumed attendant material substratum. Making a mathematical model for this medium proved quite difficult; there was a range of theories, from the dynamical formalism proposed by George Green (1793–1841), the stiff crystalline solid proposed by James MacCullagh (1809–1847), to the jellylike structure proposed by George Gabriel Stokes (1819–1903). None of these approaches, however, could explain the interaction of light with ordinary matter. Nor was it clear how large bodies—the earth, say—could easily move through a crystalline solid ether that was supposed to fill all space.

Answers were sought in electricity and magnetism. **Michael Faraday** (1791–1867) proposed that the causes of electrical and magnetic phenomena lay in the "empty" spaces—the "fields of force"—around electrical or magnetic objects. Faraday's 1845 discovery of the magneto-optical effect (the rotation of the plane of polarized light by a magnetic field) showed what many had long suspected, that there was some connection between magnetic "fields" and an optical ether. Maxwell's work in electrodynamics in the 1850s and 1860s (based on experimental work by Faraday and theoretical work by Thomson) proposed an identity: electrical and magnetic force fields were the results of motions in a single ether, the optical ether. Maxwell gave a set of equations that described the interaction of the electric and magnetic fields, based on a heuristic ether model of rotating vortices. These equations allowed wave motions in the ether that traveled at the speed of light. He thus coherently described electromagnetic interaction and optics, and his equations are in use today as the basis of classical electrodynamics.

A precise mechanical model to go with the mathematical description eluded physicists. Maxwell increasingly relied on abstract dynamical equations—clearly influenced by Thomson and Tait's *Treatise*—while never doubting the existence of a material ether. William Thomson, Joseph John Thomson (1856–1940), John Henry Poynting (1852–1914), George Francis Fitzgerald (1851–

1901), Oliver Lodge (1851–1940), Oliver Heaviside (1850–1925), and Joseph Larmor (1857–1942), as well as Continental physicists, all expanded and refined the mathematical description of the electromagnetic field. British physicists especially tried to tie the mathematics to an ether model. These theories usually had two common characteristics: (1) a rotational element, either in rotatory motion or rotational strain; (2) the expression of both matter and electricity as different manifestations of the motion of a single ether. Larmor identified the locus of rotational strain with an electric point charge, also bearing material inertia, for which he coined the word "electron," the first modern usage of the term. Though all the theories fell short, the works were a crowning achievement of Victorian physics in their sophistication, especially William Thomson's (Lord Kelvin) *Baltimore Lectures on Molecular Dynamics and the Wave Theory of Light* (delivered in 1884, published in 1904) and Larmor's *Aether and Matter* (1900).

Thermodynamic arguments were central as well to Victorian discussions of the kinetic theory of gases. Since the seventeenth century, the static theory of gases had prevailed: gases were thought to be composed of stationary particles, mutually repulsing through their atmospheres of what was called "caloric," the fluid of heat. In the 1830s the discovery of infrared radiation led to the idea that heat was transmitted as a wave, i.e., as a form of motion. One British physicist, John Herapath (1790–1868), proposed a kinetic theory, heat consisting of molecular motion: the greater the motion, the greater the heat. Clausius opened up the issue with his "On the Kind of Motion That We Call Heat" (1857). He used the laws of thermodynamics to explain the properties of gases by the motions of molecules.

Maxwell significantly expanded Clausius's work in the 1860s and 1870s into a far-reaching science, statistical mechanics. Maxwell grouped gas molecules mathematically according to their different velocities, each group given a statistical weight. A statistical profile of velocities, not a uniform average, was assumed. Using this technique, Maxwell was able to derive the known gas laws and investigate heat conduction, viscosity, and gas diffusion. The generalized approach provided the foundation of statistical mechanics, the techniques of doing the physics of large numbers of entities not directly observable.

Experimental physics concerned itself with the whole gamut of topics, often closely tied to the theoretical fields of thermodynamics, electricity and magnetism, and the behavior of gases. One field, though, in which experiment far outran theory was spectroscopy. Technical advances made possible the fine resolution of spectral lines and the identification of new chemical elements by their spectral "fingerprints." One of the most significant discoveries was by Norman Lockyer (1836–1920). He identified a new element in the solar prominences, helium, later isolated on earth.

In the literature of physics, perhaps the most significant event was Lockyer's founding in 1869 of the journal *Nature*, the premier British science journal. Thermodynamics—and especially the second law—provided the greatest inspiration for physics-based literature. In two books, *The Unseen Universe* (1875) and *Paradoxical Philosophy* (1878), Tait and Balfour Stewart (1828–1887) used the ether and the dissipation of energy to uphold a peculiar but essentially Christian world-view in the face of what they perceived as German, science-based materialism. Herbert Spencer (1820–1903) wove contemporary physical ideas into his *First Principles* (1862), although he insisted on the recoalescence of matter and energy from a condition of complete dispersal, counter to most physicists' notions of thermodynamics. William Thomson—anxious to prove the world far younger than the Darwinian-inspired geologists claimed—also demonstrated the world's relatively quick demise as "an abode fit for life" in the "heat death of the universe," a condition where all energy is uniformly distributed, the world cold and unchanging. These ideas were an inspiration in the fin de siècle mood of degeneration: *The Time Machine* (1895), by H. G. Wells (1866–1946), was set in a future that was considerably colder and dimmer than Victorian Britain.

PAUL THEERMAN

Bibliography

Cannon, Susan Faye. *Science in Culture: The Early Victorian Period.* 1978.

Harman, P. M. *Energy, Force, and Matter: The Conceptual Development of Nineteenth-Century Physics.* 1982.

Paradis, James and Thomas Postlewait, eds. *Victorian Science and Victorian Values: Literary Perspectives.* 1981.

· · · · ·

PHYSIOLOGY

Physiology, the study of animal function, emerged as an important scientific enterprise in Britain between 1870 and 1900. Originally taught with anatomy, it gradually gained separate status through educational reforms resulting from the Medical Reform Act of 1858 and the revised licensing procedures of the Royal College of Surgeons (1870). The striking progress of French and, more especially, German physiology after midcentury created an awareness in Britain of the need to establish laboratories for the teaching of experimental physiology. Michael Foster (1836–1907) was appointed praelector in physiology at Trinity College, Cambridge, in 1870. He and other intellectual heirs of William Sharpey (1802–1880) at University College, London, notably John Burdon Sanderson (1828–1905) and Edward Schäfer (1850–1935), were to bring British physiology to international preeminence by the turn of the twentieth century.

The professionalization of British physiology occurred rapidly in the 1870s. Borrowing the methodology and experimental techniques of the flourishing Continental schools, British investigators increasingly studied physiological processes in live animals. By doing so, they incurred the wrath of antivivisectionists. Burdon Sanderson's *Handbook for the Physiological Laboratory* (1873) especially provoked controversy. The Physiological Society was founded in 1876, mainly in response to the establishment of a royal commission to investigate animal abuse. The Cruelty to Animals Act of 1876 created licensing procedures and guidelines for subsequent animal research. In the last quarter of the nineteenth century, British investigators were to contribute substantially to the study of neuromuscular, brain, and cardiac function, as well as to the recognition of chemical control mechanisms in the body. They fiercely argued the importance of physiological experiments for the progress of scientific medicine.

Physiologists helped establish the place of scientific method and experimental analysis in British education. They urged the creation of teaching laboratories throughout Britain. Thomas Henry Huxley (1825–1895) directly encouraged this process. He was an outspoken publicist for the teaching of both biology and physiology in British schools. His views were shared by Sharpey and Foster who toured German physiological laboratories in 1870, studying facilities and teaching methods. Physiology at Cambridge was particularly enhanced by the interest of George Eliot (1819–1880). In 1879, she established the George Henry Lewes studentship. Lewes had been a founding member of the Physiological Society.

MERRILEY BORELL

Bibliography

Burdon Sanderson, John, ed. *Handbook for the Physiological Laboratory.* 1873.

Butler, Stella. "A Transformation in Training: The Formation of University Medical Faculties in Manchester, Leeds, and Liverpool, 1870–84." *Medical History,* vol. 30, pp. 115–132.

French, Richard. *Antivivisection and Medical Science in Victorian Society.* 1975.

———. "Some Problems and Sources in the Foundations of Modern Physiology in Great Britain." *History of Science,* vol. 10, pp. 28–55.

Geison, Gerald. *Michael Foster and the Cambridge School of Physiology: The Scientific Enterprise in Late Victorian Society.* 1978.

Rothschuh, Karl. *History of Physiology.* 1973. Trans. Guenter Risse.

Sharpey-Schafer, Edward. *History of the Physiological Society During Its First Fifty Years 1876–1926. Journal of Physiology* supplement. 1927.

Turner, James. *Reckoning with the Beast: Animals, Pain and Humanity in the Victorian Mind.* 1980.

See also BIOCHEMISTRY

. . . . .

PIANO

The pianoforte is indissolubly associated with middle-class status and feminine accomplishments. Its predominance derived not only from its versatility, but also from the cult of the virtuoso, and from engineering and manufacturing developments by such firms as Broadwood and Collard.

The piano was admirably suited to meet middle-class demands for material goods and accomplished women. A substantial and conspicuous piece of furniture even in its cheaper versions (prices ranged from 30 to 120 guineas), it nevertheless had a limited lifetime. Every piano deteriorates with age; furthermore, improvements such as the iron frame and changes in appearance, such as the shift to upright from "square" pianos, quickly made older instruments seem old-fashioned.

As an instrument for domestic music making, the piano had much to recommend it. It was capable of an impressive volume and showy effects as well as a more pathetic tone, though devotees of the plaintive might prefer the harmonium. It could be played by two or four hands and gave valuable support to singers. Awkwardness or extreme effort was not demanded of the performer; indeed, the recommended technique called for a "peaceful" wrist, the fingers being the only source of tone or power. Finally, the piano's chief virtue was its tolerance of poor playing. It is not surprising, then, that young ladies, even the unmusical, were subjected to piano lessons, despite criticism of the affectation as early as Hannah More (1745–1833) and Maria Edgeworth (1767–1849).

Although sometimes pretentious, the presence of a piano was not always a fraud. Unless music was made by the family or its guests, it simply could not be heard at home, and there exist many accounts of pleasant amateur musical evenings during which the piano was indispensable. The vogue for the piano was reinforced by Mendelssohn's pupil Queen Victoria, and by the virtuoso performances in private recitals or public halls by Clara Schumann, Liszt, Chopin, and later, Rubinstein.

Music publishers flourished, printing enormous quantities of arrangements, reductions, and original pieces, the latter chiefly short, showy, not too difficult, and strongly melodic or rhythmic. Piano manufacturers also thrived: 1851 saw 25,000 pianos made in Britain; by the century's end production had nearly tripled, and thousands more instruments were imported from abroad. Despite the introduction, toward the end of the century, of ingenious player pianos culminating in the American "Pianola," the large majority of piano buyers preferred home-made to mechanical music.

SUSAN DRAIN

Bibliography

Blom, Eric. *The Romance of the Piano.* 1928; rpt. 1969.

Hardon, Rosamond. *The Pianoforte.* 1933; rpt. 1973.

Hullah, John. *Music in the House.* 1877.

Loesser, Arthur. *Men, Women, and Pianos: A Social History.* 1954.

Mackerness, E. D. *A Social History of English Music.* 1964.

Pearsall, Ronald. *Victorian Popular Music.* 1973.

Sumner, William. *The Pianoforte.* 3rd ed., 1971.

Westerby, Herbert. *The History of Pianoforte Music.* 1924; rpt. 1971.

. . . . .

PINERO, ARTHUR WING (1855-1934)

One of the most popular and admired playwrights of the nineteenth century, Arthur Wing Pinero began his career as a "utility" actor with R. H. Wyndham's company at the Theatre Royal, Edinburgh (1874). His London debut followed in 1876 in a transferred production of Wilkie Collins's *Miss Gwilt.* From 1876 to 1881 Pinero was a member of Henry Irving's Lyceum troupe, performing both in London and on tour. Excelling in what Ellen Terry called "silly ass" roles, he appeared as Roderigo, Guildenstern, and Salarino in Irving's Shakespeare revivals. During the same period his own play *Two Hundred a Year* (1877) was given at a benefit performance at the Globe. It was followed by pieces like *The Money Spinner* (1880) and *The Squire* (1881) for which Pinero was hailed as a prom-

ising talent in William Archer's *English Dramatists of Today* (1882).

In 1885 Pinero abandoned acting to turn his full energies to playwriting and directing. He first established himself as a farceur of impressive skill with *The Magistrate* (1885), *The Schoolmistress* (1886), and *Dandy Dick* (1887), all produced by Arthur Cecil and John Clayton at the Court. A more sentimental streak appeared in *Sweet Lavender* (1888) which ran for 684 performances at Terry's Theatre. In the same year Pinero befriended Archer and began to experiment with more socially committed types of drama. *The Profligate* (1887) created a sensation when finally staged by John Hare in 1889, even though the protagonist's suicide was replaced by a conventional happy ending.

Pinero's reputation as a writer of "problem plays" was secured by *The Second Mrs. Tanqueray* (1893), a drama about a woman "with a past" who takes her own life when faced with middle-class hypocrisy and a former lover who returns to seek her stepdaughter's hand. Refused by Hare as an immoral work, the play was presented at George Alexander's St. James's Theatre, with Mrs. Patrick Campbell in the title role. It brought overnight fame to "Mrs. Pat," who went on to create the author's *Notorious Mrs. Ebbsmith* (1895), and high praise from Archer who saw in it the first stirrings of English Ibsenism. The staging also enabled Pinero to affirm his prerogatives as producer, placing himself in a line of direct descent from W. S. Gilbert and T. W. Robertson.

The decade's close brought a gracious tribute to Robertson in *Trelawny of the "Wells"* (1898) and collaboration with Arthur Sullivan on *The Beauty Stone* (1898). Pinero's association with Alexander continued into the twentieth century; *His House in Order* (1906), *The Thunderbolt* (1908), and *Mid-Channel* (1909) all received handsome productions at the St. James's. In 1909 Pinero was knighted for services to the theater, the second playwright (after Gilbert) to be so honored.

JOEL H. KAPLAN

Bibliography

Dunkel, Wilbur Dwight. *Sir Arthur Pinero: A Critical Biography with Letters.* 1941.

Fyfe, Hamilton. *Sir Arthur Pinero's Plays and Players.* 1930.

Hamilton, Clayton, ed. *The Social Plays of Arthur Pinero.* 1917-1922. 4 vols.

Lazenby, Walter. *Arthur Wing Pinero.* 1972.

Wearing, J. P., ed. *Collected Letters of Sir Arthur Pinero.* 1974.

. . . . .

PLACE, FRANCIS
(1771-1854)

Francis Place, the "radical tailor of Charing Cross," was one of the most influential workers for political reform in the early nineteenth century. He belonged to the London Corresponding Society and was instrumental in the election of Francis Burdett to Parliament, but is best known for effecting the repeal of the Combination Laws with Joseph Hume and for drafting the People's Charter with William Lovett.

Place became politically active when he unwillingly led a strike of journeyman leather breeches menders in 1793. The unsuccessful strike cost him eight months' unemployment, time he used to learn tailoring and read political philosophy. Place opened a successful tailoring shop from which he was able to retire in 1817. Although his early struggles made him sympathetic toward workers, his prosperity convinced him that self-reliance was as important as suffrage. Therefore, while his work for parliamentary representation for artisans caused conservatives to dislike him, his promotion of respectability frequently put him at odds with radical reformers.

Place preferred to work behind the scenes, but the number of people who used the library behind his tailoring shop shows his influence in various nineteenth-century social causes. A friend of Jeremy Bentham, James Mill, Robert Owen, and Joseph Lancaster, Place was involved in diverse projects such as the penny post, the British and Foreign School Society, and the publication of Jeremy Bentham's *Not Paul, but Jesus* (1823).

After he directed agitation for the Reform Bill of 1832, Place's influence declined, although he participated in the Anti-Corn-Law movement until ill health forced his retirement. Place spent the last few years of his life collecting material about working-class radicalism into scrapbooks, 182 volumes of which reside in the British Museum.

Although factionalism in the working-class movement and Place's moderate stance hurt him during his lifetime and in historians' estimations, his responsibility for the repeal of the Combination Laws alone demonstrates his influence in the first half of the nineteenth century.

NAN HACKETT

Bibliography

Thale, Mary, ed. *The Autobiography of Francis Place.* 1972.

See also CHARTISM

. . . . .

PLANCHÉ, JAMES
ROBINSON
(1796-1880)

A reformer in the areas of stage costume and setting and a prolific popular dramatist, James Robinson Planché was active steadily in the London theater from 1818 to 1856, and thereafter sporadically until 1872. He was also a respected antiquarian and authority on historical dress, holding a post in the College of Heralds from 1854.

Planché produced numerous original dramatic pieces, translations, and adaptations, including opera librettos (notably *Oberon*, 1826, for Carl Maria von Weber), melodramas, comedies, spectacles, and pantomimes. He was best known, however, for delicacy and a gentle wit, and his whimsical "extravaganzas" became a holiday institution. While Planché furnished plays to a number of houses and held various artistic and managerial posts throughout his career, he established a particularly successful working relationship with Madame Vestris and Charles Mathews at the Olympic (1831-1839), Covent Garden (1839-1942), and Lyceum (1847-1856) theaters.

In 1823 Planché designed an entire series of historically accurate costumes for Charles

Kemble's staging of *King John* at Covent Garden, a landmark antiquarian production of Shakespeare. He continued to work for unified and appropriate design of costume and setting, and during the 1830s and 1840s assisted with noteworthy Shakespearean revivals characterized by restoration of the original text.

Planché was elected a fellow of the Society of Antiquaries in 1829, and was a founding member of the British Archaeological Association (1843). An extensive list of publications includes works on heraldry, reproductions of his costume designs, and translations of French fairy tales. His *History of British Costume* (1834), long a standard source, was followed by the profusely illustrated *A Cyclopaedia of Costume or Dictionary of Dress* (1876-1879).

As a designer, Planché contributed significantly to the growing trend of verisimilitude and careful, unique mounting of each production. His extravaganzas were a widely popular form of middle-class entertainment and an important influence on the Gilbert and Sullivan Savoy operas.

KATHY FLETCHER

Bibliography

Freedley, George and Allardyce Nicoll, eds. *English and American Drama of the Nineteenth Century.* 1965.

Planché, James Robinson. *The Extravaganzas of J. R. Planché, Esq.* 1879.

————. *The Recollections and Reflections of J. R. Planché.* 1872.

See also PANTOMIME, BURLESQUE, AND EXTRAVAGANZA

· · · · ·

PLIMSOLL, SAMUEL
(1824-1898)

One cause dominated the life of this merchant, radical politician, and philanthropist: preventing loss of life at sea. Dubbed "the sailors' friend," he became identified with the mark limiting the maximum load on international shipping, the Plimsoll Load Line.

Samuel Plimsoll was born in Bristol. He pursued various careers, finally achieving success as a coal merchant. He was elected M.P. for Derby and served from 1868 to 1880. He fanatically crusaded for government regulation over the seaworthiness and safety of merchant shipping, accusing the shipping interests of villainy. Although others deserve credit for the idea and for later international implementation, the Plimsoll Load Line was always associated with his agitation and outburst in the House of Commons preparatory to passage of the Merchant Shipping Act of 1876. Allegedly, his innovative, provocative, and disruptive demonstration of July 22, 1875 became a model for later more serious incidents on the floor of Parliament. Plimsoll retired, was revered by seamen's institutions, and died at Folkestone on June 3, 1898.

Plimsoll wrote several long pamphlets including *Our Seamen* (1873), an indictment of all aspects of the shipping industry. The most consistent comment of critics on his writing was that it was "exaggerated." There are two recent unsatisfactory biographies by George Peters and David Masters.

EUGENE L. RASOR

Bibliography

Alderman, Geoffrey. "Samuel Plimsoll and the Shipping Interest." *Maritime History*, vol. 1, pp. 73-95.

Masters, David. *The Plimsoll Mark.* 1955.

Peters, George Hertel. *The Plimsoll Line.* 1975.

Times, June 4, 1898, p. 10.

· · · · ·

PLUMBING AND SEWAGE DISPOSAL

The activities of metropolitan sanitary associations during the mid-nineteenth century transformed urban life by providing arrangements for domestic plumbing, water supplies, and sewage disposal. The first **Public Health** Act (1848) recommended that "all householders must have a fixed sanitary arrangement of some kind, namely an ash-pit, privy or a water closet."

The first water closet with working parts and flushing water was invented in 1596, but the improved valves required to prevent odors (and rats) from entering houses through the waste pipe were not in use until the end of the eighteenth century. At the Exhibition of 1851, one of the exhibits was George Jennings' public urinal, although by 1891 only thirty-six towns in the country had public toilets of any sort. The domestic water closet, however, became a triumph of design between 1875 and 1900. The "National" of Thomas Twyford, which had its working parts in a wooden box, sold 100,000 units between 1881 and 1889. By the 1890s the cantilivered water closet, with a low back cistern, had been introduced, and since that time neither the workings nor the basic shape has changed.

Efficient sanitation also required the construction of sewage systems. During the first half of the century cesspools were the most common destination of wastes even in large communities. A single privy often served dozens of people, and in some rural areas and mining communities even privies were uncommon; garbage, refuse, rubbish, and the contents of chamber pots were simply tossed out into the road or piled on a midden heap outside the door. Throughout the country, water supplies were both erratic and polluted. In the 1830s The Chelsea Water Company in London had its water intake just a few feet from the outfall of the Ranelagh sewer. In fashionable areas of London's West End around Belgravia and Eton Square houses stood, according to the *Report on the Sanitary Condition of the City of London for the Years 1848-1849* by John Simon, the medical officer of health for the city, "over sewers abounding in the foulest deposits." Midcentury health authorities estimated that one-third of the deaths in any year could be traced to defective or inadequate sewers and drains.

The Metropolitan Board of Works (London) was established in 1855. Its chief engineer, Joseph Bazalgette (1819-1891) was nicknamed "the sewer king." The main sewer system was built between 1858 and 1865; during Bazalgette's twenty-year tenancy as chief engineer 1,300 miles of sewage pipes were constructed, using 318 million bricks. The development of municipal sewage systems proceeded irregularly in the rest of the country. The problem of treating sewage and purifying

wastes—rather than simply dumping them into rivers—became an important issue during the last quarter of the century.

JOHN REYNOLDS

Bibliography

Hartley, Dorothy R. *Water in England.* 1964.

Palmer, Roy *The Water Closet: A New History.* 1973.

Schoenwald, Richard I. "Training Urban Man." In H. J. Dyos and Michael Wolff, eds., *The Victorian City: Images and Realities,* vol. 2. 1973.

Stephens, John Hall. *Water and Waste.* 1967.

Wohl, Anthony S. *Endangered Lives: Public Health in Victorian Britain.* 1983.

See also ENGINEERING; ENVIRONMENTAL POLLUTION

. . . . .

PLYMOUTH BRETHREN

The Plymouth Brethren are an evangelical Christian communion founded in 1826 in Dublin. They take their name from the vigorous group formed in Plymouth by J. N. Darby (1800-1882). They underwent many divisions during the nineteenth century, and continue to break often into new groupings, both in England and in America. Millenarian and Calvinist in theology, they combine biblical fundamentalism, evangelical vigor, strict congregational government, nonclerical leadership, and denominational and cultural separatism. They eschew involvement in social schemes, preferring to institute separate helping agencies such as orphanages (Dr. Barnardo was a member of the Plymouth Brethren when he took up his work as the leading provider of homes for orphans during the Victorian era).

The membership of the group is very democratic: peers and scientists meet on common ground with laborers and businesspersons. A fair rendering of their mode of life is Edmund Gosse's novel *Father and Son* (1907), a thinly disguised autobiography featuring both Edmund (1849-1928) and his father, Philip Henry Gosse (1810-1888), a prominent scientist and opponent of Darwin's hypothesis, and leader of the Plymouth Brethren in the Devonshire area. *Father and Son* relates the narrow social life, but also the rich spiritual life, of the group, though Edmund Gosse's pervasive irony, fostered by his own early defection from the group's principles and life, occasionally makes unfair judgments on them. Though numerically small, the Plymouth Brethren were very influential in Free Church circles in the Victorian era, and have supplied to the present time a disproportionate number of excellent biblical scholars and scientists as well as administrators of charities, foreign missionaries, and leading military figures. The Plymouth Brethren are perhaps the most faithful latter-day representatives of the Puritan tradition.

GEORGE G. HARPER

Bibliography

Coad, Frederick R. *A History of the Brethren Movement: Its Origins, Its Worldwide Development and Its Significance for the Present Day.* 1968.

Irvine, William, ed. "Introduction" to *Father and Son*, by Edmund Gosse. 1965.

Rowdon, Harold H. *The Origins of the Brethren.* 1967.

. . . . .

POACHING see GAME LAWS

. . . . .

POEL (FORMERLY POLE), WILLIAM (1852-1934)

Actor and director William Poel began his stage career in 1876, taking minor parts in various touring companies. In 1881 he produced a "first quarto" *Hamlet* for the New Shakspeare Society, implementing certain innovations which would come to be associated with his future work; he abolished act breaks and presented the play after the Elizabethan fashion on an open stage unencumbered by

scenery or large properties. In 1894 Poel founded the Elizabethan Stage Society which, until its demise in 1905, presented seventeen of Shakespeare's plays as well as important revivals of pieces by Marlowe, Jonson, and Ford among others. Its productions, often played in the great halls of the Inns of Court or city guilds to the accompaniment of period music, attempted to recreate the theatrical conditions of Shakespeare and his fellows.

Throughout his career Poel advocated the return to a permanent "Tudor" set, consisting of a thrust stage, upper and lower acting areas, and concealed discovery space. (Recent scholarship has cast some doubt upon the accuracy of this reconstruction.) In 1901 Poel successfully revived the medieval morality play *Everyman*, himself taking the role of Death. With the notable exception of Bernard Shaw, few of Poel's contemporaries were sympathetic to his quest for Elizabethan authenticity. His work, however, had an important influence upon subsequent directors, including Harley Granville-Barker, Bridges Adams, and Lewis Casson.

SHEILA STOWELL

Bibliography

Lundstrom, Rinda F. *William Poel's Hamlets.* 1984.

Speaight, Robert. *William Poel and the Elizabethan Revival.* 1954.

. . . . .

POET LAUREATE

The poet laureate is the official poet of the United Kingdom, belongs to the royal household, and is expected to write poems about people—mostly royal—and about state occasions. Ben Jonson was awarded a pension by James I in 1616; the first poet laureate was appointed during the reign of Charles I; and the post was recognized as a royal office, to be automatically filled on becoming vacant, after John Dryden's appointment in 1668.

Robert Southey (1774-1843), who accepted the office when Walter Scott declined, was poet laureate when Queen Victoria came to the throne in 1837. Southey asked, and Queen Victoria agreed, to end the custom of New Year and birthday poems which had been set to music and performed in the presence of the monarch.

The first two poets laureate appointed during Victoria's reign had virtually unquestioned stature as the foremost living British poets, although William Wordsworth (1770–1850) had already passed the period of his great work by the time he was appointed in 1843. **Alfred Tennyson** (1809–1890) held the office for forty years and has become inextricably identified with Queeen Victoria's reign.

The choice was no longer so simple by 1890. Algernon Charles Swinburne (1837–1909) was put forward as Tennyson's successor. Queen Victoria agreed, but the church did not. Political unrest and three changes of government delayed the choice until 1896, when Alfred Austin (1853–1913), a comparatively minor but unexceptionable poet, became poet laureate.

ANNIE PERROTT

Bibliography

Russell, Nick. *Poets by Appointment: Britain's Laureates.* 1981.

· · · · ·

POETRY AND POETICS

Though often in sharp disagreement, several Victorian writers attempted to define the role and determine the value of the poet and of poetry itself in a society undergoing almost bewildering change. Against a background of utilitarian disdain and indifference, Victorian poets and critics first reacted against romanticism, later advocated a poetry of social engagement, and, finally, celebrated aesthetic withdrawal.

Jeremy Bentham's *Rationale of Reward* presented a case against poetry with which poets—indeed, all writers—have had to contend since its publication in 1825. Bentham's utilitarian philosophy regarded literature as "useless" except as a means of relaxation and held that if a child's game of pushpin gave more pleasure than *Hamlet*, then the game was more useful, hence better, than *Hamlet*. In his "Milton," also published in 1825, Thomas Babington Macaulay agreed with Bentham's notion that art presents a distorted view of reality but added that such distorted views are quite naturally accepted by children. The childhood of our civilization was more capable of producing imaginative literature, so it follows that "as civilization advances, poetry almost necessarily declines." Though not an isolated claim—both Hazlitt and Peacock had agreed that poetry was declining—Macaulay argued more forcefully than any of his contemporaries that the material advances of civilization had far outdistanced correlative advances by the arts.

Arthur Henry Hallam gave a more positive view of the age and its poets in "On Some of the Characteristics of Modern Poetry" (1831). Ostensibly a review of Tennyson's early verse, the essay actually delineates what Walter Houghton and G. Robert Stange in *Victorian Poetry and Poetics* labeled the two major "schools" of Victorian poetics: the "romantic" predilection for subjective, descriptive, incantatory verse; the "classical" preference for objective, moral, religious, political verse. Although Hallam was able to praise both kinds of poetry—the romantic or early Tennysonian rather more so than the classical—his two schools presented a potentially debilitating dilemma for poets. Poets might write subjective verse but seem socially isolated, even self-indulgent, or they might write objective verse but turn away from the lyric core of so much romantic and early Victorian poetry. Tennyson himself wrote examples of what Hallam labeled the subjective ("Mariana") and objective ("Confessions of a Second-Rate Sensitive Mind"), and he sometimes presented the two so-called "schools" in single poems ("The Palace of Art").

By 1833 it was clear that the age's preference seemed to be tipping toward the "objective," for in a review of Robert Browning's *Pauline* J. S. Mill wrote that its author was "possessed with a more intense and morbid self-consciousness than I ever knew in any sane human being." Several critics have felt that the review changed the course of Browning's career, and there is evidence in Browning's own words that his development of the dramatic monologue was a response to Mill's reaction against overly subjective poetry. In a prefatory note to *Dramatic Lyrics* (1842) Browning wrote that his poems "though often Lyric in expression [were] always Dramatic in principle, and so many utterances of so many imaginary persons, not mine." Though Tennyson and Browning could and did write subjective as well as objective poetry, it is fair to say that by the 1840s their dominant voice had become the objective: Browning adopted the mask of the monologue, while Tennyson, referring to the persona of his autobiographical *In Memoriam*, claimed that the "I" of the poem was "not always the author speaking of himself, but the voice of the human race speaking thro' him."

Tennyson's almost oracular position owed much to Thomas Carlyle and his lecture on "The Hero as Man of Letters." Carlyle had already warned his age against the self-absorption of the romantics—Teufelsdrockh's imperative in *Sartor Resartus* (1833) was "close thy *Byron*; open thy *Goethe*"—and in 1840 he celebrated Goethe and other writers as "a perpetual Priesthood." Moreover, said Carlyle, "the man of letters is sent hither specially that he may discern for himself, and make manifest to us, [the] Divine Idea." Much of Tennyson's laureate verse as well as the *Idylls* was influenced by Carlyle's designation of the poet as teacher and prophet. How seriously Browning regarded his role as poet may be seen in his 1855 letter to Ruskin: "A poet's affair is with God, to whom he is accountable, and of whom is his reward."

Matthew Arnold's major critical statements complement and expand on the views of Carlyle, Henry Taylor (in his preface to *Philip Van Artevelde*, 1834), and others. Arnold refused to reprint his *Empedocles on Etna* because, among other things, it presented an "allegory of the state of one's own mind"—another example of romantic social isolation and self-indulgence. The preface to his *Poems* (1853) argued that poets should address the needs of their age not by "draw[ing their] subjects from matters of present import"—a position endorsed by Arthur Hugh Clough in the July 1853 number of the *North American Review*—but, instead, by describing "those elementary feelings which subsist permanently in the race, and are independent of time." In other words, close thy Byron, open thy Aristotle. In fact, Arnold's early poetics look to classical literature for models of "unity and profoundness of moral impression"—qualities he felt were in short supply in his own time, "an age wanting in moral grandeur." Arnold's "moral" view requires careful understanding, for it is not a call

for didactic poetry. What it does mean may best be seen in his "Wordsworth" (1879) where he argues that whatever bears upon the question "how to live," is a "moral idea" and that poetry is a "criticism of life" when it applies ideas to life—when it shows us how to live. Not only did Empedocles do no such thing, but, said Arnold, too many nineteenth-century poems seemed to exist for their often glittering parts rather than for their unified wholes. This concern for a poetry of wholeness prepared the way for Arnold's claim in his "Study of Poetry" (1880) that poetry would one day fill needs once met by religion as we "turn to poetry to interpret life for us, to console us, to sustain us."

If Arnold looked to Hellenic models for inspiration and standards, Algernon Charles Swinburne looked to nineteenth-century France—particularly to Theophile Gautier. Gautier had called for the independence of art from instructional or moral intentions as early as 1835 in his *Mademoiselle de Maupin*. What came to be called "**art for art's sake**" (*l'art pour l'art*) proved especially attractive to Swinburne who, in his *William Blake* (1868), argued that art should be concerned only with aesthetic effects. To some extent Swinburne's embracing of what was increasingly recognized as "aestheticism" was one way of responding to sharply critical reviews of his *Poems and Ballads* (1866). John Morley, for one, had criticized not only the "fleshliness" of Swinburne's subjects but also his lack of "meditation" and "thought"; Robert Buchanan in 1871 would mount a similar attack against the poetry of D. G. Rossetti ("he is fleshly all over"). But Swinburne's extreme formalism had consequences beyond the matter of his self-defense. The aesthetic position rapidly became one of form for form's sake—with a correlative decline in the importance of meaning. Walter Pater claimed in "The School of Giorgione" in his *Renaissance* (1873) that "all art constantly aspires to the condition of music" because in music "form" and "matter" are indistinguishable. If the beautiful formal and sonic effects of poetry should offer no immediate instruction, that is as it should be, since art, said Pater in the conclusion to the *Renaissance*, "comes to you proposing frankly to give nothing but the highest quality to your moments as they pass, and simply for those moments' sake."

The move away from early Victorian preoccupations with literature and instruction continued in the final two decades of the century. James McNeill Whistler began his "Ten O'-Clock" lecture (1885) by confessing his "hesitation" in appearing as "The Preacher"—an ironic comment on the subject and manner of Carlyle's lectures given forty-five years earlier. Whistler takes to task, albeit obliquely, a number of Victorians who, he felt, had "maligned" art; the targets seem to be Ruskin, Arnold, and the Pre-Raphaelites. Whistler's aesthetic position is clear enough: art is "selfishly occupied with her own perfection only—having no desire to teach." In four essays collected in *Intentions* (1891), Oscar Wilde echoed Whistler's aestheticism but was more pessimistic than Whistler in his view of contemporary society. Beneath the aphorisms ("Meredith is a prose Browning, and so is Browning") and paradoxes ("Life imitates Art"), Wilde's pessimism emerges: "We ask [life] for pleasure. It gives it to us, with bitterness and disappointment in its train" ("The Critic as Artist, Part Two"). Given this grim reading, it seems appropriate for Wilde's persona Gilbert to claim that we should go to art "for everything" because art does not hurt us: "We weep, but we are not wounded. We grieve, but our grief is not bitter." Wilde would have us move, through our experiences in literature, into the artifice of eternity.

WILLIAM J. GRACIE, JR.

Bibliography

Buckley, Jerome Hamilton. *The Victorian Temper.* 1951.

Christ, Carol T. *Victorian and Modern Poetics.* 1984.

Starzyk, Lawrence J. *The Imprisoned Splendor.* 1977.

Warren, Alba H. *English Poetic Theory, 1825–1865.* 1950.

See also SERIAL LITERATURE

. . . . .

POLICE *see* LAW ENFORCEMENT

. . . . .

POOR LAW

The Victorian Poor Law aspired to ensure uniformity and efficiency in providing public relief and to promote moral reform of the pauper population. Certainly it fostered a bureaucracy and brought administrative innovations. It helped shape employment and migration patterns, and it aggravated class hostilities. Nevertheless, the Poor Law was neither uniform in its application nor notably efficient, and paupers seem to have been immune to its ideology. By the century's end many found it an embarrassing relic from a cruel and unenlightened era.

The New Poor Law (Poor Law Amendment Act) of 1834 was the product of utilitarian fervor, Ricardian economics, alarm at recent rural unrest, and a sequence of parliamentary inquiries into the perceived misapplication of poor relief. Since the Elizabethan age, poor relief had been the responsibility of each parish, which appointed its own overseers and raised funds by a rate (tax) levied on those who occupied land within the parish. Those unable to support themselves (orphans and the elderly or disabled) had a right to relief from the parish of their birth; provisions for the able-bodied were more complex although

The "Milk" of Poor-Law "Kindness"
by Joseph Kenny Meadows (1790–1874).
Punch, *January 1843.*

in theory they were required to do useful work in exchange for minimal support.

With the social dislocations of industrialization and enclosure, poor rates quadrupled between 1780 and 1820, and a series of parliamentary inquiries were mounted. Reformers agreed that outdoor allowances to the able-bodied and their families were responsible for the increase and for eroding a natural community of master and servant fixed by mutual responsibility, subordination, and industry. The bill's sponsors therefore urged that able-bodied persons should receive relief only in workhouses operated by the parish or by a union of parishes (the notorious "union workhouse" or "Poor Law Bastille"). Under the principle of "less eligibility" the standard of living provided in the **workhouse** was to be inferior to that of the lowest-paid worker. Inmates of the workhouse were to be housed in separate areas according to age and sex, married couples were separated, and until 1842 parents had no right to see their children. Between the ages of five and fourteen orphans and the children of paupers were to be lodged in separate Poor Law schools and could be hired out or apprenticed by the overseers. A further provision made mothers solely responsible for illegitimate children, replacing the earlier law which had provided a means of forcing men to contribute to the support of their bastards. The workhouse was intended as a deterrent that would drive shirkers to honest toil, promote thrift as a hedge against unemployment or illness, and discourage women from running the risk of extramarital pregnancy.

The 1834 Poor Law did not specifically mandate all of these provisions, for its framers assumed that the virtues of the universal workhouse test would be amply clear to local authorities and ratepayers. It did create a central Poor Law Commission and organized clusters of parishes into Poor Law Unions run by locally elected boards of guardians assisted by salaried officers. It applied only to England and Wales; Scotland's New Poor Law of 1845 perpetuated parish control and restricted relief to the truly destitute and disabled.

In England and Wales, administration of the New Poor Law was less uniform than its framers intended. Many of the newly elected guardians had been parish officers or members of parish select vestries under the old regime and retained their distrust of central authority. They discovered that outdoor relief was far cheaper than workhouse internment and more suited to both the seasonal labor patterns of the rural south and east and the boom-slump rhythms of the industrial Midlands and north. The cost of relief did indeed diminish, from 7 million pounds in 1831 to 4.6 million a decade later, but never were more than one-third of all able-bodied paupers in the workhouse; usually the figure was much less. As early as 1838 the commissioners backed away from imposing the workhouse test in the industrial north. Elsewhere guardians found loopholes that permitted outdoor relief to able-bodied men and women because of illness or "urgent necessity." Inevitably workhouses came to be populated by the elderly, sick, disabled, and child paupers. Eventually workhouses recognized their responsibility to these blameless poor and abandoned the "less eligibility" tenets of 1834.

The Poor Law Board (Goschen) Minute of 1869 and the Local Government Board circular of 1871 marked a renewed attack on outdoor relief, even (in the 1871 circular) for the aged and sick. But although some test workhouses were revived they did not survive the 1870s, and local relief practices depended, as before, on guardians' temperaments. Joseph Chamberlain's 1886 circular condemned the deliberately unpleasant and useless task work which often accompanied outdoor relief to the unemployed; he pronounced it degrading and urged that local authorities provide public employment without the pauper stigma.

Chamberlain's circular signaled a new attitude toward the relationship between state and citizen. Unemployment was increasingly perceived as a misfortune beyond any individual's control. Thoughtful people spoke of "poverty," not "pauperism," and demanded new remedies. The Unemployed Workmen Act of 1905 established special distress committees in urban areas to provide public works for the unemployed and set up labor exchanges. In 1909 two contradictory reports from the most recent royal commission on the Poor Laws could agree only that the Poor Law must be immediately recast. Nevertheless the Victorian Poor Law, although a discredited residual institution, lingered on until its belated abolition in 1948.

MARK NEUMAN

Bibliography

Brundage, Anthony. *The Making of the New Poor Law.* 1978.

Checkland, E. O. A. and S. G. Checkland, eds. *The Poor Law Report of 1834.* 1974.

Fraser, Derek, ed. *The New Poor Law in the Nineteenth Century.* 1976.

Henriques, Ursula R. Q. *Before the Welfare State: Social Administration in Early Industrial Britain.* 1979.

Knott, John. *Popular Opposition to the 1834 Poor Law.* 1986.

Rose, Michael E. *The English Poor Law, 1780-1930.* 1971.

———. *The Relief of Poverty, 1834-1914.* 1972.

———. ed. *The Poor and the City: The English Poor Law in Its Urban Context, 1834-1914.* 1985.

Webb, Sidney and Beatrice Webb. *English Poor Law History. Part 2: The Last Hundred Years.* 1929; rpt. 1963. 2 vols.

See also POVERTY

· · · · ·

POPULAR SHOWS AND EXHIBITIONS

In 1837 Victoria's subjects were entertained by a variety of exhibitions, ranging from the educative spectacle of the diorama to old-fashioned exploitation of human freaks and monstrous animals. By the end of her reign government-sponsored **museums** and institutes had taken over the more respectable subjects, the **music hall** captivated the multitudes, and the cinema, which began at the Empire Theatre in 1896, was clearly the coming thing. The peak years for exhibitors were between 1830 and 1860, though many offerings were duplicated as part of pleasure gardens, fairs, or theaters throughout the century. The center of the business was London; promoters then took their shows to other cities or abroad, although many successful exhibits, like those of P. T. Barnum (1810-1891), were American. A glance at one partic-

ular building, the Egyptian Hall in Piccadilly, will indicate the great variety of fare.

The Egyptian Hall, built in 1812, contained space for two to four exhibitions, with tickets for each about one shilling. The potential for profit was enormous; 35,000 pounds were paid to see Napoleon's carriage, captured at Waterloo (it was later purchased by Madame Tussaud's Wax Museum). In the 1830s exhibits included a giant model of the field at Waterloo, a mechanical reenactment of a lighthouse keeper's daughter, Grace Darling, rescuing mariners, and a band of dancing Egyptian "priestesses." (Exhibitions often allowed the religious to enjoy theatrical pleasures under the guise of education.) In 1840 the American George Catlin arrived with eight tons of Indian artifacts; after taking his show to Manchester, he added a troupe of Ojibbeway Indians, and returned to London for an extended run. Barnum arrived with his prize midget "Tom Thumb" in 1844; he then exhibited the "missing link," a creature called the "WHAT IS IT?"—but this hoax was quickly discovered. Genuine African Bushmen (1847) and two Mexican dwarfs, dubbed "Aztec Lilliputeans" (1853), demonstrated the public's interest in primitive races. But by the Queen's Jubilee (1887), when Buffalo Bill's Wild West show was the rage, "savages" had to be polished entertainers.

Other exhibits included mechanical wonders such as the "Eureka," a machine for writing Latin hexameter verses; exhibits of this kind, however, were usually found at the Polytechnic Institute, opened in 1838. Early dinosaur skeletons found a home at the Egyptian Hall in the 1840s, as did "General Washington," a gigantic horse which fell through the floor in 1845. Most exhibits depended on vigorous promotion, and showmen pioneered advertising on omnibuses and sandwich boards, and the use of half-price coupons.

Exhibitors at the Egyptian Hall and other spots, such as the "Cosmorama" (in Regent Street from 1823), occasionally found it profitable to show fine art, especially large splashy paintings of disasters or public ceremonies. Both John Martin (1789-1854) and Benjamin Haydon (1786-1846) exhibited at the hall; the latter's unhappy attempt to compete with "Tom Thumb" contributed to his suicide. More typically, a giant canvas (170 square feet! 800 portraits!) showing Parliament in

Death of the "Lion Queen," in Wombell's Menagerie, at Chatham. Illustrated London News, *19 January 1850. Library Company of Philadelphia.*

session did well in 1843, a statute of Venus followed in 1847, and heroic pictures of the soldiery in action appeared in 1860. After about 1865 the Egyptian Hall paled in comparison with newer attractions such as the Crystal Palace, the giant glass building from the Exhibition of 1851 that was moved to suburban Sydenham and enlarged; it hosted two million customers a year and was the forerunner of the modern amusement park. The Egyptian Hall remained open, however, until 1904, drawing customers to "Maskelyn and Cooke's Theatre of Mystery," a popular magic show.

The "Panorama" had been a fixture in Leicester Square since 1794; panoramas were giant circular paintings viewed from a central platform to provide maximum realistic illusion. The term was often used, however, for any large spectacle. The original Panorama (open until 1863) featured exotic cities ("Naples by Moonlight" in 1845) and topical views of battlefields, etc. Since the sole attraction was the picture, many panoramas were carefully painted. The "diorama" was the major rival; invented by Daguerre (also a pioneer of **photography**), it too required a special building. The London Diorama opened in 1823 in Regent's Park, and featured two pictures, each about 40 feet by 70 feet, that were painted on transparent cloth and subject to innovative lighting. The audience sat in a darkened auditorium that swiveled from one picture to the next. "Diorama" thus came to mean any spectacle accompanied by light and sound effects. Favorite subjects were cathedrals, picturesque landscapes, volcanic eruptions, shipwrecks, and fires; a famous "double effect" diorama depicted the alpine village of Alagna before and after an avalanche (1836). At the Royal Bazaar the "British Diorama" featured paintings by Clarkson Stanfield, R. A. (1793–1867), a leading theatrical scenepainter; at the "Colosseum" (Regent's park), a huge panorama of London from atop St. Paul's was but one of the attractions. In the 1840s and 1850s "moving panoramas"—strip-canvases unwound from spools— were popular travelogues; a 1,200 yard trip down the Mississippi caused a sensation at the Egyptian Hall in 1848. Later, storytelling showmen like Albert Smith (1816-1860) added the appeal of the stand-up comic to panoramic ascents of Mont Blanc or trips to India.

Throughout the period entertainments such as minstrel shows (the original "Jim Crow" was onstage in the 1830s), ventriloquists, and menageries had considerable appeal; fireworks were a major draw at pleasure gardens such as Vauxhall and Cremorne. The zoo was opened in 1828 in Regent's Park, and Edward Cross's Surrey Zoological Gardens combined beasts with fireworks and panoramas. In the late Victorian period, however, new institutions like the South Kensington (Victoria and Albert) Museum drew crowds away from private shows, and in the provinces, municipalities sponsored numerous exhibitions to show industrial products and puff civic pride. By the 1870s the movement for "rational recreation" provided new options for the working class, and the irrational found a new home: London in the 1870s had over 300 music halls. J. C. Merrick, the celebrated "Elephant Man" (1862-1890), spent only a short time in a freak show before finding enlightened care. Madame Tussaud's, however, remains popular today, and other descendants of Victorian shows are still found in battlefield "cycloramas," museum dioramas, and planetariums.

DAVID E. LATANÉ, JR.

Bibliography

Altick, Richard. *The Shows of London.* 1978.

Cottrell, Leonard. *Madame Tussaud.* 1951.

Fitzsimons, Raymund. *Barnum in London.* 1970.

———. *The Baron of Piccadilly: The Travels and Entertainments of Albert Smith, 1816-1860.* 1967.

Gernsheim, Helmut and Alison Gernsheim. *L. J. M. Daguerre: The History of the Diorama and the Daguerreotype.* 1968.

Luckhurst, Kenneth. *The Story of Exhibitions.* 1951.

See also AMUSEMENTS AND RECREATION: WORKING CLASS; CIRCUS; PENNY THEATERS

· · · · ·

POPULAR SONGS AND MUSIC

Popular music (that is, music requiring no special training for appreciation and little training for performance) took many forms in the Victorian period. With increasing urbanization, rural folk music was gradually absorbed into city life, expanding its subject matter accordingly. Broadside ballads became less prevalent in the second half of the century, though street singers continued to sell their topical songs. Mechanical improvements and lower prices brought the **piano** into an increasing number of middle-class homes, stimulating further demand for music suited to amateur performance. This was met from a variety of sources, including hymnals, songs from the theater and opera, drawing-room **ballads**, and other music designed for comparatively unskilled singers and players. Music publishers also began to sponsor concerts at which well-known singers were paid to introduce new songs.

Amateur music making on a larger scale was provided by many choral societies, particularly after 1840. Their work was made easier by simplified methods of music reading like the tonic sol-fa systems popularized by John Hullah (1812-1884) and John Curwen (1816-1880). Likewise, technical advances making brass and wind instruments cheaper and easier to play encouraged the formation of bands, particularly in industrial areas, where bands were sponsored by both factory owners and workers' associations.

Professional performances were also available to a wider audience. One new development was the promenade concert, resembling the concerts given at pleasure gardens and spas but modeled more directly on concerts given in Paris in 1833 by Philippe Musard (1793-1859). The first of these concerts was given in England in 1838 at the Lyceum Theatre. The most prominent figure in promoting them was the French-born Louis Jullien (1812-1860), who gave many series between 1840 and 1859. These programs included music by Beethoven and other serious composers as well as dance tunes, vocal and instrumental solos, and musical novelties. The Popular Concerts (known as the Monday and Saturday Pops), established in 1858 and continuing until 1898, were an outgrowth of the promenade concerts.

Other public musical entertainments included **music halls** and the theater. The former originated in the 1830s and 1840s in taverns with music licenses, in which communal singing was prominent, and in song and supper clubs featuring professional entertainers. The programs of ballads, minstrel acts, popular operatic selections, and comic pieces gradually expanded to include other acts. For the theater itself, in addition to providing operettas and incidental music to plays, composers wrote and arranged music for Christmas **pantomimes**, burlettas, burlesques, and parodies of successful plays and operas, and other extravaganzas.

The nineteenth century also saw the beginning of popular musical journalism. Specialized publications such as *The Singing Class Circular* (later *The Musical Times*) were established, and nonmusical magazines occasionally included a supplementary piece of music. Newspapers and other periodicals reviewed an increasing number of performances of popular as well as serious music.

JOE K. LAW

Bibliography

Disher, Maurice. *Victorian Songs, From Dive to Drawing Room.* 1955.

Lee, Edward. *Music of the People: A Study of Popular Music in Great Britain.* 1970.

Mackerness, E. D. *A Social History of English Music.* 1964.

Pearsall, Ronald. *Victorian Popular Music.* 1973.

Temperley, Nicholas, ed. *The Athlone History of Music in Britain: The Romantic Age 1800–1914.* 1981.

Vicinus, Martha. *The Industrial Muse.* 1974.

See also DANCE MUSIC; STREET MUSIC

. . . . .

POPULATION AND DEMOGRAPHICS

The most striking characteristic of nineteenth-century demography was the extraordinary increase in population. The first British census taken in 1801 counted nearly eleven million people. A hundred years later the figure stood at thirty-seven million, an unprecedented rise of more than 300 percent. Of equal importance for social, political, and economic history was the location and distribution of this expanding populace. In the early years of the century approximately 75 percent of the people lived in rural towns and villages, primarily in the agricultural south. At the end of the Victorian era virtually the same percentage lived in or around large cities, many of them in the industrial Midlands and the north, and Great Britain had become the most urbanized country in the West.

Despite the portentous warnings of Thomas Robert Malthus (1766–1834) that an unchecked population would inevitably outstrip its ability to feed itself, the British throughout most of the nineteenth century married and reproduced at an unprecedented rate. During much of Queen Victoria's reign the crude annual birthrate of her subjects in England and Wales averaged around 34.3 births per 1,000 of the population, while the fertility of married women age fifteen to forty-five averaged 288 per 1,000. These figures, which peaked in the 1870s, when the rates soared respectively to 36.3 and 304, translated into a typical family of five or six children.

Although the age at which women married gradually increased from around twenty-two to twenty-five in the second half of the century, the overall rate of marriage, which averaged 16 per 1,000 of the population annually, was higher than in most other Western countries and contributed to the rapid growth of population. If infant mortality remained depressingly high at approximately 150 per 1,000 births until the twentieth century, the general death rates fell by about 20 percent. Life expectancy correspondingly rose by nearly a third in the second half of the century, from 39.9 to 51.5 for men and from 41.9 to 55.4 for women. These aggregate trends, which varied from region to region and fluctuated at different times, added up to an increase in population that averaged nearly 14 percent a decade.

The last quarter of the century was marked demographically by the beginning of a persistent decline in the birthrate that was to last until World War II. After averaging a recorded decennial high of nearly 35.5 births per 1,000 in the 1870s the ratio steadily fell until by 1900 it hovered around 29, a fall of more than 21 percent. In the same period the number of children born each year to married women of childbearing age declined from 296 per 1,000 to under 240. The Victorian family of five or six offspring was rapidly giving way to its Edwardian successor of three or four. In the early years of the new century analysts of vital statistics calculated that somewhere between 300,000 and 500,000 fewer children were born each year than would have been the case if the birthrate had remained the same as in the mid-Victorian era.

Contemporaries were concerned by the socioeconomic differential characteristics of the decline. Throughout the first two-thirds of the century the fertility of all classes tended to be high and the differences quite modest. The unique Fertility of Marriage Census taken in 1911 showed, for example, that in the 1850s the most prolific groups in society, miners and agricultural workers, had on average only one or two more children than couples in the upper and professional middle classes. By the end of the century, however, the most fertile groups in society, primarily unskilled manual laborers, had nearly twice as many children as people in the educated classes. The inverse correlation between fertility and social status deeply troubled demographic analysts and the social critics who interpreted vital statistics to the public.

In trying to explain the declining birthrate, late Victorians looked to everything from biological to social and economic causes. Though some believed with Herbert Spencer (1820–1903) that diminishing fertility was a natural, progressive manifestation of the evolution of highly advanced civilizations and others thought it portended race deterioration and, possibly, "race suicide," most people recognized by the opening of the new century that the fall was a consequence of the rapid adoption of birth control practices. They associated "family limitation" with the economic problems and competitive challenges of the 1880s and 1890s and the desire of middle- and upper-class couples to maintain and improve their standard of living in a period of rising costs and curtailed opportunities.

Since the beginning of the decline coincided with the notorious 1877 obscenity trial of Charles Bradlaugh (1833–1891) and Annie Besant (1847–1933) for publishing an obscure **birth control** pamphlet, it was widely believed that the publicity surrounding the trial and the activites of the first birth control organization, the Malthusian League (1877–1927), which was established soon after, were somehow responsible. It now appears evident that a combination of economic, social, and cultural reasons led the last generation of Victorian men and women to turn away from the large families of their parents and grandparents and adopt a domestic pattern that continued and intensified throughout most of the twentieth century.

RICHARD A. SOLOWAY

Bibliography

Banks, Joseph. *Prosperity and Parenthood: A Study of Family Planning Among the Victorian Middle Classes*. 1954.

―――. *Victorian Values: Secularism and the Size of Families*. 1981.

Flinn, Michael. *British Population Growth 1700–1850*. 1970.

Mitchison, Rosalind. *British Population Change Since 1860*. 1977.

Soloway, Richard. *Birth Control and the Population Question in England, 1877–1930*. 1982.

Tranter, Neil. *Population Since the Industrial Revolution: The Case of England and Wales*. 1973.

Wrigley, E. A. and R. S. Schofield. *The Population History of England, 1541–1871: A Reconstruction*. 1981.

See also EMIGRATION

· · · · ·

PORNOGRAPHY

If John Cleland's *Fanny Hill* (or *The Memoirs of a Woman of Pleasure*, as it was known in 1751) denotes the classic work of pre-Victorian pornography, John S. Farmer's *The Way of a Man with a Maid* (1894?) defines the mode of Victorian pornography. There are significant differences: Cleland delights in bawdy without violence, a reciprocal round of fornication in which women play as active a role as men, but Farmer reduces the woman to a subject that is raped, beaten, and sodomized. Unlike Cleland's heroine, who always seeks redress when mistreated or deceived, Farmer's woman is routinely flogged into submission and then routinely asks for more. When the process of subjugation is complete, the female of Victorian pornography becomes the ally of her oppressor, a surrogate man like Dracula's vampires ready to assist her master in the entrapment of other women.

Although the Marquis de Sade undoubtedly inspired its rhetorical forms, Victorian pornography did not profess de Sade's philosophy of aesthetic purism and passional imperatives. The major Victorian works of pornography are singularly dull, uninspired, and derivative, consisting of little more than juxtaposed scenes of rape, singly or in groups, and the iteration of the delights of flogging. Contrary to Freud's belief that pornography was the representation of the fantasies of infantile sexual life manifested as homosexuality, there is little emphasis on homoeroticism in Victorian pornography. The first homosexual novel was *The Sins of the Cities of the Plain, or the Recollections of a Mary-Ann. With Short Essays on Sodomy and Tribadism* (1881), and specific homosexual incidents are rare in Victorian pornography.

Perhaps in response to social conditions—women's increasing demands for suffrage and marital reform, the campaign to abolish flogging in the public schools, the growing militance of trade unions—the Victorian pornographic novel establishes the absolute authority of the male protagonist. The most popular male role is the surgeon or the riding master who controls women with a knife or a whip. Women are reduced to animals and the limited imagery characterizes them as dogs or horses who must be made to take the bit and trained to show their paces.

The Victorian pornographic novel was safely kept from working-class hands by its price: 20 guineas was the average cost of a brown-wrapped volume printed in Brussels or Paris with a fake publisher's imprint and imported secretly into England. To evade the restrictions of the Obscene Publications Act (1857), considerable effort was made to conceal the authorship and place of publication. *The Amatory Experiences of a Surgeon*, for example, is stated to have been printed for the Nihilists in Moscow in 1881 although it was actually produced in Brussels. Works were often written in French by a specialist like Hugues Rebell (1868–1905) and translated into racy English by Charles Carrington's hired writers in Paris. From Paris and Brussels these works of uncompromising violence would find their way into upper-class male society in England. Similarly, salacious photographs printed in Paris or Brussels were sold for a guinea each in London.

It was not simply price that limited pornography's audience to the rich; the working class was regularly policed by a succession of social purity movements in the nineteenth century. Bawdy had been driven from the streets by clauses to the Vagrancy Act of 1824, and the Vice Society ensured that there was no open display of obscene goods. The Brighton postcard and the music hall skit became the customary form of working-class bawdy, but upper-class pornography was represented by works like *Birch in the Boudoir* and *The Romance of Lust*.

CORAL LANSBURY

Bibliography

Fryer, Peter, ed. *Forbidden Books of the Victorians.* 1970.

Lansbury, Coral. *The Old Brown Dog.* 1985.

Marcus, Steven. *The Other Victorians.* 1966.

Pearsall, Ronald. *The Worm in the Bud: The World of Victorian Sexuality.* 1969.

· · · · ·

POSITIVISM

The term "positivism" derives from the philosophical system of Auguste Comte who, in *Cours de philosophie positive* (1830–1842) and *Système de politique positive* (1851–1854), set forth a comprehensive theory of the historical development of human knowledge. Comte argued that humanity has moved through three stages of development: theological, metaphysical, and positive, having reached the scientifically based positive stage by the time of the industrial revolution. While society has progressed through these stages over the course of history, the progression is recapitulated in the mental life of each individual. Comte's positivist philosophy discounted metaphysics and revealed religion, arguing that all valid knowledge is based on verifiable propositions. Classifying the sciences in order of their complexity—mathematics as the most general, sociology (which Comte named) as the most specialized—positivists sought a complete system of empirical knowledge. Comte and his followers rejected traditional religion, substituting a "religion" based entirely on historical and sociological principles. The aim of this "religion of humanity'" was the improvement of the social condition of the human race.

Comte's influence was widespread on the Continent, but even more pervasive in England, during the last two decades of the nineteenth century. His English disciples included **John Stuart Mill**, who acknowledged his debt to Comte in his *System of Logic*, and **Frederic Harrison**, the social reformer whose essays in *The Fortnightly Review* helped popularize positivism in Britain. **G. H. Lewes** wrote one of the first books in English on Comte (1853), while positivist ideas are also evident in the work of **George Eliot** and **Harriet Martineau**. Many of those attracted to positivism were drawn by the suggestion that moral authority might be obtainable without religious belief, an idea Nietzsche critiques as "the dogma of the immaculate perception." Comte saw his own role as messianic; he was to be the first in a line of high priests of humanity.

To many Victorians, positivism represented a unified system that might explain all human knowledge: natural, social, and psychological. Comte's central principle, that the laws governing human thought and social life are merely a subclass of the laws that govern organic and inorganic nature, influenced a wide range of modern ideas, from historicism and predictive sociology to logical positivism and behaviorism. Comte's system itself, while drastically weakened by confusions and contradictions, generated a series of ideas that influenced Victorian thinking about social reorganization and human potential.

ASHTON NICHOLS

Bibliography

Lenzer, Gertrud, ed. *Auguste Comte and Positivism: The Essential Writings.* 1983.

Mill, John S. *Auguste Comte and Positivism.* 1865.

Simon, Walter M. *European Positivism in the Nineteenth Century.* 1963.

Vogeler, Martha S. *Frederic Harrison: The Vocations of a Positivist.* 1984.

· · · · ·

POSTAL SERVICES

The nineteenth century witnessed both the reform of postal rates and a massive expansion of services. Deliveries were frequent—up to twelve daily in central London where postage was two or three pence. Outside the capital, however, deliveries were fewer and rates usually based upon multiplying the number of letter sheets by distance traveled. Prepayment was less common than posting letters collect, often to the annoyance of the recipient.

In 1837 **Rowland Hill** (1795–1879), a Benthamite reformer, published *Post Office Reform*, in which he argued that cutting rates would raise volume and revenues, while promoting commerce and social communication. Parliament was persuaded, and in 1840 introduced both the adhesive postage stamp and a domestic rate of one penny for a half-ounce letter. This national "penny post" survived, with alterations in weight limit, until 1918, and was joined in 1898 by worldwide "imperial penny post."

Additional services introduced were a book post (1848), a halfpenny rate for postcards and printed papers (1870), and a parcel post (1883). Nationalization of telegraph companies in 1870 marked the beginning of the General Post Office's involvement in newer means of communication.

The growth of GPO financial services paralleled these developments. Postal money orders existed since the 1790s, but became an official service only in 1838. Cheap postal orders, payable on demand for small sums, were introduced in 1881. A successful Post Office Savings Bank was created by W. E. Gladstone (1861); life insurance and annuities were added (1864); and the GPO took over the sale of nonpostal licenses and revenue stamps (1880) and introduced a messenger service (1891).

The social and economic consequences of this transformation of postal services were widespread. Contracts to carry the mails helped subsidize the development of railway and shipping lines, while at the parochial level the local postmaster became the most visible dispenser of centralized government services.

N. MERRILL DISTAD

Bibliography

Daunton, Martin J. *Royal Mail: The Post Office Since 1840.* 1985.

Hill, Sir Rowland and George Birkbeck Hill. *The Life of Sir Rowland Hill and The History of Penny Postage.* 1880. 2 vols.

Robinson, Howard. *The British Post Office: A History.* 1948.
———. *Carrying British Mails Overseas.* 1964.

Staff, Frank. *The Penny Post, 1680–1918.* 1964.

See also PHILATELY

· · · · ·

Noel Moore. The growing market for children's books led her to revise it for publication. Rejected, it was published privately. She eventually secured as publisher Frederic Warne and Co., who produced twenty-three of her books.

Retreating to the Lake District following the death of her fiancé Norman Warne (1905), Potter used Hill Top Farm as a setting of many books. Upon her marriage to Ambleside solicitor William Heelis, she stopped writing except for occasional stories for American publishers. On her death, she bequeathed her lands to the National Trust.

CATHERINE J. GOLDEN

Bibliography

Lane, Margaret. *The Magic Years of Beatrix Potter.* 1978.

Linder, Leslie. *A History of the Writings of Beatrix Potter.* 1971.

Potter, Beatrix. *The Journal of Beatrix Potter from 1881 to 1897,* 1966. Ed. Leslie Linder.

Taylor, Judy. *Beatrix Potter: Artist, Storyteller and Craftswoman.* 1986.

· · · · ·

POTTER, BEATRIX (1866–1943)

Author and illustrator of over thirty books for young children, Beatrix Potter is best known for her first work, *The Tale of Peter Rabbit* (1901). In the best English watercolor tradition her endearing illustrations realistically depict countryside animals. Her masterpieces include *The Tailor of Gloucester* (1902) and *The Tale of Mrs. Tiggy-Winkle* (1905).

Helen Beatrix Potter was born in London on July 28, 1866. Her affluent parents were authoritarian, even by mid-Victorian standards. Writing and drawing enlivened her lonely, repressed childhood. Annual visits to Scotland and the Lake District gave her an opportunity to draw botanical specimens and even to dissect and study dead animals. Her famous story about a playfully disobedient rabbit began as a picture letter (September 4, 1893) to her former governess's ailing son,

POTTERY AND POTTERY WORKERS

Although an older historiography, following Samuel Smiles, made Josiah Wedgwood and his establishment of the Etruria factory in 1769 almost exclusively the agent of modernization in the pottery industry, the judgment is both too late and too early. From the beginning of the eighteenth century there were significant breakthroughs in the industry's technology and its ability to exploit both national and international markets. Wedgwood achieved factory manufacture but not mechanized production. He did, however, apply comprehensive logistical thought to the pottery trade. He wisely built the Etruria Factory on the banks of the Trent and Mersey Canal and applied the principle of division of labor to the potter's art. The old general laborer gave way to a series of specialists trained to perform one task only.

Wedgwood worked in earthenware, especially the improved creamware called "queensware" after 1765, black basalt, and jasper unglazed stonewares. Others sought by experiment with hard- and soft-paste porcelains to imitate imported wares from the Far East. Josiah Spode established the distinctiveness of British manufacture with his invention of bone china, the hybrid porcelain that came to dominate fine china production in Britain. Decoration by transfer print had been used since the mid-eighteenth century. In the 1840s the technology of multicolored printing was mastered, although it remained common practice to fill in outline prints by hand well into the twentieth century.

After the death of the first Josiah, Wedgwoods tended to overrely upon the achievements of the first period; not until Emile Lessore began to design for the firm in the early 1860s did Wedgwoods again take a lead in the artistic development of the pottery industry. Meanwhile standards of excellence in fine china manufacture had been set by others: Spode-Copelands, Mintons, Davenports, and the Ridgway brothers.

Useful ware was made in china, earthenware, and what would now be advertised as "oven-to-table" ironstone. Decorative ceramics were enhanced by the introduction of parian by Copelands about 1845; it was used to make figures with a marblelike finish. A little later Leon Arnoux, art director at Mintons, introduced a wide range of highly colored glazes used for decorative wares that were commonly called majolica. From the 1860s fashion favored the "art pottery" first produced by the Doulton Company and Mintons in their London studio and later taken up by William Moorcroft and other Staffordshire manufacturers.

The pottery district also produced industrial and sanitary goods. From the 1850s firms like Twyfords and Doultons manufactured plumbing fixtures in glazed earthenware. During the last third of the century, new technology brought business to the pottery industry in the form of porcelain insulators and fittings.

In the late eighteenth century Josiah Wedgwood was intent on creating a new labor force: "to make such machines of the men as cannot err." He coupled that demand with the best that paternalistic management could offer: housing, education for workers and their children, and health care (especially important in an industry where silica dust in the atmosphere and lead in the glazes both contributed to early mortality). Some were happy to accept the improvements, but other workers challenged industrial paternalism. The first potters' union emerged in 1824 to campaign against payment in truck, reductions in piecework prices, and payment limited to "good from oven" ware, but its organization was not adequate to the task. The union was resurrected in 1830, adding the issue of Martinmas hirings (which committed an employee to an employer for a year, even if no work was provided) to the list of grievances. The manufacturers overreacted and polarization of interests led to the great strike and lockout of 1836–1837. Once again the union was defeated by the united strength of the manufacturers supported by officers of the law.

In the aftermath of the Chartist-inspired Plug Plot riots of 1842, fifty-four potters and miners were sentenced to transportation. In 1843 William Evans organized the United Branches of Operative Potters. Fear of mechanization led Evans to launch a scheme for emigration to Pottersville, Wisconsin, where potters would set themselves to work as agriculturalists. Although Evans's cooperative scheme was no more successful than earlier union efforts, craft unions did survive in the separate pottery trades and in the 1850s began to protect their interests through arbitration procedures.

Unionization in the pottery trade was less successful than in other industries because of the general depression of the trade in the 1870s, increasing mechanization, and the failure of unions to admit or organize women workers, who made up some 50 percent of the total work force at the end of the century. Moreover, if unions faced a formidable task in the large factories, their difficulties in the small potbanks which came and went throughout the century were far greater.

J. H. Y. BRIGGS

Bibliography

Burchill, Frank and Richard Ross. *A History of the Potters' Union.* 1977.

Jewitt, Llewallyn. *The Ceramic Art of Great Britain*. 1878. 2 vols.

Mankowitz, Wolf and Reginald G. Haggar. *The Concise Encyclopedia of English Pottery and Porcelain*. 1957.

Owen, Harold. *The Staffordshire Potter*. 1901.

Shaw, Charles. *When I Was a Child*. 1903.

Thomas, John. *The Rise of the Staffordshire Potteries*. 1971.

. . . . .

POVERTY

Although there was a general improvement in the living conditions of the British working class in the second half of the nineteenth century, widespread poverty persisted. Its incidence varied with economic trends and the state of trade, but throughout the era poverty bore most heavily on the unskilled and was rooted in low pay and irregular employment.

Although the agricultural revolution increased food production, it also stimulated an expansion of Britain's population and made even the rural population dependent on the market for food. Enclosure deprived rural workers of their ability to adequately supplement their cash labor. During the same period, advancing industrialization led to declining possibilities for cottage labor.

In response to the misery brought about by the bad harvests of 1793 to 1795, the Berkshire justices of the peace, meeting in Speenhamland, decided to supplement workers' incomes which did not reach a minimum level with a dole that varied according to the price of bread and the size of families. The "Speenhamland system," although not universally adopted, became common in the agricultural South and West for forty years. Employers decreased wages since they would be supplemented by relief, and there was no difference between the material standards of industrious workers and slaggards. Since the amount of relief was tied to the size of the family and relief could be obtained only in one's parish of "settlement," the system aggravated rural overpopulation and immobility, two causes of poverty.

Constantly rising poor rates led to the Poor Law Amendment Act of 1834, which remained the basis of relief in Britain until World War I. In theory, although not in practice, the 1834 **Poor Law** ended "outdoor relief" for all but the "deserving poor" (i.e., the aged, blind, and orphans) and made all relief "less eligible" (that is, lower) than the lowest wages. The law punished and stigmatized the poor, who were broadly blamed for their own condition.

Many did suffer from self-inflicted wounds, of which drink was the most prominent. Although G. R. Porter undoubtedly exaggerated when, in 1850, he claimed that the lower-paid workers spent half their income on drink and more highly paid workers one third, per capita consumption of beer and spirits did rise during the nineteenth century to a peak in 1875–1876.

Poverty was, however, largely a product of economic forces and of the social environment created by those forces. The principle sources of poverty were low wages, unemployment or underemployment, and personal circumstances. Most unskilled workers experienced bouts of desperate poverty at various times in their lives: when there were a number of young children in a family, at times of illness, with the death of a principal wage earner, and during physical decline and old age.

Poverty in nineteenth-century Britain did not simply mean that workers could not save for periods of slack employment. It meant that the aggregate family income, even in good times, was either insufficient or barely sufficient to provide the family a subsistence living. Basically, it meant hunger.

Bread was for the British working class in the first half of the century the staple of life. Workers in 1840 spent an average of 17 to 39 percent of their income on bread. In addition to bread, or as a substitute for it in particularly hard times, potatoes and oatmeal completed the diet of the poorest workers. At the beginning of the Victorian era meat was seldom consumed by the unskilled. Even in prosperous times many workers could not regularly afford meat, and when consumed, it most frequently appeared only as bacon used to flavor potatoes. The wages of unskilled and casual workers and workers in declining or sweated trades were almost totally expended in paying for necessities. At the end of the century, when an unskilled worker provided a family's sole income, the family was almost invariably un-dernourished. Children might be fed for months solely on bread and a weak tea made from reused leaves. The cost of food was exacerbated by dependence on shopkeepers' credit and the necessity of purchasing food in small and therefore more expensive quantities.

Overcrowding was another persistent problem. Clearance or "ventilation" projects only drove the poor to other overcrowded and fetid slums. In the 1840s, ordinary **housing** for a worker's family in Leeds consisted of 150 square feet. It was not uncommon for seven or eight people to sleep in a single room. Inadequate sanitary provisions persisted at least through the 1880s in the overcrowded courts and back streets inhabited by the poor. At the middle of the century, in parts of Manchester, two hundred people had to share a single outhouse. Privies often overflowed and occasionally seeped into cellar dwellings. For more than half of the Victorian period, water was not easily accessible to the poor. Poorer districts of London were supplied by tanks or standpipes, making the fetching of even drinking water a burden. In these surroundings, disease ravaged the undernourished young. Of the babies born in Liverpool in 1851, only about 45 percent survived to the age of twenty. Hippolyte Taine characterized the poor Irish quarter of Liverpool in the 1860s as "the nethermost circle of Hell." His characterization could certainly be extended beyond Liverpool, and well past the 1860s.

Aggregate pauper statistics do not provide an accurate measure of the extent of poverty. Peter Stearns estimates that in 1800 as many as two-thirds of the British lived on the margins of subsistence. Many who were genuinely poor did not seek assistance or were not accorded it. The statistics are nevertheless striking. In 1802, one out of nine of England's inhabitants, one million people, were paupers or recipients of relief. Of these, 700,000 were permanently dependent upon relief, including 300,000 children, 165,000 old or disabled people, and 200,000 adults who were incapable of surviving without continual assistance. There were 3,700 workhouses which contained 83,000 individuals. In 1850, 10 percent of England's population were still classified as paupers.

The extent of poverty can be better gauged by studies that use broader criteria than re-ceipt of relief. Charles Booth, in his 1891 study, estimated that 30.7 percent of London's population lived in poverty, or serious want, having to struggle in order to obtain the necessities of life. According to Booth, the situation of 7.5 percent of the population was truly desperate; they lived in a state of chronic want. Seebohm Rowntree, in his survey of conditions in York in 1899, found that 21.5 percent of the population lived in poverty and 9.9 percent in "primary poverty." This 9.9 percent did not have enough food to maintain bare physical stamina. The recruiting statistics for the Boer War confirm the existence of this pathetic underclass: one-third of the men examined were rejected as unfit for military service.

A considerable number of working people were unable, even when fully employed, to provide their families with a consistent subsistence diet. At the beginning of the Victorian period one of the most notorious examples was that of the cotton weavers who made less than one-pence an hour. Even when fully employed, their condition was miserable. In over half of the York families categorized by Rowntree as living in "primary poverty" all working-age members of the family were regularly employed. Their earnings, however, were too meager to provide even collectively a minimum of 21 shillings a week, Rowntree's 1899 benchmark of "primary poverty" for a family of five.

In periods of economic downturn, even some artisans and skilled workers were reduced to want, and many of the unskilled became dependent on public or private assistance or went entire days without anything for the family to eat. In addition to the large cyclical movements of the economy, casual and seasonal workers were subjected to intermittent, though persistent, shortages of food.

At the end of the Victorian era, there was still widespread and deep poverty in Britain. The percentage of poor had declined significantly, to less than a third of the population. In 1901, however, in absolute numbers, there were more people in Britain who lived in poverty than in 1800.

BERNARD A. COOK

Bibliography

Booth, Charles. *Life and Labour of the People of London.* 1892–1895.

Engels, Friedrich. *The Condition of the Working Class in England*. 1845; rpt. 1958.

Fraser, Derek, ed. *The New Poor Law in the Nineteenth Century*. 1976.

Mayhew, Henry. *London Labour and the London Poor*. 1861–1862. 4 vols.

Reader, W. J. *Life in Victorian England*. 1964.

Rose, Michael E., ed. *The Poor and the City: The English Poor Law in Its Urban Context, 1834–1914*. 1895.

Rowntree, S. *Poverty: A Study of Town Life*. 1902.

Thompson, E. P. and Eileen Yeo. *The Unknown Mayhew*. 1973.

Treble, J. W. *Urban Poverty in Britain*. 1979.

See also COST OF LIVING; FOOD AND DIET; WAGES

· · · · ·

PRE-RAPHAELITE BROTHERHOOD

In September of 1848 seven young men, full of youthful idealism and critical of contemporary art and academic training, banded together to form the Pre-Raphaelite Brotherhood. Despite their youth, they were destined to become the most famous and influential movement in the history of British painting. At their first meeting two of the members, **John Everett Millais** and William Michael Rossetti, had yet to reach their twentieth birthday. Even the two oldest members, the painter James Collinson and the sculptor Thomas Woolner, were only twenty-three. Woolner, Collinson, Millais and **William Holman Hunt** had exhibited at the Royal Academy, but **Dante Gabriel Rossetti** and Frederic George Stephens had yet to finish their first painting. Woolner, Collinson and the Rossettis wrote poetry; Dante Gabriel Rossetti had even published a book of translations from early Italian poets. In W. M. Rossetti's reminiscence the members of the brotherhood "were really like brothers, continually together." The monthly meetings had a "focus of boundless companionship, pleasant and

touching to recall." The group began to dissolve as early as 1850 with the resignation of Collinson. In 1853 the regular meetings ceased and W. M. Rossetti discontinued the PRB journal in which he had documented the group's activities. The members went their separate ways, never to recapture their early closeness and camaraderie. By that time, however, the Pre-Raphaelites had won recognition, had exhibited influential, if controversial, works of art and had produced four issues of their periodical, *The Germ*. The brotherhood and their associates provided poems, stories, articles, reviews, and illustrations for this short-lived, early "little magazine."

The fact that the activities of this youthful group had an impact on art reaching well into the twentieth century is due to its three most gifted and imaginative members, D. G. Rossetti, Hunt, and Millais. Their paintings not only won attention and acclaim in their own time but continue to fascinate. Rossetti also gained recognition as a major poet and attracted followers and biographers with his charismatic personality. Although they did not achieve the same level of fame, W. M. Rossetti and Stephens helped to keep the goals of the brotherhood in the public eye through their writings about the PRB and the many art and literary reviews they wrote for major periodicals. By the late 1850s the paintings of at least a dozen young artists began to show the influence of the Pre-Raphaelites.

The goals of the Pre-Raphaelites, stated at some length in the pages of the *Germ*, lacked philosophical unity and clarity, but were expressed with a sincerity and fervor which is still endearing. Two goals emerge as the guiding precepts of all good writers and artists: the close study of nature and the genuine and heartfelt expression of ideas. They saw these precepts as a challenge to the practices of the Royal Academy schools which required students to draw from casts of the antique and to study the masters of the Renaissance. Both precepts, the brotherhood believed, had been embraced by medieval artists, but were rejected by the later artists of the Renaissance. The brotherhood wished to recapture the spirit of these early painters, a spirit closely allied to simple and sincere religious devotion. The paintings of **Ford Madox Brown**, who had studied the German Nazarenes, and the writings of John Ruskin, who also revered the close study of nature, helped to influence these goals.

The medieval subjects, the bright colors and the close attention to details—both in their meticulous delineation and their symbolic signification—differentiated the Pre-Raphaelite works from most contemporary paintings adorning the walls of the annual exhibitions. In 1849 the first paintings exhibited with the initials PRB received mild praise from the critics, but the next year, in 1850, when the meaning of the initials PRB had been revealed, the critics became more hostile. With Victorian religious controversy at its height, the medieval and religious subjects chosen by the brotherhood alerted critics to possible Tractarian and Roman Catholic sympathies. Furthermore, reviewers were bothered by the awkwardness and the unconventional appearance of the figures produced by such a close study of nature. John Ruskin came to the defense of this youthful and idealistic brotherhood beset by hostile critics, helping to explain their art and justify their goals. In the ensuing years a better understanding of the PRB, their shift to more secular and modern themes, and the decline of religious controversy allowed a greater acceptance of their work.

Although their controversial paintings gained them more attention, their drawings and graphic illustrations were just as revolutionary. Even before the formation of the PRB some of the members had met together to draw and to criticize one another's works. These sessions had led to a consistency of style in their drawings never equaled in their paintings. Hunt, D. G. Rossetti, and particularly Millais, in their innovative book and periodical illustrations greatly influenced graphic work in the 1860s and 1870s.

In 1857 a second manifestation of the Pre-Raphaelite ideals flowered in Oxford. Rossetti and six young men met to paint frescoes of medieval subjects on the walls of the Oxford Union. Among the group were **Edward Burne-Jones** and **William Morris** who, in the course of the nineteenth century, became the major progenitors of the **aesthetic movement** and the **arts and crafts movement**, both of which owed much to the original Pre-Raphaelite Brotherhood.

HELENE ROBERTS

Bibliography

Bell, Quentin. *A New and Noble School: The Pre-Raphaelites.* 1982.

Fredeman, William E. *Pre-Raphaelitism: A Bibliocritical Study.* 1965.

Hunt, William Holman. *Pre-Raphaelitism and the Pre-Raphaelite Brotherhood.* 1914.

Journal of Pre-Raphaelite Studies. 1980-.

Rossetti, William Michael. *The PRB Journal.* 1975. Ed. William E. Fredeman.

Sambrook, James, ed. *Pre-Raphaelitism: A Collection of Critical Essays.* 1974.

Tate Gallery, London. *The Pre-Raphaelites.* 1984.

Wood, Christopher. *The Pre-Raphaelites.* 1981.

See also PALGRAVE, FRANCIS TURNER

. . . . .

PRESERVATION OF MONUMENTS AND BUILDINGS

Conflicting with Victorian efforts to preserve for the public benefit important segments of Britain's historic heritage was profound respect for the sanctity of private property. Threats to prehistoric monuments, such as earthworks, burial mounds, and stone circles, entered public awareness in 1871, when the stone circle at Avebury, threatened with destruction by its owner, was purchased and saved by John Lubbock (1834–1913). Lubbock in 1873 introduced the first ancient monuments protection bill, which, as finally enacted in 1882 after restructuring by George John Shaw-Lefevre (1831–1928), allowed, but did not oblige, owners of sixty-eight listed ancient monuments, and of unlisted monuments judged similar, to place those monuments under state protection. Within eight years, the first inspector of ancient monuments, archaeologist Augustus Lane Fox Pitt-Rivers (1827–1900), Lubbock's father-in-law, had arranged with private owners for state protection of sixty-three monuments. An amending act of 1900 extended the act's provisions to any structure, no longer necessarily prehistoric, judged to be of historic or artistic interest; but not until passage of further legislation in 1913 (seventy-six years after parallel action in France) could a structure be protected without the owner's consent. Lubbock was instrumental in 1896 in launching the London County Council's survey of London, designed as a first step in identifying structures worthy of preservation, which supplied a model for work begun nationally in 1908 by the Royal Commission on Historical Monuments.

Misguided attempts at restoration were often as destructive as deliberate demolition or long-term decay, a fact behind the suggestion made to the Select Committee on National Monuments (1841) that a committee be created to advise on repair and preservation. A similar suggestion by John Ruskin in 1854, which led in the short run only to the creation by the Society of Antiquaries (1717) of an ineffective Conservation Fund, came to ultimate fruition in 1877 when William Morris (1834-1896) founded the Society for the Protection of Ancient Buildings (SPAB), familiarly known as "Anti-Scrape" to indicate their abhorrence of the common restorative practice of removing plaster from walls. The direct inspiration for the SPAB was the announcement of planned restoration at Tewkesbury Abbey by **George Gilbert Scott** (1811-1878), the architect already responsible for overzealous work on cathedrals, including Oxford, Chester, and Worcester, and numerous parish churches. The small but active, influential, and well-publicized SPAB advised architects and incumbents on methods of prolonging the useful life of medieval churches without destroying their artistic or structural integrity or removing the patina of age. Supporters of Morris, the dominant figure in the early SPAB, included the architect Philip Webb (1831-1915) and Thackeray Turner (1853-1937), executive secretary from 1883 to 1912. By the end of the Victorian period the SPAB had expanded its interest beyond ecclesiastical structures. Later it began to concern itself with Georgian and even Victorian buildings. The SPAB seldom acquired property itself, but cooperated closely with the National Trust (1895), which listed among its objectives the acquisition and preservation of buildings, in-

itially primarily medieval, of beauty or historic interest.

JOHN RANLETT

Bibliography

Evans, Joan. *A History of the Society of Antiquaries.* 1956.

Fawcett, Jane, ed. *The Future of the Past: Attitudes to Conservation, 1174-1974.* 1976.

Fedden, Robin. *The Continuing Purpose: A History of the National Trust, Its Aims and Work.* 1968.

Kennet, Wayland. *Preservation.* 1972.

• • • • •

PRESS, POLITICAL

The modern political press emerged in Britain following the repeal of the restrictive stamp tax and the duties on advertisements and paper during the period just after midcentury, and as a result of growing mass literacy and of developments in technology and distribution, including the telegraph, extensions of railways and roads, and the establishment of news agencies. As Stephen Koss notes in *The Rise and Fall of the Political Press in Britain*, these events "created a new forum for national debate by according newspapers a vastly enlarged readership and, consequently, an enhanced potential for political life" and thereby marked "the beginning of a new era in the political conduct of the press."

What followed was an enhancement in prestige for some existing newspapers (such as the *Times*) and a vast expansion of urban and provincial newspapers and periodicals which provided an unprecedented opportunity for politicians to spread their views. With the cooperation of most newspaper proprietors, editors, and journalists, politicians and political parties used (as never before) the daily and weekly press to publicize and execute party programs and to promote their political fortunes. Inevitably, this symbiotic relationship became a major factor in shaping alliances in Parliament and politics in the parliamentary constituencies, and in affecting patterns of political behavior. The alliance between politics and the press was also facilitated by the development of more comprehensive and efficient party organizations which, for self-interest or ideological reasons, attracted journalists.

For political parties and movements, newspapers provided the most convenient and effective means to convey information—and sometimes to suppress news prejudicial to the party. Thus it was deemed necessary for political groups to have the support of one or more organs of the press through which they could communicate to the electorate, to foreign governments, and to each other, and vilify their opponents. The chosen journals gained prestige and importance, since editors and journalists had the opportunity to become involved in political affairs, secrets, and even intrigue. Editors, leader writers, and newspaper proprietors were courted by politicians and became mouthpieces and apologists for their political patrons. The rewards for journalists were social acceptability, honors, and a professional status much greater than they had possessed at the beginning of the Victorian era.

Gradually, the daily and weekly press aspired to create public opinion and, as Koss asserts, achieved a "respectability" and "a heightened self-consciousness and sophistication" which it had previously lacked. As partisanship became a major feature of the Victorian press and newspapers proclaimed themselves as Tory, Liberal, radical, or socialist, the press was viewed by the public, the politicians, and itself as wielding far more power than it really had. This was more true of the London newspapers (which essentially constituted the national press) than of their provincial counterparts, which had experienced the greatest growth and generally reflected the politics of the metropolitan papers. But both the London and provincial press had overexpanded, and by the close of the century were declining in numbers and circulation.

The last two decades of the Victorian era were marked by the emergence of the "new journalism," with its sensational revelations and agitations, personal interviews, special articles, lively literary and dramatic criticism, investigative reporting, illustrations, attractive format for easy reading, and even more pronounced political partisanship. But these were also years in which newspaper proprietors (frequently members of Parliament) often financed journals from their own resources, operating at a loss in order to serve their party's interests or promote their own political aspirations. Such proprietors were able to maintain "no profit" newspapers because as sole owners they were not obliged to produce revenue for shareholders.

This situation began changing during the 1890s when more innovative proprietors (such as Alfred Harmsworth) demonstrated that a newspaper could both make a profit and accrue power and influence for its owner. Nevertheless, despite severe strains and tribulations, the partnership between press and politics forged during the Victorian decades survived well into the twentieth century.

J. O. BAYLEN

Bibliography

Boyce, George et al., eds. *Newspaper History.* 1978.

Brown, Lucy. *Victorian News and Newspapers.* 1985.

Cranfield, Geoffrey Alan. *The Press and Society from Caxton to Northcliffe.* 1978.

Herd, Harold. *The March of Journalism: The Story of the British Press from 1622 to the Present Day.* 1952.

Jones, Kennedy. *Fleet Street and Downing Street.* 1920.

Koss, Stephen. *The Rise and Fall of the Political Press in Britain: The Nineteenth Century.* 1981.

Lee, Alan J. *The Origins of the Popular Press, 1855–1914.* 1976.

Massingham, Henry William. *The London Daily Press.* 1892.

Wiener, Joel H., ed. *Innovators and Preachers: The Role of the Editor in Victorian England.* 1985.

. . . . .

PRESS, POPULAR

Between 1840 and 1900 a popular press developed in Britain. It reflected the economic and cultural changes that were slowly transforming the nation into a democracy and established the basis for twentieth-century mass journalism.

Before the mid-nineteenth century most newspapers and periodicals were conservative in makeup and content and limited in circulation. They gave extensive coverage to parliamentary news and tended to ignore feature stories. And as was true of the *Times*, the most influential of the newspapers, their leader (i.e., editorial opinion) columns occupied a large amount of space.

Changes in midcentury resulted in a great increase in readership and a revolution in the content of the press. The successful war against the **"taxes on knowledge"** led to a drastic lowering of the price of newspapers and magazines. The repeal of the remaining penny stamp duty in 1855 brought many cheap provincial and London newspapers into existence, of which the most important was the one-penny *Daily Telegraph* (1855–). Rotary printing presses increased the speed of production. The substitution of wood pulp for cotton rags brought a substantial drop in the price of newsprint. Beginning in the 1850s, use of the telegraph to transmit dispatches lowered costs and transformed news coverage. Equally important was the steady expansion of literacy. As millions of new readers emerged, it became possible to meet their demands for reading matter at prices that could still generate a profit.

The first newspapers to reflect these changes were the Sunday and weekly papers of the 1840s. The *Weekly Times*, the *News of the World*, and *Lloyd's Weekly Newspaper*, all founded during this decade, emphasized subjects of popular interest and made effective use of woodcuts. They amassed circulations in the hundreds of thousands. Then, in the 1860s, the *Daily Telegraph* gave a further stimulus to popular journalism. It featured an easy style of writing and was less serious than its chief competitor, the *Times*. Among its leading writers was **George Augustus Sala** (1828–1895), one of the best popular journalists of the age.

Yet it was not until the 1880s that the most important innovations took place. The beginnings of the "new journalism" (the term was originated by Matthew Arnold) are discernable in this decade in the pages of the *Pall Mall Gazette*, the *Star*, and other newspapers. "New journalists" like **William T. Stead**

(1849–1912) and T. P. O'Connor (1848–1929) introduced cross-headings, personal interviews, star advertising, women's columns, sports coverage, gossip, and a greater attention to crime reports. In 1885 Stead made the *Pall Mall Gazette* famous when he published a series of sensational articles about child prostitution entitled "The Maiden Tribute of Modern Babylon"; O'Connor greatly aided the *Star's* circulation by extensive coverage of the "Jack the Ripper" murders in 1888.

In the 1890s popular journalism became mass journalism. Three great press proprietors—George Newnes (1851–1910), Cyril A. Pearson (1866–1921), and Alfred Harmsworth (later Lord Northcliffe) (1865–1922)—were responsible for most of the changes that transformed the popular press into a vehicle of commercialism as well as communication. Newnes anticipated the revolution in journalism in 1881 with the publication of *Tit-Bits*, which featured potted summaries of the news and clever "stunts" designed to advertise the paper. Within a short period, this penny weekly achieved an unprecedented circulation of 900,000. Pearson established weekly and monthly magazines which owed much of their success to prize competitions. But the outstanding press lord of the century was Harmsworth. He catered to the new mass market with journals like *Answers* (modeled on *Tit-Bits*), *Comic Cuts* (for children), *Home Chat* (for housewives), and the *Daily Mail*, a halfpenny evening newspaper founded in 1896. Proclaiming itself to be the "Busy Man's Daily Journal," the *Daily Mail* had minimal parliamentary coverage; it featured political and other gossip and fiction in serialized form. It was a far cry from the stolid pages of the midcentury *Times*, and within four years its circulation had reached the threshold of nearly one million daily readers.

By 1900 the press had been wholly transformed since the beginning of Victoria's reign. Improvements in technology, as well as better methods of communicating and distributing news and newspapers, made this revolution possible. A new market for journalism existed which was representative of the nation at large. The age of the mass newspaper had begun.

JOEL H. WIENER

Bibliography

Altick, Richard D. *The English Common Reader: A Social History of the Mass Reading Public, 1800–1900.* 1957.

Boyce, George et al., eds. *Newspaper History: From the Seventeenth Century to the Present Day.* 1978.

Brendon, Piers. *The Life and Death of the Press Barons.* 1982.

Brown, Lucy. *Victorian News and Newspapers.* 1985.

Burnham, Lord. *Peterborough Court: The Story of the "Daily Telegraph."* 1955.

Cranfield, G. A. *The Press and Society: From Caxton to Northcliffe.* 1976.

Herd, Harold. *The March of Journalism: The Story of the British Press from 1622 to the Present Day.* 1952.

Lee, Alan J. *The Origins of the Popular Press, 1855–1914.* 1976.

Pound, Reginald and Geoffrey Harmsworth. *Northcliffe.* 1959.

Williams, Francis. *Dangerous Estate: The Anatomy of Newspapers.* 1957.

·　·　·　·　·

PRESS, PROVINCIAL

Provincial newspapers constitute an indispensable source for the political and social history of Victorian Britain—a history to which they made their own significant contribution. The importance of provincial cities and county society in Victorian political culture should not be underestimated. The concerns and aspirations of these communities were articulated in the columns of the hundreds of provincial dailies, and thousands of local weeklies, published in this period.

The history of the Victorian provincial press is in many respects a microcosm of the history of Victorian Britain. Provincial newspapers were beneficiaries of technological progress (steam power, railways, the telegraph), of the self-improvement ethic (taxes on the press were significantly dubbed the "**taxes on knowledge**"), and of the entrepreneurial ideal (newspapers being both an avenue for personal enrichment and a medium for advertising other ventures). The provincial press provides a paradigm of the Victorian idea of progress. The first major advance was the reduction of the newspaper stamp tax from fourpence to one penny in 1836; thereafter provincial weekly newspapers could afford larger dimensions, fuller coverage, and cheaper selling prices. The formation of the Provincial Newspaper Society in 1837 testified to the local significance, and wider aspirations, of its founding members. The stamp tax and related duties, however, still impeded the birth of a daily press in the provinces. After abolition of the advertisement duty in 1853, the stamp tax in 1855, and the paper duty in 1861 the provincial daily press made rapid progress. Established weeklies were refounded as dailies, and new dailies were launched.

Civic pride and political rivalry encouraged the proliferation of local newspapers. The Press Association, founded by leading provincial proprietors in 1868, was transformed in 1870 into a telegraphic news agency, providing comprehensive coverage of home and parliamentary news. Reuter's supplied foreign news, and the more enterprising provincial dailies used their own special correspondents and private telegraphic wires. A study of any leading provincial morning paper of the 1870s or 1880s—the *Birmingham Daily Post*, the *Manchester Guardian*, or the *Newcastle Daily Chronicle*—will reveal the very high quality of national and international news coverage, and of editorial writing, during the "golden age" of the provincial press.

The penny morning papers were soon associated with, or challenged by, provincial evening papers, commonly selling at one halfpenny. Less weighty in tone and content, these still provided a good general coverage, appealing to serious-minded working people. Proprietors and editors were men of consequence, some serving as members of Parliament. The columns of their newspapers were a potent campaign weapon, both at election times and on other occasions when "public opinion" (which, in practical terms, meant provincial press comment more than anything else) was especially aroused.

The liberal, pluralistic ideal of the press experienced severe stress in the closing decade of Victoria's reign. Spectacular advances in printing technology entailed heavy capital outlay. Individual proprietors gave way to limited companies. There were more mergers. Competition came from new morning papers (the *Daily Mail* in 1896, the *Daily Express* in 1900) which sought to become national, rather than essentially London, newspapers. Casualties ensued among provincial morning papers, but evening and weekly papers proved more resistant to the advent of the mass-circulation press.

MAURICE MILNE

Bibliography

British Library. *Bibliography of British Newspapers*. (Ongoing series of volumes, by counties.)

Dixon, Diana. "The Provincial Press: A Decade of Writings, 1972-1981." *Victorian Periodicals Review*, vol. 17, pp. 103-107.

Lee, Alan J. *The Origins of the Popular Press in England, 1855-1914*. 1976.

Milne, Maurice. *The Newspapers of Northumberland and Durham*. 1971.

Wolff, Michael, ed. *The Waterloo Directory of Victorian Periodicals, 1824-1900*. 1976.

· · · · ·

PRESS, RADICAL AND UNSTAMPED

Between 1790 and 1840 a radical and unstamped press emerged in Britain. It was part of the wider movement for political reform which characterized these decades and shaped Victorian culture by giving a stimulus to the struggle for a free press and helping to lay the foundation for popular journalism.

In the 1790s revolutionary events in France impelled British artisans and workingmen into an agitation for political and economic reform. Associations such as the London Corresponding Society (1792-1799) were formed to promote change and books such as Thomas Paine's *Rights of Man* (1791-1792) began to circulate. Amidst these turbulent events Daniel Eaton (d. 1814) and other journalists published cheap tracts and newspapers. For a time the circulation of radical journals like the *Manchester Herald* and *Politics for the People* was high. Then, with the passage of

repressive legislation by the Pitt government including the imposition of a higher stamp duty on newspapers (1797) and a requirement that printers be registered, the radical press largely disappeared.

It was revived in the years immediately after 1815, together with a renewed upsurge of political discontent. William Cobbett (1763-1835) was the foremost political journalist of these years and one of the most influential writers of the century. Cobbett's *Political Register* advocated a radical reform of taxation, an end to sinecures and corruption, and an extension of the franchise. In its twopence broadside edition (known as the "twopenny trash") it achieved an estimated weekly circulation of 40,000. Other important radical papers were the *Cap of Liberty*, the *Black Dwarf*, the *Medusa*, and the *Republican*, edited by Richard Carlile (1790-1843).

Between 1817 and 1819 the Tory government struck hard at these "blasphemous and seditious" writings. Magistrates were given increased powers to forbid the sale of radical literature and publishers were required to post bonds as sureties against a future conviction. More important, the fourpence newspaper duty was applied to all periodicals containing "news" that appeared more frequently than monthly and were sold for less than sixpence. This effectively cut off the supply of cheap journals to the poorer classes.

In the 1820s Carlile almost singlehandedly led the struggle for a free press. While a prisoner in Dorchester Gaol (1819-1825) he continued to publish the *Republican* and other cheap journals and tracts. He was assisted by members of his family and provincial volunteers like James Watson (1799-1874), who became a prominent distributor of unstamped journals in the 1830s. Several dozen of Carlile's followers were convicted of seditious or blasphemous libel. But the principle of a free press, insofar as the content of publications was concerned, was validated by this struggle.

However, the most important episode in the history of radical journalism took place during the years 1830 to 1836. The issue was whether newspapers could be published in violation of the stamp laws, that is, whether radical journals could circulate at a price of one or two pence. At stake was a popular readership as well as the ability of reformers to disseminate unpopular ideas. Henry Hetherington (1792–1849), John Cleave (1795?–1850), Watson, and other working-class journalists published hundreds of unstamped illegal journals in defiance of the laws. Many of these journals disappeared without a trace. Others, like the *Poor Man's Guardian* (1831–1835), remained in existence for the duration of the conflict. To avoid prosecution, some journalists changed the titles of their papers or issued them in a disguised format. Still, almost eight hundred vendors and publishers of unstamped periodicals were imprisoned.

In 1836 the Whig government conceded the substance of victory to a coalition of working- and middle-class reformers. The newspaper duty was reduced to onepence. In 1855 the remaining penny stamp was repealed and six years later the last of the "**taxes on knowledge**" (on paper) was removed. These events established the foundation for a penny press in Britain and for the great expansion of newspaper readers in the second half of the nineteenth century.

JOEL H. WIENER

Bibliography

Cole, G. D. H. *The Life of William Cobbett.* 1924.

Goodwin, Albert. *The Friends of Liberty: The English Democratic Movement in the Age of the French Revolution.* 1979.

Hollis, Patricia. *The Pauper Press: A Study in Working-Class Radicalism of the 1830s.* 1970.

Spater, George. *William Cobbett: The Poor Man's Friend.* 1982. 2 vols.

Thompson, E. P. *The Making of the English Working Class.* 1963.

Wickwar, William H. *The Struggle for the Freedom of the Press, 1819–1832.* 1928.

Wiener, Joel H. *Radicalism and Freethought in Victorian England: The Life of Richard Carlile.* 1983.

———. *The War of the Unstamped: The Movement to Repeal the British Newspaper Tax, 1830–1836.* 1969.

Williams, Gwyn A. *Artisans and Sans-Culottes: Popular Movements in France and Britain During the French Revolution.* 1968.

· · · · ·

PRESS, RELIGIOUS

"Creeds of almost every denomination, representing every episode of belief and unbelief, are defended by a phalanx of journals with the *Record* and the *Tablet* at the extremes, and the *Jewish Chronicle* in the rear" affirmed the anonymous author of *The Newspaper Press of the Present Day* in 1860. Seen by many as a product of British Protestantism's didactic respect for authoritative scriptures, periodical publication was but part of the profusion of religious literature in Victorian England. As late as the 1880s half of the new books published in Britain were of a religious nature.

In early Victorian England religious periodicals were both numerous (in 1860 more than 50 percent of all monthly periodicals were religious) and widely read; while the *Edinburgh Review* or *Quarterly Review* in their heyday only just reached 15,000, in the 1840s both the *Evangelical Magazine* (1793–1904) and the *Methodist Magazine* (1778–) were printing 24,000 copies a month. The success of such journals was of great importance to their promoters not only because many were produced to evangelize but also because they were partisan organs, seeking to establish influence within and between churches.

Thus the Clapham Sect promoted its views through the *Christian Observer* (1802–1877), which stood for a thoughtful Evangelicalism, as opposed to the frothy millenarianism of the *Morning Watch*. The Oxford Movement cultivated its constituency through the *British Critic* (1793–1843) and the *Christian Remembrancer* (1819–1830; 1843–1868). Ironically, J. H. Newman gave financial support to help establish the earliest religious newspaper, the *Record*, in 1828, for it was to become the fiercely Protestant organ of Evangelical hostility to Tractarianism and Liberalism. Later the *Rock* (1868–1905) and the *English Churchman* (1880–) were even more aggressively Protestant. By contrast, the High Church *Guardian* (1846–) was urbane and controlled. In the case of some small denominations like the Strict Baptists, separate churches were held together only by the periodicals they favored: there were two Strict Baptist connections, one group adhering to the *Gospel Standard* and the other to the *Earthen Vessel*.

Religious pressure groups and campaigns also made use of journals. The Liberation Society campaigned for disestablishment of the Church of England through the columns of the *Nonconformist* (1841–1879), in which a youthful Herbert Spencer's comments on "The Proper Sphere of Government" first appeared. Various facets of church life—temperance, youth work, Sunday schools—produced their own periodical literature; thus, for example, the Sunday School Union's *Sunday School Chronicle* ran from 1874.

Periodicals also became the vehicle for major theological controversies, as for example the Rivulet controversy that threatened to split the Congregational Union in 1855–1857 or the Downgrade controversy among Baptists in 1887–1888. Cardinal Manning secured the suppression of the *Rambler* (1848–1864), the organ of liberal English Catholicism. Sometimes the religious press touched on wider issues, as in February 1887 when Joseph Chamberlain placed a letter in *The Baptist* (1872–1910) which served to make the breach in the Liberal party over Home Rule permanent.

In addition to overtly ecclesiastical publications, religious interests sponsored family periodicals such as Norman Macleod's *Good Words*, the Society for the Propagation of Christian Knowledge's *Saturday Magazine* and the Religious Tract Society's *Sunday at Home* and *Women's Magazine* as well as its highly successful *Boy's Own Paper*, which secured a circulation of 160,000 a week. At the opposite extreme, parishes began to publish their own magazines, the first reputedly begun in Derby in 1859. Perhaps the most influential of all religious journals was Robertson Nicoll's *British Weekly*, which from 1886 sought to adapt the technology of the new journalism to the religious press, a process by which Nicoll came to exercise considerable political power.

J. H. Y. BRIGGS

Bibliography

Altholz, Josef L. *The Liberal Catholic Movement in England: The "Rambler" and Its Contributors, 1848–1864.* 1962.

Darlow, Thomas H. *William Robertson Nicoll.* 1925.

Ellegard, Alvar. *The Readership of the Periodical Press in Mid-Victorian Britain.* 1957.

Elliott-Binns, Leonard. *Religion in the Victorian Era.* 1936.

Kellet, E. E. "The Press." In George M. Young, ed., *Early Victorian England*, vol. 2. 1934.

Rose, E. A. *A Checklist of British Methodist Periodicals.* 1981.

Scott, P. G. "Listing Victorian Religious Periodicals." *Victorian Periodicals Newsletter*, no. 10, pp. 29–33.

———. "Victorian Religious Periodicals: Fragments That Remain." In Derek Baker, ed., *The Materials, Sources and Methods of Ecclesiastical History.* 1975.

Taylor, Rosemary. "English Baptist Periodicals." *Baptist Quarterly*, vol. 27, pp. 50–82.

Victorian Periodicals Review, vol. 14. (Special issue on religious press.)

• • • • •

PRESSURE GROUPS

Although pressure groups existed before and after the Victorian era, they took a unique role between about 1830 and 1880, in the period stretching from the unreformed Parliament to the maturation of national political parties. Organized interest groups or lobbies were able to influence public agencies through manipulating public opinion with the objective of securing specific legislation.

Victorians, especially those of the middle class, were joiners of societies, leagues, orders, and unions. Some promoted self-help, financial services, conviviality, or labor representation but did not advocate legislation. Pressure groups, on the other hand, were private, voluntary organizations organized around a single issue for the purpose of promoting reform and influencing public policy. They developed and used new tools such as statistics, fact gathering, fund raising, political organizing, and propaganda. Their activities included manipulating voting processes, publishing journals and tracts, accumulating petitions and resolutions, sponsoring speakers and lecturers, hiring agents and agitators, conducting demonstrations and mass meetings, signing and enforcing pledges, and, of course, lobbying members of Parliament and candidates.

Most pressure groups organized under a federated system of local associations which affiliated with a national center. The members tended to be middle class, professionals, radicals or liberals, and Nonconformists (especially Quakers). Many women participated. Critics and opponents called the organizations "ginger groups" and characterized their members as faddists, crotcheteers, cranks, and zealots.

Pressure groups were most active and effective during the decades around midcentury; extraparliamentary associations filled a political gap that existed during the period when parties were evolving into national organizations. The universal model and the most successful was the **Anti–Corn-Law League**, formed in 1839. Repeal was achieved seven years later. The **National Association for the Promotion of Social Science** or Social Science Association, formed in 1857, was a "union of reform groups" based on "ameliorism" and "dedicated to empirical research . . . with the objective of formulating exact social laws." The National Association for the Repeal of the Contagious Diseases Acts and the Ladies' National Association achieved their objective of repealing the regulations designed to prevent the spread of venereal diseases in the armed forces in 1886. Pressure groups formed on both sides of many controversies, as for example those organized to support and to oppose prosecution of Governor Edward Eyre for suppressing rebellion in Jamaica in the 1860s.

The range of causes was expansive. Pressure groups formed to lobby for education, temperance, protection of children and animals, the People's Charter, suffrage, women's rights, pacifism, social purity, Sunday closings, and free trade. Other groups opposed exclusive privileges of the Church of England, slavery, vaccination, vivisection, taxes on knowledge, the **white slave trade**, affinity and consanguine marriages, Sunday closings, and free trade. Around the turn of the century ultrapatriotic groups such as the Navy League and National Service League lobbied for preparation for war. Foreign policy groups agitated against Bulgarian atrocities and for imperial

preference. Pressure groups epitomized the Victorian spirit of collectivism and reform.

EUGENE L. RASOR

Bibliography

Hamer, David A. *The Politics of Electoral Pressure.* 1977.

Hollis, Patricia. *Pressure from Without in Early Victorian England.* 1974.

Malchow, Howard L. *Agitators and Promoters in the Age of Gladstone and Disraeli.* 1983.

Wootten, Graham. *Pressure Groups in Britain, 1720–1970.* 1975.

See also SOCIAL FEMINISM

. . . . .

PREST, THOMAS PECKETT (1810–1879)

Thomas Peckett Prest was one of the chief writers of popular working-class fiction during the 1840s and 1850s. Alternately described as bloods, penny dreadfuls, or Salisbury Square novels, these works were published by John Clements, J. Cunningham, John Cleave, and Edward Lloyd.

One of Lloyd's major contributors, Prest created "The String of Pearls" (1849), on which the popular play, *Sweeney Todd, the Demon Barber of Fleet Street*, is based, and imitations of Dickens's works: *The Sketch-Book* by "Bos" (1836), *The Penny Pickwick* (1838–1839), and *The Life and Adventures of Oliver Twiss, the Workhouse Boy* (1839).

Little is known of Prest's life, but he is thought to have begun his literary career adapting French farce and melodrama. In addition, he composed music hall songs and edited *The Magazine of Curiosity and Wonder* (November 5, 1835 to May 26, 1836). He is, however, best known as a writer of sensational fiction. Because many of these works were anonymous, undated, and printed in penny numbers, it is difficult to determine exactly what he wrote. He was reputed to be exceptionally prolific and is sometimes credited with as many as two hundred titles. Works often attributed to Prest include *The Maniac Father* (1842), *The Gipsy Boy* (1847), *Jack Junk* (1851), and *Varney, the Vampyre* (1847), the best-known blood. However, E. F. Bleiler argues that stylistic evidence proves that Prest did not write *Varney*.

CAROL A. SENF

Bibliography

Altick, Richard D. *The English Common Reader: A Social History of the Mass Reading Public, 1800–1900.* 1957.

Bleiler, E. F. Introduction to *Varney, the Vampyre.* 1972.

Hubin, Allen J. *The Bibliography of Crime Fiction, 1749–1975.* 1979.

Summers, Montague. *A Gothic Bibliography.* 1941.

· · · · ·

PRIME MINISTER

The evolution of the office of prime minister during Queen Victoria's reign was an outgrowth of the process that shifted political power from the Crown to **Parliament.** This transformation resulted in the magnification of the prime minister's position from head of the **cabinet** to one of the most powerful elected offices in the world. While the monarch remained the most prominent national symbol, by 1901 the constitutional position of the prime minister was clearly based on his control of the House of Commons.

The development of the cabinet from a group of royal ministers to an executive body responsible to Parliament was typical of the Victorian process of adapting existing political institutions to new conditions. As the House of Commons gained in stature, the prime minister was increasingly a member of the Commons rather than a peer. The fact that the prime minister remained in Parliament emphasized a basic distinction between the British and American systems of government. The latter maintained a separation of powers between the executive and legislature, while in Britain the two branches of govern-

ment remained closely intertwined. In addition, the prime minister was elected by a single constituency rather than a national electorate.

Public opinion was increasingly more pivotal to the political process. The prime minister was not only, as John Morley phrased it, "the keystone of the cabinet arch" but also the most important party leader and party symbol to the electorate. In 1834 **Robert Peel's** (1788–1850) Tamworth Manifesto set a new precedent by presenting the prime minister's views on a national level. It became critical that future prime ministers follow his example. This trend was encouraged by the development of the popular press, which reported political speeches in detail, and the growth of local party groups to organize new voters.

Technically, the choice of prime minister rested with the queen, but she was limited to a peer or member of Parliament who could secure a majority in the Commons. When one party had a definitive leader and a majority in the Commons, there was little room for maneuver. For example, in 1841 Peel was the clear choice, as was **William Gladstone** (1809–1898) in 1868 and 1895. Often the situation was more complicated. The 1880 general election had been dominated by Gladstone's Midlothian campaign, but Lord Granville and Lord Hartington were the official heads of the Liberal party. Queen Victoria was required to turn to them before offering Gladstone the seal of office. As the position of the leader of the opposition became institutionalized, the monarch's choice became more limited.

The office of prime minister had been developing since Walpole and Pitt's stewardship in the eighteenth century, but was not formally recognized until 1905. The prime minister had three main responsibilities. He chose his own cabinet in consultation with other party leaders and directed parliamentary and other party business; he maintained close supervision over foreign affairs; and he personally handled crises and major legislation. But how the prime minister deployed his responsibilities was largely related to his personality.

Peel, who was a well-trained administrator, was renowned for his ability to oversee the work of all departments. After the reforms of the 1840s greatly expanded the role of government, it was impossible to emulate his example. Even such strong prime ministers as Gladstone, **Benjamin Disraeli** (1804–1881), and **Lord Salisbury** (1830–1903) had trouble controlling discordant colleagues.

By the second half of the century the importance of the prime minister as party symbol was further enhanced by the rise of Gladstone and Disraeli, who were such magnetic personalities that elections became battles between the leaders of the Liberal and Conservative parties. Their alternating prime ministerships exemplified the role of personality in a prime minister's career. Disraeli, who was known for his spirited foreign policy and his glorification of empire, viewed politics as a struggle. On becoming prime minister, he announced "I have climbed to the top of the greasy pole." Gladstone had a moral conception of politics and felt that he was guided by a religious mission. His social legislation was more ideological and less paternal than Disraeli's. Although the Conservative governments of **Lord Salisbury** and **Arthur Balfour** (1848–1930) did not capture the popular imagination, they did leave their imprint on the prime ministership and revealed the role of personality in controlling the direction of government policy.

By Queen Victoria's death, the foundation of the prime minister's position had been established. The role of the monarch had been greatly reduced and it was clear that the prime minister and cabinet exercised their authority on the basis of their control of the House of Commons.

MARJORIE K. BERMAN

Bibliography

Carter, Byrum. *The Office of Prime Minister.* 1956.

Hanham, Harold John, ed. *The Nineteenth Century Constitution 1815–1914: Documents and Commentary.* 1969.

Jennings, William Ivor. *Cabinet Government.* 1936.

Le May, G. H. L. *The Victorian Constitution: Conventions, Usages and Contingencies.* 1979.

Mackintosh, John Pitcairn. *The British Cabinet.* 2d ed., 1968.

See also PARTY SYSTEM

· · · · ·

PRIMITIVE METHODIST CHURCH

A British Methodist denomination formed in 1811 by the union of Camp Meeting Methodists and Clowesites, the Primitive Methodist Church originated with the evangelistic work of Hugh Bourne (1772–1852) in 1800. Added impetus was provided in 1805 with the introduction of the "camp meeting" to English Methodism by the American evangelist Lorenzo Dow (1777–1834), resulting in the camp meeting at Mow Cop, May 31, 1807.

Expelled by the Wesleyans in 1808, Bourne and his followers, now known as the Camp Meeting Methodists, became a distinct group in 1810. William Clowes (1780–1851), an 1804 convert of Bourne, was expelled by the Wesleyans in 1810. His followers, the Clowesites, united with the Camp Meeting Methodists in 1811. On February 13, 1812, the group adopted the name "The Society of the Primitive Methodists," derived from John Wesley's statement in 1790: "I still remain a primitive Methodist."

Growth in the early decades was slow, but by 1842 an initial membership of approximately 200 had increased to nearly 80,000, with 500 traveling evangelists and more than 1,200 chapels. By 1860 membership was 132,114 and by 1875 was 165,410.

Notable for their use of women evangelists, especially in the early years, Primitive Methodists were active in the temperance movement from 1832 and provided many leaders for the trade union movement in the late nineteenth century from the ranks of its local preachers.

In 1932 the Primitive Methodists, numbering 222,021, merged with the Wesleyan Methodists and United Methodists to form the Methodist Church.

CARL W. CHEATHAM

Bibliography

Kendall, Holliday B. *The Origin and History of the Primitive Methodist Church.* 1905. 2 vols.

Petty, John. *The History of the Primitive Methodist Connexion from Its Origin to the Conference of 1860.* 1864.

Ritson, Joseph. *The Romance of Primitive Methodism.* 1909.

· · · · ·

Printing and Book Making

The art and craft of printing changed very little in its essentials during the first 350 years of its existence, but in the nineteenth century it was significantly altered by the application of mechanical power. From the time of Gutenburg, printing had been performed on a wooden press by pulling a bar that forced a sheet of paper against the inked surface of type. Around 1800 Charles, Earl Stanhope (1753-1816) built an improved hand press of iron. By the 1860s, all such presses had been outdistanced by the rapid development of power presses, although hand presses continued to be used for proofing, posters, and small editions of books.

The application of steam power to the printing press was initiated in England by Friedrich Koenig (1774-1833), a German then working in London. He employed a cylinder to press the paper against the type. The power press Koenig constructed for the *Times* in 1814 was the first to be used for a large-scale operation. In a subsequent development, printing plates were curved around a cylinder and pressed against a continuous roll of paper. Initially mechanical printing was used only for newspapers, journals, and other printed matter where volume and speed were critical.

For centuries sheets of paper had been made by hand dipping a mat or wire frame into a vat of wet pulp, the chief component of which was rags. A machine to supplant this slow and costly method was invented in France by Nicolas Louis Robert in 1798 and patented in England by the Fourdrinier brothers. Since the supply of rags could not keep up with the increasing demand for paper, experiments with other substances were intensified, and in the 1840s Friedrich Gottlob Keller in Saxony produced paper from wood pulp and ground wood. Within a decade it was in general use, greatly expanding the production of paper and decidedly reducing its quality.

Attempts to mechanize the setting of type were not entirely successful before 1880. The earliest composing machine patented in England was invented by William Church (1778-1863), but distributing type remained a problem. Two inventions in the United States had far-reaching results. In 1886 Ottmar Mergenthaler (1854-1899) brought out the Linotype machine in which a keyboard controlled the arrangement of matrices for letters and from them cast a solid line of type. In 1889 the Monotype, invented by Tolbert Lanston (1844-1913), was able to cast and set individual letters. The Linotype and the Monotype machines quickly came to account for most of the world's printing until the development of phototypesetting in the latter half of the twentieth century.

The labor of handling type had inspired William Ged of Edinburgh (1690-1749) to make in 1739 a plaster cast of type set up for printing so that it might be reproduced later without resetting. Local compositors squelched the invention at that time but Lord Stanhope revived it at the turn of the century. By 1829 the process had become the stereotype, using papier mâché instead of plaster. In 1839 the electrotype improved on this method by precipitating a copper shell of the page of type in a galvanic bath. In this way the original types were saved from wear, and the page could be reprinted whenever desired.

Two notable type designers in England were William Caslon (1692-1766) and John Baskerville (1707-1750), but they were superseded early in the nineteenth century by a "classic" letter from France which showed the use of rule and compass and was known as "Modern Face." Type founders in Victorian times made it decidedly attenuated. In 1844 the Chiswick Press in London revived a type originally cut by Caslon which received the name "Old Face." A variant, "Old Style," was issued in 1860 by another type founder. By the 1890s these three were virtually the only typefaces in England for printing books or magazines, although all manner of inventive and often flamboyant letters were designed for job printing, signs, and advertising.

Until about 1820, printers sent books unbound to booksellers (or to private customers) who had them bound in leather or paper over binders' boards. At that time William Pickering (1796-1854) introduced bindings of cloth over boards. At first Pickering attached paper labels to the spines, but in 1830 he began to stamp titles in gold leaf. The exterior of books thus began to provide designers enormous scope to express their tastes, which ranged from the restrained to the outlandish. Designs were stamped in leather; colored illustrations appeared on paper covers; decorations in gold and other colors were stamped on cloth bindings.

Victorian book design could be handsome when care was taken by concerned publishers and skilled printers, or it could be quite tasteless. An outstanding example of the former may be seen in books printed at the Chiswick Press under the collaboration of proprietor Charles Whittingham (1795–1876) and publisher William Pickering. On the other hand, the vast demand for cheap books resulted in greater quantity and decreased quality for ordinary publications. Typography was poor, title pages often were set from unrelated fonts, types were weedy, ink was pallid. In the 1880s, however, Charles Kegan Paul (1828–1902) and Joseph M. Dent (1849–1926) independently began to publish typographically attractive volumes. The *Century Guild Hobby Horse* (1884–1893), a journal of the Century Guild, showed the influence of the arts and crafts movement. At the first exhibition of the Arts and Crafts Exhibition Society in November 1888, Emery Walker (1851–1933), printer and expert on printing history, gave a lecture that inspired William Morris to design two new fonts of type in the spirit of faces cut in the fifteenth century and, subsequently, to print the volumes which he issued from his Kelmscott Press (1891–1898).

Though not the first to advocate improved book and type design, Morris's was the most influential voice. Interest in the appearance of books was shown by some publishers, notably Elkin Mathews and John Lane (1854–1925) at the Bodley Head, and by individuals who, following Morris's example, designed and printed or oversaw the printing of the books they chose to issue. A number of them used hand presses such as the Albion, and some designed their own type fonts. Among the better-known private printers of the 1890s were St. John Hornby (1867–1946) and his Ashendene Press (1894–1935), Lucien Pissarro (1863–1944) and his Eragny Press (1894–1914), and Charles Ricketts (1866–1931) and his Vale Press (1896–1903). Printing was discovered to be an art as well as a craft, and it attracted many able men and women. The private press movement, still very much alive, was an important part of what has been called "the revival of printing."

JOSEPH R. DUNLAP

Bibliography

Handover, P. M. "British Book Typography." In Kenneth Day, ed., *Book Typography 1815–1965*. 1966.

Jacobi, Charles T. *Some Notes on Books and Printing*. 1892.

McLean, Ruari. *Victorian Book Design and Colour Printing*. 2d ed., 1972.

Moran, James. *Printing Presses*. 1973.

Steinberg, S. H. *Five Hundred Years of Printing*. 3d ed., 1966.

Updike, Daniel B. *Printing Types*. 3d ed., 1962.

· · · · ·

PRISONS AND PRISON REFORM

In the eighteenth century, as Michel Foucault has noted, the nature of punishment changed. Brutal public tortures and executions gave way, gradually, to systematic plans for the reclamation of prisoners and their rehabilitation into society. In England, change came slowly; England continued to rely upon capital punishment and transportation through the early nineteenth century, but, by the end of that century, squalid prison conditions and chaotic prison management were transformed into a relatively efficient state-run system in which distinctions were drawn between children, juveniles, first offenders, and repeated offenders. As this happened, some relics of past barbarities were eradicated.

Conditions in English prisons compelled criticism early in the eighteenth century; they were the subject of parliamentary inquiry in 1730. Little action was taken, however, in part because prisons were not yet intended for long-term custody of offenders. Rather, they were holding places for prisoners awaiting trial, transportation, or execution. Capital punishment was seen as the principal deterrent against crime; public executions displayed the power of the state, punished the felon, and cautioned the public. As the eighteenth century continued, the number of capital offenses multiplied. Under Tudors and Stuarts, there had been about fifty capital crimes; under the Waltham Black Act of the

Sketch in the Clerkenwell House of Corrections: The Treadwheel.
Illustrated London News, *4 July 1874. Library Company of Philadelphia.*

late eighteenth century, that number increased to more than two hundred.

Subject to little public inspection, prisons, often owned by private contractors and run for profit, tended to be dark, foul holes in which prisoners lacked sewage and heat. Inmates, if they could not afford to purchase food and water, were dependent upon the whims of their jailers or the charity of visitors. Often, prisoners had to pay to be freed from irons. Male and female offenders, old and young, were mixed together, the women frequently giving birth on heaps of soiled straw or rags while drunks and rowdies screamed around them. On the other hand, a man of wealth could live in relative comfort in quarters segregated from the rest.

These were the conditions found by John Howard (1726?-1790) when he began his investigations in 1773, publishing his findings as *The State of the Prisons* (1777); conditions were little changed, at least in Newgate Prison, when **Elizabeth Fry** (1780-1845) began her work among women convicts in 1813. Howard's efforts were continued in the nineteenth century by the Society of Friends, and the cause of prison reform was taken up by such diverse figures as Patrick Colquhoun (1745-1820) and the novelist Charles Dickens. Much reform work was based on the thought of Cesare Bonesana, Marchese di Beccaria, whose *Crimes and Punishments* (1764) appeared in London in 1767 with a preface by Voltaire, although many English tracts were also written on the subject.

When reform came, it was largely a result of the failures of traditional measures. The increase in capital punishment for trivial offenses against property caused juries to refuse to convict. Often, juries would simply redefine the crime with which the defendant was charged, changing a capital offense to one carrying a lesser penalty. The spectacle of mass public hangings also came under criticism. By 1823, most of the Waltham Black Act had been repealed. After 1838, no one was hanged except for murder or, until 1861, attempted murder. The last public hanging occurred in 1868.

Transportation similarly failed. Begun in the early seventeenth century, transportation involved handing convicts over to private contractors who might sell the convicts' labor or hire it out, usually for a period of from seven to fourteen years. In 1776, Parliament determined, for obvious reasons, that transportation to the American colonies was increasingly fraught with difficulty, and passed an act providing that convicts be assigned hard labor at home. Before a scheme for implementation could be devised, however, the vast territory of Australia was opened and perceived as an unlimited field for convict colonization. The first convicts reached Botany Bay in January 1788, settling at Sydney. By 1832, Australian settlers were expressing grave dissatisfaction with the steady stream of convicts, while English writers questioned whether life on this new frontier, with all its opportunities for wealth, could really be construed as punishment. Transportation to New South Wales ceased in 1840. Van Diemen's Land then became inundated with convicts; transportation there had to be suspended in 1846. In 1853, the first Penal Servitude Act substituted shorter sentences of imprisonment for transportation. The sentence of transportation was abolished in 1857, although some long-term convicts continued to be sent to western Australia. The last convict ship sailed in 1868.

Regularization of the prison system accompanied this development. In the course of developing a prison system, old prisons were destroyed. Fleet and Marshalsea were demolished in 1842; the hulks, on which convicts had been stored, were razed in 1856. By 1877, Newgate Prison was used only for convicted felons who were awaiting execution. Newer prisons were designed with a view to atonement and rehabilitation, although debate continued as to the degree of silence and solitude that were necessary. As early as 1791, Jeremy Bentham (1748-1832) had planned a model prison, the Panopticon. Never constructed, his would have been a circular building with a keeper in a tower at the center; prisoners, confined to their cells for all activities, would be unable to see any other cells but would themselves be convinced that they were at all times under observation. A model prison on slightly different lines actually was constructed at Millbank, partially complete by 1816. Dartmoor, originally built in 1806 to house French prisoners of war, was rehabilitated to accommodate convicts in 1850. With the 520-cell Pentonville Prison, which was opened in 1842, the basis for early modern prison construction was set; within a half-dozen years, some fifty-four new prisons were built on the Pentonville plan.

The various steps taken toward the regularization of prisons were consolidated by the Prison Act of 1865, although only in 1877 did the ownership of all prisons pass to the home secretary. Expenses were to be met from public funds; administrative responsibility was vested in commissioners. During the next half-century, additional legislation stressed the reforming, rather than punitive, nature of penal theory. In 1853, a ticket-of-leave (parole) system was introduced and reformatories, earlier proposed, were established; in 1878, first offenders were separated from repeaters; in 1898, remission of sentences for good behavior was introduced and the use of corporal punishment was limited. Probation was established in 1907, and, in the next year, the borstal system was founded for offenders between sixteen and twenty-one, while legislation prohibited capital sentences for children. Related legislation also pointed toward the same rehabilitative end. After 1844, no one could be imprisoned for debts of under 20 pounds, and individuals were permitted to file for bankruptcy; imprisonment for **debt** was entirely abolished in 1869. The Criminal Evidence Act of 1869 allowed accused persons to testify as competent witnesses at their own trials, as could their spouses, while a Court of Criminal Appeal was introduced in 1907.

Simultaneously, legislation abolished many remnants of an early age. The public flogging of women ceased in 1817, branding in 1834, the pillory at Newgate in 1837, and, as has been noted, public executions in 1868. Even the hoisting of a black flag following an execution within prison walls was abandoned in 1902.

BETTY RICHARDSON

Bibliography

Foucault, Michel. *Discipline and Punish: The Birth of the Prisons.* 1977. Trans. Alan Sheridan.

Harding, Christopher et al. *Imprisonment in England and Wales: A Concise History.* 1985.

Hibbert, Christopher. *The Roots of Evil: A Social History of Crime and Punishment.* 1966.

Himmelfarb, Gertrude. "The Haunted House of Jeremy Bentham." In *Victorian Minds.* 1968.

Priestly, Philip. *Victorian Prison Lives: English Prison Biography, 1830–1914.* 1985.

Radzinowicz, Leon. *A History of English Criminal Law and Its Administration from 1750.* 1948–1956. 3 vols.

Webb, Sidney and Beatrice Webb. *English Prisons Under Local Government.* 1922.

· · · · ·

PROCTER, ADELAIDE ANNE (1825–1864)

The poems of Adelaide Anne Procter sold more copies in their time than the works of any other living poet except Tennyson. They are, however, largely forgotten today, despite Queen Victoria's fondness for *Legends and Lyrics* (2 series, 1858 and 1861).

The daughter of "Barry Cornwall" (the playwright and poet Barry Waller Procter), Procter lived a protected, private and intensely felt life in the midst of her family's lively literary and social circle. At the cost of her own health, she managed to achieve a measure of independence in the three causes to which she devoted her energies—religion, philanthropy, and feminism—and in her poetry, which expressed and served them all. In 1851 she avowed Roman Catholicism; two years later she first submitted her poems to *Household Words*, under the pseudonym of "Mary Berwick." Without knowing she was the daughter of his friend, Charles Dickens published and encouraged his mysterious contributor, and shared her family's surprise and pride when the modest secret was finally revealed. Her new status as a published poet enabled her to associate with such early feminists as Bessie Parkes and Barbara Smith (later Bodichon), with whom she published the anthology *Victoria Regia* (1861). The proceeds from *A Chaplet of Verses* (1862) helped support a shelter for homeless women.

Procter's poetry is limited in theme: nostalgia, spiritual growth, love won and lost, social responsibility, and heavenly reward are frequent in her lyrics. Her best poetry is narrative: retellings of legends or rearrangements of stock characters and situations, often with a supernatural element; her worst is the sentimental religious verse. Set to music, several poems survive as hymns or parlor songs, such as Arthur Sullivan's "A Lost Chord." Their lasting value, however, is as a representation of middle-class taste, and as a monument to a determined but circumscribed life.

SUSAN DRAIN

Bibliography

Julian, John. "Adelaide Anne Procter." In *A Dictionary of Hymnology.* 1892.

Maison, Margaret. "Queen Victoria's Favourite Poet." *The Listener,* April 29, 1965, pp. 636–637.

"The Poems of Adelaide Anne Procter." *The Month,* vol. 4, pp. 79–88.

Robertson, Eric. *English Poetesses: A Series of Critical Biographies with Illustrative Extracts.* 1883.

. . . . .

PROSTITUTION

In Victorian Britain, prostitution was both a major female occupation and a social issue with medical and moral dimensions. Three positions characterized the debate on prostitution: first, an older Calvinist condemnation of the prostitute as a temptress whose sin must be suppressed; second, evangelical pity for the prostitute as the victim of poverty and male lust as well as her own sin, who should be reformed; and third, the social science approach which accepted prostitution as a necessity and called for its regulation in order to safeguard public health. The debates over prostitution eventually led to the passage of the Contagious Diseases Acts in 1864. Although they were repealed in 1886, the effort to regulate prostitution ultimately changed the character of the profession.

At the beginning of the Victorian era, the definition of prostitution varied along class lines. In the fourth volume of *London Labour and the London Poor* (1862), Henry Mayhew articulated a middle-class attitude when he wrote, "Literally, every woman who yields to her passions and loses her virtue is a prostitute." Missionaries and charity officials treated common-law wives, deserted unmarried mothers, victims of rape, and streetwalkers all as "fallen women" living in sin.

In working-class communities, nonmarital cohabitation, illegitimate and premarital pregnancy, and bigamy reached high levels around midcentury. Women in these situations did not regard themselves as prostitutes, and in fact often thought of themselves as respectable, for they were not exchanging sex for money.

Sexual commerce was inextricably related to the conditions of women's work. Many women in the three major female occupations—laundry, needlework, and domestic service—did not earn enough to support themselves. If they were not supplementing a family wage, they sometimes turned to the streets to add to their income. Like other female occupations, prostitution was seasonal, rising in the winter when needlework was scarce and falling in summer, the dressmaker's busy season. Unemployed cotton mill workers turned to prostitution during the severe slump caused by the American Civil War.

A large number of full-time prostitutes were orphans or half-orphans who had been general servants. They often had their first sexual experience in their midteens and entered prostitution one or two years later. Rescue workers often characterized young prostitutes as assertive, impulsive, and rebellious girls who chafed at the restrictions of service.

Prostitution had a certain appeal to young working-class women. Unlike most workers, subjected to subordination, very low pay, and long hours of continuous work in confined conditions, prostitutes worked sporadically, earned a relatively high payment per sexual encounter, wore fine clothes, and drank and danced in pubs. In *Prostitution* (1870), **William Acton** argued that prostitutes spent a short period of their lives in the profession and moved out of it to marry or set up small businesses. A recent study of poor prostitutes in Victorian York, however, argues that their lives were in fact brief and miserable. The police harassed and imprisoned them, customers beat them, brothel keepers exploited them, and the cold, wet streets, alcohol, and disease shortened their lives.

The stereotype portrayed the fallen woman as an innocent who had been seduced by an aristocratic libertine, kept by him in luxury for some months and then abandoned, after which she engaged in a series of liaisons with wealthy men until, ravaged by disease and drink, she was reduced to a common brothel and, finally, streetwalking. Although there certainly were women who fit this pattern, each stage was actually characteristic of the class hierarchy within prostitution itself rather than part of an individual woman's progression through the ranks.

Some women lived in brothels, kept by either a man or woman. Female brothel keepers, ironically known as "mothers," presided with an iron hand, taking care to get the prostitutes into their debt for clothes. Brothels declined as a result of police prosecution, from 933 in 1841 to 410 in 1857 (in London). Far more important were the common lodging houses, to which prostitutes brought men they picked up on the street, in public houses, or in dance halls.

Male prostitution also continued throughout the period; young men and boys perambulated the same areas as their female counterparts—Regent Street and the Haymarket—and also frequented certain public houses, as well as the parks; outside of London, they followed the garrisons. They tended to be young working-class men in their teens and early twenties; post office boys in the 1880s and guardsmen throughout the century were notorious for these practices. Since their customers were often upper-class men, they had some scope to augment their earnings through blackmail. Male prostitutes sometimes continued homosexual practices throughout their lives, but many married in their twenties.

Pimps were relatively rare in England until late in the century. There were bullies, especially in rough waterside districts, but they probably inflicted most of their violence against male customers. Streetwalkers had a symbiotic relationship with thieves; a good deal of their income came from surreptitiously picking the pockets of their customers. There were, however, women who were pimped by their husbands, who had a legal right to their wives' earnings.

The majority of prostitutes' customers were working men, rather than slumming aristocrats. Men would sometimes defend prostitutes against the police, but could turn against the women if they were robbed, and popular songs reveal sexual hostility toward prostitutes. The prostitute's relations with her neighbors were also ambivalent. Commentators often noticed that in working-class neighborhoods prostitutes and respectable married women sat in music halls side by side. Poor working women might respect the prostitute for her independence and fine clothes. Yet a brothel could inspire neighborhood hostility if women perceived that their husbands, sons, and daughters were being lured into it; and married women competed with prostitutes for their husbands' wages.

Prostitution concerned the authorities as a problem of public order. The efforts to police public women must be seen in the context of other institutional attempts to control working people, such as the New Police, introduced in 1828, and the New Poor Law of 1834.

Legally, simply being a prostitute has never been an offense in Britain. Before 1839 streetwalkers could be arrested under the Vagrancy Acts as "loose, idle and disorderly persons" if they solicited men on the streets. In 1839 a new clause in the Metropolitan Police Acts introduced the notion of the "common prostitute" who could be arrested for soliciting. The police, however, were perceived as corrupt and overeager to arrest women just for being common prostitutes, so magistrates often hesitated to convict women on police evidence. Prostitutes violently resisted police attempts to repress their activities, aided by their bullies and other poor, unrespectable neighbors. Radicals also opposed the efforts of the New Police in general, and sometimes defended the rights of all women to enjoy the freedom of the streets.

The 1830s and 1840s also witnessed a resurgence of sympathy for prostitutes, whom social reformers portrayed as victims of the sweating system in dressmaking or millinery workshops. Societies for the prevention of juvenile prostitution were formed in London and Edinburgh in 1834 in response to widely publicized instances of young teenage girls being entrapped into brothels. Hundreds of female penitentiaries were also founded to rescue prostitutes. The Edinburgh institution forbade its inmates to speak with each other, and shaved their heads; as a result, two-thirds deserted it. The London Penitentiary was somewhat more successful, but it trained women only in laundry, needlework, and domestic skills, thus channeling them into the low-paying female occupations that fed the supply of prostitutes.

In the 1840s and 1850s social investigators combined new statistical techniques with the traditional religious imperative to produce several detailed studies of prostitution. In writings such as William Tait's *Magdalenism* (1840), W.R. Greg's "Prostitution" in the *Westminster Review* (1850), and William Acton's *Prostitution* (1870), these investigators acknowledged that low wages and unemployment impelled many women into prostitution, but they also stressed prostitutes' flawed moral character. Greg and Acton, more importantly, portrayed the male need for prostitution as a fact of life, and advocated that prostitutes be regulated to minimize their unhealthy effect on society.

Venereal disease thus became a public issue. The damage it caused was most evident in the military. By the 1850s and 1860s the fiascoes of the Crimean War and the subsequent investigations which revealed the poor health of the common soldier generated governmental concern. Until 1859 soldiers themselves had been inspected for venereal disease, but this was rejected as too humiliating for doctors and men alike.

As a result, the Contagious Diseases Acts were passed in 1864, and amended in 1866 and 1869. Modeled on the French system of regulation, they mandated that plainclothes policemen identify women as prostitutes and impel them to submit to examination and, if necessary, detention in a hospital for three (later nine) months. First applied to eleven garrison and port towns in England and Ireland, they were subsequently extended to five further areas. The rationalist approach to prostitution embodied in the acts appealed to many doctors, Tory supporters of the military, Liberals concerned with public sanitation, civil authorities, and the police.

The acts were effective in stigmatizing prostitutes and isolating them from their communities, for once a woman had been examined she was put on a register as a common prostitute, and the police who inspected the areas under the act scrutinized the behavior of all poor women. There is little evidence, however, that the acts had any effect on military health. Venereal disease was declining in general before the acts, and continued to do so after they were repealed, suggesting that other factors led to its control.

Furthermore, the acts aroused great public hostility because they rested on the principle that women must be regulated, examined, and treated in order to provide healthy sexual outlets for men. The National Association for the Repeal of the Contagious Diseases Acts, founded in 1869, joined together provincial Nonconformists outraged by the acts' sanction of immorality and metropolitan radicals eager to defend civil liberties against the police.

In the same year the Ladies' National Association (LNA) was also formed to campaign against the acts. Led by **Josephine Butler** (1828–1906), a charismatic feminist of strong religious convictions, the LNA gathered together women in 104 local branches across Britain by 1884. These women attacked the humiliation of women by the medical examination, which they termed "instrumental rape." Their protests—which included disrupting by-elections contested by supporters of the acts—were significant as the first independent and public agitation on the subject of sex by middle-class women in England. While they often evidenced a condescending tendency to "protect" working-class women, the members of the LNA did sometimes help women in port communities defend themselves on their own terms. The LNA also formed alliances with working-class men who perceived the acts as yet another manifestation of aristocratic sexual exploitation of poor girls.

The Liberal government continued to support the acts until 1883, when after several by-elections marked by violent public disturbances on the issue, they finally suspended the acts, which were repealed altogether in 1886.

The acceptance of prostitution as necessary to male sexual needs was further attacked in 1873, when social purity leagues were formed to advocate male as well as female continence. Unlike Josephine Butler, Jane Ellice Hopkins (1836–1904), a leader in social purity, was not particularly concerned with individual liberties. She pressed for the passage of the Industrial Schools Amendment Act in 1880, which mandated the removal of children to detention homes if they lived in a brothel, defined as a dwelling where prostitutes lodged.

In 1885 the white slavery scandal generated by W.T. Stead in his *Pall Mall Gazette* aroused an even more intense public furor about childhood prostitution. In order to expose the traffic in young women from England to France and Belgium, Stead arranged to purchase a thirteen-year-old working-class girl, Eliza Armstrong, from her mother, and had her drugged and examined for virginity. The massive outcry against the sexual exploitation of poor girls led to the foundation in 1885 of the National Vigilance Association and, in the same year, to the passage of the Criminal Law Amendment Act.

The Criminal Law Amendment Act's most important component raised the age of consent from thirteen to sixteen. Its passage through the Houses of Commons and Lords was difficult because several members objected to its restrictions on their sexual access to young girls. It also increased police powers to suppress brothels and arrest procurers, powers that were quickly used in London and the provinces. Drives against streetwalking accompanied these efforts.

Efforts to institute formal regulation of prostitution had failed, but the civil authorities, prodded by the **purity campaign**, were able to isolate prostitutes from working-class communities, stigmatize them as moral outcasts rather than casual workers, and drive them into the arms of the pimps they needed for protection against the police. Although the outcry against the **white slave trade** and the Contagious Diseases Acts had been directed against the exploitation of women and girls by police and procurers, the repressive actions of the 1890s, supported by the National Vigilance Association, were mainly directed against the prostitutes themselves.

ANNA CLARK

Bibliography

Acton, William. *Prostitution.* 1870.

Bristow, Edward. *Vice and Vigilance: Purity Movements in Britain Since 1700.* 1977.

Finnegan, Frances. *Poverty and Prostitution: A Study of Victorian Prostitutes in York.* 1979.

Gorham, Deborah. "The 'Maiden Tribute of Modern Babylon' Re-examined: Child Prostitution and the Idea of Childhood in Late-Victorian England." *Victorian Studies,* vol. 21, pp. 353–379.

Mayhew, Henry. *London Labour and the London Poor,* vol. 4, 1862.

McHugh Paul. *Prostitution and Victorian Social Reform.* 1980.

Nield, Keith, ed. *Prostitution in the Victorian Age: Debates on the Issue from Nineteenth-Century Critical Journals.* 1973.

Petrie, Glen. *A Singular Iniquity: The Campaigns of Josephine Butler.* 1971.

Storch, Robert D. "Police Control of Street Prostitution in Victorian London: A Study of the Contexts of Police Action." In David H. Bayley, ed., *Police and Society.* 1977.

Walkowitz, Judith. *Prostitution and Victorian Society: Women, Class and the State.* 1980.

· · · · ·

PROVINCIAL TOWNS AND SOCIETY

Provincial towns—that is, urban areas outside the Thames valley and smaller than the great northern cities of Manchester, Birmingham, Leeds, and Liverpool—were decisively altered by the industrial revolution. County centers and market towns, which had maintained a relatively constant population, now grew or declined drastically depending on employment opportunities and the proximity of major transportation arteries; other towns were almost instantly created by industrial needs, such as Middlesbrough, a center of coal and ironworks, and Cardiff, which provided docks for the Glamorgan coal fields in Wales.

Ancient county towns like Lincoln, Nottingham, and Leicester could often balance the development of commerce and industry. The nineteenth-century emphasis on the professions and increasing commercial activity meant that these towns held many doctors, lawyers, journalists, real-estate developers, and retailers even before the factory workers arrived. Once industry was added, such as the hosiery and leather-working industries of Leicester, a prosperous town featuring a range of social classes came into being. If such a town were on a major railway line, as Leicester was, it became an important part of the network of urbanizing Britain.

Provincial towns shared many of the problems of larger cities in adapting to mass living. Town councils were typically slow to deal with housing needs, education, sanitation and, most seriously, public health. The reluctance to impose rates on inhabitants delayed even projects acknowledged to be important, and towns often refused to institute municipal programs until forced into action by national legislation, like the Public Health Act of 1848.

Town planning was usually underemphasized, and the urban landscape reflected the industrial and commercial nature of the town, rather than the needs of its residents. Large factories and train yards usurped much of the central area of towns; working-class housing, usually slums, grew up around the factories, and the railway lines and embankments physically separated parts of the city from one another.

Middle-class residents began moving to **suburbs** by midcentury, creating a boom in building; yet overcrowding was still a problem in towns like Nottingham that were late to accept enclosure of the open fields around the old town. As a consequence, the working classes could not expand beyond the old town limits and some of the worst slums of Victorian Britain were the result.

Because town leadership tended to be middle class, utilitarian, and Dissenting, provincial government was sometimes at odds with the upper-class, conservative national leadership; provincial resistance to the Education Act of 1870, for instance, was due partly to provincial leaders' fear that Dissenting influence would be lessened if elementary education were taken out of their hands. At the same time, the transfer of real power from the aristocracy to the middle class, a process nearly accomplished by the end of the century, took place largely in provincial government.

Midcentury prosperity helped determine the forms of leisure and social activity of provincial towns. Members of the upper class being few, middle-class residents took on civic projects like the development of libraries and museums, joined self-improvement groups like literary and philosophical societies or excursion societies, and were active in philanthropy. Newspapers flourished. Mechanics' instututes offered adult education for the working class. Football and other team sports became popular and the heated rivalries between neighboring towns illustrate the increased sense of civic pride and self-identification with a town. The novels of Arnold Bennett set in the Five Towns offer a vivid picture of Victorian social life in the provinces.

By the end of the century, many pressing social problems had been dealt with: town councils had planned civic centers featuring traffic control, municipal buildings, commercial districts, public transportation, parks, and other public spaces.

LAURA NOVO

Bibliography

Briggs, Asa. *Victorian Cities.* 1963.

Everitt, Alan. *Landscape and Community in England.* 1985.

Hoskins, William George. *The Making of the English Landscape.* 1955.

Simmons, Jack. *Leicester, Past and Present*, vol. 2. 1974.

See also CLASS; GOVERNMENT: LOCAL AND COUNTY; PRESS, PROVINCIAL

. . . . .

PSYCHOLOGY

The progress of psychology during the nineteenth century was shaped and accelerated by advances in science, particularly in physiology and evolutionary biology. Where the natural pathway to psychology had previously been theology, philosophy, or sometimes medicine, now the study of mind became part of investigations of the body or of nature in general. Developments were especially significant in the study of brain structure and function, the understanding of the nervous system, the experimental investigation of sensation (sight, touch, hearing, etc.), the elucidation of abnormal psychology, and most of all in the impact of developmental ideas.

By 1800 anatomical studies had elucidated most of the human brain's major features except for the regularity of the central convolutions. Ideas of brain function, however, remained simple, if not simplistic, probably as a result of the long-held postulate that the brain was the seat of the soul. In the century's early decades, it was proposed not only that the brain was the organ of mind but also that mental function was made up of approximately thirty-three distinct faculties, each of which was subserved by a separate organ of the brain. Initially developed by Franz Joseph Gall (1758-1828), "organology" or "craniology" was imported into Britain by Johann Kaspar Spurzheim (1776-1832) and popularized as **phrenology** by George Combe (1788-1858) and many others. Phrenology, though originally based in careful anatomical research, quickly became a populist doctrine of mind and a vehicle for the diffusion of materialistic ideas. As experimental techniques improved, knowledge of brain structure and function increased: Edward Hitzig (1838-1907) showed how the stimulation of the human cortex caused eye movements, Hermann Munk (1830-1912) showed the localization of vision in the occipital cortex, and by 1876 David Ferrier (1843-1928), in his *Functions of the Brain*, was able to construct a detailed map indicating the discoveries of the "new phrenology." Important work of a similar kind was undertaken in the clinical context by Pierre Paul Broca (1824-1880) and John Hughlings Jackson (1835-1911), who implicated the cerebral convolutions in the production of epilepsy.

Careful experimental work also focused on the nervous system. Descriptions of the brain and nervous system elevated the "reflex" to a central role. The concepts of "irritability" and "sensibility" were reinterpreted and then replaced by the notion that a sensory-motor division was basic to nervous organization; this prompted the discovery of the sensory-motor division of the spinal roots by Charles Bell (1774-1842) and François Magendie (1783-1855).

Work in this domain made its greatest headway in Germany and France. In Britain, meanwhile, a school of associationist psychology based itself on the view that complex mental contents could be derived from simple sensory units. Associationism had already been presented in the work of John Locke (1632-1704), David Hume (1711-1776), and especially David Hartley (1705-1757), and in the early nineteenth century James Mill (1773-1836) and others had insinuated it into utilitarian political theory. Psychologists judged that such investigations lacked empirical support and set about to provide it. Alexander Bain (1818-1903) linked the association of ideas to neurophysiology; **Herbert Spencer** (1820-1903) reconciled associationism with heredity and in his important *Principles of Psychology* (1855) shifted the subject into the province of biology. The biological sciences provided both particular and general support to psychology—the cell theory, for instance, gave rise to the neurone theory.

Experimental psychology arose largely as an outgrowth of nineteenth-century German sensory physiology and focused on noncognitive processes, neglecting reason and other "higher" mental activities. In Britain, psychology as a separate discipline with its own organization and academic base developed later than in Germany and relatively little native work on the human senses was undertaken.

Abnormal psychology grew largely through the auspices of **mesmerism**, which thrived during the eighteenth century, then fell into disrepute, only to be revived as a therapeutic practice in Britain in the 1840s. During this decade and for some years after, mesmeric lectures were given throughout the country, clinics were established, and journals circulated widely. Contributions were made to the field by John Elliotson (1791-1868), James Esdaile (1808-1859), and James Braid (1795?-1860), whose *Neurypnology* (1843) not only provided details about the hypnotic trance but also opened the way for subsequent work on suggestion and dissociation.

Such work was pursued most energetically in France, and the greatest advances in the areas of abnormal psychology also occurred in that country. It was "moral therapy" that sank roots in English soil, an approach that devalued physical restraint and drugs in favor of reeducation and resocialization. Such ideas informed a good deal of psychiatric change and through the labors of the Tukes—William (1732-1822) and Samuel (1784-1857)—led to the establishment of asylums for managing the mentally ill. Important though such initiatives were, the optimism that inspired them was blunted as the institutions filled up with chronically incapacitated patients. Many alienists therefore felt that a judicious mixture of psychological and organic theory was required to understand mental derangement. There were flurries of interest in the work of Thomas Laycock (1812–1876) in reflex theory, J.C. Bucknill (1817–1897) on the effect of toxins on brain function, and James Cowles Prichard (1786–1848), who attempted to link **insanity** with brain inflammation and deranged nutrition.

More fruitful was the inspiration of evolutionary theory, and many took up and developed the concept of degeneration offered by B.A. Morel (1809–1873). Among the results were ideas of **social Darwinism**, a program of **eugenics**, and the criminological theories of Cesare Lombroso (1836–1909). Charles Darwin contributed to the area by emphasizing the similarity of mental processes in humans and animals in *Descent of Man* (1871) and suggesting an evolutionary interpretation of the changes of feature characteristic of major passions in *Expression of the Emotions* (1872).

More significant still was the contribution of Herbert Spencer. His *Principles of Psychology* (1855) did the most to introduce the developmental viewpoint. The work was dry, severe, and often speculative, but offered a biological psychology which many found attractive. Spencer defined life as "the continuous adjustment of internal to external relations"; psychology's task was to show in detail how this adjustment occurred. Thus associationism was given an evolutionary, even behaviorist, twist. Spencer insisted that hereditary and racial factors be prominently considered in psychological theory.

British workers made their greatest contribution to the development of nineteenth-century psychology in applying evolutionary theory to the human race. Darwin's ideas were advanced into many new arenas: the psychology of so-called primitive races (from the 1870s); the psychology of childhood (from the 1880s); and the psychology of animal behavior (from the 1890s). The science had come of age during the Victorian era; many theoretical and technical changes were to come, but psychology's ability to pose and often answer questions in almost every realm of human existence was no longer in doubt. From modest origins in theology and philosophy, psychology had become established as a science dependent on other sciences yet possessed of its own autonomy.

MICHAEL SHORTLAND

Bibliography

Boring, Edwin G. *A History of Experimental Psychology.* 2d ed., 1957.

Brett, George S. *Brett's History of Psychology.* 1962. Ed. R.S. Peters.

Chadwick, Owen. *The Secularization of the European Mind in the Nineteenth Century.* 1975.

Cooter, Roger. *The Cultural Meaning of Popular Science: Phrenology and the Organization of Consent in Nineteenth-Century Britain.* 1984.

Fancher, Raymond E. *Pioneers of Psychology.* 1979.

Flugel, John C. *A Hundred Years of Psychology, 1833–1933.* 1933.

Hearnshaw, L.S. *A Short History of British Psychology, 1840–1940.* 1964.

Mandelbaum, Maurice. *History, Man and Reason: A Study in Nineteenth-Century Thought.* 1971.

Wertheimer, Michael. *A Brief History of Psychology.* 1970.

Young, Robert M. *Mind, Brain and Adaptation in the Nineteenth Century: Cerebral Localization and Its Biological Context from Gall to Ferrier.* 1970.

——. "Scholarship and the History of the Behavioural Sciences." *History of Science,* vol. 5, pp. 1–51.

. . . . .

PUBLIC HEALTH

In the 1830s population growth combined with rapid and unprecedented urbanization to create health problems of such magnitude that new statistical tools and **engineering** techniques, as well as innovative administrative structures, were needed to solve them. By the end of the Victorian era, the environmental factors associated with disease were not eradicated, but they had been greatly alleviated by an impressive array of national health legislation aimed at improving **housing**, water, sewerage, and the control of infectious diseases.

From 1801 to 1851 the population in the principal towns and cities tripled. London soared from 958,803 to 2,362,236 inhabitants during these fifty years. Glasgow's population grew 35 percent between 1831 and 1841 and Manchester's 47 percent between 1821 and 1831. As early as 1834 these newly created urban areas were regarded both as places of opportunity and sites of enormous human suffering. The opportunity was intrinsic to the Victorian belief that industrialization would bring unprecedented progress; but progress, it was soon learned, exacted a price. The price was paid by the working classes, who were crowded into areas without adequate housing, ventilation, water supplies, or sewerage. Such urban areas were fast recognized as breeding grounds for disease and depravity.

The St. Giles district in London is an example of the conditions that prompted attention to public health. When investigated by the London Statistical Society in 1841, Church Lane in St. Giles had twenty-seven houses averaging five rooms each; 655 people lived there. Six years later the population had increased to 1,095, although the number of rooms and houses remained the same.

Crowded and unsanitary conditions were not new to the nineteenth century, but with urbanization they were magnified in scale. The old parish structure of local self-government was unable to provide adequate correctives. The Poor Law system was the first administrative structure to undergo close scrutiny. The involvement of **Edwin Chadwick** (1800–1890) in this reform provided an entry for national legislation promoting public health.

Chadwick was a disciple of Jeremy Bentham (1748–1832), whose ideas supplied the program for a close circle of his friends, including Neil Arnott (1788–1874), James Phillips Kay-Shuttleworth (1804–1877), and the influential Southwood Smith (1788–1861). The ammunition to accomplish administrative and legal reform was provided by the new science of statistics: quantification and compilation of facts.

Chadwick relied on the work of William Farr (1807–1883), which laid the foundations for the science of "vital statistics." From 1839 to 1880 Farr served as compiler of abstracts for the Registrar General's Office, which was created in 1837. Aside from issuing annual reports which contained precise details about disease and environmental squalor, Farr created a classification of common diseases for reporting the cause of death—a new and indispensable addition to the description of public health.

In 1838, when a local Poor Law board used funds to remove nuisances which were believed to be the cause of disease, auditors disallowed the expenditure. Edwin Chadwick, as Poor Law commissioner, ordered a small-scale survey in London to report the relationship of urban conditions to disease. Thus commenced an investigation which culminated in 1842 with Chadwick's *Report on the Sanitary Condition of the Labouring Population of Great Britain*. The issues presented in the 1838 surveys conducted by Doctors Arnott, Kay-Shuttleworth, and Smith were expanded upon in this report and served as a format for major reform efforts.

The report documented the correlation between disease and defective drainage, inadequate water supply, and overcrowded housing. For Chadwick, these data confirmed the theory that diseases were caused by miasmas (gases and noxious odors). The report also demonstrated the economic costs of ill health by showing that it was a leading cause of pauperism, showed a correlation with immoral habits such as intemperance, and drove home the need for administrative reform to correct problems that affected wide segments of society rather than the inhabitants of a single parish. The Public Health Act of 1848 created, for the first time, a central General Board of Health to safeguard the population.

The tasks before the General Board of Health were unprecedented, and involved years of basic development in statistical collection, map making and engineering as well as legal, administrative, and financial innovation. Before sewers could be built, for example, precise geological maps had to be drawn and experiments undertaken with various clays, pipe sizes, and levels to achieve maximum velocity of flow. Although the General Board of Health was a failure to the extent that it lacked powers of compulsion and excluded London, it made the first steps toward completing an enormous task.

In 1858 control of health policy was returned to localities and Parliament appointed the talented Dr. John Simon (1816–1904) as medical officer to the Privy Council. Local boards were created at local option. Despite this change in policy, however, centralization continued to be the operative rule in sanitary legislation. The 1866 Sanitary Act, for example, embodied the principle of compulsion by a central authority if local boards failed in their responsibilities.

By 1866 London had a major portion of its new sewer system, although no comprehensive national sanitary plan yet existed. Dr. John Simon instigated the creation of another Royal Sanitary Commission to create a long-term policy. The final report of this commission, issued in 1871, contained recommendations later embodied by three major acts. The Local Government Board Act (1871) consolidated the staffs of the Poor Law Board, the Local Government Act Office, the Registrar General's Office, and the Medical Office of the Privy Council. The Public Health Act of 1872 proposed to divide England into rural and urban sanitary districts to carry out the obligations of separate acts concerned with housing, sewage, nuisance removal, and bakehouses. Finally, the Public Health Act of 1875 consolidated and amended all of the acts related to public health.

Throughout the century, governmental action was both prompted and supplemented by voluntary organizations. Sanitary questions were frequently discussed in journals; the Ladies' Sanitary Association distributed soap and disinfecting powder and educated women about washing clothes, covering food against flies, and proper nutrition of infants. But even basic cleanliness could be extraordinarily difficult in areas where the only water available was sold at a street tap or pump, and had to be carried home by the bucketful. At midcentury, many urban areas began to establish public baths and washhouses. The Public Health Act of 1872 required local authorities to provide water supplies, though piped water was not yet universal by the end of the century.

The only successful attack on hazards to public health through strictly medical measures was smallpox **vaccination**, which became compulsory in 1853. Medical discoveries such as the identification of the **cholera** bacillus in the 1880s revealed that the theoretical underpinning of early public health measures was, in part, erroneous—but although Chadwick and his followers lacked the scientific knowledge to attack epidemic diseases directly (through innoculation, pest control, chemical purification of water, and prevention of bacterial contamination in food), the sanitary measures they recommended were nevertheless, if indirectly, effective. Overcrowded and badly ventilated housing made it easy for lice to spread typhus and for airborne bacteria to infect large numbers of people. Although "miasmas" did not cause disease, the uncleaned cesspools and faulty sewers that created the terrible smells also seeped into the water supply and spread bacterial contamination.

Medical officers of health, appointed by localities beginning in midcentury, provided a link between medical knowledge and public measures. Charged with giving advice on health to local authorities, they soon took on a multitude of functions: investigating occupational diseases and industrial pollution, inspecting schools and lodging houses, examining slaughterhouses, tracking epidemics. (Compulsory notification of infectious diseases was first required in 1889.) As it became evident that the practice of preventative medicine required legal and sociological training that general practitioners did not have, public health became legitimized as a medical specialty.

In the nineteenth century, sanitary reform was often seen as a moral cause. Edwin Chadwick's 1842 report emphasized the moral costs of slum conditions: children who slept in the same room with adults were endangered by early sexual knowledge and incest; ill health and hopelesness led to recklessness, lack of forethought, and drunkenness. Public health reformers were less apt to recognize that **poverty** itself was a primary source of ill health; people lived in overcrowded houses because they could afford no better, and malnutrition, lack of heat, inadequate clothing, and physical exhaustion caused some diseases and increased susceptibility to others.

Did the impressive public health measures undertaken during the course of the nineteenth century actually improve the people's health? Generally, statistical data indicate increased longevity for working-class persons.

Adequate sewerage and clean water supplies eliminated cholera epidemics; improved housing and ventilation had some effect on tuberculosis and other respiratory diseases. Conditions outside the reformers' control, however, also had an effect: the rise in real wages, for example, decreased the proportion of people who were seriously malnourished for much of their lives, and the availability of contraceptives stemmed the depletion of women's physical resources by repeated child-bearing. The Victorians took an enormous step in providing the physical infrastructure required for clean and healthy cities. The differential in life expectancy between the poor and the well-to-do remained as evidence of the reform yet necessary.

ROSA LYNN B. PINKUS

Bibliography

Brand, Jeanne L. *Doctors and the State: The British Medical Profession and Government Action in Public Health, 1870–1912.* 1965.

Brockington, Colin F. *Public Health in the Nineteenth Century.* 1965.

Chadwick, Edwin. *Report on the Sanitary Condition of the Labouring Population of Great Britain.* 1842; rpt. 1965.

Eyler, John M. *Victorian Social Medicine: The Ideas and Methods of William Farr.* 1979.

Lambert, Royston. *Sir John Simon, 1816–1904.* 1963.

Smith, F. B. *The People's Health, 1830–1910.* 1979.

Wohl, Anthony. *Endangered Lives: Public Health in Victorian Britain.* 1983.

Woods, Robert and John Woodward, eds. *Urban Disease and Mortality in Nineteenth-Century England.* 1984.

See also CEMETERIES AND CHURCHYARDS; EPIDEMIC DISEASES; ENVIRONMENTAL POLLUTION; PLUMBING AND SEWAGE DISPOSAL

. . . . .

PUBLIC HOUSES see BREWERIES AND PUBLIC HOUSES

. . . . .

PUBLIC SCHOOLS

British "public schools" are fee-paying institutions, generally boarding schools that educate the elite. The term was originally used to describe several boys' grammar foundations established by endowment as charitable trusts. Victorian public schools included a variety of independent institutions for boys, particularly those associated with the Headmasters' Conference.

In the eighteenth and early nineteenth centuries public schools were at a low ebb. They were characterized by poor academic and moral standards, including rebellions, drunkenness, and anarchy. But they had social prestige. During the Victorian period the old public schools reformed their image from ill-disciplined institutions to highly controlled communities. The reform spirit is associated with **Thomas Arnold**, headmaster of Rugby School between 1828 and 1842. Arnold was a religious evangelical who used moral and spiritual fervor to encourage discipline. He wanted to mold character and produce Christian gentlemen. Character training became a distinguished aspect of public schools; and Arnold was made into a legend by Thomas Hughes's *Tom Brown's School Days* (1857).

During Queen Victoria's reign, especially between 1840 and 1870, the number of public schools grew, as did the number of pupils attending. The public school system developed from three strands. First were the preeminent nine old grammar foundations: Charterhouse, Eton, Harrow, Merchant Taylors', Rugby, St. Paul's, Shrewsbury, Westminster, and Winchester. Second, other old endowed grammar schools, such as Repton, Sherborne, and Uppingham, were transformed, usually by ambitious young headmasters. Edward Thring, for example, developed Uppingham from a school of twenty-five boys to one of over three hundred between 1853 and 1888. Third, new foundations were established to meet increasing middle-class demand. For example, Marlborough (1843) catered to the sons of clergy and Epsom (1855) to doctors' sons. Many public school boys entered military or colonial service.

Although each public school was proud of its unique character, they shared common traits. All were religious in tone, with the chapel playing an important part in school life. Many masters were Anglican clerics. In 1860, for instance, fourteen of the eighteen masters at Rugby were clergymen. Next, the curriculum was dominated by the classics. Before the 1860s, at least three-quarters of class time was spent on Latin and Greek. Although "modern" subjects were added at most schools, the classics continued to dominate; science and technology were neglected. At Harrow in 1875 well over half the masters were in classics. A knowledge of Latin and Greek became a social indicator. Attending a public school enabled sons of the nouveau riche to become gentlemen. Public school boys were trained for leadership and many developed a lasting social network.

A further common characteristic was the development of athleticism. Team sports became an important part of school life. Games were viewed as building moral character, manliness, and team spirit. They also used energies that might otherwise be diverted into aggression or sexual activity.

Public schools were not above criticism. The Clarendon Commission (1861–1864) investigated the nine "great" schools and discovered many abuses in the use of endowments. Between 1864 and 1868 the Taunton Commission examined the other 791 endowed schools and made a revolutionary proposal to pool endowments and create a national system of secondary education with a modern curriculum—but nothing came of the scheme. Indeed, the ensuing Endowed Schools Act (1869) assisted some schools to revise their statutes and gain public school status. Furthermore, fear of state intervention led to the creation of the Headmasters' Conference (1869), which helped to forge an exclusive public school club.

More recently, public schools have been accused of aiding the decline of Britain by producing leaders ignorant of science and technology, absorbing the entrepreneurial spirit of the middle classes, and reasserting a traditional gentry culture. The public schools not only produced the class that governed the nation and the empire but also permeated the entire culture via books and comics. In addition, state secondary schools were created in the public school image. The public school ethos thus helped perpetuate the class gulf and shape Britain in the twentieth century.

OLWYN M. BLOUET

Bibliography

Bamford, Thomas William. *Rise of the Public School.* 1967.

Chandos, John. *Boys Together: English Public Schools, 1800–1864.* 1984.

Gathorne-Hardy, Jonathan. *The Old School Tie: The Phenomenon of the English Public School.* 1978.

Simon, Brian and Ian Bradley, eds. *The Victorian Public School.* 1975.

Wiener, Martin J. *English Culture and the Decline of the Industrial Spirit, 1850–1980.* 1981.

See also EDUCATION, SECONDARY

. . . . .

PUBLISHING AND PUBLISHERS

Before the Victorian period, publishers were generally also printers and booksellers; some had been editors and authors as well. As the century passed, such diversity became less common. Publishing became a full-time occupation, requiring heavy capital investment; consolidation and partnerships increased and the great family firms took in members of the third and fourth generation.

During the first half of the century printing costs were high. New works were published in very small editions, primarily for sale to libraries, although noncopyright books and standard religious and educational works were produced in various cheap forms. William and Richard Chambers of Edinburgh and Charles Knight of London built a strong trade during the 1830s with inexpensive editions of improving works. With the success of *Pickwick Papers* in 1836, publishers learned that new works could be successfully sold to a much wider audience when broken into monthly parts. Technological advances helped bring down printing costs but required the capital to buy new machinery and a publishing program that would keep it fully occupied and make the investment worthwhile. The firm of Bradbury and Evans, which acted as both printer and publisher, kept the presses rolling by establishing *Punch* and printing the novels of Dickens and Thackeray. Chapman and Hall pioneered the Christmas book (1843), the cheap collective reissue of living novelists (1847), and various "libraries" of standard and recent works in cheap reprint editions.

Most of the great Victorian publishing houses were family concerns whose founders had begun as self-educated apprentices to printers or booksellers. During the first half of the century, a great many publishers were established. The middle decades were a period of consolidation: new generations came into family firms; partnerships were formed and expanded; and publishers diversified by beginning magazines and developing strong lists of bread-and-butter works such as grammars, encyclopedias, cookbooks, and standard libraries. London was increasingly the center of the trade, though such strong firms as Chambers, Blackwoods, and Nelson remained in Edinburgh. Most publishers were operated as partnerships, so that individual partners retained financial and editorial control and houses developed a distinct personality. By the late 1850s almost all quality fiction was published by seven firms: Chapman and Hall, Bradbury and Evans, Macmillan's, Longman's, Richard Bentley, Blackwood's, or Smith, Elder.

John Murray, originally Byron's publisher, was no longer primarily interested in literature. Its Victorian authors tended to be those with prestige in natural sciences: Charles Lyell, Roderick Murchison, Edward Whymper, Henry Layard and, of course, Charles Darwin. Murray also published Samuel Smiles (*Self-Help*), David Livingstone, many travel guides, and the *Quarterly Review.*

Edward Moxon, himself a poet, published Alfred Tennyson's *Poems* of 1833 and 1842, *The Princess, In Memoriam, Idylls of the King,* and other works. He also published the early Robert Browning, Mary Shelley's edition of Shelley's *Poetical Works,* and Landor, Sou-

they, and Swinburne. His richly illustrated editions of Tennyson and Rogers were particularly elegant.

Edward Chapman and William Hall published the early works of Charles Dickens, but a dispute over *Martin Chuzzlewit* alienated Dickens for fifteen years. (He returned to Chapman and Hall for *Great Expectations, Our Mutual Friend,* and *Edwin Drood.*) Other major authors were Thomas Carlyle, Robert Browning (*Christmas Eve and Easter Day, Men and Women,* and *Dramatis Personae*), Elizabeth Barrett Browning, Elizabeth Gaskell, Anthony Trollope, A.H. Clough, Leigh Hunt, and W.H. Hudson. George Meredith, a reader for the firm, published *Modern Love, Richard Feverel,* and *Diana of the Crossways* with them. Chapman and Hall also published *Fortnightly Review.*

Another firm of major literary significance, George Smith and Alexander Elder, published all of Ruskin's important early works, much of Browning, including *The Ring and the Book;* Charlotte Brontë; much of Matthew Arnold; major novels by Thackeray; *Robert Elsmere* and other novels by Mary Ward; Hardy's *The Trumpet Major;* Gissing's *New Grub Street* (about publishing); and works by Robert Bridges, Harriet Martineau, Humphry Davy, Richard Jefferies, George Meredith, Sydney Dobell, and J.A. Symonds. The firm's *Cornhill Magazine* and *Pall Mall Gazette* were closely associated with Thackeray.

Bradbury and Evans published Dickens, Thackeray, and *Punch.* William Blackwood and Sons had George Eliot and *Blackwood's Edinburgh Magazine* as well as Bulwer-Lytton, Margaret Oliphant, Charles Reade, Richard Blackmore, Anthony Trollope, and Joseph Conrad's *Lord Jim.* Alexander Macmillan, who became acquainted with the young Christian socialists when they frequented his bookshop in Cambridge and became Charles Kingsley's publisher, gained prominence toward the latter half of the century with Palgrave's *Golden Treasury, Alice in Wonderland,* Kipling's prose fiction, and the early novels of Henry James. Richard Bentley, a rather notorious skinflint best known for Bentley's Standard Novels (120 volumes, 1833–1855) and *Bentley's Miscellany* (edited for a time by Dickens), had an eye for very popular middlebrow fiction; he published much of Ainsworth and the fantastically successful novels of Ellen Price Wood, including *East Lynne*, which he took after two other publishers had turned it down.

Publishing novels required that a firm have the resources to tie up its capital in a fairly substantial outlay for typesetting, paper, and advertising, and be willing to wait for reviews and word-of-mouth publicity, which could make a new book slow to take hold. Unknown authors could be victimized by "payment against profits" schemes that left them owing money to the publisher even if the book were moderately successful. Among the firms that were willing to take chances—but often did not serve their authors well—were Tinsley Brothers (who did the early Thomas Hardy) and T.C. Newby (*Wuthering Heights*).

During the late Victorian period, the book trade became increasingly organized, leading in 1896 to the establishment of the Publishers' Association. Major firms bought out booksellers and lesser rivals. Some transformed their partnerships into companies with boards of directors and, inevitably, surrendered some of their editorial independence. The new firms that entered the field often had distinctive interests to promote. Elkin Matthews and John Lane (together and separately) published books by a number of avant-garde authors; Ruskin's later works were published by George Allen, a firm he helped found; William Morris and the Kelmscott Press created beautifully crafted editions of Renaissance and nineteenth-century poets and inspired the small press movement of limited editions for choice audiences. Other firms came increasingly to specialize in a particular area: medical books, juvenile literature, religious materials, and schoolbooks. Large firms devised special imprints for particular lines and began to originate major projects such as George Smith's *Dictionary of National Biography*. The old method of selling to the trade with lavish dinners hosted by a publisher was abandoned in favor of the new system of travelers or publishers' representatives. From the 1870s, professional literary agents began to represent authors and their interests. The distinctively personal nature of publishing was increasingly replaced by purely business arrangements.

DENNIS R. DEAN

Bibliography

Altick, Richard D. *The English Common Reader.* 1957.

Curwen, Henry. *A History of Booksellers.* 1873; rpt. 1968.

Feltes, Norman N. *Modes of Production of Victorian Novels.* 1986.

Mumby, Frank A. *Publishing and Bookselling.* Rev. ed., 1974.

Sadlier, Michael. *Nineteenth Century Fiction: A Bibliographical Record.* 1951.

Sutherland, J. A. *Victorian Novelists and Publishers.* 1976.

See also CHILDREN'S LITERATURE; TAUCHNITZ EDITIONS; YELLOWBACKS

· · · · ·

PUGIN, AUGUSTUS WELBY NORTHMORE (1812–1852)

The most articulate, versatile architect of the early **Gothic revival**, A. W. N. Pugin was both a prolific designer and author. Among his notable commissions were St. Chad's Cathedral, Birmingham (1839–1841); St. Giles's, Cheadle (1840–1846); and his underacknowledged collaboration in the late 1830s with **Charles Barry** on the Houses of Parliament, for which he provided the decorative detail. A born polemicist, Pugin also wrote numerous articles and eight profusely illustrated books arguing the merits of medieval architecture and society, including *Contrasts* (1836, revised 1841), *The True Principles of Pointed or Christian Architecture* (1841), and *An Apology for the Revival of Christian Architecture in England* (1843).

Pugin received his unorthodox professional training mainly by assisting his father, an architectural illustrator and publisher, and by designing furniture and stage scenery. He formally began his architectural career in 1835, converting to Roman Catholicism that same year. A steady stream of commissions followed, ranging from church restorations and estate remodelings to his work with Barry; he also established workshops to produce tile, metalwork, wallpaper, and other architectural furnishings.

Pugin's writings, however, were more broadly influential. In *The True Principles* he enunciated Gothic's functional characteristics of truthfully expressed materials, structure, and ornament that later revivalists would extol. In *Contrasts*, through satirically juxtaposing in text and picture medieval and Victorian settings, he contended that Gothic architecture organically embodied a Catholic society and that to revive the style successfully, medieval religion must also be restored.

Although his passionate advocacy was silenced by madness and premature death, Pugin helped move the Gothic revival away from archaeologically correct imitation to free adaptation of the style's underlying principles, while his Catholic interpretation of the Gothic style, though it alienated Protestants, nonetheless encouraged among later critics a holistic view of building in which social context and moral judgment became essential elements.

KRISTINE OTTESEN GARRIGAN

Bibliography

Belcher, Margaret. *A. W. N. Pugin: An Annotated Bibliography.* 1985.

Ferrey, Benjamin. *Recollections of Pugin.* 1861.

Gwynn, Denis R. *Lord Shrewsbury, Pugin and the Catholic Revival.* 1946.

Stanton, Phoebe. *Pugin.* 1971.

Trappes-Lomax, Michael. *Pugin, A Medieval Victorian.* 1932.

· · · · ·

PURITY CAMPAIGN

Emerging during a realignment of various pressure groups associated with the campaign to repeal the Contagious Diseases Acts and evolving from the rescue (of prostitutes) societies earlier in the nineteenth century, the social purity movement aimed for a single standard of sexual morality for men and women. The movement is an example of the transfor-

mation late in the century of the tenets of political liberalism, from laissez faire to state intrusion and intervention. The most identifiable leader was Ellice Hopkins (1836–1904).

There had been social purity movements previously (e.g., in the 1690s and c. 1800), crusades on behalf of pure standards of public morality and chaste private sexual behavior. During the nineteenth century the focus was initially upon "rescue," a systematic process of reclaiming prostitutes. Rescue societies formed and conducted "midnight missions." Individual men and women would venture out at night into the "harlot districts" of urban areas and attempt to persuade prostitutes to abandon their practices. The societies, often funded by wealthy evangelicals, sponsored Magdalen Homes for temporary voluntary confinement until the unfortunate women could "be returned to their friends." Prime Minister William Gladstone personally conducted such midnight perambulations in London for over four decades.

Passage of the Contagious Diseases Acts (CDA) during the 1860s and subsequent opposition campaigns increased the level of interest and activity to influence Parliament and public opinion by means of pressure groups. The acts applied only to the locale of eighteen military and naval bases, and the primary purpose was to reduce the incidence of venereal diseases in the armed forces. Opponents complained that the acts represented the epitome of the double standard, and women, especially poor women, were victimized. One consistent manifestation of all of these movements was the increased participation of women of all classes in social and political activities. The most identifiable leader of the anti-CDA campaign was **Josephine E. Butler** (1828–1906).

The other event that accelerated activism was the sensational series of newspaper articles of July 1885 in the *Pall Mall Gazette* entitled "The Maiden Tribute of Modern Babylon." The author, William T. Stead (1849–1912), and Butler actually completed a transaction of selling a young English girl to a Continental brothel, the process dubbed the **white slave trade.** This and the repeal of the Contagious Diseases Acts caused a realignment within a number of pressure groups advocating "vigilance" and moral reform. Notable leaders at this crucial period were

Hopkins, Butler, William Shaen (1820–1887), and William A. Coote (1842–1919).

For half a century after 1870, a number of pressure groups arose superseding the old rescue societies and anti-CDA groups. The evolution was complex and was marked by schism, amalgamation, and consolidation. "Alliances" and "unions" abounded. Prominent ones included the National Vigilance Association, the Social Purity Alliance, the Moral Reform Union, the White Cross League, and, finally, in 1915, the Association of Moral and Social Hygiene, uniting social purity and medical forces. Emerging later was the Josephine Butler Society and its journal, *The Shield*, which first appeared in 1870 as the organ of anti-CDA.

Josephine Butler was the glorified heroine of the social purity movement and, later, the modern pressure group was named for her. She continued to campaign against regulation in India and on the Continent. However, she opposed some of the extreme measures such as public attacks against prominent persons such as Charles Dilke and Charles Stewart Parnell based on moral judgments. Butler represented that segment of the movement that stressed individual rights and opposed government regulations.

Ellice Hopkins founded several moral purity groups. She was primarily concerned about the degradation of women and focused much of her efforts on the maintenance of moral purity in men. Her White Cross Army and later White Cross League solicited pledges of chastity from young men (15,000 in 1885) and harked back to the times of medieval chivalry.

Some of these associations adopted even more extreme objectives. To eradicate prostitution and the double standard the National Vigilance Association sought "to create a universal ethic of chastity, for all men and women alike." William Shaen wrote the platform for the Moral Reform Union which called for suppression of sexual intercourse and legal sanctions against seduction. W.A. Coote advocated "social purification" and the establishment of a "totally purified society." The single standard appeared to be absolute chastity for all.

Modern scholars have assessed characteristics of the social purity movement as demonstrative of a new type of liberal reform: activist, coercive, interventionist, calling for extension of state authority and for state intrusion into matters of morality. Public attacks on immorality led to the destruction of promising political careers. Such practices have been dubbed "militant righteousness," "sexual Puritanism," and "the new inquisitorial society."

EUGENE L. RASOR

Bibliography

Bristow, Edward J. *Vice and Vigilance.* 1977.

Coote, William A., ed. *A Romance of Philanthropy.* 1916.

Jeffreys, Sheila. *The Spinster and Her Enemies: Feminism and Sexuality, 1880–1930.* 1985.

Pivar, David J. *Purity Crusade.* 1973.

See also PROSTITUTION

· · · · ·

PUSEY, EDWARD BOUVERIE (1800–1882)

Edward Bouverie Pusey, Regius professor of Hebrew at Oxford University, led the Oxford Movement in the **Church of England** with John Keble and J.H. Newman. Pusey, Keble, and Newman argued in *The Tracts for the Times* (1833–1841) that the established church was not the Protestant Church of England but the Catholic church in England, and thus the Oxford Movement was the beginning of a Catholic revival within the worldwide Anglican communion.

To Victorians, Pusey and "Puseyism" were terms of disapprobation and mockery, suggesting troglodytic crankiness and unpatriotic oddity. Today Pusey can be seen as one who related liturgical worship in the Catholic tradition to the process by which human beings were adapting to the social circumstances of industrialization. In 1833 Pusey, who had grown up among the landed aristocracy, took the unprecedented step of advocating that a church be constructed every day of the year amid the brutal social conditions of the mill towns. By reviving parish worship and constructing new churches, Pusey opposed those who attacked the sacraments and proclaimed that Evangelical or Nonconformist preaching should be at the heart of Christian worship.

Against the Puritan spirituality which had deprecated the body and its senses and portrayed material externals as signs of hypocrisy in religion, Pusey held up the sacramental-liturgical life as the Church of England's noble heritage. For his adherents, known as Puseyites, eucharistic worship celebrated with incense, vestments, and processions gave new significance to earth as well as to eternity, to matter as well as to spirit. More than fifty Puseyite parishes in industrial cities established funds for workers' compensation, funds for burial, and distribution centers for clothing, food, and other necessities.

Though in one sense the future lay with the Puseyites—throughout the world the eucharist began to supplant morning prayer and evensong as the chief form of Anglican worship—in another sense it did not. The Tractarians, advocates of the principles of the Oxford Movement, had dreamed of a popular Catholic revival, but by the end of the Victorian era in most areas of English life the Church of England had been reduced to a tangential formality.

R. W. FRANKLIN

Bibliography

Brilioth, Yngve. *The Anglican Revival.* 1933.

Butler, Perry, ed. *Pusey Rediscovered.* 1983.

Chadwick, Owen. *The Mind of the Oxford Movement.* 1960.

Franklin, R. W. *Nineteenth Century Churches: The History of a New Catholicism in Württemberg, England, and France.* 1987.

———. *The Nineteenth Century Liturgical Movement.* (Forthcoming)

———. "Pusey and Worship in Industrial Society." *Worship,* vol. 57, pp. 386–412.

Liddon, Henry Parry. *Life of Edward Bouverie Pusey.* 1893–1897. 2d ed., 4 vols.

Lough, R. G. *Dr. Pusey, Restorer of the Church.* 1981.

Presitge, Leonard. *Pusey.* 1933.

· · · · ·

QUAKERS see FRIENDS, SOCIETY OF

· · · · ·

RACE

During the Victorian period "race" was a classification covering any grouping of natural objects linked by shared descent or origin. Although the term continued to have wide parlance and reference throughout the nineteenth century, by the 1840s its use had been appropriated by ethnologists to designate a division of humankind united by common morphology and culture. Race was the basic unit of ethnological analysis and a subject of intense social and political interest.

Carl von Linnaeus (1707–1778), an eighteenth-century Swedish systematist, had divided humanity into four families, or races, based upon skin color. A fifth category was added by the comparative anatomist Johann Friedrich Blumenbach (1752–1840) in the 1780s. Blumenbach's classification—American, Caucasian, Ethiopian, Malayan, and Mongolian—became the standard basis for subsequent taxonomy. Later theorists subdivided Blumenbach's categories into varieties or stocks, based on body size and shape, hair color and form, and facial characteristics. The varieties—often themselves referred to as races—had distinct cultural and physical histories. The British population was hypothesized to be the result of racial mixture between numerous racial subgroups, including Iberians, Celts, Anglos, Saxons, Jutes, Frisians, and Normans.

European colonization in Africa, Asia, and the Americas during the eighteenth and nineteenth centuries had caused a precipitous decline in numbers among aboriginal populations, while stimulating interest in their origins and history. Controversy over slavery and self-rule, particularly regarding Africans in the New World, had also given rise to an increased demand for information about the character and capabilities of primitive peoples. As a consequence, numerous ethnological societies were formed in the 1830s to gather information on the history and cultures of non-European peoples. Data collecting often was directed toward solution of the "origins" problem: Were different races distinct species, or only varieties, and did they have one or multiple origins (monogenesis versus polygenesis)?

During the second half of the century political disruptions within the empire, including the Sepoy Rebellion in India (1857), the Jamaican rebellion (1865), and continuing troubles in Ireland had a hardening effect upon British public opinion. Direct rule was increasingly imposed upon subject peoples. Political disruption was attributed to undesirable social attributes not yet eliminated by evolutionary advance. Political pragmatism among colonial administrators was theoretically justified by reference to the tenets of a nascent evolutionary anthropology. Different races had distinct psychological characterists and varying evolutionary potential. A racial hierarchy that placed Europeans at the top of a scale of evolutionary development also implied their responsibility to help direct races whose social advance had been retarded.

DAVID K. VAN KEUREN

Bibliography

Bolt, Christine. *Victorian Attitudes to Race.* 1971.

Curtis, Lewis P. *Anglo-Saxons and Celts: A Study of Anti-Irish Prejudice in Victorian England.* 1968.

Stocking, George, ed. *Race, Culture, and Evolution.* 1982.

See also ANTHROPOLOGY;
ETHNOLOGY

· · · · ·

RACING AND RACEHORSES

Racing was popular throughout the nineteenth century, both with breeders and owners of racehorses and with spectators, many of whom were from the working class.

Horse racing in Britain, using horses especially bred for the purpose and competing for prizes, had been established long before Victorian times. The thoroughbred horse as a distinct breed developed in the eighteenth century from selective crosses of imported Arabian horses and English mares. Breeding records had been kept since the late seventeenth century, and were recorded and published in the *General Stud Book* from 1793.

Records for the various established distances at which horses raced were lowered significantly in the nineteenth century. However, it is not clear whether this was a result of breeding better horses or of improvements in the conditions of racing. Faster racing surfaces, refined timing techniques, superior equine physiology and veterinary care, and even athletic riding styles all contributed to faster races.

The Jockey Club, in existence by the mid-eighteenth century, became the governing authority for British racing in the 1860s and 1870s under the leadership of Lord George Bentinck and Admiral Henry John Rous. The development of railways made racing accessible to the British public on a large scale. The enclosure of courses, which began in 1875, helped control crowds and provide income for promoters. Transportation of racehorses by rail made more frequent racing possible, replacing the time-consuming and tiring system of walking horses from one track to another. The railways offered special fares on major race days, encouraging crowds of up to 80,000 on bank holiday meets by the end of the century. Although Victorians were disturbed by the rowdiness and **gambling** involved, the British upper classes both supported and participated in racing, and the working classes attended in great numbers. Although there were relatively few women spectators until late in the century, a few women owned or bred racehorses, and everyone gambled.

ELLEN B. WELLS

Bibliography

Blew, William C. A. *A History of Steeple-Chasing.* 1901.

Cook, Theodore A. *A History of the English Turf.* 1901-1904. 3 vols.

Loder, Eileen P. *Bibliography of the History and Organisation of Horse Racing and Thoroughbred Breeding in Great Britain and Ireland.* 1978.

Longrigg, Roger. *The History of Horse Racing.* 1972.

Seth-Smith, Michael. *The History of Steeplechasing.* 1968.

Vamplew, Wray. *The Turf: A Social and Economic History of Horse Racing.* 1976.

Willett, Peter. *The Thoroughbred.* 1970.

· · · · ·

RADICAL CARTOONS

Nineteenth-century radical cartoons look back to the work of James Gillray (1757–1815), arguably the greatest English caricaturist. Gillray himself was a conservative. His admirer and disciple **George Cruikshank** (1791–1878), while politically ambivalent, teamed up with William Hone (1780–1842) in the conflict surrounding Peterloo and the Queen Caroline scandal of 1819–1821 to direct brilliant and effective visual attacks against the government.

The most important of these were *The Political House that Jack Built*, published in December 1819 and selling an estimated 100,000 within a year, *The Queen's Matrimonial Ladder* (1820), and *The Political Showman* (1821). Cruikshank combined the fantastic imagination typical of Gillray's work with parodies of popular genres—the nursery rhyme, the newspaper, wild-beast shows, children's printed toys. In such work Cruikshank and his fellow cartoonists exploited popular iconography both to ridicule their opponents and to embody the class struggle in such images as the "tree of liberty."

The work of Charles Jameson Grant, published largely in *Cleave's Weekly Police Gazette* (1834–1836), used the crude but effective style of street broadsheet woodcuts. L. Lewis Marks moved from licentious lampoons of Regency scandal to agitation for the Reform Bill in *The Chronologist* (1831–1832). *Figaro in London* (1831–1839) used caricatures by Robert Seymour (1800–1836) and "Paul Pry" (William Heath, c. 1795–1840) to attack both Whigs and Tories. *Figaro*, at first based on the Parisian *La Caricature*, soon changed its style and became the forerunner of the middle-class *Punch*. In spite of the importance of caricature in pamphlet

warfare, the radicals found no successor to Cruikshank.

"Ally Sloper" was conceived as a low-life character by Charles Ross in 1867 and developed by William Giles Baxter into the hero of *Ally Sloper's Half-Holiday* (1884–1923). Sloper, a boozing grotesque, moved through all levels of his society, slyly subverting Victorian values and pretensions. William Morris hailed *Ally Sloper's Half-Holiday* as "the poor man's *Punch*," and it was the Victorian forerunner of the twentieth-century popular "comic." However, the earnest tenor of the British working-class movement in the later Victorian period prevented radical cartoons from flourishing in Britain as they did in continental Europe, and Sloper's political import was only incidental.

LOUIS JAMES

Bibliography

Bailey, Peter. "Ally Sloper's Half-holiday: Comic Art in the 1880's." *History Workshop*, vol. 16, pp. 4–31.

George, M. Dorothy. *English Political Caricature.* 1959.

Gould, Ann. *Masters of Caricature.* 1981.

James, Louis. *Print and the People, 1819–1851.* 1976.

Low, David. *British Caricaturists.* 1942.

Rickwood, Edgell. *Radical Squibs and Loyal Ripostes.* 1971.

Wardroper, John. *The Caricatures of George Cruikshank.* 1977.

· · · · ·

RADICAL POLITICS

The term radicalism, describing those wishing for extensive political or social change, was applied to popular agitators from about the 1770s. Working-class popular movements brought artisan societies into alliance with middle-class reformers, among whom Dissenters, particularly Unitarians, were prominent. The French Revolution in 1789, *The Rights of Man* (1792) by Thomas Paine (1737–1809), as well as the economic distress caused by the Napoleonic Wars, gave impetus to radical demands. By the 1820s emergent trade unionism (though still legally constrained) and provincial newspapers such as the *Leeds Mercury, Sheffield Independent,* and *Manchester Guardian* were giving further expression to radical aims. Radical agitation after 1816 took the form of mass meetings, petitions for parliamentary reform, demands for relief from economic distress, calls for lower taxation, and the reemergence of political clubs. In Parliament Joseph Hume (1777-1855), **Francis Place** (1771-1854), and a group of radical M.P.'s strongly influenced by **Utilitarianism**, known as "Philosophical Radicals," added to the demand for fundamental political change. Although radicalism took a variety of forms, a deep loathing of the aristocratic ideal and the oligarchic assumptions that framed even Whig notions of liberty brought radicals together. It continued to do so, with varying degrees of success, throughout the nineteenth century during campaigns to repeal the Corn Laws, extend the franchise, and reform land law.

The climax of agitation for parliamentary reform during 1830-1832 showed the strength of middle-class radicalism among professionals and manufacturers. After 1832 parliamentary radicals, a group of about 100-120 M.P.'s, including Philosophical Radicals such as George Grote (1794-1871), J. A. Roebuck (1801-1879), and William Molesworth (1810-1855), who were supported by John Stuart Mill (1806-1873) through the *Westminster Review* and by **Daniel O'Connell's** (1775-1847) Irish M. P.'s, sought extension of the political change apparently signaled by the 1832 Reform Act. But despite the Lichfield House Compact of February 1835, which brought Whig and radical M. P.'s together, a lack of effective organization and leadership disappointed many radicals. The rise of **Chartism**, led by William Lovett (1800-1877) and Francis Place, and the **Anti–Corn-Law League**, led by C. P. Villiers (1802-1898) and **Richard Cobden** (1804-1865), revitalized parliamentary radicalism after 1839 and revived the alliance of artisan and middle-class agitation.

From the Anti–Corn-Law league emerged the "**Manchester school**" headed by Cobden and **John Bright** (1811-1889) who saw the triumph of their **free trade** ideals with repeal

of the Corn Laws in 1846. While the free trade economic doctrine of Manchester school radicalism became widely accepted, Cobden and Bright's criticism of British foreign policy during the Crimean War, arguing for a moral internationalism instead of power politics based on national interest, proved, in the short term, ineffective. Other radicals voicing an older eighteenth-century radical patriotism, such as Roebuck, Edward Baines (1800-1890), A.H. Layard (1817-1894), and David Urquhart (1805-1877), denounced Cobden and Bright, although Manchester school advocacy of nonintervention and disarmament did become part of political debate later in the nineteenth century.

The 1860s witnessed a strong revival of radicalism. Parliamentary reform returned as a major issue. The Reform Union, formed in 1864, called for household suffrage, and the Reform League (1865) demanded more extensive reforms. Radicals such as Thomas Milner Gibson (1806-1884), C. P. Villiers, and Layard became part of the leadership of the **Liberal party.** In the universities a progressive intelligentsia emerged centered around figures such as Henry Fawcett (1833-1884), A. V. Dicey (1835-1922), Goldwin Smith (1823-1910), Leslie Stephen (1832-1904), and James Bryce (1838-1922). John Stuart Mill continued to provide intellectual weight to radical aims, though untypical in his support for proportional representation and women's suffrage.

With the 1867 Reform Act, the Liberal government of 1868-1874, and the realization of some radical economic and political aims, religion came to the fore in radical thinking. Increasingly the moral zeal of Nonconformity became the sustaining inspiration for radical activity. It prompted campaigns over church rates, education, and disestablishment, as well as a temperance movement. It influenced municipal activism, the local social welfare reforms that in the early 1870s formed part of the "civic gospel" of Birmingham and other provincial cities, and contributed to the activity of the National Liberal Federation. Between 1874 and 1885, 70 percent of radical M.P.'s were Nonconformists. Through militant and often dogmatic pressure groups, such as the Central Nonconformist Committee, the Liberation Society, the National Education League, and the United Kingdom Alliance, organized popular opinion was allied with electoral pressure.

From a background of provincial Nonconformity and municipal activism **Joseph Chamberlain** (1836–1914), M.P. for Birmingham from 1876, formed the National Liberal Federation in 1877 to channel radical energies toward the reconstruction of the Liberal party. As leader of the radical section Chamberlain became a member of the Liberal cabinet from 1880 to 1885. In the spring of 1885 he proposed an "Unauthorised Programme" for the extension of democracy and betterment of the working classes. Chamberlain's espousal of the Unionist cause after 1886 was a damaging blow as most radicals supported W. E. Gladstone (1809–1898) in Home Rule for Ireland.

In 1891 radicals supported the "Newcastle Programme" calling for Irish Home Rule, Welsh disestablishment, land tax, and local government reform, and a reduction of the House of Lords' powers. Despite a period of division and recrimination after 1895, radicals saw, by 1914, the realization of most of the objects contained in the "Newcastle Programme."

ANGUS HAWKINS

Bibliography

Adelman, Paul. *Victorian Radicalism: The Middle Class Experience 1830–1914*. 1984.

Chamberlain, Joseph. *The Radical Programme*. 1885, ed. David A. Hamer, 1971.

Emy, Hugh Vincent. *Liberals, Radicals and Social Politics, 1892–1914*. 1975.

Hamburger, Joseph. *Intellectuals in Politics: John Stuart Mill and the Philosophic Radicals.* 1965.

Hamer, David A. *The Politics of Electoral Pressure.* 1977.

Heyck, Thomas W. *The Dimensions of British Radicalism: The Case of Ireland, 1874–95.* 1974.

Maccoby, Simon. *English Radicalism, 1872–1914.* 1935–1955. 5 vols.

——. *The English Radical Tradition.* 1957.

Thomas, William. *The Philosophic Radicals.* 1979.

· · · · ·

RAGGED SCHOOLS

Although there is disagreement as to who opened the first ragged school—the Congregationalist, Thomas Cranfield, in Camberwell in 1810 or the Unitarian, John Pounds, in Portsmouth some ten years later—there is no doubt that in the next two decades they spread rapidly. The establishment of the Ragged Schools Union (RSU) in 1844 secured a wide coalition of religious interests under evangelical leadership to provide basic education for children so dirty, wild, and uncared-for that no other school would take them.

The education was initially on Sundays only, provided by middle- and upper-class volunteers. It later extended to weekday evenings and, with the coming of some paid agents, to the daytime as well. By 1849 there were 11,000 Sunday scholars and 8,000 day/evening students. The latter category rose to a peak of 25,000–30,000 scholars in 1869, with over 400 paid teachers. By the 1850s the movement had spread to towns and cities throughout the United Kingdom. **Mary Carpenter** became known for her work in the Bristol area. One calculation suggests that ragged schools were in touch with some 40,000 scholars in the later 1860s. Their work was justified not only on compassionate grounds but also on those of social expediency: it represented an attempt to integrate into society those who otherwise would turn to crime and violence.

The RSU quickly discovered that it was impossible to limit its activities to education. "Intellectual teaching is feeble in the work of reformation," affirmed John Macgregor. "The hand and the eye must be taught to work as well as the head stored with book-learning." Macgregor inspired the Shoeblack Brigade, created for the Exhibition of 1851, which offered ragged school graduates their first sheltered and disciplined employment. Later there were hostels, employment in other trades, and an emigration scheme with a parliamentary grant secured by Shaftesbury to send ragged school graduates to Australia. Meals for ragged children, penny banks, infant nurseries, clothing clubs, and excursions and holidays for the poor all became part of the program.

In the 1870s ragged schools had to reassess their activities because of environmental im-

Dinner-time at the Clare-Market Ragged School. Illustrated London News, *25 December 1869.*
Library Company of Philadelphia.

provement in many cities and because of the 1870 Education Act. Some schools closed and others became board schools, although others continued their old work. Schooling was not universally compulsory until 1880 or free until 1891. In 1893 the RSU was relaunched as the Shaftesbury Society, concentrating on work with disabled children, practical instruction of destitute boys on the training ship *Arethusa*, and missions catering to the whole family in downtown areas.

J.H.Y. BRIGGS

Bibliography

Garwood, John. *The Million Peopled City: Or One Half of the People of London Made Known to the Other Half.* 1853.

Heasman, Kathleen. *Evangelicals in Action.* 1962.

Laqueur, Thomas W. *Religion and Respectability: Sunday Schools and Working Class Culture, 1780–1850.* 1976.

Macgregor, John. *Ragged Schools: Their Rise, Progress and Results.* 1853.

Manton, J. *Mary Carpenter and the Children of the Streets.* 1976.

Montague, C. J. *Sixty Years in Waifdom, or the Ragged School Movement in English History.* 1904.

Schupf, H. W. "Education for the Neglected: Ragged Schools in Nineteenth Century England." *History of Education Quarterly*, vol. 12, pp. 162–183.

. . . . .

RAGLAN, LORD FITZROY JAMES HENRY SOMERSET (1788–1855)

Lord Raglan commanded the British forces in the East from the outbreak of the **Crimean War** in 1854 until his death from cholera (June 28, 1855). At the time of his death, Raglan was greatly maligned by the English press for the failure of the allies to capture the Russian naval fortress at Sebastopol and for the suffering the British troops had endured during the previous winter.

Nonetheless, Raglan's military career was distinguished. Born in 1788 the youngest son of Henry, fifth duke of Beaufort, and educated at Westminster, Raglan served as the duke of Wellington's aide-de-camp and military secretary (1808–1815), as secretary at the British embassy in Paris (1815–1818), and at the Ordnance (1818–1827). Subsequently he was military secretary at the Horse Guards (1827–1852) until his appointment as master-general of the Ordnance (1852). In 1814 he married Wellington's niece Emily Harriet, daughter of the third earl of Mornington.

Raglan was the logical choice as commander of the expeditionary force. He had an intense pride and a profound sense of duty and honor. His tact and even temper were greatly admired; at times, however, he was too generous, and his greatest fault was his uncritical nature. He was unwilling to see the shortcomings of his staff, and too infrequently intervened to resolve critical problems. By frequently deferring to the French commanders, Raglan placed the British troops in a dangerous position on the heights before Sebastopol, a situation that prolonged the siege and increased the losses and suffering among the troops. But Raglan himself was a victim of England's unreadiness for war, and his death added to the misfortunes of the Crimean campaign.

F. DARRELL MUNSELL

Bibliography

Gibbs, Peter. *Crimean Blunder*. 1960.

Hamley, Sir Edward. *The War in the Crimea*. 1890.

Hibbert, Christopher. *The Destruction of Lord Raglan*. 1963.

Kinglake, A. W. *The Invasion of the Crimea*. 6th ed., 1877–1888. 9 vols.

Life of Field-Marshal Lord Raglan: With a Review of the Military Operations in the Crimea. 1855.

· · · · ·

RAILWAYS

Growing to 6,621 miles of line in 1850, 11,789 in 1875, and 15,195 in 1900, railways accounted for an increase of about 10 per cent in the national wealth of mid-Victorian England. Their role in Victorian society is suggested by the average of thirty railway journeys per person undertaken in 1900.

True railways had evolved from tramways for moving freight. Far along the evolutionary path was the Stockton and Darlington railway (1825); shippers, who used their own wagons often pulled by horses, paid tolls (as on turnpikes) for access to the carriageway. By contrast, the Liverpool and Manchester (1830) railway was powered entirely by steam with company-operated trains, both passenger and freight, which ran on a fixed schedule. The overwhelming success of the Liverpool and Manchester railway as a technology, as an investment, and as a service to industry and the general public, made it a model for hundreds of lines constructed after 1830.

The burst of railway construction in the mid-1830s was followed by the "railway mania" of the mid-1840s, when 8,652 miles of new line were authorized in three years. By 1850 English railways, already employing 56,000 men, linked London with Dover, Brighton, Bristol and Exeter, Birmingham, Liverpool and Manchester, Leeds, York, and East Anglia. The west coast line to Scotland was in operation, the line to Holyhead for communication with Ireland was opened in March, and the east coast route to Scotland was nearing completion. Two lines had bored under the Pennines to supply service between Lancashire and Yorkshire. On all these routes an intensive passenger and freight service was operated. Almost as striking as the extent of the railway evolution was the speed at which it was accomplished. As Charles Dickens wrote in *Dombey and Son* (1848), parliamentarians who had laughed at railways in the late 1820s had, within twenty years, woven them thoroughly into the fabric of their lives.

Four men—three engineers and one financier—were associated most fully in the public mind with England's adoption of railways. George Stephenson (1781–1848), a self-taught engineer from the Tyneside (where basic railway technology had first evolved), supervised construction of both the Stockton and Darlington and the Liverpool and Manchester railways and developed the "Rocket" (1829), the prototype locomotive for the Liverpool and Manchester railway, in concert with his son Robert Stephenson (1803–1859), who was engineer of lines connecting London with Birmingham and Chester with Holyhead. **Isambard Kingdom Brunel** (1806–1859) built the opulent Great Western from London to Bristol, later extended into Devon and Cornwall, and experimented in the late 1840s with the atmospheric railway, a theoretical triumph but practical failure, on which trains were propelled by the force of atmospheric pressure pushing a piston in a vacuum tube between the rails. Brunel's lines were built with the rails seven feet apart, allowing more commodious (and expensive) rolling stock and locomotives than those mandated by the four foot eight-and-a-half-inch gauge used by the Stephensons. Since equipment could not be interchanged, expensive transshipment of goods was necessary at break-of-gauge points. Because the timid Regulation of Gauge of Railways Act (1846) failed to implement fully the royal commission's recommendation that the Stephenson gauge be adopted as standard, the wide gauge was not entirely eliminated until 1892.

The problem of incompatible gauges would not have arisen had the Stephensons and Brunel recognized the potential of a unified nationwide railway system as early as did George Hudson (1800–1871), "the railway king," who promoted lines radiating from York and, by the late 1840s, controlled something like a quarter of England's railway mileage. Hudson thought in terms of an integrated network, rather than discrete and independent lines, but his questionable financial methods led to his downfall in 1849. With Hudson's departure, any possibility of uniform operation and interchangeable traffic through centralized ownership evaporated. To the extent that later Victorian railways operated as a unit, they did so through the agency of the Railway Clearing House (1842), a vast bookkeeping organization which distributed revenues of multiline shipments among the various companies involved and moved the railways toward standardized signaling systems, working practices, and classification of goods.

English railways were almost unique worldwide in being planned, built, and operated by private investors with a minimum of state involvement. Each railway company began life with an act that authorized investors to form themselves into a joint stock, limited liability company, empowered to acquire, by compulsory purchase, land on which to construct its proposed line. Legislation established minimal safety standards, but for the most part competition was expected to ensure safety and create route structures best meeting the country's requirements. An act of 1844 contemplated eventual nationalization to begin piecemeal as early as 1865, although in fact the railways remained under private ownership until 1948.

By 1870 the fifteen largest railway companies, representing 80 percent of total railway capital, earned 83 percent of gross railway traffic revenue. Those operating from London included the London and North Western, running from Euston Station to Birmingham, Manchester, Liverpool, and north toward Scotland; the Great Western, fanning out from Paddington Station to cover an arc drawn from Chester to Cornwall; the Midland, from St. Pancras Station north to Sheffield, Leeds, Manchester, and, by an expensive moorland line constructed in the 1870s, Carlisle; the Great Northern, from King's Cross through Doncaster on the east coast route toward Scotland; the impecunious Great Eastern, serving East Anglia with proverbially slow and late trains from Liverpool Street; the London and South Western from Waterloo Station, serving the south coast from Portsmouth to Devon; the London, Brighton, and South Coast, operating from both Victoria and London Bridge Stations; and the South Eastern and the London, Chatham, and Dover, which competed (until conclusion of a working union in 1899) in providing largely duplicate services from Victoria, Charing Cross, Cannon Street, Holborn Viaduct, and London Bridge to the major towns in Kent and the channel ports. Companies beyond the metropolis included the Lancashire and Yorkshire; the North Eastern, which held virtually a territorial monopoly north and east of York; and the Manchester, Sheffield, and Lincolnshire, which changed its name to the Great Central in 1899 upon opening an unnecessary trunk line south from Nottinghamshire to Marylebone Station in London.

Railway employment in 1873 numbered 275,000—3 percent of the male labor force. By 1875 total capital invested in railways was 630 million pounds, greater than the sum invested in the cotton industry, and annual gross revenue generated by the railways in the 1870s averaged about 52 million pounds, double the revenue of the coal industry. In 1900 railways employed about 440,000 workers and carried 425 million tons of freight. Freight traffic generated 53 percent of railway receipts in 1870 and 51 percent in 1900.

From the mid-Victorian period, travel in England was normally railway travel, road services being used only to reach the nearest railway station, of which there came to be some 9,000. Frequency of passenger service was notable; in 1888 there were twenty-nine express trains daily between London and Manchester and fifty-seven between Liverpool and Manchester, while intervals of only two or three minutes separated trains on some sections of the London underground railway system, which had first offered service in 1863. Even most rural lines carried four or five trains daily. Passengers, choosing between first- and third-class accommodation (the second class having been phased out from the 1870s), numbered 540.7 million in 1880 and 992.4 million in 1900.

JOHN RANLETT

Bibliography

Freeman, Michael and Derek H. Aldcroft. *The Atlas of British Railway History*. 1985.

Hawke, G. R. *Railways and Economic Growth in England and Wales, 1840–1870*. 1970.

Ottley, George. *A Bibliography of British Railway History*. 1965.

Pollins, Harold. *Britain's Railways: An Industrial History*. 1971.

Simmons, Jack. *The Railway in England and Wales 1830–1914*. Vol. 1: *The System and Its Working*. 1978.

See also STEAM ENGINE

· · · · ·

READE, CHARLES (1814–1884)

For three decades (1850s–1870s), both as a playwright and a novelist, Charles Reade practiced a social realism which he called "matter-of-fact romance" and which focused on topics like prison abuse, bigamy, labor unions, private insane asylums, insurance fraud, and women's entry into the medical profession. He researched his topics in a manner that has been compared to that of Emile Zola. Drama critics accused him of salaciousness; reviewers labeled his novels "too theatrical." Like Wilkie Collins, a close friend, he was branded a writer of sensation novels. Yet consensus acknowledges that *The Cloister and the Hearth* (1861) remains one of the finest historical novels in the English language.

Reade matriculated at Magdalen College, Oxford (1831), when he received a demyship. He took a third in Greats (1835) and an M. A. (1838); he also entered Lincoln's Inn (1836) and was called to the bar (1842). In that year he obtained a Vinerian fellowship at Magdalen, retaining it throughout his life. Except for personal and family litigation, he never practiced law.

He began his literary career in 1851 when he privately printed *Peregrine Pickle*, a play dedicated to Fanny Stirling, then at the Olympic. For her he adapted such plays as *The Ladies' Battle* (1851) from the French. His initial success, *Masks and Faces* (1852), was his first collaboration with **Tom Taylor**. Increasingly, he adapted plays from his own novels, often taking them on provincial tours. He persuaded Ellen Terry to return to the stage as Philippa Chester in *The Wandering Heir* (1874). His most profitable theatrical venture, *Drink* (1879), was taken from Zola's *L'Assomoir*.

Reade transformed *Masks and Faces* into a novel, *Peg Woffington* (1852), and then wrote *Christie Johnstone* (1853). His first major novel was *It Is Never Too Late to Mend* (1856). *Hard Cash* (1863, serialized in Dickens's *All the Year Round*), *Griffith Gaunt* (1866), *Put Yourself in His Place* (1870), *A Terrible Temptation* (1871), *A Simpleton* (1873), and *A Woman-Hater* (1877) followed. His greatest popularity occurred in the United States, where James T. Fields and Harper were his publishers. Ernest A. Baker called Reade "a brilliant story-teller" and praised his "incomparably vivid style"; Walter C. Phillips wrote of his "vivid dramatic method." Yet many critics agree that Reade relied on "outward behavior" instead of "inner processes" in his characterizations.

Baker declared Griffith Gaunt to be "nothing but a creature of instinct and impulse," a phrase describing the characters of many French and American literary naturalists. Reade probed the social ills of his period in a manner dramatizing "here-and-now" scenes. Victorian England rejected such realism, although *The Cloister and the Hearth* was immediately praised. Amusingly, the subplot of *Foul Play* (1868)—the hero and heroine marooned on a Pacific island—created a storyline imitated by British writers well into the twentieth century.

THOMAS D. CLARESON

Bibliography

Burns, Wayne. *Charles Reade: A Study in Victorian Authorship.* 1961.

Elwin, Malcolm. *Charles Reade: A Biography.* 1931.

Phillips, Walter C. *Dickens, Reade, and Collins: Sensation Novelists.* 1919.

Scott, Kenneth W. *Wilkie Collins and Charles Reade: A Bibliography of Critical Notices and Studies.* 1949.

· · · · ·

REFORM BILL see ELECTIONS AND THE FRANCHISE

· · · · ·

RELIGIOUS ORDERS

The Reformation destroyed English monasticism, but circumstances early in the nineteenth century encouraged its revival. Refugee priests escaping the French Revolution and Wesleyan emotionalism softened the prejudices against brotherhoods. But it was the Oxford Movement that gave renewed impetus to the monastic ideal. John Keble and Edward Bouverie Pusey praised practices such as celibacy and communal living. John Henry Newman, however, emerged as the spokesman for monasticism. Newman idealized its history and believed it could strengthen the Anglican church. In 1840 he established a brotherhood based on monastic principles at Littlemore.

Other factors also encouraged the growth of brotherhoods: the praiseworthy work of Anglican nuns such as Marian Hughes and Priscilla Sellon, the encouragement of convocation and church congresses, and the exoneration of religious orders by a House of Commons Select committee in 1871. Ritualism and Anglo-Catholicism supplied theological support.

In 1865 Richard Meux Benson established the Society of St. John the Evangelist, the Cowley Fathers. This brotherhood emphasized communal prayer, but also engaged in missionary and educational apostolates. Charles Gore founded the Community of the Resurrection in 1892. Gore attempted to reconcile traditional principles of religious life to modern society. The brotherhood's main work was evangelization, and it opened the College of the Resurrection at Mirfield, Yorkshire, to train its members for work in England and Africa. In 1893 Father Herbert Kelly established the Society of the Sacred Mission for evangelization abroad. Education and communal life prepared the future missionary. Aelred Carlyle's Anglican Benedictines of Caldey Island, by contrast, followed a strict and literal interpretation of monasticism, but the community converted to Roman Catholicism in 1913.

The 1897 Lambeth Conference suggested the following guidelines for Anglican brotherhoods: the local bishop, as official visitor, must give permission for a community to settle in his diocese and he must approve its constitutions; the Book of Common Prayer must be used exclusively; and the ownership of property must be vested in the established church.

RENE KOLLAR

Bibliography

Allchin, Arthur M. *The Silent Rebellion: Anglican Religious Communities, 1845–1900.* 1958.

Anson, Peter. *Abbot Extraordinary.* 1958.

———. *The Call of the Cloister: Religious Communities and Kindred Bodies in the Anglican Communion.* 1964.

Attwater, Donald. *Father Ignatius of Llanthony.* 1931.

Benson, Richard Meux. *Instructions on the Religious Life.* 1951.

Bull, Paul. *The Revival of the Religious Life for Men.* 1900.

Kelly, Herbert. *England and the Church.* 1902.

Mozley, Anne, ed. *Letters and Correspondence of John Henry Newman.* 1890.

Sockman, Ralph. *The Revival of the Conventual Life in the Church of England in the Nineteenth Century.* 1917.

Wand, J. W. C. *Anglicanism in History and Today.* 1961.

Weller, Reginald. *Religious Orders in the Anglican Communion.* 1909.

Woodgate, Mildred. *Father Benson: Founder of the Cowley Fathers.* 1953.

See also SISTERHOODS

· · · · ·

RESTAURANTS

Restaurants in England are essentially a post-1850 development indicative of more adventurous eating habits, changing leisure patterns, and increased acceptance of women appearing in public. Previously dining in public was a matter of beef, potatoes, and beer (or port) stolidly consumed over a newspaper in significantly named "eating houses" or "dining rooms." For anything more elaborate one dined privately, in a club or at home. A dining guide for visitors to the Exhibition of 1851 lists only a half-dozen places, all quite expensive, claiming the title restaurant; the oldest was Verrey's on Regent Street. But by the 1860s foreign immigrants, particularly in Soho, were beginning to open Continental-style restaurants which were taken up by bohemian journalists like Blanchard Jerrold, G. A. Sala, and E. S. Dallas, who publicized them. The most famous beneficiaries of their patronage were the Café Royal (1865) and Romano's (1874). Their wider variety of food and more welcoming, leisurely ambience caught on, and by the mid-1870s English catering entrepreneurs like Frederick Gordon and Spiers and Pond had opened restaurants like the Holborn (1873) and Criterion offering excellent cooking, Continental or English style, at reasonable prices and in opulent surroundings, complete with music. Moreover, the new American-style grand hotels that were springing up at the time usually had large restaurants open to nonresidents.

Most importantly, these new restaurants welcomed women. Previously women simply did not dine in public, though some early restaurants had private rooms where escorted women were served (the exception was confectioners' shops, where women could get a light midday meal). The growing fashion for dining out as an evening entertainment was stimulated by the fashion for dining later, and by the increasing respectability of theatergoing—the Criterion and Gaiety restaurants adjoined theaters. By the 1890s the best London restaurants met the highest Continental standards. At the Savoy in the 1890s high society dined on the cuisine of Escoffier while Johann Strauss conducted the orchestra.

At a more modest level, tea shops, like the ABC chain (1880), flourished on the patronage of women shoppers, shop assistants, and clerical workers. Here at last were places where a respectable women could dine alone. Department store restaurants also competed for women shoppers. Increasingly restaurants also employed women as waitresses. (A. J. Munby's diary provides an interesting glimpse of the problems of pioneer waitresses.) Tipping was general, a penny per shilling (8 percent) being usual. Waiters were often entirely dependent on tips and in some places even paid their employers.

CHRISTOPHER KENT

Bibliography

Boniface, Priscilla. *Hotels and Restaurants: 1830 to the Present Day.* 1981.

Borer, Mary Cathcart. *The British Hotel Through the Ages.* 1972.

Deghy, Guy and Keith Waterhouse. *Café Royal: Ninety Years of Bohemia.* 1955.

Grant, James. *Lights and Shadows of London Life.* 1842.

Newnham-David, Nathaniel. *Dinners and Diners.* 1899.

See also CLUBS, GENTLEMAN'S

. . . . .

REYNOLDS, GEORGE WILLIAM MACARTHUR (1814-1879)

Author of *The Mysteries of London* (1844-1846)—the biggest best seller of nineteenth-century England—G. W. M. Reynolds was also a leading figure in the development of the popular press, founding and editing *Reynolds Miscellany* (1846-1869) and *Reynolds Weekly Newspaper* (1850-1969), one of the first and the longest-lived English radical working-class newspaper.

Reynolds was born into an upper middle-class family and educated at Sandhurst. In 1830 he took his inheritance to France where he became involved in radical politics and learned an antiaristocratic, anticlerical republicanism that stayed with him until he died. In 1839, having lost his money in publishing ventures, he returned to England where he wrote for and edited a variety of popular newspapers and magazines, including the radical *Weekly Dispatch* (1842) and the penny weekly *London Journal* (1845-1846). In 1844, he began to publish his best-known novel, *The Mysteries of London* (modeled on Eugene Sue's *Mystères de Paris*). Its combination of sensational, even pornographic material with radical political sentiments is his hallmark as a popular writer, and brought him notoriety and a large fortune.

Reynolds was prolific, producing some forty-odd novels over a twenty-year period. The most characteristic, in addition to *The Mysteries of London* and its sequel *The Mysteries of the Court of London* (1848-1855) are *Mary Price; or the Memories of a Servant-Maid* (1851-1852), *The Soldier's Wife* (1852-1853), *The Massacre of Glencoe* (1852-1853), and *The Seamstress* (1853).

Reynolds was active in Chartist politics for a short time (1848-1852), but his main political influence came through his editing and writing for *Reynolds Weekly Newspaper* from 1850 until the 1870s. This newspaper had a large working-class readership and it consistently supported Chartist goals and working-class causes. The popular "Notices to Correspondents" column, in which the editor responds to a wide variety of questions from readers, gives insight into the interests and concerns of readers of the popular press.

Reynolds reflects many of the characteristic contradictions in popular culture, especially its combination of sensationalism and politics, exploitation and education. The mass circulation of his journals and the huge sales of his novels make him a crucial figure in the history of popular writing.

ANNE HUMPHERYS

Bibliography

Bleiler, E. F. Introduction and bibliography in *Wagner the Wehr Wolf*, by G. W. M. Reynolds. 1975.

James, Louis. *Fiction for the Working Man.* 1963.

——. and John Saville. "G. W. M. Reynolds." In Joyce M. Bellamy and John Saville, eds., *Dictionary of Labour Biography*, vol. 3. 1976.

. . . . .

RHODES, CECIL JOHN (1853-1902)

Cecil John Rhodes is notable in two significant respects. First, he is an outstanding example of a self-made man who amassed a huge fortune. Second, he was a central figure in the age of imperialism which spanned the last quarter of the nineteenth century. He became personally involved in the "scramble" for Africa.

Rhodes, the son of an Anglican clergyman, was educated at Bishop Stortford grammar school. In 1870, for health reasons, he joined his brother, Herbert, in Natal on a cotton farm, but soon became involved in diamond mining at Kimberley. In 1873 he entered Oriel College, Oxford, and, after intermittent residence, gained his degree in 1881.

At Oxford Rhodes developed his ideas about the British empire in his first will, the "Confession of Faith" (1877). He discussed colonial expansion, the development of a federated empire, the recovery of the United States into the fold, his belief in Anglo-Saxon virtue, and his plan for a secret society to uphold the empire.

Rhodes made his fortune in diamonds. By 1891 his De Beers Consolidated Company controlled 90 percent of world diamond production. After the discovery of gold in the Rand in 1886, Rhodes formed the Consolidated Goldfields Company. In 1889 Rhodes obtained a charter for the British South Africa Company, which was afforded trading and administrative powers over a huge area, north of the Transvaal to the Zambesi. Local peoples, such as the Ndebele under King Lobengula, were subjugated (1893 and 1896). The territory was soon known as Rhodesia. Part of Rhodes's objective was to thwart potential Boer or German expansion in South Africa.

Rhodes translated wealth into power. Elected to the Cape Parliament in 1880, Rhodes became prime minister ten years later. In office, he stimulated agricultural and railroad development, and tightened voting regulations by adding an educational requirement. The Glen Grey Act (1892) set aside land and established local African councils. Those Africans living on the reservation had no representation in the Cape Parliament.

By 1895 Rhodes was at the height of his power. He was made a privy councillor. Shortly afterwards, Rhodes was implicated in the infamous Jameson Raid (1895), a scheme to overthrow the government of Paul Kruger in the Transvaal. The raid failed, Rhodes resigned as prime minister, and British and Boer opinion polarized. The Boer War erupted in 1899 and lasted until 1902, the year of the Rhodes's death. In 1910 the Union of South Africa was formed, but the Boer (Afrikaner), rather than British, elements gained political ascendancy.

Some of Rhodes's ideas live on. His will made provision for students from the United States and other territories to win scholarships to Oxford University. Rhodes directed that neither race nor religion should influence the selection of candidates. He wanted to foster international understanding and "British ideals" in the context of a federated empire.

OLWYN M. BLOUET

Bibliography

Flint, John. *Cecil Rhodes.* 1974.

Galbraith, John S. *Crown and Charter: The Early Years of the British South African Company.* 1974.

Lockhart, John G. and C.M. Woodhouse. *Cecil Rhodes: The Colossus of Southern Africa.* 1963.

Roberts, Brian. *Cecil Rhodes: Flawed Colossus.* 1987.

Wheatcroft, Geoffrey. *The Randlords: The Men Who Made South Africa.* 1985.

· · · · ·

THE RHYMERS' CLUB (1890–1896)

Although sometimes linked with the **decadence** of the 1890s, the Rhymers' Club—a group of poets who met to read and discuss their works—stood for no single school or movement, but included a variety of poets: John Davidson (1857–1909), who did not contribute to the Rhymers' books, Ernest Dowson (1867–1900), Edwin Ellis (1848–1916), George Greene (1853–1921), Arthur Hillier (b. 1858), Lionel Johnson (1867–1902), Richard Le Gallienne (1866–1947), Victor Plarr (1863–1929), Ernest Radford (1857–1919), Ernest Rhys (1859–1946), Thomas Rolleston (1857–1920), Arthur Symons (1865–1945), John Todhunter (1839–1916), and William Butler Yeats (1865–1939). The Rhymers usually met at the Cheshire Cheese, a London tavern, but the exact dates and frequency of their meetings are uncertain, and the club had no officers or formal rules. Their two anthologies—*The Book of the Rhymers' Club* (1892) and *The Second Book of the Rhymers' Club* (1894)—show diverse approaches and uneven quality; they include both major and negligible poems.

Although Yeats was the only Rhymer to achieve greatness, there were other notable figures in the group. Plarr, a minor poet, is still worth reading; Le Gallienne was a prolific reviewer and critic; Rhys went on to edit the Everyman series. Davidson, although sharing an interest in music halls with Symons, objected to the decadent artificiality which he associated with the Rhymers, and was perhaps the group's most anomalous member. Davidson did not succeed in his attempt to write a new poetry, but in poems like "Thirty Bob a Week" (1894) he effectively used a vigorous, realistic idiom. Symons, influenced by French decadents and Walter Pater, defended art's artificiality as true to modern urban life. Symons's exact, uncluttered language, in his poems about dancers and lovers, focuses on details rather than ideas, and renders intense, fleeting impressions. He celebrates not an ideal love, but "just enough to last one night." In contrast, Johnson longs for an ideal past, for the immortal thinkers and writers of Oxford, or the dignity and grace of the Stuarts in "By the Statue of King Charles at Charing Cross" (1892). Intellectual and detached, Johnson uses restraint even when expressing his inner conflicts, as in "The Dark Angel" (1894). The poet usually identified as most characteristic of the Rhymers is Dowson, whose "Cynara" poem—"Non Sum Qualis Eram Bonae Sub Regno Cynarae" (1891)—with its desperate search for passion and the world's pleasures and its haunting sense of innocence lost, is perhaps the poem most often cited as representative of the transitional poetry of the 1890s.

Although the Rhymers' Club was more of a loose assembly than a bonded community of poets, it enabled its diverse members—traditionalists and impressionists, decadents and antidecadents—to debate their art when it was in an uncertain passage between Victorian and modern forms. The two anthologies provided an outlet for new voices. And despite their differences, the best of the Rhymers shared a common desire to dispense with abstractions and inflated rhetoric. Thus they helped change the language of poetry.

RICHARD BENVENUTO

Bibliography

Alford, Norman. *The Rhymers' Club*. 1980.

Beckson, Karl. "Yeats and the Rhymers' Club." *Yeats Studies*, no. 1, pp. 20-41.

Fletcher, Ian. Introduction to *The Collected Poems of Lionel Johnson*. 1982.

Flower, Desmond and Henry Maas, eds. *The Letters of Ernest Dowson*. 1967.

Longaker, John Mark. *Ernest Dowson*. 1967.

Nelson, James G. *The Early Nineties: a View from the Bodley Head*. 1971.

Stanford, Derek. *Poets of the 'Nineties: A Biographical Anthology*. 1965.

Thornton, R.K.R. *The Decadent Dilemma*. 1983.

Yeats, W.B. *The Autobiography of William Butler Yeats*. 1953.

· · · · ·

RIDDELL, CHARLOTTE COWAN (1832-1906)

Charlotte Cowan Riddell was a novelist, short story writer, and magazine editor. Some of her work was published under the pseudonyms R. V. Sparling and F. G. Trafford. Although many of her works deal with everyday life in the city and with family situations, she is best remembered for her ghost stories. Riddell wrote four supernatural novels: *The Uninhabited House* (1874), *The Haunted River* (1877), *The Disappearance of Mr. Jeremiah Redworth* (1878), and *Fairy Water* (1873), which has been reprinted as *The Haunted House at Latchford* in *Three Supernatural Novels of the Victorian Period*. These novels all appeared originally in *Routledge's Christmas Annual*. Among her fourteen supernatural short stories, "The Open Door" (1882) and "Nut Bush Farm" (1882), two of the most effective, were first printed in *Weird Stories* (1885), a collection of six ghostly tales that Riddell considered to be her best.

Riddell was born near Belfast. In 1855, after her father's death, she went to London to make a living as a writer. She married Joseph Hadley Riddell in 1857. Her struggle with poverty influenced almost all of her literature including the supernatural tales; not until the publication of *George Geith of Fen Court* (1864) did she achieve any real financial success. This struggle gives her ghost stories a sense of realism. The supernatural events in her tales are always placed amid the events of everyday life. Although Riddell never achieved great fame, the verisimilitude of her writing was important to the development of the ghost story as a genre.

JO ANN CHRISTEN

Bibliography

Bleiler, E. F., ed. *The Collected Ghost Stories of Mrs. J. H. Riddell.* 1977.

Ellis, Stewart M. *Wilkie Collins, Le Fanu and Others.* 1951.

See also SUPERNATURAL FICTION

. . . . .

RIOTS AND DEMONSTRATIONS

Riots and demonstrations, planned or unplanned, as well as rowdiness and drunkenness, had long been a part of British history before the Victorian age. Although some rioting was spontaneous, directed protests were frequently the only avenues open to redress what were perceived as infringements of rights, or assaults on traditional habits and pleasures. These responses were part of a long heritage of lower-class protest and resistance to authority. In the nineteenth century there were Reform Bill and Chartist disturbances in the 1830s and 1840s. There were demonstrations in London over the regulation of shopping and drinking hours in 1855, which saw the police clash with crowds in Hyde Park, resulting in a royal commission to investigate police excesses. Also in Hyde Park in 1862 there were ethnic and religious clashes—the so-called Garibaldi riots—and even ritualist riots in churches during the 1840s and 1850s. In the later 1860s, Reform Bill demonstrations in London resulted in violence between the police and crowds. In the 1880s London's Trafalgar Square was the scene of socialist demonstrations that brought the crowds into conflict with the police and military. These were only the more conspicuous disturbances, all the more so if they occurred in London.

With police reform in the boroughs and the counties from the 1830s and 1840s, the unpaid constables, the few town watchmen, the volunteer militia, and the army gave way to professional, uniformed police as the first line of defense for preventing disorders before they got out of hand, as well as regulating behavior in public places. Public order in its broadest sense, not riot control specifically, was the reason for the formation of police forces, but it quickly became clear that police armed with wooden batons (truncheons) could, if deployed at the correct time, disperse a crowd without the lethal violence that might result from the introduction of armed soldiers. Memories of the "Peterloo Massacre" of 1819 were still fresh. A well-disciplined police force was usually mroe than a match for a much larger, heterogeneous crowd.

In general the Victorian propertied classes harbored no great anxieties over the revolutionary potential of the masses, as they had early in the century. By the 1840s their concerns about crime were more narrowly focused on the so-called "criminal classes," or "dangerous classes," the shiftless, unemployed, semicriminal poor, as distinct from the respectable employed. Also, English crowds were relatively restrained, especially by Continental or American standards, and the disturbances in the second half of the century, whatever the stated purpose, often involved some degree of protest over the use of parks or other public places for demonstrations.

The Victorian bureaucratic state increasingly drew its mandate from a wider constituency, and its responses to pressures from below ultimately took the form of some accommodation, not confrontation or naked repression. By mid-Victorian years, the increasing use of the word "demonstration" reveals the changes in collective action that came about as groups sought to apply pressure to the body politic in socially accepted, nonriotous ways: by parades, banners, election rallies, through trade unions and the strike, and through peaceful protests and demonstrations. Ultimately, England's success in avoiding the likes of the "June Days" in Paris in 1848 lay very much in the restraint and flexibility of the British government and its willingness to make concessions. Also evident was the acceptance by the British people of the rule of law and the various social disciplines thrust on them by a modern society that placed increasing emphasis on orderly behavior. This in turn helped reduce the instances of rioting and other serious public disorder in the nineteenth century.

PHILLIP THURMOND SMITH

Bibliography

Gilley, Sheridan. "The Garibaldi Riots of 1862." *The Historical Journal*, vol. 16, pp. 697–732.

Harrison, Brian. "The Sunday Trading Riots of 1855." *The Historical Journal*, vol. 8, pp. 219–245.

Mather, F. C. *Public Order in the Age of the Chartists*. 1959.

Miller, Wilbur. *Cops and Bobbies: Police Authority in New York and London, 1830–1870.* 1977.

Richter, Donald. *Riotous Victorians*. 1981.

Silver, Allan. "The Demand for Order in Civil Society." In David J. Bordua, ed., *The Police: Six Sociological Essays*. 1967.

Smith, Phillip Thurmond. *Policing Victorian London: Political Policing, Public Order, and the London Metropolitan Police*. 1985.

Stevenson, John. *Popular Disturbances in England, 1700–1870*. 1979.

See also BLOODY SUNDAY;
CHARTISM

· · · · ·

RITCHIE, ANNE THACKERAY (1837–1919)

Daughter and editor of Victorian novelist William Makepeace Thackeray and aunt to modernist author Virginia Woolf, Anne Thackeray Ritchie bridged their two worlds in life and art. Ritchie wrote impressionistic fiction that prefigured the twentieth-century stream-of-consciousness novel, and her reminiscences captured the spirit of her father's friends, her own contemporaries, and the emerging generation.

Ritchie began writing under her father's tutelage, but she went on to infuse her fiction, critical introductions, and memoirs with her own brand of impressionism. Her first two novels, *The Story of Elizabeth* (1863) and *The Village on the Cliff* (1867), initially ap-

peared in *The Cornhill Magazine*. Quickly gaining a following, she proceeded to write about various women authors, including Mme. de Sévigné, Maria Edgeworth, Jane Austen, Elizabeth Gaskell, and George Eliot. Completing *Records of Tennyson, Ruskin, and Robert and Elizabeth Browning* (1892) and *Chapters from Some Memoirs* (1894) encouraged Ritchie to tackle Thackeray's life story in a series of biographical introductions (1898–1899 and 1910–1911) to his canon. She became Lady Ritchie in 1907 when her husband was knighted. Lady Ritchie was elected a fellow of the Royal Literature Society (1911), and she served as president of the English Association (1913).

In her *TLS* obituary notice, Woolf suggested that Ritchie was a "transparent medium" through which we would know the Victorian age. As she looked ahead to a new era, Ritchie also heralded her niece's feminism and narrative innovations.

CAROL HANBERY MacKAY

Bibliography

Gérin, Winifred. *Anne Thackeray Ritchie: A Biography*. 1981.

Ritchie, Hester Thackeray, ed. *Thackeray and His Daughter: The Letters and Journals of Anne Thackeray Ritchie*. 1924.

The Two Thackerays: Anne Thackeray Ritchie's Centenary Biographical Introductions to the Works of William Makepeace Thackeray. 1988, Intro. by Carol Hanbery MacKay. 2 vols.

· · · · ·

RITUALISM AND ANTIRITUALISM

Ritualism refers to the movement within the Anglican church that emulated the liturgies and devotions of medieval Christianity or Roman Catholicism. The origins of Victorian ritualism can be found in the **High Church** theology of the seventeenth century, the writings of the Tractarians, and the interest in architecture and liturgy generated by the Cambridge Camden Society.

The Six Points expressed the views of the ritualists: eastward position, eucharistic vestments, the mixing of water and wine in the chalice during Holy Communion, altar lights, unleavened bread, and incense. Some clerics, such as Alexander Heriot Mackonochie, Charles Lowder, and George Rundle Prynne, believed that ritualist practices would enliven urban parishes and aid in evangelization. These "slum priests" also encouraged auricular confession. Others, such as Lord Shaftesbury, argued that ritualism was a departure from traditional Anglican teaching and even encouraged conversions to Rome. Opposition often took the form of violence, such as in the riots at St. George's-in-the-East during 1859.

The English Church Union, founded in 1860, championed the High Church cause. In addition to the Six Points, it advocated reunion with Rome. Its foe, the Church Association, was established in 1865. Its lawyers successfully prosecuted Mackonochie and John Purchase for ritual offense under the Church Discipline Act of 1840.

The Public Worship Regulation Act of 1874 attempted to control clerical disobedience and the spread of alleged Roman practices. Drafted by the archbishop of Canterbury, Archibald Tait, it established a court to hear ritual cases. The uproar caused by the imprisonment of five clerics (Arthur Tooth, Thomas Dale, Richard Enraght, Sidney Green, and Bell Cox) for contempt of court and the use of the episcopal veto to halt proceedings destroyed its force.

In 1890 the archbishop of Canterbury, Edward Benson, heard the case of Edward King, the bishop of Lincoln, accused of liturgical improprieties. Benson forbade the mixing of water and wine during the service and the sign of the cross at absolution; and he ordered that the manual acts during the consecration must be visible to the congregation. But the following were permissible: eastward position, candles, mixed chalice, the *Agnus Dei* after the consecration, and ablution. The Lincoln Judgment effectively ended ritual prosecutions and confirmed the comprehensiveness of Anglican liturgy.

RENE KOLLAR

Bibliography

Bentley, James. *Ritualism and Politics in Victorian Britain: The Attempt to Legislate for Belief.* 1978.

Chadwick, Owen. *The Victorian Church.* 2 vols. 1966-1970.

Davies, Horton. *Worship and Theology in England.* Vol. 3. 1690-1850. 1961.

———. *Worship and Theology in England.* Vol. 4. 1850-1900. 1962.

Ellsworth, L. E. *Charles Lowder and the Ritualist Movement.* 1982.

Embry, J. *The Catholic Movement and the Society of the Holy Cross.* 1931.

Rowell, Geoffrey. *The Vision Glorious: Themes and Personalities of the Catholic Revival in Anglicanism.* 1983.

· · · · ·

ROBERTSON, THOMAS WILLIAM (1829-1871)

Actor and playwright Thomas William Robertson represented a new note of realism amid the often maudlin chorus of mid-Victorian theater. In social comedies such as *Society* (1865), *Ours* (1866), *Caste* (1867), *Play* (1868), and *M. P.* (1870), he demonstrated a sustained attention to naturalistic detail in every element from acting to set design. Though many critics derisively referred to his innovations as "cup-and-saucer" drama, Robertson earned the respect of such disparate contemporaries as Shaw, Wilde, and W.S. Gilbert.

Born into a theatrical family, Robertson settled in London in 1848 and took odd jobs teaching, acting, and writing for newspapers. His early plays, principally melodramas and farces, were not successful. Failure as a playwright, however, ended with the production of *David Garrick* (1864), which marked the beginning of his long association with Squire Bancroft and the Prince of Wales Theatre. *Society* and *Ours*, which treated contemporary issues and concerns, fully established Robertson's reputation.

Caste, long considered Robertson's finest work, was also his fullest examination of a stratified society. In this story of a marriage between an aristocrat and the daughter of a lower-class drunkard, Robertson exhibited all of his most striking characteristics: minutely realistic stage settings (including the much-maligned teacup), restrained dialogue, ensemble acting, and a gradual, rather than catastrophic, evolution of character. In particular, the simultaneously staged conversations attempted to achieve a naturalism that went beyond external verities.

The author of twenty-two plays, Robertson died at the age of forty-two, a scant seven years from the date of his first theatrical triumph. Although he returned briefly to melodrama, the best of Robertson's later work adhered to the principles and production values established in his earlier successes. His orthodox social views, reflected in his plays' themes, prevent him from being seen as a revolutionary figure in nineteenth-century drama. His attempts at dramatic realism, however, opened up important new avenues in the theater. Thus Robertson must be accorded a pivotal position in the move toward modernism.

LAUREN SMITH

Bibliography

Pemberton, Thomas E. *The Life and Writings of T. W. Robertson.* 1893.

Savin, Maynard. *Thomas William Robertson: His Plays and Stagecraft.* 1950.

See also THEATERS AND STAGING (*illus.*)

. . . . .

ROBINSON, HENRY CRABB (1775–1867)

Henry Crabb Robinson was the indefatigable friend of many public (mainly literary) men and women and a supporter of liberal and educational causes. His diaries and letters are a mine of information about the period and its famous figures. He contributed to journals including the *Monthly Repository* and the *Westminster Review*, but thought himself incapable of creative work.

Robinson's anecdotes appear in his diary (begun in 1811 and continued until within days of his death), reminiscences written up from the diaries, thirty volumes of travel journals, and voluminous correspondence. Only selections are printed, but the manuscripts have been searched for information on the Wordsworths, Coleridge, Lamb, Goethe, and many lesser figures.

From a middle-class Dissenting family, Robinson was largely self-educated. He bought an early share in London University, "as a sort of debt to the cause of civil and religious liberty," and served many years on its senate. He deliberately cultivated the famous but became their genuine friend. Except to say that he talked too much, contemporaries spoke no ill of him, and his Sunday breakfasts were an institution. His early studies at Jena made him among the first to spread a knowledge of German literature and philosophy in England. He was briefly foreign correspondent and then foreign editor of the *Times*; between the ages of thirty-six and fifty he made enough money as a barrister to retire to books, causes, famous friends, and the initial sifting of his papers.

SHELAGH HUNTER

Bibliography

Baker, John M. *Henry Crabb Robinson of Bury, Jena, The Times, and Russell Square.* 1937.

Brown, Eluned, ed. *The London Theatre 1811–1866: Selections from the Diary of Henry Crabb Robinson.* 1966.

Morley, Edith J. *The Life and Times of Henry Crabb Robinson.* 1935.

———, ed. *Henry Crabb Robinson on Books and Their Writers.* 1938.

Sadler, Thomas, ed. *Diary, Reminiscences, and Correspondence of Henry Crabb Robinson.* 1869.

. . . . .

ROMAN CATHOLIC CHURCH

When the nineteenth century opened, the Roman Catholic church in England was a small and feeble body of survivors from the days of the penal laws. The church underwent a tremendous revival during the century, aided by converts from High Church Anglicanism and the influx of Irish immigrants; it became a strong, hierarchically disciplined church with a working-class base, the only church to continue growing into the twentieth century. The Catholic church in Ireland, always a church of the majority, also experienced institutional and devotional maturation in the course of the century.

At the end of the eighteenth century, the Roman Catholics of England were a small unobtrusive group, numbering about 100,000, shaped by the experience of two centuries of persecution and disabilities and the consciousness of the invincible Protestantism of the English people, who could easily be roused by a "no popery" cry. Although most disabilities (other than political) were repealed by acts of 1778 and 1791, the hereditary "old Catholics" remained quiescent under the traditional leadership of a core of aristocrats and gentry. The achievement of **Catholic emancipation** in 1829, which removed nearly all political disabilities, was due not to the English but to the more vigorous Irish Catholics, led by Daniel O'Connell (1775–1847). Even then the "cismontane" English Catholics sought to deemphasize the Roman aspect of the church in government and devotion. The Roman authorities treated England as a missionary country, with mission stations instead of parishes and vicars-apostolic (in episcopal orders but with no independent authority) instead of diocesan bishops. The vicars-apostolic quarreled with each other and with the religious orders.

Nonetheless there were signs of revival and growth in the new century. Natural increase, a growing trickle of Irish immigration, and some conversions yielded a membership of about 250,000 by 1840, when the number of vicars-apostolic was raised from four to eight to meet the larger needs. Schools that had been formed on the Continent in penal days returned to England after the French Revolution, and there were signs of a revival of intellectual life. **Nicholas Wiseman** (1802–1865), then rector of the English College in Rome, visited England in 1835–1836 to stimulate his fellow Catholics (founding the *Dublin Review* in 1836), to promote Roman devotions and to reach out to sympathetic Anglicans.

Two events of the 1840s changed the face of Roman Catholicism in England. The first was the conversion, beginning in 1845, of significant numbers of High Church Anglicans, led by **John Henry Newman** (1801–1890), who had become convinced that the only true seat of ecclesiastical authority was in Rome. They were self-converted and somewhat aggressive in their Romanism, but the unmarried exparsons soon became priests who would be sorely needed, and in Newman they offered English Catholicism instant intellectual eminence. The other event was the Irish famine in 1845 and subsequent years, which led to the emigration in a short time of some one million Irish people, with more following steadily throughout the century; several hundred thousand of these went to England, and many others to Scotland. The Irish provided the English Catholic church with the bulk needed for it to achieve major importance in England. They also brought social problems: almost all were poor, and they had to be reintegrated into Catholicism in an unfriendly land by a church hardly ready for such an effort. Henceforth, the majority of Catholics in England would be non-English in ethnic origin and lower-class in social status. By recapturing the immigrants and accepting a mission to the working class, Roman Catholicism ensured that it would be a growing force in England.

The new importance and visibility of English Catholicism produced a demand for an ordinary hierarchy of bishops with dioceses. In 1850 Pope Pius IX (1846–1878) erected a hierarchy of one archbishop and twelve bishops, headed by Wiseman as cardinal and archbishop of Westminster. Hailed as a "second spring" of the church and a "restoration" of the hierarchy, this was in fact a mere administrative reorganization. The new sees were carefully named so as not to duplicate Anglican bishoprics. Nonetheless, this so-called "papal aggression" provoked a storm of anti-Catholic agitation, stimulated by Lord John Russell (1792–1878) with his letter to the bishop of Durham. Popular protest forced the passage of an Ecclesiastical Titles Act in 1851, forbidding the use of territorial titles; but the act was never enforced and was eventually repealed. If anything, the incident stimulated a more vigorous assertion of Catholicism in England. It should be noted, however, that Rome still regarded England as a mission land, kept under the tight control of the Congregation of Propaganda until 1908.

Wiseman succeeded in implementing the organization of the new hierarchy, although his administrative ineptitude made his primacy a series of quarrels with bishops and clergy. His true achievement was to bring to England the Roman devotions and the ultramontane spirit which characterized the Catholic revival on the Continent in the nineteenth century. Unfortunately, this brought him into conflict with a promising liberal Catholic movement, designed to bridge the gap between Catholicism and the leading secular ideas of the day, led by the young Sir John (later Lord) Acton (1834–1902). Rome, under the threat of political liberalism, adopted a siege mentality which involved opposition to much modern thought. Under official disapproval, Acton's *Rambler* and *Home and Foreign Review* were extinguished, and with them went Catholic intellectualism.

Wiseman's promotion of ultramontanism was continued after 1865 by his successor at Westminster, **Henry Edward Manning** (1808–1892), a convert from Anglicanism who was rapidly promoted and who became a cardinal in 1875. Manning's merit was to recognize that the Catholic Church in England was mostly Irish and working class and to reorient the church to meet the needs of this constituency. This drew him into social Catholicism and won him the respect of the workers: Roman Catholicism was the only denomination that did not lose the working class. A complete system of denominational schools and charities was developed. Manning left his church sufficiently secure that his successor, **Herbert Vaughan** (1832–1903), could erect the impressive Westminster Cathedral as a monument to its success.

In Ireland, Roman Catholics had always been in the majority, and the diocesan structure of the church had been kept up. However, the eighteenth century was the nadir of Irish Catholicism. The effect of severe penal laws had been to eliminate the Catholic aristocracy and gentry, leaving a Catholic body consisting almost entirely of depressed peasants with no leadership except their priests. After the repeal of the penal laws, a small Catholic middle class emerged which provided the political leadership that brought about Catholic emancipation. In Ireland, religion and politics were intermixed, and the political interests of Irish Catholics were largely absorbed by nationalism and the land question; the disestablishment of the Anglican Church of Ireland in 1869 practically ended the religious issue, except for educational matters which were never fully resolved. The Catholic bishops remained a political force but could devote their attention to religious matters. In fact, the Catholicism of most Irish people was little more than formal at the beginning of the nineteenth century; moral and devotional standards were deplorably low. The rapid rise of population made it difficult for the clergy to keep up until the great famine reversed the trend. Then, under the leadership of Paul Cullen (1803–1878), archbishop of Dublin from 1852 and later cardinal, the bishops took firm control of their clergy and developed a disciplined church, which in turn stimulated an intense devotion and a puritanical morality among the laity. This "devotional revolution" shaped the religious character of the Irish people and the Irish diaspora throughout the world.

JOSEF L. ALTHOLZ

Bibliography

Altholz, Josef L. *The Liberal Catholic Movement in England.* 1962.

Beck, George A., ed. *The English Catholics, 1850–1950.* 1950.

Bossy, John. *The English Catholic Community, 1570–1850.* 1975.

Holmes, J. Derek. *More Roman than Rome.* 1978.

Larkin, Emmet. *The Historical Dimensions of Irish Catholicism.* 2d ed., 1984.

Norman, Edward. *The English Catholic Church in the Nineteenth Century.* 1984.

Schiefen, Richard J. *Nicholas Wiseman and the Transformation of English Catholicism.* 1984.

Thureau-Dangin, Paul. *The English Catholic Revival in the Nineteenth Century.* 1914. 2 vols.

Ward, Bernard. *The Sequel to Catholic Emancipation.* 1915. 2 vols.

Ward, Wilfrid. *The Life and Times of Cardinal Wiseman.* 1897. 2 vols.

. . . . .

ROMANTICISM

Themes and habits of mind inherited from the English poets of the romantic movement permeate Victorian novels, poetry, and argumentative prose, although Victorian writers expand and adapt romantic ideas, offering them as solutions to problems of their own society.

Many major Victorian novelists look back to the romantic decades for settings, a retrospective habit which is itself romantic. They often regard the romantic period as an ideal time whose lost virtues are needed by a more complex modern age. With darkly luxurious word portraits suggesting John Constable's painting, the opening chapter of George Eliot's *Felix Holt, the Radical* (1866) describes the graceful vistas and provincial charm of a past lost to the anxious, industrial present. These nostalgic rural vignettes constitute Eliot's own Wordsworthian mergence through memory with the harmonies of the earlier age.

The Victorians sustain the romantic belief in the holiness of the heart's affections and the efficacious guidance—creative and moral—given by the spontaneous overflow of powerful feeling. Victorian sentimentality, earnestness, and exuberance about prospects for personal completion have their origin in the romantic value of emotional release and the hopeful expectation of "something evermore about to be" (Wordsworth, *The Prelude*, 1805).

Victorian writers reaffirm the romantic faith in nature's moral and emotional efficacy. In works ranging from Matthew Arnold's "The Scholar-Gipsy" (1853) to Charles Dickens's *Hard Times* (1854), nature is presented as an antidote for the bleakness of the industrial city. Victorian attitudes toward the city also intensify the romantics' aversion. Following the tradition of Blake's "London" (1794) and book seven of Wordsworth's *Prelude*, novels like Charles Kingsley's *Alton Locke* (1850) and Dickens's *Bleak House* (1853) depict the city as a hellish wasteland which destroys its inhabitants emotionally and morally.

Although the Victorian middle class valued conformity and respectability, many Victorian authors inherit the romantic impulse toward individuality and nonconformity. Unconventional characters like Heathcliffe of *Wuthering Heights* (1847) and Professor Teufelsdrockh of Thomas Carlyle's *Sartor Resar-*

tus (1833–1834) protest against conformity and shallow propriety, as does the third chapter of John Stuart Mill's *On Liberty* (1859). An archetypal romantic rebel, Robert Browning's Fra Lippo Lippi (1855) is governed by such ideals as freedom from customary perspectives and independence of the creative imagination. Through such romantic types, Victorian authors declare the value of transcending the commonplace and of a restless intellect absorbed in the quest to comprehend life and eternity. Their conception of human worth thus incorporates the romantic ideal of process and constant personal development, as seen in Wordsworth's "Tintern Abbey" (1798) and Keats's *The Fall of Hyperion* (1819).

The **Gothic revival** in architecture, the Oxford Movement in religion, and the **Pre-Raphaelite Brotherhood** in art are diverse manifestations of another romantic interest carried forward by the Victorians: **medievalism.** Victorian authors often wish to revive medieval conditions and states of mind as foundations for a perfect nineteenth-century commonwealth, as in Carlyle's *Past and Present* (1843), Benjamin Disraeli's *Sybil* (1845), or William Morris's *News from Nowhere* (1891).

Victorian novelists and essayists amplify the romantic assumptions that the writer is a critic of society and that literature is a powerful instrument in the service of social and political reform. Romantics like Blake and Wordsworth emphasized the reform of human nature, believing that social reform would follow from the renovated human mind. Victorians called for the change of institutions—Parliament, the electoral process, the Church of England, the schools, universities, and courts—because institutions direct the regeneration of human nature and society. Victorian authors, however, continued to believe that reform will be accomplished not through specific platforms or simple institutional changes but through the exercise of imagination and the renovation of the nation's mind and character.

For Dickens in *Hard Times* the life of imagination, embodied in Sleary's circus, mitigates the ruthless industrialism of Bounderby and the soulless utilitarianism of Gradgrind. For Arnold in *Culture and Anarchy* (1869) Hellenism—openness to new ideas, love of contemplation, cultivation of the inner life—

must be disseminated to oppose "Doing as One Likes," evangelical quarrelsomeness, and other sources of anarchy. For Eliot in *Middlemarch* (1872) humanity's elevation proceeds from the inner apocalypse of specific individuals; the "growing good of the world" depends on "unhistoric acts" and "living faithfully a hidden life," on the intellectual transformations and unobtrusive spiritual growth of people like Dorothea Brooke. The interpersonal relationships in *Middlemarch* further show that empathic participation in others' consciousness, the Keatsian ability to feel what is in other minds, is necessary for human solidarity and happiness.

EDWARD DRAMIN

Bibliography

Abrams, M. H. *Natural Supernaturalism: Tradition and Revolution in Romantic Literature.* 1971.

Ball, Patricia. *The Central Self: A Study in Romantic and Victorian Imagination.* 1968.

Brantlinger, Patrick. *The Spirit of Reform: British Literature and Politics, 1832–1867.* 1977.

Dramin, Edward. *Light in a Dark Place: Romanticism in the Victorian Social-Political Novel, A Critical Anthology.* 1987.

Houghton, Walter. *The Victorian Frame of Mind, 1830–1870.* 1957.

Johnson, Edward D. H. *The Alien Vision of Victorian Poetry.* 1952.

Mill, John Stuart. *On Bentham and Coleridge.* 1950, ed. F. R. Leavis.

Willey, Basil. *Nineteenth Century Studies.* 1949.

See also WORDSWORTHIANISM
· · · · ·

ROSEBERY, FIFTH EARL OF (ARCHIBALD PHILIP PRIMROSE) (1847–1929)

Foreign secretary (1886 and 1892–1894), prime minister (1894–1895), and leader of the **Liberal party** (1894–1896), Archibald Primrose succeeded as fifth earl of Rosebery in 1868.

Rosebery came to prominence as Gladstone's principal supporter in the Midlothian campaign (1879–1880). Unlike many Liberal aristocrats, he supported Gladstone in the Home Rule crisis (1886), becoming foreign secretary. He was the first chairman of the London County Council (1889). As foreign secretary in Gladstone's last ministry he went his own way, consulting the cabinet little. When Gladstone retired, Rosebery was preferred as his successor over the head of the irascible William Harcourt, chancellor of the Exchequer. However, worn down by insomnia, Rosebery conducted a short-lived and disastrous ministry, riven by personal acrimony.

Rosebery strove to set a new direction for Liberalism after Gladstone. Known as Liberal imperialism, this involved an element of collectivism and a "clean slate" with regard to Irish Home Rule, and led to his estrangement from the mass of the party during the Boer War (1899–1902). A brilliant and fascinating personality, he seemed to be the brightest star in Liberal politics. However, his effectiveness was diminished by his indecision and aloofness, which led to his eventual political isolation.

STUART BALL

Bibliography

Hamer, David A. *Liberal Politics in the Age of Gladstone and Rosebery.* 1972.

James, Robert R. *Rosebery.* 1963.

Matthew, Henry C. G. *The Liberal Imperialists.* 1973.

Stansky, Peter. *Ambitions and Strategies: The Struggle for the Leadership of the Liberal Party in the 1890s.* 1964.

· · · · ·

ROSS, JANET (1842–1927)

Janet Anne Duff Gordon Ross descended from a remarkable line of intelligent and literate women: Susannah Taylor of Norwich (1755–1823), Sarah Austin (1793–1867), and her mother, Lucie Duff Gordon (1821–1869). She is remembered chiefly for her edition of their correspondence, *Three Generations of Englishwomen* (1888; enlarged 1892), and for her own memoirs, *The Fourth Generation* (1912); she was, however, also the editor, translator, or author of some twenty other volumes.

Ross as a dashing young woman inspired the heroines of two of George Meredith's novels, *Evan Harrington* (1861) and *Harry Richmond* (1871). She married Henry James Ross (1820–1902) in 1860 and proceeded with him to Egypt, where he was a partner in Briggs' Bank. In Alexandria she was correspondent for the *Times* (1863–1864) and bore a son, Alexander (1862), who was rapidly given up to the care of Ross's great-aunt. After commercial failure in Egypt, the Rosses moved to Italy (1866). Tuscany supplied subjects for Ross's sketches of peasant life, an edition of popular songs (1890), translations of the Medici letters (1910), and histories of Pisa (1909), Lucca (1912), and the villas and palaces of the district. Ross was also an indefatigable translator and editor, while her most often reprinted work was *Leaves from Our Tuscan Kitchen* (1899), a vegetable cookbook.

Ross was at home in four languages and did painstaking archival research, but lacked the historian's ability to generalize and to subordinate. Her work remains valuable as a quarry of information, especially because she had the gift for friendship with both eminent and common people. Ross herself, amusingly portrayed by her niece Lina Waterfield in *Castle in Italy* (1961), became famous as an English eccentric in her high-handed old age.

JEAN O'GRADY

. . . . .

ROSSETTI, CHRISTINA GEORGINA
(1830–1894)

The poet Christina Rossetti is best known for her love lyrics and religious poetry. Her writings include six books of poems, one of short stories, three of rhymes and tales for children, and seven books of devotional verse and prose. Her first book, *Goblin Market and Other Poems* (1862) won her immediate recognition as a skilled and original poet. Much of her finest work appeared in this volume and in *The Prince's Progress and Other Poems* (1866).

Educated at home amid a family whose men were intellectual, political, and artistic, and whose women were devoutly religious, Rossetti lived in London with them nearly all her life. Her father, a political exile from Italy, was a professor at King's College. One brother, William Michael, was an editor, translator, and art critic; her other brother, Dante Gabriel, a renowned artist and poet. As children, she and her brothers wrote journals together, and her brothers later criticized and edited her work. Christina Rossetti has sometimes been called the "high priestess of Pre-Raphaelitism."

Equally important to her development was another midcentury movement. Like her Anglo-Italian mother and her sister Maria, who became an Anglican nun, Rossetti was greatly influenced by the Oxford Movement, which sought to bring into the Anglican church early Catholic doctrines and rituals. So strict was her devotion that she allegedly twice rejected marriage proposals because her suitors' religious beliefs were not precisely congruent with her own. While Rossetti's poetry has the fresh pictorial quality and the erotic luxuriousness of Pre-Raphaelite art, much of its distinctiveness arises from combining the sensual with the ascetic, and the erotic with the renunciatory. Although her family history accounts to some extent for these opposing tendencies, she remains nonetheless an enigmatic literary figure about whom there is little biographical or critical agreement.

The discrepancy between the passionate intensity of Rossetti's poetry and her quiet, retiring life has obsessed many of her biographers. Yearning, loss, and balked desire are major themes in her writing, and melancholy its most dominant tone. Her poems give such direct immediacy to love's frustrations and desires that several biographers have been tempted to posit various "lost lovers," or to view her poetry as pitting woman against saint or sacrificing one to the other. Others argue against the rigidity of regarding art as dependent upon lived (as opposed to imagined) experience. They see in Christina Rossetti a complex rather than a "divided self," and one that includes the eccentricity, whimsical ingenuity, and delicate wry humor also revealed in much of her poetry.

Though highly regarded in her own time, Christina Rossetti received little critical attention in the decades after her death. While her highly wrought verse forms were recognized as finely crafted, her lucid images, simple diction, and clear style created for many readers the illusion of a simple surface. Others were put off by her subject matter. More recently, revisionist essays have explored how Rossetti's poetry negotiates between her own experience and the social conventions and literary traditions she inherited, and have uncovered in her severe Christianity a modest and oblique, yet critical, radicalism. These revaluations have given new pertinence to Virginia Woolf's evaluation of Christina Rossetti: "Modest as you were, still you were drastic, sure of your gift, convinced of your vision."

SUZANNE GRAVER

Bibliography

Battiscombe, Georgina. *Christina Rossetti: A Divided Life.* 1981.

Blake, Kathleen. "Christina Rossetti's Poetry: The Art of Self-Postponement." In *Love and the Woman Question in Victorian Literature.* 1983.

Crump, Rebecca W. *Christina Rossetti: A Reference Guide.* 1976.

——, ed. *The Complete Poems of Christina Rossetti: A Variorum Edition.* 1979. 3 vols.

Harrison, Anthony H. *Christina Rossetti in Context.* 1988.

Kent, David A., ed. *The Achievement of Christina Rossetti.* 1988.

McGann, Jerome. "Christina Rossetti's Poems: A New Edition and a Revaluation." *Victorian Studies,* vol. 23, pp. 237–254.

——. "The Religious Poetry of Christina Rossetti." *Critical Inquiry,* vol. 10, pp. 127–144.

Packer, Lona Mosk. *Christina Rossetti.* 1963.

Rosenblum, Dolores. *Christina Rossetti: The Poetry of Endurance.* 1986.

Woolf, Virginia. "'I Am Christina Rossetti.'" In *Virginia Woolf, The Second Common Reader.* 1932.

· · · · ·

ROSSETTI, DANTE GABRIEL (1828–1882)

A founder of the **Pre-Raphaelite Brotherhood**, Dante Gabriel Rossetti was a poet-painter whose work presents an iconoclastic and personal mythology in which art and eroticism mediate spiritual redemption. Representative are poem-painting pairs such as *The Blessed Damozel* (1870; 1879), symbolic portraits such as *Beata Beatrix* (1863), and the sonnet sequence, *The House of Life* (1881).

Born Gabriel Charles, Rossetti changed his name in response to his father's studies of Dante's politico-moral allegories. His own translations of Dante and of medieval courtly love lyrics provided sources for the iconography and metaphor in his mature work.

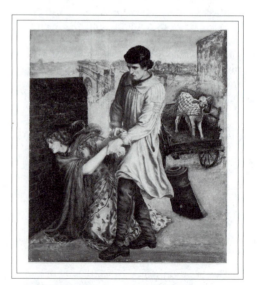

Found (c. 1853, unfinished)
by Dante Gabriel Rossetti.
Reproduced courtesy of the Delaware Art Museum.

Beata Beatrix (c. 1863)
by Dante Gabriel Rossetti.
Reproduced courtesy of the Tate Gallery,
London.

Studying art with Ford Madox Brown and William Holman Hunt in the 1840s, Rossetti was influenced by the German Nazarenes, Dürer, and John Ruskin. With Brown, Hunt, and John Everett Millais, Rossetti formed the Pre-Raphaelite Brotherhood in 1848, revolting against neoclassical conventions in art. His first oils, *The Girlhood of Mary Virgin* (1849) and *Ecce Ancilla Domini* (a.k.a. *The Annunciation*, 1850), exemplify Pre-Raphaelite flattened perspective, "fidelity to nature," typological details, mannerist figures, and illuminated colors. Despite Ruskin's support, *The Germ* (1848–1850), the journal of Pre-Raphelite literature and art, which included Rossetti's aesthetic manifesto, "Hand and Soul," failed and the brotherhood disbanded.

From c. 1850 to her suicide in 1862, Rossetti lived with and eventually married the poet-artist, Elizabeth Siddal, his model for scenes from Dante's *Vita nuova*, a series of watercolors on Arthurian themes, and many portrait drawings. Rossetti identified himself and Lizzie with the tragic lovers in the famous oil, *Beata Beatrix* (c. 1863), which shows Lizzie as Beatrice gazed upon by Dante in an ambiguous vision of "death-in-love," also a theme in Rossetti's sonnets. The eroticized Christian symbolism in *Beata Beatrix* also characterizes the narrator's ironic dream-vision in the famous poem, "The Blessed Damozel" (c. 1846–1870) and its painted version (c. 1871–1879). From c. 1858 onwards, Rossetti was also in love with Fanny Cornforth, the model for the "fallen woman" who rejects her fiancé's call to duty in the controversial painting, *Found* (1853–1882, unfinished). Rossetti's most important work of social realism, *Found*, and its companion sonnet suggest a deep ambivalence over sexuality, Victorian moral codes, and women's rights which also pervades the dramatic monologues, "Jenny" (c. 1846–1870) and "A Last Confession" (c. 1846–1870).

Rossetti soon became known for his book designs, picture frames, stained glass, and his illustrations in Tennyson's *Poems* (1870). Edward Burne-Jones and William Morris joined Rossetti in the second phase of Pre-Raphaelitism, emphasizing a highly stylized medievalism and the coordination of literature and the arts, partly inspired by William Blake. During the late 1860s, Rossetti fell in love with Morris's wife, Jane Burden, who acted as his favorite model for the "femme fatale" type that his patrons often commissioned. Rossetti's monumental oils of dreamy or threatening women, dressed in historical costumes against decorative or mystic backgrounds, suggest his increasing difficulties with sexuality and faith, as in *Monna Vanna* (1866) and *Astarte Syriaca* with its sonnet (1877). Rossetti mastered the "double work of art," or sonnet-painting pairs, such as *Lady Lilith* (1864–1868). His *Poems* (1870) were attacked by Robert Buchanan in the "fleshly school" controversy. *Ballads and Sonnets* (1881), including the final version of the sonnet sequence, *The House of Life*, however, was well accepted. Celebration of the power of love—"Thy soul I know not from thy body, nor / Thee from myself, neither our love from God"—and of art—the "moment's monument"—over doubt and death is central to Rossetti's work.

As a poet-painter, Rossetti definitively influenced Oscar Wilde and the English aesthetic movement, the arts and crafts movement, and Continental art nouveau. Rossetti's metaphoric and symbolic style of writing also molded that of Walter Pater and W.B. Yeats, among others.

THAÏS E. MORGAN

Bibliography

Ainsworth, Maryan Wynn, ed. *Dante Gabriel Rossetti and the Double Work of Art.* 1976.

Doughty, Oswald. *A Victorian Romantic: Dante Gabriel Rossetti.* 1960.

—— and John R. Wahl, eds. *Letters of Dante Gabriel Rossetti.* 1965–1967. 4 vols.

Fennell, Francis L., ed. *Dante Gabriel Rossetti: An Annotated Bibliography.* 1982.

Fredeman, William E., ed. "Dante Gabriel Rossetti: An Issue Devoted to the Works." *Victorian Poetry,* vol. 20.

Hilton, Timothy. *The Pre-Raphaelites.* 1970.

Nochlin, Linda. "Lost and *Found*: Once More the Fallen Woman." *Art Bulletin,* vol. 60, pp. 139–153.

Riede, David G. *Dante Gabriel Rossetti and the Limits of Victorian Vision.* 1983.

Rossetti, William Michael, ed. *The Works of Dante Gabriel Rossetti.* 1911.

Sambrook, James, ed. *Pre-Raphaelitism: A Collection of Critical Essays.* 1974.

Sonstroem, David. *Rossetti and the Fair Lady.* 1970.

Surtees, Virginia. *Dante Gabriel Rossetti: 1828–1882. The Paintings and Drawings: a Catalogue Raisonné.* 1971. 2 vols.

· · · · ·

ROTHSCHILD FAMILY

The Rothschild family of bankers and financiers rose to great prominence in Europe during the nineteenth century and were particularly successful in England. Of German-Jewish descent, the Rothschilds created a unique advantage for themselves by establishing sons of the house in business in a number of European countries, thus providing a network of international contacts that enabled the family firm to handle business well beyond the scope of most competitors.

Baron Nathan de Rothschild (1777–1836) founded the English branch of the family. N. M. Rothschild and Sons became one of the most highly respected institutions in the City of London and a major creditor for the British government; it arranged financing to reimburse slave owners when slavery was abolished in the British dominions (1834), to relieve the Irish famine (1844–1846), and to purchase the Suez Canal (1875).

Younger members of the family quickly became influential in both political and social life. Lionel de Rothschild (1808–1879) was responsible for relieving Jews of one of their most burdensome disabilities: the inability to sit in the House of Commons without first swearing "on the true faith of a Christian." Ferdinand (1839–1898) created one of the wonders of the world when he built Waddeson Manor. Nathaniel (1840–1915) became the first Jewish peer in 1885. Two generations of the family, moreover, were close personal friends as well as influential advisors of the Prince of Wales.

SHEILA MONNET

Bibliography

Cowles, Virginia. *The Rothschilds: A Family of Fortune.* 1973.

Morton, Frederic. *The Rothschilds: A Family Portrait.* 1962.

Roth, Cecil. *The Magnificent Rothschilds.* 1939.

· · · · ·

ROYAL ACADEMY OF ARTS

The Royal Academy of Arts, founded in the eighteenth century as a private society of artists under the patronage of George III and the presidency of Joshua Reynolds (1723–1792), became the most powerful arbiter of public taste in the fine arts in Victorian times. It both reflected and fostered the public enthusiasm for art which followed widespread popular education and the emergence of wealthy middle-class patrons. Its free training school helped to train some of the best painters of the age, including John Millais (1829–1896) and Dante Gabriel Rossetti (1828–

1882). Although best known for its painters, the academy also admitted engravers, sculptors, and architects, who exhibited with the painters. The Royal Academy's most significant influence was, however, its May exhibition.

The May exhibition marked the opening of the London social season with banquets and private views for the rich or influential. The artists and general public waited for the official opening to see which works had been selected. Before the Victorian era, artists had worked largely through private commissions, opening their studios only to patrons who would order works, but the nineteenth century's new breed of buyer did not have the social power to penetrate such private enclaves. Instead, the newly rich manufacturers from the Midlands went to the Royal Academy exhibition to choose their works, often relying, in the absence of trained taste, on the art critics' selection of "picture of the year."

A general enthusiasm for the arts among the general public further intensified interest in the academy exhibition, causing semiriots before such "paintings of the year" as Frith's *Derby Day* (1858) and *Railway Station* (1877). By the end of the 1880s more than 400,000 people attended the annual exhibition. As a result, prices rose dramatically, and artists could realize additional profit from cheap popular engravings which sold in the thousands.

Even artists lucky enough to have work chosen for exhibition could not be sure that it would be properly seen by the art-buying public. Due to limitations of space, the hanging committee placed paintings from floor to ceiling on all walls for the exhibition, which was first held at the National Gallery and, after 1867, at its present site, Burlington House in Picadilly. Since a member of the academy might have up to eight works automatically hung "on the line" at eye level, outsiders often found their work either "skied" to the ceiling or accessible only on hands and knees.

With so much resting on the decisions of the hanging committee, which chose 2,000 or so works from the 12,000 submitted, there were inevitably charges of bias, particularly from younger artists who felt, with some justice, that older academicians not only gave themselves preferential treatment but also actively discriminated against the work of prom-

ising newcomers. Several royal commissions investigated these charges, but little was done until the 1870s, when the opening of powerful rival galleries such as the Grosvenor Gallery gave artists a real alternative to the academy.

MEGAN J. NELSON

Bibliography

Forbes, Christopher. *The Royal Academy, 1837–1901, Revisited.* 1975.

Graves, Algernon. *The Royal Academy of Arts: A Complete Dictionary of Contributors and Their Work, 1769-1904.* 1905-1906. 8 vols.

Hutchison, Sidney C. *The History of the Royal Academy 1760-1968.* 1968.

Lamb, Walter Rangeley Maitland. *The Royal Academy: A Short History of Its Foundation and Development to the Present Day.* 1935.

· · · · ·

ROYAL FAMILY

The Victorian royal family was the first ruling family in England to warrant the modern use of the term "family." Although Queen **Victoria**'s description of babies as "froglike" is well known, and although she wrote to her daughter that childbirth made her feel "like a dog or a cow," Victoria and **Albert** felt a great deal of affection toward their nine children, and encouraged a family life that would have seemed foreign to Victoria's Hanoverian ancestors. During the early years of her marriage to Prince Albert, Victoria regularly spent time with her children and often had a baby brought to her for as much as an hour and a half at luncheon. The warm relationship continued after the children were grown. Although Victoria felt some jealousy toward the relationship between Albert and their eldest child, "Vicky" (Victoria, the Princess Royal, 1840-1901, later Crown Princess of Prussia and Empress Frederick of Germany), the queen wrote her daughter intimate letters at least twice each week after her marriage in 1858. In these letters, Victoria spoke openly about many intimate details of family and personal life, and clearly regarded her married daughter as one of her closest confidants. In later years, her daughter Beatrice (1857–

1944), though herself the mother of four children, devoted most of her time to her mother, serving as her companion and unofficial secretary.

Victoria and Albert's relationship with their most prominent child was somewhat more strained. Albert Edward, Prince of Wales (1841–1910, "Bertie" to the family, later King Edward VII), was educated by private tutors according to a rigorous plan devised by his father. Albert had clear notions of training his son to be fit, intellectually and morally, for the job that would someday be his. Although he was provided with several carefully selected boys of his own age to be his companions (Albert did not believe that a monarch could afford the luxury of friends), it was not until his tour of Germany in 1857 that the prince first experienced close companionship outside the confining royal family circle. Thereafter he was torn between the duty that had been inculcated in him as a child and the love of pleasure that was to be his best-known trait until he ascended the throne in 1901.

In 1861, the prince had the first of his celebrated love affairs, with the actress Nellie Clifden. Queen Victoria always believed that the death of her beloved Albert, later that same year, had been brought on by the pain of Bertie's affair becoming public, and never fully forgave her son. The prince was excluded from the inner circles around the queen and given no important state functions to perform. As a result he was able to devote himself more fully to the pleasures of travel, gambling, and romance. In 1863, he married Alexandra (1844–1925), daughter of Prince Christian of Schleswig-Holstein (later King Christian IX of Denmark). Because of the withdrawal of the queen into seclusion following the death of Albert, the Prince and Princess of Wales became the acknowledged leaders of English society. In the latter years of Victoria's reign, the prince began to use his love of travel and his genuine interest in foreign affairs in order to increase English popularity abroad, particularly in France.

The roles of the other royal children were not so well defined as that of the future king, and providing suitable marriages and futures occupied the minds of both the queen and Prince Albert. Victoria, their eldest child, was destined early to make a glittering marriage and assume a throne. In 1844, when she was not quite four years old, Albert was already contemplating a possible marriage between her and Frederick, the future crown prince of Prussia. The marriage took place in 1858, and she lived the rest of her life in Germany. She visited England frequently, but her desire for close relations between England and Germany could do nothing to overcome the differences that existed between the two countries. Alfred ("Affie," 1844–1900), the second son and fourth child of Victoria and Albert, was the only other of their children for whom a future was foreseen at birth. Albert intended that Alfred would succeed his (Albert's) brother as duke of Saxe-Coburg-Gotha. In the meantime he was educated for the navy, in which he served. In 1862 he was offered the vacant throne of Greece, but he was compelled by English diplomatic interests to refuse. In 1874 he married Grand Duchess Marie, daughter of Alexander II, czar of Russia. In 1893, he succeeded his father's brother as duke of Saxe-Coburg-Gotha, and renounced his privileges as an English peer.

The remaining children led varied lives. Alice (1843–1878) studied nursing and was interested in social welfare. She is probably best known, however, for her progeny. She married Louis IV, grand duke of Hesse-Darmstadt, and was the mother of Alexandra, last czarina of Russia, grandmother of Lord Louis Mountbatten, and great-grandmother of Prince Philip, duke of Edinburgh. Her marriage and the marriage of her sister Victoria linked the British royal family to all the major ruling families of Europe, and led to Queen Victoria's nickname, "the grandmother of Europe." Like her mother and her sisters Victoria and Beatrice, she was a transmitter of hemophilia. Helena ("Lenchen," 1846–1923) married the penniless Prince Christian of Schleswig-Holstein and lived an uneventful life in England. Louise (1848–1939), later the duchess of Argyll, was a sculptor, author under the pseudonym "Myra Fontenoy," and advocate of women's education. Arthur, duke of Connaught (1850–1942), Victoria's favorite son, married Princess Louise of Prussia and was a soldier all his life. Leopold, duke of Albany (1853–1884), the first of Victoria's children at whose birth chloroform was used, was a hemophiliac, married Princess Helena of Waldeck-Pyrmont, and interested himself in artistic and literary matters. The last child,

Beatrice (1857-1944), married Prince Henry of Battenberg, and devoted herself to her mother. After Victoria's death, it was Beatrice who edited the queen's diaries.

It is difficult to assess the precise significance of the royal family to the country. The heavy expenses incurred by some of them contributed to the antimonarchical sentiment that was present at least until Victoria's well-managed emergence from seclusion under the tutelage of Benjamin Disraeli and the celebration of her two Jubilees in 1887 and 1897. The traditional role of royal children, the cementing of diplomatic alliances through marriage, was clearly out of date by the nineteenth century. If anything, the marriages of Victoria's children complicated British foreign policy more than they smoothed its path. In the end, it may be that the greatest function served by the royal family was the mutual comfort of its members, the function served by most families today.

DAVID C. ITZKOWITZ

Bibliography

Fulford, Roger, ed. *Dearest Child: Letters Between Queen Victoria and the Princess Royal, 1858-1861.* 1964.

James, Robert Rhodes. *Prince Albert: A Biography.* 1984.

Longford, Elizabeth. *Queen Victoria: Born to Succeed.* 1964.

Magnus, Philip. *King Edward VII.* 1964.

· · · · ·

RUGBY FOOTBALL

Rugby football developed as a separate game from soccer essentially because the graduates of Cheltenham, Marlborough, and Rugby refused to accept the rules drawn up by the Football Association in 1863. A small cluster of clubs, led by Blackheath, continued to employ their own rules before, in 1871, establishing the Rugby Foothball Union which catered largely to bourgeois and aristocratic participants who insisted on handling the ball and hacking the ball carrier and who also frowned upon the use of working-class professionals.

To the majority of late Victorians, Rugby football seemed too violent. It never therefore enjoyed the universal popularity of **soccer**, but it did attract a loyal following throughout the British Isles before spreading to New Zealand and South Africa. In Lancashire and Yorkshire, Rugby football attracted many working-class players who eventually established their own league when the union refused to modify its stance on the question of professionalism. Despite this split, the game has survived and international Rugby football competition has flourished since the 1870s. Perhaps the greatest of the Victorian stars was Len Stokes who represented England from 1875 to 1881 and set a record of seventeen conversions which lasted for more than a century.

KEITH A.P. SANDIFORD

Bibliography

Dunning, Eric and Kenneth Sheard. *Barbarians, Gentlemen and Players: A Sociological Study of the Development of Rugby Football.* 1979.

Griffiths, John. *The Book of English International Rugby, 1871-1982.* 1982.

Owen, Owen L. *The History of the Rugby Football Union.* 1955.

Walvin, James A. *The People's Game: A Social History of British Football.* 1975.

· · · · ·

RUSKIN, JOHN
(1819-1900)

A major aesthetic and social critic, prose writer John Ruskin was the late-born only child of a prosperous sherry merchant and his devoutly Evangelical wife, who strictly but devotedly nurtured their son's genius. His father's wealth provided for the early travels that inspired Ruskin's interest in Gothic architecture and Italian painting; for the drawing instruction that enabled him to illustrate many of his books; and above all, for the luxury of regularly publishing his controversial views, expressed in a style of extraordinary eloquence. Ruskin's eclectic works run to thirty-nine heavy volumes in the standard edition, yet they manifest a clear organic evolution.

Ruskin's earliest books were on art. Outraged by some critics' disdain for J. M. W. Turner's impressionistic later oils, he sought to defend the great English painter in what would eventually become the five volumes of *Modern Painters* (1843-1860). Though Ruskin's aesthetics developed complexly, the concerns of *Modern Painters'* opening volumes underlay his thinking lifelong. He insisted that the artist accurately depict nature, less in terms of literally faithful reproduction (though this was important) than in the inspired apprehension of a vital energy infusing natural form. All great artists are great moral teachers, whose visual truths educate viewers to revere divine creation; society's encouragement of such artists indicates its moral health. Turner, whose vision Ruskin came increasingly to characterize as tragic, was the only "modern" painter fully evincing this greatness. (Ruskin's hopes for the Pre-Raphaelite Brotherhood, whom he championed during the 1850s, were disappointed.)

After two volumes of *Modern Painters* appeared, Ruskin temporarily shifted his energy to his major architectural writings, *The Seven Lamps of Architecture* (1849) and *The Stones of Venice* (1851-1853). Continuing to fuse the aesthetic and moral, he exalted French and Italian Gothic because he believed its honestly expressed structure, its integrity of materials, and especially its richly carved natural decoration symbolized a healthy society. But he significantly expands his view of artistic creation by stressing Gothic's "imperfection," a concept he explicitly defines in the famous *Stones of Venice* chapter "The Nature of Gothic." Unlike classical or Renaissance architecture with its proudly rational symmetries, Gothic building promoted and incorporated the creative effort of the humblest individual artisans, who thus found joy and wholeness in their labor—rewards denied to divided, alienated modern workers. The very irregularity of Gothic embodies and ultimately harmonizes the aspirations of a spiritually unified civilization.

By the late 1850s the social criticism latent in his earlier work became overt—and passionate. Convinced that he had failed as an aesthetic interpreter, repelled by contemporary architects' incapacity to revive Gothic style, and depressed by upheavals in his personal life (including in 1854 the scandalous annulment of his marriage and in 1858 his temporary but extended loss of Christian faith), he determined that beauty could only flourish after he had reformed society itself. Thus in 1860 he began a sequence of essays in *Cornhill Magazine*, brilliantly attacking Victorian laissez faire economics. When reader outrage forced their cancellation, Ruskin published them as a book, *Unto This Last* (1862). Thereafter, virtually all his writings, whatever their ostensible subjects (crystals, mythology, war, flowers, monasticism, and feminine roles, among others)—even his lectures delivered while Slade professor of art at Oxford (1870-1878, 1883-1885)—contained indictments of Victorian materialism.

An especially important work was *Fors Clavigera* (1871-1884), a series of ninety-six letters addressed to English workers, commenting on national life and reporting the activities of the unsuccessful utopian society he founded in 1871, Saint George's Guild. Ironic, topical, often wrenchingly confessional, *Fors* permitted him to go on teaching despite growing mental instability; his first breakdown came in 1878. Frustrated in his public schemes for reform and privately by his harrowing courtship of a young Irish woman, Rose LaTouche, who died in 1875, he became convinced that England's skies were progressively darkening as a judgment on the nation's vanity and greed, a theory promulgated in *The Storm-Cloud of the Nineteenth Century* (1884). Only in the luminous fragments of his uncompleted autobiography *Praeterita* (1885-1889) did he briefly achieve peace before madness silenced his remaining years.

Ruskin's influence was complicated and protean. He expanded the audience for art, teaching readers to see empirically, unhampered by fashion and academic convention; his architectural writing widened public acceptance of the **Gothic revival** and helped inspire the **arts and crafts** and preservation movements. His insistence that the concept of a self-interested economic man is false and dehumanizing led him to enunciate radically anticompetitive proposals and to carry out myriad practical applications, exhausting his inheritance. He would affect later figures as diverse as William Morris, Leo Tolstoy, Marcel Proust, Frank Lloyd Wright, and Mahatma Gandhi. With his manic energy, impassioned moral concern, and tragically flawed nobility,

John Ruskin was the prototypical Victorian critic.

KRISTINE OTTESEN GARRIGAN

Bibliography

Cook, E. T. and Alexander Wedderburn, eds. *The Works of John Ruskin*. 1903-1912.

Fitch, Raymond. *The Poison Sky: Myth and Apocalypse in Ruskin*. 1982.

Garrigan, Kristine Ottesen. *Ruskin on Architecture: His Thought and Influence*. 1973.

Helsinger, Elizabeth. *Ruskin and the Art of the Beholder*. 1982.

Landow, George. *The Aesthetic and Critical Theories of John Ruskin*. 1971.

Leon, Derrick. *Ruskin, the Great Victorian*. 1949.

Rosenberg, John. *The Darkening Glass: A Portrait of Ruskin's Genius*. 1961.

Sherburne, James Clark. *John Ruskin, or The Ambiguities of Abundance*. 1972.

Walton, Paul. *The Drawings of John Ruskin*. 1972.

· · · · ·

RUSSELL, LORD JOHN
(1792-1878)

Lord John Russell was a major political figure for most of his lifetime. He served for more than sixty years in either the House of Commons (1813-1861) or, after being created an earl in 1861, the House of Lords (1861-1873); held principal cabinet offices for about twenty-five years; and was twice prime minister (1846-1852, 1865-1866). The long-term advocacy of civil and religious liberty and parliamentary reform made Russell's extended political career notable.

A favorite subject for caricaturists because of his small stature, frail body, and large head, "little Johnny Russell" was the third son of the duke of Bedford. He attended Edinburgh University (1809-1812) but left without taking a degree and was elected to the House of Commons in 1813 for the family borough of Tavistock while abroad and not yet of age. His early career was devoted to pressing for parliamentary reform. He was successful in his support for the repeal of the Test and Corporation Acts (1828), which helped open local and national governmental office to Protestants who did not conform to the established Anglican Church. Russell also supported the entry of Roman Catholics into civil and military office and Parliament through the Catholic Emancipation Act (1829).

When the **Whig party** finally emerged from years in the wilderness of opposition, Russell was included as paymaster of the forces in Earl Grey's government (1830). He became a leading member of the four-man committee that drafted the original version of the Reform Act of 1832, which stands as Russell's greatest achievement.

In the government formed by Lord Melbourne in 1835, Russell served as home secretary (1835-1839) and colonial secretary (1839-1841). His major accomplishment during this administration was passage of the Municipal Corporations Act (1835). Although Russell led the Whig/Liberal/Radical opposition to Robert Peel's 1841-1846 Conservative government, he supported Peel's repeal of the Corn Laws in 1846.

In June 1846, Russell became prime minister. His first administration was not outstanding. His government lacked a party majority in the House of Commons, and his handling of the **Irish famine** (1845-1849) was ineffective: Russell left famine relief largely to the mercies of a free market because of his dogmatic belief in laissez faire. His administration did, however, pass a major Public Health Act (1848). The closing years of Russell's first government were weakened by his increasing rivalry with Lord Palmerston, the foreign secretary. In the coalition government headed by the Peelite Lord Aberdeen, Russell was foreign secretary (1852-1853) and leader of the House of Commons (1852-1855). He resigned from this government on the question of its mismanagement of the Crimean War.

Having lost the leadership of the Whig party to Lord Palmerston, Russell served as colonial secretary for five months in Palmerston's government (1855) and was then out of office for four years. He returned as foreign secretary in Palmerston's second administration in 1859. While Palmerston lived, however, reform was dead. Russell's 1860 reform bill perished for want of interest and in 1861 he accepted a peerage and went to the House of Lords. As foreign secretary he promoted Italian unification. His policy of neutrality in the American **Civil War**, however, was compromised by the failure to prevent the sailing of the Confederate *Alabama*.

After Palmerston's death in October 1865, Russell again became prime minister. With Gladstone as leader in the House of Commons, the Russell government introduced a bill extending the franchise. His own party split over the measure and Russell resigned in 1866, although a second installment of parliamentary reform was achieved in 1867 under Lord Derby and his principal lieutenant, Benjamin Disraeli.

ROBERT S. FRASER

Bibliography

Gooch, George Peabody, ed. *The Later Correspondence of Lord John Russell, 1840-1878.* 1925. 2 vols.

Prest, John. *Lord John Russell.* 1972.

Russell, John. *Recollections and Suggestions, 1813-1873.* 1875.

Russell, Rollo, ed. *Early Correspondence of Lord John Russell, 1805-1840.* 1913. 2 vols.

Walpole, Spencer. *The Life of Lord John Russell.* 1889. 2 vols.

See also ELECTIONS AND THE FRANCHISE

· · · · ·

RUSSELL, WILLIAM HOWARD (1820-1907)

William Howard Russell was one of Britain's first and most distinguished war correspondents. His reports from the Crimea (1854-1856) established his reputation, and he later covered the Indian Mutiny (1858-1859) and the American Civil War (1861-1862). He was knighted in 1895.

Born and educated in Ireland, Russell read law and practiced it sporadically at the Middle Temple. His more important work as a journalist began in 1841 when he reported on the

Irish elections for the *Times*. During the Crimean War Russell revealed the mismanagement of the British war effort under Lord Raglan and described the suffering of troops who lacked adequate supplies and proper medical care. These graphic reports probably contributed to the fall of the Aberdeen ministry (1855) and also inspired Florence Nightingale to volunteer her services. At the battle of Balaclava (1854), Russell first used the now famous phrase "the thin red line" to describe the British infantry. In 1858 Russell's reports on the rebellion in India continued to arouse public opinion. After his reports from Cawnpore, the government began to moderate its punishment of the mutineers.

In 1861 Russell went to the United States as a reporter for the *Times*. Although the *Times* supported the Confederate states, Russell strongly opposed slavery. Nevertheless, he soon became unpopular in the North because of his candid description of the Union retreat at the first battle of Bull Run (1861) and his predictions that the South would eventually win the war. Russell turned in his later years to travel writing and published accounts of trips to the Near East (1869), India (1875-1876), and North America (1881).

As a journalist Russell was sometimes guilty of inaccuracies, but, like his friend Charles Dickens, he excelled in portraying scenes of great drama or human suffering. These reports touched his readers and sometimes influenced government policy.

ALBERT E. WILHELM

Bibliography

Atkins, John. *The Life of Sir William Howard Russell: The First Special Correspondent.* 1911.

· · · · ·

RUTHERFORD, MARK (WILLIAM HALE WHITE) (1831-1913)

Both the novels and the life of William Hale White, who published as "Mark Rutherford," expressed the Victorian preoccupation with doubt and faith at its most extreme pitch. A lapsed Calvinist who turned to literature as an anodyne for the dread of facing a universe devoid of intelligible meaning, he was author of five compelling novels which paradoxically define a mood of desperate uncertainty and spiritual disorientation in prose of chiseled clarity and classical restraint. Haunted by a sense of personal unworthiness and tormented by a spirit enamored of perfection, Rutherford translated his gropings, frustrations, and desires into nervous characters who search for meaning and purpose in the spheres of social reform or personal relationships.

The *Autobiography* (1881) and *Deliverance* (1885) are the most famous and influential of his novels. Thematically concerned with the opposition between spiritual aspiration and personal limitations, these books are among the most important examples of "confessional" literature in the Victorian age.

In his subsequent books—*The Revolution in Tanner's Lane* (1887), *Miriam's Schooling* (1890), *Catharine Furze* (1893), and *Clara Hopgood* (1896)—Rutherford continued to depict his spiritual drama through characters preoccupied with the problem of living a responsible and committed existence in the light of ethical principles not subject to the modern world's corrosive scepticism. His writings combine a sense of the uniqueness and incommensurability of specific moral dilemmas with a desire to sustain a demythicized version of Christianity capable of holding human egotism in check. Among twentieth-century writers who have acknowledged his influence are Andre Gide, D. H. Lawrence, and John Middleton Murray.

STEPHEN GURNEY

Bibliography

Maclean, Catherine M. *Mark Rutherford: A Biography of William Hale White.* 1955.

Stock, Irwin. *William Hale White: A Critical Study.* 1956.

Stone, Wilfred. *The Religion and Art of William Hale White.* 1954.

Willey, Basil. *More Nineteenth Century Studies.* 1956.

· · · · ·

RYE, MARIA
(1829-1903)

A pioneer of child emigration, Maria Rye was the first to send significant numbers of British children to Canada, commencing in 1869. She began her humanitarian activities among London's poor and later became interested in expanding opportunities for middle-class women. A founder of the Women's Employment Society, she responded to the scarcity of jobs in England by launching the Female Middle-Class Emigration Society in 1861. Its aim was to place girls as domestic servants in Canada and Australia.

The economic crisis of 1866-1867, the outbreak of cholera in England, and Charles Loring Brace's scheme of placing destitute New York City children with Midwest farm families converged to turn Rye's attention to child emigration. Supported by the Church of England, by philanthropic organizations, and by parishes that agreed to finance passage for workhouse children, she bought an old jail in Niagara-on-the-Lake, Ontario ("Our Western Home"). By the mid-1870s she had placed over 5,000 children, mostly young girls, in Canadian homes, either for adoption or as indentured servants.

Rye's lack of organizational skills coupled with minimal inspection or supervision of the children after they had been placed led to a storm of controversy in England, culminating in a highly critical government inquiry (1874-1875)—although she was for the most part defended by Canadian authorities and editorial writers. Her work in the field was soon overshadowed by Annie Macpherson and **Thomas Barnardo**, but the debate she engendered set the stage for reforms in agencies responsible for sending unaccompanied children overseas.

TREVOR J. PHILLIPS

Bibliography

Turner, Wesley B. "Miss Rye's Children and the Ontario Press, 1875." *Ontario History*, vol. 68, pp. 169-203.

Wagner, Gillian. *Children of the Empire.* 1982.

See also CHILD SAVING

· · · · ·

SALA, GEORGE AUGUSTUS (1829-1895)

Journalist and novelist George Augustus Sala is best known for his column (later expanded to a full page) "Echoes of the Week," which ran in the *Illustrated London News* from 1862 to 1887, and for his leaders and special correspondent's reports in the *Daily Telegraph* from 1857 until just before his death. All but one of his five novels were written by 1863, when, as he put it, he abandoned literature for journalism. The most important is *The Baddington Peerage* (1860).

Sala first made his mark as a regular contributor to Dickens's magazine *Household Words* from its inception in 1851 until 1856; according to John Forster, Dickens considered him the ablest and most interesting of his "young men." He is a probable model for Adolescens Leo, representative of the "young lions" (the turgid philistines of the *Daily Telegraph*) in Matthew Arnold's *Friendship's Garland* (1871), which also mentions Sala by name. He claimed, in his autobiography *The Life and Adventures of George Augustus Sala* (1895), that after 1863 his annual income from journalism never fell below 2,000 pounds; but his alcoholism and bohemianism often left him notoriously short of funds, as well as unreliable in meeting deadlines and completing novels. *Twice Round the Clock* (1859) contains lively journalistic sketches of London, including discreet glances at its unsavory nightlife. His novels *The Baddington Peerage* (1860) and *The Seven Sons of Mammon* (1862), though sloppily written and egotistical like much of his journalism, retain some interest as perhaps the closest English imitations of Balzac and Eugène Sue. The thirteen travel books made up largely of his special correspondent's reports to the *Daily Telegraph* offer some useful source material for the study of contemporary life and events both in western Europe and in more far-flung countries like Russia, the United States, and Australia.

P.D. EDWARDS

Bibliography

Straus, Ralph. *Sala: The Portrait of an Eminent Victorian.* 1942.

· · · · ·

SALISBURY, THIRD MARQUIS OF (ROBERT GASCOYNE-CECIL) (1830-1903)

The Conservative politician who served as secretary for India (1866-1867 and 1874-1878), foreign secretary (1878-1880, 1885-1886, 1887-1892, and 1895-1900), prime minister (1885-1886, 1886-1892, and 1895-1902), and leader of the **Conservative party** (1885-1902) was known as Lord Robert Cecil (1830-1865), Viscount Cranborne (1865-1868), and Lord Salisbury (1868-1903).

Salisbury's significance lies in two areas. First, he dominated the formulation of foreign policy in the late nineteenth century. Second, in domestic politics, he was the most successful Conservative leader of modern times.

Becoming foreign secretary in 1878, Salisbury brought clarity, consistency, and firmness of purpose to British policy in the Eastern crisis, then at its height. This led to success at the Congress of Berlin (1878). Salisbury was repeatedly concerned with problems in four regions: the Near East, India's northern frontier, the Far East, and Africa. The first three were the most important, and all involved conflict with Russian ambitions. Between 1878 and 1893 the emergence of the European alliance systems constricted Salisbury's policy. He sought to avoid committing Britain to either of the two groupings. This led to the policy described as "isolation," but it did not necessarily imply British weakness. Salisbury took a firm stand against Russian expansion in Afghanistan in the 1880s and forced France to accept British control of the Nile Valley in the Fashoda crisis (1898). He sought to avoid entangling commitments. Salisbury opposed the negotiations for an Anglo-German agreement (1901), and was uncertain about the Anglo-Japanese alliance (1902), preferring limited pacts such as the Mediterranean Agreements (1887).

In domestic politics, Salisbury was a passionate defender of the status quo. He resigned from the cabinet in disapproval of the Second Reform Act (1867), but was later reconciled to Disraeli's leadership. On the latter's death he succeeded to the Conservative leadership in the House of Lords, and formed the first of four governments in 1885. Between 1883 and 1887 he defeated a challenge from Lord Randolph Churchill. In the Home Rule crisis (1885–1886) Salisbury outmaneuvered the moderate centrists, emerging as leader of the Unionist forces. His greatest achievement was holding these together, culminating in the coalition ministry formed in 1895, with Lord Hartington and Joseph Chamberlain serving under him. He established the doctrine of the mandate, strengthening the powers of the House of Lords in the 1890s.

Salisbury was motivated by strong religious convictions, intellectual vigor, and a profound pessimism. He feared the advent of class conflict, and promoted social legislation designed to forestall it. He looked on his task as defensive: to hold back and diminish the forces of change. In this respect, as well as in winning three out of five elections, he must be considered successful in his own terms.

STUART BALL

Bibliography

Cecil, Gwendolen. *Life of Robert, Marquis of Salisbury.* 1921–1932. 4 vols.

Grenville, John A. S. *Lord Salisbury and Foreign Policy.* 1964.

Marsh, Peter. *The Discipline of Popular Government: Lord Salisbury's Domestic Statecraft, 1881–1902.* 1978.

Taylor, Robert. *Lord Salisbury.* 1975.

. . . . .

SALVATION ARMY

In 1865 William Booth (1829–1912), an itinerant evangelist who had been a Methodist preacher, founded the Christian Mission in London's East End. This mission to the poor was reorganized in 1878 along military lines, with the preachers known as officers and Booth as the general superintendent. It then became known as the Salvation Army, whose aim was to evangelize the poorest and most outcast of the urban masses. The Salvation Army was also noted for giving women equal responsibility with men for preaching and welfare work; Booth is credited with having

exclaimed, "My best men are women!"

Initiation of the Salvation Army's Social Services for Men in 1887 was Booth's acknowledgment that without adequate material resources the masses would be unable to respond to the gospel. *In Darkest England and the Way Out* (1890) was his blueprint for rehabilitating the unemployed by processing them through a series of colonies to be located in towns, the countryside, and overseas. Booth hoped to raise 100,000 pounds by public donation to finance the project, but the salvationists were strongly criticized for giving help indiscriminately. The "Darkest England" scheme was never completely established, although the publicity surrounding its inauguration enhanced the Salvation Army's reputation as one of Victorian England's foremost charities.

Recent scholarship has challenged the reputation of the Salvation Army as the poor people's church. It appears that the majority of officers were not reformed drunkards but rather men and women in steady employment who saw membership in the Salvation Army as a means of confirming their status and enhancing their self-image as respectable—not rough—working people. There was also indifference (which sometimes became hostility) toward the Salvation Army in working-class districts, typified by attacks on their meetings by gangs known as the "skeleton army."

While the Salvation Army's acceptability to the working-class community needs to be seen in a more limited perspective, the role of women must also be evaluated. The practice of giving women the same responsibilities as men was entirely due to the influence of William Booth's wife, Catherine Booth (1829–1890). A woman of deep religious conviction, as well as great intellect and independence of mind, Catherine Booth believed that women were equal to men in their being, but inadequate education and social custom made them intellectual inferiors. In this she echoes the ideas of many liberal feminists, as does her contention that barriers against women preaching resulted purely from prejudice. Her argument that women had a special responsibility to spread the gospel implies a moral mission for womankind similar to that proposed by Evangelical feminists. Catherine Booth, however, lacked sympathy with those who would alter women's social and domestic position. There is no evidence that she was influenced by the writings of other Victorian feminists. Her inspiration was personal experience and her own reading of theology, which explains both the scope and limitation of her ideas.

Through Catherine Booth's influence the Salvation Army provided women with a variety of roles. Women were seen as independent moral agents capable of choosing good over evil. They were to make these moral choices as preachers, as workers (particularly in their capacity as servants), and as wives and mothers. While most women who became officers in the Salvation Army were working class, some single middle-class women were prominent in organizing the Women's Social Services, founded in 1884. One of the Salvation Army's more significant contributions, furthermore, was in promoting the ideal that married women should combine domestic duties with responsibilities outside the home.

The Salvation Army was an important agent of the social **purity campaign**, particularly through its participation with William Stead in the "Maiden Tribute" campaign of 1885. Studies of its welfare work for women suggest a degree of negotiation between helper and recipient. The Salvation Army's rescue programs concentrated on young women. Some of them were without economic support, but about a third chose to enter the homes for other reasons, and very few had actually been prostitutes. However, in both the women's and men's social services help was seldom offered without charge. Where the Salvation Army did differ from the Charity Organization Society was in its insistence that help should be extended to all, and not merely to the "deserving poor." This conviction won it a reputation for compassion, and by the end of the nineteenth century the Salvation Army had become the embodiment of respectability and sincerity.

GILLIAN BALL

Bibliography

Bramwell-Booth, Catherine. *Catherine Booth.* 1970.

Ervine, St. John. *God's Soldier: General William Booth.* 1934. 2 vols.

Higginbotham, Ann R. "Respectable Sinners: Salvation Army Rescue Work with Unmarried Mothers, 1884-1914." In Gail Malmgren, ed., *Religion in the Lives of English Women, 1760-1930.*

Sandall, Robert. *The History of the Salvation Army.* 1947. 4 vols.

See also BANDS AND BAND MUSIC

. . . . .

SAVOY OPERAS

The comic **operettas** with librettos by William Schwenk Gilbert (1836-1911) and music by **Arthur Sullivan** (1842-1900) are generally referred to as the Savoy operas; **Richard D'Oyly Carte** (1844-1901) built the Savoy Theatre (opened in 1881), the first in the world to be electrically lit throughout, purposely for their production. After initially commissioning Gilbert and Sullivan to write *Trial by Jury* (1875), D'Oyly Carte was responsible for their continuing collaboration and for staging their works. These are *The Sorcerer* (1877), *H.M.S. Pinafore, or the Lass That Loved a Sailor* (1878), *The Pirates of Penzance, or the Slave of Duty* (1879), *Patience, or Bunthorne's Bride* (1881), *Iolanthe, or the Peer and the Peri* (1882), *Princess Ida, or Castle Adamant* (1884), *The Mikado, or the Town of Titipu* (1885), *Ruddigore, or the Witch's Curse* (1887), *The Yeomen of the Guard, or the Merryman and His Maid* (1888), *The Gondoliers, or the King of Barataria* (1889), *Utopia Limited, or the Flowers of Progress* (1893), and *The Grand Duke, or the Statutory Duel* (1896). One additional joint work, *Thespis, or the Gods Grown Old* (1871), was not produced by D'Oyly Carte.

Although some of the Savoy operas are lesser works of art than others, they must be seen as one of the most remarkable cultural phenomena of the Victorian period. They have been translated into numerous languages and continue to be presented, in their original form or variously adapted, by commercial theatrical companies and by amateur Gilbert and Sullivan societies all over the world.

The initial intentions of Gilbert and Sullivan were modest: to create profitable and tasteful shows that burlesqued the dramatic and musical productions that cluttered London's stages and concert halls. But *The Mikado* is not specifically a parody and *Patience*, for example, continues to be appreciated by audiences altogether unfamiliar with the target of its satire (the aesthetic movement). Because they all reflect the cast of Gilbert's mind and also because they began to be composed for a specific company of singers, they are somewhat formulaic, but each operetta's relative closeness to the formula seems only to have established and ensured its degree of popularity.

The music more than the words keeps the Savoy operas in performance, and Sullivan's stature as a creative artist was and remains greater than Gilbert's. But the operettas are essentially Gilbertian: many rework material from his earlier writings, nearly all reflect his taste for "topsyturvydom," and all fit his definition of humor ("All humor properly so called is based upon a grave and quasirespectful treatment of the ridiculous"). Moreover, whereas Sullivan was anxious during most of his years in the partnership to turn to more serious composing, Gilbert's knowledge that the operettas were his only opportunity for immortality caused him to care intensely that they be as perfect as he could make them. Among the consequences of this ambition is the standard of stage direction Gilbert introduced into the British theater, a standard that by itself must be considered a significant artistic contribution.

DENNIS CHALDECOTT

Bibliography

Baily, Leslie. *Gilbert and Sullivan and Their World.* 1973.

Jones, John Bush, ed. *W. S. Gilbert: A Century of Scholarship and Commentary.* 1970.

Williamson, Audrey. *Gilbert and Sullivan Opera: An Assessment.* Rev. ed., 1982.

· · · · ·

SCHREINER, OLIVE (1855-1920)

A pacifist feminist born in South Africa, Olive Schreiner wrote numerous articles against colonialism, war, and unemployment. She is known primarily for *The Story of an African Farm* (1883) and *Woman and Labour* (1911), the "bible" of the militant suffrage movement. Although Schreiner advocated marriage and maternity, many people in England considered her the first and most outspoken of the fin de siècle "New Women."

The daughter of German missionaries, Schreiner was influenced by the writings of Ralph Waldo Emerson (from whose name she derived her pseudonym "Ralph Iron"), Herbert Spencer, and Charles Darwin. When her father's mission failed, she became a governess and began writing her first novel, *Undine* (published in 1929), set in an unreal England of endless forests and perpetual snowfall. With *African Farm* Schreiner stayed closer to her own experience; she took the manuscript when she left for England in 1881. Centered around the heroine's vision of sexual equality, *African Farm* argues that differences between men and women are not natural but constructed by society. Schreiner was unable to complete her most ambitious novel, *From Man to Man* (1926), about the failure of marriage and its links to prostitution. *Man to Man*, like *The Life* (1924) and *The Letters of Olive Schreiner* (1924), was radically edited and published posthumously by her husband, Samuel Cronwright-Schreiner.

In London Schreiner lived with prostitutes, gathering information for her novel and for friends in the Men and Women's Club, an elite group that met weekly to discuss socialism and sexuality. Schreiner became friends with group leader Karl Pearson and with self-proclaimed "sex radicals" Havelock Ellis and Edward Carpenter. During this period she wrote the short, visionary pieces collected in *Dreams* (1890) and *Dream Life and Real Life* (1893).

Schreiner returned to South Africa in 1889. After her marriage in 1894, she wrote primarily political tracts, writings shaped by her experience of the Boer War. *Trooper Peter Halket of Mashonaland* (1897) is a parody of Cecil Rhodes and British racism. Schreiner's criticism of antinative policies in *An English South African's View of the Situation* (1899) and *Thoughts on South Africa* (1923) was quite radical for its time. Schreiner left the Cape Colony Women's Enfranchisement League when it refused to support suffrage for native men and women as well as white women.

Expanding Mary Wollstonecraft's *A Vindication of the Rights of Woman* (1792), *Woman and Labour* argues that men and women will benefit equally from women's improved economic status, and that equality will lead to improved sexual relations between men and women. Schreiner was the first South African woman novelist and she remains a major influence on the novels of black and white South Africans and on the contemporary feminist movement.

CAROL BARASH

Bibliography

Barash, Carol, ed. *The Olive Schreiner Reader: Writings on Women and South Africa.* 1987.

Beer, Gillian. *Darwin's Plots: Evolutionary Narrative in Darwin, George Eliot and Nineteenth-Century Fiction.* 1983.

Beeton, Ridley. *Olive Schreiner: A Short Guide to Her Writings.* 1974.

First, Ruth and Ann Scott. *Olive Schreiner.* 1980. (Includes primary bibliography.)

Showalter, Elaine. *A Literature of Their Own: British Women Novelists from Brontë to Lessing.* 1977.

Smith, Malvern V. W. and Don Maclennan. *Olive Schreiner and After: Essays on Southern African Literature in Honour of Guy Butler.* 1983.

Walkowitz, Judith. "Science, Feminism and Romance: The Men and Women's Club, 1885-89." *History Workshop*, no. 21, pp. 37-59.

· · · · ·

SCIENCE

The term "science" acquired its present meaning and connotations during the Victorian period. In the previous century, although it included the study of nature, the word still referred to any body of systematic knowledge. By the time of the foundation of the British Association for the Advancement of Science in 1831, "science" began to apply more narrowly to knowledge of the physical world. This process met with some opposition, and when

William Whewell (1794-1866) coined the word "scientist," S. T. Coleridge regretted the demise of the more general and synthetic natural philosophy in which "men of science" moved across several fields of natural knowledge and related them to moral and theological issues. By 1900 "science" generally referred to the specialized knowledge of nature produced by professional practitioners in academic institutions or research laboratories; its discoveries were seen to affect many areas of life, and its inquiries were regarded as the product of a method that could be extended to social and political questions.

The increasing specialization of science was accompanied by a popularization of scientific knowledge. This took place in a variety of publications including the mathematically informed textbooks on astronomy and mechanics by **Mary Somerville**, learned articles in the successive editions of the *Encyclopaedia Britannica*, and shorter and more accessible entries in publications aimed at a broader readership such as Chambers's *Cyclopaedia*, the *Penny Cyclopedia*, and Charles Dickens's *Household Words*. But there was a tension between these two processes because the growing complexity of particular disciplines, although still within the reach of leisured amateurs, became more difficult to disseminate among wider audiences. Leading scientists feared that popularization would produce a superficial image of science and, consequently, debates over the cultural significance of science involved a number of controversial distinctions—between experts and amateurs, between the content of science and its method, between "pure" science and technology, and between scientific and religious or metaphysical knowledge.

In the first half of the century many of the advanced scientific debates of the day were covered, and indeed conducted, in major periodicals such as the *Edinburgh Review* and its conservative rival, the *Quarterly Review*. In 1869, with the appearance of the first issue of *Nature*, the scientific community possessed a weekly journal specifically devoted to science and to the promotion of the scientific enterprise. Although general periodicals such as *The Nineteenth Century* still contained material on science and its philosophical implications, the establishment of *Nature* was indicative of the fact that detailed understanding of recent scientific developments had passed beyond the competencies of the educated public.

While the response to **Charles Darwin's** theory of **evolution** undoubtedly gave science a high public profile, the debates it inspired, such as the confrontation between T. H. Huxley and Samuel Wilberforce in 1860, illustrated the increasing gap between specialist expertise and lay comprehension of technical scientific issues. Wilberforce, the bishop of Oxford, coached by the comparative anatomist Richard Owen, entered the debate under the assumptions of a passing age in which the moral and theological implications of a scientific theory were appropriate criteria in its assessment. Similarly, in an earlier controversy, the reaction of the scientific community to **Robert Chambers's** anonymous *Vestiges of the Natural History of Creation* (1844) highlighted a conflict between amateur speculation and the more rigorous procedures of scientific method. Chambers attacked the narrow specialization of scientific disciplines and their failure to provide the unified theory of the natural world demanded by the public; on the other hand, his critics ridiculed the inadequate grasp of technical concepts and evidence allegedly betrayed by his best-selling book. If this was popular science, the experts on both sides of the evolutionary debate were agreed about its deleterious effects on public appreciation of proper science.

This was the context in which the issue of scientific subjects in popular education was considered. Whig reformers such as Henry Brougham asserted the utility, both moral and practical, of the scientific knowledge directed toward the members of mechanics' institutes from the 1820s. Other commentators pointed to the fact that such instruction of the lower classes necessitated at least an equal acquaintance with science on the part of the more educated classes. The *Westminster Review,* under the editorship of the utilitarians in the 1820s and 1830s, lampooned the antiquated undergraduate training of Oxford and Cambridge, where the sons of the aristocracy could emerge from a university education without a trace of modern science. The place of science in both popular and university education raised important questions about the defining features of science.

While **geology** in the early decades of the century exploded the biblical time scale and evolutionary theory later challenged the Victorians' view of man's place in nature, the other dominant cultural impact of science was produced through its perceived association with technology. The success of contemporary **engineering** was cited as a sign of human understanding and control of nature. Thus in his novel *Yeast* (1851), Charles Kingsley wrote that "The spinning jenny and the railroad, Cunard's liners and the electric telegraph, are to me . . . signs that we are, on some points at least, in harmony with the universe. . . ." In the same year, the Great Exhibition at the Crystal Palace celebrated the wonders of modern machinery; future technological innovation was thought to be the guarantee of material and political supremacy. But some leaders of the scientific community feared that the emphasis on applied science would weaken public appreciation of abstract research that did not promise immediate utility. They argued that popular education had stressed factual information and the material benefits of science to the exclusion of theoretical principles and reasoning. In 1849 a writer in the *Edinburgh Review,* commenting on the recent rush to patent mechanical inventions, admonished those who "risk their livelihood in search of inventions when they are not sufficiently educated to know the limits of the scientifically possible." This was the message of **Charles Babbage** and later Lyon Playfair, who argued for the importance of abstract research as a basis for subsequent technology.

The debate over the reform of university education also involved questions about the relationships between science and technology. The influential ideal of a liberal education as independent of practical concerns about career meant that a close association with the image of useful technology would damage the chance of including science in the curriculum. Accordingly, boundaries were drawn between technology, with its artisan and commercial connotations, and the concept of "pure" science as a pursuit fitted, like Latin and Greek, to train the minds of gentlemen. Scientists of different generations, such as the astronomer **John Herschel** and the physicist **James Clerk Maxwell**, agreed that science was a facet of human speculation which should not be curtailed by pragmatic criteria. Partly as a result of this attitude, academic science in Britain, more so than in Germany or the United States, was divorced from the technological demands of industry; and by the end of the century the first industrial nation had lost its initial advantage.

On the issue of general science education boundaries were also drawn, but in this case between the content of science and its method. The specialization of science and the perceived inadequacy of popularization encouraged the view that an appreciation of scientific method could bridge the gap between science and the public. Although this suggestion was problematic, it was reinforced by the conviction that the method of science could be transferred to other areas of inquiry. By the end of the century disciplines such as history, **psychology**, and **anthropology** claimed the status of "sciences," and "scientific" approaches were urged in subjects such as fishing, boxing, swimming, and life itself. In his *The Grammar of Science* (1892), Karl Pearson asserted the cultural authority of science over theology and philosophy, and pronounced the scientific habit of mind as the guarantee of a stable society. While in the early decades of the century natural science shared links with other areas of thought, by the end of the Victorian period it aspired to intellectual dominance, setting the model against which other subjects were judged. Norman Lockyer, the editor of *Nature*, effectively predicted this in 1870 when he looked ahead to the time in which the average person would be "made to feel that Science dogs him at every footstep, meets him at every turn, and twines itself round his life." It is now possible to recognize that the phenomenon he described was one of the most profound legacies of the Victorian era.

RICHARD R. YEO

Bibliography

Eisen, Sydney and Bernard V. Lightman. *Victorian Science and Religion: A Bibliography.* 1984.

MacLeod, Roy M. and Peter Collins, eds. *The Parliament of Science: The British Association for the Advancement of Science, 1831–1981.* 1981.

Morrell, Jack and Arnold Thackray. *Gentlemen of Science: Early Years of the British Association for the Advancement of Science.* 1981.

Turner, Frank M. "Public Science in Britain, 1880–1919." *Isis*, vol. 71, pp. 589–608.

Yeo, Richard. "Science and Intellectual Authority in Mid-Nineteenth-Century Britain: Robert Chambers and *Vestiges of the Natural History of Creation*." *Victorian Studies*, vol. 28, pp. 5–31.

· · · · ·

SCIENCE FICTION

Science fiction, speculative fiction with a basis in plausible, if untested, scientific theory, emerged alongside the tremendous advances made in science and industry in the nineteenth century. Victorian science fiction—called scientific romance, a term originally applied to the early works of **H. G. Wells** (1866-1946)—shows the writers' fascination with the possibilities inherent in new scientific discoveries while simultaneously reflecting a certain despair concerning the potentially destructive results of such investigations. This despair is evident in three concerns of early science fiction: travel in time and outer space; world cataclysm; and scientific breakthroughs resulting in transformations or adaptations of the human physique and psyche.

Wells's *The Time Machine* (1895) and *The First Men in the Moon* (1901) are largely responsible for inspiring the tidal wave of twentieth-century science fiction employing time and space travel. In these novels, technology replaces gods and chance, which had determined earlier quest literature.

Similarly, spiritual condition, which in earlier literature determines the abnormal physique of beings such as Grendel in *Beowulf* or Duessa in *The Faerie Queene* (1590) is replaced by scientific method or mistake in novels such as Wells's *The Island of Dr. Moreau* (1896), in which the title character creates humans out of animals, and Arthur Conan Doyle's (1859-1930) "The Los Amigos Fiasco" (1892), in which a criminal is accidentally given superhuman vitality and longevity when administered an overdose of electric shock.

The knowledge that enables science fiction protagonists to effect these transformations is typical of earlier Faustian heroes such as those in Christopher Marlowe's *Doctor Faustus* (1593), Ann Radcliffe's *The Italian* (1797), and Byron's "Manfred" (1817). Mary Shelley's *Frankenstein* (1818), in which the title character assembles and gives life to a man, and her "The Mortal Immortal" (1834), in which the central character gains an unnaturally prolonged youth through drinking a potion, constitute forerunners of the human transformation theme in Victorian science fiction; Shelley's protagonists achieve their ends through science, unlike earlier Faustian characters whose supernatural knowledge and power is given them by demonic spirits. Like Shelley's Frankenstein, the title character in Doyle's *The Doings of Raffles Haw* (1891) makes his discovery—a formula for creating gold—through pure scientific investigation. And like Winzey in "The Mortal Immortal," Dr. Jekyll, who in **Robert Louis Stevenson**'s (1850–1894) *The Strange Case of Dr. Jekyll and Mr. Hyde* (1886) creates a separate individual out of the pleasure-seeking and destructive side of his own mind, effects his self-transformation through drinking a potion.

The strain of early science fiction that deals with high technology and end-of-the-world cataclysms probably draws on the tradition of epic battles. Matthew Phipps Shiel (1865–1947) was a forerunner of science fiction's world cataclysms. His *Yellow Danger* (1898) and *The Lord of the Sea* (1901) both envision future high-technology battles between major political powers. In Shiel's *The Purple Cloud* (1901), almost the entire world population is killed by the release of gasses from beneath the earth's surface.

LYNN HAMILTON

Bibliography

Lundwall, Sam. *Science Fiction: What It's All About.* 1971.

Moskowitz, Sam. *Explorers of the Infinite: Shapers of Science Fiction.* 1963.

Philmus, Robert. *Into the Unknown: The Evolution of Science Fiction from Francis Godwin to H.G. Wells.* 1970.

Suvin, Darko. *Victorian Science Fiction in the United Kingdom.* 1983.

See also FANTASY LITERATURE; UTOPIAN FICTION

· · · · ·

SCOTLAND, CHURCH OF see CHURCH OF SCOTLAND

· · · · ·

SCOTS LAW

Scots in the Victorian period, instead of being subject to the English common law that prevailed elsewhere in the United Kingdom, lived under a separate and distinct legal system guaranteed to them forever by the Act of Union (1707). The system derived from four sources: ancient Scottish custom; feudal custom; the canon law of the medieval church; and Roman, or civil, law, which had been generally adopted and imposed in many western European states in the sixteenth century. The updated version of civil law embodied in France's Napoleonic Code, however, had no impact because of Britain's wars with Napoleon; and Scotland made no major reforms of the law or courts in the nineteenth century comparable to those in England.

Probably the best-known difference between Scots and English law was Scotland's use of a criminal trial jury of fifteen, a bare majority of whom could render a verdict of "guilty," "not guilty," or "not proven." In civil cases, the use of a jury of twelve had been introduced by statute in 1815. All Scottish courts administered both law and equity and, unlike in England, the Crown could be sued. Although writs of habeas corpus were unknown, a statute of 1887 required that an accused person be brought to trial within 110 days or be released. Free legal aid was available to the poor. Almost all lands, except for land owned by the church, was held by feudal tenure; and subinfeudation was still common. Since the seventeenth century, however, nearly every kind of land conveyance had to be made in writing. Divorces could be obtained, by custom, for adultery and also, by a 1573 statue, for desertion. Because Scots law regarded as legally valid and binding an "irregular marriage," in which the man and woman simply made a declaration of their intention before witnesses, the village of Gretna in Dumfriesshire, just across the border from England, became a popular destination for eloping English couples in the early Victorian period. But an 1857 statute imposed a prior residence requirement of twenty-one days in Scotland.

The Scottish legal profession, like the English, was divided into two categories: advocates (barristers) and law agents (attorneys or solicitors). Admission to the bar was controlled by the Faculty of Advocates, while would-be law agents had to qualify for admission to one of the recognized societies, of which the Writers to Her Majesty's Signet, headquartered in Edinburgh, was the oldest and best known. The lord advocate, who performed the functions of attorney general and chief prosecutor, was a political appointee of ministerial rank and the most powerful government official in Victorian Scotland.

Scotland's highest civil court, the Court of Session, sat in the old Parliament Hall in Edinburgh. It consisted of an Outer House, presided over by the lord president, whose seven judges individually tried cases in the first instance; and an Inner House, under the lord justice clerk, whose two divisions of four judges each heard cases on appeal. Although it was the supreme court for Scotland, its decisions had been appealable to the House of Lords at Westminster since 1711. The highest criminal court was the Court of Justiciary, staffed by the Court of Session judges who also served as commissioners of justiciary, periodically traveling on circuit to the cities and principal towns to try cases of treason, murder, and other very serious crimes. Though no appeals were allowed in criminal cases, difficult questions of law could be referred to a special panel of two or three of the commissioners.

At the county level the sheriff's court, presided over by the sheriff-substitute (an advocate), exercised a comprehensive civil jurisdiction and also tried all but the most serious criminal cases. The sheriff-principal (usually a leading Edinburgh advocate) customarily visited a county sheriff's court two or three times a year to hear cases on appeal. At the lowest local level the justice of the peace courts (rural) and the burgh police courts (urban) had jurisdiction over both petty crimes and small-claims cases involving sums of no more than five pounds.

Most Scots were proud of their legal system, which they considered generally superior to England's. It is probably no coincidence that many active advocates of **law reform** in nineteenth-century England, notably Lord Brougham, came from Scottish backgrounds.

MICHAEL De L. LANDON

Bibliography

Gibb, Andrew Dewar. *A Preface to Scots Law.* 1964.

Kolbert, Colin F. and N. A. M. Mackay. *History of Scots and English Land Law.* 1977.

Smith, Thomas B. *Scotland: The Development of Its Laws and Constitution.* 1962.

· · · · ·

SCOTT, GEORGE GILBERT (1811–1878)

George Gilbert Scott specialized in the design and restoration of ecclesiastical buildings. The most prolific (if not the most original) architect of the **Gothic revival**, Scott was responsible for some 730 buildings and earned a knighthood for the Albert Memorial (1862). William Morris, however, saw him as a vandal whose church and cathedral restorations destroyed the fabric of the past.

Scott was the fourth of thirteen children. His father was a perpetual curate at Gawcot in Buckinghamshire and his mother a relative of "Capability" Brown, the eighteenth-century landscape designer. In 1827 he became articled to the evangelical architect James Edmeston (1791–1867). One of Scott's first tasks was the design of workhouses (often referred to as "Bastilles") erected after the passage of the Poor Law Amendment Act of 1834. In 1848 he married Caroline Oldrid (1811–1872); they had five sons, of whom two became architects. He was elected to the Royal Academy in 1861.

Scott's Albert Memorial (1862) is the apogee of secular Victorian Gothic. He also designed the St. Pancras Hotel complex (1868–1877), the Foreign Office and other government buildings in Whitehall (1862–1873), the

Martyrs' Memorial at St. Giles in Oxford (1841) and a number of college and university buildings.

Scott is best known, however, for his ecclesiastical work. Early in his career, he won a competition to build the Nickolaikirke in Hamburg (1844–1863), and in 1849 he became architect to the dean and chapter of Westminster Abbey. He designed the Anglican cathedral in St. John's, Newfoundland, did restoration work on the English cathedrals at Ely, Lichfield, Hereford, Ripon, and Salisbury, and built or restored a vast number of parish churches. Scott's work was in such demand that he had nearly thirty assistants working for his practice in the 1860s. Those who admired the patina of age were incensed by Scott's practice of restoring colors to their medieval brilliance, removing paneling that had been added in intervening centuries, repairing weathered surfaces, and adding Gothic elements to non-Gothic churches. William Morris and others led a movement that became known as "Anti-Scrape" and, in 1877, founded the Society for the Protection of Ancient Buildings. Scott, however, fervently defended his Gothic practices and pointed out that it was often impossible to shore up the cracked and crumbling fabric of centuries-old walls without removing the layers of plaster and wood that had been added more recently.

JOHN REYNOLDS

Bibliography

Bayley, Stephen. *The Albert Memorial: The Monument in Its Social and Architectural Context.* 1981.

Cole, David. *The Work of Sir Gilbert Scott.* 1980.

Scott, George Gilbert. *Personal and Professional Recollections.* Ed. G. Gilbert Scott. 1879; rpt. 1977.

· · · · ·

SCULPTURE

Victorian sculpture has long been critically neglected. Before the 1880s Britain lacked a sculptor of genius and the scale of patronage and collecting did not compare with that in France. Although the impetus for innovation was accordingly lacking, the period nevertheless produced much competent, and some very good, work.

The influence of Francis Chantrey (1781–1841) and John Gibson (1790–1866) long persisted. Chantrey's mastery of fleshy textures and pragmatic adaptation of form and costume to the sitter's appearance were continued by his assistant, Henry Weekes (1807–1877), later professor of sculpture at the Royal Academy. Gibson, who spent most of his career in Rome, produced classically inspired, exquisitely finished sculpture. His *Tinted Venus* (1851–1856; Walker Art Gallery, Liverpool), so called because he colored the marble with wax, was derived from the *Venus de'Medici.* The work of John Henry Foley (1818–1874) developed from idealized classicism to the self-confident, timeless realism of the *Prince Albert* (1868–1874; Albert Memorial, London). The Pre-Raphaelitism of Thomas Woolner (1825–1892) and Alexander Munro (1825–1871) is evident in the scrupulously rendered flowers of Woolner's Wordsworth monument at Grasmere (1851) and

The Tinted Venus (*1851–56*).
by John Gibson.
Liverpool, Walker Art Gallery.

The Mower (*1884*)
*by William Hamo Thornycroft.
Liverpool, Walker Art Gallery.*

Munro's visionary, Rossettilike *Paolo and Francesca* (1851).

Alfred Stevens (1817–1875) remains the most admired sculptor before 1880, largely because his groups for the Wellington Monument (1857–1912) in St. Paul's Cathedral are a sensitive interpretation of Michelangelo. Stevens was a bridge between earlier Victorian and what later became known as the "New Sculpture," which flourished from about 1880 to 1905. Other influences on the new movement included Frederic (later Lord) Leighton (1830–1896), a sculptor as well as a painter, patron, and president of the Royal Academy; the teaching of Jules Dalou (1838–1902) which introduced French modeling techniques to British students; and the lively, realistic portraiture of Joseph Edgar Boehm (1834–1890), sculptor-in-ordinary to Queen Victoria.

Edmund Gosse (1849–1928), the champion of the New Sculpture, characterized it as obediently following nature. This quality is displayed in the work of Hamo Thornycroft (1850–1925), whose *Mower* (1884) reveals

another important characteristic of the movement: the revival of early Renaissance sculpture (in this instance Donatello's *David*). Treatment of surface became livelier and the range of subjects broadened. The latter is apparent in the symbolism of Alfred Gilbert (1854–1934) and his contemporaries, who included George Frampton, Harry Bates, and Onslow Ford. The ideals of the arts and crafts movement were reflected in architectural sculpture, the distinctions between carving and sculpture being largely eliminated.

Recent reassessment of the New Sculpture establishes its revolutionary nature but much research remains to be done, particularly in balancing the achievement of the "old" sculpture with that of the "New."

MARK STOCKER

Bibliography

Beattie, Susan. *The New Sculpture.* 1983.

Dorment, Richard. *Alfred Gilbert.* 1985.

Manning, Elfrida. *Marble and Bronze: The Art and Life of Hamo Thornycroft.* 1982.

Read, Benedict. *Victorian Sculpture.* 1982.

· · · · ·

SEAMSTRESSES, DRESSMAKERS, AND MILLINERS

Technically, a dressmaker made dresses, a milliner made headgear, and a seamstress made any type of clothing; however, most businesses dealt in both clothing and headgear, so the terms came to be used interchangeably. People who worked at home on a free-lance or piecework basis were usually referred to as slop workers.

According to R.D. Grainger's report to the Children's Employment Commission of 1842, in London alone 15,000 women (most of them between the ages of 16 and 25) were employed as milliners and dressmakers; by 1863 there were 17,500. The large number of women in the dress trade was primarily due to two factors: the demand for seamstresses and the limited employment opportunities for women.

With the industrial revolution fabric became abundant and inexpensive, allowing women of the middle and upper classes to follow changes in fashion. Greater mobility and the growing number of newspapers and magazines meant that changes in fashion were more widely and quickly disseminated. Thus the demand for seamstresses increased dramatically. But even more dramatic was the increase in the number of women who entered the dress trade. For middle-class women forced to find employment, needlework was a way to earn a living without seeming to sacrifice respectability. Since girls of all classes were taught needlework and the occupation did not involve working in a factory, it was considered a relatively genteel occupation in an extremely limited range of possibilities.

Adding to the number of seamstresses was the belief that for an ambitious working-class or lower middle-class girl, dressmaking was a way to step up in the world. It seemed to give entry into the world of fashion and refinement and provided, at least in theory, a career with definite prospects and the possibility of one day having one's own business.

Despite the seemingly genteel nature of the profession, the seamstress's life was hard. Usually a girl served as an apprentice for two or three years, beginning at age fourteen or fifteen. She, or her family, would pay a premium (often 20 pounds or more) and she would receive her room and board but no salary. A woman then became an "improver," usually receiving a minimal wage; however, if she moved to a new house she had to pay another premium, although usually lower than that for an apprentice. A seamstress then moved to third, second, or first hand, with the work changing from simple seaming to cutting and fitting to, finally, supervising and instructing. Many girls were kept in ignorance of the finer techniques to prevent their moving on or up, since a third hand earned between 12 and 16 pounds a year, a second hand between 20 and 25 pounds, and a first hand between 30 and 80 pounds.

Aside from her minimal pay, a seamstress often had to work long hours with poor ventilation and light. Before a major social event it was not unheard-of for a seamstress to be kept at work for seventy-two hours, breaking only for tea with bread and butter. Often the workroom's ventilation was a window which was usually shut to prevent drafts. Thus the workrooms were often either hot and airless or cold and drafty. Light was provided by tallow candles, sometimes needed both day and night when windows were few and located at ceiling level. These working conditions caused illness, loss of vision, and early death from consumption. In his 1842 report to the Children's Employment Commission, Grainger concludes that, with the exception of overtly dangerous occupations such as needle grinding, "there are no occupations . . . in which so much disease is produced as in dressmaking, or which present so fearful a catalogue of distressing and frequently fatal maladies."

LYNN M. ALEXANDER

Bibliography

Chadwick, Edwin. *Report on the Sanitary Condition of the Labouring Population of Great Britain.* 1965. Ed. M. W. Flinn.

Grainger, R. D. "Report to the Children's Employment Commission (1842)." *British Parliamentary Papers.* 1968.

Hammerton, A. James. *Emigrant Gentlewomen: Genteel Poverty and Female Emigration, 1830–1914.* 1979.

Hellerstein, Erna Olafson, Leslie Parker Hume, and Karen M. Offen, eds. *Victorian Women: A Documentary Account of Women's Lives in Nineteenth-Century England, France, and the United States.* 1981.

Johansson, Sheila Ryan. "Sex and Death in Victorian England: An Examination of Age- and Sex-specific Death Rates, 1840–1910." In Martha Vicinus, ed., *A Widening Sphere.* 1977.

Kestner, Joseph. *Protest and Reform: The British Social Narrative by Women, 1827–1867.* 1985.

"A London Dressmaker's Diary." *Tait's Edinburgh Magazine,* vol. 9, 709–718.

Neff, Wanda. *Victorian Working Women.* 1929.

Pinchbeck, Ivy. *Women Workers and the Industrial Revolution, 1750–1850.* 1930.

Walkley, Christina. *The Ghost in the Looking Glass: The Victorian Seamstress.* 1981.

See also CLOTHING AND FASHION; SWEATSHOPS

. . . . .

SEELEY, JOHN ROBERT
(1834–1895)

John Robert Seeley is most noted as a publicist for British imperialism, a reputation that rests on his wide-selling book *The Expansion of England* (1883). Seeley also played a role in the development of history as a discipline.

Seeley, the son of a publisher, was born in London in 1834. He studied classics, graduating from Cambridge in 1857. Before becoming Regius professor of modern history at Cambridge in 1869, he spent six years as professor of Latin at University College, London. His *Ecce Homo* (1865) stressed the political significance of religion.

As Regius professor his philosophy of history developed. First, history and political science were wedded: history was "the school of statesmanship," and could teach lessons. Seeley encouraged the teaching of modern political history, and published *The Life and Times of Stein* (1878), a book about the rise of the Prussian state. Second, history teaching should foster national unity. Therefore, he promoted educational reform, such as university extension.

The Expansion of England illustrated that modern British history was dominated by imperial expansion. Seeley remarked that the empire had developed "in a fit of absence of mind," but if the empire were to survive, a common sense of nationality was essential to Britain and the settlement colonies such as Canada and Australia. His thesis was that great-power status rested on imperial federation, resulting in a transoceanic state that could coexist with Russia and America.

OLWYN M. BLOUET

Bibliography

Seeley, John Robert. *The Expansion of England.* 1971. Ed. John Gross.

Wormell, Deborah. *Sir John Seeley and the Uses of History.* 1980.

. . . . .

SENIOR, JANE ELIZABETH HUGHES
(1828–1877)

Jane Elizabeth Hughes Senior was a social scientist and the first woman to serve as an inspector of workhouses and pauper schools. She was appointed by the Gladstone government in 1873 and reported the following year to the local government board on the effects of pauper school education on girls. Recognizing the relationship of institutional design to social outcome, Senior recommended breaking up the larger pauper schools, boarding orphans with local families, and creating special programs to keep poor girls in school. Her report is an excellent example of a nineteenth-century survey research study analyzing empirical data. Senior, who was the sister of author Thomas Hughes and the daughter-in-law of economist Nassau William Senior, died in 1877.

BARBARA ALLEN

Bibliography

Senior, Jane Elizabeth. "Report of Mrs. Nassau Senior as to the Effect on Girls of the System of Education in Pauper Schools." *House of Commons Sessional Papers.* 1874.

"The Late Mrs. Nassau Senior's Work." *The Spectator*, vol. 50, pp. 436–437.

. . . . .

SENIOR, NASSAU WILLIAM
(1790–1864)

Nassau William Senior achieved distinction both as a key theorist in the development of economics between Ricardo and Jevons and as a statesman who tackled such social problems as Poor Law reform and trade unionism. His abstinence theory of interest has been recognized as his most significant contribution to the corpus of economic science. Although he was attacked by Marx for his analysis of the marginal productivity of labor and his theory of wages ("Senior's Last Hour," in *Capital*), Senior can be considered an important example of the engaged intellectual. He believed that economic theory was a deductive science, while legislation was an art that drew information from many sources, including theory.

Senior was educated at Oxford and called to the bar in 1819, but his interest in political economy soon drew him from legal practice to legal reform. He returned to Oxford as first Drummond professor of political economy from 1825 to 1830, a post he occupied again from 1847 to 1852. Senior served on the Poor Law Commission of 1833 and authored the report upon which the 1834 **Poor Law** was based, although he later found fault with the new law's design. He subsequently served on royal commissions on factories (1837), handloom weavers (1841), the Irish Poor Law (1844), and education (1857).

A frequent contributor to the *Edinburgh Review*, the *Quarterly Review*, and the *London Review*, Senior found more favor as a writer on economic than on literary subjects, although William Makepeace Thackeray described Senior's review of *Vanity Fair* (*Edinburgh Review*) as of great importance to the growth of his reputation.

BARBARA ALLEN

Bibliography

Bowley, Marian. *Nassau Senior and Classical Economics.* 1937.

· · · · ·

SENSATION NOVEL

"Sensation novel" is a popular generic term, usually disparaging, for crime, mystery, and horror novels, particularly of the 1860s and 1870s. A writer in the *Literary Budget*, November 1861, asserted that the term originated in America; its widespread use in Britain began with the publication, in quick succession, of **Wilkie Collins**'s *The Woman in White* (1860), **Ellen Price Wood**'s *East Lynne*

(1861), and **Mary Elizabeth Braddon**'s *Lady Audley's Secret* (1862). In addition to Collins (1824–1889), Wood (1814–1887), and Braddon (1837–1915), leading exponents of the sensation novel included **Charles Reade** (1814–1884), **Edmund Yates** (1831–1894), and **Joseph Sheridan Le Fanu** (1814–1873).

The most distinctive sensation novels are characterized by an exciting amalgam of such subjects as bigamy, murder, arson, blackmail, madness, and persecuted innocence (usually young and female), acted out in the most ordinary and respectable social settings and narrated with ostentatious care for factual accuracy and fullness of circumstantial detail. Because of their seamy subjects and what Henry James called their "thorough-going realism" (*Nation*, November 9, 1865), they were accused by conservative critics and moralists of libeling mid-Victorian society and instilling an un-Christian sense of fatalism, of ubiquitous evil and danger. Novels with an overt moral and ethical purpose, such as Collins's *No Name* (1862) and *Armadale* (1866) and Reade's *Hard Cash* (1863), incurred the heaviest opprobrium; but the novels of Braddon, who believed that people read novels simply for "amusement," and to a lesser extent those of Wood, also aroused widespread social concern.

In particular there was vague, but understandable, suspicion that the rash of "bigamy novels" which *East Lynne* and *Lady Audley's Secret* were blamed for initiating represented an underhand circumvention of the "prudery" enforced upon Victorian novelists: even when the bigamy was unintentional, as in *East Lynne* and *Lady Audley's Secret*, it effectively enabled a man and women to enjoy the sweets of adultery, and when the bigamist was a young and beautiful woman like Lady Audley or the eponymous heroine of Braddon's *Aurora Floyd* (1863), the erotic piquancy of the situation could hardly be missed. By concentrating on the external effects and evading the moral causes of deviant or unconventional behavior, the sensation novelists enabled themselves to hint at all sorts of forbidden passions, especially female passions, without actually naming them. Thus it is never quite acknowledged that the restless urge for action that leads the "horsey" Aurora Floyd to marry her father's groom or Collins's Magdalen Vanstone (the heroine of *No Name*) to contrive and execute a devious revenge against the man who has cut her out of her inheritance constitutes a specifically sexual rebellion, a purposeful rejection of patriarchal rules; and the homicidal furies of Lady Audley and of Wood's Charlotte Carleton St. John (in *St. Martin's Eve*, 1866) are ascribed, ultimately, not to any psychosexual or social causes—as might have been expected—but to an hereditary taint of insanity.

Social and literary-critical opinion about the methods and aims of the sensationists was sharply divided, roughly along the same lines as opinion about the respective merits of Dickens and Thackeray. Though Dickens's example was widely invoked in defense of the sensation novel, and though he obviously influenced it, his own art was almost invariably recognized as of a higher order. Margaret Oliphant, in one of the most systematic and trenchant attacks on the sensationists ("Novels," *Blackwood's Magazine*, September 1867), saw Charlotte Brontë to blame for their reckless, rebellious heroines; and certainly the recipe of bigamy, murder, arson, and insanity in novels like *Lady Audley's Secret* and *St. Martin's Eve* does recall *Jane Eyre*. The sensation novel also has affinities to the Gothic and the Newgate novel, Richardson's *Pamela* and *Clarissa*, and the novels of Balzac and Eugène Sue. Braddon herself suggested parallels between her beautiful but fiery, even demonic, heroines and the style of female beauty popularized by the Pre-Raphaelites.

In the wake of the sensation novel, analogous sensationalism was detected not only in art, in poetry (Swinburne), and religion (Moody and Sankey), but also in such unexpected areas as diplomacy, auction sales, science, and sport. Seen at the time as a concerted attack on the national nervous system, the phenomenon now appears as part of an inevitable and growing reaction against mid-Victorian stodginess and prudery.

P. D. EDWARDS

Bibliography

Edwards, P. D. *Some Mid-Victorian Thrillers: The Sensation Novel, Its Friends and Its Foes.* 1971.

Fahnestock, Jeanne. "Bigamy: The Rise and Fall of a Convention." *Nineteenth-Century Fiction*, vol. 36, pp. 47–71.

Hughes, Winifred. *The Maniac in the Cellar: Sensation Novels of the 1860s.* 1980.

Phillips, Walter C. *Dickens, Reade, and Collins: Sensation Novelists.* 1919.

Wolff, Robert Lee. *Sensational Victorian: The Life and Fiction of Mary Elizabeth Braddon.* 1979.

· · · · ·

SERIAL LITERATURE

Serial literature—works that pursue their stories over an extended period of time with formal interruptions in the text due to the publication format—became a central literary form in the Victorian age. Serial literature includes the monthly publication of separate parts in paper wrappers in the 1830s; by the 1860s, installments more often appeared in monthly and weekly literary periodicals. If serial literature owed its origin to marketing strategies, the result was a pervasive literary medium which created distinctive—and significant—aesthetic effects.

The impetus behind serial literature was commercial: the growing and increasingly literate middle class could purchase cheap parts when expensive bound volumes were beyond their means. Publication of works in individual numbers, especially histories, the Bible, religious tracts and encyclopedias, began in the late eighteenth century. But not until the enormously popular *Pickwick Papers* appeared in parts in 1836–1837 did the installment format begin to become a medium for much of the age's best literature. Charles Dickens popularized the serial novel through such classics as *David Copperfield* (1849–1850), *Bleak House* (1852–1853), and *Great Expectations* (1860–1861). Other great serial novels include William Makepeace Thackeray's *Vanity Fair* (1847–1848), George Eliot's *Middlemarch* (1871–1872), Thomas Hardy's *The Return of the Native* (1878), Henry James's *The Portrait of a Lady* (1880–1881), and Joseph Conrad's *Lord Jim* (1899–1900). Major serial poems include Coventry Patmore's *Angel in the House* (1854–1863), Arthur Hugh Clough's *Amours de Voyage* (February–May 1858), Alfred Tennyson's *Idylls of the King* (1859–1885), Robert Browning's *The Ring and the Book* (1868–1869), William

Morris's *The Earthly Paradise* (1868-1870), and Hardy's *The Dynasts* (1904-1908). Nonfiction prose works, such as Thomas Carlyle's *Sartor Resartus* (1833-1834), John Henry Newman's *Apologia Pro Vita Sua* (1864), Matthew Arnold's *Culture and Anarchy* (1867-1868), and virtually all of John Ruskin's major works, also appeared serially.

Traditional study of serialization has emphasized ways authors overcame the inherent restrictions of Victorian publishing formats. More recently, attention has focused on the economic and ideological factors that shaped serialization. Reader-response criticism illuminates the distinctive aesthetics of serial texts. The weeks, months, or years between installments of serial works provided opportunity for reaction, interpretation, and involvement before a work had been completed. Furthermore, the sheer duration of a novel or poem read over many months and even years had a significant impact on the way in which Victorian literature was understood, encouraging a blending and interaction among the worlds of literature, current events, and personal life.

An additional reason for serial literature's popularity was its affinity with other Victorian intellectual frameworks, particularly the ethos of process and progress. The theory of evolution, for example, encouraged a world view of creations slowly unfolding over time, instead of (as the catastrophic school—or Genesis—maintained) in single, full-blown acts of creation. Similarly, the Victorian Bildungsroman, as seen in David Copperfield's difficult, nineteen-month evolution from naive, troubled childhood to mature, productive adulthood, became a familiar pattern to the age. An analogue is Patmore's *Angel in the House* (1854-1863), where the titles of individual volumes—"The Betrothal," "The Espousals," "Faithful for Ever," and "Victories of Love"—reveal the slow growth and development of spousal love. Serial literature also accorded with Victorian notions of history. The Victorians' serial conception of historical progression informs not only such monumental studies as Thomas Babington Macaulay's *History of England* (1849-1861) but also Browning's *The Ring and the Book* (1868-1869), Eliot's *Romola* (1862-1863), and Tennyson's *Idylls* (1859-1885).

A major resource for investigating the impact of serial literature is contemporary Victo-

rian periodicals. The major literary and political monthlies and quarterlies reviewed serial texts, usually at the end of their publication runs. In regular columns labeled "Serials," more widely read weekly papers like the *Weekly Dispatch*, *Sunday Times*, and *Illustrated London News* reviewed individual installments of ongoing novels and long poems.

Beyond its economic origins and effects, then, the serial format is an element of meaning in many nineteenth-century texts. Victorians regularly engaged the major literary productions of their time (and formed lasting impressions of their significance) in small, discrete units with extended time for reflection (even reinterpretation) before proceeding. While there are many variations in installment formats in the nineteenth century—weekly, monthly, annual, and less regular issue—all share the factors of a continuing story and extended reading time. The serial context of many major literary works of the last century is an important source of their power as they affected and shaped the imagination of Victorian culture.

LINDA K. HUGHES
MICHAEL LUND

Bibliography

Altick, Richard D. *The English Common Reader.* 1957.

Beaty, Jerome. *Middlemarch: From Notebook to Novel.* 1960.

Butt, John and Kathleen Tillotson. *Dickens at Work.* 1957.

Vann, J. Don. *Victorian Novels in Serial.* 1985.

——— and Rosemary T. VanArsdel. *Victorian Periodicals: A Guide to Research.* 1978, 1988.

See also FICTION SYNDICATION

· · · · ·

SERVANTS

Domestic service was the largest single source of employment for women and girls in the nineteenth century, and with increasing affluence and rising standards of living in the middle class the number of servants employed—both male and female—grew steadily. In 1851, 13.3 percent of the employed population (taking both sexes together) were domestic servants. By 1881 the proportion had risen to 15.9 percent. During the middle and late Victorian period, about one-third of all women between ages fifteen and twenty were in domestic service. The duties and conditions of work varied enormously, from the virtual slavery of a young maid-of-all-work employed by a lodging-house keeper to the specialized skills and the elaborate "downstairs" social life in an aristocratic household.

Domestic work required heavy manual labor in the age before household appliances. The duties of a woman servant in a middle-class household might include cooking, cleaning, sewing, washing, ironing, child care, filling and cleaning lamps, carrying coal and tending the open grates that heated individual rooms, hauling water up to bedrooms and slops down, going on errands, carrying parcels and luggage, walking the ladies of the household to social functions and waiting to accompany them home (particularly after dark), ordering food and household supplies, dealing with tradespeople, and keeping the books. Simply producing daily meals, in the absence of refrigeration or prepared foods, involved daily or near-daily marketing, baking, preserving, and so forth.

The most common variety of servant—and the lowest rung on the ladder of domestic employment—was the maid-of-all-work, often employed in the families of tradespeople or skilled workers. Sometimes an orphan from the workhouse, the maid-of-all-work might be employed from age twelve or thirteen. Her work was essentially solitary; she was often forbidden to have visitors; she was the first up (in order to make the fires and heat water for bathing) and went to bed only when her employers did, with duties that could keep her on call throughout a seventeen-hour day. She might sleep on a pallet on the floor of a basement kitchen and suffer from the consequences of undernourishment and the damp, smoky atmosphere in which she labored.

The domestic manuals and housewives' guides of the period provide exhaustive, prescriptive, and no doubt oversystematized descriptions of duties of specialized servants. In the midrange of the middle class, a suitable establishment consisted of three servants, generally a cook, a housemaid, and either a parlourmaid or nursemaid (depending on the presence and ages of children). Keeping a horse required adding a man or boy to the staff of servants, as did grounds that called for substantial outside work.

The country estates and great townhouses of the wealthy and aristocratic were served by a large and structured staff; in the servants' hall rigid lines of procedure echoed the etiquette that governed life above stairs. At the head of the indoor staff were a butler, a housekeeper, and a head cook. Under these three came footmen, assistant cooks, parlourmaids, housemaids, nurserymaids, kitchenmaids, scullerymaids, dairymaids, laundresses, a boot-boy, and a doorkeeper or watchman who attended also to fires and fueling. At meals in the servants' hall, the upper ranks were served by a youth (often referred to as the steward's boy) or a maid. Each member of the team—females under the housekeeper's orders, males under those of the butler—was trained and supervised. The head cook received orders directly from the mistress of the house; she was also generally responsible for the keys to the cupboards, where staples and supplies were kept locked up until needed for the preparation and serving of meals. Wines were stored, and poured at table, by the butler. He also had charge of the silverware, which was washed and polished in his pantry. Ladies' maids and gentlemen's valets were responsible for maintaining clothing and providing personal attendance. Outdoor staff—gardeners, grooms, coachmen, and carpenters—were overseen generally by a factor or agent of the master of the house.

Even the duties of a lady's maid—which young servants often saw as the most "dainty" and desirable post—called for heavy labor as well as specialized skills. Isabella Beeton's *Book of Household Management* (1859–1861) indicates that care of a lady's wardrobe involved not only laying out the mistress's clothes and helping her to dress but also removing spots, mending, ironing, washing and repairing lace, and packing and unpacking as required. Other duties of the lady's maid included lighting fires and sweeping in the dressing room and bedroom, managing baths, and emptying slops. Beeton suggested that the lady's maid should be a reasonably expert milliner, dressmaker, and hairdresser, and enough of a chemist to prepare cosmetics and home remedies.

Employment in substantial households could provide a high degree of job and financial security, although moral lapses and theft were punished by summary dismissal without appeal. (Legislation governing conditions of employment in agriculture and industry offered no protection to domestic servants, whose lot remained unregulated.) Most employers preferred servants from the country; they were thought to be healthier and less likely to have distracting suitors and unsavory local contacts. The daughters of agricultural laborers often began their life in service with a relatively low-paid position near their homes at age twelve or thirteen, which they kept only long enough to gain some training and save enough money to buy clothing suitable for getting a job in a town.

The great variation in domestic servants' age, skill, and working conditions makes generalizations about wages difficult. Wages generally included food and lodging; some employers paid an extra allowance for tea, sugar, and beer instead of supplying them, thus protecting against waste and immoderate consumption. Some servants had to provide their own clothing and pay for washing; others were supplied with uniforms or livery. A table in one domestic manual for 1861 suggests wages in the range of 25 to 50 pounds per year for butlers, valets, and housekeepers; 12 to 25 pounds per year for a lady's maid; 15 to 30 pounds for a cook or head nurse; and 9 to 14 pounds for a maid-of-all-work. The junior posts in a large household (nurserymaid, scullerymaid, stableboy), which were held by young teenagers, might pay as little as 5 or 6 pounds a year.

Even though wages had risen substantially by the end of the century, other kinds of work—work that provided defined tasks, a workday limited by law or union contract, and the freedom of not living twenty-four hours a day under the employer's supervision—became increasingly attractive. First menservants and then women became harder to find. Although domestic service was still the largest single employment for women at the end of Victoria's reign, there were already fewer servants in proportion to the number of families than there had been twenty years previously.

SALLY MITCHELL

Bibliography

Beeton, Isabella. *The Book of Household Management.* 1861.

Hartcup, Adeline. *Below Stairs in the Great Country Houses.* 1985.

Horn, Pamela. *The Rise and Fall of the Victorian Servant.* 1975.

Stanley, Liz, ed. *The Diaries of Hannah Cullwick, Victorian Maidservant.* 1984.

Waterson, Merlin. *The Servants' Hall.* 1980.

See also HOUSEWORK AND DOMESTIC TECHNOLOGY; MUNBY, A.J. AND HANNAH CULLWICK

. . . . .

SETTLEMENT MOVEMENT

Settlements were educational enterprises of an experimental nature, designed and staffed by resident academics and clergymen to help solve social problems in urban working-class districts. The conventional starting point for the movement is the founding of Toynbee Hall at Whitechapel, East London, in 1884. By 1900 university and church settlements had spread throughout urban Britain and to other parts of the Western world.

The movement's origins can be traced to the activities of F. D. Maurice, one of the early leaders of English Christian socialism. In 1854 Maurice founded the Working Men's College in London, recruiting his teachers primarily from the ranks of young university graduates. In the following two decades, an increasing number of university teachers and students became interested in improving the lot of the laboring masses through instruction, advice, and example. John Ruskin, a professor of fine arts at Oxford who also taught drawing and art history at the Working Men's College, inspired a generation of undergraduates with his idea of bringing beauty and culture to the industrial city. T. H. Green, professor of moral philosophy, also encouraged Oxford students to spend time in the slums in order to practice good citizenship by giving practical assistance to the underprivileged. Eventually this missionary activity led to the establishment of regular residency in the slums, first practiced by Edward Denison in 1867 and later by Arnold Toynbee in the early 1880s. Shortly after Toynbee's death in 1883, his friend the Reverend Samuel Barnett (vicar of the slum parish of St. Jude's, London) founded the first university settlement in Toynbee's name.

Barnett encouraged university men to remain in residence at Toybee Hall, teaching and administering to various educational, cultural, and social needs of the East London working classes. The primary object was to build bridges between classes in the belief that contact would enrich both parties, would benefit the poor more than almsgiving, and would create social harmony.

Though Toynbee Hall's origins were linked to the **Broad Church**, its purpose was religious only in a general sense. Oxford House, an Anglican settlement with a more pronounced clerical element, was established at Bethnal Green a year later by a group of Tractarians. Before long many Nonconformist and a few Roman Catholic settlements were founded in London and other cities. Women's settlements, established by the new women's colleges or through other voluntary agencies, emphasized child centers, prenatal care, girls' clubs, and other practical services.

While education remained the focus of settlement work, activities included clubs, recreation, and involvement in local government. Although settlement leaders would sometimes join in campaigns to urge Parliament to pass benevolent legislation, settlements were not, on the whole, overtly political. At the turn of the century there were about fifty-six settlements in England and Wales. The most impressive expansion had taken place in the United States, where over two hundred settlements had been established by that time.

PAUL T. PHILLIPS

Bibliography

Briggs, Asa and Anne Macartney. *Toynbee Hall: The First Hundred Years.* 1984.

Inglis, Kenneth S. *Churches and the Working Classes in Victorian England.* 1963.

Meacham, Standish. *Toynbee Hall and Social Reform, 1880-1914: The Search for Community.* 1987.

Nettleship, L. E. "William Fremantle, Samuel Barnett and the Broad Church Origins of Toynbee Hall." *Journal of Ecclesiastical History*, vol. 33, pp. 564-579.

Picht, Werner. *Toynbee Hall and the English Settlement Movement.* 1914.

Vicinus, Martha. *Independent Women: Work and Community for Single Women, 1850-1920.* 1985.

· · · · ·

SEWELL, ANNA (1820-1878)

Anna Sewell's celebrity rests entirely on her only book, *Black Beauty* (1877). Told in the first person by Black Beauty, and written to encourage humane treatment of animals and workers, the book became the best-known animal tale of the nineteenth century and a children's classic.

Sewell's parents were Quaker, and her mother, Mary Wright Sewell (1797-1884), wrote religious and children's books. Anna Sewell was a lifelong invalid who got about much of the time in a pony cart.

The horse in *Black Beauty* serves as a spokesman for all beasts of burden and burdened workers. The book teaches that animals and humans should be treated with kindness in return for obedience, patience, and a desire to please. *Black Beauty*'s gospel of work and acceptance of class make it a conservative work, but the rage against cruelty and injustice that it directs at the insensitive and intemperate of all classes carries its own program for reform. The book became a favorite text of animal protectionists, temperance societies, and educational and religious reformers. It was as popular with working-class readers as with the rich. Although *Black Beauty* is today regarded as a children's classic, it was in its own time part of the consciousness and literature of the age. The book's power grows from the gentle irony of the narrative voice and from readers' willing empathy for the horse. *Black Beauty* has sold many millions of copies and spawned numerous imitations.

SUZANNE GRAVER

Bibliography

Chitty, Susan. *The Woman Who Wrote Black Beauty: A Life of Anna Sewell.* 1971.

Lansbury, Coral. *The Old Brown Dog: Women, Workers, and Vivisection in Edwardian England.* 1985.

. . . . .

Bibliography

Colby, Vineta. *Yesterday's Woman: Domestic Realism in the English Novel.* 1974.

Foster, Shirley. *Victorian Women's Fiction: Marriage, Freedom and the Individual.* 1985.

Sewell, Eleanor L., ed. *The Autobiography of Elizabeth M. Sewell.* 1907.

. . . . .

SEWELL, ELIZABETH MISSING (1815–1906)

The author of over forty devotional and literary works, Elizabeth Missing Sewell is best known for her first book, *Amy Herbert* (1844). Sewell's novels with a High Church flavor, including *Gertrude* (1846) and *Margaret Percival* (1847), were written for educated, middle-class Anglican girls. Concentrating on girls' educational reform post-1860, she wrote *The Principles of Education* (1865) and founded a church school.

Sewell lived her entire life on the Isle of Wight. Suffering serious privations at boarding school, she became committed to improving girls' education and, due to geographical isolation, turned to writing to convey her religious and moral teachings. *Amy Herbert* and *Laneton Parsonage* (1846–1848), written for younger girls, contain direct religious instruction. Her books for older girls, similar to those of Charlotte Mary Yonge, combine instruction and fiction. Her heroines are serious of purpose, obedient, and devout. *The Principles of Education* provides an idealized account of how girls from middle-class homes should be prepared to assume a broad range of suitable employment. In 1852 she took in private pupils and in 1866 opened St. Boniface Diocesan School for middle-class girls, which she supervised until her death.

Sewell's books, never achieving the popularity of Yonge's, are rarely read today. Though didactic and uneventful, her novels written during the Anglican revival offer a portrait of the ideal Victorian middle-class girl and her model Christian home.

CATHERINE J. GOLDEN

SEWING MACHINES

The modern sewing machine was an American invention, first introduced into British clothing manufacture in the 1850s, and into people's homes for domestic use in the 1860s. It stimulated the growth of the ready-made clothing trade. In respectable households, dresses, shirts, and underwear had traditionally been made at home; by 1900, they were more commonly bought ready-made.

Elias Howe (1819–1867), the American inventor generally credited with promoting the first successful lockstitch sewing machine, brought his invention to London in 1847, though practical machines only became available in Britain in the early 1850s. Because of patent restrictions, the trade flourished first in Scotland, where English patents did not apply. The first domestic machines were introduced by William Newton Wilson (1827–1894) in 1858. Imported American machines competed with British machines and, from the 1870s onward, cheap German machines. Sewing machines were principally made in and around Manchester, Birmingham, and Coventry. The most important English makers were Bradbury and Jones, but the largest factory in Britain at Clydebank near Glasgow belonged to Singer. The demands of sewing machine manufacture fostered the adoption of many American factory practices, such as the intensive use of gauges to ensure interchangeability of parts. American machine tools were a common feature in British sewing machine factories.

Sewing machines were seldom used for fashionable clothes, but they were enthusiastically adopted by the makers of ready-made clothing. Their use changed the design of the ubiquitous corset, and in the boot and shoe trade, they put an end to child labor. The sewing machine helped bring cheap, well-made clothing within the reach of ordinary British people.

RAY BATCHELOR

Bibliography

Cooper, Grace Rogers. *The Sewing Machine: Its Invention and Development.* 1976.

Head, Carol. *Old Sewing Machines.* 1982.

· · · · ·

SEX EDUCATION

Young Victorians gained carnal knowledge by avoiding their usual sources of education—family, church, and school—and conversing with friends, observing animals, and trying to extract information from books. The anonymous male author of *My Secret Life* described how (in early Victorian times, when he was an adolescent) he first mutually masturbated with schoolfellows and then imagined having intercourse: "it set me reflecting, that delicate, handsome ladies, should allow pricks to be thrust up them, and nasty stuff ejected into them. I read Aristotle, tried to understand it, and thought I did, with the help of much talk with my schoolfellows; yet I only half believed it."

"Aristotle" referred to *Aristotle's Masterpiece*, which had been in existence since the seventeenth century, and which was probably the most widely read sex manual in nineteenth-century England. It described female anatomy, conception, pregnancy, and the delivery of the child, but gave little in the way of detail about sexual relations. Reticence about intercourse was the rule in sex manuals, which also contained misinformation and confusion. Dr. Samuel Solomon's widely read *A Guide to Health, or Advice to Both Sexes* (1800) stated that, although intercourse was enjoyable, "over-indulgence" caused mental and physical exhaustion and "convulsions of all the senses." Books and articles by physicians expressed a variety of opinions about the effects of masturbation.

Dr. Harry Campbell, in *Differences in the Nervous Organisation of Man and Woman: Physiological and Pathological* (1891), admitted that there were divergent views among medical men on the subject of sexual desire among women. After conducting his own survey he concluded that the sexual instinct is much less in women than in men, the view supported by the prominent physician **William Acton** and other gynecological authorities. Although women did not always feel sexually inferior to men, neither could they ever feel entirely free from this male view of them. The ideology expected men to learn about sex by having early sexual experiences, while it encouraged women to wait passively or to have mental conflicts if they made sexual advances to men.

Although Victorians differed in their carnal knowledge and sexual morals, they sometimes agreed on the need for better sex education. In 1870 the physician James Paget commented that "ignorance about sexual affairs seemed to be a notable characteristic of the more civilised parts of the human race." In her *Autobiography* (1893), the freethinker Annie Besant wrote that ignorance about sex had been a "fatal blunder" in her early life. And the Reverend Edward Lyttleton, headmaster of Eton, observed in his *Training of the Young in the Laws of Sex* (1900): "there is a huge amount of woeful and preventable waste of married happiness, due to debased thought and ignorance, which is the direct result of the prevailing reticence on sexual questions." Despite these admonitions, changes in sex education did not come until many years after the end of Victoria's reign.

RALPH COLP, JR.

Bibliography

Gay, Peter. *The Bourgeois Experience: Victoria to Freud.* Vol. 1: *Education of the Senses*; Vol. 2: *The Tender Passion.* 1984, 1986.

Hare, E. H. "Masturbatory Insanity: The History of an Idea." *Journal of Mental Science*, vol. 108, pp. 2–25.

Jeffreys, Sheila. *The Spinster and Her Enemies: Feminism and Sexuality 1880–1930.* 1985.

Marcus, Steven. *The Other Victorians: A Study of Sexuality and Pornography in Mid-Nineteenth-Century England.* 1966.

My Secret Life. Complete and unexpurgated edition, 1966.

Petersen, M. Jeanne. "Dr. Acton's Enemy: Medicine, Sex, and Society in Victorian England." *Victorian Studies*, vol. 29, pp. 569-590.

Smith, F. Barry. "Sexuality in Britain, 1800-1900: Some Suggested Revisions." In Martha Vicinus, ed., *A Widening Sphere: Changing Roles of Victorian Women*. 1980.

Stearns, Carol Z. and Peter N. Stearns. "Victorian Sexuality: Can Historians Do It Better?" *Journal of Social History*, vol. 18, pp. 625-634.

Woodward, John and David Richards, eds. *Health Care and Popular Medicine in Nineteenth Century England: Essays in the Social History of Medicine*. 1977.

See also PORNOGRAPHY

· · · · ·

SEXUAL VIOLENCE

The sexual danger faced by women and girls greatly concerned Victorians of all classes, but they often confused rape and seduction, portraying the victim of violence as herself dangerous. Chastity was thought to be the most important element in a woman's character, and it mattered little to the Victorians whether a "fallen women" had lost her virtue through rape or seduction.

In the decade before Victoria's coronation, publicity about the sexual danger women faced in public places intensified; the newly expanded popular press reported indecent assaults with the injunction that no respectable women could safely traverse London streets. Such publicity contributed to the fear of crime which was used to justify the formation of the New Police in 1828, but the New Police constables themselves often harassed women out alone at night, treating them like prostitutes, refusing to help them if they were assaulted, or telling them to go home.

In the 1830s and early 1840s, reformers also identified factories and mines as the site of sexual danger to women, although they portrayed mill girls as themselves sexually depraved. Working-class activists seized upon the image of the factory master sexually exploiting his female workers, both as a justification for legislation controlling the work of women and children, and as a metaphor for class exploitation. Radical newspapers such as the *Weekly Dispatch* printed many examples of masters raping their female domestic servants to underline this point.

The available statistics demonstrate, however, that these stereotypes are misleading. Most victims of rape were assaulted by men of their own class—more than half by men they knew. While incidents of sexual harassment of female workers by supervisors were reported in factory districts, there were many more incidents of assaults on female domestic servants and agricultural workers. The latter often worked alone in homes and fields, while female factory hands worked in large groups and could protect each other. Furthermore, within working-class culture young women faced the danger of rape by gangs of young men, and there is some evidence of rape in courtship, usually termed "forcible seduction."

It is impossible, however, to determine changes in the incidence of sexual violence. First, the introduction of the New Police in 1828 increased the reporting and prosecution of all crimes. Second, the vast majority of sexual assaults were never prosecuted; the prosecution procedure was difficult and expensive and the police unsympathetic, and a rape trial was a humiliating experience for women. Although precedent held that a woman's bad sexual reputation did not excuse rape, in practice judges allowed victims' characters to be impugned. The conviction rate for rape was always low, although when the death penalty for rape was amended to transportation for life in 1841 the conviction rate increased from 10 percent between 1836 and 1840 to 33 percent between 1841 and 1845.

The next important change in the law came in 1885 with the Criminal Law Amendment Act, which raised the age of consent from thirteen to sixteen for girls, and included a watered-down clause which made sexual harassment of a chaste girl by a guardian or master an assault. This act was passed in response to W. T. Stead's campaign against juvenile prostitution, or "white slavery," and the related social **purity campaigns.** The sexual abuse of children had always aroused popular fury, and in this period many feminists also made it an issue, both by agitating for the change in the age of consent and by helping girls and women who had been assaulted. At the same time, however, gynecologists and police surgeons considered women and children who accused men of sexual assaults to be lying, hysterical, and malicious. Even some of the social purity campaigns viewed abused girls as "contaminated," and in fact they were usually sent to detention homes. It took until 1908 for incest to be made illegal.

The Victorian age, then, became increasingly concerned with sexual danger, but the response was usually to control the lives of its victims in order to "protect" them.

ANNA CLARK

Bibliography

Clark, Anna. *Women's Silence, Men's Violence: Sexual Assault in England, 1770–1845.* 1987.

Cobbe, Frances Power. "Wife-Torture in England." *Contemporary Review,* vol. 53, pp. 55–87.

Edwards, Susan. *Female Sexuality and the Law.* 1981.

Jeffreys, Sheila. *The Spinster and Her Enemies: Feminism and Sexuality, 1880–1930.* 1985.

Lambertz, Jan. "Sexual Harassment in the Nineteenth-Century English Cotton Industry." *History Workshop,* no. 19, pp. 29–61.

Walkowitz, Judith. *Jack the Ripper's London.* (Forthcoming.)

. . . . .

SHAFTESBURY, LORD (ANTHONY ASHLEY COOPER) (1801–1885)

Elevated to his ancestral title as seventh earl in 1851, Lord Shaftesbury was acknowledged during his lifetime as a leading parliamentarian, social reformer, and Church of England Evangelical. He entered Harrow (1813) and then Christ Church, Oxford (1819), where he became a serious student and took a first class in classics (1822). Following the requisite grand tour of Europe and several years as a country gentleman, he was elected Tory M. P. for Woodstock in 1826. He married Lady

Emily ("Minny") Cowper in 1830, and with her raised nine children.

Although Shaftesbury's choice of a career in politics was not unusual for an heir to an earldom, the seriousness with which he took this vocation marked him out as a potential leader from 1826. He sat on four committees his first year in the House of Commons, the last being the Committee on Lunacy which was formed in 1827 to probe into the scandalous state of English asylums. His visits to asylums, which later developed into frequent and rigorous tours of areas of social blight, convinced him that most of England was unaware of the appalling conditions in which the inmates were kept. His efforts led to his appointment as chairman of the permanent commission (1829), a position which he maintained almost continuously until his death. He submitted further reform bills on the creation and inspection of asylums, and was consulted throughout his life as the leading Victorian expert on English asylums.

Shaftesbury's involvement in industrial reform began in the early 1830s. Correspondence with the poet laureate, Robert Southey (1774–1843), roused his concern for the thousands of children working twelve, fourteen, or more hours a day in the mills of the north. When approached by the operatives of Yorkshire and Lancashire in 1833 to take up the leadership of their cause from Michael Sadler, a defeated M. P., Shaftesbury took on the challenge as a summons from God and very quickly submitted the Ten Hours Bill (1833). Melbourne's Whig government, however, passed its own bill which lowered the suggested age of protection from eighteen to thirteen years, and soon proved unenforceable. Shaftesbury made several frustrating attempts to see through a stricter bill under both Whig and Tory governments over the following seventeen years. In his last effort to change legislation, he consented to a compromise (1850) that was to add one half-hour to the ten-hour demand but prevent the "relays" (split shifts spread over long days) that had circumvented the intention of previous legislation regarding children.

The years 1846–1851 brought tremendous change to Shaftesbury's life. He resigned his parliamentary seat in 1846 when the droughts in England and Ireland convinced him to abandon his pro–Corn Law stance. Although he was out of Parliament for less than two years, his focus began to move from legislation to **philanthropy**. Shocked by his experience of the London slums, he took on the presidency of the **Ragged School** Union (1846), which he promoted vigorously until his death. He was returned to the House of Commons as a Tory in 1848, but his accession to the House of Lords (1851) encouraged his movement away from the center of political power. Although he continued to call for commissions and submit new bills on a wide variety of issues, his leadership of Evangelical missionary organizations, such as the Church Missionary Society, burgeoned as did his involvement in a bewildering number of self-improvement societies and his gifts to various social causes. He was also more frequently identified as the leading articulator of Evangelical concerns.

Shaftesbury's social interests extended beyond those of most Victorian reformers. He brought before the government—and a startled public—the pitiful condition of women and children in the mines (1840), the plight of the chimney sweeps (1840), the terrible conditions of urban boarding houses (1851), and the urgent need for urban sanitation reform (1846–1851), to name but a few. In each case he worked enthusiastically to change the conditions, often against considerable initial opposition.

Although Shaftesbury has been described as a conscientious rural aristocrat who rebelled against both the social chaos of industrial society and socialist solutions, his religious conviction had an equal part in steering his rather unpredictable career. Through childhood exposure to evangelical Christianity by an affectionate maid and close friendships with prominent Evangelicals, particularly Edward Bickersteth, and (after 1850) Alexander Haldane, Shaftesbury's compassion and sense of religious responsibility for the "brutalized" were sharpened by a premillennial urgency to do God's will. This mind set also played a major part in his frequent refusal of government office and in his subjection of party loyalty—and even of Britain's interests—to moral principle (in, for example, the Opium Wars). Although some contemporaries disliked the bias that this frame of mind brought

to Shaftesbury's disputes over *Essays and Reviews* (1860) and to his "bishop-making" under his father-in-law Lord Palmerston, most Victorians were convinced at his death that he had served faithfully as the conscience of the nation.

PAUL H. FRIESEN

Bibliography

Battiscombe, Georgina. *Shaftesbury: A Biography of the Seventh Earl.* 1974.

Best, Geoffrey F. A. *Shaftesbury.* 1964.

Cooper, Anthony Ashley. *Speeches of the Earl of Shaftesbury.* 1868.

Finlayson, Geoffrey B. A. M. *The Seventh Earl of Shaftesbury.* 1981.

Hammond, John L. and Barbara Hammond. *Lord Shaftesbury.* 1923.

Hodder, Edwin. *The Life and Work of the Seventh Earl of Shaftesbury.* 1886. 3 vols.

. . . . .

SHARP, WILLIAM (1855-1905)

The Scottish poet, editor, and biographer William Sharp (1855-1905) wrote five volumes of commonplace poetry and published adequate biographies of Dante Gabriel Rossetti (1882), Percy Bysshe Shelley (1887), Heinrich Heine (1888), and Robert Browning (1890). His real success as a writer went unrecognized until his identity as Fiona MacLeod was revealed after his death. Writing as Fiona MacLeod, the Highland author of dreamy Celtic verse and prose, he published *Pharais: A Romance of the Isles* (1894), *The Mountain Lovers* (1895), *The Sin Eater* (1895), *The Washer of the Ford* (1896), *Green Fire* (1896), *From the Hills of Dreams* (1897), *The Dominion of Dreams* (1899), and *Where the Forest Murmurs* (1906).

Sharp's interest in early Celtic stories, myths, and poetry prompted him to write imitations of Ossianic verse that are marked by quaintness and anachronism in language and style and replete with subjects from pre-Christian Highland lore and nature worship. Ostensibly written in trancelike states or as the records of dreams, the "Fiona" literature is a curiosity of the romantic revival in late Victorian times and rests on the edge of the Celtic renaissance.

JOHN J. CONLON

Bibliography

Alaya, Flavia. *William Sharp—"Fiona MacLeod."* 1970.

Sharp, Elizabeth. *William Sharp (Fiona MacLeod): A Memoir Compiled by His Wife.* 1910.

Sharp, William. *Selected Writings of William Sharp.* 1912. 5 vols.

———. *The Writings of Fiona MacLeod.* 1909–1910.

. . . . .

George Bernard Shaw in a Jaeger suit. Reproduced courtesy of Jaeger.

SHAW, GEORGE BERNARD (1856–1950)

Bernard Shaw, genius of wit and comedy, abandoned his native Ireland for England at twenty and devoted himself to rousing and dazzling the British public with his unorthodox and socialist views, ultimately set forth in over fifty plays, including *Man and Superman* (1903), with its theory of an evolutionary life force; *Major Barbara* (1905); *Pygmalion* (1913), which became the musical *My Fair Lady* (1956); *Heartbreak House* (1919); *Back to Methuselah* (1921); and *St. Joan* (1923). In his long apprenticeship, Shaw wrote five unsuccessful novels, most notably *An Unsocial Socialist* (1887); developed a formidable talent as a public speaker; served as music critic for the *Star* (1888–1890) under the pseudonym Corno di Bassetto, and as theater critic for the *Saturday Review* (1895–1898); and discovered in his first play, *Widowers' Houses* (1892), on slum landlordism, a natural medium and playground for his ideas.

Born in Dublin, the son of a whimsical, often drunk civil servant, Shaw clerked for an estate agent before settling in London with his sister and mother, a singer and teacher of music. Almost penniless, he ghosted music

criticism and rid himself of agonizing shyness by speaking on every possible occasion—in debating societies, on street corners, in public houses. Joining the **Fabian Society** in 1884, he found a socialist platform consonant with his vision of evolutionary progress, his interest in economics having been fired by hearing Henry George speak in 1882 and by reading Marx. In the mid-1880s William Archer, Ibsen's translator, secured him posts as music critic for the *Dramatic Review*, art critic for the *World*, and book reviewer for the *Pall Mall Gazette*, and supplied him with the plot and subject for *Widowers' Houses*. By 1898, when he entered into his reputedly unconsummated marriage of companionship with Charlotte Payne-Townshend, Shaw was a celebrated critic and Fabian spokesman, having rendered both Ibsen and Wagner as socialists in *The Quintessence of Ibsenism* (1891) and *The Perfect Wagnerite* (1898). The Shaw persona—intimidatingly authoritative, brilliantly lucid, instructing while it amused with cap-and-bell antics—was firmly established in the public mind and endured provocative as ever until Shaw's death at ninety-four.

Shaw had little response from producers or audiences for his new drama with its talkiness, clash of ideas, witty reversals of expectation, and shocking frankness. J. T. Grein's Independent Theatre Club performed *Widowers' Houses* privately in 1892, but delayed until the turn of the century performances of *Mrs. Warren's Profession* (1893) on prostitution and *The Philanderer* (1893) with its "New Woman," an autobiographical account of Shaw's own philandering. His only play to be performed publicly in Victorian London was the delightful debunker of romanticism *Arms and the Man* (1894), written for Florence Farr's repertory season at the Avenue Theatre. Though well received, it lost money. The actor Richard Mansfield took it and *The Devil's Disciple* (1897) to New York where the latter was a hit.

Upon joining the *Saturday Review* in 1895, Shaw laid siege to nineteenth-century theater with its irrelevance to contemporary problems and thought, and promoted Ibsen. He published his first nine plays in *Plays Pleasant and Unpleasant* (1898) and *Three Plays for Puritans* (1901), collections that contain such winning theater as *Candida* (1895), *You Never Can Tell* (1898), and *Caesar and Cleopatra* (1901). But Shaw was not acclaimed as a playwright until the Vedrenne and Granville-Barker management at the Royal Court produced ten of his plays in repertory in 1904–1907.

Far from being mere vehicles for ideas, the early plays, like most of his work, sparkle with wit and paradox like the man himself. Shaw, the champion of workers and women's rights, also admired entrepreneurs and dictators, and rejected sex from fear of female dominance. A realist in assessing social problems and behavior, he was also a visionary, foretelling a human victory over self-destructive tendencies. The plays are Mozartian in their point and counterpoint style and organic unity, while the prefaces to them show a mastery of dialectical prose. Shaw received the Nobel Prize in 1925.

TAMIE WATTERS

Bibliography

Bentley, Eric. *Bernard Shaw: A Reconsideration.* 1947.

Ervine, St. John. *Bernard Shaw: His Life, Work, and Friends.* 1956.

Henderson, Archibald. *George Bernard Shaw: Man of the Century.* 1956.

Laurence, Dan H., ed. *Bernard Shaw: A Bibliography.* 1983.

Morgan, Margery. *The Shavian Playground.* 1972.

Shaw, Bernard. *Collected Letters.* 1965–. Ed. Dan H. Laurence. 4 vols.

Weintraub, Stanley, ed. *Shaw: An Autobiography.* 1969, 1970. 2 vols.

. . . . .

SHAW, RICHARD NORMAN (1831–1912)

Richard Norman Shaw created a distinct late Victorian architectural style using vernacular, medieval, and eighteenth-century elements. He is particularly associated with the "Old English" style, used mostly in country houses, and the "Queen Anne" style of urban structures.

Shaw was born in 1831, and after a period of apprenticeship and Continental travel, entered the office of George Edmund Street in 1858. Shaw and William Eden Nesfield (1835–1888) began working together on commissions in early 1863; they were partners from 1866 to 1869. In the 1860s Shaw developed his Old English style, which utilized half-timbering, massive chimneys, tiles, leaded windows, and other elements found in Elizabethan and Jacobean farmhouses, manors, cottages, and town buildings. Shaw, practicing alone, made use of these distinct elements at Cragside, Northumberland (1870), Grim's Dyke, Harrow Weald (1870–1872), and many other country houses during the next three decades.

At roughly the same time, Shaw also gained fame as an urban architect. The New Zealand Chambers, Leadenhall Street, London (1872; destroyed) combined Georgian windows; brick; gables, sashes, and moldings found in vernacular buildings of Germany and Holland; and distinctive oriels. The use of vernacular elements more or less dating from the early eighteenth century is typical of the style that came to be called Queen Anne. Shaw used this architectural vocabulary in Lowther Lodge, Kensington (1875), the Albert Hall Mansions (1879), houses in Melbury Road,

Queen's Gate, Chelsea, and Cadogan Square (1876ff), the first Alliance Assurance Building, Pall Mall (1882) and New Scotland Yard (1887–1890). Shaw's Queen Anne style had the picturesque compositions of earlier Gothic revival buildings, but used classical architectural elements in multiple combinations rather than purely Gothic ones. His late work, such as the second Alliance Assurance Building, St. James Street (1903), and the rebuilding of Regent Street (1905), was more strictly classical (in a grand and heroic mode) than his earlier work.

Shaw's classicism was viewed by his biographer Reginald Blomfield as his great contribution to late Victorian architecture. Nikolaus Pevsner saw Shaw as a precursor of modernism because of the freedom with which he combined elements. Although subsequent generations did not imitate him, Shaw was widely influential in his own time, and is the figure most responsible for the popularity of the Old English and Queen Anne styles in the late nineteenth century.

FLOYD W. MARTIN

Bibliography

Blomfield, Reginald. *Richard Norman Shaw, R. A., Architect, 1831–1912.* 1940.

Pevsner, Nikolaus. "Richard Norman Shaw." In Peter Ferriday, ed., *Victorian Architecture.* 1963.

Saint, Andrew. *Richard Norman Shaw.* 1976.

· · · · ·

SHIPPING AND SEAMEN

In 1837, British ships were generally inferior to those built in North America, but during the Victorian era the merchant marine of Great Britain developed into the largest and most powerful in the world. Shipbuilding and sea transport experienced dramatic technological advance and expansion. Advances in **engineering** coupled with the steady income provided by government mail contracts enabled British shipyards to recapture their leading position. Merchant seamen slowly became professionals. The government touted free trade while gradually intervening and guiding these trends.

Merchant shipping incorporated a broad range of endeavors: the design, architecture, engineering, and construction of ships; the development and maintenance of sea transport, communication, and other maritime services (both coastal and international); the recruiting, training, and maintenance of crews; and the creation of essential management, financial services, insurance, and support facilities on a worldwide basis. Throughout the era all of these activities increased again and again. By 1914, 60 percent of the world's merchant ships and 40 percent of its total ship tonnage were built in Great Britain; 50 percent of the total trade of the world and 67 percent of British imperial trade were in ships operating under the British flag.

The Clyde River area was the most active shipbuilding center, especially after the transformation to metal hulls and steam propulsion. The products of this virtual shipbuilding monopoly dominated coastal and world trade and commerce. There were three categories of commercial oceangoing ships: tramp steamers (unscheduled bulk carriers), more regularized cargo vessels, and passenger liners.

The life of merchant seamen improved very slowly. Although no longer subject to impressment, seamen were victimized by crimping. When a ship arrived in port, it was met by "crimps" who offered food and lodging on credit until the crew were paid off a few days later. By that time the seaman was often so deep in debt that he was virtually a hostage to the crimp, who then accepted a commission from the master of an outgoing ship and provided him with hands who were broke and ready to ship out. Seafaring tended to be a trade of last resort. Because of the long absences from home and the wretched conditions on board ship, seamen often came from economically depressed areas where there was no other work—or were men who, for personal or legal reasons, preferred to disappear from their usual haunts. Several prisoners' aid societies specialized in finding work at sea for discharged convicts.

Unhealthy conditions on board ship made a seaman's useful life short; most were broken in health by age thirty-five or forty. Boys went to sea as young as eleven or twelve. The masters of tramp and cargo ships sometimes rose from the forecastle and might be illiterate, navigating only by rule of thumb. On passenger ships, especially in the East India trade, officers were better educated and had generally been apprenticed as midshipmen. Proposals to improve the seaman's lot were regularly defeated due to the influence in Parliament of shipping interests. An act in 1844, however, did provide some regulations about the payment of wages, require that certain medicines be carried on board, and specify the amount and potency of the lime juice to be given daily to prevent scurvy among the crews of oceangoing ships.

Voluntary examinations in seamanship and navigation for masters and mates were introduced in 1845 and made compulsory in 1851. Increasingly sophisticated navigation instruments, the establishment of the Meteorological Office (1854) to provide storm warnings, and the publication of well-researched books on routes brought increased safety. Other technological changes affected the types and numbers of men at sea. Engineers and firemen were added to the mates and seamen. Several reformers and philanthropists were active on seamen's behalf. **Samuel Plimsoll** (1824-1898), the "sailor's friend" and radical politician, agitated for safety measures; Thomas, Earl Brassey (1836-1918) campaigned against crimping; and Dame Agnes Weston (1840-1918) created Sailors' Rests to provide crimp-free lodging and other social services in important ports.

Steam propulsion made schedules more predictable, stimulated expansion, and encouraged the formation of shipping companies. The old East India Company and family concerns were transformed into giant corporations such as the Peninsular and Orient (P & O), Cunard, and Royal Mail lines. From 1834, Lloyd's *Register of Shipping* provided information about all known British and foreign ships above a certain tonnage and rated their condition, age, and safety. By the mid-nineteenth century the loose association of insurers that had developed in Edward Lloyd's coffeehouse during the reign of Charles II had become the center of underwriting for the world's marine insurance.

Although the Victorian era is known as a period of free trade, the state and the shipping companies became mutually dependent through subsidies, mail contracts, monopolistic shipping conferences, and even official sanction of the opium trade. In the decades between 1870 and 1890, the British proportion of the world's tonnage was at its peak. P & O bragged that it was "the unofficial fleet of the British Empire." Not until the twentieth century, however, did seamen have a viable trade union or statutory regulation to provide an adequate diet, and their typical monthly pay, which was five pounds in 1914, tripled during World War I.

EUGENE L. RASOR

Bibliography

Brown, Antony. *Hazard Unlimited: The Story of Lloyd's of London.* New ed., 1978.

Course, Alfred G. *The Merchant Navy: A Social History.* 1963.

Gibbs, Charles R. V. *British Passenger Liners of the Five Oceans.* 1963.

Jackson, Gordon. *The British Whaling Trade.* 1978.

Kirkaldy, Adam W. *British Shipping: Its History, Organization and Importance.* 1914; rpt. 1970.

Palmer, Sarah. *Charted and Uncharted Waters.* 1981.

Pollard, Sydney. *The British Shipbuilding Industry, 1870-1914.* 1979.

Thornton, Roland Hobhouse. *British Shipping.* 2d ed., 1959.

. . . . .

SHIPS AND SHIPBUILDING

Ship design underwent revolutionary changes during the nineteenth century, as the products of industrialism were allied with the quest for greater speed, capacity, reliability, and safety. Thus, sails gave way to steam power, wooden hulls to iron and (after c. 1880) steel; the early paddle wheels yielded to more powerful screw propulsion; and the size of ships increased several fold.

Unlike wooden ships, iron ships had no practical size limit, allowed more stowage per ton, were safer from fire, did not consume scarce timber supplies, employed smaller crews, and could withstand the vibrations of steam engines. Although experimental iron barges appeared in the eighteenth century, regular iron shipbuilding began only in the 1830s, most notably at the Thames yard of William Fairbairn (1789-1874). The first practical steamboat, the *Claremont*, built in 1807 by the American, Robert Fulton (1765-1815), was suitable only for inland waterways. Only in 1819 did a paddle steamer, the *Savannah*, venture an Atlantic crossing, and that mostly under full sail. In 1829 the *William Fawcett* began a regular mail packet service across the Irish sea. From this sprang the Peninsular and Oriental Steam Navigation Company, which began carrying the mails to Egypt and India in 1840, the same year that Samuel Cunard (1787-1865), a Halifax, Nova Scotia shipowner, began a regular transatlantic steamship mail and passenger service.

In 1838 two paddle steamers, the *Sirius* and the *Great Western*, raced across the Atlantic in under twenty days. The latter vessel, sponsored by the railway of the same name, was designed by the great engineer **Isambard Kingdom Brunel** (1806-1859), who became the most influential ship designer of the era. His next design, the *Great Britain* (launched in 1843), combined an iron hull with screw propulsion to create a watershed vessel that has survived to this day.

The science of hydrodynamics developed rapidly in the mid-nineteenth century, thanks to the efforts of men like John Scott Russell (1808-1882), who studied wave disturbance patterns, and William Froude (1810-1879), who pioneered the study of ship models in testing tanks. Advances in hydrodynamics led to more efficient designs, and the replacement of the shipwrights' old length-to-beam ratio of four or five to one by new, scientifically derived ratios of eight or nine to one.

Russell and Froude collaborated with Brunel on his third and last ship design, the colossal *Great Eastern* (launched 1858, and originally named "Leviathan"), which, though commercially unsuccessful (except as a cable layer) pointed to the future. At more than 25,000 tons when loaded, the *Great Eastern* was more than five times larger than Brunel's previous design. Despite both screws and paddle wheels, with separate engines for each, the *Great Eastern* was underpowered. Later the development of more efficient engines allowed builders such as Alfred Yarrow (1842-1932) to supply enormously powerful triple-and quadruple-expansion engines for the largest vessels. Finally, the old reciprocating engines were rendered obsolete by the steam turbine, demonstrated by its inventor, Charles Parsons (1854-1931), when his high-speed launch *Turbina* disrupted the Queen's second Jubilee naval review at Spithead in 1897.

Paralleling the evolution of the steamship, and its gradual shedding of masts and sails, was the development of the pure sailing ship to its highest level of both efficiency and beauty. Beginning with the designs of the American, David MacKay (1810-1880) in the 1850s, and culminating in the famous British tea clippers of the China trade in the 1860s and 1870s, the square-rigged pure sailing ship reached its apogee. With the adoption of metal hulls, masts, and rigging, and such equipment as Henry Cunningham's topsail reefing gear (patented in 1850), the sailing ship continued to provide economical long-distance haulage, primarily of freight, well into the twentieth century. Late in the nineteenth century Parliament legislated against the worst safety abuses of shipowners such as overloading. These reforms had been promoted for years by **Samuel Plimsoll**, M. P. (1824-1898).

Ever conservative in clinging to wooden ships, Britain's Royal Navy did finally consent to install steam engines, if only as auxiliary power, in its ships of the line, once the screw proved its superiority over paddle wheels, which were too vulnerable to gunfire to be practical. A tug-of-war in 1845 between two otherwise identical frigates, in which the screw-propelled H.M.S. *Rattlesnake* towed away the paddle wheeler H.M.S. *Alecto*, settled the issue. However, the burning of a wooden Turkish fleet by the Russian Navy's explosive shells at Sinope in 1853 sounded the death knell of the wooden warship. The French navy responded with *La Gloire*, launched in 1859, a wooden ship covered with iron plates. In 1860 the Royal Navy launched H.M.S. *Warrior*, designed by J.S. Russell and Isaac Watts. This first iron-hulled warship mounted guns on a single deck that spanned its 380-foot length, and displaced more than 9,000 tons. Ironically, the last wooden three-decker, the obsolete H.M.S. *Victoria*, had been launched only the year before. The appearance of the first iron turret ship, the

U.S.S. *Monitor*, designed by John Ericsson (1803–1889), in successful combat in the American Civil War, rendered the broadside mounting of guns obsolete. Over the next several decades the technical development of warship design proceeded rapidly, and plagued the great powers with their first great international arms race.

N. MERRILL DISTAD

Bibliography

Brinnin, John Malcolm. *The Sway of the Grand Saloon: A Social History of the North Atlantic.* 1971.

Brodie, Bernard. *Sea Power in the Machine Age.* 1941.

Dugan, James. *The Great Iron Ship [Great Eastern].* 1953.

Emmerson, George S. *John Scott Russell, A Great Victorian Engineer and Naval Architect.* 1977.

Pole, William, ed. *The Life of Sir William Fairbairn, Bart.* 1877; rpt. 1970.

Robb, A. M. "Ship-Building." In Charles Singer et al., eds, *A History of Technology.* Vol. 5: *The Late Nineteenth Century,* c. 1850–c. 1900. 1958.

Rolt, L. T. C. *Isambard Kingdom Brunel: A Biography.* 1957.

Rowland, K. T. *Steam at Sea: A History of Steam Navigation.* 1970.

Yarrow, Eleanor, Lady. *Alfred Yarrow, His Life and Work.* 1923.

See also NAVY

. . . . .

SHIRREFF, EMILY (1814–1897) and MARIA SHIRREFF GREY (1816–1906)

The Shirreff sisters were crusaders for female education. Their major polemical works are *Thoughts on Self-Culture, Addressed to Women* (1850), which they coauthored, and *Intellectual Education and Its Influence on the Character and Happiness of Women* (1858) by Emily Shirreff. Maria Shirreff Grey made important contributions to secondary education, founding the Women's Education Union (1871), the Girls' Public Day School Company or GPDSC (1872; later Trust), and the Maria Grey Training College for Teachers (1878). Shirreff's main contributions were to early childhood education. Both published numerous books and pamphlets.

The Shirreff sisters were largely self-educated. Apart from publishing books, they led private lives until they reached middle age. Their public careers began in the 1870s when Grey founded the Women's Education Union, which launched the GPDSC and teachers' college. Shirreff supported the organizations her sister founded, serving as council member of the GPDSC(T), editor of the *Journal of the Women's Education Union,* and honorary secretary of the union. Shirreff was also briefly mistress of Girton College (1871) and a lifelong member of its council. Her main focus, however, was the Froebel Society, which created a national kindergarten system and a teachers' training college to sustain it. Shirreff was president of the society from 1875 to 1897.

Much of Shirreff's and Grey's work suggests that women should develop their intellectual powers in conjunction with their spiritual and domestic role. Grey's views, particularly, became gradually more feminist, but there remained within them a conflict between women's right to self-development and her duty to be of service to others. This tension, however, is itself representative of much nineteenth-century feminist thought.

By 1900 the GPDST provided academically rigorous and relatively inexpensive secondary education to some seven thousand girls in thirty-six schools nationwide. The schools were nondenominational and financed through shareholdings, while the curriculum was modeled on Frances Mary Buss's at North London Collegiate. The GPDST laid the foundation for a national secondary education system for girls.

SUZANNE GRAVER

Bibliography

Ellsworth, Edward W. *Liberators of the Female Mind: The Shirreff Sisters, Educational Reform, and the Women's Movement.* 1979.

Girls' Public Day School Trust. *Centenary Review, 1872-1972.* 1972.

Grey, Maria. *Memorials of Emily A. E. Shirreff, with a Sketch of Her Life.* 1897.

Kamm, Josephine. *Indicative Past: A Hundred Years of the Girls' Public Day School Trust.* 1971.

· · · · ·

SHOPS AND SHOPPING

In early Victorian times, a shop could be anything from the front room of a cottage where an old woman made and sold sweets and pickled onions to an elegant establishment where discreet attendants displayed goods individually to a patron comfortably seated in the showroom. Regent Street (completed in 1820) was designed as a fashionable shopping promenade, and included "warehouses" or "workrooms" devoted to such items as silks, velvets, shawls, gloves, fans, parasols, and ribbons. In between—and accounting for most retail sales—were market stalls and the shops of those who followed a craft or trade. In the latter case, goods were produced on the premises and sold at retail from the front. New patterns of retail selling emerged as a consequence of mass production and urban development, although the older forms also persisted throughout the century.

Early in Victoria's reign, **street traders** accounted for a large proportion of the sales of foodstuffs and perishable goods. Some were very marginal, simply investing a few pence in goods that could be carried on a tray around the neck. Others had established routes or fixed locations, or appeared regularly in those towns and neighborhoods that had a market day. Most retail shops were small, so there were large numbers in proportion to the population. The 1851 census listed 52,673 tailors, 85,913 grocers, 14,320 greengrocers and fruiterers, and 67,691 butchers. Many who had their own premises also had the parliamentary vote after 1832, and used their influence in local politics to impose by-laws against obstruction, nuisance, and Sunday trading. Laws such as these led to the closure of many street markets. The fixed, covered markets that were sometimes built in their place let stalls to established tradespeople and to the more prosperous itinerant vendors.

In the 1850s, as public transportation improved, large retail outlets began to be built in city centers. Clothing stores, earlier in the century, had been primarily workrooms; the customer looked at a model, chose a fabric, and contracted to have the item made. By the 1860s some ready-made clothing was available. The term "department store" came into use to describe large shops that sold several varieties of goods (such as cloaks, mourning, children's clothing, curtains, carpets, and housewares). The "Bazaar" that opened in Manchester in 1831 was a forerunner; various departments were let to separate traders, but the Bazaar's organizer required that all goods be displayed with prices attached. The ability to walk around, see what was available, and make comparisons before speaking to a shop assistant was a novel feature.

Haggling over prices was never as common in Britain as elsewhere, and the better class of shop before midcentury had generally maintained discreet silence. Prosperous people ordered goods sent to their homes or sent servants out to do marketing without any money changing hands; bills were submitted monthly by tradespeople and annually by those who sold durable and fashionable goods. Shops in working-class neighborhoods also extended credit to regular customers, though they generally demanded payment weekly on whatever day wages were paid. Department stores, on the other hand, usually sold only for cash. The no-credit policy, fixed prices, and the economies of scale made possible by ordering large quantities of mass-produced goods gave firms such as Marshall and Snelgrove, Lewis's, Kendall Milne, and Swan and Edgar a reputation for good value and attracted a great many customers, especially from the middle classes.

Cooperative retail stores that sold a wide variety of goods to members only also developed in the latter half of the century. Those that grew from working-class movements were more common in industrial areas of the north and Midlands; the Civil Service Supply Association (1866) and the Army and Navy Stores (1871) sent orders to members throughout the empire and also sold from premises in London. Specialists such as Thomas Burberry (waterproof clothing) and Arthur Liberty (British-made fabrics of Oriental design) began with single shops and developed numerous branches.

Outside the urban centers things changed more slowly. In the suburbs there were still many producer/dealers, some street markets, and a variety of hawkers, hucksters, and costers until the 1860s. Many of the latter were casual workers needing supplementary income when their seasonal work stopped. The stall holders, itinerant traders, and general dealers were gradually replaced by local specialist shops. In the 1880s shopping arcades or parades occupied by these specialists and by branches of multiple grocery, clothing, and footwear chains were built.

In cities, towns, and suburbs the omnibus and tram helped shops expand beyond the small, family-run unit, although the working classes tended to live near their work and shop informally at neighborhood outlets that offered evening hours. In villages access to rail services came slowly, and carrier networks continued to operate. Carriers traveled through villages to a market town, taking commissions along the route and bringing goods back on the return; the drivers often worked from 6 a.m. to 10 p.m. The availability of cheap factory goods made deep inroads on the trade of local shoemakers, tailors, millers, bakers, saddlers, and so forth when transportation improved and access to market towns became easier. By 1900 agricultural workers, when they could afford it, could eat tinned corn beef and sardines, use condensed milk rather than fresh, and wear clothing indistinguishable from that of town dwellers. The very small village shops and their counterpart in poorer urban neighborhoods, which had limited stocks but dealt in a variety of goods from pickles to shoelaces, began to disappear; the 1891 census recorded a decline in the number of persons engaged in general and informal retailing.

ANNIE PERROTT

Bibliography

Adburgham, Alison. *Shops and Shopping, 1800–1914.* Rev. ed., 1981.

Davis, Dorothy. *Fairs, Shops and Supermarkets: A History of English Shopping.* 1966.

Winstanley, Michael J. *The Shopkeeper's World, 1830–1914.* 1983.

· · · · ·

SHOPWORKERS

In the course of the Victorian era, shopworkers experienced a marked decline in living and working conditions. At the start of the century, many shop assistants served an apprenticeship in exchange for being taught a particular retail trade. They often worked in small, specialized shops in close relation to their employer. Although they received little or no salary, they were provided with food and lodging in the employer's home. Most apprentices aspired to establish their own business. Industrialization greatly altered this traditional arrangement. Mass production, urbanization, and the rise in consumers' purchasing power transformed the retail trades. The apprenticeship system was replaced by a more impersonal relationship, and the skilled apprentice gave way to the unskilled worker.

As shopworkers' status deteriorated, women were employed in ever-growing numbers. Women from the lower middle class considered shopwork less arduous and more respectable than factory work. Employers were able to pay women on average only half the salary demanded by their male counterparts. As unskilled, underpaid, unorganized, and increasingly female employees, shopworkers were easily exploited. Although conditions varied considerably from shop to shop, assistants were often forced to work sixty to eighty hours a week for wages of perhaps one or two pence per hour. Wages were further reduced by fines for infractions of shop rules and by mandatory deductions for such things as health care and library dues.

One of the shopworkers' worst grievances was the living-in system. Assistants were frequently required to reside in dormitories owned and operated by their employer and to take meals in the shop's cafeteria. Employers provided this arrangement in lieu of part of the worker's salary—at a cost far less than paying full wages.

In an effort to improve their situation, shopworkers began organizing in 1889. Unionization proved difficult. Shopworkers perceived themselves as middle class and felt that unions were for the working class. They often remained isolated in small or medium-sized establishments, making solidarity hard to achieve. In addition, an invisible caste system dictated, for intance, that an employee of a West End haberdashery was "better" than an assistant to a greengrocer in Bermondsey. Unity was also undermined by the working hours, which made meetings difficult to arrange. Nevertheless, in 1891, the shopworkers formed a union that admitted men and women equally, thus distinguishing itself from other contemporary unions. The National Amalgamated Union of Shop Assistants, Warehousemen and Clerks represents one of the first examples of the successful organization of unskilled workers.

Shopworkers won some small measure of protection under the Truck Act of 1896, but its provisions were inadequate to secure significant improvement. Not until the Shops Act of 1912 was any limitation imposed on working hours. The living-in system was ultimately made unprofitable by the social and economic changes wrought by World War I.

DONNA PRICE PAUL

Bibliography

Bondfield, Margaret. *A Life's Work*. 1948.

Fabian Society. *Shop Life and Its Reform*. 1897.

Hallworth, Joseph and Rhys Davis. *The Working Life of Shop Assistants*. 1910.

Hoffman, Philip C. *They Also Serve: The Story of the Shop Workers*. 1949.

Holcombe, Lee. *Victorian Ladies at Work: Middle-Class Working Women in England and Wales, 1850-1914*. 1973.

· · · · ·

SILVER-FORK NOVEL

The silver-fork novel, also called the fashionable novel, the aristocratic novel, the society novel, and the novel of high life, dominated popular fiction in the 1820s and 1830s. Often set in the Regency period, these books presented a world of fashionable extravagance, peopled by characters whose necks glittered with jewels, their pedigrees with peerdoms, and their conversation with aphorisms and French phrases. The settings were great country estates, foreign spas, gambling rooms, opera houses, Belgrave Square mansions, and Almack's at the height of the London Season; the typical plot featured romance, glamorous vice, a smattering of politics, the appearance of well-known public figures, a great many social occasions, and a good deal of idle talk. Detailed descriptions of furnishings, costumes, and cuisine sometimes included plugs for the chic merchants who supplied the heroine's bonnet or the hero's cigar. These novels were sold in sumptuous editions to the wealthy as well as leased out by lower-class libraries at a penny a volume; aristocratic readers enjoyed seeing themselves and their friends flattered and satirized, middle-class readers sought instruction in the manners of the class they aspired to enter, and lower-class readers relished both the vicarious experience of wealth and the presentation of the wealthy as shallow and corrupt.

Some nine-tenths of the silver-fork novels were published and promoted by Henry Colburn (d. 1855), who also published that other resource of the social climber, Burke's *Peerage*. As the appeal of the type derived in part from the gossipy pleasures of its supposedly accurate portrayal of high life, Colburn printed some writers, such as Lady Charlotte Susan Maria Campbell Bury (1775–1861) and the Countess of Blessington (1789–1849), whose novelistic talents were rather less brilliant than their connections in society. The major early examples of the type were **Benjamin Disraeli**'s *Vivian Grey* (1826–1827), which traced the social and political career of a charming, unscrupulous youth, and **Edward Bulwer-Lytton**'s *Pelham* (1828), the Bildungsroman of an intellectual dandy. The latter reputedly set the fashion of black evening clothes for men. Disraeli's later novels such as *Coningsby* (1844) and *Sybil* (1845), which show their heroes first in high society and then in reaction against it, demonstrate the shift away from fashion and toward politics in the 1840s, which lessened the popularity of the silver-fork genre. But the form was continued through that decade by Catherine Grace Frances Moody Gore (1799–1861), by far the most prolific of the fashionable novelists and the most successful woman novelist of the era. Gore's light, witty satire is most successful in *Mrs. Armytage, or Female Domination* (1836) and the 1841 set, *Cecil, or The Adventures of a Coxcomb* and *Cecil, a Peer*, in which she follows her Regency fop from childhood to middle age, by way of Oxford, the Foreign Office, the Peninsular wars, the grand tour, and the prince regent's court.

From its beginnings, the fashionable novel was criticized and caricatured. The "silver-fork" tag comes from "The Dandy School," William Hazlitt's 1827 review of *Vivian Grey* and Theodore Edward Hook's *Sayings and Doings* (1824-1828), in which he deplored the materialism, snobbery, and vulgarity of the school. Carlyle attacked *Pelham* in the "Dandiacal Body" chapter of *Sartor Resartus* (1833-1834), and Thackeray savaged Gore in *Punch's Prize Novelists* (1853). But Thackeray's *Vanity Fair* (1847-1848), with its exposure of folly and corruption at the highest levels of society, can be seen as the culmination of the silver-fork tradition.

NAOMI JACOBS

Bibliography

Rosa, Matthew. *The Silver-Fork School: Novels of Fashion Preceding Vanity Fair.* 1936.

. . . . .

SIMCOX, EDITH (1844-1901)

Edith Jemima Simcox was a social reformer and a writer (occasionally under the pseudonym H. Lawrenny). She was also the most devoted of George Eliot's "spiritual daughters."

Simcox's public life was devoted to social reform. As a member of the London School Board (1879-1882), she advocated compulsory education for all children. Active in labor reform, she promoted cooperative ventures and unionism. She helped to start and manage a small cooperative of shirtmakers (1875-1883) and to launch the Shirt and Collar Makers Union (1875) and also attended the national Trades Union Congress and several international labor conferences. In addition, Simcox worked for women's rights.

Simcox wrote three books and contributed articles and reviews to leading newspapers and journals on such subjects as ethics, economics, history, art, literature, biography, education, women, and the working classes. Her writings include two autobiographical pieces, the disguised *Episodes in the Lives of Men, Women, and Lovers* (1882) and the confessional but unpublished "Autobiography of a Shirt Maker," both expressions of her adoration for George Eliot.

Twenty-five years younger than Eliot, Simcox's relation to her was reverential to the point of idolatry, and highly passionate and tormented. Simcox felt that all her books were inspired by Eliot, who treated Simcox kindly but with reserve, and who was not nearly as radical, politically and sexually. Despite Simcox's work as writer and reformer, her interest for modern scholars has been primarily through her relation to Eliot.

SUZANNE GRAVER

Bibliography

Haight, Gordon S., ed. *The George Eliot Letters*, vol. 9. 1978. (Contains sections from ms. of Simcox's autobiography.)

McKenzie, K. A. *Edith Simcox and George Eliot.* 1961; rpt. 1978.

. . . . .

SINCLAIR, CATHERINE (1800-1864)

Catherine Sinclair was a popular author who wrote fiction for children as well as novels for adults. From the age of fourteen she acted as secretary for her father, John Sinclair (1754-1835), a prominent politician and prolific writer. After his death she began publishing stories she had been telling her niece and nephew.

Holiday House (1839), Sinclair's most popular work, combines an adventurous but sentimental story line with fairy-tale character types—naughty but well-meaning children, a loving uncle and grandmother, a witchlike nanny—and a witty if didactic writing style. *Beatrice, or The Unknown Relatives* (1852), a popular novel written for an adult audience, is flawed in its use of character types drawn from melodramas; in its plot (a series of intrigues); and especially in its theme, presented as a motto at the end of the preface: "BEWARE OF ROMANISM." Fortunately, there was more to Sinclair's religious ethic than paranoid anti-Catholicism; *Beatrice* demonstrates that the poor succumb to the wiles of priests and nuns because the selfish Protestant aristocracy contributes nothing to their welfare. Sinclair was herself a determined and active philanthropist.

Holiday House is significant in being the first work of children's fiction in English that included realistically human child characters and was intended to entertain as well as instruct; modern literature for children has followed the course Sinclair established. Her quirky, individualistic characters, sense of humor, and incipient feminism give Sinclair's works lasting value.

ELIZABETH J. DEIS

Bibliography

Darton, Frederick Joseph Harvey. *Children's Books in England: Five Centuries of Social Life.* 1932.

Green, Roger Lancelyn. *Tellers of Tales: Children's Books and Their Authors from 1800 to 1964.* 1965.

Lurie, Alison. Preface to *Holiday House*, by Catherine Sinclair. 1976.

· · · · ·

SINGLE WOMEN

Victorian novels and popular literature portray unmarried women as faded lonely spinsters, self-sacrificing maiden aunts performing unpaid domestic tasks in the homes of their relatives, or genteel but ignorant **governesses**, patronized by unfriendly employers. This fictional representation expresses the fact that following the 1851 census, single women were identified as a social problem—"superfluous women"—indicating much about nineteenth-century ideas concerning the role of middle-class women and the institution of marriage. Although the "surplus" of unmarried women in the total population belonged largely to the lower classes,

public debate centered on the middle-class spinster.

Underlying the idea that unmarried middle-class women were "redundant" was the belief that only marriage and motherhood fulfilled women's biological, social, and divinely appointed destiny and complemented men's worldly work. Although single (and married) working-class women engaged in waged work, often as domestic servants, middle-class women lost their status as "ladies" by engaging in paid work. The ubiquitous governess or ladies' "companion," living as part of the household, could keep a tenuous hold on gentility, while a wage earner could not. Feminists disputed this restricted view of women's role, arguing that there was much public and educational work for which women were suited, should be paid, and which would not detract from their status as ladies. Feminists nevertheless highlighted the economic importance of marriage. If a middle-class woman had no income or earnings, and no financial support from kin, she needed a husband. Marriage became a career, and its true moral and religious significance was forgotten.

While not challenging the centrality of marriage to social stability, feminists argued that paid work became an economic necessity for many women, making a sound education and training imperative to ensure financial independence for all middle-class women, should the need arise. But feminists also believed that for some women work provided a freely chosen alternative to marriage and motherhood. Many of the women who deliberately renounced marriage to become pioneer doctors, headmistresses, teachers, educators, administrators, reformers, social workers, and writers were motivated and sustained by a sense of religious calling and commitment. Amongst these were Dorothea Beale, Constance Maynard, Mary Carpenter, Frances Power Cobbe, Emily Davies, Florence Nightingale, and Sophia Jex-Blake. Some of these women earned professional fees and salaries, but possession of a private income enabled others to remain independent. Much of their work expanded conventional domesticity and caring into more public domains, but much also aimed at improving facilities for women themselves. Such women provided a network and community of support for others and role models for younger women who were able to utilize the greater opportunities created. The "**New Woman**" of the 1880s and 1890s reflected the success of earlier pioneering single women as well as the expansion of the professional, white-collar, and service sectors of the economy which made marriage less of an economic necessity for women.

ROSAMUND BILLINGTON

Bibliography

Hammerton, A. James. *Emigrant Gentlewomen: Genteel Poverty and Female Emigration, 1830–1914.* 1979.

Holcombe, Lee. *Victorian Ladies at Work: Middle-Class Working Women in England and Wales, 1850–1914.* 1973.

Jeffreys, Sheila. *The Spinster and Her Enemies: Feminism and Sexuality, 1880–1930.* 1985.

Vicinus, Martha. *Independent Women: Work and Community for Single Women, 1850–1920.* 1985.

——, ed. *A Widening Sphere: Changing Roles of Victorian Women.* 1980.

See also SISTERHOODS; WOMANHOOD; WOMEN'S FRIENDSHIPS

. . . . .

SISTERHOODS

The midcentury religious revival which stirred High and Low Church reformers with the desire for a purified Christianity also inspired the formation of sisterhoods and deaconess groups. Whatever their doctrinal disputes, Church of England prelates, Dissenters, and Evangelicals were instrumental in founding charitable women's **religious orders** to teach and care for the sick and poor.

Anglican sisterhoods for the most part represented an English response to Roman Catholicism. Groups like the Sisters of the Holy Cross (1845), Sisters of All Saints (1851), and Sisters of St. John the Baptist (1851) promised fidelity to the order, lived in convent houses, wore religious costumes, and were answerable to mother superiors. Although they led lives immersed in prayer, ritual, and

caritative or reform work, gentlewomen attracted to this life achieved in return freedom from the constraints of genteel Victorian family life.

Low Church deaconess groups distrusted the sisterhoods' convent life and simplified their members' religious observances. These groups were more often composed of women from the lower classes (who would have been admitted only as "lay sisters" in an Anglican order) yet required obedience to religious authority and, later in the century, some form of commitment to the communal life.

Protestant sisterhoods contributed some of the first professional English nurses. One of the early nurses' training institutes, St. John's House, founded as an order of the Anglican Church (1848), provided the entire nursing staff for King's College Hospital in London. St. John's House sisters joined Protestant nurses and Roman Catholic nuns to aid Florence Nightingale's pioneering efforts in the Crimean War. Also important to nursing history was a member of the Christ Church Sisterhood, Sister Dora of Walsall (Dora Pattison), who in the 1860s did for English industrial workers what Nightingale had done for soldiers in the Crimea.

By the end of the century, sisterhoods numbered over fifty orders with at least a thousand members and had founded hospitals, schools, orphanages, and houses of refuge. The less numerous deaconesses worked in settlement houses and missions. Research is only beginning to assess the achievement of sisterhoods and allied women's religious groups, but it is clear that they supplied vocations for women which combined spirituality and social utility, and provided a measure of independence from constricting Victorian ideologies of womanhood.

LAURA HAPKE

Bibliography

Allchin, Arthur M. *The Silent Rebellion: Anglican Religious Communities, 1845–1900.* 1958.

Anson, Peter F. *The Call of the Cloister: Religious Communities and Kindred Bodies in the Anglican Church.* 1956.

Arnstein, Walter. *Protestant Versus Catholic in Mid-Victorian England: Mr. Newdegate and the Nuns.* 1982.

Austin, Anne L. *History of Nursing Source Book.* 1957.

Bennett, Alice Horlock. *Through an Anglican Sisterhood to Rome.* 1949.

Bolster, Evelyn. *The Sisters of Mercy in the Crimean War.* 1964.

Hill, Michael. *The Religious Order: A Study of Virtuoso Religion and Its Legitimation in the Nineteenth-Century Church of England.* 1973.

Jameson, Anna. *"Sisters of Charity" and "The Communion of Labour": Two Lectures of the Social Employment of Women.* 1859.

Manton, Jo. *Sister Dora: The Life of Dorothy Pattison.* 1971.

Vicinus, Martha. *Independent Women: Work and Community for Single Women, 1850–1920.* 1985.

. . . . .

SLAVE TRADE

From the fifteenth to the second half of the nineteenth centuries between 9.5 and 12 million African slaves were shipped to the Americas. Slaves, mostly from west and central Africa, were an important commodity in the growth of the Atlantic economy, and their labor helped to produce wealth.

In the eighteenth century England was the most prominent nation involved in this slave trade. Merchants based in London, Bristol, and Liverpool successively dominated the trade. From the 1780s abolitionist feeling mounted, culminating in the abolition of the British slave trade in 1807. Other nations also banned the trade, but it continued illicitly. During the nineteenth century the Royal **Navy** policed the seas, and diplomacy was used to persuade other nations to enforce anti–slave trade measures. Despite British activity, approximately two million slaves were transported across the Atlantic in the nineteenth century, mostly to Brazil and Cuba, where slavery lingered longest. The traffic was effectively suppressed in the 1860s.

With the gradual decline of the Atlantic trade Victorian attention shifted to the Ottoman slave trade. Slaves, mostly from central and east Africa, were destined for the Islamic world. British policy involved naval action, treaties with European and African powers, and substituting legitimate commerce for the slave trade. The exploits of such antislavery heroes as David Livingstone and Charles Gordon captured Victorian attention, and the Anti-Slavery Society kept the issue in the public eye. Suppression of the slave trade afforded moral justification for intervention in Africa. British action culminated in persuading the major European powers that were partitioning Africa to repress the trade in the Brussels Act of 1889/90.

OLWYN M. BLOUET

Bibliography

Curtin, Philip. *The Atlantic Slave Trade: A Census.* 1969.

Miers, Suzanne. *Britain and the Ending of the Slave Trade.* 1975.

Rawley, James A. *The Transatlantic Slave Trade: A History.* 1981.

Toledano, Ehud R. *The Ottoman Slave Trade and Its Suppression, 1840–1890.* 1982.

See also ANTISLAVERY MOVEMENT

. . . . .

SMALLPOX see VACCINATION

. . . . .

SMILES, SAMUEL (1812–1904)

Through his best-selling books, Samuel Smiles promoted the self-made man who achieved success through diligence, temperance, and thift. His name became a catchword for Victorian optimism and self-reliance.

Although active in the Anti–Corn-Law League and an advocate of state-supported education and public libraries, Smiles opposed Chartism. He edited the *Leeds Times* from 1838 to 1842, competing with Feargus O'Connor's radical *Northern Star*. Lectures on self-education given to Leeds working-class institutions later evolved into his most famous book, *Self-Help* (1859).

After 1845, Smiles worked as secretary for railway companies while he wrote for popular periodicals, primarily *Eliza Cook's Journal.* Combining his interests, he wrote a biography of George Stephenson, developer of the railroad locomotive, published in 1857. Smiles repeated the motif of a self-educated man rising from poverty and ignorance in later biographies, including *Life of a Scotch Naturalist, Thomas Edward* (1876), *Robert Dick, Baker . . . Geologist and Naturalist* (1878), and *Josiah Wedgwood* (1894). In *Self-Help, Lives of the Engineers* (1861–1862), *Character* (1871), *Thrift* (1875), and *Duty* (1880), Smiles used biographical anecdotes to preach his gospel of industry, diligence, and self-denial. These inspirational books were immensely popular in Britain and abroad.

Smiles's message lost popularity as it became fashionable to scoff at Victorian earnestness or to fear that it impeded passage of social legislation. However, Smiles was not simply reactionary or self-serving; he admitted that diligence did not automatically bring wealth or fame. Smiles's heroes such as George Stephenson and Josiah Wedgwood were men whose inventions he felt benefited society. In his unflagging industry and optimism, he embodied the spirit of the Victorian age in his books and personal life.

NAN HACKETT

Bibliography

Briggs, Asa. "Samuel Smiles and the Gospel of Work." In Asa Briggs, *Victorian People.* 1955.

Green, Thomas B. *Life and Work of S. Smiles.* 1904.

Smiles, Aileen. *Samuel Smiles and His Surroundings.* 1956.

Thornton, A.H. *Samuel Smiles and Nineteenth Century Self-Help in Education.* 1983.

· · · · ·

SMOKING AND TOBACCO

The Victorian period witnessed the "modernization" of tobacco use. Snuff, with its elegant paraphernalia of snuff boxes, silk handkerchiefs, etc.—the only fashionable way of taking tobacco in the eighteenth century—went into a rapid decline in the early nineteenth century. Smoking returned to favor in high society with the Spanish cigar, popularized by veterans of the Peninsular campaigns. By 1823 Lord Byron was celebrating its "naked beauties" in *The Island*, and the cigar's Freudian career was well launched. It was of course intensely masculine, unlike the androgynous snuff which women could also take. Indeed, W. M. Thackeray claimed that women's opposition to cigars was due to jealousy. The return to smoking was resisted in polite society, not least by Queen Victoria; but assisted by the Prince of Wales, an avid smoker, it had broken out of the smoking room by the end of the century. However, as late as 1885 Baedeker's *Handbook for London* warns tourists that smoking is not so universal in England as in America or on the Continent and is prohibited in many places where other countries allow it.

The commonest method of tobacco use remained pipe smoking (chewing was virtually unknown, being much derided as a nasty American habit) with the briar pipe, introduced in the 1860s, replacing the traditional clay. Pipe smoking was considered vulgar and was not indulged in by gentlemen except in bohemian circles where it was a mild gesture of social defiance—Tennyson, William Morris, D. G. Rossetti, Charles Kingsley, and J. E. Millais were all ardent pipe smokers. Cigar or pipe smoking was widely celebrated by Victorian men of letters as a means of relaxation. Mid-Victorian clubs had opulent smoking rooms, and railways introduced smokers' carriages in 1868. The 1860s also witnessed the introduction of the cigarette. Again at first a smart military fashion following the Crimean War, it was one that women—albeit only very "fast" ones—could share. The revolution came with the Bonsack cigarette-making machine, monopolized by the Wills tobacco firm whose aggressively marketed "Woodbine" brand at five for a penny brought cigarettes to the masses. By 1901 cigarette sales had exploded from 1 percent to 17 percent of tobacco sales in only a decade, and by the end of World War I cigarettes were dominant.

CHRISTOPHER KENT

Bibliography

Alford, B. W. E. *W. D. and H. O. Wills and the Development of the U. K. Tobacco Industry 1786-1965.* 1973.

Apperson, G. L. *The Social History of Smoking.* 1914.

. . . . .

SMUGGLING

The smuggling of goods to avoid payment of duty had been endemic on the coasts of Britain since the Middle Ages. The imposition of new and higher duties in the eighteenth century inaugurated an era of widespread smuggling by large, well-organized bands, such as the notorious Hawkhurst Gang, who often fought pitched battles in confrontations with authorities. The nineteenth century, however, witnessed changes both in the pattern of smuggling and in the government's means of combating it.

Smuggling flourished during the Napoleonic Wars, but in 1817 the Royal Navy established the Coast Blockade system to deal with smugglers, as well as to provide a reserve of able-bodied seamen for service in the event of war. In 1831 the Coast Blockade was superseded by the Coastguard under the authority of the Customs Department, but in 1856 responsibility for the Coastguard was itself transferred to the Admiralty.

In the face of this greatly improved enforcement, smugglers gradually switched from employing armed force to more ingenious methods of concealment. Their use of false bottoms and hidden compartments became even more sophisticated with the introduction of steam propulsion and iron ships. However, the steady introduction of a policy of **free trade**, beginning in the 1840s, gradually reduced the number of commodities that offered any incentive to smugglers. Where smugglers had once purveyed everything from tea and brandy to silks and playing cards, after 1860 their activities were largely confined to tobacco and liquor, upon which significant duties remained in force.

N. MERRILL DISTAD

Bibliography

Bowen, Frank C. *His Majesty's Coastguard.* 1928.

Carson, Edward. *The Ancient and Rightful Customs: A History of the English Customs Service.* 1972.

Chatterton, Edward Keble. *King's Cutters and Smugglers, 1700-1855.* 1912; rpt. 1971.

Smith, Graham. *King's Cutters: The Revenue Service and the War Against Smuggling.* 1983.

Teignmouth, Henry N. Shore, Lord. *Smuggling Days and Smuggling Ways; or, the Story of a Lost Art.* 1892; rpt. 1972.

. . . . .

SOCCER

The most popular game in the world took shape between the late 1840s and the early 1860s. This period witnessed the stabilization of competitions, the creation of the professional footballer, and the formation of football's commercial structure.

It is impossible to say when football began. The Greeks played a version called *episkyros*. During the Middle Ages people devoted a whole day (usually Shrove Tuesday) to a match. In some regions married men played against single men; in others married women played against single women. For centuries kings and clergymen tried to suppress the game because it was a source of injury and public disorder.

The game as it is known today dates from the athletic revival of the 1840s, when organized games became part of the curriculum at public schools. Over the years the number of players was reduced, the size of the field defined, and rules introduced to simplify the game and control the violence. The Eton tradition featured "dribbling" the ball while Rugby allowed "handling" it; the Cambridge Rules, compiled in 1848, combined various rules so that men from different schools could play together.

Football clubs sprang up like mushrooms during this period: Sheffield F. C. (1857) and Forest F. C. (1859) were among the first. In 1863 a committee formulated the more streamlined Cambridge University Football Rules, which restricted handling and forbade pushing and tripping. In the same year the Football Association was formed. At first it was devoted to establishing standards for amateur football, but as the recreation of a few became the pursuit of thousands, the Football Association began to regulate professional football. (The expansion of football coincided with the growth of railways and the introduction of labor legislation that shortened the work week.) The first professional clubs included Notts County (1862), Stoke City (1863), and Nottingham Forest (1865). In 1885 the Football League was formed to control the professional matches. Exceptional players like Nicholas Ross, the captain of Everton, and Charles Athersmith, the outside-right of Aston Villa, earned between 10 and 30 pounds a month.

During this period England exported association football (or soccer) to all parts of the world. The International Football Association Board was formed in 1885. By 1900 many European countries (including Austria, Belgium, France, Germany, and the Netherlands) had adopted the rules governing association football.

ROBERT M. SEILER

Bibliography

Young, Percy M. *A History of British Football.* 1968.

See also RUGBY FOOTBALL

. . . . .

SOCIAL DARWINISM

The Darwinian hypothesis was stimulated by the work of social analysts and parent to much social thinking that hoped to secure the patronage of science. Beyond that, Charles Darwin's impact on social science is more illusory: the inspiration for much of the social theory comes not from Darwin but from **Herbert Spencer**, a "social evolutionist" who saw human progress in terms of pre-Darwinian physical and biological models.

Social Darwinists took Darwin to mean that struggle for existence in the natural world gives birth to an evolutionary process that can be identified with progress, therefore justifying struggle as a means of hastening human progress. "The survival of the fittest," the principal rallying cry of social Darwinists, was originally employed in Spencer's 1852 "Essay on Population" and was not used by Darwin until the fifth edition of *The Origin of Species* in 1869. The phrase is open to multiple interpretations. Competition between individuals apparently legitimizes laissez faire and individualistic self-help; competition between classes would provide a scientific rationale for class warfare. Chauvinism, militarism, and imperialism may be defended on the basis that progress arises from competition between nations.

Contrasting attitudes to **race** also plundered Darwinian theory to advantage: the concept of a single primordial form might reinforce an integrationist position—or so thought Asa Gray—but others took the "favoured races" language to legitimize segregation. Elsewhere Darwinism was taken to support environmentalism, as when Bernard Shaw claimed that biological theory "implied that street arabs are produced by slums not by original sin" thus throwing "the authority of science on the side of the Socialist." But others condemned social welfare programs for stifling individual initiative and protecting or even multiplying the weaker stock within a nation.

Darwin's own relationship to the social Darwinists remains enigmatic. Some social deductions from his work alarmed him: witness his indignation that he had proved that "might is right" and therefore that "Napoleon is right and every cheating tradesman is also right." But social Darwinist judgments can be found in his own later writings, as for example his opinion that "the more civilized so-called Caucasian races have beaten the Turkish hollow in the struggle for existence."

The simultaneous emergence of evolutionary themes in natural science and social science in the nineteenth century represent parallel developments. That political, social, and economic theorists should seek corroboration from the natural sciences, however, marks a significant intellectual change.

J.H.Y. BRIGGS

Bibliography

Burrow, J. W. *Evolution and Society.* 1966.

Flew, Anthony G. N. *Evolutionary Ethics.* 1968.

Himmelfarb, Gertrude. *Victorian Minds.* 1975.

Hofstadter, Richard. *Social Darwinism in American Thought.* Rev. ed., 1955.

Oldroyd, D.R. *Darwinian Impacts.* 1980.

See also EUGENICS

. . . . .

SOCIAL FEMINISM

In the late nineteenth century, women formed political pressure groups to improve the economic and social status of their sex through social reform. While outside the mainstream of political power because they did not have the parliamentary franchise, these women, sometimes working with male allies, were not content to wait for the vote before establishing a publicly recognized connection between social reform and women's rights. Social feminism parallels women's efforts to gain political emancipation.

The groups that formed in the 1880s and 1890s and in the early years of the twentieth century, such as the Women's Cooperative Guild (1883), the Women's Industrial Council (1894), the National Union of Women Workers (1895), the Scottish (or Glasgow) Council for Women's Trades (1895), the Liverpool Women's Industrial Council (by 1896), the Hastings and St. Leonard's Women's Industrial Council (c. 1899-1900), the Women's Labour League (1906), and the Fabian Women's Group (1908) built upon earlier efforts at social reform by advocates of women's rights. By the late nineteenth century, social feminist women found a framework for their demands that the public recognize women's economic and social rights and needs in the milieu that included the revival of Socialism, "new unionism," the investigative work of Charles Booth, and the heightened agitation for women's suffrage.

As the groups developed, social feminists had a network of support and public forums from which they could express their views and exert pressure on public officials. They championed a wide range of industrial and family issues, including the plight of sweatshop workers, technical training for girls, women's unemployment, and recruitment of women

as factory and sanitary inspectors. They also saw the necessity of the franchise. **Clementina Black** (1853-1922), a founder of the Women's Industrial Council and its longtime leader, was an active suffragist; Margaret Irwin (d. 1940) of the Scottish Council emphasized the importance of the vote for women workers.

Although the various groups had separate structures and slightly different objectives, all sought legislative remedies and relied upon investigative work as a method of gaining credibility for their programs. They joined forces at various times in their efforts to help women, and their memberships—especially among leaders—often overlapped. For example, Catherine Webb of the Women's Cooperative Guild served as honorary secretary of the Women's Industrial Council in its early years; Margaret MacDonald (1870-1911), who was involved with the council and the National Union of Women Workers, helped form the Women's Labour League. The groups often cut across class lines and were proponents of trade unions for women; both the Women's Industrial Council and the Scottish Council for Women's Trades evolved out of efforts to organize women into **trade unions.**

The impact of social feminist activity continued in the early years of the twentieth century. The 1880s and 1890s set the stage for women who became public figures even before they had the vote. Their experience within their own groups enabled them to influence the social policies developed by the "new liberals."

ELLEN F. MAPPEN

Bibliography

Banks, Olive. *Faces of Feminism: A Study of Feminism as a Social Movement.* 1981.

Evans, Richard. *The Feminists: Women's Emancipation Movements in Europe, America and Australasia, 1840-1920.* 1977.

Hollis, Patricia. *Women in Public, 1850-1900: Documents of the Victorian Women's Movement.* 1979.

Lewis, Jane. *Women in England, 1870-1950: Sexual Divisions and Social Change.* 1984.

Mappen, Ellen. *Helping Women at Work: The Women's Industrial Council, 1889-1914.* 1985.

Murray, Janet, ed. *Strong-Minded Women and Other Lost Voices from Nineteenth-Century England.* 1982.

. . . . .

SOCIAL PROBLEM NOVEL

The social problem novel is a fictitious narrative depicting the situation of workers during the industrial revolution. The authors who worked in this tradition wrote for two reasons: to expose abuses and to promote legislative reform of these abuses. The content of this literature involves a variety of industrial situations: the kinds of workers (men, women, children), the hours of work, the conditions of the work environment, the abuse of workers by overseers or middlemen, the workers' domestic lives, the habits of the working class (including financial imprudence, alcoholism, and sexual profligacy), and the relationships between middle-class factory owners and their lower-class "hands." Social problem novels generally focus on one particular industry or trade. An important aspect of social problem novels is their use of sources, which range from personal observation to Blue Books (the published results of parliamentary investigations) to commissioners' field reports.

The social problem novel arose as a response to the processes of the industrial revolution, which was marked by a difficult and rapid transition from a cottage system of production to a factory system and from an agriculturally based to an industrially based economic system. Social problem narratives (including some novellas or short stories as well as novels) are concerned with the consequences of this transition. The authors generally wrote other types of fiction in addition to their protest narratives. Most of the important social novels appeared during the 1840s and 1850s, although a few of the significant texts in the tradition appeared earlier or later.

The most important novels in the tradition are: Charlotte Brontë, *Shirley* (1849); Dinah Mulock Craik, *John Halifax, Gentleman* (1856); Charles Dickens, *The Chimes* (1845) and *Hard Times* (1854); Benjamin Disraeli, *Coningsby* (1844) and *Sybil* (1845); George Eliot, *Felix Holt, the Radical* (1866); Eliza-beth Gaskell, *Mary Barton* (1848), *Ruth* (1853), and *North and South* (1855); Geraldine Jewsbury, *Marian Withers* (1851); Julia Kavanagh, *Rachel Gray* (1856); Charles Kingsley, *Yeast* (1848) and *Alton Locke* (1850); Fanny Mayne, *Jane Rutherford; or the Miners' Strike* (1853); Harriet Martineau, *The Rioters* (1827), *The Turn-out* (1829), *A Manchester Strike* (1832), and *The Hill and the Valley* (1832); Paul Pimlico, *The Factory Girl* (1849); G. W. M. Reynolds, *The Seamstress* (1850); Elizabeth Stone, *William Langshawe, the Cotton Lord* (1842) and *The Young Milliner* (1843); Charlotte Elizabeth Tonna, *Combination* (1832), *Helen Fleetwood* (1839-1841), and *The Wrongs of Woman* (1843-1844); and Frances Trollope, *Michael Armstrong, the Factory Boy* (1840) and *Jessie Phillips* (1844). Earlier novels anticipating some themes of the social problem novel include Maria Edgeworth's *Castle Rackrent* (1800) and *The Absentee* (1812). Some notable short tales in the tradition include the anonymous "Ellen Linn, the Needlewoman" (1850) and "A London Dressmaker's Diary" (1842); Elizabeth Gaskell, "Libbie Marsh's Three Eras" (1847) and "Lizzie Leigh" (1850); Eliza Meteyard ("Silverpen"), "Lucy Dean; The Noble Needlewoman" (1850); and Camilla Toulmin, "The Orphan Milliners" (1844) and "A Story of the Factories" (1846). Early short tales anticipating the themes of social problem novels include Hannah More's "Village Politics" (1793) and "A Lancashire Collier Girl" (1795) and John Galt's "The Seamstress" (1833).

Authors of social problem novels were similar only in concentrating on working-class suffering and on workers' relationships with the managerial classes. Their common emphasis was on the plight of the disenfranchised in the new industrial era and the need for reform in such areas as housing, labor legislation, sanitation, access to employment, and education. Their political ideologies differed considerably, as revealed in the solutions they offered to workers' problems. Harriet Martineau opposed state intervention as strenuously as Charlotte Tonna advocated its necessity. Some novelists, such as Elizabeth Stone, had no specific political ideology; others had a platform to advance. Charles Kingsley proposed Christian socialism; G. W. M. Reynolds espoused a radical position; Benjamin Disraeli supported the conscientious aristocratic paternalism of Young England.

The writers also differed in their sources of information. Elizabeth Gaskell relied primarily on detailed personal observation of the city of Manchester. Charlotte Tonna used Blue Books (from which she had compiled an anthology, *The Perils of the Nation*, 1843), often quoting verbatim in her texts. Disraeli likewise made use of government reports. Frances Trollope, on the other hand, used *A Memoir of Robert Blincoe* (1828) as a source for *Michael Armstrong*. Charlotte Brontë did extensive research in newspaper accounts of the Luddite movement for *Shirley*. Charles Kingsley wrote a treatise, *Cheap Clothes and Nasty* (1850), analyzing the situation of the tailoring trade, before he published his novel on the subject, *Alton Locke*.

Just as these writers differed in their political ideologies and their use of sources, they also differed in emphasis. Some concentrated on the rise of the new industrialist or captain of industry, as in *William Langshawe, John Halifax*, or *Marian Withers*. Others focused on a specific trade: dressmaking and seamstressing in *The Wrongs of Woman, The Young Milliner, The Seamstress, Rachel Gray*, and "Lucy Dean"; the metals trades in *Sybil*; mining in *Jane Rutherford*; textiles in *A Story of the Factories, Michael Armstrong*, and *Helen Fleetwood*; tailoring in *Alton Locke*; agriculture in *Yeast*. Several writers (such as Tonna) concentrated on the abuse of women or on child labor, as in the case of Trollope.

Social problem fictions appeared in a variety of forms. The short tale facilitated immediacy of impression; the diary of "A London Dressmaker's Diary" is particularly effective in suggesting the mind of a suffering worker. Some novels were published as single volumes (*The Young Milliner, The Rioters, The Turn-Out*) to increase their impact and intersect with contemporary events. Other works appeared in two-volume format (*Mary Barton*) or three-volume sets. The long serialized novel deployed suspense to increase reader involvement in such works as *Jane Rutherford, Helen Fleetwood, Hard Times, The Factory Girl*, or *The Seamstress*. Other works appeared in parts, as with the four parts of Tonna's *The Wrongs of Woman*. The social problem writers experimented with a variety of narrative strategies, including diaries and first-person and third-person accounts, in an attempt to achieve the greatest impact on readers.

The social problem narrative developed and changed over the period in which it flourished. Edgeworth and More concentrated on the lower classes; Edgeworth pioneered in the use of dialect. In the 1820s and 1830s, novelists like Martineau and Trollope began using the social novel to promote legislative reform; Trollope's *Michael Armstrong* denounces child labor laws and advances the cause of the ten hours movement, while *Jessie Phillips* protests the New Poor Law's bastardy provisions. In the 1840s novelists concentrated on exposing evils in specific trades. Some works focused on a single solution for a specific problem; "Lucy Dean," for example, promotes female emigration. In the 1850s the interest shifted to questions of assimilation of the rising managerial classes.

The social problem novel aroused public attention and disseminated information that might otherwise have been ignored because it translated dry sociological and parliamentary data into fictional form for mass consumption. In this way disenfranchised citizens (women, and many men) could bring indirect pressure to bear on lawmakers. The form declined after the early 1860s for several reasons: the Crimean War refocused attention to foreign affairs; the legislation of the 1840s and 1850s removed some of the worst abuses; the Second Reform Bill (1867) enfranchised many men of the middle class. When this form of novel was revived in the 1880s its focus had shifted from the "industrial problem" to the "urban" problem, concentrating once more on the lower classes but without the emphasis on the factory system and specific trades that had marked the social problem novel in the middle decades of the century.

JOSEPH KESTNER

Bibliography

Brantlinger, Patrick. *The Spirit of Reform*. 1977.

Cazamian, Louis. *The Social Novel in England, 1830–1850*. 1903.

Gallagher, Catherine. *The Industrial Reformation of English Fiction, 1832–1867*. 1985.

Himmelfarb, Gertrude. *The Idea of Poverty.* 1984.

Kestner, Joseph. *Protest and Reform: The British Social Narrative by Women, 1827–1867.* 1985.

Kovacevic, Ivanka. *Fact Into Fiction.* 1975.

Melada, Ivan. *The Captain of Industry in English Fiction.* 1970.

Smith, Sheila. *The Other Nation.* 1980.

Webb, Igor. *From Custom to Capital.* 1981.

See also WORKING-CLASS NOVELISTS

. . . . .

SOCIAL SEASON

In Victorian Britain national social life revolved around a three-month period in early summer termed "the season." Large numbers of people from the upper classes came to London during these months to participate in a wide variety of social activities. One major purpose for taking part in the season (which disrupted daily life and could entail vast expense) was to provide opportunities for young men and women of suitable backgrounds to meet. These meetings, in the hothouse atmosphere of the short-lived season and under the strict constraints of social sanction, provided the basis for the Victorian marriage market.

"Society," defined by the *Oxford English Dictionary* as the "aggregate of leisured, cultured, or fashionable persons regarded as forming a distinct class or body," referred also to the social pattern ingrained in the upper classes, who alone could afford to engage in Society's activities, and in whose hands were concentrated national political, economic, and social power.

The bulk of Society's activities were conducted in London during the three months of May, June, and July. This period originally coincided with the sitting of Parliament (when the political elite would have been in London anyway) and ended formally on August 12,

Regent Street in the Season. Illustrated London News, *21 April 1866.*
Library Company of Philadelphia.

the beginning of the grouse-shooting season. Other people unconnected with Parliament bore the expense of a London season because it was the thing to do. It was during the season that, as Anthony Trollope said in *Can You Forgive Her?* (1864), one saw one's friends.

Victorian Society developed in response to the dislocations resulting from the industrial revolution. In a time in which the population grew rapidly, national wealth expanded, and the distribution of wealth shifted dramatically (with the concomitant increase in social mobility and political change), Society served several critical functions. Throughout the century Society assumed increasing influence over the conduct of upper-class public and private life. Social life became more formalized and ritualized; so did the activities appropriate to the season. Events in genteel life occurred at proper times and places. During the season the great entertainments—balls and parties—took place, important quasi-sporting and/or artistic events such as racing at Ascot, viewings at the **Royal Academy**, and attendance at the opera occurred, and less-structured but equally important social events such as riding in the Row and engaging in charity work transpired. Social events beyond the season, such as grouse and partridge shooting, hunting, and country house parties also had their own appropriate times, places, and modes of conduct.

Society's increasing attention to the minutiae of social life enabled its members to find touchstones in a rapidly changing environment and to share not only common pursuits but also a common outlook. Society, said Lady Frances Balfour, was "composed of people who knew how to behave, were well bred, and felt their obligations to live according to the position in which they were placed." And she added, "there was . . . much ease among the inner circle, the ease of equality of station which everyone recognized, and behaved according to an unwritten but perfectly understood code of manners. Certain things were 'not done,' certain people were 'not received,'" and so forth.

Representatives of the new forms of wealth and achievement needed certain prerequisites to pass through the funnel of Society. One classic way to gain access to higher social status had always been through marriage. The Victorians utilized the machinery of Society to facilitate the amalgamation of new money with old social elites. Marriage and its preliminaries, like other important activities, were conducted within the compass of Society's rules, manifested in the term "marriage market." The commercial connotation indicates the economic as well as the social and sexual importance of marriage. Especially for upper-middle-class girls without personal fortunes, marriage was the only vocation that would provide economic security. In addition, marriage gave upper-class women status; spinsterhood was equated with failure. "What," asked Trollope in *Phineas Finn* (1869) "can a woman become if she remains single?"

Because of the importance of marriage and because of the possibility of using it to gain access to the social and political elite, Society regulated courtship with great care. The marriage market was organized under extensive chaperonage within the confining activities of the season, starting with balls or parties where a girl would meet eligible young men. Unofficial but universally recognized time restraints imposed great pressure on a marriageable girl. Considerable prestige was attached to a girl who became engaged in her first season; she and her mother were considered successful. On the other hand, a girl was generally considered to have failed if she were not engaged by her second or third season. And the economic reality of the marketplace of marriage had its effects: parents, unless they were quite rich, would be loath to go to the expense of season after season to no avail, especially if there were other daughters to dispose of. A further economic consideration was the notion of scarcity, that is, the widespread belief that there were more women available than men. Substantial numbers of men delayed marriage or remained single because of the need to have sufficient income to maintain a suitable style of life—a place in Society—which would cost exponentially more for a man with a family than for a single man. The disparity was augmented by the tendency of Victorian men to marry much younger women.

The social season and the marriage market, accordingly, were important realities in Victorian Britain. They provided the social, political, and economic elite—"Society"—with an opportunity to see their friends and be seen by them. They also provided Society's members with sanctioned opportunities to show off their daughters to the right sort of men. Society and the season gave the upper classes a way to regulate social life so as to provide a comfortable pattern in confusing and rapidly changing times. With the marriage market, they also provided a way to control access to status positions—to the highest and most visible social circles and also to the centers of economic and political power.

ESTHER SIMON SHKOLNIK

Bibliography

Balfour, Lady Frances. *Ne Obliviscaris: Dinna Forget.* 1930.

Crathorne, Nancy. *Tennant's Stalk.* 1973.

Davidoff, Leonore. *The Best Circles: Society, Etiquette and the Season.* 1973.

Evans, Hilary and Mary Evans. *The Party That Lasted 100 Days: The Late Victorian Season.* 1976.

Lewis, Jane. *Women in England 1870–1950: Sexual Divisions and Social Change.* 1984.

Pless, Mary T. *Daisy, Princess of Pless.* 1928.

Shkolnik, Esther Simon. *Leading Ladies: A Study of Eight Late Victorian and Edwardian Political Wives.* 1987.

See also ARISTOCRACY AND GENTRY; COUNTRY SOCIETY; COUNTRY SPORTS; SOCIETY, ETIQUETTE AND CUSTOMS OF

· · · · ·

SOCIALISM

During the nineteenth century, socialism developed a uniquely British character. A robust popular heritage, emphasizing the primacy of moral choice, bound together socialists of varying hues. The earliest British socialists inspired later generations with a vision of a morally regenerated society in which all classes would benefit.

Industrialist and philanthropist Robert Owen (1771–1858) argued that circum-stances and not nature determined human character; thus, in order to improve society, one needed first to improve conditions for individuals. Since Owen believed that the industrial revolution had produced social disharmony by promoting competition and materialism, he advocated social and economic cooperation by all segments of society to create a just community.

Owenite socialism commanded for a time a strong base of support among both men and women of the working class. In the envisioned cooperative society, women would share active and equal partnership. Within Owenite thought, an early feminism combined with a moral socialism to forge an alliance that would not reappear until the 1880s. The luster of the Owenite vision dimmed by 1829, after several efforts to establish utopian communities failed. Owen himself, however, maintained an influential position throughout the 1830s and 1840s, largely because his precepts were adapted to the working-class causes of **trade unionism**, the **cooperative movement**, and **Chartism.**

Some historians argue that by the 1830s a class consciousness had been created in England. The advent of Chartism in 1838 signaled the first true working-class campaign on a mass scale. The charter that adherents sought to press upon Parliament made six political demands: universal manhood suffrage, annual parliaments, the secret ballot, equal electoral districts, payment of members of Parliament, and abolition of the property requirement for M. P.'s. Chartist support fluctuated, with peaks at times of severe unemployment and economic distress. Although Chartism did not produce a uniform social critique or advance a plan for economic change or social reconstruction, it provided an unprecedented example of a popular movement that developed a specifically working-class consciousness.

Following the complete demise of Chartism by 1850, Britain entered an era of unparalleled economic growth and social stability. Socialism retreated into the preserve primarily of the intellectual elite. Though pockets of working-class radicalism remained, most workers seemed to lose interest in political activism. Despite the social quiescence, these were the years during which Karl Marx, residing in London, formulated his massive critique of capitalism and theories of scientific socialism. Though Marx's concepts remained virtually unknown in Britain until the early 1880s, all modern varieties of British socialism had to confront and ultimately to adapt Marxism to the British experience.

The first such adapter was H.M. Hyndman (1842–1921), a journalist and stockjobber who read the French translation of *Capital* in 1880. He seized on the economic aspects of Marxism—the labor theory of value, the concept of surplus value, the collective ownership of means of production—and added indigenous traditions such as utilitarianism, Chartism, and radical thought. In 1881 he founded the Democratic Federation to promulgate his new philosophy.

By 1884 Hyndman's group had adopted an entirely socialist agenda and renamed itself the Social Democratic Federation (SDF). However, disagreements erupted within the group. The disaffected members followed William Morris (1834–1896), the artist and poet, into the short-lived Socialist League, which stressed a moral and aesthetic vision of socialism. Hyndman's organization never attracted much support beyond a small coterie of predominantly middle-class sympathizers. Their advocacy of class struggle, antipathy to trade unions, and calls for the forceful reconstruction of the state were repugnant even to many within the socialist camp.

The year 1884 witnessed the birth of another celebrated socialist organization, the **Fabian Society**. Sidney Webb, a middle-level civil servant, was the leading light amid a collection of remarkable men and women, including George Bernard Shaw, Annie Besant, and Beatrice Potter, who later married Webb. Like the SDF, the Fabians remained a small group composed essentially of educated middle-class converts to socialism. While the Fabians accepted the basic socialist demand for common ownership of the means of production, they rejected such Marxist concepts as the exploitation of the working class, the class struggle, and the labor theory of value. Webb replaced the latter with his "law of rent," based heavily upon the theory advocated by the economist David Ricardo (1772–1823), which stated that land and not labor creates wealth. Webb extended this notion to include all forms of capitalist production, which he believed shared the character of rent in that they also possessed the potential

for "differential advantage." According to Webb, persons who accumulate and control these differential advantages, or surplus products, do so at the expense of the rest of the nation, not just of one class.

The Fabians did not believe in fomenting revolutionary change; rather they encouraged gradual reform. They insisted that socialism would best be served by extending democracy, not by subverting the parliamentary system. Fabians sought to work within the system and its major political parties through tactics such as rational arguments, extensive research, educational campaigns, and appeals to fairness and justice.

The socialist revival of the 1880s spawned a plethora of groups, cults, individual popularizers, and readily accessible propaganda sounding the call for a new social order. The interest in socialism was encouraged by the confluence of several social trends. Beginning in the mid-1870s, the British economy faltered badly. Unemployment rose, as did trade union membership. The era of "new unionism" in the 1880s recruited many unskilled and hitherto unorganized workers. Industrial conflicts increased in frequency. The first strike to mobilize unskilled workers was the matchgirls' strike in London in 1888. The men quickly followed the women's lead with triumphant strikes in 1889 by London gasworkers and dock workers.

The new ethical socialism of the late 1880s embraced the practical concerns of the labor movement while also representing the moral and aesthetic notions of William Morris. The heritage of religious Nonconformity mixed with the almost religious socialist fervor exhibited by journalist Robert Blatchford (1851–1943). His common-sensical explanations of socialism in his widely read newspaper, the *Clarion*, drew numerous disciples. Many women activists joined the ethical socialist movement, thanks to its demands for the equality of all citizens and its pleas for social justice and reform. As a result, socialism and feminism renewed their alliance of the Owenite years.

Ethical socialism found its organizational voice with the formation of the Independent Labour party (ILP) in 1893. The ILP was influenced strongly by the Fabians and to a lesser extent by the SDF. Both groups sent delegates to the founding conference of the new party but neither affiliated with it. The Fabians were initially skeptical of the need for a workers' party, preferring their policy of influencing the existing political machinery. The SDF continued its doctrinal stridency and contempt of trade unions and "labourism" for advocating nonsocialist pursuit of working-class interests. The ILP, on the other hand, actively recruited working-class members, agitated on behalf of social reforms that would benefit workers or their families, and specifically sought the cooperation of unions. Much of the party's direction came from **Keir Hardie** (1856–1915), a former miner, new unionist, and recently elected Independent Labour member of Parliament.

The ILP won the support of the older, established unions after a series of employer offensives and adverse legal decisions undermined the position of workers. The result was an alliance among the unions and the socialist societies to seek direct labor representation in Parliament; and thus, in 1900, the Labour Representation Committee (LRC) was formed. After the election of twenty-nine of its candidates to the House of Commons in 1906, the LRC changed its name to the **Labour party** and socialism in Britain entered a new era.

DONNA PRICE PAUL

Bibliography

Beer, Max. *A History of British Socialism.* 1919–1921. 2 vols.

Cole, G. D. H. *A History of Socialist Thought.* 1953–1960. 5 vols.

Hunt, E. H. *British Labour History, 1815–1914.* 1981.

Pierson, Stanley. *British Socialists: The Journey from Fantasy to Politics.* 1979.

———. *Marxism and the Origins of British Socialism.* 1973.

Taylor, Barbara. *Eve and the New Jerusalem: Socialism and Feminism in the Nineteenth Century.* 1983.

Thompson, E. P. *The Making of the English Working Class.* 1963.

Webb, Sidney. *Socialism in England.* 2d ed., 1893.

See also CHRISTIAN SOCIALISM

· · · · ·

SOCIETY, ETIQUETTE AND CUSTOMS OF

Victorian society was dominated by an elite class clearly distinguished by its etiquette and social customs. New knights and peers were formally admitted to society, while others might sometimes gain informal entry to society's exclusive ranks.

Women controlled and regulated society. If a woman was presented at court, her family was officially considered society. Aristocratic families had an inherited right to presentation; other debutantes were presented if their mothers had succeeded in making the right social contacts.

"Morning" calls were actually made in the late afternoon. A call was required when a family moved into the neighborhood or left it, or arrived or departed from London. Calls were also made to acknowledge events such as a birth, death, or marriage, and after parties and balls. Calls could also be merely friendly.

The lady making a call would deliver calling cards to the door for herself, her eligible daughters, and her husband. If the servant indicated that the mistress was "at home," she would be admitted for a fifteen-minute visit. A lady did not, however, have to admit to being "at home." Often printed on the cards were the "at home" days, when a lady would expect to receive visitors.

People refused calls and invitations while in deep mourning, although one could gain social advantage by judiciously invoking or abandoning mourning. Bereaved families wore black and crepe, and servants and distant relatives wore black armbands. Children and parents mourned for one year, widows for three years.

Society maintained exclusiveness by the "cut." In public areas such as Hyde Park, one simply could refuse to recognize someone. The "cut" severed acquaintances one no longer wished to continue. The practice dated from earlier times when public gathering places like Bath and Vauxhall were fashionable.

Victorians, however, preferred private parties. Dinner guests arrived at 6:30, with dinner served half an hour later. The host escorted in to dinner the lady guest whose social rank was highest. The numerous courses were accompanied with elaborate rituals for taking wine. After fruit was served and the tablecloth removed, the hostess rose from the table and led the ladies from the room while the men remained to smoke and drink port or brandy. Later the men would join the ladies in the drawing room for conversation, coffee, card games, or musical entertainment.

Chaperoned young ladies at balls were not to accept more than two dances with the same gentleman. At private balls a young lady could not refuse any gentleman who asked her to dance, but at public balls she was correct to dance only with gentlemen with whom she was acquainted. Dancing and assisting a lady to her carriage were two of the few rituals that permitted any physical contact between the sexes.

Many families followed the custom of morning prayers before breakfast. Servants and children assembled in the dining room while the head of the household read a brief scripture and led the prayers. The upper classes maintained a "correct" distance between parents and children by sequestering children in nurseries and schoolrooms and by sending boys away to preparatory school and public school.

Gentlemen were to treat ladies correctly and were expected to know how to ride and to shoot. Society ranked gentlemen by their birth and education, as well as by their horsemanship and their London clubs.

Society's drawing rooms were the scenes of significant political influence in addition to social ritual. However, the rise of a civil service governed by merit and the broadening of the franchise diminished the power of society from the 1880s onwards.

KARLA KRAMPERT WALTERS

Bibliography

Balfour, Lady Frances. *Ne Obliviscaris: Dinna Forget.* 1930.

Beeton, Isabella. *The Book of Household Management.* 1861.

Besant, Walter. *Fifty Years Ago.* 1887.

Davidoff, Leonore. *The Best Circles: Society, Etiquette and the Season.* 1973.

Lambert, Angela. *Unquiet Souls: The Indian Summer of the British Aristocracy, 1880–1918.* 1984.

Mason, Philip. *The English Gentleman: The Rise and Fall of an Ideal.* 1982.

See also ARISTOCRACY AND GENTRY; CLUBS, GENTLEMEN'S; COUNTRY SOCIETY; DEATH AND FUNERALS; SOCIAL SEASON; SOULS, THE

. . . . .

SOCIETY FOR PSYCHICAL RESEARCH

The Society for Psychical Research was founded in 1882 to conduct scientific inquiries into occult phenomena, especially the possibility of survival after death. Belief in the supernatural was never a condition of membership in the SPR, which included skeptics as well as spiritualists. The organization followed rigorous standards of investigation and exposed several phony mediums, such as the Theosophist H. P. Blavatsky (1831–1891). The prime objective of the SPR, however, was to reconcile science and religion—to prove, by controlled experiment, the existence of an immortal human soul.

Because the SPR filled the vacuum left by the decline of Victorian religion, it acquired a following with impressive intellectual credentials. The Cambridge philosopher Henry Sidgwick (1838–1900) served as president, and was succeeded by A. J. Balfour (1848–1930) in 1893. The membership lists included Leslie Stephen (1832–1904), Lewis Carroll (1832–1898), Andrew Lang (1844–1912), and Arthur Conan Doyle (1859–1930), as well as such eminent physicists as William Crookes (1832–1919), Lord Rayleigh (1842–1919), Oliver Lodge (1851–1940), and J. J. Thomson (1856–1940).

The psychologists William McDougall (1871–1938), William James (1842–1910), and Henri Bergson (1859–1941) were also officers of the SPR, whose experiments in hypnotism and trances were bound up with the investigation of the subconscious mind. Edmund Gurney (1847–1888) and the poet F. W. H. Myers (1843–1901) wrote at length on the subject of multiple personalities. In the

June 1893 number of the SPR *Proceedings*, Myers published the first British account of the work of Sigmund Freud (1856-1939), who later became a corresponding member of the society. Myers himself suggested, in his posthumously *Human Personality and Its Survival of Bodily Death* (1903), that the psyche normally consisted of several independent "streams of consciousness," one of them conscious, the rest "subliminal."

JONATHAN ROSE

Bibliography

Cerullo, John. *The Secularization of the Soul: Psychical Research in Modern Britain.* 1982.

Oppenheim, Janet. *The Other World: Spiritualism and Psychical Research in England, 1850–1914.* 1985.

. . . . .

SOCIOLOGY

An understanding of the development of sociology in Victorian England provides insight into the dynamic yet static response of Victorians to the turmoil and change that surrounded them. The term "sociology" was first coined by the French philosopher Auguste Comte (1787-1857), who defined the new field in 1837 as a premier, all-encompassing science of society. **Herbert Spencer** (1820-1903), the independently wealthy and controversial English theorist, modified Comte's ideas to meet the demand of his cultural milieu. It is through an examination of both the overwhelming popularity of Spencer's work and its final demise that one can best appreciate the contributions to sociology made by Victorian intellectuals.

Comte's sociology appealed to Spencer because it combined two traditionally opposing aspects of Western philosophical thought: organicism and positivism. Organicism is anchored in idealism and is usually espoused by radical reformers. Essentially, it views society as analogous to the human body: an integrated whole, with each part related to the others. It is thus linked to romantic notions of the self and to the belief that the whole is greater than the sum of its parts and can be intuitively known. Positivism, on the other hand, is associated with science; its followers are most often conservative in nature. Positivists believe that knowledge of the world is gained through experience and that experience is recorded in fact. Comte, in combining these traditions in his science of sociology, created a discipline with a built-in tension. This appealed to Spencer's view of life and enabled him to recognize radical change within a framework of order and progress.

Victorian society promoted such an all-encompassing theory replete with contradiction. Urbanization, industrialization, and democratization were progressively undercutting the traditional patterns of status, belief, authority, and community. Rule by central monarchy and support by religious authority and family bonds were all dissipating by 1830. The visible and increasing squalor and poverty of the laboring classes, the persistence of old and the appearance of new diseases, and the continued technological revolution encouraged contemporaries to seek an explanation of events beyond the sphere of individual actions.

Advances in the natural sciences, particularly biology, suggested that the laws that governed society were also knowable. The social sciences (as they came to be called) of sociology, anthropology, and psychology developed in response to the quest for new knowledge. Spencer's contribution to sociology is of special interest because his work depicts so accurately the intellectual and social fabric of English society during the reign of Queen Victoria.

Spencer was an evolutionist whose theories predated Darwin yet matured in a post-Darwinian environment. In his first book, *Social Statics* (1851), he coined the phrase "survival of the fittest" and laid the groundwork for his praise of laissez faire and his acceptance of its social consequences. Spencer viewed societies (indeed, individuals and institutions as well) as evolving from homogeneous to heterogeneous (specialized and differentiated) entities. Industrialization was the way to this progress in the urban sphere. Within the predictable framework of progress, the survival principle was held accountable for the poverty, disease, and hardship that accompanied change. For sociology to be a science, it had to be value free. Spencer's evolutionary approach, influenced by Jeremy Bentham's utilitarianism, satisfied this requirement.

Not all English sociologists were grand theory builders. A nexus of social reformers, statisticians, humanitarians, philanthropists, and journalists contributed to the empirical aspect of sociology. This contribution is still regarded as significant. Charles Booth, Henry Mayhew, Edwin Chadwick, Beatrice and Sidney Webb, and others concentrated on accumulating statistics for reform purposes. They were problem-oriented investigators who recorded urban squalor, disease patterns, and the conditions of the laboring poor. Akin to Spencer in their undaunted belief in progress, they differed from him in their use of statistical descriptions to provide government with "grounded theories" for active reform.

Empirical studies such as these and Spencer's prolific general theoretical contributions represented two trends within the new field of sociology. Events, however, caused some to doubt whether a science of sociology existed at all. Intrusions and exceptions to evolution such as the depression of 1876–1896, colonization, and the rise of a professional civil service and compulsory primary education demanded an explanation. To provide one, Spencer had to admit to significant exceptions which weakened his theory to the point of uselessness.

Influential as Spencer's original work was, it has traditionally been seen as too narrowly conceived in time and place to represent a permanent contribution to sociological theory. Recent reevaluations of his work point to the complexities of his argument and to his increased dismay with laissez faire in later years. In any case, Spencer's work provided his contemporaries—both lay and professional—with an intellectual response to the tension that resulted from their attempt to attain certainty amid a diversity of social facts. His theory was replaced in England by that of the sociologist L. T. Hobhouse, who regarded the uncertainties of the 1830s as commonplace and accepted that reform measures could ease the poverty and hardships that accompanied industrialization. Progress, in this context, took on a less dogmatic form as the new sociology broke with the predictable drive of evolution and accepted an incrementalist approach to change.

ROSA LYNN B. PINKUS

Bibliography

Abrams, Phillip. *The Origins of British Sociology, 1834–1914.* 1968.

Burrow, J. W. *Evolution and Society: A Study in Victorian Social Theory.* 1970.

Jones, Greta. *Social Darwinism and English Thought.* 1980.

Martindale, Don. *The Nature and Types of Sociological Theory.* 1960.

Peel, J. D. Y. *Herbert Spencer: The Evolution of a Sociologist.* 1971.

Spencer, Herbert. *Principles of Sociology.* 1851.

———. *The Study of Sociology.* 1873.

Turner, Jonathan H. *Herbert Spencer: A Renewed Appreciation.* 1985.

. . . . .

SOMERSET, ISABEL (1851–1921)

Isabel Caroline Somers-Cocks, who later became Lady Henry Somerset, was a temperance leader, suffrage worker, philanthropist, and sometime editor and journalist.

She was eldest daughter of Charles Somers-Cocks, Viscount Eastnor (later the third and last Earl Somers) and his wife Virginia Pattle, and succeeded to the estate on her father's death in 1883. She had married Lord Henry Somerset in 1872 and given birth to a son in 1874, but the marriage effectively ended with a separation in 1878. After a protracted legal battle, she was awarded custody of their son and Henry Somerset left England, apparently to avoid prosecution for homosexual offenses.

Lady Henry retired to her home, Eastnor Castle (near Ledbury) to work among the village poor, where she was moved by the poverty, lack of education, and drunkenness that she encountered. In 1885 she joined the British Women's Temperance Association and spoke to audiences throughout England. In 1890 she succeeded Margaret Bright Lucas as national president. Meanwhile, in 1889, she joined the British Woman's Suffrage Society, seeking to unite temperance and suffrage in one great cause for women.

In 1891, Somerset attended the first convention of the World Women's Christian Temperance Union at Faneuil Hall, Boston, and was elected vice-president. She became fast friends with Frances Willard, the organization's president; after the meeting they traveled widely in the United States. On Willard's death in 1898, Somerset became president until she retired from public life in 1906.

From April 1892 to December 28, 1893 Somerset assisted Christine J. Bremer with editorial chores for the *Woman's Herald.* Simultaneously, she initiated the *Journal* (June–December 1893) which became the *Woman's Signal* on January 4, 1894. It continued under her editorship until she relinquished it to Florence Fenwick Miller in September 1895.

Somerset's private philanthropy gave her more personal satisfaction, perhaps, than any of her public work. On her property near Reigate she founded Duxhurst (1895), a farm colony for female alcoholics, the first in England, where women were treated as patients rather than outcasts. She founded also a training home for workhouse children and the Children's Village at Duxhurst.

ROSEMARY T. VAN ARSDEL

Bibliography

Bolton, Sarah K. "Lady Henry Somerset." In *Famous Leaders Among Women.* 1895.

Fitzpatrick, Kathleen. *Lady Henry Somerset.* 1923.

Strachey, Ray. *Frances Willard, Her Life and Work.* 1912.

· · · · ·

SOMERVILLE AND ROSS

Edith Somerville (1858–1949) and Martin Ross (1862–1915) were Anglo-Irish cousins who collaborated on novels, short stories, travel books, and essays between 1887 and 1915. As the unwed daughters of great Anglo-Irish families, Somerville and Ross supplemented their spinster's incomes by chronicling both the serious and gay sides of **Anglo-Irish society.** In their realistic novels, comic short stories, and essays they write of life among the Anglo-Irish in late nineteenth-century rural Ireland. After Martin Ross's death Edith Somerville continued writing fiction, but she never achieved the success that appeared so effortless and unstrained in her collaboration with Martin Ross.

Although the three volumes of Somerville and Ross's celebrated Irish R. M. stories—*Some Experiences of an Irish R. M.* (1906), *Further Experiences of an Irish R. M.* (1908), and *In Mr. Knox's Country* (1915)—were originally read as comic sporting fiction, they surpass this limiting view. Ironic, witty and, by implication, irreverent regarding the British authority in Ireland, the stories present a world that continually subverts the dignity of the queen's resident magistrate whose assignment it is to hear charges and mete out justice in this occupied land. More directly critical of Anglo-Irish society and values is their distinguished novel *The Real Charlotte* (1894). Through a plot juxtaposing the material, sexual, and social ambitions of a ruthless spinster to the effortless male conquests and apparent indifference to wealth or rank of her lovely young cousin and dependent, *The Real Charlotte* exposes varieties of oppression and decadence in Anglo-Irish society.

Their biographers suggest that Martin Ross possessed keener judgment and a more acute skepticism than Edith Somerville who, in turn, contributed immense vitality, humor, and a painter's eye to the partnership. That they never wrote a second novel to rival *The Real Charlotte* is probably due to the popular demand for more and more Irish R.M. stories as well as to Martin Ross's early death. Their unusual collaboration, extraordinarily specific social background, and geographical isolation prevent comparisons with other contemporary writers; however, as with so many writers of Anglo-Irish fiction, Maria Edgeworth (1767–1849) and her *Castle Rackrent* (1800) appear to have been influential.

VIRGINIA K. BEARDS

Bibliography

Cronin, John. *Somerville and Ross.* 1972.

Hall, Wayne E. *Shadowy Heroes: Irish Literature of the 1890s.* 1980.

Lewis, Gifford. *Somerville and Ross: The World of the Irish R. M.* 1986.

Powell, Violet. *The Irish Cousins: The Books and Background of Somerville and Ross.* 1970.

Robinson, Hilary. *Somerville and Ross: A Critical Appreciation.* 1980.

Somerville, Edith. *Irish Memories.* 1917.

· · · · ·

SOMERVILLE, MARY FAIRFAX GREIG (1780–1872)

Hailed as the "queen of nineteenth-century science," Mary Somerville through her writings and scientific and social connections had a profound influence on the definition of "physical sciences" and on the exchange and spread of certain important scientific ideas. Born in Jedburgh, Scotland on December 26, 1780, the daughter of an English admiral and his Scottish wife, she passed the first third of her life in Burntisland and Edinburgh, the second in London, and the last in Italy. Largely self-educated, she developed an early interest in mathematics. In 1804 she married a cousin, Captain Samuel Greig of the Russian navy (1777–1807), and after his death an army doctor, William Somerville (1771–1860), also a cousin. By these marriages three children survived to maturity.

In London the Somervilles were at the center of the foremost English scientific society. Encouraged by her husband and numerous eminent British and French scientific friends, Mary Somerville became well acquainted with the latest science of the day and published four scientific papers and four widely praised books: *The Mechanism of the Heavens* (1831); *On the Connexion of the Physical Sciences* (1834); *Physical Geography* (1848); and *On Molecular and Microscopic Science* (1868). Her autobiography, *Personal Recollections of Mary Somerville* (1873), drastically edited by her daughter Martha, appeared the year after Somerville's death.

To her contemporaries Somerville represented a unique personality, a woman superbly gifted in science but displaying also every attribute they admired in a lady, wife, and mother. She supported many liberal causes, including women's rights and higher education for women.

ELIZABETH C. PATTERSON

Bibliography

Patterson, Elizabeth C. *Mary Somerville, 1780–1872.* 1979.

———. *Mary Somerville and the Cultivation of Science, 1815–1840.* 1983.

· · · · ·

SONGS

The main categories of song in Victorian culture are partly delimited by social class. **Folk music** is what people sing for themselves without professional help, and is generally anonymous and passed on by oral transmission; in Victorian times it was practiced chiefly by the rural and urban working classes. **Popular song** is a commercial product, composed and performed by professional musicians, which caters to the common denominators of the class for which it is intended. Working-class popular song is typified by the **music hall** song, middle-class popular song by the drawing-room **ballad**. These types of song are treated in separate articles.

Art song aspires to the status of a work of art, building on a classical tradition, and by a degree of originality providing some intellectual challenge to an educated audience. In Victorian times art songs were performed in concerts by professional singers, normally with orchestral accompaniment. They were also cultivated at home by amateurs, with piano, harp, or guitar. Although there was a strong preference for Italian, German, and French art songs over English ones, a school of English song composers achieved some success. Its leading exponents were Edward James Loder (1813–1865), William Sterndale Bennett (1816–1875), Charles Hubert Hastings Parry (1848–1918), and Charles Villiers Stanford (1852–1924). The songs of Parry and Stanford laid the foundation for a considerable flowering of English art song in the early twentieth century.

NICHOLAS TEMPERLEY

Bibliography

Banfield, Stephen. *Sensibility and English Song.* 1985.

Bush, Geofrrey and Nicholas Temperley, eds. *English Romantic Songs, 1800–1860.* Musica Britannica, vol. 43. 1979. (Anthology.)

. . . . .

SOULS, THE

A talented company of witty men and women favored by birth, wealth, and good looks, the Souls formed in the early 1880s and numbered forty at George Curzon's famous Bachelors' Club dinner for them in 1889. Anti-Philistine in their taste for art, literature, and cycling, these friends called themselves "the Gang"; they were dubbed "the Souls" because they considered their souls superior and talked incessantly about them. They occasionally enhanced the Marlborough set of the Prince of Wales, but, having their Shakespeare by heart, preferred poetry to fox hunts, charades and pencil games to cards. Wilfrid Blunt (1840–1922) found in their society "all that . . . was most intellectually amusing and least conventional" (*Diaries*, 1891).

Leading men among the Souls were Arthur Balfour (1848–1930), a future prime minister; his handsome private secretary George Wyndham (1863–1913); Harry Cust (1861–1917), poet, editor, and heartbreaker; and Curzon (1859–1925), later viceroy of India. But paramount were the women: the hostesses Lady Desborough (1867–1952) and Lady Elcho (1861–1937); the beauty and artist Violet Manners, duchess of Rutland (1856–1937); and Laura Tennant (1862–1886) and Margot Tennant (1864–1945), who galvanized the Souls into being. At the Glen in Peebleshire, these two youngest daughters of Sir Charles Tennant, M.P., enthralled male guests by holding midnight discussions of literature while propped up in bed, pillows on the floor for attenders. Widely read, with reams of memorized poetry, they had their minds sharpened by family games and their brother Edward's Etonian friends. The sometimes bizarre Margot was satirized in E. F. Benson's *Dodo* (1893), but in the following year she married H. H. Asquith (1852–1928), later prime minister.

The Souls were tightly knit by birth, marriage, their children's marriages to each other, and love affairs not always platonic (Cust reputedly fathered Diana Manners Cooper). Their golden days came to an end with World War I and the loss of their sons. Full of zest and sparkle, they were an ornament to the leisured classes of late Victorian and Edwardian England.

TAMIE WATTERS

Bibliography

Abdy, Jane and Charlotte Gere. *The Souls.* 1984.

Lambert, Angela. *Unquiet Souls.* 1984.

. . . . .

SOUTH AFRICA

At the beginning of Victoria's reign South Africa was in great turmoil. Slavery had just been abolished and repercussions among the South African Boers were immediate. The Boers, a dour Calvinistic farming people of Dutch ancestry, justified slavery by biblical interpretation. With the passage of the Slavery Emancipation Act of 1833, the Boers resisted in every way possible. Placing "Hottentots and Kaffirs" on an equal legal footing was, said one Boer woman, "contrary to the laws of God and the natural distinction of race and religion." When the British made treaties with the various tribal groups, the Boers became increasingly fearful. By 1835, therefore, many Boers decided to cross the Orange River beyond the frontier of British jurisdiction.

Thus began what became known as the "Great Trek," an epic march north into Natal and what became the Orange Free State and the Transvaal. The Boers immediately came into conflict with the indigenous native populations and there were a series of "Kaffir wars." The British government then had to decide whether to abandon the "Boertrekkers" or attempt to protect a population fleeing from its jurisdiction. Finally British law was extended to a line north of modern Pretoria. Natal was then annexed in 1843. Expansion in the area between the Orange and Vaal rivers continued through the 1840s until, in the 1850s, the government decided that the cost of maintenance was too high. In 1852 and 1854 British control was relaxed by the Sand River and Bloemfontein Conventions.

For the next decade there was relative calm in the Boer areas of South Africa. In 1867 diamonds were discovered in Griqua tribal areas bordering on the Boer Orange Free State. By 1871 the British had annexed Griqualand, to the annoyance of the Free State Boers. British policy floundered as colonial secretaries groped for a South African policy. Prime Minister Gladstone had no real interest in expansion, while Disraeli was of little help. "Do what you think wisest," was his only advice to his colonial secretary.

In 1878 the British colonial secretary failed to keep a rein on the aggressive policies of South African governor Bartle Frere. A border conflict with the Zulu tribe erupted. Although the colonial secretary urged Frere to accommodate the Zulus, Frere instead sent them an ultimatum which led to the disastrous Zulu War of 1879, which saw the battle of Isandhlwana—the British army's worst defeat at the hands of a native army.

By the end of Victoria's reign trouble had been brewing for considerable time between the Boers of South Africa and the British authorities. In 1877 the British government decided to federate all white communities in South Africa and annexed the Transvaal. Boer protests led to an initial military skirmish in 1881. Following Gladstone's Midlothian campaign of 1879, the Boers presumed that the annexation would be revoked. When it was not, a brief military campaign in 1881 resulted in a British embarrassment at Majuba Hill and the retrocession of the Transvaal. Conditions in South Africa festered through the remainder of the 1880s and early 1890s.

After the discovery of gold in the Transvaal in 1886, relations between the Boers and Britain changed irrevocably. Overnight the Boer pastoral economy was swamped by an influx of thousands of gold-hungry immigrants ("*uitlanders*," most of whom were British citizens). The Boer treatment of these *uitlanders* was of particular concern to **Cecil Rhodes**, prime minister of the Cape Colony. They paid substantial taxes and could be conscripted, but were not allowed to vote or hold any seats in the Volksrad. Rhodes and his friends planned, therefore, overthrowing the Transvaal government of President Paul Kruger by force. The plan was scarcely a secret in Cape

Town, or even in London. Evidence indicates that Colonial Secretary **Joseph Chamberlain** conspired actively with the plotters. The resulting raid on the Boers, led by Dr. **Leander Starr Jameson** in December, 1895, was a fiasco. Four days after it began, six hundred invaders surrendered ignominiously to Boer troops.

In 1897 Chamberlain appointed **Alfred Milner** as governor of Cape Colony and high commissioner for South Africa. With this appointment, compromise became virtually impossible. Milner possessed an unswerving commitment to imperialism and Anglo supremacy. By 1898 Chamberlain was comparing the position of *uitlanders* with Spartan Helots, and a crisis rapidly began to build. In May, 1899 there was a South African "summit" at Bloemfontein which solved nothing. After Milner expressed British demands for the accommodation of *uitlanders*, Kruger replied: "It is our country that you want." Even after Boer concessions were offered in August, Milner refused to be swayed. Chamberlain and the dispirited cabinet of Lord Salisbury convinced themselves that war was inevitable. British forces were moved to the Boer borders on October 9; Kruger demanded that they be removed; on October 11, 1899, war was begun.

The South African war tarnished the concluding years of Victoria's reign—it damaged Victoria's personal image and that of British imperial supremacy. For three bitter years British military strength was unable to defeat two tiny republics whose population, as war critic David Lloyd George so vividly stated, "did not exceed that of Flintshire or Denbighshire." The South African Boers, although numbering no more than 50,000–60,000 amateur soldiers, proved to be excellent marksmen, were in possession of the latest German military equipment, and were a formidable enemy. They were finally defeated only by sheer weight of numbers and supplies; the final victory was neither glorious nor cheap.

During the initial stages of the war the Boers maintained the upper hand and initiated much of the offense. After invading both Cape Colony and Natal, they besieged the strategic garrisons of Kimberley, Mafeking, and Ladysmith. There was a "black week" in December 1899 during which many observers expected the Boers to secure victory. It was not until February 1900 that British reinforcements began to reverse the tide. By June 1900 both Boer capitals had been occupied and British victory was guaranteed, although the Boers resorted to hit-and-run tactics by small irregular groups called "commandos." In this way the war continued for another year and a half. British frustration led to drastic tactics such as a scorched-earth policy and the expedient of rounding up Boer women and children and herding them into internment camps. By war's end over 26,000 had died of disease, and government critics were characterizing the policy as "methods of barbarism."

The war dragged on, Britain isolated and friendless diplomatically, until May 31, 1902, when the treaty of Vereeniging was concluded. The terms provided that Boers who took a loyalty oath were to be released, their language was to be safeguarded, and self-government was to be restored. Voting rights for blacks in South Africa were not to be considered until the stated terms had been implemented. When British South Africa and Boer South Africa were united in 1910 into the Union of South Africa, such voting rights were, of course, excluded.

NEWELL D. BOYD

Bibliography

Chamberlain, Muriel E. *The Scramble for Africa.* 1974.

De Kiewiet, Cornelius W. *British Colonial Policy and the South African Republics.* 1929.

———. *The Imperial Factor in South Africa.* 1937.

Eldridge, C. C. *England's Mission, 1868–1880.* 1973.

Grenville, J. A. S. *Lord Salisbury and Foreign Policy.* 1964.

Marais, Johannes. *The Fall of Kruger's Republic.* 1961.

Robinson, Ronald E. and John Gallagher. *Africa and the Victorians: The Official Mind of Imperialism.* 1961.

Wilson, Monica and Leonard Thompson. *The Oxford History South Africa.* 1971. 2 vols.

See also BOER WAR

. . . . .

SPASMODIC POETRY

After the publication of *Festus* (1839) by Philip James Bailey (1816–1902), a school of "spasmodic poetry" flourished for about twenty years. These were lengthy poems (up to 40,000 lines) that depicted the universe from heaven to hell; they used the dramatic form of Goethe's *Faust*, the guilty rhetoric of Byron's *Manfred*, and Milton's theology. While unread today, *Festus* and company were highly praised by many Victorian critics as well as by poets like Alfred Tennyson and Elizabeth Barrett Browning.

Festus was followed by J. Westland Marston's *Gerald* (1842) and Richard H. Horne's *Orion* (1843). Horne (1803–1884) declared in his essay on *Festus* that the poet should "soar away towards the illimitable heavens, unknown ecstasies, and the eternal mysteries of the Divine" (*New Spirit of the Age*, 1844), and Bailey added a "Proem" to *Festus* to make clear that "Poetry is itself a thing of God." The incredible popularity of *Festus* may be ascribed to its combination of overblown romanticism and a comforting message about salvation. The second wave of spasmodic poems were more relevant to secular society; two of these were "A Life-Drama" (in *Poems*, 1853) by Alexander Smith (1830–1867), and *Balder* (1854) by Sydney Dobell (1824–1874). *Balder*, which ends when the poet-hero murders his mad wife as an act of mercy, clearly shows the connection of the genre to the sensation novels popular in the 1860s. This poem provoked a literary controversy culminating in a famous hoax. William Edmondstoune Aytoun (1813–1865), a *Punch* satirist, penned an anonymous attack in *Blackwood's* (May 1854) on an unpublished poem, *Firmilian, a Spasmodic Tragedy* by T. Percy Jones. Supporters of Dobell and Smith came to the rescue of *Firmilian*, but when the poem appeared it turned out to be a parody composed by Aytoun himself. The subsequent laughter spread the name "spasmodic poetry" and effectively ended its vogue.

Spasmodic poetry reflected the need of a growing reading public for both profound and sensational matter coupled with an orthodox moral. In its treatment of contemporary problems and psychological abnormalities, however, it influenced such fine poems as Tennyson's *Maud* (1855) and Barrett Browning's *Aurora Leigh* (1857).

DAVID E. LATANÉ, JR.

Bibliography

Buckley, Jerome H. *The Victorian Temper: A Study in Literary Culture.* 1951.

Weinstein, Mark A. *William Edmonstoune Aytoun and the Spasmodic Controversy.* 1968.

· · · · ·

SPENCER, HERBERT (1820–1903)

Little read though it is today, Herbert Spencer's work represents an impressive attempt to build a metaphysical system on naturalist principles. Spencer's naturalism, which typifies a signficant current in Victorian opinion, was expressed most prominently in the studies of biology, sociology, and ethics which made up his "System of Synthetic Philosophy" (1862–1893). *First Principles* (1862) set out "primordial truths" arrived at by deduction from the "elementary datum of consciousness."

Spencer was born in Derby, the son of an eccentric Nonconformist teacher, and was formally schooled for only three months. He became a railway engineer in 1837 and engaged extensively in journalism. Appointed subeditor of *The Economist* in 1848, he left five years later to assume the life of an independent scholar: his writing was popular enough to provide a reasonable income. He worked unremittingly until overcome by chronic illness toward the end of his life; he never married ("I was never in love") and spent most of his years in hotels and boarding houses, paying quite consciously for his intellectual commitment with an almost total lack of intimate companionship. He did, however, form some powerful, if cerebral, friendships with renowned figures, including Thomas Carlyle, J. S. Mill, T. H. Huxley, and George Eliot, with whom he once considered marriage.

Spencer was diverse in his interests and drew on the popular Nonconformist theology of his day, on the work of Thomas Malthus, Jean-Baptiste Lamarck, and Charles Lyell,

and on certain principles of physics such as the conservation of energy. Nevertheless, Spencer's guiding ideas were formed early in his life, after which he admitted few others.

His ultimate goal was to articulate a coherent, logical, necessary system of general ideas in terms of which every element of experience could be interpreted. Philosophy's function was to unify the sciences; the sciences (each in its circumscribed area) were to discover laws or regularities in phenomena. Spencer's system is philosophical and also evolutionary, for as set out in his celebrated essay "Progress: Its Law and Cause" (1857), Spencer's evolutionism is universal. Defined as passage from a "relatively indefinite, incoherent homogeneity to a relatively definite, coherent heterogeneity," evolution was the key to understanding all phenomena, whether organic, inorganic, or "super-organic" (that is, social).

Spencer found evolution at work everywhere and many linked his name indissolubly with Charles Darwin's; biological Darwinism was widely supposed to inform Spencer's ethical, political, and economic beliefs. Though this was not, strictly speaking, so, Spencer gained much prestige by popular association with *The Origin of Species* (1859). Darwin confessed that he could not fathom Spencer's metaphysics—an understandable reaction to what was in the main a difficult amalgam buried in a hideous style. Only in some political essays, in his first book in defense of laissez faire, *Social Statics* (1851), and in his *The Study of Sociology* (1873) did Spencer manage a more accessible and pleasing idiom.

In additon to his statement and development of a theory of general evolution, Spencer's chief claim to fame was as the thinker (after Auguste Comte) most responsible for founding **sociology**. As expressed in his *Principles of Sociology* (1876–1896), societies, like organisms, undergo life-and-death cycles. Spencer was little interested in solid historical detail; he worked on an abstract level and proposed a typology of social structures.

Spencer's concern with issues of priority has made it difficult to gauge influences upon him. His utilitarian ethics and his religious agnosticism were informed by contemporary debates, but his evolutionary *Principles of Psychology* (1855) were independent and original. His *Autobiography* (1904) provides a detailed, it not always accurate, account of the genesis and chronology of his thought. That thought covered too broad a field to win many intellectual converts, and it was too synthetic to win other admirers. Nevertheless, Spencer's writings offer a deep probe into Victorian social, scientific, political, ethical, and philosophical life.

MICHAEL SHORTLAND

Bibliography

Andreski, Stanislav, ed. *Herbert Spencer: Structure, Function and Evolution.* 1972.

Burrow, J. W. *Evolution and Society: A Study in Victorian Social Theory.* 1966.

Duncan, David. *Life and Letters of Herbert Spencer.* 1908.

Greene, John C. "Biology and Social Theory in the Nineteenth Century: Auguste Comte and Herbert Spencer." In Marshall Clagett, ed., *Critical Problems in the History of Science.* 1969.

Hudson, William H. *Herbert Spencer.* 1908.

Medawar, P. B. *The Art of the Soluble.* 1967.

Peel, J. D. Y. *Herbert Spencer: The Evolution of a Sociologist.* 1971.

Rumney, Jay. *Herbert Spencer's Sociology: A Study in the History of Social Theory.* 1934.

Wiltshire, David. *The Social and Political Thought of Herbert Spencer.* 1978.

See also PSYCHOLOGY

· · · · ·

SPIRITUALISM

Spiritualism, a phenomenon whereby the living communicate with the dead through a medium, was brought to England from America by such practitioners as the Fox sisters and Daniel D. Home. Characterized by knockings, rappings, spirit writings, materializations, and levitation, spiritualism, which was introduced into England in 1852, was well received. The same milieu that entertained mesmerism fervently supported materialism. Doubting the God they could not empirically affirm, but athirst for faith in an afterlife, many Victori-

ans readily welcomed contact with "departed spirits."

In Britain spiritualism had its detractors, but it had also a sizable following. Though Charles Dickens, Robert Browning, and Havelock Ellis, for example, scoffed at the notion of séances attended by table-rapping ghosts, the believers included Elizabeth Barrett Browning, Edward Bulwer-Lytton, Arthur Conan Doyle, and the crusading journalist William Stead. Even Queen Victoria participated in a séance. Many proponents of spiritualism came to view it as a religion. Other considered it a spiritual science, a means to investigate the existence and survival of the human soul.

Although the best-known figure associated with spiritualism was a man, D.D. Home, women took a more active and visible role in spiritualism than they were able to achieve in churches. Many, like the famous Florence Cook, were mediums. Others recorded and defended the movement: Catherine Crowe, in *Spiritualism and the Age We Live In* (1859), argued for open-mindedness on the subject; Emma Hardinge Britten's *Modern American Spiritualism* (1870) recorded the progress of the spiritualist movement in the United States; Sophia de Morgan's *From Matter to Spirit* (1863) schooled readers about the functions and kinds of mediums.

Spiritualism empowered individuals because it emphasized personal connections to the spirit world and because it had no authoritative scripture or organizational hierarchy. **Florence Marryat** wrote both fiction and nonfiction that declared spiritualism to be a religion for the oppressed and the bereaved. In the latter part of the nineteenth century, the powerful and dazzling **Madame H. P. Blavatsky** founded the **Theosophical Society** to spread the tenets of spiritualism.

VANESSA D. DICKERSON

Bibliography

Brandon, Ruth. *The Spiritualists: The Passion for the Occult in the Nineteenth and Twentieth Centuries.* 1983.

Oppenheim, Janet. *The Other World: Spiritualism and Psychical Research in England, 1850–1914.* 1985.

Porter, Katherine H. *Through a Glass Darkly: Spiritualism in the Browning Circle.* 1958.

See also SOCIETY FOR PHYSICAL
RESEARCH; WATTS, ANNA MARY
HOWITT

· · · · ·

SPORT

The Victorians were among the most sports
minded of all societies. They glorified play,
and almost transformed it into work, because
they sincerely believed that sports and games
were necessary for the development of tough
mental fiber as well as a powerful physique.
They became almost obsessed with brawn because they did not think that a feeble body
could possibly support a vigorous mind. They
abhorred physical weakness since they
thought that it could be eliminated by exercise and discipline—hence the popularity of
sports and games in nineteenth-century Britain. But sports were also deliberately used by
the British cultural and political elite as effective forms of social control.

Academic institutions, voluntary associations, and religious organizations gave whole-
hearted encouragement to sports and combined to establish a host of clubs, leagues, and
associations throughout Britain. In keeping
with the authoritarian character of Victorian
society, central bodies emerged to control individual sports and to codify their laws and
regulations. Thus, for instance, the Marylebone Cricket Club became the dominant
force in **cricket**, the Football Association in
soccer, and Wimbledon in **tennis.**

These central authorities were rendered
necessary by the process of industrialization
which had upset traditional sporting patterns.
Emerging towns had brought together heterogeneous migrants from various rural districts
and necessitated the standardization of athletic rules. Improved transportation had led
also to interregional competitions which rendered imperative the establishment of national codes of conduct. Urbanization also
seemed to require more rigid and formal controls than had been necessary in the agrarian
past.

Victorian sports were not only influenced
by the coming of a new material order, but
also reflected the new morality of evangeli-

cals, who put more stress than the Georgians
had done on sobriety, moderation, and the
Puritan work ethic. Thus gambling and corruption were considerably reduced after
1830. Blood sports were also frowned upon
and, by the 1840s, many of the traditional
diversions, like animal baiting and cockfighting, had been eradicated both by custom and
parliamentary statute.

Whereas the Georgians had been more
rambunctious and individualistic in their
play, the Victorians tended to exalt team
games which they considered more suitable
for the inculcation of civic virtues such as
loyalty and patriotism. Cricket and football
thus became supreme at the public schools
and the universities where, by the 1860s, they
were regarded as integral features of the curriculum. Even Queen Victoria thought it necessary to hire a professional to coach her sons
at cricket.

Although sports were generally used as
agents of socialization, they did little to bridge
the gap between the classes during the nineteenth century. It is true that bourgeois and
aristocratic patrons kept sports clubs alive at
every level, but working-class teams were
forced to compete mainly among themselves
because of the persistence of older forms of
snobbery. Some sports, too, were so expensive that they excluded the middle and lower
orders. Horses and yachts, for example, could
be purchased only by a small minority. Sports
thus served quite often as an index of socioeconomic status. Soccer and track and field
were the cheapest forms of athletic activity
and naturally came to be dominated by the
proletariat.

The sports mania of the age led thousands
of spectators to boxing bouts, cricket
matches, soccer games, and track and field
contests. Clubs erected huge pavilions and
stadiums, charged admission fees, and thus
commercialized most sports. This is only one
example of the pervasive influence the Victorians had on modern sports. They not only
taught the world how to play and to commercialize games, but they established important
ground rules in such sports as archery, **athletics**, badminton, bowls, boxing, canoeing,
cricket, cycling, dog racing, field hockey, golf,
horse **racing**, polo, rowing, Rugby, soccer,
swimming, tennis, and yachting. The Victorians also made significant athletic progress.

The British record for the mile, for instance, was 4.33 in 1862, but was under 4.13 by the end of the century. It took the best swimmers almost 75 seconds to cover 100 yards in the 1870s, but the record for that distance had dropped to 60 seconds by 1892.

KEITH A.P. SANDIFORD

Bibliography

Haley, Bruce. *The Healthy Body and Victorian Culture.* 1978.

Harris, Harold A. *Sport in Britain: Its Origins and Development.* 1975.

Malcolmson, Robert W. *Popular Recreations in English Society, 1700–1850.* 1973.

Mangan, J. A. *Athleticism in the Victorian and Edwardian Public School.* 1981.

Mason, Tony. *Association Football and English Society, 1863–1915.* 1980.

Vamplew, Wray. *The Turf: A Social and Economic History of Horse Racing.* 1976.

Watman, Melvyn F. *History of British Athletics.* 1968.

See also COUNTRY SPORTS; RUGBY FOOTBALL; SPORTS AND GAMES, WOMEN'S; SPORTING LITERATURE

. . . . .

SPORTING LITERATURE

The literature of **sports** and sporting life proliferated in the Victorian age. There was a continuation of the Regency's passion for physical activity, which had virtually mythologized hunting and glorified the shared interests of lower-class men and sporting aristocrats for racing and pugilism. Victorian medievalism led to the revival of archery, falconry, and bowls and contributed to the evolution of newer variants, as in the case of lawn tennis. The influence of the military and of the universities and public schools, which insisted on fitness as a part of education, promoted athletics, cricket, and Rugby football. To these causes must be added the concern

with general health, the vogue for periodicals and annuals, and the Victorian love of codification which produced so many sporting manuals. Facets of these impulses are to be found in all types of Victorian literature, both fictive and expository, prose and poetry.

The elder Pierce Egan (1772–1849), whose influence on Charles Dickens is well noted, was the outstanding sporting novelist of the early nineteenth century. The only comparable writer of the following generation was Robert Smith Surtees (1803–1864). Of his hunting novels, the best remembered are *Mr. Sponge's Sporting Tour* (1853), which occasioned his introduction to his great friend William Makepeace Thackeray; *Handley Cross* (1843); and *Jorrock's Jaunts and Jollities* (1838). The latter two detailed the adventures of the sporting grocer, Mr. John Jorrocks, sometimes hailed as the prototype of Mr. Pickwick. Surtees's novels are still read for their humor, social criticism, and comic detail of the life of the time.

Closely allied in outlook and appeal is "Nimrod," or C. J. Apperley (1779–1843), whose sporting memoirs and reminiscences included *The Chace, the Turf and the Road* (1837) and *The Life of a Sportsman* (1842), which is partly fiction and partly social history. The success of Surtees and Apperley was enhanced by the wonderful illustrations of John Leech and Henry Alken.

Sporting scenes, both as background and satire, recur in the novels of Dickens, Thackeray, Anthony Trollope, George Meredith, and a host of minor writers, while short stories with sporting motifs abound. However, the majority of fictional pieces with sporting content are found among schoolboy stories. Thomas Hughes's *Tom Brown's School Days* (1857) and Talbot Baines Reed's *The Fifth Form at St. Dominic's* (1887) are representative of the best in a domestic setting. R. M. Ballantyne's *The Gorilla Hunters* (1861) is more typical of the exotic adventure tale. Verse with sport as a subject, both serious and comic, was produced by such diverse and unexpected writers as Lewis Carroll ("The Deserted Parks") and Francis Thompson ("At Lord's").

In periodical literature, the more important sporting journals were the *Sporting Magazine* (1792–1870), sometimes known as "the Old Warwick Coach," Surtees and Ackermann's

New Sporting Magazine (1831–1870), and the *Sporting Review* (1839–1870). The same period saw the start of *The Field* (1853), the *Sporting Times* ("the pink 'un", 1865), and *Country Life* (1895). A new innovation was the annual digest of statistics and scores. The venerable survivor, *John Wisden's Cricketers' Almanack*, is one example which began in 1864 and continues almost unchanged in its aims.

Other nonfiction writings include recollections, autobiographies, anecdotes, letters, biographies, and a great many general-interest volumes on sports of all kinds. Historical surveys linked contemporary activities with romantic pastimes supposedly typical of "Merrie England." Other books and articles sketched regional and rural sports, especially those of the Highland Scots.

Treatises offering instruction were as popular then as now, from the cricketing classic *Felix on the Bat* (1845) to Richard F. Burton's *The Book of the Sword* (1884). *The Badminton Library of Sports and Pastimes* (1885–1896), twenty-eight volumes of information on a wide spectrum of topics from big game shooting to swimming to the poetry of sport, was characteristic of a penchant for sets of books that made rounded, general knowledge available for the gentleman and gentlewoman of leisure.

In its sporting literature lies a unique opportunity to see the whole pattern of Victorian attitudes and manners revealed at their most relaxed and unselfconscious, allowing even social barriers to be transcended on occasion, and illumined on the stage of an era that began with coaches and coursing and concluded with cycling and motors.

C. GORDON-CRAIG

Bibliography

Bovill, E. W. *The England of Nimrod and Surtees, 1815–1854.* 1959.

Darwin, B. "Sporting Writers of the Nineteenth Century." In *Essays Mainly on the Nineteenth Century Presented to Sir Humphrey Milford.* 1948.

Haley, Bruce. *The Healthy Body and Victorian Culture.* 1978.

Higginson, Alexander H. *British and American Sporting Authors: Their Writings and Biographies.* 1951.

Neumann, Bonnie Rayford. *Robert Smith Surtees.* 1978.

Slater, J. H. *Illustrated Sporting Books: A Descriptive Survey.* 1899.

Welcome, John. *The Sporting World of R. S. Surtees.* 1982.

. . . . .

SPORTS AND GAMES, WOMEN'S

The Victorian image of the ideal woman was antithetical to sport. Passive, gentle, and delicate, she lacked the strength and inclination to undertake strenuous exercise and competitive games. From midcentury, however, powerful forces of economic and social change spawned a sporting revolution and a feminist movement that challenged the ideal and sought women's admission into spheres traditionally dominated by men. Women's gradual entry into sports activities was somewhat removed from the centers of feminist controversy, but it was fundamental to female emancipation.

Women's sport emerged partly from the campaign for improved education. Its leaders believed women had a right to strengthen their bodies as well as their minds, and a pressing need to do so to refute medical arguments that higher learning would damage reproductive organs. They also held that games, particularly team games, would impart valuable moral qualities, such as honor and courage, that had previously been ascribed exclusively to males. The result was that from their earliest days in the 1870s women's university colleges and girls' public schools encouraged students to participate in sport. By the end of the century a diverse array of facilities and intra- and interinstitution competitions were in place; and students participated, competitively or noncompetitively, in hockey, cricket, lacrosse, netball, rounders, lawn tennis, golf, archery, croquet, fencing, swimming, riding, walking, running, cycling, boating, shooting, fives, rackets, ice-skating, jujitsu, drill, and Swedish gymnastics.

Women's sport also developed outside educational settings. In 1895, for example, representatives of private clubs joined those from

Newnham College, Cambridge, Hockey Team, 1894–5. Reprinted by permission of the Principal and Fellows of Newnham College.

colleges and schools to found the All England Women's Hockey Association, under whose aegis hockey rapidly developed into the premier women's team game. A few women also played cricket, a playful form of which was popular on country house lawns in the 1870s. In 1887 some aristocratic Yorkshire women formed the first women's club, but few others followed suit, so there was no national organization until 1926. A minor aberration were the Original English Lady Cricketers, two teams of female professionals created in 1890 by male entrepreneurs who anticipated making money from exhibitions in major centers. Following a successful first season, the teams disbanded when the managers absconded with the profits.

In the apparently more ladylike realm of individual sports, riding and fox hunting predated the nineteenth century, but it was croquet in the 1860s that first spurred the en-

trance of substantial numbers of women into competitive sport. When leisured society turned to the relatively more thrilling game of lawn **tennis** the following decade, ladies were most enthusiastic. The All-England Croquet and Lawn Tennis Club allowed female members from 1883, and in 1884 sponsored the first ladies' singles championship. Ladies' doubles and mixed doubles were officially added to the championship program in 1913, by which time few towns or villages in England lacked a ladies' tournament, and changes in clothing and attitudes had converted the original patball style of play into more skillful and vigorous action.

Golf was tennis's only serious rival. Women began to play in the 1860s and the first two ladies' clubs were established in 1867 and 1868. For years, however, fashion, propriety, inadequate facilities, and male scorn inhibited development. In 1893, when the Ladies'

Golf Union was founded and the first open championship held, there were only 20 women's clubs in England, and membership averaged less than 50. Thereafter, advances were rapid. By 1905, fully three decades before the men, the LGU had established a national handicapping system, while by 1914 courses and quality of play had improved markedly, and the LGU represented over 20,000 players and 460 clubs.

It was, however, **bicycling**, a national passion in the 1890s, that provided women's most significant sporting experience. Despite predictions of damage to health and femininity, thousands took to the "wheel," discovering that it gave them an exhilarating sense of independence and brought the sexes together on relatively equal terms. Because of its public nature and remarkable extent, cycling more than any other activity focused attention on women's right, desire, and need to participate in outdoor exercise; it promoted dress reform; and it symbolized the **New Woman**'s determination to challenge social controls and participate more fully in national life.

By the end of the Victorian age the range of women's sports was in marked contrast to the earlier severe constraints. While it must be noted that except in the case of cycling the numbers of sportswomen were relatively limited and derived almost entirely from the middle and upper classes (working-class women lacked the leisure, means and education to participate), in addition to the major activities, women swam, fenced, rode, hunted, shot, fished, yachted, boated, punted, ice- and roller-skated, skied, hiked, played badminton, climbed mountains, and drove motor cars.

There remained, however, a strong belief that sport was a basically masculine phenomenon and that female involvement, particularly in "unsexing" activities, was aberrant and physically dangerous. Thus the gradual acceptance of sport as compatible with the socialization of women required protracted negotiations and compromises to reconcile the apparent conflict between games and womanliness, and produced limitations that protected male dominance and female modesty. At the same time sport proved a powerful deviant activity through which women expressed hostility to constraining social norms. It provided unique opportunities to compete, acquire skills, and be physically active. It

heightened women's consciousness of their own bodies and offered a means of greater body control. Finally, it presented women in nontraditional roles and contributed substantial modifications to the feminine ideal and to definitions of women's rights, nature, and abilities.

KATHLEEN E. McCRONE

Bibliography

Atkinson, Paul. "Fitness, Feminism and Schooling." In Sara Delamont and Lorna Duffin, eds., *The Nineteenth-Century Woman: Her Cultural and Physical World*. 1978.

——. "Strong Minds and Weak Bodies: Sports, Gymnastics and the Medicalization of Women's Education." *British Journal of Sports History*, vol. 2, pp. 62-71.

Fletcher, Sheila. *Women First: The Female Tradition in English Physical Education 1880-1980*. 1984.

Hargreaves, Jennifer A. "'Playing Like Gentlemen While Behaving Like Ladies': Contradictory Features of the Formative Years of Women's Sport." *British Journal of Sports History*, vol. 2, pp. 42-50.

Mangan, J. A. and Roberta J. Park, eds. *From 'Fair Sex' to Feminism: Sport and the Socialization of Women in the Industrial and Post-Industrial Eras*. 1987.

McCrone, Kathleen E. *Sport and the Physical Emancipation of English Women, c. 1870-1914*. 1988.

Rubinstein, David. "Cycling in the 1890s." *Victorian Studies*, vol. 21, pp. 47-71.

· · · · ·

STAINED GLASS

Eighteenth-century English stained glass relied almost entirely on the enamel painting of a picture onto regularly shaped panes of clear glass. Early nineteenth-century glass painters began to rediscover the art of medieval and Renaissance glass: the use of colored glass (produced by adding metal oxides to molten glass) and of lead channeling to joint the pieces and produce outline drawing.

In Victorian times, the glass pieces were cut smaller and selected with more care; thicker and more irregular glass produced richer and more varied tints; small pieces of white glass were used to enhance color and design; and figures often simulated the flatness of medieval designs. By the end of the century British glass was widely recognized as preeminent. The number of workers engaged in the industry had risen during Victoria's reign from fewer than one hundred to several thousand.

The revival of antiquarian and craft interest in stained glass and the great expansion of demand can be attributed to the building of new churches to serve the rapidly growing population of cities and manufacturing towns; the **Gothic revival** in architecture; and the restoration (often amounting to rebuilding) of medieval and Tudor churches and cathedrals.

The strict Gothicist views of **A.W.N. Pugin**, who designed much of the glass for his churches, are presented in his own publications and in *The History of Stained Glass* (1848) by his associate, William Warrington. A more thorough exposition of the views common to the Gothicists is *An Inquiry Into the Difference of Style Observable in Ancient Glass Paintings* (1847) by Charles Winston. Ruskin's letters to Edmund Oldfield (1844) reflect similar views, based on his central principle of truth to materials.

In the 1850s demanding Gothicist architects such as Butterfield, Street, and Burges and prolific ones such as G. G. Scott commissioned stained glass from the new firms Clayton and Bell; Heaton, Butler and Bayne; and Lavers and Barraud; and from the older general glass-making firm of James Powell and Sons. Improved glass became available through the enterprise of Winston, who had medieval glass analyzed by a chemist and replicated by Powell's.

William Morris's new firm, Morris, Marshall, Faulkner and Co. (later Morris and Co.) exhibited successfully at the 1862 Exhibition. Their early work varied from the dramatic vigor of **Ford Madox Brown** to be the flat-footed stillness of Morris. **Edward Burne-Jones** gradually became the chief designer. He ventured into large-scale Italian High Renaissance pictorialism, quite different from the canopied Gothic style of the early work. Other artists influenced by Morris included Henry Holiday and Charles Kempe.

The arts and craft movement of the 1880s encouraged a return to Ruskinian principles of the artist-craftworker and away from the production-line distinction between designer and worker characteristic of the large firms, including Morris's. The figure designers such as Selwyn Image and Christopher Whall followed the Pre-Raphaelite tradition, their backgrounds being inspired by Morris's patterned foliage.

In the next generation stained glass became lifelessly imitative until the 1950s.

KEN GOODWIN

Bibliography

Harrison, Martin. *Victorian Stained Glass.* 1980.

Sewter, A. C. *The Stained Glass of William Morris and His Circle.* 1974, 1975. 2 vols.

· · · · ·

STAINER, JOHN (1840–1901)

A cathedral organist, composer, and musicologist, John Stainer's compositions include upwards of fifty anthems, several cathedral services, oratorios, cantatas, hymn tunes, and organ pieces. His best-known work is *The Crucifixion* (1887), an extended meditation on the Passion of Christ for soloists and choir with organ. His scholarly editions and writings include *Music of the Bible* (1879), *Dufay and His Contemporaries* (1898), *Early Bodleian Music* (1901), and, with William Alexander Barrett (1834–1891), *A Dictionary of Musical Terms* (1876).

Stainer was a boy chorister at St. Paul's Cathedral. In 1856 he became organist of the Church and College of St. Michael in Tenbury whose founder, Frederick Ouseley (1825–1889), greatly influenced his scholarly predilections. He became organist of Magdalen College, Oxford, in 1859 and obtained the degrees of B.Mus. (1860), B.A. (1864), D.Mus. (1865), and M.A. (1866). In 1872 he became organist of St. Paul's Cathedral and was knighted on his retirement in 1888. In 1889 he succeeded Ouseley as professor of music at Oxford.

Stainer was modest about his abilities as a composer, and his reputation suffered unduly from the extreme anti-Victorian reaction earlier in this century. Even so, his best works—e.g., the anthems "I saw the Lord" (1858), "Drop down, ye heavens" (1866), and the Evening Service (No. 3) in B-flat—are among the most estimable in the cathedral repertory. He effected significant improvements in music both at St. Paul's and Oxford.

WILLIAM J. GATENS

Bibliography

Charlton, Peter. *John Stainer and the Musical Life of Victorian Britain.* 1984.

Edwards, Frederick George. "John Stainer." *The Musical Times,* vol. 42, pp. 297–309.

Gatens, William J. *Victorian Cathedral Music in Theory and Practice.* 1986.

· · · · ·

(1916, with Cecil Forsyth), and *Interludes: Records and Reflections* (1922).

Recent years have seen a marked renewal of interest in Stanford's music, but he is best remembered as a teacher. Among his most prominent pupils were Ralph Vaughan Williams, Gustav Holst, John Ireland, Herbert Howells, and Frank Bridge.

JOE K. LAW

Bibliography

Fuller-Maitland, J. A. *The Music of Parry and Stanford.* 1934.

Howes, Frank. *The English Musical Renaissance.* 1966.

Norris, Gerald. *Stanford, the Cambridge Jubilee, and Tchaikovsky.* 1980.

· · · · ·

STANFORD, CHARLES VILLIERS (1852-1924)

Composer, teacher, conductor, and writer, Charles Villiers Stanford was professor of composition at the Royal College of Music (1883-1924) and at Cambridge (1887-1924). He was knighted in 1902.

After early training in his native Dublin, he studied at Queen's College, Cambridge (1870-1874), and then for two years in Leipzig (with Carl Reinicke) and Berlin (with Friedrich Kiel). In addition to teaching at Cambridge and the Royal College of Music, Stanford conducted the London Bach Choir (1885-1902) and the Leeds Triennial Festival (1901-1910).

A prolific composer, Stanford produced nine completed operas, seven symphonies, three piano concertos, and six Irish rhapsodies. He also composed many choral pieces, part songs, and solo songs, including arrangements of Irish songs. His best-known large works are *The Revenge* (1886), *Songs of the Sea* (1904), and *Songs of the Fleet* (1910), all for chorus and orchestra. Several of his anthems and services are still in frequent use. Among his books are *Musical Composition* (1911), *Brahms* (1912), *A History of Music*

STANLEY, HENRY MORTON (1841-1904)

As an explorer, journalist, and writer, Henry Morton Stanley became an internationally acclaimed figure. He is best remembered for remarking, "Dr. Livingston, I presume," upon finding the famous Scottish missionary-explorer in 1871. Stanley was knighted in 1899.

Born John Rowlands in the Welsh town of Denbigh, the future explorer spent his early years in a workshop, from which he escaped at fifteen. He worked his way to New Orleans where he met a merchant, Henry Morton Stanley, who became his foster father and whose name he acquired. After serving on both sides during the American Civil War, he covered Indian wars in the West as a newspaper correspondent. In 1869 the New York *Herald* commissioned him to find **David Livingston**, who was believed lost in Central Africa. Late in life he retired to England, married Dorothy Tennant, and served briefly in Parliament.

The search for Livingston was the turning point in his life. After finding him at Ujiji, a village on Lake Tanganyika, Stanley spent the rest of his career as an African explorer. In three subsequent expeditions, he crossed Africa from east to west (1874–1877), worked to open the Congo River Basin (1879–1885), and commanded a mission to relieve Emin Pasha, the governor of the Sudan province of Equatoria (1887–1889).

Stanley's accomplishments were significant. He mapped Lake Victoria and Lake Tanganyika and settled the question of the Nile River's source. By signing treaties, surveying, building roads, and establishing trading posts, he was instrumental in opening the Congo Basin area to the West. Through his explorations, lecturing, and vivid writing he did more than anyone else to introduce much of Central Africa to the world's knowledge.

Judgments about Stanley and his work, however, varied during his lifetime as they have since his death. Much of the criticism concerns his methods. His expeditions were larger and better financed than those of other African explorers. He displayed a single-minded discipline and could be ruthless; he was a hard taskmaster compared to Livingston (and critics frequently made the comparison). If at times he was sympathetic, even respectful, toward African people and their leaders, at other times he was unyielding. He relied heavily on his armed strength. Furthermore, some consider him one of the enablers of the Western scramble to partition Africa. Nevertheless, his leadership, personal courage, and contributions to geographical knowledge and to exciting the Western imagination about Central Africa are generally recognized. He ranks as one of the greatest of that breed of explorers who, for better or worse, penetrated Africa in the nineteenth century.

JAMES D. STARTT

Bibliography

Bennett, Norman R., ed. *Stanley's Dispatches to the New York Herald, 1871–1872, 1874–1877.* 1970.

Farwell, Byron. *The Man Who Presumed.* 1957.

Hird, Frank. *H. M. Stanley: The Authorized Life.* 1935.

Maurice, Albert, ed. *H. M. Stanley: Unpublished Letters.* 1957.

Stanley, Lady Dorothy, ed. *The Autobiography of Sir Henry Morton Stanley.* 1909.

Stanley, Henry M. *In Darkest Africa.* 1890.

——. *Through the Dark Continent.* 2 vols., 1878.

Stanley, Richard and Alan Neame, eds. *The Exploration Diaries of H. M. Stanley.* 1961.

· · · · ·

STATISTICS

Queen Victoria's reign began during a period of unprecedented interest in economic and demographic data. In 1832 the Board of Trade created a Statistical Department to organize and publish information. Civil registration of births, marriages, and deaths began in 1837. Statistical societies were established in London and other cities with the intent of creating a science of society by collecting information from which (as in the phsycial sciences) general laws could be deduced. Toward the century's end an attention to theory advanced the development of statistics as a mathematical science.

British rulers ever since the Norman conquest had intermittently collected information in response to immediate practical problems. *Natural and Political Observations on the Bills of Mortality* (1662) seems to be the earliest attempt to draw inferences from the numbers that were available. In the second half of the eighteenth century the life insurance business began to develop actuarial methods. The decennial census—at first a very crude instrument—was inaugurated in 1801. Collections of data were valued for their economic information and because numbers gave support to political causes. The report of criminal statistics begun in 1810, for example, was related to the campaign to reduce the number of capital offenses.

Most members of the Statistical Society of London, established in 1834, were liberal reformers. The founders included Poor Law commissioner **Nassau Senior**, the radical **Francis Place**, the mathematician **Charles Babbage**, and the aging Thomas Malthus. The society's stated purpose was to establish statistics as a separate science of accumulating and arranging facts, to deduce from them general principles that affect human life (excluding all opinion and theory), and to focus on the social and moral condition of the wage-earning classes. Later in the decade, the society began to attract younger members whose careers in insurance or the civil service gave them some sophistication in handling numbers and used its political contacts to improve governmental information gathering. When civil registration of deaths was made compulsory in 1837, for example, a standardized form provided columns for sex, age, profession, and cause of death. The census of 1841 was the first to use a printed return and ask detailed questions about age and occupation.

The goal of early enthusiasts was often overtly political. The Manchester Statistical Society conducted a major survey of the working population which included questions on schooling and books but neglected to ask about income. Miserable living conditions could therefore be correlated with lack of education—but not with low wages. Early papers of the London Statistical Society asked interesting questions but drew conclusions on wholly inadequate evidence: one calculated the influence of occupation on health from gross mortality figures without inquiring into the number of workers in each occupation.

Among the new members drawn into the London Statistical Society in 1839 was William Farr (1807-1883), a medical practitioner who was to serve for forty years in the Registrar General's Office and become the most accomplished practical statistician of the period. In addition to valuable work in epidemiology and other aspects of public health, Farr created standardized classifications to report occupation on the census form and cause of death on the registry of vital statistics. Furthermore, his work made the number of deaths per thousand of population a standard method for comparing various areas or occupational groups.

In statistical theory, Britain lagged behind the Continent until the closing decades of the century, when important contributions were made by two eugenicists. **Francis Galton** (1822-1911) developed the concept of regression analysis and provided the means to cope with problems involving more than one variable. Karl Pearson (1837-1936) created the standard formula for the coefficient of correlation. By 1900 most government departments contained a division to generate and analyze statistical returns, and professional

education in the field was provided by the London School of Economics.

SALLY MITCHELL

Bibliography

Annals of the Royal Statistical Society, 1834-1934. 1934.

Cullen, Michael J. The Statistical Movement in Early Victorian Britain: The Foundations of Empirical Social Research. 1975.

Eyler, John M. Victorian Social Medicine: The Ideas and Methods of William Farr. 1979.

Kendall, M. G. and A. G. Doig. Bibliography of Statistical Literature Pre-1940. 1986.

MacKenzie, Donald A. Statistics in Britain, 1865-1930: The Social Construction of Scientific Knowledge. 1981.

· · · · ·

STEAD, WILLIAM THOMAS (1849-1912)

During the 1880s, W. T. Stead enlivened the Pall Mall Gazette with techniques that came to be called "the new journalism," making it into one of England's most controversial and influential papers. A man of vast energy, strong moral convictions, and a gift for self-promotion, he edited the Darlington Northern Echo (1871-1880), the Pall Mall Gazette (1883-1889), and the monthly Review of Reviews (1890-1912), promoting such causes as social purity, women's suffrage, universal military service (for both women and men), world peace, the Salvation Army, antivivisection, and spiritualism. His published works include a translation of the Oberammergau Passion Play (1891), If Christ Came to Chicago! (1894), and various "spirit writings" transmitted from those "beyond the veil."

The son of a Congregational minister, Stead was educated primarily by his father and apprenticed to a merchant at age fourteen. At twenty-two he was made editor of the Darlington Northern Echo and in 1880 became assistant to John Morley at the Pall Mall Gazette. When Morley was elected to Parliament in 1883, Stead succeeded him as editor.

Under Stead, the *Pall Mall Gazette* moved steadily in the direction of making news, rather than simply reporting speeches and events. The new journalism featured banner headlines; shorter paragraphs and a more readable style, with crossheads to break up long columns; illustrations, diagrams, and maps; interviews and human interest stories; and signed articles. Most of these devices were already used by the American or sensational press; Stead put them together in a respectable paper. As an interviewer, he learned how to pressure subjects and get answers—and also how to develop sources. He remarked in the *Contemporary Review* (November 1886) that "it is better to be intimate with the confidant of a Minister than to be merely on friendly terms with the Minister himself."

Stead's major tool for influencing government and public opinion was the mounting of campaigns. He kept a subject in the public eye by writing leaders that used investigative material and then, over the following weeks, pursuing the topic in news stories, reports of speeches, letters to the editor, and human interest features. The most famous of these campaigns was the series on juvenile prostitution published in 1883 under the title "The Maiden Tribute of Modern Babylon." Others included agitations for a stronger navy in 1884 and against police brutality in response to Bloody Sunday.

Leaving the *Pall Mall Gazette* at the end of 1889, Stead launched the *Review of Reviews*, a sixpenny monthly which printed a review of the news (written with Stead's own inimitable bias), articles on his current crusades, a "Character Sketch" of a prominent personality, summaries of leading articles in major British and foreign periodicals, and a highly condensed version of a new novel.

Stead's moral fervor led him into campaigns that often seem contradictory. He was a close friend of Cecil Rhodes, wrote an interview with General Charles Gordon that perhaps made possible the expedition to Khartoum, and supported the Jameson Raid. In 1899, however, he founded a Stop the War Committee and was reviled as pro-Boer. In the latter years of his life he promoted Anglo-American reunion, became increasingly involved with spiritualism, and worked for arms limitation. In March 1912 he received a cable-gram inviting him to share the platform at a Carnegie Hall peace crusade with President Taft, William Jennings Bryan, and Booker T. Washington, and booked passage on the *Titanic*. Those who pulled away from the ship in the final lifeboats reported seeing him standing upright on the deck in an attitude of prayer.

Stead's support of women's rights may have been fueled by the overspill of his intense (and, according to Havelock Ellis, rigidly repressed) sexual energy. A good friend of Josephine Butler and Millicent Garrett Fawcett, he also served as Annie Besant's coeditor for a few weeks to get the *Link* established, corresponded with Olive Schreiner, promoted Sarah Grand's *The Heavenly Twins* by condensing it in the *Review of Reviews*, and was proud to be the first editor in England to engage women on exactly the same pay and terms as men. Yet it is also evident that the "Maiden Tribute" investigation served his own prurient interests and that he habitually touched and kissed women who came into his office. His reputation has also suffered from his ignorance—or deliberate neglect—of the unwritten laws of politics, journalism, dress, and gentlemanly behavior, and from the dedication of fellow spiritualists who continued to publish his "works"—communicated through various mediums—for several decades after his death.

Before taking the post at *Pall Mall Gazette* Stead wrote in his diary of the possibility it offered him to become "the most powerful man in England." His prodigious energy, rigid moralism, and personal ambition helped turn the press in directions that were imitated by many editors in the generations that followed.

SALLY MITCHELL

Bibliography

Baylen, Joseph O. "W. T. Stead and the 'New Journalism.'" *Emory University Quarterly*, vol. 21, pp. 1–13.

———. "W. T. Stead as Publisher and Editor of the *Review of Reviews*." *Victorian Periodicals Review*, vol. 12, pp. 70–83.

Robson, Ann. "The Significance of 'The Maiden Tribute of Modern Babylon.'" *Victorian Periodicals Newsletter*, vol. 11, pp. 51–57.

Schults, Raymond L. *Crusader in Babylon: W. T. Stead and the "Pall Mall Gazette."* 1972.

Stead, Estelle W. *My Father.* 1913.

Whyte, Frederic. *The Life of W. T. Stead.* 1925; rpt. 1971. 2 vols.

See also WHITE SLAVE TRADE

· · · · ·

STEAM ENGINE

When Queen Victoria came to the throne in 1837, the steam engine as pioneered by Thomas Newcomen for pumping water out of deep mines had already been established for over a hundred years. Improved by James Watt, Richard Trevithick, and other engineers, it had been widely adopted to provide rotary action in many industrial processes. From the 1820s it made an indispensable contribution to the success of the **railways** and emerged as the innovation that was to transform marine transport.

The Victorian period thus coincided with the apotheosis of the steam engine. In the second half of the nineteenth century steam became the dominant source of power in industrial production, coal and metal mining, the public services, and both land and sea transport. By the end of the century other sources of power such as the internal combustion engine and electricity had begun to challenge the steam engine's supremacy, but these innovations made more initial progress in America and in continental Europe, where steam technology was less strongly entrenched than it was in Britain. In a very real sense, therefore, the Victorian period was the age of steam.

The early steam engines had been "atmospheric" engines: that is, their power stroke relied on the weight of the atmosphere when steam was condensed below the piston in a vertical cylinder to produce a partial vacuum. They had also been cumbersome, with the piston connected to a heavy swinging beam which actuated the pumping rods. The application of steam's expansive energy, and then of high-pressure steam, combined with improved machine making and the use of metal throughout, made more compact units possible. Steam engines assumed a remarkable variety of forms, including arrangements with cylinders placed horizontally or in the "inverted vertical" form (that is, with the piston driving downwards rather than upwards). Compactness also gave a capacity for mobility and led thus to the development of the steam locomotive.

The possibility of using high-pressure steam at several stages as the pressure fell in order to increase the engine's power led to the development of "compound" engines, with high- and low-pressure cylinders, and to triple- and quadruple-expansion engines. Some very large steam engines were built to drive the machines in cotton mills and iron rolling mills, with engines of 2,000 horsepower becoming common by the century's end. The invention of the steam turbine by Charles Parsons (1884) marked a significant new departure in steam technology (it passed the steam through a series of blades to provide direct rotary action) which, because it came to be widely used in the generation of electricity and in marine engines, displaced the reciprocating steam engine from many applications in the twentieth century. Despite continued technical improvement with high-speed forced-lubrication and "uniflow" designs (in which the steam was exhausted through ports in the middle of the horizontal cylinder to avoid repeated heating and cooling of the valves), the reciprocating steam engine steadily lost ground to its rivals and never again enjoyed the supremacy it had during the Victorian period.

R. A. BUCHANAN

Bibliography

Buchanan, R. A. and George Watkins. *The Industrial Archaeology of the Stationary Steam Engine.* 1976.

Cardwell, Donald S. L. *From Watt to Clausius: The Rise of Thermodynamics in the Early Industrial Age.* 1971.

Dickinson, Henry W. *A Short History of the Steam Engine.* 2d ed., 1963.

Watkins, George. *The Stationary Steam Engine.* 1968.

· · · · ·

STEPHEN, LESLIE
(1832-1904)

Editor, biographer, literary critic, Alpinist, and agnostic, Leslie Stephen reflects two dominant characteristics of the age—evangelicalism and rationalism. A respected "higher" journalist in his day, his major achievements remain his literary and agnostic essays, his studies in the history of ideas, and the *Dictionary of National Biography*.

The son of James and Jane Venn Stephen, he was educated at Eton, King's College, London, and Trinity Hall, Cambridge, where he was an ordained fellow and tutor (1855-1864). In the early 1860s he lost his faith, resigned his tutorship, and began a career in London journalism. In 1865 he was elected president of the Alpine Club; he later edited the *Alpine Journal* (1868-1872) and published a set of mountaineering essays. Stephen edited the *Cornhill Magazine* (1871-1882), to which he contributed the literary studies collected in *Hours in a Library* (rev. ed., 1892). For George Smith, he edited (1882-1891) the *Dictionary of National Biography*, writing 378 lives himself. After 1880 he devoted much time to biography: *Life of Henry Fawcett* (1885), *The Life of Sir James Fitzjames Stephen* (1895), *Studies of a Biographer* (1898-1902), and, for Morley's *English Men of Letters*, *Samuel Johnson* (1878), *Alexander Pope* (1880), *Swift* (1882), *George Eliot* (1902), and *Hobbes* (1904).

Stephen's *Essays on Freethinking and Plainspeaking* (1873) and *An Agnostic's Apology* (1893) claim that the age was essentially post-Christian. The *Science of Ethics* (1882) attempts to establish a Darwinian basis for morality. His intellectual histories, *History of English Thought in the Eighteenth Century* (1876) and *The English Utilitarians* (1900), pioneer the concept of social change as the basis for intellectual change.

Stephen married twice: Harriet Marian, Thackeray's youngest daughter, and Julia Jackson Duckworth. The second marriage produced, notably, Virginia Woolf and Vanessa Bell.

MARK REGER

Bibliography

Annan, Noel. *Leslie Stephen: The Godless Victorian.* 1984.

Maitland, Frederic W. *The Life and Letters of Leslie Stephen.* 1906.

. . . . .

STEVENSON, ROBERT LOUIS
(1850-1894)

Novelist, short story writer, poet, and essayist, Robert Louis Stevenson was a prolific and versatile writer of the late Victorian period. His work includes travelogues, personal and literary essays collected in *Virginibus Puerisque* (1881), adventure stories such as *Treasure Island* (1883), Gothic horror stories such as "The Body Snatcher" (1884), the children's poems of *A Child's Garden of Verses* (1885), historical romances including *Kidnapped* (1886) and *The Black Arrow* (1888), and psychological studies of human nature. Stevenson's devotion to his craft won him the early admiration of such writers as William Ernest Henley and Henry James. After the popular success of *The Strange Case of Dr. Jekyll and Mr. Hyde* (1886), Stevenson became one of the celebrated writers of his time.

Born in Edinburgh and captivated by Scottish history all of his life, Stevenson lived mostly abroad because of his poor health. In France, in 1876, he met Fanny Vandegrift Osbourne (1840-1914), a married woman with two children, whom (after her divorce) he married in California in 1880. After further travels in Europe and America, Stevenson settled in the South Pacific, where his Samoan neighbors called him "Tusitala," or tale teller.

After *Treasure Island*, which he called an adventure novel because it subordinates character to incident, Stevenson combined adventure with history to explore the conflicts in Scotland between Highlander and Lowlander, Jacobite and Whig. The two protagonists of *Kidnapped* and its sequel, *David Balfour* (1893; British title: *Catriona*) become attached to each other yet retain separate values. *Jekyll and Hyde*, a brilliantly written mystery, remains Stevenson's most celebrated portrait of the divided personality, but the theme is developed more fully in *The Master of Ballantrae* (1889), a story of opposition between two brothers, told by a narrator with divided feelings. *The Ebb-Tide* (1894), a powerful late novella, explores the darkness of human nature and the evil consequences arising from a lack of inner restraint with a realism that anticipates Joseph Conrad.

Usually associated with the late Victorian revival of Gothic and romance, Stevenson was a disciplined artist who strongly defended the power of illusion and imagination, and who insisted that fiction should render the truths that make life significant, as opposed to the trivial or mundane. His finely wrought stories made an important contribution to the development of modern English fiction.

RICHARD BENVENUTO

Bibliography

Balfour, Graham. *The Life of Robert Louis Stevenson.* 1901.

Calder, Jenni. *Robert Louis Stevenson: A Life Study.* 1980.

Colvin, Sidney, ed. *The Letters of Robert Louis Stevenson.* 1911. 4 vols.

Eigner, Edwin. *Robert Louis Stevenson and the Romantic Tradition.* 1966.

Furnas, Joseph C. *Voyage to Windward: The Life of R. L. Stevenson.* 1951.

Kiely, Robert. *Robert Louis Stevenson and the Fiction of Adventure.* 1964.

Morris, David. *Robert Louis Stevenson and the Scottish Highlanders.* 1929.

Smith, Janet Adam, ed. *Robert Louis Stevenson: Collected Poems.* 2d ed., 1971.

Swearingen, Roger. *The Prose Writings of Robert Louis Stevenson: A Guide.* 1980.

· · · · ·

STILLMAN, MARIE SPARTALI (1844-1927)

Marie Spartali Stillman was a celebrated Pre-Raphaelite beauty who became a successful painter in her own right.

Daughter of Michael Spartali, a wealthy and cultured merchant who served as Greek con-

sul-general in London, she and her sister captivated artists of the 1860s with their classical beauty. Stillman was painted by D. G. Rossetti (*A Vision of Fiammetta*) and by Edward Burne-Jones (*Danae and the Brazen Tower*), and photographed by Julia Margaret Cameron. In 1871 she married William James Stillman, former American consul in Rome and Crete, founder of the art journal *The Crayon*, and foreign correspondent for the *Times*. Despite the responsibilities of raising a large family, Stillman continued to paint and to maintain friendships in artistic circles.

After receiving art lessons at home, Stillman persuaded Ford Madox Brown to take her on as a student in 1864. She began to show her watercolors in 1867 at the Dudley Gallery; she also exhibited at the Royal Academy, the Grosvenor, the New Gallery, and at several galleries in the United States. Working primarily in small-scale watercolors, she shows Rossetti's influence in choosing medieval subjects, such as *Sir Tristram and La Belle Iseult* (1873) and *The Pilgrim Folk* (1914), a Dantean scene displayed with a sonnet from *La Vita Nuova*. Stillman also did solitary female figures, such as *Lady Prays—Desire* (1867); late in her career, she produced some lovely landscapes, including *Kelmscott Manor* (1905).

ROBIN SHEETS

Bibliography

Christian, John. "Marie Spartali: Pre-Raphaelite Beauty." *Antique Collector*, vol. 55, pp. 42–47.

Elzea, Rowland. *The Samuel and Mary R. Bancroft, Jr. and Related Pre-Raphaelite Collections.* 1984.

Ormond, Richard. "A Pre-Raphaelite Beauty." *Country Life*, vol. 138, pp. 1780–1781.

Rossetti, William Michael. "English Painters of the Present Day." *Portfolio*, vol. 1, pp. 117–118.

· · · · ·

STOKER, BRAM (1847-1914)

Although Bram Stoker wrote other novels of suspense and terror, including *The Jewel of Seven Stars* (1903), *The Lady of the Shroud*

(1909), and *The Lair of the White Worm* (1911), and created a collection of stories entitled *Dracula's Guest* (1914), his literary fame rests upon a single Gothic novel: *Dracula* (1897).

Stoker was born in Dublin. Graduating from Trinity College, he spent time as an Irish civil servant and as drama critic and editor for the *Dublin Mail.* He also devoted twenty-eight years of his life to managing Henry Irving's acting career, until Irving died in 1904.

Stoker's Count Dracula builds upon the vampire lore of literary forerunners such as Lord Ruthven in Polidori's *The Vampyre* (1819), Sir Francis Varney in Prest's or Rymer's *Varney the Vampyre* (1847), and Carmilla in Le Fanu's novella (1872). However, as critics point out, Stoker's vampire also draws from romantic myth, Transylvanian folklore, and historial fact. With first-person letters and journals, carefully structured suspense, and powerful scenes of struggle between Dracula and his opponents (Van Helsing and the Harkers), this novel is the most powerful literary portrayal of vampirism in Victorian and modern times. *Dracula* ushers in the troops of vampires in film, stage, and fiction, all of whom pale in comparison with the original.

Some scholars explain Dracula's popularity with the Victorian audience as a function of sociopsychological factors such as repressed sexuality, the inversion of Christianity, and the victory of middle-class values over the aristocratic, but the impact of *Dracula* persists because of its elegant eroticism and psychological terror.

BETTE B. ROBERTS

Bibliography

Ludlam, Harry. *A Biography of Dracula: The Life Story of Bram Stoker.* 1962.

McNally, Raymond and Radu Florescu. *In Search of Dracula.* 1972.

Ronay, Gabriel. *The Truth About Dracula.* 1974.

Twitchell, James B. *The Living Dead: A Study of the Vampire in Romantic Literature.* 1981.

Wolf, Leonard. *A Dream of Dracula: In Search of the Living Dead.* 1972.

· · · · ·

STONE, ELIZABETH WHEELER (1803–1858?)

Novelist Elizabeth Wheeler Stone was born in Manchester. She was the daughter of John and Mary Wheeler; John Wheeler was publisher of the *Manchester Chronicle.* Her novels suggest that she married in the 1830s and lived for some period in London. Her brother James Wheeler published a *History* of Manchester (1836) and edited an anthology *Manchester Poetry* (1838) which influenced her.

Stone's earliest published work is *The Art of Needle-Work* (1840), which anticipates her interest in milliners. *William Langshawe, the Cotton Lord* (1842) and *The Young Milliner* (1843) are important **social problem novels.** The first deals with captains of industry; the second records the plight of a young seamstress. Stone also published a three-volume novel *Miss Pen and Her Niece* (1843), dealing with the early eighteenth century. Included in the third volume is the novella *Sir Eustace de Lucie*, which derives from Wordsworth's poem *The Horn of Egremont Castle* (1807). Later works include *Mr. Dalton's Legatee* (1850) and *God's Acre* (1858), the latter an investigation of churchyard monuments.

JOSEPH KESTNER

Bibliography

Kestner, Joseph. "A Manchester Woman's Wordsworth: Elizabeth Stone and *The Horn of Egremont Castle." Wordsworth Circle,* vol. 14, pp. 107–108.

———. *Protest and Reform: The British Social Narrative by Women, 1827–1867.* 1985.

· · · · ·

STREET, GEORGE EDMUND (1824–1881)

London's Law Courts building (1866–1880) is the monument to George Edmund Street, the mid-Victorian architect most committed to the structure and grandeur of the Gothic style. With concern for polychromy, truth to materials, craftsmanship, and an awareness of spatial volumes, Street remade the forms and ideals of the medieval past for the Victorian world.

Street developed an enthusiasm for medieval architecture while growing up in Essex. Appointed architect to the diocese of Oxford in 1850, he became active in the Ecclesiological Society and considered forming an architectural society similar to the Pre-Raphaelite Brotherhood. From 1850 until his death he traveled to the Continent every year but two to study Gothic architecture.

In 1853 Street produced designs for the Theological College at Cuddesdon and for the East Grinstead Sisterhood. Two years later he competed to design Lille Cathedral and won second place to William Burges, as he did also in the competiton for the Crimean Memorial Chapel in Constantinople in the same year. That commission, however, was subsequently given to Street (1857). St. James the Less, Westminster (1858) illustrates Street's ability to bring Continental medieval influences into British design. *The Ecclesiologist* (vol. 19, 1861) applauded St. James as more than the repetition of medieval forms: each part was clearly part of a systematic construction, and brick was used to integrate the building into London's fabric.

Street entered two competitions in 1866, for a new National Gallery and for the Law Courts. The former amounted to little, but the latter turned out to be the crowning achievement of his career. A great deal of imagination is evident in the structure's design, particularly in the exteriors that reveal numerous carvings, decorations, and moldings. Although the building's medieval design was somewhat out of fashion by the time it officially opened in 1882, there is now a growing appreciation of Street's ability to create an enormous structure that blends well with its surroundings.

FLOYD W. MARTIN

Bibliography

Brownlee, David. *The Law Courts: The Architecture of George Edmund Street*. 1984.

Goodhart-Rendel, H. S. *George Edmund Street*. 1953; rpt. 1983.

King, Georgiana Goddard, ed. *George Edmund Street: Unpublished Notes and Reprinted Papers*. 1916.

Street, Arthur Edmund. *Memoir of George Edmund Street, R.A., 1824-1881*. 1888.

Street, George Edmund. *Brick and Marble in the Middle Ages: Notes of a Tour in the North of Italy*. 1855.

Summerson, John. *Victorian Architecture: Four Studies in Evaluation*. 1970.

See also GOTHIC REVIVAL

. . . . .

STREET MUSIC

The street music of Victorian England derived from a long tradition, but acquired its own peculiar character. Among the most venerable forms were the cries of itinerant vendors; these could become quite elaborate, drawing on alternation between speaking and singing or on harmonic by-play between several different singers. Leigh Hunt praises the street cries of Chelsea in the 1830s, referring to a tradition that they had been composed by Purcell. The waits—Christmas music performed by street musicians in the hope of gratuities—also thrived, inspiring Pierce Egan Jr.'s Dickensian fable (*The Waits*, 1857).

Street music, however, was not just an incidental or seasonal occupation. Henry Mayhew estimates that there were 1,000 instrumentalists, 50 "Ethiopian serenaders" (mostly whites made up as blacks), and 250 balladeers at work in London. He also divides street musicians into "the skilful and the blind," the latter belonging "generally to the rudest class of performers" and living on a level of desperation that he conveys vividly. Soloists might perform on the hurdy-gurdy, the violin, the bagpipe, the guitar, the Irish pipes, or the East Indian tom-tom. Ethnic origin varied almost as much as instruments.

Street balladeers had their own specialized niche. Their ballads or broadsides were sung—in streets or public houses—so that they might be sold. The usual price was a halfpenny, the buyer almost always one of the poor. Subjects included politics, sex, crime, and the royal family. This emphasis on current events distinguishes broadsides from the more traditional eighteenth-century chapbooks; broadsides anticipate the tabloid newspapers which replaced them. A popular broadside could sell 2.5 million copies.

After the 1830s, street music seems to have become more and more exclusively identified with working-class culture. William Harvey gives a nostalgic account of street music early in the century, before middle-class musical life had all gone indoors to the concert hall. In *Dombey and Son* (1848), itinerant musicians hope to be bought off before Dombey's wedding. An 1864 campaign against street music resulted in the Metropolitan Police Act of the same year, establishing grounds—though not always practical grounds—for prosecution of musicians. Carlyle, Tennyson, and Babbage were among those supporting the bill; in his last account of street music, even Mayhew caught the tone of the times, noting that "the humbler and more filthy the passenger," the great the noisemaking privilege.

RICHARD MAXWELL

Bibliography

Harvey, William. *London Scenes and London People.* 1863.

Mayhew, Henry. *London Characters.* 1870.

———. *London Labour and the London Poor.* 1861–1862. 4 vols.

Neuberg, Victor. "The Literature of the Streets." In H. J. Dyos and Michael Wolff, eds., *The Victorian City.* 1973.

Scholes, Percy and Peter Gammond. "Street Music." In Denis Arnold, ed., *The New Oxford Companion to Music.* 1983.

· · · · ·

STREET TRADERS

In the mid-nineteenth century there were still many nonshop outlets—including fairs, markets, and hawkers—for perishable produce and small household goods. Itinerant hawkers varied in prosperity. The lowest were the beggars who sold pins, thread, and other such items. The "cheap jack," at the other extreme, was an entrepreneur who traveled around with a horse and cart, usually dealing in hardware and crockery. The most famous street traders were London's costermongers, who not only filled an important need by selling produce and foodstuffs at the hours and localities accessible to working people, but also developed a colorful culture distinctly their own.

Henry Mayhew's edited oral histories provide many examples of the puff and patter used by hawkers, who peddled virtually anything for which a market could be generated: foodstuffs, tinware, birds, cutlery, fireworks, patent medicines, toys, flypaper, tobacco, coal, printed material, and so forth. Some goods were bought largely from motives of charity. Old women sold tape and cotton, blind people peddled bootlaces, disabled tailors sold needles. Flower girls—who tended to be very young, ragged, and barefoot—went to Covent Garden early in the morning and made up bunches from flowers they bought or found discarded. Their profits might come to sixpence a day.

Stalls and barrows required a moderate capital and some permanence. The largest street markets took place on Saturday night and Sunday morning, when working people had their pay and time to spend it. In some areas hundreds of stalls sold food for Sunday dinner and all varieties of new and second-hand merchandise. Sellers of prepared foods were patronized by working people who had no wife at home to cook (or no lodging with cooking facilities). Wares included coffee, sandwiches, pea soup, fried fish, baked potatoes, pastries, sweets, hot eels, meat pies, and luxuries such as pineapples and ices.

The largest class of London street sellers were the costermongers, who resold fish, fruit, and vegetables from the wholesale markets such as Billingsgate and Covent Garden. According to Mayhew, some 30,000 men, women, and children belonged to the class. Some sold from stationary stalls, while others—using handbarrows or donkey carts—made rounds in suburban neighborhoods poorly served by shops. Known by their flashy clothing and their distinctive slang, costermongers formed cohesive family clans, with children often selling on their own from the age of seven or so. Their earnings were irregular—depending on season and chance—but might run up to 30 shillings a week, somewhat above average for the working class.

JOHN REYNOLDS

Bibliography

Mayhew, Henry. *London Labour and the London Poor*, vol. 1, 1851.

. . . . .

STRETTON, HESBA (1832-1911)

Hesba Stretton was the pseudonym of Sarah Smith, an evangelical writer whose lifelong concern for the conditions of slum children was demonstrated by her involvement in founding the London Society for the Prevention of Cruelty to Children (1884) and by the themes and settings of her juvenile tract fiction.

Her fifth children's book, *Jessica's First Prayer*, was published in 1867 by the Religious Tract Society. By her death in 1911, over one and a half million copies had been sold. It was translated into a variety of Asian and African languages for the use of missionaries, as well as into every European language and into Braille. The story, with its emphasis on self-improvement and on the evangelical conversion of adults by an innocent waif, was enormously appealing to the Victorians.

Altogether Stretton wrote over sixty stories, many of which appeared in such periodicals as *All the Year Round* (edited by Dickens), *Leisure Hour, Sunday at Home,* and *The Day of Rest.* Her most popular books after *Jessica* were *Little Meg's Children* (1868) and *Alone in London* (1869). Together with *Jessica,* they established the pattern for the street arab genre, opening whole new vistas for Victorian tract writers.

Although she was principally interested in her adult novels, which included *David Lloyd's Last Will* (1869) and *The Doctor's Dilemma* (1872), and began to write tract fiction only to supplement her income, the tracts, far more than the adult novels, demonstrate Stretton's commitment to reform and her literary skill.

JILL SHEFRIN

Bibliography

Bratton, J. S. "Hesba Stretton's Journalism." *Victorian Periodicals Review*, vol. 21, pp. 60-70.

———. *The Impact of Victorian Children's Fiction.* 1981.

Cutt, Margaret Nancy. *Ministering Angels: A Study of Nineteenth-Century Evangelical Writing for Children.* 1979.

Mortimer, Margaret. Preface to *Little Meg's Children,* by Sarah Smith. 1970.

Salway, Lance. "Pathetic Simplicity: An Introduction to Hesba Stretton and Her Books for Children." *Signal,* vol. 1, pp. 20-28.

. . . . .

STRIKES

Before the industrial revolution, strikes in Britain were infrequent and limited to small and specialized groups of workers. Strikes grew in frequency with the industrial revolution, and in the nineteenth century became, in contrast to the riot of premodern times, the dominant form of British social conflict. Although strikes became intermeshed with political objectives during the Chartist era, they were before 1850 primarily defensive. After 1850 strikes were utilized with greater success both to advance as well as to defend the interests of the working class.

The Combination Acts of 1799-1800 outlawed both trade unions and strikes and allowed justices of the peace to deal out summary imprisonment. Unions were driven underground, and workers occasionally turned to violent forms of resistance such as machine breaking, incendiarism, and assault. Despite their illegality, however, open strikes did take place. London carpenters in 1810 successfully withheld their labor for five weeks and won a wage increase of four shillings a week. Glasgow cotton weavers had less success in 1812; although 40,000 workers struck for six weeks, they gave in when their leaders were imprisoned. The 14,000 stocking makers in Leicester who struck in 1819 after their employers cut wages received wide public support. Even the lord lieutenant of the county subscribed to the strike fund, and the "exemplary" conduct of the workers helped to win sympathy. Not all strikes were so pacific. When seamen in England's northern ports struck in 1815 for improved wages and larger crews, naval vessels, 500 marines and four regiments were sent to the Tyne to restore order.

A flurry of strike activity greeted the repeal of the Combination Acts in 1824. Strikes subsided, however, when amendments forbidding them were enacted in 1825 and an economic downturn induced irregular employment. The 1824–1825 legislative package allowed workers to organize but prohibited breach of contract and "molestation" or "obstruction" of employers.

Amid working-class disappointment with the limited Reform Bill of 1832, the Grand National Consolidated Trades Union, inspired by the ideas of Robert Owen, was founded in October 1833. Although the new national union suffered from inadequate leadership and an insufficiently developed base, it spawned much enthusiasm, and the enthusiasm led to premature strikes. Employers and the government responded. In Derby 1,500 mill workers were locked out by their employers for refusing to renounce the union. Early in 1834, six **agricultural laborers** were arrested in Tolpuddle, Dorsetshire, for administering a secret oath while organizing for the Friendly Society of Agricultural Labourers and were sentenced to seven years' transportation. A massive demonstration organized by the Grand National Union at London's Copenhagen Fields helped win the freedom of most of the Tolpuddle martyrs. The Grand National Union, however, did not survive the combination of its own weaknesses and the assaults of its enemies. By 1835 it had collapsed.

Agricultural workers in the 1830s were too weak and vulnerable to profit from unionization. The threat to employment posed by threshing machines spurred them to direct action. The most serious uprising, the Swing riots (1830), spread westward from Kent until twenty counties were affected. Violence was directed primarily at threshing machines, but subsequent hangings and transportation engendered widespread incendiarism and cattle maiming. Sporadic reactive violence, largely the work of a young and unattached minority, continued into the next decades.

With the collapse of the Grand National Union, the Chartist movement attracted many workers. Although there was some talk of a national insurrection to win acceptance of the charter, the only armed movement of any significance was the Newport uprising of 1839. Several thousand miners marched on Newport before being dispersed by the gunfire of a small number of soldiers. The miners' leaders, including John Frost, a former mayor, were convicted of high treason and sentenced to death, but ultimately transported instead.

William Benbow's call for a general strike won considerable support. In July 1842, after the rejection of the second Chartist petition, workers in the Lancashire centers of Ashton, Stalybridge, and Hyde met and decided to strike. By August 9, the strike had spread to Manchester. For a week, no work went on within a 50-mile radius. Original demands centered on wages, but an August 7 meeting at Mottram Moor affirmed that there would be no work until the charter was enacted. By early September, however, the strike was broken. The military occupied many Lancashire towns, and 1,500 labor leaders were imprisoned.

With the decline of Chartism, workers once again pinned their hopes on **trade unions.** In April 1844, Durham miners attempted to throw off the traditional eleven-month bond, which tied them to their jobs. Lord Londonderry responded by locking them out and hiring strikebreakers; the miners stripped the strikebreakers and threw their clothes and tools down the pit shafts. A general lockout was also employed in 1853 when spinners at some Preston mills struck for a wage increase.

In the 1850s miners and skilled workers successfully began to form national organizations. Most of the engineers' strikes were in defense of their craft rights to do certain types of work in the face of competition from semi-skilled machine tenders. The members of small craft societies in the Sheffield cutlery trades used violence against interlopers. After continuing for some time, the violence reached a crescendo in 1866 and was dubbed the "Sheffield outrages."

Other crafts attempted to win recognition of their rights by demonstrating their moderation and respectability. The conservative leaders of the London carpenters, iron founders, bricklayers, and shoemakers formed the "Junta" to work for conciliation as the path to improvement. Conciliation, however, required enlightened cooperation from employers and almost infinite patience from the rank and file. Enlightenment was not a widespread virtue of business in this era, and workers were impatient for relief.

In 1859, when London building workers campaigned for a nine-hour day, contractors informed their workers that they would employ only men who signed a document repudiating union membership. Twenty thousand refused. After six weeks, 14,000 were still on strike and receiving three shillings and six pence a week from the contributions of other workers. The strike dragged on into 1860 as malnutrition and disease took an increasing toll. By the latter part of the strike, the nine-hour issue had been displaced by the workers' concern for their right to belong to a union. The antiunion pledge was removed on February 6, 1860, and the men still resisting went back to work.

Engineering workers, through a very important strike, gained the nine-hour day in 1871. By successfully challenging the employers' absolute right to establish conditions of employment, the engineers inspired other workers. Although a gasworkers' strike for a shorter day failed in 1872, the organization and economic clout of unskilled workers were significantly abetted by legalization of the right to strike in 1875. Beckton gasworkers struck in 1889 for an eight-hour day. Their struggle succeeded and, in turn, led to the formation of the Gas Workers' and General Labourers' Union on March 12, 1889. Within a few months, nearly 30,000 gas stokers had joined. The success of the gas stokers and of the matchgirls, who had in 1888 won a strike for better conditions and wages, inspired other unskilled workers.

The greatest victory for the unskilled was the strike of London dock workers in 1889: 10,000 workers went out for four weeks and won a wage of sixpence an hour, extra pay for overtime, and the end of piecework. The London Dock Strike was one of the most significant in the history of the British trade union movement. It served as catalyst for the organization of unskilled workers, 200,000 of whom joined unions in 1890. It also set the stage for the development of a national labor movement and the conduct of both strikes and collective bargaining on the national level.

Employers counterattacked by using professional strikebreakers, and were supported by the police, the military, and the press.

Soldiers were called out during miners' strikes in 1893 and 1898. At Featherstone, Yorkshire, striking miners were fired on and several were killed.

The 1902 strike by workers on the Taff Vail Railway in South Wales led to a disastrous decision by the House of Lords holding unions responsible for damage due to a strike. This debilitating measure contributed to the development of the **Labour party**, and with labor's growing political clout the decision was revoked in 1906. A great crescendo of strike activity developed in the years immediately preceding World War I. The mounting campaign, which many hoped would lead to a national general strike, was abruptly terminated by the outbreak of the war.

BERNARD A. COOK

Bibliography

Cole, G. D. H. *A Short History of the British Working-Class Movement, 1789-1947.* 1948.

Cronin, James E. *Industrial Conflict in Modern Britain.* 1979.

———. "The Peculiar Pattern of British Strikes Since 1888." *The Journal of British Studies,* vol. 18, pp. 118-141.

Foster, John. *Class Struggle and the Industrial Revolution: Early Industrial Capitalism in Three English Towns.* 1974.

Fraser, W. Hamish. *Trade Unions and Society: The Struggle for Acceptance, 1850-1880.* 1974.

Frow, Ruth, E. and Michael Katanka. *Strikes: A Documentary History.* 1971.

Hobsbawm, Eric J. *Labour's Turning Point: 1880-1900.* 1974.

McCord, Norman. *Strikes.* 1980.

Webb, Sidney and Beatrice Webb. *The History of Trade Unionism.* 1920.

· · · · ·

SUBURBS AND PLANNED COMMUNITIES

The suburban movement represented a major change in the way Victorians and their descendants lived. Separate from but always linked socially and economically to cities, the suburbs featured homes separated from workplaces and major cultural institutions, an emphasis on family life in a healthful, even bucolic setting, and freedom from urban overcrowding and industrial defilement with their resulting social ills, including crime. "Suburbia" was a state of mind developed in the early nineteenth century by the upper middle class; by the end of Victoria's reign it had been passed down the social scale. Ideally suburbs were bourgeois utopias.

Although suburbs were formed in various ways, the usual practice was for the owner of a sizeable piece of land to contract with a builder to construct a "housing estate" with restrictions imposed by the landowner. Tenants did not own but secured long-term—often ninety-nine-year—leases, unless construction was sponsored by a freehold land society. Churches, schools, and public houses were usually encouraged to locate within the estate. Essential was the provision of **transportation**, at first by omnibuses, later by tramways and railways. Transportation determined which social classes might become suburbanites, for until the end of the century the lower middle class and especially the working classes could not afford to commute by railway, in spite of Parliament's encouragement with its Cheap Trains Act in 1883. From London, for example, those classes were channeled to the northeast by the availability of workingmen's fares not to be found on railways leading west.

The ideal suburban house was a freestanding villa of which architect John Nash's at Park Villages (1824) on the edge of London's Regent's Park was the prototype. Over the years the favored architectural style varied from Gothic revival and Italianate to Queen Anne and Arts and Crafts. Preferably the house had a pastoral site on extensive grounds. But although all cities had land available near their edges, by the 1840s semidetached and terraced houses began to appear on smaller lots. Nor did all suburbs continue to attract the class of resident for whom they were originally intended. And by the 1880s some novelists and journalists had begun to speak disparagingly of the dullness of life in "villadom."

Thus in the 1890s a number of developers were ready to attempt the kind of planning already instituted by a few industrial and landed philanthropists. In 1853–1863 alpaca manufacturer Titus Salt erected Saltaire, near Bradford, with a mill, community buildings, and houses in a variety of sizes. In 1839 **Joseph Paxton** and John Robertson designed Edensor, a farming estate at Chatsworth, Derbyshire, for the sixth duke of Devonshire. This kind of contribution, along with a nostalgia for cottage architecture and the values of a country village produced the late nineteenth-century "garden suburb," a carefully designed, low-density, parklike neighborhood of tree-lined streets which followed land contours, with churches, clubs, stores, and recreation grounds.

England's first garden suburb, Bedford Park, appeared in 1875–1876 on London's western edge. Its brick and tile houses surrounded by low walls and white pale fences, mostly designed by **Norman Shaw**, were small but its aesthetic appearance, along with the mildly bohemian behavior of its residents (they played tennis on Sundays) drew attention to it. Much larger was Bournville, built near Birmingham by Quaker cocoa processors, the Cadburys, begun in 1878 but completed after 1895 by architect W. Alexander Harvey. Since only half of its residents worked at the adjacent factory, it was not quite a company town. Often visited was the Lever Brothers' Port Sunlight, Merseyside, planned in 1888 by William and Segar Owen, a highly paternalistic soap company suburb of such quality that only a few could afford to imitate its construction features. But this kind of community was most successfully realized only in the twentieth century by Dame Henrietta Barnett, Raymond Unwin, Barry Parker, and **Edwin Lutyens** at Hampstead Garden Suburb, Middlesex, after 1906.

Also beyond Victoria's reign was the first "garden city," a self-contained, hygienic town which included both workplaces and homes. Invented in 1898 by Ebenezer Howard, the concept soon became confused with "garden suburb." It was first attempted at Letchworth, Hertfordshire in 1903.

HARRY SCHALCK

Bibliography

Dyos, H. J. *Victorian Suburb: A Study of the Growth of Camberwell.* 1966.

—— and D. A. Reader. "Slums and Suburb." In H. J. Dyos and Michael Wolff, eds., *The Victorian City: Images and Realities*, vol. 1. 1973.

Olsen, Donald J. "House Upon House: Estate Development in London and Sheffield." In H. J. Dyos and Michael Wolff, eds., *The Victorian City: Images and Realities*, vol. 1. 1973.

Richards, James M. *The Castles on the Ground: The Anatomy of Suburbia*. 2d ed., 1973.

Stern, Robert A. M. and John M. Massengale, eds. *The Anglo-American Suburb*. 1981.

Thompson, F. M. L., ed. *The Rise of Suburbia*. 1982.

See also EDINBURGH; HOUSING

· · · · ·

SUEZ CANAL (1859-1901)

The Suez Canal is 107 miles long, linking Port Said on the Mediterranean Sea with the port of Suez in the Gulf of Suez. From 1869 to 1900 the canal proved a vital trade route between Britain and India.

Canal construction commenced in 1859 and was completed in 1869 by the French-owned Universal Canal of Suez Maritime Company, headed by Ferdinand de Lesseps (1805-1894). Britain initially opposed the canal, fearing a threat to its existing trade route to India, since the waterway would be largely French owned. Yet by the close of the first year of operation, 289,234 of the 436,609 tons passing through the Suez Canal were British. In 1870 the Egyptian Khedive, Ismail (1830-1895), unsuccessfully urged Britain to purchase the still unprofitable canal.

By 1874 British merchant trade accounted for 74 percent of Suez Canal traffic. This prompted Prime Minister Benjamin Disraeli—who believed ownership of the canal to be vital to Britain's imperial defense and commercial trade—to send the banker Nathaniel de Rothschild (1840-1915) to inquire about purchasing de Lesseps's interest in the canal. The Frenchman's price was said to have "astounded even a Rothschild" and the matter was dropped.

In November 1875, amid outrage by British merchants over rising canal tolls, and at the suggestion of the British journalist, Frederick Greenwood (1830-1909), Britain purchased 176,602 Suez Canal Company shares from the insolvent Ismail for 4 million pounds borrowed from Baron Lionel de Rothschild (1808-1879). The British press praised the purchase, lauding the waterway both as a commercial highway and as a barrier against Russian designs on a warm-water port in the Near East. In 1882 British troops occupied the canal during nationalist uprisings in Egypt. A year later, angered by French management of the canal, William Gladstone's ministry discussed construction of a second canal through Palestine, but took no action. With the occupation of Egypt in 1883, however, Britain's hold on the canal tightened. In 1888 Britain was a signatory to the Convention of Constantinople (October 29, 1888) which guaranteed the neutrality of the canal to the end of the century.

BERYL I. DIAMOND

Bibliography

El-Benhawy, Mohamed A. "The Suez Canal: A Descriptive Bibliography." Ph.D. dissertation, University of Michigan, 1964.

Farnie, D. A. *East and West of Suez: The Suez Canal in History, 1854-1956.* 1969.

Hallberg, Charles W. *The Suez Canal: Its History and Diplomatic Importance.* 1974.

Marlowe, John. *World Ditch: The Making of the Suez Canal.* 1964.

· · · · ·

SUFFRAGE, WOMEN'S

The Victorian movement for the enfranchisement of women had its roots in both **feminism** and the agitation to expand the franchise for men. Although the parliamentary vote for women was not achieved until after World War I, the suffrage struggle shaped and reflected the period's argument over women's rights, and by the last quarter of the nineteenth century had become virtually the sole focus of the organized women's movement.

The suggestion that women might vote goes back at least to Mary Wollstonecraft's *A Vindication of the Rights of Woman* (1792), but in fact women were not explicitly excluded from the franchise until the Reform Bill of 1832. Although few women had been able to exercise the right implied by the previous statutory use of the term "person," the Reform Bill's express restriction of the vote to men codified existing practice—and also prompted the first formal introduction in Parliament of the demand for women's suffrage. An 1832 petition from Mary Smith of Yorkshire was sponsored by Henry Hunt, who argued that women who paid taxes ought to be allowed to vote. Like most early parliamentary debates on women's suffrage, Hunt's proposal was met with ridicule.

Although most early radical and socialist groups automatically incorporated women's suffrage into their platforms, the influential Chartist movement removed the demand from their People's Charter of 1838, thus setting the stage for the often bitter conflict between women's and working-class men's rights. Popular movements to alter the franchise came to focus almost exclusively on the reduction or removal of property qualifications for men.

The argument against women's suffrage remained essentially unchanged throughout the Victorian period. Women were, it was claimed, sufficiently represented by the male voters in their families; there was thus no need for women to vote and they would not, in any case, vote differently from their husbands and fathers. It was also argued that women were unfit for public life and that politics would contaminate their innocence and violate the domestic sphere. Prosuffrage arguments were based on objections to taxation without representation, on the realization that women might have political interests different from men's, and on concepts of abstract justice and individual rights.

By midcentury women had begun to organize. Serious parliamentary consideration of women's suffrage began in 1867 when **John Stuart Mill** introduced an amendment substituting the word "person" for "man" in the Second Reform Bill's description of those entitled to the franchise. The proposal was overwhelmingly defeated, but Mill's sponsorship forestalled much of the ridicule that had greeted previous attempts to enfranchise

women. Although subsequent bills in 1870, 1883, and 1892 also failed, interest in the issue increased rapidly. Candidates for Parliament began to promise support for women's suffrage and enlist suffragists' help in their campaigns, although many reneged immediately upon election.

While suffrage activists concentrated principally on the national franchise, municipal voting rights were achieved long before the final parliamentary capitulation. In 1869 unmarried women who paid property taxes gained the right to vote in municipal elections. The Education Act of 1870 established local school boards and permitted women both to vote and to be elected. By 1888 single and married women were able to vote in both municipal and county elections. The Local Government Act of 1894 stipulated that "no person shall be disqualified by sex or marriage from being elected . . . or being an elector" in the district and parish councils that came under its provisions. These concessions helped to pave the way for the parliamentary vote, but they were also used by antisuffragists, who argued that local voting rights were a natural extension of women's interest in domestic and family affairs while the national vote represented an inappropriate leap into public concerns.

Although public attention to the suffrage movement (and early historical accounts) focused on London-based middle-class leaders and activities, working-class women were active from the beginning, particularly in regional organizations. Women involved in trade union activism and the struggle for rights in the workplace also demanded the vote, and working women in Manchester and other manufacturing centers saw suffrage as but one part of their campaign to improve women's lives.

As interest in women's suffrage grew, divisions developed between those feminists who saw the vote as the most important goal and those who concentrated on issues of education and employment. To some extent the intense public focus on suffrage probably led to the collapse of a visible feminist movement after World War I, since many activists had relied on the demand for the vote as their rallying point, paying less attention to other issues or to underlying questions of women's position.

Although it took some time for organized opposition to develop, public protests against the suffrage movement began in 1889 with a letter in *Nineteenth Century* signed by over one hundred prominent women, including **Mary Ward** (1851–1920). Ward gradually became the leader of the antisuffrage movement, working energetically against the expanded franchise until 1918.

In 1897 the various prosuffrage organizations came together under the umbrella of the National Union of Women's Suffrage Societies (NUWSS), headed by **Millicent Garrett Fawcett** (1847–1929), and lobbying of Parliament became more intense. By the end of the Victorian period, dozens of local and national groups had been formed to advance the cause. Although the movement split around 1903 between "constitutional" suffragists (headed by Fawcett) and militant activists or "suffragettes," headed by **Emmeline Pankhurst** (1858–1928), all had the same goal. The two wings of the movement differed primarily on the question of means: the militants preferred dramatic demonstrations (and occasional violence) while the constitutionalists used parliamentary petition and lobbying. Both groups, however, demanded universal enfranchisement of women, without regard to marital status or property qualifications.

While achieving the vote (for women thirty and over in 1918, and for women of twenty-one in 1928) was its most obvious accomplishment, the suffrage movement empowered women in other ways. The necessity for public speaking, parliamentary lobbying, and clearly defined strategies forced women to educate themselves about the political process and to overcome Victorian restrictions on their public behavior. Suffrage rallies provided many women with their first experiences of public speaking. Middle-class women steeled themselves to override cultural and personal taboos (and often to alienate family and friends) in order to solicit funds and signatures, argue with opponents, and march in demonstrations. In the suffrage movement, furthermore, women of all classes worked together for a cause that affected the lives of all.

LAURA STEMPEL MUMFORD

Bibliography

Blackburn, Helen. *Women's Suffrage: A Record of the Women's Suffrage Movement in the British Isles.* 1902.

Liddington, Jill and Jill Norris. *One Hand Tied Behind Us: The Rise of the Women's Suffrage Movement.* 1978.

Reiss, Erna M. *Rights and Duties of Englishwomen.* 1934.

Rover, Constance. *Women's Suffrage and Party Politics in Britain, 1866–1914.* 1967.

Strachey, Ray. *The Cause.* 1928; rpt. 1978.

See also ELECTIONS AND THE FRANCHISE

· · · · ·

SUICIDE

In Victorian England suicide was both illegal and touched with the taint of insanity. Most Victorians felt that felo-de-se, the legal term for deliberate self-murder, was immoral and disgraceful, and suicides were often concealed by the victims' families. Nevertheless attitudes toward suicide altered considerably as the Victorian era unfolded.

Until 1823 it was legally possible to bury suicides at crossroads with a stake through the heart. The law allowing for this atrocity dated from the tenth century when civil law required not only ignominious burial but also forfeiture of personal and real property to the Crown. Reasons for this kind of severity were supposedly moral. The felo-de-se was to be impaled and buried outside of consecrated ground because suicide was thought to be the one unrepentant crime against God, life being considered a commission from God and the taking of it God's prerogative only. The loss of goods and property was mandated in the belief that suicide could be prevented if people knew of the harsh and inevitable consequences for their heirs. It was only if a suicide could be proved insane at the time of the act that forfeiture was not demanded, at least until 1870 when forfeiture became illegal. In 1823 suicides were given the right to a more decent burial but privately, at night, and without Christian rites.

Because of such legal severity, coroner's juries were by the 1830s heavily utilizing the loophole in the law: they found more and more suicides "temporarily insane," a verdict that saved already aggrieved families the further ignominy of poverty. Yet the stigma of **insanity** in a family was little better than that of suicide, and growing concern over the meaning of "temporary" insanity called out the physicians. They were consulted by the courts to help determine cases of suicidal insanity and became embroiled in a controversy over the connection between suicide and insanity. In order to clarify their thinking, men like Daniel Hack Tuke (1827–1895) pioneered in scientific studies of insanity and helped establish "mental science" as a province of medicine.

Meanwhile nonprofessional attitudes toward suicide revealed deep-seated public discomfort over self-destruction. Suicide became a topic of considerable interest, but aside from professional discussions and sensational newspaper accounts of dramatic suicides like several from the Monument (between 1839 and 1842), it was not openly discussed. Instead the Victorians addressed this fearful interest obliquely, through displacement. The literature of the period shows this well: except when dishonored, mainstream middle-class males were rarely depicted as suicidal. They were too close to the center of Victorian society. But figures from the past like Matthew Arnold's Empedocles in *Empedocles on Etna* (1852), fallen women like those of the melodrama, and misfits and outsiders like Charles Dickens's Quilp in *The Old Curiosity Shop* (1841) killed themselves openly and came under intense scrutiny. Through literature, motives were questioned and reasons posited for self-destruction.

Underlying all this was a profound sense of insecurity that increased as the Victorian age approached the 1870s and 1880s. The will to live, so well-buttressed in the early Victorian period by literary works like Thomas Carlyle's *Sartor Resartus* (1833–1834), was undermined by a strong sense of despair. In September of 1877, the prestigious periodical *Nineteenth Century* published an article by W.H. Mallock (1849–1923) entitled "Is Life Worth Living?" Subsequent discussion of this frightening question revealed that suicide was increasingly thought to be pitiable and understandable rather than execrable. In 1879 and 1882 came two further legal revisions. No longer could suicide be considered as homicide, so that the minimum sentence for at-

tempted suicide would be reduced to two years; and suicides were at last granted the right to burial in daylight hours. Thus suicide law like other Victorian attitudes toward suicide became a barometer of Victorian mores and concerns, revealing both anxiety and a liberalizing of rigid morality. By the end of the century suicide prevention and the social significance of suicide dominated a freer discussion of self-destruction both in England and on the Continent and led toward the first generation of suicidologists like Emile Durkheim (1858–1917) in France.

BARBARA T. GATES

Bibliography

Douglas, Jack D. *The Social Meaning of Suicide.* 1967.

Durkheim, Emile. *Suicide: A Study in Sociology.* 1951.

Fedden, Robin. *Suicide: A Social and Historical Study.* 1938.

Morselli, Enrico A. *Suicide: An Essay on Comparative Moral Statistics.* 1881.

Sprott, Samuel E. *The English Debate on Suicide from Donne to Hume.* 1961.

Strahan, Samuel A. K. *Suicide and Insanity.* 1894.

Tuke, Daniel Hack. *Chapters in the History of the Insane in the British Isles.* 1882.

Westcott, William Wynn. *Suicide: Its History, Literature, Juris-Prudence, Causation, and Prevention.* 1885.

Winslow, Forbes. *The Anatomy of Suicide.* 1840.

· · · · ·

SULLIVAN, ARTHUR SEYMOUR (1842–1900)

Arthur Seymour Sullivan was the foremost composer of the Victorian age. Apart from the imperishable **Savoy operas** created with William Schwenck Gilbert between 1875 and 1896, his serious work in many other branches of music commands increasing respect.

Sullivan entered the Royal Academy of Music while still a boy chorister at the Chapel

Royal (1854) and won the First Mendelssohn scholarship to the Leipzig Conservatory (1858–1861). His rise to fame was rapid after the production of his music to *The Tempest* (Crystal Palace, 1862) and his cantata *Kenilworth* (Birmingham Festival, 1864). His first stage work, *Cox and Box* (libretto by Frank C. Burnand), was produced in 1867.

The famous series with Gilbert began with the one-act, all-sung *Trial by Jury* (1875), but the other twelve were full-length operas with spoken dialogue. *H.M.S. Pinafore* (1878) and *The Mikado* (1885) have been most popular, especially in the U.S.; connoisseurs of Sullivan's music tend to favor *Iolanthe* (1882) and *The Yeomen of the Guard* (1888), while *Patience* (1881) and *Princess Ida* (1884) are inimitable satires on the aesthetic and women's movements respectively. Musically speaking, the Savoy operas were a product of the native English opera tradition, elements from French operetta, and a strong German influence, primarily of Mendelssohn and Schubert.

After his quarrel with Gilbert in 1890, Sullivan was never again able to find his feet. Their two remaining collaborations were relative failures. Sullivan's one grand opera, *Ivanhoe* (1891), has a splendid score, but has never found a secure place in the repertory.

Sullivan also produced a series of boldly conceived oratorios and cantatas. *The Martyr of Antioch*, commissioned for the 1880 Leeds Festival, rises above the conventional religiosity of Victorian oratorio. Sullivan's mastery of the orchestra is displayed in incidental music to five Shakespeare plays, several concert overtures, and the "Irish" Symphony (1866). His large output of songs, part songs, and church music is mostly forgotten, except for two pieces that still demonstrate his flair for reaching the larger public: his ballad "The Lost Chord," and his tune ("St. Gertrude") for the hymn "Onward, Christian Soldiers."

NICHOLAS TEMPERLEY

Bibliography

Jacobs, Arthur. *Arthur Sullivan: A Victorian Musician.* 1984.

Pearson, Hesketh. *Gilbert and Sullivan.* 1935.

Young, Percy. *Sir Arthur Sullivan.* 1971.

· · · · ·

SUNDAY SCHOOLS

A central feature of working-class life, the Sunday school movement originated in the late eighteenth century. Promoted by the philanthropic concern born out of the evangelical revival, its precise beginnings are now debated. Robert Raikes, editor of the *Gloucester Journal*, who started a Sunday school there in 1780, was one of several early pioneers. His object was to get young people off the streets on the sabbath and to teach them the catechism, some basic Christian duties, and how to read. The scholars were then dismissed to make way for others, for Raikes and his colleagues were responding to a particular crisis and had no idea of founding an enduring institution.

Sunday schools came into being in various ways: through the action of church bodies, by the resolution of town meetings in the north and Midlands, through the enthusiasm of individuals, both lay and ordained, or by the joint action of interdenominational consortia. They appeared in the period when churches acted together in common response to the ferment in English social life provoked by the French Revolution, but before long a tighter denominationalism replaced the common evangelical urgency. The Wesleyans sought greater denominational control of the schools with which they were associated and came out against teaching writing on Sundays. Anglican clergy were worried about lay leadership in the schools. In dissenting bodies that were not Wesleyan, however, lay initiative and the teaching of nonreligious subjects continued well after midcentury. Early schools had paid teachers, but after 1800 teachers increasingly volunteered their services.

The Sunday School Union (eventually a national organization) was established in 1803, though initially its activities were confined to London. It produced periodicals and teaching materials, nurtured the idea of training, set out what amounted to a model constitution, and encouraged the establishment of new schools. By 1828 it had a missionary working in the provinces where previously autonomous unions began to refer to the London body as the "parent" union. By this time, in the view of Thomas Laqueur, the movement had become a thoroughly working-class institution, attended, staffed, and often managed by the community which it served.

By 1851 there were more than 23,000 Sunday schools in England, only 45 percent of which were Anglican; the enrollment was just short of 2.1 million. Few working-class children, except perhaps in London, escaped at least some contact with Sunday school. The movement reached its peak in the 1880s with just short of 6 million enrolled, or some 19 percent of the population of England, Wales, and Scotland. In the manufacturing centers, about half of those who received any education at all secured it for an average of between three and five years from Sunday schools, which thus made a significant contribution to mass literacy.

Indeed, it has been argued that they were more successful in this respect than in acting as recruitment agencies for the churches. Sunday schools did, however, sustain a basic Christian culture among working-class children. If they operated as agencies of social control, then the discipline was self-imposed and offered immediate benefits to scholars and their families. There is little evidence of coerced attendance, which would have been difficult to enforce in communities that were mostly pluralistic in religion.

By the 1870s Sunday school curricula had become wholly religious, but their social, leisure, and training functions on weeknights included Bands of Hope (juvenile temperance organizations), recreation (with special Sunday School Holiday Homes for the needy), Boys and Girls Life Brigades (uniformed organizations exercising a paramilitary pattern of discipline), the Christian Endeavour Society (for training in active church membership), and a branch of the International Bible Reading Association. Interdenominational and international, the Sunday school movement was one of the agencies that pioneered ecumenical relationships among Protestant churches.

J.H.Y. BRIGGS

Bibliography

Booth, Frank. *Robert Raikes of Gloucester.* 1980.

Cliff, Philip B. *The Rise and Development of the Sunday School Movement in England, 1780-1980.* 1986.

Ferguson, John, ed. *Christianity, Society and Education.* 1981.

Laqueur, Thomas W. *Religion and Respectability: Sunday Schools and Working Class Culture, 1780-1850.* 1976.

Newby, Catherine R. *The Story of Sunday Schools: Robert Raikes and After.* 1930.

Ward, William R. *Religion and Society in England, 1790-1850.* 1972.

· · · · ·

SUPERNATURAL FICTION

Supernatural fiction flourished in Victorian England; authors wrote about every weird phenomenon from spectral presences to clairvoyance. Short stories, novels, and novellas on the inexplicable or the otherworldly coexisted with and countered the period's empiricism, skepticism, and scientism. As technological and scientific advances called into question accepted truths, supernatural fiction offered, at the least, a circumvention of sticky issues of faith and spirituality and, at most, a safe mode of confronting empirically challenged beliefs about the soul, about God, about afterlife, and even about the substantiality of the self.

From Walter Scott to Oscar Wilde, many major authors tried their hand at the genre. Charlotte Brontë's *Jane Eyre* (1847) and Emily Brontë's *Wuthering Heights* (1847) can be classified as supernatural works. George Eliot's short and uncanny story about the horrid psychic experiences of Latimer in "The Lifted Veil" (1859) is her most sustained excursion into the realm of the unknown, though touches of supernaturalism surface in novels like *Adam Bede* (1859) and *Romola* (1863). Elizabeth Gaskell wrote a number of supernatural tales of which the most anthologized is "The Old Nurse's Story" (1852). Charles Dickens's *A Christmas Carol* (1843) is one of the best-known haunted fictions; indeed, in his capacity as writer and editor, Dickens is largely responsible for making the supernatural tale a Christmas staple. At the end of the age, the supernatural tale was successfully executed by such writers as Robert Louis Stevenson, Thomas Hardy, and Henry James, who declared in a preface to *The Altar of the Dead* (1895) that the ghost story possessed a "neatness without which representation" and "beauty" are lost.

Popular writers also felt the attractions of the genre. Joseph Sheridan Le Fanu made the ghost story, which apparently spoke to his psyche, his specialty. Tales like "Green Tea" (1869) and "Carmilla" (1872) have justly earned him recognition as a master of the supernatural story. Catherine Crowe's fascination with the supernatural led her to collect supposedly factual accounts of spectral phenomena, accounts that have been called some of the best in the British storehouse of ghost stories. Indeed, women writers were notably drawn to the supernatural. Margaret Oliphant, Charlotte Riddell, Amelia B. Edwards, and Florence Marryat are only a few of the popular writers who worked in the genre, especially toward the end of the century. Though the reasons for this marked interest are complex, women's assigned role as spiritual guide helps account for their identification with the otherworldly. Finally, both men and women wrote supernatural tales because they were marketable, especially at Christmas with its spiritual overtones and its invitations to suspend disbelief.

During the century uncanny phenomena such as mesmerism and spiritualism came into vogue and the Society for Psychical Research was founded. Supernaturalism served a purpose during the Victorian age. Eerie fiction not only entertained, it also reaffirmed. Tensions brought about by change could be examined or neutralized, and a sense of the being and vitality of things spiritual could be rediscovered at a time when materialism, scientism, and dogmatism threatened to snuff out the numinous.

VANESSA D. DICKERSON

Bibliography

Briggs, Julia. *Night Visitors: The Rise and Fall of the English Ghost Story.* 1977.

Penzoldt, Peter. *The Supernatural in Fiction.* 1952.

Scarborough, Dorothy. *The Supernatural in Modern English Fiction.* 1917.

Sullivan, Jack. *Elegant Nightmares.* 1978.

Wagenknecht, Edward. *Cavalcade of the English Novel: From Elizabeth to George VI.* 1943.

See also GOTHIC NOVEL

· · · · ·

SURGERY AND SURGEONS

The most significant advances in the practice of medicine during the nineteenth century came in the field of surgery. **Anesthesia** and antisepsis led to dramatic improvements in surgical technique and in the survival of patients, thus transforming surgery from a dangerous and desperate last resort into a positive measure for restoring health. As a consequence, the prestige of surgeons relative to physicians was significantly altered.

The surgeon had emerged as a respectable practitioner only at the end of the eighteenth century. Ties with the craft guild of barber-surgeons had been severed sixty-five years earlier; in 1800 the College of Surgeons was allowed to add the preface "Royal." By custom and law, however, surgical practice also included the nonsurgical treatment of "outward diseases" such as syphilis and skin ailments. The surgeon did bloodletting and bonesetting, drew teeth, treated scalds, burns, ulcers, tumors, and sore breasts. Most members of the Royal College of Surgeons in the first half of the nineteenth century held a second qualification from the Society of Apothecaries and functioned as general practitioners. In rural areas surgeons with lesser qualifications also treated animals.

Surgical operations were primarily emergency measures: amputation made necessary by accident or osteomyelitis, removal of gross tumors, and other procedures performed as a last resort on patients already moribund. Thus although the death rate was extremely high, it might be more appropriate to speak of the survival rate: operations did sometimes prevent almost certain death. Any injury that broke the skin was liable to serious infection. A person with a compound fracture or ragged wounds to a limb might be saved by amputation and cautery. Speed was the major component of a surgeon's skill; in operations on a conscious patient the surgeon who was strong and quick could best minimize pain, shock, and loss of blood.

Anesthesia dramatically altered the practice of surgery by providing relief to patients and giving surgeons time. Ether was successfully used in 1846 and chloroform (which became the most common surgical anesthetic in Britain for the next sixty years) in 1847. At first patients were simply rendered unconscious before the operation began, but over the next ten years continued administration of chloroform was made safe. The Royal College of Surgeons had laid the foundations for the emergence of highly qualified surgical specialists by instituting a rigorous examination for fellows in 1844. Once patients could be kept under anesthesia, surgeons rapidly expanded the range and sophistication of their techniques.

As the number of constructive repairs and voluntary operations on patients who were not already on the verge of death grew, however, the rate of postoperative mortality from infection became increasingly apparent. "Pyaemia" (caused by staphyloccus bacteria) was endemic in hospitals and epidemics of (streptococcal) "hospital infection" would occasionally sweep the wards. Although surgeons had as yet no understanding of the bacterial causes, they perceived the need for cleanliness and fought postoperative infection by dressing wounds with such agents as zinc permanganate (Condy's fluid), chlorine, cold boiled water, and bread poultices. When epidemics of "hospital infection" were particularly severe, wise surgeons closed their theaters and refused to operate. Surgical mortality rates for this period are extremely difficult to calculate and subject to wide variation. Contrary to popular mythology, however, most infections were probably not caused by the surgeon's hands or by dirty instruments. Studies of deaths following amputation show that the rate was highest after traumatic injuries, when patients were brought into the hospital already contaminated by rough-and-ready bandaging and dung-strewn streets.

Antiseptic techniques were originated by Joseph Lister, who was in 1865 professor of surgery at Glasgow. Reading Louis Pasteur's *Researches on Putrefaction*, Lister immediately perceived that the germ theory explained surgical infection. He theorized that postoperative infections could be prevented if germs already in the wound were destroyed, if everything touching it was scrupulously disinfected, and if the air itself was purified so that it could not deposit any organisms into the site of the operation. Lister chose carbolic acid as the most suitable antiseptic agent; in 1867 he began using it for dressings and cleaning instruments and by 1871 had devised a spray that he believed could kill airborne germs in the operating room. Resistance to the germ theory and inability to understand and duplicate Lister's scrupulous perfectionism retarded acceptance of the antiseptic method, but by the 1880s its essential elements were in wide use. (Lister himself abandoned the continuous spray—the most problematic feature of his method—by 1887.) During the 1890s steam sterilization of linens, boiling of instruments, systematic scrubbing, and the donning of surgical gloves, caps, gowns, and ultimately masks slowly replaced the heavy use of tissue-damaging carbolic.

Efforts to prevent shock from blood loss were not quite so successful. Blood transfusions had first been performed early in the nineteenth century by James Blundell, who had some success in cases of women who had collapsed from postpartum hemorrhage. In the third quarter of the century, better equipment was invented and transfusions became more common—which led to the realization that unexpected fatalities made the procedure very risky. By this time, however, the effectiveness of saline injections to restore the fluid volume had been demonstrated; transfusion was abandoned until the mystery of blood groups was solved in the twentieth century.

By the last two decades of the Victorian era, surgeons dared to open the thorax, the abdomen, and even the skull. Cesarean section was no longer performed only to snatch the infant of a woman already dead or dying, but gave some hope of saving both mother and child. Advances in surgical pathology provided materials for improved diagnosis. Skin grafts, colostomies, repair of congenital orthopedic defects such as clubfoot, removal of ovarian cysts, excision of cancers in the digestive tract, and appendectomies entered the repertoire of surgical procedures. The French physiologists who mapped the brain's functions made it possible to localize tumors and abscesses within the skull, although the death rate was much higher in brain surgery than in other fields. Surgeons were using X-ray photographs to locate foreign objects in the body and examine broken bones within months after their discovery was published in *Lancet* in 1896.

No comparable advances in the physician's craft took place until the twentieth century, when antitoxins and chemical therapies would provide the means to fight many diseases. The significant medical improvements of the nineteenth century arose from the preventative measures of the public health movement and from the anesthesia and antisepsis that transformed surgery and the surgeon's role.

SALLY MITCHELL

Bibliography

Cartwright, Frederick F. *The Development of Modern Surgery.* 1967.

Wangensteen, Owen H. and Sarah D. Wangensteen. *The Rise of Surgery: From Empiric Craft to Scientific Discipline.* 1978.

Youngson, A. J. *The Scientific Revolution in Victorian Medicine.* 1979.

See also HEALTH; MEDICAL PRACTICE; MEDICAL SCIENCE

· · · · ·

SUTTEE

The term "suttee" (or *sati*), meaning "truthful or virtuous woman," denotes both the Hindu practice of immolating—usually by burning—a widow at or after the funeral of her husband, and also the woman so sacrificed. The abolition of suttee by the British was but one event in a century of struggle over the direction of social reform in both countries. But the British reformers shared with their Indian subjects a view of the predominantly sexual function of women, and a belief that high-status but "unprotected" (unmarriageable) women constituted a social problem.

Although originally considered a perquisite of very high status, by the beginning of the nineteenth century suttee had spread far through the Indian social structure. For "respectable" Hindus, the death of the husband before his wife was held to be unnatural and caused by the latter's unchastity (in a previous life if not in the present); marriage of widows was eschewed; and the surviving widow was treated as a penitent sinner, unlucky even to look at. (The word "widow" was often used to connote "prostitute.") Suttee was considered not a punishment, but rather a statement that

the wife who "followed" her dead husband had been faithful to him.

In the early decades of the nineteenth century, under missionary pressure, British officials began to monitor suttee ceremonies, attempting to ensure that they were, as prescribed, voluntary. At once, the number of suttees increased dramatically. In 1829, after convincing himself that abolition would not provoke a mutiny among the native army, the governor-general, Lord William Bentinck, declared suttee illegal in Bengal, and the other British-ruled territories soon followed suit.

The abolition of suttee was followed by efforts to rehabilitate widows. Thus, an age of consent (twelve, as in England at the time) both within and without marriage, was instituted, and attempts were made to encourage the remarriage at least of virgin widows. The problem of unmarriageable widows, however, remained intractable, and philanthropic efforts turned to the opening of schools and hostels where, it was hoped, those who were cast off by both family and in-laws could be taught useful skills so they could earn a living. These efforts paralleled schemes to assist impoverished English ladies to emigrate in the hope that they would marry male colonists, and the establishment of hostels, asylums, and benevolent societies to assist "distressed gentlewomen."

DOROTHY STEIN

Bibliography

Ahmed, Aly F. Salahuddin. *Social Ideas and Change in Bengal, 1818–1835.* 1965.

Hammerton, A. James. *Emigrant Gentlewomen.* 1979.

Natarajan, Dandapani. *Age and Marital Status.* Census of India Centenary Monograph No. 8. 1971.

Ramabai, Sarasvati. *The High-Caste Hindu Woman.* 1901.

Stein, Dorothy K. "Women to Burn: Suttee as a Normative Institution." In Jagdish P. Sharma, ed., *Individuals and Ideas in Modern India.* 1982. (A shortened version appeared in *Signs,* vol. 4, pp. 253–289.)

Thompson, Edward J. *Suttee.* 1928.

· · · · ·

SWEATSHOPS

Sweatshops were work premises (often a room in a worker's home or a garret, basement, or backroom) characterized by overcrowding, unsanitary conditions, and low wages, and where irregular and long hours of straining and monotonous work prevailed. The number of these unregulated premises increased throughout most of the Victorian era as manufacturers in certain trades used sweatshop production as a cheap way of meeting market fluctuations and as a means of weakening organized labor. Sweatshop workers, often known as "sweated workers" (or "outworkers"), were largely helpless victims of exploitation by their employers and by one another. Union and state regulatory action failed to end the system; only when the women's industrial rights movement pushed the state to enact a minimum wages law (1909) did production begin to move out of the sweatshop into the factory.

Sweatshops were common in early nineteenth-century handloom weaving, framework knitting, and lacemaking and, later, in nail and chain making, box making, some of the metal trades, hosiery, furniture, and in the clothing and footwear trades—particularly in London, but also in Leeds, Sheffield, Newcastle, Manchester, and Glasgow. In some trades (e.g., handloom weaving) the sweatshop was the mark of an industry in decline, while in others, especially clothing, it accompanied an industry in rapid growth.

Although sweatshops existed in a variety of other trades, including the London baking industry, they were most common in industries prone to subdivision and subcontract of labor, and thus usually only a portion of the manufacturing process took place in the sweatshop. Most typically, sweatshop work was "given out" by a factory owner, artisan shop, or retailer. While this decentralized system had all but disappeared in the textile trades by the 1850s, it expanded in other trades—particularly clothing and footwear—where unions were weak or nonexistent or where employers wished to escape factory and workshop laws. New, inexpensive, and portable machines (e.g., the sewing machine) could be set up in basements, bedrooms, and the like. Further, sweatshops grew because of the availability of large numbers of women who needed an alternative to poverty and of immigrant eastern European Jewish workers who entered Britain between 1880 and 1914.

The system, which was organized by "middlemen" (or women) subcontractors, was highly competitive, and forced workers to travel frequently and for some distance to secure the pieces to be "worked up." Sweated workers, the most wretchedly exploited sector of the labor force, made up a notable proportion of the workforce in a number of cities. Although many sweatshop workers were left out of the census and other reports, it is probable that in 1900 at least half of the London clothing trades workers worked in sweatshops.

Beginning in the 1880s, sweating was energetically attacked by unions (e.g., the Women's Trade Union League, the Women's Industrial Council), public and private groups (including a House of Lords committee), and through state regulatory legislation, but without success. It was only with the establishment of a National Anti-Sweating League and then with the nation's first modern minimum wage legislation (the Trade Boards Act of 1909) that sweatshop production became unprofitable.

JAMES ANDREW SCHMIECHEN

Bibliography

Bythell, Duncan. *The Sweated Trades: Outwork in Nineteenth Century Britain.* 1978.

Parliamentary Papers, House of Commons. *Reports of the Select Committee on Homework.* 1907.

——, House of Lords. *Reports of the Select Committee on Sweating.* 1888–1889.

Schmiechen, James A. *Sweated Industries and Sweated Labor: The London Clothing Trades, 1867–1914.* 1984.

See also BLACK, CLEMENTINA; DOMESTIC INDUSTRY

· · · · ·

SWINBURNE, ALGERNON CHARLES (1837–1909)

Algernon Charles Swinburne is notorious for his erotic and blasphemous *Poems and*

Ballads (1866) and his iconoclastic activities in London during the 1860s and 1870s. However, this popular legend overlooks Swinburne's influential career as a serious poet, dramatist, and critic.

Son of aristocracy, Swinburne began writing at Oxford (1856-1860) where he met Dante Gabriel Rossetti and briefly joined the Pre-Raphaelite circle. Although his first classicist tragedy, *Atalanta in Calydon* (1865), was praised, *Poems and Ballads, Series #1* (1866) caused a great scandal. The dramatic monologues "Anactoria," "Laus Veneris," "Dolores," and "Hymn to Proserpine" ironically associate Christianity with sadomasochism, while "The Triumph of Time," "The Leper," and "Les Noyades" are necrophiliac parodies of romantic love, perhaps hinting at Swinburne's relations with his cousin, Mary Gordon. In "Notes on Poems and Reviews" (1866), Swinburne wittily exposes his critics' moral hypocrisy and asserts a doctrine of "l'art pour l'art" modeled on Théophile Gautier and Charles Baudelaire.

At his peak during the 1860s and 1870s, Swinburne published several history plays, a landmark study of William Blake (1868), and a series of essays on French and English contemporaries that influenced later aesthetes, especially Walter Pater. In Paris, Swinburne met leading symbolists and impressionists whose aesthetics shaped his ideas. *Songs Before Sunrise* (1871) espouses the radical republicanism of Percy Bysshe Shelley, Victor Hugo, and Giuseppe Mazzini. Swinburne's two novels, *A Year's Letters* (also known as *Love's Cross-Currents*, 1905) and *Lesbia Brandon* (unfinished, 1952), reflect his gift for satire as well as his homoeroticism and taste for flagellation **pornography** (which he also wrote on the side). Attacked with Rossetti in Robert Buchanan's essay, "The Fleshly School of Poetry" (1871), Swinburne shot back with a parodic invective, "Under the Microscope" (1872). He also debated with Thomas Carlyle, John Ruskin, and Ralph Waldo Emerson over morality in art. At the same time, Swinburne was a respected scholar, as shown by his collaboration on Bemjamin Jowett's translations of Plato, his studies of Elizabethan dramatists and metaphysical poets, and his second classicist tragedy, *Erechtheus* (1871).

After a severe breakdown in 1879, Swinburne left London to reside with his friend, the critic Theodore Watts-Dunton, in rural Putney, where he continued to write. *Songs of the Springtides* (1880) includes a romantic autobiography, "Thalassius," and a long lyric, "On the Cliffs," in which Swinburne's use of fragments of classical myths anticipates T. S. Eliot. Besides completing a trilogy about Mary Stuart, Swinburne finished his lyrical masterpiece, *Tristram of Lyonesse* (1882), an erotic and Wagnerian reply to Alfred Tennyson's *Idylls of the King*.

A candidate for poet laureate in 1892, Swinburne strongly influenced later Victorians such as Thomas Hardy, aesthetes such as Oscar Wilde, and early moderns, including W. B. Yeats, James Joyce, and Ezra Pound.

THAÏS E. MORGAN

Bibliography

Beetz, Kirk H. *Algernon Charles Swinburne: A Bibliography of Secondary Works, 1861-1980.* 1982.

Gosse, Edmund and Thomas J. Wise, eds. *The Complete Works of Algernon Charles Swinburne.* 1925-1927. 20 vols. (Expurgated, with lacunae and corrupt texts; vol. 20 contains Wise's discredited bibliography of Swinburne's works.)

Henderson, Philip. *Swinburne: The Portrait of a Poet.* 1974.

Hughes, Randolph, ed. *Lesbia Brandon, by Algernon Charles Swinburne.* 1952.

Hyder, Clyde K. *Swinburne's Literary Career and Fame.* 1933.

Lang, Cecil Y., ed. *Letters of Algernon Charles Swinburne.* 1959-1962. 6 vols.

McGann, Jerome J. *Swinburne: An Experiment in Criticism.* 1972.

Riede, David G. *Swinburne: A Study of Romantic Mythmaking.* 1978.

Sypher, Francis J., ed. *A Year's Letters by Algernon Charles Swinburne.* 1974.

Thomas, Donald. *Swinburne: The Poet in His World.* 1979.

· · · · ·

SYMONDS, JOHN ADDINGTON (1840–1893)

John Addington Symonds was a poet, critic, travel writer, translator, and the author of a seven-volume history of the Italian Renaissance. He was also a homosexual who confronted the social and moral strictures of Victorian England.

Symonds wrote and published poetry but received harsh critical reviews in the press. His own critical works fared better, although many readers found his prose too impressionistic. His works of literary criticism include *An Introduction to the Study of Dante* (1872), *Studies of the Greek Poets* (2 vols., 1873–1876), *Shakespeare's Predecessors in the English Drama* (1884), and *Walt Whitman: A Study* (1893). His most successful work is his *Renaissance in Italy* in seven volumes (1875–1886). In this work Symonds focuses less on economic and historical forces than on literature and culture. It has been compared to Jacob Burckhardt's *History of the Renaissance in Italy* (originally published in German in 1860). Symonds also translated the *Life of Benvenuto Cellini* (1888) and the *Memoirs of Count Carlo Gozzi* (1890), and wrote a *Life of Michelangelo Buonarroti* (1893).

Symonds began writing his own *Memoirs* in 1889. The *Memoirs* focus primarily on the psychological and social turmoil he experienced because of his **homosexuality.** Here Symonds describes his theory of an ideal, refined homosexual love. He also expresses his hope for more tolerant social attitudes. The *Memoirs* were suppressed after his death but were finally published in 1984. They provide an important first-hand account of what it was like to be homosexual in Victorian England. For modern readers it is the *Memoirs*, along with the *Renaissance in Italy*, that establish the importance of Symonds.

OWEN SCHUR

Bibliography

Babington, Percy Lancelot. *Bibliography of the Writings of John Addington Symonds.* 1925.

Grosskurth, Phyllis. *John Addington Symonds: A Biography.* 1964.

——— , ed. *The Memoirs of John Addington Symonds.* 1984.

Reade, Brian, ed. *Sexual Heretics: Male Homosexuality in English Literature from 1850–1900.* 1970.

Schueller, Herbert M. and Robert L. Peters. *The Letters of John Addington Symonds: 1840–1893.* 1967–1969. 3 vols.

· · · · ·

TALBOT, WILLIAM HENRY FOX (1800–1877)

William Henry Fox Talbot, squire of Lacock manor, Wiltshire, applied his resources and Cambridge education to a life of research. Although only one-third of his twelve patents dealt strictly with **photography**, he is best remembered for his pioneer work in that field. His publications include *The Antiquity of the Book of Genesis* (1839), *Sun Pictures in Scotland* (1845), *English Etymologies* (1847), five other books, and some 150 papers.

From the 1820s onward Talbot had an interest in numbers theory and curve analysis. His papers on optics and light assisted the early development of spectroscopy. In 1842 he proposed the production of cheaper but improved reflecting telescopes and in 1871 suggested spectral analysis to reckon distances of some fixed stars. He was among the first English scholars to decipher cuneiform inscriptions from Nineveh. Cameras at excavations, he believed, would provide accurate and quick copies of inscriptions.

In 1834 Talbot began photographic experiments at Lacock. His sensitized paper, placed under lace or leaf and exposed to sunlight, produced negative images which a strong saline solution made moderately permanent. By 1835 these photogenic drawings were made in small cameras. He then produced positive prints and also experimented in photomicrography. News of Daguerre's invention caused Talbot to publicize his process at the Royal Institution's exhibit on January 25, 1839 and, six days later, with a paper to the Royal Society. Calotype/Talbotype prints, products of his vastly improved 1840 process, illustrated his *The Pencil of Nature* (1844), the first book published for profit to contain photographs. Talbot's wife Constance was probably the first woman photographer.

At age twenty-two Talbot became the youngest member of the Royal Astronomical Society. By 1831 he was a member of the Royal Society. In 1838 he received the Royal Medal for research in integral calculus and the Rumford Medal in 1842 for his contributions to photography.

JOHN J. WOODS

Bibliography

Arnold, Harry J .P. *William Henry Fox Talbot: Pioneer of Photography and Man of Science*, 1977.

Booth, Arthur H. *William Henry Fox Talbot: Father of Photography*. 1965.

Lassam, Robert. *Fox Talbot, Photographer*. 1979.

Newhall, Beaumont. *The History of Photography from 1839 to the Present*. 1982.

Ward, John and Sara Stevenson. *Printed Light: The Scientific Art of William Henry Fox Talbot and David Octavius Hill with Robert Adamson*. 1986.

· · · · ·

TAUCHNITZ EDITIONS

From 1841 to 1943 the Leipzig firm of Bernhard Tauchnitz published serially in English a "Collection of British and American Authors," comprising the more significant work of some 750 writers in 5,370 volumes, and eventually achieving a total issue exceeding 40 million copies distributed throughout the world. By private agreements in 1843 and later by Continental copyright provisions, the first Baron Tauchnitz (1816-1895) often secured from Dickens, Bulwer-Lytton, Trollope, and others advance proofs of work then at press and thus occasionally produced variant texts preceding those customarily regarded as "first editions." At other times (e.g., with Meredith's *Ordeal of Richard Feverel*, 1875) the firm originally issued the first revised text, or commissioned work specially "corrected"or otherwise altered for Continental readers.

Apart from this general production Tauchnitz published a number of limited series now rarely encountered, including one for young readers (30 vols., 1860-1883), another of German authors in English translation (51 vols., 1867-1892), and two with abridged English texts and accompanying German commentary for use in schools (41 vols., 1886-1917; 52 vols., 1926-1939). To further its literary or pedagogic activity, and to maintain its own foreign monopoly, the firm also produced numerous bilingual dictionaries (English-German, French, Italian, Spanish, Russian), thus advancing by this means an appreciation of English literature beyond all national frontiers.

Upon the destruction of the original establishment in 1943 successive postwar firms were started in Hamburg (1946), Milan (1951), and Stuttgart (1952); but none of these prevailed against increasing competition from other publishers.

WILLIAM B. TODD

· · · · ·

TAXES AND TARIFFS

Victorian fiscal policy was characterized by a movement from indirect to direct taxation and by a progressive simplification of both taxes and tariffs. These lines of development, established by Peel in the 1840s, were not decisively interrupted until the early twentieth century when increased spending on defense and social welfare led Lloyd George to seek new sources of revenue, notably in his "People's Budget" (1909). In addition to taxes imposed by central government, local taxation, in the form of rates on buildings and land, provided funds for poor relief, public health and, after 1870, education.

Sidney Smith's dying Englishman, burdened by various taxes on items of personal consumption from medication to marble headstones and expiring in the arms of an apothecary licensed at 100 pounds "for the privilege of putting him to death," caricatured the complexity of the early nineteenth-century fiscal system and its capacity to vex the individual taxpayer. State revenue was derived largely from customs and excise supple mented by a haphazard array of direct taxes. These included levies on specific professions and trades; legacy, probate, and stamp duties; and assessed taxes on, for example, horses, manservants, and windows. Assailed by free-traders and by radicals seeking remission of taxes that fell heavily on the necessary expenditure of the poor, the system proved insufficiently flexible when trade was slack, leaving the Whigs embarrassed by four successive budget deficits after 1838.

Peel's 1842 budget initiated a new era of fiscal policy. Its twin objectives were to eliminate the deficit by enhancing revenue and to remove restrictions on trade. Income tax, previously imposed during the French wars but abandoned in 1816, was reintroduced at seven-pence on the pound on all incomes above 150 pounds per annum. By increasing direct taxation in this way Peel was free to begin a reform of the tariff. Duties were reduced on 750 articles and maximum rates of 5 percent, 12 percent and 20 percent applied on raw materials, semimanufactured, and manufactured goods respectively. Further reductions followed in 1845 including the abolition of all export duties and the removal of duties on many imported raw materials, notably cotton.

After the repeal of the **Corn Laws** (1846) and Gladstone's **free trade** budgets (1853, 1860), the shape of the Victorian fiscal system was clarified. Indirect taxes, raised for revenue purposes only, continued to fall on a range of mainly imported commodities such as coffee, tea, tobacco, wines, and spirits. The notoriously complex assessed taxes were reformed from the late 1860s to facilitate convenient payment and economical administration. Chancellors came to rely on income tax as a permanent resource, varying the rate to meet annual requirements. The demands of war were satisfied by a rate of one shilling and fourpence in 1855–1856 while Gladstonian stringency and booming trade permitted a short-lived reduction to twopence in 1874. At the start of the twentieth century income tax receipts became the largest single item in gross public revenue.

By late twentieth-century standards Victorian taxation was modest, reflecting Gladstone's view that money should be allowed "to fructify in the pockets of the people." But with central government expenditure doubling be-

tween 1870 and 1910, chancellors were forced to widen the tax base. Graduated estate duties, dating from Harcourt's 1894 budget, increased significantly the yield payable at death while introducing the principle that taxes should be levied in proportion to the ability to bear them. This radical innovation opened the way for Lloyd George whose 1909 budget embraced not only new impositions on landowners but also graduated income tax and some differentiation between earned and unearned income. Though free trade was maintained, a point of departure from the Victorian fiscal tradition had been reached.

DILWYN PORTER

Bibliography

Kynaston, David. *The Chancellor of the Exchequer.* 1980.

Roseveare, Henry. *The Treasury: The Evolution of a British Institution.* 1969.

Sabine, Basil. *A History of Income Tax: The Development of Income Tax from 1799 to the Present Day.* 1966.

Shehab, Fakhri. *Progressive Taxation: A Study in the Development of the Progressive Principle in the British Income Tax.* 1953.

· · · · ·

TAXES ON KNOWLEDGE

The "taxes on knowledge" involved a series of financial exactions and restrictions on publishing during the eighteenth and nineteenth centuries. After effective agitation, they were reduced during the 1830s and repealed by 1860.

Beginning in 1712, Parliament imposed several types of taxes and duties on paper, printing, publications (especially newspapers), and advertisements. Stamps of varying amounts were required for every copy, even those unsold. One purpose was to raise revenue—but another was to control circulation. The stamp tax on newspapers was fourpence between 1815 and 1836, which meant that only the prosperous could afford newspapers.

In the 1830s a number of illegal, unstamped, and usually radical-oriented newspapers were published. Over 200 titles have been identified and over 1,100 cases of selling unstamped publications went before the London magistrates. Henry Hetherington, publisher of the *Poor Man's Guardian* (1831–1835), went to prison twice. G. J. Harney and Bronterre O'Brien were other radical publishers of this "Pauper Press."

The advertisement duty was reduced in 1833 and the newspaper tax in 1836. Late in the 1840s, encouraged by the successful campaign against the Corn Laws, two significant pressure groups were formed: the Newspaper Stamp Abolition Committee and the Association for the Repeal of Taxes on Knowledge. Prominent leaders were members of Parliament William Ewart and Thomas Milner-Gibson, and the popular radical, **Francis Place.**

The advertisement duty was repealed in 1853, the newspaper stamp tax in 1855, and the excise duty on paper in 1861. The successful campaign to repeal the taxes on knowledge, in conjunction with improved technology for paper and printing and innovations in journalism, made possible the rise of a mass press and the introduction of widely circulated periodicals (especially women's magazines) that were largely supported by advertising revenues, rather than purchase price.

EUGENE L. RASOR

Bibliography

Collet, C. D. *History of the Taxes on Knowledge.* 1899. 2 vols.

Hollis, Patricia. *The Pauper Press.* 1970.

Wiener, Joel H. *The War of the Unstamped.* 1969.

See also *LAWS OF PUBLIC WORSHIP, SPEECH, AND THE PRESS; PRESS, RADICAL AND UNSTAMPED*

· · · · ·

TAYLOR, CLEMENTIA DOUGHTY (1818-1908)

Clementia Doughty Taylor was a leader of the women's suffrage movement. The daughter of Mr. and Mrs. John Doughty of Brockdish, Norfolk, she was governess to the daughters of the Taylor family. In 1842 she married Peter Alfred Taylor (1819-1891), the older brother of her charges.

Clementia and P. A. Taylor shared radical political views. P. A. Taylor was elected to Parliament in 1862 where he represented Leicester until he retired in 1884. Clementia Taylor was a close friend and correspondent of Giuseppe Mazzini (1805-1872) and an active member of the Society of Friends of Italy. Like her husband she sided with the North in the American Civil War. Clementia Taylor founded the Aubrey Evening Institute, a school that provided free classes to working women. She served on the Executive Committee of the Married Women's Property Committee from 1876 to 1882. She was also well known as a political hostess for liberal causes at Aubrey House, the Taylors' home in Kensington. Her close friendship with George Eliot continued undiminished after Eliot and George Henry Lewes established their household together.

Clementia Taylor is best remembered as a leader of the women's suffrage movement. She signed the petition presented by J. S. Mill to Parliament in 1866, and served as treasurer and briefly as honorary secretary of the London National Society for Women's Suffrage in 1867. Taylor advocated votes for married women as well as widows and spinsters, which put her at odds with many other suffragists. In 1890 she joined the council of the short-lived Women's Franchise League, which pressed for votes for women regardless of marital status.

MARY LYNDON SHANLEY

Bibliography

Blackburn, Helen. *Women's Suffrage: A Record of the Women's Suffrage Movement in the British Isles with Biographical Sketches of Miss Becker.* 1902.

Gladstone, Florence. *Aubrey House, Kensington, 1698-1920.* 1922.

Haight, Gordon, ed. *The George Eliot Letters.* 1954-1978. 9 vols.

Times, April 14, 1908.

· · · · ·

TAYLOR, TOM
(1817–1880)

Known primarily as a dramatist, Tom Taylor also had a career that included journalism, art criticism, the law, university teaching, and public service. His best plays, *Masks and Faces* (1852), *Plot and Passion* (1853), *The Fool's Revenge* (1859), *The Ticket-of-Leave Man* (1863), and *New Men and Old Acres* (1869) helped establish him as the most popular English dramatist of the period 1845–1870.

Taylor, the son of a wealthy brewer, was educated at the University of Glasgow and at Trinity College, Cambridge, graduating with a distinguished record. In 1844 he moved to London and began to prepare for a legal career and to write satirical columns for *Punch*. (He was to become its editor in 1874.) Appointed as professor of English language and literature at the University of London in 1845, Taylor held the post for two years. He was also admitted to the bar in 1846. In 1850, when he was appointed assistant secretary to the Board of Health, he gave up the law permanently, and remained as a public servant until 1871.

Though engaged in public activities, Taylor wrote plays continuously. His first success was a one-act farce, *To Parents and Guardians*, performed at the Lyceum Theatre (1846), but it was his collaboration with **Charles Reade** in *Masks and Faces* that made his reputation as a writer of comedy. From 1853 to 1860 he wrote chiefly for the Haymarket and Olympic theaters; the former was known for its repertoire of eccentric comedy and the latter, under the management of Alfred Wigan, for its sophisticated French adaptations.

By 1860 Taylor's plays were vehicles for popular performers on both sides of the Atlantic. His comic writing was admired for its plot construction, and his melodramas for accurate and richly detailed domestic realism. In 1861 his play *Our American Cousin*, with E. A. Sothern playing Lord Dundreary, became the most fashionable comedy in London, running for over four hundred performances. *The Ticket-of-Leave Man* was his most enduring melodrama. His best comedy is probably *New Men and Old Acres*, written in collaboration with Augustus Dubourg.

Increasingly from 1870 Taylor's reputation began to be questioned and his reliance on French models of the "well-made play" deni-grated. Nevertheless, he continued to write, even if less successfully: the verse dramas *Twixt Axe and Crown* (1870), *Jeanne d'Arc* (1871), and *Ann Boleyn* (1876), and a prose drama, *Lady Clancarty* (1874), which was his last major success.

Taylor was a conservative playwright who at the same time was keenly aware of his audience's tastes and its toleration of new ideas. He popularized and applied French techniques of plot construction on the English stage. His plays continued to be revived into the early twentieth century, but with the advent of Ibsen and the new drama, Taylor's works came to be unjustly regarded as old-fashioned and derivative.

VICTOR EMELJANOW

Bibliography

Emeljanow, Victor. *Victorian Popular Dramatists.* 1987.

Taylor, Tom. *Plays: Selections.* 1985. Ed. Martin Banham.

Tolles, Winton. *Tom Taylor and the Victorian Drama.* 1940.

• • • • •

TEACHERS' EDUCATION AND TRAINING

Formal training of teachers began in the United Kingdom in the early nineteenth century when education was extended to the lower classes. Instructors of the privileged continued to lack any special preparation other than a knowledge of the subject or (particularly in the case of governesses) a background of "good breeding."

The training of elementary teachers for the poor evolved from the monitorial system, which was independently developed by Andrew Bell (1753–1832) for his (Church of England) National Society schools and by Joseph Lancaster (1778–1838) for his (Dissenting) British and Foreign Society schools. A single teacher could handle a great many children in one large classroom by teaching the lesson to a few older children ("monitors") who then instructed groups of younger pupils. Still dominant in the 1840s, the monitorial system was criticized by **James Kay-Shuttleworth** (1804–1877), secretary of the committee established in 1839 to oversee governmental grants to education. Under the pupil-teacher or "simultaneous" system instituted by Kay-Shuttleworth's committee in 1846 and revised during subsequent years to 1860, promising children remained at elementary school until age eighteen, earning money from thirteen while teaching the younger children in the daytime and receiving further instruction in the evenings. At eighteen these young people entered a teachers' training college; after an average stay of twenty-one months they were examined and certified.

By the 1850s there were some forty elementary school teachers' training colleges in England and Wales. Kay-Shuttleworth himself founded the Battersea Normal School (1840). He believed that prospective elementary school teachers should be given the equivalent of a secondary education as well as professional training. The general view, however, was that teachers of the poor were becoming too educated; the Newcastle Commission (appointed in 1858) concluded that teachers who came from the training colleges were overqualified, could not really do their work, and wanted excessive pay. The Revised Code of 1862 dealt a severe blow to teachers' training by reducing the grants to training colleges and lowering their examination standards.

The Elementary Education Act of 1870, mandating the establishment of many more elementary schools (the "Board Schools"), created an enormous demand for new teachers and eventually raised the standard of training. In the 1880s, daytime training colleges began to be established which were connected to university colleges (where the students could receive general education) rather than to elementary schools (where they would spend most of their days practice teaching). By the end of Victoria's reign teachers in elementary schools were beginning to have a sense of professional status and were increasingly women from the middle or lower-middle class rather than the working-class boys and girls who had stayed on in their elementary schools as pupil-teachers.

Toward the end of the century, when the need for secondary schools for the poor began to be evident, the concept of professional training for teachers in such schools was not welcomed. The tradition remained among the "educated classes" that secondary school and university teachers needed only to know their subjects and be of good character. In 1876, however, chairs of education were established at the universities of Edinburgh and St. Andrews, and within ten years both Oxford and Cambridge began to consider treating education as a university subject. The universities at first merely examined and certified prospective secondary school teachers, although some lectures on the history, theory, and practice of education were delivered at Cambridge. The first training colleges for secondary teachers were established as a part of the effort to upgrade the education of middle-class girls, since the women who were to teach in the new academic schools for girls had no adequate access to university education. The earliest such college, the Maria Gray College, opened in 1878. Comprehensive and systematic training of teachers for Britain's secondary schools was not, however, established until the state began to provide secondary education in the twentieth century.

DENNIS CHALDECOTT

Bibliography

Holcombe, Lee. *Victorian Ladies at Work.* 1973.

Rich, R. W. *The Training of Teachers in England and Wales During the Nineteenth Century.* 1933.

Tropp, Asher. *The School Teachers: The Growth of the Teaching Profession in England and Wales from 1800 to the Present Day.* 1957.

Widdowson, Frances. *Going up Into the Next Class: Women and Elementary Teacher Training, 1840–1914.* 1980.

See also **BEALE, DOROTHEA;**
EDUCATION

. . . . .

TECHNOLOGY AND INVENTION

Victorian Britain was acknowledged to be "the workshop of the world," as symbolized by the **Exhibition of 1851,** when visitors came from all over the world to admire the products of British manufacture and commerce assembled in the Crystal Palace. Encouraged from the outset by Albert, the prince consort, and opened by Queen Victoria, the exhibition displayed the prodigious progress achieved by Britain as a result of the rapid industrialization of the previous hundred years. The scale of the achievement makes it appropriate to describe this process as the "industrial revolution."

Contemporary observers of the national achievement represented by the Great Exhibition recognized that it derived from a remarkable accession of technological inventions. New sources of inanimate power, new machines, and new processes had transformed the heavy industries and textile industries into large-scale enterprises producing massive wealth. Coal, iron, and cotton had all responded to the stimulus of technological innovation with dramatic increases in productivity. The **steam engine** had developed from a crude pumping machine into a versatile prime mover used as a winding engine in the coal mines, as a source of power for spinning and weaving machines, as the driving force for rolling engines and steam hammers in the iron and engineering industries, and as a radically new form of transport in the shape of the **railway** steam locomotive and the steamship. By the middle of the nineteenth century, only Britain, among all the nations of the world, had experienced the transforming effect of this industrial revolution.

The success of this industrial revolution encouraged governments, in Britain and elsewhere, to commit themselves to what has been called "the invention of invention." This was the institutionalization of invention: the process whereby potential inventors were assisted in the exercise of their talents by the provision of suitable inducements and rewards. It was in the Victorian period especially that this institutional approval was given to the innovative process of technology and invention, confirming the continuing renewal and transformation of industrial society.

Prominent among the inducements provided for innovation was the development of patent law in order to ensure that the inventor received adequate financial reward for a successful invention. Not all inventions were capable of successful development, so investment in a new idea could be very risky. The reinforcement of patent law gave inventors some legal protection while they attempted to exploit their ideas and thus encouraged inventors and their financial backers to take chances in the expectation of receiving ample returns on their investment.

Another inducement was the reform of restrictive legislation for the control of manufacturing and commercial organizations in order to encourage entrepreneurs and general investors to put their resources into the development of new inventions. This was done primarily through the device of limited liability in company law, but in some countries an important part was played by special banking and credit facilities in helping to set up new enterprises. These measures proved to be very effective in drawing large amounts of investment into new industrial processes, thus consolidating the institutionalization of invention.

Of more general application as an inducement to continuing innovation was the social ethos of *Self-Help*, made popular in the best-selling work of that title by Samuel Smiles which was first published in 1859. This ethic was a stimulus to hard work and persistence in trying out new ideas, because success in such ventures guaranteed both wealth and social approval. The great inventors like James Watt became household models of successful self-help, so that young people in Victorian Britain were brought up in an environment that provided a positive spur to invention.

This social ethic was incorporated into the educational system. Education in Britain was frequently criticized for its tardiness in accepting the need for thorough technical instruction, and with a long-standing and successful tradition of apprenticeship—learning through work—Britain was certainly later than France or Germany in equipping itself with systematic theoretical education in the new technologies. But such a system did emerge in the second half of the nineteenth century, supplying both basic instruction for artisans and high-level technical theory in university courses for potential engineers and managers. The effect of this educational revolution was to integrate technology into the scholarly disciplines, and to make continuing invention a universal assumption.

One aspect of these educational developments was the reconciliation of technology and science. Technology has traditionally been concerned with practicalities, with making and doing things rather than with the speculative reflection which has been more characteristic of science. Most of the earlier inventions of the industrial revolution such as the spinning and weaving machines, the coke smelting of iron, and the atmospheric steam engine of Thomas Newcomen, had been primarily the products of the craft tradition of trial and error. Some contribution had been made by more speculative men such as the scientists of the Royal Society who had encouraged Papin and others to demonstrate the results of their researches on the power of steam, but the relationship remained underdeveloped.

As the process of innovation became increasingly sophisticated, however, the interest of scientists in the theoretical implications of machines like the high-pressure steam engine grew and produced a novel understanding of the nature of heat, energy, and work, which was embodied in the new science of thermodynamics. Similarly, the research of organic chemists into the range of useful materials that could be derived from coal tar, and of electrical scientists into the practical applications of electricity as a new source of power, acquired profound technological significance. The result was an increasing integration of science and technology, which aided the recognition of technology as an academic discipline.

This achievement of the "invention of invention" produced a subtle transformation in the quality of inventions. Some certainly remained fairly simple and many were still the result of a single inspired inventor. More generally, however, the innovations that stemmed from the increasingly scientific technology after the Exhibition of 1851 tended to incorporate a significant amount of scientific theory and more often than not they were the result of teamwork, although this was not always acknowledged. For instance, W.H. Perkin is often given the credit for having discovered the first aniline dye in 1856, but he could not have done so without having studied the latest research in organic **chemistry** at the Royal College of Chemistry, where the director was the German scientist A.W. Hofman, whose work did much to inspire the artifical

dyes, synthetic textiles, plastics, and high explosives industries in Germany.

The increasing role of scientific technology in invention was apparent in many industries by the end of the nineteenth century. The heavy chemical industry had been transformed by the Solvay process (1861) for producing soda much more economically than the earlier Leblanc process. The iron and steel industry was given a tremendous boost by the "converter" process of Henry Bessemer and the Siemens "open-hearth" process (both 1856), but both required the scientific research of Percy Gilchrist and S.G. Thomas with their "basic steel" process (1875) in order to fulfill their enormous potential for mass producing cheap steel. The electrolytic process for the recovery of aluminum from its ores (1886) was but one application of the new electrical science, which was producing innovations of massive importance in power technology, with dynamos for the mechanical generation of **electricity** and electric motors for converting this energy into power for machines and vehicles. The application of electrical science led also to the telephone (1876), radio (1885), and the modern electronics industry. It also produced striking discoveries in radioactivity and X-rays (1895) which profoundly altered the scientific understanding of the nature of matter and opened up the way to the exploration of the atom and to atomic power. The internal combustion engine was refined by Rudolf Diesel with thermodynamic science to produce a wonderfully versatile engine (first British patent, 1892), and early in the new century the achievement of powered flight by the Wright brothers (1903) became the focus for the concentrated application of aerodynamic science. Even the steam engine underwent development inspired by scientific technology such as that incorporated in the "Uniflow" engine (1908), as well as in the steam turbine of Charles Parsons (1884) and others.

In these and many other respects, the Victorian period demonstrated an impressive shift toward scientific technology. Of course, as the processes of industrialization spread and other countries began to share the benefits of increased productivity and a higher standard of living, Britain forfeited its position as the "workshop of the world." What had been unique to Britain in 1851 had become widely shared in Europe and North America by the end of the century. Britain, however, retained a leading position for industrial innovation: the principle of the "invention of invention" had been thoroughly learned, and technology had been fully integrated with science in a progressive ethos which placed Britain, together with the other industrialized nations, on the brink of an exciting range of new developments at the beginning of the twentieth century.

R. A. BUCHANAN

Bibliography

Buchanan, R. A. *History and Industrial Civilization.* 1979.

———. *Technology and Social Progress.* 1965.

Cardwell, Donald S. L. *The Organisation of Science in England.* Rev. ed., 1972.

———. *Technology, Science and History.* 1972.

Derry, T. K. and Trevor I. Williams. *A Short History of Technology.* 1961.

Ferguson, Eugene S. *Bibliography of the History of Technology.* 1968.

Jewkes, John, David Sawers, and Richard Stillerman. *The Sources of Invention.* 1958.

Mumford, Lewis. *Technics and Civilization.* 1934.

Pacey, Arnold. *The Maze of Ingenuity: Ideas and Idealism in the Development of Technology.* 1974.

Rosenberg, Nathan, ed. *The Economics of Technological Change.* 1971.

Smiles, Samuel. *Self-Help.* 1959.

Usher, Abbott P. *A History of Mechanical Inventions.* 2d ed., 1954.

See also EDUCATION, TECHNICAL; PATENTS

. . . . .

The Great Telegraphing Room at the New Offices of the Electric and International Telegraph Co., Bell Alley, Moorgate Street. Illustrated London News, *31 December 1859. Library Company of Philadelphia.*

TELEGRAPH AND TELEPHONE

The modern age of telecommunications began in 1837 when Charles Wheatstone in England and Samuel Morse in America patented the first telegraph equipment. Morse's system became more successful, but Wheatstone is credited with developing several improvements in telegraphic communication.

The first British telegraph lines were used for railway signaling. By midcentury companies were offering service to the public and during the 1850s the inland network rapidly expanded and links were established to France (1851) and across the Irish and North seas. Civil and military authorities and journalists quickly took advantage of the telegraph. The government temporarily took over the system during the Chartist disturbances of 1848. In 1851 Paul Reuter brought his news service to London and both the press and the military extensively used the telegraph during the Crimean War. The **Atlantic cable** was completed in 1866 and by 1870 London was linked with Bombay. The telegraph drastically reduced the size of the world and altered the conduct of business, government, and public discourse. General dissatisfaction with service by the press and public led to takeover of the inland system by the post office in 1870.

The telephone, invented in America in 1876, quickly emerged as a competitor to the telegraph and in 1880 the post office by court decision obtained control over its development. By 1890 the National Telephone Company shared a virtual monopoly on service with the post office and the system had expanded slowly to about 50,000 subscribers. Restrictive post office policies, the company's difficulties in obtaining wayleaves, and chronic uncertainty in government policy all served to retard development of the British telephone system. Nevertheless, after 1890 increased demand produced more rapid growth while general dissatisfaction with the system resulted in a gradual takeover by the post office completed in 1911.

FREDERICK E. LAURENZO

Bibliography

Baldwin, Francis G. C. *The History of the Telephone in the United Kingdom.* 1925.

Hemmeon, J. C. *History of the British Post Office.* 1912.

Kieve, Jeffery L. *The Electric Telegraph: A Social and Economic History.* 1973.

· · · · ·

TEMPERANCE MOVEMENT

Although the drink problem is as old as alcohol, the temperance movement in Britain began in the nineteenth century. Around 1830 increasing optimism about human nature and the visibility of drunken urban workers aroused reformers to organize temperance societies and make public pledges against drinking alcoholic beverages. Temperance became part of Victorian respectability, particularly for Nonconformist artisans, clerks, and shopkeepers in the north and west of England and in Wales and Scotland.

Temperance meant different things to different people. The first reformers advocated an antispirits pledge which allowed drinking wine and the most popular British drink, beer, in moderation. In 1832 Joseph Livesey (1794–1884) led seven Preston workingmen in a total abstinence pledge. By the 1840s temperance usually meant teetotalism. Some teetotalers demanded the long pledge in which abstainers promised not to provide alcohol to others, but few temperance societies insisted upon it.

The strength of the temperance movement lay in the network of local organizations which provided a teetotal subculture for those who rejected the dominant drinking culture. National organizations typically existed as federations of independent societies. There were two such large national teetotal organizations: the London-based National Temperance Society (formed 1842) which became the National Temperance League in 1856, and the predominantly provincial British Association for the Promotion of Temperance (1835) which became the British Temperance League in 1854. Gradually the temperance ethic entered popular culture, as exemplified by the drawings of George Cruikshank (1792–1878): *The Bottle* (1847), *The Drunkard's Children* (1848), and *The Worship of Bacchus* (1862).

Neglected by Their Parents, Educated Only in the Streets and Falling into the Hands of Wretches Who Live Upon The Vices of Others, They Are Led to the Gin Shop, to Drink at That Fountain Which Nourishes Every Species of Crime (plate I of The Drunkard's Children) *by George Cruikshank, 1848. Reproduced from* Graphic Works of George Cruikshank, ed. Richard A. Vogler, Dover Publications Inc.

A vision of a temperance reformation, with total abstinence reshaping society, inspired the first teetotalers. Early teetotalism flourished among sociopolitical radicals who preached a belligerent form of "self-help." Independent-minded workers often adopted teetotalism out of the same motives that drove them to organize adult education classes and trade unions or agitate for Chartism. At first only the smaller, more revivalistic Nonconformist denominations welcomed the teetotal movement. When teetotalers demanded unfermented wine in the eucharist, traditionalists denounced them as troublemakers. The most celebrated clerical advocate of teetotalism was, atypically, an Irish Catholic priest, Father Theobald Mathew (1790–1856), who pledged uncounted thousands in Ireland in the 1840s.

By the 1860s moral reform had largely displaced social reform in teetotal ideology, and living life free from alcohol became objective enough. The churches began to swallow up the teetotal movement, and by the 1870s most denominations started their own temperance societies. Most younger Nonconformist ministers abstained from drink as did an important minority of clergymen in the established church. Gospel temperance, imported from the United States in 1878, tightened the bonds between religion and teetotalism. A good Christian had a religious duty to abstain. Gospel temperance also introduced the blue ribbon as the badge of the teetotaler.

The regalia and ritual of fraternal temperance orders added color to the temperance movement, and lodge life strengthened the sense of community. The Rechabites were organized in 1835, the Sons of the Phoenix in 1844, while the Sons of Temperance migrated from the United States in 1847, as did the Good Templars in 1868.

In 1876 Good Templar women helped found the British Women's Temperance Association which made the white ribbon its badge. Schism divided the organization in 1893. Those who wanted to confine their efforts to temperance created the Women's Total Abstinence Society, while the majority who favored a broad program of reform organized the National British Women's Temperance Association. Although never as important as the Woman's Christian Temperance Union in America, the British women had two notable presidents, **Isabella Somerset** (1851–1921) and **Rosalind Howard, countess of Carlisle** (1845–1921).

Specialized societies sprang up for sailors, soldiers, police, railroad workers, commercial travelers, physicians, and other occupational groups. Temperance societies for children enjoyed great numerical success. The **Band of Hope**, founded in 1847, could claim more than three million members by the end of the century. Irish Catholic children joined the Pioneer Total Abstinence Association of the Sacred Heart (1898).

Personal abstinence and moral suasion did not satisfy those who saw drink as a national crime and sin. In 1853, inspired by the enactment of prohibition in the American state of Maine, the Quaker reformer Nathaniel Card (1805–1856) helped organize the United Kingdom Alliance for the Immediate and Total Legislative Suppression of the Traffic in All Intoxicating Liquors. Four years later the alliance retreated to a policy of prohibition by local option referendum, known as Local Veto. The alliance, headquartered in Manchester, took the Anti-Corn-Law League as its model. An efficient system of alliance agents rallied temperance opinion, pressed test questions upon parliamentary candidates, raised money, and published a weekly newspaper, the *Alliance News*. In 1864 Wilfrid Lawson (1829–1906) introduced the Permissive Prohibitory Bill in the House of Commons. In 1879 he replaced the bill with a more vaguely worded resolution which the Liberal party leadership supported in 1883. In 1891 William Gladstone endorsed the Newcastle Programme, which included Local Veto. The so-called advanced temperance party, led by the alliance and the National Temperance Federation (1884), became closely aligned with the Liberals, while the drink trade became allied with the Conservatives.

By the 1880s temperance reform enjoyed support on medical and economic grounds as well as on those of morality and Christian humanitarianism. Sunday closing was enacted for Wales in 1881, and in most places licensing justices permitted few new public houses. Abstainers were a substantial minority in the country, at least a tenth of the United Kingdom's adult population when Victoria died. Moderate drinkers too condemned drunkenness, and middle-class opinion welcomed legislation that restricted the licensing of the sale of drink. This broad support for reform did not mean agreement on what reform should be. For instance, the Church of England Temperance Society (1862; reorganized with teetotal and nonabstinence sections, in 1873) disliked Local Veto, preferred reducing the number of licensed premises as a method of reform, and believed that those who lost their licenses deserved some kind of compensation. The majority and the minority reports of the (Peel) Royal Commission on the Licensing Laws endorsed reduction in numbers in 1899. Another approach to reform, the so-called Gothenburg scheme, named after the Swedish port where it was pioneered, removed private profit from the retail sale of drink. At the end of Victoria's reign most temperance reformers worked to limit and reform the sale of drink, not prohibit it.

DAVID M. FAHEY

Bibliography

Harrison, Brian. "Drink and Sobriety in England, 1815–1872: A Critical Bibliography." *International Review of Social History*, vol. 12, pp. 204–276.

———. *Drink and the Victorians: The Temperance Question in England, 1815–1872*. 1971.

Shiman, Lilian Lewis. *Crusade Against Drink in Victorian England*. 1988.

· · · · ·

TENNIEL, JOHN (1820–1914)

Long associated with **Lewis Carroll**'s Alice books, John Tenniel's illustrations are recognized even by people who have never read *Alice's Adventures in Wonderland* (1865) and *Through the Looking-Glass* (1872). Although well known to the Victorian middle-class audience as a *Punch* cartoonist, it is for his Alice illustrations that Tenniel is remembered today.

Tenniel was born in London where he lived all his life. He became *Punch's* chief artist when John Leech died in 1864 and held that position until 1901. Prior to his *Punch* assignment, Tenniel illustrated *Aesop's Fables* (1848) and Thomas Moore's *Lalla Rookh* (1861). Married in 1852 but widowed two years later, he lived quietly, allowing the *Punch* roundtable to serve as his club. He was virtually self-taught, never used models because of his shyness and a self-proclaimed memory for detail, and aspired to high art but found his niche in illustration and political caricature.

Lewis Carroll had originally considered using his own illustrations for *Alice's Adventures in Wonderland* but was convinced to seek Tenniel's help. The two men worked closely, although not without acrimony, over the forty-two illustrations. Close parallels can be seen between Carroll's drawings and Tenniel's, but Tenniel's tend to be more realistic and more detailed. In addition, as Michael Hancher demonstrates, Tenniel reused characters and backgrounds from his *Punch* illustrations. For example, Tweedledum and Tweedledee look remarkably like the John Bull character in an April 1861 *Punch* cartoon. Much of the humor in Tenniel's illustrations is lost on modern audiences unfamiliar with *Punch* satires of such subjects as fashions or the Pope.

Alice in Wonderland is noted not only for freeing children's literature from didacticism but also for the quality of publication. Tenniel labored to assure that the drawings were finely detailed and correctly positioned with the text. Border, cut-in, and L-shaped illustrations were employed to match text and picture. Tenniel insisted that the first printing be recalled because he was displeased with the reproductions of his art.

Tenniel agreed only with reluctance to illustrate the second Alice book, and he and Carroll argued over details such as the crinolines on the queen. But Carroll took Tenniel's advice, altered his text, and omitted the "Wasp in the Wig" chapter. The book was the last that Tenniel illustrated.

LOUISA SMITH

Bibliography

Hancher, Michael. *The Tenniel Illustrations to the "Alice" Books.* 1985.

. . . . .

TENNIS

During the second half of the nineteenth century many preindustrial recreations became organized as economic change gave rise to a mass consumer society with growing leisure time. Lawn tennis emerged as a popular Victorian middle- and upper-class pastime for family participation. The game became a feature of country house life, and tennis clubs were founded by the middle classes. Tennis appealed to middle-class women and helped emancipate them.

Lawn tennis is an adaptation of several racket sports including real (royal) tennis, an indoor game originally played by monks, monarchs, and aristocrats. The invention of the lawn mower enabled tennis to move outdoors.

Victorian pioneers and popularizers of the game include Major T. H. Gem, who established the first lawn tennis club in 1872 at Leamington Spa, and Major W. C. Wingfield, who tried to patent a racket game called "sphairistiké," played on an hourglass shaped court, in 1874. Players from public schools were important in the development of the game. The Marylebone Cricket Club (MCC), as the governing body of real tennis and rackets, drew up regulations for lawn tennis in 1875.

Croquet had led the way as a lawn and female sport. The All England Croquet Club, founded in 1869 at Wimbledon, soon added tennis to its title and organized the first men's tennis championship (1877), specifically to raise funds. A women's singles event was played in 1884. The All England club modified the MCC rules and codified the game.

Tennis spread rapidly to Europe and North America, and was soon played on surfaces other than grass. The first international competition was the Davis Cup between Great Britain and the United States (1900).

OLWYN M. BLOUET

Bibliography

Arlott, John, ed. *The Oxford Companion to World Sports and Games.* 1975.

Baker, William J. *Sports in the Western World.* 1982.

Walvin, James. *Leisure and Society, 1830-1950.* 1978.

See also SPORTS AND GAMES, WOMEN'S

. . . . .

TENNYSON, ALFRED (1809-1892)

Alfred Tennyson, one of the most popular and prolific Victorian poets and an accomplished literary craftsman, became poet laureate in 1850. His major works include *Poems* (1842), *The Princess* (1847), *In Memoriam* (1850), *Maud* (1855), and *Idylls of the King* (1859-1874; printed in one volume in 1889). Using literary and mythological sources and experimental or relatively unfamiliar verse forms (idyl, monodrama, medley, dramatic monologue), his works explore madness, a self divided between action and regression, the search for solid grounds for religious faith, troubled sexuality, the romance of the past, and the artist's mission.

During a painful childhood in a family plagued by genteel poverty, alcoholism, drug abuse, and madness, Tennyson devoted himself to poetry. *Poems, Chiefly Lyrical* (1830) provides early evidence of his ability to suggest psychological states through lushly sensual description of the physical world.

While at Cambridge University (1827–1829) Tennyson associated with the Cambridge Apostles and befriended the aspiring poet and critic Arthur Hallam, who encouraged the shy Tennyson to publish. *Poems* (1832) contains early versions of some famous works which explore the dilemma of the artist: "The Palace of Art," "Oenone," "The Lotos-Eaters," and "The Lady of Shalott." Several critics attacked this volume for its stylistic affectation.

Wounded by the hostile reviews and overwhelmed by Arthur Hallam's sudden death (1833), Tennyson exorcised his grief over the next ten years by writing: he produced a series of elegies tracing the phases of his sorrow, poems on the Arthurian materials, and revisions of the 1833 poems. *Poems* (1842) includes these revisions; new poems like "Morte D'Arthur" and "Ulysses," which indirectly reflect on Hallam's loss; and a collection of "English Idyls," depictions of Victorian domestic life using a remodeled classical verse form. Tennyson addressed the debate on women's proper sphere in *The Princess: A Medley.* Highly elaborate in form, employing narrative frames, several narrators, and a mix of story and song, the verse itself embodies the poem's theme; the need for a "medley" in every person of masculine and feminine traits.

The 1840s, a decade of poverty, nervous collapse, and failed romance, yielded to the 1850s in which marriage, financial security, fame, and the position of poet laureate came Tennyson's way. Three major works mark the decade. *In Memoriam,* a loosely structured cycle of elegies for Hallam, departs from the traditional English elegy form and broadens the subject matter to include not only the stages of grief and the artist's struggle to transform pain into poetry but also key Victorian concerns like the bases of religious faith and the implications of evolutionary theory. *Maud: A Monodrama* depicts contemporary social and economic injustice through the eyes of a neurotic narrator who ranges from lyrical exaltation to hysterical ranting in extraordinary poetry that registers the modulations in his voice.

The *Idylls of the King,* on the other hand, examines mid-Victorian England through the vehicles of **Arthurian legend** and a self-conscious, sophisticated verse form derived from Alexandrian poetry. Epic in scope, the *Idylls* trace the rise and fall of a state based on Christian ideals, examining how individual moral and psychological problems erode the social fabric.

In his last twenty years Tennyson wrote historical dramas and four volumes of poetry: *Ballads and Other Poems* (1880), *Tiresias and Other Poems* (1885), *Locksley Hall Sixty Years After* (1886), *Demeter and Other Poems* (1889), and *The Death of Oenone, Akbar's Dream, and Other Poems* (1892). Long regarded primarily as a lyricist given to overt moralizing, Tennyson now is seen as a poet of great technical sophistication, psychological insight, and a modern sense of ambivalence and loss.

CATHERINE BARNES STEVENSON

Bibliography

Beetz, Kirk K. *Tennyson: A Bibliography, 1827–1982*. 1984.

Buckley, Jerome H. *Tennyson: The Growth of a Poet*. 1960.

Lang, Cecil Y. and Edgar F. Shannon, eds. *The Letters of Alfred Lord Tennyson*. 1981–.

Martin, Robert B. *Tennyson: The Unquiet Heart*. 1980.

Ricks, Christopher, ed. *The Poems of Tennyson*. 1968.

· · · · ·

TERRY, ELLEN
(1847–1928)

In addition to her warmth and charm as an actress, Ellen Terry was notable for her lengthy associations with Henry Irving and George Bernard Shaw. Born to a well-established acting family, she made her debut at the age of nine as Mamillius in Charles Keane's production of *The Winter's Tale* (1856). She left the stage at sixteen to marry the painter **G. F. Watts.** When this unhappy alliance ended, Terry returned to acting, most notably as Katherine to Irving's Petruchio in *The Taming of the Shrew* (1867).

Terry's career was interrupted a second time when she again left the stage to live with architect and theatrical designer Edward Godwin. Neither this relationship, nor subsequent marriages to Charles Kelly (1839–1885) and James Carew (1876–1938), proved as enduring as her career. At the instigation of author Charles Reade, Terry staged a successful comeback as Philippa in *The Wandering Heir* (1874), and followed it by appearances as Portia in the Bancroft's production of *The Merchant of Venice* (1875) and the title role of Olivia in John Hare's adaptation of Goldsmith's *The Vicar of Wakefield* (1878).

At the age of thirty-one Terry began a theatrical partnership with Irving which was to last

for a quarter of a century. Although her dramatic skills were not of the highest, Terry lent her undeniable glamour and vivacity to the wide range of Shakespearian plays which they staged at the Lyceum, as well as to contemporary plays by authors such as Tennyson and Ibsen. Her famous correspondence with Shaw, published in 1931, is remarkable for its brilliant wit and insight; Shaw reciprocated by writing a number of parts specifically for her. She was made a dame of the British Empire in 1925.

LAUREN SMITH

Bibliography

Auerbach, Nina. *Ellen Terry, Player in Her Time.* 1987.

Manvell, Roger. *Ellen Terry.* 1968.

· · · · ·

TEXTILE INDUSTRY

Textiles, mining, metal manufactures, and engineering were the staple industries of Victorian Britain. In the early Victorian period, textiles employed more than one industrial worker in every four, produced 10 to 15 percent of British national income, and accounted for 60 to 70 percent of the value of British exports.

As it had been from the late eighteenth century, cotton continued to be the most dynamic branch of the industry. The number of cotton workers exceeded the combined total of those working in the other three major branches—wool, linen, and silk. The concentration of cotton workers in Lancashire, already heavy at the beginning of Victoria's reign, became progressively greater at the expense of Scotland and other regions of the British Isles. By the end of the century, over 90 percent of the total employment in the cotton industry could be found in Lancashire and the neighboring parts of Yorkshire, Derbyshire, and Cheshire.

The typical Victorian cotton firm had to adapt in various ways to changing circumstances. In the 1830s many were hereditary firms owned by descendants of the industrial pioneers. From the 1860s onward increased capital requirements spurred the growth of limited liability companies (often called "Oldham limiteds" after the town in which they became most prominent). Technical innovations were common during the early and mid-Victorian periods. Water wheels were increasingly eclipsed by steam engines as sources of power, and domestic handloom weavers were replaced by powerloom weavers in factories. Toward the end of the century, however, entrepreneurs became more reluctant than their leading foreign rivals to innovate, especially in adopting ring spinning and automatic loom weaving. This began to slow the growth of workers' productivity. Home demand began to slacken after 1860, and since traditional outlets in Europe and North America were also drying up, British producers confronted increasingly sharp competition for markets in Asia and Latin America.

Many of the general developments found in cotton also appeared in the other branches of the textile industry. Geographic concentration became increasingly prominent, with woolen and worsted production located in the West Riding of Yorkshire and linen manufacture in northern Ireland. Most hand processes gave way to mechanized factory production. The increased power required for machines was provided primarily by the installation of new steam engines. In the wool, linen, and silk branches combined, steam power increased nearly sevenfold from 1838 to 1871.

By the end of Victoria's reign, signs of relative decline in the textile industry became increasingly apparent. With mounting foreign competition and shifting marketing patterns, the annual rate of growth in the forty years after 1857 was considerably less than half of what it had been in the preceding forty years. The peak of employment in wool factories occurred in 1890, in flax and related factories in 1874, and in silk factories as early as 1856. Exports of woolen and linen goods declined precipitously during the last three decades of the century.

In the meantime, however, the remarkable increase in the number of textile factories and the size of the factory work force had contributed to at least three major sociopolitical developments. First, an important new type of legislation, the **Factory Act**, was inaugurated in 1833. Applying only to textile factories at first, it signaled the government's willingness to regulate private industry by using a professional bureaucracy and, simultaneously, its desire to improve the health and education of child workers. Second, the concentration of factories in urban centers facilitated the formation of **trade unions.** Textile unions typically differentiated themselves by craft (admitting only spinners or weavers or machine makers, for example) and they almost invariably excluded women. Third, many factories became centers of social and cultural events for workers. These might feature friendly societies, sporting clubs, factory bands, and some activities designed to advance the factory owner's political beliefs. In myriad ways, therefore, the Victorian textile industry provided an important symbol of the new industrial age.

ROBERT GLEN

Bibliography

Ashley, William J., ed. *British Industries.* 1903.

Chapman, Stanley D. *The Cotton Industry in the Industrial Revolution.* 1972.

Farnie, D. A. *The English Cotton Industry and the World Market, 1815–1896.* 1979.

Howe, Anthony. *The Cotton Masters, 1830–1860.* 1984.

Jenkins, D. T. and K. G. Ponting. *The British Wool Textile Industry, 1770–1914.* 1982.

Joyce, Patrick. *Work, Society and Politics: The Culture of the Factory in Later Victorian England.* 1980.

Ward, John T. *The Factory Movement, 1830–1855.* 1962.

Warner, Frank. *The Silk Industry of the United Kingdom.* 1921.

See also DOMESTIC INDUSTRY

. . . . .

THACKERAY, WILLIAM MAKEPEACE (1811–1863)

William Makepeace Thackeray gained his celebrity as a novelist and satirist, but his early journalism, art and theater criticism, travel books, and lectures, as well as the density of topical and topographical detail in his novels, make him a great chronicler and social historian of his age. He was the most versatile of Victorian men of letters, being skilled with both "pen and pencil." Moreover, as self-styled "moral philosopher" and "weekday preacher" he served his first readers as a high popularizer of culture and ideas.

Thackeray was born in Calcutta to Anne Becher and Richmond Thackeray, secretary to the Bengal Board of Revenue. His father died when Thackeray was four, and his mother married a suitor of her youth, Henry Carmichael-Smyth, then an ensign in the Bengal Engineers. Thackeray was sent to England at the age of six to be educated, and was later joined there by his mother and stepfather. He was a student at Charterhouse (referred to as "Slaughterhouse" in some of his stories because of its location in Smithfield) and attended Trinity College, Cambridge (February 1829–June 1830), leaving without taking a degree.

During his early youth he was something of a drifter, living the life of an affluent dilettante. He spent nine months at Weimar (July 1830–March 1831) where he met Goethe and absorbed the literary and theatrical life there (recalled in the Pumpernickel section of *Vanity Fair*). Subsequently he read law at the Middle Temple (scene of some of the episodes of *Pendennis*). The loss of a good part of his inheritance through a bank failure in India forced on him the necessity of making a living. At first he hoped to become an artist, studying intermittently in Paris from 1833 to 1837 at the Ecole des Beaux Arts and at various ateliers, as well as in London studios (an experience recollected in *The Newcomes*). Recognizing that he could not become a first-rate artist, Thackeray turned to journalism, but his studies stood him in good stead as an art critic, and more importantly as illustrator for a number of his own books. Early journalistic ventures included a partnership in the *National Standard* (the *Museum* of *Lovel the Widower*), which he also served as Paris correspondent (May 1833–August 1834) and Paris correspondent for the *Constitutional* (September 1836–July 1837). The failure of these enterprises, together with financial burdens brought on by his marriage to Isabella Shaw (August 20, 1836) and early fatherhood, steered him into the hackmanship of his early years. The two principal journals he was asso-

ciated with were *Fraser's Magazine* (1834–1847) and *Punch* (1842–1851). (This phase of his career is recapitulated in his last completed novel, *The Adventures of Philip*). His first commercially successful novel, *Vanity Fair* (1848), freed him from the necessity of "magazinery" to which he did not return until he became editor of *Cornhill* in 1859.

Thackeray's literary sensibility was fed largely by eighteenth-century writers, notably the essayist-journalists Addison and Steele (who appear in *Henry Esmond*), the novelists Fielding and Smollett, and the historian Gibbon. Among Continental writers, Montaigne was a lifelong favorite. His intellectual outlook was much influenced also by a French educator-philosopher Victor Cousin whose *Cours d'Histoire* he first came upon as an art student in Paris. Cousin's system of thought, known as eclecticism, held that the primary function of the philosopher in the modern world was to reconcile different positions, no one set of beliefs containing the whole truth, and he therefore enjoined on his followers the study of psychology, "universal sympathy," and tolerance of human error. This cosmopolitanism is reflected in the shifting mental perspectives of Thackeray's novels and in their tempered skepticism.

Most of Thackeray's fiction can be linked with periodicals. To *Fraser's*, noted for its slashing iconoclasm, belong *The Yellowplush Papers* (1838), a black comic exposé of sham aristocrats and pretenders to learning; as well as the parodic novels *Catherine* (1838–1839; published posthumously as a book in 1869), a satire on popular crime novels, and *Barry Lyndon* (1844), which guys then-popular sentimental Irish novels. His principal contributions to *Punch*, a journal noted for its blend of sanative satire and serious social criticism, were the delightful series of parodies "Punch's Prize Novelists" (1853; later published as *Novels from Eminent Hands*) and *The Book of Snobs* (1848; first appeared as "The Snobs of England by One of Themselves"). These led into the panoramic *Vanity Fair* and its successor, the more autobiographic *Pendennis* (1849–1850).

Thackeray's main activity during the 1850s aside from writing was two series of historical lectures delivered in England, Scotland, and the United States, resulting in the books *The English Humourists of the Eighteenth Cen-*

tury (1853) and *The Four Georges* (1861). He took to the platform mainly to provide a nest egg for his two daughters, Anny and Minny, for whose care he had sole responsibility owing to the early insanity of his wife (she had to be confined from 1845 until her death in 1893). The lectures proved lucrative, if deleterious to Thackeray's health. Their fictional by-products were the historical novels *Henry Esmond* (1852) and its sequel *The Virginians* (1859). His great *Familienroman* of this decade, *The Newcomes* (1855), which some consider his masterpiece, also takes on the coloration of the historian and popular lecturer (it is narrated by Thackeray's alter ego Arthur Pendennis). Also belonging to this period is the greatest of Thackeray's Christmas stories, *The Rose and the Ring* (1854), which he labeled "A Fireside Pantomime for Great and Small Children."

Thackeray's last works appeared in *Cornhill Magazine* which he edited, at the invitation of the publisher George Smith, from 1859-1862. His outstanding contribution to *Cornhill* was the series of essays modeled on his beloved *Spectator*, entitled *The Roundabout Papers* (published as a book in 1863). However, the preoccupations of these papers—the past recalled, the changes wrought by time, the fallibility of human judgment, the subtlety of civilized evil—are also embedded in the textures of the novels that first appeared in *Cornhill: Lovel the Widower* (1861); *The Adventures of Philip* (1862), which completes the Pendennis sequence, and in which Thackeray reviews his career; and *Denis Duval*, a lively adventure story unfortunately left unfinished at Thackeray's death (posthumously published in book form in 1864). Thackeray was found dead in his last home at Palace Green, Kensington on Christmas night, 1863, at the age of fifty-two. He is buried in Kensal Green Cemetery.

The Library Edition of Thackeray's works was published by Smith, Elder in twenty-four volumes, 1867-1869. Other important editions are the Biographical Edition (1898) and the Centenary Biographical Edition (1910-1911), both supervised by his daughter **Anne Thackeray Ritchie** who provided important biographical introductions.

ROBERT A. COLBY

Bibliography

Colby, Robert A. *Thackeray's Canvass of Humanity.* 1979.

Costerus. Thackeray Issue. 1974.

Harden, Edgar F. *The Emergence of Thackeray's Serial Fiction.* 1979.

——. *Thackeray's English Humourists and Four Georges.* 1985.

McMaster, Juliet. *Thackeray: The Major Novels.* 1971.

Phillipps, Kenneth C. *The Language of Thackeray.* 1978.

Ray, Gordon N. *The Age of Wisdom.* 1958.

——. *The Uses of Adversity.* 1955.

——, ed. *The Letters and Private Papers of William Makepeace Thackeray.* 1945-1946. 4 vols.

Studies in the Novel, vol. 13. (Thackeray Special Number. Spring–Summer 1981.)

Sutherland, John. *Thackeray at Work.* 1974.

Tillotson, Geoffrey. *Thackeray the Novelist.* 1954.

——. and Donald Hawes, eds. *Thackeray: the Critical Heritage.* 1968.

See also CLOTHING AND FASHION (illus. by Thackeray); SILVER-FORK NOVEL

· · · · ·

THEATERS AND STAGING

The development of the nineteenth-century playhouse is largely the story of how the intimate Georgian stage with its shutters, grooves, and apron platform yielded to the elaborately illusionistic theaters of the mid and late Victorians.

In the first decades of the century, the patent houses of Covent Garden and Drury Lane were rebuilt. Both theaters had been greatly enlarged during the 1790s, a practice reaffirmed after the fires of 1808 and 1809. The Covent Garden and Drury Lane that opened their doors in 1809 and 1812 each held some three thousand spectators. In expanding the pit and multiplying the tiers to accommodate

Ours *at the Prince of Wales's* (*set by Charles Stanfield James*). Illustrated London News,
20 October 1866.

such numbers, both theaters effectively altered the relationship of actors and audience. Not only did the sheer distances involved have an impact upon performance style, but at Drury Lane the diminished forestage made necessary by an enlarged pit caused the proscenium doors to be removed. Players were compelled to make entrances from the wings rather than upon a stage apron—a procedure so unnerving that the doors were temporarily replaced.

The expansion was intended to attract a large if unfashionable public with an insatiable appetite for melodrama, farce, and pantomime. Such tastes were already being catered to by a host of so-called minor theaters licensed for "burlettas" rather than legitimate plays. On the bankside, Astley's Ampitheatre with its ring for equestrian entertainments had been a popular haunt since the 1780s. Its rebuilding in 1803 ushered in a period of unprecedented success that included the staging of military campaigns and (during the

1830s) Andrew Ducrow's productions of Shakespeare on horseback. Under the management of Robert Elliston (1774–1831) the Royal Circus in Blackfriars Road was reconstructed as a nonequestrian playhouse called the Surrey. It became a celebrated home for nautical melodrama including, in 1829, Douglas Jerrold's wildly popular *Black-Eyed Susan*. The (Royal) Coburg in Waterloo Road, opened in 1818, was soon nicknamed the "Blood Tub" for the excesses of its stage displays. Christened the Royal Victoria in 1833, the playhouse eventually became the home of the Old Vic.

North of the river the principal minors were the Olympic in Wych Street, built from the timbers of a French Seventy-Four, and the Sans Pareil in the Strand, both opened in 1806. The latter seems to have been the first theater to replace tiered boxes with open galleries; redubbed the Adelphi in 1819 it gave its name to a series of particularly sensational melodramas known as "Adelphi screamers."

During the flurry of building that took place in the 1830s these theaters were joined by, among others, the New City (1832), the Strand (1832), the St. James's (1835), the Grecian in Hoxton (1832), and the City of London in Norton Folgate (1837).

In the year of Victoria's accession **William Charles Macready** (1793–1873) assumed the management of Covent Garden (1837–1839) and subsequently transferred his activities to Drury Lane (1841–1843). Attempting to win back middle-class audiences, Macready championed what might be called a unity of style most apparent in his restored texts of Shakespeare. Viewing each play as an opportunity for creating a sequence of stage pictures, he drew upon painters like Clarkson Stanfield to provide dioramas for imposing transition effects. Contemporaries especially praised the moving seascape used to illustrate Henry V's crossing to France. For *King John*, presented at Drury Lane in 1842, William Telbin designed an impressively roofed throne room constructed by setting flats diagonally across the stage grooves. Macready also experimented with more subtle forms of illumination. His use of limelight capitalized on the system of gas jets that had replaced oil and candles at both houses two decades earlier.

Many of Macready's reforms had been anticipated by **Madame Vestris** (1797–1856) at the Olympic during the early 1830s. In a repertory limited by the restrictions of a "burletta" license, Vestris trained her eye for detail on the domestic interiors of farce and light comedy. Olympic productions used real carpets, practicable blinds, and doorknobs that turned, while properties formerly painted on canvas gave way to three-dimensional stage furniture. Vestris's husband and business partner, comedian Charles Mathews, Jr. (1803–1878), has left a record of "drawing-

Interior of Astley's Amphitheatre, 1843. Illustrated London News, *1 April 1843.*

rooms fitted up like drawing-rooms, and furnished with taste and care." Whether such innovations included a box set is a matter of debate. Early critics maintained that Vestris's "more perfect enclosure [gave] the appearance of a private chamber infinitely better than the old contrivance of wings." Yet the often-cited evidence for three walls and a ceiling cloth provided by a contemporary engraving of William Bernard's *The Conquering Game* (1832) remains ambiguous. Nevertheless, these Olympic stagings represent a signal step in the search for verisimilitude, while Vestris's use of multiple traps to preset entire scenes antedates Fechter's Lyceum work by some quarter of a century.

The Theatre Regulation Act (1843) effectively ended the monopoly of the patent houses. As it turned out, however, the minor theaters initially made few changes in their repertories. A notable exception was Sadler's Wells, where from 1844 to 1862 Samuel Phelps (1804-1878) presented thirty-four of Shakespeare's plays in handsome and often innovative revivals. During the early part of the century, the "Wells" had been best known for aquatic spectacles staged in a large water tank fed by the New River. Phelps aimed at subtler stuff, and to this end collaborated with designer Frederick Fenton, whose atmospheric gauzes offered an alternative to Macready's more illustrative Shakespeare. Contemporaries were impressed by "the foul and filthy air" of Phelps's *Macbeth* (1847) and praised the elegant diorama—clouds shifting behind a simultaneously moving wood—which Fenton designed to effect scene changes in *A Midsummer Night's Dream* (1853).

In a similar fashion, **Charles Kean** (1811-1868) raised the Princess's Theatre to respectability. Known earlier as a bazaar, concert hall, and opera house, the Princess's in Oxford Street became, under Kean's direction (1850-1859), one of London's most fashionable playhouses, offering audiences a steady diet of Shakespeare and genteel melodrama. Indulging his passion for antiquarianism, Kean joined an obsession with archeological detail to Macready's visual effects. Painstaking research into period sources surfaced in interpolated scenes included for their educational value—William Cuthbert's view of Iona (*Macbeth*, 1853) or Thomas Grieve's panorama of Tudor London (*Henry VIII*, 1855)—

while Shakespeare's text had to dance attendance upon the long intervals needed to shift such scenery. The most important of Kean's non-Shakespearean stagings were Byron's *Sardanapalus* (1852), for which Frederick Lloyds contrived an obliquely drawn "Hall of Nimrod" based upon Layard's Assyrian excavations, and Dion Boucicault's *Corsican Brothers* (1852), which introduced the "ghost glide" (or "Corsican trap")—a device that enabled an actor to rise through the stage while passing mysteriously across it.

Neither Phelps nor Kean was as radical as French tragedian Charles Fechter (1824-1879), who guided the fortunes of the Lyceum during the 1860s. Abolishing that theater's system of grooves, wings, and borders, Fechter installed a compartmentalized counterweighted stage similar in principle to the multiple traps Vestris had used to preset furniture at the Olympic. For outdoor scenes he devised an early form of sky cloth or cyclorama and (building upon Fenton's work at Sadler's Wells) refined the use of gauze to facilitate disappearing effects. Such reforms, however, did not survive Fechter's departure; after 1867 the Lyceum's grooves and shutters were reinstalled.

More immediately influential were the activities of actress Marie Wilton (1839-1921) and her future husband **Squire Bancroft** (1841-1926). Refurbishing the shabby Queen's Theatre (popularly known as the "Dust Hole"), the Bancrofts managed to create in unfashionable Tottenham Street a relatively comfortable playhouse catering to a West End clientele. Reopened as the Prince of Wales's in 1865, the new house boasted elegant fittings, plush carpets, and lace coverings for stalls seats. On its stage the domestic realism of Vestris's Olympic was perfected. Indeed, a link between the two managements appears in playwright T. W. Robertson (1829-1871), who had been Vestris's prompter. For the Bancrofts he wrote the sequence of cup-and-saucer comedies—*Society* (1865), *Ours* (1866), *Caste* (1867), and *School* (1869)—for which he has remained best known. Not only did Robertson's stage directions justify the use of richly detailed interiors, but his insistence upon a fully integrated stage picture enabled designers like Charles Stanfield James to contrive intricately understated special effects: a sunset reflected in the windows of a West End square, leaves falling from an avenue of trees, or shadows lengthening by the light of a full moon.

Such attention to detail became a house style at the Prince of Wales's. Its apogee was reached in Sardou's *Peril* (1876), which displayed a great hall so elaborately built that a smaller boudoir set had to be constructed inside it. In 1880, when the Bancrofts assumed management of the Haymarket, they carried their notion of pictorial stagecraft to its logical end, abolishing what remained of the forestage and placing a gilt frame around the proscenium. They also replaced what was left of the pit with opulent (and expensive) stalls seating, preparing the way for the more intimate theaters that would soon grace inner London.

The century's final decades were characterized by a proliferation of actor-managers. The foremost was **Henry Irving** (1838–1905), whose regime at the Lyceum (1878–1899) transformed that playhouse into "a temple of the arts." Believing firmly in the theater as a place of mystery and wonder, Irving took advantage of contemporary technology to present a program at once conservative, romantic, and spectacular. Scenery was designed by the likes of Burne-Jones (*King Arthur*, 1895), Ford Madox Brown (*Lear*, 1892) and Alma-Tadema (*Cymbeline*, 1896), while mechanical innovations included the final replacement of grooves and shutters with braced flats which could be set at oblique angles. To focus attention upon the stage, Irving employed a black false proscenium and initiated the practice of regularly lowering house lights during performances. He rejected electricity, which had been introduced at D'Oyly Carte's Savoy in 1881, largely because he preferred the subtleties of limelight. Contemporaries applauded Irving's integration of the elements of his art and the sumptuous, often sculptural quality of his *mise en scène*. At the newly built Her Majesty's (1897), **Herbert Beerbohm Tree** (1853–1917) trafficked in similar effects; his *Midsummer Night's Dream* of 1900 sported a carpet of real grass and (it is said) real rabbits.

It was, however, in the playhouses of **Charles Wyndham** (1837–1919) and **George Alexander** (1858–1918) that the reforms begun by Vestris and the Bancrofts were brought to completion. In 1883 Wyndham refitted the underground Criterion in Piccadilly Circus, turning what had been "a stuffy band-box" into an elegant playhouse with coterie ambitions. Among his improvements was the addition of incandescent lighting. During the 1890s the Criterion meticulously staged the society comedies written for Wyndham by Henry Arthur Jones (1851–1929). Alexander's management of the St. James's (1891–1919) reversed the temporarily lean fortunes of a playhouse that had gained a reputation for polite audiences and fastidious technique during the regime of John Hare and the Kendals. Under Alexander—and in a repertory that included Jones, Pinero, and Wilde—the playhouse itself became a prominent fixture of the London season, presenting turn-of-the-century spectators with a seemingly endless round of well-wrought drawing rooms and country estates.

JOEL H. KAPLAN

Bibliography

Booth, Michael R. *Victorian Spectacular Theatre: 1850–1910*. 1981.

Glasstone, Victor. *Victorian and Edwardian Theatres: An Architectural and Social Survey*. 1975.

Leech, Clifford and T. W. Craik, gen. eds. *The Revels History of Drama in English*. Vol. 6: 1750–1880; vol. 7: 1880–Present. 1975, 1978.

Mander, Raymond and Joe Mitchenson. *The Lost Theatres of London*. 1968.

——. *The Theatres of London*. New ed., 1975.

Rosenfield, Sybil. *A Short History of Scene Design in Great Britain*. 1973.

Rowell, George. *Theatre in the Age of Irving*. 1981.

——. *The Victorian Theatre: 1792–1914*. Rev. ed., 1978.

Sherson, Errol. *London's Lost Theatres of the Nineteenth Century*. 1925.

Southern, Richard. *The Victorian Theatre: A Pictorial Survey*. 1970.

See also CARTE, RICHARD D'OYLY; PANTOMIME, BURLESQUE, AND EXTRAVAGANZA

. . . . .

THEOLOGY

Theological developments in the nineteenth century focused on five areas of debate: religion and science; **biblical criticism**; the nature of the church; the theology of society; and God and the afterlife.

At the beginning of the nineteenth century, the defense of Christianity was still entrusted to such works as Bishop Butler's *Analogy of Religion, Natural and Revealed*, published in 1736 to refute the deists, and the writings of William Paley, whose *Natural Theology* (1802) sought to sanctify the conclusions of seventeenth-century science with the "argument from design."

But there was already dissatisfaction with such arguments. In his *Aids to Reflection* (1825), Samuel Taylor Coleridge (1772–1834) attacked "books of natural theology, physico-theology, demonstrations of God from nature and the like." In *The Grammar of Assent* (1870), **John Henry Newman** (1801–1890) argued in like fashion that in practical affairs men do not wait upon scientific proof but act because conviction demands it. Both Coleridge and Newman insisted on the discontinuity between theology and other forms of knowledge. For Coleridge, apprehension rather than comprehension was the appropriate vehicle for approaching God, while for Newman it was the "illative sense" that had to be cultivated to perceive the deepest realities. Paley's line of argument had made theology vulnerable to scientific change; Coleridge and Newman argued that religion's verities could not be supported by science and, by the same token, could not be contraverted by it.

There were other responses to the new science. Conservatives such as Samuel Wilberforce, bishop of Oxford (1805–1873) defended the received interpretations of Genesis. Others, including Charles Kingsley (1819–1875) and Henry Drummond (1851–1897), welcomed the new thinking as indicating a more profound pattern of creation. In *Natural Law in the Spiritual Life* (1883) Drummond argued that science was the essential analogy that unlocked the meaning of Christianity. The new biology and the new geology, however, were forerunners of other intellectual challenges to be presented by history, philosophy, comparative religion, and psychology.

The Aufklärung in Germany gave birth to a thoroughgoing scrutiny of Protestant theology and also to biblical criticism, which was thus from the first associated with advanced theological positions. In England at the beginning of the century, little was yet known of these developments, but other forces were already attacking the inerrancy of the Scriptures. In the 1820s, Dean Buckland's geological researches led him to question the Genesis narrative. Dean Milman's naturalistic *History of the Jews* (1830) gave offense by treating them as any other Oriental tribe. Thomas Arnold, who was familiar with German developments, thought that the Book of Daniel was written much later than the prophet's period. In his *Essay on the Right Understanding of the Scriptures* (1831) Arnold insisted that issues of faith must be separated from technical issues of criticism.

In 1846, eleven years after its publication in German, George Eliot translated Strauss' *Leben Jesu* into English. Strauss held that all miraculous elements in the life of Christ had to be ascribed to the "myth" which arose within the Christian community between Christ's death and the writing of the Gospels. Strauss was a product of the Tubingen school, founded by F. C. Baur, who believed that New Testament documents reflected a Hegelian process in which the Gospels represented a Catholic synthesis of conflicting Petrine (Jewish) and Pauline (Gentile) elements. The New Testament seemed open to the same kind of critical dissection that was already being applied to the Old.

Essays and Reviews (1860) attempted to introduce the Church of England to the critical and historical study of the Bible. **Benjamin Jowett** (1817–1893), master of Balliol, contributed an important essay which applied both his textual acumen and his Platonic philosophical perspective: "The critic took men to the letter, the philosopher urged men to rise above it. . . . When interpreted like any other book, the Bible will be found to be unlike any other book." Even in 1860, the invitation to such new thought was deemed too abrupt. The bishops joined in a declaration which amounted to a censure of the volume.

In the latter years of the century the techniques and conclusions of biblical criticism applied to both the Old and New Testaments became domesticated. Informed opinion began to accept such conclusions as the complex authorship of the Pentateuch, the late dating of the Law in its priestly form, and the non-Davidic authorship of many of the Psalms. In 1881, however, Robertson Smith (like Samuel Davidson of the Lancashire Congregational College almost a quarter of a century earlier) was deposed from his chair at the Free Church College in Aberdeen for his views of Pentateuchal authorship. He defended himself by arguing that the Bible was the Word of God only in the sense that it contained the Word of God, a position in line with the teaching of the reformers who advanced no doctrine of verbal infallibility.

The evangelical revival of the previous century not only produced a new family of churches in Methodism but, together with the teaching of Jonathan Edwards, amended the hyper-Calvinism into which much of old dissent had lapsed. Edward Williams for the Congregationalists and Andrew Fuller for the Baptists wrote revisionist treatises on moderate or evangelical Calvinism which led to the founding of the modern missionary movement and thus raised further questions about the nature of the church, its ministry, and its sacramental practice. The issue of church order was raised when Anglican Evangelicals split over charismatic and adventist emphases in the 1820s; and even more profoundly when some erstwhile Evangelicals, including J. H. Newman, joined with a group of High Churchmen to create the Oxford Movement.

The Oxford men feared for the security of the church in an age of prevailing liberalism. Newman believed that the second generation of Evangelicals had little power to defend the church. The source of faith, still of critical importance, was no longer located in a threatened Bible but in an authoritative church, and mediated by a sacramental priesthood ordained in apostolic succession. When his teaching was condemned by his bishop, Newman's own logic compelled him to leave the Church of England. His way into the Roman church was aided by a theory of the development of doctrine which persuaded him that the contemporary Roman Catholic church was in fact the legitimate successor of the apostolic church. Notwithstanding this loss, the surviving Oxford men developed a more elaborate ritual, created the Anglo-Catholic

school in the Church of England, and more generally aroused higher standards of churchmanship.

Coleridge's essay *On the Constitution of Church and State* (1830) laid the foundation of a broader social mission for the church. More significantly, **F. D. Maurice** (1805–1872) provided the theological basis for the **Christian socialist** movement. He diagnosed "the great disease of our time, that we talk about God and about our religion and do not confess Him as a Living God." In opposition to narrow churchly or partisan concerns, Maurice insisted that the gospel proclaimed (in the title of his first major work) *The Kingdom of Christ* (1838). "Economy and politics," he wrote, "must have a ground beneath themselves . . . in God. The Kingdom of Heaven is to me the great practical existing reality which is to renew the earth."

Christ's incarnation, according to Maurice, was the heart of revelation; it sanctified common life as well as initiated religion. To be faithful to such an incarnation, the church must work for unity. For Maurice, religious experience was necessarily corporate and never solitary; its governing principle was God's grace and not the sin that other groups seemed to make normative through their emphasis on the Fall. Moreover, the Kingdom instituted by the incarnation included all humankind and was to be experienced not only in the hereafter but now. The corollary of the notion that eternal life could begin now was that eternal death did not mean everlasting punishment, a conviction that cost Maurice his chair at King's College, London, in 1853. His thinking, however, became widely influential.

Explorations in Christology must be set against the historic battles with Unitarianism and the hostile reception accorded to Strauss. The anonymous *Ecce Homo*, published in 1865 and written by **J. R. Seeley**, was called by Lord Shaftesbury, "the most pestilential volume ever vomited forth from the jaws of Hell." Others found its undogmatic reconstruction refreshing. Although reductionist Christologies were not widespread in England, many found the relationship between the divine and the human natures of Christ helpfully expressed in terms of the "kenotic" theory, which held that the incarnate Christ accepted the mental limitations of a first-century man while retaining his moral perfection. Such a view was embraced by A. M. Fairbairn's *The Place of Christ in Modern Theology* (1893).

The older view of the atonement through a penal substitution came to be seen as a challenge to the unity of the Father and the Son. While some theologians simply made the incarnation the definitive act, two free-church leaders, R. W. Dale and Scott Lidgett, sought to combine the sacrificial element in the crucifixion with the affirmation that Christ, in so suffering, acted as the moral head and representative of the human race.

Throughout the century there was also debate about the afterlife. Long before Maurice lost his chair in 1853, Thomas Malthus (1766–1834) had adopted the position that came to be known as conditional immortality. In 1846, Edward White's *Life in Christ*, advocating such a view, caused embarrassment and was partly responsible for his resignation from his pastorate. By 1887, times had changed so greatly that White was able to win the support of R. W. Dale and election to the chair of the Congregational Union. Some even regarded his views as too cautious, and like J. Baldwin Brown and Alexander Mackennal embraced the "Larger Hope" of universalism.

J. H. Y. BRIGGS

Bibliography

Chadwick, Owen. *The Victorian Church*. 1966, 1970. 2 vols.

Cockshut, A. O. J., ed. *Religious Controversies of the Nineteenth Century: Selected Documents*. 1966.

Davis, Horton. *Worship and Theology in England*, vols. 3 and 4. 1961, 1962.

Eisen, Sydney and Bernard V. Lightman. *Victorian Science and Religion: A Bibliography with Emphasis on Evolution, Belief, and Unbelief*. 1984.

Elliott-Binns, Leonard F. *English Thought 1860–1900: The Theological Aspect*. 1956.

Storr, Vernon Faithfull. *The Development of English Theology in the Nineteenth Century*. 1913.

Vidler, Alexander R. *The Church in an Age of Revolution*. 1961.

Wood, Herbert George. *Belief and Unbelief Since 1850*. 1955.

See also BIBLICAL CRITICISM

. . . . .

THEOSOPHY

Derived from Greek "theos" (god) and "sophia" (wisdom), theosophy is a synthesis of religion, philosophy, and science which attempts to offer authoritative knowledge of God, the universe, and the purpose of life by direct mystical tradition, philosophical inquiry, or both. The term refers to a broad spectrum of occult and mystical philosophies, often pantheistic in nature, which hold that knowledge does not reside in a set of beliefs superimposed upon practitioners but unfolds from within the human spirit.

Early examples of theosophic thought exist in the Hindu Vedas. The *I Ching* (Book of Changes) of Confucianism and *Tao Te Ching* (Book of the Virtuous Way) of Taoism also contain theosophic elements. Western influences include Pythagoras, Plato, and second-century heretical Christian gnosticism. The writings of Nicholas of Cusa, Phillippus Aureolus Paracelsus, and Giordano Bruno reflect a Renaissance fusion of mysticism and materialism. Platonism and Neoplatonism expanded to an interest in the Kabbala. Significant names associated with later theosophic thought are Jacob Boehme, Friedrich von Schelling, and Emanuel Swedenborg.

The Victorian revival of theosophical thought began with the establishment of the Theosophical Society in 1875 by Helena Petrovna **(Madame) Blavatsky**, Henry Steel Olcott, and William Q. Judge. Theosophic doctrine contains three propositions: (1) God is infinite, absolute, unknowable, and source of both spirit and matter; (2) reincarnation governs all growth by laws of justice or karma, and it is through successive embodiments in physical form that spirit finally attains to godhood; and (3) there is a fundamental identity of all souls with the universal oversoul. Theosophy appealed to some Victorian freethinkers and social reformers by suggesting that all souls are the same in essence, varying only in degrees of development, and that human talents are earned by individual effort and merit.

MARIAN R. FISHER

Bibliography

Campbell, Bruce F. *Ancient Wisdom Revived: A History of the Theosophical Movement.* 1980.

Holden, Pat, ed. *Women's Religious Experience.* 1983.

Kannan, A. *Impact of Theosophy and Science: Modern Thought in the Light of Theosophy.* 1971.

Webb, James. *The Occult Establishment.* 1976.

———. *The Occult Underground.* 1974.

Winner, Anna Kennedy. *The Basic Ideas of Occult Wisdom.* 1970.

. . . . .

THOMPSON, FRANCIS (1859-1907)

Along with Coventry Patmore and Gerard Manley Hopkins, Francis Thompson is considered one of the three major Catholic poets of Victorian England. The son of a physician who was a Catholic convert, Thompson first endeavored to follow his father's career but, owing to bad health and skittish nerves, found himself unfit for medical practice. Years of drifting, poverty, depression, and hardship were finally overcome when Thompson's work came to the attention of Wilfrid and Alice Meynell. The Meynells succored Thompson and provided the stability and support that he was unable to bring to his own life.

Thompson's poetry was highly regarded in Catholic circles of his own day, but, following the general devaluing of Victorian verse in the early twentieth century, has failed to recover its critical reputation. Thompson wrote in an ornate, diffuse, and rhapsodic manner—adapting the atmospheric imagery of Shelley, the lush density of Keats, and the mystical yearnings of the metaphysicals to a verse that endeavors to sustain a uniformly high emotional pitch. The lavish diction, overripe imagery, and sustained intensity are not al-

ways successful. His two most famous poems are "The Hound of Heaven" and "The Kingdom of Heaven." The first forcefully conveys the sense of God's pursuit of the errant and fleeing soul; the second is an ecstatic affirmation of God's sacramental presence in the whole of creation: "O World invisible, we view thee,/O world intangible, we touch thee,/O world unknowable, we know thee,/Inapprehensible, we clutch thee!"

In addition to his poetry, Thompson composed several prose essays. The one on Shelley has become a staple in critical bibliographies of that poet. "Paganism Old and New" affirms the belief that the meaning and significance of classical myth becomes fully apparent only when seen from the perspective of Christianity.

STEPHEN GURNEY

Bibliography

Megroz, R. L. *Francis Thompson: The Poet of Earth in Heaven.* 1927.

Meynell, Wilfrid, ed. *The Works of Francis Thompson.* 1913.

Reid, John C. *Francis Thompson, Man and Poet.* 1960.

Thompson, John. *Francis Thompson, Poet and Mystic.* 1923.

Wright, Rev. Thomas H. *Francis Thompson and His Poetry.* 1927.

. . . . .

TICHBORNE CLAIMANT

The "Tichborne claimant" generated a controversial series of trials after 1866 when, in Australia, he assumed the identity of Sir Roger Charles Doughty Tichborne, Bart., (b. 1829), heir to rich estates in Hampshire, who was presumed lost at sea in 1854. While the corpulent claimant stood in marked contrast to the thin Sir Roger, he did possess sufficient resemblance and intimate family knowledge to win over the dowager Lady Tichborne. The claimant's memory was otherwise unpersuasive.

A suit against the Tichborne estate trustees led to a long civil trial (1871-1872), which the claimant lost, after which he was arrested on a criminal charge of perjury. In his much longer second trial (1873–1874) the claimant was found guilty, declared to be Arthur Orton (1834–1898), son of a butcher in Wapping, and sentenced to fourteen years penal servitude. Edward Kenealy, the claimant's legal counsel, was disbarred for his pains, but continued to fight the case in Parliament and in his newspaper, *The Englishman*. The claimant served ten years, and died in penury in 1898.

The Tichborne case was a judicial and journalistic landmark. The claimant generated endless sensational press copy, attracted the support of people willing to advance him considerable sums of money against his expectations of inheritance, and also won a large following of people eager to imagine a conspiracy to defraud a legitimate heir.

Kenealy's enormous edition of the perjury trial proceedings is biased on the claimant's behalf. Atlay and Maugham assume the claimant's guilt throughout their books. Woodruff presents the most impartial account.

N. MERRILL DISTAD

Bibliography

Atlay, James Beresford. *The Tichborne Case*. Notable British Trials Series. 1912.

Kenealy, Edward Vaughan Hyde. *The Trial at Bar of Sir Roger C. D. Tichborne, Bart., in the Court of Queen's Bench . . . for Perjury*. 1875–1880. 8 vols.

Maugham, Frederic Herbert. *The Tichborne Case*. 1936.

Woodruff, Douglas. *The Tichborne Claimant: A Victorian Mystery*. 1957.

. . . . .

TIMES, THE

Founded in London in 1785, by the midnineteenth century the *Times* reached a level of influence unprecedented in the history of journalism, distinguishing itself equally by the accuracy of its news and the independence of its opinions.

John Walter (1738/9–1812) started the *Daily Universal Register* primarily to advertise his printing business. In 1788 he renamed it the *Times*. Under his proprietorship, the *Times*, like other daily journals, accepted government subsidies in return for support of official policy. In 1803 Walter's son, John Walter II (1776–1847), assumed control of the newspaper and, in addition to transforming production with the first steam-driven press (1814), gradually established the paper's independence from external control. From 1806 he fought the system of party and government subsidies, braving the frequent threat of legal action. When in 1819 leading articles critical of the Peterloo massacre drew official protest, the *Times* defended itself as "a free journal, unattached to any other cause than that of truth, and given to speak boldly of all parties" (October 22, 1819). In 1817 Walter appointed as editor Thomas Barnes (1785–1841), who during his reign of twenty-four years earned for the *Times* the nickname "The Thunderer." Barnes, together with Edward Sterling (1773–1847), penned leading articles that "thunder[ed] for reform" (January 29, 1831). By appealing to the force of public opinion, in language that bullied and castigated, the *Times* established itself as the voice of the rising middle class.

After succeeding Barnes as editor in 1841, John Thadeus Delane (1817–1879) and John Walter III (1818–1894), chief proprietor from 1847, led the *Times* to the zenith of its influence during the Crimean War (1854–1856). Pledged "to investigate truth and to apply it on fixed principles to the affairs of the world" (February 6, 1852), the *Times* printed passionate articles that exposed military and governmental incompetence as well as the deplorable state of medical aid provided British soldiers. These detailed reports contributed significantly to the reformation of medical care under Florence Nightingale (1820–1910) and the fall of Aberdeen's ministry. During the war the *Times* also flourished financially; by 1855 its circulation exceeded 50,000, more than four times that of its major competitors combined.

From these heights the *Times* declined during the remainder of the century. Chief among reasons for the falling off was the abolition of the newspaper stamp tax in 1855, which financially enabled other newspapers to offer the *Times* its first serious competition in a generation. By 1870 the circulation of the *Times* had risen to 70,000, but by then the

Daily News sold 150,000 and the *Daily Telegraph* 250,000. The *Times* did not appeal to the newly literate lower middle and working classes, groups that found the political opinions of the *Times* alien to their aspirations. In the late century the *Times* spoke conservatively on political issues, opposing further extension of the franchise and Irish Home Rule. The paper steadily lost financial ground as well as prestige, damaged seriously by the publication in 1887 of what were afterward discovered to be forged letters linking **Charles Stewart Parnell** (1846-1891) to the political murders in Phoenix Park (1882).

The history of the *Times* in the Victorian era in many ways reflects that of the educated upper middle class for which it spoke, the class empowered by the passing of the first Reform Bill. Never radical but strongly, if cautiously, reformist in the 1820s and 1830s, the newspaper, as it became an established institution, found its opinions less influential as the lower middle and working classes gained political strength. By the century's end the *Times* remained a powerful voice, but like Victoria herself, it had aged. Most British readers turned elsewhere for their news as for their politics.

LOWELL T. FRYE

Bibliography

Desmond, Robert W. *The Information Process: World News Reporting to the Twentieth Century.* 1978.

Hudson, Derek. *Thomas Barnes of* The Times. 1944.

Times. The History of the Times. 4 vols. 1935–1952.

Walker, Martin. *Powers of the Press: Twelve of the World's Influential Newspapers.* 1983.

· · · · ·

TONNA, CHARLOTTE ELIZABETH (1790-1846)

Novelist Charlotte Elizabeth Browne Phelan Tonna was born in Norwich in 1790, the daughter of a rector, Michael Browne, and became almost totally deaf by the age of ten.

She is remembered for her social protest in such works as *Combination* (1832), *Helen Fleetwood* (1839-1841), and *The Wrongs of Woman* (1843-1844). She married George Phelan in 1813 and separated from him about 1824 because he physically abused her; she published under the pseudonym "Charlotte Elizabeth" to prevent claims against her income. After Phelan's death in 1837 she married Louis H. J. Tonna.

Tonna was a strong Low Church Evangelical. She opposed Catholic emancipation in 1829, denounced popery, and opposed the Tractarian movement in such works as *Conformity* (1841), *Falsehood and Truth* (1841), and *The Church Visible in All Ages* (1844). She was the editor of several periodicals, most importantly the *Christian Lady's Magazine*, which she edited from 1834 until her death.

Tonna's work falls into four categories: protest fiction, religious-historical novels, children's tales, and travel accounts. She discussed the dangers of trade unionism in *Combination*, protested slavery in *The System* (1827), and denounced factory conditions in *Helen Fleetwood*. In 1842 she began work on *The Perils of the Nation* (published anonymously in 1843), a compilation of material from parliamentary investigatory reports about children in industry. These she used in her four-part study of women's work, *The Wrongs of Woman*.

Tonna's religious-historical works supporting the Protestant cause include *Derry* (1833), about Ireland in 1688, and *The Rockite* (1829), on the persecution of Irish Protestants in 1825. Her most important travel work is *Letters from Ireland* (1838), where she had lived from 1819 to 1824. *The Happy Mute* (c. 1832) concerns her training of a deaf boy, John Brett, whom she adopted in 1823.

Tonna was a pioneer in investigating industrial conditions and researching women's labor. Her protests advanced the cause of child labor legislation. The diversity of her work as editor, author, mission worker in London, and protester gives her writing an impressive range.

JOSEPH KESTNER

Bibliography

Fryckstedt, Monica Correa. "Charlotte Elizabeth Tonna and *The Christian Lady's Magazine*."

Victorian Periodicals Review, vol. 14, pp. 43–51.

Gallagher, Catherine. *The Industrial Reformation of English Fiction, 1832–1867.* 1985.

Kestner, Joseph. "Charlotte Brontë and Charlotte Elizabeth Tonna: A Possible Source for *Jane Eyre*." *Papers on Language and Literature*, vol. 20, pp. 96–98.

——. *Protest and Reform: The British Social Narrative by Women, 1827–1867.* 1985.

Kovacevic, Ivanka. *Fact into Fiction.* 1975.

—— and S. Barbara Kanner. "Blue Book Into Novel: The Forgotten Industrial Fiction of Charlotte Elizabeth Tonna." *Nineteenth-Century Fiction*, vol. 25, pp. 152–173.

Kovaleski, Elizabeth. "The *Personal Recollections* of Charlotte Elizabeth Tonna." *Tulsa Studies in Women's Literature*, vol. 1, pp. 141–155.

• • • • •

TOYS AND GAMES

Victorian children's toys and games reflected not only children's own interests and needs but also (and sometimes primarily) adult culture, both in the recreations offered and in contemporary attitudes toward those recreations. Through the Victorian period, the number and variety of manufactured toys and games increased dramatically for a number of reasons: rising affluence, scientific developments, increased interest in and concern for children, and the effects of industrialization, commercialization, and mass production. By the period's end most toys and games were directed specifically toward children rather than to a mixed market of children and adults.

At the period's beginning the traditional toys—the Noah's Ark (the only toy suitable for Sundays in strict households), balls, marbles, hoops, tops, and dolls—were still basic for most children. To these, however, had been added several recent innovations.

Toy theaters, celebrated by Robert Louis Stevenson in his 1884 essay "Penny Plain and Two-Pence Coloured," were miniature printed reproductions of the characters, scenes, and stages of early nineteenth-century plays. The best-known producers of toy theaters were Benjamin Pollock (1856–1937), after whom a London toy museum is named, and Martin Skelt (1835–1872). Skelt bought other printers' old engravings, dropped the quality and price, and distributed his theaters throughout Britain. Toy theaters had originally been souvenirs or advertisements for adults, but by Skelt's time they had become toys for children.

Other toys followed a similar pattern. Scientific developments, for example, were rapidly adapted for adult recreations and then (especially with the advent of mass production) for children's toys. Magic lanterns (1840s) and other by-products of discoveries in optics such as the Phenakisticope and the zoetrope were first produced as amusements for all but gradually became identified with children. Dolls, which had often been used as models of adult fashion, were completely appropriated by children by the end of the century.

Part of this process of appropriation derived from the developing toy industry. Children represented a huge market: 36 percent of England's population in the second half of the nineteenth century was under fifteen. A competitive market gave manufacturers and merchants the incentive to make their stock fresh, attractive, and inexpensive. Trains, velocipedes, and magnetic gadgets were all available for children soon after their invention.

Most of these toys were manufactured in Germany, France, and Switzerland. Not until the end of the century did such firms as William Britain and Sons (c. 1880), Lines Brothers (from 1858), and Chad Valley (established in 1897) challenge the dominance of Continental manufacturers of wooden and metal toys. Printed board games and dissected puzzles (jigsaws), on the other hand, were almost entirely produced in England. Until midcentury, inventing and printing games was a sideline for mapmakers and printmakers. By the century's end specialized toy manufacturers had generally taken over. Early games were printed from plates, but could be produced more cheaply with the advent of lithography from about 1839.

The predominance of moralistic and didactic board games eased through the century, despite such games as "The Cottage of Content or The Right Roads and Wrong Ways" (William

Spooner, 1848) and "English Grammar" (John Betts, before 1875). Evangelicals and reformers were still concerned about children's leisure occupations but by 1870 the emphasis on spiritual growth was largely replaced by attention to children's physical and economic welfare, and a more liberal yet more organized notion of children's play evolved.

In the matter of sports, for example, early evangelicals had tried to suppress football because of the rowdiness, drunkenness, and gambling that surrounded free-for-all village matches. By the mid–Victorian period, however, the more violent forms of football still held sway only in badly-run public schools. After the reforms of Thomas Arnold and others, football and cricket emerged from the public school milieu as organized national sports associated with qualities necessary to the empire: character, loyalty, obedience, discipline, group identity, and physical fitness. By the century's end girls were also urged to take up wholesome physical recreations like croquet, cycling, and gymnastics.

The transformation of games to organized sports, combined with the marketing of manufactured toys and games and the rise of leisure "industries" such as pantomimes and circuses, caused some Victorians to feel that the old "organic" culture of England was being lost to a new, unhealthy mass culture. Much contemporary writing about children's play is actually antiquarian nostalgia searching for remnants of vanished folklore.

In fact, given the number and profundity of the changes affecting Victorian society, children's informal play was extraordinarily consistent through the period. Traditional games of hunting, daring, chasing, and the like were ubiquitous, as were the simpler, sometimes improvised, children's toys. The real change was the rising sentimentality that caused middle- and upper-class children to be sequestered in their own cloistered and sometimes claustrophobic worlds.

ROBIN M. SUNDSTROM

Bibliography

Haining, Peter. *Movable Books: An Illustrated History*. 1979.

Hannas, Linda. *The English Jigsaw Puzzle, 1769–1890*. 1972.

King, Constance Eileen. *The Encyclopedia of Toys*. 1978.

Opie, Iona and Peter Opie. *Children's Games in Street and Playground*. 1968.

Speaight, George. *The History of the English Toy Theatre*. 1969.

Walvin, James. *A Child's World: A Social History of English Childhood, 1800–1914*. 1982.

White, Gwen. *Antique Toys and Their Background*. 1971.

Whitehouse, F. R. B. *Table Games of Georgian and Victorian Days*. 1951.

See also CHILDHOOD; SPORT; SPORTS AND GAMES, WOMEN'S

· · · · ·

TRACK AND FIELD
see ATHLETIC SPORTS

· · · · ·

TRACTS

One feature of the evangelical revival of the late eighteenth and early nineteenth centuries was the publication and distribution of religious tracts. Concerned about social disorder, the danger of growing literacy among the lower orders, and the influence of such radical and antireligious writers as Tom Paine, religious tract societies used the form and methods of cheap popular literature in an attempt to spread the message of social deference and Christian salvation to the poor and working classes. As the century progressed the effort was concentrated particularly on the young; the Religious Tract Society became one of the more important publishers of literature for children of all classes.

The Cheap Repository Tracts (1794), which pioneered the use of fiction with Hannah More's work, and the Anglican Society for the Promotion of Christian Knowledge (founded in 1698) tended to emphasize the social messages of obedience, deference, honesty, and humility. The Religious Tract Society (1799) was explicitly evangelical, with a strongly religious message. It served both Anglicans and

Nonconformists, though various denominations later formed their own organizations, including the Wesleyan Methodist Tract Society (1822), the Friends Tract Association (1828), and the Baptist Tract Society (1841). Secular movements such as the British Temperance League also published tracts.

Tracts, like the ballads and chapbooks peddled by hawkers, were often illustrated with woodcuts and featured both sensational material and gritty details of life among the poor. Frequently they were aimed at a specific trade (sailors, servants, prostitutes). Nonconformists tended to distrust fiction; a typical tract in the first half of the nineteenth century was a real or pretended biography, narrated in the first person, giving details of a sinful life and dramatic conversion or of a pious life (under distressing circumstances) and holy death. The language, however, was often vigorous and direct. Although a great many tracts were sold to ladies and gentlemen, who distributed them free along with (or in lieu of) other charity, the tract societies also used the secular network of ballad and chapbook sellers, cleverly setting the wholesale price so that tracts were cheaper than commercial products. A tract's narrative of sordid crime and urgent repentence was, in fact, little different from sensational "last dying confessions" sold to the crowds at public executions.

In the Victorian period the tract societies turned increasingly to juvenile literature. In 1824 the Religious Tract Society began a series of stories for young children and launched a monthly Sunday school magazine, the *Child's Companion.* They were concerned particularly with the lack of reading material that was suitable and yet not too simple, so that children with limited formal schooling would continue to read. By midcentury the society's catalogue classified books in two categories: those suitable for families and boarding schools, and those for Sunday, National, and common day schools. For middle-class children it published historical adventures, family stories, and fiction set in exotic parts of the empire. For poor children, writers such as Hesba Stretton developed the "street arab" or "city arab" tale about homeless, ill-treated waifs—tales that sometimes closed with a bathetic deathbed, but nevertheless grappled with real problems of poverty, abuse, and exploitation.

By the end of the century the Religious Tract Society published two extremely popular juvenile periodicals—the *Boy's Own Paper* (from 1879) and the *Girl's Own Paper* (1880)—which had almost no explicitly religious content. Tract fiction and tract distribution were easy to satirize (as in Thackeray's Lady Emily Sheepshanks) and rightfully angered many poor people who knew their distress had social and economic, rather than moral, causes. Tract writers, however, produced some vigorous works and provided affordable reading matter for many who might otherwise not have progressed beyond minimal literacy.

SALLY MITCHELL

Bibliography

Bratton, J. S. *The Impact of Victorian Children's Fiction.* 1981.

Clarke, W. K. Lowther. *A History of the S.P.C.K.* 1959.

Cutt, Margaret Nancy. *Ministering Angels.* 1979.

Green, S. G. *The Story of the Religious Tract Society.* 1899.

Hewitt, Gordon. *Let the People Read.* 1949.

James, Louis. *English Popular Literature, 1819-1851.* 1976.

———. *Fiction for the Working Man.* 1963.

• • • • •

TRADE UNIONS

Trade unions developed slowly from small guilds of artisans and craftsmen—tailors, carpenters, masons, printers, shoemakers—who, because they were skilled, could command concessions from employers. Unionism in the nineteenth century advanced through three stages: its origins in the proliferation of small local clubs; the midcentury development of large, amalgamated groups more interested in improving conditions for current members than in attracting new ones; and finally the political and social establishment of labor unionism. By 1900 a large number of unskilled workers had joined the ranks.

Late in the eighteenth century, laissez-faire

government and the breakup of guilds led more and more workers to seek combination for protection against economic uncertainty. Development was slow, however, because skilled workers were primarily interested in maintaining their own status and because many people perceived combination as a threat to public order. The Combination Acts of 1799 and 1800 made most union activity illegal. Though enforced irregularly, such laws nevertheless evidence the government's distrust and suspicion of workers. Their repeal in 1824 prompted the establishment of numerous small, autonomous clubs, each restricted to skilled workers in a single occupation.

Though several early attempts to form federations of trade societies suffered from unsuccessful strikes and a confusion of union and cooperative aims, they do indicate a nascent labor consciousness. Worker dissatisfaction with the Reform Act of 1832 briefly fueled the movement. Most groups shunned radicalism, but some like John Doherty's National Association for the Protection of Labour (1830) were more aggressive. Disputes quickly doomed the Operative Builders Union (1832–1834), which had invested heavily in cooperative production. Robert Owen's Grand National Consolidated Trades Union (1833) pushed immediately for an eight-hour day, but craft unions considered its methods reactionary and violent. Its members included some women's groups, such as the Lodge of Female Tailors, although women (like child factory workers) were difficult to organize beause they were so easily replaced. Owen claimed 800,000 members but only a small percentage paid dues. Unable to provide support for striking member unions, the Grand National collapsed inside a year. Its demise ended the uneasy alliance between cooperation and unionism. The idea of uniting unions of different trades was for a time abandoned. Over the next twenty years, gains were made primarily by smaller groups of craftsmen and engineers.

By midcentury, improved transportation and industrial growth resulted in larger markets, more unyielding employers, and increased efforts to unionize. Under the aggressive but practical leadership of Martin Jude, the Miners Association of Great Britain (1842) helped raise workers' living standards

and improve mining safety. It claimed 100,000 members before its dissolution in 1848. Miners' unions spread rapidly in the north in the 1850s. Alexander MacDonald's National Miners Association led the fight for safety reforms.

In the same period, Manchester textile unions formed groups that eventually became the Amalgamated Association of Operative Cotton Spinners (1853). Textile workers, however, were relatively slow to unionize because they were variously skilled, a larger labor force was available, and a high proportion were women. More successful were the engineers, who generally survived the 1848 depression in good stead. Though its members were mostly from the north, the Amalgamated Society of Engineers set up a national headquarters in London. Led by William Allan, the centralized ASE grew in strength by offering its member societies sound fiscal assistance. In 1853, even after conducting an unsuccessful twelve-week strike, the ASE was able to retain its membership and continue growing.

During the 1860s and 1870s, the legal status of unions improved and several large and influential union groups developed. These centralized bodies had full-time leaders who sought good relations with employers, a better public image, and more favorable union legislation. In London, the building unions formed the Amalgamated Society of Carpenters and Joiners, modeled after the ASE. Building worker strikes in 1859–1860 led to the London Trades Council, a permanent committee to mediate disputes and coordinate union activities. Some delegates of the various LTC unions, Robert Applegarth, William Allan, Edwin Coulson, and George Odger—known as the "Junta"—gained considerable influence. The National Reform League (1865) and George Potter's more radical London Working Men's Association campaigned to increase labor representation in Parliament and secure the franchise for working men. Thomas Dunning's pamphlet *Trade Unions and Strikes* (1860) and W. T. Thornton's *On Labour* (1869) also helped shape public opinion.

In 1869 the newly formed Trades Union Congress created its standing Parliamentary Committee, and within a few years power shifted from the LTC Junta to the new TUC, which soon spoke for organized labor. In 1871 the Trade Union Act granted legal status to unions, but during the 1874 election the TUC's Parliamentary Committee successfully influenced voters to reject the Liberal government, which was also responsible for the hated Criminal Law Amendment Act. Although the new Conservative government repealed this law and made several unionist concessions, unionists perceived that the Liberal party was, after all, more responsive to their needs, and their alliance flourished.

As secretary of the Parliamentary Committee from 1875 to 1890, Henry Broadhurst, a Liberal and supporter of Gladstone, tried to maintain the position of unions in a period of great economic and political change caused by depression and growing international markets. Many unions failed, but women and unskilled workers became more active. Joseph Arch's National Agricultural Labourers Union (1872) grew to 100,000 members within a year but dwindled and eventually collapsed, the victim of declining British agriculture. **Emma Paterson** founded the Women's Protective and Provident League (1874) to protect female combination and egalitarian legal reform. As the first woman delegate to the TUC at a time when the congress sought to restrict female employment, she often took feminist rather than unionist positions. By the time she died in 1886, her organization, its name changed to the Women's Trade Union League, had grown to include thirty affiliated societies representing women in numerous trades. These groups led to the National Federation of Women Workers (1906), a genuine trade union whose important work would go far beyond the largely propagandist activities of its predecessors.

Radical elements criticized the conservative policies of older unions and renewed demand for the eight-hour day, the minimum wage, and the regular employment guarantee. A new generation of socialist-inspired unions offering lower membership fees and easier entrance requirements attracted many unskilled workers who were generally younger and more aggressive than their skilled counterparts. One was the Matchmakers Union formed by Annie Besant in the wake of a strike by women factory workers in 1888. Her socialist supporters included George Bernard Shaw. The highly publicized five-week strike

by London dock workers in 1889 was another sign that labor, as opposed to trade, unions had arrived. More and more women, seamen, gasworkers, domestic servants, municipal workers, and other unskilled and semiskilled laborers joined unions; membership doubled between 1888 and 1891.

"General" unions—those accepting members without regard to their employment—spread rapidly in the London area. A schism developed between the older trade unions and the new labor unions, which were influenced by varying degrees of socialism, but the differences diminished within a few years. Meanwhile, the Liberal party's alliance with labor showed signs of strain. The first Independent Labour member of Parliament, the socialist James Keir Hardie, lobbied to convince a broad spectrum of working-class groups that the existing political parties did not adequately serve their needs. His Independent Labour party, although otherwise ineffective, did lead to the Labour Representation Committee (1900), the start of the British **Labour party.**

Throughout most of the century union activity had less effect than one might imagine on the living standards of workers and on the labor market in general. Even when membership was high, worker participation was uneven. Eventually, though, better work conditions, fewer instances of "collective bargaining by riot," more political clout, and a developing working-class consciousness were the fruits of union growth. In 1800 the middle class, the government, and most workers viewed unionism with considerable suspicion. A century later the movement was a viable social, economic, and political force.

STEVEN N. CRAIG

Bibliography

Cole, G. D. H. *A Short History of the British Working Class Movement.* 1948.

Frow, Ruth et al. *The History of British Trade Unionism: A Select Bibliography.* 1969.

Hunt, Edward H. *British Labour History: 1815–1914.* 1981.

Pelling, Henry. *A History of British Trade Unionism.* 1963.

Webb, Sidney and Beatrice Webb. *History of Trade Unionism.* 1920.

See also LABOR LAWS; SOCIAL FEMINISM; STRIKES

. . . . .

TRAGEDY

Victorians considered that tragedy was a verse drama of the past, usually involving spectacle. Until 1843 the Licensing Bill (1737) permitted only three theaters to perform drama; these theaters were so large as to encourage spectacle instead of drama and elocution instead of acting. Shakespeare formed a large part of the repertoire.

After 1843, when many licensed theaters were allowed to produce spoken drama, the emphasis on repertoire hindered new developments. Attempts at tragedy were almost always an imitation of earlier drama. The general tendency in Victorian tragedy was to present abstraction rather than living character, and the past rather than the present. Bulwer-Lytton and Tennyson tried to write historical tragedy and were commercially successful. Others saw the error of slavishly imitating the past and attempted domestic tragedy. John Westland Marston's *The Patrician's Daughter* (1841) demonstrates the problem a serious dramatist faced. Marston gave his play a contemporary setting but kept the blank verse of earlier English tragedy. The play failed because the audience could not accept verse in a contemporary setting, nor could they understand a modern character who exhibited a tragic flaw. Victorian tragedy could not evolve on the stage and had virtually died by the middle of the era.

However, the attempts to write domestic tragedy led to a significant evolution in theory. In his preface to the 1841 edition of *The Patrician's Daughter*, Marston speaks authoritatively of treating contemporary life tragically, of recognizing the "hero in undress." Reviewing *The Patrician's Daughter*, George Henry Lewes also stressed the tragic potential in modern culture, but, unlike Marston, Lewes insisted on prose instead of poetry. Other critics—most notably Thomas Doubleday, Thomas de Quincey, and Eneas Sweetland Dallas—emphasized the importance of using modern realities rather than archaic models as the basis of tragedy.

Because public taste and literary tradition stifled the development of serious drama in Victorian England, the real inheritor of the evolving theory of tragedy was the novel. Both George Eliot and Thomas Hardy achieved the heights of great tragedy. Eliot's novels manifest a dialectic of good in conflict with good and fulfill many patterns of Hegelian tragic theory while still consciously working in the Aristotelian mode. Hardy used patterns of Sophoclean, Euripidean, and modern social tragedy in his novels. Many of the Victorian issues about the character of the hero and the effect of realistic events still fuel debates about the possibility of modern tragedy.

DENNIS GOLDSBERRY

Bibliography

Bailey, James O., ed. *British Plays of the Nineteenth Century.* 1966.

Thomson, Fred C. "A Crisis in Early Victorian Drama: John Westland Marston and the Syncretics." *Victorian Studies*, vol. 9, pp. 375-398.

. . . . .

TRANSPORTATION (PENAL) see PRISONS AND PRISON REFORM

. . . . .

TRANSPORTATION, URBAN

The predominant feature of urban transportation in the nineteenth century was the horse, which pulled carriages, buses, and cabs, was used as a pack animal, and was also a means of recreation. Road surfaces were abysmal; streets were smelly and congested; horses slipped on hills and in icy weather; and traffic jams were commonplace, although road engineers such as Thomas Telford (1757-1834) and John MacAdam (1756-1836) had begun to bring some sense to road-building techniques. Mechanized public transportation within **cities** began to make headway late in the century, and the automobile made a hesitant appearance among the rich in the 1890s.

Although readers of Dickens often imagine that Victorian roadways bustled with heavy long-distance coaches, the heydey of coaching was in the fifty years between 1780 and 1830. The **railways'** advantages of speed, comfort, and relative cheapness quickly put an end to the days of coaching and coaching inns. The swaying and unheated coaches had been uncomfortable even for the inside passengers, and the "outsiders," who paid a lesser fare to ride on the coachman's box, were in danger from the weather, the jolting over unimproved road surfaces, and the bursts of speed on good sections of toll roads. The typical coach fare was in the range of sixpence a mile, while twopence a mile became common for moderate railway accommodations.

For travel over shorter distances, only the well-to-do could afford to keep a private carriage, which required feeding and stabling horses and hiring one or more male servants to drive and care for them. Within London, the three main methods of travel at midcentury were Hackneys, cabs, and omnibuses. Hackney carriages were expensive, dirty, and disease ridden; they often doubled as hearses, ambulances, or prison vans. The lighter one-horse cabs—their name derived from the *cabriolet*—were introduced from Paris at the beginning of the nineteenth century. The "hansom safety cab," famous for its method of construction, was patented in 1834. Cabs were licensed and fares enjoyed some standardization.

The horse-drawn omnibus was introduced to England in 1829 by George Shillibeer (1797–1866). The earliest carried 22 persons, all seated inside the vehicle, which was drawn by three horses. A smaller version introduced in 1849 carried 12 passengers inside and two outside. Omnibuses were hard on horses: in 1840 the average life of an omnibus horse was seven years, which was reduced to four years by 1894. In 1901 the main company, the London General Omnibus Company (founded 1855) ran 16 million route miles, carrying 101,109,572 passengers at an average cost of about a penny a mile. The first motor 'bus, with a horse-bus body on a Cannstall-Daimler chassis, appeared in October 1899.

Urban tramways became possible in the 1860s with the patenting of the crescent rail, which was sunk flush with the road surface, although legal disincentives incorporated in the Tramways Act (1870) helped make tramways less common in Britain than in many other countries. A naturalized English citizen, Karl Willhelm Siemens (1823–1883), first successfully applied electricity to the running of a tramroad in 1883. Although tramways required a substantial initial investment, working expenses were far less than on horse-drawn cars, and fares could be very low. Blackpool, the Lancashire seaside resort, had a fixed fare of twopence for any journey; Glasgow, which had a fine, efficient tram service, gave passengers 2¼ miles for a penny.

The London underground railroad system was made possible by two types of construction. The earliest, "cut and cover," was used for the Metropolitan, District, and Circle lines, which began as steam-hauled routes. Construction was begun in 1854 and the Metropolitan Line opened for passengers in January 1863. The first line using "tube" construction—wholly underground, in deep tunnels—was built in 1890 and used electric locomotion instead of steam. It ran between King William Street in the City of London and Stockwell in south London, and is now part of the Northern Line.

Trackless self-propelled vehicles were first regulated in the "Red Flag Act"—properly the Locomotive and Highways Act (1861)—which required that steam engines (such as threshing machines, fairground engines, and steamrollers for road repairs) move at a speed no higher than 4 mph through towns and 2 mph in the countryside and be attended by three persons, one of whom had to walk 60 yards in front carrying a red flag during daylight hours and a red lantern at night. The act remained in force until 1896—by which time it was also applied to automobiles.

The most noteworthy of the pioneer British motorcar manufacturers, F. W. Lanchester (1868–1946) built three experimental machines in 1895 and opened his Ladywood works in Birmingham soon thereafter. The story of motorized urban transportation, however, belongs to the twentieth century rather than the nineteenth.

JOHN REYNOLDS

Bibliography

Nokes, George A. *Locomotion in Victorian London.* 1938.

Ransom, Philip J. G. *The Archaeology of the Transport Revolution.* 1984.

See also HORSES AND CARRIAGES

· · · · ·

TRAVEL AND EXPLORATION

The eighteenth and nineteenth centuries formed a second great age of European—and especially British—exploration and imperial expansion. By the end of Queen Victoria's reign so little of the earth remained geographically unexplored that the traveler as explorer had almost completely given way to the traveler as tourist. Improved transport and other innovations meant that travelers were often more comfortable and nearly as safe as they were at home. Moreover, the literature of exploration joined with new discoveries and attractions to stimulate the impulse for recreational travel.

According to a popular phrase, the traditional motives of out-of-the-way travel were "for God, Gold, and Glory." This was generally true of travel for pilgrimage, commerce, or conquest, whether in the classical world and Middle Ages or in the first great age of European exploration and expansion in the fifteenth and sixteenth centuries. In the eighteenth century, however, a new motive emerged and inaugurated an age of government-sponsored exploration seeking to widen scientific knowledge of the earth as a whole. Britain played a leading role because it had a large navy, the bulk of which was without work between major wars, and a ready surplus of skilled seamen and navigators. James Cook's three voyages to the Pacific, though not the earliest, provided models of organization and execution for all later voyages of discovery, including the wide-ranging *Beagle* expeditions (1826–1830 and 1831–1836) under Philip King (1793–1856) and Robert Fitzroy (1805–1865), and the United States Exploring Expedition (1838–1842) under Charles Wilkes (1798–1877). Major roles were also played by the Royal Society (chartered in 1662), by the Royal Navy's Hydrographic Office (the first hydrographer was appointed in 1795) and by the Royal Geographical Society (founded in 1830).

The new scientifically oriented expeditions recruited naturalists to observe and record flora, fauna, and other aspects of natural history. Three of the greatest naturalists of all time eagerly participated in expeditions: Joseph Banks (1743–1820) accompanied Cook on his first voyage (1768–1771); the German scientist Baron Alexander von Humboldt (1769–1859) explored in the Americas (1799–1804) and in Asiatic Russia (1829); and Charles Darwin (1809–1882) accompanied Fitzroy on the second voyage of the *Beagle* (1831–1836). These journeys led to major scientific discoveries. Geographical exploration was abandoned only during times of war; one expedition provoked another until virtually no coastline had escaped charting and no blank spaces remained on the terrestrial globe.

Several major geographical challenges had beckoned to explorers at the beginning of the nineteenth century. The first was the search for the elusive Northwest Passage between the Atlantic and the Pacific. John Franklin (1786–1847) led three major expeditions into the arctic wilderness, on the last of which he and all his crew perished. This disaster led to several rescue expeditions and intensified exploration of the region. Although a passage does exist, it soon became clear that the climate rendered it of little practical value.

A second challenge was presented by the interior of Africa, where the young Scot, Mungo Park (1771–1806) explored the Niger on two expeditions, the second of which ended tragically. He was succeeded in the continuing exploration of West Africa by Hugh Clapperton (1788–1827), who explored much of the interior of Nigeria, by David Denham (1786–1828), who explored the region between Timbuctoo and Lake Chad, and by Richard Lander (1804–1834), on whose last and ill-fated expedition, accompanied by his brother John (1807–1839), the question of the course and outlet of the Niger was finally settled. Elsewhere in Africa the ancient riddle of the source of the Nile attracted the attention of many leading British explorers, including **Richard Burton** (1821–1890), John Hanning Speke (1827–1864), James Grant (1827–1892), Samuel Baker (1821–1893), **David Livingstone** (1813–1873), and **Henry Morton Stanley** (1841–1904)—and also sparked much controversy among them. European exploration of Africa continued throughout the nineteenth century.

A third challenge lay in the interior of the Arabian peninsula, where—as in West Africa—a harsh climate and terrain were allied with a hostile Muslim culture to impede the passage of outsiders. Nonetheless, a notable succession of explorers, including Richard Burton, William Palgrave (1826–1888), and Charles Doughty (1843–1926), made significant inroads. A fourth challenge lay in the interior of Australia, where Charles Sturt (1795–1869) on two expeditions located and named the River Darling, navigated the length of the Murray, and searched in vain for an inland sea. Later the ill-fated Burke and Wills Expedition (1860–1861) succeeded in crossing the continent from Melbourne in the south to the Gulf of Carpenteria in the north, but came to grief in the wilderness on the return journey. The fifth and sixth challenges were the oceanographic exploration of the world under the sea and the conquest of the North and South Poles; in each case the final chapters remained to unfold in the twentieth century.

Another form of exploration that came into its own in the nineteenth century was that of the archaeologist who sought to uncover the remains of lost cities and civilizations. In the late eighteenth century Johan Joachim Winckelmann (1717–1768) began to uncover the cities of Pompeii and Herculaneum, buried by the eruption of Mount Vesuvius in 79 A.D. During the course of the nineteenth century the popular imagination was fed and the museums of Europe filled with antiquities. Austin Henry Layard (1817–1894) excavated the ruins of Nineveh; Heinrich Schliemann (1822–1890) located the historic site of legendary Troy; John Lloyd Stephens (1805–1852) explored the ancient rock city of Arabia Petraea and later the lost Mayan cities in the jungles of the Yucatan; George Dennis (1814–1898) described the cities and cemeteries of

Etruscan Italy; and Jean-Francois Champollion (1791–1832), Giovanni Belzoni (1778–1823), John Gardner Wilkinson (1797–1875), Flinders Petrie (1853–1942), and others deciphered and explained the monuments and wonders of ancient Egypt.

Travel was greatly facilitated by many nineteenth-century fruits of the industrial revolution. Improved sailing ships, steam propulsion, and the conversion to iron and steel hulls, along with the introduction of regularly scheduled service, rendered ocean voyages a more certain means of travel. On land, improved roads, the extension of mail and stagecoach services, and the development of railways gave travelers hitherto undreamed-of mobility. The opening in 1830 of the first public rail line between Liverpool and Manchester inaugurated a worldwide frenzy of railroad construction, which led to the spanning of Europe, Russia, the United States, Canada, and Australia by transcontinental lines.

This process of linking the continents and the oceans in a grid of regularly scheduled transport services shrank distances and reduced the discomfort and expense of travel, which led in turn to the rise of the travel agent and the conducted tour. Thomas Cook began his celebrated career in 1845 when he organized a church-sponsored railroad excursion to the seashore. In 1865 he relocated his firm to London, and soon owned an entire fleet of steamers on the Nile. Thomas Cook and Sons, Ltd. was commissioned by the government to organize transport for the expedition to relieve General Gordon at Khartoum in 1884. "Cook's Tours" became synonymous with well-organized travel.

On the Continent, George Nagelmackers (1845–1905) formed the Cie. Internationale des Wagons Lits in 1872 to exploit the railway sleeping cars invented by the American George Pullman (1831–1897). Nagelmackers offered European travelers dining car service in 1882 and in 1883 inaugurated the famous Orient Express service between Paris and Constantinople. Splendid new grand hotels provided further incentives to travel; some, such as Shepheard's Hotel in Cairo, were built in exotic locales. Travel was also facilitated by major engineering feats. The St. Gotthard tunnel (opened in 1882) linked Italy and the Adriatic ports by rail with northern Europe.

The Suez Canal (opened in 1869) subtracted thousands of miles from voyages to India and the Far East. Better preservation of food improved eating standards on journeys of all kinds; the firm of Fortnum and Mason's served as provisioners to both intrepid explorers and mere excursionists.

As travel grew both easier and cheaper all but the poorest people could indulge in holidays away from home. But as the common people made the seaside holiday their own, the higher classes abandoned it in favor of the European continent and the exotic East. There was a widespread romantic enthusiasm for Italy and Greece, for the Near and Far East with their antiquities, for mountain holidays (and Alpine climbing as a sport), and for taking the cure in Continental spas such as Marienbad, Leukerbad, or Baden Baden, which entered their heyday catering for wealthy foreign tourists in the later nineteenth century.

All of these developments were reflected in the publications of the period. While travel literature had always been extremely popular, in the nineteenth century cheap editions of voyages and travels flooded the market. Archaeological accounts often became best sellers. The Royal Navy's Hydrographic Office made admiralty charts prized the world over for their high standards of cartography. In 1851 Cook's began to promote their conducted tour business through the pages of a periodical entitled *The Excursionist*. A new business grew up for firms such as Bradshaw's in the publication of timetables for railroads and steamships. In addition, the tourist guidebook emerged as a major literary genre.

Upper-class travelers had a long tradition of turning their travel diaries and letters into formal publications, but such accounts were quite distinct from the literature of scientific exploration. As a result of the many changes that eased the hardships of travel for both explorers and tourists in the latter part of the nineteenth century, the distinction between the two kinds of journeying began to blur. Samuel Baker could take his bride on a honeymoon exploring the headwaters of the Nile, a journey that produced a classic volume in the literature of African discovery, and **Mary Kingsley** (1862-1900) wrote of her explorations in West Africa with a matter-of-fact tone more appropriate to a Cook's excursion in

Europe. The celebrated series of guides issued by the firm of John Murray included one by Richard Ford (1796-1858), the *Handbook for Travellers in Spain* (1845) which, with its sequel *Gatherings from Spain* (1846), made a lasting contribution to the literature on that country. Murray's series of guidebooks spawned many imitators, and a vastly expanding tourist market enabled another of Murray's authors, Augustus J. C. Hare (1834-1903), to earn his living from the production of guidebooks.

Where the factual literature of travel and exploration left off, authors of romantic fiction such as **Henry Rider Haggard** (1856-1925) and Jules Verne (1828-1905) were quick to supply their own fancy. Verne's "Voyages extraordinaires" series captured the popular imagination and enthusiasm for the wonders of science and exotic travel. *Around the World in Eighty Days* (1874), which was dramatized to great acclaim in Paris, only slightly exaggerated the realities of travel in the late Victorian world and—fittingly—featured an eccentric Englishman as its hero.

N. MERRILL DISTAD

Bibliography

Brosse, Jacques. *Great Voyages of Discovery: Circumnavigators and Scientists, 1764-1843.* 1985.

Cameron, Ian. *The History of the Royal Geographical Society, 1830-1980: To the Farthest Ends of the Earth.* 1980.

Ceram, C. W. *Gods, Graves, and Scholars: The Story of Archaeology.* 1952.

Newby, Eric. *Mitchell Beazley World Atlas of Exploration.* 1975.

Pimlott, J. A. R. *The Englishman's Holiday: A Social History.* 1947.

Schivelbusch, Wolfgang. *The Railway Journey: Trains and Travel in the Nineteenth Century.* 1979.

Stafford, Barbara. *Voyage into Substance: Art, Science, Nature and the Illustrated Travel Account, 1760-1840.* 1984.

Swinglehurst, Edward. *The Romantic Journey: the Story of Thomas Cook and Victorian Travel,* 1974.

Sykes, Percy. *A History of Exploration from the Earliest Times to the Present Day.* 1934; 2d ed., 1926; 3d ed. with appendix, 1949–1950; reissued with new introduction, 1961.

See also ARCTIC AND ANTARCTIC EXPLORATION; NATURAL HISTORY; OCEANOGRAPHY

· · · · ·

TRAVEL AND TOURISM

Foreign travel in the Victorian period became commonplace for the middle classes. The railway and steamship greatly increased the speed and comfort of travel and reduced its cost, while Thomas Cook's organized excursions popularized tourism.

In the eighteenth century a one- to three-year grand tour of Europe was considered the finish of a wealthy gentleman's education. After the Napoleonic Wars, the British middle class began to travel on the Continent in large numbers, and the grand tour was replaced by the commercialization of pleasure travel. Indicative of this change was the development of guidebooks listing hotels, places of interest, costs, timetables, and advice to travelers. The most popular was Mariana Starke's one-volume *Guide for Travellers on the Continent* (1832). Also used extensively were guidebooks by the English publisher John Murray and the German publisher Karl Baedeker.

Some travelers from the 1820s to the 1840s followed the route of the classic grand tour. France had special allure, but Italy was considered the climax. Genoa, Florence, Rome, and Venice were the main cities to be visited; antiquities, Renaissance art, and landscapes were the focus of interest. Italy had perennially been favored by literary-minded travelers, and the sojourns of Byron, Shelley, and Keats helped popularize it for middle-class tourists. Several hundred English families set up permanent residence in Italy by the 1860s, which added to its aura as the most relished destination for tourists.

Switzerland became so fashionable for travelers by the 1850s and 1860s that it was referred to as "the playground of Europe." Besides its views of the Alps, and mountaineering, Switzerland offered spas with mixed bathing (in voluminous costumes). By 1853 this country of 2.5 million had 14,500 inns. The winter sports holiday developed in the 1890s when skiing as a sport was introduced.

The interest of Carlyle and Coleridge in German writers helped popularize travel in Germany. The Rhineland had once been part of the return route from the South, but now steamer trips on the Rhine became fashionable. By the 1860s and 1870s steamers on the Rhine could handle 800,000 passengers a year. Many tourists also went to German spas such as Baden Baden and Weisbaden to drink and bathe in the mineral waters. Pastimes at the spas included gambling. In the 1870s the casinos moved to Monte Carlo and the Mediterranean.

America was a favored destination in the first half of the Victorian period to the adventurous and liberal-minded traveler interested in the democratic government. After the Civil War luxury hotels and improved rail service attracted the pleasure traveler who came to see New York, Boston, Niagara Falls, Washington, and New Orleans; take a trip up the Mississippi and Ohio Rivers; or by the end of the century, travel by rail to California.

The opening of the Suez Canal in 1869 and the work of English archaeologists created tourist interest in Egypt. The climate was prescribed for health cures, and in the 1880s and 1890s, steamer trips on the Nile and side trips to the Holy Land (organized by Thomas Cook) made Egypt the premier winter resort.

The **railway** and steamship revolutionized travel. A trip from England to Rome took twenty-one days in 1843 and only two and a half days in 1860. Passage to America could take two to eight weeks by sailing vessel, but only five days by steamship in 1889.

What technology made possible, Thomas Cook made popular. He introduced group excursion rates, the round-trip ticket, hotel coupons, and traveler's checks. After getting his start by offering a twenty-six-mile trip to a temperance rally, Cook arranged group excursions from the provinces to London, Paris, and the Continent, and finally, in 1872, around the world. Cook's seaside trips to France made it possible for working people to have a foreign holiday. His European tours were popular with women who were thus able to travel unescorted. The "Cookites," as they were called, could spend a few days in Paris or take a twenty-one-day tour of Switzerland for 20 pounds in 1863.

Victorian tourists were notorious for taking their English manners with them, and they were often seen as being both polite and condescending. Guidebooks of the period provide insights into taste, and numerous travel accounts document individual experiences.

SUSAN SCHOENBAUER THURIN

Bibliography

Berger, Max. *The British Traveller in America, 1836–1860.* 1964.

Delgado, Alan. *The Annual Outing and Other Excursions.* 1977.

Lambert, Richard S., ed. *Grand Tour: A Journey in the Tracks of the Age of Aristocracy.* 1935.

Löschburg, Winfried. *History of Travel.* 1979.

Premble, John. *The Mediterranean Passion.* 1987.

Pimlott, John A. R. *The Englishman's Holiday.* 1947.

Pudney, John. *The Thomas Cook Story.* 1953.

Swinglehurst, Edmund. *Cook's Tours: The Story of Popular Travel.* 1982.

Turner, Louis and John Ash. *The Golden Hordes.* 1975.

· · · · ·

TRAVEL LITERATURE

Seven years before Victoria ascended the throne, the Royal Geographical Society was born and exploration became institutionalized. The great era of imperialism and scientific discovery offered broad fields of action and research to soldiers, scientists, missionaries, diplomats, writers, and many others. Books by travelers took several forms, including letters, diaries, journals, narratives, and sketches. Because they satisfied the Victorian appetite for both fact and romance, they enjoyed a popularity rivaling that of the novel.

The enthusiasm for Orientalism found an outlet in travel to the Arab countries of the Near East, the Middle East, and North Africa.

In *Eastern Life: Present and Past* (1848) the keen social critic Harriet Martineau exploded the romantic myth of the harem. **Richard F. Burton**'s *Personal Narrative of a Pilgrimage to El-Medinah and Meccah* (1855–1856) became the archetype for Arabian adventure stories. The later traveler R. B. Cunninghame Graham, acting in the Burton tradition, disguised himself as an Arab in order to enter a Moroccan holy city. *Mogreb-el-Acksa* (1898) is his spirited record of the failure of this charade. Two Eastern narratives elevated the literary status of the travel book: Charles Doughty's prose masterpiece *Travels in Arabia Deserta* (1888) and Alexander Kinglake's *Eothen* (1844), a uniquely personal, impressionistic tour of the Holy Land.

The search for the source of the Nile generated several exploration journals, notably Burton's encyclopedic *The Lake Regions of Central Africa* (1860). Other popular accounts included those of John Hanning Speke, Henry Morton Stanley, and Samuel White Baker. *Missionary Travels and Researches in South Africa* (1857), David Livingstone's moving record of his transcontinental trek, became a best seller. Finally, the most sensitive and eloquent Victorian appraisal of the African is contained in **Mary Kingsley**'s *Travels in West Africa* (1897).

Charles Darwin's *Voyage of the Beagle* (1839) belongs to a tradition of South American naturalist journals. Inspired by Darwin, Henry Walter Bates published an account of his eleven-year exploration of the Amazon River system. At the end of the century, William Henry Hudson's *Idle Days in Patagonia* (1893) transformed the travel book into a voyage inward into the human mind.

An important historical resource, the Anglo-Indian travel book was often the product of many years' residence. While Burton's four valuable, far-ranging works went almost unnoticed at their publication, Emily Eden's two volumes of letters continue to enjoy a following. Marianne Postans Young was remarkable for her sympathetic appreciation of the native Indian. William Henry Sleeman's accounts are exceptionally acute and complex responses to Indian culture.

Although Dickens and Ruskin left influential sketches of the Italian cities, romanticism was steering earnest travelers from the popular watering places of Europe. George Borrow's boisterous *The Bible in Spain* (1842) describes his attempt to distribute the scriptures during a dangerous Spanish civil war. Edward Lear illustrated his travel journals with his landscapes of Calabria, Corsica, Greece, and Albania. Leslie Stephen entitled his widely read mountain-climbing account *The Playground of Europe* (1871). Samuel Butler's *Alps and Sanctuaries* (1881) inspired twentieth-century travelers to Italy.

Another visitor to Italy was Frances Trollope, notorious for her inflammatory *Domestic Manners of the Americans* (1832). Accounts of American travel covered the spectrum from rugged Western adventure stories to studious analyses of Eastern social institutions. Like many Britons, Charles Dickens became disillusioned with the United States; his *American Notes* (1842) is a record of how he was both impressed and disappointed. Other eminent literary travelers to America included Martineau, Thackeray, Kipling, Wilde, Matthew Arnold, Anthony Trollope, and Charles Kingsley.

Several globe-trotters made a career of recording their experiences abroad. Burton wrote forty-three volumes of travel. The most celebrated Victorian woman travel writer was **Isabella Bird,** best remembered for *A Lady's Life in the Rocky Mountains* (1879); in her thirty-year travel career, she visited Hawaii, North America, India, and the Near and Far East. Robert Louis Stevenson's finely crafted accounts of his travels in Europe, the United States, and the South Seas are among the most evocative and entertaining of the period.

Travel freed Victorian women: abroad in remote areas they became the professional equivalents of Victorian men. Their motives were various. Poor health sent Lucie Duff Gordon to Egypt. Kate Marsden was driven by a sense of mission to minister to Siberian lepers. Marianne North's botanical paintings and Amelia Edwards's Nile researches reveal a scientific interest. Curiosity impelled Anna Brassey on a world cruise and Constance Cumming on tours of China and Japan. To satisfy a thirst for adventure, Anne Blunt penetrated the Saudi peninsula and Florence Douglas Dixie tackled Patagonia and the Transvaal. Many accompanied their husbands only to find a theater for their own talents. Often, they surpassed their men in their responsiveness to native cultures. Whatever their motives, women travel writers left accounts marked by superior wit, perception, and compassion.

JOAN CORWIN

Bibliography

Assad, Thomas J. *Three Victorian Travellers: Burton, Blunt, Doughty.* 1964.

Dyson, Ketaki Kushari. *A Various Universe: A Study of the Journals and Memoirs of British Men and Women in the Indian Subcontinent, 1765–1856.* 1978.

Fedden, Robin. *English Travellers in the Near East.* 1958.

Hamalian, Leo, ed. *Ladies on the Loose: Women Travellers of the Eighteenth and Nineteenth Centuries.* 1981.

Kirkpatrick, F. A. "The Literature of Travel 1700–1900." In *The Cambridge History of English Literature,* vol. 14. 1917.

Middleton, Dorothy. *Victorian Lady Travellers.* 1965.

Moorehead, Alan. *The White Nile.* 1960.

Rotberg, Robert I., ed. *Africa and Its Explorers: Motives, Methods, and Impact.* 1970.

Shattock, Joanne. "Travel Writing Victorian and Modern: A Review of Recent Research." In Philip Dodd, ed., *The Art of Travel: Essays on Travel Writing.* 1982.

Stevenson, Catherine Barnes. *Victorian Women Travel Writers in Africa.* 1982.

Tidrick, Kathryn. *Heart-Beguiling Araby.* 1981.

Van Orman, Richard A. *The Explorers: Nineteenth Century Expeditions in Africa and the American West.* 1984.

Van Thal, Herbert, ed. *Victoria's Subjects Travelled.* 1951.

. . . . .

TREE, HERBERT BEERBOHM (1853–1917)

As an actor, Herbert Beerbohm Tree excelled in the type of eccentric characterization exemplified by his role as Svengali in

George Du Maurier's *Trilby* (1895). As a manager, he followed in the stylistic footsteps of Henry Irving by staging lavish productions of Shakespeare, as well as contemporary plays by Wilde, Ibsen, and Shaw. Though both his acting and his production values tended toward romantic excess, Tree's enormous commercial success, coupled with his efforts to raise the standards of the English stage, made him a significant figure in late Victorian theater.

Half-brother of noted author and caricaturist **Max Beerbohm**, Tree began his career in amateur theatricals. During the period 1880–1887 he appeared on stage professionally in a wide variety of roles, achieving particular renown as Paolo Macari in *Called Back* (1884). In 1887 he undertook the management of the Haymarket Theatre and, in the ensuing decade, staged a long string of financially successful productions. Notable among them were the melodrama *Captain Swift* (1888), *The Merry Wives of Windsor* (1889), Wilde's *A Woman of No Importance* (1893), and Ibsen's *An Enemy of the People* (1893).

The substantial profits generated by *Trilby*, a play that Tree revived a number of times, enabled him to build Her Majesty's Theatre in 1897. Together with his wife, actress Helen Maud Holt (1863–1937), he produced eighteen Shakespearian plays over a period of twenty-six years, each, it seemed, more elaborate than the one preceding it. While *Julius Caesar* (1898) and *Henry VIII* (1910) demonstrated Tree's accomplished use of spectacle, his fondness for stagey, rather than staged, effects often diminished the critical value of his productions. Nevertheless, in *Richard II* (1903), to which his acting talents were more ideally suited, he achieved a genuine coherence of vision.

Tree went on to produce, under Shaw's direction, *Pygmalion* (1914), playing Henry Higgins to Mrs. Patrick Campbell's Eliza Doolittle. Always an advocate for actors, he sought to raise the standards of the profession by founding the Royal Academy of Dramatic Art in 1904. He was knighted in 1909.

LAUREN SMITH

Bibliography

Pearson, Hesketh. *Beerbohm Tree: His Life and Laughter.* 1956.

· · · · ·

TROLLOPE, ANTHONY (1815–1882)

Best known for the "Chronicles of Barsetshire" (*The Warden*, 1855; *Barchester Towers*, 1857; *Doctor Thorne*, 1858; *Framley Parsonage*, 1861; *The Small House at Allington*, 1864; and *The Last Chronicle of Barset*, 1867) and for the "Palliser" novels (*Can You Forgive Her?*, 1864; *Phineas Finn*, 1869; *The Eustace Diamonds*, 1873; *Phineas Redux*, 1874; *The Prime Minister*, 1876; and *The Duke's Children*, 1880), Anthony Trollope is generally ranked below Dickens and George Eliot, but more or less on a level with other major mid-Victorian novelists such as Charlotte and Emily Brontë, Thackeray, and Elizabeth Gaskell.

Trollope's *An Autobiography* (1883) gave a moving but unsentimental account of his humiliations as a penniless, unkempt dayboy at Harrow School and of his delight at winning social success and popularity along with the fame and money that his novels brought him—particularly after the appearance of *Framley Parsonage*, which was serialized in the opening numbers of the *Cornhill Magazine* under Thackeray's editorship. Between 1841 and 1859 Trollope lived mainly in Ireland, working as a postal surveyor and contracting his lifelong passion for hunting. By the time he retired from the post office in 1867, he had become a senior official and had been entrusted with several missions overseas. He claimed credit for having introduced the pillar-box into rural England. Several of his novels, including the first two, are set in Ireland and have recently found admirers, but his best and most popular novels deal with English middle- and upper-class life.

Both in his own day and since, Trollope has especially been praised for his "realism" and for what Henry James called his "eye for the moral question," in particular the casuistries of conscience. The subtlety of social and psychological observation, the comic verve, and the freshness of moral outlook that characterized his studies of the rural clergy and landed gentry in the Barsetshire novels (and others) were never unmixed with a degree of cynicism and pessimism, but the note of satire (which he professed to deplore) became sharper in the Palliser novels, dealing mainly with the political and social high life of London, and in

The Way We Live Now (1875), his massive indictment of the "commercial profligacy" he saw invading all walks of life—nowadays often regarded as his masterpiece. In *He Knew He Was Right* (1869) he achieved the most impressive and disturbing of several studies of psychological derangement, and in *Mr. Scarborough's Family* (1883) he radically questioned the legal and ethical codes on which Victorian society rested. But even in these novels Trollope's tolerance and equanimity, his "strenuous moderation" in assigning praise and blame, seldom desert him for long. His novels stand out from those of most of his contemporaries by their avoidance of both false heroics and melodramatic villainy, both sentimental idealism and exaggerated moral rigor.

P. D. EDWARDS

Bibliography

apRoberts, Ruth. *The Moral Trollope.* 1971.

Edwards, P. D. *Anthony Trollope, His Art and Scope.* 1977.

Hall, N. John, ed. *The Letters of Anthony Trollope.* 1983. 2 vols.

Kincaid, James R. *The Novels of Anthony Trollope.* 1977.

Lyons, Anne K. *Anthony Trollope: An Annotated Bibliography of Periodical Works by and About Him in the United States and Great Britain to 1900.* 1985.

McMaster, Juliet. *Trollope's Palliser Novels.* 1978.

Sadleir, Michael. *Trollope, A Bibliography.* 1928.

———. *Trollope, A Commentary.* 1927.

See also CARICATURE *(illus.)*
. . . . .

TROLLOPE, FRANCES
(1779-1863)

Although she wrote thirty-four novels, Frances Trollope is better known as the mother of **Anthony Trollope** and the author of *Domestic Manners of the Americans* (1832) than for her achievements in fiction. Yet she significantly expanded the art of fiction with her controversial social reform novels and her many works featuring a new, strong kind of heroine.

Born Frances Milton, she was educated by her father, a Bristol clergyman. Her union with Thomas Anthony Trollope produced seven children in eight years. When, after eighteen years of busy domestic life, bankruptcy loomed, Frances Trollope embarked on a scheme in utopian living in the United States with her friend Frances Wright, who had founded a colony for the education and emancipation of slaves. The venture collapsed, and Trollope went to Cincinnati where her business and cultural scheme—the famous Cincinnati Bazaar—also failed. At fifty-two, she returned to England and published *Domestic Manners of the Americans,* which became highly controversial for its attacks on many of America's most prized beliefs about itself.

Even the success of her first book and the earnings from subsequent travel books and several popular novels could not rescue the Trollopes' finances. Fleeing to Belgium, where Mr. Trollope could not be sued by his creditors, Frances Trollope wrote to support her family while nursing several of her children who were dying of tuberculosis. Of necessity, she forged the spartan writing habits later emulated by her son Anthony.

The first of Trollope's social reform novels grew out of her strong revulsion for American slavery. *The Life and Adventures of Jonathan Jefferson Whitlaw* (1836) told the story of a cruel overseer, anticipating by fifteen years the more famous *Uncle Tom's Cabin* by Harriet Beecher Stowe. *The Vicar of Wrexhill* (1837) attacked evangelical excesses and their unfortunate effects upon women. For *The Life and Adventures of Michael Armstrong, the Factory Boy* (1839)—the first novel by a woman author published in monthly parts—Trollope embarked on a fact-finding mission to Manchester, where she interviewed radical leaders and visited factories and slums. The novel's realistic settings were powerful and its theme original: Trollope placed no hope in individual benevolence but looked instead to legislation to relieve the poor. Her purpose was to awaken the national conscience on behalf of factory children. She followed with an equally offensive topic in *Jessie Phillips* (1843), the narrative of a fallen woman who is destroyed by her society as well as by her seducer.

In the middle 1840s Trollope began increasingly to write of determined, intelligent, and willful girls having difficulty in marital ventures. Although the primary heroines were conventional, Trollope drew sympathetically a series of strong female characters including fortune hunters, villainesses, sirens, and unhappy wives. In these novels, women longed for excitement as well as security.

Her final fictional innovation was a group of novels in which heroines noted for their sturdy, even aggressive, independence confront tyrannical fathers or cope with marriages to weak or evil men and emerge victorious. Her last book, *Fashionable Life: Or, Paris and London* (1856), presents a vision of a community of women living in peace, harmony, and cooperation.

Although her literary achievements have been overshadowed by her heroic breadwinning and the fame of her son, Frances Trollope helped revitalize the travel book by concentrating on people rather than landscape and, even in her lighter fiction, was instrumental in breaking down the nineteenth-century stereotypes of the heroine. Her novels of social reform introduced a whole range of new subjects into what had been called "the fairyland of fiction."

HELEN HEINEMAN

Bibliography

Heineman, Helen. *Frances Trollope*. 1984.

———. *Mrs. Trollope: The Triumphant Feminine in the Nineteenth Century*. 1979.

Johnston, Johanna. *The Life, Manners and Travels of Fanny Trollope: A Biography*. 1978.

Trollope, Frances Eleanor. *Frances Trollope: Her Life and Literary Work from George III to Victoria*. 1895.

· · · · ·

TUBERCULOSIS

Tuberculosis was the leading cause of death throughout the nineteenth century. Although romantically associated with creative genius (and the delicate fragility of idealized feminine beauty), it struck hardest among those subject to malnutrition, crowded dwellings, and ill-ventilated workplaces. Until the discovery of the tubercule bacilli by German scientist Robert Koch in 1882 the disease was generally thought to be hereditary. It remained incurable; the decrease in tuberculosis mortality over the last half of the century was due to improvements in diet and housing rather than to any medical advance.

In 1838, one-sixth of all deaths in England and Wales were due to tuberculosis. Although mortality roughly halved in the last half of the century, the very ubiquity of the disease masked its contagious nature. The word itself first came into medical usage at about mid-century. The chronic pulmonary form, which takes a few months to several years to run its course, was generally referred to as "consumption." The late stage, with expectoration of pus from the lungs, was often called "phthisis." "Scrofula," marked by swollen glands and skin ulcerations, was recognized as a variety of tuberculosis by the 1860s. Tubercular infections could also be dismissed as "grippe" or confused with typhus (as in the case of the two eldest Brontë sisters). The nonmedical term "decline" and the medical diagnoses of asthenia, tabes, inflammation of the lungs, hectic fever and gastric fever are also common designators for illnesses that were probably tubercular.

Even when correctly diagnosed, tuberculosis was underreported. The belief that it was hereditary aroused terror in relatives and made it difficult for them to obtain life insurance. Advice manuals urged young women to inquire into a suitor's family history and declared that men with consumptive tendencies were unfit for marriage because of the risk to their children and the hardship to a family whose breadwinner suffered a lengthy illness. Exercise, hard work, study, and mental strain were said to endanger adolescent girls, whose susceptibility to anemia gave them a "consumptive look." Many minor vices were thought to open doors for the disease to enter, including immodest dress, rich food, alcoholic beverages, waltzing, tight lacing, excessive emotion—and, of course, disappointment in love.

The romantic mythography of tuberculosis blossomed during the Victorian period. Its

identification with poets, artists, and bohemianism was intensified; even medical literature suggested that the fires of creative genius
wasted and consumed the body. In literature,
consumptives such as Paul Dombey were spir-
itualized and purified as they declined. The
languid paleness of tubercular Pre-Raphaelite
models contributed to a standard of feminine
beauty which dominated fashion magazines
through much of the twentieth century.
George Du Maurier's *Trilby* (1894) was only
one in the long line of sexual victims beatified
(and beautified) through suffering.

Literary and artistic convention avoided
both the ugly manifestations of the disease
and the recognition that it was more likely to
attack workhouse children, domestic servants,
miners, seamstresses, potters, and disproportionate numbers of married women. In fact,
the higher mortality rate of females as compared to males during the nineteenth century
was not, as is commonly supposed, directly
related to the dangers of childbirth. At midcentury, about half of all deaths in women
between fifteen and thirty-five were due to
some form of tuberculosis. The overall female
advantage in mortality arose when the excess
of female deaths from tuberculosis declined.
Women's greater susceptibility was probably
due to dietary disadvantage and to the overcrowding and poor ventilation of homes and
workplaces in which women spent most of
their time. Females aged between five and
nineteen were the last to achieve a consistently lower death rate than their male counterparts.

Medical treatments for tuberculosis included bleeding, blisters, cod liver oil, cal-
omel, and stimulants. Opium was used to
quiet coughing and relieve diarrhea. Rest,
quiet, and good diet offered some hope of
remission. Hospitals generally rejected tubercular patients as incurable; they were cared
for at home or in the workhouse infirmary.
The wealthy sought refuge in the sun: Nice
was most fashionable; the Trollopes and the
Brownings went to Florence; Cannes, Torquay, and the Isle of Wight were known as
winter resorts for consumptives. Others
pinned their hope on long sea voyages or,
from the late 1860s, on the high mountain air.

SALLY MITCHELL

Bibliography

Dubos, Rene and Jean Dubos. *The White Plague:
Tuberculosis, Man and Society.* 1952.

Johansson, Sheila Ryan. "Sex and Death in Victorian England." In Martha Vicinus, ed., *A Widening Sphere.* 1977.

King, Lester Snow. *Medical Thinking: A Historical
Preface.* 1982.

Smith, F. B. *The People's Health, 1830–1910.* 1979.

. . . . .

TUCKER, CHARLOTTE MARIA
(1821–1893)

Charlotte Maria Tucker, missionary and author of popular didactic children's fiction
under the pseudonym A.L.O.E. ("A Lady of
England"), devoted her life and talents to promoting Christianity.

Educated at home, Tucker spent her early
adulthood teaching younger siblings, visiting
the poor at Marylebone Workhouse, and taking part in social life with the political and
intellectual figures entertained by her father,
St. George Tucker (1771–1851), chairman of
the East India Company. She began her writing career at age thirty-two, after her father's
death. Besides publishing numerous books,
Tucker contributed tract fiction to *The Children's Paper* (1855–1925) and other religious
magazines.

Though Tucker's tales always conclude with
a pointed lesson, she underplayed religion, relying instead on a mix of humor, fact, and
earnestness. *The Story of a Needle* (1858), *Old
Friends with New Faces* (1858), *Crown of
Success* (1863), *Fairy Know-a-Bit* (1866), and
Fairy Frisket (1874) epitomize her secular approach to evangelizing. *The Rambles of a Rat*
(1857) combines adventure with religion and
fact to promote ragged schools. *War and
Peace* (1862) contains escapes, sieges, and violence to show "the power of faith to give *peace*
even in the midst of tumult and *war.*" From
1875 to her death in 1893, Tucker did missionary work in India and wrote allegorical Christian tales that were translated into Urdu, Pun-
jabi, Hindi, Bengali, and Tamil.

Tucker presents the conventional catalogue of vices and virtues: pride, sloth, avarice, and folly versus faith, charity, honesty, thrift, and good works. But her contemporary settings and characters, skillful narration, and sense of the absurd endeared her to children of all classes. Her works demonstrate midcentury ideas on religious and practical education and reveal the assimilation of utilitarian and secular values in tract fiction.

SUSAN NARAMORE MAHER

Bibliography

Bratton, J. S. *The Impact of Victorian Children's Fiction.* 1981.

Cutt, Margaret Nancy. *Ministering Angels: A Study of Nineteenth-Century Evangelical Writing for Children.* 1979.

Giberne, Agnes. *A Lady of England: The Life and Letters of Charlotte Maria Tucker.* 1895.

Oliphant, Margaret et al. *Women Novelists of Queen Victoria's Reign.* 1897.

Times, December 29, 1893.

. . . . .

TURNER, JOSEPH MALLORD WILLIAM (1775-1851)

Joseph Mallord William Turner is generally acknowledged to have been Britain's greatest painter. Extremely prolific, he produced during his long career over five hundred works in oil and thousands of watercolors, drawings, and sketches, in addition to numerous prints executed personally or by engravers. A true romantic in his personal response to the beauty and power of nature, he also gave expression to the advent of modern industrialism in such famous paintings as *The Fighting "Temeraire"* and *Rain, Steam and Speed.*

Born in London's Covent Garden district, Turner developed quickly as an artist, producing his first drawings in the 1780s. He exhibited his first watercolor in 1790 and his first oil, *Fishermen at Sea,* in 1796, both at the Royal Academy. In 1799 he was elected associate of the Royal Academy, with elevation to full membership following in 1802. Turner's genuine interest in the fashionable styles of classicism, the picturesque, and the sublime, his versatility in working with ideal and topographical landscape, marine subjects, and genre and history painting—in fact almost every form save portraiture—won him sufficient patronage to achieve lifelong financial security. The supreme impetus for his art was nature. He painted its soft, nurturing beauty in *Crossing the Brook* (1815), its grandeur in the watercolor *Upper Fall of the Reichenbach* (c. 1810), and its dangerous turbulence in *Calais Pier* (1803). It was nature that stimulated his romanticism, that expressive style through which he communicated his personal response to phenomena and his understanding of the underlying power of the environment. This is most evident in such paintings as *Norham Castle, Sunrise* (c. 1835-1840), a canvas ablaze with the sun's hot light, enveloping and blurring everything in its proximity. His personal and intuitive approach, characterized by bold color and loose brushwork, coincided also with his interest in the cataclysmic and destructive power of the natural elements, as portrayed in *Snow-Storm, Avalanche and Inundation* (1837) and other works.

Turner often depicted contemporary events and concerns in his paintings, for example *The Battle of Trafalgar* (1806), *The Burning of the Houses of Lords and Commons* (1835), and *Slavers Throwing Overboard the Dead and Dying* (1840), the last a vivid condemnation of the then rampant slave trade. Industrial and technological forms also appeared in his art. Early in his career he painted *Limekiln at Coalbrookdale* (c. 1797) and later captured the grim activity of industrial towns in such watercolors as *Leeds* (1816), *Newcastle-on-Tyne* (c. 1823), *Dudley, Worcestershire* (c. 1830-1831), and *Coventry, Warwickshire* (c. 1832). In *The Fighting "Temeraire"* (1839) he underscored the reality of modern change in the form of a black steam tug towing a great but obsolete ship of the line to the wreckers. In *Staffa—Fingal's Cave* (1832) the new technology battles nature as a storm threatens a coastal steamer, and in *Snow-Storm—Steam-Boat off a Harbour's Mouth* (1842) human invention is rendered helpless in a terrible vortex of snow, wind, and sea. Perhaps his most famous technological subject is *Rain, Steam and Speed—the Great Western Railway*

(1844), a wonderful vision of speeding mechanical power.

Turner's individualism of style lost him support during the last years of his life, a time when fashion was moving toward meticulous detail and sentimental symbolism in the arts. Yet one notable Victorian rose to his defense: in 1843 the first volume of John Ruskin's *Modern Painters* was devoted largely to celebrating Turner's greatness.

Turner was one of the most accomplished artists of his age. His watercolors were unsurpassed in technique and conception while his oils, in their use of dynamic color and free application of paint, were so far in advance of their time that they prefigure, in some instances, modern abstract art.

WILLIAM S. RODNER

Bibliography

Butlin, Martin and Evelyn Joll. *The Paintings of J.M.W. Turner*. Rev. ed., 1984.

Finberg, Alexander J. *The Life of J. M. W. Turner, R. A.* 1961.

Gage, John, ed. *Collected Correspondence of J. M. W. Turner*. 1979.

Lindsay, Jack. *J. M. W. Turner: His Life and Work: A Critical Biography*. 1966.

Rawlinson, William G. *The Engraved Work of J. M. W. Turner, R.A.* 1913.

Wilton, Andrew. *J. M. W. Turner: His Art and Life*. 1979.

. . . . .

TWINING, LOUISA (1820–1912)

Louisa Twining originated workhouse reforms that raised the standard of Poor Law administration and demonstrated women's ability to manage social services.

Twining, the youngest child of Richard Twining, a prosperous tea merchant, was born in London in 1820. An Evangelical Anglican with a powerful sense of religious mission, she began visiting workhouses in 1853 and soon committed herself to eradicate the shocking conditions she found, although she never questioned the Poor Law's validity or the deterrent principle behind it.

Over the next several decades, alone and in conjunction with societies such as the **National Association for the Promotion of Social Science**, the talented, determined, practical, and well-connected Twining pressured authorities to allow systematic workhouse visiting, to improve the quality of workhouse life and nursing, and to appoint and allow the election of female inspectors and guardians. Appropriately, she was elected to the Kensington and Tunbridge Wells boards of guardians in 1884 and 1892.

In addition to Poor Law reform Twining was involved in other causes: temperance, workingmen's colleges, a home for art students, and refuges for convalescent cholera victims and newly released mental patients. Although she justified her public work on the grounds that caring for the disadvantaged was a traditional female duty, she also supported women's rights. Twining was a progressive conservative, who failed fully to comprehend the roots of poverty and sexual discrimination, but her example and activities produced significant social changes.

KATHLEEN E. McCRONE

Bibliography

McCrone, Kathleen. "Feminism and Philanthropy in Victorian England: The Case of Louisa Twining." *Canadian Historical Papers* (1976), pp. 123–139.

Prochaska, F. K. *Women and Philanthropy in Nineteenth-Century England*. 1980.

Twining, Louisa. *Recollections of Workhouse Visiting and Management During Twenty-Five Years*. 1880.

———. "Women as Official Inspectors." *Nineteenth Century*, vol. 35, pp. 489–494.

———. "Women as Public Servants." *Nineteenth Century*, vol. 28, pp. 950–958.

———. *Workhouses and Women's Work*. 1858.

. . . . .

TYPEWRITER

The modern typewriter was invented by an American, Christopher L. Sholes, and the manufacture and distribution of the machine in Victorian Britain was primarily an American achievement. The firearms manufacturer, E. Remington and Sons, began producing Sholes's machine in 1874 and brought out the prototype of all modern machines in 1878. In 1886 Remington Typewriter Company became an independent firm and established its first dealership in Britain. During the 1880s typewriters rapidly invaded British offices. Courses of instruction were devised immediately and in 1890 the Union of Lancashire and Cheshire Institutes introduced certification examinations in typewriting. By 1894 the post office found it necessary to create the new civil service grade of "women typists."

The invasion of American machines was accompanied by an influx of young women into a previously exclusive male world. From the beginning, typewriting positions were monopolized by women. Offices were rapidly expanding in size and number and the typewriter provided an ideal vehicle by which women could be introduced into the growing number of clerical jobs. Typewriters and female typists made possible the increasing flow of documents that characterized twentieth-century offices. Moreover, they strongly reinforced trends toward the routinization of office work, the creation of office hierarchies, and the erosion of the salaries and status of clerical workers. By 1900 the typewriter was common to all but the smallest offices and until 1914 it remained one of the primary mechanical imports from America, being surpassed in value only by agricultural machinery.

FREDERICK E. LAURENZO

Bibliography

Current, Richard N. *The Typewriter and the Men Who Made It.* 1954.

Davies, Margery W. *Woman's Place Is at the Typewriter: Office Work and Office Workers, 1870–1930.* 1982.

Mares, George Carl. *The History of the Typewriter.* 1909.

See also CLERKS AND CLERICAL WORK

· · · · ·

UNITARIANISM

The theological position in Protestant Christianity which denies the Trinity and affirms the single personality of God is known as Unitarianism. In the Victorian period, under the leadership of **James Martineau** (1805–1900) and his sister **Harriet Martineau** (1802–1876), Unitarians were chiefly notable for advocating social reform, especially the abolition of slavery in the British Empire and in the United States, rather than for theological controversy.

The background of Victorian Unitarianism is the long history of dispute among Christians about the divinity of Jesus. The Roman Catholic and Anglican churches were both staunchly Trinitarian and relentlessly persecuted Unitarian theology until the early seventeenth century. The last men to die in England for religious heresy were disbelievers in the Trinity who were executed by James I in 1612. Nevertheless, such prominent thinkers as John Milton, John Locke, and Isaac Newton held Unitarian views.

The first Unitarian church in England was founded in London in 1774 by Theophilus Lindsey (1723–1808), and in the nineteenth century Unitarian congregations developed mainly in such large industrial cities as Manchester, Birmingham, and Leeds. Their membership was not working class but managerial, composed largely of educated and often powerful people. The numbers remained small (229 congregations with about 30,000 members in 1851, compared to 2,789 Baptist congregations, for example), but their influence was large, owing to the prominence of Unitarians in British industry (the Wedgwoods in pottery, the Tates in sugar) and in Parliament. Independent in spirit, the Unitarians were never tightly organized as a religious body, nor was their observance severe or puritanical: they could dance, play cards, and attend the theater. They held strongly to fundamental Christian principles and values, but urged and practiced toleration on theological and doctrinal questions.

The father of English Unitarianism was the scientist Joseph Priestley (1733–1804), a Presbyterian minister of Leeds and later Birmingham who founded the Unitarian Society for Promoting Christian Knowledge in 1791.

His major contribution to Unitarian thought was his *Letters . . . on the History of the Corruptions of Christianity* (1792), which argued that the primitive church was unitarian in theology. This unpopular view, coupled with his support of the French Revolution in its early stages, made Priestley a highly controversial figure in England. After the Birmingham riots of 1791 he emigrated to the United States, where he was warmly welcomed by the increasingly influential Unitarian community in America.

The leadership of English Unitarianism was assumed by Thomas Belsham (1750–1829), one of the first English religious thinkers to accept and approve the new methods of **biblical criticism** developed in Germany (the "higher criticism"). A member of Belsham's church, William Smith (1756–1835), introduced into Parliament the Trinity Bill of 1813, which abolished the legal penalties for nonbelief in the Trinity. Emancipated, Unitarians formed new congregations, published tracts, established domestic and foreign missions, and consolidated a national leadership in the British and Foreign Unitarian Association (1825).

James Martineau, the leading English Unitarian of the middle and later nineteenth century, was a theological liberal who sought to release Unitarianism from its traditional reliance on Scripture. "Reason," he argued, "is the ultimate appeal, the supreme tribunal, to the test of which even Scripture must be brought" (*The Rationale of Religious Enquiry*, 1836). Martineau was a powerful speaker and writer whose views became increasingly influential and were supported by other prominent Unitarian thinkers such as John James Tayler (1797–1869) and John Hamilton Thom (1808–1894).

Victorian Unitarians strenuously supported movements for prison reform, temperance, peace, education, and women's rights. They were instrumental in moving through Parliament the Emancipation Act of 1833, which abolished slavery throughout the British Empire. In the 1840s and 1850s attention turned to slavery in the United States. Harriet Martineau became a fervent abolitionist and supporter of the American William Lloyd Garrison (1805–1879). Her book *Society in America* (1837) did much to rally British public opinion against slavery in the United States. Robert Hibbert (1770–1849), whose trust fund established the Unitarian *Hibbert Journal*, was a gradualist on this issue.

In the Victorian era, English Unitarians, having achieved their own legal emancipation in 1813, gradually strengthened their domestic position, expanded their foreign missions, increased somewhat their always limited numbers, refined their traditional Bible-centered theology, and campaigned successfully for a variety of social reforms.

JAMES HAZEN

Bibliography

Davies, Horton. *Worship and Theology in England: From Newman to Martineau.* 1962.

Holt, Raymond. *The Unitarian Contribution to Social Progress in England.* Rev. ed., 1952.

Stange, Douglas. *British Unitarians Against American Slavery.* 1984.

Watts, Michael. *The Dissenters.* 1978.

Wilbur, Earl Morse. *A History of Unitarianism.* 2 vols. 1945–1952.

· · · · ·

UTILITARIANISM

The term "utilitarianism" commonly describes a moral philosophy, also known as Benthamism or Philosophical Radicalism, that flourished in England between the mid-eighteenth and the late nineteenth centuries. Derived principally from the thought of Jeremy Bentham (1748–1832) and his protégé James Mill (1773–1836), it exercised a vigorous influence on English political, social, economic, and legal thought during the middle years of the century, and its advocates frequently became leaders in political and social reform movements. Utilitarianism shaped the thought of **John Stuart Mill** (1806–1873) and engendered forceful opposition from such thinkers as Thomas Carlyle, John Ruskin, John Henry Newman, Charles Dickens, and Matthew Arnold.

With the celebrated opening sentences of *An Introduction to the Principles of Morals* and *Legislation* (1789), Bentham stated the cardinal tenets of utilitarianism. "Nature has placed mankind under the governance of two sovereign masters, pain and pleasure," he wrote. "It is for them alone to point out what we ought to do, as well as to determine what we shall do." According to Bentham, who believed he had uncovered a scientific theory of human nature and legislation, the pleasure/ pain principle is both the fundamental cause of individual and collective human behavior and the criterion of utility by which such behavior may be measured. Because humans are rational and self-interested creatures, they seek to maximize their pleasures and minimize their pains; a morally correct or right action, accordingly, results in the greatest possible pleasure within a set of given circumstances. When Bentham endeavored to establish the criteria by which actions could be judged, he produced one of his less happy ideas, the "felicific calculus" or moral arithmetic. These criteria considered all pleasures equal in quality, thus emphasizing (as John Stuart Mill and other critics observed) the quantity of pleasure over its quality.

Together with the "greatest happiness principle," English utilitarianism embraced a broad range of ideas, including initially an acceptance of the laissez-faire position with regard to state intervention in economic and social matters. While the utilitarians remained staunch individualists and advocates of laissez faire in the economic sphere, their attitude toward the state evolved to a position that endowed it with an active social responsibility. "The business of government," Bentham had written in the *Introduction*, "is to promote the happiness of society, by punishing and rewarding." Because he distrusted the state and sought to ensure that government would act not only benevolently and rationally but also in the interest of the greatest number, Bentham became an advocate of democratic and representative government, and he championed such political reforms as universal manhood suffrage, annual parliaments, and the secret ballot. By promoting democracy, supporting a positive role for the state, and encouraging peaceful social change through the political process, Bentham and the utilitarians helped lay the foundation for the creation of the welfare state in Great Britain.

Other characteristics of utilitarianism in-

clude its typically English emphasis on rationalism and efficiency, its ahistorical empiricism, and its distrust of metaphysical speculations and abstract concepts. Notably absent from most utilitarian thought is any sympathy for the emotional and aesthetic side of life and for the arts and poetry, a lack distressingly evident to John Stuart Mill. In all, an optimistic philosophy in the secular tradition of the Enlightenment, utilitarianism asserted confidently that humans can master their social, political, and economic environment and that they can shape it according to their vision of the good life.

Although the name of Jeremy Bentham is frequently identified with the doctrine of utilitarianism, he was hardly an original thinker and he borrowed ideas from a heritage of hedonistic thought that reaches back to Epicurus. Nevertheless, utilitarianism emerged chiefly from a tradition in English moral philosophy that dates from the seventeenth and eighteenth centuries, and owes a little to Thomas Hobbes and John Locke and much to David Hume. Other important English precursors of utilitarianism include Richard Cumberland (1631–1718); Francis Hutcheson (1694–1746), who used the phrase later adopted by the Benthamites, "the greatest happiness of the greatest number" in the fifth edition of his *An Inquiry Into the Original of Our Ideas of Beauty and Virtue* (1753); Joseph Priestley (1733–1804); the associationist psychologist David Hartley (1705–1757); the laissez-faire economist Adam Smith (1723–1790); and the religious utilitarian William Paley (1743–1805).

Because it provided a seemingly scientific standard of utility by which to measure the performance of political and legal institutions, utilitarianism appealed to the reformers who did so much to humanize and rationalize English institutions in the decades following Waterloo. Bentham's rejection of the natural rights tradition, which many in England associated with the French Revolution and Jacobinism, likewise enhanced its attractiveness. Nevertheless, questions remain concerning both the influence of utilitarianism on the history of nineteenth-century Britain and the content of Bentham's ideas about the proper role of government.

Bentham's ideas spread widely after 1815, largely through the efforts of a loosely organized group of followers, through the voluminous writings of Bentham and the two Mills, and through articles by sympathizers in the periodical press. Among the first admirers were **Francis Place** (1771–1854), David Ricardo (1772–1823), and Samuel Romilly (1757–1818). A second important group, the Philosophical Radicals, composed of intellectuals and members of Parliament influenced by James Mill, flourished between 1817 and 1841: it included John Arthur Roebuck (1801–1879), George Grote (1794–1871), and William Molesworth (1810–1855). John Stuart Mill's Utilitarian Society met between 1822 and 1826. The *Edinburgh Review* and then the *Westminster Review* (founded 1824) helped stimulate discussion of utilitarian ideas, as did articles in the *Morning Chronicle* and the *Examiner* and James Mill's essays in the *Encyclopaedia Britannica*. For the few who wished to read Bentham in the original, John Bowring published a collected works between 1838 and 1843.

Students of Victorian governmental development who have investigated how utilitarian philosophy in general and Bentham's unfinished *Constitutional Code* (published in 1830–1841) in particular relate to the genesis of the Victorian administrative state have reached opposite conclusions concerning the role of utilitarian ideas in this revolutionary transformation. The traditional viewpoint, with origins largely in A. V. Dicey's *Lectures on the Relation Between Law and Public Opinion in England During the Nineteenth Century* (1905), ascribes much of the impetus to Bentham and his followers. By crusading for sweeping legal reforms as well as for the creation of a rational, efficient, and humane government, the argument runs, Benthamite disciples and sympathizers in Parliament, in the salons of influential Whig leaders, in the press, and in academic chairs played important roles in the passage of reform legislation. The Poor Law Amendment Act of 1834 serves as a convenient example. **Edwin Chadwick** (1800–1890), once Bentham's private secretary, and **Nassau Senior** (1790–1864) prepared the ground for its passage with a commission report of 1832 that pointed out gross deficiencies in the administration of poor relief. The act passed in 1834 prescribed the centralized administration of poor relief, and the government machinery it established resembled proposals for the development of a professional administration outlined in the *Constitutional Code*. Other reform measures said to bear the imprint of utilitarianism include the Factory Act of 1833, the Prison Act of 1835, the Municipal Corporation Act (1835), the establishment of the Committee on Education in 1839, the Lunacy Act of 1842, and the Public Health Act of 1848. Additionally, it has been argued, utilitarian ideas helped fashion British colonial policy in India and other possessions.

Challenging this interpretation, Oliver Mac-Donagh, David Roberts, and others have argued that, even without the presence of Bentham and the utilitarians, the Victorian administrative state would have been created, owing largely to the necessities imposed by accelerated economic and social change; that the impetus for administrative reform originated within the administrative process itself; and that these reforms were made as ad hoc responses to immediate problems. While most Victorian reforms would probably have occurred without the pressure applied by utilitarian ideas, it may yet be contended that Bentham and his followers helped mold the structure of British public administration.

Reformers moved by utilitarian ideas did not restrict themselves to the political, administrative, and legal fields. Heeding the teachings of Bentham, who sketched a utilitarian scheme of education in *Chrestomathia* (1816), and of James Mill, they called for the reform of existing educational institutions and demanded that education be made accessible to all levels of society. Men influenced by utilitarian ideas advocated the rejuvenation of the British university system and the adoption of a curriculum more suited to the needs of business and industry and to the stimulation of political and economic progress; in this regard, they had a part in founding the University of London (1828) and University College (1836). Utilitarians also participated in the mechanics' institutes and in the work of the Society for the Diffusion of Useful Knowledge (1827) and the Society for the Diffusion of Practical Knowledge (1833).

As the influence of utilitarian ideas spread during the first half of the nineteenth century, critics appeared from both within and without the utilitarian tradition. Of the former, the most notable is John Stuart Mill. Raised by his father in accord with the strictest utilitarian principles, the younger Mill wrote articles promoting the Benthamite cause during the 1820s and edited Bentham's *Rationale of Judicial Evidence* (1827). Then followed his celebrated mental crisis, so eloquently narrated in the *Autobiography* (1873), from which Mill emerged critical of utilitarian ideas, his new position appearing in essays on Bentham and Coleridge in 1838 and 1840. In these essays and in *Utilitarianism* (1863), Mill, who recognized that his upbringing had left him without the ability to express emotions and devoid of an aesthetic sense, sought to humanize utilitarianism by stressing the quality, not just the quantity, of pleasure and by recognizing that such "social feelings" as altruism, not just self-satisfaction, bring happiness. These qualifications notwithstanding, the utilitarian influence in Mill's work remained pervasive, as for example in *On Liberty* (1859).

While John Stuart Mill criticized utilitarianism from a position of sympathy, others attacked it directly. These critics associated it with the worst evils of the industrial revolution, with excessive rationalism, with the mechanization of human life, and with a contemptuous disregard for the individual. Thomas Gradgrind, "a man of facts and calculations," in Charles Dickens's *Hard Times* (1854) is the most famous example; in other novels, such as Benjamin Disraeli's *Coningsby* (1844) or Frederick Denison Maurice's *Eustace Conway* (1834), appeared similar denunciations of the utilitarian frame of mind. Thomas Carlyle in "Signs of the Times" (1829), *Sartor Resartus* (1833–1834), and *Past and Present* (1843) fulminated against utilitarianism, as did John Ruskin in *Unto This Last* (1862). Others chastised the utilitarians for advocating democracy, notably Thomas Babington Macaulay (1800–1859) in three essays published by the *Edinburgh Review* in 1829. All in all, Benthamism, or more precisely a disparate compilation of ideas labeled Benthamism by those who heartily disliked them, generated a powerful and articulate opposition. Nevertheless, the utilitarian tradition in nineteenth-century English thought did not die out.

By the close of the nineteenth century, utilitarianism had found wide acceptance as an ethical philosophy, but the tradition of reform that had originated with Jeremy Bentham had lost much of its vigor. Henry Sidgwick (1838–1900), whose *Methods of Ethics* first appeared in 1874, has been called the last of the traditional utilitarians. What followed were not new philosophical works but histories of a movement of thought. Leslie Stephen's three-volume *The English Utilitarians* appeared in 1900, followed a year later by Ernest Albee's *A History of English Utilitarianism*.

ROBERT W. BROWN

Bibliography

Albee, Ernest. *A History of English Utilitarianism.* 1901.

Brantlinger, Patrick. *The Spirit of Reform: British Literature and Politics, 1832–1867.* 1977.

Cromwell, Valerie. "Interpretations of Nineteenth-Century Administration: An Analysis." *Victorian Studies,* vol. 9, pp. 245–255.

Finer, Samuel E. "The Transmission of Benthamite Ideas, 1820–1850." In Gillian Sutherland, ed., *Studies in the Growth of Nineteenth-Century Government.* 1972.

Halévy, Elie. *The Growth of Philosophic Radicalism.* 1928.

Hamburger, Joseph. *Intellectuals in Politics: John Stuart Mill and the Philosophic Radicals.* 1965.

Mazlish, Bruce. *James and John Stuart Mill: Father and Son in the Nineteenth Century.* 1975.

Plamenatz, John. *The English Utilitarians.* 2d ed.; rpt. 1966.

Roberts, David. "The Utilitarian Conscience." In Peter Marsh, ed., *The Conscience of the Victorian State.* 1979.

Stephen, Leslie. *The English Utilitarians.* 1900. 3 vols.

Thomas, William. *The Philosophic Radicals: Nine Studies in Theory and Practice, 1817–1841.* 1979.

· · · · ·

UTOPIAN FICTION

Utopias present a community whose social organization and relationships seem superior to those of the author's society and have satiric implications for the society that produces them. The most articulate Victorians were keenly aware that alternative societies could be imagined. The temporal depth of Asia and Africa stimulated "lost race" novels like Rider Haggard's, and their vast environments suggested more spectacular "noble savages" like Kipling's Mowgli. If Asia and Africa were "decadent" or "barbaric," the United States was a self-confident "society of the future," of racial pluralism, social leveling, and high technology.

Utopian debate questioned democracy, monarchy, establishmentarianism, leadership, the family, and especially women's role. Older influences such as Rousseau's *Contrat Social* and Paine's *Rights of Man* were set beside Saint-Simon, Fourier, Cabet, Robert Owen, Marx, J. S. Mill's *On Liberty*, and Kropotkin's *Mutual Aid*. Actual utopian communities were attempted and discussed. Like such eighteenth-century philosophical romances as *Candide, Rasselas*, and *Gulliver's Travels*, Victorian utopias employ innocent, well-intentioned male explorers, representative (though estranged) Victorians. The protagonist enters Utopia bewildered and explores it bemusedly. The book ends when he is removed from it—sometimes by strenuous plotting.

Some awful visions of the future, not seriously dystopian, predicted the conquest of Britain by invasion (usually, after 1870, by Germany) or radical violence. The first, *The Battle of Dorking* (1871), by George Tomkyns Chesney (1833–1895), typically has little civilian social content. The finest of its innumerable progeny, *The War of the Worlds* (1898), by H. G. Wells, and *The Inheritors* (1901), by Joseph Conrad and Ford Madox Hueffer, employ chilling utopian ironies. The latter warns of ruthless Dimensionalists, who shall inherit the earth by breaking down the social order. Their representative, Miss Granger, dispassionately describes their perfection, "with no ideals, prejudices, or remorse; with no feeling for art and no reverence for life, free from any ethical traditions; callous to pain, weakness, suffering and death, as if they had been invulnerable and immortal."

Many male Victorians felt a deep, half-conscious guilt about the caricatures of womanhood their society "believed." Tennyson's *The*

Princess (1847) and W. S. Gilbert's travesty of it, *Princess Ida* (1884), exemplify this fascinated guilt and some flimsy male self-reassurances. In *The Coming Race* (1871), by Edward Bulwer-Lytton (1803–1873), intellectually and physically superior women dominate the Ana's subterranean civilization. Through the power of *vril*, combining *aqua vitae*, electricity, and nuclear energy, their race will annihilate us. Lytton's ambiguous ironies sometimes invert Victorian convention—women court the coy males—but the maid who marries her blushing groom doffs forever the mighty wings that were her recreation, adornment, and art. Lytton is witty on children, who, being violent, perform any violence needed. Only in small utopias can individuals feel valued; the Ana rely on teenage emigration and colonization for population control.

Erewhon (1872), by Samuel Butler (1835–1902), is a satiric travesty of English society. Erewhonians reject all machines, and their reasoning parodies Darwinian natural selection: humanity took a million years to dominate the environment, but machines are progressing many times faster, so "mechanical consciousness" is inevitable. Victorian expectations are brilliantly overturned by Erewhonian medicine; the diseased are criminal, the criminal are "ill." Swiftian in detail, *Erewhon* is poorly plotted. Higgs is memorable as explorer of wild New Zealand, and tolerable as Erewhon's commentator, but his love affair and escape are shoddy. *Erewhon Revisited* (1901) focuses mainly on religious credulity.

The finest female-centered utopia is *A Crystal Age* (1887), by W. H. Hudson (1841–1922). The protagonist awakes in a distant future, somewhere in South America, and is cared for by an agrarian but conservationist community in a huge country house ruled by a wise, adored Mother. The prose is graceful and thoughtful, the environmental detail miraculous. Mystical music and holy silences, a version of telepathy, and the serenity of matriarchal love, all are threatened by the protagonists' infectious Victorian "true love."

News from Nowhere (1890), by William Morris (1836–1896), was stimulated mainly by two books. *After London, or Wild England* (1885), by Richard Jefferies (1848–1887), foretells the reversion of England to violent barbarism, yet is utopian in celebrating the destruction of hideous cities, drowning the Thames Valley in loving detail. Morris was infuriated by the big-city, automated, credit-card mechanism of the American Edward Bellamy's *Looking Backward* (1888), which helped to make utopias a fashion in the 1890s.

In Morris's Nowhere, late twenty-first-century England, cities have become village, garden, field, and forest. Human cooperation has survived capitalism, politics, and money; its sophisticated communism aims at simplicity, though inconspicuous technology exists. The "neighbours" delight in nature and fear only that they should run short of worthwhile work. Morally, they are free and affectionate, though violence remains.

Nowhere is the only utopia interesting to live in; it is "an Epoch of Rest" with major challenges foreshadowed. Ellen, a beautiful Nowherian, determines to learn from the grim past the protagonist represents; her people are forgetting history, but old dangers may reappear. Morris was the first Communist to posit spiral recurrence rather than straight-line historical inevitability; thus Nowhere is charmingly fourteenth-century, yet the "Neighbours" combine bronze age lustiness with childlike brightness.

Guest, who dreams Nowhere, is an embodied awful warning, and the chief source of the vigor, pain, and integrity of *News from Nowhere*. Guest is Morris, and this open secret gives Nowhere emotional immediacy; the places he visits are his own beloved places, many of the "Neighbours" his own descendants. His estrangement from them is paradoxically complete. His response to Ellen and community makes his return poignant and stirring, inevitable and bracing. Morris fought his contemporary society with stubborn courage, and his utopia gives the best reasons for change, to celebrate how people might live.

NORMAN TALBOT

Bibliography

Armytage, W. H. G. *Yesterday's Tomorrows: A Historical Survey of Future Societies*. 1968.

Bailey, J. O. *Pilgrims Through Space and Time: Trends and Patterns in Scientific and Utopian Fiction*. 1947.

Jameson, Frederic. "Introduction/Prospectus: To Reconsider the Relationship of Marxism to Utopian Thought." *Minnesota Review*, vol. 6 (n.s.), pp. 53–58.

Manuel, Frank, ed. *Utopias and Utopian Thought*. 1966.

Morton, Arthur Leslie. *The English Utopia*. 1952.

Sargeant, Lyman Tower. *British and American Utopian Literature, 1516–1975: An Annotated Bibliography*. 1979.

· · · · ·

VACCINATION AND SMALLPOX

Over the course of the nineteenth century the incidence of smallpox in Britain declined as a consequence of a public health campaign that included the development and widespread use of an effective vaccine. As the frequency of this highly contagious and often fatal viral disease waned, there emerged in its place a controversy concerning the wisdom of compulsory vaccination.

In 1798 Edward Jenner (1749–1823), an English country doctor, published a report that described a means of inducing immunity to smallpox. He had found that introducing cowpox matter to the bloodstream gave protection without the risk imposed by the current practice of variolation (inoculation with live smallpox virus); he called his operation "vaccination." News of Jenner's discovery spread across Europe and his cowpox vaccination became a common procedure, replacing most variolation.

Although the rate of smallpox in Britain quickly declined, periodic outbreaks of the disease continued to occur, particularly among the poor, who had little understanding of sanitation, little access to vaccination, and a reluctance to abandon folk remedies. In the wake of the severe epidemic of 1837–1840, however, Parliament passed the Vaccination Act of 1840, which both provided free vaccination to the lower classes under the Poor Law and forbade the practice of variolation.

Following the Vaccination Act of 1853, which introduced a compulsory requirement, social opposition to the procedure began to emerge. An antivaccination movement opposed the compulsory law, dismissing vaccination as neither safe nor effective as a life-long protection against smallpox. In response to these claims, which had some validity, the advocates of vaccination labored steadily to improve the quality of their vaccine and to promote periodic revaccination. Such was the persistence of the antivaccinationists, however, that by the end of the century the compulsory vaccination law had been modified to accommodate conscientious objectors. The cherished principle of individual rights had prevailed against the legislated imperatives of public health.

JAMES HILL

Bibliography

Cartwright, Frederick F. *Disease and History.* 1972.

Dixon, Cyril W. *Smallpox.* 1962.

Hopkins, Donald R. *Princes and Peasants: Smallpox in History.* 1983.

Smith, F. B. *The People's Health 1830–1910.* 1979.

. . . . .

VAUGHAN, HERBERT ALFRED (1832–1903)

Herbert Vaughan, third archbishop of Westminster, attempted to reconcile Roman Catholicism with the social, educational and religious climate of Victorian England. Through the influence of Cardinal Manning (1808–1892), Vaughan was appointed bishop of Salford in 1872, and succeeded Manning at Westminster in 1892. In the following year, Leo XIII named him a cardinal.

Vaughan received his education in England and abroad. Ordained in 1854, he soon recognized the need for foreign missionaries. Through his efforts, St. Joseph's College opened in 1866 to train the Mill Hill Fathers, founded by Vaughan, for work among blacks in America. After a fight with the Jesuits in Salford, he appealed to Rome and secured a decision that championed the authority of bishops over religious orders. Vaughan also led campaigns against intemperance, sup-

ported sanitation and housing improvements, and began a crusade to rescue Catholic children from poverty and indifference.

As archbishop Vaughan established Oscott as a central seminary, secured permission from the Vatican for Roman Catholics to attend Oxford and Cambridge, and supported the Education Act of 1902, which extended government support to voluntary schools. Theologically an ultramontane, he worked to secure the condemnation of Anglican orders in 1896. Vaughan's major project was the construction of Westminster Cathedral (1895–1903), which would serve as the religious center for English Roman Catholics.

To his clergy, Vaughan seemed aloof and rigid. A political conservative, he approached social problems with a sense of paternalism. He demonstrated his real genius in administration and financial matters.

RENE KOLLAR

Bibliography

Holmes, J. Derek. *More Roman Than Rome: English Catholicism in the Nineteenth Century.* 1978.

Leslie, Shane, ed. *Letters of Herbert Cardinal Vaughan to Lady Herbert of Lea, 1867–1903.* 1942.

McCormack, Arthur. *Cardinal Vaughan: The Life of the Third Archbishop of Westminster.* 1966.

Norman, Edward. *The English Catholic Church in the Nineteenth Century.* 1984.

Snead-Cox, John G. *The Life of Cardinal Vaughan.* 1910. 2 vols.

. . . . .

VENEREAL DISEASE

Nineteenth-century scientific investigations raised new fears about venereal disease in Victorian England. Philip Ricord in 1837 established the differences between syphilis and gonorrhea, and soon afterwards described the three phases of syphilis. Joseph-Pierre Martin found that syphilis was still contagious in its second phase and in the early latent period, while Rudolph Virchow demonstrated the systematic nature of the disease. By the 1870s cardiovascular syphilis had been identified, as had the sequelae of paralysis and insanity. In William Osler's words, the result was to add "terror to an already terrible disorder."

Adding further terror was the realization that syphilis crossed the placental barrier; children could be born with syphilis and even infect the wet-nurse who nursed them. Philandering partners could bring syphilis and gonorrhea home to innocent spouses, and venereal diseases could be spread nonsexually in the workplace (as among glassblowers who used the same blowpipe).

Gonorrhea, though regarded as somewhat less dangerous, was found to cause sterility in women. It could be spread even though a carrier was asymptomatic. It was also realized that an infant infected with gonorrhea as it passed through the birth canal would in all likelihood become blind. There were no cures for either disease.

The result was to give impetus to ideals of sexual morality, to emphasize the dangers not only of venereal disease but also of sex outside the marriage bond. Both the fear of venereal disease and the medical emphasis on the danger of uncontrolled sexual activity fueled campaigns against **prostitution.** The military was concerned because gonorrhea in males often produced disabling cystitis at key periods. Although the military ultimately turned to advocating prophylactics, the campaign against venereal disease must be regarded as a major formative factor in Victorian attitudes toward sexuality.

VERN L. BULLOUGH

Bibliography

Bullough, Vern L. and Bonnie Bullough. *Prostitution: An Illustrated Social History.* 1978.

Bullough, Vern L. *Sexual Variance.* 1980.

Fournier, Alfred. *Syphilis and Marriage.* 1881. Trans. Prince A. Morrow.

Pusey, William Allen. *The History and Epidemiology of Syphilis.* 1933.

Tempkin, Owsei. "Therapeutic Trends and Treatment of Syphilis Before 1900." *Bulletin of the History of Medicine,* vol. 39, pp. 309–316.

• • • • •

VESTRIS, MADAME (LUCY ELIZABETH BARTOLOZZI) (1797–1856)

As an operatic contralto and ballad-singing comedienne, Madame Vestris gained overnight popularity in the "breeches" title role of W. T. Moncrieff's 1817 burlesque *Giovanni in London.* It is, however, for her later work as impresario and stage manager that she is best known today.

Born in London, Lucy Elizabeth Bartolozzi was married in 1813 to Auguste Armande Vestris, who deserted her four years later. From 1831 to 1839 Madame Vestris guided the fortunes of the Olympic Theatre on Wych Street, transforming it into one of London's most important and influential minor playhouses. One-third the size of Covent Garden and Drury Lane, and limited in its repertoire by its burletta license, the Olympic provided a genial home for domestic comedy—principally from French sources—and for a series of mythological and fairy extravaganzas planned and written by **J. R. Planché.**

While there is some controversy over whether Vestris first introduced English playgoers to the box set, her attention to detail and passion for accuracy took her interiors well beyond the expected flats and wings of the period. As her business partner and second husband, light comedian Charles Mathews, Jr. (1803–1878), noted in his autobiography, under her supervision "drawing-rooms were fitted up like drawing-rooms, and furnished with taste and care." Additional reforms included the use of multiple traps for presetting scenes, and performance times geared to the schedules of the middle-class spectators Vestris wished to attract to her theater.

Many of these innovations were pursued by Vestris and Mathews during their management of Covent Garden (1839–1842)—a tenancy that saw the first production of Boucicault's *London Assurance* (1841) as well as an important revival of *A Midsummer Night's Dream* (1840)—and, after the monopoly of the patent houses was broken, at the Lyceum (1847–1855). Vestris's early championing of a closely observed bourgeois comedy bore fruit during the 1860s in the cup-and-saucer plays of the Olympic's erstwhile prompter T. W. Robertson.

SHEILA STOWELL

Bibliography

Appleton, William W. *Madame Vestris and the London Stage.* 1974.

Williams, Clifford John. *Madame Vestris: A Theatrical Biography.* 1973.

· · · · ·

VICTORIA, QUEEN OF ENGLAND (1819–1901)

From 1837 until 1901 Victoria reigned as queen of the United Kingdom of England, Scotland, and Ireland and of British possessions overseas. From 1877 on she also held the title of empress of India. In addition to serving as a symbol of domestic propriety and British power, she exercised genuine political influence.

Born on May 24, 1819, Victoria was the only child of Edward Duke of Kent (the fourth son of King George III) and of a widowed German princess, Victoria of Saxe-Coburg. She was baptized Alexandrina Victoria (after Czar Alexander I of Russia and her mother respectively), but she ceased to use her Russian name once she became queen. Her father died when she was eight months old, and she was raised in the Germanic piety of her mother and of her governess, Baroness Lehzen, the daughter of a Lutheran pastor. She was tutored privately at Kensington Palace, and she displayed a gift for languages—she spoke French and German as fluently as English—as well as singing, dancing, and sketching. Except for well-chaperoned annual "progresses" from 1832 on, she was carefully secluded from society and better acquainted with the company of dolls and dogs than of other children; until she became queen, she slept in her mother's bedroom. During her adolescence she began to keep a daily journal, a custom she maintained until the final weeks of her life. Since the three eldest sons of George III had no legitimate children who survived them, she became queen on June 20, 1837, on the death of her uncle, King William IV.

During her first years on the throne, her political and constitutional mentor was the urbane but grandfatherly Whig prime minister, Lord Melbourne. Her poise and ingenuousness at her first privy council meeting (1837) and her coronation (1838) contrasted happily with the scandals and extravagance associated with her "wicked uncles," but in 1839 "scandal" affected her own court. It was tarred as a hotbed of intrigue when a lady-in-waiting, Flora Hastings, was suspected of pregnancy (rather than of the malignant tumor from which she subsequently died). When Melbourne's shrinking parliamentary majority caused him to resign in 1839, the Tory leader, Robert Peel, in forming a new government, asked Victoria to replace some of the ladies of her household. She stubbornly refused this request as both an infringement of her prerogative and a reflection on their (and her) morality; in due course Melbourne returned for two more years as prime minister. Victoria's life changed dramatically on February 10, 1840, when she married her first cousin, Prince Albert of Saxe-Coburg-Gotha, the son of an elder brother of her mother. Before the year was out she became a mother for the first time, and a few months later a decisive general election compelled her to replace Melbourne with Peel.

For the next twenty years it becomes difficult to distinguish Victoria's domestic or political influence from that of her husband. They had nine children: Victoria (1840), Edward (1841), Alice (1843), Alfred (1844), Helena (1846), Louise (1848), Arthur (1850), Leopold (1853), and Beatrice (1857). During the last two confinements, Victoria popularized the use of anesthetics in childbirth. Albert and Victoria sought to create the model family in the land, but the attempt to transform their sociable but idle son into a carbon copy of his sober and learned father proved counterproductive. Her children came to look upon the queen as a firm and demanding matriarch. Their marriages and those of her grandchildren were to link Victoria with the major Continental dynasties as "grandmother of Europe."

Under Albert's influence, Victoria largely forsook London in favor of Windsor Castle, Osborne House on the Isle of Wight (as winter palace), and Balmoral in the Scottish Highlands (as summer palace and favorite holiday resort). Albert became the queen's private secretary and drafted numerous memoranda in her name. His ideal was a constitutional monarchy that transcended political party distinctions but brought an independent influence to bear. During the years 1846–1859, when no single party could claim an overall majority in the Commons, the royal couple helped determine the makeup of several ministries, and in 1851 (on grounds both of policy and of failure to consult the monarch) they secured the dismissal of Lord Palmerston as foreign secretary. Despite his success in organizing the Great Exhibition of 1851 and his absorption in public causes, Albert (whom Victoria named prince consort in 1857) never became truly popular in his adopted land, but Victoria was passionately devoted to him, and her grief at his death from typhoid in December 1861 all but overwhelmed her.

During the fifteen years after 1861, Victoria ceased to perform almost all public functions other than unveiling memorials to Albert. She saw her prime monarchical duty as that of reading dispatches and advising her ministers (largely by mail). During the later 1860s her popularity waned: there was a short-lived republican movement and unsubstantiated rumors linked her to her favorite Scottish servant, John Brown, either as his lover or secret wife. Her popularity had been reestablished by the time of her Golden Jubilee (1887) and Diamond Jubilee (1897).

During Victoria's reign the monarch took formal action only upon the advice of her ministers; they in turn were responsible to a House of Commons chosen by an increasingly democratic electorate. When a party had no obvious leader, however, the queen could choose; e.g., she named Lord Rosebery as prime minister in 1894. She also influenced or "vetoed" the appointment of particular cabinet ministers, foreign envoys, and Anglican bishops, and she inspired specific statutes like the Anti-Vivisection Act of 1876. When Parliament was in session, her prime ministers wrote to her daily. Victoria defined herself as a liberal and, as an advocate of free trade, religious toleration, and constitutional

government, she was one, but during the second half of her reign she favored the policies of the Conservative party (led by Benjamin Disraeli and Lord Salisbury) far more often than those of the Liberal party (led by William Ewart Gladstone). In her eyes, the Liberals were insufficiently concerned with national defense and with resisting Russian aggression in the Near East, too eager to appease Irish nationalism, and far too eager to tamper with established institutions like the House of Lords. Victoria used her behind-the-scenes influence to slow the process of change more effectively than most contemporaries suspected.

The queen was an apostle of moral propriety, good manners, and domesticity, and she condemned high society for its frivolity and laxity. She set forth her belief in the simple virtues in *Leaves from the Journal of Our Life in the Highlands* (1868) and *More Leaves . . .* (1884). Despite the anomaly of her own position, Victoria believed that men and women occupied separate social spheres, and she opposed efforts to extend suffrage and opportunities for higher education to women. In religion, her undogmatic piety made her Broad Church, and she opposed the Sabbatarianism and teetotalism of the Low Church as much as the ritualism of the High Church. Under her influence, the Public Worship Act (1874) was passed to curb Roman Catholic practices within the Church of England. Although formal head of the latter, she personally preferred Presbyterian services in Scotland, and she became the first monarch to name a professing Jew a peer and to employ a professing Moslem as a personal servant. She became keenly conscious of the fact that she headed a multireligious as well as a multiracial empire. Britain's imperial mission, she believed, was "to protect the poor natives and advance civilization," and she sought to promote such aims by becoming empress of India in 1877. During her reign, the monarchy became the single most obvious link that held together the world's largest empire; by the 1890s one person in four on earth was a "subject" of Queen Victoria. By the time of her death at Osborne on January 22, 1901, she had become a symbol of empire, of British power, and of personal longevity as well as personal morality. Understandably, her death (and burial with Albert in the Frogmore Mausoleum in Windsor Great Park) seemed to mark the end not only of an individual but also of an age.

WALTER L. ARNSTEIN

Bibliography

Arnstein, Walter L. "Queen Victoria and Religion." In Gail Malmgreen, ed., *Religion in the Lives of English Women, 1760-1930*. 1986.

Benson, A. C. et al., eds. *Letters of Queen Victoria, 1837-1901*. 1907-1932.

Connell, Brian. *Regina Versus Palmerston*. 1961.

Duff, David. *Victoria Travels*. 1970.

Fulford, Roger, ed. The private correspondence of Queen Victoria and the German crown princess published in five volumes: *Dearest Child, 1858-1861*; *Dearest Mama, 1861-1864*; *Your Dear Letter, 1865-1871*; *Darling Child, 1871-1878*; and *Beloved Mama, 1878-1885*. 1964-1981.

Guedalla, Philip, ed. *The Queen and Mr. Gladstone*. 1933. 2 vols.

Hardie, Frank. *The Political Influence of the British Monarchy, 1868-1952*. 1970.

Longford, Elizabeth. *Victoria R. I.* 1964.

Warner, Marina. *Queen Victoria's Sketchbook*. 1979.

Weintraub, Stanley. *Victoria: An Intimate Biography*. 1987.

Woodham-Smith, Cecil. *Queen Victoria: From Her Birth to the Death of the Prince Consort*. 1972.

See also ALBERT, PRINCE CONSORT; ROYAL FAMILY

. . . . .

VIVESECTION see ANIMAL PROTECTION

. . . . .

VOYNICH, ETHEL BOOLE (1864-1960)

The first novel of Ethel Voynich, *The Gadfly* (1897), has been a continual best seller in Russia for eighty years: cosmonauts Yuri Ga-garin and Valentina Tereshkova asserted its early influence on them. Although it is now seldom read in Britain and the United States, G. B. Shaw, D. H. Lawrence, and Bertrand Russell, among others, praised it highly. Voynich's other novels, *Jack Raymond* (1901), *Olive Latham* (1904), *An Interrupted Friendship* (1910), and *Put Off Thy Shoes* (1945) never achieved comparable success.

Voynich was born in Cork of Irish-Huguenot ancestry, the youngest of five daughters of eminent mathematician **George Boole** and Mary Everest Boole. From 1887 to 1889 she was a governess in St. Petersburg, and on her return to London worked in the editorial office of *Free Russia*, the journal of the emigre Russian revolutionary Narodniks. She married the Polish revolutionary Wilfrid Michael Voynich, who later became a noted bibliophile and bookseller. They emigrated to the United States in 1920. Voynich also translated from Russian, Polish, and French and taught and composed music.

The Gadfly expresses a romantic view of revolution: it is set in the Italy of the Risorgimento where an English seminarian, Arthur Burton, renounces his Catholicism, flees Italy, suffers immense physical and mental hardship, and returns to promote revolution in Italy as the Gadfly, a brilliant satirist. *An Interrupted Friendship* and *Put Off Thy Shoes* elaborate on Arthur Burton's background. *Olive Latham* is the only novel that deals directly with Voynich's own Nihilist background.

Voynich was a maverick among women writers of the 1890-1910 period. She obsessively emphasizes the moral and psychological effect of physical pain, and her women characters are strong-minded and idealistic but more concerned with social revolution than with more common and limited concerns such as suffrage.

BARBARA GARLICK

Bibliography

Kettle, Arnold. "E. L. Voynich: A Forgotten English Novelist." *Essays in Criticism*, vol. 7, pp. 163-174.

Kennedy, James G. "Voynich, Bennett, and Tressell: Two Alternatives for Realism in the Transition Age." *English Literature in Transition*, vol. 13, pp. 254-286.

. . . . .

WAGES

The question of wages cannot be separated from the issue of the standard of living, which has become the most debated point in recent British economic history. Though there is general agreement that wages rose in the second half of the nineteenth century, controversy continues to surround the status of the working class in the first half of the century.

Average money wages in Britain declined, or were at best stagnant, for most of the period from 1815 to 1850. Those who argue for an increase in real wages contend that the decrease in prices more than compensated for the fall in wages. There may have been some rise in average real wages after 1820, but estimates running as high as 40 percent for the period from 1824 to 1850 clearly need to be tempered.

Insufficient data make it impossible to provide a comprehensive picture of real wages and the distribution of income early in the century. Wages varied by area, date, and industry, and must be adjusted for the unemployment, underemployment, and short time that many workers faced during a year. Data about prices are also imperfect. Most are drawn from institutional accounts and do not reflect the higher rates that workers paid to purchase in small quantities. In the quarter of a century after Napoleon's defeat, high taxes on articles of common consumption, which fell with disproportionate severity on the working class, must also be taken into consideration in assessing the standard of living.

Wages were somewhat improved through the upgrading of jobs. The wage differential between higher- and lower-paid workers increased dramatically between 1815 and the 1850s. Since factory work paid better than agricultural labor, many people came to the factories and towns to escape grinding poverty in the countryside. Industrial work, however, was filled with insecurity. Cyclical unemployment and underemployment plagued the lives of workers. In many sorts of employment the number of working hours fluctuated from week to week and even from day to day. Occupations such as dock work and the millinery trade experienced seasonal slowdowns. For unskilled laborers, in particular, periodic recourse to charity and the pawnshop were regular features of life. In the 1850s the vast

majority of pawnshop pledges were for minuscule amounts; 60 percent of the pledges at pawnbrokers in Liverpool were for five shillings or less, and 27 percent were for sixpence or less.

Conditions undeniably deteriorated for certain categories of workers. The one million **agricultural laborers**, especially those in the South and East, and workers in occupations that were severely impacted by new technologies suffered obvious declines. Between 1805 and 1833 the weekly earnings of the half-million handloom weavers fell from 23 shillings to 6 shillings 6 pence. In 1833 coarse-grade cotton weavers did not receive more than 1 pence an hour. In the late 1840s fancy cotton weavers in western Scotland made between 5 and 7 shillings a week. A considerable portion of British workers did not, even when fully employed, earn enough to ensure a subsistence diet.

After the 1840s, however, the standard of living for most British workers improved. Maturing industries could afford higher wages, and railways increased workers' mobility, thus allowing them to move more easily from low-wage areas. Finally, the development of trade unionism was stimulated after 1875 when picketing became legal and combined actions in disputes with employers were decriminalized. Though trade unions did not enroll a majority of the workers, they had a pace-setting effect upon industrial wages.

Although real wages increased significantly between 1850 and 1902, the rate of increase was uneven. There were stagnant periods in the 1850s, the early 1860s, and between the mid-1870s and mid-1880s. The greatest gains occurred between 1868 and 1875, when wages rose by an average of 30 percent. The improvement was less dramatic after 1886, but the general rise continued until 1902.

Over the entire period from 1850 to 1902 the average increase in real wages was around 50 percent. It has been estimated, however, that workers who were able to take advantage of shifts in the occupational structure and enter a more skilled or better-paying job experienced real wage gains of 80 percent. By 1900 the average weekly wage was 40 shillings for skilled workers, 30 shillings for the semi-skilled, and 20 shillings for the unskilled. In 1867 the average for the 15 percent of the working class categorized as skilled had been

28–40 shillings; the unskilled, who were in the majority, earned 10–12 shillings per week.

This improvement, however, must be tempered by comparing wages to the minimal physical requirements for a family. According to Seebohm Rowntree, a family at the turn of the century needed 26 shillings a week to avoid chronic want. Anything below 21 shillings for a family meant desperate poverty. Since 59 percent of British adult male workers in 1900 earned less than 25 shillings a week, most families needed more than one wage earner to achieve anything approaching a decent standard of living.

The wages paid to women who worked at home making trousers or shirts were insufficient even for subsistence. While some in London made as much as 15 shillings during good times, most made between 7 and 12 shillings a week when fully employed. Some home shirtmakers put in thirteen hours a day six days a week to earn 7 shillings. Net earnings as low as 2 shillings and 6 pence a week were not uncommon at the beginning of the twentieth century. In 1893 most outworking boxmakers made less than 6 shillings a week, while 28 percent made between 2 and 4 shillings. Male sewing machine operators in factories were better paid, earning up to 10 shillings a week in Glasgow in 1857. By 1888 comparable workers during peak times could make 18 shillings a week, and in the 1890s the best operators earned as much as 8 shillings a day.

In the construction trades, Glasgow carpenters were earning 36 shillings for a fifty-one-hour week in 1892, and Liverpool masons 30 shillings a week. The elite among unskilled laborers, who serviced these craftsmen, could earn 18 shillings during busy summer weeks in Manchester in the 1830s; by 1902, in Glasgow at peak times, they could make 24 shillings a week and in Birmingham as much as 31 shillings. Shipbuilding, foundry, and engineering laborers did not do as well. Manchester engineering laborers made 16 shillings a week in 1834, 15 in 1849, 18 in 1872, 17 in 1888, and 21 in 1893. Tyneside shipyard workers rose from 18 shillings a week in 1888 to 21 in 1899. Unskilled women in the factory work force fared far worse. In Birmingham in 1901 they made around 10 shillings a week, while in Manchester in 1907, 7 shillings a week was not unusual. Lon-

don charwomen made more, rising from 6 shillings and 7 pence a week in the 1840s to 15 shillings in the early 1900s.

Thus although real progress in wage rates was evident by 1900, a large proportion of the British working class remained in a precarious economic situation even when fully employed and could be plunged into desperate straits with the loss of even a few days' earnings through illness, short time, or failure to find work.

BERNARD A. COOK

Bibliography

Deane, Phyllis and W. A. Cole. *British Economic Growth, 1688–1959: Trends and Structure.* 1962.

Hobsbawm, Eric J. *Industry and Empire.* 1968.

Levi, Leone. *Wages and Earnings of the Working Classes.* 1855; rpt. 1971.

Mokyr, Joel. *The Economics of the Industrial Revolution.* 1985.

Treble, James H. *Urban Poverty in Britain.* 1979.

See also COST OF LIVING; MINING AND MINERS; SERVANTS; SHOPWORKERS; WOMEN'S EMPLOYMENT

· · · · ·

WALES AND WELSH NATIONALISM

The designation of Wales (Welsh, *Cymru*) as an English principality stems from Edward I's act of naming his first-born son and heir, born in Caernarvon castle in 1284, the "Prince of Wales." With the Statute of Rhuddlan (1284) and the Act of Union (1536), English subjugation of Wales was essentially completed, most effectively by the proscription against the use of the Welsh language in any legal or administrative context. The last serious and sustained Welsh revolt against English rule ended with the defeat of Owain Glyndŵr in 1409. That Henry VII (1485–1509) was of Welsh birth further aligned the interests of the Welsh gentry with the English court, with centers of English learning (primarily Jesus College, Oxford, founded in 1571), and with the Inns of Court. The Welsh supported the royalist cause in the Civil War, and throughout the eighteenth and nineteenth centuries Wales was regarded as essentially a province or region of the United Kingdom. The industrial expansion of the nineteenth century turned Wales, particularly the southeast sector, into a major supplier and exporter of coal and iron products.

There was no strong Welsh "Home Rule" movement like the one in Ireland. Important events in Welsh national life in the nineteenth century include the revival of the Eisteddfod (1819), the founding of the University of Wales in Aberystwyth (1872), and religious controversy leading to the disestablishment of the Church in Wales, not finally accomplished until 1914. Sporadic actions such as the Merthyr Tydfil labor riots (1831) and the rural Rebecca Riots against toll gates (1840s) were more economic than nationalist in motivation. Considerable resentment was generated by the 1847 report of a parliamentary commission on education in Wales. The effect of educational expansion and reform was to discourage, if not forbid, the use of Welsh in the schoolroom. These measures, coupled with massive English immigration to the industrial South, hastened the decline in use of the Welsh language. While the population of Wales almost quadrupled during the century, the proportion of those speaking Welsh declined to approximately 50 percent.

By the twentieth century Wales was itself divided between the largely rural and Welsh-speaking northern and western regions and the industrial and English-speaking South. It was, and remains, predominantly Nonconformist in religion (Calvinist-Wesleyan) and Liberal (more latterly Labour) in politics. The Welsh Liberal David Lloyd-George, prime minister from 1916–1922, did not use his office to further Welsh independence, and the General Strike of 1926 and sustained economic depression forced mass emigration. Welsh nationalist sentiment, closely affiliated with the reassertion of the distinct cultural nationalism of language, has had its most visible success since 1945.

SAMUEL REES

Bibliography

Jones, R. Brinley, ed. *Anatomy of Wales*. 1972.

Roderick, Arthur J., ed. *Wales Through the Ages.* 1959. 2 vols.

Williams, A. H. *An Introduction to the History of Wales*. 1962. 2 vols.

Williams, David. *A Short History of Modern Wales*. 1962.

See also ANGLO-WELSH LITERATURE; CELTIC REVIVAL

· · · · ·

WALKER, FREDERICK (1840–1875)

Frederick Walker was an illustrator, watercolorist, and genre painter. Key works include the oil paintings *The Lost Path* (1863), *The Wayfarers* (1866), *The Bathers* (1867), *The Vagrants* (1869), *The Harbour of Refuge* (1872), and *The Right of Way* (1875); and the watercolors *Strange Faces* (1862), and *Philip in Church* (1864). The latter was worked up from one of his illustrations in *Cornhill Magazine* for W. M. Thackeray's serialized novel *The Adventures of Philip* (1862).

Walker was born in London. His father was a jeweler, his mother a professional embroiderer. He briefly attended art school at Leigh's Academy and at the Royal Academy. Apprenticed in 1858 to Josiah Wood Whymper (1813–1903), the wood engraver, Walker learned the techniques that enabled him to become one of the foremost illustrators of the 1860s. After about 1865 he did little illustration, devoting himself instead to watercolor and oil painting. Walker's watercolor technique was greatly admired for its frescolike finish and tiny multicolored dots of luminous color, a style similar to the work of William Henry Hunt (1790–1864) and Myles Birket Foster (1825–1899). His subject matter often evoked a poetic vision of idealized rural life.

Although Walker died young, his sphere of influence was enormous. His work enjoyed a cultlike following among critics and fellow artists alike, and the rural sentiment of his style flourished through the end of the nineteenth century in the art of such followers as Helen Allingham (1848–1926). Walker is enshrined in Victorian literature as the model for Little Billee in **George Du Maurier**'s *Trilby* (1894).

LEE M. EDWARDS

Bibliography

Black, Clementine. *Frederick Walker*. 1902.

Carr, J. Comyns. *Some Eminent Victorians*. 1908.

Marks, John George. *Life and Letters of Frederick Walker, A.R.A.* 1896.

Phillips, Claude. *Frederick Walker and His Works.* 1894.

· · · · ·

WALLACE, ALFRED RUSSEL (1823–1913)

One of the leading biologists and naturalists of the nineteenth century, Alfred Russel Wallace was a co-originator with **Charles Darwin** of the theory of **evolution.** In addition, Wallace was a keen critic of nineteenth-century social life and maintained an active interest in spiritualism.

Wallace received little formal education, and until the 1850s was outside the professional scientific community. In 1854, after completing an expedition to South America, he embarked on a journey to the Malay Archipelago. During the next four years, he collected specimens and began to develop theories on the evolution of species which culminated in the composition of his essay "On the Tendency of Species to Depart Indefinitely from the Original Type" (1858). The essay was read along with a selection from Charles Darwin's unpublished work on natural selection at a meeting of the Linnean Society of London in 1858. Wallace returned to Britain in 1862 with his reputation as one of the nation's leading biologists firmly established. He began to publish essays on the distribution of plants and animals and the limitations that geography placed on the spread of species.

Wallace also advocated applying the methods of evolutionary biology to the study of humans. In 1864 he read papers before the London Ethnological Society and the Anthropological Society employing natural selection as the means to explain racial characteristics of the inhabitants of different zones of the Malay Archipelago. He argued for a much greater antiquity for the human species than ethnologists and anthropologists commonly asserted in order to explain the variety of human types found in the region. By 1869, however, Wallace was arguing that natural selection alone could not account for the moral and intellectual faculties in human beings. Wallace explained their appearance as the result of the intervention of a "higher intelligence" in the evolutionary process.

Wallace's belief in a higher intelligence complemented his increasing involvement with spiritualism. In the mid-1860s Wallace became a vigorous proponent of his new belief. In 1882 he joined the **Society for Psychical Research**, and though he several times refused the offer of its presidency, he frequently spoke on the society's behalf. Wallace's involvement with psychical research harmed his reputation within the scientific community and was responsible for his failure to gain paying positions in scientific societies. He ceased his association with spiritualism by 1890, but the flirtation left a permanent stain on his reputation.

Wallace was active in social reform from the mid-1860s until the end of his life. Henry George's *Progress and Poverty* (1879) affected him profoundly, and in 1881 Wallace became head of the Land Nationalization Society, a land reform body concerned especially with Irish matters. By 1890 Wallace openly characterized himself as a socialist.

In his later years Wallace wrote on a wide variety of subjects including evolution, social questions, and philosophy. Wallace was a model of humanity and compassion, and playing on the title of his *The Wonderful Century* (1898), Frank M. Turner has characterized him as the wonderful man of the wonderful century.

GEORGE MARIZ

Bibliography

Fichman, Martin. *Alfred Russel Wallace*. 1981.

George, Wilma. *Biologist Philosopher: A Study of the Life and Writings of Alfred Russel Wallace.* 1964.

Ghiselin, Michael T. *The Triumph of the Darwinian Method.* 1969.

Marchant, James. *Alfred Russel Wallace: Letters and Reminiscences.* 1916. 2 vols.

McKinney, Henry Lewis. *Wallace and Natural Selection.* 1972.

Turner, Frank M. *Between Science and Religion: The Reaction of Scientific Naturalism in Late Victorian England.* 1974.

Wallace, Alfred Russel. *My Life: A Record of Events and Opinions.* 1905.

· · · · ·

WARD, GENEVIEVE
(1838-1922)

Genevieve Ward was born in New York and died in London. Though she began her career as an opera singer, it was as a dramatic and tragic actress that she was best known. She was particularly noted for her performance as Stephanie de Mohrivart in Herman Merivale's *Forget Me Not* (1879), a role she first played opposite the young Forbes Robertson and in which she subsequently appeared throughout the world. Though often seen as an actress whose techniques appeared increasingly old-fashioned, she was courageous enough to attempt the "new drama" of Ibsen, playing Lona Hessell in *The Pillars of Society* (1889) and Mrs. Borkman in *John Gabriel Borkman* (1897).

Ward's career as a dramatic actress began at the Theatre Royal, Manchester, as Lady Macbeth (1873). She made her London debut in the Adelphi melodrama *The Prayer in the Storm* (1874) and was praised for her "power" and "mastery of elocution," which were to be her strengths for the rest of her long career.

Ward's acting was much admired by critics like Clement Scott and William Winter. It seems to have been more suited to a declamatory Shakespearean style and to strong situational melodrama than to Ibsen, where she appeared—at least in Shaw's opinion—to be out of her element. Ward was responsible for helping to launch the careers of Beerbohm Tree and Forbes Robertson and retained a lifelong interest in actor training.

VICTOR EMELJANOW

Bibliography

Scott, Clement. *The Drama of Yesterday and Today.* 1899.

Winter, William. *The Wallet of Time.* 1913. 2 vols.

· · · · ·

WARD, LESLIE
(1851-1922)

Leslie Ward, with Carlo Pellegrini ("Ape"), was one of the two famous caricaturists associated with the society magazine *Vanity Fair* (1868-1914). His caricatures and formal portraits established Ward's reputation during a long productive life which, in 1918, earned him a knighthood.

Ward was the son of Edward Matthew Ward, the historical painter, and Henrietta Ward, artist and teacher. He attended a private school before Eton and later studied architecture under Sidney Smirke. Ward joined the staff of *Vanity Fair* in 1873 and contributed more than half of the magazine's 2,300 caricatures before retiring in 1911. He married Judith Mary Topham-Watney in 1899 and had one child.

Because of his family, education, and social position, Ward belonged to the right clubs, knew prominent persons, and enjoyed the benefits of Victorian society. In addition to his caricatures for *Vanity Fair* and other magazines, including *The Graphic* and *Mayfair*, Ward painted portraits and, on occasion, exhibited at the Royal Academy. His major contributions, however, were in the popular arts, specifically the caricatures which appeared under his *nom de crayon*, "Spy," in *Vanity Fair*.

Although Carlo Pellegrini established the standards and format of the *Vanity Fair* caricature, Leslie Ward perpetuated and insured the caricature's unique style. His fame rests more on his conventional interpretations and sustained productivity than on originality or artistic gifts. Nonetheless, he captured the mood and sense of his times, and his sketches are among the most accurate and insightful studies of certain Victorians, including Anthony Trollope, John Stuart Mill, and Lord Roberts.

ROY T. MATTHEWS

Bibliography

Gombrich, Ernst and E. Kris. *Caricature.* 1940.

Low, David. *British Cartoonists, Caricaturists and Comic Artists.* 1942.

Matthews, Roy. "Spy." *British History Illustrated,* vol. 3, pp. 50–57.

Ward, Leslie. *Forty Years of "Spy."* 1915.

See also CARICATURE *(illus.)*

· · · · ·

WARD, MARY ARNOLD (1851–1920)

Mary Augusta Arnold Ward, who wrote under the name Mrs. Humphry Ward, gained international recognition with her 1888 novel *Robert Elsmere,* and also left an impressive legacy as a journalist, translator, religious scholar, founder of Oxford's Somerville College, social reformer, and war correspondent. More controversially, she was also chief architect for the women's antisuffrage campaign.

Granddaughter of Dr. **Thomas Arnold** of Rugby and niece of **Matthew Arnold**, Ward and her seven younger siblings were excluded from many economic privileges of their Arnold heritage when their father Thomas converted to Catholicism in 1856. When her family moved to Oxford in 1865, Ward compensated for her mediocre education in girls' schools by studying at the Bodleian and under the tutelage of several Oxford mentors. In 1872, she married Thomas Humphry Ward, tutor at Brasenose College and later art critic for the *Times.* She bore three children, in contrast to her mother's eight and her grandmother's nine. While a newlywed, Ward was a founding member of Oxford's Lectures for Ladies, established in 1873. It was the germ for the Association for the Education of Women (1877), which in turn established Oxford's first two colleges for women in 1879. Ward was a moving force behind the Nonconformist Somerville Hall.

Recognized for her work in Spanish and church history, Ward became a regular reviewer for *Macmillan's,* the *Pall Mall Gazette,* the church *Guardian,* the *Oxford Chronicle,* and the *Times.* Though her first novel, *Miss Bretherton,* was published in 1884, it was her second novel, *Robert Elsmere,* that made Ward an overnight celebrity. Ward eventually wrote twenty-five novels.

Ward's wealth and fame as a novelist enabled her to found in 1890 a London settlement house which by 1899 had become the Passmore Edwards Settlement House (PES); after her death it became the Mary Ward Centre, an establishment still in operation. Aside from her executive and financial skills, among Ward's most significant personal initiatives at PES was the Invalid Children's School established in 1899. Her political organizing spearheaded legislation that made such education available to all handicapped children, first in London and eventually throughout the country. Ward also initiated the Children's Recreation School and PES Vacation School. Designed to care for children of working parents, the PES programs were again adopted first citywide and then nationally.

Ward split with the nineteenth-century women's rights movement over suffrage. While she advocated women's franchise in local elections and even urged women to run for local offices, she adamantly opposed women's suffrage in national elections. Ward drafted the first published women's antisuffrage statement in 1889, helped organize the Women's National Anti-Suffrage League, and chaired its first meeting in 1908. For the next decade she was one of its most articulate and energetic spokespersons.

During World War I Ward was swept into the British propaganda machinery. She toured the front three times, as well as other places carefully selected by the government, before writing *England's Effort* (1916), *Towards the Goal* (1917), and *Fields of Victory* (1919).

A remarkable woman whose achievements are staggering, Ward has not been honored in the later twentieth century as she was in the nineteenth. Her antisuffrage stand obliterated many of her other accomplishments in the eyes of later generations. She stood firmly in a tradition of social reformers whose progressive ideas improved the lives of women and poor people and whose intellectual courage permitted dialogue on religious questions. Her political conservatism surfaced in international issues of suffrage and war. Compared to Eliot, Sands, and James in her day, Ward can now be seen as an important minor novelist whose twenty-five novels are a revealing record of Victorian, and early twentieth-century middle- and upper-class life.

CARYN McTIGHE MUSIL

Bibliography

Colby, Vineta. *The Singular Anomaly: Women Novelists of the Nineteenth Century*. 1970.

Jones, Enid Huws. *Mrs. Humphry Ward*. 1973.

Knoepflmacher, U. C. "The Rival Ladies: Mrs. Humphry Ward's *Lady Connie* and D. H. Lawrence's *Lady Chatterly's Lover*." *Victorian Studies*, vol. 4, pp. 141–158.

Paterson, William S. *Victorian Heretic: Mrs. Humphry Ward's "Robert Elsmere."* 1976.

Smith, Esther M. G. *Mrs. Humphry Ward*. 1980.

Trevelyan, Janet P. *The Life of Mrs. Humphry Ward, by Her Daughter*. 1923.

· · · · ·

WARS AND MILITARY ENGAGEMENTS

Following the battle of Waterloo in 1815 Britain entered the forty-year period known as the "great peace." However, while the nation was involved in no major conflict until the **Crimean War** (1854–1856), it was engaged in numerous small wars overseas. Similarly, during the post-Crimean decades of "splendid isolationism" from European entanglements, these small-scale campaigns continued unabated until the **Boer War** of 1899–1902—a major conflict which revealed fundamental British military weaknesses. These weaknesses had much to do with the Victorian "small war mentality" associated with the some seventy-four small wars fought against non-European enemies. First, because the troops available for duty at home or in Europe were diverted largely for this purpose and for colonial defenses, the British army came to be viewed as essentially a colonial force. Second, the use of traditional military tactics was perpetuated by their success against non-Europeans. Third, the record of success furthered national complacency about the military establishment. Finally, because the non-European enemies were so varied in military technology and tactics it seemed essential to approach warfare from the perspective of pragmatism and improvisation, which discouraged planning strategy and developing military "intellect," furthering instead the emphasis on military "character."

Consistent with the pragmatic "muddling through" perspective, no systematic study of the subject was undertaken until the publication in 1896 of *Small Wars: Their Principles and Practice* by Captain Charles E. Callwell. Callwell grouped these campaigns into three categories in terms of their political objectives: expeditions to punish an offender for an insult or wrong; campaigns to suppress insurrections and restore order; and campaigns of conquest or annexation. In practice, however, there was much overlap: the first two were frequently associated with the expansion of British territory. Additionally, the army's role of defending overseas bases that were essential to the navy's control of trade routes or were needed as strategic outposts could and often did become offensive and expansionist.

During the period of "informal empire" associated particularly with Lord Palmerston's dominance, the sphere of free trade was not always expanded by peaceful means. The "opium war" of 1839–1842, for example, imposed an open-door trading policy upon the Chinese and also secured the ceding of Hong Kong to Britain.

Historians no longer make a rigid distinction between the "old imperialism" of indirect rule and the "new imperialism" of territorial expansion once associated with Benjamin Disraeli. The integral relationship between the two, and the role of small wars in furthering both, can be seen in British India. Retaining this profitable colony gave rise to countless military engagements on the borders of British territory with Indian potentates who threatened security of trade. These motives led, for example, to the conquest of Sind (1841–1863) and the Sikh wars of 1846–1847 and 1848–1849. The conquest of the Sikh state resulted in Britain's annexation of the Punjab and brought the British frontier to the Indus. But the ruthlessness of the territorial seizures helped bring about the **Indian Mutiny**, as did the 1856 General Service Enlistment Act which followed the Second Burmese War (1851–1853). The British relied upon the Indian Army to make up for the consistently understrength British army, but found it difficult to persuade the sepoy soldiers to undertake even garrison duty in Burma. The 1856 act, intended to create a more uniform and useful Indian Army, introduced reforms that threatened the caste system and helped cause the mutiny—ironically creating a need for still more British troops to be stationed in India. The Burmese War itself, however, led to the British annexation of Burma and completed British conquest of the Indian subcontinent.

In most of these campaigns victory over the native enemies was won with relative ease by the discipline, firepower, and leadership of the British troops. That these factors might prove ineffectual against a European enemy with a large army and modern military tactics and technology was hidden by the record of colonial success and by the British focus on the Near East.

The need to protect the Near Eastern route to India via the Mediterranean and Red Sea and anxiety about Russian encroachments along that route led to numerous campaigns such as the Second Afghan War (1878–1880), a conflict marked by Major-General Roberts's relief of Kandahar after a march of some three hundred miles through arid and difficult terrain. Increasing British involvement in the Near East also led to nationalist reactions such as Arabi Pashi's revolt; the revolt itself led a reluctant William Gladstone to accept that the ensuing Egyptian War (1882) would result in Egypt's becoming a British protectorate. The commander of this campaign, Garnet Wolseley (like Roberts and Herbert Horatio Kitchener), became a national hero on the basis of his military success. He was also popular because of the success of his troops in the 1873–1874 war against the Ashanti threat to British interests in West Africa—a campaign which, like many others, encouraged the belief that conventional maneuvers such as the "square" and volley firing remained effective.

Success in this case was also based on the construction of a road through the rough jungle. Indeed, the British military was most impressive in these small wars for the engineering feats performed to transport men and supplies through miles of unfamiliar terrain ranging from the jungles of tropical Africa to

the dense forests of Canada (as in the 1869–1870 expedition to crush the Red River rebellion). But British military involvement in the self-governing colonies was increasingly replaced by colonial self-defense, and by 1870 all British troops had left Australia, New Zealand, and Tasmania. At the same time, the nation's involvement in Africa increased from the 1880s on, both as a continuation of past entanglements and as part of the "scramble for empire."

The Sudanese War (1884–1885) ended with the fall of the Sudanese capital of Khartoum and the death of General Charles Gordon. The reconquest of the Sudan was achieved in the 1896–1899 campaign led by Kitchener, while the victorious 1898 battle of Omdurman against the Egyptian troops again argued for the efficacy of improvisation, traditional military tactics, collective discipline, and individual heroism. The Anglo-Boer Wars created the first serious challenge to that perception.

British security in **South Africa** was seen as essential to protect the Cape Colony and the Cape route to India. The Zulu War of 1879, for example, tried to end the threat to British Natal posed by this powerful warrior people. But the Dutch settlers known as Boers powerfully rejected Britain's claim to paramount authority in South Africa. Following Britain's annexation of the Transvaal, the Boers' attempt to regain their independence led to the first Anglo-Boer War (1880–1881), and to the humiliating British defeat at Majuba Hill. The legacy of Majuba together with the discovery of massive gold fields in the Transvaal led to the Second South African War of 1899–1902.

The defeats suffered in this major Anglo-Boer war finally exposed Britain's fundamental military weaknesses, but the Victorian faith that military success was ultimately assured by the traditional moral virtues of heroism and "character" only died, if at all, in the trenches of World War I. The small war mentality of the officer class allowed the British to believe that warfare was something quite remote from business as usual.

PATRICIA MORTON

Bibliography

Barnett, Correlli. *Britain and Her Army, 1509–1970*. 1970.

Bond, Brian, ed. *Victorian Military Campaigns.* 1967.

Harries-Jenkins, Gwyn. *The Army in Victorian Society.* 1977.

Higham, Robin, ed. *A Guide to the Sources of British Military History.* 1971.

Holt, Edgar. *The Opium Wars in China.* 1964.

Jordan, Gerald, ed. *British Military History: A Supplement to Robin Higham's Guide to the Sources.* 1988.

Padfield, Peter. *Rule Britannia: The Victorian and Edwardian Navy.* 1981.

Pakenham, Thomas. *The Boer War.* 1979.

Robinson, Ronald and John Gallagher. *Africa and the Victorians.* 1961.

Spiers, Edward. *The Army and Society, 1815-1914.* 1980.

Symons, Julian. *England's Pride: The Story of the Gordon Relief Expedition.* 1965.

· · · · ·

WATER CURE

Flourishing between 1840 and 1870, the water cure centered on Malvern, Matlock, and Ilkley, but hydropathic institutions priced for all classes existed in many towns. The water cure or hydropathy was developed by an Austrian, Vincent Priessnitz (1799–1851). It originally consisted of using cold water internally and externally to regulate the body, and was employed in the treatment of many diseases. Hydropathy was used in residential institutions together with a regime of rest, simple diet, abstinence from alcohol, and regular exercise. It became popular as an alternative to the prevailing medical practice of prescribing large quantities of drugs. Hydropathy also provided a "rest cure" by which Victorians could recover from problems brought on by stress. Initially opposed by doctors, hydropathy was modified and extended by such qualified physicians as James Gully (1808–1883), but lay people did much to popularize and commercialize the treatment.

LOUIS BILLINGTON

Bibliography

Metcalfe, Richard. *The Rise and Progress of Hydropathy in England and Scotland.* 1906.

Price, Robin. "Hydropathy in England 1840–1870." *Medical History*, vol. 25, pp. 269–280.

Rees, Kelvin. "Medicine as a Commodity: Hydropathy in Matlock." *The Society for the Social History of Medicine Bulletin*, no. 36, pp. 24–27.

· · · · ·

WATERCOLORS

Victorians considered watercolor painting a British discovery. Although they were incorrect, English artists did develop new techniques, colors, and subject matter for watercolors. Most importantly, they established methods of exhibiting and marketing their works, and literally taught England to paint.

Unlike oil paints, watercolors are relatively simple to use, water soluble, and cheap. By the nineteenth century, they were available in three dozen colors, in hard cakes or in liquid form (packaged in fold-up tubes, much like modern toothpaste tubes). Watercolors were easy to carry in a pocket or small case.

Professional watercolor painters fought a hard battle to gain recognition. In 1804 eminent watercolorists formed the Water-Colour Society (which eventually became the Old Water-Colour Society); in 1832 other disgruntled artists formed the New Society of Painters in Water Colours, which attracted popular book illustrators like **Kate Greenaway** (1846–1901) and **Randolph Caldecott** (1846–1886).

Watercolorists often painted landscapes or architecture, a legacy from the eighteenth century. Samuel Prout (1783–1852) contributed illustrations to *The Landscape Annual*; his *Rudiments of Landscape in Progressive Studies* (1813) was one of the most influential books on watercolors. An eminent landscape artist, James Duffield Harding (1797–1863), taught John Ruskin (1819–1900) watercolor painting. Many artists, like Clarkson Stanfield (1793–1867) and Henry Moore (1831–1895), concentrated on seascapes.

The Pre-Raphaelite example caused many watercolorists to forsake simple translucent colors and quiet landscapes. **Edward Lear** (1812–1888), who traveled extensively, published *Journals of a Landscape Painter in Albania* (1851). William Henry Hunt (1790–1864) changed his originally subdued style to match the popular taste for detail. Edward Burne-Jones (1833–1898), a fervent Pre-Raphaelite, mixed media like pastels and watercolors. Some artists, like Frederick Walker (1840–1875) and John William North (1842–1924), held on to eighteenth-century methods, while others, like James Abbott McNeill Whistler (1834–1903), followed French innovations.

Most well-educated Victorians knew how to paint in watercolors because it formed part of their standard education. Under male tutelage, girls practiced watercolor painting to develop their "gentle" grace and "quiet" motor skills. Victorian novels, such as Charlotte Brontë's *Jane Eyre* (1847) and Wilkie Collins's *The Woman in White* (1871), are full of passionate women watercolorists. Watercolor painting quickly developed a visual language accessible to reasonably intelligent Victorians, thereby becoming the most "British" art form.

JULIA M. GERGITS

Bibliography

Bayard, Jane. *Works of Splendor and Imagination: The Exhibition Watercolor, 1770–1870.* 1981.

Binyon, Laurence. *English Water-Colours.* 1933.

Clarke, Michael. *The Tempting Prospect: A Social History of English Watercolours.* 1981.

Hardie, Martin. *Water-Colour Painting in Britain.* 1966.

. . . . .

WATERHOUSE, ALFRED (1830–1905)

A brilliant use of materials and extensive attention to planning mark the architecture of Alfred Waterhouse. His most important works are London's Natural History Museum (1868–1880), his plan for the Law Courts (1866), and the head London office of the Prudential Assurance Company (1876).

Born near Liverpool to a wealthy Quaker family, Waterhouse was apprenticed to an architect in Manchester, the city in which he first set up practice. In 1859 he won the competition for the Manchester Assize Courts (destroyed), a well-planned structure with a striking Ruskinian Gothic facade. Waterhouse entered the London Law Courts competition (1866). His plan was best liked by the lawyers, but the commission went to George Edmund Street. Possibly due to the magnificence of his entry, Waterhouse in the same year was appointed to carry on the design of the Natural History Museum. The winning design for the museum, decided in an earlier competition, was by Captain Francis Fowke, who had died in late 1865. The government intended Waterhouse to carry out Fowke's designs, but new plans were submitted in 1868, and approved in 1871. When the museum opened in 1881, only the front portion was built; Waterhouse's plans for side and rear ranges were never built. The museum design integrates German Romanesque detailing, an interior of baroque grandeur, and ironwork that parallels that used in contemporaneous railway stations. Planned much like a medieval cathedral, the building was, and remains, a temple to natural history, with carvings of animals (living and extinct), and colored terra cotta decoration.

Waterhouse also remodeled Eaton Hall, near Chester (1870–1882, now mostly destroyed) for the duke of Westminster. It was an enormous Gothic structure that included a magnificent bell and clock tower.

Later, Waterhouse did work on Cambridge and Oxford colleges, and designed the Prudential Assurance Company offices in London. Built in four stages between 1877 and 1897, this structure incorporates terra cotta decoration over steel construction. He built twenty-four other Prudential offices between 1877 and 1901. Waterhouse had great sensitivity for color, planning, and picturesque elements in his design and used various historical forms to achieve these ends.

FLOYD W. MARTIN

Bibliography

Fawcett, Jane, ed. *Seven Victorian Architects.* 1976.

Girouard, Mark. *Alfred Waterhouse and the Natural History Museum.* 1981.

Maltby, Sally, Sally McDonald, and Colin Cunningham. *Alfred Waterhouse, 1830–1905.* 1983.

See also GOTHIC REVIVAL *(illus.)*

. . . . .

Bibliography

Howitt, Margaret, ed. *Mary Howitt: An Autobiography.* 1889.

Walker, Mary Howitt. *Come Wind, Come Weather: A Biography of Alfred Howitt.* 1971.

Woodring, Carl Ray. *Victorian Samplers: William and Mary Howitt.* 1952.

. . . . .

WATTS, ANNA MARY HOWITT (1824–1884)

Anna Mary Howitt Watts was a painter, novelist, and poet associated with the Pre-Raphaelites and English feminists in the 1850s. After 1859 she ceased painting professionally and became known as a maker of "spirit drawings."

Watts was the daughter of the popular writers **William and Mary Howitt.** From 1850 to 1852 she worked informally in the Munich studio of Wilhelm von Kaulbach. In 1852 Watts formed, with Barbara Leigh Smith Bodichon and Bessie Rayner Parkes, the Pre-Raphaelite Sisterhood to support its members' writing and painting activities. Watts was also a member, along with Dante Gabriel Rossetti and John Millais, of the Portfolio Club. From 1854 to 1856 she exhibited several paintings, including *Faust's Margaret Returning from the Fountain* (1854) and, at the Royal Academy, *The Castaway* (1854).

However, increasing mental instability, mixed critical response to her work, and a negative appraisal from John Ruskin of her *Boadicea* (1856) produced in Watts a mental breakdown and a turn to **spiritualism.** After 1859 she devoted all her artistic efforts to drawings allegedly done at the behest of spirits, and to her researches and writings on spiritualism, including *Aurora* (1875), a volume of poems written by Watts and her husband Alaric Alfred Watts, and *Pioneers of the Spiritual Reformation* (1883), a biography of the spiritualists William Howitt and Justinus Kerner.

Watts's experiences reflect the pressure exerted by external conditions on Victorian women seeking careers in the arts as well as her own psychological makeup.

LENORE BEAKY

WATTS, GEORGE FREDERIC (1817–1904)

George Frederic Watts was widely regarded as the greatest English painter of his era. A romantic fascination with beauty's vulnerability to death runs through his work. His portraits of Victorian intellectuals, such as *Tennyson* (1864), combine an ennobled exterior likeness with a feeling for the spiritual essence of the subject. In symbolic pictures such as *Hope* (1866), inspired by Michelangelo's Sistine ceiling, Watts sought to distill the salient ideas of the Victorian age into an emblematic form. He was also a sculptor of note. *Physical Energy* (1870–1904), in Kensington Gardens, is his best-known statue.

Watts entered the public eye in 1843 when his cartoon of *Caractacus* won a competition to select artists to fresco the newly built Houses of Parliament. From 1843–1847 he lived in Florence. Upon his return he experimented briefly with depictions of contemporary destitution in paintings like *Found Drowned* (1849). In the late 1850s and early 1860s his style came momentarily under Pre-Raphaelite influence, as in *Choosing* (1864), a portrait of his first wife, **Ellen Terry.** He played a leading role in the late Victorian revival of interest in the nude and in Hellenic subjects. He was associated with the Grosvenor Gallery. Although he was elected to the Royal Academy in 1867, he continued to consider himself an outsider.

Watts's determination to paint "ideas, not things" aligns him with the European symbolists. He compared the suggestive effects of his paintings to sonorous music. The subjects and style of his late work, such as *The Sower of Systems* (1902), became increasingly abstract.

MARILYNN LINCOLN BOARD

Bibliography

Barrington, Mrs. Russel. *G. F. Watts: Reminiscences.* 1905.

Blunt, Wilfrid. *England's Michelangelo: A Biography of George Frederic Watts, O.M., R.A.* 1975.

Minneapolis Institute of Arts. *The Victorian High Renaissance.* 1978.

Watts, Mary. *George Frederic Watts.* 1912. 3 vols.

· · · · ·

WEBB, BEATRICE POTTER (1858-1943) and SIDNEY JAMES (1859-1947)

Beatrice and Sidney Webb were leaders of the **Fabian Society**, influential socialist reformers, and authors of a number of important works of social and political history, among them *The History of Trade Unionism* (1894), *Industrial Democracy* (1897), and the nine-volume *English Local Government* (1903-1929).

Although the Webbs shared a number of political and intellectual interests when they met in 1890, their social backgrounds were radically different. Beatrice Webb's father was a railway magnate and lumber merchant who presided over a household of nine daughters in Gloucestershire, and her mother was a learned woman devoted to the study of languages and political economy. Sidney Webb's parents kept a hairdressing and millinery shop in London, and his father was an ardent supporter of John Stuart Mill.

While Sidney Webb worked his way up through the civil service to the Colonial Office (1883) and took an external law degree at London University (1886), Beatrice Potter struggled to make a life for herself outside of marriage. She found a vocation as social investigator when she assisted her cousin **Charles Booth** in his pioneering study of poverty, *Life and Labour of the People in London* (1889-1903). She was attracted to Fabianism by reading *Fabian Essays in Socialism* (1889), edited by George Bernard Shaw and containing Sidney Webb's essay on the "historic basis" of socialism. The essay's reliance on the evolutionary social philosophies of Herbert Spencer and Auguste Comte appealed to her, as did Sidney Webb's emphasis on research and investigation within the Fabian Society.

In the first decades of their marriage the Webbs produced most of their major works of research, formulated plans for the London School of Economics, founded the *New Statesman* (1913), and waged a hard and unsuccessful campaign for the reform of the Poor Law (1906-1909). Although they accepted the new Labour party with reluctance, Sidney Webb joined the party executive (1915), was returned as Labour M.P. from Seaham (1922), and served in the cabinets of both Labour governments (1924 and 1929). Meanwhile, Beatrice Webb wrote *My Apprenticeship* (1926), the autobiography she had begun in the throes of a personal crisis during World War I. A second and less personal volume of autobiography, *Our Partnership*, was published posthumously in 1948.

Because of what has been regarded as the Webbs' mechanistic and positivist notions of social change and their latter-day attraction to Soviet communism, they have earned the disapprobation of Marxists and anti-communists alike. They have also been the subject of a number of satirical portraits, most notably in H. G. Wells's *The New Machiavelli* (1911), as well as of some laudatory biographies by friends and political allies. In recent years historians have begun to acknowledge the religious impulse behind their political thought. The Webbs and other early Fabians reflected the late Victorian need for a secular faith to guide collective life. For them Fabianism was no mere utilitarian philosophy but a creed to govern society and their own lives. The Webbs' attraction to Soviet communism owed as much to their ongoing and frustrated search for this all-embracing creed as to their elitist and technocratic tendencies.

DEBORAH EPSTEIN NORD

Bibliography

Adam, Ruth and Kitty Muggeridge. *Beatrice Webb: A Life.* 1967.

Cole, Margaret. *The Story of Fabian Socialism.* 1961.

———, ed. *The Webbs and Their Work.* 1949.

Hobsbawm, Eric. J. "The Fabians Reconsidered." In Eric J. Hobsbawm, *Labouring Men: Studies in the History of Labour.* 1964.

MacKenzie, Norman, ed. *The Letters of Sidney and Beatrice Webb.* 1978. 3 vols.

——— and Jeanne MacKenzie, eds. *The Diary of Beatrice Webb.* 1982–1985. 4 vols.

McBriar, A. M. *Fabian Socialism and British Politics, 1884–1918.* 1962.

Nord, Deborah Epstein. *The Apprenticeship of Beatrice Webb.* 1985.

Wolfe, Willard. *From Radicalism to Socialism: Men and Ideas in the Formation of Fabian Socialist Doctrines, 1881–1889.* 1975.

· · · · ·

WEBSTER, AUGUSTA DAVIES (1837–1894)

Augusta Webster was an accomplished translator, poet, dramatist, essayist, educator, and advocate of women's rights. She began publishing under the pseudonym Cecil Home: *Blanche Lisle and Other Poems* (1860), *Lilian Gray* (a poem, 1864), and a three-volume novel, *Lesley's Guardians* (1864). In 1866 and 1868, translations of Aeschylus's *Prometheus Bound* and Euripides's *Medea*, published under her own name, were praised by Greek scholars. Reprints of her essays in the *Examiner* on women's rights were used by the Women's Suffrage Society. In 1878 Webster published *A Housewife's Opinions*, essays on various topics including her ideas as a democratic educator. She served several terms on the London School Board.

Webster's career as a dramatist began in 1872 when she published the poetic drama *The Auspicious Day. In a Day* (1882) was successfully produced and reviewed at Terry's Theatre, London, in 1890. The three-act tragedy *The Sentence* (1887) was considered her best play.

Her volumes of poetry include *Dramatic Studies* (1866), *A Woman Sold and Other Poems* (1867), and *Yu-Pe-Ya's Lute: A Chinese Tale in English Verse* (1874). *A Book of Rhymes* (1881) introduced the Italian song form *rispetti* into English poetry. The posthumous *Mother and Daughter* (1895), an unfinished sonnet sequence, was introduced by William Michael Rossetti.

Webster's notable contribution to poetry is the feminist use of the dramatic monologue to incite empathy for women's social plight as second-class citizens, as in "Tired" and "A Castaway," which rivals Dante Rossetti's "Jenny" as an exposé of Victorian prostitution. In "Circe" and "Medea in Athens," her dramatic technique demands a reevaluation of the evil cunning of historically demonic women.

SHELLEY J. CRISP

Bibliography

Miles, Alfred Henry et al. *The Poets and Poetry of the Nineteenth Century.* 1905–1907.

· · · · ·

WELLINGTON, DUKE OF (ARTHUR WELLESLEY) (1769–1852)

The hero of the Peninsular War (1808–1814), the conqueror of Napoleon at the battle of Waterloo (June 18, 1815) and the most acclaimed public figure of his day, the duke of Wellington rose to his great eminence from the lower reaches of the Irish aristocracy by military genius and dedication to his profession in the long wars against France that followed within six years of his first commission in the army in 1787. When he finally returned to England in 1818 he entered the cabinet as master general of the ordnance (to 1827) and played a leading role in politics until the end of his life. In 1827 he was (twice) briefly commander in chief of the army. From 1828 to 1830 he was prime minister; then Conservative leader in the House of Lords until 1846; foreign secretary in 1834–1835; and commander in chief again from 1842 to his death.

Wellington's career made him seem the very embodiment of the Victorian virtues of discipline, hard work, and selfless public service. Living much in the public eye, he was immediately recognized by his famous hooked nose, abrupt manner, and customary military salute. He appeared indifferent to fame and his austerity was legendary. His laconic sayings, genuine or apocryphal, were treasured as epitomizing good sense. Though Wellington opposed most reforms, his conviction that strong government and avoiding civil war were more important than preserving the existing order led him to play an important if reluctant part in the major legislative changes of the period, from **Catholic emancipation** (1829) to the repeal of the Corn Laws (1846). This pragmatic conservatism made him a leading example of the Victorian synthesis of stability and adaptation. In a time of rapid transformation he was a reassuring symbol of continuity and public safety. His elaborate public funeral was as much a landmark and celebration of the Victorian age as was the Crystal Palace exhibition of the previous year.

NEVILLE THOMPSON

Bibliography

Longford, Elizabeth. *Wellington: Pillar of State.* 1972.

——. *Wellington: The Years of the Sword.* 1969.

Thompson, Neville. *Wellington After Waterloo.* 1986.

· · · · ·

WELLS, HERBERT GEORGE (1866-1946)

More than any other writer, H.G. Wells prodded Britain into thinking about the future. He invented most of the major themes that have since dominated **science fiction**, including time travel in *The Time Machine* (1895), interplanetary combat in *The War of the Worlds* (1898), and an Orwellian dystopia in *When the Sleeper Wakes* (1899). Going beyond the gadgetry of Jules Verne, Wells used science fiction as a vehicle for moral, philosophical, and social criticism.

Wells was the son of a failing Bromley shopkeeper and a domestic servant. In 1884 he won a state scholarship to the Normal School of Science, where he studied under T. H. Huxley. That celebrated Darwinist taught Wells the darker implications of evolutionary theory: that man is brother to the ape, and might someday revert to his bestial origins. Wells's early novels are haunted by the specter of reverse evolution: the simian Morlocks of *The Time Machine*, the half-humans of *The Island of Dr. Moreau* (1896), the "paeleolithic" killer of *The Invisible Man* (1897), and the squid-like Martians of *The War of the Worlds*.

Huxley, however, also taught that through scientific knowledge and sheer ethical will, humankind could achieve genuine moral progress. Reading Plato had already suggested to Wells that society might be reorganized along more rational lines. As a student, Wells frequented socialist meetings at William Morris's Kelmscott House, where he heard several Fabian socialists speak.

Wells found work as a teacher and, in 1891, he married his cousin, Isabel Mary Wells (1866-1931). She proved to be a conventional and (hence) incompatible wife. Two years later he eloped with one of his students, Amy Catherine Robbins (1872-1927).

By 1893, Wells had decisively broken into popular journalism. In a literary career that spanned more than half a century, he averaged better than two books a year, in addition to a torrent of ephemeral journalism. He was driven to extraordinary productivity first by the need to earn a living, and later by an obsessive impulse to convert the world to his schemes for social planning. Henry James, in a long correspondence with Wells (1898-1915), paid him many compliments but also criticized his work as slipshod.

Wells's prose does lack polish, but it has remarkable energy and punch. Ingeniously, he made science fiction seem thoroughly believable; see the vivid description of a lunar civilization in *The First Men in the Moon* (1901). Wells was, as Joseph Conrad proclaimed, a "Realist of the Fantastic." He also wrote convincingly about the everyday struggles of the lower middle class, as in his novel *Love and Mr. Lewisham* (1900).

The foreboding of Wells's fin-de-siècle novels lightened in the Edwardian years. In *Anticipations* (1901) he offered some optimistic predictions for the coming century. Having been catapulted out of the lumpenbourgeoisie, Wells now found a new class to identify with: a class of scientists and engineers whom he called the "New Republicans." For the rest of his life, Wells would exhaustively argue that these specialists, armed with their indispensable expertise, could take control of society. Much like Plato's Guardians, they could establish a technocratic dictatorship, introduce scientific social planning and eugenic controls, and thus abolish war and poverty. The Fabian socialists, who were thinking along similar lines, took a sharp interest in *Anticipations*. With the encouragement of Bernard Shaw, Sidney and Beatrice Webb, and Edward Pease, Wells joined the Fabian Society in 1903.

JONATHAN ROSE

Bibliography

Hammond, John R. *Herbert George Wells: An Annotated Bibliography of His Works.* 1977.

MacKenzie, Norman and Jeanne MacKenzie. *H. G. Wells.* 1973.

Smith, David C. *H. G. Wells, Desperately Mortal.* 1986.

· · · · ·

WESLEY, SAMUEL SEBASTIAN (1810–1876)

A cathedral organist and composer, Samuel Sebastian Wesley's principal musical publications were the *Cathedral Service in E* (1845); *Twelve Anthems* (1853), including works dating from the early 1830s onward; and *The European Psalmist* (1872); as well as numerous separate anthems, smaller-scale liturgical compositions, and organ pieces. His published writings are an extended preface to the *Service in E* and two tracts: *A Few Words on Cathedral Music* (1849) and *Reply to the Inquiries of the Cathedral Commissioners* (1854).

He was the illegitimate son of Samuel Wesley (1766–1837) and thus a descendant of the founders of Methodism, though his entire ca-

reer was spent in the service of the Anglican church. Wesley was a boy chorister of the Chapel Royal, after which he held several minor organist positions before the five major appointments that account for the bulk of his career: Hereford Cathedral (1832), Exeter Cathedral (1835), Leeds Parish Church (1842), Winchester Cathedral (1849), and Gloucester Cathedral (1865). He earned the degrees of B.Mus. and D.Mus. from Oxford University in 1839 and tried unsuccessfully to gain musical professorships at Edinburgh, Oxford, and Cambridge.

Wesley was, on the whole, an unhappy and self-pitying man, with a volatile temper and a reputation for being difficult. He was, nevertheless, the most celebrated English organist and cathedral composer of his day. He brought a then unaccustomed breadth, grandeur, and romantic expressiveness to his larger choral works. His compositional style is highly distinctive.

WILLIAM J. GATENS

Bibliography

Chappell, Paul. *Dr. S. S. Wesley.* 1977.

Gatens, William J. *Victorian Cathedral Music in Theory and Practice.* 1986.

Hiebert, Arlis J. *The Anthems and Services of S. S. Wesley.* 1965.

Horton, Peter. "Samuel Sebastian Wesley at Leeds: A Victorian Church Musician Reflects on His Craft." *Victorian Studies*, vol. 30, pp. 99–111.

Routley, Erik. *The Musical Wesleys.* 1968.

· · · · ·

WESLEYAN METHODIST CHURCH

In the decades between the death of John Wesley in 1791 and the opening of the Victorian era the main body of Methodism was transformed from an evangelical "connexion" within the Church of England into an independent denomination. Wesleyan membership grew, from about 87,000 in 1801 to nearly 285,000 in 1850 and about 412,000 in 1901. Concentrated in the textile and mining districts of the north and in Wales and Cornwall, Methodism remained weak in London and declined in rural areas over the century. Wesleyan membership as a percentage of the total adult population hovered around 2 percent throughout the century, and the combined total of all branches of Methodism never reached above 4 percent. In contrast to the dynamism of its first century, Methodism experienced steady but decelerating growth in the Victorian period.

By midcentury Methodism had entered a new phase. An ambitious (and expensive) program of chapel and school construction was in progress, with a preference for imposing neo-Gothic structures, built to last and to impress. Two new seminaries were opened in the 1840s, and Wesleyan ministers were better paid and better educated than before.

The freewheeling, revivalist practices of earlier days—camp meetings, cottage gatherings, extemporaneous prayer and exhortation—were abandoned in favor of more orderly chapel services. Centralizing tendencies enhanced the power of circuit leadership, and final authority over a wide range of denominational affairs lay with the Annual Conference (which admitted no lay members until 1878).

Early nineteenth-century data suggest that women constituted a majority of Methodist membership—a sizable majority in the more urban centers. It is likely that this ratio increased through the century. Yet for women the new orthodoxy meant a narrowing of their role in chapel life. Female preaching, which had flourished briefly with Wesley's encouragement, died out, and women had to content themselves with Sunday-school teaching, sick visiting, and informal support services. Later in the century foreign missions, the founding of Methodist girls' schools, and the recruitment of deaconesses for inner-city mission work offered new opportunities for a determined few.

Not surprisingly, the shift toward denominationalism brought protests from laypeople and from some ministers who bemoaned the loss of revivalist fervor and favored more lay involvement. In consequence, the Wesleyans suffered a series of major defections, culminating in the formation of the rival United Methodist Free Churches in the early 1850s.

But new-style Methodism offered some fresh channels for both lay and clerical energies. Important measures of religious emancipation, including the repeal of the Test and Corporation Acts in 1828, the voluntarization of the church rate in 1853, and the opening of Oxford and Cambridge degrees to non-Anglicans in 1854, bolstered the social and political confidence of all branches of dissent. Setting aside both Wesley's Toryism and the political quietism urged by his successor, Jabez Bunting, Victorian Methodism became more willing to challenge the establishment and more and more closely identified with political Liberalism. All the Wesleyans elected to Parliament in the nineteenth century sat as Liberals. Through its strong appeal to sections of the skilled working class, Methodism also contributed several generations of chapel-trained leaders to the developing trade union movement.

To be sure there were issues—for example, Irish Home Rule—on which most Methodists parted company with official Liberalism. Wesleyanism's most powerful spokesman of the 1880s and 1890s was Hugh Price Hughes (1847–1902), a dynamic preacher, indefatigable fund raiser, and brilliant publicist who succeeded in making the "Nonconformist conscience" a force in national politics. In the columns of the *Methodist Times* and through his platform oratory Hughes roused public indignation over the Parnell scandal, inveighed against Anglican control of education, and enlisted Methodist support for Liberal imperialism. A proponent of the social gospel, he urged the establishment of Methodist city missions and denominational associations devoted to temperance and social purity.

Having outgrown its revivalist origins, Victorian Wesleyan Methodism successfully accommodated in various respects to the mainstream of British society. In so doing it also entered into direct competition with Anglicanism for the allegiance of the respectable elements of that society, and its influence in shaping the Victorian conscience far outweighed its numbers.

GAIL MALMGREEN

Bibliography

Currie, Robert et al. *Churches and Churchgoers: Patterns of Church Growth in the British Isles Since 1700.* 1977.

Davies, Rupert et al., eds. *A History of the Methodist Church in Great Britain*, vols. 2 and 3. 1978, 1983.

Davis, Horton. *Worship and Theology in England from Newman to Martineau, 1850–1900*. 1962.

Gilbert, Alan D. *Religion and Society in Industrial England: Church, Chapel and Social Change, 1740–1914*. 1976.

Hempton, David. *Methodism and Politics in British Society, 1750–1850*. 1984.

Townsend, W. J. et al. *A New History of Methodism*. 1909. 2 vols.

Ward, W. R. *Religion and Society in England, 1790–1850*. 1972.

Wearmouth, Robert F. *Methodism and the Struggle of the Working Classes, 1850–1900*. 1954.

See also NONCONFORMITY; PRIMITIVE METHODIST CHURCH

· · · · ·

WEST AFRICA

British policy in West Africa for the first three-quarters of the nineteenth century was shaped by humanitarian pressure to thwart the **slave trade.** British traffic in slaves was outlawed by the statute of 1807, and the British presence in West Africa was a vital deterrent to slavers from other countries. Thus Britain established forts in Sierra Leone (1808), the Gambia (1816), and the Gold Coast (1821) to serve as commercial bases and to clear the coast of slave traders.

Attempts to develop profitable colonies failed, however, and in 1865 the House of Commons urged general withdrawal from the West African colonies—a policy stymied by humanitarian worries about the slave trade. Tribal wars contributed to the instability of the area, and the Gold Coast colony was established in 1874 to protect the coastal Fanti from the Ashanti of the interior. Yet despite the government's best efforts, West Africa remained a considerable nuisance: the Foreign Office took no real interest in the area but at the same time did not want to abandon it to French exploitation.

Farther south, British traders penetrated the deltas of the Congo and the Niger to further their profitable trade in palm oil. The merchants were happy to stay on the coast, but Palmerston's policy in the 1850s of exporting civilization through trade led to the annexation of Lagos in 1861 and to extensive probing up the Niger. In the late 1870s, however, the situation became too problem-ridden to justify the expenditures necessary to bring order to the areas upriver. Furthermore, fierce commercial competition in the palm oil trade drove prices down and left British merchants hanging on tenuously in a region the government was beginning to despair of.

By 1880 France had begun to expand its domain in Senegal, putting pressure on Gambia and Sierra Leone and leading to an agreement with England on demarcation lines in 1881. The British occupation of Egypt in 1882, however, disturbed the balance of European powers and led to France's expansion of its trading interests in West Africa. British trade in the Congo delta suffered in the early 1880s from French and Belgian exploration in the area. Britain responded by signing a treaty with Portugal in 1884, acknowledging Portuguese rights in the Congo in return for commercial privileges. France solicited resistance to the treaty from Germany, and Bismarck in effect began the partition of West Africa by establishing protectorates over Togoland and the Cameroons.

Confronted by this setback, Britain chose to defend its interests along the Niger River. From 1880 until the end of the century, George Goldie Taubman (later Sir George Taubman Goldie) played a central role in the Niger region with his National African Company, which bought out competing French firms and concluded treaties with the local chiefs. Goldie's enterprise gave England control of the lower Niger, and in 1886 Goldie received a government charter to do business as the Royal Niger Company. Goldie's ambition was hampered, however, by contention with competing interests in Liverpool and by German complaints about his de facto monopoly in the area. To settle the issues, England created the Niger Coast Protectorate in 1893, financing its administration by customs duties paid by the disgruntled Liverpool traders.

By 1890 Sierra Leone and Gambia had been isolated by French advances in the area, and Salisbury was content to submit to the French in West Africa as a means of placating them about Egypt. The Gold Coast hinterlands were similarly abandoned to German intrusions into the area. Only in the upper Niger where Goldie's company was strong did Britain enjoy any hegemony, and even there the government was solely interested in preventing the French from establishing routes between West Africa and the Red Sea.

With the installation of Joseph Chamberlain in the Colonial Office in 1895, British official policy toward West Africa became more aggressive. Chamberlain was intent on involving the British taxpayer in imperialism rather than leaving West African interests to the merchants, and he immediately moved to subdue the Ashanti on the Gold Coast and to introduce railways and land reform to the neglected outposts. Chamberlain's ambitions clashed with Salisbury's in the middle 1890s, as the prime minister was concerned with British objectives along the Nile and regarded West Africa as a pawn in his game with the French. To confront France directly in the Niger region, Chamberlain formed a West Africa Frontier Force in 1897 and faced the French army on the Niger the next year. Salisbury's policy of conciliation prevailed, however, and the Niger Convention of 1898 granted France access to the Niger and left Britain essentially where it had been at the beginning. Thus the century ended with a generally peaceful partition of West Africa.

FRANK DAY

Bibliography

Cook, Arthur N. *British Enterprise in Nigeria.* 1943.

Robinson, Ronald, John Gallagher, and Alice Denny. *Africa and the Victorians: The Climax of Imperialism.* 1961.

· · · · ·

WEST INDIES

When Queen Victoria ascended the throne in 1837 the once valued British West Indian sugar islands were undergoing a major transition from slavery to freedom. The British Parliament abolished slavery in the empire in 1833. The white planters, many of them absentee owners, were allotted 20 million pounds in compensation for loss of property. A brief apprenticeship period was designed to prevent immediate withdrawal of labor. Many missionary groups heightened their efforts to Christianize and educate the blacks before full emancipation went into effect in 1838.

The 1840s saw bankruptcies and financial loss for many planters. Sugar production fell, as did sugar prices. In West Indian colonies such as Trinidad and Guiana, where there was plenty of undeveloped land, blacks left plantations, established free villages, and became smallholders. The consequent labor shortage resulted in efforts to introduce indentured labor from China and the Indian subcontinent. Lord John Russell called it "a new system of slavery." East Indian groups were to become significant minorities in the West Indian setting, making up approximately one quarter of the population of British Guiana, and about one third that of Trinidad, by the 1880s. But in islands like Barbados where plantations occupied most land, there was little alternative for blacks but to continue working on sugar estates. East Indian ethnic groups were not introduced.

The rise of a free trade philosophy was a major blow to the British West Indian islands. After the abolition of the Corn Laws in 1846, the floodgates of free trade were opened and preferential duties favoring colonial sugar were dismantled between 1846 and 1854. British markets were opened up to sugar grown in foreign colonies, including the slave-grown sugar of Cuba. Sugar beet presented added competition. In the late nineteenth century sugar prices fell dramatically and the percentage of British colonial sugar imported into the mother country declined. Sugar continued to be grown but did not regain its former importance. Other crops, such as citrus fruits, coffee, bananas, and cocoa, gave some diversity to export-oriented agriculture.

Constitutionally the islands did not move toward democracy or self government; quite the reverse. The old representative system, characterized by governors, appointed councils, and elected assemblies, gave way to the Crown Colony system of strong executive government everywhere except in Barbados. A proposal to federate the West Indies in 1876 led to rioting in Barbados and the plan was abandoned. The West Indian colonies did not develop responsible government of the type achieved in Canada, Australia, and New Zealand.

The West Indian event that attracted the most attention during Queen Victoria's reign became known as the Governor Eyre controversy. In 1865 riots erupted in St. Thomas Parish, Jamaica, occasioned by economic hardship, partly due to drought and the impact of the American Civil War. Religious revivalism, especially associated with the Baptists, added to the electric atmosphere. During the riots several whites were killed, and Governor **Edward Eyre**, fearing a rerun of the Indian Mutiny (1857) declared martial law. The military tried to restore order and several hundred blacks were court-martialed and summarily executed. The most famous victim was George William Gordon who, although not present at the riot, was a political agitator and enemy of the governor. The incident polarized opinion in England. Figures such as John Stuart Mill, Thomas Hughes, Herbert Spencer, and Thomas Huxley saw the governor as a tyrant. They organized the Jamaica Committee and tried, unsuccessfully, to bring Eyre to trial. Conservatives, including Thomas Carlyle, Alfred Tennyson, and John Ruskin, championed the governor. Much of the public viewed Eyre as a hero who had saved the whites from certain massacre. Racial sentiments were unleashed. The controversy raised the issue of whether an empire was compatible with the development of liberal democracy inside England.

Toward the end of Victoria's reign a royal commission examined West Indian conditions (1897). There were serious economic hardships characterized by the continual decline of the sugar industry. Joseph Chamberlain, the colonial secretary, established the Imperial Department of Agriculture for the West Indies (1898) in an effort to assist the agricultural situation. But many West Indians, searching for better opportunities, migrated to areas such as New York and Panama.

During the Victorian years the British West Indies were swimming against the tide of English historical development. They initially depended on slavery when free labor was fueling the industrial revolution. The sugar economy relied on protection when free trade was making England great. The governments reverted to Crown Colony administration when democracy was evolving in England and self-government was developing in many colonial territories.

OLWYN M. BLOUET

Bibliography

Bolt, Christine. *Victorian Attitudes to Race.* 1971.

Froude, J. A. *The English in the West Indies.* 1888.

Green, William A. *British Slave Emancipation.* 1976.

Levy, Claude. *Emancipation, Sugar, and Federalism: Barbados and the West Indies, 1833–1876.* 1980.

Morrell, W. P. *Colonial Policy of Peel and Russell.* 1930.

Parry, J. H. and Philip Sherlock. *A Short History of the West Indies.* 3d ed., 1971.

Semmel, Bernard. *Democracy Versus Empire.* 1969.

. . . . .

WHIG PARTY

Originally a derogatory term, the label "Whig" came into use in the 1670s to describe those opposed to the succession of James II to the throne. Whigs saw Parliament as a crucial constraint on royal prerogative. By the early eighteenth century they also argued for toleration of Nonconformist dissenters. Civil and religious liberty became a Whig catch phrase, and party organization in Parliament became the venerated means of safeguarding the national interest and controlling royal power. By the 1790s, under the leadership of Charles James Fox (1749-1806), Whigs such as Earl Grey (1764-1845) were calling from the opposition benches for reform of Parliament and the removal of the political disabilities of dissenters. Responsible reform, Whigs believed, would preserve the respect, gratitude, and loyalty of the lower social ranks for the propertied and the aristocracy. Thus a commitment to due deference within a firm social hierarchy framed Whig notions of moderate reform and liberty realized through a party of aristocratic lineage in Parliament. Ambivalent in their relations with extraparliamentary radicalism, Whigs received increasing support in the early nineteenth century from industrial interests in northern England, as well as from the middle classes and commerce. Though briefly in office as members of the "Ministry of All the Talents" from 1806–1807, Whigs remained an opposition party until 1830.

By the 1820s Whigs were focusing parliamentary debate on taxation, **Catholic emancipation**, and parliamentary reform. In 1828 the young Whig **Lord John Russell** (1792–1878) proposed abolition of the Test and Corporation Acts; in the following year Catholic emancipation removed the political disabilities of Catholics. In November 1830 Earl Grey formed a Whig government committed to parliamentary reform. The predominantly aristocratic Whig cabinet, including Lord John Russell, **Lord Durham** (1792–1840), Lord Althorp (1782–1845), and Henry Brougham (1778–1868), also contained liberal Tories such as Lord Stanley (1799–1869), Lord Palmerston (1784–1865), and Sir James Graham (1792–1861). Despite the opposition of the House of Lords and the reluctance of William IV (1765–1837), the parliamentary reform bill introduced by Russell in March 1831 became law in July 1832. The 1832 Reform Act heralded a series of Whig reforms. In 1833 slavery was abolished, and a Factory Act passed alleviating harsh working conditions and child labor. In 1834 the New Poor Law centralized the administration of poor relief, restricted outdoor relief, and required ablebodied men on relief to live in workhouses. The Whig government was weakened in June 1834 by the resignations of Stanley and Graham. In July 1834 Earl Grey resigned as prime minister. He was succeeded by **Viscount Melbourne** (1779–1848), but in November 1834 William IV dismissed the Whig ministry.

The Lichfield House Compact of February 1835 brought Whig, radical, and Irish M.P.'s together in political alliance. Thereafter, Whig and Liberal became increasingly synonymous terms. Indeed, some would assign the foundation of the **Liberal party** to February 1835, although the Willis's Rooms meeting of 1859 remains the more commonly accepted date. In April 1835 Melbourne formed a new Whig

government which passed a Municipal Corporation Act, reforming local government, the Tithe Act of 1836, and the Registration Act of 1837, which released dissenters from the obligation to be baptized, married, and buried in an Anglican church. It also commissioned the Durham report on Canada which proposed a colonial policy of responsible government and based the ties of empire upon consent rather than coercion. During the 1830s the Birmingham lawyer Joseph Parkes (1796–1865), as party manager, extended Whig extraparliamentary organization, aided by the founding of the Reform Club in 1836. The 1841 general election, however, proved a demoralizing defeat for the Whig party.

After an abortive attempt to form a government in November 1845, and following the Corn Law crisis, Russell formed a Whig ministry in June 1846. Enjoying few substantial achievements, this government did consolidate the move toward free trade by repealing the Navigation Acts (1849) as well as increasing the state grant for education in 1847 and passing the Public Health Act in 1848. In response to the Irish famine Russell pursued a laissez-faire policy founded on a Malthusian diagnosis of the disaster. In December 1851 the foreign secretary, **Lord Palmerston**, was forced to resign because of policy differences with his colleagues, and in February 1852 retaliated by helping to bring down Russell's government.

A number of Whigs, including Russell and Palmerston, joined the coalition ministry formed by the Peelite leader, the earl of Aberdeen (1784–1860), in December 1852. Before its fall in February 1855, however, the Aberdeen coalition was dogged by the growing and bitter rivalry between Russell and Palmerston, and embarrassing revelations of mismanagement in the Crimean War. In February 1855 Palmerston formed a Whig-Liberal government pursuing a policy preoccupied with foreign affairs and the defense of British interests abroad. Upon the fall of Palmerston's ministry in February 1858 (ironically for not defending British honor with sufficient vigor), the Whig party was deeply divided.

In June 1859 Whigs reunited in alliance with radicals and former Peelites, under the leadership of Palmerston, who formed his second government. This event marks the foundation of the Liberal party, in which aristocratic Whigs continued to provide both leadership and a tradition of administrative progressivism. Following the Home Rule crisis of 1886 many Whigs, led by Lord Hartington (1833-1908), moved over to the Conservative and Unionist party.

ANGUS HAWKINS

Bibliography

Brock, Michael. *The Great Reform Act.* 1973.

Kriegel, Abraham D. "Liberty and Whiggery in Early Nineteenth-Century England." *Journal of Modern History,* vol. 52, pp. 253-278.

——, ed. *The Holland House Diaries, 1831-1840.* 1977.

Southgate, Donald. *The Passing of the Whigs, 1832-1886.* 1965.

Vincent, John R. *The Formation of the British Liberal Party, 1857-1868.* 2d ed., 1976.

· · · · ·

WHISTLER, JAMES McNEILL (1834-1903)

James Abbot McNeill Whistler was one of the foremost painters of his century. His achievements include the etchings of *The French Set* (1858) and *The Thames Set* (1860-1861), the paintings of *La Princesse du Pays de la Porcelaine* (1864), the four *Symphonies in White* (1862, 1864, 1867, 1868-1869), *Arrangement in Grey and Black, No. 1: The Artist's Mother* (1872), *Arrangement in Grey and Black, No. 2: Thomas Carlyle* (1873), the *Nocturnes* (chiefly 1870s), and the decoration of *The Peacock Room* (1876-1877).

Born in Lowell, Massachusetts, Whistler became a citizen of the world, residing principally in Paris (1855-1860) and London (1860-1903) and making expeditions for etching and painting to Chile and throughout western Europe. At Paris he studied in the studio of Charles Gleyre and was influenced by the works of Velasquez, Courbet, Rembrandt, and Hals as well as by his French contemporaries who insisted that line,

number, proportion, and color held supremacy over the subject of the painting.

Whistler sounded a new note in painting by using musical terms for the titles of his works—arrangements, notes, nocturnes, and symphonies. One nocturne, *The Falling Rocket: Nocturne in Black and Gold* (1875) earned the wrath of the preeminent art critic of the age, John Ruskin (1819-1900) in *Fors Clavigera* (1877), which led to the celebrated civil action, *Whistler* vs. *Ruskin* (1878), described in Whistler's *The Gentle Art of Making Enemies* (1890).

Whistler's early, more traditional method of the 1850s was soon replaced by an impressionism that was distinctly his own. Like many of his contemporaries he had an Oriental phase in which he did not entirely imitate Oriental techniques but included Oriental objects, costume, and decoration in his works. One notable achievement of the Oriental period was *The Peacock Room* he decorated for Frederick R. Leyland. Another was the adoption of his monogram in the shape of a butterfly for signing his works.

Whistler did much to publicize his art and art in general. His "Ten O'Clock" lecture (1885) proclaimed an artistic creed asserting the primacy of art and the artist. As president of the Society of British Artists (1866-1888) and of the International Society of Sculptors, Painters and Engravers (1898-1903) his promotion of art (and self) found unique, if controversial, expression. As one who lived his iconoclastic life in public, Whistler epitomized the stereotype that artists are above the conventions of society. He also served the artistic community by helping to establish the tenet that artists have a right to their own work in the action of *Sir William Eden* vs. *Whistler* (1895), described in Whistler's *The Baronet and the Butterfly* (1899).

JOHN J. CONLON

Bibliography

Gregory, Horace. *The World of James McNeill Whistler.* 1959.

Pearson, Hesketh. *The Man Whistler.* 1978.

Pennell, Elizabeth R. and J. Pennell. *The Life of James McNeill Whistler.* 1911.

——. *The Whistler Journal.* 1921.

Sutton, Denys. *Nocturne: The Art of James McNeill Whistler.* 1964.

Weintraub, Stanley. *Whistler: A Biography.* 1974.

Whistler, James McNeill. *The Baronet and the Butterfly.* 1899.

———. *The Gentle Art of Making Enemies.* 1890.

Young, Andrew McLaren et al. *The Paintings of James McNeill Whistler.* 1980.

See also AESTHETIC MOVEMENT

· · · · ·

WHITE SLAVE TRADE

The slave trade, slavery, and white slavery were all the focus of organized campaigns in Great Britain during the nineteenth century. In chronological sequence, the campaigns to abolish the slave trade took place early in the century, slavery from the 1840s to the 1860s, and white slavery during the last quarter of the century. In all cases pressure groups participated in the various campaigns; often there were close links with abolitionist groups in America. After 1900 the movement expanded into an international effort for a legal ban on all slavery.

The terms "white slavery" and "white slave trade" were first used in the 1830s. The association was with the Continental or French system of state regulation of **prostitution.** Regulation entailed state-sponsored brothels, a special "morals" police, and periodic registration and medical examination of "inscribed women" (called reglementation). This system functioned in France and the Low Countries, among other places. Anglo-Saxons (especially the English and Americans) denounced sanctioning legalized vice. However, little effort was made to control prostitution. Authorities were restricted from prosecuting brothel keepers, and the age of consent remained at twelve until 1875, when it was raised to thirteen and then in 1885 to sixteen.

In fact, regulation and reglementation were implemented on a limited scale in Great Britain. During the 1860s commanders of the armed forces became alarmed at the dramatic increase in the incidence of venereal diseases, and they prevailed upon Parliament to pass the Contagious Diseases Acts (1864, 1866, and 1869). In the locale of eighteen military and naval facilities all women designated as prostitutes were required to undergo medical examination periodically and submit to treatment if necessary. Special police enforced the acts. Some "regulationists" advocated the extension of the provisions of the acts to all of the population.

Opposition to the Contagious Diseases Acts surfaced in about 1870 when pressure groups were formed, one exclusively by and for women, to lobby for repeal. Leaders of the repealers, who called themselves the "new abolitionists," included **Josephine E. Butler** (1828-1906) and James Stansfeld (1820-1898). After an extended campaign, and despite the fact that no women could vote, repeal was achieved in 1886.

Associated with these new abolitionists were some who favored abolition of prostitution, which they deemed "a great injustice to women and a moral and legal wrong." They claimed that because of the peculiar legal situation in Great Britain, notably the low age of consent (it was twenty-one on the Continent), young English virgins were being sold into slavery to Continental brothels. An official investigation conducted by the House of Lords (1882) found some corroboration. Butler and the renowned sensationalist journalist **William T. Stead** (1849-1912) sought to provoke public opinion. In July 1885 Stead published a series entitled "The Maiden Tribute of Modern Babylon" in his newspaper, the *Pall Mall Gazette.* The articles recounted an actual transaction and, almost immediately, the previously neglected Criminal Law Amendment Act (1885) was passed. These newspaper articles are now seen as a formative event in the development of "yellow journalism." Judith Walkowitz, the most recent scholarly reviewer of these events, claims that the evidence of an international white slave trade was thin and that the accusations were a "myth."

The campaign revived in about 1900, led by William A. Coote (1842-1919). International pressure groups concentrated their efforts on condemnation of the traffic and the formulation of international legal controls against "trade and traffic in young girls." An international congress was held in London in 1913.

EUGENE L. RASOR

Bibliography

Coote, William A. *A Vision and Its Fulfilment.* 1910.

Gorham, Deborah. "The 'Maiden Tribute of Modern Babylon' Re-examined: Child Prostitution and the Idea of Childhood in Late-Victorian England." *Victorian Studies*, vol. 21, pp. 353–379.

Scott, Benjamin. *A State Iniquity.* 1890; rpt. 1968.

Terrot, Charles. *Traffic in Innocents.* 1959.

Walkowitz, Judith R. *Prostitution and Victorian Society.* 1980.

. . . . .

WILBERFORCE, SAMUEL (1805-1873)

Anglican prelate Samuel Wilberforce was a notable preacher, educator, and church administrator. The son of antislavery philanthropist William Wilberforce, he gained an Oxford first in mathematics and a second in classics. He was successively curate at Checkendon, rector of Brighstone, rector of Alverstoke, dean of Westminster, bishop of Oxford (1845–1869), and bishop of Winchester.

Wilberforce's chief work was in church administration and in education of the clergy. He founded a theological college at Cuddesdon in 1854. Committed to the well-being of his church in relation to secular power, he sought to reconcile the differences between contending factions (especially Tractarians and Evangelicals), but this sometimes led to vacillation and to his displeasing all parties. Leaning somewhat toward the Anglo-Catholic Tractarians of the Oxford Movement, he nevertheless strongly opposed Roman Catholicism.

An amateur naturalist, he participated in the evolutionary debates, but overreached himself in his rhetoric at the British Association in 1860 and is reckoned to have "lost" the encounter with the Darwinian T.H. Huxley. However, in his review of *The Origin of Species* (*Quarterly Review*, 1860), Wilberforce showed significant deficiencies in Darwin's argument. More immediately important for the church was the controversy over the liberal *Essays and Reviews* (1860), which

Wilberforce also reviewed in *Quarterly Review*, restating the traditional view of a divinely inspired Bible—the source of moral authority for Christians.

Typifying mainstream Anglican thinking in the midcentury, Wilberforce initiated revision of the King James Bible, which led to the publication of the Revised Version (1881–1885). His dexterity ("slipperiness") in ecclesiastical politics earned him the sobriquet "Soapy Sam."

DAVID OLDROYD

Bibliography

Ashwell, Arthur R. and Reginald G. Wilberforce. *Life of the Right Reverend Samuel Wilberforce.* 1880–1882. 3 vols.

Meacham, Standish. *Lord Bishop: The Life of Samuel Wilberforce, 1805–1873.* 1970.

. . . . .

WILDE, OSCAR (1854-1900)

Author, wit, and an early adherent of the doctrine of **art for art's sake**, Oscar Wilde first attracted attention by his aesthetic appearance and exquisite taste. He began to gain notice as a writer with *The Happy Prince and Other Tales* (1888), and in the next seven years produced most of his major works—including *The Picture of Dorian Gray* (1890); such essays as "The Critic as Artist" (1890) and "The Soul of Man Under Socialism" (1891); and his best-known plays: *Lady Windermere's Fan* (1892), *Salomé* (1894), and *The Importance of Being Earnest* (1895). *The Ballad of Reading Gaol* (1898) shows a marked improvement over the earlier *Poems* (1881) and is Wilde's last major work. *De Profundis*, the important apologia that Wilde wrote in 1897, is published in full in Rupert Hart-Davis's edition of Wilde's letters.

Born in Ireland, Wilde went from Trinity College, Dublin, to Oxford, where he graduated in 1878. He lectured in America, including in the West, on aestheticism in 1882; married Constance Lloyd (1857–1898) in 1884; and began a two-year editorship of *Woman's World* in 1887. By then Wilde's homosexuality had appeared, eventually leading him to frequent contacts with the homosexual underworld. His association with Lord Alfred Douglas (1870-1945) resulted in a bitter quarrel with Douglas's father, the marquis of Queensberry. In 1895, after a spectacular series of trials, Wilde was sentenced to prison for two years. He died in Paris.

The diversity of Wilde's work—ornate, derivative poems, simple moral allegories, comic satire—suggests his use of different masks to reveal himself. Wilde is often identified with his cleverly ironical, amoral wits and dandys. The wits tend to speak in paradox and epigram, analyzing life to reveal its pleasures and absurdities, its lack of anything worthy of belief. Rational, cynical, "modern," they value art over nature, and concern themselves more with fashion—the proper knot of a tie—than morality. Yet a strong moral impulse is seen in the Puritans of Wilde's plays and in the fairy tales which teach the need for Christlike love and charity for the poor. Hedonism is also strong in Wilde—in the sensuous luxuriance of his early poems, the purple passages of *Dorian Gray*, the fascination with corruption of *The Sphinx* (1894), and such characters as Dorian and Salomé. These conflicting attitudes create a complex, polyphonic art, one in which Wilde can espouse both sides of an idea.

Though he is still controversial, Wilde's fame is now greater than was predicted by contemporaries who were offended by the artificiality of his art and by his sexual excesses. He played a major role in the revival of English drama; he satirized the differences between social conventions and society's real values; and even while asserting the uselessness of art, he defended the role of the artist in a materialistic world.

RICHARD BENVENUTO

Bibliography

Beckson, Karl, ed. *Oscar Wilde: The Critical Heritage.* 1970.

Chamberlin, J. E. *Ripe Was the Drowsy Hour: The Age of Oscar Wilde.* 1977.

Cohen, Philip K. *The Moral Vision of Oscar Wilde.* 1978.

Ellmann, Richard. *Oscar Wilde.* 1988.

Fletcher, Ian and John Stokes. "Oscar Wilde." In Richard J. Finneran, ed., *Anglo-Irish Literature: A Review of Research.* 1976.

Gagnier, Regina. *Idylls of the Marketplace: Oscar Wilde and the Victorian Public.* 1986.

Hart-Davis, Rupert, ed. *The Letters of Oscar Wilde.* 1962.

Hyde, H. Montgomery. *Oscar Wilde: A Biography.* 1975.

Mikhail, E. H. *Oscar Wilde: An Annotated Bibliography of Criticism.* 1978.

Nassaar, Christopher S. *Into the Demon Universe: A Literary Exploration of Oscar Wilde.* 1974.

San Juan, Epifanio, Jr. *The Art of Oscar Wilde.* 1967.

Shewan, Rodney. *Oscar Wilde: Art and Egotism.* 1977.

· · · · ·

WILDLIFE PROTECTION

Victorian decisions affecting the protection of wildlife depended more upon a species' appeal to popular sentimentalized anthropomorphism, balanced against the political and social influence of its human predators, than upon scientific evaluations. Britain's first act designed to protect wildlife, the Sea Birds Preservation Act (1869), established a closed season to protect breeding sea birds. It was inspired by an uneasy alliance of the Royal Society for the Prevention of Cruelty to Animals (1824), the British Association for the Advancement of Science (1831), which had been interested in bird preservation by Cambridge ornithologist Alfred Newton (1829-1907), and a movement founded by the anti-Darwinian clergyman-naturalist Francis Orpen Morris (1810-1893) in reaction to the slaughter that lower-class day trippers from the Yorkshire industrial towns perpetrated against birds nesting on East Riding sea cliffs. The Wild Birds Protection Act (1872) applied similarly to land birds. By 1896 five additional bird protection acts had created a body of legislation seldom enforced not only because of its inconsistent nomenclature and complexity, but also because of lingering nostalgia for bird nesting as a traditional rite of boyhood, and an abiding rural impression that birds, rather than the insects they ate, were prime culprits in the destruction of crops. Legislation concerned solely with the deliberate destruction of wildlife ignored totally the greater depredations wrought by increased cultivation, agricultural drainage projects, and continuing residential and industrial development.

Founded initially to fight the use of bird plumes as hat decorations, the Selborne Society (1886) rapidly expanded its concerns to include the preservation of plants and wild animals. It published a chatty, essentially nonscientific nature study magazine, *Nature Notes*, and conducted countryside rambles. By 1904, with 1,700 members in branches throughout England, it considered itself Britain's foremost proponent of the conservation of wildlife and the natural environment. The Selborne Society cooperated with the Bands of Mercy, founded in 1875 by Catherine Smithies (1795–1877), in attempting to indoctrinate children with a sense of compassion for animals. The Society for the Protection of Birds (1889), which was allowed to preface "Royal" to its title in 1904, was founded by Emily Williamson (1856–1936) in Didsbury, but moved to London in 1891. By 1898 it claimed 20,000 members and 152 branches. Prominent early officials included the popular naturalist William Henry Hudson (1841–1922), barrister Montague Sharpe (1856–1942), and Margaretta Louisa Lemon (1860–1953), who conducted the society's day-to-day business.

Only late in the Victorian era did sanctuaries for birds and animals begin to emerge. In 1888 a bird preserve was founded in the Norfolk Broads at Breydon. During the 1890s the London County Council experimented with nature walks and small preserves. The National Trust (1895) began to acquire land for a nature reserve at Wicken Fen, near Cambridge, in 1899. In 1902 the Selborne Society established its preserve for wildlife and plants at Perivale, in west London. But there were few sanctuaries until 1912 when, in exasperation with the National Trust's random and slowly paced acquisitions, professional naturalists founded the Society for the Promotion of Nature Reserves.

JOHN RANLETT

Bibliography

Allen, David Elliston. *The Naturalist in Britain: A Social History*. 1976.

Ranlett, John. "'Checking Nature's Desecration': Late-Victorian Environmental Organization." *Victorian Studies*, vol. 26, pp. 197–222.

Sheall, John. *Nature in Trust: The History of Nature Conservation in Britain*. 1976.

Stamp, Laurence Dudley. *Nature Conservation in Britain*. 1969.

Thomas, Keith. *Man and the Natural World: A History of the Modern Sensibility*. 1983.

· · · · ·

WILSON, CHARLOTTE (1854–1944)

Charlotte Mary Martin Wilson, a pioneer of early British anarchism, was born in 1854 at Kemerton, near Tewkesbury, and attended Merton Hall, Cambridge (later Newnham College) in 1873–1874. In 1876 she married a London stockbroker, Arthur Wilson, and settled at "Wyldes," a farmhouse near Hampstead Heath which she soon used for political gatherings. In 1884 she was the only woman elected to the first executive committee of the **Fabian Society**, where she formed a discussion group to study the works of Continental socialists, including Marx and Proudhon. The Fabians' chief proponent of anarcho-socialism, she wrote extensively for *Justice* (1884), *The Anarchist* (1885), *Practical Socialist* (1886), *Present Day* (1886), and *Fabian Tracts* (1886), and a sample of her work may be found in *Three Essays on Anarchism* (1979). In 1886 she cofounded *Freedom*, the most significant and durable English anarchist journal, with the recently arrived Peter Kropotkin; she continued to publish and edit *Freedom*, with pauses for ill health, until 1901. She founded a Fabian Woman's Group in 1908 to support women's suffrage, emigrated to the United States after her husband's death, and died in New York at ninety in April 1944.

Wilson shared Morris's and Kropotkin's hopes for anarchist/socialist education and an effective general strike, and the ethical qualities of her visionary communism emerge clearly in her theory of human development: "When each person directs his own life . . . throws his whole soul into the work he has chosen, and makes it the expression of his intensest purpose and desire, then, and then only, labour becomes pleasure, and its produce a work of art."

Charlotte Wilson was an ardent and isolated figure, almost unique in the male-dominated political landscape of late nineteenth-century England. John Henry Mackay's contemporary tribute to her in *The Anarchists* (1891) provides an appropriate epigraph: "whoever knew her, knew also that she was the most faithful, the most diligent, and the most impassioned champion of Communism in England."

FLORENCE S. BOOS

Bibliography

Blagg, Helen M. and Charlotte Wilson. *Women and Prisons*. 1912.

Walter, Nicholas, ed. *Three Essays on Anarchism.* 1979.

· · · · ·

WISEMAN, NICHOLAS PATRICK STEPHEN (1802–1865)

A theologian, linguistic scholar, and ecclesiastical administrator, Cardinal Wiseman influenced Newman and the Tractarians and was a leader of the Roman Catholic revival in England.

Wiseman studied for the priesthood in Rome, became rector of the English College in 1828, and returned to England in 1840 as president of St. Mary's College, Oscott, and coadjutor to Bishop Thomas Walsh, whom he succeeded as vicar apostolic of the London district in 1849. At the restoration of the Roman Catholic hierarchy in England (September 29, 1850), Wiseman was created a cardinal and first archbishop of Westminster. His impetuously indiscreet pastoral letter "From Out the Flaminian Gate" (1850) caused a storm of hostile opposition in England.

A notable preacher and lecturer, Wiseman was a founding editor of the *Dublin Review* (1836) and author of *Fabiola* (1855), a novel about the early Christian Church. His later years were clouded by ill health and many conflicts. The English bishops saw him as the embodiment of Vatican autocracy, and older English Roman Catholics continued to distrust him as too Romanized and dangerous to the traditionally delicate position of Roman Catholics in England.

He was, however, respected by intellectuals and popular with the Roman Catholic masses of the larger cities. Through force of personality, bold public image, and persuasive abilities, Wiseman raised the prestige of the Roman Catholic church in Victorian England.

C. GORDON-CRAIG

Bibliography

Ward, Wilfrid. *The Life and Times of Cardinal Wiseman*. 1897. 2 vols.

· · · · ·

WOMANHOOD

Victorians described the ideal of womanhood in a stream of etiquette books, sermons, educational tracts, manuals on domestic economy, popular poems, and novels. The virtues they admired—purity, honor, gentle and selfless accommodation to the needs of others—were derived from Enlightenment theorists and given moral intensity under evangelicalism. Working from assumptions regarding woman's biological weaknesses, a matter of natural law at the beginning of the century and of evolutionary science at the end, Victorians discussed sexual difference in terms of oppositions: men were strong, active, and intellectual, while women were fragile, passive, and emotional. Prescribed gender roles were consistent with these supposedly innate qualities and with the changed living conditions of the industrial revolution. New methods of production had separated the workplace from the home, taking men to the time discipline of factories while leaving women the task-oriented duties of child care and household management. For the rising middle classes, the ideal woman would be a worthy companion for her husband, a loving educator of her children, and a competent manager of her household.

Discussion of women's duties centered on the concepts of "mission," "sphere," and "influence." Woman's mission was to begin the moral regeneration of society by displaying the principles of Christianity in all her daily activities; her sphere was the home, a shelter for her own innocence and a sanctuary for her husband when he returned from the brutally competitive world of commerce. Within the domestic sphere, she could exercise her influence, a moral and spiritual force so strong that it was said to obviate the need for political power. Guiding her children's education and guarding her husband's integrity, she served as the conscience of the family and the state. Extolled as "the angel in the house" by poet Coventry Patmore and mythologized as a queen "of higher mystery" by essayist John Ruskin, she seemed to be a suprahuman figure.

Social critics such as Anna Jameson argued that the celebrated ideals were inconsistent with legal reality and irrelevant to single and working-class women. Theorists Harriet Martineau and John Stuart Mill attacked the scheme as an artificial construct enforcing women's subordination. Indeed, throughout the century, conservatives invoked the rhetoric of mission, sphere, and influence to restrict women's activities, especially in politics.

Although prescriptive literature may not be a reliable indicator of actual practice, the widespread popularity of books on conduct, child rearing, and household management suggests that they addressed the needs of middle-class women anxious to define their roles in a changing society. Victorian women were urged to see themselves, their daily responsibilities, and their moral destiny with great seriousness. Moreover, activists realized that the new ideal could be an argument for change. Those who sought improved rights for women in education, work, and politics often began by insisting on the need to take women's noblest qualities—integrity, charity, and patience—beyond the home and into society.

ROBIN SHEETS

Bibliography

Auerbach, Nina. *Woman and the Demon: The Life of a Victorian Myth.* 1982.

Bell, Susan Groag and Karen M. Offen. *Woman, the Family, and Freedom: The Debate in Documents.* 1983. 2 vols.

Berman, Sandra. *Fit Work for Women.* 1979.

Burstyn, Joan N. *Victorian Education and the Ideal of Womanhood.* 1980.

Crow, Duncan. *The Victorian Woman.* 1971.

Gorham, Deborah. *The Victorian Girl and the Feminine Ideal.* 1982.

Helsinger, Elizabeth K., Robin Lauterbach Sheets, and William Veeder, eds. *The Woman Question: Society and Literature in Britain and America, 1837–1883.* 1983. 3 vols.

Klein, Viola. *The Feminine Character: History of an Ideology.* 1949.

Taylor, Gordon R. *The Angel-Makers: A Study in Psychological Origins of Social Change, 1750–1850.* 1974.

Vicinus, Martha, ed. *Suffer and Be Still: Women in the Victorian Age.* 1972.

—— , ed. *A Widening Sphere: Changing Roles of Victorian Women.* 1977.

See also ELLIS, SARAH STICKNEY; FAMILY; GENTLEMAN; SPORTS AND GAMES, WOMEN'S

. . . . .

WOMEN IN ART

Although the Victorian period produced many women artists, their opportunities and progress were limited considerably by their gender. Because women were traditionally identified with the amateur "accomplishment art" appropriate to genteel feminine upbringing and with so-called minor genres and media such as miniature painting and **watercolor**, they had difficulty being taken seriously as professionals. Moreover, Victorian notions of female decorum operated to restrict their subject matter; women artists were expected to produce work that was delicate and chaste: floral paintings, portraits, nature studies, sentimental domestic scenes.

Their most daunting impediment, however, was achieving adequate formal instruction.

Usually taught in segregated classes, they were not routinely permitted to draw from life and certainly not from nude models, though such training was essential if they were to produce the historical and narrative paintings so popular with the Victorians. Establishments like the Female School of the Government Schools of Design, opened in London in 1843, were specifically oriented toward commercial and decorative rather than fine arts. Not surprisingly, therefore, many of the most successful women artists came from either wealthy or artistic families who could supply private tutelage and encouragement.

A formidable barrier to professional validation was the **Royal Academy.** Women were informally excluded from its schools, the most prestigious venue for professional education, until 1860, when Laura Herford was inadvertently admitted, having signed her entry with initials rather than her full name. Still, women students there increased only gradually in number, and they continued to suffer discriminatory treatment. For example, they were not allowed to draw from undraped male models until 1893 nor to work in coeducational classes until 1903. Even then, life classes remained segregated.

Partly because paintings were submitted anonymously for jurying, some women did, however, exhibit regularly in the annual Royal Academy shows, especially in the last third of the century. But no women were elected to full membership in the association between 1819 and 1936. Thus they remained outside the network of established power and were deprived of opportunities to develop or assert professional authority.

In reaction to these patterns of exclusion, various women's groups were founded to help provide training, exhibition space, and moral support for women artists, such as the Society of Female Artists, which was organized in 1857 and prospered in various forms for the rest of the century under aristocratic sponsorship. Yet this separation in some ways only reinforced women's secondary status, subjecting them to continuing critical double standards in media, subject matter, and technique.

Despite these obstacles, a number of artists in varied areas won modest and occasionally spectacular success, including the first woman to attend a Royal Academy lecture, the history painter Henrietta Ward (1832-

1924); the literary portraitist Margaret Gillies (1803-1887); the genre painters Emily Osborn (b. 1834; fl. 1851-1908) and Sophie Anderson (1823-c. 1898); the illustrators **Kate Greenaway** (1846-1901) and Mary Ellen Edwards (b. 1839; fl. 1862-1908); the botanical artist Marianne North (1830-1890); **Elizabeth Thompson Butler** (1846?-1933), famed for her dramatic military panoramas; and the sculptors Susan Durant (182?-1873) and Mary Thornycroft (1814-1895). Ward, Osborn, Butler, Durant, and Thornycroft all received royal patronage.

Women who sought careers as scholars rather than creators of art likewise encountered hindrances. Although the founding of many new museums, the opening of private collections to the public, and the development of a new class of untutored patrons produced opportune conditions for research and critical writing in the emerging discipline of art history, women were generally barred from institutional employment. They also typically lacked the funds and mobility for foreign travel, so necessary at a time when satisfactory art reproductions were not yet readily available. Thus they often took on the underpaid, low-prestige tasks of writing guidebooks or translating and editing art documents—work that accorded them relatively little authority yet was important to the advance of scholarship.

Among women who nevertheless were able to make serious contributions during the century were Mary Merrifield (1804/5-1889), whose translations of historical texts on painting techniques remain in print; Elizabeth Rigby, later **Lady Eastlake** (1809-1893), noted for her translations of German art historical works and for her periodical criticism; Mary Margaret Heaton (1836-1883), who translated the writings and produced the first English biography of Albrecht Dürer; and Emily F.S. Pattison, later Lady Dilke (1840-1904), the author of rigorously researched contextual studies of the arts and their patronage in France from the Renaissance to 1800.

The most influential woman scholar in this period was the prolific **Anna Jameson** (1794-1860), who has been called England's first professional art historian. Basically self-taught, she moved from early general writings, including travel literature, to specialization in art with the publication of her *Hand-*

book to the *Public Galleries of Art in and Near London* (1842) and a companion volume on private collections two years later. Writing in a graceful, readable style, she widened and educated the audience for art through works like her series of forty-five articles on the then undervalued Italian "primitive" artists that appeared in the *Penny Magazine* from 1843 to 1845 and were collected as *Memoirs of the Early Italian Painters* (1845). Her most ambitious work was her imposing study of Christian iconography, *The Poetry of Sacred and Legendary Art*; volumes appeared in 1848, 1850, and 1852, the series being completed posthumously by Jameson's literary executor Lady Eastlake. In this as in her other writings she combined objectivity and sympathy, emphasizing the historical contexts and functions of art.

KRISTINE OTTESEN GARRIGAN

Bibliography

Clayton, Ellen C. *English Female Artists*. 1876.

Harris, Ann Sutherland and Linda Nochlin. *Women Artists: 1550–1950*. 1977.

Holcomb, Adele M. "Anna Jameson: The First Professional English Art Historian." *Art History*, vol. 6, pp. 171–187.

Nunn, Pamela Gerrish. "Ruskin's Patronage of Women Artists." *Woman's Art Journal*, vol. 2, pp. 8–13.

Sherman, Claire Richter, ed., with Adele M. Holcomb. *Women as Interpreters of the Visual Arts, 1820–1979*. 1981.

Wood, Christopher. *Dictionary of Victorian Painters*. 2d rev. ed., 1978.

Yeldham, Charlotte. *Women Artists in Nineteenth-Century France and England*. 1984.

See also ARTISTS' MODELS

· · · · ·

WOMEN'S EMPLOYMENT

Approximately one-third of the workers in Victorian Britain were female. Most of these were household servants, but many women worked in agriculture, industry, and com-merce. Women's share in the labor force declined slightly from 34 percent in 1861 to 30 percent in 1911. Industrialization dramatically altered the type of work women did; although many women still worked as **servants,** by the beginning of the twentieth century opportunities had arisen for women in business, industry, and **civil service.**

Industrialization created a stronger distinction between home and workplace than had previously existed. In preindustrial Britain, women tended crops, mined coal, created textiles at home, and made and marketed agricultural products. Census records from 1841 onward reveal that women still helped produce the food and goods that fed and clothed Victorian Britain. However, continuous technological change made people less able to support themselves by working at home. Hired **agricultural laborers** and machinery replaced the small holding, and manufactured textiles rendered much **domestic industry** obsolete. Before 1850 families relying on the income of both husband and wife found that men's wages did not rise as rapidly as women's work declined. Having to work away from home made women's employment more difficult if they had children.

Between 50 percent and 70 percent of working-class single women worked outside the home. Census figures seldom accurately reported married women's piecework or part-time employment, yet the census of 1911 reveals that 10 percent of married women and 30 percent of widows worked; in London's working-class districts, 20 percent of married women and 50 percent of widows worked. Wives abstained from paid employment if the family was sufficiently prosperous, but reentered the work force when widowed or if the husband's wages proved inadequate.

Employers saw women as an enormous supply of relatively inexpensive labor. Men might become unemployed when women could be hired more cheaply. Thus male-dominated **trade unions** tried to achieve male monopoly in certain trades. They were aided by the belief, popular among the middle class, that work involving heavy physical labor was not "suitable" for women. For example, in 1851 agriculture had 199,000 female workers (and 1,284,000 male workers); by the 1880s it was becoming rare to see women working in fields. Machinery was increasingly used, while the Agricultural Trades Union, established in 1872, raised the wages of male workers enough for rural families to rely on one breadwinner's income.

Reforms helped alleviate the poor working conditions of many women. The Mines and Colliery Act (1842) prohibited women and children from working in mines. Between 1844 and 1850 Parliament regulated the hours of women working in factories. Such legislation also protected male workers, for in practice men's hours were reduced as well. Women's long hair and flowing dress were hazardous around machinery; laws requiring machinery to be encased reduced everyone's accident risks.

Some "women's work" was transformed into "men's work" when made sufficiently remunerative. Men's wages rose in coal mining and agriculture as women left these lines of work. Highly paid skilled labor was deemed neither economical nor "suitable" for unskilled females. J. Ramsay MacDonald's *Women in the Printing Trades: A Sociological Study* (1904) reported that typesetting continued to be predominately male and well paid under the typesetters union; but that in bookbinding (which became mechanized during the nineteenth century), wages fell as the percentage of women binding books increased from fewer than 25 percent in 1841 to more than 50 percent in 1881.

Few Victorians considered household service "unsuitable" for women, although servants worked long hours and carried heavy burdens. Servants, 90 percent of whom were women, were the largest category of workers in Victorian Britain; household service increased from 13 percent to 16 percent of the labor force during the nineteenth century. In 1871, 1,336,534 women worked as servants. Unless they employed three or more servants, housewives did varying amounts of their own housework, although laundry was customarily hired out. As Elizabeth Gaskell illustrated in *Cranford* (1853), fastidious class distinctions made middle-class women pretend that they did not cook or clean even when they did these tasks.

Female employments declining under industrialization included spinning, weaving, and lacemaking. Abrupt changes in fashion disrupted the glove making and millinery trades; basket weaving disappeared when less expensive imports flooded the market. Even-

tually the sewing machine displaced **seamstresses**, although clothing "sweatshops" continued to employ many women.

Women rarely entered certain lines of employment. In 1861, out of 38,991 people working as lawyers, law court officers and law stationers, only twenty-one were women. Similarly, out of 38,441 physicians, surgeons, and druggists, only 2,426 were women. Few women worked in railroads, chemicals, building, or iron and steel, although these were the leading industries.

Women's wages were much less than men's. In the 1830s single men working in agriculture earned 25 pounds per annum while women earned five pounds, and cotton mills in Lancashire paid women from 6 to 9 shillings while men were paid 10 to 20 shillings per week. In the worsted industry, men's wages rose 66 percent between 1855 and 1865 while women's wages rose only 6 percent. In the London clothing trades, women made half of what men made, even though the proportion of women tailors rose from 38 percent to 51 percent. In 1906 women in these trades earned 15 shillings a week or less, and despite inflation, their wages had not changed since 1886. By the end of the century women held 70 percent of all teaching appointments below the university level; yet in 1914 a certificated male head teacher earned 176 pounds per year, while a female head teacher earned 122 pounds.

Some new occupations offered women new opportunities. Under Florence Nightingale, **nursing** evolved into a more respectable profession. Retailing saw many family-operated shops replaced by larger establishments with hired shop assistants. Female **shopworkers** in the 1880s earned 50 pounds per year, 20 percent less than male shop assistants. As civil service grew, so did women's share: in 1851 only 2,169, or 4 percent of central government employees were women; by 1911 the number of women was 39,773, or 21 percent of central government employees. Most of these were post office workers or telephone and telegraph operators. Clerical work increased: in 1861 only 279 women were **clerks**; in 1901, 57,736 women represented 11 percent of all clerical workers. By 1911, 18 percent of clerks were women. Over 90 percent of these women were secretaries or typists in business or commerce.

Some of these new occupations appealed to middle-class women who had traditionally not only regarded most female occupations to be beneath their status, but also cherished the leisure of gentlewomen, believing firmly that while a "woman" might work, a "lady" does not. Farmers' wives and tradesmen's wives gladly abandoned the dairy or shop if they could afford to do so. Yet as many as one-third of middle-class Victorian women were unmarried and unemployed; many lacked income. In "Female Industry," in the *Edinburgh Review* (1859), Harriet Martineau argued that women's work of all kinds needed to be better valued and better paid. John Stuart Mill in *The Subjection of Women* (1869) and John Duguid Milne in *The Industrial Employment of Women in the Middle and Lower Ranks* (1870) argued that employment be made more available and more socially acceptable for single middle-class women. However, William Rathbone Greg's "Why Are Women Redundant?" in *Literary and Social Judgments* (1873), which probably more nearly represented the prevailing opinion, criticized proposals to employ middle-class women. Although women of the working classes always labored, it was not until late in the century that nursing, civil service, office work, and secondary schools for girls created opportunities for middle-class women who sought employment.

KARLA KRAMPERT WALTERS

Bibliography

Davidoff, Leonore and Belinda Westover, eds. *Our Work, Our Lives, Our Words: Women's History and Women's Work.* 1986.

Holcombe, Lee. *Victorian Ladies at Work: Middle-Class Working Women in England and Wales.* 1973.

John, Angela. *Unequal Opportunities: Women's Employment in England, 1800-1918.* 1986.

Neff, Wanda. *Victorian Working Women: An Historical and Literary Study of Women in British Industries and Professions 1832-1850.* 1966.

Pinchbeck, Ivy. *Women Workers and the Industrial Revolution, 1750-1850.* 1930.

Richards, Eric. "Women in the British Economy Since About 1700: An Interpretation." *History*, vol. 59, pp. 337-357.

Schmiechen, James. *Sweated Industries and Sweated Labor: The London Clothing Trades, 1860-1914.* 1984.

Tilly, Louise and Joan Scott. *Women, Work and Family.* 1978.

See also *FACTORIES; GOVERNESSES; LACEMAKERS; LANGHAM PLACE CIRCLE*

· · · · ·

WOMEN'S FRIENDSHIPS

Friendships among women constitute a subculture of Victorian society which illuminates the separate spheres of the two sexes and indicates the complexity of women's contribution to Victorian life. The bonding of women occurred within the family structure during the crises of childbirth, marriage and death, and outside the biological family when women formed communities for their economic and spiritual self-development. The Victorians lauded female friendships because women were considered morally superior to men; hence the ties among women catalyzed social transformation, cutting across class boundaries to achieve the Victorian ideal of society as a family.

Diaries and letters show that women formed networks of affective relationships which included the extended family as well as close friends, often lasted a lifetime, and provided emotional and physical support during the female rituals of courtship, marriage, birth, nursing, menopause, and death. Letters written between sisters mitigated the pain of pregnancy and the fear of childbirth just as diaries passed among cousins reassured young women about to marry. Separated from the world of men, women gained prestige and support from nurturing other women both within and without the family structure. **Philanthropy** provided women with a sense of purpose, later manifested in the development of social services, as upper- and middle-class women campaigned against prostitution, provided food and clothing to the poor, and conducted classes in hygiene and child care.

Charity might bind together women of different classes but women's communities also formed around educational and religious institutions. Boarding school friendships catalyzed adolescent closeness, and bonds formed during the school years gave women who chose not to devote themselves to their families a network of professional and emotional support. The Victorians' concept of women as self-sacrificing underscored women's commitment to the Church and heightened women's sense of themselves as pure and more spiritual than men. The Victorian ideal of service permeated women's communities, yet its foundation in the closeness of the mother-daughter bond and its manifestation in women's friendships threatened male hegemony. Women authors built a literary tradition of their own by reading the works and personal correspondence of other women, used female bonding to create fictional communities, and established maternal relationships with their audience. The pervasiveness, strength, and durability of women's friendships during the Victorian age highlights the many-faceted roles within and without the family played by women in their domestic, economic, spiritual, and social contributions to the diversity of Victorian society.

CYNTHIA HUFF

Bibliography

Auerbach, Nina. *Communities of Women: An Idea in Fiction.* 1978.

Faderman, Lillian. *Surpassing the Love of Men: Romantic Friendships and Love Between Women from the Renaissance to the Present.* 1981.

Moers, Ellen. *Literary Women: The Great Writers.* 1977.

Prochaska, Frank K. *Women and Philanthropy in Nineteenth-Century England.* 1980.

Showalter, Elaine. *A Literature of Their Own: British Women Novelists from Brontë to Lessing.* 1977.

Vicinus, Martha. *Independent Women: Work and Community for Single Women, 1850–1920.* 1985.

See also HOMOSEXUALITY;
SINGLE WOMEN; SISTERHOODS

· · · · ·

WOOD, ELLEN PRICE
(1814–1887)

Popularly known as Mrs. Henry Wood, Ellen Price Wood was one of the most phenomenally successful writers of the nineteenth century. Wood was the daughter of a glove manufacturer and the wife of a prominent member of a banking and shipping firm. After more than ten years of contributing short stories to *New Monthly Magazine* and *Bentley's Miscellany*, she published her first novel in 1860. Written in twenty-eight days, *Danesbury House* won a prize of 100 pounds offered by the Scottish Temperance League. Her unprecedented commercial and popular success began with *East Lynne* (1861), a prototype of the **sensation novel**, which became a best seller after it was favorably reviewed by the *Times* (January 25, 1862).

In 1867 Wood became editor and proprietor of the *Argosy*, a monthly magazine that printed the bulk of her later writing, including the "Johnny Ludlow stories" (reprinted in six series, 1874–1899), often considered her best work. Among the other more notable novels produced during her remarkably prolific career are *Mrs. Halliburton's Troubles* (1862), *The Channings* (1862), *The Shadow of Ashlydyat* (1863), which was Wood's own favorite, *Lord Oakburn's Daughters* (1864), and *A Life's Secret* (1867), which contained such a hostile portrait of strikes and trade unions that an angry mob besieged the publisher's offices.

Despite the sensational and the supernatural which figure largely in her work, Wood's art, like her life, was firmly grounded in middle-class values and attitudes. Wood has been called the most intrinsically representative woman novelist of the mid-Victorian era.

MARILYN J. KURATA

Bibliography

Elliott, Jeanne B. "A Lady to the End: The Case of Isabel Vane." *Victorian Studies*, vol. 19, pp. 329–344.

Elwin, Malcolm. *Victorian Wallflowers.* 1934.

Hughes, Winifred. *The Maniac in the Cellar: Sensation Novels of the 1860s.* 1980.

Sergeant, Adeline. "Mrs. Henry Wood." In *Women Novelists of Queen Victoria's Reign.* 1897.

Wood, Charles W. *Memorials of Mrs. Henry Wood.* 1894.

· · · · ·

WOOD ENGRAVING

The era of mass-produced woodblock illustration very nearly coincided with Queen Victoria's reign. Blocks made from the endgrain of boxwood were first used for woodcuts late in the eighteenth century. Boxwood is hard enough to let the artist use fine details, and it could withstand the force of mechanical presses. Although other methods of reproduction were available, woodblock's comparative cheapness made it the most common means of **illustration** until it was superceded by photomechanical processes in the 1890s. As high-speed presses and cheaper paper made it possible to produce art for the millions, many of the period's eminent artists created drawings for wood engraving, and noted illustrators worked almost entirely in the medium. Wood engraving illustrated books, periodicals, catalogues, and advertisements, and it made possible the new innovation of pictorial journalism.

The first book to use engravings done on the endgrain of boxwood was *The General History of Quadrupeds* (1790), by Thomas Bewick (1753-1828). Bewick's white line illustrations were actually drawn on the wood with engraving tools, and his followers, through the early Victorian period, were also artist-artisans who engraved their own designs.

In the commercial era that followed, labor was divided: artists produced the drawings, and engravers incised them on woodblocks. Stereotyping and later electrotyping (first used in 1839) could make multiple copies of the same block for high-speed presses. In the 1860s it became possible to print photographs directly on woodblocks; the engraver would then cut away the white areas and use various hatching and stippling techniques to reproduce the photograph's tones and shades.

One of the engraving firms noted for its high-quality work was Dalziel Brothers. (The four active "brothers" were actually George, Edward, Margaret, and John). George Dalziel engraved the first drawing John Leech (1817-1864) did for *Punch* and made blocks for the

initial number of the *Illustrated London News*. The Dalziel Brothers' Camden Press (founded in 1857) was the choice of many artists who did illustrated books. Other noted engravers included the radical **William James Linton** (1812-1897) and Henry Vizetelly (1820-1894), who drew up the prospectus for the *Illustrated London News* and later helped found its slightly less successful competitor, the *Pictorial Times* (1843-1848).

The *Illustrated London News* (1842-) was the pioneer of pictorial journalism. Although some sensational illustrations owed more to imagination than observation, its staff artists roamed the world to send back sketches of battles, explorations, and courtroom dramas which were then rapidly transferred to woodblocks by a large corps of engravers.

In the 1860s a number of magazines became noted for the quality of their illustrations, including *Good Words, Cornhill*, the *Sunday Magazine*, and *St. Paul's*. The Frenchman Gustave Doré (1832-1833) produced an extraordinary record of the contrasts between wealth and poverty in *London: A Pilgrimage* (1872). Techniques for the commercial reproduction of colored pictures done from wood blocks (first established in the 1850s) expanded the medium and made the illustrations of children's books a growing field.

In the 1890s, newspaper illustrators were largely replaced by photographers, and photographic techniques could also reproduce art. Wood engraving, shorn of its major commercial uses, passed back into the hands of artist-artisans, largely through the influence of the arts and crafts movement. William Morris's Kelmscott Press (1891) was the forerunner of the private presses which continued, into the twentieth century, to use wood engraving as an artistic medium.

SALLY MITCHELL

Bibliography

Bliss, Douglas Percy. *A History of Wood Engraving.* 1964.

de Maré, Eric. *The Victorian Woodblock Illustrators.* 1981.

Engen, Rodney K. *Dictionary of Victorian Wood Engravers.* 1985.

Lindley, Kenneth. *The Woodblock Engravers.* 1970.

Linton, William J. *Wood Engraving: Manual of Instruction.* 1884.

·　·　·　·　·

WOOD, JOHN GEORGE (1827-1889)

From 1851 until his death, John George Wood produced popular illustrated books and articles on **natural history** which were repeatedly reprinted and sold widely in English-speaking countries. His publications and lectures were the fruit of personal experience, correspondence and contacts with biologists, and a thorough acquaintance with the literature.

Educated at Oxford University and ordained as a minister in the Church of England, Wood supported a large family by writing. His best-known books are *Common Objects of the Sea-Shore* (1857), *Common Objects of the Microscope* (1861), *The Illustrated Natural History* (1859-1863), *Homes Without Hands* (1864-1865), and *Insects at Home* (1871-1872). From 1897 he gave annual lecture tours in England, visiting the United States in 1883 and 1884. Wood illustrated the lectures with colored chalk sketches on a canvas.

Wood's articles appeared in many popular magazines, including *Leisure Hour, Good Words, Once a Week,* and *Sunday Magazine,* as well as leading children's periodicals. In his articles he focused almost exclusively on British natural history topics, in a lively and relaxed manner. In the late 1870s and 1880s he must have written at least one article a month.

Although Wood did not contribute to the science of natural history, he interpreted it to a very wide audience. Some of his readers would become the biologists of the next generation.

ELLEN B. WELLS

Bibliography

Crosland, Newton. *Rambles Round My Life: An Autobiography 1819-1860.* 1898.

Wood, Theodore. *The Reverend J. G. Wood.* 1890.

·　·　·　·　·

WORDSWORTHIANISM

Followers of the poet William Wordsworth (1770-1850) were known, often pejoratively, as "Wordsworthians." They were more interested in Wordsworth as a personal model and faithful guide to life than in his poetry per se. The most prominent, who attended Oxford and Cambridge in the 1830s when Wordsworth's reputation stood highest, offered personal homage to the older poet. Wordsworthianism was most in the public eye from 1830-1845 and 1870-1885.

Henry Taylor (1800-1886), who met Wordsworth in 1823, championed him against both the poetry of the younger romantics and the philosophy of the Benthamites; his much-discussed preface to *Philip van Artevelde* (1834) defined a Wordsworthian poetics. It was through Taylor that John Stuart Mill, who revealed his admiration for Wordsworth's healing powers in his *Autobiography* (1873), met the poet in 1831. Taylor also introduced Aubrey de Vere (1814-1902); de Vere demonstrated his veneration by making yearly pilgrimages to Wordsworth's grave in the 1850s.

In 1829 John Wilson complained in *Blackwood's* that some young "disciples" of Wordsworth talked of his poetry as "actual revelation." An early strain in Wordsworthianism was the need for religious consolation: many young Wordsworthians, like Frederick Faber (1814-1863), participated in the Oxford Movement. Another Wordsworthian of High Church sympathies was William Gladstone, the future prime minister; he studied classics with Charles Wordsworth (1806-1892, the poet's nephew) at Oxford, and later entertained Wordsworth in London. In the 1830s Gladstone read Wordsworth before speeches in the Commons, and he used his influence with Robert Peel to help Wordsworth receive a pension in 1842. One of the leaders of the Oxford Movement, John Keble, presented Wordsworth with an honorary degree in 1839.

By the 1870s Wordsworthians felt that their poet's teachings were being eclipsed and made greater efforts to popularize him. Stopford Brooke (1832-1916) devoted nine lectures in *Theology in the English Poets* (1874) to Wordsworth, and Leslie Stephen's "Wordsworth's Ethics" (*Cornhill Magazine,* 1876) extends the case for Wordsworth as a philosopher. Matthew Arnold, whose father was intimate with Wordsworth, argues in his introduction to an edition of Wordsworth's poems (1879) that Wordsworth must be rescued from his admirers, and that "we cannot do him justice until we dismiss his formal philosophy." Arnold confesses, however, that he too is a "Wordsworthian."

In 1880 Wordsworthians gathered at Grasmere to found the Wordsworth Society. Charles Wordsworth was the first president, and others included Matthew Arnold and James Russell Lowell, then American ambassador to Britain. After sponsoring numerous publications, the society amiably voted to dissolve in 1886, when their original goals had been met. Wordsworthians were subjected to ridicule by Victorians who favored more vigorous poets (like Byron) or more up-to-date bards (like Browning). By the turn of the century they were considered old-fashioned; Ezra Pound anachronistically described a stuffy Roman in "Homage to Sextus Propertius" (1919) as an "ancient, respected, Wordsworthian" with the confidence that postwar audiences would get the joke.

DAVID E. LATANÉ, JR.

Bibliography

Arnold, Matthew. *Essays in Criticism: Second Series.* 1888.

Logan, James. *Wordsworthian Criticism: A Guide and Bibliography.* 1961.

Peek, Katherine. *Wordsworth in England: Studies in the History of His Fame.* 1943.

· · · · ·

WORKHOUSE

The deterrent workhouse was the chief instrumentality of the New **Poor Law** (Poor Law Amendment Act) of 1834. This legislation was supposed to drive the able-bodied poor to labor by encouraging a system of uniform workhouses run on the punitive principle of "less eligibility," and by prohibiting outdoor relief. These stern conditions were not realized and in the seventy years that followed workhouses were transformed, haltingly and unevenly, from "Bastiles" intended to punish the able-bodied into places of refuge for the aged, the sick, and deserted, orphaned, and illegitimate children.

The workhouse policy of 1834 failed because the new Poor Law Commission was not empowered to require the building and maintenance of uniform workhouses, and because the effective prohibition of outdoor relief to the able-bodied was never possible. No more than a third of all able-bodied paupers on relief were ever actually in the workhouse. Most inmates were genuinely impotent, and the proportion of these old, sick, and child paupers increased over time. To these blameless poor the principle of deterrence was not supposed to apply. But ambivalence persisted on this point and hindered the transformation of the workhouse into a national system of residential care.

Over the second half of the century various factors helped change many workhouses from punitive to service institutions. In new buildings encouraged by civic pride and easier financing, workhouse doctors raised the standard of their infirmaries and struggled to focus administrative energies upon the specialized needs of a largely ailing inmate population. The growing status of the medical profession, and consequently workhouse doctors' greater freedom from lay control, encouraged these tendencies. From the 1880s a new awareness of the root causes of unemployment helped erase vestiges of the deterrence ideology and workhouse discipline relaxed; amenities, even entertainments, might be permitted. Better understanding of nutrition meant an improved diet. By 1900 workhouse schools had nearly disappeared; the children attended local elementary schools. But these gains were not easily, or evenly, won. Even after 1900 many small rural workhouses harbored the residue of deterrence; their infirmaries were places of passive cruelty, their food unpalatable at best. The legend of the early Victorian workhouse, its lurid exaggerations around a core of truth, found an echo in these lingering indignities.

MARK NEUMAN

Bibliography

Crowther, M. A. *The Workhouse System, 1834–1929: The History of an English Social Institution.* 1981.

New Ward for the Casual Poor at Marylebone Workhouse. Illustrated London News,
28 September 1867. Library Company of Philadelphia.

Digby, Anne. *Pauper Palaces.* 1978.

Webb, Sidney and Beatrice Webb. *English Poor Law Policy.* 1910; rpt. 1963.

. . . . .

WORKING-CLASS CLUBS AND ASSOCIATIONS

The growth of the manufacturing population in the nineteenth century caused an explosion of voluntary guilds, fraternities, clubs, and societies that contributed to the political, social, and economic advancement of the working class.

Social movements, trade unionism, and politics spawned many associations. In 1821 **Owenite socialism** led the printer George Mudie to found the London Cooperative Society, the first of many such associations. The National Association for the Protection of Labour (1831) made an early attempt, with some success, to unite all trade societies under its banner. Irish reformers galvanized their opposition to British authority through Daniel O'Connell's Catholic Association (1823), and radical political societies like the London Working Men's Association (1836) attracted great public support by calling for universal male suffrage, annual parliaments, and secret ballots. One notable result of the activities of such associations, and of the many that followed, was the granting of the franchise to town workers in 1867. Less successful were later attempts to make adult education available to the working class, though Ruskin College (1899) and the Workers' Education Association (1903) were initially well received.

Hundreds of informal, social clubs met in local pubs, which served as centers of working-class social life by providing numerous activities, informal opportunities for business contacts, and frequent opportunities for social drinking and dining. It was such conviviality that ultimately ritualized the popular roast beef and ale dinner. Retreatlike alternatives to the more boisterous alehouses were offered by The Working Men's Club Movement, founded in 1862 by the Unitarian minister Henry Solly. The movement, which established a network of clubs that provided members with cheap food and quiet reading rooms, was promoted by clergymen anxious to encourage temperance and inculcate workers with middle-class values of respectability.

Most club members came from the better-paying occupations and were almost exclusively male. However, after overcoming some initial skepticism and resistance, female clubs representing most interests soon sprang up, at first as counterparts to local male clubs. Though often plagued by a poverty of funds and a more volatile membership, once accepted such clubs multiplied quickly.

Friendly Societies, nonpolitical, nonreligious organizations that provided members with various kinds of insurance, were the most important working-class associations to experience rapid development in the nineteenth century. By 1874 some 32,000 societies at home and abroad claimed over four million members. Many small, local clubs eventually became affiliated with one of the centralized "orders," which often boasted huge memberships. In 1884, for example, the Manchester Unity of Oddfellows served half a million members in over 4,000 lodges. The Female Foresters, the Odd Sisters, and the Ancient Shepherdesses were a few of the many Friendly Societies available to women.

Though initially suspected of subversive aims and sometimes criticized for encouraging excessive drinking, working-class clubs and societies generally improved the welfare of their members. By fostering small labor communities, such societies contributed to the formation of a working-class consciousness, which in itself helped guarantee a continuation of broad social reform.

STEVEN N. CRAIG

Bibliography

Baernreither, Josef M. *English Associations of Working Men.* 1893.

Bailey, Peter. *Leisure and Class in Victorian England.* 1978.

Gosden, P. H. J. H. *The Friendly Societies in England, 1815–1875.* 1961.

Taylor, J. *From Self-Help to Glamour: The Working Men's Club, 1860–1970.* 1972.

· · · · ·

WORKING-CLASS LITERATURE

Working-class literature emerged with the social changes surrounding urban industrialization that brought into being the term "working class" (first used in 1813 by Robert Owen). It is estimated that literacy increased fivefold between 1780 and 1830; cheaper methods of papermaking, printing, and distribution were developed, and in the social revolutions of the early nineteenth century, printed matter assumed a central role for self-improvement, political organization, and entertainment. Earlier popular literature, produced for a largely rural population, had taken the form of **broadsheets**, chapbooks, and serial "number books." Working-class literature developed from these roots and, in particular, exploited the potential of cheap periodicals.

William Cobbett (1763–1835) was a pioneer in the field. The self-educated son of a farm laborer, he combined vigorous plainness of style with radical sentiments, and his prolific writings helped form the new audience. His *Political Register*, reduced to twopence, sold an estimated 200,000 copies in two months and provoked the government into taxing cheap periodicals (the Seditious Publications Act, 1816). A war against the "taxes on knowledge" ensued. Henry Hetherington's illegal *Poor Man's Guardian* (1831–1836) campaigned for the 1832 Reform Act and its success helped secure the reduction of the tax in 1836. Feargus O'Connor's Chartist *Northern Star* (1837–1852) may be seen as the last major journal of this heroic phase, although *Reynolds's Weekly Newspaper* (1850–1962) maintained radical views in a Fleet Street dominated by commercial concerns, and smaller left-wing periodicals, such as *The Bee-hive Newspaper* (1861–1876), continued to the end of the century.

Educational literature was pioneered by the utilitarian Society for the Diffusion of Useful Knowledge with the *Penny Magazine* (1842–1846). Although the **Penny Magazine** soon became associated with the educated artisan class, cheap informational material established itself as an important sector of working-class literature, from the publications of William and Robert Chambers (some 170,000 sets of *Chambers' Information for the People* were sold 1833–1870), through cheap reprints of standard poets issued by William Milner of Halifax, to John Dicks's huge English Library of Standard Works, begun in 1883.

Out of this serious readership emerged working-class writers of autobiography, poetry, journalism, and fiction. Samuel Bamford's *Autobiography* (collected edition, 1968) and William Cobbett's *Rural Rides* (1830) remain major literary achievements. In the north, the emergence of dialect literature, as exampled in *Ben Brierley's Journal* (1869–1885), overlapped with dialect performance poetry and the development of the music hall culture. More derivative were a succession of working-class poets, including **Thomas Cooper** (1805–1892), Gerald Massey (1818–1907), and the Northumberland poet, Joseph Skipsey (1832–1903).

The working-class audience also sought the entertaining literature increasingly provided by a commercialized press. Street ballads, published by James Catnach and his rivals until the 1860s, came under increasing competition from journals and the penny issue fiction introduced by Edward Lloyd. His plagiarism of Dickens's novel as *The Penny Pickwick* (1837–1839) by "Bos" (probably Thomas Peckett Prest) may well have sold more than the original, and J. M. Rymer's *Ada the Betrayed* (1845) was one of many successors. *The Mysteries of London* (1846–1848), a radical narrative focusing on urban contrasts between rich and poor, and other prolific writing earned **G.W.M. Reynolds** (1814–1879) the obituary title of "the most popular writer in England."

By the 1860s penny issue fiction had degenerated into ostensibly juvenile "blood and thunder" (which nevertheless retained a significant adult readership), with titles like *The Wild Boys of London* (suppressed by the police in 1865). The working-class literature of the early decades was being taken over by mass-circulation journals, ranging from the penny *London Journal* (1845–1942) and *Reynolds's Miscellany* (1846–1869) to the more "genteel" *Family Herald* (1843–1939) and Dickens's *Household Words* (1850–1859). This literature was directed toward family and in particular female readers. Each weekly issue typically included a miscellany of information, entertainment and—in particular—serialized fiction. Although its sensationalism could be cruder than middle-class reading, it is increasingly difficult to identify such literature as "working class," in part because by the late nineteenth century the divisions between classes were easing. The 1870 Education Act, in particular, brought a more uniform literacy, and mass publication pulps such as George Newnes's *Tit-Bits* (1881–) were aimed at a broad audience. Middle-class prejudices against cheap publications waned; working-class readers bought popular editions of writers such as **Marie Corelli**, Florence Barclay, and **Ellen Price Wood**. If working-class literature developed out of popular tradition, in the 1870s it merged with publications for a mass market.

LOUIS JAMES

Bibliography

Altick, Richard D. *The English Common Reader: A Social History of the Mass Reading Public, 1800–1900.* 1957.

Dalziel, Margaret. *Popular Fiction a Hundred Years Ago.* 1957.

Hodgart, M. J. C. *The Ballads.* 2d ed., 1962.

Hollis, Patricia. *The Pauper Press: A Study of Working Class Radicalism in the 1830s.* 1970.

James, Louis. *Fiction for the Working Man, 1830–1850.* Rev. ed., 1973.

Leavis, G. D. *Fiction and the Reading Public.* 1939.

Mitchell, Sally. *The Fallen Angel: Chastity, Class and Women's Reading, 1835–1880.* 1981.

Neuberg, Victor. *Popular Literature: A History and a Guide.* 1972.

Turner, E. S. *Boys Will Be Boys*. Rev. ed., 1957.

Vicinus, Martha. *The Industrial Muse: A Study of Nineteenth-Century British Working-Class Literature*. 1974.

Vincent, David. *Bread, Knowledge and Freedom: A Study of Nineteenth Century Working Class Autobiography*. 1981.

Webb, R. K. *The British Working Class Reader, 1790–1848*. 1935.

See also PERIODICALS: CHEAP AND POPULAR

· · · · ·

WORKING-CLASS NOVELISTS

In the **social problem novel** of the 1840s and 1850s, middle-class writers responded to the unemployment, urban migration, hunger, and despair among the poor and working classes. Even though the purpose of writers such as Elizabeth Gaskell (1810–1865), Charles Dickens (1812–1870), and Charles Kingsley (1819–1875) was to arouse sympathy among middle-class readers, paternalism and a fear of revolution or violence by the masses often restrained their intentions. Actual working-class novelists of the 1840s were found among the Chartists, who aimed to create a class-based, socialist literature which would depict triumph over the cruel aristocracy, eliminate the materialistic middle class, and elevate the miserable working classes. Melodramatic plots and an overriding interest in the history of Chartism shape the works of Ernest Jones (1819–1869) and Thomas Martin Wheeler (1811–1862). Although political tracts thinly disguised as novels, Jones's *De Brassier* (1851–1852) and Wheeler's *Sunshine and Shadow* (1849–1850) signal the first major fiction by a vocal and organized working class.

A second group of social problem writers associated with middle-class interests were active in the 1880s—George Gissing (1857–1903), Walter Besant (1836–1901), and Rudyard Kipling (1865–1936). Less well known were the journalists who often sensationalized working-class conditions for their middle-class audiences and the Christian and temperance reformers whose moralizing sometimes blamed the poor for alcohol, prostitution, and laziness. Some individuals of working-class origin—like William Pett Ridge (1860–1930), Edwin Pugh (1874–1930), and Richard Whiteing (1840–1928)—found careers in the middle class as writers. Belonging to the "cockney school," their novels sentimentalized the communal life of London's East End using dialect and memorable characters. The cockney as a stock figure had been comic in early Victorian novels, was rendered tragic by Gissing, and became a regional type (on the order of Scottish, Irish, or Yorkshire characters) in later Victorian fiction. The cockney school's intention to ameliorate the reputation of violent working-class life and mold the poor into admirable personalities unfortunately backfired when their heroes became stereotypes.

Late in the century some novelists began to endorse the growing power of trade unionism. Workers, newly portrayed as exploited and victimized, served as subjects for novels that demanded either parliamentary resolution or a fundamental restructuring of political institutions. In these works, collective action replaces the personal focus of middle-class fiction, and class solidarity replaces philanthropy. Notable are William Edward Tirebuck's (1854–1900) *Miss Grace of All Souls* (1895), cited by Tolstoy as one of the best examples of modern English fiction, and *City Girl* (1887) by "John Law"—a pseudonym for **Margaret Harkness** (1861–1923). In an April 1888 letter, Friedrich Engels defined realism as the faithfulness with which Harkness portrayed the working classes: "besides truth of detail, the truthful reproduction of typical characters under typical circumstances." Although novelists who focused on working-class life generally adopted a realistic mode, almost all of them—regardless of their own class origins—tended to subordinate the feelings, culture, and wide range of people among the working classes to their own didactic purposes and class viewpoints.

READE W. DORNAN

Bibliography

Brome, Vincent. *Four Realists: Arthur Morrison, Edwin Pugh, Richard Whiteing, William Pett Ridge*. 1965.

Eagleton, Mary and David Pierce. *Attitudes to Class in the English Novel from Walter Scott to David Storey.* 1979.

Keating, P. J. *The Working Classes in Victorian Fiction.* 1971.

Klaus, H. Gustav. *The Literature of Labour: Two Hundred Years of Working-Class Writing.* 1985.

———. *The Socialist Novel in Britain: Toward the Recovery of a Tradition.* 1982.

Vicinus, Martha. *The Industrial Muse: A Study of Nineteenth Century British Working-Class Literature.* 1974.

Williams, Raymond. *Writing in Society.* 1983.

See also DIALECT WRITING
· · · · ·

WORKING-CLASS POETS AND POETRY

The Burnett-Vincent-Mayall bibliography of nineteenth-century working-class autobiographies lists more than a hundred poets—about one of every eight autobiographers. There were probably thousands of Victorian laborers who published in the poetry columns of provincial and labor newspapers.

A few poetic artisans and agricultural workers had attracted the attention of the literate classes in the Georgian period. The farm laborer John Clare (1793–1864) continued to write verse even after he was placed in a lunatic asylum in 1837. The industrial working class as such produced no great bards in the Victorian era. The best-remembered Victorian worker-poet, the Scottish weaver William McGonagall (1830–1902), is read today for the hilarious badness of his work.

Many northern industrial towns did, however, boast some rousing balladeers. The Bradford brickmaker Reuben Holder (1797–?) and the Barnsley collier George Hanby (1817–1904) could be relied on to produce commemorative verses for temperance meetings, great fires, or any other local happenings. By midcentury the balladeer was already giving way to union versesmiths like the Durham "pitman's poet" Tommy Armstrong

(1848–1919). Coal miners' unions used songs and poems as propaganda, to promote self-help and solidarity and to denounce employers and blacklegs. The most widely read radical worker-poet was the "Corn Law rhymer," **Ebenezer Elliott** (1781–1849).

The Chartist movement also produced a number of militant poets. The London wood engraver **William James Linton** (1812–1897) wrote Shelleyesque revolutionary hymns and, later in life, romantic love poetry. Gerald Massey (1828–1907) won striking critical acclaim with *The Ballad of Babe Christabel* (1854) and served as a model for George Eliot's Felix Holt. **Thomas Cooper** (1805–1872), an amazingly well-read shoemaker, aspired to produce proletarian epics in the style of Spenser and Milton, but his work was too pretentious to appeal to working-class or middle-class readers.

The Northumberland collier Joseph Skipsey (1832–1903) ranged from elegies for mine disasters to etherial spiritual and nature poems. He also edited the Canterbury Poets series, including volumes of Burns, Blake, and Shelley. (These three, together with Shakespeare and Milton, were the most revered models for working-class poets.)

Workers who attempted romantic or classical poetry were apt to fall between two audiences. Alienated from their fellow laborers (who could not afford books of poetry), they usually failed to break into the London literary marketplace. Patronage was sometimes available—the Pre-Raphaelites found subsidies and jobs for Joseph Skipsey—but few worker-poets flourished in that hothouse atmosphere.

Dialect poets from the northern counties could find a paying market in local newspapers, almanacs, and penny readings; they also attracted the attention of distinguished folklorists and philologists. Benjamin Brierley (1825–1896) and Edwin Waugh (1817–1890) were among the founders of the Manchester Literary Club (1862), which brought together businessmen and proletarian authors. Brierley and Waugh inspired a whole generation of dialect poets. Waugh sat on the board of the English Dialect Society and received a civil list pension of 90 pounds a year in 1886.

Women worker-poets were very few and quite obscure. Ellen Johnston (b. 183?), a Scottish powerloom weaver, published her work in local newspapers. Mary Smith (1822–1889), a domestic servant and schoolmistress, brought out two volumes of poetry.

The great variety of working-class poetic voices can be heard in the work of Joseph Burgess (1853–1934), who edited several Lancashire labor newspapers. Burgess drew on his experience as a piecer to produce a bitter dialect verse, "Ther's Nowt Loike Spinnin' Shoddy" (1874). But he could also use elevated standard English to compose a conventional nature sonnet, "The Sun and the Sky" (1872). He was properly rhetorical in eulogizing Disraeli and Czar Alexander II, and then later produced the rollicking doggerel of "The Ballads of Betty Twigg." (This last series he wrote for the *Workman's Times*, spinning out eight hundred words of verses each week in an hour or two.)

JONATHAN ROSE

Bibliography

Burnett, John, David Vincent and David Mayall, eds. *The Autobiography of the Working Class: An Annotated, Critical Bibliography.* Vol. 1: 1790–1900. 1984.

Maidment, Brian E., ed. *The Poorhouse Fugitives.* 1987.

Vicinus, Martha. *The Industrial Muse: A Study of Nineteenth Century British Working-Class Literature.* 1974.

See also DIALECT WRITING

· · · · ·

WORKING HOURS

On the threshold of industrialization, the workday in Britain generally ran from 6 a.m. to 6 p.m. with two and a half hours off for meals and rest. Industrialization increased the hours and intensity of labor, but during the course of the nineteenth century, as a result of worker agitation, philanthropic concern, and economic change, working hours were gradually restored to and, in a some cases, pushed below their preindustrial level.

Factories, particularly cotton mills, assaulted traditional patterns of work. Cottage laborers had subjected themselves to frenzied and protracted periods of labor punctuated by days of leisure. Artisans and other workers, as well as cottage laborers, sometimes observed "holy Monday," and valued their traditional holidays and half- or short Saturdays. The pace of prefactory work also differed from machine-dictated labor. Furthermore, with access to gardens and commons, most workers had not yet been subjected to a total dependency on wages.

Beginning in the late eighteenth century, the working day in cotton mills was extended far beyond the traditional ten hours of actual labor. Water-powered spinning mills, often worked with parish apprentices, usually had two shifts of twelve hours, eleven of which were spent in labor. Workers in hand-powered mills were often forced to work thirteen hours, spread over a fourteen-hour shift. Saturdays were stretched to ten or more hours although "free" mill workers retained a devotion to "holy" Mondays.

With the introduction of steam power, mills moved to the cities. Shift work, though continuing in small communities, was usually dropped, and hours were extended to keep the expensive machinery in use. Parish apprentices were replaced by women and free children, who constituted 75 percent of the work force in cotton mills. Hours generally ran from 6 a.m. to 7 p.m. with an hour for lunch, although in 1816 workers in the mills around Manchester worked thirteen and a half hours, the longest regular mill hours in England.

Philanthropic opposition produced legislation to limit the workday in textile mills. An 1802 act, which was never enforced, prohibited the employment of parish apprentices in cotton mills at night or for more than twelve hours during the day. Subsequent acts limited hours for all children and developed the rudiments of enforcement. The act of 1833 stabilized the working hours in all textile mills at twelve. The day generally ran from 6 a.m. to 7 p.m., with an hour off for meals.

Most other industries had retained the traditional twelve-hour day, with one and a half or two hours for meals, thus establishing ten or ten and a half hours of actual work. In the early 1830s there was pressure on workers to extend their normal hours, but in most cases resistance was effective. Cottage laborers persisted in their irregular habits but were forced to respond to declining pay by increasing their hours. For many workers, however, actual hours of labor often exceeded normal hours of labor. Work could, at the employer's demand, extend throughout the day and into the night. Particularly in the clothing districts, workers could not refuse to put in extra hours during periods of high demand.

The act of 1847, passed in response to Chartist agitation and the unemployment that accompanied a serious slump, reduced the actual hours of labor in the textile industry to ten per day, and the 1850 Factory Act required textile workers' days to end at 2 p.m. on Saturdays. This legislation eventually had wider impact: it was first in Manchester, the cotton center, that the short Saturday came to prevail in most trades.

By 1870 the majority of the London trades had a ten-hour day with a 4 p.m. Saturday, and in the early 1870s craft unions were able to take advantage of prosperity and low unemployment to win a substantial reduction in working hours. Employers' opposition was diminished because of their desire to regulate competition through standardized hours, and because of the introduction of hourly pay. As the campaign for shorter hours spread, most organized workers made substantial gains. By 1875 a work week of fifty-four to fifty-six and a half hours was the norm.

The success of the craft unions helped inspire the "new unionism" of the 1880s. The "new unions" of the unskilled or semiskilled were able to disrupt work temporarily by striking, but lacked the leverage craft unions could exert through the scarcity of their skills. Thus the new unions sought to establish the eight-hour day through legislation. Between 1893 and 1900, 53,000 workers, many of them shift workers in continuous-process industries, achieved the eight-hour day. Government, however, was responsible for over half of the reductions in hours between 1890 and 1902. In 1894, 43,000 government employees were granted an eight-hour day, and in 1902 Parliament reduced the hours of textile workers by an hour a week. Government again, under pressure from the rising Labour party, acted in 1909 to limit the workday in mines to eight hours.

BERNARD A. COOK

Bibliography

Bienefeld, M. A. *Working Hours in British Industry: An Economic History.* 1972.

Cole, G. D. H. *A Short History of the British Working-Class Movement, 1789–1947.* 1948.

Hammond, John L. and Barbara Hammond. *The Town Labourer.* 1917.

See also CHILD LABOR

. . . . .

WRIGHT, THOMAS (c. 1840–1892)

Thomas Wright, a working-class essayist, journalist, and novelist, wrote as the "Journeyman Engineer" and the "Riverside Visitor" from the late 1860s through the 1880s. A working engineer, Wright sought to portray the working classes clearly and fairly to the rest of English society. In *Some Habits and Customs of the Working Classes* (1867), *The Great Unwashed* (1868), *Our New Masters* (1873), and other works, he analyzed working-class living and working conditions, amusements, reading, education, culture, political beliefs, and trade union activities.

Born in about 1840 in a large seaport, Wright attended school until he was about fourteen, served a seven-year apprenticeship, and became a journeyman engineer about 1860. His earliest known articles appeared in *Chambers's Journal, All the Year Round,* and the *Star* (1866–1868). Wright wrote about all types of workers, but his best pieces concerned artisans, whom he described as hardworking, proud, caring, anxious for education, but still ignorant and uncultured. His understanding of working-class culture is especially acute in "On a Possible Popular Culture," (*Contemporary Review,* July 1881) and "Concerning the Unknown Public," (*Nineteenth Century,* February 1883).

Wright is one of a handful of authentic Victorian working-class voices. His sensitive depictions of the working classes, reasoned defense of trade unions, sophisticated analyses of cheap, popular literature, and careful delineations of the various groups within the working classes stand as remarkable and uniquely reliable documents. Barely remembered today, Wright is far too little read and appreciated.

EVELYN D. ASCH

. . . . .

WYNDHAM, CHARLES (1837–1919)

A principal actor-manager of the late Victorian period, Charles Wyndham initially prepared for a medical career and served briefly as a federal army surgeon during the U.S. Civil War. Returning to England in 1865, he established himself as an actor on the provincial circuit and in London, where he was engaged at the Royalty, St. James's, and Queen's theaters. After touring the United States with his own company in 1871–1873 (the first of many such visits), Wyndham introduced English audiences to *Brighton* (1874), a clever adaptation of Bronson Howard's *Saratoga*. The piece helped make his reputation as London's leading light comedian.

In 1876 Wyndham assumed management of the recently completed Criterion Theatre, fulfilling expectations with farces like James Albery's *Pink Dominos* (1877) and appearing in revivals of T. W. Robertson's costume drama *David Garrick* (1864), a play that became his signature piece. During the 1890s Wyndham abandoned "rattling farce" for smart comedy, creating the *raisonneurs* in a number of society plays by Henry Arthur Jones. The worldly-wise Sir Richard Kato, Q. C. (*The Case of Rebellious Susan*, 1894) and Col. Sir Christopher Deering (*The Liars*, 1897) enabled the actor to reconcile his comedic talents and advancing years.

In 1899 Wyndham and Mary Moore—his leading lady, business partner, and (after 1916) second wife—opened Wyndham's Theatre in Charing Cross Road, where both played in a repertoire that included the comedies of Hubert Henry Davies and the most considerable of Jones's society dramas, *Mrs. Dane's Defence* (1900). Wyndham's knighthood, conferred in the coronation ceremonies of 1902, made him the third actor so honored.

JOEL H. KAPLAN

Bibliography

Moore, Mary. *Charles Wyndham and Mary Moore*. 1925.

Pemberton, T. Edgar. *Sir Charles Wyndham: A Biography*. 1904.

Rowell, George. "Wyndham of Wyndhams." In Joseph W. Donohue, ed., *The Theatrical Manager in England and America*. 1971.

Shore, Florence Teignmouth. *Sir Charles Wyndham*. 1908.

Trewin, Wendy. *All on Stage: Charles Wyndham and the Alberys*. 1980.

. . . . .

YATES, EDMUND (1831–1894)

Journalist, novelist, poet, and dramatist, Edmund Hodgson Yates owned and edited the enormously successful weekly *The World* from 1874 to 1894. His *Edmund Yates: His Recollections and Experiences* (1884) is among the richest and liveliest records of Victorian literary and theatrical life, particularly its bohemian side. *Broken to Harness* (1864), his first and best novel, amusingly exploits the vogue of the "fast woman" and the "pretty horse-breaker." Most of his seventeen other novels cater generously to the fashionable appetite for "sensation," but the best of them—*Land at Last* (1866), *Kissing the Rod* (1866), and *Wrecked in Port* (1869)—rise above the ruck of **sensation novels** by virtue of their racy and topical pictures of London's bohemia.

Yates came to prominence as one of "Dickens's young men" on the staff of *Household Words*. With his column "The Lounger in the Clubs" (*Illustrated Times*, 1855–1863) he claimed to have inaugurated the new style of "personal journalism" based on titbits of often malicious social and artistic gossip that later made *The World* so successful and became a dominant feature of twentieth-century popular journalism. After editing several minor journals between 1855 and 1860, some in collaboration with G.A. Sala and Henry Vizetelly (1820–1894), he became editor of the *Temple Bar* (1860–1867), initially under Sala's nominal editorship.

Yates achieved undeserved notoriety first when expelled from the Garrick Club for an allegedly ungentlemanly article on Thackeray (1858) and later when convicted and imprisoned for a criminal libel published, but not written, by him in *The World* (1884–1885); his diary, now in the British Library, movingly records his rapid mental and physical deterioration while in prison. Yates's reputation also suffered from private allegations, not published until after his death, that several of his novels were partly or wholly written by Frances Cashel Hoey (1830–1908). The allegations are unlikely to be true but have never been proved false.

Apart from a few of his novels and some comic verse that is still anthologized, Yates is best remembered for his journalistic innovations and for his percipience in employing men like William Archer (1856–1924) and George Bernard Shaw (1856–1950) on *The World*.

P. D. EDWARDS

Bibliography

Edwards, P. D. *Edmund Yates: A Bibliography.* 1980.

———. *Frances Cashel Hoey: A Bibliography.* 1982.

· · · · ·

YEATS, WILLIAM BUTLER (1865–1939)

William Butler Yeats, leader of the Irish literary revival and one of the foremost modern poets, had firmly established himself as a literary figure by the end of the nineteenth century. His first characteristic verse appeared in *The Wanderings of Oisin and Other Poems* (1889), followed by *Poems* (1895) and *The Wind Among the Reeds* (1899). His early play, *The Countess Cathleen* (1892), and subsequent dramatic poem, *The Land of the Heart's Desire* (1894), were followed by prose collections, the Irish tales of *The Celtic Twilight* (1893) and the symbolist stories of *The Secret Rose* (1897).

Yeats was born in Dublin in 1865, son of the painter John Butler Yeats and Susan Pollexfen. The family moved between Dublin, Sligo, and London during the poet's youth. Yeats settled in London in 1887, where his poetry soon came to reflect elements of Pre-Raphaelitism and aestheticism. He joined the **Rhymers' Club**, a group whose members included Arthur Symons, Lionel Johnson, and Ernest Dowson. Yeats's aestheticism, however, was tempered by his growing Irish nationalism, the vigorous energy of his Irish themes, and his ongoing interest in mythology, Irish folklore, and spiritualism. He traveled to France, where he met Mallarmé and Verlaine. By 1900 Symons was referring to Yeats as the "chief representative" of the symbolist movement in Britain. In 1896 he met Lady Augusta Gregory and, together with George Moore and Edward Martyn, they founded the Irish Literary Theatre. Yeats ended the 1890s with the first performance of *The Countess Cathleen* (1899) and the publication of the volume of his early verse most suggestive of his later powers.

Yeats's career as a poet awaited the twentieth century for its fullest development, but his poetic themes and principles were clearly set down in the twilight of Victorianism. He combined an interest in the traditions and folklore of Ireland with aesthetic aspects of Pre-Raphaelitism and his own brand of symbolist spiritualism to produce a poetic voice that possesses, for all its modernity, undeniable resonances of its Victorian origins.

ASHTON NICHOLS

Bibliography

Bloom, Harold. *Yeats.* 1970.

Ellmann, Richard. *The Identity of Yeats.* 1954.

———. *Yeats: The Man and the Masks.* 1948.

Marcus, Phillip L. *Yeats and the Beginning of the Irish Renaissance.* 1970.

Parkinson, Thomas. *W. B. Yeats, Self-Critic: A Study of His Early Verse.* 1951.

Yeats, W. B. *Autobiographies.* 1955.

See also **IRISH LITERATURE**

· · · · ·

YELLOWBACKS

Frequently called "railway novels," yellowbacks were a publishing phenomenon that emerged in the late 1840s, with the establishment of the first railway bookstalls, and continued until the end of the century. By about 1855 they had assumed their characteristic format: a cover of glazed paper (usually, but not always, yellow) over boards with an eye-catching illustration in two or three colors on the front, a decorative spine, and advertisements for other books or commercial products on the back. Selling for two shillings or less, they were considerably cheaper than most books of the time.

Yellowbacks were usually reprints, sometimes representing a fourth stage of publishing after magazine serialization, a "three-decker" first edition, and a one-volume clothbound reprint. The work of such popular novelists as Ouida and Mary Elizabeth Braddon predominated, and there was a trend to more sensational subject matter from the 1870s on. Some early detective novels appeared first as yellowbacks. Nonfiction titles were generally limited to current events, amateur natural history, and sports. Well-known illustrators were employed to design the covers, many of which were printed by the wood engraver Edmund Evans (1826–1905). Though relatively few survive, yellowbacks were published in vast numbers: one series alone, Routledge's Railway Library, begun in 1849, had reached 1,300 titles by 1898, with printings as high as 5,000 copies.

The Victorian yellowback shares with the modern mass-market paperback the characteristics of cheapness, availability, and popular appeal. Seldom of textual importance, it reflects the reading tastes of its day and demonstrates the interrelation of publishing and social change.

ELIZABETH HULSE

Bibliography

Evans, Edmund. *The Reminiscences of Edmund Evans.* 1967.

Rogerson, Ian, ed. *Yellowbacks: An Exhibition.* 2nd ed., 1984.

Sadleir, Michael. *Nineteenth Century Fiction: A Bibliographical Record Based on His Own Collection,* vol. 2, 1951.

———. "Yellow-backs." In John Carter, ed., *New Paths in Book Collecting.* 1934.

Walbank, Alan. "Railway Reading." *Book Collector,* vol. 9, pp. 285–291.

· · · · ·

YONGE, CHARLOTTE MARY (1823–1901)

Although she wrote over two hundred books, Charlotte Yonge's enduring accomplishment is the two dozen novels dramatizing middle-class life within the spiritual discipline of the Oxford Movement. She won popular success with *The Heir of Redclyffe* (1853), a novel that strongly influenced William Morris and Edward Burne-Jones. Subsequent achievements include *The Daisy Chain* (1856) and its sequel, *The Trial* (1864); *Hopes and Fears: Or Scenes from the Life of a Spinster* (1860); *The Clever Woman of the Family* (1865); *The Pillars of the House* (1873); and *The Three Brides* (1876). The charm of these novels and their psychological penetration into the springs of domestic affection and anxiety continue to attract readers who are indifferent to Yonge's religious views.

Yonge lived in the village of Otterbourne near Winchester. **John Keble**, rector of the neighboring village of Hursley, prepared her for confirmation and tutored her in church history and theology. When her interest in devising stories and her ear for dialogue became apparent, she resolved to devote her talents to the Church of England.

In *The Heir of Redclyffe*, young Guy Morville's hereditary violent temper, high spirits, and sacrificial death delighted readers of the 1850s, but the more subtly drawn character is his cousin Philip, who is racked by social and sexual jealousies he dare not admit to himself. Two novels about the May family, *The Daisy Chain* and *The Trial*, use as continuing theme the family's determination to build a church (with its accompanying social services) in an impoverished hamlet; the drama comes from the growth of eleven motherless children. Ethel May, a sallow, angular, scholarly adolescent, matures into a character of great humor and force; to many readers she

has seemed a prototype for Louisa May Alcott's Jo March (who is, early in *Little
Women*, discovered in her attic munching
apples and reading *The Heir of Redclyffe*).
With *The Clever Woman of the Family*,
however, Yonge's delicate touch fails; the strident Rachel Curtis is humiliated in her attempts to assist exploited child lacemakers
because she goes about her laudable purpose
without appropriate masculine, clerical guidance.

Some of Yonge's historical works for children, such as *The Little Duke* (1854) are still
read. *A History of Christian Names* (1863)
was a significant contribution to the discipline
of onomastics. She also wrote stories of village
life intended primarily for "cottagers' daughters." *Langley School* (1850) and its sequels
are the best of these.

From 1851 to 1894 Yonge edited *The
Monthly Packet of Evening Readings for
Members of the English Church*. She serialized many of her own novels in the *Monthly
Packet* and filled it with contributions on history, literature, and science. She provided numerous educational materials for parents and
Sunday school teachers, such as *Scripture
Readings for Schools, with Comments*
(1871-1879). Her *Cameos from English History* (1868-1899), written for adolescents,
are well researched and richly detailed; she
also wrote "nursery" histories.

Yonge was a professional writer with great
respect for her readers. Critical comments in
her journalism and letters reveal her interest
in the craft of fiction. Although her great subject is Victorian domestic life, she seldom
presents conventional two-parent families. Instead, widowed parents, stepparents, and
older siblings acting as parents populate her
fiction. Her observational facility and skill
with dialogue allow her to extract dramatic
interest from "the daily round, the common
task" which her mentor John Keble hymned
in *The Christian Year* (1827).

BARBARA J. DUNLAP

Bibliography

Battiscombe, Georgina. *Charlotte Mary Yonge:
The Story of an Uneventful Life*. 1943.

——— and Marghanita Laski, eds. *A Chapelet for
Charlotte Yonge*. 1965.

Brownell, David. "The Two Worlds of Charlotte
Yonge." In Jerome H. Buckley, ed., *The Worlds
of Victorian Fiction*. 1975.

Colby, Vineta. *Yesterday's Woman: Domestic
Realism in the English Novel*. 1974.

Coleridge, Christabel R. *Charlotte Mary Yonge, Her
Life and Letters*. 1903; rpt. 1969.

Mare, Margaret L. and Alicia C. Percival. *Victorian
Best-Seller: The World of Charlotte M. Yonge*.
1947; rpt. 1970.

Tillotson, Kathleen. "*The Heir of Redclyffe*." In
Geoffrey and Kathleen Tillotson, eds., *Mid-Victorian Studies*. 1965.

· · · · ·

YOUNG ENGLAND

Young England was a small political coalition within the Tory party in the early 1840s.
Led by **Benjamin Disraeli** (1804-1881), it
reacted against the rationalistic utilitarianism
of its time, as well as against what it saw as the
unprincipled compromises of the Tory prime
minister, Robert Peel (1788-1850).

Young England originated in the friendship
of several young aristocrats, particularly
George Smythe (1818-1857) and Lord John
Manners (1818-1906). Both were influenced
by Frederick Faber (1814-1863), a disciple of
John Henry Newman and an Oxford Movement devotee. Although Manners, Smythe,
and Alexander Baillie-Cochrane had been in
political sympathy for some time, the movement crystalized around Disraeli when in autumn of 1843 the four agreed to sit together in
Parliament and speak and vote in concert.
They formed the inner circle of a slightly
larger group of like-minded Tories restive at
Peel's attempts to tighten party control and
his supposed compromise of the central
tenets of Toryism (particularly the interests of
the landed classes). Young England opposed
Peel on issues including factory legislation
and tariff reform. The movement foundered
on the Maynooth Grant Bill (1845), in which
Peel proposed a permanently increased grant
to the Roman Catholic seminary at Maynooth
in Ireland. The logic of Young England principles, sympathetic to the Roman Catholic faith,
demanded support of the measure; Disraeli,

however, apparently could not miss the chance to attack Peel, and thus broke with his cohorts. Although the formal coalition disintegrated, Smythe and Manners continued to support Disraeli's political career.

Young England's reputation was and is out of proportion to its actual accomplishments in Parliament, mainly due to the idealized depiction in Disraeli's novels *Coningsby* (1844) and *Sybil* (1845). The movement embodied on a political level much of the romantic medievalism that infused literary and religious movements of the time. Its sources were diverse— Samuel Taylor Coleridge's social theory, the Oxford Movement, the novels of Walter Scott, and Kenelm Digby's moralizing treatise, *The Broad Stone of Honour* (1822), which sought to revive medieval notions of chivalry. Young England was innovative in diagnosing the ills attendant upon unchecked economic individualism, but nostalgic in the cure it prescribed. The restoration of a benevolent hierarchy, a central tenet of Young England, was to be realized in a neofeudal coalition of aristocracy and (as Disraeli liked to call it) peasantry under the guidance of a resuscitated monarchy, with the Church of England as "the spiritual and intellectual trainer of the people."

Some of its more extreme rhetoric (most notoriously, Manners's couplet, "Let wealth and commerce, laws and learning die,/But leave us still our old Nobility") rendered Young England vulnerable to attack, and writers such as Dickens and Thackeray quickly seized the opportunity for parody. Practically, Young England failed; imaginatively, it symbolized the desire for a unified and ordered society, an ideal community able to withstand the pressures that would separate the social and religious sensibility.

MARK S. LOOKER

Bibliography

Blake, Robert. *Disraeli.* 1966.

Morris, Kevin. *The Image of the Middle Ages in Romantic and Victorian Literature.* 1984.

Saintsbury, George. *Collected Essays and Papers,* vol. 3. 1923.

Whibley, Charles. *Lord John Manners and His Friends.* 1925.

· · · · ·

YOUNG IRELAND

Young Ireland was a movement of Irish middle-class intellectuals that represented the same romantic aspirations as Young Poland, Young Italy, and Young England—all opposed Enlightenment rationalism and industrial materialism and espoused a romantic revolutionary nationalism. Young Ireland constructed its cultural nationalism on indigenous Irish myths, legends, and symbols.

Young Ireland became prominent in 1842 with the founding of its newspaper *The Nation* by Thomas Osbourne Davis, Charles Gavan Duffy, and John Blake Dillon. By subordinating art to the politics of nationalism, advocating the deanglicization of Ireland, preaching a revolutionary means to obtain Irish freedom, and attempting to create a unique Irish culture out of the country's Gaelic past, Young Ireland in the pages of *The Nation* created a vision of an ideal independent Ireland dominated by peaceful nonsectarianism and devoted to preserving the Irish language and folklore. With a regular audience of a quarter of a million, Young Ireland conveyed its definition of Irish cultural nationalism in essays, poetry, ballads, and lyrics praising the superior virtue and spirituality of the Irish race.

Young Ireland rejuvenated Daniel O'Connell's repeal campaign in 1843, but cooperative efforts ceased because Young Ireland supported nondenominational education and perceived violence as a viable means to obtain independence. Young Ireland then created its separate organization, the Irish Confederation, and engineered an unsuccessful revolt in 1848. Although disbanded a year later, Young Ireland's legacy inspired the Fenians, Sinn Fein and the Easter 1916 Rebellion as well as the Gaelic revival and the Irish literary renaissance.

TIMOTHY JEROME SARBAUGH

Bibliography

Brown, Malcolm. *The Politics of Irish Literature.* 1972.

Duffy, Charles Gavan. *A Short Life of Thomas Davis.* 1985.

———. *Young Ireland.* 1896.

Gwynn, Denis. *O'Connell, Davis, and the Colleges Bill.* 1948.

———. *Young Ireland and 1848.* 1949.

McCaffry, Lawrence. *Daniel O'Connell and the Repeal Year.* 1966.

Nowlan, Kevin. *The Politics of Repeal.* 1965.

O'Broin, Leon. *Charles Gavan Duffy: Patriot and Statesman.* 1967.

See also GAELIC CULTURE; IRISH LITERATURE; IRISH NATIONALISM

. . . . .

ZANGWILL, ISRAEL (1864–1926)

Deservedly the best known of the Anglo-Jewish novelists, Israel Zangwill also wrote short stories, plays, and essays. Of his twelve novels, the very popular *Children of the Ghetto* (1892) and *The King of Schnorrers* (1894) examine Anglo-Jewish life, as do his three volumes of short stories: *Ghetto Tragedies* (1893; American edition: *They That Walk in Darkness*, 1899), *Dreamers of the Ghetto* (1898), and *Ghetto Comedies* (1907). These works are the first sympathetic explorations of the frequently anguishing choices immigrant Jews made as they adapted to life in a liberal society.

Zangwill believed that Judaism was intellectually dead and that it would eventually blend with Christianity. Nonetheless, along with Theodore Herzl, Zangwill championed a homeland for Jews, and he worked to resettle Jews who left eastern Europe at the century's end. With the exception of *The King of Schnorrers*, a witty presentation of the prized Jewish traditions of education and charity, Zangwill's fiction seriously portrays the difficulties of living as an Orthodox Jew in a non-Jewish society, the process of assimilation, and the generation gap between immigrant parents and their English-born children.

Zangwill is the first to depict fully all aspects of Anglo-Jewry without didacticism and to portray the intellectual divisions in the Anglo-Jewish community—indeed, in Judaism—at the century's end. Zangwill's achievement was to create the modern **Anglo-Jewish novel.**

LINDA GERTNER ZATLIN

Bibliography

Adams, Elsie Bonita. *Israel Zangwill.* 1971.

Fisch, Harold. "Israel Zangwill." In *Encyclopedia Judaica,* vol. 16.

Wohlgelernter, Maurice. *Israel Zangwill: A Study.* 1964.

. . . . .

RESEARCH MATERIALS FOR
VICTORIAN STUDIES

The following annotated bibliography describes some of the principal reference works useful to the researcher in Victorian studies. Though most of the titles focus primarily on the Victorian period, some are general works of basic importance to library research. The list is organized by type of resource and the annotations indicate the scope and organization of the work.

ARCHIVES AND MANUSCRIPTS

British Library. Department of Manuscripts. *Index of Manuscripts in the British Library.* Cambridge: Chadwyck-Healey, 1984.

This alphabetical index replaces over thirty catalogues and covers all manuscript collections acquired by the British Library up to 1950. It allows the user to identify an individual item, the collection in which it belongs, its number within the collection, and its folio or article number. This last number can be used for ordering photocopies and microfilms. New cross-references have been added to those from the original catalogues and are a great aid to finding main entries.

Foster, Janet and Julia Sheppard. *British Archives: A Guide to Archive Resources in the United Kingdom.* Detroit: Gale, 1982.

This guide is an alphabetical listing, by location, of all types of archival materials; 708 entries are included. The book is well organized, with an index to collections, a key subject-word index, a list of repositories, by county and alphabetically, a list of useful addresses for institutions not included, and a selected bibliography of books on archival and manuscript research.

Hammer, Philip M., ed. *A Guide to Archives and Manuscripts in the United States.* Compiled for the National Historical Publications Commission. New Haven: Yale University Press, 1961.

A listing of more than one thousand archival agencies, historical societies, libraries, and other organizations with archival holdings, this book is organized by state, city, and institutional name. The index includes subjects specifically mentioned in the descriptive list.

United States. National Historical Publications and Records Commission. *Directory of Archives and Manuscript Repositories in the United States.* Washington, D.C.: National Archives and Records Service, General Services Administration, 1978.

This government guide describes manuscript repositories and archives in the United States. Organized by state and city.

BIBLIOGRAPHIES

Chaudhuri, Brahma, ed. *Annual Bibliography of Victorian Studies.* Edmonton, Alberta: LITIR Database, 1976–.

The main emphasis of this cross-disciplinary listing of the year's work on Victorian studies is on literary studies, but other topics are given extensive attention. Sections include: General and Reference Works; Fine Arts; Philosophy and Religion; History; Social Sciences; Science and Technology; and Language and Literature, with listings for individual authors. Subject, author, title, and reviewer indexes are included. The volume for 1976 was published in

1981. This is probably the most comprehensive of the annual Victorian bibliographies.

Chaudhuri, Brahma, ed. *A Comprehensive Bibliography of Victorian Studies, 1970-1984.* 3 vols. Edmonton, Alberta: LITIR Database, 1984.

Following the same organization and format as Chaudhuri's *Annual Bibliography of Victorian Studies,* this bibliography extends coverage back to 1970 and adds items missed in the annual volumes. Some items have been reassigned to subject sections different from their places in the annual volumes.

Bibliographies of Studies in Victorian Literature. Urbana: University of Illinois Press, 1945–1967. New York: AMS Press, 1981–.

These reprints of the annual bibliographies begun in *Modern Philology* and continued in *Victorian Studies* begin with 1932-1944 and then proceed by ten-year periods. The first volume includes only an index of the Victorian authors covered. The later volumes index the names of authors, scholars, and general topics.

Faxon, Frederick W. *Literary Annuals and Gift Books: A Bibliography 1823-1903.* Reprinted with supplementary essays by Eleanore Jaimieson and Iain Bain. Pinner, Middlesex: Private Libraries Association, 1973.

Faxon's bibliography of annuals and gift books is reprinted with useful additional material, including Jaimieson's essay on binding styles and Bain's on illustrations.

"Guide to the Year's Work on Victorian Poetry." *Victorian Poetry.* Annual, vol. 1, 1963–.

Each year since its first issue in 1963, *Victorian Poetry* has included in its fall issue a bibliographic essay on the year's scholarship on Victorian poetry. The growth and increasing specialization in the field is evident; in 1963, R.C. Tobias wrote the entire essay, covering eight pages. In 1984, Tobias covered only the general material; specialists wrote separate essays on major figures and the entire survey covered fifty-three pages. A valuable scholarly source.

Kanner, Barbara. *Women in English Social History, 1800-1914: A Guide to Research.* 3 vols. New York: Garland, 1987.

This work deals with issues in English social history, with the focus on matters central to women. The

Introductory essay covers the status of research and publication in the various subject areas, neglected questions, current perspectives and approaches, and possible new approaches. Organization is by broad subject areas (Marriage and Family; Sickness and Health Care), with subsections on narrower topics.

Madden, Lionel and Diana Dixon. *The Nineteenth-Century Periodical Press in Britain: A Bibliography of Modern Studies, 1901-1971.* New York: Garland, 1976.

This bibliography of studies of the nineteenth-century periodical press includes listings of books, pamphlets, periodical articles, dissertations, and theses appearing between 1901 and 1971. It includes sections on bibliographies, general history, individual periodicals and newspapers, and studies and memoirs of those connected with Victorian journals. Originally published as a supplement to volume 3 of *Victorian Periodicals Newsletter,* the bibliography contains minor errors; use cautiously.

Nicholls, David. *Nineteenth-Century Britain, 1815-1914.* Folkstone, Kent: Dawson; Hamden, Conn.: Archon, 1978.

Aimed at nonspecialists, this bibliography offers an annotated listing of books on various topics in Victorian history. Sections are: General; Political and Constitutional; Foreign, Imperial, and Defense; Economic; Social; Education; Religion; Wales; Scotland and Ireland; and Literary and Cultural. Very basic.

Nineteenth Century Short Title Catalogue: Extracted from the catalogue of the Bodleian Library, the British Library, the Library of Trinity College, Dublin, the National Library of Scotland, and the University Libraries of Cambridge and Newcastle. Newcastle-upon-Tyne: Avero, 1984–.

This project will eventually cover British books printed between 1801 and 1918. It should include all books published in Britain, its colonies and the United States, all books in English wherever published, and all translations from English. The first series, based on the holdings of the libraries listed, covers 1801-1815. The second series covers 1816-1870 and the third 1871-1918. As the introduction warns, the texts themselves have not been examined; this is a listing of these libraries' holdings according to their catalogues. Inconsistencies of entry therefore exist, but extensive cross-references have done much to remedy problems. A subject index based on the Dewey Decimal Classification and an imprint index are included.

Vann, J. Don. *Victorian Novels in Serial*. New York: Modern Language Association, 1985.

An interesting introduction covers the history of serialization and its effects on authorship and on the endings of parts. The main section of the book lists the serialized novels of sixteen Victorian novelists. Each entry gives the place of publication, dates, and the chapters that appeared on each date. Notes at the end of some entries provide information about such matters as the date when the book appeared as a volume and peculiarities in its publishing history. An invaluable aid to studies on the serialization of the novel.

"Victorian Bibliography." *Victorian Studies*. Annual, vol. 1, 1957–.

The "Victorian Bibliography" in *Victorian Studies* is a continuation of an earlier annual bibliography published in *Modern Philology*. It appears in the summer issue. Prepared by a committee of experts, the bibliography covers books published in the previous year having a bearing on the Victorian period. Selected items from earlier years missed in previous bibliographies are also included. The bibliography is divided by broad subject categories. Each entry includes bibliographic information and, where possible, a listing of reviews that have appeared on that item. Of central importance to both specialized subject research and more general work on the period.

Wodehouse, Lawrence. *British Architects, 1840–1976: A Guide to Information Sources*. Detroit: Gale, 1978.

This book is an uneven but useful guide to modern British architects. Architects who have not been evaluated by critics are excluded, as are theorists such as Morris and Ruskin. Brief biographical sketches are included for many entries. The index includes the heading "Victorian Architecture," thereby facilitating period research.

BIOGRAPHY

Banks, Olive. *The Biographical Dictionary of British Feminists*. Vol. 1: 1800–1930. New York: New York University Press, 1985.

The introduction offers a useful essay on the varieties of feminism. The entries are lengthy enough to give unusually complete information and include brief but often comprehensive bibliographies. Information on many of the figures listed here is not easily available elsewhere.

Baylen, Joseph and Norbert J. Gossman, eds. *Biographical Dictionary of Modern British Radicals*. Vol. 2: 1830–1870. Sussex: Harvester Press, 1984.

This volume contains almost two hundred biographies of important figures in British radicalism between 1830 and 1870. Articles were written by about eighty contributors and are signed. It is indexed by names and by topic. The third volume (as yet unpublished) will cover 1870 to 1914, completing a unique source of information for Victorian studies.

Dictionary of Literary Biography. Detroit: Gale.
    Vol. 18: *Victorian Novelists After 1885*. Ed.

Ira B. Nadel and William E. Fredeman. 1983.
    Vol. 19: *British Poets, 1880–1914*. 1983. Ed. Donald E. Stanford.
    Vol. 21: *Victorian Novelists Before 1885*. Ed. Ira B. Nadel and William E. Fredeman. 1983.
    Vol. 32: *Victorian Poets Before 1850*. Ed. William E. Fredeman and Ira B. Nadel. 1984.
    Vol. 35: *Victorian Poets After 1850*. Ed. William E. Fredeman and Ira B. Nadel. 1985.
    Vol. 55: *Victorian Prose Writers Before 1867*. Ed. William B. Thesing. 1987.
    Vol. 57: *Victorian Prose Writers After 1867*. Ed. William B. Thesing, 1987.

The Dictionary of Literary Biography as a whole deals with a broad range of authors from various periods and schools of British, Canadian, and American literature. The five volumes listed are the ones thus far devoted to Victorian writers. They provide lengthy biographical essays by subject specialists, often including critical insights as well as purely biographical material. Articles are attractively illustrated and include listings of the author's major works and a brief bibliography including the standard edition of the author's works and the location of the author's papers.

The Dictionary of National Biography. Ed. Sir Leslie Stephen and Sir Sidney Lee. London: Oxford University Press, 1908–. Reprinted 1921–1922, 1937–1938, 1949–1950, 1959–1960, 1963–1964. First supplement 1901, 2d supplement 1901–1911, 3d supplement 1912–1921, 4th supplement 1922–1930, 5th supplement 1931–1940, 6th supplement 1941–1950, 7th supplement 1951–1960, 8th supplement 1961–1970. Index and Epitome. Ed. Sir Sidney Lee. London: Smith, Elder, 1903–1913. 2 vols.

This set needs no description. The most important user aid is the cumulative index in each supplement covering all entries from 1901.

Pettys, Chris et al. *Dictionary of Women Artists: An International Dictionary of Women Artists Born Before 1900.* Boston: G.K. Hall, 1985.

This biographical dictionary covers more than 21,000 women painters, sculptors, printmakers, and illustrators born before 1900. Photographers, architects, craftsworkers, and designers are included only if they are also associated with the above art forms. Each entry lists, to the extent available, name, including maiden and/or married name, pseudonyms, dates and places of birth and death, media and subject matter, places of residence and/or activity, identification of other artists in family, schools and teachers studied under, exhibition record, and bibliographical references.

Wood, Christopher. *Dictionary of Victorian Painters: With Guide to Auction Prices, 300 Illustrations, and Index to Artists Monograms.* Woodbridge, Suffolk: Antique Collectors' Club, 1971.

This dictionary covers artists active between 1837 and 1901. Entries include biographical information, recent auction prices or a probable price range if no auction records are available, and a detailed bibliography. It also includes an index to monograms used by artists and a section of black and white illustrations of major works.

DISSERTATIONS

Altick, Richard D. and William R. Matthews, comps. *Guide to Doctoral Dissertations in Victorian Literature, 1886–1958.* Urbana: University of Illinois Press, 1980.

Though sadly out of date, this is a useful guide to early dissertations. It lists dissertations dealing wholly or in part with British literature from 1837 to 1900 and includes European, English, and American dissertations.

Comprehensive Dissertation Index. Ann Arbor, Mich.: Xerox University Microfilms, 1973–. 1861–1972, 1973–1982, and annual supplements.

This set listing American dissertations is compiled from various sources, including *DAI, American Dissertation Index,* and Library of Congress records. It includes subject listings by key word and an author index. Entries give the original source and the UMI order number when it exists. A convenient and close to comprehensive listing of American dissertations.

Index to Theses Accepted for Higher Degrees in the Universities of Great Britain and Ireland. London: Aslib, 1950–.

This index to British and Irish dissertations is arranged by broad subject, with indexes by author and by more specific subject based on key words in dissertation titles.

GUIDES TO RESEARCH

DeLaura, David J. *Victorian Prose: A Guide to Research.* New York: Modern Language Association, 1973.

This collection of bibliographic essays includes both major and secondary Victorian prose writers. Bibliographies are complete through 1971, with a few items from 1972. Vital to beginning research in this field but in need of an update.

Faverty, Frederic E. *The Victorian Poets: A Guide to Research.* 2d ed. Cambridge, Mass.: Harvard University Press, 1968.

The second edition of this guide is complete to the end of 1966. The first edition is still useful for the critical insights of critics who are not in the second edition. A third edition is badly needed.

Ford, George H., ed. *Victorian Fiction: A Second Guide to Research*. New York: The Modern Language Association, 1978.

An updating of Lionel Stevenson's 1966 *Victorian Fiction*, this volume is as useful as its predecessor. It adds several authors, and the critics writing the bibliographic essays are often different from those in the previous volume. Because of these differences, it should be used as a supplement and not as a replacement.

Madden, Lionel. *How to Find Out About the Victorian Period*. Oxford: Pergamon Press, 1970.

An invaluable and exhaustive guide to general reference sources and to sources specifically on the Victorian period. It is divided by broad subject field and includes sample pages from major sources. An updated version is needed.

Stevenson, Lionel, ed. *Victorian Fiction: A Guide to Research*. Cambridge, Mass.: Harvard University Press, 1966.

An indispensable guide to research on Victorian fiction. Bibliographic essays on general materials and on major authors evaluate the literature in the fields through 1962. Updated by Gerald Ford's *Victorian Fiction: A Second Guide to Research* but not superceded by it.

Storey, Richard and Lionel Madden. *Primary Sources for Victorian Studies: A Guide to the Location and Use of Unpublished Materials*. London: Phillimore, 1977.

This guide is directed to students starting primary source research in Victorian studies. The emphasis is on archives and repositories in Great Britain, but some attention is given to the problem of finding material outside Britain.

Vann, J. Don and Rosemary T. Van Arsdel. *Victorian Periodicals: A Guide to Research*. New York: Modern Language Association, 1978.

This guide provides an excellent starting point for research on periodicals. It gives information on locating and using materials and a bibliography of works on this often elusive field.

INDEXES

Boyle, Andrew. *An Index to the Annuals, 1820–1850*. Vol. 1: *The Authors (1820–1850)*. Worcester: Andrew Boyle, Ltd., 1967.

This index to annuals and gift books published between 1820 and 1850 lists authors by the name signed to the article. Pseudonyms are not identified; some but not all initials are. There are separate listings for "Author of" signatures and anonymous works. Deficiencies limit its usefulness, and subsequent volumes have not appeared.

Houghton, Walter E. *The Wellesley Index to Victorian Periodicals, 1824–1900*. Toronto: University of Toronto Press; London: Routledge and Kegan Paul, 1979–.

As of volume 3, thirty-five periodicals have been indexed. The set is to be complete with volume 4, when forty-eight monthlies and quarterlies will have been indexed. Each volume indexes a major Victorian periodical, with a full listing of each volume's

contents. The most valuable feature is the identification of anonymous authors whenever possible.

Palmer's Index to the "Times" Newspaper, 1790–June 1941. London: Palmer, 1868–1943. (Reprint, New York: Kraus, 1965.)

This quarterly subject index to the *Times* is the main source of access to this important material. It includes lists under "Deaths" that are useful sources of biographical information.

Poole, William Frederick and William I. Fletcher. *Poole's Index to Periodical Literature*. Gloucester, Mass.: Peter Smith. Vol. 1, Rev. ed. 1802–1881, 2 parts, 1953; 1st supplement, 1882–1886, 1938; 2d supplement, 1887–1891, 1938; 3d supplement, 1892–1896, 1938; 4th supplement, 1897–1901, 1938; 5th supplement, 1901–1906, 1938.

Cumulative Author Index for Poole's Index to Periodical Literature, 1802–1906. Comp. and ed. by C. Edward Wall. Ann Arbor, Mich.: Pierian Press, 1971.

Poole's is a subject index to 479 English and American periodicals published between 1802 and 1906. Articles having no nonfiction subject, such as sto-

ries, poems, and plays, are listed under the first word of the title which is not an article. Reviews of literary works are entered under the name of the author reviewed; reviews of nonfiction are listed under the subject of the reviewed book. Some English periodicals listed in volume 1 are incompletely indexed.

LIBRARY CATALOGS

Ash, Lee and William G. Miller, comps. *Subject Collections: A Guide to Special Book Collections and Subject Emphases as Reported By University, College, Public, and Special Libraries and Museums in the United States and Canada.* 6th ed., rev. and enl. New York: Bowker, 1985.

The title describes the contents. Organization is by subjects based on the Library of Congress subject heading and then alphabetically by abbreviated state name. Arrangement is then by city and then name of library. Though the book offers important material, it would be much more useful if some indexing was provided, including institutions listed. Increased use of cross references has made subject

searching easier. "See also" references would be a further improvement.

The British Library General Catalogue of Printed Books to 1975. London: Clive Bingley, 1979.

These volumes replace the *General Catalogue of Printed Books* of the British Museum. It lists the more than 8,500,000 volumes of the British Library and is an invaluable bibliographic source. Items are listed under main entry and some cross references are supplied. The amount of information included in an entry varies according to the time in which it was originally catalogued. Subsequent editions will keep the catalogue up to date, with the volumes covering 1976–1982 and 1982–1985 now available.

MICROFORM PROJECT

The Nineteenth Century. R.C. Alston, editorial director. Cambridge: Chadwyck-Healey, 1987–.

This project proposes to republish on microfiche nineteenth-century English language books and pamphlets of research value, especially those published after 1845 and in danger of loss through deterioration of book stock. The set will be produced over the next thirty years and will include a general collection and a number of specialist collections, with emphasis on scarce materials not available in other forms. The General Collection will cover British, Colonial, and international political studies, social studies, economics, transport and communication, commerce and industry, philoso-

phy and aesthetics, beliefs and religion, education, the law and society, entertainment and leisure, and the family. Specialized sets now available are linguistics and publishing, the book trade, and diffusion of knowledge. Art and architecture and music are forthcoming, with other specialist collections to be added during the course of the project. Machine-readable cataloguing is being produced for each item published and these records will be searchable through the Research Library Group's database, RLIN, and through the OCLC database. This project promises to preserve much endangered material and has great promise in facilitating access to rare research materials.

PARLIAMENTARY DEBATES

Ford, Percy and Grace Ford. *Select List of British Parliamentary Papers, 1833–1899.* Shannon, Ireland: Irish University Press, 1969.

This useful guide is arranged by subject with an alphabetical order. It "includes the report and all other materials issued by committees and commissions or similar bodies of investigation into economic, social, and constitutional questions, and matters of law and administration."

Great Britain. Parliament. *Parliamentary Debates.* Vols. 1–41 (1803–1820) London; n.s. vols. 1–25 (1820–1830) London; 3d series vols. 1–356 (1830–1890/91) London; 4th series vols. 1–199 (1892–1908) London.

Generally cited as Hansard. A general index covers the first and second series (London: Baldwin, 1834). The remaining series must be approached through sessional indexes. The indexes list debates both under the names of speakers and under the subject of their addresses. These indexes are made difficult to use by a lack of cross-references. Entries in the index are to column numbers, with volume numbers in brackets. The four series covering the Victorian period are not official transcripts and are not complete.

PERIODICAL LISTS

The Times. London. *Tercentenary Handlist of English and Welsh Newspapers, Magazines, and Reviews.* London: The *Times,* 1920.

This list begins with the year 1620 and goes through 1919. Section 1 covers the London and suburban press, section 2 the provincial press. Organization is by the date of the earliest copy which has been found for examination. Information includes number and date of the earliest issue, date of discontinuance if known, and, in some cases, printer, editor, distributor, and a reference to the library or collection if it is other than the British Library's general collection. It claims to be nearly exhaustive for the nineteenth century.

Wolff, Michael, John S. North, and Dorothy Deering. *The Waterloo Directory of Victorian Periodicals, 1824–1900.* Phase 1. Sponsored by The Research Society for Victorian Periodicals and Waterloo Computing in the Humanities. Waterloo, Ontario: The University of Waterloo, 1977.

This is an alphabetical listing of newspapers and periodicals published in England, Ireland, Scotland, and Wales between 1824 and 1900.

STATISTICS

An Almanack; 1869–. London: Whitaker, 1869.

For the late Victorian period, few sources are better than *Whitaker's Almanac* for statistical and other types of information. The index (in the front of each volume) gives detailed subject access to the contents.

Great Britain. Board of Trade. *Statistical Abstract for the United Kingdom.* Vols. 1–83, 1840–1923. London: Printed for Her Majesty's Stationery Office by Eyre and Spottiswoode (Reprint, Vaduz: Kraus Reprint Lts., 1965.)

Each volume contains statistics for the previous five years. Subjects covered vary slightly from volume to volume, with the emphasis on demographic and commercial information.

Mitchell, B. R., with the collaboration of Phyllis Deane. *Abstract of British Historical Statistics.* Cambridge: Cambridge University Press, 1962.

Mitchell, B. R., and H. G. Jones. *Second Abstract of British Historial Statistics.* Cambridge: Cambridge University Press, 1971.

The *Abstract* contains demographic and economic statistics going back to 1199. However, emphasis is on the eighteenth and nineteenth centuries. Because of the wide areas of both time and subject covered, statistical information is very general. It does regularize the information given in the *Statistical Abstract of the United Kingdom.* The *Second Abstract's* chief purpose is to continue information from the earlier volume's cut-off date of 1938 to 1965 or 1966. However, some new subjects are added, and these have pre-1938 figures.

Mitchell, B. R. *European Historical Statistics, 1750–1970.* New York: Columbia University Press, 1975.

The statistics recorded here are excellent for comparative purposes. The figures for the United Kingdom for the Victorian period are drawn from the *Statistical Abstract, Annual Statement of the Trade of the U.K.,* and *Tables of Revenue, Population, Commerce, etc.*

SHARON W. PROPAS

CONTRIBUTORS

LYNN M. ALEXANDER   Upper Iowa
University
   Seamstresses, Dressmakers, and
    Milliners

BARBARA ALLEN   Indiana University
   Senior, Jane Elizabeth Hughes
   Senior, Nassau William

JOSEF L. ALTHOLZ   University of
Minnesota
   High Church
   Broad Church
   Church of England
   Evangelical Movement
   Jowett, Benjamin
   Newman, John Henry
   Roman Catholic Church

NANCY FIX ANDERSON   Loyola University
of New Orleans
   Family
   Linton, Eliza Lynn

DAVID E. ANSELL
   Cemeteries

WALTER L. ARNSTEIN   University of
Illinois
   Victoria, Queen of England

EVELYN D. ASCH   Loyola University of
Chicago
   Wright, Thomas

JOEL W. ATHEY   Oklahoma State
University
   Boole, George
   Hamilton, William
   Logic

DOROTHY ATKINS   Loras College
   Inheritance

ZELDA AUSTEN   Long Island University
   Eastlake, Elizabeth Rigby

PETER BAILEY   University of Manitoba
   Music Hall

HOWARD C. BAKER
   Cholera

STUART BALL   University of Leicester
   Balfour, Arthur James
   Cabinet
   Labour Party
   Rosebury, Fifth Earl of (Archibald
    Philip Primrose)
   Salisbury, Third Marquess of (Robert
    Gascoyne-Cecil)

CAROL BARASH   Rutgers University
   Schreiner, Olive

JAMES J. BARNES AND PATIENCE P.
BARNES   Wabash College
   Copyright

JOAN BASSIN   New York Institute of
Technology
   Architectural Competitions

RAY BATCHELOR   Royal College of Art,
London
   Sewing Machines

J. O. BAYLEN   Georgia State University
   Jameson, Leander Starr
   Press, Political

STEVEN BAYME   American Jewish
Committee
   Abrahams, Israel
   Adler, Nathan
   Jewry and Judaism
   Montefiore, Moses H.

LENORE BEAKY   LaGuardia Community
College
   Watts, Anna Mary Howitt

VIRGINIA K. BEARDS   Pennsylvania State
University
   Anglo-Irish Life and Society
   Somerville and Ross

CYNTHIA F. BEHRMAN   Wittenberg
University
   Governesses
   Nursery and Nanny

SCOTT BENNETT   Northwestern University
Library
   Penny Magazine

RICHARD BENVENUTO   Michigan State
University
   Decadence
   Morrison, Arthur
   Rhymers' Club
   Stevenson, Robert Louis
   Wilde, Oscar

MARJORIE K. BERMAN   Community
College of Aurora
   Parliament
   Prime Minister

LOUIS BILLINGTON   University of Hull
   Water Cure

ROSAMUND BILLINGTON   Humberside
College of Higher Education
   Education, Women's
   Beale, Dorothea
   Pankhurst, Emmeline Goulden
   Single Women

OLWYN M. BLOUET   Texas A & M
University
   Gordon, Charles George
   Kay-Shuttleworth, James Phillips
   Kitchener, Horatio Herbert
   Livingstone, David
   Missionaries
   Ordnance Survey
   Public Schools
   Rhodes, Cecil John
   Seeley, John Robert
   Slave Trade
   Tennis
   West Indies

MARILYNN LINCOLN BOARD   SUNY
Geneseo
   Watts, George Frederic

DAVID R. BOONE   Harpeth Presbyterian
Church
   Church of Scotland
   Free Church of Scotland

FLORENCE S. BOOS   University of Iowa
   Morris, William
   Browning, Elizabeth Barrett
   Wilson, Charlotte

MERRILEY BORELL   Tufts University
School of Medicine
   Physiology

NEWELL D. BOYD   Houston Baptist
University
   Boer War
   Canada
   Chamberlain, Joseph
   Government: Colonies and Empire
   Milner, Alfred
   South Africa

JOHN H. Y. BRIGGS   University of Keele
   Baptists
   Pottery and Pottery Workers
   Press, Religious
   Ragged Schools
   Social Darwinism
   Sunday Schools
   Theology

MONIKA BROWN   Pembroke State
University
   Blackmore, Richard Doddridge
   Craik, Dinah Maria Mulock
   Hobbes, John Oliver
   Literacy and the Reading Public
   Literary Criticism
   Manning, Anne

ROBERT W. BROWN   Pembroke State
University
   Utilitarianism

HALLMAN B. BRYANT   Clemson University
   Hunt, William Holman
   Landseer, Edwin
   Millais, John Everett

R. A. BUCHANAN   University of Bath
   Engineering
   Steam Engine
   Technology and Invention

LAURIE E. BUCHANAN   Central Michigan
University
   Gaskell, Elizabeth Cleghorn

VERN L. BULLOUGH   SUNY College,
Buffalo
   Venereal Disease

ELIZABETH A. CAMPBELL   Oregon State
University
   Hopkins, Gerard Manley

KEN CARLS University of Illinois
Mackintosh, Charles Rennie and
Margaret MacDonald

CYNTHIA CARLTON-FORD University of
Minnesota
Death and Funerals

CHERYL M. CASSIDY University of
Michigan
Eyre, Edward John

DENNIS CHALDECOTT California State
University, San Jose
Savoy Operas
Teachers' Education and Training

CARL W. CHEATHAM Faulkner University
Labour Church
Primitive Methodist Church

JO ANN CHRISTEN Southern Illinois
University at Edwardsville
Riddell, Charlotte Cowan

THOMAS D. CLARESON The College of
Wooster
Reade, Charles

ANNA K. CLARK Rutgers University
Prostitution
Sexual Violence

MICAEL M. CLARKE Loyola University of
Chicago
Advice Manuals
Norton, Caroline Sheridan

REBECCA COCHRAN Iowa State University
Medievalism

ALFRED COHEN Trenton State College
Hardie, James Keir
O'Connor, Feargus Edward

MICHAEL COHEN Murray State University
Egg, Augustus Leopold

ROBERT A. COLBY Queens College, CUNY
Fiction Syndication
Thackeray, William Makepeace

VINETA COLBY Queens College, CUNY
Oliphant, Margaret Oliphant Wilson

RALPH COLP, JR., M.D. Columbia
University
Darwin, Charles Robert
Ellis, Henry Havelock
Sex Education

JOHN J. CONLON University of
Massachusetts-Boston
Art Nouveau
Early English Scholarship and
Criticism
Haggard, Henry Rider
Harris, Frank
Henley, William Ernest
Morley, John
Naturalism
Sharp, William
Whistler, James McNeill

BERNARD A. COOK Loyola University,
New Orleans
Agricultural Laborers
Agriculture
Mining and Miners
Poverty
Strikes
Wages
Working Hours

JOAN CORWIN
Bird, Isabella
Kingsley, Mary
Travel Literature

RICHARD A. COSGROVE University of
Arizona
Chancery and Doctors' Commons
Common Law
Judicial System

MOUREEN COULTER Northeast Missouri
State University
Patents

DON RICHARD COX University of
Tennessee
Doyle, Arthur Conan
Jack the Ripper
Mystery and Detective Fiction

ROBERT M. CRAIG Georgia Institute of
Technology
Architecture
Jekyll, Gertrude
Landscape Architecture and Design
Lutyens, Edwin Landseer
Paxton, Joseph

STEVEN N. CRAIG Illinois State University
Cooperative Movement
Holyoake, George Jacob
Trade Unions
Working-Class Clubs and Associations

SHELLEY J. CRISP   University of North Carolina
- *Blind, Mathilde*
- *Coleridge, Mary Elizabeth*
- *Greenwell, Dora*
- *Levy, Amy*
- *Webster, Augusta Davies*

DAVID DANIELS
- *Board and Table Games*

FRANK DAY   Clemson University
- *Anglo-Indian Literature*
- *Egypt*
- *Palestine*
- *West Africa*

DENNIS R. DEAN   University of Wisconsin-Parkside
- *Dinosaurs*
- *Landscape Painters*
- *Learned Societies*
- *Lyell, Charles*
- *Publishers and Publishing*

ELIZABETH J. DEIS   Hampden-Sydney College
- *Farce*
- *Sinclair, Catherine*

CHRISTINE DEWAR
- *Jerrold, Douglas*

BERYL I. DIAMOND
- *Suez Canal*

VANESSA D. DICKERSON   University of Virginia
- *Crowe, Catherine Stevens*
- *Marryat, Florence*
- *Spiritualism*
- *Supernatural Fiction*

N. MERRILL DISTAD   University of Alberta
- *Burton, Richard Francis*
- *Firearms*
- *Food and Diet*
- *Milnes, Richard Monckton*
- *Munby, Arthur Joseph and Hannah Cullwick*
- *Oceanography*
- *Postal Services*
- *Ships and Shipbuilding*
- *Smuggling*
- *Tichborne Claimant*
- *Travel and Exploration*

READE W. DORNAN   University of Michigan-Flint
- *Working-Class Novelists*

SUSAN DRAIN   Mount Saint Vincent University
- *Choral Music*
- *Elliott, Ebenezer*
- *Gatty, Margaret*
- *Hood, Thomas*
- *Journalism and Journalists*
- *Oxford English Dictionary*
- *Piano*
- *Procter, Adelaide Anne*

EDWARD DRAMIN   Iona College
- *Romanticism*

THOMAS L. DRUCKER   Dickinson College
- *Mathematics*

CHARMAZL DUDT   West Texas State University
- *Meynell, Alice Thompson*
- *Meynell, Wilfrid*

BARBARA J. DUNLAP   City College Library, CUNY
- *Yonge, Charlotte Mary*
- *Civil War, United States*
- *Infant Feeding*

JOSEPH R. DUNLAP   City College of New York
- *Printing and Book Making*

LEE M. EDWARDS   New York University
- *Genre Painting*
- *Herkomer, Hubert von*
- *Walker, Frederick*

P. D. EDWARDS   University of Queensland
- *Clive, Caroline*
- *Sala, George Augustus*
- *Sensation Novel*
- *Trollope, Anthony*
- *Yates, Edmund*

STEPHEN ELWELL
- *Illustration*

VICTOR EMELJANOW   University of Newcastle, New South Wales
- *Actors and the Acting Profession*
- *Hare, John*
- *Taylor, Tom*
- *Ward, Genevieve*

DAVID M. FAHEY   Miami University
   Temperance Movement

JOHN E. FINDLING   Indiana University
   Southeast
   Philately

MICHAEL FINK   University of Texas, San
   Antonio
   Elgar, Edward

BENJAMIN FRANKLIN FISHER IV
   University of Mississippi
   Molesworth, Mary Louisa

LEONA W. FISHER   Georgetown University
   Lemon, Mark

MARIAN FISHER
   Blavatsky, Madame Helena
   Theosophy

KATHY J. FLETCHER   University of
   Maryland, Baltimore County
   Pantomime, Burlesque and
      Extravaganza
   Planché, James Robinson

PAULINE FLETCHER   Bucknell University
   Gardens and Parks

EVELYN L. FORGET   University of
   Winnipeg
   Banking
   Economics

R. W. FRANKLIN   St. John's University
   Pusey, Edward Bouverie

ROBERT S. FRASER   University of
   Wisconsin-Eau Claire
   Churchill, Lord Randolph Henry
      Spencer
   Home Rule
   Melbourne, Second Viscount (William
      Lamb)
   Palmerston, Lord (Henry John
      Temple)
   Parnell, Charles Stewart
   Peel, Robert
   Russell, Lord John
   Durham, Earl of

PAUL H. FRIESEN   Wycliffe College,
   Toronto
   Shaftesbury, Lord (Anthony Ashley
      Cooper)

LOWELL T. FRYE   Hampden-Sydney
   College
   The Times

BARBARA GARLICK   University of
   Queensland
   Voynich, Ethel Boole

KRISTINE OTTESEN GARRIGAN   DePaul
   University
   Gothic Revival
   Pugin, Augustus Welby Northmore
   Ruskin, John
   Women in Art

WILLIAM J. GATENS   Church of St. Luke
   & the Epiphany, Philadelphia
   Cathedral Music
   Music and Morals
   Stainer, John
   Wesley, Samuel Sebastian

BARBARA T. GATES   University of
   Delaware
   Suicide

JOAN MICKELSON GAUGHAN   Washtenaw
   Community College
   Australia
   Cardigan, Seventh Earl (James
      Thomas Brundel)
   East Africa
   East India Company
   Eden, Emily
   Far East
   New Zealand

JULIA M. GERGITS   Illinois Institute of
   Technology
   Butler, Elizabeth Thompson
   Embroidery
   Home Furnishings and Decoration
   Housework and Domestic Technology
   Needlecrafts
   Watercolors

ROBERT GLEN   University of New Haven
   Manchester
   Owenite Socialism
   Textile Industry

MARTHA GOFF-STONER   Michigan State
   University
   Christmas

CATHERINE J. GOLDEN   Skidmore College
   Ainsworth, William Harrison
   Cruikshank, George

Potter, Beatrix
Sewell, Elizabeth Missing

DENNIS GOLDSBERRY College of
Charleston
Du Maurier, George
Fitzgerald, Edward
Lewes, George Henry
Tragedy

K. L. GOODWIN University of Queensland
Stained Glass

C. GORDON-CRAIG University of Alberta
Patmore, Coventry
Sporting Literature
Wiseman, Nicholas Patrick Stephen

NORBERT J. GOSSMAN University of Detroit
Bridges, Robert

WILLIAM J. GRACIE, JR. Miami University
Poetry and Poetics

SUZANNE GRAVER Williams College
Anderson, Elizabeth Garrett
Blackwell, Elizabeth
Browne, Hablot Knight
Buss, Frances Mary
Eliot, George
Field, Michael
Hill, Octavia
Sewell, Anna
Shirreff, Emily, and Maria Shirreff
Grey
Simcox, Edith
Rossetti, Christina Georgina

BRIAN GRIFFIN National University of
Ireland
Gaelic Culture

ELIZABETH GRUBGELD Oklahoma State
University
Carleton, William
Ireland
Moore, George Augustus

STEPHEN GURNEY Bemidji State
University
Arnold, Matthew
Rutherford, Mark
Thompson, Francis

NAN HACKETT St. Lawrence University
Autobiography
Place, Francis
Smiles, Samuel

KAREN I. HALBERSLEBEN SUNY College
at Oswego
Antislavery Movement
Philanthropy

LYNN M. HAMILTON Huntington College
Science Fiction

A. JAMES HAMMERTON LaTrobe
University
Emigration

LAURA HAPKE Pace University
Sisterhoods

GEORGE GRAHAM HARPER Calvin
College
Plymouth Bretheren

ANGUS HAWKINS Loyola Marymount
University
Conservative Party
Irish Party
Liberal Party
Liberal Unionists
Party System
Radical Politics
Whig Party

JAMES HAZEN University of Nevada at Las
Vegas
Unitarianism

HELEN HEINEMAN Framingham State
College
Trollope, Frances

SARA A. HELLER College of Charleston
Horses and Carriages

SHEILA R. HERSTEIN City College
Library, CUNY
Bodichon, Barbara Leigh Smith
English Woman's Journal,
Englishwoman's Review
Faithfull, Emily
National Association for the
Promotion of Social Science

KATHLEEN HICKOK Iowa State University
Bevington, Louisa Sarah
Fane, Violet
Nesbit, Edith

ANN R. HIGGINBOTHAM Eastern
Connecticut State University
Abortion
Day Nurseries
Infanticide

JAMES HILL
Vaccination and Smallpox

GEORGE W. HILTON   UCLA
Breweries and Public Houses

ELISABETH HIRSCHHORN   Brown
University
Comedy

WILSON J. HOFFMAN   Hiram College
Barry, Charles
Brunel, Isambard Kingdom
Factories
Lloyd, Marie

TERRENCE E. HOLT
Myth

DAVID HOPKINSON
Class
Education, Secondary

CRAIG HOWES   University of Hawaii at
Manoa
Periodicals: Comic and Satiric

CYNTHIA HUFF   Georgetown University
Diaries and Diarists
Dogs and Dog Shows
Women's Friendships

LINDA K. HUGHES   Texas Christian
University
Serial Literature

ELIZABETH HULSE
Yellowbacks

ANNE HUMPHERYS   Lehman College,
CUNY
Mayhew, Henry
Reynolds, George William MacArthur

SHELAGH HUNTER
Adams, Sarah Flower
Hall, Anna Maria and Samuel Carter
Martineau, James
Robinson, Henry Crabb

DAVID ITZKOWITZ   Macalester College
Gambling
Royal Family

NAOMI JACOBS   University of Maine
Periodicals: Monthly Magazines
Silver-Fork Novel

LOUIS JAMES   University of Kent
Radical Cartoons
Working-Class Literature

ROSEMARY JANN   Geroge Mason
University
Carlyle, Thomas
Froude, James Anthony
History and Historians

DALE A. JOHNSON   Divinity School,
Vanderbilt University
Congregational Church
Disestablishment
Nonconformity

SIDNEY JOHNSON
Aristocracy and Gentry
Chadwick, Edwin
Country Society
Epidemic Diseases

JOEL H. KAPLAN   University of British
Columbia
Alexander, George
Jones, Henry Arthur
Melodrama
Pinero, Arthur Wing
Theaters and Staging
Wyndham, Charles

RICHARD KELLY   University of Tennessee
Carroll, Lewis

RICHARD S. KENNEDY   Temple University
Collins, Wilkie
Hardy, Thomas

THOMAS C. KENNEDY   University of
Arkansas
Friends, Society of

CHRISTOPHER A. KENT   University of
Saskatchewan
Smoking and Tobacco
Clubs, Gentlemen's
Restaurants

JOSEPH A. KESTNER   University of Tulsa
Social Problem Novel
Stone, Elizabeth Wheeler
Tonna, Charlotte Elizabeth

BRUCE L. KINZER   University of North
Carolina at Wilmington
Elections and the Franchise
Gladstone, William Ewart

ALISA KLAUS
Baby Farming
Infant Mortality

RENE KOLLAR Saint Vincent Archabbey
  Religious Orders
  Ritualism and Antiritualism
  Vaughan, Herbert Alfred

NEIL KUNZE Northern Arizona University
  Housing

MARILYN J. KURATA University of
Alabama at Birmingham
  Insanity
  Wood, Ellen Price

MICHAEL DE L. LANDON University of
Mississippi
  Scots Law

RICHARD LANDON University of Toronto
  Butler, Samuel
  Maginn, William

CORAL LANSBURY Rutgers University—
Camden
  Pornography

DAVID E. LATANÉ, JR. Virginia
Commonwealth University
  Graphic Arts
  Macready, William Charles
  Popular Shows and Exhibitions
  Spasmodic Poetry
  Wordsworthianism

FREDERICK E. LAURENZO University of
Mississippi
  Clerks and Clerical Work
  Electricity
  Telegraph and Telephone
  Typewriter

JOE K. LAW University of Texas-Arlington
  Macaulay, Thomas Babington
  Mackenzie, Alexander Campbell
  Mulready, William
  Novello, Clara
  Parry, Charles Hubert Hastings
  Popular Songs and Music
  Stanford, Charles Villiers

EUGENE D. LeMIRE Flinder University of
South Australia
  Bloody Sunday

TREVOR H. LEVERE University of Toronto
  Arctic and Antarctic Exploration

BERNARD LIGHTMAN York University
  Agnosticism

SHARON LOCY Loyola Marymount
University
  Mudie, Charles Edward
  Periodicals: Cheap and Popular

MARK S. LOOKER Concordia College
  Church of England Parish Life
  Keble, John
  Young England

ABIGAIL A. LOOMIS Northern Illinois
University
  Libraries and Librarianship

LUND, MICHAEL Longwood College
  Serial Literature

LARRY LUTCHMANSINGH Bowdoin
College
  Arts and Crafts Movement
  Ashbee, Charles Robert
  Brown, Ford Madox
  Burne-Jones, Edward
  Cole, Henry
  De Morgan, William
  Jones, Owen
  Linton, William James
  Mackmurdo, Arthur Heygate

CAROL HANBERY MacKAY University of
Texas
  Ritchie, Anne Thackeray

RAYMOND N. MacKENZIE Cray Research,
Inc.
  Periodicals: Reviews and Quarterlies

LORALEE MacPIKE California State
University
  Childbirth
  Midwives

E. D. MACKERNESS University of Sheffield
  Drama Criticism
  Musical Comedy
  Music Criticism
  Oratorio
  Orchestras

DIANNE SACHKO MacLEOD University of
California, Davis
  Art Criticism

SUSAN NARAMORE MAHER University of
Nebraska-Omaha
  Childhood
  Tucker, Charlotte Maria

GAIL MALMGREEN   Columbia University
   Carpenter, Mary
   Wesleyan Methodist Church

DEBRA N. MANCOFF   Beloit College
   Academic Painting
   History Painting
   Hughes, Arthur

ELLEN F. MAPPEN   Douglass College
   Black, Clementina
   Social Feminism

GEORGE MARIZ   Western Washington
University
   Caird, Edward
   Education, Higher
   Oxford and Cambridge Local
      Examinations
   Wallace, Alfred Russel

CAROL A. MARTIN   Boise State University
   Howitt, Mary Botham and William

FLOYD W. MARTIN   University of Arkansas
at Little Rock
   Cameron, Julia Margaret
   Photography
   Shaw, Richard Norman
   Street, George Edmund
   Waterhouse, Alfred

PAUL MARX   University of New Haven
   Manchester School

ROY T. MATTHEWS   Michigan State
University
   Caricature
   Ward, Leslie

RICHARD MAXWELL   Valparaiso University
   Bicycle
   Egan, Pierce
   National Gallery
   Philology
   Street Music

LAWRENCE J. McCAFFREY   Loyola
University of Chicago
   Catholic Emancipation

KATHLEEN E. McCRONE   University of
Windsor
   Sports and Games, Women's
   Twining, Louisa

LYLE A. McGEOCH   Ohio University
   Clarendon, Fourth Earl (George
      Villiers)

ALLYSON F. McGILL   Indiana University
   Oxford Novel

DONALD J. McGRAW
   Bacteriology

SUSAN JARET McKINSTRY   Carleton
College
   Brontë, Emily Jane

EILEEN M. McMAHON   Loyola University
of Chicago
   Dublin
   O'Connell, Daniel

DIANE McMANUS   Temple University
   Dance and Ballet

IVAN MELADA   University of New Mexico
   Industry

LYNN L. MERRILL
   Natural History

DAVID PHILIP MILLER   University of New
South Wales
   Astronomy

MAURICE MILNE   Newcastle Polytechnic
   Press, Provincial

JoANNA STEPHENS MINK   Illinois State
University
   Brontë, Anne
   Langtry, Lillie

DENNIS J. MITCHELL   Jackson State
University
   Cost of Living
   Cross, Richard Assheton
   Factory Acts
   Labor Laws
   Money
   Opium

SALLY MITCHELL   Temple University
   Broadsides and Chapbooks
   Burdett-Coutts, Angela Georgina
   Circus
   Country Sports
   Education, Adult
   Gissing, George
   Gypsies
   Lister, Joseph
   Medical Education
   Pawnshops
   Servants
   Statistics
   Stead, William Thomas

Surgery and Surgeons
Tracts
Tuberculosis
Wood Engraving

SHEILA ANNE MONNET
Booth, Charles
Rothschild Family

JAMES R. MOORE   The Open University
Naden, Constance Caroline Woodhill

THAÏS E. MORGAN   Arizona State
University
Rossetti, Dante Gabriel
Swinburne, Algernon Charles

PATRICIA MORTON   Trent University
Wars and Military Engagements
Army

PRUDENCE ANN MOYLAN   Mundelein
College
Government: Local and County

MARIE MARMO MULLANEY   Caldwell
College
Butler, Josephine Grey
Marx, Eleanor

SHIRLEY A. MULLEN   Westmont College
Besant, Annie Wood
Bradlaugh, Charles
Freethought

LAURA STEMPEL MUMFORD
Caird, Mona Alison
Egerton, George
Fawcett, Millicent Garrett
Feminism
Feminist Writing
Grand, Sarah
New Woman
Suffrage, Women's

F. DARRELL MUNSELL   West Texas State
University
Crimean War
Irish Famine
*Raglan, Lord (Fitzroy James Henry
Somerset)*

CARYN McTIGHE MUSIL   LaSalle
University
Ward, Mary Arnold

VALERIE GROSVENOR MYER
Bulwer-Lytton, Edward George

MEGAN NELSON   University of British
Columbia
Palgrave, Francis
Royal Academy of Arts

MARK NEUMAN   Bucknell University
Beggars and Vagrants
Poor Law
Workhouse

ASHTON NICHOLS   Dickinson College
Positivism
Cambridge University
Yeats, William Butler

DEBORAH EPSTEIN NORD   Harvard
University
*Webb, Beatrice Potter and Sidney
James*

LAURA NOVO   Columbia University
Antiquarianism
Archaeology
Domestic Industry
Education, Elementary
Local History
Provincial Towns and Society

CYNTHIA J. NOWAK   University of Toledo
Art for Art's Sake
Fin de Siècle

JEAN O'GRADY   University of Toronto
Press
Game Laws
*Laws of Public Worship, Speech, and
the Press*
Ross, Janet

ROBERT O'KELL   University of Manitoba
Disraeli, Benjamin

DAVID R. OLDROYD   University of New
South Wales
Chemistry
Wilberforce, Samuel

JOHN V. ORTH   University of North
Carolina School of Law
Legal Profession

HANS OSTROM   University of Puget Sound
Horne, R. H.

FRANK JOHN PAPATHEOFANIS   University
of Illinois College of Medicine
Anesthesia
Biochemistry

JAMES PARADIS   Massachusetts Institute of
Technology
Huxley, Thomas Henry

GRAHAM PARKER   Osgoode Hall Law
School, Toronto
Law Reform

SANDRA PARKER   Hiram College
Clough, Arthur Hugh
Housman, Alfred Edward

ANDREW PARKIN   University of British
Columbia
Boucicault, Dion
Campbell, Mrs. Patrick
Farr, Florence

ELIZABETH C. PATTERSON   Albertus
Magnus College
Somerville, Mary Fairfax Greig

DONNA PRICE PAUL   University of North
Carolina
Lacemakers
Matchworkers
Shopworkers
Socialism

ANNIE PERROTT
Poet Laureate
Shops and Shopping

M. JEANNE PETERSON   Indiana University
Acton, William
Medical Practice
Paget, James

JOHN PFORDRESHER   Georgetown
University
Beardsley, Aubrey Vincent

PAUL T. PHILLIPS   St. Francis Xavier
University
Manning, Henry Edward
Settlement Movement

TREVOR J. PHILLIPS   Bowling Green State
University
Barnardo, Thomas
Child Saving
Rye, Maria

ROSA LYNN PINKUS   University of
Pittsburgh School of Medicine
Health
Medical Science
Public Health
Sociology

DILWYN PORTER   Worcester College of
Higher Education
Free Trade
Taxes and Tariffs

DIANA POSTLETHWAITE   St. Olaf College
Chambers, Robert
Mesmerism
Phrenology

LINDA RAY PRATT   University of
Nebraska—Lincoln
Gonne, Maud

SHARON W. PROPAS   University of
Cincinnati Libraries
Research Materials for Victorian
Studies

JOHN RANLETT   Potsdam College, SUNY
Animal Protection
Commons and Open Spaces
Environmental Pollution
Preservation of Monuments and
Buildings
Railways
Wildlife Protection

EUGENE L. RASOR   Emory and Henry
College
Forster, William Edward
Hill, Rowland
Navy
Plimsoll, Samuel
Pressure Groups
Purity Campaign
Shipping and Seamen
Taxes on Knowledge
White Slave Trade

ALAN RAUCH   Rutgers University
Education, Technical
Lear, Edward
Paleontology

SAMUEL REES   University of Alberta
Anglo-Welsh Literature
Wales and Welsh Nationalism

MARK REGER
   Dictionary of National Biography
   Stephen, Leslie

JOHN REYNOLDS   Somerset
Archaeological and Natural History
Society
   Cockerell, Charles Robert
   Debt, Imprisonment for
   Educating the Deaf and Blind
   Juvenile Crime
   Lighting
   Plumbing and Sewage Disposal
   Scott, George Gilbert
   Street Traders
   Transportation, Urban

BETSY COGGER REZELMAN   St. Lawrence
University
   Newlyn School

BETTY RICHARDSON   Southern Illinois
University at Edwardsville
   Firefighting
   Law Enforcement
   Martineau, Harriet
   Prisons and Prison Reform

KENNETH A. ROBB   Bowling Green State
University
   Historical Novel
   Marryat, Frederick

BETTE B. ROBERTS   Westfield State
College
   Gothic Fiction
   LeFanu, Joseph Sheridan
   Stoker, Bram

HELENE E. ROBERTS   Fogg Art Museum,
Harvard University
   Clothing and Fashion
   Pre-Raphaelite Brotherhood

BONNIE JEAN ROBINSON   University of
Virginia, Charlottesville
   Aesthetic Movement
   Pater, Walter

ANN P. W. ROBSON   University of Toronto
   Mill, Harriet Hardy Taylor

JOHN M. ROBSON   University of Toronto
   Mill, John Stuart

WILLIAM S. RODNER   Pennsylvania State
University, Altoona Campus
   Turner, Joseph Mallord William

ELLIOT ROSE   University of Toronto
   Ewing, Juliana Gatty
   Hughes, Thomas

JONATHAN ROSE   Drew University
   Barrie, J. M.
   Carpenter, Edward
   Carte, Richard D'Oyly
   Fabian Society
   Graham, Robert B. Cunninghame
   Operetta
   Society for Psychical Research
   Wells, Herbert George
   Working-Class Poets and Poetry

KEITH A. P. SANDIFORD   University of
Manitoba
   Athletic Sports
   Cricket
   Foreign Relations
   Grace, William Gilbert
   Sport
   Rugby Football

TIMOTHY JEROME SARBAUGH   Gonzaga
University
   Young Ireland

GAIL L. SAVAGE   Pennsylvania State
University
   Civil Service
   Gentleman
   Henty, George Alfred

HARRY SCHALCK   West Chester University
   Suburbs and Planned Communities

NANCY ENGBRETSEN SCHAUMBURGER
Manhattanville College
   Dickens, Charles

WILLIAM H. SCHEUERLE   University of
South Florida
   *Amusements and Recreation: Middle
   Class*

JAMES ANDREW SCHMIECHEN   Central
Michigan University
   Sweatshops

NATALIE SCHROEDER   University of
Mississippi
   Newgate Novel

OWEN SCHUR   University of New Orleans
   Museums and Galleries
   Periodicals: Women's
   Symonds, John Addington

JOEL S. SCHWARTZ   College of Staten
Island, CUNY
  Evolution

BEVERLY SEATON   Ohio State
University—Newark
  Flowers, Language of

ROBERT M. SEILER   University of Calgary
  Oxford University
  Soccer

CAROL A. SENF   Georgia Institute of
Technology
  Birth Control
  Brontë, Charlotte
  Cobbe, Frances Power
  Irving, Henry
  Prest, Thomas Peckett

MARY LYNDON SHANLEY   Vassar College
  Bright, Ursula Mellor
  Divorce
  Elmy, Elizabeth Wolstenholme
  Marriage Law
  Married Women's Property
  Paterson, Emma Smith
  Taylor, Clementia Doughty

ANNE DHU SHAPIRO   Colorado College
  Folk Music

WILLIAM CHAPMAN SHARPE   Barnard
College
  Cities

ROBIN SHEETS   University of Cincinnati
  Davies, Emily
  Ellis, Sarah Stickney
  Jameson, Anna Brownell Murphy
  Marsh, Anne
  Stillman, Marie Spartali
  Womanhood

JILL SHEFRIN   Osborne Collection,
Toronto Public Library
  Children's Literature
  Stretton, Hesba

LILIAN LEWIS SHIMAN   Nichols College
  Band of Hope
  Howard, Rosalind, Countess of Carlile

ESTHER SIMON SHKOLNIK
  Social Season

MICHAEL SHORTLAND   University of
Oxford
  Babbage, Charles
  Biological Science
  Faraday, Michael
  Geology
  Maxwell, James Clerk
  Mechanics' Institutes
  Psychology
  Spencer, Herbert

LLOYD SIEMENS   University of Winnipeg
  Annuals and Gift Books

CAROLE SILVER   Stern College, Yeshiva
University
  Fairy Lore

LAUREN SMITH   University of British
Columbia
  Bancroft, Squire, and Marie Wilton
  Melba, Nellie
  Robertson, Thomas William
  Terry, Ellen
  Tree, Herbert Beerbohm

LOUISA SMITH   Mankato State University
  Crane, Walter
  Caldecott, Randolph
  Children's Illustrated Books
  Greenaway, Kate
  Tenniel, John

PHILIP THURMOND SMITH   St. Joseph's
University
  Atlantic Cable
  Chartism
  Crime
  Exhibition of 1851
  Riots and Demonstrations

W. JOHN SMITH   University of
Manchester
  Child Labor
  Children
  London

RICHARD A. SOLOWAY   University of
North Carolina at Chapel Hill
  Population and Demographics

RICHARD FRANCIS SPALL, JR.   Ohio
Wesleyan University
  Anti-Corn-Law League
  Bright, John
  Cobden, Richard
  Corn Laws

WARD STANLEY   Philadelphia College of
the Arts

JAMES D. STARTT   Valparaiso University
Empire and Imperialism
Irish Nationalism
Stanley, Henry Morton

DOROTHY STEIN   Institute of Historical
Research
Dowry
Lovelace, Ada
Suttee

CATHERINE B. STEVENSON   University of
Hartford
Tennyson, Alfred

WILLIAM STOCKDALE   University of
Western Ontario
Harney, George Julian

MARK STOCKER   University of Canterbury,
New Zealand
Sculpture

SHEILA STOWELL   University of British
Columbia
Archer, William
Kean, Charles John
Poel, William
Vestris, Madame

ROBIN M. SUNDSTROM
Toys and Games

JAN SUSINA   Wheaton College
Fairy Tales
Folklore
Hemyng, Bracebridge
Ingelow, Jean

HERBERT L. SUSSMAN   Northeastern
University
Novel

PHILIP SWAN   Humberside College of
Higher Education
Apothecaries
Drugs and Patent Medicines
Hospitals
Nursing

EILEEN SYPHER   George Mason University
Harkness, Margaret Elise

NORMAN TALBOT   University of Newcastle
(Australia)
Utopian Fiction

BEVERLY TAYLOR   University of North
Carolina
Carey, Rosa Nouchette
Cook, Eliza
Gilbert, John
Harrison, Jane Ellen
Kavanagh, Julia
Landor, Walter Savage
Lyall, Edna

PHILIP M. TEIGEN   National Library of
Medicine
Green, John Richard
Osler, William

NICHOLAS TEMPERLEY   University of
Illinois
Balfe, Michael William
Ballad, Drawing-Room
Bands and Band Music
Bennett, William Sterndale
Bishop, Henry Rowley
Conductors
Dance Music
Hymns
Loder, Edward James
Macfarren, George Alexander
Music
Music Education
Music Publishers
Musical Scholarship
Opera
Philharmonic Society
Songs
Sullivan, Arthur Seymour

PAUL THEERMAN   Smithsonian Institution
Edinburgh
Physics

ELIZABETH BOYD THOMPSON   Purdue
University
Meredith, George

NEVILLE THOMPSON   University of
Western Ontario
Wellington, Duke of (Arthur Wellesley)

DOUGLAS THORPE
Fantasy Literature
Macdonald, George

SUSAN SCHOENBAUER THURIN
University of Wisconsin-Stout
Travel and Tourism

WILLIAM B. TODD   University of Texas
Tauchnitz Editions

W. CRAIG TURNER   Mississippi College
    Conrad, Joseph
    Kipling, Rudyard

GILLIAN TYLER
    Salvation Army

LARRY K. UFFELMAN   Mansfield University
    Christian Socialism
    Harrison, Frederic
    Kingsley, Charles
    Lind, Jenny

ROSEMARY T. VAN ARSDEL   University of
Puget Sound
    Allen, Grant
    Banks, Isabella Varley
    Becker, Lydia Ernestine
    Blackburn, Helen
    Jex-Blake, Sophia Louisa
    Somerset, Isabel

DAVID K. VAN KEUREN   Naval Research
Laboratory, Washington, D.C.
    Anthropology
    Ethnology
    Nature versus Nurture
    Race

MARTHA VICINUS   University of Michigan
    Nightingale, Florence

CHARLES L. VIGUE   University of New
Haven
    Eugenics
    Galton, Francis

PHYLLIS E. WACHTER   Community
College of Philadelphia
    Lee, Vernon

NANCY MADDEN WALCZYK   University of
Wisconsin-Milwaukee
    Celtic Revival
    Irish Literature

KARLA KRAMPERT WALTERS   California
Polytechnic State University, San Luis
Obispo
    Society, Etiquette and Customs of
    Women's Employment

E. CLEVE WANT   Texas A & M University
    Biblical Criticism
    Maurice, Frederick Denison

CHRIS WATERS   Stanford University
    Amusements and Recreation: Working
    Class

    Cooper, Thomas
    Homosexuality
    Penny Theaters

TAMIE WATTERS
    Albert, Prince Consort
    Arnold, Thomas
    Braddon, Mary Elizabeth
    Broughton, Rhoda
    Cholmondeley, Mary
    Clough, Anne Jemima
    Corelli, Marie
    Jewsbury, Geraldine Endsor
    Kemble, Fanny
    Ouida
    Pattison, Mark
    Paxton, Joseph
    Shaw, George Bernard
    Souls, The

BARBARA WEISS
    Bankruptcy

ELLEN B. WELLS   Smithsonian Institution
Libraries
    Racing and Racehorses
    Wood, John George

MURIEL WHITAKER   University of Alberta
    Arthurian Legend

BRUCE A. WHITE   Gallaudet University
    Fry, Elizabeth

WILLIAM WHITLA   York University
    Browning, Robert
    Classical Scholarship
    Literary Prizes and Honors

JOEL H. WIENER   City College of New
York
    Press, Popular
    Press, Radical and Unstamped

ALBERT E. WILHELM   Tennessee
Technological University
    Frazer, James George
    Russell, William Howard

ANITA C. WILSON   Miami University
(Ohio)
    Mozley, Harriet Newman

JOHN J. WOODS   Rosemont College
    Herschel, John Frederick William
    Talbot, William Henry Fox

DIANE WORZOLA   University of Wisconsin
    Langham Place Circle
    Parkes, Bessie Rayner

EDGAR WRIGHT   Laurentian University
  Dialect Writing

PAUL A. B. WRIGHT
  Artists' Models

RICHARD YEO   Griffith University
  (Australia)
  Science

LYNN ZASTOUPIL   University of Minnesota
  India
  Indian Mutiny

LINDA GERTNER ZATLIN   Morehouse
  College
  Aguilar, Grace
  Farjeon, Benjamin
  Zangwill, Israel
  Anglo-Jewish Novel

INDEX

Principal entries are in boldface type. In general, page references
are to the entire article in which a topic appears.